The Routledge Companion to the Study of Religion
Second Edition

The Routledge Companion to the Study of Religion is a major resource for courses in Religious Studies. It begins by explaining the most important methodological approaches to religion, including psychology, philosophy, anthropology and comparative study, before moving on to explore a wide variety of critical issues, such as gender, science, fundamentalism, ritual, and new religious movements. Written by renowned international specialists, this new edition:

- includes eight new chapters on post-structuralism, religion and economics, religion and the environment, religion and popular culture, and sacred space
- surveys the history of religious studies and the key disciplinary approaches
- explains why the study of religion is relevant in today's world
- highlights contemporary issues such as globalization, diaspora and politics
- includes annotated reading lists, a glossary and summaries of key points to assist student learning.

John R. Hinnells is Emeritus Professor at Liverpool Hope University and Honorary Research Professor at SOAS where he was founding head of the Department for the Study of Religion. He is also a Senior Member of Robinson College, Cambridge, and life member of Clare Hall, Cambridge. His main works on Zoroastrianism are *Zoroastrians in Britain* (OUP 1996); *Zoroastrian and Parsi Studies* (2000) and *The Zoroastrian Diaspora* (2005). He edited the *New Penguin Dictionary of Religions* and the *New Penguin Handbook of Living Religions* (1997 and 1998). He is editor of the Routledge series Library of Religious Beliefs and Practices.

Contributors: Douglas Allen, Gregory D. Alles, William Sims Bainbridge, Michael Barnes, Jeremy Carrette, Thomas Dixon, David F. Ford, Judith Fox, Paul Gifford, Roger S. Gottlieb, Garrett Green, Rosalind I. J. Hackett, John R. Hinnells, Lawrence Iannaccone, Darlene Juschka, Richard King, Kim Knott, Mary Ellen Konieczny, Gordon Lynch, Luther H. Martin, Seán McLoughlin, Chad Meister, Dan Merkur, George Moyser, Henry Munson, William E. Paden, Martin Riesebrodt, Robert A. Segal, Eric J. Sharpe, Donald Wiebe and John Wolffe.

The Routledge Companion to the Study of Religion

Second edition

Edited by John R. Hinnells

Routledge
Taylor & Francis Group

LONDON AND NEW YORK

First published 2010
by Routledge
2 Park Square, Milton Park, Abingdon, Oxon OX14 4RN

Simultaneously published in the USA and Canada
by Routledge
711 Third Ave, New York, NY 10017

Routledge is an imprint of the Taylor & Francis Group, an informa business

© 2010 John R. Hinnells for selection and editorial materials. The
contributors for their contributions.

Typeset in Goudy by
HWA Text and Data Management, London

British Library Cataloguing in Publication Data
A catalogue record for this book is available from the British Library

Library of Congress Cataloging-in-Publication Data
A catalog record for this book has been requested

ISBN10: 0-415-47327-6 (hbk)
ISBN10: 0-415-47328-4 (pbk)
ISBN10: 0-203-86876-5 (ebk)

ISBN13: 978-0-415-47327-9 (hbk)
ISBN13: 978-0-415-47328-6 (pbk)
ISBN13: 978-0-203-86876-8 (ebk)

Contents

Contributors

Douglas Allen is Professor of Philosophy at the University of Maine. He served as President of Society of Asian and Comparative Philosophy, 2001–2004, and is Series Editor of Lexington's Studies in Comparative Philosophy and Religion. Author and editor of thirteen books and over 100 book chapters and journal articles, his most recent books are *Comparative Philosophy and Religion in Times of Terror*, and *The Philosophy of Mahatma Gandhi for the Twenty-First Century*.

Gregory D. Alles is Professor of Religious Studies at McDaniel College, Westminster, MD, USA. A past president of the North American Association for the Study of Religion, he is the editor of *Religious Studies: A Global View* (Routledge, 2008). He has recently been engaged in fieldwork among *ādivāsī* (indigenous) people in eastern Gujarat, India.

William Sims Bainbridge is the author of fifteen books, four textbook-software packages, and about 200 shorter publications in the social science of technology, information science, religion and culture. In 2006 he published *God from the Machine*, applying artificial intelligence techniques to understand religious cognition, and in 2007 he published *Across the Secular Abyss* and *Nanoconvergence* about the tensions between religion, cognitive science, social science, and emerging technologies.

Michael Barnes is Senior Lecturer and Reader in Interreligious Relations at Heythrop College in the University of London. He has written several books and a number of articles on Christianity and other faiths, notably *Theology and the Dialogue of Religions* (Cambridge: CUP 2002). He lives and works in Southall, West London, where he runs a small dialogue centre.

Jeremy Carrette is Professor of Religion and Culture and Head of Religious Studies at the University of Kent, UK. He is the author of numerous works on Foucault, William James and the politics of religious knowledge, including *Selling Spirituality* (London: Routledge, 2005), co-authored with Richard King. His most recent work is *Religion and Critical Psychology: Religious Experience in the Knowledge Economy* (London: Routledge, 2007) and he is the author of a forthcoming text *William James: Belief, Experience and Truth* (Equinox Press).

Thomas Dixon is Senior Lecturer in History at Queen Mary University of London. His publications include *From Passions to Emotions: The Creation of a Secular Psychological*

Category (2003), *The Invention of Altruism: Making Moral Meanings in Victorian Britain* (2008), and *Science and Religion: A Very Short Introduction* (2008).

David F. Ford is Regius Professor of Divinity at the University of Cambridge. He is the author of numerous books, including *Christian Wisdom: Desiring God and Learning in Love* (2007), *Theology: A Very Short Introduction* (2000), *Self and Salvation: Being Transformed* (1999), *The Shape of Living* (1997), *Meaning and Truth in 2 Corinthians* (1988, 2008, with Frances M. Young), and *Barth and God's Story: Biblical Narrative and the Theological Method of Karl Barth in the Church Dogmatics* (1981, 2008). He also serves as Director of the Cambridge Inter-Faith Programme and is a member of the editorial board of *Modern Theology* and *Scottish Journal of Theology*.

Judith Fox has a PhD in the Sociology of New Religious Movements and taught at the School of Oriental and African Studies in London. She presently lives in Hyde Park, Chicago, raising one-year-old Zachary with her husband Richard.

Paul Gifford is Professor of African Religion at the School of Oriental and African Studies (SOAS) of the University of London. Among his publications are *African Christianity: its Public Role* (1998), *Ghana's New Christianity: Pentecostalism in a Globalising African Economy* (2004), and *Christianity, Politics and Public Life in Kenya* (2009).

Roger S. Gottlieb is Professor of Philosophy at Worcester Polytechnic Institute (USA). He is the author or editor of fourteen books and over 100 articles on political philosophy, ethics, religious studies, environmentalism, and spiritual life, including *Marxism 1844–1990*; *Joining Hands: Politics and Religion Together for Social Change*, and *A Spirituality of Resistance: Finding a Peaceful Heart and Protecting the Earth*.

Garrett Green is the Class of 1943 Professor Emeritus of Religious Studies at Connecticut College (New London, Connecticut). He is the author of *Imagining God: Theology and the Religious Imagination* (1989, 1998) and *Theology, Hermeneutics, and Imagination: The Crisis of Interpretation at the End of Modernity* (2000). He translated and introduced Karl Barth, *On Religion: The Revelation of God as the Sublimation of Religion* (2006).

Rosalind I. J. Hackett is Professor of Religious Studies and adjunct in anthropology at the University of Tennessee. She has published widely on religion in Africa; her latest book is *Proselytization Revisited: Right Talk, Free Markets, and Culture Wars* (ed.) (Equinox 2008). In 2005 she was elected President of the International Association for the History of Religions (until 2010).

John R. Hinnells is Emeritus Professor at Liverpool Hope University and Honorary Research Professor at SOAS where he was founding head of the Department for the Study of Religion. He is also a Senior Member of Robinson College, Cambridge and life member of Clare Hall, Cambridge. His main works on Zoroastrianism are *Zoroastrians in Britain* (OUP, 1996); *Zoroastrian and Parsi Studies* (Ashgate 2000) and *The Zoroastrian Diaspora* (OUP, 2005). He edited the *New Penguin Dictionary of Religions* and the *New Penguin Handbook of Living Religions* (1997 and 1998). He is editor of the Routledge series Library of Religious Beliefs and Practices.

Laurence R. Iannaccone is Professor of Ecoonomics at Chapman University. In more than fifty publications, Iannaccone has applied economic insights to study denominational growth, church attendance, religious giving, international trends, and many other aspects of religion and spirituality. He is currently writing two books on the economics of religion.

Darlene Juschka is Associate Professor in Women's and Gender Studies and Religious Studies. Several of her more recently published articles include 'Deconstructing the Eliadean Paradigm: Symbol.' In Willi Braun and Russell T. McCutcheon, eds. *Introducing Religion: Essays in Honor of Jonathan Z. Smith*, 163–177. London: Equinox Publishers, 2008. Released in 2001 was her anthology *Feminism in the Study of Religion: a Reader*, while her newest text *Political Bodies, Body Politic: The Semiotics of Gender* is scheduled for release in the fall of 2009 through Equinox Press.

Richard King is Professor of Religious Studies at Vanderbilt University in Nashville, Tennessee (USA). He is a specialist of classical Hindu and Buddhist thought, postcolonial approaches to the study of religion and the comparative study of mysticism. He is the author of four books: *Early Advaita Vedanta and Buddhism* (State University of New York Press, 1995), *Orientalism and Religion, Postcolonial Theory, India and 'the Mystic East'* (Routledge, 1999); *Indian Philosophy. An Introduction to Hindu and Buddhist Thought* (Edinburgh University Press, 1999) and (co-authored with Jeremy Carrette) *Selling Spirituality. The Silent Takeover of Religion* (Routledge, 2005).

Kim Knott is Professor of Religious Studies at the University of Leeds and Director of Diasporas, Migration and Identities, a strategic research programme funded by the UK Arts and Humanities Research Council. Her books include *Hinduism: A Very Short Introduction*, translated into a dozen languages, and *The Location of Religion: A Spatial Analysis*. She is currently working, with Seán McLoughlin, on an edited collection on *Diasporas: Concepts, Identities, Intersections*, and, with Thomas A. Tweed, on a sourcebook for the geography of religion.

Mary Ellen Konieczny is Assistant Professor of Sociology in the Center for the Study of Religion and Society at the University of Notre Dame. Her book manuscript (in progress), *The Spirit's Tether: Religion, Work, and Family among American Catholics*, is an ethnographic study exploring how religion shapes perceptions and practices of gender relations, sexuality and childrearing among middle class Catholics.

Gordon Lynch is Professor of Sociology of Religion and Director of the Centre for Religion and Contemporary Society at Birkbeck College, University of London. He was one of the founders of the UK Research Network for Theology, Religion and Popular Culture. He is the author and editor of a number of books and articles on religion and contemporary culture, including *Understanding Theology and Popular Culture* (Blackwell, 2005) and *Between Sacred and Profane: Researching Religion and Popular Culture* (ed., IB Tauris, 2007).

Luther H. Martin is Professor of Religion at the University of Vermont. He is the author of *Hellenistic Religions* (1987) and of numerous articles in this area of his historical specialization. He has also published widely in the field of theory and method in the study of religion, most recently, in the area of cognitive theory and historiographical method. In this latter area, he is co-editor of *Past Minds: Studies in Cognitive Historiography* (in press). He is currently President of the International Association for the Cognitive Science of Religion.

Seán McLoughlin is Senior Lecturer in the department of Theology and Religious Studies at the University of Leeds, UK. He has published numerous journal articles, book chapters and reports on religion and ethnicity, diaspora and identity amongst the Pakistani and Kashmiri heritage Muslims in Britain. Most recently, Dr McLoughlin has been the Principal Investigator on a UK Arts and Humanities Research Council network, *From Diaspora to Multi-Locality: Writing British-Asian Cities* (2006–2009), and is presently preparing a related co-edited volume. He is the co-editor of *European Muslims and the Secular State* (Ashgate, 2005).

Chad Meister is Professor of Philosophy at Bethel College. His written and edited books include *Introducing Philosophy of Religion* (Routledge), *The Routledge Companion to Philosophy of Religion* (Routledge), *The Philosophy of Religion Reader* (Routledge), *The Oxford Handbook of Religious Diversity* (Oxford University Press, 2010), and *Evil: A Guide for the Perplexed* (Continuum, forthcoming).

Dan Merkur is a psychoanalyst in private practice in Toronto and a Visiting Scholar in the Study of Religion at the University of Toronto. He has taught religious studies at five universities and published eleven books in the history and/or psychoanalysis of religion, including *Psychoanalytic Approaches to Myth* (Routledge, 2005).

George Moyser is Professor and Chair of the Department of Political Science at the University of Vermont in the United States. He has published several books and numerous articles on the relationship of religion and politics in Europe including, *Politics and Religion in the Modern World* (Routledge), *Church and Politics in a Secular Age* (The Clarendon Press) (with Kenneth Medhurst), and *Church and Politics Today* (T and T Clark).

Henry Munson is a Professor of Anthropology at the University of Maine. He is the author of *The House of Si Abd Allah: The Oral History of a Moroccan Family, Islam and Revolution in the Middle East*, and *Religion and Power in Morocco*, all published by Yale University Press. His essays on the comparative study of militant religious conservatism have appeared in *Daedalus, Religion, Religion Compass, Britannica Online, The Routledge Companion to the Study of Religion*, and *The Blackwell Companion to the Study of Religion*.

William E. Paden is Professor, Department of Religion, at the University of Vermont. He is the author of *Interpreting the Sacred: Ways of Viewing Religion* (second edn, 2003), and *Religious Worlds: The Comparative Study of Religion* (second edn, 1994), as well as numerous articles on theory and method.

Martin Riesebrodt is Professor of Sociology at the University of Chicago. His earlier work has focused on fundamentalist movements and the sociology of Max Weber. Recently he has published an interpretative theory of religion (*The Promise of Salvation. A Theory of Religion*. Chicago: University of Chicago Press, 2009).

Robert A. Segal is Sixth Century Chair in Religious Studies, University of Aberdeen. He is the author of, among other books, *Theorizing About Myth* (Massachusetts, 1999), and *Myth: A Very Short Introduction* (Oxford, 2004). He is the editor of, among other books, *The Blackwell Companion to the Study of Religion* (Blackwell, 2006), and *Myth: Critical Concepts* (Routledge, 2007).

Eric J. Sharpe, in his early career, taught at the Universities of Lancaster and Manchester. In 1977 he was appointed to the First Chair of Religious Studies in Australia, at the University of Sydney, which he held until his retirement in 1996. His publications in the fields of religious studies and missiology include *Comparative Religion: A History* (1975), *Understanding Religion* (1983), *Karl Ludvig Reichelt, Missionary, Scholar and Pilgrim* (1984) and *Nathan Söderblom and the Study of Religion* (1990). Eric Sharpe died on 19 October, 2000.

Donald Wiebe is Professor of Philosophy of Religion in the Faculty of Divinity at Trinity College, University of Toronto. He is a co-founder of the North American Association for the Study of Religion and of the recently established Institute for the Advanced Study of Religion. His publications include *Truth and Religion, Beyond Legitimation, The Irony of Theology and the Nature of Religious Thought*, and *The Politics of Religious Studies*.

John Wolffe is Professor of Religious History at the Open University, where he has contributed to numerous courses, and edited *Religion in History: Conflict, Conversion and Coexistence* (Manchester UP, 2004). His other publications include *God and Greater Britain: Religion and National Life in Britain and Ireland 1843–1945* (Routledge, 1994) and *The Expansion of Evangelicalism: The Age of Wilberforce, More, Chalmers and Finney* (InterVarsity Press, 2006).

Introduction

Religions do not exist, nor are they studied, in a vacuum. While the first edition of this book was being prepared, major international events have rocked societies and their religions: the attack on the Twin Towers in New York and on the Pentagon on 9/11; the wars in Iraq and Afghanistan, ever more brutal battles between Palestinians and Jews appear to have pitched Christianity, Islam and Judaism against each other. Bombs in Bali, Kenya and London, terrorist attacks in Mumbai, wars in Sudan and Somalia, crisis in Zimbabwe and the global credit crunch have turned societies upside down as fears of nuclear war grow with tensions rising and falling between India and Pakistan and with developments in North Korea and Iran, the world appears under threat. With the break up of the old Soviet Union, countries have been opened up to Christian missionaries and New Religious Movements, so religions have become more prominent on the world stage.

This book looks at the many perspectives from which religion may be viewed. The first edition (2005) was well received but this second edition is larger with eight new chapters as well as revisions and updating to the others. It starts by looking at different answers to the question 'Why study religion?' It is important to know how we got to where we are in the subject and how scholars have theorized about religion. The chapter by Eric Sharpe maps the historical picture of the growth of religious studies down to the 1960s and the chapter by Greg Alles covers the period since then. Contrary to popular opinion there are many approaches and disciplines involved in the study of religions; each is discussed here in a separate chapter. Robert Segal discusses theories of religion. The obvious routes into the subject are theology and religious studies, though there is much debate about the relationship between the two. In America there are signs of a growing difference whereas in Britain the two appear to be coming together as can be seen in the chapters by David Ford and Don Wiebe. The historical approach is clearly an important one in the study of religions and is discussed here by John Wolffe. Philosophy of religion is a well established route in many cultures, which is discussed by Chad Meister. A very different approach is the phenomenology of religion – where the term phenomenology is used differently from wider philosophy as discussed by Douglas Allen. There are various social and/or scientific ways of studying religion. The sociological study of religion is of growing importance and is discussed here by Martin Riesebrodt and Mary Ellen Konieczny. Authors were asked to look particularly at recent developments in their subjects; Rosalind Hackett exemplifies this in her chapter on anthropology by avoiding the all-too-common tour of nineteenth-century theorists. 'Psychology of religion' is an umbrella term for a number of approaches which are discussed by Dan Merkur. Many different approaches are used in the comparative study of religion as discussed by William Paden.

Whichever methodological approach one pursues there are a number of key issues addressed by scholars involved with religions. Gender is obviously an important subject and is addressed here by Darlene Juschka. An issue which is often discussed is the problems caused by insider and outsider perspectives as discussed by Kim Knott. Jeremy Carrette discusses some of the key developments in post structuralist theories of religion. 'Orientalism' has been a subject of recent debate and the issues related to religions are discussed by Richard King who also discusses issues concerning mysticism and spirituality. Theories of secularization and studies of New Religious Movements are discussed by Judith Fox. Contrary to what 'rationalist' approaches to society might have expected, fundamentalism (often a misused term) seems to have become more prominent in various cultures and countries (Henry Munson). Myths and rituals are interpenetrating and central to religions and cultures (Robert Segal). The question of authority is a major feature in most traditions, both in the sense of religious individuals and their charisma, and in the sense of authoritative texts (Paul Gifford). Of course texts are not static; the words may not change, but their interpretation does – an issue at the heart of hermeneutics (Garrett Green). Religions do not exist in a vacuum so there are chapters on how religions have been involved in, interacted with or been seen through the prism of politics (George Moyser), popular culture (Gordon Lynch), the financial world (Larry Iannaccone and William Bainbridge), advances in scientific discoveries and thought (Thomas Dixon) and environmental concerns (Roger Gottlieb). Increasingly scholars have become interested in the notion of sacred space (Kim Knott). The chapter on religion and cognition by Luther Martin looks at one of the most challenging forms of current approaches to religious studies. Back in the 1960s and 1970s international migration increased dramatically. It was assumed by many that migrants would, over a couple of generations, 'assimilate' and leave their religion behind. The reverse has happened, resulting in the growth of the study of diasporas (Sean McLoughlin). As religions have met and interacted – and sometimes experienced tensions – so religious pluralism has become an issue that many people have had to address (Michael Barnes).

There have been numerous debates about definitions and presuppositions in the study of religion. Many scholars have questioned whether there is any such 'thing' as religion, there are only the religions. But some have gone further and questioned the value of the terms 'religion' at all. In various languages, Sanskrit for example, there is no word for 'religion'. Is 'religion' a Western construct imposed on various cultures as a part of intellectual imperialism? It has been said that words mean what we want them to. My own opinion is that the word 'religions' is useful, but should be used with caution.

The ease of travel, large migrations to and from many countries and the growth of the internet and the media have resulted in the interaction of cultures at a global level. The 'other' is encountered more often, more closely and by more people than ever before. Whereas some religions were remote and exotic, now they are part of the local scenery for many.

Students on many courses become fretful when studying theory and method. However, the more complex the subject, the more important such issues are. When the subject is one as full of sensitivities, presuppositions and prejudices as the study of religions is, then it is essential, from the outset, the student is alerted to debates and doubts and that key issues, motives, aims and academic beliefs are fore-grounded – that is why my own assumptions and interests are articulated frankly and explicitly in the first chapter. I spent much time reflecting on the value of a section on the definition of such important terms as 'religion', but others, such as Mark Taylor, have done that, and for shorter articles students can consult my *New Penguin Dictionary of Religions*. I thought this book should be on theoretical approaches and key issues at the heart of debates in the study of religions. There is no one 'right' way to study religions. One 'wrong' way is dogmatism – that does not appear in this volume. Not only are there different approaches, there are also different opinions and emphases and much enthusiasm for the subjects (the singular is best avoided!). The publishers suggested that I indicate how the book may be used by students on courses. Had it been available during the forty years in which I taught the subject at undergraduate level, I would have woven a seminar around each chapter; if it were at (post)graduate level I would have required students to have read the relevant chapter before a lecture or seminar. However it is used, I hope students find it useful.

In planning the book, authors were invited who are specialists and leaders in their field, on the basis that an introduction to a subject can be the most influential literature a student ever reads. It is often the person who has real command of the subject who is the person with the vision to give the best overview. Each author received the same author's brief on length, treatment of material and bibliography. Inevitably some kept 'closer' to the brief than others; equally inevitably some have different perceptions of what are the appropriate issues and levels for students in their first year of studying religions. Such are the facts of life for every editor. Nor is it necessarily a bad thing. The students using the book will be different and it is foolish to invite senior scholars to contribute and then to put them all into a straitjacket. Furthermore, some topics are better handled in one way rather than another. But all authors have been willing to discuss and amend their text.

The structure of the book follows broadly the structure of the introductory course I taught at the School of Oriental and African Studies in London University, some of the time with one of the contributors, Dr Judith Fox; she joined the course to the benefit and delight of both myself and the students. It has been amended in the light of discussions with Professors Rosalind Hackett and Don Wiebe in the early stages, and Professor Robert Segal has helped considerably on several occasions. I am indebted to all of them, although I take responsibility for any failing in the overall conception and execution of the book. I would like to dedicate my work in this book to Eric Sharpe, a long-standing close friend, who finished his chapter for this book only a few days before his death.

John R. Hinnells

Chapter 1

Why study religions?

John R. Hinnells

Introduction

Are the study of theology and religious studies only for religious people? If you are religious, should you not get on and practise your religion rather than study it? If you are studying religions, should you not get on with that – studying them – rather than discussing abstract theories and debates on methods? The answer to each of these questions is 'no'. Obviously many people do wish to study religion if they are religious, because they want to know more about their own religion, or be able to see their religion in the context of others. Some people find studying religion helps to develop their own spiritual journey, be they Christian, Jewish, Buddhist, Zoroastrian or whatever. Students in most fields object to starting a subject by lectures on theory and method. But it is necessary to be aware of the different disciplinary perspectives used, and to be alert to some of the key issues that affect basic presuppositions.

But why study religions if you are not religious and/or do not want to become religious? As a professor of the comparative study of religion, the first question I am commonly asked when meeting people is – 'which religion do you belong to?' Those who know me to be an atheist, often ask why I spend most of my life studying something I believe to be wrong? Indeed one might go further. I incline to the view that religions are dangerous because more people have been tortured and killed for religious reasons than for any other motive. Persecution, the torture and killing of heretics and people of other religions have been major themes running through much of world history. At a personal level a religion can be helpful, supportive and even joyous for many people. But equally many are tortured by feelings of guilt or shame because they cannot live according to the ideals of their religion, or cannot in conscience accept doctrines they are expected to hold.

Of course one does not have to agree with something in order to study it. Students of the Holocaust do not have to agree with Hitler and his followers. One can learn something about history, about oneself, from studying even evil forces. But why have whole departments of theology and religious studies? Why have such financial and human resources been invested in the subject if it is harmful or marginal, and for which one has no attachment? Increasingly sociology, psychology, history, philosophy departments in the twentieth and twenty-first centuries have moved religious studies towards the margins of their subject. One does not have to be ill to become a doctor but one does have to want to care for and aid the sick to be a doctor – why study religions if one does not wish to encourage people to be religious? Some universities have it in their constitution that they shall not teach or research religion – University College London and Liverpool are two examples in Britain.

Despite my own non-religious position, however, I want to argue that the study of religions is vital and not only for 'the Hitler principle' that one should never ignore forces for destruction (nor is it because religions have sometimes been forces for good), but because of the massive power that religions have wielded, something that no one can deny. I question whether one can understand any culture and history – political or social – without understanding the relevant religions. This is true not only of 'the Holy Roman Empire' or the Islamic conquest of Iran, i.e. in past history; it is true in the twenty-first century as well. Although the situation in Northern Ireland is complex it cannot be denied that there are strong religious motives involved in the conflict there; there is sectarian hatred. Christian Serbians were killing Muslims in the former Yugoslavia; Muslims in many countries believe that the West is anti-Muslim and many fear that if there is another World War it will be between Islam and the Christian world.

Originally my intention had been to write a standard survey of academic arguments for and against such studies. Obviously one only writes an Introduction to a book when all the material is in. Having read all the chapters it is clear that there are several scholarly and well-written articles in this book surveying the field. So I concluded that this should be a personal piece based on forty years of university teaching, also to make explicit my motive in producing the book and why it is structured with certain emphases. It means that most examples will be taken from my specialist field – the Parsis and their religion Zoroastrianism. There is no single argument for why and how one studies religions. Many readers will reject my arguments completely and that is perfectly reasonable; maybe where this book is used for a course an early seminar discussion on the subject may be 'why study religions?' The basic question to be addressed is: why should an atheist want to study religions? First, it is necessary at the start of a book of this nature to discuss what one means by the term 'religion'.

Defining religion

There have been endless discussions of the definition of 'religion'. Indeed recently some scholars have argued for avoiding the word 'religion' as meaningless and have argued instead for the term 'culture'. This introduction is not a place for extensive debate, but rather as a place for explaining where I am 'coming from' as editor of this book, but it would be a mistake not to indicate my position on this primary issue of saying what is meant by the word 'religion'. In my opinion there is no such thing as 'religion', there are only the religions, i.e. those people who identify themselves as members of a religious group, Christians, Muslims, etc. An act or thought is religious when the person concerned thinks they are practising their 'religion'. Organizations are religious when the people involved think they are functioning religiously. In some societies in East Asia a person may have, say, a Christian initiation, a Buddhist wedding and a Chinese funeral; in my understanding, at the moment they are acting, say, in a Christian way, then at that moment they are a Christian. Of course the boundaries of those groups are fluid – so some people who claim to be, say, Muslims are not accepted by the majority of that religion as being 'true' Muslims. My general position in discussing religions is that people are what they believe they are. I am cautious about replacing 'religion' with 'culture' (Fitzgerald 2000, see also McCutcheon 2001) partly because that simply moves the debate on to the question of what is meant by 'culture'. But many others see culture as something that includes religion, but that also has much wider connotations. The Parsis, for example, have what they see as their culture in addition to their religion. The equivalent term is *Parsi panu* (Parsi-ness), and it includes non-religious dress (e.g. the Parsi style of a sari in contrast to the religious garments, the sacred shirt and cord, *sudre* and *kusti*), drama (*nataks* – in Gujarati, rather bawdy but huge fun – and never on religious themes) and their own highly distinctive way of cooking *dhansak*. All these are Parsi favourites, common not only in the old country but also in the diaspora. They would interpret such items as parts of Parsi culture but not part of their Zoroastrian religion. Parsis who say they are not Zoroastrians (either because they are not religious or if they have converted to, say, Christianity) are still likely to enjoy *Parsi panu*. Some of my colleagues disagree with the use of the phrase 'the religious dimension' of a situation or event. I do not wish to imply that there is any 'thing' out there that is religious. But events, like people, are complex, and can have both religious and secular dimensions; having one does not exclude the other. An act is a religious act when the person involved believes it to be associated with their religion. A religious thought is a thought which the thinker thinks is Zoroastrian (Christian, etc.). Of course I recognize that the situation is far from clear-cut. What of 'cultures' that have no word for 'religion', as in Sanskrit, and where the term for a religion is anachronistic, for example the term 'Hinduism', which is a modern West-imposed label for a plethora of different groups, beliefs and practices across a large continent with some purely local phenomena. 'Hinduism' exists in the diaspora communities because of compliance with use of Western categories, e.g. to obtain charitable status. Ninian Smart's use of the term 'world views' has some merits, but prioritizes the belief aspect of religion that is inappropriate elsewhere, e.g. Parsis for whom 'religion' is to do with individual identity; it is something in the blood or genes, to do with community boundaries and associated practices but with little or no reference to beliefs. In the case of Zoroastrianism, 'religion' is appropriate since there is a term (*den*) that it is reasonable to translate as 'religion'. All 'labels' have limitations and these must be accepted, so 'religion' is a useful but potentially misleading term.

Religions and politics

The former British Prime Minister, Margaret Thatcher, once argued strongly that religion was a private matter of belief (therefore bishops should not get involved in political debates as they were doing). But I believe that in this assertion she was completely wrong. Religions and religious leaders have rarely been outside politics, be they Jesus, Muhammad or Gandhi. Christianity was a driving force in Spanish, Portuguese and British empire-building. With the first two there was a powerful urge for converts as well as fortunes. The British came to stress 'the white man's burden' of 'civilizing the natives' (though fortunes and converts were also welcome!).

Partition in South Asia in 1947 sought to create separate Muslim and Hindu nations. These countries have been to war, or on the brink of it, many times in the following decades (though, now that there are more Muslims in India than in Pakistan, the religious divisions no longer follow the original policy). The showing and sales of videos of the two Indian epics, the *Ramayana* and the *Mahabharata* stoked (probably unwittingly) the fires of Indian nationalism, and the radical BJP (Bharatiya Janata Party) party came to power. A touchstone was the Hindu claim to the site of the mosque at Ayodhya, which they claimed was built over an important Hindu temple (Van der Veer). Many looked on in horror at the Hindu attacks on Muslims, the mob violence and the torching of Muslim homes in Bombay and Gujarat by Hindu militants in the early 1990s. The sorry tale of religious violence extends over all continents.

In the contemporary world the various religions seem to be even more prominent: the Israeli conviction that the land of Israel is God's gift to them has led to attempts to eject or impose themselves over the Palestinians (who respond with suicide missions). The reason why it is thought American governments ignore Israel's breaking of UN resolutions is due to the powerful Jewish lobby in the US; rightly or wrongly many Muslims believe it be an anti-Islam stance. The Shah was overthrown in 1979 for various reasons, but a major factor was the popular uprising led by Ayatollah Khomeini on the grounds that American influence had become more important to the government than Islam. It is difficult to believe that the invasion of Iraq in 2003/4 is legitimately explained simply by the terrible massacre of thousands in the destruction of the Twin Towers in New York on 9/11. It is not only that there is little evidence of Iraqi government involvement in al Qaeda activity; it is highly unlikely because Saddam Hussein was not a particular ally of a movement that opposed his secularizing tendencies. President Bush and Prime Minister Blair, both of whom have made public their Christian religious position, sought 'regime change' through invasion or 'a crusade' as Bush called it. For Muslims in many countries this was seen as a Christian assault on Islam and the consequences will almost certainly be with us for many years and may well have brought al Qaeda's ideology into Iraq and provoked more militant Muslims in many countries. Many fear it might bring nearer a war between the Christian 'West' and Islam. Terrorist activity in America, England, India and Spain, for example, has increased since 9/11 and increases the concern about such a war, and the invasion of Afghanistan raises wider concerns prompting some Muslims to see this as a further Christian–Western invasion of Muslim countries.

Some writers suggest such acts are not the outcome of 'real' or 'true' Christianity/Islam, etc., rather they suggest this is people using a religion to justify their violence; it is not, they say, that religion is the cause of the problems. Even the fighting in Northern Ireland between Catholics and Protestants is often put down to other causes. Doubtless there are a variety of factors in most conflicts, but religions are often potent factors in the explosions of violence. Of course religions can also be at the forefront of movements for peace and justice; for example Gandhi's non-violent campaign; Archbishop Desmond Tutu in South Africa; the Reverend Martin Luther King with his dream in America; and the bishops' stand taken against the corrupt dictators in South America with 'Liberation theology'. How can anyone doubt the importance of studying religions when they are such potent forces?

Religion and culture

Is it possible to understand another culture without looking at the appropriate religion practised there, be that in ancient Egypt or modern America? (It should be noted that the term 'culture' is a contested one, see Masuzawa in Taylor 1998: 70–93.) It is often difficult to say which came first, the religion or the values and ideals – but basically it does not matter; they are now part of an intricate network. In pre-modern times most artwork was produced for use in the relevant religion. How can one study the art without understanding its use and context? Whether the student/teacher/writer is religious or not, one cannot – should not – fail to study the religion of the culture. A study of the history of Gothic churches or of artefacts from primal societies in North America or Africa or the Pacific without setting them in their religious context is inevitably going to fail to understand their importance and 'meaning'. The artist may or may not have been inspired by the religion of his region but it is important to know something of the culture in which the object was produced and used, and religions are commonly an important part of that culture.

In the contemporary world, interaction with other cultures is inevitable, with trade, in the news, when travelling or just watching television; meeting a different cultural tradition is inevitable for most people. To understand a religion, it is essential to have an awareness of the different sets of values and ideals, customs and ethical values. Even if the people one meets from the 'other' culture are not religious, nevertheless their principles, values and ideals will commonly have been formed by the religion of their culture. Although an atheist, I have no doubt that my value system has been formed by Christianity, specifically Anglican Christianity. My attitudes to gender relations, prioritizing one set of values over another, what I consider to be 'good and bad', have all been affected by my general background of which Christianity was a major part.

Racial and religious prejudices are major issues in the contemporary world. They are often interwoven so it is not clear whether someone is discriminated against for being, say, from Pakistan or because of prejudice against Islam, and either can be the excuse for violence. In the 1980s and 1990s I undertook a survey questionnaire among Zoroastrians in America, Australia, Britain, Canada, China, East Africa and Pakistan, and conducted a series of in-depth interviews with Zoroastrians in France and Germany. Many respondents believed that they had faced prejudice, especially in Canada, but there they said they had faced it mainly in obtaining a first job. Once you had shown that you were good at your work, they said, you were accepted. In America one-third of my respondents said that they had experienced discrimination, but what they feared even more was the threat of the 'melting pot' eroding their identity. Some scholars describe the 'melting pot' as a myth, and there have been different terms used, e.g. a 'salad bowl' of cultures. American respondents and informants thought that the 'melting pot' was a threatening reality. The countries in which most people said that they frequently faced discrimination were Germany and Britain – especially in schooling (Hinnells 2005). One major motive for me in pursuing the comparative study of religions (usually abbreviated, conveniently if unfortunately, to comparative religion) is to encourage knowledge and understanding between religions and cultures, based on the assumption that prejudice will be overcome if each knows more about the other. The media and many sections of society have stereotypical images of 'the other'. I hope that knowledge will result in understanding, and thereby better relations between peoples. Above all my 'quest' as a teacher is to enable students to 'see through the spectacles' of another culture. I do not believe that there is a block of knowledge that has to be conveyed. If someone can develop an empathetic understanding of one other culture, the result will be that they are more ready to empathize with other cultures as well. But am I wrong? Is it necessarily the case that the more you know about the other religion, the more you will think positively about people from that religion? Some might be alienated from it. Would people respect Hitler more if they knew more about him? Maybe my motives are 'woolly liberalism'. If I thought that, then I would feel I had wasted much of my academic life.

Some common presuppositions

Writers have a tendency to think that 'real' Islam is found in the Middle East and in Arabic texts; or 'real' Hinduism is found in Sanskrit texts. R. C. Zaehner, for example, wrote his widely used book *Hinduism*, without ever having been to India (when he went there he did not like it!). What resources he thought he needed to write about Hinduism were his books in his study and in the Bodleian library in Oxford. His methodological assumptions were shared by many of his contemporaries. Of course textual studies are important, both the 'sacred' texts but also their hermeneutical interpretation by later generations. One problem, however, is that these texts are commonly the domain of the intellectuals and the literary few – widespread literacy is a modern phenomenon, and still not present in many countries. Archaeology can yield important information, but by definition most of the artefacts unearthed tend to be those which were most durable, costly and therefore often came from the domain of the wealthy and powerful, not from the wider population. That is one reason why in this chapter I have stressed the importance of studying various art forms, both 'pop' and 'high' art. Meeting people from the religion studied (where possible) can be very important even if a student is studying ancient texts. It changes one's attitude when seeing how the religious literature is used. The study of religions needs to be 'polymethodic'.

There is a common tendency in religious studies to think of religions as monolithic wholes. It is now quite common to question if there is any such thing as Hinduism, but the same is less true of the study of other religions. For example, is there any such 'thing' as Christianity, or are there are many Christianities? Are Primitive Welsh Methodists a part of the same religion as the Russian Orthodox? Where does one draw the boundary of Christianity – does it include the Mormons or 'The Children of God' (now known as 'The Family'), a group which sought to express the love of God and Jesus through the practice of 'flirty fishing' following the Biblical injunction to become fishers of men (that practice has ceased but the movement remains active and somewhat 'unconventional' – see Van Zandt). Some American tele-evangelists seem to be from a very different religion from that practised in St Peter's in Rome – the Northern Ireland politician and preacher, the Reverend Ian Paisley, thinks so, judging by his tirades against the Pope. If a religious movement calls itself 'Christian' should it not be treated as part of Christianity – or one of the Christianities?

The new growth in religion: some key questions

In the 1960s many of us forecast that religions would gradually decline, especially, but not only, in the West – we were wrong! In studying religions it is important to ask why things happen and to understand why change comes about.

- In many Western cities, especially in America and the Middle East, but also in the new Russia, in Korea, in Mumbai, religious groups have become more prominent. Why?
- As far as Christianity is concerned, growth is pre-eminently among evangelicals and charismatic groups. Why?
- Whereas secularization was the theme of the 1960s and 1970s, there has been an increase in the number of New Religious Movements (NRMs). It is impossible to estimate the number of people involved, because many of the movements are small, and dual membership also happens. But the number of movements has increased. Why?
- The broad pattern of recruits to NRMs are middle aged, middle class, generally well educated – and often people who had sought but not found religious fulfilment in established religious groups. Why?
- The aspect of various religions that have become more prominent is what is labelled as 'fundamentalism'. Why?

In the 1970s and 1980s sociologists wrote from an entirely secular perspective about migration and diaspora groups in the West. The religion of the migrants and subsequent generations was ignored; they were simply labelled as Hindus, Muslims, etc., but there was rarely any discussion of patterns of religious change and continuity, nothing about how Hinduism/Islam, etc. have been shaped in the diaspora. Because the scholars were not themselves religious, they tended to look past the religion of the subjects they were writing about. The discussions were about prejudice, housing, working patterns – all, of course, issues of great importance, but writers ignored that which meant most for many migrants – religion.

There was another factor. Writing as someone involved in an aspect of government policy relating to migration in the 1960 and 1970s, frankly it was assumed that migrants' religions would fade over the years and generations as they assimilated. It was assumed that they had left their religion behind back in the old country. These ideas were completely wrong. Studies of transnational or diaspora communities at the turn of the millennium commonly found that migrants tend to be more religious after migration than they were before, because their religion gives them a stake of continuity in a sea of change. Further, recent studies are finding that what might be called the second generation's 'secular ethnicity' – their Pakistani/ Indian/Bangladeshi, etc. culture is not as meaningful to the young, who prefer to see themselves as Muslims/Hindus/Zoroastrians, etc. (see for example Williams 2000; Hinnells 2005). Religion is becoming the marker that many young people are taking up. Further, there was an assumption that migrants and their youngsters would be more liberal than the orthodox people back in the old country. This is not necessarily so. The religions of people in South Asia move on (I am less familiar with the literature on South East and East Asians in America); their religions are dynamic and change or 'evolve'. There the changes are often greater than among people in the diaspora, for, in the latter, continuity matters in individual or group identity. An example of this would be the militancy among Sikhs in Britain, and especially in Canada, which was stronger than it was in India following the attack on the Golden Temple. The diaspora impacts on the old country. Since the 1970s the biggest source of income for Pakistan was money sent 'home' by families working overseas.

One common question in many religions is that of authority. To use a Parsi example again: in 1906 in a test case in the Bombay High Court it was decided that the offspring of a Parsi male married out of the community could be initiated, but not the offspring of an intermarried woman because Parsi society was a patrilineal one (there were also some caste-like debates). That judgement continues to be followed by most Parsis in post-colonial, independent India – and by many Parsis in the diaspora. Technically the authority of the High Priests (*Dasturs*) in India is within the walls of their temples (*Atash Bahrams*). But among the traditional/orthodox members in the diaspora their judgements carry considerable weight. These issues came to a head in the 1980s over an initiation in New York of a person neither of whose parents were Zoroastrians. When the furore erupted, opinions in America were evenly divided over whether the authority of a 1906 Bombay High Court judgment in the days of the British Raj, and of the priests 'back' in India, was binding over groups in the West in the third millennium. Lines of authority become complex as religious people adapt to new social, legal and cultural settings.

There is another vitally important factor in the study of religions in their diasporas, namely the implications of religious beliefs and practices of transnational groups for public policy in their new Western homes. Some obvious examples are the implications for healthcare. Since attitudes to pain and suffering are different in different religions or cultures, it can be essential that doctors and nurses are sensitive to, and are therefore knowledgeable about, values, and the priorities of their patients (Hinnells and Porter 1999; Helman 1994). The problems are even more acute in the case of psychiatric illness because what might seem 'abnormal' behaviour in one society may not in another (Rack 1982; Bhugra 1996; Littlewood and Lipsedge 1997; Honwana 1999 on the damage which 'Western' psychological practice can inflict on – in this case – African peoples who had experienced the trauma of the massacres in Mozambique). Perhaps the instance where informed sensitivity relating to religious/cultural values is of greatest need surrounds death and bereavement. Having 'a good death', the 'proper' treatment of the body and support for the bereaved all matter hugely to people of any culture. 'Doing the right thing' is emotionally vital and that commonly involves religious beliefs and practices even for those who do not consider themselves religious. (Spiro *et al.* 1996; Howarth and Jupp 1996; Irish *et al.* 1993, the last of these is particularly good on a wide range of minority groups in America, e.g. Native Americans.)

The presence of a huge range of religious groups, be that in Australia, Britain, Canada or the USA and elsewhere, has serious implications for social policy and national laws, problems both for the minorities and for governments because many religious traditions evolved outside a Western legal orbit (and others which have not, e.g. the Mormons and polygamy). The obvious example is concerning gender issues where some traditions are in conflict with Western concepts of human rights (Nesbitt 2001; Hawley 1994; Sahgal and Yuval Davis 1992; Gustafson and Juviler 1999). Policymakers concerned with schools and educational policy, crime and punishment all have a need to pay serious attention to the religions in their midst, the values, priorities and principles (see Haddad and Lummis 1987) especially at times such as the start of the twenty-first century, when Muslim feelings run high and where governments all too readily stigmatize minorities; when there is violence, invasion and wars; when there is a breakdown in aspects of human rights, for example the rights of prisoners. Ignoring religious issues and feelings can be exceedingly dangerous.

Change in the new world

Not only do religions change, so too do the countries to which people migrate. Perhaps the country which has changed the most is the USA. Prior to the Hart-Cellar Act of 1965 migration was only from Northern Europe and was mostly of English speakers. Gradually South and East Europeans were allowed in, but from the 1970s Asians were admitted, providing they fitted the criteria of US interests, admitting in particular the highly educated, especially scientists and people in the medical profession. There have long been migrants, many illegal, from Mexico to undertake menial tasks, but with the arrival of educated Asians, perceptions of 'the other' began to change. Black settlers from the days of slavery became accepted in a way hardly imaginable in the early 1960s; so that 'People of Color' can occupy places of high office, including Obama becoming President of the USA. Attitudes to Asian cultures had changed briefly in the 1890s with the Parliament of World Religions in Chicago and in particular the teaching 'missions' of Swami Vivekananda. But it was mainly from the 1960s that interest in Asian religions began, with Rajneesh, the Maharishi, Reverend Moon and the work of the Krishna Consciousness movement. Many American cities have their China towns. In California there are 'villages' of nationalities, for example the Iranians settled near Los Angeles (in an area popularly known as 'Irangeles'). Refugees are not always the poor; many Iranians, for example, after the fall of the Shah brought their substantial wealth with them (see Naficy 1991). In the 1990s interest in 'Native' American religions grew. Hindu temples were built following the designs and bearing the images crafted by skilled traditional artists from India. The religious landscape of the US changed dramatically in some forty years (Eck 2000, 2002; Haddad 1991, 2000; Williams 1988, 2000; Warner and Wittner 1998). It, and the landscapes in Australia, Britain and Canada have all changed further in the third millennium (see Hinnells 2010).

In countries where there is substantial religious pluralism, inter-faith activity has been important. What has yet to be adequately studied is the impact of these activities. There are of course many benefits in developing active communications between groups, but I fear there may be problems not yet identified. On the Christian side it tends to be the Protestant churches who are involved, less so the Catholics who are numerically the biggest Christian denomination in the world. From the minority groups' side it tends to involve not necessarily the typical Hindu, Muslim, Zoroastrian, etc., rather those leaders whose linguistic and social skills enable them to interact with the 'outside world'. These 'gatekeepers' of the communities often emphasize the aspects of their religion that will find the most ready acceptance in the outside world, so with Zoroastrians they will emphasize the ancient (indeed the prophet Zoroaster's) emphasis on 'Good Thoughts, Good Words and Good Deeds' rather than, say, the purity laws. In time this sanitized version of the religion may impact back into the community. I read in one book of minutes from a Canadian Zoroastrian Group where the managing committee made a conscious decision to change the translation of an Avestan (roughly 'scriptural') text so that it would not offend Muslim guests. This is an issue which merits further study.

What of theology?

So far this chapter has focused on religious studies and comparative religion because this book is likely to be used mostly in the study of religions. For a member of any religion, its theology is important – the word is usually applied just to Christian thought, but there is comparable activity in most religions, certainly in Islam, Judaism and Zoroastrianism for example. (The late Ninian Smart often referred to Buddhology – and that may not be inappropriate.) 'Theologizing' is particularly important in many mystical groups, not least in Islam in the West (see Hinnells and Malik 2006). The Mullahs in Iraq and Iran have been prominent in recent times, exercising considerable influence over national politics with their teachings. For the billions of active religious people in the world, working out the implications of their crucial religious teachings for their daily life is of vital importance. Geography is far more important in the study of religions than is generally appreciated. Religious beliefs and ideas, symbols and practice, are naturally affected by social and geographical conditions in which the theology is elaborated. Religion in central New York is bound to have different symbols or images to cater for the different needs from those in a remote village in northern Scotland, which is in turn different in the deserts of Saudi Arabia or in India and Korea. I am fascinated by the differences between urban and rural patterns of religion. It is inevitable that if a theology is to be meaningful to a person, if it is 'to speak to that person', as many Christians would say, then it has to be different from that in a different environment. Such issues have probably been pursued more in the study of Buddhism, Hinduism or Islam than they have with Christianity (a notable exception is Ford 1997).

Can an atheist see the point in studying theology? Its value is that it addresses the big questions which many people want to ask – Who am I? Where do I come from? Where am I going? Why do the innocent suffer? What non-theologians often overlook with theology is the wide range of subjects involved – textual studies and languages, archaeology, philosophy, ethical issues, history and through applied theology there is an engagement with local communities. If theology was restricted to theological colleges and madressas, etc., the consequence would almost certainly be an increase in sectarian prejudice. But of course many people are religious, though they do not belong to a formal church yet they believe in a God.

A lot of people outside the churches, the mosques, temples, etc. yearn for a 'spiritual' life and to them the study of theology and religious studies can be fulfilling. Secularism may be strong in Britain, but in many other countries religion is alive and well, not least in America.

The comparative study of religions

I am convinced by Max Müller's dictum: 'He who knows one knows none', that is if you only study one religion, you are not studying religion, but just, say, Christianity (or Zoroastrianism, or Islam, etc.). It is only through some element of comparison that we appreciate just what is, and is not, characteristic of religions generally and what is specific to that religion. The term 'comparative study of religion' is widely suspected, because it was used by particular Western academics, mainly in the nineteenth century, who were trying to prove that Christianity was superior to other religions. Some huge theories about 'religion' were constructed by writers who ranged widely across different religions – from the comfort of their armchairs and without the necessary first-hand knowledge of texts in the original language or without knowing people from that religion. The term 'comparative religion' has also been associated with superficiality because you cannot 'really' know much about a range of religions. But if comparative linguistics and comparative law, etc. are valid subjects then so, surely, 'the comparative study of religion' can be too. Of course I reject any idea of trying to compare to show the superiority of any one religion. When one is comparing it is essential to compare what is comparable, so should we compare the whole of one religion with the whole of another? In my study of the Parsi diaspora, it was helpful to compare the Parsi experience with that of Jews, or Hindus or Sikhs, etc. in that same context, which usually, but not necessarily, means in the same city or region. It has also been helpful to compare Parsis in different countries, e.g. Britain, Canada and the US, or their experience in different cities in the US (e.g. Houston and Chicago). My theoretical question was 'how different is it being a religious Parsi, say, in Los Angeles or in London, or in Sydney or Hong Kong?' (Hinnells 2005). It is regrettable that there are not more comparative studies of diaspora religions in different countries so that we might discover what is, or are, *the* American (British/Australian/Canadian) experience(s). It can also be helpful to compare the theology of different religions, e.g. on issues of attitudes to the body partly for doctors and nurses, or for the understanding of social groups (Law).

Obviously the comparative study of religion should not be concerned only with the modern world. Earlier in my career I was passionately interested in the Roman cult of Mithras (first to fourth centuries CE). In order to understand what was significant about Mithraism it was important to learn about contemporary religious beliefs and practices in the Roman Empire. There was such a rich diversity of religious cults; Mithraism shared features with some (e.g. early Christianity) and not with others. In fact the key breakthrough in the study of Mithraism came when Gordon and Beck began to look at the contemporary Roman ideas on astrology (Beck). By taking a blinkered look at just one cult, it would have been impossible to interpret the archaeological finds of temples and statues (especially difficult because there are virtually no Mithraic texts, only inscriptions and the comments of outsiders). One of the things which disturbs me about some work in New Testament studies and in research on Christianity's early developments is that so much of the evidence is looked at only through the lens of the Judaeo-Christian traditions. Can one really understand the development of the liturgy of the Mass/Eucharist/Lord's Supper without looking at the role of sacred meals in the contemporary Roman religions? Nothing exists in a vacuum. It seems odd that so many books and courses on the philosophy of religion look at key figures such as Hume and Kant without looking at their contemporary world; or studying the Biblical work of Bultmann without looking at the anti-Semitic culture in which he lived and worked and which many would say coloured his account of Judaism. Taking the context seriously, comparing other related phenomena, is crucial.

Bias

What of the theme of insider/outside? Can a person outside the religion really understand what it is like to be a Zoroastrian – or whatever? Even after thirty-five years of living with and studying Zoroastrians I think it is impossible for me to understand them and their religion fully. I may get close to it, but as an outsider my instincts, my basic thoughts and aspirations, etc. are, for better or worse, English. Ultimately we cannot change our basic conditioning; we cannot step outside our identity. We may – should – seek to go as far as possible in empathy and with understanding but we are all products of our own history.

It is vital that students and scholars should be conscious of their own motivations or biases – because we all have them. It is the ones we are not aware of that are the most dangerous: to illustrate the point with a story against myself. I am currently writing a book about the Parsis of Bombay in the days of the Raj. The book's structure seemed clear: defining key periods, important individual and social groupings; having worked on the history of temples, doctrinal changes, visited India many times over thirty years, and having worked with a high priest and each of us having the other as a house guest, I felt close to the community. Then a book came out which collected the oral histories of a broad spectrum of Parsis; some highly educated some not, some famous others not, about their personal private religious feelings (Kreyenbroek with Munshi 2001). It made me realize that with my atheistic attitude, despite my contacts with many Parsis, I had completely failed to look at the widespread belief in the miraculous powers of prayer; the importance of mantras to preserve people from misfortune and to bless and aid them in a project, i.e. the reality of miracles for many people. I had failed to look for what I don't believe in.

There is, of course, the alternative danger of being biased in favour of your subject. One can normally tell the denomination of a Church historian, or a theologian, from his/her writings. Authors rarely draw conclusions at variance with the teaching in their denomination. The same can be true of internal accounts of other religions, for example Orthodox and Liberal accounts of Judaism. There is often an honourable desire when making a university teaching appointment to look for someone who knows the tradition from the inside, be (s)he Muslim, Jewish, Sikh, Hindu, etc. Of course they can have a depth of insight that is beyond the outsider. But, as with Christianity, in principle the appointment should be solely on academic grounds. Many of those grounds, e.g. linguistic facility, may well make an insider the right appointment. But in recent years there have been difficult cases where such an appointee has been summoned to their religious council of elders and reprimanded for not teaching a particular perspective. There have been cases where an insider from one section of a religion has denied the others were true believers, but were heretics. This has happened in Christianity also when in recent years some theologians had papal support withdrawn and were not allowed to teach in a Catholic institution because they had 'deviated' from authorized Church teaching. There can be difficulties with insiders, as well as with outsiders.

Some time ago a publisher asked me to write a book on Zoroastrianism and the Parsis for English schools. It began to be used by Parsis in their Sunday schools and in some adult education classes. When the English edition lapsed, the Parsis in Bombay reprinted it and still sell it there and in some other centres around the world. At first it seemed to be the greatest possible compliment. Gradually however I began to worry. When I visited some communities my own words were coming back at me. With plant photography one must take great care never to break or destroy anything that is being photographed. How much greater care should one take with a living religion (especially one that is declining numerically at a great rate)? Should you affect the people you study? Can you get too close to your 'field'? Is it fanciful to think that you can avoid having an impact? What is the impact of a group of students going to a mosque or temple? Does it change an act of worship if there is an 'audience' of outsiders watching?

Using the right words

There are numerous debates about the meaning of key terms such as 'religion', 'culture', 'race', etc. This section is not about these important terms (a useful book for that is Taylor 1998), but rather it is concerned with terms that raise religious issues.

The first is to do with translations for key religious concepts. An obvious one is: should one write 'Allah', or 'God'? My vocabulary changes according to the audience. With Zoroastrians and students I use 'Ahura Mazda' (Pahlavi: Ohrmazd) rather than 'God'. The danger is of unconsciously importing Christian notions into the concept of the ultimate. However, if talking to the general public or perhaps in a lecture that is not essentially about theology the word 'God' may be appropriate, otherwise there are so many technical words that the listener (or reader) will switch off. But there are some technical words that it is essential to use because their obvious equivalent Western term would give a misleading impression. For example the terms 'spirit and flesh' are inappropriate for the Zoroastrian concepts of *menog* and *getig*. The *menog* is the invisible, intangible, the realm of the soul, *getig* is the visible and tangible world, but the *getig* world is not a subordinate or 'lower' world; it is almost the fulfilment of the *menog* – it is its manifestation. There is nothing of the Hellenistic 'spirit and flesh' dualism. A Zoroastrian could never make the connection 'the world, the flesh and the devil' for the *getig* world is the Good Creation of Ohrmazd. Misery, disease and death are the assault of the evil force, Ahriman, on the Good Creation; human duty is to fight evil and protect the Good Creation so that at the renovation *menog* and *getig* will come together to form the best of all possible worlds. Zoroastrians do not use the term 'the end of the world' for that would be Ohrmazd's defeat; instead they refer to the 'renovation', the time when all will be restored or refreshed and again becomes perfect as it was before the assault of evil. 'Spirit and flesh' therefore involve a different cosmology from *menog* and *getig*.

Sometimes scholars use Christian terms for concepts or practices in order to help the reader but it can lead to misrepresentation. For example, Zaehner uses the word 'sacrament' to describe one of the higher Zoroastrian ceremonies, the *Yasna* in which the *haoma* (*soma* in Hinduism) plant is pounded with pestle and mortar. The ceremony is led by two priests and can be performed at a time of death or for blessings. Laity may attend but rarely do so for the priests offer it on their behalf. This is Zaehner's description of the rite:

> The Haoma … is not only a plant … it is also a god, and the son of Ahura Mazdah. In the ritual the plant-god is ceremonially pounded in a mortar; the god, that is to say is sacrificed and offered up to his heavenly Father. Ideally Haoma is both priest and victim – the Son of God, then offering himself up to his heavenly Father. After the offering

priest and faithful partake of the heavenly drink, and by partaking of it they are made to share in the immortality of the god. The sacrament is the earnest of everlasting life which all men will inherit in soul and body in the last days. The conception is strikingly similar to that of the Catholic Mass.

(Zaehner 1959: 213)

Of course the Catholic convert, Zaehner, intended this as a very respectful account of the rite. But it bears no resemblance whatever to the Zoroastrian understanding of the ritual. There is a huge danger in failing to see the religion through the insider's spectacles.

An earlier writer, J. H. Moulton, is another good example of well-intentioned scholarly misrepresentation of another religion. Moulton was a Professor of New Testament Studies but took a keen interest in Zoroastrianism. He was also a Methodist Minister. In his Hibbert Lectures in 1912, he applied contemporary Protestant methods of Biblical scholarship to the study of Zoroastrianism. He applied the contemporary assumption that religions are divided between the priestly or prophetic forms; the former being associated with superstition and the latter with visionary, personal religious experience. He argued that since Zoroaster was clearly a prophet he could not have been a priest, so when Zoroaster refers to himself as a priest (which he explicitly did) then Moulton concluded he must have been speaking metaphorically. He concluded:

That Zarathushtra is teacher and prophet is written large over every page of the Gathas [the poetic passages deriving from Zoroaster himself]. He is perpetually striving to persuade men of the truth of a great message, obedience to which will bring them everlasting life … He has a revelation … There is no room for sacerdotal functions as a really integral part of such a man's gospel; and of ritual or spells we hear as little as we expect to hear …

(p. 118)

A traditional Zoroastrian (or a Catholic Christian for that matter) would not make such a distinction between priestly and prophetic religion. These are but two examples of a widespread trend to impose Western ways of thinking, or methods of analysis, on non-Western phenomena. Misrepresentation does not arise only from prejudice against a religion, but can come equally from the well-intentioned scholar. Many scholars find it helpful to draw a typology of religions and these can be useful in classifying data, but they can also result in trying to fit data into a false dichotomy; it has to be 'either this, or that or that', etc. It rarely allows for 'this and that' – in Moulton's case either a prophet or a priest, but Zoroaster could be described as 'both … and'.

Some of the most common words used in writing about religion are inappropriate or at least demand substantial clarification. 'Praying' and 'prayers' are words used in many religions, for example, in Christianity and Zoroastrianism. But the activities they refer to are somewhat different. In Western Christianity, prayers are in the vernacular and it is thought important to know what the words mean. Be the prayers intercessions or thanksgiving, there is an element of conversation with God. Prayers in Zoroastrianism are rather different. They should be in the ancient 'scriptural' Avestan language in which it is believed Zoroaster prayed to Ohrmazd. It does not matter if the worshipper does not understand them, indeed orthodox Parsi priests in India argue that it is unhelpful to understand the words, for if you do then you think about what they mean and thereby limit yourself to mere human conceptual thought. By praying in

Avestan one seeks to share something of the visionary experience of the prophet, the purpose of prayer is to achieve direct experience of Ohrmazd in a trance-like state.

There are numerous terms in common usage which have presuppositions that merit questioning. The term 'faith community' implies that 'faith', i.e. a set of beliefs, is what defines a community and that is a Christian and intellectual understanding of the 'other'. For Jews and Parsis religion is to do with identity, a question of community boundaries, it is to do with who or what you are, something that is in the blood, the genes. For Parsis in particular, identity, far more than any set of beliefs, is what matters. For Muslims also it is a questionable term, since 'just' believing is inadequate, Islam is a way of life.

Another term in common usage which can cause religious offence is 'Old Testament'. Orthodox Jews object to it for it implies old, redundant, replaced. Most say that they have become accustomed to this Christian abuse of their scripture. Their preferred term though is 'Hebrew Bible'. The usual Christian reaction is to point out that a part (but only a very small part) is in Aramaic. But should students of religion use terms and phrases that can cause religious offence? The question becomes sharper when the word is used in the naming of university departments, of academic societies and books.

Conclusion

Whether one is religious or not, the study of religions is a key to understanding other cultures; religions have been powerful forces throughout history in any country, sometimes working for good and sometimes working to destroy. They have inspired some of the greatest and most noble of acts; equally they have inspired some of the most ruthless brutality. They have been the patrons – and the destroyers – of arts and cultures. But they are central to much social and political history. Scholars who have left religions out of their pictures when writing about various societies, be they Hindus in Britain or Muslims in America, are excluding a key element from their study. It is essential to know the values, ideals and priorities of those from another culture or religion with whom one comes into contact. Globalization makes such contact with 'the other' common. Religions might be compared to diamonds; they have many facets; they can be seen from many angles, but the pictures are too complex for any one writer to see the whole. This book looks at a range of approaches to these diamonds.

Bibliography

Beck, R. 1984, 'Mithraism Since Franz Cumont', in Temporini, H. and Haase, W. (eds), *Aufstieg und Niedergang der Romischen Welt*, II, 17, 4, Berlin: Walter De Gruyter, pp. 2002–115.

Bhugra, D. 1996, *Psychiatry and Religion: Context Consensus and Controversies*, London: Routledge.

Coward H., Hinnells, J. R. and Williams, R. B. (eds) 2000, *The South Asian Religious Diaspora in Britain, Canada, and the United States*, Albany: State University of New York Press.

Eck, D. 2000, 'Negotiating Hindu Identities in America', in Coward *et al.* 2000, pp. 219–37.

—— 2002, *A New Religious America*, San Francisco: Harper Collins.

Fitzgerald, T. 2000, *The Ideology of Religious Studies*, Oxford: Oxford University Press.

Ford, D. 1997 (3rd edition 2005), *The Modern Theologians: An Introduction to Christian Theology in the Twentieth Century*, Oxford: Blackwells.

Gustafson, C. and Juviler, P. (eds) 1999, *Religion and Human Rights: Competing Claims?*, New York: M. E. Sharpe publishers.

Haddad, Y. Y. 1991, *The Muslims of America*, New York: Oxford University Press.

—— 2000, 'At Home in the Hijra: South Asian Muslims in the United States', in Coward *et al.* 2000, pp. 239–58.

—— and Lummis, A. T. 1987, *Islamic Values in the United States*, New York: Oxford University Press.

Hawley, J. S. (ed.) 1994, *Fundamentalism and Gender*, New York: Oxford University Press.

Helman, C. G. 1984 (3rd edn 1994), *Culture, Health and Illness*, Oxford: Butterworth-Heinemann.

Hinnells, J. R. 1996, *Zoroastrianism and the Parsis*, Mumbai: Zoroastrian Studies.

—— 1998, in Hinnells, *The New Penguin Handbook of Living Religions,* London: Penguin Books, pp. 819–47.

—— 2000, *Zoroastrian and Parsi Studies: Selected Works of John R. Hinnells*, Aldershot: Ashgate Publishing (esp. Chapters 16–18 for this chapter).

—— 2005, *The Zoroastrian Diaspora: Religion and Migration*, Oxford: Oxford University Press.

—— ed. 2007, *Religious Reconstruction in the South Asian Diaspora: from One Generation to Another*, Basingstoke and New York: Palgrave Macmillan.

—— (ed.) 2010, *The New Penguin Handbook of Living Religions of the World*, London: Penguin Books (a third edition with four new chapters on religions in the third millennium).

—— and King R. (eds), 2007, *Religion and Violence in South Asia, Theory and Practice*, Abingdon and New York: Routledge.

—— and Malik, J. (eds), 2006, *Sufism in the West*, Abingdon and New York: Routledge.

—— and Porter, R. (eds) 1999, *Religion, Health and Suffering*, London: Kegan Paul International.

Honwana, A. M. 1999, 'Appeasing the Spirits: Healing Strategies in Post War Southern Mozambique', in Hinnells and Porter (eds) 1999, pp. 237–55.

Howarth, G. and Jupp, P. C. 1996, *Contemporary Issues in the Sociology of Death, Dying and Disposal*, Basingstoke: Macmillan Press.

Irish, D. P., Lundquist, K. F. and Nelsen, V. J. (eds) 1993, *Ethnic Variations in Dying, Death, and Grief*, Washington DC: Taylor and Francis.

Kreyenbroek, P. with Munshi, Shahnaz N. 2001, *Living Zoroastrianism: Urban Parsis Speak About Their Religion*, Richmond: Curzon Press.

Law, J. M. (ed.) 1995, *Religious Reflections on the Human Body*, Bloomington: Indiana University Press.

Lewis, P. 2007, *Young, British and Muslim*, London and New York: Continuum.

Littlewood, R. and Lipsedge, M. 1982 (3rd edn 1997), *Aliens and Alienists: Ethnic Minorities and Psychiatry,* London: Routledge.

McCutcheon, R. 2001, *Critics not Caretakers: Redescribing the Public Study of Religion*, Albany: State University of New York Press.

Melton, J. G. 1991, *The Encyclopaedia of American Religions*, New York: Triumph Books, (3 vols).

Moulton, J. H. 1913, *Early Zoroastrianism*, London: Williams and Norgate.

Naficy, H. 1991, 'The Poetics and Practice of Iranian Nostalgia in Exile', *Diaspora*, 1:3, pp. 285–302.

Nesbitt, P. D. (ed.) 2001, *Religion and Social Policy*, Walnut Creek/Lanham: Altamira Press.

Rack, P. 1982, *Race, Culture and Mental Disorder*, London: Tavistock Publications.

Sahgal, G. and Yuval-Davis, N. (eds) 1992, *Refusing Holy Orders: Women and Fundamentalism in Britain*, London: Virago.

Spiro, H. M., McCrea Curnen, M. and Wandel, L. P. (eds) 1996, *Facing Death: Where Culture, Religion and Medicine Meet*, New Haven: Yale University Press.

Taylor, M. C. (ed.) 1998, *Critical Terms for Religious Studies*, Chicago: Chicago University Press.

Van de Veer, P. 1994, *Religious Nationalism: Hindus and Muslims in India*, Berkeley: University of California Press.

Van Zandt, D. E. 1991, *Living in the Children of God*, Princeton: Princeton University Press.

Warner, R. S. and Wittner, J. G. 1998, *Gatherings in Diaspora: Religious Communities and the New Immigration*, Philadelphia: Temple University Press.

Williams, R. B. 1988, *Religions of Immigrants from India and Pakistan*, Cambridge: Cambridge University Press.

—— 2000, 'Trajectories for Further Studies', in Coward *et al.* 2000, pp. 277–87.

Zaehner, R. C. 1959, 'Zoroastrianism' in Zaehner, R. C. (ed.), *Encyclopaedia of Living Faiths*, London: Hutchinson Books.
—— 1966, *Hinduism*, Oxford: Oxford University Press.

Suggested reading

Hadad, Y. Y. 1991, *The Muslims of America*, New York: Oxford University Press.
Hinnells, J. R. (ed.) 2007, *Religious Reconstruction in the South Asian Diaspora*, BJP.
Hinnells J. R. (ed.) 2010, *A New Handbook of the World's Living Religions*, London: Penguin, especially the last four chapters.
Lewis, P. 2007, *Young, British and Muslim*, London and New York: Continuum.

Chapter 2

The study of religion in historical perspective

Eric J. Sharpe

Motive, material, method

The academic study of anything requires that those involved should consider at least three questions: why, what and how? The first demands that we examine our *motive*; the second makes us consider our *material* – what do we accept as admissible evidence? The third, and most difficult, level of inquiry is concerned with *method*: how do we deal with the material we have at hand? How do we organize it, and with what end in view ('motive' again)? A century ago, it was not uncommon to speak in this connection of 'the science of religion' (German: *Religionswissenschaft*) – a form of words no longer current in English. What has been identified as the foundation document carried the title *Introduction to the Science of Religion* (Friedrich Max Müller 1873). According to Müller, such a science of religion was to be 'based on an impartial and truly scientific comparison of all, or at all events, of the most important religions of mankind' (1873: 34). It was, then, to be impartial and scientific by the standards of the age and based on the best material available at the time.

The history of the study of religion since the Enlightenment can never be told in full. There is simply too much of it, and it is subdivided in too many ways: by period, by geographical and cultural area and by the 'disciplines' cherished by most academics. The one history can be described as being made up of many smaller histories – for instance the history of the study of everything from Animism and Anabaptism to Zoroastrianism and Zen Buddhism. The field may be divided by subject matter; along national lines; depending on where in the world the tradition of study has been pursued; in relation to events in world and local history; and so on, virtually ad infinitum. No one can cover the whole of the area.

The words 'the study of religion' obviously convey different meanings to different people. For most of human history and in most cultures, they would have conveyed no meaning at all. To 'study' in the sense of standing back to take a coolly uncommitted view of anything, was not unknown in the ancient world, but it was uncommon, being cultivated by 'philosophers' – lovers of wisdom – but hardly elsewhere. Similarly, where what we call 'religion' is concerned: gods, goddesses, spirits, demons, ghosts and the rest, people knew and generally respected them (along with what it was hoped was the right way to please, or at least not to offend them); 'religion' they did not.

These supernatural beings – who were they? In the ancient world, they were envisaged in human terms: a hierarchy reaching all the way from a royal family down through nobles and artisans to mischief-makers: imps and demons of the sort who spread disease and curdle milk. There were the ghosts of the departed, still in many ways close at hand and with their remains buried nearby. (The unburied tended to turn into peculiarly nasty ghosts.) Sun, moon and stars watched; storms rampaged; forests and mountains brooded; powerful animals marked out their territories. 'Power' was perhaps the key to the world as archaic man saw it – power of heat over cold, light over darkness, life over death – and those who knew how to control that power became themselves powerful.

The process must have begun at some point in time, somewhere in the world, but we have no way of knowing when or where that point might have been (absolute origins of anything are always out of reach). When our records, such as they are, begin – numerical dates are worse than useless in such matters – we are already able to sense the presence of something or someone like a proto-shaman: at one and the same time a ruler and a servant of the spirits, a controller of rituals and an interpreter of laws and customs. From what we know of later shamanism, it would seem that such persons were servants of their respective societies by virtue of their knowledge of the spirit-world and their ability to establish and maintain contact with it. Shamanism 'proper' belongs in the context of hunter-gatherer societies, and as the structure of human societies changed, so too did the function of mediation between the tangible, everyday world and the unseen forces that were believed to control it.

The shaman was chosen and prepared for his (or in some cases, her) work, by aptitude, discipline and application, and by initiation – a pattern that survived most tenaciously in the trade guilds and those of the learned professions, which (untypically in the modern West) treasured their own past. In more complex societies – that of the agriculturalists and fisherfolk in their settled environments, that of the city-dwellers within their walls, and so on down to our own day and its bizarre preoccupation with economics – the functions of the shaman (serving the people by mediating between one order of being and another) have multiplied and diversified in an intriguing way.

This is not to say that the Pope or the Archbishop of Canterbury, or for that matter the Chief Rabbi or the Dalai Lama, or the Shankaracharya of Puri, are crypto-shamans: merely that their training on the one hand and their functions on the other, are of a kind one recognizes. (How well or how indifferently individuals may fill high offices has no bearing on the question.) Each has a position in an ongoing tradition, and is responsible for its continuation. Here we have the first, and the dominant, sense in which what we call 'the study of religion' functions. It is appropriate to call this a *discipline* in the strictest sense, an apprenticeship in which a pupil (*discipulus*) is taught by a master (*magister*) inside the bounds of a system, within the frontiers of which both knew precisely what was to be taught to whom, and why. Since the wellbeing of individuals and societies depended in large measure on the maintenance of what it is perfectly proper to call 'law and order', much of what had to be learned was concerned with these concepts and their ramifications.

In many cultures, 'law' (in Sanskrit, *dharma*, in Hebrew, *torah* and in Latin, *religio*, even the much misunderstood Australian Aboriginal word 'dreaming') and 'religion' are almost synonymous. What one supposes began as habit hardened first into custom and eventually into law, on the basis of which boundaries could be set up and wars fought. In the ancient world, no one expected laws, or religions, to be all of one kind. The 'when in Rome ...' principle was, and often still is, no more than common sense: deities, like humans and animals, were to some extent territorial, and to pay one's respects to a *genius loci* was no more than courtesy. Customs differed in much the same way as languages differed, and normally even the learned would know very little of what went on outside the family. 'Study' was for the most part concerned only with the family's (tribe's, nation's) traditions, history, sacred places and the rituals associated with them. In time, as more of this material was committed to writing, the study of those writings assumed a central place in the student's apprenticeship: often through memorization and constant repetition and chanting, in a setting in which the student's submissive obedience was simply taken for granted. This pattern of education is still operative today, though unevenly; generally speaking, Judaism, Islam, the ancient traditions of the East – varieties of Hinduism and Buddhism – have held fast to the method where instruction in the secular West has not.

What did the student make of other peoples' traditions, their deities, their rituals and their laws? In the ancient world, there were, roughly speaking, three alternatives: to ignore them altogether (the majority view), to observe them as curiosities, without taking them too seriously, and to condemn them as evil. Let us consider the second and third of these.

Greek and Roman 'philosophers' and historians were in many cases intrigued by the customs of the various peoples they met around the Mediterranean and as far afield as northern Europe. Perhaps they did not take their own national myths and rituals too seriously. At all events, the Greek and Roman historiographers, beginning with Herodotus (died approx. 420 BCE) showed a certain amount of interest in other people's behaviour where gods and the like were concerned. Berosus and Manetho (both third century BCE) wrote about ancient Egypt and Mesopotamia, Herodotus having previously written about the Persians. In the second century BCE Pausanias compiled an extensive and invaluable account of rituals and places of worship in his native Greece. The Romans for their part made fewer contributions, though special mention may be made of the accounts of the customs of the Celtic and Germanic tribes contained in 'war reports' like Caesar's *De bello Gallico* and Tacitus' *Germania*. Such writings as these (and there were many more) were compiled as information and entertainment, and to some extent propaganda: not as systematic accounts of anything. Tacitus 'studied' Celtic and Germanic tribes because they were troublesome to the Roman legions, and that was all.

The Hebraic attitude to such things could not have been more different. Israel knew all about 'the nations' and their deities, and trusted none of them. To the extent that other people's religion appears in the Hebrew Scriptures/Old Testament, it does so under a black cloud. Egypt and Mesopotamia – oppression. Canaan – apostasy. Persia – a brief glimpse of light. Rome – more oppression, this time apparently terminal, as the Temple was laid waste and the people scattered. Understanding? What was there to understand, except that the gods of the nations were impostors, small-time crooks, perhaps not without local influence, but entirely incapable of any act of creation. Least of all could they create a world, as Yahweh had done. They were mere 'idols', man-made and powerless. It is all summed up in two verses, 'For all the gods of the peoples are idols; but the Lord made the heavens' (Ps. 96:5); and 'The gods who did not make the heavens and the earth shall perish from the earth and from under the heavens' (Jer. 10:11).

There was the additional frightening possibility that 'idols' were nests of 'evil spirits' – unseen vermin whose existence was never properly explained, but whose malevolence no one in the ancient world seriously have doubted.

We find a partial relaxation of this uncompromising attitude in respect of the worship of natural phenomena – sun, moon and stars. These were at least God's creations, and not man-made objects, and may therefore be admired for the sake of their Creator, to whom ideally they ought to point the way. Human beings, however, are incorrigibly obtuse, and go off in pursuit of 'idols' even so. A classical statement of this attitude is to be found in Paul's Letter to the Romans (1:20–23):

Ever since the creation of the world his invisible nature, namely, his eternal power and deity, has been clearly perceived in the things that have been made … [but to no avail] Claiming to be wise, they became fools, and exchanged the glory of the immortal God for images resembling mortal man or birds or animals or reptiles …

All of this carried over into early Christianity, later Judaism and later still, Islam. There is one God, who has created, and will ultimately judge, the world; he has made his will known to humanity through his servants the Prophets, though his power may be recognized in what he has created. To 'study' in this connection was to know and obey the will of God, as set forth in successive writings – historical records, prophecies, hymns, statutes and apocalyptic, visionary writings. We have no need to enter into further details, except to point out that in Judaism the heart of the matter is the Law (Torah) itself, in Christianity the person and work of Jesus Christ, and in Islam again the Law, as revealed afresh to Muhammad; in all three traditions, the dividing line between truth and falsehood was sharply marked (in some modern versions of Judaism and especially Christianity, it has grown less so, modernism and Islam meanwhile remaining largely irreconcilable).

All this stands out in sharp contrast to the spirit of detached inquiry we find in Greek philosophy. Where the Classical cultures had philosophers, the Judaeo-Christian-Muslim tradition had prophets and their disciples, whose business was less to inquire than to obey. The tension between them has been felt repeatedly in Western religious and intellectual history, and it is well that we recognize where it all began. On the one side there are the conservatives, who love and respect tradition and continuity; on the other there are the inquirers, the radicals, the freethinkers (or however else fashion may label them). The terminology is constantly changing, but today's alternatives would seem to be 'fundamentalist' (meaning conservative) and 'pluralist' (which may mean anything, but is obviously anti-fundamentalist).

What of the Orient in all this? Here we must be brief, but in the Hindu and Buddhist traditions, to 'study religion' has always meant to place oneself under spiritual guidance, either by private arrangement with a guru, or as a member of a community of monks or nuns. In either case, the disciple's relationship to a guru has always been paramount: to be accepted as a disciple, or a novice, is to be prepared to show unquestioning obedience to the guru in everything, however trivial or apparently unreasonable. Not until you have made your submission in faith (Sanskrit: *shraddha*) to a teacher, can you begin to be taught. *What* is to be taught, it is entirely up to the guru to decide. The process of teaching and learning is strictly one-way, from the guru to the disciple, whose role is generally limited to the asking of respectful questions and absorbing the teacher's answers, either in writing or (more often) by memorization – a method still common enough in our own day, despite repeated attempts to discourage it.

We who live in the age of information, with every conceivable fact instantly available to anyone capable of pressing the right computer keys in the right order, find it hard to imagine a time when very little was known about our world and its inhabitants, and what little was known, had to be fitted into existing paradigms. At the end of the first millennium, the West divided religion into four categories, and only four: Christendom, Jewry, Islam and 'paganism'– an *omnium gatherum* for everything that did not sort under the first three. As to the study of religion, one studied within the framework of one's own tradition. To be sure, there was a certain curiosity value in other people's customs: travellers' tales have never lacked an audience, and although the genre invited exaggeration and a concentration on the previously unknown and the bizarre, world literature between the fifth and the fifteenth centuries (the 'dark ages' of Western culture) was full of fresh information concerning people's beliefs and customs, myths and rituals.

In his fascinating book *The Discoverers* (1983) Daniel Boorstin wrote that:

> The world we now view from the literate West – the vistas of time, the land and the seas, the heavenly bodies and our own bodies, the plants and animals, history and human societies past and present – had to be opened for us by countless Columbuses …
>
> (p. xv)

Discoveries are not inventions. One discovers what is already there to be discovered; one invents what is *not* already there. Discovery is in a sense the archaeology of ideas, the finding afresh of what, somewhere and at some time, was once common knowledge but which the world has since forgotten. But having discovered, one has to find some way of incorporating the new information into one's existing frames of reference. In the Christian West, that meant in practice sorting each new wave of information into the categories set forth in the Bible, with occasional footnotes supplied by 'the ancients'. There were true and false gods and goddesses; there was the sin of idolatry; there were sacrifices offered to 'demons' and various related abominations. This was the only viable principle of measurement: by reference to the (so far) unquestioned and unquestionable data of revelation, as stated in Holy Writ and interpreted by the Holy Church. Not until the advent of evolutionary theory toward the end of the nineteenth century did the would-be student of religion have an alternative method to fall back upon.

'Discoveries' came thick and fast, once navigation had become a tolerably exact business, and exploration by sea (as distinct from the overland treks of antiquity) developed. Judaism and Islam were already known, though little understood – in Islam's case, against a background of fear fuelled by the Crusades. The Enlightenment (German, *Aufklärung*) was more interested in China and its (apparently) rational approach to religion than in alternative monotheism or pagan superstitions. Most of the Enlightenment's information about China came directly from the reports of Jesuit missionaries, among whom the first was Matteo Ricci (1552–1610), who idealized Chinese 'religion' as a system without 'priestcraft' (the bugbear of the Age of Reason), but in possession of high moral virtues. At much the same time other Jesuits were writing about the indigenous peoples of north America in similar terms; the phrase 'the noble savage' seems to have been coined by John Dryden (1631–1700) in his *Conquest of Granada* (1670), the point being that virtue can and does flourish beyond the boundaries of Western urban civilization. The 'noble savage' was (or seemed to be) the antithesis of modern urban man – an image which has since proved remarkably resilient.

What manner of religion might 'the noble savage' have known and observed? On this point, the unorthodox Western intelligentsia in the seventeenth and especially the eighteenth century were of one mind. Ruling out supernatural revelation and its (supposed) manifestations as a matter of principle, but retaining a core of belief in a divine moral order, there was proposed a system of basic religion, resting on five 'common notions': that there is a God, a supreme power; that this power is to be worshipped; that the good order or disposition of the human faculties is the best part of divine worship; that vices and crimes must be eliminated through sorrow and repentance; and that there is a future life, in which virtue will be rewarded and vice punished. This was 'natural religion', later known as 'deism'. First formulated in the early seventeenth century by Lord Herbert of Cherbury (1583–1648) in his

De Veritate (1624), and restated with variations ever since, 'natural religion' of this kind was passionately anti-ecclesiastical and contemptuous of rites and rituals, doctrines and dogmas, which it dismissed as 'priestcraft'. Its adherents long found access to faculties of theology/divinity practically impossible, but they were able to exercise an indirect influence on the study of religion from elsewhere in the academy.

The nineteenth century

Betweeen 1801 and 1901 the Western world passed through a time of unprecedented intellectual change. At the dawn of the century, Napoleon, having failed to conquer Egypt, was on the point of trying to impose his will on Europe; the formality of what Tom Paine called 'The Age of Reason' had begun to lose ground to those who valued the spontaneous more than the coolly calculated, and the natural more than the artificial. The Romantic movement (as it came to be called) left its mark on literature, music (where Beethoven and Berlioz were the greatest romantics of all) – and on both the practice and the study of religion. It did not begin in 1801. Romanticism had been years in the preparation among those for whom the dry categories of order for order's sake had no appeal.

Where the practice of religion in the West was concerned, little in 1801 differed greatly from what it had been a century earlier, except perhaps the new factor of Protestant revivalism which had begun with the Wesleys in England in the 1730s, and which in the nineteenth century was to lead to the Protestant missionary movement, and indirectly to the making available of vast quantities of material (of unequal value, naturally) for scholars to work on. Otherwise there were Protestants, Catholics and freethinkers; outside, there were Jews, Muslims and assorted pagans, about whom little was known other than by rumour and hearsay. A massive work like William Hurd's *New Universal History of the Religious Rites, Ceremonies and Customs of the Whole World* (1788) is instructive in this regard, representing as it does what the educated but non-specialist reader might find of religious interest in the foundation year of the New South Wales penal colony. It was not the only compilation of its kind: the putting together of encyclopaedias was common enough in the eighteenth century. But it is instructive in its concentration on 'rites, ceremonies and customs', on the externals of religion in the non-Christian world. Often it was wildly inaccurate, sometimes to the modern reader (of whom I suspect I may be the only one) reminiscent of *Indiana Jones and the Temple of Doom*. In those days the heathen were expected to perform bizarre rituals and carry out abominable sacrifices in the name of their idols – the Bible said so! What else there might be behind the rituals, very few in the West knew.

The tide was about to turn, however. China, the West knew after a fashion. Before, almost until the end of the eighteenth century, India was a mystery within an enigma within a locked box. The Muslim north was known in part. Its official language was Persian before it was English; and it was through the medium of Persian that the West first gained a limited access to, first, Hindu laws (Halhed, *A Code of Gentoo Laws*, 1776, collected in Sanskrit, translated into Persian, then retranslated into English), and later, a number of *Upanishads*, this time from Sanskrit to Persian to Latin. Then in 1785 there appeared Charles Wilkins' translation of the *Bhagavadgita*, followed four years later by William Jones' translation of Kalidasa's play *Sakuntala* (1789), both this time directly from Sanskrit to English. No 'temple of doom' here. Instead, an India heavy with the scent of jasmine and sandalwood and a home, not of grotesque ceremonies but of timeless wisdom.

In the early years of the nineteenth century, while the fearsome figure of Napoleon was rampaging around Europe, India was coming to serve Europe and America as a landscape of the mind, and an antidote to the crass materialism that had emerged in the wake of the industrial revolution. This was not the 'real' India at all, but it served its purpose. And when it transpired that there was more to Indian thought than caste, cow-worship and suttee, India grasped and held the romantic imagination. One thing, however, was lacking: knowledge of Hindusm's most ancient scriptures, known collectively as the Veda (meaning knowledge), of which the oldest part, a collection of over a thousand ritual texts, was the *Rigveda*. Long kept secret from outsiders, its Sanskrit text was finally published, at the East India Company's expense, between 1849 and 1862, under the editorship of a German scholar working in Oxford, Friedrich Max Müller (1823–1900).

Müller was a pivotal figure in the study of religion in the West during the second half of the nineteenth century. He belonged firmly within the orbit of German Romanticism (his father wrote the poems set to music by Schubert as *Die schöne Müllerin* and *Winterreise*); he was a good friend of Ralph Waldo Emerson, and is said to have been a fine pianist. In religious terms he was (for want of a better word) a broad-church liberal Christian. One thing he was not: he was not a Darwinian.

Between 1801 and 1860 the raw material on which the study of religion is based multiplied at an extraordinary rate. What most of all captured the attention of a broader public was that involving the 'truth' of the Bible, and especially its chronology. We have no need to go into detail, though we may need to remind ourselves that in these years (before 1860), the study of religion sorted into two separate compartments: that which related to the world of the Bible (Egypt, Mesopotamia, Canaan, Iran, Greece and Rome); and that which did not (the rest), with Islam somewhere in between.

The Victorian anthropologists

Those who persist in believing 'the Victorian Age' to have been a time of smug self-satisfaction in matters of religion, delude themselves. For one thing, it was a very long period of time, and little of what was taken for granted in the 1830s still held good in 1900. No doubt there were smug and self-satisfied individuals, then as always, human nature being what it is. But with regard to religion, the second half of the nineteenth century saw practically everything called into question, somewhere, by someone. Then, as later, the chief focus of controversy was the word of the Bible: was it, or was it not, 'true' and therefore infallible, or at least authoritative? And if not, what leg has faith left to stand on?

On the negative side, some controversialists quite clearly said and wrote what they did chiefly to challenge the authority of the Church. The world could not have been created as described in Genesis, in 4004 BC. There had never been an Adam and Eve, a flood, a parting of the Red Sea. Further on, there had been no Virgin Birth, no Resurrection – the existence of Jesus himself was at least doubtful, and so on.

There was nothing new about this, battles having been fought over precisely this territory since the days of Lord Herbert of Cherbury and the deists in the early seventeenth century. But a blanket condemnation of 'miracles' and the supernatural was one thing; proposing a plausible alternative was another matter entirely. Before the middle years of the nineteenth century, though there was no shortage of fresh material, there was no comprehensive method with which to treat it, once one had abandoned the hard-and-fast 'truth-versus-falsehood' categories of Christian tradition. *Evolution* filled that gap from the 1880s on.

Say 'evolution' and one thinks at once of Charles Darwin and his epoch-making book *On the Origin of Species* (1859). Darwin had very little to say directly about religion, either for or against (Ellegård 1958). Some of his contemporaries were however less cautious. The most widely read of those writing in English was the popular philosopher Herbert Spencer (1820–1904), who took Darwin's biological theory and made it into a universal explanation of life on earth and its social institutions – government, language, literature, science, art and of course religion. All these things began with simple forms: *homo sapiens* had evolved out of something prior to and simpler than man (exactly what, no one knew, though the hunt for 'fossil man' was pursued with diligence); religion had therefore evolved out of something cruder than *Hymns Ancient and Modern*. What that 'something' might be, no one could possibly know (Trompf 1990). Conjecture was inevitable. Of the various theories put forward in the late nineteenth century, that labelled 'animism' has stood the test of time better than most. The term was launched by the Oxford anthropologist E. B. Tylor, in his important book *Primitive Culture* (1871), who declared that religion began with 'a belief in Spiritual Beings', prompted by reflection on the phenomena of dream and death. Suppose that I dream about my father, who died in 1957 (I do, as it happens): is that evidence that he is still alive in some other order of being? If majorities count, most of the world's population has always believed so. There is then at least some reason to inscribe 'animism' on religion's birth certificate, as indeed those wanting religion without revelation urged.

But might there perhaps be some even earlier stage, less explicit than animism? Tylor's successor at Oxford, R. R. Marett, thought there was, and called it 'pre-animism', without dreams and reflections on the mystery of death, but with a sense of the uncanny and of supernatural power (Polynesian/Melanesian *mana*). Marett's book *The Threshold of Religion* (1909) set out the arguments.

A quite different attack on the animistic theory came from the Scottish man of letters Andrew Lang (1844–1912), who had begun as a classicist and specialist on Homer, was for a time a disciple of Tylor, but in the end struck out on his own. From his Tylorian years comes his first anthropological book, *Custom and Myth* (1884). *Myth, Ritual and Religion* (1887) marks a transition, and his mature position was stated in *The Making of Religion* (1898). Lang's final argument was that there was no way in which animism was capable of evolving into ethical monotheism. Again and again the anthropological evidence had recorded belief in 'high gods' – conceptions of a Supreme Being, divine rulers and creators – which the evolutionists had simply chosen to ignore or dismiss as proof of 'the missionaries' tampering with the evidence. Lang tried to let the evidence speak for itself. He never claimed to have cracked the code, merely that '… alongside of their magic, ghosts, worshipful stones … most of the very most backward races have a very much better God than many races a good deal higher in civilization …' (Sharpe 1986: 63).

Lang was a public figure only in what he wrote. Having resigned his Oxford fellowship on his marriage, he held no farther academic position, living entirely by his pen. His versatility was extraordinary – historian, novelist, minor poet, psychic researcher, biographer, translator of Homer: he was sometimes ironical and often inaccurate, but never dull. His anthropological investigations were undertaken almost in his spare time, though he once confessed that given the opportunity, he might have devoted more time to anthropology. As it was, his hints and suggestions proved extremely fruitful. When he died in 1912, the Austrian ethnologist Wilhelm Schmidt had just published the first volume of his massive work *Der Ursprung der Gottesidee* (in the end twelve volumes in all), in which Lang's 'high gods' were taken very seriously indeed.

Another celebrated Scottish anthropologist to leave his mark on the study of religion was James George Frazer (1854–1951), still remembered as the tireless and unworldly author of *The Golden Bough* (1922), a compendium of practically everything sorting under what was then called 'primitive' religion, including folklore (domestic anthropology). For many years now, Frazer has been branded the archetypal 'armchair anthropologist', all of whose material was second-hand, having been raked together by casual observers whose motives were variable and whose accuracy was open to question. The criticism was justified up to a point, but Frazer did what he could to verify his sources, and was well aware of the risks he was running. In any case, the task of pulling together the growing bodies of evidence concerning archaic and vernacular religions needed to be undertaken by someone.

Frazer might well have become the first professor of comparative religion in the UK. In 1904 he was approached with a view to taking up such a post at the University of Manchester, but in the end declined, on the grounds that he was not a fit and proper person to instruct young men preparing for the Christian ministry. One wonders what might have become of the study of religion at Manchester, had Frazer's scruples been overcome!

The history of religion school

Between about 1890 and the outbreak of the First world War in 1914, a prominent position in Protestant religious scholarship was occupied by a group of fairly young biblical scholars, most of them Germans, known collectively as *die Religionsgeschichtliche Schule* (the history of religion (not 'religions') school). Their leaders were Wilhelm Bousset on the New Testament and Hermann Gunkel on the Old Testament side, and their chief theorist was Ernst Troeltsch (1865–1923), who, almost alone of the group, is still read today, thanks largely to his book *Die Absolutheit des Christentums und die Religionsgeschichte* (1902, belated Eng. tr. *The Absoluteness of Christianity and the History of Religions*, 1971). The principles of the movement were threefold: first, to focus on religion rather than on theology; second, to concentrate on popular expressions of religion rather than on high-level statements *about* religon; and thirdly, to examine closely the environment of the Old and New Testaments, rather than merely treating them as the free-floating (and divinely inspired) texts of orthodox tradition. The productivity of the young men making up the movement was remarkable, though relatively little of their work found its way into English. The trouble was that, like the Deists of the seventeenth and eighteenth centuries, they were generally political radicals, socialists and populists at a time and in a country where socialism was held to be only one step removed from treason.

To the members of the school, the world or scholarship nevertheless owes a great deal, for liberating the study of the Bible from its dogmatic straitjacket, for opening up the worlds of 'later Judaism' and the Hellenistic mystery religions, and for demonstrating that conspicuous piety is no substitute for sound scholarship where the study of religion is concerned. Special mention may be made of their work on the religious traditions of ancient Iran, Egypt and Mesopotamia. Iran was important mainly because of the towering figure of the prophet Zoroaster/Zarathustra (perhaps c.1200 BCE), whose teachings seemed to anticipate those of the Judaeo-Christian tradition at a number of points, in particular eschatology (death, judgement and the future life). Also, there were myriad points of contact between Iran and India. There emerged a new label, 'Indo-European', as an alternative to 'Aryan' as a blanket term for everything from the languages of north India to those of northern Europe. (The sinister overtones of 'Aryan' as the equivalent of 'non-Jewish' came later.)

Other advances that were registered toward the end of the nineteenth century in the academic study of religion concerned Egypt and Mesopotamia, thanks in both cases to the decipherment of what had previously been unreadable scripts, hieroglyphic and cuneiform respectively. We cannot go into details, but in both cases sober history and wild surmise combined. In Egypt's case, speculation went all the way from the bizarre theories of the Mormons (invented before the hieroglyphs had been deciphered) to the Egyptian origins of monotheism, which Sigmund Freud wrote about and may even have believed in, and the universal diffusionism of the Australian Grafton Elliot Smith, which claimed Egypt as the cradle of the whole of western civilization. A controversial expression of what came to be called 'pan-Babylonism' was a series of lectures on 'Babylon and the Bible' (*Babel und Bibel*), delivered in Berlin by Friedrich Delitzsch in 1902–5, which claimed that everything of value in the Old Testament was copied from Babylonian sources – the creation and flood narratives, the Sabbath, the notion of sin and much more.

The 'father' of the history of religion school (as distinct from its propagandists) had been the great historian Adolf (von) Harnack (1851–1930). In 1901 Harnack, also lecturing in Berlin, had argued *against* the widening of the theological curriculum to include non-biblical religions, chiefly on the grounds that the result would be dilettantism and superficiality. If comparative religion were to be taught at the universities, it should be in faculties of arts/humanities, and not under the aegis of theology. (Eventually, this was more or less what happened.) A somewhat different point of view was that of the Swedish scholar Nathan Söderblom (1866–1931), who argued in his Uppsala inaugural lecture of 1901 that there should be no artificial barrier between biblical religion and the rest, and that comparative religion (*religionshistoria*) should be an essential part of the theological curriculum. Three years later comparative religion in fact became an integral though subordinate part of the theological programme of the University of Manchester.

The trouble, though, was that often, the advocates of *Religionsgeschichte* (comparative religion) were at best indifferent and at worst hostile to theology as the churches understood it and the faculties taught it. And of course vice versa. Hence in most universities the study of 'other religions' came to be scattered around departments of history, anthropology, classics, Semitic studies and the like, and kept separate from theology. So it remained until the onset of 'the religious studies movement' in the 1960s.

Psychology and the mystics

The years around the turn of the nineteenth to twentieth century saw the emergence of many new 'sciences', among them 'the science of religion'. Within that science there were soon sub-sciences, of which the psychology of religion and the sociology of religion were the most significant. If two books were to be picked out as foundation documents of these sub-sciences, they might well be William James' *The Varieties of Religious Experience* (1977) on the psychological side, and Émile Durkheim's *The Elementary Forms of the Religious Life* (1915) on the sociological, though neither marks an absolute beginning. The difference between them is easily stated. Whereas the psychology of religion was, to begin with, concerned only with the individual's mental processes as they relate to religion, the sociology of religion saw (and still sees) religion as a collective, social phenomenon.

In both cases the formative years were the 1890s. This has nothing to do with the character of religion itself, which has always involved individuals and societies in equal measure. In psychology's case, the initial question concerned the mechanism by which the individual comes to experience sensations and feelings that he or she identifies as supernatural, and the consequences to which this may lead. The old alternatives had been divine inspiration on the one hand, and demonic deception on the other (speaking here in Judaeo-Christian terms). But suppose there were nothing supernatural involved. What then?

Interestingly enough, a number of the first psychologists of religion were Americans. Religious individualism was endemic in nineteenth-century America, especially among the heirs of the Enlightenment, such as Emerson and the New England Transcendentalists. 'Individualism ... was common enough in the Europe of the nineteenth century; in America, it was part of the very air men breathed' (Nisbet 1965: 4). This was due in part to the importance of the individual 'conversion experience' as the major criterion by which the genuineness of religion was judged. Sectarian extremism was also common, some parts of America even coming to resemble a menagerie of frequently warring sects. Add to this the impact of phenomena as diverse as exploration, industrialization, migration, half-understood Darwinism and not least the Civil War, and it is not hard to grasp the fascinated energy with which intellectuals tackled religious questions. Here an important book was Andrew Dickson White's *A History of the Warfare of Science with Theology in Christendom* (1955). White, the first President of Cornell University, was writing too early to incorporate psychology into his account; he was not irreligious, but was passionately opposed to the imposition of 'theological' limits on free enquiry.

The first psychologists of religion in America are all but forgotten today – Granville Stanley Hall, James H. Leuba and Edwin D. Starbuck among them. Starbuck is worth a special mention as the first to work with questionnaires as a means of gathering material. How do you find out what people experience as 'religion'? Simple: ask them! The results of his enquiries took shape in his book *The Psychology of Religion* (1899). Starbuck also taught a course in the psychology of religion at Harvard in 1894–5. The major emphasis of his questionnaires was on 'religious experience' in general, and the experience of conversion in particular. The method as such was deeply flawed, but won approval as a means of breaking away from the crude choice between divine inspiration and demonic deception as explanations of 'the conversion experience'.

Starbuck's material was used (and duly acknowledged) by his Harvard teacher William James in preparation for the lectures delivered in Scotland and published in 1977 as *The Varieties of Religious Experience* – one of the few religious classics of the twentieth century. William James, (1842–1910), the elder brother of the novelist Henry James, came of Swedenborgian stock, though his personal religion was an undogmatic theism. He trained as a doctor, but never practised medicine. Then he became fascinated by the infant science of psychology, and for years worked on his one and only book, *The Principles of Psychology* (1890) – all his later publications were tidied-up lectures, *Varieties* being his unquestioned masterpiece.

James was writing (or rather, speaking) as what he called a 'radical empiricist', a pragmatist who was convinced that where religion was concerned, judgement is possible only on a basis of the results to which it leads – religion is what religion does, not what it claims to be able to do. He drew a famous distinction between two religious temperaments: that of the 'healthy-minded' – positive, optimistic, relatively unconcerned with the problem of evil – and that of 'the sick soul' – obsessed with the sense of its own unworthiness, inadequacy and (in Christian terms) sin. 'Let sanguine healthymindedness do its best with its strange power of living in the moment and ignoring and forgetting, still the evil background is really there to be thought of, and the skull will grin in at the banquet' (James 1977: 140).

James also anticipated in *Varieties* what in the 1960s was to become one of the bugbears of the study of religion, by introducing the subject of artificially induced 'religious' experience through drugs, even going so far as to experiment himself with nitrous oxide ('laughing gas') and to suggest that if there should be supernatural revelation, the 'neurotic' temperament might be better able to receive it than the well-adjusted.

There were major flaws in James' approach to his subject, and this may be the time to mention them briefly. One was entirely deliberate, namely, his exclusion of religion's social dimension from his inquiry: 'religion' he limited to 'the feelings, acts, and experiences of individual men in their solitude, so far as they apprehend themselves to stand in relation to whatever they may consider the divine' (James 1977: 31). How far individuals feel, act and experience because of the environment in which they live, with all its precedents, images, taboos, expectations and the rest, he does not discuss. More important was the assumption, shared by all those who have ever used questionnaire material, that the individual actually *knows*, fully consciously, what he or she believes and why – and this is not always safe, as Freud and Jung were shortly to show.

Lectures XVI and XVII in *Varieties*, James devoted to the subject of 'Mysticism', which we might perhaps characterize as religious experience at its most intensive. Wisely, he did not attempt to define this notoriously slippery word, but identified 'ineffability', 'noetic quality' (the quality of self-authenticating knowledge), 'transiency' and 'passivity' as a 'mystical group' of states of consciousness (James 1977: 380–2). Whether mysticism is therefore to be welcomed or avoided had long been disputed territory. *Mystik* had long been regarded by theologians (especially those of the Catholic tradition) as something entirely positive, a mark of divine favour; *Mysticismus* was the word used by German-speaking rationalists to denote irrationality and delusion in religion, in practically the same sense as 'enthusiasm'. The English language was in the unfortunate position of having only one word to cover both senses. Either way, 'mysticism' came in the years around the turn of the century to serve as a catch-all term for all that sorted under the categories of visions, voices, trances and what today we call 'altered states of consciousness'; but also to label religious intensity. At the back of all this was what was the mystic's desire to achieve oneness with the Ultimate Reality – or alternatively, a mental disorder of some kind, depending on one's presuppositions.

One cannot 'study' mystics, except to the extent that they are prepared to write or speak about their experiences. There was however no lack of such material, and beginning in the years around the turn of the century there appeared a number of significant works on the subject. The first of these was W. R. Inge's *Christian Mysticism* (1899), followed by, among others, James' *Varieties*, Nathan Söderblom's *Uppenbarelsereligion* (*The Religion of Revelation*, 1903, which drew the important distinction between theistic and non-theistic expressions of religious faith), Friedrich von Hügel's massive *The Mystical Element of Religion* (1908), Rufus Jones' *Studies in Mystical Religion* (1909) and Evelyn Underhill's *Mysticism* (1940). At the end of this line we may perhaps place J. B. Pratt's *The Religious Consciousness* (1920). It is perhaps worth noting that the last four authors mentioned were Roman Catholic, Quaker, uneasy Anglican and Unitarian respectively: clearly religious experience bore no particular relation to Christian denominationalism. Pratt's horizon was however wider: he had a lively interest in India, writing with regard to Buddhism that he had '… tried to enable the reader to understand a little *how it feels to be a Buddhist*' (Sharpe 1986: 115f. emphasis in original).

It was slightly ironical that Pratt's book should have been called *The Religious Consciousness*, since by the time it appeared, Freud, Jung and their respective bands of followers had most effectively called in question the very idea of consciousness as a decisive factor in human conduct. The new psychologists, wrote Sir John Adams in 1929, '… know exactly what they want and are quite clear about the way they propose to attain it. There is a lion in their path; they want that lion killed and decently buried. This lion is Consciousness …' (Sharpe 1986: 197). The Freudians, the Jungians and the rest of the psychoanalytical establishment did not pretend to scholarship in the area of religion, and some of their ventures into the field were quite bizarre; their profession was medicine, after all. But whereas Freud and his followers treated religion as part of the problem where mental health was concerned, the Jungians took a more positive view of religious mythology and symbolism. The psychoanalytical cause became fashionable in the years following the insanity of the First World War, not least in America, and cast a long shadow.

As an example, we may quote the case of the American anthropologist Margaret Mead (1902–1978), author of the celebrated *Coming of Age in Samoa* (1928), which proved, entirely to its author's satisfaction, that adolescence can be practically pain-free, once the sexual restraints imposed by society have been relaxed. Mead was a protegée of Franz Boas, a determined Freudian. Margaret Mead was no more than 23 when she did the field-work on which her book was based, and many years later one of her chief Samoan informants confessed that the girls who had supplied her with material had been pulling her leg (Freeman 1983). It did not matter. Her teacher Franz Boas wrote that: 'The results of her painstaking investigation confirm the suspicion long held by anthropologists, that much of what we ascribe to human nature is no more than a reaction to the restraints put upon us by civilisation' (Mead 1928: viii). 'Field-work' was of the essence, no matter how poorly equipped the investigator – an attitude which passed in the course of time to the study of religion.

Psychoanalysis aside, other issues divided students of religion in the early years of the twentieth century. Another relatively new science was the science of sociology – collective, rather than individual human behaviour. A key concept in this connection was 'holiness/ sacredness' (the adjectives 'sacred' and 'holy' are generally interchangeable; 'the sacred' and 'the holy' are on the other hand abstractions).

There were two alternatives: on the psychological (and often the theological) side, what was up for investigation was 'what the individual does with his/her own solitariness'; on the sociological side, what communities do under the heading of 'religion'. At the time when William James was most influential, there was a strong current of thought flowing in precisely the opposite direction: toward the assessment of religion's social functions, past and present. Out of the second of these there emerged *the sociology of religion*, which over the years was to assume a more and more dominant role as an academic sub-discipline.

One can do sociology in two different but connected ways. First, as an evolutionary science. Although Darwin was first and foremost a biologist, it was not long before his admirers applied the evolutionary model to (among much else) the development of human societies. Here the prophetic voice was that of the popular philosopher Herbert Spencer (1820–1904), whose *First Principles* (1862) argued that 'the law of organic evolution is the law of all evolution' in every field of human activity, and not just in biology: 'this same advance from the simple to the complex, through successive differentiations, holds uniformly' (Spencer 1862: 148). Spencer held that the simplest, and therefore the earliest, form of religion had been the worship (or at least fear) of the dead, especially those who had been powerful during their lifetimes: 'The rudimentary form of all religion is the propitiation of dead ancestors …' (Spencer 1901). This 'ghost theory' (as it came to be called) has the merit of sometimes being at least partly true. Examples are not hard to come by. But it leaves out too much to serve as a general theory of the origin of religion.

Shortly before Spencer's death, there had been published a centenary edition of an influential book by the German theologian Friedrich Schleiermacher (1768–1834), *Über die Religion: Reden an die Gebildeten unter ihren Verachtern* (1799; Eng. tr. *On Religion: Speeches to its Cultured Despisers*, 1893). It was important on two counts: first, because it argued that the only way to study religion adequately is not in terms of the bloodless intellectual abstractions of 'natural religion' (which is in actual fact neither natural nor religion), but in and through the religious beliefs and practices of actual living human beings – a point made many years earlier by Charles de Brosses, but taken insufficiently seriously since. And second, because to Schleiermacher, the heart of religion was to be found, not in rules and regulations, hierarchies, hassocks and hymnbooks, but in the individual's experience of (or sense of) and dependence upon a power infinitely greater than his own. The reissue of Schleiermacher's *Über die Religion* in 1899 could not have come at a more opportune moment. Darwinism was all very well; the rule of law was an efficient sergeant-major in an unruly world, but left little room for creative individuality. It was however Schleiermacher's editor who made the greater long-term impression.

Rudolf Otto (1869–1937) was a philosopher and theologian by training and temperament, with Indology as another area of interest and expertise. Today however he tends to be remembered for only one book, *Das Heilige* (1917; Eng. tr. *The Idea of the Holy*, 1923), which argued that what is essential in religion is the individual's experience of 'the holy', even at one point requesting that the reader who has had no such experience to read no further! But experience of what, precisely? Trying to explain, Otto coined the word 'numinous' (*das Numinose*), a sense of the presence of a *numen* (deity, supernatural being). This in its turn gives rise to a perception, or apprehension, of a *mysterium* which is both *tremendum* (scary) and *fascinans* (intriguing).

The words 'holy' and 'sacred' are adjectives, which need to be related to someone or something if they are to make sense, and are not easily turned into nouns ('holy scripture', 'holy mountain', 'holy day', 'sacred cow', 'sacred site' make sense as the abstract nouns 'the holy' and 'the sacred' do not.

A few years before the appearance of Otto's book there appeared in France Émile Durkheim's *Les Formes Élémentaires de la Vie Religieuse* (1912; Eng. tr. *The Elementary Forms of the Religious Life*, 1915). Here we have the opposite argument: that (put crudely) religion is a social phenomenon, resting not on the individual's feeling-states but on the needs of the community. Families, tribes and nations set up symbols of their own collective identity – from totem poles to national flags – which are 'sacred' through their associations.

On this view, every human community invents its own sacred symbols. The supernatural does not enter into it, the closest approximation being 'power' (the Melanesian/Polynesian *mana* and similar power-words, which Durkheim mistakenly believed to be impersonal, but which always turn out to be associated with spiritual beings who possess them). It is therefore the community which decrees what is, and what is not, 'sacred' in its own cultural terms.

The phenomenology of religion

Between the outbreak of the First World War in 1914 and the end of the second in 1945, the study of religion in the West became fragmented. The old idealism had been shattered in the trenches of the battlefield, and in 1920, religion itself, let alone the study of religion, seemed to have no future worth speaking of. On the Christian theological front, the tradition of scholarship was maintained by a very few idealists in the face of growing opposition from the disciples of Karl Barth, Emil Brunner and the other 'dialectical' theologians, in whose eyes 'religion' was as dust and ashes compared to the Gospel, and who declined to study it further. The conservatives were what they had always been: intent on doing battle with 'the world' on as many fronts as possible. Meanwhile, the anthropologists, Orientalists, philologists and the rest cultivated their respective gardens.

Comparative religion had been trying to compare religions as totalities, as systems, as competing solutions of the world's problems. This was unsound. Religions are totalities only in the pages of textbooks, and what believers actually believe, and how they believe, may bear little resemblance to what they are supposed to believe and do. The student, intent on examining religions and writing their histories, was faced with an impossible task. One alternative was to divide the field functionally, by themes and characteristics, and to attempt on that basis limited comparisons: prayer with prayer, sacrifice with sacrifice, images of deity with images of deity. In all this it was important to examine, not what the textbooks say, but what is actually there to be observed, the *phenomena* involved in the business of religion. The point had been made by Charles de Brosses in the 1760s and by Friedrich Schleiermacher in 1799: that the student of religion must concentrate, not on what people might do, ought to do or what the textbooks say they are supposed to do, but on what they actually do, and the ways in which they actually behave. But people do, and have done, so many things. How can anyone grasp the field as a whole?

It was with an eye to resolving this difficulty that the term 'the phenomenology of religion' was pressed into service. As we have said, limited comparisons were still possible, provided that they were based on either reliable information or careful observation. However, in the early years of the twentieth century, 'phenomenology' acquired another set of meanings, having to do less with the material than the mind-set of the observer. The name of the philosopher Edmund Husserl is often mentioned in this connection, though his contribution to the study of religion was at best indirect. 'Philosophical' phenomenology aimed at the elimination of subjectivity (and hence dogmatic bias) from the inquirer's process of thought. As such, the ideal was and is unattainable, and it was unfortunate that for a time in the 1970s, a few phenomenological catch-words (*epoché*, the suspension of judgment, and *eidetic vision*, the gift of seeing things as wholes, as well as 'phenomenology' itself) found their way into the vocabulary of the study of religion. In the inter-war years, the trend was best represented by the Dutch scholar Gerardus van der Leeuw (1890–1950), author of *Phänomenologie der Religion* (1933; Eng. tr. *Religion in Essence and Manifestation*, 1938).

Practically all the first phenomenologists of religion were Protestant Christian theologians – Chantepie de la Saussaye, Nathan Söderblom, Rudolf Otto, Edvard Lehmann, William Brede Kristensen ('... there exists no other religious reality than the faith of the believers ...') and C. Jouco Bleeker. An exception was the enigmatic German scholar Friedrich Heiler, whose chaotic book *Erscheinungsformen und Wesen der Religion* (1961) rounded off the series. In all these cases, phenomenology was a religious as much as a scholarly exercise. Those making up the between-the-wars generation of scholars we now call phenomenologists were deeply committed to the principle that the causes of sound learning and sound religion were not two causes, but one. The enemies of sound learning were all too often captive to *unsound* religion – unsound because (among other things) unhistorical and therefore almost inevitably authoritarian. Faced with such a configuration, one may distance oneself altogether from religious praxis; or one may try to bring the religious community (that is, the faculties of theology) round to one's way of thinking. Most opted for the first of these alternatives; the very few who chose the latter, though they won a few battles, ultimately lost the war – not because of the innate superiority of theological thinking, but due to the corrosive influence of secularization on religious thought in general.

Tools of the trade

Over the past century or so, the study of religion has gradually acquired an extensive body of reference material for the use of students. The idea that it might be possible to bring together all the world's knowledge and publish it in encyclopaedia form belongs to the Enlightenment. Today we are more modest, but the genre has survived. As far as religion is concerned, an important landmark was James Hastings' *Encyclopaedia of Religion and Ethics* (1908–26); in German, there was *Die Religion in Geschichte und Gegenwart* (1909–13), a fourth edition is currently in preparation. The *Encyclopedia of Religion* (16 vols, edited by Mircea Eliade) appeared in the US in 1987. Given the new situation created by the Internet, it is unlikely that there will be any more.

Compact dictionaries and handbooks are by now legion, as are 'world religions' textbooks for student use. Special mention may be made of *The New Penguin Dictionary of Religions* (1997) and *The New Handbook of Living Religions* (1998), both edited by John R. Hinnells. On the textbook front, Ninian Smart's *The World's Religions* (1989, an updated version of a book first published in 1969 as *The Religious Experience of Mankind*) has proved an excellent *gradus ad parnassum* for generations of religious studies students.

Concerning scholarly journals, we must be brief. They have never been other than variable in quality, and though these days every effort is made to guard professional standards, the level of readability is often depressingly low. There is the additional factor that the fragmentation of the study of religion in recent years has resulted in more and more specialist journals, which can only be read with profit by fellow specialists. Among the best 'general' journals in English are *Religion* (UK/US), *Journal of the American Academy of Religion* (US), *Journal of Religion* (US) and *Numen* (international).

Congresses, conferences, consultations

In 1993 there was celebrated the centenary of the Chicago 'World's Parliament of Religions', though this time relabelled 'Parliament of World Religions' – a shift in meaning no one bothered to examine at all closely. Both were propaganda exercises, but for different causes: 1893 for religious oneness (monism), 1993 for religious diversity (pluralism). There would be little point in listing even a selection of the myriad conferences, congresses and consultations that have punctuated the years between, increasingly frequently since the advent of air travel in the 1960s. Opinions differ as to their importance, though it is probably true to say that the best are the smallest (the most satisfying conference I have ever attended numbered no more than thirty-five or so participants). It would however be churlish to deny their social function or the opportunity they provide for younger voices to make themselves heard among their peers.

Bibliography

Boorstin, D. J., *The Discoverers*. New York, Vintage Books, 1983.

Capps, W. H., *Religious Studies: The Making of a Discipline*. Minneapolis MN, Fortress Press, 1995.

Cook, S. A., *The Study of Religions*. London, A. & C. Black, 1914.

Daniel, G., *The Idea of Prehistory*. Harmondsworth, Penguin, 1964.

De Vries, J., *The Study of Religion: A Historical Approach*. trans. K. W. Bolle, New York, Harcourt, Brace & World, 1967.

Durkheim, É., *The Elementary Forms of the Religious Life*. Trans. J. W. Swain, London, George Allen & Unwin, 1915.

Eliade, M. (ed.), *Encyclopedia of Religion*. 16 vols, New York, Macmillan, 1987.

Ellegård, A., *Darwin and the General Reader*. Göteborg (Gothenburg, Sweden), Acta Universitatis Gothoburgensis 7, 1958.

Evans-Pritchard, E. E., *Theories of Primitive Religion*. Oxford, Clarendon Press, 1965.

Feldman, B. and Richardson, R. D., *The Rise of Modern Mythology, 1680–1860*. Bloomington, Indiana, Indiana University Press, 1972.

Frazer, J. G., *The Golden Bough*. Abridged edn, London, Macmillan, 1922.

Freeman, D., *Margaret Mead and Samoa: The Making and Unmaking of an Anthropological Myth*. Cambridge, MA, Harvard University Press, 1983.

Hastings, J. (ed.), *Encyclopaedia of Religion and Ethics*. Edinburgh, T. & T. Clark, 1908–1926.

Heiler, F., *Erscheinungsformen und Wesen der Religion*. Stuttgart, publisher unknown, 1961.

Hinnells, J. R. (ed.), *The New Penguin Dictionary of Religions*. London, Penguin, 1997.

—— (ed.), *A New Handbook of Living Religions*. Harmondsworth, Penguin, 1998.

Hügel, F. von, *The Mystical Element of Religion*. 2 vols, London, Dent, 1908.

Hurd, W., *New Universal History of the Religious Rites, Ceremonies and Customs of the Whole World*. London, publisher unknown, 1788.

Inge, W. R., *Christian Mysticism*. London, Methuen, 1899.

James, W., *The Principles of Psychology*. 2 vols, New York, H. Holt & Co., 1890.

—— *The Varieties of Religious Experience*. The Gifford Lectures 1901–2, reprinted Glasgow, Collins, 1977.

Jones, R. M., *Studies in Mystical Religion*. London, Macmillan & Co., 1909.

Lang, A., *Custom and Myth*. London, Longmans & Co., 1884.

—— *Myth, Ritual and Religion*. 2 vols, London, Longmans & Co., 1887.

—— *The Making of Religion*. London, Longmans & Co., 1898.

Leeuw, G. van der, *Religion in Essence and Manifestation: A Study in Phenomenology*. Trans. J. E. Turner, London, George Allen & Unwin, 1938.

Marett, R. R., *The Threshold of Religion*. London, Methuen, 1909.

Mead, M., *Coming of Age in Samoa*. New York, Morrow, 1928.

Müller, M. F., *Introduction to the Science of Religion*. London, Longmans, Green and Co., 1873.

Nisbet, R. A., *Émile Durkheim*. Englewood Cliffs, NJ, Prentice-Hall, 1965.

Otto, R., *The Idea of the Holy*. Trans. J. W. Harvey, London, Humphrey Milford, 1923.

Pratt, J. B., *The Religious Consciousness: A Psychological Study*. New York, Macmillan, 1920.

Schiele, F. M. (ed.), *Die Religion in Geschichte und Gegenwart*. 5 vols, Tübingen, publisher unknown, 1909–13.

Schleiermacher, F., *On Religion: Speeches to its Cultured Despisers*. Trans. John Oman, London, publisher unknown, 1893.

Schmidt, W., *The Origin and Growth of Religion: Facts and Theories*. London, Methuen, 1931.

Sharpe, E. J., *Understanding Religion*. London, Duckworth, 1983.

—— *Comparative Religion: A History*. London, Duckworth, 1975. Second edition, London, Duckworth, and La Salle, Open Court, 1986.

Smart, N., *The World's Religions*. Cambridge, Cambridge University Press, 1989.

Smith, H., *The Religions of Man*. New York, Harper & Row, 1964.

Spencer, H., *First Principles*. London, Williams & Norgate, 1862.

—— *Essays: Scientific, Political and Speculative*. 3 vols, London, Williams & Norgate, 1901.

Starbuck, E. D., *The Psychology of Religion: An Empirical Study of the Growth of Religious Consciousness*. London, Scott, 1899.

Trompf, G. W., *In Search of Origins*. London, Oriental University Press, 1990.

Underhill, E., *Mysticism: A Study in the Nature and Development of Man's Spiritual Consciousness*. 13th edn, London, Methuen, 1940.

Waardenburg, J., *Classical Approaches to the Study of Religion: Aims, Methods and Theories of Research*. 2 vols, The Hague and Paris, Mouton, 1973–4.

White, A. D., *A History of the Warfare of Science with Theology in Christendom*. 2 vols, London, Arco, 1955.

Chapter 3

The study of religions: the last 50 years

Gregory Alles

In one sense, the study of religions is as old as religion itself, or at least as the first human beings who looked at their neighbours or themselves and wondered what they were doing when they did what we have come to call religion. In another sense, in most parts of the world the study of religions in a narrower, more technical sense, as the non-theological study of religion in the context of higher education, did not begin in earnest until after the Second World War. In the same period, the academic study of religions expanded greatly in Europe, which already had firm if small traditions of such study. In those parts of the world that had traditions of teaching theology, such as North America and colonial Africa, the development of the study of religions was largely a shift in emphasis from examining the world through a lens shaped by religious conviction to examining it through one shaped by perspectival pluralism, religious uncertainty, or anti-religious naturalism, usually an uneven mixture of all three. The shift rarely satisfied everyone. In other parts of the world, such as East Asia, it involved building an academic enterprise around an imported foreign category, 'religion'.

Although the expansion and internationalization of the study of religions began in earnest after the Second World War, an exact starting point is impossible to determine. As the preceding chapter demonstrates, the academic study of religions had a long prehistory and history in Europe, and the global move to study religions academically had neither a single founder nor a founding moment. Nevertheless, it is clear that as Europe and Japan rebuilt, as Europe gradually divested itself of its colonies, as much of the rest of the world tried its hand at self-government, and as the Cold War divided up the world between two and later three great powers vying for influence, the United States, the Soviet Union, and the People's Republic of China, universities and colleges in many parts of the world instituted programmes for the study of religions.

From the point of view of history, it is just becoming possible to assess the earliest of these events. Their lasting significance – the significance that makes people in later periods want to remember them and transmit them to succeeding generations as history – will not be apparent until those later periods come into being. At the same time, one should not ignore them, even if it is tempting for older generations to dismiss some developments as retrograde. They are the movements that shape the study of religions today.

The study of religion in context

There were probably many reasons for the expansion and internationalization of religious studies after the Second World War. Some of them were truly global in scope.

One reason was the vast expansion of both the world's population and of tertiary education. In 1900 the world's population was 1.65 billion (10^9). In 1950 it was 2.5 billion; by 1999 it was almost 6 billion. With all other factors constant, the number of scholars studying religions worldwide should have increased four-fold during the course of the twentieth century, most of the growth taking place after the Second World War. Other factors did not, however, remain constant. After the Second World War, countries in Europe and the European diaspora generally shifted from elite to mass universities, giving a much higher percentage of their populations access to higher education and employment within it. Furthermore, in both the de-colonizing world and in nations attempting to demonstrate the viability of an alternative political ideology, such as the People's Republic of China, the establishment and promotion of tertiary educational institutions allowed governments to stake claims to quality. A government that fostered a system of universities and colleges deserved loyalty and respect. Under such conditions even a field of study that loses a moderate amount of market share will actually expand (cf. Frank and Gabler 2006).

Such statistics alone do not, however, explain the expansion and internationalization of the study of religions after the Second World War. Significant global technological and cultural developments probably played a role, too. Among them one might mention infrastructural factors such as the introduction in the late 1950s of commercial jet aircraft – the de Havilland Comet 4 and the more successful Boeing 707 in October 1958, the Douglas DC–8 in September 1959; and the launch of communication satellites – Sputnik 1 in October 1957, Project SCORE in December 1958, Telstar in July 1962. Commercial jet air transportation gave increasing numbers of people, including scholars, ready access to more distant parts of the world. Satellites enabled the transmission of higher volumes of auditory and visual communication throughout much of the world. Both had the effect of stimulating curiosity about places elsewhere, creating demand for knowledge about religions, among other topics, and providing affordable means to meet that demand. At least in some people, they also had the effect of undercutting older, locally defined loyalties, including assertions of exclusive claims to religious Truth associated with traditional approaches to theology.[1] For the pluralists, the space programmes of the 1960s and early 1970s, especially images of the earth from space, such as the earth rising over the moon shot from Apollo 8 in 1968 and the whole-earth view shot from Apollo 17 in 1972, provided visual icons. There is also some evidence that the events of the Holocaust and the Second World War themselves made parochial definitions of Truth seem more untenable within an academic context (Frank and Gabler 2006: 67).

In addition to global factors, local factors probably also contributed to an expansion in the volume of the study of religions as well as to a shift in its emphases in various parts of the world. For example, in the 1950s, during the Cold War against godless Communism, religiosity and, in some circles, religious plurality became markers of identity for the United States. (Significantly, the study of religions had very different trajectories in nations under the influence of the Soviet Union.) In 1963 the US Supreme Court noted in a ruling that although government institutions could not teach students to be religious, they could and probably should teach students about religions (*School District of Abington v. Schempp* 374 US 225 [1963]). As the Vietnam War and public opposition to it intensified, interest in Asian religions grew, because the experience of the war and its aftermath provided more intimate contact with what often seemed strange religions; consider the impact of Thich Quang Duc's self-immolation on June 11, 1963. That interest also grew because religions like Buddhism and Hinduism could be promoted as alternatives to a seemingly stifling and bellicose Christianity. In 1965, the United States also changed its immigration laws, allowing limited numbers of Asians, previously barred, to enter the country, eventually creating a new religious demographic.

Expansion and internationalization[2]

These factors and others as well combined in the decades following the Second World War to create a general shift toward a more pluralistic conception of religious studies as well as the establishment of new academic units and positions. Until the 1960s many state universities in the United States had largely avoided the study of religions. In the 1960s state universities began to found academic units for it. The most significant of these was the department of religious studies at the University of California–Santa Barbara, established in 1964. Although Friedrich Max Müller (1867) had announced the birth of the science of religion while working at Oxford, the United Kingdom had lacked academic units devoted to its study. That changed, too, as Great Britain began to institute such programmes, especially in its new universities. The way was led by Ninian Smart, who founded the first British department of religious studies in Lancaster University in 1967. Earlier, in 1960, the fifth section (*Sciences religieuses*) of the École Pratique des Hautes Études in Paris expanded to include 29 chairs. It has since grown to roughly twice that size and is the largest single unit devoted to the study of religions in Europe. In orientation its work has tended to be more exactingly historical and philological than is often the case in religious studies departments in other countries.

At the other end of the Eurasian land mass, the People's Republic of China founded the Institute for World Religions in Beijing in 1964, although the Cultural Revolution (1966–1976) severely disrupted its work. In Korea and Japan the study of religions was promoted through academic appointments and the establishment of new academic units, such as the chair of religious studies at the University of Tsukuba, founded in 1973. In New Zealand (Aotearoa), the University of Otago established a chair in the phenomenology of religion in 1966; Victoria University, Wellington, established a chair in religious studies in 1971. The Universities of Queensland and Sydney, Australia, established Departments of Studies in Religion in 1974 and 1977, respectively. Meanwhile, in Africa, especially those parts of Africa formerly under British rule, programmes in religious studies were founded as newly independent African nations established national universities. Nigeria was and remains particularly active in the study of religions, beginning with the founding of the department of religious studies at the University of Ibadan in 1949. In addition to local African professors, African programmes in religious studies have benefited from the services of many leading scholars of European and, less frequently, North American origin, such as Geoffrey Parrinder, J. G. Platvoet, James Cox, Rosalind Hackett, and David Chidester.

Scholarship involves more than academic units in universities. It also involves professional associations and other structures that facilitate scholarly communication and research. These structures, too, map the growth of religious studies during the last fifty years. Among the new professional associations founded after the Second World War were the International Association for the History of Religion (established 1950), followed (or in some cases preceded) by the founding of national associations in many European countries, the American Academy of Religion (the new name given to the National Association of Bible Instructors in 1963), the Korea Association for Studies of Religion (1970), later revived as the Korean Association for the History of Religions; the Society for the Sociology of Religion (a Japanese association founded in 1975; the Japanese Association for Religious Studies has been founded in 1930); the Australian Association for the Study of Religion (1975); the New Zealand Association for the Study of Religion (1978); the [mainland] Chinese Association of Religious Studies (1979), and the African Association for the Study of Religion (1992). Similarly, a host of new journals came into being, including, to name only a few: *Numen* (journal of the IAHR, 1954), *Przeglad Religioznawczy* (Poland, 1957), *History of Religions* (US, 1961), *Temenos* (Finland, 1965), *Journal of Religion in Africa, Religion en Afrique* (Africa, 1967), *Religion* (UK and North America, 1971), *Japanese Journal of Religious Studies* (Japan, 1974), *Shijie Zongjiao Yanjiu* (China, 1979), *Jongkyo Yeongu* (Korea, 1986), *Journal for the Study of Religion* (Southern Africa, 1988), *Method and Theory in the Study of Religion* (North America, 1989), *Zeitschrift für Religionswissenschaft* (Germany, 1993), *Religio. Revue pro Religionistiku* (Czech Republic, 1993), *Archaevs: Studies in the History of Religions* (Romania, 1997), and *Bandue* (Spain, 2007). Space does not permit mentioning the many book series and text books, reference works, and anthologies that appeared, but one might note the publication of two editions of two major encyclopaedias in this period: *Religion in Geschichte und Gegenwart* (1957–1965, 1998–2005) and *The Encyclopedia of Religion* (1987, 2005).

It would be misleading to suggest that after the Second World War religious studies emerged equally in every part of the world. In the Soviet sphere of influence, the study of religions was under severe political pressure, and some scholars, such as Kurt Rudolph, an expert in Gnosticism and Mandaeism at the University of Leipzig, left for the West. Since the fall of European Communism, vigorous programmes in religious studies have arisen in places such as the Czech Republic, Hungary, Romania, and Bulgaria, with recent promising beginnings in Russia itself. Aside from Israel, universities in the Middle East still tend to teach 'theology', or rather, Islamic law, although a non-theological study of religions has begun to emerge in some countries, such as Turkey. In South America, other academic units, such as history, anthropology, sociology, and psychology, generally study local religions. In South Asia there are very few programmes in religious studies, but sociology, introduced into Indian universities in the 1960s, has produced very fine scholarly work on religions, such as the work of T. N. Madan (1976, 2004, 2006).

Theoretical beginnings

Despite the wide geographical expanse of the study of religion, theoretical work in the field has tended to be done in Europe or countries associated with the European diaspora. That hardly means, however, that only people of western European ancestry have been theoretically influential. A dominant influence in the first part of the period under review was the 'Chicago school', associated above all with the names of three professors at the University of Chicago, none of whom was western European in the common usage of the term: Joseph M. Kitagawa, Charles H. Long, and Mircea Eliade.

In many ways the Romanian-born scholar, Mircea Eliade (1907–1986), defined the study of religions throughout much of the period under consideration. That is true both for his admirers and for his many critics, who reacted by deliberately contrasting their work with his. Although Eliade is closely associated with the name 'history of religions', the designation was in some sense a relic of Romanian and French terminology as well as of earlier terminology at the University of Chicago. Rather than history, Eliade's thinking represented perhaps the last grand flourishing of the phenomenology of religion. Rejecting approaches that sought to explain religion in terms of something that was not religious, such as society or the human psyche, he attempted to develop what he called a morphology of the sacred. That is, he wanted to identify the basic forms through which the sacred manifested itself in human consciousness. He was particularly interested in cosmogonies (myths of origin) and their ritual re-enactment, which he interpreted as an attempt to return to the time or origins and live in close proximity to the sacred. He developed these ideas in full form in *Patterns in Comparative Religion* (1949b; Eng. trans. 1958) and *The Myth of the Eternal Return* (1949a; Eng. trans. 1954), then repeated them tirelessly in a series of more popular books. He was also particularly known for his studies of yoga (1954; Eng. trans. 1958) and shamanism (1951; Eng. trans. 1964).

Ninian Smart (1927–2001) had a different background and a different approach to the study of religions. He also occupied a different sphere of influence. A Scotsman, he read philosophy and classics at Oxford. As noted above, he founded the department of religious studies at Lancaster University in 1967. Eventually he also took a position in the United States at the University of California–Santa Barbara. While Eliade's notion that the sacred manifests itself as a structure of human consciousness can be read in a religiously committed sense, Smart (1973) insisted that scholars of religions needed to adopt a methodological agnosticism: as scholars they should be non-committal in the matter of religious truth. Instead of developing a grand theory of religious content, as Eliade did, Smart identified six, later seven, dimensions constitutive of religion: doctrinal, mythological, ethical, ritual, experiential, institutional, and material. He also famously noted the similarity between Marxism, for example, and more traditional religions and suggested that the study of religions is properly the study of worldviews (Smart 1983). Like Eliade, he, too, was a popularizer, but in a broader range of media. A notable example was his series 'The Long Search' on BBC television (Smart 1977).

One final figure anticipated much work in the study of religions that was to follow, the Canadian Wilfred Cantwell Smith (1916–2001), a professor at Harvard, among other universities. An Islamicist who taught in Lahore prior to Pakistani independence, Smith (1963) critically interrogated the central category on which religious studies is based, 'religion' itself. The term, he contended, was a modern invention that did not correspond to what was found empirically throughout most of human history. He recommended replacing it with the terms 'faith' and 'cumulative tradition'. In addition, he objected to an objectivizing, 'us' and 'them' mentality, which he saw underlying religious studies. He envisioned a time when the peoples of the world would come together to talk with each other about themselves (Smith 1959: 34). If Smart advocated a methodological agnosticism and Eliade provided a grand statement of the content allegedly underlying all religions, Smith took a different approach and eventually moved *Towards a World Theology* (1981).

These three thinkers were not the only leading figures in the study of religions at the beginning of the period under consideration. There were many other important scholars as well. Arguably those who did careful historical and philological work contributed just as much if not more substance to the study of religion than these three figures did. Among such scholars one might name, to include only a few, Hideo Kishimoto (1903–1964) and Ichiro Hori (1910–1974) in Japan, P. V. Kane (1880–1972) in India, Raffaele Pettazzoni (1883–1959) in Italy, Annemarie Schimmel (1922–2003) in Germany, Henri-Charles Puech (1902–1986) and Marcel Simon (1907–1986) in France, S. G. F. Brandon (1907–1971) in the United Kingdom, and Okot p'Bitek (1931–1982) in Uganda, generally known for his contributions to literature but also important for his contributions to the study of African traditional religions. Nevertheless, the prominence of the institutions with which Eliade (Paris, Chicago), Smart (Lancaster, Santa Barbara), and Smith (Harvard, Dalhousie) were associated gave them unparalleled importance for scholars of religions who aspired to be more than philologists or historians in the strictest sense of the words. They served to define three major sub-communities within the study of religions.

Second thoughts

Figures like Eliade, Smart, and Smith provided starting points for the study of religions during the last fifty years. It is striking, however, how little of the work that has been done has directly developed their ideas. Most theoretical directions in the study of religion have been set from the outside as scholars reacted to the writings of Eliade, Smart, and Smith, especially Eliade. Although some have wanted to see the study of religion as a discipline, defined by a particular method, in practice it has been an undisciplined, polymethodic field largely planted with seeds from elsewhere. Many heirloom cultivars – ideas of earlier scholars such as Émile Durkheim, Sigmund Freud, and Max Weber – have continued to produce rich crops. Among the most important sources of new seeds have been anthropology, literary studies, cultural studies, and in recent days, the social sciences.

An anthropological turn

A central claim in Eliade's theory of religion was that 'archaic' peoples were the prime representatives of *homo religiosus*, religious humanity. It should not come entirely as a surprise, then, that in the last fifty years scholars of religions have turned to the field that once took such 'archaic' peoples as its object of study, anthropology. Initially they used anthropology as a means to assess and critique Eliade's claims. Then they returned to it repeatedly as a well from which to draw the freshest methodological waters. This is not the place to recite the history of anthropology over the last fifty years, but some names are unavoidable.

While Eliade had sought to identify the content of religious thought, the French anthropologist Claude Lévi-Strauss took a different approach, articulated in several books from the mid-1950s to the early 1960s (1955, 1958, 1962a, 1962b; Eng. trans. beginning 1961). Under the inspiration of structural linguistics, he tried to describe the logical patterns according to which the mind worked, along with their implications. The resulting structuralism, which made heavy use of binary oppositions to identify the language underlying religious 'utterances' rather than the meaning of the utterances themselves, became a major movement within the study of religions. Lévi-Strauss himself applied the method at length to the elucidation of myth. Wendy Doniger, who studies Hindu mythology, applied it to good effect in her early work on the god Śiva (1973). Hans Penner (1989, 1998) has continued to be a vigorous spokesperson for the possibilities of structuralism.

Other anthropologists also exercised profound influence on the study of religions beginning in the 1960s. The American, Clifford Geertz (1926–2006) sought to effect a paradigm shift in anthropology away from a structural-functionalist anthropology that sought causal explanations toward a hermeneutical anthropology that sought to understand the meaning of symbols. Among his most influential contributions to the study of religions are his programmes of 'thick description', identifying local knowledge, and 'reading' culture as a text, as well as his account of 'religion as a cultural system' (Geertz 1973, 1983). Another important anthropologist from the same period, Victor W. Turner (1920–1983), adapted Arnold van Gennep's analysis of rites of passage to many other cultural areas, exploring the anti-structural phase of 'liminality' in activities such as pilgrimage (Turner 1967, 1969,

1974). Mary Douglas (1921–2007) rose to prominence because of her book *Purity and Danger* (1966), which, inspired by structuralism, argued that dirt and pollution were not the result of natural experiences but rather reflected an inability to fit certain items into established categories. Each of these anthropologists was extremely influential on work in the study of religions. For example, Victor Turner is in some ways a founding figure for the later field of ritual studies.

The names Geertz, Turner, and Douglas hardly exhaust the anthropologists from the 1960s who had an impact on the study of religion. Among his many writings, the structuralist Edmund Leach (1966) published a harsh critique of Eliade. One might also mention Melford Spiro (1970) and Stanley Tambiah (1970, 1981), who worked on Burmese and Thai Buddhism, respectively. Spiro has been particularly important for a definition of religion that he published at the same time that Geertz published 'religion as a cultural system': religion is 'an institution consisting of culturally patterned interaction with culturally postulated superhuman beings' (Spiro 1966: 96).

Eventually this new generation of anthropologists came in for harsh criticism. Their successors found them vulnerable on a number of grounds, including an overly systematic view of culture, an inattention to the political dimensions of cultural activity, and a propensity to over-interpret the data. For scholars of religions, however, they had the effect of calling important paradigms into question, especially those associated with Eliade. Specifically, a grand synthesis of religious content such as Eliade and the other phenomenologists had attempted to provide seemed untenable and irresponsible to the complexities of cultural data.

Within the study of religions itself this kind of critique is probably best represented and furthered by a younger colleague of Eliade's at Chicago, Jonathan Z. Smith (1978, 1982, 2004). A specialist in Greco-Roman religions who has been more a writer of essays than of monographs, Smith has been particularly interested in issues of definition, classification (taxonomy), difference, and relation. A careful reader and relentless critic, Smith anticipated much future criticism by seeing Eliade's views as reflecting an overly conservative political orientation, emphasizing locative, normative aspects of religion while ignoring utopian, radical dimensions. Among Smith's other distinctive ideas is the claim that definitions should not be rooted in essential features, as in Spiro's definition mentioned above, but 'polythetic', loose bundles of features any one of which might not be present in a specific instance of religion. He has also insisted that the study of religion consists in translating the unknown into the known and of redescribing the original in terms of other categories. His favourite example of such translation is Émile Durkheim's *Elementary Forms of the Religious Life*, which translates the religious into the social.

Inspired in part by Smith as well as the anthropological turn, scholars of religion have largely abandoned the older phenomenological enterprise and turned instead to detailed studies informed by theoretical issues but carefully delimited in terms of geographical, temporal, cultural, and linguistic extent. They have also felt less comfortable than a scholar such as Eliade did about discussing religions of communities whose languages, history, and culture they do not themselves have a good working knowledge of. Such reluctance led Eliade and others with similar sentiments to lament the loss of the *grande oeuvre* and the fragmentation of the field into a great variety of subspecialties. From the other side, such limitations seemed a prerequisite for responsible scholarship.

Critical modes

Smith's work intersects with anthropological theory, but it intersects with more work as well. It also addresses issues of interest to various modes of critique that became common in the 1970s and 1980s. These modes – postmodern, post-structural, post-colonial, feminist – are most closely associated with literary and cultural studies. A number of French thinkers from the late 1960s were influential in their development, among whom the most famous are Jacques Derrida (1930–2004) and Michel Foucault (1926–1984). In some quarters these approaches are quite controversial.

The postmodern

Derrida's work is notoriously difficult, but perhaps one may say that it explores the limits of human speech and, implicitly, human conceptualization. For Derrida, human attempts to make definite utterances always ultimately fail; indeterminacy is implicit within them. If the goal of one kind of academic discourse is to construct meaningful accounts – or in Smith's terms, to translate the unknown into the known – the goal of an alternative kind of discourse is to deconstruct such accounts, to show that, ultimately and irredeemably, they miss out. This can often be done through creative rhetorical means that call into question the pretensions of the discourse at hand, for example, by responding to earnest attempts at precise definition by deliberately playing with words, blurring their boundaries and obscuring their meanings. Although Derrida's brilliance at such deconstruction is readily acknowledged, it is not clear that some of his epigones have not devolved into silliness.

The major impact of postmodernism has been not so much on the study of religion in the narrow sense as on theology. This makes sense, both because postmodernism rejects the 'modernist' project that an 'objective' study of religions would seem to presume, and because contemporary naturalist discourse often seems entirely at odds with theological claims. (Recently theologians and scientists have begun to explore a possible merger of the two.) In vulgar terms, if God can no longer be found in rational accounts, as in the days when philosophers of religion claimed to be able to prove God's existence by reason alone, perhaps intimations of God can be found in the inevitable limitations of naturalist discourse. Leading post-modern theologians include John D. Caputo, John Milbank, and Mark C. Taylor. Within the study of religions more narrowly, perhaps the best representative of this approach is Tomoko Masuzawa (1993, 2005), who has reread the history of the study of religion from a postmodern perspective.

Post-structural, post-colonial, and feminist currents

Many postmodern thinkers have tended to concentrate on language. For some of them, language in fact creates the world, and there is no world outside language. Such an orientation does not necessarily preclude social and ethical reflection, but other critical modes, post-structural, post-colonial, and feminist, arose with a more distinct orientation toward social criticism. Perhaps the leading thinker for this line of thought was Michel Foucault.

Among other concerns, Foucault examined the manner in which knowledge and power are mutually implicated. Powerful institutions and persons create knowledge in such a way that it perpetuates and extends their power. At the same time, those who possess knowledge also possess power. Power-knowledge exercises its governance through defining the marginal and controlling it in a number of ways. Foucault pursues the theme through the examination of institutions such as psychiatric treatment, hospitals, and prisons, as well as by looking at how what counts as knowledge, the various conditions for knowledge, have changed over the centuries. Although Foucault himself did little with religion *per se*, it should be fairly apparent that these ideas provide a rich set of possible themes for the study of religions to explore. Parallel currents of thought particularly important for the study of religion were post-colonialism and feminism.

Derrida and Foucault largely thought within the horizons of Europe. In her well-known article, 'Can the Sub-Altern Speak?', the Indian thinker and translator of Derrida, Gayatri Spivak (1988), famously re-directed his line of thinking in a post-colonial direction to talk about the marginalization of colonized people, especially women. Even larger was the impact of Edward Said's *Orientalism* (1978), which in some ways extended Foucault's project beyond the European frontier. The book examines the various ways in which Orientalism as a discourse, including the academic field known by that name, has imagined the people of the Middle East. According to Said, these imaginations are not accurate representations so much as the creation of images of an 'other' to the European self that serves the European self's own ideological purposes. Simultaneously, many women, who had largely been excluded from higher education prior to the twentieth century, began to examine the many ways in which academic discourse, including academic discourse about religions, had been narrowly centred on men. Once identified, such discourse easily appears as an instrument of control. Linking all of these approaches together is a perspective on human activity that emphasizes the social construction of reality and identity, political dominance and cultural hegemony, and society as a location for suppression, appropriation, and exploitation.

Post-structural, postcolonial, and feminist thought each had enormous impact upon the study of religion. It is fairly obvious that religion has served to subordinate and exclude women. For examples, one need only consider the hiring practices of almost all churches prior to the feminist critique or of the Roman Catholic Church and Orthodox synagogues still today. Many early feminist thinkers addressed issues of religion directly. Many of them also worked within Christian institutions or in explicit rejection of those institutions, and they were often theologians as much as scholars of religions. Among other names one may note Rosemary Radford Ruether (1983, 1992), Elisabeth Schüssler Fiorenza (1983), and, on the more radical side, Mary Daly (1973, 1978). Feminism has not, however, been limited to Christianity, and in many religious communities important women thinkers, such as Rita Gross (1993) in Buddhism and Judith Plaskow (1990) in Judaism, have emerged to criticize androcentrism and patriarchal authority, to re-read inherited traditions, and to reformulate their communities' teachings and practices. Their work has also had a salutary impact on the study of religions. If at the beginning of the period under consideration it was acceptable to equate men's religious activity with the religious activity of the entire community, it is no longer so today. A large number of publications have appeared devoted to women's religious lives. In addition, steps have been taken to encourage women's full participation in the academic community. One example is the Women Scholars Network of the International Association for the History of Religions, organized by Rosalind Hackett and Morny Joy.

Like feminism, post-colonial thought has had a major impact upon the study of religion. Said's *Orientalism* unleashed a reconsideration and critique of traditional representations not only of Arabs, Islam, and the Ancient Near East but also of people in Asia more generally. Similar dynamics can be found in writing about religions throughout the world. Writing on Islam and Christianity, Talal Asad (1993) famously critiqued Clifford Geertz's notion of to negotiate the crisis of representation is to write not about others, or only about others, but to write about themselves. Again, autobiographical reflection is hardly new to scholars of religions. Religious autobiography has a history that goes back, at least in the Christian context, to Augustine's *Confessions*. It is also a topic on which scholars of religions have done considerable work. Before television made experiences overseas more visibly accessible, scholars, including theologians and scholars of religions, often recounted their experiences abroad to a wider audience. In addition, a scholar as influential as Mircea Eliade wrote his autobiography at some length (Eliade 1981, 1988).

Nevertheless, under the impact of the crisis of representation, some scholars have abandoned the once standard divide between their scholarly work and their autobiographies. They have used autobiography as a presentational mode within their academic writings to a variety of rhetorical effects, one of them being to interrogate the authoritative gaze of the academic expert. In her study of Mama Lola, a Vodou priestess in New York, the American scholar, Karen McCarthy Brown (1991) provided an account not only of her own conversion experiences but also a fictionalized account of her subject's biography. While not exactly a work in religious studies, Amitav Ghosh's semi-autobiographical *In an Antique Land* (1992) contains much reflection on religion while reconstructing the geography of the Indian Ocean in medieval times. Robert Orsi, a recent president of the American Academy of Religion, has written an account that interweaves personal autobiography and family narrative with reflections on his situation as a scholar of religions studying the Catholicism in which he grew up (Orsi 2005). Autobiographical and other narrative forms have proven extremely useful for elucidating 'lived religion'.

Science returns

From their beginnings the social sciences have studied religions, but their interest in religion has waxed and waned. Perhaps twenty years ago psychologists found many other topics much more interesting than religion. Today there is considerable work being done on the psychology of religion from a variety of perspectives. Such work, however, is usually housed in other academic units than religious studies. It often does not make its way into the 'study of religions' narrowly conceived.

Within the study of religions more narrowly, science has occupied a tenuous place, in part because to some extent the field grew from theological roots. A standard trope, which received much impetus from Mircea Eliade, was the insistence that the study of religions should be hermeneutical, that is, an attempt at understanding other people's meanings, not explanatory, that is, engaged in providing reductive causal explanations of religion. Nevertheless, throughout much of the period under discussion, a few voices have championed the need for reductive explanations. They include Hans Penner and Edward Yonan in an important article from 1972, Robert Segal (1992) in an open debate with Daniel Pals, and Don Wiebe (1981, 1998).

Beginning in the 1990s, two scientific currents have begun to grow within the study of religions. The first seeks to explain religion in the terms of rational decision making, especially as employed in economic thinking. Bearing some resemblance to Adam Smith's discussion of religion in *The Wealth of Nations*, this direction began theoretically with Rodney Stark and William Sims Bainbridge's *A Theory of Religion* (1987). It is most widely associated with the work of Rodney Stark and younger colleagues such as Laurence Iannaccone and Roger Finke (Stark and Finke 2000). Stark *et al.* tend to address sociological topics, such as religious reaffiliation and conversion (explained by combining network theory with religious capital theory) and the positive effects of a free religious 'market' on religious practice. Other scholars, such as Ilkka Pyysiäinen in Finland and Joseph Bulbulia in New Zealand, are beginning to approach the economics of religion from somewhat different perspectives.

A second scientific approach to religion is beginning to receive widespread international attention: cognitive science, a burgeoning subject in many fields at the beginning of the twenty-first century, and a popular one as well. Some scholars have investigated the ways in which physiological processes in the brain lead either to mystical experiences or to notions of God. Among them are Michael Persinger (1987), who has explored the relationship between temporal lobe epilepsy and religious experience, James Austin (1998), who has analysed brain states among Zen practitioners, and Andrew Newberg (Newberg, d'Aquili, and Rause 2001), who has developed a theory of how intense meditation and prayer unusually arouse certain systems within the brain. Another approach works on the level of concepts, among other topics exploring the alleged competitive advantage that religious concepts have as 'memes'. Leading representatives of this approach include Pascal Boyer (2001), Robert McCauley and Thomas Lawson (2002), Justin Barrett (2004), and Harvey Whitehouse (Whitehouse and Laidlaw 2007).

Some popular authors, such as Richard Dawkins and Daniel Dennett, have employed a cognitive-scientific emphasis in explicit, high-profile attacks on religion. Nevertheless, both economic and cognitive-scientific analyses have been of great interest to some theologians as well as to scholars of religions. Indeed, some leading researchers in the field, such as Andrew Newberg and Justin Barrett, have explicit theological agendas.

At the time of writing, scholars of religions seem to be divided between two camps, one camp favouring critical cultural studies, the other favouring more scientific approaches. Although there have been some attempts to synthesize these two orientations, they are in their very beginning phases.

Final reflections

In her award-winning novel, *The Inheritance of Loss*, Kiran Desai (2006: 269) notes that we still inhabit a world 'where one side travels to be a servant, and the other side travels to be treated like a king'. The words 'servant' and 'king' are rather harsh, but the disparities that they point to are very real. The current chapter divides into two parts. The first part, the contextual, discusses the internationalization of the study of religion. The second part, the theoretical, reads as if the study of religion were mostly something undertaken by people living in Europe and the countries of the European diaspora, most notably, the United States and Canada. In part this division reflects the inadequacies of the author, whose primary base is in the United States. That inadequacy may itself reflect, however, certain realities about the study of religions today.

Compared to their colleagues in the natural sciences, scholars of religions in Europe and the countries of the European diaspora are very poorly funded. Compared with their colleagues in other parts of the world, particularly Africa, they have a wealth of resources at their disposal. Scholars from the rest of the world frequently do advanced study in Europe and the United States; the reverse is not often the case, and when it is, those scholars often find it difficult to get their degrees recognized at home, unless they also come with other degrees in hand. The theories that scholars most cite tend to be European and North American. For example, Chinese, Korean, and Japanese scholars have been actively discussing the work of, for example, Mircea Eliade and Jonathan Z. Smith. By contrast, many scholars from Europe or European diaspora countries who are not China experts might find it difficult to name a single Chinese theoretician who has been important in their work. Similarly, throughout the world, publication in the United States or Europe is often taken as a mark of professional quality. Publication in journals or with presses located elsewhere is generally less highly valued, and often results in less visibility. Gifted scholars from other parts of the world often jump at the chance to teach in Europe or the United States. Among many possibilities are, from Africa, the Nigerians Jacob Olupona (Harvard) and Afe Adogame (University of Edinburgh), and from India, where there are few programmes in religious studies, many members of the subaltern studies group: Ranajit Guha (UK, Vienna), Partha Chatterjee (Columbia, but also Calcutta), Gyan Prakash (Princeton), Dipesh Chakrabarty (Chicago), Sudipta Kaviraj (Columbia), and Gayatri Spivak (Columbia). In other words, when scholars from other parts of the world are taken seriously in the so-called West, they often move there.

Inasmuch as these disparities reflect disparities in wealth, access to resources, and political and social power, it may be difficult to change them through direct action within religious studies alone. They may change only as other parts of the world assume prominence on the global stage, as China appears to be doing. One also suspects that changes in theoretical hegemony within the study of religions are not leading but lagging changes. That is, they will occur only as a result of, and therefore after, shifts in social, political, and economic power. At the same time, the study of religions continues to globalize. At the 2005 Congress of the International Association for the History of Religions in Tokyo, Japan, new societies from Greece, Romania, South and Southeast Asia, and Turkey affiliated with the international body.

There are several tensions within the study of religion today. One has already been briefly noted, the tension between those who favour critical cultural studies and those who favour natural science. Another concerns the tired but apparently unavoidable division between theology and religious studies. As the preceding survey indicates, not all who count as scholars of religions have refrained from religious reflection in their work. As new scholars enter discussions within the study of religions, whether from other parts of the world or from other parts of the academy, such as the neurosciences, the question of the place of religious commitment and conviction within academic work continues to resurface. Indeed, some scholars have adopted that ultimate harbinger of contemporaneousness, the prefix 'post-', and begun to speak of a 'post-secular' age. The issue of religious commitment becomes especially important when religiously committed people with access to significant amounts of private money attempt to direct research in directions that they find attractive. This has happened in the case of the social and cognitive scientific study of religion (Templeton Foundation) and the study of Hinduism (Infinity Foundation).

Another location of tension is in the relationship between scholars of religions and the broader public. At the beginning of the twenty-first century, it is often easy to forget just how contentious work in the study of religions once was in Europe. The historical-critical study of the Bible is a good example. In 1839 David Friedrich Strauss received a chair at the University of Zurich, but his *Life of Jesus* was so controversial that he could never assume it. In recent years, committed religious practitioners from other traditions have begun to pay attention to what scholars of religions are saying about them, and they are not always happy. The most notorious case may be the criticism by traditional Hindus, led by Rajiv Malhotra, of scholars who use Freudianism to examine Hinduism, notably Wendy Doniger, Paul Courtright, and Jeffrey Kripal (Ramaswamy, de Nicolas, and Banerjee 2007). There have, however, been other instances of tension between tradition-minded, politically active Hindus and scholars of Hinduism, as well as between scholars and practitioners of other religions, such as Sikhs and Native Americans. Unfortunately, these debates have not always been conducted according to the norms of academic, or for that matter non-academic, civility. They have at times led not only to threats of violence but also to physical assault and caused scholars either to switch specializations, as Sam Gill has done, or to abandon academia altogether.

There is yet another reason why relationships between scholars of religions and the broader public would seem to be crucial at the beginning of the twenty-first century. With the shift from elite to mass universities came a shift away from cultural education rooted in the humanities towards advanced technical training rooted in the natural and social sciences. University students from privileged backgrounds once had the luxury of studying art, poetry, and religion. Now students all over the world enter higher education looking to improve their job prospects. The place of the humanities in this setting is precarious, and the study of religions perhaps more precarious than other fields. At the same time, events at the end of the twentieth and the beginning of the twenty-first centuries would seem to indicate that even for persons with limited interest in higher education as an end in itself, an understanding of religions is useful. Such persons may, however, find that usefulness in political and commercial purposes to which academics themselves object.

In any case, scholars of religions have begun to take serious steps to address audiences outside the academy. They have served as expert witnesses in courts of law. They have consulted for news agencies and the communications media. They have begun to give significant attention to the ways in which religion is studied in primary and secondary education. They have even begun to wonder why governments do not consult them more often. It is too early to tell what the eventual outcome of these various activities will be.

Notes

1 Liberal theologians had already abandoned such exclusive claims, while others were still able vigorously to assert traditional religious loyalties, as they began to do in the 1970s.
2 For specific information in this section, readers might consult the various chapters of Gregory D. Alles, ed., *Religious Studies: A Global View* (London: Routledge, 2008).

Bibliography

Asad, T., *Genealogies of Religion*, Baltimore, Johns Hopkins University Press, 1993.
Austin, J. H., *Zen and the Brain*, Cambridge, MIT Press, 1998.
Barrett, J. L., *Why Would Anyone Believe In God?* Walnut Creek, AltaMira Press, 2004.
Boyer, P., *Religion Explained*, New York, Basic Books, 2001.
Brown, K. M., *Mama Lola*, Berkeley, University of California Press, 1991.
Daly, M., *Beyond God the Father*, Boston, Beacon Press, 1973.
—— *Gyn/ecology*, Boston, Beacon Press, 1978.
Desai, K., *The Inheritance of Loss*, New Delhi, Penguin Books, 2006.
Doniger, W., *Asceticism and Eroticism in the Mythology of Śiva*, London, Oxford University Press, 1973.
Douglas, M., *Purity and Danger*, New York, Praeger, 1966.
Dubuisson, D., *Mythologies du XXe siècle*, Villeneuve-d'Ascq, Presses universitaires de Lille, 1993.
—— *L'Occident et la religion*, Bruxelles, Editions Complexe, 1998.
—— *Impostures et pseudo-science. L'œuvre de Mircea Eliade*, Villeneuve d'Asq, Presses universitaires du Septentrion, 2005.

Eck, D. L., *Encountering God*, Boston, Beacon Press, 1993.

Eliade, M., *Le mythe de l'éternel retour*, Paris, Gallimard, 1949.

—— *Traité d'histoire des religions*, Paris, Payot, 1949.

—— *Le chamanisme et les techniques archaïques de l'extase*, Paris, Payot, 1951.

—— *Le yoga. Immortalité et liberté*, Paris, Payot, 1954.

—— *1907–1937, Journey East, Journey West*, San Francisco, Harper & Row, 1981.

—— *Exile's Odyssey, 1937–1960*, Chicago, University of Chicago Press, 1988.

Faure, B., *The Rhetoric of Immediacy*, Princeton, Princeton University Press, 1991.

—— *Chan Insights and Oversights*, Princeton, Princeton University Press, 1993.

Fitzgerald, T., *The Ideology of Religious* Studies, New York, Oxford University Press, 2000.

—— *Discourse on Civility and Barbarity*, New York, Oxford University Press, 2007.

Frank, D. J., and J. Gabler, *Reconstructing the University*, Stanford, Stanford University Press, 2006.

Geertz, C., *The Interpretation of Cultures*, New York, Basic Books, 1973.

—— *Local Knowledge*, New York, Basic Books, 1983.

Ghosh, A., *In an Antique Land*, London, Granta Books, 1992.

Gill, S. D., *Mother Earth*, Chicago, University of Chicago Press, 1987.

Gross, R. M., *Buddhism After Patriarchy*, Albany, State University of New York Press, 1993.

Leach, E. R., 'Sermons by a Man on a Ladder,' *New York Review of Books* 7, no. 6 (20 October 1966).

Lévi-Strauss, C., *Tristes tropiques*, Paris, Plon, 1955.

—— *Anthropologie structurale*, Paris, Plon, 1958.

—— *La pensée sauvage,* Paris, Plon, 1962a.

—— *Le totémisme aujourd'hui*, Paris, Presses universitaires de France, 1962b.

Lincoln, B., *Discourse and the Construction of Society*, New York, Oxford University Press, 1989.

—— *Authority: Construction and Corrosion*, Chicago, University of Chicago Press, 1994.

—— *Religion, Empire, and Torture*, Chicago, University of Chicago Press, 2007.

Lopez, D. S., *Prisoners of Shangri-La*, Chicago, University of Chicago Press, 1998.

Madan, T. N., *Images of the World, Essays on Religion, Secularism, and Culture*, New Delhi, Oxford University Press, 2006.

Madan, T. N. (ed.), *Muslim Communities of South Asia*, New Delhi, Vikas, 1976.

—— *India's Religions*, Delhi, Oxford University Press, 2004.

Marcus, G. E., and M. M. J. Fischer, *Anthropology as Cultural Critique*, Chicago, University of Chicago Press, 1986.

Masuzawa, T., *In Search of Dreamtime*, Chicago, University of Chicago Press, 1993.

—— *The Invention of World Religions*, Chicago, University of Chicago Press, 2005.

McCauley, R. N., and E. T. Lawson, *Bringing Ritual to Mind*, Cambridge, Cambridge University Press, 2002.

McCutcheon, R. T., *Manufacturing Religion*, New York, Oxford University Press, 1997.

Müller, F. M., *Chips from a German Workshop*, vol. 1, London, Longmans, Green, 1867.

Newberg, A. B., E. d'Aquili, and V. Rause, *Why God Won't Go Away*, New York, Ballantine Books, 2001.

Orsi, R. A., *Between Heaven and Earth*, Princeton, Princeton University Press, 2005.

Penner, H. H., *Impasse and Resolution*, New York, P. Lang, 1989.

Penner, H. H. (ed.), *Teaching Lévi-Strauss*, Atlanta, Scholars Press, 1998.

Penner, H. H., and E. A. Yonan, 'Is a Science of Religion Possible?' *Journal of Religion* 52, no. 2 (April 1972): 107–133.

Pennington, Brian, 2005, 'Introduction: A Critical Evaluation of the Work of Bruce Lincoln,' *Method and Theory in the Study of Religion* 17, 1–7.

Persinger, M. A., *Neuropsychological Bases of God Beliefs*, New York, Praeger, 1987.

Plaskow, J., *Standing Again at Sinai*, San Francisco, Harper & Row, 1990.

Ramaswamy, K., A. de Nicolas, and A. Banerjee (ed.), *Invading the Sacred*, New Delhi, Rupa, 2007.

Ruether, R. R., *Sexism and God-talk*, Boston, Beacon Press, 1983.

—— *Gaia & God*, San Francisco, HarperSanFrancisco, 1992.

Said, E. W., *Orientalism*, New York, Pantheon Books, 1978.

Schüssler Fiorenza, E., *In Memory of Her*, New York, Crossroad, 1983.

Segal, R. A., *Explaining and Interpreting Religion*, New York, P. Lang, 1992.

Smart, N., *The Science of Religion & the Sociology of Knowledge*, Princeton, Princeton University Press, 1973.

—— *The Long Search*, Boston, Little, Brown, 1977.

—— *Worldviews, Crosscultural Explorations of Human Beliefs*, New York, Scribner's, 1983.

Smith, J. Z., *Map Is Not Territory*, Leiden, Brill, 1978.

—— *Imagining Religion*, Chicago, University of Chicago Press, 1982.

—— *Relating Religion*, Chicago, University of Chicago Press, 2004.

Smith, Wilfred Cantwell 1959, 'Comparative religion – Whither and Why?' in Eliade, Mircea, and Kitagawa, Joseph M. (eds), *The History of Religions, Essays in Methodology*, Chicago, University of Chicago Press, pp. 31–58.

—— *The Meaning and End of Religion*, New York, Macmillan, 1963.

—— *Towards a World Theology*, Philadelphia, Westminster, 1981.

Spiro, M. E., 'Religion, Problems of Definition and Explanation,' in Michael E. Banton (ed.), *Anthropological Approaches to the study of Religion*, London, Tavistock, 1966, pp. 85–126.

—— *Buddhism and Society*, New York, Harper & Row, 1970.

Spivak, G., 'Can the Subaltern Speak?' in C. Nelson and L. Grossberg (eds), *Marxism and the Interpretation of Culture*, Urbana, University of Illinois Press, 1988, pp. 271–313.

Stark, R., and W. S. Bainbridge, *A Theory of Religion*, New York, P. Lang, 1987.

Stark, R., and R. Finke, *Acts of Faith*, Berkeley, University of California Press, 2000.

Strenski, I., *Four Theories of Myth in Twentieth-Century History*, Basingstoke, Hampshire, Macmillan, 1987.

Tambiah, S. J., *Buddhism and the Spirit Cults in North-East Thailand*, Cambridge, Cambridge University Press, 1970.

—— *A Performative Approach to Ritual*, London, British Academy, 1981.

Turner, V. W., *The Forest of Symbols*, Ithaca, Cornell University Press, 1967.

—— *The Ritual Process*, London, Routledge & K. Paul, 1969.

—— *Dramas, Fields, and Metaphors*, Ithaca, Cornell University Press, 1974.

Whitehouse, H., and J. Laidlaw, *Religion, Anthropology, and Cognitive Science*, Durham, Carolina Academic Press, 2007.

Wiebe, D., *Religion and Truth*, The Hague, Mouton, 1981.

—— *The Politics of Religious Studies*, New York, St. Martin's Press, 1998.

Suggested reading

Alles, G. D. (ed.), *Religious Studies: A Global View*, London, Routledge, 2008.
An attempt to map the study of religions worldwide.

Antes, P., A. W. Geertz, and R. R. Warne (eds), *New Approaches to the Study of Religion*, Berlin, Walter de Gruyter, 2004.
Recent chapters on the study of religions, with several on the history of the study of religions in different parts of the world.

Doležalová, I., L. H. Martin, and D. Papoušek (eds), *The Academic Study of Religion during the Cold War*. New York, P. Lang, 2001.
Especially important for its detailed accounts of the study of religions in parts of Europe under Soviet influence.

Strenski, I. *Thinking about Religion*, Malden, MA, Blackwell, 2006.
A good historical, contextual account of the study of religions, although mostly devoted to the period before the Second World War.

Chapter 4

Religious history

John Wolffe

Introduction

Religious history is both one of the oldest and also one of the most recent approaches to the study of religion. Sometime in the later first century CE the Christian writer of the Gospel of Luke announced his intention 'to write an orderly account' of 'the things that have been fulfilled among us' in order that his readers might 'know the certainty of the things you have been taught' (NIV 1982: Luke 1:1–4). The intention was to compile a work of history, in the general sense of describing past events, but it was a history that had an explicit religious purpose in enabling readers to 'know … certainty', a certainty that was implicitly assumed to be self-evident from the narrative that followed. Some nineteen centuries later when Sidney E. Ahlstrom embarked on his seminal survey, *A Religious History of the American People*, he claimed that his theme was 'one of the most intensely relevant subjects on the face of the earth', but he did not profess to offer any 'certainty' for religious believers. On the contrary he was at pains at the outset to point out that religious history

> enjoys no rights of sanctuary, no immunity from the demands for evidence and plausibility that are made on historians generally. The historian cannot claim supernatural or divinely inspired sources of insight; nor on such grounds can he place one body of holy scripture above another.
>
> (Ahlstrom 1972: xiv)

Ahlstrom went on to insist that religious history should also include the study of 'secular' religiosity and moral seriousness; that it must attend to the 'radical diversity' of actual religious movements and experience; and that the social context of religious activity 'must ever be borne in mind'. These aspirations, foundational to the critical academic study of religious history as it developed in the later twentieth century, would have seemed very alien to the mindset of religiously-motivated historians at the time that the Gospel of Luke was written.

The scope of the concept of 'religious history' is a matter of significant confusion and debate. It is possible to discern a broad trend over time from the history with a religious purpose of the Gospel of Luke and other foundational ancient texts to the detached objective investigation of the religious dimensions of 'the larger frame of world history' (Ahlstrom 1972: xiv) that characterizes the contemporary academic discipline. Aspects of the older approach persist however, for example in the view of the editor of a collection of essays on

Historians of the Christian Tradition that 'for the sovereign God of Scripture, history is a tool for His own purposes' and his definition of religious historians as those who deal with 'people, ideas and events in a theologically informed fashion' (Baumann and Klauber 1995: 3, 11). For Ahlstrom, theology is subordinate to history, with theological developments presented in a 'historically conditioned' context, but for Baumann and Klauber the interpretation of history remains subordinate to their underlying theological convictions.

Alongside approaches in which history and theology are primary, is what might be characterized as the religious studies approach to the past, originating in the development in Germany around the turn of the twentieth century of the concept of *Religiongeschichte*. This word is normally translated into English as 'comparative religion' or 'history of religion(s)'. One leading British practitioner of religious history has pithily remarked that 'The academic subject called "The History of Religions" turns out to have nothing to do with the discipline of history' (Collinson 1999: 154). Central to the *Religiongeschichte* approach is the comparative study of different religious traditions, identifying commonalities and contrasts. The history of *religions* (in the plural) acknowledges the distinctive historic characteristics of various religious traditions, whereas implicit in the history of *religion* (in the singular) is a perception of religion as a universal human phenomenon in which the similarities between different traditions and cultural and geographical manifestations ultimately are more significant that the differences. Both approaches though yield results that are very different from the religious history written by scholars such as Ahlstrom and Collinson, who were trained as historians, and are concerned much more with understanding the detailed historical context of religious activity in a specific time and place, than with making comparisons across traditions, cultures and societies. A further difference of emphasis between history of religion(s) and religious history lies in the tendency of the former to give considerable attention to the origins and early history of religious traditions, whereas the latter is focused primarily on their later development. Nevertheless, as in relation to the explicitly theological history advanced by Baumann and Klauber, the issue is confused by fluid use of the term 'religious history'. For example the English translation of Hans Kippenberg's survey of the development of the discipline of comparative religion, *Entdeckung der Religiongeschichte*, was given the title *Discovering Religious History in the Modern Age* when 'Discovering the History of Religions ...' would have given a more accurate representation of its content (Kippenberg 2002).

A broad understanding of religious history thus overlaps significantly with other approaches to the study of religion, with theology on the one hand, and with the comparative study of religion on the other. In this chapter, however, a narrower working definition will be adopted, in concentrating particularly on that approach to the study of religion that is essentially a branch of the discipline of History, analogous for instance to anthropology of religion as a branch of Anthropology or sociology of religion as a branch of Sociology.

Religious history is founded on the historical methodology of rigorous analysis of the printed and archival records of the past in awareness of their cultural, political and social context. Institutional and official records (such as censuses) yield fascinating insights not only into organizational developments, but also into the grassroots realities of religious practice, especially when studied in conjunction with more personal documents such as letters, diaries, and oral history recordings. As in any branch of history the outcomes of such investigation have to be interpreted, and such interpretation will more or less subtly reflect the presuppositions of the particular scholar. However the underlying aspiration to reconstruct a specific *milieu* in the past as fully and objectively as possible distinguishes religious history from the overt confessional commitments of what might be termed theological history and the broader comparative ambitions of history of religion(s). It must be stressed, however, that methodological boundaries remain fluid, and that it is more useful to think in terms of a spectrum of different approaches to the study of religion in the past than of hard and fast distinctions.

Before turning to discuss the development of religious history in its modern form from the eighteenth century onwards, and more particularly during the second half of the twentieth century, it will be useful to provide a brief survey of much more longstanding traditions of theological history.

Antecedents

The uses of theological history

The term 'theological history' is used here in a general comparative sense to denote historical writing in any tradition that explicitly articulates or is clearly shaped by its underlying religious ideas. An early example of the genre was the ancient Chinese *Spring and Autumn Annals*, reputedly the work of Confucius (c551–479 BCE) and infused by Confucian morality and beliefs about the interplay of earthly events and heavenly judgements on them (Ng and Wang 2005: x). Probably broadly contemporary with Confucius were the historical books of the Hebrew Bible which recounted the chequered spiritual record of the people of Israel in their dealings with the Almighty (Halpern 1996). Half a millennium later the historical books of the Christian New Testament gave accounts of the life and ministry of Jesus of Nazareth, his death and resurrection, and the subsequent initial development of the Christian Church. While the extent to which such texts record actual objective historical events has been much debated (for contrasting perspectives see Brettler 1995; Wright 1992), their importance in shaping the consciousness of their respective religious traditions is undeniable (Sterling 1992: 17). The historical approach of such Jewish and Christian writings, locating events within a particular chronological timeframe, contrasts with the great Hindu epics, the *Mahabharata* and the *Ramāyāna*. Although many believe that the events recounted in them actually took place – as was apparent when in 1992 Hindu militants demolished the Babri Mosque at Ayodhya because it was believed to be on the site of a temple built by Lord Ram – their religious power arises from a perceived timelessness that transcends chronological specificity (Frykenberg 1996: 166, 173; Kurien 2007: 170).

As the passage of time gave Christianity a past of its own, it began to acquire its own historians, most notably Eusebius of Caesarea (c260–c340), who recounted the history of the church from its beginnings to his own times in the reign of Constantine, and Bede (c673–735), who described the early history of the church in England. The histories of Eusebius and Bede were both shaped by their strong theological vision of divine providence and redemption, but they also provided much factual information that would otherwise have been lost to posterity. Meanwhile in *The City of God*, written between 413 and 426, Augustine of Hippo provided a seminal work of theological history, profoundly influencing subsequent Christian thought about the overall shape of the past, but saying little about the detail of specific events (Bauman and Klauber 1995: 59–116.)

The emergence of Islam in the seventh century CE in due course gave rise to a particularly rich tradition of historical writing. Although the Qu'rān itself is a work of prophecy not history, Muhammad transmitted to his followers a strong sense of his own place in history, a perception reinforced by the dramatic expansion of Muslim power in the decades after his death (Rosenthal 1968: 26, 129). Early Islamic historical writing was fragmentary in character, but al-Tabari (*d.* 923 CE), who lived in what is now Iraq, achieved both an impressive synthesis of earlier sources, and a theological vision of 'the idea of the integration of all prophetic missions in history, and also the idea of the unity of the *umma*'s experiences' (Duri 1983: 159). Al-Biruni (973–1048 CE) compiled his *Chronology of Ancient Nations*, a strikingly evenhanded gathering of information regarding the ritual calendars and religious development of Christianity, Judaism and other non-Muslim traditions of his time, as well as of Islam itself (Sachau 1879). From the eleventh century CE onwards theological concerns came increasingly to shape Islamic historiography, but there was also an enduring capacity to provide valuable factual accounts of contemporary events, as for example in Ibn Shaddād's vivid narrative of the siege of Acre in 1191 (Rosenthal 1968: 143; Robinson 2003: 147–8).

Religious conflict, both within and between traditions, also left a strong imprint on historical writing. Some of the earliest quasi-historical narratives from early Christianity are accounts of martyrdoms, which were accorded great religious significance because of the analogy they presented with the death of Jesus himself (Musurillo 1972). Similarly, 'the divisive history of martyrdom' dating back to the death of al-Husayn at Karbala in 680 has dominated Shi'ite historical consciousness and operated as a major factor perpetuating separation from the majority Sunni Muslim community (Cook 2001: 58–9). Christian and Muslim accounts of the events of the Crusades perpetuated rival interpretations of their religious purpose and meaning (Gabrieli 1969; Peters 1971). The division of Western Christianity in the sixteenth century gave a major stimulus to historical writing because the legitimacy of the Protestant Reformers depended on interpreting the past to claim that they were seeking to restore the purity of apostolic times that had been corrupted by the Catholic Church. Such a perspective was presented by writers such as Heinrich Bullinger (1504–75), Lucas Osiander (1534–1604), and John Foxe (1516–87), whose *Acts and Monuments… of the Church* linked a Protestant reading of Christian history to accounts of the sufferings of the martyrs under Queen Mary, and a patriotic assertion of special role of the English people in the purposes of God (Cameron 2005: 122–40; Bauman and Klauber 1995: 117–38). The Roman Catholic response was led by Caesar Baronius (1538–1607) who in his *Ecclesiastical Annals* sought to marshal historical evidence for the continuity and validity of Catholic beliefs and practices (Cameron 2005: 141–4).

Theological history provides otherwise irrecoverable evidence of the distant past and an awareness of the place of religion in a wider historical landscape. Such texts can also be invaluable for understanding the outlooks of writers and their contemporaries: for example Foxe's very widely read work played a major role in shaping the religious and political culture of early modern England (Haller 1963). Contrasts and fluctuations in the historical activity of religious communities are also revealing. The widespread perception that Buddhists and Hindus lacked a sense of history is belied by texts such as the *Mahāvamsa*, which developed in Sri Lanka from the sixth century CE onwards (Frykenberg 1996: 152–3; Maraldo 2004: 332–3), but, outside China, levels of activity and interest in South and East Asia were low relative to the strong Christian and Islamic traditions of historical writing. There was also relatively little historical writing in diaspora Judaism between the second and fifteenth centuries CE, except when a need was felt to record the bitter experience of persecution (Myers 1997).

The impact of the Enlightenment

The origins of later approaches to the writing of religious history are to be found in the eighteenth century. Leading historians of that period represented a wide spectrum of personal religious beliefs, from the overt scepticism of David Hume (1711–76), through the measured cynicism of Edward Gibbon (1737–94) to the committed but moderate Protestantism of Johann Lorenz von Mosheim (c 1694–1755) and William Robertson (1721–93). They were all, however, inspired by a characteristic Enlightenment aspiration to rational detachment, which although imperfectly achieved, still represented a significant break from polemical theological history.

Edward Gibbon's *Decline and Fall of the Roman Empire* (1776–88) is an established classic of secular historiography, but it was also a seminal work of religious history that gives due weight to the role of Christianity, but eschews Christian triumphalism and gives extensive attention to other religious traditions. Thus a penetrating analysis of the development of Christianity and its relationship to the Roman government (Chapters 15 and 16) is balanced by a sympathetic account of the attempt of the Emperor Julian to restore paganism (Chapter 23), and a critical judgement on the eventual suppression of paganism under Theodosius (Chapter 28). Gibbon gave an Enlightenment cast to the usual Protestant polemic against Roman Catholicism, by representing the subsequent 'degeneracy' of the Catholic Church as an assimilation of residual polytheism and pagan 'superstition'. A later chapter (50) provides a full assessment of the ministry of Muhammad and its immediate aftermath, with judgements that are mixed but overall by no means negative (Gibbon 1998).

Mosheim sought to write '*unpartheiischen und gründlichen*' (impartial and thorough) church history. His work was translated into English in 1765 and was widely read in the English as well as German-speaking world. He attacked historians who imposed their own value judgements on the past, but though he eschewed the traditional prejudices of his Lutheran heritage he manifested the newer prejudices of the Enlightenment in readiness to characterize religious practices he disliked as 'irrational', 'superstitious' or 'fanatical' (Cameron 2005: 149–52). Robertson was similarly highly critical of earlier historians. In his *History of Scotland* (1759) he wrote with reference to the reign of Mary Queen of Scots:

> But as the same passions which inflamed parties in that age have descended to their posterity; as almost every event … has become the object of doubt or of dispute; the eager spirit of controversy soon discovered, that without some evidence more authentic and more impartial than that of such historians, none of the points in question could be decided with certainty.

> (Robertson 1996a: vi)

He went on to list the original sources that he had himself consulted. For him too, however, a Protestant polemic against the pre-Reformation Church as false religion was replaced by an Enlightenment characterization of it as bigoted, superstitious and illiberal (Robertson 1996a: vol. 1, 145–57). He also retained a strong sense of underlying divine providential purpose in the unfolding of human history and the progress of Christian civilization (Robertson 1996a: vol. 1, lix). In paradoxical contrast to his sceptical friend David Hume, Robertson emphasized the political rather than religious character of the Reformation, whereas Hume in his *History of England* (1754–9) portrayed it as a religious movement, whose very excesses were an implicit argument against religion itself (Fearnley-Sander 1990: 331).

Robertson also endeavoured to develop an objective understanding of non-Christian religious traditions. Thus in his *History of America* (1777) he observed that most of the evidence currently available regarding native American religion came from priests and missionaries, who, he suggested, 'engrossed by the doctrines of their own religion, and habituated to its institutions, are apt to discover something which resembles those objects of their veneration in the opinions and rites of every people' (Robertson 1996b: vol. 2, 181). In his own analysis he emphasized the non-theistic nature of pre-Columbian religion. Similarly, in his last work on India (1791), he urged his readers to suspend their own incredulity towards Hinduism, and to recognize the integrity of its adherents (Robertson 1996c: 313, 434).

Enlightenment approaches initially co-existed with theological ones. For example *The History of the Church of Christ* (1794–1809) by Joseph and Isaac Milner was shaped by the authors' commitment to demonstrating the historical continuity of their own Evangelical Protestant convictions (Walsh 1959). Competing and selective readings of the past played an important role in fuelling the internal conflicts of the early nineteenth-century Church of England (Nockles 2007). On the other side of the Atlantic the copious historical writings of Philip Schaff (1819–93) were shaped by his conviction that the United States had a special providential role to give birth to the Christianity of the future (Conser and Twiss 1997: xi–xii).

Even where explicit theological agendas were muted, a belief in inexorable human 'progress' was central to historical writing in the English-speaking world in the nineteenth century. It shaped the secular scholarship of Thomas Babington Macaulay as well as the work of a significant school of 'Liberal Anglican' historians, which included Thomas Arnold (1795–1842), Henry Hart Milman (1791–1868) and Arthur Penrhyn Stanley (1815–81). Nevertheless Milman's principle of 'accommodation', the idea that belief systems are not fixed for all time, but are shaped by and to their particular historical context, represented a significant step towards a more modern approach to religious history (Forbes 1952: 76–8). Milman applied this approach in successive works, the *History of the Jews* (1829), *History of Christianity* (1840), and *History of Latin Christianity* (1854), with his ability to rise above traditional prejudices evident in his balanced treatment of the Middle Ages, and his insistence that Christians should overcome historic antipathies through a better understanding of the Jews. Stanley, who became Regius Professor of Ecclesiastical History at Oxford University in 1856, articulated an expansive understanding of his discipline, which, he argued, should be quite as much concerned with the abolition of the slave trade as with the niceties of liturgical vestments:

> Never let us think that we can understand the history of the Church apart from the history of the world, any more than we can separate the interests of the clergy from the laity, which are the interests of the Church at large.
>
> (Stanley 1861: xxxiii)

In his subsequent *Lectures on the History of the Eastern Church* he gave significant attention to Muhammad, affirming the positive qualities of Muslims which he said 'no Christian can regard without reverence' (Stanley 1861: 334).

In the medium term, however, intellectual trends worked against Stanley's broad ambitions for the subject. In the late nineteenth and early twentieth centuries the consolidation of History and Theology as separate academic disciplines marginalized theological history, and left even objective work on religious history in an uncomfortable no man's land. The difficulty was exacerbated by a growing culture of academic specialization which made the confident generalizations of an earlier age appear suspect (Cameron 2005: 156), and by the tendency of increasingly embattled churches to look inwards rather than outwards for reassurance of their own significance. Technical scholarly standards, in respect particularly of detailed even-handed sifting of evidence, improved, but breadth of vision contracted. Thus Norman Sykes, one of the leading British church historians of the first half of the twentieth century, was notable for penetrating analysis of the inner dynamics of eighteenth-century Anglicanism, but displayed an innocence of religious worlds beyond the Church of England, let alone beyond Christianity (Kent 1987: 7, 99–103). Similarly Peter Guilday, the 'most significant historian of American Catholicism' in the same period, devoted his career to the writing of biographies of bishops, for which he was at pains to get approval from their living successors (Dolan 1993: 152–3). Conversely, standard general histories, at least of periods subsequent to the Reformation, usually had little to say about religion.

The rise of the new religious history

It is a significant irony that the very year, 1963, in which, according to Callum Brown, 'organised Christianity [began] a downward spiral to the margins of social significance' (Brown 2001: 1), also saw the publication of a book that has had a seminal influence in stimulating a return to much more widespread intellectual interest in religious history. Edward Thompson's *Making of the English Working Class* shocked the devout by its negative and in some respects gratuitously offensive interpretation of the impact of Methodism during the Industrial Revolution. However, in a not dissimilar way to the work of Gibbon and Hume two centuries earlier, it made a compelling case that religion had to be taken seriously as an historical phenomenon even by those who rejected its ontological claims. Moreover Thompson's own Left-wing credentials ensured that other British socialist historians were encouraged to move away from the simplistic analysis of religion suggested by Marxist theory into a much more subtle appreciation of its role in social and political history. A similar process in relation to an earlier period was stimulated by Christopher Hill, another leading historian strongly associated with the Left, who elucidated the role of religion in the turbulent political and social history of the seventeenth century (for example Hill 1964; Hill 1970). The readiness of socialist historians to take religion seriously was further advanced by the changing nature of Roman Catholicism in the wake of Vatican II which shook previous stereotyped perceptions of its past (Obelkevich *et al.* 1987: 5–7).

Meanwhile the cultural and spiritual ferment of the 1960s contributed to a growing historical interest in forms of religious activity outside the structures and conventions of organized Christianity, evident in 1971 in the publication, to great critical acclaim, of Keith Thomas's *Religion and the Decline of Magic*. In this book, Thomas, drawing on insights from social anthropology, sought to elucidate the diverse belief systems of early modern England, including astrology, magic, witchcraft, prophecy, ghosts and fairies, and their ambivalent relationships to organized Christianity. His approach has been emulated in significant comparable studies of other societies and periods (notably Butler 1990, Connolly 1982, Devlin 1987, Hutton 1996, Obelkevich 1976).

In the United States too the 1960s and 1970s saw the beginnings of new directions in religious history, symbolized above all by the publication of Ahlstrom's massive and still unsuperseded survey in 1972. The intellectual dynamics of the process were somewhat different from those in Britain, with a lack of influential figures in 'secular' history such as

Hill and Thompson, who became centrally interested in religion. Rather, the rise of the 'new social history' in America initially seemed to be an irrelevance to established practitioners of religious history who framed their subject in terms of intellectual history and theology rather than social history (Stout and Taylor 1997: 17). Nevertheless the subject was developing fresh dynamism. A central representative figure has been Martin Marty (b. 1928), professor of modern Christian history at the University of Chicago from 1963 to 1998. Like A. P. Stanley a century before, Marty has perceived an expansive role for his discipline, characterizing himself not as a church historian but as a historian of American religion (Bauman and Klauber 1995: 581). In his prolific writings on American religious history, culminating in a three-volume study of the twentieth century (Marty 1986–1995), his central preoccupation has been with the diversity and pluralism of the nation's religious life:

> … in the face of the most jumbled and competitive mélange of religiosities the world has ever known, my project almost naturally came to focus around the philosophical theme of the one and the many.
>
> (quoted Dolan and Wind 1993: p. ix)

Although Marty's personal influence has been substantial it should not be exaggerated (Stout and Taylor 1997: 23), but by the 1980s a similar agenda came to dominate American religious history. The copious publications of the decade showed both a convergence between social and religious history and a fascination with 'outsiders' rather than mainstream Christian denominations (Marty 1993).

Alongside Britain and the United States, the country with the most active intellectual community of religious historians is France, something of a paradox in view of the country's rapid dechristianization, and its traditions of secular education (Hilaire: 2004: 3). Whereas in America interest in religious history might be explained as a byproduct of contemporary religious resurgence, in France as to a lesser extent in Britain, scholarly fascination with religion in the past has increased even as the influence of Christianity has declined in the present. Its appeal seems to lie in the ability of researchers to move well beyond the preoccupations of unfashionable institutions and clerical elites, to consider the religious life of ordinary people. In the introduction to their three-volume *Histoire Religieuse de la France Contemporaine* (1985–8), covering the period since 1880, Gerard Cholvy and Yves-Marie Hilaire defined their subject as

> *Religious history* and not the history of the adherents of a single church. We aim to take account of many dimensions of religious activity: beliefs, practices, understandings and impulses, whether orthodox or not, whether faith known or faith lived, whether unbelief or a way of believing differently.
>
> (Cholvy and Hilaire 1985–8: I, 6, translated)

Cholvy and Hilaire's statement of their ambitions provides a good summary of the scope of the new religious history. It is impossible in this short survey to reference, let alone discuss, even a cross-section of the rich flowering of publications that appeared in the 1980s and 1990s, but the survey articles listed in the bibliography will provide a starting-point for readers who want to explore the literature further. It will be useful, however, to list some of its salient characteristics. First, religion is treated primarily in a social and cultural context rather than a theological and intellectual one. Micro-studies of particular localities are a common approach, but they move away from the traditional genre of narrative church histories to explore communities in the round. It follows, second, that methodology owes more to the social sciences, particularly anthropology and sociology, than it does to theology. Third, there is an aspiration to reconstruct the religious worlds and experiences of 'ordinary' people, rather than present official ecclesiastical perspectives. Thus, fourth, although the broad frame of reference has been Christian, the nature of 'Christianity' is often redefined and reinterpreted and considerable space given to forms of belief that are anything but 'orthodox'. Finally, there is an endeavour to illuminate the religious histories of hitherto-neglected groups, notably women, black people, 'pagans' and native Americans. A representative sample of influential practitioners, in addition to those already mentioned, might include Catherine Albanese (Native American religion); Jay Dolan (American Catholicism); Eamon Duffy (sixteenth-century English Catholicism); Catherine Hall (gender, class and religion); Nathan Hatch (popular Christianity in the early American republic); David Hempton (Methodism in Britain, Ireland and America); Ronald Hutton (British paganism and popular ritual); Hugh McLeod (religion and society in modern Britain and continental Europe), Alfred Raboteau (African American religion) and Michel Vovelle (dechristianization in France).

The advance of the new religious history was rather slower in other English-speaking countries and in continental Europe outside France. South Africa's intellectual isolation during the apartheid era was conducive to the persistence of a traditional Protestant white-dominated church history, although since 1993 there has been cross-fertilization with earlier pioneering endeavors to give due weight to the religious history of black people. This has enabled a more balanced and richer synthesis (Elphick and Davenport 1997). In Australia, although the 1980s and 1990s saw numerous publications of a conventional denominational history kind, only a handful of scholars began to produce the kind of religious history now widespread in the northern hemisphere (Carey et al. 2001). Nevertheless, by the turn of the millennium, the Australian-based *Journal of Religious History* was showing itself receptive to more innovative approaches.

Similarly it was not until the 1990s that religious history began to gain ground in Germany and, significantly, a key pioneering book was the work of an Englishman, David Blackbourn (Blackbourn 1993; Williamson 2006: 139). Since then, however, substantial advances have been made, notably in the work of Lucien Hölscher, Thomas Nipperdey, and Hartmut Lehmann. A particular preoccupation of German religious history has been with exploring the political implications of the country's distinctive religious composition, with a Protestant majority, a large Catholic minority (35 percent of the total population in 1900), and (until the Holocaust) a small but particularly high profile Jewish minority. To what extent did religion, religious division (or conversely the rejection of religion) contribute to the tensions that gave birth to Nazism and the Holocaust? (Williamson 2006).

In the Netherlands the Research Centre Religion and Society at the University of Amsterdam has played a valuable role in stimulating interactions between historians and social scientists (for example see Van der Veer 1996), but here as in Scandinavia the dominant approach has continued to be the study of church history in theological faculties. The situation in these historically predominantly Protestant countries is mirrored in Spain, where mainstream historians have remained reluctant to engage with religion, while ecclesiastical historians have been preoccupied with the internal dynamics of the Catholic Church (Pellistrandi 2004: ix–xi). The fall of the Soviet Union opened the door to new approaches to the study of Russian religious history, but the quality of work has hitherto been mixed (Husband 2007).

Recent decades have, however, seen significant transitions in the way historians write about Christianity in the non-Western world. A longstanding tradition of history written from the perspective of Western missionaries reached its culmination in 1964 with a survey by Bishop Stephen Neill (Neill 1964). In the 1960s and 1970s more secularly minded scholars developed a much more critical counter-narrative of the missionary as cultural imperialist villain rather than Christian evangelistic hero. Both approaches, however, were unsubtle in their understanding of relationships between missions and empire which were assumed, whether for better or worse, to be closely bound up with each other. They also lacked appreciation of the dynamics of non-Western societies and cultures, apt to be perceived as passive beneficiaries or victims of missionary attention, rather than as active agents in their own religious and cultural development (Peterson and Allman 1999: 1–2). More recent books, notably by Brian Stanley (1990) and Andrew Porter (2004), have portrayed missionaries as in a much more ambivalent relationship to empire, sometimes working in concert with imperialistic forces, but maintaining their own religious agendas, and sometimes through their sympathy with indigenous peoples working against the advance of empire, or even sowing some of the seeds of its subsequent disintegration. In the meantime, engagement with the social sciences has contributed to a much more nuanced understanding of African, Asian and Latin American Christianities in their indigenous contexts rather than merely as a narrative of European and North American evangelization. In relation to Africa a seminal work was a study of nineteenth-century missionaries among the Tswana people by the anthropologists, John and Jean Comaroff (1991), while for Latin America, a book by the sociologist, David Martin (1990), has had a similarly extensive influence.

Such approaches are reflected in surveys of African Christianity by Elizabeth Isichei (1995), of India by Robert Frykenberg (2008), and in a collection of essays arising from the Currents in World Christianity project (Lewis 2004). There has also been an explicit endeavour by African historians 'to tell the story of African Christianity, not Christianity in Africa, as an African story, by intentionally privileging the patterns of African agency' (Kalu 2005).

Towards a history of religious diversity

Despite the richness and vitality of the new religious history its obvious limitation, from a Religious Studies perspective, was the retention of primarily Christian frames of reference even when Christian confessional commitments and institutional preoccupations receded. Such a criticism must be moderated by the acknowledgement that historical scholarship relating to North America and Western Europe naturally reflected the religious make-up of those societies in the period studied. Except in the far distant and the very recent past, their organized religious composition was a predominantly Christian one, with Jews and Native Americans representing the only significant longstanding visible minorities. If a historical narrative of Christian predominance in periods before the later twentieth century is to be questioned, the most plausible basis for doing so lies not in according exaggerated importance to small minorities from other religions, but in questioning the extent to which Christianization was ever complete in the face of the arguable long-term persistence of indigenous pre-Christian and pagan belief systems (Stark 2001). On the other hand representatives of other religious traditions in the West were sometimes noteworthy links to very different worlds, or significant forerunners of later developments, so their almost complete historical invisibility needed to be redressed.

Historical scholarship on Judaism and on religion outside the West pointed something of a way forward, because the bifurcation between 'church' and 'secular' history that occurred in the Christian historiographical world in the earlier twentieth century was alien to most other religious traditions and cultures. While the absence of distinctions between the history of Jews as an ethnic group and the history of Judaism as a religious tradition brings its own conceptual difficulties, it means that works such as Salo Wittmeyer Baron's monumental *Social and Religious History of the Jews* (Baron 1952–83) were in some respects forerunners of the wider trend to integrate the history of religion with 'secular' developments (Myers 1997). W. Montgomery Watt in his studies of Muhammad published in the early 1950s also found it essential to integrate the investigation of religion and ideology with 'the economic, social and political background' (Watt 1953: xi).

From the 1970s the trends apparent in the religious history of Christian societies were being paralleled elsewhere. In analysing nineteenth-century Sri Lankan Buddhism, Kitsiri Malalgoda combined sociological training with historical methodology (Malalgoda 1976). In his study of early Islam, Fred Donner took religious inspiration very seriously while also providing a richly detailed analysis of the political and military factors that contributed to the rapid expansion of Muslim power in the decades after Muhammad's death. Islam, Donner concluded, 'provided the ideological underpinnings for this remarkable breakthrough in social organization' (Donner 1981:9).

Barbara Metcalf's study of Islamic revival in India under British rule in the later nineteenth century offered a penetrating analysis of the interplay of religious and political factors in a very different historical context, of considerable importance for understanding the dynamics of subsequent Muslim resurgence in the West in the South Asian diaspora of the twentieth century (Metcalf 1982). Hitherto there have only been isolated attempts to write systematic religious histories of Asian societies, but James Huntley Grayson's study of Korea, first published in 1989, was a distinguished achievement. It covers a wide chronological span and weaves together analysis of the major world religions – Buddhism, Confucianism, Islam and Christianity – that have had a presence in the peninsular with an assessment of the enduring influence of Korean traditional religion (Grayson 2002). James Thrower undertook a similar assignment for Central Asia, in a book that focused particularly on the nineteenth and twentieth century religious transitions associated with Russian imperialism, Soviet oppression, and the eventual reconstruction of Islam in the region following the fall of the Soviet Union (Thrower 2004).

Hindu religious history has developed in particularly close association with the wider history of India. This linkage has at times been problematic insofar as it has led to subordination to ideological agendas deriving from colonialism and postcolonialism on the one hand and Indian nationalism on the other (White 2006: 122–30). On the other hand some of the publications of the influential Subaltern Studies school, which highlights the study of previously neglected groups such as women and the poor, have pointed the way towards a more evenhanded integration of religious and social history. Romila Thapar's authoritative survey of early Indian history gives extensive attention to religion (Thapar 2003). Thapar has also developed a penetrating critique of ideologically committed readings of the Indian religious past (Thapar 2005), an approach paralleled for the modern era in the work of Sumit Sarkar (Sarkar 2002). Sikh religious history has also engendered significant tensions between ideologues and serious scholars (McLeod 2007: 7–8) but important contributions have nevertheless been made (for example McLeod 2007; Oberoi 1994).

In Western religious history, however, even in the 1980s religious traditions other than Christianity and Judaism tended to be very much an afterthought. Thus in their three volume work of well over a thousand pages on modern French religion, Cholvy and Hilaire assigned them merely a part of one chapter of twenty-nine pages on 'Migration' after ten pages on Christian migration, and six on Jews (Cholvy and Hilaire 1985–8: III, 401–29). Only in the final chapter of a two-volume collection of essays, *Religion in Victorian Britain*, produced by the Open University, was 'The impact of other religions' discussed (although earlier chapters gave substantial coverage to Judaism and secularism) (Parsons 1988). A *festschrift* for Martin Marty, published in 1993 and entitled *New Dimensions in American Religious History* did not find much room for 'new dimensions' that were not primarily Christian ones (Dolan and Wind 1993).

Nevertheless other currents of enquiry were already flowing, and were given increased impetus in the 1990s by events such as the Rushdie affair of 1989 that raised the profile of minority religious communities in the West. Moreover as these communities matured there was a growing recognition that they had a religious history of their own stretching back several generations and sometimes considerably further. Thus a pioneering study published in 1984 and reissued in 1997 provided evidence of enduring commitment to Islam among some African slaves forcibly brought to North America in the eighteenth and nineteenth centuries (Austin 1997). In a number of books and edited volumes in the late 1980s and 1990s Yvonne Yazbeck Haddad mapped out the history of Muslims in America (for example Haddad 1991). Thomas Tweed's account of American encounters with Buddhism, first published in 1992, took the story back well into the nineteenth century, even though he concluded that conditions were then not conducive to Buddhism taking root in the United States (Tweed 2000). For Richard Seager, the watershed came with the World's Parliament of Religions in Chicago in 1893, which signalled 'the end of the era of Protestant triumphalism in America and the beginnings of a new twentieth century world of religious pluralism' (Seager 1995: x). When in 1993 and 1994 the Open University produced a companion collection of essays on religion in Britain since 1945, traditions other than Christianity received extensive coverage (Parsons 1993–4). A supplementary volume on Victorian religion, published in 1997, contained a substantial chapter by Gwilym Beckerlegge tracing the nineteenth-century roots of their presence in Britain (Beckerlegge 1997). Also in 1997, in a review essay, it was possible for Tweed to characterize the history of Asian religions in the United States as now an 'emerging subfield' (in Conser and Twiss 1997: 189–207). A further notable advance came in 2001 with Peter Van der Veer's study of religious and cultural interactions between Britain and India, which demonstrated the potential for scholarship to move away from the paradigms of Christian mission history to explore religious encounters in a more even-handed fashion (Van der Veer 2001).

Literature in the field expanded rapidly in the 1990s and early 2000s, especially in relation to Buddhism and Islam. Islam has been shown to have had a long history in the Americas, not only among African Americans (Gomez 2005), but also attracting white converts, such as Alexander Russell Webb, who ran a Muslim Mission in Manhattan in the 1890s (Abd-Allah 2006). A British counterpart to Webb, William Henry Quilliam, led the Liverpool Muslim Institute during the same decade (Beckerlegge 1997: 243–65).

In 2004 Humayun Ansari published a detailed scholarly history of British Islam (Ansari 2004), and although other traditions and national contexts have yet to receive such systematic treatment, the necessary foundations for such achievements are being laid (for example by Kay 2004, Kurien 2007).

The impact of such historical recognition of religious diversity remained patchy even in the early years of the twenty-first century. For example even a book as innovative in other respects as Callum Brown's *Death of Christian Britain* (Brown 2001) remained anchored to the premise that secularity was the only viable alternative to Christianity in the later twentieth century, with other religions notably absent from the analysis. At one level the growing historical attention given to non-Christian traditions can thus be seen as an important rebalancing of the weight of scholarship, but it also potentially has more profound implications for how religious history is researched and studied (cf Tweed 1997, Leonard *et al.* 2005). Given the contemporary and near-contemporary nature of much of the material under review, it naturally fosters a yet closer interdisciplinary engagement between historians, scholars of religion and social scientists. There is also the prospect of a future religious history in which the internal history of any tradition receives less attention than connecting themes, such as the multi-layered and sometimes contested religious associations of particular localities, for example Ayodyha, Glastonbury, Jerusalem and Uluru. Religious identities, and the nature of religion itself, are likely to be perceived as malleable and changing rather than as fixed points of reference. Study of the various forms of encounter between religious traditions will probably loom large, with contemporary experience, both of conflict and of coexistence, stimulating re-examination of much earlier periods (Fletcher 2003; Wolffe 2004). The challenge for future scholars will be to keep such exciting newer lines of enquiry in creative tension with continuing endeavours to understand the internal history of particular religious traditions, while interpreting past patterns of belief and practice in a manner that respects their integrity and avoids anachronism.

Bibliography

Abd-Allah, U.F. (2006), *A Muslim in Victorian America: The Life of Alexander Russell Webb*, New York: Oxford University Press.

Ahlstrom, S.E. (1972), *A Religious History of the American People*, New Haven, CT and London: Yale University Press.

Ansari, H. (2004), '*The Infidel Within': Muslims in Britain since 1800*, London: Hurst & Co.

Austin, A.D. (1997), *African Muslims in Antebellum America: Transatlantic Stories and Spiritual Struggles*, New York: Routledge (first published 1984, New York: Garland).

Baron, S.W. (1952–83), *A Social and Religious History of the Jews*, 2nd edition, 18 vols, New York: Columbia University Press.

Baumann, M. and Klauber, M.I. (1995), *Historians of the Christian Tradition: Their Methodology and Influence on Western Thought*, Nashville: Broadman and Holman.

Beckerlegge, G. (1997), 'Followers of "Mohammed, Kalee and Dada Nanak": The Presence of Islam and South Asian Religions in Victorian Britain', pp. 221–67 in J. Wolffe, ed., *Religion in Victorian Britain V: Culture and Empire*, Manchester: Manchester University Press.

Blackbourn. D. (2003), *Marpingen: Apparitions of the Virgin Mary in Nineteenth-Century Germany*, Oxford: Oxford University Press.

Brettler, M.Z (1995), *The Creation of History in Ancient Israel*, London: Routledge.

Brown, C.G. (2001), *The Death of Christian Britain: Understanding Secularisation 1800–2000*, London: Routledge.

Butler, J. (1990), *Awash in a Sea of Faith: Christianizing the American People*, Cambridge, MA: Harvard University Press.

Cameron, E. (2005), *Interpreting Christian History: The Challenge of the Churches' Past*, Oxford: Blackwell.

Carey, H.M. *et al.* (2001), 'Australian Religion Review, 1980–2000, Part 2 Christian Denominations', *Journal of Religious History*, 25: 56–82.

Cholvy, G. and Hilaire, Y-M (1985–8), *Histoire Religieuse de la France Contemporaine*, 3 vols, Toulouse: Privat.

Collinson, P. (1999), 'Religion, Society and the Historian', *Journal of Religious History* 23: 149–167.

Comaroff, J. and J. (1991), *Of Revelation and Revolution: Christianity, Colonialism and Consciousness in South Africa*, Chicago: University of Chicago Press.

Connolly, S.J. (1982), *Priests and People in Pre-Famine Ireland, 1780–1845*, Dublin: Gill and Macmillan.

Conser, W.H. and Twiss, S.B. (1997), *Religious Diversity and American Religious History: Studies in Traditions and Cultures*, Athens: University of Georgia Press.

Cook, D. (2007), *Martyrdom in Islam*, New York: Cambridge University Press.

Devlin, J. (1987), *The Superstitious Mind: French Peasants and the Supernatural in the Nineteenth Century*, New Haven: Yale University Press.

Dolan, J.P. (1993), 'New Directions in American Catholic History', pp.152–174 in J.P. Dolan and J.P. Wind, eds., *New Dimensions in American Religious History: Essays in Honor of Martin E. Marty*, Grand Rapids: Eerdmans.

Donner, F.M. (1981), *The Early Islamic Conquests*, Princeton: Princeton University Press.

Duri, A.A., trans. L.I. Conrad (1983), *The Rise of Historical Writing Among the Arabs*, Princeton: Princeton University Press.

Elphick, R. and Davenport, R., eds. (1997), *Christianity in South Africa: A Political, Social and Cultural History*, Cape Town: David Philip.

Fearnley-Sander, M. (1990) 'Philosophical History and the Scottish Reformation: William Robertson and the Knoxian Tradition', *Historical Journal* 33: 323–38.

Fletcher, R. (2003), *The Cross and the Crescent: Christianity and Islam from Muhammad to the Reformation*, London: Penguin.

Forbes, D. (1952), *The Liberal Anglican Idea of History*, Cambridge: Cambridge University Press.

Frykenberg, R.E. (1996), *History and Belief: The Foundations of Historical Understanding*, Grand Rapids: Eerdmans.

Frykenberg, R.E. (2008), *Christianity in India: From Beginnings to the Present*, Oxford: Oxford University Press.

Gabrieli, F., trans E.J. Costello (1969), *Arab Historians of the Crusades*, London: Routledge and Kegan Paul.

Gibbon, E. (1998), ed. A. Lentin and B. Norman, *The Decline and Fall of the Roman Empire*, selected chapters, Ware: Wordsworth.

Gomez, M.A. (2005), *Black Crescent: The Experience and Legacy of African Muslims in the Americas*, New York: Cambridge University Press.

Grayson, J.H. (2002), *Korea – A Religious History*, revised edition (first published 1989), London: Routledge Curzon.

Haddad, Y.Y. (1991), ed., *The Muslims of America*, Oxford: Oxford University Press.

Haller, W. (1963), *Foxe's Book of Martyrs and the Elect Nation*, London: Jonathan Cape.

Halpern, B. (1996), *The First Historians and History*, University Park: Pennsylvania State University Press (paperback edn., first published 1988).

Hilaire, Y-M (2004), 'État des lieux: France', pp. 3–13 in B. Pellistrandi, ed. *L'histoire religieuse en France et en Espagne*, Madrid: Casa de Velázquez.

Hill, C. (1964), *Society and Puritanism in Pre-Revolutionary England*, London: Secker and Warburg.

Hill, C. (1970), *God's Englishman: Oliver Cromwell and the English Revolution*, London: Weidenfeld and Nicholson.

Husband, W.B. (2007), 'Looking Backward, Looking Forward: The Study of Religion in Russia after the Fall', *Journal of Religious History*, 31: 195–202.

Hutton, R. (1996), *The Stations of the Sun: A History of the Ritual Year in Britain*, Oxford: Oxford University Press.

Isichei, E. (1995), *A History of Christianity in Africa*, London: SPCK.

Kalu, O.U., ed. (2005), *African Christianity: An African Story*, Pretoria: Department of Church History, University of Pretoria.

Kay, D.N. (2004), *Tibetan and Zen Buddhism in Britain: Transplantation, Development and Adaptation*, London: Routledge Curzon.

Kent, J. (1987), *The Unacceptable Face: The Modern Church in the Eyes of the Historian*, London: SCM.

Kippenberg, H.G. (2002), *Discovering Religious History in the Modern Age*, Princeton: Princeton University Press.

Kurien, P.A. (2007), *A Place at the Multicultural Table: The Development of American Hinduism*, New Brunswick (NJ): Rutgers University Press.

Leonard, K.I. *et al.*, ed. (2005), *Immigrant Faiths: Transforming Religious Life in America*, Walnut Creek: Altamira.

Lewis, D.M., ed. (2004), *Christianity Reborn: The Global Expansion of Evangelicalism in the Twentieth Century*, Grand Rapids: Eerdmans.

McLeod, W.H. (2007), *Essays in Sikh History, Tradition and Society*, Oxford: Oxford University Press.

Malalgoda, K. (1976), *Buddhism in Sinhalese Society 1750–1900: A Study of Religious Revival and Change*, Berkeley and Los Angeles: University of California Press.

Maraldo, J.C. (2004), 'History', pp. 332–6 in E. Buswell, ed., *Encyclopedia of Buddhism*, New York: Thomson Gale.

Martin, D. (1990), *Tongues of Fire: The Explosion of Protestantism in Latin America*, Oxford: Basil Blackwell.

Marty, M. (1986–95), *Modern American Religion*, 3 vols, Chicago: University of Chicago Press.

Marty, M. (1993), 'American Religious History in the Eighties: A Decade of Achievement', *Church History*, 62: 335–77.

Metcalf, B.D. (1982), *The Islamic Revival in British India: Deoband 1860–1900*, Princeton: Princeton University Press.

Musurillo, H. (1972), *Acts of the Christian Martyrs*, Oxford: Clarendon Press.

Myers, D.N. (1997), 'Historiography', pp. 326–8, in R.J.Z. Werblowsky and G. Wigoder, *The Oxford Dictionary of the Jewish Religion*, Oxford: Oxford University Press.

Neill, S. (1964), *A History of Christian Missions*, Harmondsworth: Penguin.

Ng, O-C and Wang Q.E. (2005), *Mirroring the Past: The Writing and Use of History in Imperial China*, Honolulu: University of Hawaii Press.

NIV (1982), *The Holy Bible: New International Version*, London: Hodder and Stoughton.

Nockles P. (2007), 'Recreating the History of the Church of England', pp. 233–289 in N.Yates, ed., *Bishop Burgess and His World*, Cardiff: University of Wales Press.

Obelkevich, J. (1976), *Religion and Rural Society: South Lindsey 1825–1875*, Oxford: Oxford University Press.

Obelkevich, J., Roper, L. and Samuel, R, eds (1987), *Disciplines of Faith: Studies in Religion, Politics and Patriarchy*, London: Routledge & Kegan Paul.

Oberoi, H. (1994), *The Construction of Religious Boundaries: Culture, Identity and Diversity in the Sikh Tradition*, Delhi: Oxford University Press.

Parsons. G. (1988), *Religion in Victorian Britain, Vol 1 Traditions, Vol II Controversies*, Manchester: Manchester University Press.

Parsons, G. (1993–4), *The Growth of Religious Diversity: Britain from 1945, Vol I Traditions, Vol II Issues*, London: Routledge.

Pellistrandi, B., ed. (2004), *L'histoire religieuse en France et en Espagne*, Madrid: Casa de Velázquez.

Peters, E. (1971), *The First Crusade: The Chronicle of Fulcher of Chartres and Other Source Materials*, Philadelphia: University of Pennsylvania Press.

Peterson, D. and Allman, J. (1999), 'New Directions in the History of Missions in Africa', *Journal of Religious History* 23: 1–7.

Porter, A. (2004), *Religion versus Empire? British Protestant Missionaries and Overseas expansion, 1700–1914*, Manchester: Manchester University Press.

Robertson, W. (1996a), *The History of Scotland*, London: Routledge/Thoemmes Press (reprint of 1794 edn).

Robertson, W. (1996b), *The History of America*, London: Routledge/Thoemmes Press (reprint of 1792 edn).

Robertson, W. (1996c), *Historical Disquisition Concerning the Knowledge which the Ancients had of India*, London: Routledge/Thoemmes Press (reprint of 1791 edn).

Robinson, C.F. (2003), *Islamic Historiography*, Cambridge: Cambridge University Press.

Rosenthal. F. (1968), *A History of Muslim Historiography*, Leiden: Brill.

Sachau, C.E. (1879), trans., *The Chronology of Ancient Nations*, London: W.H. Allen & Co.

Sarkar, S. (2002), *Beyond Nationalist Frames: Relocating Postmodernism, Hindutva, History*, Delhi: Permanent Black.

Seager, R.H. (1995), *The World's Parliament of Religions: The East/West Encounter, Chicago, 1895*, Bloomington and Indianapolis: Indiana University Press.

Stanley, A.P. (1861), *Lectures on the History of the Eastern Church with an Introduction on the Study of Ecclesiastical History*, London: John Murray.

Stanley, B. (1990), *The Bible and the Flag: Protestant Missions and British Imperialism in the Nineteenth and Twentieth Centuries*, Leicester: Apollos.

Stark, R. (2001), 'Efforts to Christianize Europe 400–2000', *Journal of Contemporary Religion*, 16:105–23.

Sterling, G.E. (1992), *Historiography and Self-Definition: Josephus, Luke-Acts and Apologetic Historiography*, Leiden: Brill, 1992.

Stout, H.S. and Taylor, R.M., 'Studies of Religion in American Society: The State of the Art', pp. 15–47 in H.S. Stout and D.G. Hart, eds., *New Directions in American Religious History*, New York: Oxford University Press.

Thapar, R. (2003), *The Penguin History of Early India*, London: Penguin.

Thapar, R. (2005), *Somanatha: The Many Voices of a History*, London: Verso.

Thomas, K. (1971), *Religion and the Decline of Magic: Studies in Popular Beliefs in Sixteenth and Seventeenth Century England*, London: Weidenfeld & Nicolson.

Thompson, E.P. (1963), *The Making of the English Working Class*, London: Victor Gollancz.

Thrower, J. (2004), *The Religious History of Central Asia from the Earliest Times to the Present*, Lewiston: Edwin Mellon Press.

Tweed, T.A. (2000), *The American Encounter with Buddhism 1844–1912: Victorian Culture and the Limits of Dissent*, Chapel Hill: University of North Carolina Press (first published 1992).

Van der Veer, P., ed. (1996), *Conversion to Modernities: The Globalization of Christianity*, London: Routledge.

Van der Veer, P. (2001), *Imperial Encounters: Religion and Modernity in India and Britain*, Princeton: Princeton University Press.

Walsh, J.D. (1959), 'Joseph Milner's Evangelical Church History', *Journal of Ecclesiastical History*, 10: 174–87.

Watt, W.M. (1953), *Muhammad at Mecca*, Oxford: Clarendon Press.

White, D.G. (2006), 'Digging Wells While Houses Burn? Writing Histories of Hinduism in a Time of Identity Politics', *History and Theory* 45: 104–31.

Williamson, G.E. (2006), 'A Religious Sonderweg? Reflections on the Sacred and the Secular in the Historiography of Modern Germany', *Church History*, 75: 139–56.

Wolffe, J., ed. (2004), *Religion in History: Conflict, Conversion and Coexistence*, Milton Keynes and Manchester: The Open University/Manchester University Press.

Wright, N.T. (1992), *The New Testament and the People of God*, London: SPCK.

Suggested reading

This section highlights items surveying the methodology and development of religious history: for examples of the genre in practice see the references.

Brooke, C. *et al.* (1985), 'What is Religious History?', *History Today*, 35 (August 1985): 43–52.

Cameron, E. (2005), *Interpreting Christian History: The Challenge of the Churches' Past*, Oxford: Blackwell.

Conser, W.H. and Twiss, S.B. (1997), *Religious Diversity and American Religious History: Studies in Traditions and Cultures*, Athens, GA: University of Georgia Press.

Cox, J., Howard, T.A., Kselman, T and Williamson, G.S. (2006), 'Modern European Historiography Forum' (survey articles on Britain, France and Germany), *Church History*, 75: 120–62.

Kent, J. (1987), *The Unacceptable Face: The Modern Church in the Eyes of the Historian*, London: SCM.

Shaw, D.G. *et al.* (2006), Theme issue on history and religion, *History and Theory*, 45:4 (December 2006).

Part I

Key approaches to the study of religions

Chapter 5

Theories of religion

Robert A. Segal

Theories of religion go all the way back to the Presocratics. Modern theories come almost entirely from the modern disciplines of the social sciences: anthropology, sociology, psychology, politics, and economics. Pre-social scientific theories came largely from philosophy and were speculative rather than empirical in nature. What John Beattie writes of modern anthropological theories of culture as a whole holds for theories of religion, and for theories from the other social sciences as well:

> Thus it was the reports of eighteenth- and nineteenth-century missionaries and travellers in Africa, North America, the Pacific and elsewhere that provided the raw material upon which the first anthropological works, written in the second half of the last century, were based. Before then, of course, there had been plenty of conjecturing about human institutions and their origins; to say nothing of earlier times, in the eighteenth century Hume, Adam Smith and Ferguson in Britain, and Montesquieu, Condorcet and others on the Continent, had written about primitive institutions. But although their speculations were often brilliant, these thinkers were not empirical scientists; their conclusions were not based on any kind of evidence which could be tested; rather, they were deductively argued from principles which were for the most part implicit in their own cultures. They were really philosophers and historians of Europe, not anthropologists.
>
> (Beattie 1964: 5–6)

Origin and function

A theory of religion is an answer to at least two questions: what is the origin and what is the function of religion? The term 'origin' is confusing because it can refer to either the historical or the recurrent beginning of religion. It can refer either to when and where religion first arose or to why religion arises whenever and wherever it arises. According to convention, nineteenth-century theories focused on the origin of religion, whereas twentieth-century theories have focused on the function of religion. But 'origin' here means historical origin. Nineteenth-century theories in fact sought the recurrent origin of religion at least as much as any historical one, yet no more so than twentieth-century theories have done. Conversely, nineteenth-century theories were concerned as much with the function of religion as with the origin, and no less so than twentieth-century theories have been. Furthermore, the historical origin proposed by nineteenth-century theories was not that of a single time and place, such as the Garden of Eden, but that of the earliest *stage* of religion – any time and anywhere. Therefore even the 'historical' origin was as much recurrent as one-time.

The questions of recurrent origin and of function are connected, and few theories theorize about only the recurrent origin or only the function. Ordinarily, the answer to both questions is a need, which religion arises and serves to fulfill. Theories differ over what that need is. Any theories that do concentrate on only the recurrent origin or on only the function typically either attribute the origin of religion to an accident or else make the function a byproduct. Yet 'accident' and 'byproduct' really refer to the means, not the ends. Unless religion, however accidental its origin or coincidental its function, serves a need, it surely will not last and surely will not continually re-arise. Still, origin and function are distinct issues, and to argue on the basis of the sheer fulfillment of a need that religion arises *in order* to fulfill the need is to commit the fallacy of affirming the consequent.

The issues of origin and function can each be divided into two parts: not only *why* but also *how* religion arises or functions. In explaining the ends of religion, theories do not thereby automatically explain the means. Some theories explain how religion arises, others how religion functions, others both, still others neither.

For example, the Victorian anthropologist E. B. Tylor (1871), who epitomizes the purportedly nineteenth-century focus on origin, roots religion in observations by 'primitives' of, especially, the immobility of the dead and the appearance in dreams and visions of persons residing far away. The 'why' of origin is an innate need to explain these observations, which trigger the need rather than implant it. The 'how' of origin is the processes of observation, analogy, and generalization. Independently of one another, primitive peoples the world over create religion by these means and for this end. Later stages of humanity do not re-invent religion but instead inherit it from their primitive forebears. They perpetuate religion because it continues to satisfy in them, too, the need to explain observations. Similarly, religion changes not because the need changes but because believers revise their conceptions of God. Religion gives way to science not because the need changes but because science provides a better, or at least more persuasive, means of satisfying it. The 'why' of function is the same as the why of origin: a need to explain observations. The 'how' of function is the one issue that Tylor ignores.

Truth

Most twentieth-century theorists forswear the issue of the truth of religion as beyond the ken of the social sciences. One exception is the sociologist Peter Berger, who ever since *A Rumor of Angels* (1969) has been prepared to use his theory to confirm the truth of religion (see Segal 1992: 6–7, 16, 117–18). Most nineteenth-century theorists were not at all reluctant to take a stand on the issue of truth. But they based their assessment on philosophical grounds, not on social scientific ones. Instead of enlisting the origin and function of religion to assess the truth of religion, they assessed the truth on an independent basis and, if anything, let their conclusion about it guide their theorizing about origin and function (see Segal 1992: 15–17). They thereby circumvented the possibility of committing either the genetic fallacy or what I call the functionalist fallacy: arguing that either the origin or the function of religion refutes – necessarily refutes – the truth of it. But Sigmund Freud, in *The Future of an Illusion* (1964 [1961]), did offer a way of using the origin of religion to argue against the truth of religion without committing the genetic fallacy (see Segal 1989: ch. 7). And the philosopher and psychologist William James tried to use the function, or effect, of religious mysticism to argue *for* the truth of religious mysticism without committing the functionalist fallacy (see Segal 2005).

Theories from religious studies

The key divide in theories of religion is between those theories that hail from the social sciences and those that hail from religious studies itself. Social scientific theories deem the origin and function of religion nonreligious. The need that religion arises to fulfill can be for almost anything. It can be either physical – for example, for food, health, or prosperity – or intangible – for example, for explanation, as for Tylor, or for meaningfulness, as in the highest stage of religion for Max Weber. The need can be on the part of individuals or on the part of society. In fulfilling the need, religion provides the means to a secular end.

By contrast, theories from religious studies deem the origin and function of religion distinctively religious: the need that religion arises to fulfill is for the experience of God. There really is but one theory of religion from religious studies. Adherents to it include F. Max Müller, C. P. Tiele, Gerardus van der Leeuw, Raffaele Pettazzoni, Joachim Wach, and Mircea Eliade.[1] For all of these 'religionists,' religion arises to provide contact with God. Like many social scientists, many religionists confine themselves to the issues of origin and function and shy away from the issue of truth. Just as social scientists entrust the issue of truth to philosophers, so religionists entrust it to theologians.

For religionists, human beings need contact with God as an end in itself: they need contact with God because they need contact with God. To ask why humans need that contact is to miss the point. An encounter with God may yield peace of mind and other beneficial byproducts, but the need is still for the encounter itself. The need is considered as fundamental as the need for food or water. Without the contact, humans may not die, but they will languish. Because the need is for God, nothing secular can substitute for religion. There may be secular, or seemingly secular, *expressions* of religion, but there are no secular *substitutes* for religion. Religionists consider the need for God not only distinctive but also universal. To demonstrate its universality, they point to the presence of religion even among professedly atheistic moderns.

Strictly speaking, there are two versions of the one religionist theory. One is the form just described: religion originates within human beings, who seek contact with God. The exemplar of this form is Eliade, who stresses the yearning for God or, so he prefers, the sacred: 'But since religious man cannot live except in an atmosphere impregnated with the sacred, we must expect to find a large number of techniques for consecrating space' (Eliade 1968: 28). Sacred places, or spaces, are one venue for encountering God. Religious sites, such as churches and mosques, are built on those spots where God is believed to have appeared – the assumption being that wherever God has once appeared, that God, even if formally omnipresent, is more likely to appear anew. Sacred times, or time, is the other venue for encountering God. Myths, which describe the creation by God of physical and social phenomena, carry one back to the time of creation, when, it is believed, God was closer at hand than God has been ever since: 'Now, what took place "in the beginning" was this: the divine or semidivine beings were active on earth... Man desires to recover the active presence of the Gods ... [T]he mythical time whose reactualization is periodically attempted is a time sanctified by the divine presence ...' (Eliade 1968: 92).

This version of the religionist theory bypasses the issue of the existence of God. The theory is committed to the existence of only the *need* for God, not to the existence of God. The catch is that if religionists claim that religion actually fulfills the need – and why else would they advocate religion? – then God must exist. Religionists thus prove to be theologians. Still, the emphasis is on the need itself.

The other version of the religionist theory, epitomized by Müller, roots religion not in the need for God but in the experience of God. However indispensable the experience of God may be for human fulfillment, religion originates not in the quest for God but in an unexpected encounter with God. Müller himself singles out the sun and other celestial phenomena as the main locale where God or, for Müller, the Infinite is encountered: 'Thus sunrise was the revelation of nature, awakening in the human mind that feeling of dependence, of helplessness, of hope, of joy and faith in higher powers, which is the source of all wisdom, the spring of all religion' (Müller 1867: 96).

The two versions of the religionist theory are compatible. The quest for an encounter with God may be fulfilled by an uninitiated encounter, and an uninitiated encounter can lead to a quest for further encounters. Still, the approaches differ. One starts with a need; the other, with an experience. Deriving religion from a need for God makes the religionist theory more easily comparable with social scientific theories, since nearly all of which do the same.

Social scientific theories

Religionists commonly assert that social scientists, in making religion a means to a nonreligious end, are less interested in religion than they. This assertion is false. Social scientists are interested in religion for exactly its capacity to produce anthropological, sociological, psychological, and economic effects. Many social scientists consider religion a most important means of fulfilling whatever they consider its nonreligious function. Some even make it the key means of doing so.

Moreover, for religion to function nonreligiously, it must be operating *as* religion. The nonreligious effect comes from a religious cause. The power that religion has, let us say, to goad adherents into accepting social inequality stems from the belief that God sanctions the inequality, that God will one day remedy the inequality, or that the inequality is a merely worldly matter. Without the belief, religion would have no social effect. Undeniably, the social sciences approve or disapprove of religion for its anthropological, sociological, psychological, or economic consequences. Undeniably, religion is admired only when it inculcates culture, unites society, develops the mind, or spurs the economy, not when it makes contact with God. But the nonreligious benefit of religion presupposes the efficacy of religion as religion.

Put another way, religion for social scientists functions as an independent variable, or as the cause of something else. In *origin* religion is indisputably a dependent variable, or the effect of something else, as it, like anything else, must be, unless it creates itself *ex nihilo*. But in *function* religion is an independent variable. Even if it is the product of nonreligious causes, it is in turn the cause of nonreligious effects. If religion could not be an independent variable in its effect because it was a dependent variable in its origin, there would be few independent variables around.

Contemporary social scientific theories

Religionists often assert that contemporary social scientists, in contrast to earlier ones, have at last come round to seeing religion the way the religionists do. Contemporary social scientists are consequently embraced by religionists as belated converts. The figures embraced most effusively are Mary Douglas (1966, 1973), Victor Turner (1967, 1968), Clifford Geertz (1973, 1983), Robert Bellah (1970), Peter Berger (1967, 1969), and Erik Erikson (1958, 1969). These social scientists are pitted against classical ones like Tylor (1871), Frazer (1922), Durkheim (1965), Malinowski (1925), Freud (1950), Jung (1938), and Marx (1957).

What is the difference between classical and contemporary social scientists? The difference cannot be over the importance of religion. Classical social scientists considered religion at least as important a phenomenon as any of their contemporary counterparts do. The power of religion is what impelled them to theorize about it. Similarly, the difference cannot be over the utility of religion. While for Frazer, Freud, and Marx, religion is incontestably harmful, for Tylor, Jung, and Durkheim it is most helpful. For these three, religion is one of the best and, for Durkheim, the best means of serving its beneficial functions. Contemporary social scientists grant religion no greater due.

The difference between contemporary and classical social scientists must be over the nature of the function that religion serves. In contrast to classical theorists, for whom the functions of religion are nonreligious, contemporary theorists purportedly take the function of religion to be religious. But do they? Where religionists attribute religion to a yearning for God, contemporary social scientists attribute it to a yearning for, most often, a meaningful life. Contact with God may be one of the best means of providing meaningfulness, but even if it were the sole means, it would still be a means to a nonreligious end. For Douglas, humans need cognitive meaningfulness: they need to organize their experiences. For Turner, Geertz, Bellah, Berger, and Erikson, humans need existential meaningfulness: they need to explain, endure, or justify their experiences. Existential meaningfulness as the function of religion is not even new and goes back to at least Weber, who, to be sure, limits the need for meaningfulness to the 'higher' religions (see Weber 1963: Chapters 8–13). But even if this function were new, the need would remain secular. In short, the divide between social scientific theories of religion and the religionist theory remains (see Segal 1989: Chapter 4).

The religionist argument

What is the case for the religionist theory? The case tends to be presented negatively. It appeals to the inadequacy of social scientific theories, which should properly include contemporary theories. All social scientific theories are supposedly inadequate because in deeming the origin and function of religion nonreligious, they necessarily miss the religious nature of religion. Only the religionist theory captures the religious nature of religion.

In actuality, social scientific theories do not miss the religious nature of religion. On the contrary, it is what they mean *by* religion. The religious nature of religion is the starting point of their theorizing. It is the datum to be theorized about. Far from somehow failing to perceive that adherents pray to God, sacrifice to God, and kill others in the name of God, social scientists take for granted that adherents do so. The question for social scientists is why they do so. The religious nature of religion is the starting point of theorizing. It is not the end point. If social scientists somehow missed, let alone denied, that Christians go to church, sing hymns, take sacraments, read the Bible, and devote their lives to God, and do all of these things because they believe in God, they would be left with nothing to explain. Religiosity, far from being overlooked, is the preoccupation of social scientists.

Against social scientists and others, religionist Eliade, in a famous passage, declares that 'a religious phenomenon will only be recognized as such if it is grasped at it own level, that is to say, if it is studied *as* something religious. To try to grasp the essence of such a phenomenon by means of physiology, psychology, sociology, economics, linguistics, art or any other is false' (Eliade 1963, p. xiii). But Eliade conflates description with explanation, not to mention description with metaphysics (essence). No social scientist fails to recognize religion as religion. That is why there exists the anthropology of *religion*, the sociology of *religion*, the psychology of *religion*, and the economics of *religion*. There would be no social scientific theories of *religion* if the distinctiveness of religion went unrecognized. But the *recognition* of religion as religion does not mean the *explanation* of religion as religion.

It is as believers in God that Christians go to church, but it is also, for example, as members of a group that they do so. While acknowledging the difference between a religious group and a team, a family, or a gang, sociologists explain religion in the same way that they explain a team, a family, and a gang: as a group.

At the same time no sociological account of religion can be exhaustive. There is a point at which any sociological account must cease – the point at which a religious group differs from any other kind of group. But to acknowledge a stopping point for sociology is not to dismiss a sociological approach. Sociology can account for religion to whatever extent religion does constitute a group. How fully religion constitutes a group, it is up to sociologists to establish. The more group-like they show religion to be, the more successful their account. Sociologists are to be commended, not condemned, for attempting to account as fully as possible for religion sociologically. Their inevitable inability to account for it entirely sociologically marks the limit, not the failure, of the sociology of religion.

Religionists would reply that the attempt to 'sociologize' is inherently futile, for the origin and function of religion can only be religious. Otherwise religion ceases to be religion and becomes society. But this conventional rejoinder, offered like a litany, misses the point. Nobody denies that religion consists of beliefs and practices directed toward God rather than toward the group. But Durkheim, for example, is not thereby barred from matching a believer's experience of possession by God with an individual's experience of participation in a group. Durkheim is not barred from asserting that the euphoria and power which individuals feel when they amass precede religious experience, parallel religious experience, and thereby account for religious experience. Participants, thinking their state of mind superhuman, attribute it to possession by God, but Durkheim attributes it to 'possession' by the group.

Still, Durkheim is not maintaining that religion originates exclusively through group experience. After all, the group is not itself God, just god-like. The concept of God and attendant practices must still be created.[2] Durkheim offers his account of religion as a necessary but not quite a sufficient one. What must yet be accounted for is precisely the step from group to God. But to concede that there is more to an account of religion than the group is not to concede that religiosity is all there is to an account. For Durkheim, religion is to be accounted for sociologically *and* 'religionistically' – with the sociological element predominant. For all other social scientists the same is true: a predominantly sociological, anthropological, psychological, or economic account of religion must be supplemented by a religionist one.

The final religionist rejoinder is the appeal to symmetry. If the effect is religion, the cause must be religionist. There must be a match between cause and effect. A sociological cause can produce only a sociological effect. Explained sociologically, the product is the group, not religion.

This rejoinder, too, misses the point. Of course, there must be symmetry between cause and effect. Causes must be similar enough to their effects to be capable of producing them. But a sociological account of religion does not purport to account for the nonsociological aspects of religion, only for the sociological ones. To reply that the sociological aspects are aspects of the group and not of religion is to commit a double fallacy: excluding the middle and begging the question. A sociological account of religion is not an account of something *other than* religion. It is an account of aspects *of* religion. To limit religion to its religionist aspects is to beg the question at hand: what *is* the nature of religion?

To be sure, the claim that sociology can explain anything of *religious* beliefs and practices might seem to be asserting that sociology can explain something *nonsociological*. But this concern is misplaced. Sociology takes *seemingly* nonsociological aspects of religion and transforms them into sociological ones, which it only then accounts for. Durkheim matches atttributes of God – God's power, God's overwhelming presence, God's status as the source of values and institutions – with attributes of the group whose God it is. The symmetry between cause and effect is preserved by sociologizing the effect. A gap remains between the sociological cause and the *religious* effect: the group is still just a group, not a God. But symmetry is not intended to mean identity.

To take an example from another field, Freud contends that a believer's relationship to the believer's father matches the believer's relationship to God. He contends that believers' feelings toward their fathers precede their feelings toward God, parallel those feelings, and therefore cause the feelings. But he proposes only a necessary, if also largely sufficient, cause of religion. No more than Durkheim does he propose, to use a redundancy, an altogether sufficient one. What must still be supplied is the step from father to God. The father for Freud, like the group for Durkheim, is God-like but not God. God may be human-like, but no human being is omnipotent, omniscient, or immortal. God is 'father' of the whole world, not just of a family. The adult conception of God may derive from a child's 'idolization' of the child's own father, but the conception transforms a God-like figure into a God. Even when Freud brashly declares that 'at bottom God is nothing other than an exalted father' (Freud 1950: 147), he is still distinguishing a father from an exalted, deified father. The closer the link that Freud draws between father and God, the more convincing is his account, but he, like Durkheim and all other social scientists, takes for granted a limit to the link, and does so even while ever trying to tighten that link. Again, symmetry does not mean identity.

The mind–body analogy

One way of exposing the fallacy in the religionist argument that only identity between cause and effect can account for the effect is to appeal to the grand philosophical issue of the relationship between the mind and the body. There are four possible relationships. (1) Only mind exists, and the body (matter) is an illusion (idealism). (2) Only the body exists, and the mind (spirit) is an illusion (materialism, or reductionism). (3) Both mind and body, spirit and matter, exist, but they operate independently of each other (parallelism). (4) Both mind and body, spirit and matter, exist, and either one causally affects the other (interactionism). Alternatively, the two causally affect each other.

Religionists never go so far as to espouse the equivalent of idealism: claiming that only religiosity exists and that the mind, society, and culture are illusory. Rather, they assume as their options the equivalents of either parallelism or materialism/reductionism. Parallelism clearly constitutes no threat, for it preserves religiosity. Religionists assume that the sole threat comes from materialism/reductionism, which they seek to counter by arguing that religion is other than mind, society, and culture. They often assume – falsely – that the social sciences are outright materialistic.

Religionists overlook the interactionist option. Interactionism grants religion partial autonomy but not immunity. On the one hand it does not, like reductionism, dissolve religion into sheer mind, society, or culture.[3] On the other hand it does not, like parallelism, preclude the impact of the mind, society, or culture on religion.

Nemeses of religionists like Durkheim, Freud, and Marx espouse interactionism rather than, as defined here, reductionism or, obviously, parallelism. They seek to account for religion, not to deny (reductionism) or to isolate (parallelism) it. If they denied religion (reductionism), they would have nothing to account for. If they isolated religion (parallelism), they would be unable to account for it. Because Durkheim, Freud, and Marx no more reduce religion entirely to society, mind, or economy than philosophical interactionists reduce the mind entirely to the body, they do not claim to be accounting wholly for it. They claim only to be accounting significantly for it. They claim that one cannot account for religion apart from society, mind, or economy. Furthermore, the interactionism is for them two-way: religion, here as an independent variable, accounts considerably for society, mind, and the economy, just as society, mind, and the economy account considerably for religion.

Postmodernism

A postmodern approach to religion might seem to offer religionists solace by its opposition to generalizations and therefore to theorizing, but in fact it does not. Religionists theorize as much as social scientists. Contrary to postmodernists, both sides vaunt precisely the universality of their formulations. Contrary to both religionists and social scientists, postmodernists insist that theories *cannot* apply universally, not merely that they *may* not – a point scarcely denied by theorists on either side.

The postmodern refutation of theory takes several forms. One form is the uncovering of the origin – the historical, one-time origin – of theories. The assumption is that a theory does not merely arise in a specific time and place but is bound by that time and space. Where, for most of us, testing may show that a theory is in fact limited in its applicability, postmodernists assume *a priori* that any theory is so limited, and on the grounds that it originates in a specific time and place. But how can the sheer origin of a theory undermine – necessarily undermine – the theory? The argument blatantly commits the genetic fallacy. Reducing the scope of theories to the occasion of their origin fails to allow theorists any capacity to think. It reduces theorists to mere mirrors of their times. It conflates discovery with invention, creativity with construction. For an example of this variety of the postmodern attack on theory, see many of the contributions to *Critical Terms for Religious Studies* (Taylor 1999).

Another form of the postmodern attack on theory comes from Derrida. Here theories are undermined by the presence of contrary currents in the texts that present the theories. The most brilliant application of Derridean deconstructionism to theories of religion is Tomoko Masuzawa's *In Search of Dreamtime* (1993), the subtitle of which is *The Quest for the Origin of Religion*. Masuzawa assumes that classical theories of religion sought above all the historical, one-time origin of religion. She lumps religionist theories with social scientific ones and takes as her prime targets Durkheim, Freud, Eliade, and Müller. Against them, she argues that their own texts undermine their intentions. Like Pirandello's characters, their texts take on a life of their own.

For example, Durkheim's definition of the sacred as the ideal society is supposedly undermined by the continual appearance in *The Elementary Forms of the Religious Life* of another definition: the sacred as the opposite of the profane. Freud's attribution, in *Totem and Taboo*, of the origin of religion to the sons' rebellion against their tyrannical father is supposedly undercut by Freud's own characterization of this would-be historical deed as fantasy. Contemporary theorists of religion, epitomized by Eliade, may reject the quest for the origin of religion as unsolvable, but we are told that they remain obsessed with believers' own quest for the origin of everything, including religion. That quest is in turn undone by the locating of the origin of everything outside history, in mythic time, and is undone still more by the attempt through myth to override history by recovering the past, by making the past present.

Masuzawa's argument is tenuous. As noted, classical theorists sought the recurrent more than the historical origin of religion. Declares Durkheim near the outset of his *Elementary Forms*:

> The study which we are undertaking is therefore a way of taking up again, *but under new conditions*, the old problem of the origin of religion. To be sure, if by origin we are to understand the very first beginning, the question has nothing scientific about it, and should be resolutely discarded. There was no given moment when religion began to exist, and there is consequently no need of finding a means of transporting ourselves thither in thought ... But the problem which we raise is quite another one. What we want to do is to find a means of discerning the ever-present causes upon which the most essential forms of religious thought and practice depend.
>
> (Durkheim 1965: 20)

Even Freud, who in *Totem and Taboo* comes closest to seeking the historical origin of religion, seeks only the first stage of religion. Moreover, classical theorists, as noted, were as much after the function of religion as after the origin, recurrent or historical. Contemporary theorists are no different.

The presence in theories of inconsistencies argues for the provisional state of the theorizing, not for any systematic undermining of the effort. Furthermore, far more egregious inconsistencies in these theories have long been recognized. In Durkheim, sometimes society is the recurrent source of religion, but sometimes religion is the recurrent source of society. Freud himself sheepishly recognizes the seeming inconsistency between his account of religion in *Totem and Taboo* and his account of it in *The Future of an Illusion*. There may be irony, but there is no inconsistency in Eliade's abandonment of the quest for the historical origin of religion on the one hand and his interpretation of myth as a return to the historical, or prehistorical, origin of everything in the world on the other.

Masuzawa's approach is postmodern in the conclusion she draws: that the quest for historical origin, for her the key concern of at least classical theorizing, must be abandoned, in which case so presumably must theorizing itself, at least of a classical variety. The rejection of historical origin is meant to be part of the deconstruction of epistemological foundations. The study of religion must acknowledge its fault lines.

But even suppose that all classical theorists outright failed in a common quest for the historical origin of religion. What would follow? That subsequent theorists dare not try? Does the failure of even all quests to date doom all future ones? Does the quest for the historical origin of religion become impossible rather than merely difficult and become improper as well as impossible?

The final postmodern rejection of theory derives from Foucault. Here the political end to which theories are put is sought – as if the use of a theory refutes the theory. This tactic commits what I dub the functionalist fallacy – the counterpart to the genetic fallacy. The fullest application of a Foucauldian analysis of religion is Russell McCutcheon's *Manufacturing Religion* (1996). Rather than attacking all theories of religion like Masuzawa, McCutcheon attacks only the religionist theory. There is nothing postmodern in much of his attack, which concentrates on Eliade. Cataloguing standard objections, McCutcheon argues that Eliade attributes religion exclusively to a distinctively religious need, thereby dismisses nonreligious needs as irrelevant, and thereby isolates religion from the rest of life. McCutcheon is less Foucauldian than Marxist when he argues that religion arises to sanction oppression, as in using a myth of the origin of social inequality to justify the perpetuation of the inequality.

McCutcheon follows Foucault in targeting less religion than the religionist theory, or 'discourse,' and targeting it for its political effects. He objects to Eliade's theory not simply because Eliade ignores the nonreligious origin and function of religion but even more because, in so doing, Eliade supposedly sanctions whatever political effect religion in fact has. McCutcheon denies that the political consequence is unintended. Citing Eliade's own well-documented alliance with the fascistic Romanian Iron Guard, he asserts that the conception of religion as otherworldly is a calculated method of masking how worldly in both origin and function religion really is. The religionist discourse 'manfactures' the theory of religion not merely to give religiosity autonomy, as has conventionally been argued, but to deflect attention away from the political origin and function of religion. McCutcheon even suggests that religionist theorists manufacture religion to benefit themselves: to give themselves a discipline and, with it, jobs. Knowledge is power, as Sophists back in fifth-century Athens proclaimed.

As delightfully iconoclastic as McCutcheon's claim is, he falls far short of proving it. One must do more than show that religion has a political side, and McCutcheon himself offers only a handful of examples. One must also show that religion has no religionist side, lest, as for even reductionists, the religionist theory still holds, albeit less than monopolistically. To do so, McCutcheon must account for all of religion nonreligiously. Showing who benefits from religion hardly suffices, for there can be multiple effects of religion, which, like much else in life, can be overdetermined. And the nonreligious effects can surely, as for Weber and other theorists, be coincidental rather than intentional. In trying to replace rather than to supplement a religionist account of religion with a political one, McCutcheon thus ventures beyond both classical and contemporary social scientific theorists, whose accounts of religion are, again, proffered as less than sufficient. Indeed, McCutcheon's one-sided view ventures beyond that of even some religionists, not all of whom insist, like Eliade, that religion is exclusively religionist in origin and function.

In postmodern fashion, McCutcheon ties his repudiation of the religionist theory to an opposition to theorizing itself. Somehow the attribution of religion to a spiritual need makes all religions the same – the prerequisite for a theory. Yet somehow the attribution of religion to a political need makes all religions different – and thereby impervious to generalization. When McCutcheon insists on 'contextualizing' religion, he means rooting religion not simply in political and other material conditions generally but in the material conditions particular to each religion. Yet his mechanical quest for the material beneficiary of each religion seemingly makes all religions the same. In place of the 'totalizing' religionist theory, he puts an equally totalizing materialist theory.

Postmodern criticisms of theories of religion arise in conspicuous ignorance of contemporary philosophy of social science and the sociology of natural science. Absent is the consideration of logical problems like those of induction, falsification, and relativism. Absent is the mention of the various alternatives proposed to the standard models of scientific explanation worked out by, above all, Carl Hempel, who himself allows for merely probabilistic explanations. Postmodernism dismisses theorizing per se, and on the most illogical of grounds, of which the worst is the declaration that 'we live in a postmodern world.'

In postmodern approaches to religion, one never encounters discussions of the ramifications of, above all, radical, contemporary sociology of science. For example, the Edinburgh 'strong programme' pioneered by David Bloor (1991), Barry Barnes, and Steven Shapin offers a comprehensive rationale for the activity that should make postmodernists salivate: the contextualizing of theories. According to the program, the holding of all beliefs, true and rational ones no less than false and irrational ones, is to be accounted for sociologically rather than intellectually. Where McCutcheon and the contributors to *Critical Terms* either ignore the issue of truth, limiting themselves to the issues of origin and function, or else conflate the issues, the Edinburgh sociologists distinguish the issues, take on truth as well as origin and function, and argue that all evaluations of scientific theories are dictated by nonintellectual factors. Would-be intellectual justifications purportedly mask sociological imperatives, including ideological ones. Epistemology becomes sociology. The boldness of this nonpostmodern approach to theorizing in science makes the postmodern approach to theorizing in religion rather tame.

Overall, theorizing about religion, whether by religionists or by social scientists, remains safe from the postmodern attack, just as social scientific theorizing about religion remains safe from the religionist attack. May social scientists continue to make sense of religion.

The category 'religion'

One issue that has come, or come back, to the fore in recent decades is that of the term, or category, religion itself. Traditionally, the question raised has been whether proffered definitions of religion fit all cases. The difficulty with this procedure is that whoever offers the definition can reject cases that do not fit on exactly the grounds that they are not cases of religion. The argument is conspicuously question-begging since it presupposes rather than supports the appropriateness of the definition at hand. Yet equally question-begging is the criticism, for it, too, rests on some definition that must first be established. As circular as these debates go, some of the greatest works on theories of religion, notably Tylor's *Primitive Culture* (1871) and Durkheim's *Elementary Forms of the Religious Life* (1912), begin their analyses of religion by rejecting existing definitions of religion – usually on the grounds that the definitions are too narrow – and substituting their own.

This traditional challenge to the category religion has been succeeded by a different one, one shaped by postmodernism. One form of this new challenge has been an appeal to the time and place of the origin of the category as an argument against its applicability beyond that time and place. Daniel Dubuisson's *The Western Construction of Religion* (2003 [1998 in French]) is the finest example so far of this argument.

Dubuisson's approach can best be appreciated by contrasting it to a work of only a decade earlier that takes for granted the suitability of the category religion and that celebrates the gradual extension of it to ever more cases: J. Samuel Preus' excellent *Explaining Religion* (1987). For Preus, 'religion' identifies more or less obvious characteristics of a worldwide phenomenon. Where Dubuisson writes to *challenge* the universal applicability of the category religion, Preus writes to explain how the category has come to *acquire* its justifiably universal applicability. Where Dubuisson spurns the category religion on the grounds that it in fact never gets beyond its Christian origins, Preus touts the category on the grounds that it eventually comes to encompass even Christianity. Where Dubuisson scorns the social scientific study of religion as theology in disguise, Preus glories in the social scientific study of religion as liberation from theology.

Preus traces the step-by-step emergence of the social scientific 'paradigm' out of the theological one. Initially, all religions got accounted for irreducibly religiously (Bodin, Herbert of Cherbury). Next, all religions save Christianity – or save Judaism and Christianity – got accounted for nonreligiously (Fontenelle, Vico). Finally, all religions got accounted for nonreligiously (Hume, Comte, Tylor, Durkheim, and Freud). The social scientific paradigm is at last complete, though of course ever subject to revision.

Preus credits the social sciences with forging the comparative approach that overcame Christian ethnocentrism and thereby allowed for the recognition of the universality of religion. For Preus, the identification of the universal category religion led to universal explanations of religion. In other words, it led to theorizing. For Dubuisson, who never cites Preus, there has been no progress, so that there is nothing to celebrate. Dubuisson insists that even those theorists who have prided themselves on breaking with what Preus calls the theological paradigm have in fact not escaped from it. Theology has continued to 'set the agenda' for the study of religion. Therefore the only solution is the elimination of the category religion itself.

Dubuisson begins by posing three questions:

- Is Christianity [not simply] the special form taken in the West by something that has always existed and that similarly exists elsewhere, if not everywhere, namely, religion or the religious phenomenon?
- As the legitimate daughter of Christianity, is religion not rather than an element wholly unique to Western civilization, one of its most original creations?
- Should we not, moreover, go somewhat farther and ask whether religion is not effectively the West's most characteristic concept, around which it has established and developed its identity, while at the same time defining its way of conceiving humankind and the world? (Dubuisson 2003: 9)

His answers to these three questions are clear: (1) no, (2) yes, and (3) yes. To cite one of his many summary statements of his position:

> Whatever term we choose – *weltanschauung*, cosmography, vision, conception, figuration of the world, and so on – the fact remains that all global conceptions of the world, all utopias, all messianic movements, all theologies, all the imaginary worlds that the West has conceived of (and eventually tried to impose) have always been realized by taking as model (whether it was admired, envied, hated, imitated, deformed, or denigrated) that or those promoted by the Christian religion in its capacity of appearing to offer the most complete, most hegemonic conception of the world.
>
> (Dubuisson 2003: 37–38)

Dubuisson's claim prompts many questions. For example, if Christianity is the common model on which modern theorists have blindly based their conception of religion, why have they differed with one another so sharply on their conception of religion? How constricting can deference to Christianity be when theorists who purportedly all defer to it castigate one another's definitions?

If Christianity is the common model on which theorists have ethnocentrically based their conception of religion, how have they managed to find so many other cases of religion? One would think that a model so particularistic – as Dubuisson's answer to his first question claims – would never fit any other case, let alone hundreds of other cases.

Conversely, if Christianity is the common model on which theorists have blithely based their conception of religion, why, as Preus shows, did it take them so long to find commonality? One would think that a model so readily presumed to be universal would easily fit, or be taken easily to fit, every other case.

If Christianity is the model on which theorists have based their conception of religion, why have so many theorists emphasized the *differences* between Christianity and other religions? Similarly, if theorists have based their conception of religion on a single religion, why have so many theorists stressed the differences between kinds and between stages of religion? For Tylor, primitive religion is materialist, explanatory, and amoral, whereas modern religion is spiritual, metaphysical, and moral. For Tylor, primitive religion is like science, and modern religion is unlike it. For Durkheim, the change from mechanical to organic solidarity makes for changes in the nature of religion. For Weber, primitive, or magical, religion has scant gods, no priests, no ethics, and no metaphysics, and is concerned with immediate, worldly ends, whereas higher religion has gods, priests or prophets, ethics, and metaphysics, and is ultimately preoccupied with the need for meaningfulness. How are these theorists any less attentive to differences *within* the category of religion than is Dubuisson in his proposed replacement of 'cosmographical formations' for religions?

While Dubuisson, to his credit, does not take the postmodern route of dispensing altogether with categories, or similarities, his criticism of the category religion does appeal to the litany-like argument made by particularists against comparativists. Dubuisson asks rhetorically, 'Does the fact that a human being – a Benedictine monk, a Roman augur, or Tungus shaman – addresses a supernatural suffice to authorize us to speak of a common religious phenomenon?' (Dubuisson 2003: 13). But this argument is tautological: of course, similarities cannot identify differences, for if similarities could, they would not be similarities. But this argument is also question-begging: only if one *presupposes* that differences are somehow deeper than similarities can one dismiss similarities as superficial. If one were to presuppose that differences are trivial, then they would become superficial. Moreover, similarities are by no means confined to the surface. They often lie beneath the surface. An emigré to a foreign country is typically struck first by the differences between it and home, and only later comes to notice the similarities. And apparent differences can turn into underlying similarities.

At the same time similarities do not mean identities. Similarities mean just similarities. Similarities allow for differences, and exactly at the point at which no further similarities can be found. No one claims that Christianity is identical with Buddhism or Christianity of one time and place identical with Christianity of another. Rather, the claim is that they are akin, and sufficiently akin to be categorized as cases of religion and in turn explicable in the same way.

Finally, what is the force of the claim, made by Dubuisson and so many others, that the category religion is 'constructed'? What is the alternative: revealed? Unless the category was already in the world when humans arrived, of course it was created. And of course it was created by someone at some time or place. Are scientific theories, which Dubuisson contrasts to social scientific ones, any less constructed? The issue is not the specificity of the origin of a category or a theory but the applicability of the category or theory beyond its origin. Automatically to restrict applicability to the time and place of origin is to commit the genetic fallacy. It is to collapse discovery into invention. To take a common example, Freud generalized from the cases of largely middle-class Viennese Jewish women at the turn of the twentieth century. The issue is whether his generalization nevertheless holds universally. To assume that it does not simply because of the ineluctably constricted origin of any category or theory is fallacious. To avoid the genetic fallacy, Dubuisson must actually prove, not simply assert, the following claim:

> the history of religions ... was itself a unique historical construction, intimately tied to the ideas of its time, on which it was dependent at every stage of development ... The study of its first syntheses, drawn up in the second half of the nineteenth century, reveals, among the intellectual factors that surrounded its birth, the constant presence of the most ordinary prejudices of that period.
>
> (Dubuisson 2003: 147)

Commendably, Dubuisson seeks to prove this claim and thereby sidesteps the fallacy.

If one version of the new challenge to the category religion has been an appeal to the time and place of the origin of the term, another has been an appeal to the political use to which the term has been put. This challenge is even more fervently postmodern since it appeals to the authority of Foucault and to that of his partial follower, Edward Said, author of the 1978 classic *Orientalism* (1991).

Among the most discussed books of this form of the challenge have been Talal Asad's *Genealogies of Religion* (1993) and *Formations of the Secular* (2003), Timothy Fitzgerald's *The Ideology of Religious Studies* (2000) and recent *Discourse on Civility and Barbarity* (2007), and Richard King's *Orientalism and Religion* (1999). There are differences among these authors. Asad follows Foucault. Fitzgerald follows Said. King follows both, and also Asad. Still, none of the three is uncritical of whomever he follows. Fitzgerald concentrates on the category 'religious studies,' which he wants replaced by 'cultural studies.' Asad concentrates on the category religion. King concentrates on Indian religion as a case of Orientalism. But for all three, knowledge – here the knowledge of religion – is power. That line is a crude slogan for Foucault's position. While King's book is the most derivative of the ones named, it is also the most accessible and will serve as an example of this kind of challenge to the category religion.

King begins with the term 'mystical.' This term, like religion, is 'a social construction' (King 1999: 14). The term has a changing meaning. The meaning reflects the time and place of its origin. Therefore no meaning can apply to all times and places. Above all, the term has never been merely academic but has always been political:

> [T]he way one defines 'the mystical' relates to ways of establishing and defining authority. This is obvious in the pre-modern context since anyone claiming direct experiential knowledge of God or the ultimate reality is in effect claiming unmediated authority to speak the truth. In a traditional Christian context, for instance, such a claim might be seen as undermining the claim of the Church to mediate between heaven and the divine. Defining mysticism then is a way of defining power. One's answers to the questions 'What is mysticism?' and 'Who counts as a mystic'?' reflect issues of authority.
>
> (King 1999: 9–10)

If one replies that in modern times mysticism is seen as otherworldly and therefore apolitical, King answers that 'the separation of the mystical from the political is itself a political decision'

(King 1999: 10). He might have replied as Fitzgerald would surely have done: that the 'de-politicizing' of mysticism, as of religion in general, serves exactly to rob it of political power.

King then turns to the application of Said's notion of Orientalism to India. King claims that the West has concocted a false, stereotyped, monolithic, and demeaning conception of India and claims that that conception has served its colonial interests. Western scholars have ignored the myriad, contradictory religions actually found in India and have instead created a single religion called Hinduism, which is then equated with all of Indian culture. The West has created 'a romantic and exotic fantasy' of Indian religion 'as deeply mystical, introspective and otherworldly' (King 1999: 142). Unchanging, passive, feminine India then gets contrasted to the worldly, active, manly West. This characterization of India has served politically to justify colonialism:

> Thus works that purport to explain the 'Oriental mind-set' or the 'Indian mentality', etc., presupposes that there is a homogeneous, and almost Platonic 'essence' or 'nature' that can be directly intuited by the Indological expert. … [This] 'essentialism' [is objectionable] not just because it misrepresents the heterogeneity of the subject matter, but also because of the way in which such essentialism results in the construction of a cultural stereotype that may then be used to subordinate, classify and dominate the non-Western world.
>
> (King 1999: 91–92)

King's thesis, like Dubuisson's, is tenuous. First, a definition – here of mysticism or of Hinduism – either holds or fails to holds, regardless of the political ends to which it is put. Second, a definition either holds or fails to hold, regardless of the time and place of its origin. Third, a definition either holds or fails to hold, regardless of the number of past definitions that have been offered. Fourth, a definition either holds or fails to hold, regardless of who invents it – here Westerners or Indians. Fifth and last, a definition is either useful or useless, not right or wrong. If it succeeds in identifying similarities among the range of cases it encompasses, it is useful. The legitimate objection to the Orientalist definition should be that it is erroneous or useless, not anything else.

Tomoko Masuzawa's *Invention of World Religions* (2003) is a wonderfully bold attempt to uncover the origin and function of the idea of 'world religions.' Masuzawa shows that by the nineteenth century the religions of the world had been conventionally divided into four groups: Christianity; initially Judaism, later Buddhism; Islam (or Mohammedanism); and everything else, which was labeled paganism, heathenism, idolatry, or polytheism. Early in the nineteenth century this categorization began to be challenged, and by the early twentieth century it had been replaced by 'world religions', which now numbered a dozen or so. This categorization remains in place today, and is taken as no less natural than the prior one was. So argues Masuzawa.

The conventional view of the concept of 'world religions' is that it evinces the multicultural, empathetic spirit of contemporary scholars. God forbid that any religion should be overlooked, misunderstood, or criticized. That a dozen religions are considered worthy of the epithet 'world' is vaunted as evidence of the ecumenical vision of today's scholars.

Masuzawa spurns this self-congratulatory view. She does not merely observe, as others before her have done, that the basis for inclusion is not quite self-evident. Instead, she argues that, despite the tolerance seemingly epitomized by the concept of multiple world religions, the concept ironically originated as a way of preserving the uniqueness and superiority of

Christianity. She denies that the 'advent' of world religions marks 'a turn away from the Eurocentric and Eurohegemonic conception of the world, toward a more egalitarian and lateral delineation' (Masuzawa 2003: 13).

Masuzawa rightly ties the scientific study of religion to the comparison of religions. But where Preus argues that the scientific, comparative 'paradigm' for studying religion arose to replace the Christian-centered theological one, Masuzawa argues that the scientific study of religion arose within theology itself. She even demonstrates that the field that forged the topic of world religions was comparative theology. The grouping together of 'great religious systems' was intended to highlight the uniqueness of Christianity, which alone achieved the common goal of universality and transcendence. The comparative method was thus used to show differences, not similarities: 'comparative theology would not compromise the unique and exclusive authority of Christianity' (Masuzawa 2003: 81). Masuzawa devotes separate chapters to Buddhism and Islam, the religions that most threatened Christianity.

The retention of the superiority of Christianity faced one special obstacle: the emergence in linguistics of the divide between Indo-European and Semitic languages. Linguistic families were racial categories, as the synonym for Indo-European – Aryan – attests. Since Hebrew is a Semitic language, and since Christianity evolved out of Judaism, was Christianity not thereby a Semitic language and consequently a Semitic rather than European (or Indo-European) religion and culture and race? Masuzawa shows, as others before her have done, that Christianity was severed from Judaism and regrouped with Hellenism. Masuzawa shows how even the efforts of comparative theologians to pit Christianity against other religions to parade its superiority was attacked by yet more conservative theologians. While barely mentioned by her, the scholar who suffered most was William Robertson Smith, who dared to argue that Christianity arose from primitive religion, even while transcending it.

Masuzawa makes clear that she is not, like Dubussion, Asad, or Fitzgerald, writing about the term 'religion' or the term 'religious studies.' She confines herself to the term 'world religions.' But what she writes of it parallels what they have claimed of 'religion' and of 'religious studies.' Both Dubuisson and Fitzgerald have consequently called for the outright abandonment of their terms. Masuzawa does not explicitly go this far, though clearly for her the term is irretrievable.

Like the others' books, Masuzawa's book prompts questions. First, why did the category of 'world religions' become so prominent if the goal was to defend the uniqueness of Christianity? Second, does the retention of the term today dictate the retention of its original use? Third, does the use of the term in introductory courses and textbooks really evince the thinking of scholars? Finally, is the term in fact objectionable? Surely some religions, unlike most others, do transcend national or regional boundaries. As long as the criteria used for the category are explicit, and as long as the category identifies significant aspects of religion, why not still employ it?

In sum, the arguments made to date for the abandonment of the category 'religion,' 'mysticism,' or 'world religions' are considerably less decisive than their proponents assume.

Notes

1 I exclude Rudolf Otto because he does not account for religion but instead simply defines religion as an encounter with God.

2 Furthermore, the group comes together in the first place for religious reasons – one of the circularities in Durkheim's argument. Thus Australian aboriginal clans, Durkheim's test case, amass to 'celebrate a religious ceremony' (Durkheim 1965: 246).

3 Reductionism here means complete, or eliminative, reductionism. The reduction is ontological. By contrast, the reduction in social scientific accounts of religion is only methodological. Social scientists deny not that religious beliefs and practices exist but that those beliefs and practices generate and sustain themselves. Religious beliefs and practices are not considered hallucinatory. The 'hallucination' is the assumption that they create and perpetuate themselves.

Bibliography

Asad, Talal 1993 *Genealogies of Religion*. Baltimore, MD: Johns Hopkins University Press.

Asad, Talal 2003 *Formations of the Secular*. Stanford, CA: Stanford University Press.

Beattie, John 1966 [1964] *Other Cultures*. London: Routledge & Kegan Paul; New York: Free Press.

Bellah, Robert N. 1970 *Beyond Belief*. New York: Harper & Row.

Berger, Peter L. 1967 *The Sacred Canopy*. Garden City, NY: Doubleday. (Also published as *The Social Reality of Religion*. London: Faber and Faber, 1969.)

Berger, Peter L. 1969 *A Rumor of Angels*. Garden City, NY: Doubleday.

Bloor, David 1991 *Knowledge and Social Imagery*. 2nd edn (1st edn 1976). Chicago: University of Chicago Press.

Douglas, Mary 1966 *Purity and Danger*. New York and London: Routledge.

Douglas, Mary 1973 *Natural Symbols*. 2nd edn (1st edn 1970). New York: Vintage Books; London: Barrie and Jenkins.

Dubuisson, Daniel 2003.*The Western Construction of Religion*, trans. William Sayers. Baltimore, MD: Johns Hopkins University Press.

Durkheim, Émile 1965 [1912] *The Elementary Forms of the Religious Life*, trans. Joseph Ward Swain. New York: Free Press.

Eliade, Mircea 1963 [1958] *Patterns in Comparative Religion*, trans. Rosemary Sheed. Cleveland: Meridian Books.

Eliade, Mircea 1968 [1959] *The Sacred and the Profane*, trans. Willard R. Trask. New York: Harvest Books.

Erikson, Erik H. 1958 *Young Man Luther*. New York: Norton.

Erikson, Erik H. 1969 *Gandhi's Truth*. New York: Norton.

Fitzgerald, Timothy 2000 *The Ideology of Religious Studies*. New York and Oxford: Oxford University Press.

Fitzgerald, Timothy 2007 *Discourse on Civility and Barbarity*. Oxford and New York: Oxford University Press.

Frazer, J. G. [James George] 1922 *The Golden Bough*. Abridged edn. London: Macmillan.

Freud, Sigmund 1950 *Totem and Taboo*, trans. James Strachey. London: Routledge & Kegan Paul.

Freud, Sigmund 1964 [1961] *The Future of an Illusion*, trans. W. D. Robson-Scott, rev. James Strachey. Garden City, NY: Doubleday Anchor Books.

Geertz, Clifford 1973 *The Interpretation of Cultures*. New York: Basic Books.

Geertz, Clifford 1983 *Local Knowledge*. New York: Basic Books.

Jung, C. G. 1938 *Psychology and Religion*. New Haven, CT: Yale University Press.

King, Richard 1999 *Orientalism and Religion*. London and New York: Routledge.

McCutcheon, Russell 1996 *Manufacturing Religion*. New York and Oxford: Oxford University Press.

Malinowski, Bronislaw 1925 'Magic, Science and Religion,' in Joseph Needham, ed., *Science, Religion and Reality* (New York and London: Macmillan), 20–84.

Marx, Karl, and Friedrich Engels 1957 *On Religion*. Moscow: Foreign Languages Publishing.

Masuzawa, Tomoko 1993 *In Search of Dreamtime*. Chicago: University of Chicago Press.

Masuzawa, Tomoko 2003 *The Invention of World Religions*. Chicago: University of Chicago Press.

Müller, Friedrich Max 1867 'Comparative Mythology' (1856), in his *Chips from a German Workshop*, vol. 2 (London: Longmans, Green), 1–141.

Preus, J. Samuel 1987 *Explaining Religion*. New Haven: Yale University Press.

Said, Edward 1991 *Orientalism*. 3rd edn (1st edn 1978). Harmondsworth: Penguin.

Segal, Robert A. 1989 *Religion and the Social Sciences*. Atlanta: Scholars Press.

Segal, Robert A. 1992 *Explaining and Interpreting Religion*. New York: Peter Lang.

Segal, Robert A. 2005 'James and Freud on Mysticism,' in Jeremy Carrette, ed., *William James and 'The Varieties of Religious Experience'* (London and New York: Routledge), 124–32.

Taylor, Mark C., ed. 1998 *Critical Terms for Religious Studies*. Chicago: University of Chicago Press.

Turner, Victor H. 1967 *The Forest of Symbols*. Ithaca, NY: Cornell University Press.

Turner, Victor H. 1968 *The Drums of Affliction*. Oxford: Clarendon Press.

Tylor, E B. [Edward Burnett] 1871 *Primitive Culture*. 2 vols. London: Murray.

Weber, Max 1963 *The Sociology of Religion*, trans. Ephraim Fischoff. Boston: Beacon Press.

Suggested reading

Because theories of religion come mainly from the social sciences, the most useful overviews are of the application of these disciplines to the study of religion. Edited by Robert A. Segal, *The Blackwell Companion to the Study of Religion* (Oxford, UK, and Malden, MA: Blackwell, 2006) contains lucid chapters on 'Anthropology of Religion' (Fiona Bowie), 'Economics of Religion' (Rodney Stark), 'Psychology of Religion' (Roderick Main), and 'Sociology of Religion' (Grace Davie).

Chapter 6

Theology

David F. Ford[1]

Definitions of theology and academic theology

Theology at its broadest is thinking about questions raised by, about and between the religions. The name 'theology' is not used in all religious traditions and is rejected by some. It is a term with its own history, which will be sketched below. Yet there is no other non-controversial term for what this chapter is about, so it is used here in full recognition of the disputes and diverse associations surrounding it. Theology has many analogues or comparable terms such as 'religious thought', 'religious philosophy', various technical terms for the teaching and deliberative dimension of particular religions and even 'wisdom'. Indeed, wisdom (though itself a complex idea with different meanings and analogues in different traditions) is perhaps the most comprehensive and least controversial term for what theology is about. Wisdom may embrace describing, understanding, explaining, knowing and deciding, not only regarding matters of empirical fact but also regarding values, norms, beliefs and the shaping of lives, communities and institutions. The broad definition of theology given above could be refined by reference to wisdom. The questions raised by, about and between the religions include some that are not necessarily theological, and many of these are formative for the disciplines covered in other chapters in this volume. One helpful (if still quite vague) further determination of the nature of theology by reference to wisdom is: at its broadest, theology is thinking and deliberating in relation to the religions with a view to wisdom.

This chapter is mainly about the narrower subject of academic theology as pursued in universities and other advanced teaching and research institutions, especially in settings variously called departments of religion, religious studies, theology and religious studies, theology or divinity. The primary focus is on this academic theology in its European history and its present situation in universities that are in continuity with that tradition and its expansion beyond Europe. There have been numerous traditions of theology (or its analogues) originating in other parts of the world and in various religious traditions, some of which are increasingly significant within contemporary universities; but an appropriate way of portraying academic theology within one chapter is to concentrate on its characteristics in the academic tradition that generated the field called in other chapters the study of religion or religious studies.

In that tradition, as will be seen, theology is an inherently controversial discipline because of its subject matter, because of its history, because of the relations of other disciplines to religious issues and because of the nature of modern universities and the societies that support them. Academic theology is distinguished from theology in general mainly by its relation to the various disciplines of the academy. So a preliminary definition of academic theology (and analogues of theology) is that it *seeks wisdom in relation to questions, such as those of meaning, truth, beauty and practice, which are raised by, about and between the religions and are pursued through engagement with a range of academic disciplines.*

The final preliminary definition to be considered is that of religion. This too is a contested concept, as other chapters in this volume make clear. For the purposes of this chapter it is sufficient to identify religion in a low-key, non-technical way through a number of generally accepted examples. Religion, it is assumed, includes such ways of shaping human life in communities and their associated traditions as are exemplified by Buddhism, Christianity, Hinduism, Islam and Judaism. This is not an exclusive definition; it simply limits the scope of reference of this chapter, while allowing that much of what it says could be applied to other instances of religion and to traditions (such as cultures, philosophical schools, or secular worldviews and ways of living) which might not be included in a particular definition of religion. It is also a definition that does not entail any particular position on such disputed matters as the essence, origin and function of religion.

Before focussing on the discipline of academic theology it is important first to say more about theology and its analogues in the broadest sense.

Theology beyond the academy

The religious communities mentioned in the definition above all place a high priority on learning and teaching. An immense amount of time and energy is spent on such activities as the study and interpretation of key texts, and instruction in tradition, prayer and ethics. Much learning happens through imitation, and the adoption of habits of thought, imagination, feeling and activity, which are assimilated through participation in a community's life. Such learning and teaching have been important in helping those traditions survive and develop over many generations.

It is, however, never simply a matter of repeating the past. The texts and commentators raise questions that require consideration afresh by each generation; each period and situation raises new issues; there are conflicts, splits and challenges from inside and outside the tradition. Even when the verdict is that what is received from the past ought to be repeated and imitated as closely as possible in the present, that is a decision which cannot be arrived at without some deliberation. Thinking about appropriate ways to understand and act in the context of a particular tradition comes under my broad definition of theology. Such thought is pervasive and usually informal, and teaching usually aims at turning its basic features into implicit, taken-for-granted assumptions in the light of which questions are faced and behaviour shaped. Yet, because of the many factors which prompt internal and external questioning, explicit thought may also be provoked, and theological inquiry, in the sense described above, may be generated. What is the right interpretation of this text? How should children be educated in this tradition? What is the right response to legal or political injustice? Does God exist? If so, what sort of God? What about death, creation, salvation, gender issues? What, if any, is the purpose of life? How should those with very different traditions and conceptions be treated? Such questions may give rise to theological inquiry.

Yet it is not only those who identify with a particular community and its traditions who ask such questions. Religions provoke inquiry in many beyond their own members; and some of their own members may dissociate themselves from their community but may still (sometimes even more energetically) pursue such questions. In addition, there are public debates about every major area of life – medicine, politics, economics, war, justice and so on – which raise religious issues and require deliberation and decision. Such debates display various types of theological thinking, both implicit and explicit.

Therefore theology in the broad sense is practised not only within religious communities but also by many who are beyond such communities or in an ambivalent relationship with them; and it is also present between religious communities and in public debates, both within and between nations.

Finally, theological questions arise at all levels of education. They may be focussed in religious or theological education, but, because of the considerations discussed above, they are also distributed through other subjects, and they are relevant to overall educational policy and practice.

Overall, it is important to remember that only a very small part of the theology going on in the world is taught and learnt in the university settings that are the main concern of this chapter.

Academic theology: early history in Europe

The Greek word *theologia* meant an account of the gods, and it was taken over by the early Christian church to refer to the biblical account of God's relationship to humanity. This close relationship to scripture was maintained through the Middle Ages in western Europe, when theology in the narrower sense of a specific discipline studied in universities arose with the development of universities in the early thirteenth century. It is significant that these universities themselves had many characteristics in common with Islamic institutions from which Christian scholars learnt a great deal.

Before the foundation of universities, theology had been nurtured in the many monasteries around Europe and in associated rural schools. Theology was there inseparable from the duties of worship and prayer, pervaded by the life of the cloister. In the cities the cathedral schools, founded for training diocesan clergy, were important theological centres. In addition, theology in the cities became part of the guild-oriented activity of a new rising class of freemen, both students and teachers, who responded favourably to new forms of argument and teaching and to the rediscovery of forgotten writings of the past. Here theology in schools (hence the label 'scholastic') was becoming a specialty subject for professional, philosophically trained dialecticians. Anselm of Canterbury (1033–1109), based in a monastery, brought fresh systematic and argumentative rigour to theology, and described it as 'faith seeking understanding'. Peter Abelard (1079–1142) represented the new sort of teacher and dialectician. In Paris, the new religious movement embodied in the Augustinian canons of St Victor mediated between the claims of the monastery and the schoolroom. This was an age of discovery, compilation and integration, which culminated in producing what became (in addition to the Bible) the standard theological text for discussion in the university schoolrooms of Europe during the next four centuries. This was the *Sentences* of Peter the Lombard (d. 1160), a collection of four books of the theological wisdom of Scripture and of the early Fathers of the church.

After the formal establishment of the first universities in the first part of the thirteenth century, scholastic theology developed under a new influence, the mendicant religious orders of Franciscans and Dominicans. Both flourished in the new University of Paris. Thomas Aquinas (1225–1274) among the Dominicans and Bonaventure (1221–1274) among the Franciscans developed distinctive ways of doing theology within the new universities. They drew on traditional monastic resources such as Augustine and Pseudo-Dionysius, and, especially in Thomas's case, on newly discovered texts of Aristotle as well. Their disputation-dominated educational environment produced several major theological syntheses, which remain classic texts. One persistently contentious issue remained the nature of theology. Whereas all agreed that it was a form of *sapientia* (wisdom) there was dispute about its status as a *scientia* (branch of rational knowledge relying on its own first principles).

In the later Middle Ages theology split into distinct 'ways' based on the religious orders. After 1450, as the Renaissance and other changes occurred in Europe, the dominance of Parisian theology was broken as many European universities established theology faculties. The largely Dominican faculty at Salamanca replaced Lombard's *Sentences* with Thomas Aquinas's *Summa Theologiae* as the basic text for classroom commentary. The Salamancan theologian Melchior Cano (1509–1560) produced a systematic treatise combining various kinds of authoritative texts, scriptural, scholastic and Renaissance humanist, including historical and scientific, covering the main theological *loci* (places). This gave birth to systematic theology in the modern sense.

By this time, humanist scholarship, especially represented by Desiderius Erasmus (1466–1536), together with the initiation of the Protestant Reformation by a professor at the University of Wittenberg, Martin Luther (1483–1546), had begun a reaction against a scholastic theology that had become highly specialized and abstruse. The humanist and Protestant emphasis was on recovering the original sense of scripture and of early Christian writers. They produced scholarly editions of the texts based on the best possible manuscript evidence, and they interpreted the 'plain sense' of the texts with the intention of approximating as near as possible to what the authors meant. The result in Protestant universities was that the main task of theology became the interpretation of scripture studied in Hebrew and Greek.

Catholic theology continued to be scholastic in form, with Thomas Aquinas dominant, though often understood through the medium of later interpreters and summaries in manuals. Polemics between Catholics and Protestants increasingly shaped both sides, as they developed systematic statements of their positions and counterpositions. A further dimension was apologetics defending theological positions against an increasing number of critiques and challenges, some of which made a sharp distinction between 'revealed' and 'natural' religion and theology. During the eighteenth century, theology began to lose its role as the 'leading science' whose word carried authority for other faculties. The rise of sovereign states, whose practical demands were less theological than legal, gave pre-eminence to the law faculties. These in turn were superseded by the 'new sciences' that entered the curriculum, studying the 'book of nature'. Many of the ideas that had most effect on later discussion of theological issues were generated by those outside theology faculties, whether Protestant or Catholic.

During these centuries, theology also became increasingly differentiated into branches. By the twentieth century the main branches had become: systematic (or dogmatic or doctrinal or constructive) theology; historical theology; biblical theology; moral theology (or theological ethics); philosophical theology; practical (or pastoral) theology and mystical theology (or spirituality).

Academic theology in the modern university

A formative event in the shaping of the modern academic tradition of Christian theology in the nineteenth and twentieth centuries was the foundation of the University of Berlin in 1809, which became for many the archetypal modern university (see Frei 1992: 95ff.). There was considerable debate about whether theology ought to be included in it. Some (such as the philosopher J.G. Fichte) argued that it had no place in a university committed to modern standards of rationality. The position which won was that of the theologian F.D.E. Schleiermacher, who affirmed the role of rationality in the university without allowing it either to dictate to theology or to be in competition with theology. He saw theology as a positive science or discipline (*Wissenschaft*), by which he meant that it was not included within any one theoretical discipline but that it related to several disciplines with a view to the practical task of educating those who would lead the Christian church. The usual pattern of theological faculties in the German university became that of the state overseeing and paying for a faculty which both owed allegiance to general standards of rationality (*Wissenschaft*) that presuppose academic freedom, and also was committed to training clergy for the state Protestant church. Two consequences of this make modern German theology a specially good focus through which to study the discipline in modernity.

First, it meant that theology was carried on in an environment where it was continually in engagement with and informed by other academic disciplines in their most advanced forms. Christianity became the religion that was most thoroughly examined, explained, critiqued and argued about in the nineteenth-century European university.

Second, the attempt to hold together the requirements of academy and church built into theology the tendency towards a tension between 'reason' and 'faith'. This tension is one way of approaching the task of describing basic types of modern Christian theology (see Frei 1992; Ford 2005). These types are of wider relevance than to the German or the Christian context, and developing them will provide a helpful framework later in this chapter.

The German pattern might be described as confessional theology (in the sense of theology according to the belief and practice of one religious community or 'confession' of faith) funded by the state. This continues to be the norm in Germany and other countries which follow its pattern, and some universities contain both Roman Catholic and Protestant faculties of theology. In addition, some German universities teach religious studies or 'history of religions', and there is a fluid situation as regards the relations with theology.

Elsewhere, different patterns have emerged. Those in North America and England exemplify the main contrasting ways in which the discipline is present in universities today.

In North America the tendency has been to separate theology from religious studies. Theology has often been understood as a confessional discipline (whereas the description given above includes confessional theology but is not limited to it) and has been largely taught in institutions affiliated to a Christian church or group of churches. The main location of theology has therefore been the 'seminary' or 'divinity school', sometimes attached as a professional school to a non-state university. Because of the separation of church and state, theology has rarely been taught, except as intellectual history, at state-funded universities, but many church-affiliated universities have departments of theology. Departments of religious studies exist in many state and private universities. These embody various understandings of the discipline, ranging from a few which integrate theology with religious studies, to others which define religious studies over against theology (a position that has been represented controversially by Don Wiebe, the author of Chapter 8). Judaism, numerically far smaller than Christianity, displays a comparable range of relationships in the institutionalization of its theology or (to use a term which is preferred by many Jews) its religious thought.

In Britain university theology has become largely state-funded, and has developed from being exclusively Christian and Anglican to embracing, first, other Christian traditions, and then, in the later twentieth century, other religions. Departments in British universities are called variously theology, religious studies, theology and religious studies, and divinity. Whatever the name, most now embrace both theology and religious studies.

Most universities in other parts of the world roughly correspond to the German (confessional theology), American (separation of theology and religious studies) or British (integration of theology with religious studies) models for the field, and both within countries and internationally there is a continuing debate about which is to be preferred. The next section will outline the main issues in the debate.

Theology in distinction from religious studies

Theology has advanced reasons why it should be separate from religious studies; religious studies has likewise had reasons for being separate from theology; and there have been advocates of integration who refuse to accept such separation. We will consider each set of reasons in turn, while recognizing that there are also those who interpret the reasons on one or both sides as rationalizations of religious, political or economic interests intent on maintaining or gaining power and influence.

Theology's reasons for favouring separation centre on three related considerations.

- First, especially in the Abrahamic faiths (Judaism, Christianity and Islam) there is the role of God in knowing God, and of faith and commitment in doing theology. If theology includes knowing God (or analogues of God), and if knowing God depends on responding in faith and obedience (or on some other form of self-involving practice) to God's initiative, then surely those who are not believers cannot do theology?

- Second, moving beyond the possible individualism of the first point, there is the relation of theology to a community and its tradition. If a particular theology is intrinsically connected to a particular community, then surely it can only be genuinely pursued in the context of that community? The logic of these points is to confine genuine theology to confessional faculties, seminaries, divinity schools or other institutions in affiliation with the community whose theology is being studied.

- Third, there has been some theological suspicion of the very category of 'religion'. Whereas, for example, God in Jewish, Christian or Muslim belief can be understood as relating to and transcending all creation, religion has often been seen as one domain of human existence among others. The objection of theology to being paired with religious studies is that this constricts the scope of theology. The effect of the Enlightenment (not least through inventing the modern sense of the word 'religion') tended to be to privatize religion, so that it became a matter of private discretion with its proper sphere in human interiority. Where religion's public role was concerned, the tendency was to limit its power and to deny its contribution to public truth. Its competitors in the public sphere included not only nationalism, capitalism and communism, but also new understandings of the universe, humanity, history and society which were closely associated with various academic disciplines. When these disciplines focussed on their limited concepts of religion, theology did not find that they could do justice to its questions of meaning, truth, beauty and practice.

Religious studies in distinction from theology

Religious studies, for its part, has been aware that its origins in European and American universities lay partly in a desire for academic freedom for the study of religion without being answerable to religious authorities. Institutional separation from theology had a political point.

Academically, the key issue concerned knowledge and the methods which lead to it. The study of religion developed as a loose alliance of disciplines whose main concerns were elsewhere. It has never had a generally agreed method or set of methods, despite many proposals. In one of the most comprehensive accounts of the field, Walter H. Capps finds its fragile coherence in an Enlightenment tradition stemming from Descartes and Kant in its conception of knowledge and method (Capps 1995). Religious studies has focussed on questions such as the essence and origin of religion, the description and function of religion, the language of religion and the comparison of religions. But, in dealing with those questions through disciplines such as philosophy, psychology, sociology, phenomenology and anthropology, Capps suggests that the most fundamental feature of the field has been a broadly Kantian epistemology (if that can be taken as allowing for both empiricist and hermeneutical developments). The concern for academic autonomy in line with that tradition has often persuaded it to prefer separation from theology, except where theology (or its analogues) is willing to accept its terms. Capps is hospitable to theology, which is willing to find a role contributing to his conception of religious studies, but he also recognizes the need to go beyond his own paradigm. The next section offers one conception of how that might be achieved.

The question about knowledge and methods is a mirror-image of the problems, mentioned above, which theology has with religious studies. Religious studies has usually wanted to bracket out, for example, any conception of God being involved in the knowing that goes on in the field; and its pursuit of questions of meaning, truth, beauty and practice has tended to be limited to the methods of its constituent disciplines. It prefers to use such methods in rigorous pursuit of what can be known and justified to dealing with larger or more synthetic issues without those methods or beyond them. Overall, therefore, a basic concern of religious studies has been that of the academic integrity of the field.

Theology integrated with religious studies

Those who advocate the integration of theology with religious studies rarely suggest that all theology and religious studies should be institutionally combined. They recognize that religious communities will want to have their own academic institutions in which confessional theology (or its analogues) would be the norm; and that many universities will want to specialize in their religious studies (e.g. by focussing on a few disciplines such as sociology, anthropology or phenomenology) so as to exclude theology as well as some other disciplines. There are many factors (historical, religious, political, economic, cultural) other than the overall conception of the field which help determine its shape in a particular institution. Their main point for integration is the academic case in principle for the inseparability of the two. One version of the case is as follows.

First, theology is not in competition with religious studies but needs it. If theology is to be rigorous in its pursuit of questions of meaning, truth, beauty and practice then it needs to draw on work in other disciplines. This will not just be a matter of using their results when they are congenial, but rather of entering into them from the inside and engaging both critically and constructively with their methods and results. Academic theology has done this much more thoroughly in some areas than in others. It has been most widely practised in relation to philosophy, textual scholarship and history. In each of these fields there are many practitioners who integrate their discipline with theology, and also many who do not. This gives rise to considerable debate about issues that are not likely to be conclusively resolved (a common situation in philosophy, textual interpretation and history). The argument is that for the health of the field it is desirable to have some settings where such debates can be carried on as fully as possible.

Second, theology is not just pursued by those who identify with a particular community, and it can be studied in many ways other than confessionally. Universities are obvious settings for those who wish to pursue theological questions in such ways. For the members of particular religious communities there can also be advantages in doing theology in dialogue with academics and students of other faith traditions and of none.

Third, religious studies need not be in competition with theology. Certain definitions of the field exclude certain definitions of theology, but other definitions of religious studies open it towards integration with theology. A key issue is how far questions intrinsic to the field may be pursued, and whether some answers to those questions are to be ruled out in advance. For example, is the question of truth concerning the reality of God as identified by a particular tradition allowed to be pursued and then answered in line with that tradition? If so, then the way is opened for critical and constructive theology within a religious studies milieu. If not, what reasons can be offered for cutting off inquiry and disallowing certain answers? Such cutting off and disallowing either appears arbitrary or it relies on criteria that are themselves widely contested and debated within the field. The irresolvability of the dispute over boundaries and criteria has been intensified by similar disputes, often bitter, in other disciplines with which religious studies and theology engage, such as literary studies, philosophy, history and the human sciences.

Fourth, the three main responsibilities of theology and religious studies can be argued to converge and so make integration appropriate for them in university settings. The first is their responsibility towards the academy and its disciplines. The requirement is excellence in the study and teaching of texts, history, laws, traditions, practices, institutions, ideas, the arts and so on, as these relate to religions in the past and the present. This involves standards set by peer groups, work within and collaboration between disciplines and a worldwide network of communication. The second is their responsibility towards religious communities. This includes the tasks of carrying out their academic responsibilities critically and constructively, educating members of religious communities as well as others, and providing forums where religious traditions can engage in study, dialogue and debate together. Universities have increasingly become centres of such interfaith engagement in which theological concerns with, for example, questions of truth and practice, go together with the use of a range of academic disciplines. The third is their responsibility to society and the realm of public life. Issues in politics, law, the media, education, medicine and family life often raise questions which require complex interdisciplinary, interreligious and international collaboration. These questions embrace theological as well as other matters.

Fifth, in the light of the above four points, the case for a fundamental dualism in the field is undermined. It is still appropriate to have institutions with particular emphases and commitments, but the overall intellectual and ethical 'ecology' of the field embraces theology and religious studies.

Types of Christian theology

How can the field of academic theology be described so as to do justice to the range of theologies and their different ways of relating to other disciplines? One typology worked out in relation to Christian theology is that of Frei (1992). It takes account of the importance of institutional contexts both historically and today. Frei takes the University of Berlin as his historical point of departure, and his typology also relates to the American situation of theology and religious studies. He recognizes that there are very different types of theology, some of which are more at home in universities than others. His typology therefore grows out of the academic tradition with which this chapter is mainly concerned and it is limited to Christian theology; but it can also be developed in relation to other religious traditions. Its attempt to do descriptive justice to the current state of the field results in allowing both for the separation of theology and religious studies and for their integration.

There are five types on a continuum, of which the two extremes will be described first.

Type 1

This type gives complete priority to some contemporary philosophy, worldview, practical agenda or one or more academic disciplines. In its academic form it subjects Christian theology to 'general criteria of intelligibility, coherence, and truth that it must share with other academic disciplines' (Frei 1992: 2). Immanuel Kant (1724–1804) is seen as the main historical exemplar of this in modernity. He applied his criteria of rationality and morality to theology and offered an understanding of religion 'within the bounds of reason alone'. In terms of the previous discussion, a Kantian Type 1 is in line with a conception of religious studies which insists on a particular set of epistemological criteria being met by any theology that is to be admitted to the academy. It therefore excludes other types of theology mentioned below. It also gives philosophy (of a particular type) priority as the main cognate discipline of theology.

Other versions of Type 1 use different external criteria to judge theology – for example, an ecological worldview, or a feminist ethic, or a political programme or an imaginative aesthetic.

Type 5

This type takes Christian theology as exclusively a matter of Christian self-description. It is the 'grammar of faith', its internal logic learnt like a new language through acquiring appropriate conceptual skills. It offers a scriptural understanding or a traditional theology or version of Christianity as something with its own integrity that is not to be judged by outside criteria. All reality is to be seen in Christian terms, and there is a radical rejection of other frameworks and worldviews. Examples include some types of fundamentalism (such as those seeing the Bible as inerrant and all-sufficient for theology) and also more sophisticated conceptions of a religion as a distinctive and embracing 'language game' or 'world of meaning'. In terms of the previous discussion, Type 5 is in line with a conception of theology which prefers separation from religious studies and other disciplines.

The two extremes of Types 1 and 5 can be seen to come together in their tendency to see everything in terms of some given framework (whether Christian or non-Christian) and to cut off the possibilities for dialogue across boundaries.

Types 2, 3 and 4

Between the two extremes come three types that in various ways incorporate dialogue.

Type 2 tries to correlate general meaning structures with what is specifically Christian. It interprets Christianity consistently in terms of some contemporary philosophy, idiom or concern, while trying to do justice to the distinctiveness of Christianity. One example is the German theologian Rudolf Bultmann (1884–1976), who reconceived the Christian Gospel in terms of existentialist philosophy. The overall integration is biased towards the general framework, and so this type is close to Type 1.

If Type 2 moves in the other direction towards a correlation which does not attempt a comprehensive integration, then it becomes Type 3. This non-systematic correlation is a thoroughly dialogical form of theology. Theological questions, methods and positions are continually being correlated with other questions, methods and positions. Theology can learn a great deal from other disciplines and positions without giving a single one overarching significance, and it is only from within the process of dialogue that judgements can be made. Schleiermacher is an example of this type, as is Paul Tillich (1886–1965) who correlated fundamental questions about life and history with the meaning offered by Christian symbols and ideas.

Type 4 gives priority to Christian self-description, letting that govern the applicability of general criteria of meaning, truth and practice in Christian theology, yet nevertheless engaging with a range of disciplines and with other worldviews and theological positions in *ad hoc* ways. It does not go to the extreme of Type 5, but still insists that no other framework should be able to dictate how to understand the main contents of Christian faith. It is 'faith seeking understanding', basically trusting the main lines of classic Christian testimony to God and the Gospel, but also open to a wide range of dialogues – not least because God is seen as involved with all reality. The Swiss theologian Karl Barth is of this type, resisting the assimilation of Christian faith to Western culture and ideologies, especially that of the Nazis. Type 4 sees Type 3 as inherently unstable: there can be no neutral standpoint from which to carry on dialogues, and therefore there has to be a basic commitment for or against Christian faith – which yet needs to be tested in encounters with other positions. A favoured cognate discipline of this type of theology as practised in Britain and North America is the more descriptive (rather than explanatory) types of social science.

Assessment of the types

Any complex theology is not likely to fit neatly into a single type, and the purpose here is not to set up neat pigeonholes enabling all theologians to be labelled. Many will display subtle blends and uncategorizable positions which resist easy description. Rather, the aim is to portray a range of types which spans the field and enables a judgement about theology in relation to other disciplines, including those embraced in religious studies. The judgement is that, while Type 5 is likely to be least at home in the university and Type 1 least at home in the Christian community, Types 2, 3 and 4 can, in different ways and with different points of tension, be at home in both. There are Christian communities that would exclude the first four types, and there are universities that would exclude the last four types, but these ways of drawing boundaries are controversial and many institutions are more inclusive. The practical conclusion is that an overview of the discipline of theology, as it has developed in universities carrying forward the European tradition, argues for a definition that can embrace all five types. This in turn supports the argument above in the previous section that it makes academic as well as theological sense to see the field as whole, embracing theology and religious studies. The different types of theology construe the field in widely varying ways, and particular institutions and traditions need to take fundamental decisions about which types they embrace – but that is the case in many other fields too.

Beyond Christian theology

The above typology has been deliberately tradition-specific. The next question is whether something like those types do justice to the other religious traditions which are the examples being used in this chapter: Judaism, Islam, Hinduism and Buddhism. There was a blossoming of the study of these and other religious traditions in the universities of Europe and the US in the nineteenth century, though apart from the special case of Judaism the study was mostly outside theological faculties. A major factor in the rise of the field of religious studies was an attempt to do fuller academic justice to religions other than Christianity. From a standpoint at the beginning of the twenty-first century it is possible to see that attempt as having two main phases, the second still in progress and provoking much debate.

The first phase involved the establishment of religious studies over against theology (usually against confessional Christian theology). The main concern was for properly academic study through disciplines such as the others described in this Companion.

The second phase has accompanied the multiplication of universities around the world and the growth of the study of theology and religious studies in them. The last half of the twentieth century has seen an unprecedented expansion in higher education and of the disciplines and subdisciplines that study religions. One crucial feature of this second phase has been that considerable numbers of academics and students in universities now study their own religion as well as the religions of others. This has led to debates similar to those which have surrounded Christian theology in the European tradition. How far is it appropriate to be a Jew and pursue critical and constructive Jewish thought in a university? If a Buddhist academic is discussing ethical issues, how far is it appropriate to develop Buddhist positions? Increasingly, the answer has been that it is appropriate; then the debate moves on to consider the criteria of appropriateness. But, once it is granted that members of traditions can contribute in such ways to academic discussions and utilize a range of disciplines in doing so, then what has been defined above as academic theology is being practised. The result is that the type of religious studies which defined itself against Christian confessional theology is now being challenged to 're-theologize'. Can it recognize the academic validity of inquiries, debates and dialogues which are theological (in the sense of seeking wisdom about questions of meaning, truth, beauty and practice relating to the religions and the issues they raise), which use various academic disciplines, and which relate to other traditions besides Christianity?

The impetus towards such theology has been strengthened by suspicion directed towards the ways in which religions have been studied by Western academics. For example, the accounts of Judaism by non-Jews (especially Christians) have been subjected to thorough critique (especially by Jews); Islam, Buddhism and Hinduism have struggled to resist the imposition of 'orientalist' identities projected by Western scholars; and Christians have often judged accounts of their faith to be distorted by post-Enlightenment academic presuppositions and criteria. In particular there has been a rejection of 'ideologies of neutrality' and associated positions such as the dichotomy between fact from value, or the separation of knowledge from ethics and faith. The key point has been: 'no one stands nowhere', and it is desirable that religious traditions (together with genders, races, classes and cultures) have their own academic voices that can speak from where they stand. Huge questions of epistemology, ethics, theology and the meaning of 'academic' are at stake here and are likely to remain in contention; but once they have been raised they are hard to suppress, and many institutions have created the settings for pursuing them. One such setting is the integrated field of theology and religious studies.

The typology suggested by Frei is an attempt to devise a conception of the field that fits such a setting. It is applicable to religions besides Christianity insofar as each is a tradition (or set of traditions) whose traditional identity can be rethought and developed in the present according to the five types. For example, there are those who assimilate Buddhist ideas and practices to a variety of non-Buddhist frameworks (Type 1); others are 'fundamentalist', or convinced of the self-sufficiency of a particular set of traditional Buddhist ideas and practices (Type 5); and others arrive at more dialogical identities which balance differently between those extremes (Types 2, 3 and 4).

Yet each of the sample religions with which this chapter is concerned has a distinctive history in relation to theology or its analogues. In line with this chapter's limited scope (focussing on theology in the university tradition begun in western Europe in the Middle Ages, continued today in research universities that are successors to that tradition in and beyond Europe and America, and concerned especially with the relation between theology and religious studies) it is not possible to discuss the history of each tradition in detail. What are offered below are some considerations from the standpoint of each of the five traditions as they take part in theology and religious studies in contemporary universities. Most space is given to Judaism as the tradition which has, besides Christianity, been most intensively engaged with academic study and thought in the universities of Europe, North America and more recently Israel.

Judaism

The term 'theology' is often considered suspect among Jewish thinkers. This is partly because theology is sometimes seen as being about the inner life of God, which has not usually been a Jewish concern. Partly it has been a reaction of a minority against oppressive and dominant confessional theology: it has not been safe for Jews to condone public or university theological talk, since Christians (or others) could use it to seek domination or to proselytize. Partly, too, theology has been seen as abstractive, intellectualizing and even dogmatizing (in the bad sense) instead of practice-oriented discussion about community-specific behaviour. Perhaps the most acceptable term is Jewish religious thought.

The main institution for articulating Jewish religious thought has been the rabbinic academy, whose origins are in the 'yeshivah', a centre of learning and discussion going back to the Mishnaic period in Palestine, and continuing in the Talmudic academies of Palestine and Babylonia, and later in centres spread around the diaspora. The discourse of these centres combined study of biblical texts (with a view to expounding both its plain sense and also its relevance to traditional and current issues), ethical discussion, jurisprudence, literary interpretation, folk science and much else. The rabbinic academy is still the normative institution for the religious thought of most orthodox Jewish communities, and there are equivalents in other forms of Judaism – for example, rabbinical seminaries, Jewish colleges and other institutes.

There have been other non-university centres of Jewish religious thought besides the rabbinical academies. Beginning in the late Persian or Second Temple period, sages, and later rabbis and textual scholars, included devotees of the esoteric circles that generated Jewish mystical practice and literature or 'kabbalah'. These kabbalistic circles conducted 'theology' in the sense of studying the inner life of God, or at least those dimensions of God that are processual and descend into levels of human consciousness. Hasidism is a large, popular movement of lived kabbalah, and some contemporary Jewish academics are paying increasing attention to kabbalistic study.

One influential tradition in Jewish thought has been sustained by intellectuals, scientists and statesmen working in a succession of empires and civilizations – Persian, Greek, Roman, Islamic, Christian, modern European and American. They have been social and cultural brokers in statecraft, finance, medicine, the sciences and scholarship, and have produced much sophisticated and often influential thinking which mediates between Jewish and non-Jewish interests and understandings and which might be categorized under Types 2, 3 and 4 above. Examples include Moses Maimonides (1125–1204) in medieval Spain, the Jewish doctors, mystics, scientists, scholars and diplomats of Renaissance Italy, the Jewish intelligentsia in twentieth-century New York, and communities of lively religious thought which flourish outside the universities in Israel.

Jews were long excluded from the Christian-dominated university tradition of Europe, but since their entry into these academic settings they have, considering their small numbers, been disproportionately influential in many disciplines. Some have approximated to Types 1 and 2 above, attempting to accommodate Jewish religious traditions to the categories of Western thought. This was developed in German universities in the nineteenth century, Moses Mendelssohn (1729–1786) being a major figure. Others studied Judaism according to the canons of *Wissenschaft*, with a strong historicist tendency. This tradition, known in German as *Wissenschaft des Judentums*, remains the strongest influence on Jewish academic religious study. At its heart is the study of Jewish texts by explaining how and in which contexts they were composed, and what their sentences meant to those who composed and received them. This study is 'theological' in the sense used in this chapter insofar as it sometimes argues that the religious meaning of the texts is exhausted by what can be elicited through its methods.

Out of this tradition of *Wissenschaft* have come more complex forms of interaction, brokerage or dialogue with various types of academic inquiry, perhaps best labelled 'humanistic Jewish studies'. The study of texts has been opened up by such approaches as hermeneutical theory, structuralism and deconstruction, and the range of human and natural sciences has been related to Jewish concerns. In terms of the types above, it has most affinities with Type 3, but relates happily to any of the first four.

Finally, a recent development has called itself 'postcritical' or 'postliberal', sometimes welcoming the label 'Jewish theology'. Influenced by literary studies, postmodernism, and twentieth-century Jewish philosophies originating in Germany, France and America, these thinkers try to integrate three elements: philosophical inquiry; academic studies of texts, society and history; and traditional forms of rabbinic text study and practice. Its main affinities are with Type 4 in its concern to maintain a community-specific identity while learning from a wide range of dialogues – including dialogues with other religious traditions.

Islam

Islamic theology shares some of the strategies and concerns of Christian and Jewish discourse about God, since all three traditions are rooted in ancient Semitic narratives of a just and merciful Creator, and have historically evolved under the influence of Greek thought. For some three centuries after the death of the Prophet Muhammad (632 CE) the theology of the new religion was stimulated by encounters with several eastern Christian traditions, a debt which was later to be repaid when Avicenna, Ghazali and Averroes exercised profound influence on theologians of the Latin west in the Middle Ages. In spite of these convergences, however, the term 'theology' has no one Arabic equivalent, and theology in the sense used in this chapter has been pursued across many of the traditional Islamic disciplines.

One such subject area is Islamic jurispurdence (*usul al-fiqh*), which incorporates discussions of moral liability, natural law, the status of non-Muslims and other topics which received exhaustive treatment of a theological nature.

Sufism, Islam's highly diversified mystical and esoteric expression, also included systematic expositions of doctrine and cosmology in which mystical and exoteric teachings were juxtaposed, frequently in order to justify speculative or mystical insights to literalists.

A further discipline of great historic moment was Islamic philosophy (*falsafa* or *hikma*), which inherited late Greek philosophical syntheses and developed them into multiple religious systems. Many of these were regarded as too unscriptural and were therefore frequently confined to the status of private belief systems among elite circles.

Interacting with all these disciplines was *kalam*, conventionally translated as 'Islamic theology'. This is primarily a scriptural enterprise, applying forms of reasoning of Greek origin to the frequently enigmatic data of revelation. Ghazali (d. 1111) and Shahrastani (d. 1153) incorporated aspects of the *falsafa* tradition to shape *kalam* into a highly complex and rigorous Islamic worldview. Their tradition, known as Ash'arism, is still taught as Islam's orthodoxy in most Muslim countries. Orthodox status is also accorded to Maturidism, a theology which prevails among Muslims in the Indian subcontinent, Turkey, Uzbekistan and the Balkans. The debates between these schools are due mostly to the greater weight attached to rationality by Maturidism over against the comparatively more scriptural Ash'arism.

There have been various institutional settings for these types of theology, perhaps the most distinguished being Al-Azhar University in Cairo. In the twentieth century there have been many new universities. Those in Saudi Arabia, for example, have rejected the forms of reasoning from scripture found in both Ash'arism and Maturidism in favour of a strict literalism. These 'fundamentalists' (*Salafis*) are in a polemical relationship with traditional institutions such as Al-Azhar, and it may be that this engagement has become a more significant and widespread activity than the engagement with the discourses of modernity. In terms of the types used in this chapter, the main debates are between a Type 4, which inhabits and interprets the Qur'an with the aid of traditional Greek-influenced rationality, and a Type 5, which finds the Qur'an self-sufficient.

So far there has been comparatively little Muslim theology analogous to Types 1, 2 or 3. This is partly because of the widespread acceptance of the divinely inspired status of the Qur'anic text, and a rejection of the relevance of text-critical methodologies. There are some modern Muslim theologians open to post-Kantian approaches to metaphysics, found in more secular institutions such as Dar al-Ulum, a faculty of Cairo University or the Islamic Research Academy of Pakistan. Perhaps partly because the Qur'an contains comparatively little cosmological or other material that might clash with modern science, the defining controversies in modern Islam concern the extent of the relevance of medieval Islamic law to modern communities. So it is in matters of behaviour rather than belief that the greatest range of types is found.

It is in universities in the European tradition that some of the potentially most far-reaching developments are now taking place. Due to the establishment of large Muslim communities in Europe and North America, making it now the second largest religion in the West, Muslim scholars and theologians are increasingly present in faculties of theology and religious studies. The study of Islam has shifted there away from 'oriental studies', and new forms of dialogue and interpretation are being developed.

Hinduism and Buddhism

Hinduism and Buddhism both have long and complex intellectual traditions of thought in many genres and many types of institutions. As with the other religious traditions, the university plays only a small role in contributing to Hindu and Buddhist religious or theological thought in the sense of a pursuit of wisdom. 'Hinduism' and 'Buddhism' themselves are terms which became popular due to Western interpreters in the nineteenth century but which mask the deeply plural phenomena that more developed understanding of these traditions now suggests. Nineteenth century university studies often approached these from the angle of philology, with more systematic studies of the religious dimensions frequently shaped by colonial concerns. The earlier conceptualizations of Hinduism concentrated on the Sanskritic (Brahmanical or elitist) forms as representative, with continuing repercussions.

India in the twentieth century has been one of the most important countries for dialogue between religious traditions, including Hinduism, Buddhism, Christianity and Islam. This dialogue has been deeply affected by Hindu and Buddhist approaches that insisted not only on theoretical and doctrinal discussion and disputation, in which argument (*tarka*) based on textual exegesis (*mimamsa*) plays a prominent part (and where the argumentation has been vigorously intra- and inter-religious in both traditions), but also on experience or realization of the goal (*anubhava/saksat-kara*, *dhyana*, ultimately *moksa/nirvana*), in what is an integrated grasp of truth-in-life.

This in turn encouraged suspicion of Western academic study applied to religion, especially the stress on the 'objectivity' of truth and knowledge and the tendency to separate understanding from practice. In Indian universities, the secular constitution led to religious traditions being studied mainly in departments of philosophy in ways similar to the more 'neutralist' approaches to religious studies in the West, and this reinforced the alienation of universities from the more wisdom-oriented inquiries of those concerned with the contemporary development of religious traditions and dialogue between them. In other countries of the East, however, there are other patterns – in Thailand, for example, where Buddhism is for all practical purposes the state religion, the study of Buddhism is privileged in the universities.

The numbers of Hindus and Buddhists living in diaspora in the West, together with large numbers of Westerners who now practise versions of these faiths, has begun to transform the situation of Hinduism and Buddhism in Western universities, where the late twentieth century saw a blossoming of posts related to them. The pattern has been repeated of a move from 'oriental studies' to 'religious studies' to a pluralist situation where oriental studies and religious studies continue, but there are also Hindus, Buddhists and others engaged in deliberating about questions of meaning, truth, beauty and practice with a view to wisdom for the contemporary situation.

Christianity

So far, Christian theology has been dealt with mainly in its history as a discipline, its relation to religious studies and its types. The contemporary situation of Christian theology is described using the five types in Ford 2005.

Of the traditions described above, the closest parallel is with Judaism, and there are analogies in Christian theology for most of the strands in Jewish theology. There is rapid growth at present in studies and constructive contributions to 'theology and ...' topics, the accompanying fields including notably philosophy, ethics, politics (leading to 'theologies of liberation'), the natural and human sciences, culture and the arts, gender (leading to feminist and womanist theologies), race, education, other religions and postmodernity. The German and other European and North American academic traditions continue strongly, but the most obvious new development in the twentieth century has been that of theological traditions in other countries and cultures. African, Asian, Latin American and Antipodean theologies have all emerged (often displaying acute tensions between the types described above), and many of these are networked in transregional movements.

At the same time, major church traditions have undergone theological transformations, most noticeably the Roman Catholic Church through the Second Vatican Council. At present the Orthodox Church in countries formerly Communist is having to come to intellectual (and other) terms with exposure to massive global and local pressures; and the Pentecostal movement (reckoned to number over 300 million) is beginning to develop its own academic theology. Between the churches there have developed ecumenical theologies and theologies advocating or undergirding common action for justice, peace and ecological issues. As with other religious traditions, the spread of education has meant that far more members of churches are able to engage with theology, and there are local and international networks with university-educated laypeople addressing theological issues in relation to the Bible, tradition, and contemporary understanding and living.

The future of theology

Viewed globally, the vitality of theology in the twentieth century was unprecedented: the numbers of institutions, students, teachers, researchers, forms of theology and publications expanded vastly. It is unlikely that this vitality will diminish. Questions of meaning, truth, beauty and practice relating to the religions will continue to be relevant (and controversial), and the continuing rate of change in most areas of life will require that responses to those questions be constantly reimagined, rethought and reapplied. Higher education is likely to continue to expand, and there is no sign that the increase in numbers in members of the major religions is slowing. The convergence of such factors point to a healthy future, at least in quantitative terms.

Theology in universities is likely to continue according to a variety of patterns, such as the three mainly discussed in this chapter. Quantitatively, the main setting for theology or religious thought will continue to be institutions committed to particular religious traditions. There will also continue to be university settings in which religious studies are pursued without theology. My speculation is that the nature of the field, including its responsibilities towards academic disciplines, religious communities and public discourse, will also lead to an increase in places where theology and religious studies are integrated. The history of the field in recent centuries has not seen new forms superseding old ones (religious studies did not eliminate theology in universities) but the addition of new forms and the diversifying of old ones. Beyond the integration of theology and religious studies, further diversification is imaginable as theology engages more fully with different religions and disciplines and attempts to serve the search for wisdom through each.

Within the university it is perhaps the theological commitment to wisdom that is most important and also most controversial. Seeking wisdom through pursuing fundamental questions in the context of dialogue between radical commitments is never likely to sit easily within universities. Yet in a world where the religions, for better and for worse, shape the lives of billions of people, there is a strong case for universities encouraging theological questioning and dialogue as part of their intellectual life.

Note

1 I am indebted to four other scholars who are joint authors of parts of this chapter: John Montag, SJ on the early history of theology in Europe, Timothy Winter on Islam, Julius Lipner on Hinduism and Buddhism (all from the University of Cambridge); and Peter Ochs on Judaism (University of Virginia).

Bibliography

Capps, Walter H., *Religious Studies. The Making of a Discipline* (Fortress Press, Minneapolis 1995).

de Lange, Nicholas, *Judaism* (Oxford University Press, Oxford and New York 1986).

Ford, David F., 'Faith and Universities in a Religious and Secular World' in *Shaping Theology: Engagements in a Religious and Secular World* (Blackwell, Oxford 2007), 115–42.

Ford, David F. with Muers, Rachel (ed.), *The Modern Theologians. An Introduction to Christian Theology since 1918* 3rd edn (Blackwell, Oxford 2005).

Frei, Hans W., *Types of Christian Theology*, eds George Hunsinger and William C. Placher (Yale University Press, New Haven, CT and London 1992).

Harvey, Peter, *An Introduction to Buddhism. Teachings, History and Practices* (Cambridge University Press, Cambridge 1990).

Keown, Damien, *Buddhism: A Very Short Introduction* (Oxford University Press, Oxford 2000).

Lipner, Julius, *Hindus: their Religious Beliefs and Practices* (Routledge, London 1998).

Martin, R.C., Woodward, M. and Atmaja, D., *Defenders of Reason in Islam* (Oneworld, Oxford 1997).

Montgomery Watt, W., *Islamic Philosophy and Theology* (Edinburgh University Press, Edinburgh 1985).

Pelikan, Jaroslav, *The Christian Tradition: A History of the Development of Doctrine* 5 vols (Chicago University Press, Chicago 1989).

Waines, David, *An Introduction to Islam* 2nd edn (Cambridge University Press, Cambridge 2003).

Wiebe, Donald, *The Politics of Religious Studies: The Continuing Conflict with Theology in the Academy* (St Martins Press, New York 1999).

Winter, Tim, *The Cambridge Companion to Classical Islamic Theology* (Cambridge University Press, Cambridge 2008).

Suggested reading

de Lange, Nicholas, *Judaism* (Oxford University Press, Oxford and New York 1986).
   A lucid overview, with chapters on theology and eschatology, and other chapters on further aspects of thought (Torah and tradition, law, ethics and mysticism), which are embraced in the definition of theology used in this chapter.

Ford, David F. (ed.), *The Modern Theologians. An Introduction to Christian Theology since 1918* 3rd edn (Blackwell, Oxford 2005).

Covers the main Christian theologies of the period, both individual thinkers and movements, as well as the debates and critical questions about them.

Frei, Hans W., *Types of Christian Theology*, eds George Hunsinger and William C. Placher (Yale University Press, New Haven, CT and London 1992).
Frei's own account of the very useful typology of modern theologies, sensitive to historical and institutional contexts, which is described briefly in this chapter.

Harvey, Peter, *An Introduction to Buddhism. Teachings, History and Practices* (Cambridge University Press, Cambridge 1990).
Perceptive and comprehensive, especially good on religious thought and its relation to practice.

Lipner, Julius, *Hindus: their Religious Beliefs and Practices* (Routledge, London 1998).
Perhaps the best comprehensive introduction to Hinduism.

Winter, Tim, *The Cambridge Companion to Classical Islamic Theology* (Cambridge University Press, Cambridge 2008).
An authoritative and up-to-date overview of the major themes and developments in pre-modern Muslim theology.

Chapter 7

Philosophy of religion

Chad Meister

Philosophy of religion is the philosophical study of the meaning and nature of religion. Such study includes careful analyses of religious concepts, beliefs, terms, arguments, and practices of religious adherents. Philosophical reflection on religion is by no means a new endeavor; it has been part and parcel of the philosophical enterprise from the earliest times in both the east and the west. However, historically much of the work done in philosophy of religion has been primarily focused within the various theistic religions. More recent work often involves a broader approach – taking into consideration a plethora of religious traditions and topics from across the religious spectrum.

There are a number of themes which fall under the domain of philosophy of religion as it is commonly practiced in philosophy of religion departments, but the focus here will be limited to five: (1) religious belief and language; (2) religious diversity; (3) philosophical theology; (4) arguments for and against the existence of God; and (5) problems of evil.

Religious belief and language

Philosophy, especially in the analytic tradition, prides itself on precision of terms and clarity of concepts. Religious language, however, is often imprecise and veiled in mystery. This imprecision was challenged in the mid-twentieth century with the rise of logical positivism. Logical positivists were philosophers who used a principle of verifiability to reject as meaningless all non-empirical claims; only the tautologies of mathematics and logic, along with statements containing empirical observations or inferences, were considered meaningful. Many religious statements, however, such as claims about the transcendent, are neither tautological nor empirically verifiable. So certain fundamental religious claims and beliefs (such as "Yahweh is good," or "Atman is Brahman," or "Nirvana is beyond Ultimate Reality") were taken by the positivists to be cognitively meaningless utterances. Positivism became a dominant philosophical approach and for a time, for this and related reasons, philosophy of religion as a discipline became suspect.

In the latter half of the twentieth century, however, the philosophical tide began to turn with respect to religious language. Many philosophers argued that the positivists' empiricist criteria of meaning were unsatisfactory and problematic. Due to the philosophical insights on the nature and meaning of language provided by the later Ludwig Wittgenstein (1889–1951), the rise of a pragmatic version of naturalism offered by W. V. O. Quine (1908–2000), and other factors, logical positivism began to wane. For these reasons, along with the exemplary work of such analytic philosophers of religion as Alvin Plantinga (1932–), Richard

Swinburne (1934–), John Hick (1922–), and others, by the 1970s discussions about religious (and metaphysical and ethical) concepts were revived and soon became accepted arenas of viable philosophical and religious discourse.

With the collapse of positivism, two different streams emerged in philosophy of religion: realism and non-realism. Probably the vast majority of religious adherents are religious realists – defined here as those who hold that their beliefs are about what really exists (or are so believed to exist) independent of the human beings who are having those beliefs. Assertions about Allah, for example, or Brahman, or Yahweh, are true if there are actual referents for them. While they are in the minority, there are also religious non-realists – those who hold that religious claims are not about realities which transcend human language, concepts, and social forms; religious claims are not about something "out there." Sigmund Freud (1856–1939), for example, believed that there are no referents for religious beliefs about transcendent entities such as God, the dao, and so forth. Instead, religion is an illusion and religious beliefs are merely manifestations of this illusion. Belief in God, for him, is simply the projection of a father image.

Other non-realists have been more favorable toward religion. Ludwig Wittgenstein, for example, took religion very seriously. He was, however, opposed to natural theology – the attempt to demonstrate the existence of God from evidence in the natural world – and to the development of religious doctrines. He was more interested in religious symbol and ritual. In his later works, Wittgenstein understood language to be not a fixed structure directly corresponding to the way things actually are, but rather to be a human activity susceptible to the vicissitudes of human life and practice. Language does not offer a picture of reality, he argued, but rather is a set of activities which he described as "language games." In teaching language, one needs to be able to respond to words in certain contexts; speech and action work together. In many cases, then, the meaning of a word is its use in the language. For Wittgenstein, this is true in religious discourse as it is elsewhere. Thus in speaking of God or Brahman or nirvana or the dao, the meanings of such words have more to do with their use than with their denotation. The language games of the religions reflect the practices and forms of life of the various religious adherents, and so religious claims should not be taken as providing literal pictures of reality which somehow lie beyond those activities.

Religious non-realists often note the alleged failure of realism to provide evidences for the objective truth of any particular religion, or of religion in general. Whether referring to arguments for the existence of God, or evidences for resurrection or reincarnation, for example, non-realists argue that such projects in natural theology are abject failures. Non-realists are convinced that since there are no conclusive reasons to believe that a particular religion is true, a better way of approaching religious claims and beliefs is to understand them non-realistically.

Another point made by non-realists is that religious claims, beliefs, and practices exist within a given social context and involve human language and concepts. Since religious claims and activities are always within a particular human context, and since the mind structures all perception within that context, the meanings of these claims are determined and limited by that context. A person is simply unable, it is argued, to posit objective, transcendent realities beyond human language and cognition.

Realists have responded to these claims in different ways. Regarding the claim that there is no rational justification for religious beliefs, some realists (such as the fideists noted below) agree. Nevertheless, they claim that religion does not require evidence and justification; religion is about faith and trust, not evidence. Other realists, as we will see, disagree and claim that while faith is crucial to religion (at least to some religions), there are in fact good arguments and evidences for religious truth claims.

With respect to the point that religious claims, beliefs, and so on exist only within a given social context, some realists have responded by noting that while much of what occurs in religious discourse (and practice) is of human origin, one need not affirm a reductionist stance in which all religious meanings and symbols are reducible to human language. And some even argue that there are solid reasons and arguments for believing that religious claims are true, and that there are objective referents for their claims. Several of these arguments will be explored below.

Religious diversity

Philosophy of religion in the western context has emphasized themes related to Ultimate Reality understood *theistically* – themes such as the nature and existence of God, challenges to the existence of God, language about God, and so on. In recent times there has been a growing interest in religions and religious themes beyond the scope of the theistic traditions. This should not be surprising given the influx of religions in the west and the growing awareness of the wide variety of non-theistic religious traditions. While awareness of religious diversity is not a new phenomenon, philosophers of religion from both the east and the west are becoming increasingly more aware of and interactive with religious others. It is now fairly common to see contributions in western philosophy of religion literature on Hinduism, Buddhism, Daoism, Confucianism, and African religions, for example.

This rising interest in eastern religion and in comparative religion by philosophers in the west has brought about a deeper understanding of and appreciation for the different non-theistic religious traditions. But it has also brought to the fore an awareness of the many ways the different traditions conflict. Consider some examples: for the Advaita Vedantan, the concept of Ultimate Reality is pantheistic monism in which only Brahman exists, whereas Muslims affirm theistic dualism in which Allah – the one and only God – exists as distinct from human beings and the other created entities; for the Christian, salvation is the ultimate goal whereby human beings are united with God forever in the afterlife, while the Buddhists' ultimate goal is nirvana – an extinguishing of the individual self and complete extinction from all suffering. Numerous other examples could be cited as well.

How is one to respond to this diversity of fundamental beliefs? Different answers have been offered. One response to diversity is to deny or minimize the doctrinal conflicts, or to maintain that doctrine itself is not as important for religion as religious experience and that the great religious traditions are equally authentic responses to Ultimate Reality. This is one form of religion pluralism. John Hick, a leading defender of pluralism, denies the claim (widely held by atheists and others) that religion is solely a human projection. Utilizing Immanuel Kant's (1724–1804) distinctions of noumena (things as they are in themselves) and phenomena (things as they are experienced), Hick argues that a person's experiences – religious and non-religious – depend on the interpretive frameworks and concepts through which one structures and understands them. Thus, while some people experience and understand Ultimate Reality in personal, theistic categories (as Allah or Yahweh, for example), others do so in impersonal, pantheistic ways (as nirguna Brahman, say). Yet others experience and understand Ultimate Reality as non-personal and non-pantheistic (as with the Tao). One common illustration of the pluralist view of experiencing God uses the Hindu parable of the blind men and the elephant to capture this point. In this parable God is like an elephant surrounded by several blind men. One man touches the elephant's tail and believes it is a rope. Another touches his trunk and believes it is a snake. Another touches his leg and believes it is a tree. Yet another touches his side and believes it is a wall. Each of them are experiencing the same elephant but in very different ways from the others. In our experiences and understandings of Ultimate Reality, we are very much like the blind men, for our beliefs and viewpoints are constricted by our enculturated concepts.

Hick argues for the pluralistic hypothesis – that Ultimate Reality or the "Real" is ineffable and beyond the understanding of our conceptual systems. Nevertheless, the Real's presence can be experienced (in various forms) through various spiritual practices and linguistic systems. He uses analogies to describe his hypothesis, including an ambiguous picture of a duck-rabbit which Ludwig Wittgenstein used in his influential work, *Philosophical Investigations*. A culture that has ducks but no familiarity with rabbits would see the ambiguous diagram as a duck. People in this culture would not even be aware of the ambiguity. So too with the culture that has rabbits but no familiarity with ducks. People in this culture would see the diagram as a rabbit. Hick's point is that the ineffable Real is experienced in the different traditions *as* Yahweh, or *as* Allah, or *as* Vishnu, or *as* the Tao, etc., depending on one's religious concepts through which his or her individual experiences occur.

An objection to the pluralistic hypothesis is that it stands over the traditions and makes an exclusive (non-pluralistic) claim about the Real and salvation/liberation; namely, that the Real is experienced equally legitimately among the different traditions and that they each offer valid expressions of the soteriological goal. None of them is correct in contrast to the others; rather, they are all in a sense true. This claim, some have argued, is self-contradictory, for in asserting that no religious position in reference to the Real and the soteriological goal is superior to or truer than another, one has done just that – asserted that this pluralistic view is truer than and superior to all others.

Another way of responding to the conflicting claims of the different traditions is to remain committed to the truth of one set of religious teachings while at the same time agreeing with some of the central concerns raised by pluralism. One way of accomplishing this is through what Joseph Runzo calls "religious relativism," whereby the correctness of a religion is relative to the worldview of its community of adherents. On this view the different religious traditions are comprised of various experiences and mutually incompatible sets of truth claims, and the traditions are themselves rooted in distinct worldviews that are incompatible with, if not contradictory to, the other worldviews. Runzo maintains that these differing experiences and traditions emerge from the plurality of *phenomenal* divine realities experienced by the adherents of the traditions. On this relativistic view, a person's worldview (that is, her total cognitive web of interrelated concepts and beliefs) determines how she comprehends and experiences Ultimate Reality. Furthermore, there are incompatible yet adequate truth claims which correspond to the different worldviews, and the veracity of a religion is determined by its adequacy to appropriately correspond to the worldview of which it is subsumed. Thus, an important difference between the religious relativist and the pluralist is that for the former, and not for the latter, truth itself is understood to be relative.

While relativism may offer a more accurate account than pluralism of the actual cognitive beliefs of religious adherents, it is sometimes argued that it nevertheless falls short of their *actual* beliefs. Muslims, for example, have not historically held that Allah is the true God *only within the Islamic religion*. To the contrary, for Muslim adherents the claims about Allah (as well as all other claims) described in the Koran are taken to be unequivocally and objectively true. For the Islamic believer, then, Allah is the one and only true God regardless of what one's religion or worldview happens to be – regardless of whether a person believes it or not. So too among the other major faith traditions; their beliefs are typically understood to be true in an objective and absolute sense. In effect, adherents of the major religious traditions have historically been exclusivists rather than relativists (or pluralists), and this leads to yet another response to religious conflict.

A third response to the apparent conflicting truth claims of the religions is exclusivism. As with pluralism and relativism, there are different meanings of the term "exclusivism" when used in religious discourse. The major element in this context is that the central tenets of one religion are true and any claims which are incompatible with those tenets, including those of other religions, are false. For example, from the exclusivist perspective, if the Jewish claim that Yahweh is the one true God who literally spoke to the biblical prophets in space and time is true, then the Advaita Vedantan claim that Brahman (God) is *nirguna* – without attributes – must be false, for these two understandings of Ultimate Reality are contradictory. This does not mean that exclusivists are not self-critical of their own beliefs, nor does it rule out the practice of dialoguing with or learning from religious others. But it does mean that religious differences are real and that there are intractable disagreements among religious adherents. Some form of religious exclusivism is historically the most widely held position among the adherents of the major world religions, although pluralism and relativism are currently on the rise.

Responses to exclusivism include moral objections (such as that the exclusivist is arrogant, dishonest, oppressive, or the like) and intellectual or epistemic objections (including claims that the exclusivist holds unjustified or irrational beliefs).

Philosophical theology

Though the terms "philosophy of religion" and "philosophical theology" have sometimes been used interchangeably in past times, more recently they have developed distinct connotations. As already noted, philosophy of religion is philosophical reflection on religious ideas, concepts, and practices. Philosophical theology has come to mean the philosophical examination of the nature of Ultimate Reality and the various doctrines within the religions, most especially the theistic religions.

There are both theistic and non-theistic understandings of God, or Ultimate Reality. Monotheism, or what is sometimes referred to as "Ethical Monotheism," is the doctrine or belief that God exists as a perfect being and that God's nature can be at least partly described as having attributes that set God apart from human beings. Traditionally, these attributes have included omniscience (being all-knowing), omnipotence (being all-powerful), omnibenevolence (being morally perfect), and timelessness (being eternal), among others. This is the view of God traditionally held by adherents of the three major monotheistic religions: Judaism, Christianity, and Islam, as well as a longstanding theistic tradition within Hinduism. Much of the work in philosophical theology, then, focuses on the broadly theistic topics of the divine attributes, miracles, revelation, death and immortality, and others. It also commonly includes specific Christian theological issues such as the doctrines of the Trinity, the Incarnation and Atonement, sin and salvation, and heaven and hell.

The coherence of theism is yet another major topic of discussion in philosophical theology. The logical consistency of each of the divine attributes of classical theism has been challenged, and in the last few decades the objections to them have come from both adherents and non-adherents of theism. Take the divine attribute of omniscience, for example. If God has exhaustive knowledge of all future events, including human actions, how could one freely choose to do those actions? A recent position known as "open theism" defends a view of God's knowledge which, unlike the historical concept of omniscience defended by Boethius, Anselm, Aquinas, and other traditional believers, posits a future that is undetermined, open, and uncertain. Adherents of open theism argue that their view allows for human freedom without denying God's omniscience and thus maintains an element of orthodoxy and yet avoids the contradictions which arise from the traditional view of divine knowledge.

The challenges to the classical view of God are taken even further by Christian and Jewish scholars who hold to a position known as "process theism." For process theologians and philosophers, many of the divine attributes as traditionally understood are denied. As these thinkers argue, many of the historic attributes of God are derived from ancient Greek philosophy and are not found in the Hebrew and Christian Bibles. This process view, they maintain, in which God has persuasive power and not coercive power, for example, better fits the descriptions of God as described in the scriptures. Furthermore, they argue, God is not a substance in the classical sense of the term but rather is involved within the spatiotemporal world as an active participant – a *process* that is at work in and beyond the world.

While there have been many challenges to the classical attributes of God, there are also contemporary philosophers and theologians who have defended each of the attributes as traditionally understood. And there is much lively discussion currently underway by those defending both the classical and neo-classical views of God. But not all philosophers and theologians have believed that the truths of religious beliefs can be or even should be rationally justified, as noted above. Fideists, such as Søren Kierkegaard (1813–1855), for example, maintain that religious faith does not need the support of rational arguments. For fideists, attempting to prove one's religious faith may even be an indication of a lack of faith. Natural theologians, on the other hand, maintain that faith can be supported by rational arguments and that God's very existence can be demonstrated through the use of reason unaided by special revelation.

Arguments for and against the existence of God

Adherents of the theistic religions, as with adherents of non-theistic religions, do not typically affirm their religious convictions *because of* well-articulated, rational reasons or arguments in support of those convictions. Nevertheless, such reasons and arguments have historically been used by many believers to defend and advance their views. For over two millennia arguments have been offered in support of the belief that God exists. The God to which the conclusion of the various classical arguments points is the God of the theistic religions, primarily Judaism, Christianity, and Islam. Three of the arguments which have been prominent historically and still receive special attention in contemporary philosophy of religion discussions are the ontological, cosmological, and teleological arguments.

Ontological arguments, first developed by St Anselm of Canterbury (1033–1109), take a variety of forms. The common theme among them is that they begin a priori – proceeding from the mere concept of God – and conclude that God must exist; in other words, if successful, ontological arguments demonstrate that God's non-existence is impossible. They are unique among the traditional arguments for God's existence in that they are a priori arguments, for they are based on premises that can allegedly be known independently of experience of the world.

Anselm begins his argument in a prayer to God, claiming that he knows that God is "a being than which nothing greater can be conceived". He also knows that it is one thing to exist in the mind (in the understanding) and another to exist outside the understanding (outside one's thoughts; in reality). He then asks which is greater, to exist in the mind or in reality. He concludes the argument this way:

> Therefore, if that, than which nothing greater can be conceived, exists in the understanding alone, the very being, than which nothing greater can be conceived, is one, than which a greater can be conceived. But obviously this is impossible. Hence, there is no doubt that there exists a being, than which nothing greater can be conceived, and it exists both in the understanding and in reality.
>
> (*Proslogion*, Chapter II, 54)

Thus, by the mere analysis of the concept of God, since it would be a contradiction to affirm that the greatest possible being does not exist in reality but only in the mind (because existing in reality is greater than existing in the mind), one is logically drawn to the conclusion that God must exist.

There have been many objections to this a priori argument for God. One of the most famous is based on the analogy of the greatest possible island and was developed by Anselm's fellow monk, Gaunilo. Utilizing a *reductio ad absurdum*, he argued that if we affirm Anselm's ontological argument, we must also affirm that the greatest possible island exists. Since that conclusion is absurd, so too is Anselm's conclusion. Another important objection was offered by Immanuel Kant that existence is not a real predicate. Since existence does not add to the concept of a thing, and in Anselm's argument existence is treated as a real predicate, the argument is flawed.

More recent modal versions of the argument have been construed that avoid the objections to Anselm's original formulation, including one proposed by Alvin Plantinga. But their soundness has also been challenged on multiple fronts, including debates about the role modal logic should play in metaphysical discussions such as this one.

Cosmological arguments begin by examining some empirical or metaphysical fact of the universe, from which it then follows that something outside the universe must have caused it to exist. There are different types of cosmological argument, and its defenders include some of the most prominent thinkers spanning the history of philosophy: Plato, Aristotle, ibn Sina, al-Ghazali, Maimonides, Aquinas, Descartes, and Leibniz, to name a few. Three versions of the argument that have received much attention are the Thomistic contingency argument, the Leibnizian sufficient reason argument, and the kalam argument.

Regarding the Thomistic contingency argument (named after the medieval Christian theologian/philosopher Thomas Aquinas), the claim is made that contingent things exist in the world – "contingent things" ostensibly referring to those things which begin to exist and cease to exist. It is next argued that not all things can be contingent, for if they were there would be nothing to *ground* their existence. Only a necessary thing (or being) can account for the existence of contingent things – "necessary thing" ostensibly referring to a thing which never began to exist and which cannot cease to exist. This necessary thing (or being) is referred to as God.

A second kind of cosmological argument is the Leibnizian sufficient reason argument, so named after the German thinker Gottfried Wilhelm Leibniz (1646–1716). In this version, an answer is sought to the question, "Why is there something rather than nothing?" For

Leibniz, there must be an explanation, or "sufficient reason," for anything that exists, and the explanation for everything that exists must lie either in the necessity of its own nature or in a cause external to itself. The argument concludes that the explanation of the universe must lie in a transcendent God since the universe does not have within its own nature the necessity of its existence.

One objection raised against both the Thomistic and the Leibnizian arguments is that they are demanding unnecessary explanations. If every individual thing in the universe can be explained (even an infinite set of things), why does the whole itself need a further explanation? Furthermore, an explanation must at some point come to an end – a brute fact. So why not end with the universe? Why posit some further transcendent entity?

A third type of cosmological argument is the kalam argument (the term "kalam" coming from medieval Islamic theology which came to mean "speculative theology"). The claim of this argument is that there must be a transcendent first cause of the universe which brought it into existence given that the following two premises are true: (1) whatever begins to exist needs a cause, and (2) the universe began to exist. This version of the cosmological argument has arguably been bolstered in recent times by empirical evidences from astrophysics and cosmology. For example, on one interpretation of the standard Big Bang cosmological model, the time-space universe came into being *ex nihilo* approximately 13.7 billion years ago. Such a beginning is best explained, argue kalam defenders, by a transcendent cause – namely God.

The premise that the universe began to exist is also argued philosophically in two ways. First, it is argued that an actual infinite set of events cannot exist, for actual infinities lead to metaphysical absurdities. Since an infinite temporal regress of events is an actual infinite set of events, such a regress is metaphysically impossible. Thus, the past cannot be infinite; the universe must have had a temporal beginning. A second approach begins by arguing that an infinite series of events cannot be formed by successive addition (one member being added to another). The reason for this is that when adding finite numbers, one after the other, the new number is also finite. The addition of yet another finite number, ad infinitum, will never lead to an actual infinite. Since the past is a series of temporal events formed by successive addition, the past could not be actually infinite in duration. The universe must have had a beginning.

A number of objections have been raised against the kalam argument. For example, with respect to the alleged scientific evidence for a beginning of the universe, there are interpretations of the Big Bang model other than those which entail an *ex nihilo* beginning. There are also other cosmological models of the universe besides the Big Bang model, including eternal universe theories – views more in keeping with Hindu cosmologies than with traditional theistic concepts of the cosmos. In addition, responses have been offered to the philosophical challenges of an eternal universe as well, including the utilization of set theory and mathematical systems which employ actual infinite sets.

Teleological, or design, arguments extend back at least two millennia. In the east, as far back as 100 CE, the Nyāya school in India argued for the existence of a deity based on the order found in nature. In the west, Plato, Aristotle, and the Stoics offered arguments for a directing intelligence of the world given the order found within it. There is an array of teleological arguments, and a common theme among them all is the claim that certain characteristics of the natural world reflect design, purpose, and intelligence. These features of the natural world are then used as evidence for an intelligent, purposive designer as opposed to naturalistic explanations. One version of the design argument is based on the apparent fine-tuning of the cosmos.

Fine-tuning arguments include the claims that the laws of nature, the constants of physics, and the initial conditions of the universe are finely tuned for conscious life on planet Earth. For example, several dozen "cosmic constants," such as the following, are offered as evidence for fine-tuning: (1) If the strong nuclear force (the force that binds protons and neutrons in the atom) had been either stronger or weaker by just 5 percent, life would be impossible; (2) If neutrons were not roughly 1.001 times the mass of protons, all protons would have decayed into neutrons, or visa versa, and life would be impossible; 3) If gravity had been stronger or weaker by one part in 10^{40}, life-sustaining stars (such as the sun) could not exist; thus life would most likely be impossible. While each of the individual calculations of such constants may be in error, it is argued that the number of them, coupled with their independence from one other, provides strong evidence of their being intentionally set with life in mind.

There have also been several important objections raised against fine-tuning arguments. According to an anthropic principle objection, if the laws of nature and physical constants were not finely tuned, there would be no observers to note this fact. Given that such observers exist, it should not be surprising that the laws and constants are just so. One way of accounting for such observers is the many-worlds hypothesis. On this view, there are very many universes, perhaps an infinite number of them, each with their own fundamental physical parameters. Most of these universes would include life-prohibiting parameters, but at least a minimal number of them would probably include life-permitting ones. As a result, it should not be surprising that one of them at least – ours, for example – is such. Much of the current fine-tuning discussion turns on the plausibility of the many-worlds hypothesis and the anthropic principle.

Other versions of the teleological argument have also been proposed which focus not on fundamental parameters of the cosmos but on different aspects of living organisms, including the emergence of living organisms, alleged irreducibly complex systems within living organisms, information intrinsic within the DNA of living organisms, and the rise of consciousness, in an attempt to demonstrate intelligent, purposive qualities of the world. At this time these biological and noological design arguments have not generally received as much attention as the fine-tuning argument by those engaged in natural theology or by the broader philosophical community. While a number of philosophers of religion hold that such scientific and philosophical evidences as offered by the cosmological and teleological arguments provide support for belief in a transcendent deity, there are also many who maintain that the evidence favors naturalism. Naturalism, as used here, is the view that natural entities have only natural causes, and that the world can be fully described and explained by the physical sciences. This view removes the need for a transcendent being to explain the world, and it denies that there are solid reasons or evidences to believe in such a being. And just as there are arguments for God's existence, there are also arguments against the existence of God and for naturalism. The most prominent of these arguments are of three types: responses to the positive arguments for God, arguments that theism is incoherent, and problems of evil.

One common objection to the traditional arguments for God's existence as a whole (cosmological, teleological, ontological, moral, arguments from religious experience, etc.) is that even if they are successful, they do not prove the existence of the God of any particular religion. Even if successful, the cosmological argument only provides evidence for a transcendent first cause of the universe, nothing more; at best, the teleological argument provides evidence for a purposive, rational designer, nothing more; and so on. But this is a far cry from the God (or gods) depicted in the Koran, or the Bible, or the Vedas.

Nevertheless, natural theologians maintain that the central aim of these arguments is not to offer a full-blown proof of any particular deity, but rather to provide some evidence or warrant for belief in a creator, or a designer, or a moral lawgiver, or the like. Some natural theologians argue that it is best to combine the various arguments in order to provide a cumulative case for theism. Cosmological arguments provide insight into God's creative providence; teleological arguments provide insight into God's purposive nature and grand intelligence; moral arguments provide insight into God's moral nature and character, etc. Taken together, they argue, the classical arguments offer a picture of a deity not unlike the God of the theistic religious traditions. Furthermore, they maintain, even if this approach does not prove the existence of any particular deity, it does nonetheless lend support to theism over naturalism.

Philosophical challenges to theism have also included the claim that the very concept of God makes no sense – that the attributes ascribed to God are logically incoherent (either individually or collectively). Much of this criticism has focused on God as understood in Judaism, Christianity, and Islam, but it is also relevant to the theistic elements found within Mahayana Buddhism, Hinduism, Confucianism, and certain forms of African and Native American religions. The question of whether theism is coherent is an important one not only because of what may be learned about the divine attributes but also because if there is reason to believe that theism is incoherent, then theistic belief is, in an important sense, undermined.

One important set of problems which arises from discussions of the coherence of theism has to do with the existence of evil and suffering.

Problems of evil and suffering

It is widely recognized by philosophers and theologians (both eastern and western) that there are problems for one who affirms the existence of an omnipotent and omnibenevolent God on the one hand and the existence of evil on the other. Since most streams of Hinduism and Buddhism do not have such a God, they do not have the problems of evil that the theistic traditions do. They do have the related problem of suffering, and offer their own responses to it as discussed below, but those traditions which affirm the existence of a good and all-powerful God are confronted with some troubling conundrums. Philosopher David Hume (1711–1776 CE), quoting the ancient Greek thinker Epicurus (341–270 BCE), expressed one of the problems this way:

> Is he [God] willing to prevent evil, but not able? then he is impotent. Is he able, but not willing? then he is malevolent. Is he both able and willing? whence then is evil?
>
> (*Dialogues Concerning Natural Religion*, Part X, 63)

This is one version of the problem which is often construed as a logical problem of evil. For the logical problem, it is asserted that the two claims, (1) an omnipotent and omnibenevolent God exists and (2) evil exists, are *logically incompatible*. Since evil ostensibly exists, the argument goes, God (as traditionally understood) must not.

Despite its historical sway, it is now widely acknowledged by philosophers of religion that the logical problem has been successfully rebutted. One reason for this is as follows. Claims (1) and (2) are not explicitly contradictory. If they are implicitly contradictory, there must be hidden premises or unstated assumptions which make them so. But what might those be? The two assumed premises/assumptions appear to be these: (a) an omnipotent God could create any world, and (b) an omnibenevolent God would prefer a world without evil over a world with evil. Given these two claims, (1) and (2) would be logically incompatible. However, it turns out that (a) and (b) need not be true, even on a classical theistic account. It could be that a world which has creatures with free will is more valuable than a world which has no free creatures. And it could be that such free creatures cannot be *caused* or *determined* to do only what is morally right and good – even by God. If this is so, in order for God to create beings who are capable of moral good, God had to create beings who are capable of moral evil as well. If this scenario is a logical possibility (and it seems to be so), then assumption (a) is not necessarily true: God cannot create just any world. Furthermore, assumption (b) is not necessarily true either. For all we know, God could use evil to achieve some good end. As long as (a) and (b) are possibly false, the conclusion of the argument is no longer necessarily true, and so it loses its deductive force. This response to the logical argument from evil is called a *defense*, which is distinguished from a *theodicy*. A defense is an attempt to demonstrate that anti-theistic arguments from evil, such as the one just mentioned, are unsuccessful on their own terms. A theodicy, on the other hand, is an attempt to justify God given the evil in the world. Both defenses and theodicies have been used by theists in responding to the various problems of evil.

However, even granting that the logical problem of evil has been rebutted, this does not solve every problem related to evil for the theist. One of the most discussed problems in recent times is the evidential problem of evil in which it is argued that the vast amount and horrific nature of the many evils which exist make it unlikely or improbable that an omnipotent and omnibenevolent God exists.

When assessing arguments of this sort, some important questions for consideration are these: what is the claim probable or improbable with respect to? And what is the relevant background information with respect to the claim? For example, the plausibility of the claim "God's existence is improbable with respect to the evil in the world" considered alone may well be very different from the plausibility of the claim "God's existence is improbable with respect to the evil in the world" when considered in conjunction with, say, one or more of the arguments for God's existence noted earlier. Furthermore, the theist can offer other hypotheses which may raise the probability of evil given God's existence. For example, the major theistic traditions affirm the belief that God's purposes are not restricted to this earthly life but extend on into an afterlife as well. In this case, there is further opportunity for God to bring moral good out of the many kinds and varieties of evil in this life. Thus the full scope of the considerations and evidences for and against theism may well raise the probability of God's existence above that of taking into account only a part.

Besides theistic considerations of evil, non-theistic religions have also offered accounts of its nature and existence, specifically with respect to suffering, and for Hindus and Buddhists these considerations are rooted in karma and reincarnation. In its popular formulations, reincarnation is the view that the conscious self transmigrates from one physical body to the next after death. Each human being has lived former lives, perhaps as another human being or maybe even as another kind of organism. Reincarnation is connected to the doctrine of *karma*. Karma (Sanskrit for "deed" or "action"), as typically understood within Hinduism and Buddhism, is a concept of cause and effect in which all actions are shaping past, present, and future events. It is, in effect, the idea that one reaps the good and bad consequences of her or his actions, either in this life or in another.

Those who affirm reincarnation and karma often point to a difficulty they see with the theistic religions: it seems exceedingly unfair that one child is born healthy into a wealthy, loving family, for example, whereas another child is born sickly into a poor, cruel environment. If there is a Creator God who brought these two persons into the world, such a God seems to be unloving and unjust. However, if the two children are reaping the consequences of actions they performed in previous lives, this seems to provide a justification for the inequalities. The effect of one's karma determines the circumstances of our past, present, and future lives; we reap what we sow.

A number of objections have also been raised against the doctrine of karma. For one, does it really offer a plausible explanation for the inequalities found in this life? According to the karmic law of cause and effect, a person's present life circumstances are explained by her actions in a previous life. And her life circumstances in that life are explained by her life circumstances in a life previous to that one. And so on indefinitely. So the solution we hoped for regarding inequalities seems to never come to an end; it ends up being relegated to the dustbins of the infinite past. Furthermore, does it really seem fair that when a person who has lived a long life dies and is reincarnated, she must start all over again as a baby with her maturity, life experiences, wisdom, and memories completely gone? As with the theistic replies to evil, they may be helpful at some level, but they nevertheless leave one with less than complete solutions to the variety of problems of evil.

The field of philosophy of religion is flourishing and expanding in new and exciting directions. Beyond those areas noted, there are many other significant currents emerging and developing as well, including feminist and continental approaches to philosophy of religion, emphases on religion and the environment, race and ethnicity, science and faith, religious experience, and religious rites.

Bibliography

Adams, Marilyn McCord. *Horrendous Evils and the Goodness of God*. Ithaca, NY: Cornell University Press, 1999.
  A careful analysis of evil and the goodness of God.

Anderson, Pamela Sue. *A Feminist Philosophy of Religion: The Rationality and Myths of Religious Belief*. Oxford: Blackwell, 1998.
  A prolegomenon to feminist philosophy of religion in the Anglo-American context.

Anselm of Canterbury ([1077–1078] 1962) *St. Anselm: Basic Writings*. LaSalle, IL: Open Court Publishing.
  Includes Anselm's *Proslogium*, which contains his famous ontological argument.

Bowker, John. *Problems of Suffering in Religions of the World*. Cambridge: Cambridge University Press, 1970.
  An elucidation and comparison of the varying perspectives of evil and suffering as understood within the world religions.

Craig, William Lane. *The Cosmological Argument from Plato to Leibniz*. Eugene, OR: Wipf and Stock, 1980.
  Analyzes the cosmological arguments of thirteen major proponents.

Davis, Stephen T. *Christian Philosophical Theology*. Oxford: Oxford University Press, 2006.
  Discusses central topics in philosophical theology, including creation, revelation, the Incarnation, resurrection, redemption, karma and Grace.

Everitt, Nicholas. *The Non-Existence of God*, London: Routledge, 2004.

An introduction and critical assessment of arguments for God, including some of the most recent arguments.

Gellman, Jerome. *Mystical Experience of God: A Philosophical Inquiry*. London: Ashgate, 2002.
Discusses the validity of mystical experiences of God.

Hick, John. *An Interpretation of Religion: Human Responses to the Transcendent*. 2nd ed. New Haven, CT: Yale University Press, 2004.
The classic work on religious pluralism and a defense of the pluralistic hypothesis.

Hick, John. *Evil and the God of Love*. New edition. London: Palgrave Macmillan, 2007.
A modern classic on the problem of evil from a theistic perspective.

Hume, David. *Dialogues Concerning Natural Religion*. Second edition. Richard H. Popkin, ed. Indianapolis/Cambridge: Hackett Publishing, 1998.
A classic critique of the design argument.

Meister, Chad and Paul Copan, eds. *The Routledge Companion to Philosophy of Religion*. London: Routledge, 2007.
A collection of newly commissioned essays by leading philosophers of religion on a host of significant topics.

Oppy, Graham. *Arguing About Gods*. Cambridge: Cambridge University Press, 2006.
Examines contemporary arguments for and against God and argues that none of them are persuasive.

Phillips, D. Z. *Religion and the Hermeneutics of Contemplation*. Cambridge: Cambridge University Press, 2001.
Argues that philosophers would best see their task not as being for or against religion, but rather as understanding it.

Plantinga, Alvin. *Does God Have a Nature*. Milwaukee, WI: Marquette University Press, 1980.
A work in philosophical theology which focuses on God's nature, sovereignty, and God's relation to properties.

Sharma, Arvind. *A Hindu Perspective on the Philosophy of Religion*. New York: St. Martin's Press, 1990.
Presents the philosophy of religion from a non-western, Hindu perspective.

Soskice, Janet M. *Metaphor and Religious Language*, Oxford: Oxford University Press, 1984.
Provides an account of metaphor and language for understanding talk of God and for scientific discourse.

Swinburne, Richard. *The Coherence of Theism*. Oxford: Clarendon Press, 1977.
Examines whether belief in God as traditionally understood in the Christian tradition is coherent.

Swinburne, Richard. *Faith and Reason*. Second edition. Oxford: Clarendon, 2008.
An analytic approach to the implications of religious faith.

Taliaferro, Charles. *Contemporary Philosophy of Religion*. Oxford: Blackwell, 1998.
An engaging and comprehensive introduction to contemporary philosophy of religion.

Ward, Keith. *Religion and Revelation*. New York: Oxford University Press, 1994.
Examines the concept of revelation as it relates to five major world religions.

Suggested reading

Griffiths, Paul J. *Problems of Religious Diversity*. Oxford: Blackwell, 2001.
Analyzes a number of philosophical questions raised by religious diversity.

Hume, David. *Dialogues Concerning Natural Religion*. Second edition. Richard H. Popkin, ed. Indianapolis/Cambridge: Hackett Publishing, 1998.
A classic critique of the design argument.

Meister, Chad. *Introducing Philosophy of Religion*. London: Routledge, 2009.
A concise introduction to many of the central topics in philosophy of religion; includes diagrams, charts, and other pedagogical features.

Taliaferro, Charles. *Evidence and Faith: Philosophy and Religion since the Seventeenth Century*. Cambridge: Cambridge University Press, 2005.
An excellent and accessible overview of philosophy of religion from the modern period to the present; focuses on developing views of faith and evidence.

Chapter 8

Religious studies

Donald Wiebe

The problematic idea of religious studies

Including the notion of 'religious studies' as one discipline among many for description and analysis in a volume like this suggests that there is broad agreement among those who study religion in the modern Western university as to the meaning of the term. Unfortunately, this is not the case. There is a vast literature committed to providing an understanding of the nature and value of the enterprise, but, as I shall show, there is little agreement to be found among those who have put their hand to the task. Not only is the term 'religious studies' ambiguous with respect to the enterprise it designates, but the very idea of 'a discipline' is itself vigorously contested; and it is quite obvious that whether or not religious studies can justifiably be called a discipline depends wholly upon the understanding of 'discipline', which is operative. As one scholar has put it, the term is used with more passion than precision (Benson 1987: 91). There is, moreover, considerable debate about the nature of the modern university within which 'religious studies' as 'a field of study' exists, so that to equate 'religious studies' with 'the academic study of religion' provides little – if any – clarification as to the nature or structure of this venture beyond information about its institutional location. Indeed, depending upon the assumptions one makes about the *raison d'être* of the modern university, there is no guarantee that 'religious studies' as 'the academic study of religion' can even be clearly differentiated from the scholarly study of religion carried on in other institutions, including religious institutions. It is no surprise, therefore, that some who have attempted to set out the meaning of the term 'religious studies' have remarked that perhaps the clearest thing that can be said about it is that it 'appears to be the designation of choice for the academic study of religion in the college and university setting' (Olson 1990a: 549). There is, perhaps, equal agreement that this designation for the study of religion, 'legitimated' by virtue of inclusion in the curriculum of the university, came into use only after the Second World War; primarily since the 1960s. Providing a singular, overarching definition of 'religious studies' as it is carried out in the modern university, therefore, is hardly possible; at the very least, such an exercise is unlikely to be either persuasive or helpful. To understand 'religious studies' is to understand the diverse and nuanced way in which the term is used. And in a sense, one must follow the principle that to understand a concept it is important to be familiar with its history. This is not to say that no generalization is possible, but it does require that a thorough knowledge of the debate over the use of the term is essential before proposing one use of the concept over another. Much of this essay, therefore, will consist of a critical examination of the diverse ways in which the notion is understood in the reflective methodological literature in the field. Given the proliferation of relevant publications, however, this review cannot hope to be comprehensive. Accordingly, I restrict my analyses to Anglo-American (including Canadian) treatments of the subject, beginning with the attempts to provide a definitive statement on the notion in representative encyclopedias and encyclopedic dictionaries. Despite the diversity of views that will emerge in this analysis of the literature about the study of religion as it is currently carried out in colleges and universities, I shall attempt in the conclusion to draw out some warrantable generalizations about 'religious studies' that may assist those coming new to the field.

Encyclopedic treatment of the notion of religious studies

Encyclopedic treatments of 'religious studies' consider the term to refer to a new kind of study of religious phenomena – that is an exercise free from narrow ecclesiastical interference and more general religious influence. Religious studies, that is, is often taken to be other than a religious quest or undertaking and, unlike earlier scholarly studies within the framework of the academy (colleges and universities), seems to work on the assumption of religion's status as a purely social phenomenon. There is agreement not only that there existed a scholarly study of religion in the university prior to the emergence of religious studies departments in the modern university, but also that it was religious or theological in character. ('Theology' is often used in the literature to refer not only to a particular discipline but also, more generally, to denote any kind of confessional or religious orientation.) Indeed, not only was it religious, it was parochial, exclusivist, and therefore sectarian and ideological. As I show here, however, the encyclopedia portraits are not internally coherent in their accounts of this enterprise and therefore leave much to be desired with respect to defining the term.

Those who consult the new *Encyclopedia of Religion* (Eliade 1987) for enlightenment on the notion of 'religious studies' (Vol. XII: 334) will find the cross-reference 'Study of Religion, article on Religious Studies as an Academic Discipline' (Vol. XIV) – an entry that consists of essays by Seymour Cain ('History of Study'), Eric J. Sharpe ('Methodological Issues'), and Thomas Benson ('Religious Studies as an Academic Discipline'), the last of which purports to trace 'the development of religious studies as part of the liberal arts curriculum of secular and sectarian institutions of higher learning during the latter half of the twentieth century' (64). According to Benson, religious studies is a scholarly or academic undertaking aimed at 'fostering critical understanding of religious traditions and values' (89) as opposed to a religious exercise designed to nurture faith. It is therefore a new enterprise, distinct from an earlier style of 'faith-based' study of religion in the university that is usually referred to as 'theology.'

Harold Remus, in the *Encyclopedia of the American Religious Experience* (1988, Vol. III), claims that the development of new academic disciplines, such as sociology, anthropology, and psychology, applied to the study of religion at the end of the nineteenth century, 'led eventually to the development of an academic field designated *religion* or *religious studies* that was dedicated in principle to the academic study of religion ...' (1658). There is a clear line of demarcation, he insists, between this new discipline and its forerunner (the religiously committed study of religion). Religious studies, he warns, must not be confused with religious education which, like theology, is confessional in nature. 'Religious studies,' he writes, 'does not seek to inculcate religious doctrines or specific religious values, to strengthen or win commitment to a religious tradition or institution, or to provide instruction preparatory to professional training for the ministry or rabbinate' (1653). For Remus, therefore, religious studies cannot involve instruction *in* religion but can nevertheless teach *about* religion (1657).

Alan Olson presents a similar picture of 'religious studies' in the *Encyclopedia of Religious Education* (1990a), insisting that such studies are 'to be distinguished from theological studies programs at the some two hundred and fifty seminaries and divinity schools in the United States and Canada' (549). For more than a century, he claims, religious studies has been trying to differentiate itself from religious and theological enterprises as a study that excludes personal belief. In his view, 'religious studies is meant to identify an objective, scientific, non-biased study of religion as distinct from 'theological' and/or 'confessional' study for the purpose of increasing the faith, understanding, and institutional commitment of individual degree candidates in a particular religion' (549–50). Thus, according to Olson, whereas the academic study of religion in the US had been primarily in the care of religiously founded institutions until well into the twentieth century – and, therefore, had been essentially religious in character – by the 1950s it became more scientific and 'emerged as an important interdisciplinary, polymethodological, and cross-cultural area of academic inquiry' (551).

The entry by Ninian Smart on 'Religious Studies in Higher Education' in John Hinnells' *The New Penguin Dictionary of Religions* (1997) echoes Olson's description. After acknowledging the existence of long-standing traditional approaches to the study of religion in institutions of higher learning, Smart maintains that 'Religious Studies as a new multidisciplinary subject incorporating history of religions, cross-cultural topics, social-scientific approaches and ethical and philosophical reflections … came to prominence chiefly in the 1960s and early 1970s' (420). The significance of the new 'discipline,' it is suggested, is that the academic study of religions in the modern university made possible a variety of scholarly approaches different from those sanctioned up to then by the traditional theological framework. Smart argues that this shift of approach clearly broadened the scope of studies in religion.

Despite the advent of a new and clearly defined scholarly approach to religious studies, that new study does not consistently reflect the neutral status of an objective science. Benson points to this, for example, arguing that even though admitting religious studies results from secularizing forces in society, what lies behind the emergence of this new field is not primarily a scientific impulse. Religious studies programs, he notes, have usually been created in response to student and community interests, so that, even though such studies of religion are not as overtly religious as they once were, they are nevertheless concerned with more than scientific knowledge, for they are often touted as an important element in the 'liberal education' dedicated to the cultivation of the self. As he puts it, religious studies is 'generally influenced by pluralistic assumptions and [has] tended toward global perspectives on the nature and history of religion' (1987: 89). As a consequence, religious studies, even while bringing a broader curriculum to the religion department and considerably undermining the traditional seminary model, has unfortunately held the door open to 'a crazy quilt of courses encompassing many disciplines, eras, regions, languages, and methods of inquiry' (91) – including traditional seminary-type offerings of Christian history, theology, biblical studies, religious ethics, religious thought, and religious education. The survival of religious studies in the US, he suggests, is therefore tied not to the social sciences but rather to the fate of the humanities which are, like theology in the past, directed not only toward providing knowledge about the human estate, but to the search for meaning, the inculcation of values, and the formation of the character of students. Recognizing this, Benson points to the vestigial religious overtones to 'religious studies' in the university context, noting that in the publicly funded university, the study of religion occasionally raises apprehension 'concerning church–state relations and the constitutional status of state-funded religious studies' (89). Objections to such studies in the public university context, he suggests, have eased in the light of court decisions that have distinguished teaching about religion (even with the overtones described) from religious indoctrination, implying that only self-ascribed sectarian religious education need be excluded from the field. In Benson's estimation, therefore, religious studies seems to connote a broadly liberal religious education directed toward the formation of character and the betterment of society rather than scientific study aimed at knowledge and explanation of religious phenomena. He admits that in the 1960s there was deep interest in gaining disciplinary status for religious studies, but not on the grounds of its being a science. Rather, such status was sought on the basis of scholarly interest in a common subject matter: 'the nature and diverse manifestations of religious experience' (91). But this, he declares, is not sufficient to warrant its recognition as a discipline, because it clearly does not have a method peculiar to itself. 'Religious studies are, perhaps, best understood,' he therefore concludes, 'as a community of disciplines gathered around the complex phenomenon of religious belief and practice' (92).

Although Remus argued for a line of demarcation between instruction *in* religion and teaching *about* religion, he also noted that such teaching *about* religion is of particular importance to liberal education (1988: 1658). And in so doing, he seems to suggest that religious studies is more than merely a scientific undertaking, despite his insistence that it is not the task of liberal education to make the university a religious place (1658). He claims, for example, that it is not only the emergence of the social sciences that provided an impetus to the development of this new field, but that a 'decline in institutional religions has also been a factor in enrolment in religious studies courses ...' (1658), suggesting thereby that the new enterprise has become in some sense a surrogate religion. Courses available in the new departments, that is, provide students with 'opportunities to pursue some of the basic human issues – such as freedom, justice, love, evil, death – that universities were often bypassing in favor of technical and analytical study' (1659). Thus, although not intending to indoctrinate, the new religious studies department nevertheless constitutes an element in the student's search for meaning in life; it is not simply concerned with obtaining empirical and theoretical knowledge about religion.

Olson's demarcation of religious studies from a religio-theological study of religion is at least as ambiguous. For Olson, however, the reasons no such clear demarcation is possible are connected to the nature of science rather than to the nature of either religion or religious studies. A proper understanding of 'science,' Olson insists, will be seen to exclude all possibility of providing a fully naturalistic explanation for religion. 'Religious studies,' he writes, 'has greatly contributed to the growing awareness that *true science* does not have to do with the development of a monolithic discipline, but with the collective efforts of a community of scholars illuminating one or more facets of the truth' (1990a: 551, emphasis added). In an article on the university in the same encyclopedia (1990b), Olson's notion of religious studies is further clarified in his claim that the discipline is an important element in the humanities because it provides sustained attention to religious values, making knowledge alone an insufficient goal of the enterprise. Consequently for Olson – although he does not spell it out in great detail – a scientific study of religion that seeks to study religion wholly objectively is little more than an ideology of secular humanism.

The essay by Smart in Hinnells' *The New Penguin Dictionary of Religions* also acknowledges that the so-called new religious studies is not altogether new; in fact, it offers programs that often parallel those offered in divinity schools and departments of theology. It is acknowledged, moreover, that, at least in part, religious studies is fuelled by 'a growth in questing and questioning' rather than by the ideal of obtaining objective knowledge about religion (1995: 420–1). Thus, even though involving the sciences in the study of religion, the new religious studies is not unambiguously scientific in intent or in practice. Not only is it determined by a religious or theological agenda, it is also shaped, Smart argues, by other ideological agendas. Since its emergence in the 1960s it has been profoundly affected by newer, non-objectivist approaches to the understanding of human phenomena such as feminism and postmodernist theorizing (421). Smart then concludes by pointing out how important religious studies is to the humanities – and by implication – to the humanist (and 'liberal education') agenda: 'Religious Studies is in one sense a branch of social science but has also begun to play a vital role in the humanities, both because of its cross-cultural commitments and because of its serious consideration of diversity of human world-views' (421).

In light of this analysis of the encyclopedists' efforts to provide an account of 'religious studies' – of the academic study of religion in the university context – scholars will have to acknowledge, as does Adrian Cunningham (1990), that 'perhaps "religious" [in the phrase "religious studies"] may still carry hints of its earlier usage to describe adherents, and of the ambiguities of "religious education" …' (30). Michael Pye (1991) makes the same point more forcefully, arguing that 'the adjective "religious" can easily suggest, and sometimes may be intended to suggest, that these "studies" are supposed to be religious in orientation and not simply studies *of* religion …' (41). The term is often used, he maintains,to designate those subjects and activities which in the past have constituted theological enterprises, and must therefore be taken for 'camouflage for theology' (42).

The lack of clarity and precision in the encyclopedia definitions of 'religious studies' is not surprising for it reflects current practices in the enterprise as it is observed in college and university departments around the world. A critical review of the self-reflective literature on "religious studies" as it is carried on in Canada, Great Britain, the United States of America, and elsewhere in the world will, I suggest, lend credence to Cunningham's and Pye's assessment that the field fails to live up to the implicit ideal of it as a scientific rather than a religious undertaking found in the encyclopaedic accounts.

'Religious studies' in Canada

The character of the academic study of religion is thoroughly analysed in the ambitious state-of-the-art reviews of religious studies in Canadian universities directed by Harold Coward. Six volumes of the study have appeared between 1983 and 2001, covering the provinces of Alberta (Neufeldt 1983), Quebec (Rousseau and Despland 1988), Ontario (Remus *et al.* 1992), Manitoba and Saskatchewan (Badertscher *et al.* 1993), British Columbia (Fraser 1995), and New Brunswick, Prince Edward Island, Nova Scotia, and Newfoundland (Bowlby 2001).

Although entitled '*The Study of Religion* in Canada/Sciences Religieuses au Canada,' the projected study is described in the editor's introduction to each volume as 'A State-of-the-Art Review of *religious studies* in Canada' (emphasis added), which seems to identify 'religious studies' in university departments very broadly with any and every type of study of religion carried on in institutions of higher learning. The ambiguity of the project description, in fact, provides other authors in the series all the encouragement needed for dealing not only with the academic study of religion in the university setting but also with the religious and theological study of religion in other post-secondary educational institutions from bible schools to seminaries. Brian Fraser, for example, entitles his state-of-the-art review not 'Religious Studies in British Columbia' but *The Study of Religion in British Columbia* (1995), and makes it very clear early on in the volume that he believes the ambiguity of the project title leaves room for argument to the effect that the kinds of study carried on in these very different institutions are not only complementary but in some fundamental sense the same. 'In the other volumes in the Canadian Corporation for the Study of Religion (CCSR) series on the study of religion in Canada,' he writes, 'the focus has been on religious studies in the secular university, with minimal attention being paid to various approaches of theological studies' (viii). As there is only one department of religious studies in universities in British Columbia (UBC), and because Fraser works, as he puts it, from a 'vocational base in theological studies,' he chose 'to focus on the broader subject indicated by the original designation of the series as a whole, i.e. the study of religion' (viii–ix). A comprehensive review of the state-of-the-art in that province, he insists therefore, 'requires that appropriate attention be paid to both religious studies and theological studies' (ix). This, in his view, moreover, is not mandated simply by the fact that two radically different kinds of study of religion exist in institutions of higher education. It exists also because they have complementary interests, so that a proper study of 'religious studies' requires that this fact be recognized. According to Fraser, for example, both types of study of religion exact an element of commitment aside from that found in religious institutions; for while religious institutions of higher learning are committed to enhancing 'participation in and contribution to religious traditions and communities that govern the institutions in which the study takes place' (viii), the so-called neutral and non-advocative study of religion in the university is also directed toward results 'that intend to elucidate the questions of human existence that religions have always tried to confront' (viii). Religious studies, therefore, even though having 'nothing whatsoever to do with the professional training of ministers' (20), seems to be a kind of non-sectarian civil religion or general theology fit for 'a public and pluralistic institution' (viii) because it engages fundamental questions of meaning in human existence. His views in this regard are clearly exhibited in his praise for the work of the Centre for Studies in Religion and Society at the University of Victoria, which, he claims, emerged in part as 'the result of the need for an expanded view of studies in religion' (109) wherein the 'interdisciplinary nature of its commitment brings together the various voices of the scholarly worlds, while not ignoring the community at large, [to address] major challenges of global concern ...' (109). And it is in light of this kind of project that Fraser expresses the hope for an integration of the various approaches 'to the study of religion and the religions themselves[,] and for the development of a [university-based] doctoral program in *religious/theological studies*' (109, emphasis added).

Had Fraser consulted the first volume in this series, he would not have needed to provide justificatory argument for his study of religious and theological programs of study in British Columbia's religious institutions. For in Ronald W. Neufeldt's (1983) account of 'religious studies' in Alberta he acknowledges that some scholars 'expressed some opposition to the inclusion of theological colleges and bible colleges and institutions' (xi) but nevertheless in his study proceeded to support such an expanded notion of the field – as has every subsequent study.

In all of the programs described in the Canadian studies, only that of the University of Regina is (in theory at least) purely epistemic in orientation. And its view about the nature of the discipline clearly places it in a minority. There were some early indications that religious studies would be identified primarily with a non-religious, scientific approach to understanding religion (Anderson 1972), but, as the state-of-the-art studies make clear, such views did not have a significant impact on the development of the field in Canada. Charles Davis's essay on 'The Reconvergence of Theology and Religious Studies' (1974–5) better captures the aims and desires of those involved in Canadian university departments of religion, as is clearly evident in the majority of the contributions to the more recent volume of essays, *Religious Studies: Issues, Prospects and Proposals* (1991), edited by Klaus Klostermaier and Larry Hurtado. While recognizing something new in contemporary religious studies, the editors nevertheless pointedly invited participants to the conference 'to consider the study of religion at public universities *as a continuation of the intellectual examination of religion which goes back over the ages*' (ix, emphasis added). This is also clearly evident in the character of the research activities of the majority of those who contribute to the Canadian journal *Studies in Religion/Sciences Religieuses*, whose pages are for the most part filled with religious and theological research rather than with scientific studies of religion (Riley 1984). Indeed, as I have shown elsewhere, religious studies in Canada, for the most part, has been more concerned with a 'learned practice of religion' rather than with seeking a scientific explanation of it (Wiebe 2006).

'Religious Studies' in Great Britain

Although there are no other state-of-the-art reviews of the field of religious studies as extensive as that undertaken by the Canadians, the festschrift for Geoffrey Parrinder, edited by Ursula King and entitled *Turning Points in Religious Studies* (1990), provides a comparable one-volume review of the emergence, development, and current state of religious studies in Great Britain. This volume is of particular interest because it unequivocally presents itself as providing an account of religious studies as a new discipline, clearly distinguishable from the theological approaches to the study of religion that had until recently characterized university scholarship. As the fly-leaf notice about the volume puts it: 'Religious Studies was first introduced as *a new discipline* in various universities and colleges around the world in the 1960s. This discipline brought about a *reorientation of the study of religion*, created new perspectives, and influenced all sectors of education' (emphasis added). The clarity of this brief statement about a new discipline that has re-orientated scholarship in religion, however, is quickly effaced by the editor's general introduction to the essays intended to document both the emergence of the new discipline and the major turning points in its evolution. For King speaks here not of a *discipline*, but rather of a *field* of study which 'found wider recognition from the 1960s and 1970s onwards when the term "Religious Studies" came first into general use' (15). But as a field, religious studies cannot be characterized methodologically, for fields of study involve a multiplicity of disciplinary approaches to a particular subject matter of interest. Her introduction to the essays on the institutional growth of religious studies in the universities of England, Scotland, and Wales, moreover, compromises the claim that the so-called new discipline brought about a re-orientation of the study of religion already in existence prior to the 1960s. These essays, she writes, 'show how much the course of Religious Studies and the history of its programmes have been intertwined with and often curtailed by earlier institutional developments in the study of theology, so that it has often been difficult to maintain the distinctiveness of Religious Studies' (16). Having acknowledged this, King then goes on to claim that religious studies cannot really 'be fully understood without looking at the closely associated developments in religious education and practical issues in interfaith dialogue …' (16), suggesting that religious studies is – and ought to be – more than an academic (scientific) discipline. Thus she includes in the volume not only essays on the development of the 'new discipline' but also on the role of religious studies in relation to developments in religious education, interreligious dialogue and philosophy of religion. For King, these 'concerns' characterize distinct approaches to the subject matter of religious studies and are therefore some of the disciplines that characterize the field as multidisciplinary; but all of them clearly reflect the traditional religious and theological concerns of the scholarly study of religion which 'Religious Studies' ought to have superseded. As Robert Jackson points out in his essay on 'Religious Studies and Developments in Religious Education' (1990), for example, religious education embodies not only an epistemic or scientific concern about religion, but also sees religion itself as a form of knowledge and a distinct realm of experience (107); and religious education, therefore, as directed to awakening 'a unique spiritual dimension of experience' in children (110). The *raison d'être* of religious education, therefore, is not only epistemic but formative; aimed at helping children exercise their spiritual curiosity, and encouraging 'in them an imaginative openness to the infinite possibilities of life' (110). W. Owen Cole's discussion of 'The New Educational Reform Act and Worship in County Schools of England and Wales' (1990) similarly confirms the judgement that religious education is concerned not only with gaining knowledge about religion but also with nurturing religious growth and development. As Cole puts it: 'Some kind of collective gathering is considered desirable by most teachers *for a number of purposes* including the collective exploration of and reflection upon values and beliefs …' (129–30, emphasis added). The fact that philosophy holds the same kind of religious and theological import as one of the disciplines that make up the multidisciplinary enterprise of religious studies is clearly evident in Keith Ward's 'The Study of Truth and Dialogue in Religion' (1990). For Ward, philosophy's value to religious studies is to be found in its concerns with the meaning and truth of religion (230).

Interestingly (if not ironically), only Marcus Braybrooke – Chairman of the interfaith movement 'World Congress of Faiths' – appears to assume that religious studies is a genuinely new approach to the study of religion. Braybrooke writes: 'The underlying hope of the interfaith movement, *although not of the academic study of religions*, is that in some way religions are complementary or convergent' (1990: 138, emphasis added). He nevertheless seems to believe that a positive complementarity exists between religious studies and interfaith development. And Eleanor Nesbitt's article on Sikhism (1990) presents a similar proposal for encouraging a positive relationship between the modern student of religion and the religious devotee.

The descriptions of the emergence of religious studies in the universities in England (Adrian Cunningham), Scotland (Andrew F. Walls), and Wales (Cyril Williams), it must be noted, claim (or suggest) that it achieved status in the university as an autonomous discipline by virtue of its differentiation from religion and theology. Their claims, however, seem to be undermined by the editor of the volume in which they appear, for they are found in the context of numerous other contributions of the kind just described, as well as an essay by Ninian Smart – 'Concluding Reflections on Religious Studies in Global Perspective' (1990) – that argue a contrary case. It is true that neither Smart nor the other essayists argue specifically against undertaking scientific analyses of religion and religions. Smart does argue, however, against what he calls a scientifically purist stance in religious studies. As with the other essayists, Smart insists that religious studies can only properly be understood as a polymethodic and multidisciplinary enterprise which embraces 'as much as possible of the scholarship of all sorts going on in the world … [w]hether it is neutral and objective or religiously committed'

(305, 300). As a non-purist study, religious studies, he claims, will triumph because it can 'be a force for permitting deeper conversations between religions, without reverting into a simple exchange of pieties' (305). In this light, it is ironic that Cunningham should remark, as I have already noted, that even though the designation 'religious studies' for the study of religion carried on in university departments has an honourable history, 'perhaps "religious" may still carry hints of its earlier usage to describe adherents, and of ambiguities of "religious education," and it would be better for the university area to be simply called religion"' (30).

Given Ninian Smart's widespread influence on the development of university studies of religion over the formative period under review here, not only in the UK but also in Canada, Australia, New Zealand, South Africa, and the US, it may be helpful to elaborate more fully his views on the nature and structure of 'religious studies.' In 'Some Thoughts on the Science of Religion' (1996), Smart clearly differentiates between the scientific study of religion and religious studies, with the former being associated with a multiplicity of disciplines, including history, comparative religions, and other social scientific approaches to the study of religious phenomena (16). It is possible, Smart admits, to take 'religious studies' to be fully described as the scientific study of religion, but he thinks such an understanding falls short of the view of that enterprise held by the majority of those engaged in it. Thus he argues for a broader view of 'religious studies' that will include not only scientific studies but also 'reflective studies' (19). By 'reflective studies' Smart means the examination of philosophical questions about the meaning and value of religion, in the same sense presented by Keith Ward (1990). Smart admits that such a reflective religious studies involves itself in 'presentational concerns,' by which he means engagement with the questions of truth and meaning, yet he denies that this amounts to merging religious studies with theology (19). This on two grounds: first, that which he calls 'extended pluralistic theologizing' is clearly distinguishable from traditional theology; and second, that 'certain reductionistic views of science are themselves ideological positions that are not clearly distinguishable from traditional theology' (20). He argues, therefore, that talk of the science of religion as the core of religious studies is wholly reasonable, but only if it remains non-reductionist. As such, the science of religion would then allow for critical reflection on the meaning, truth, and value of religion insofar as it is not simply identified with traditional theology, which, he claims, 'is tainted by arrogance, colonialism and a usual lack of pluralism' (19). As he puts it, '[I]f Religious Studies is to take on board reflective studies, and with that get involved with any presentational concerns with theology or ideology, it is only with Extended Pluralistic Theologizing … that it should blend' (19). For him, therefore, '[t]o be genuinely scientific and objective we need to be able to steer a middle channel between the Scylla of secret theology and the Charybdis of reductionism' (20), which requires a blend of non-reductionistic scientific studies of religion with reflective, extended theology. Both traditional theology and scientific purism are excluded.

In his contribution to Jon R. Stone's *The Craft of Religious Studies* (1998), Smart reiterates his concern about 'scientific purism,' even though he acknowledges that what is called modern religious studies arose only after the 1960s with the merger of the history of religions with the social sciences (18). The new discipline, he insists, must be both speculative and philosophically reflective, although he warns against its being used as as mere 'clothing for a religious worldview' (24). It is little wonder, therefore, that Smart characterizes religious studies here as a quest (ix). But neither should it come as a surprise, therefore, that many in the academic world, as Smart himself puts it, have categorized religious studies 'as some form of tertiary Sunday School, … [and so] resist and despise it' (24). There is sufficient confusion about the notion of 'religious studies,' he judiciously notes, that 'the outside world in academia may be forgiven for misunderstanding what the field of Religious Studies is all about …' (24). But it does not appear to me that his own characterizations of the field have helped dispel the confusion; indeed, his own work seems to contribute to a view of religious studies as a religious exercise.

Subsequent studies on the character of 'religious studies' in the UK confirm that the dominant conception of the study of religion in British universities is essentially as a religious exercise. The volume *A Century of Theological and Religious Studies in Britain* (Nicholson 2003), for example, treats essentially Christian topics from a Christian point of view, and *Fields of Faith: Theology and Religious Studies for the Twenty-first Century* (Ford *et al.* 2005) attempts to show the interplay of the two fields in relation to a range of topics in Christian theology and thereby establish ground for a future in which theology and religious studies are pursued together.

'Religious Studies' in the United States of America

That this kind of confusion about the nature of religious studies also exists in the American context is clearly acknowledged in the report of the Committee on 'Defining Scholarly Work' of the American Academy of Religion (AAR). In a report entitled 'Religious Studies and the Redefining Scholarship Project,' the committee notes: 'Religious Studies, however defined or wherever located, remains suspect in the eyes of many within the rest of the academy and continually finds itself marginalized or otherwise obscured due to the fact and/or perception of blurred boundaries between studying religion and being religious, or between education about and education in religion'(Myscofski and Pilgrim *et al.* 1993: 7).

The suspicion in which religious studies is held in the US academic context, therefore, is due primarily to the confusion of what is proposed as an academic (and therefore scientific) enterprise with a religious or theological undertaking. As in Canada and Great Britain, scholars in the US claim that a significant transformation in the nature of the study of religion in the university context occurred after the Second World War. In *God's People in the Ivory Tower: Religion in the Early American University* (1991), Robert S. Shepard claims that the study of religion in US colleges and universities briefly flirted with the idea of creating a science of religion but remained essentially a kind of 'Christian *Religionswissenschaft*' that was essentially moralistic and apologetic in intent and practice. As such it was unable

> to separate [itself] from the theological and professional concerns of the nascent university, particularly the rising seminary within the university. A theological agenda accompanied the entrance of comparative religion in American higher education despite the arguments, some rhetorical and some sincere, that the new discipline was objective, scientific, and appropriate as a liberal arts subject. (129)

Nevertheless, claims Shepard, the academic study of religion in US colleges and universities experienced a renaissance after the Second World War and within a very short period of time gained disciplinary status within the academic context. D. G. Hart (1992) comes to a similar conclusion in his analysis of the field of religious studies. While not unaware of the fact that the rapid growth of the field was stimulated by the cultural crisis generated by the Second World War, and that such studies were aimed at ensuring college and university students received an education that included 'values-training' and moral formation (209), he nonetheless insists that the development of the American Academy of Religion (AAR) transformed the field into a scientific discipline. These changes, he insists, constitute a watershed in the history of the study of religion in the US, because they involved the substitution of scientific explanations of religious phenomena for the earlier quest for religious, theological, and humanistic accounts of religion. 'The new methods of studying religion advocated by the AAR,' he writes, 'signalled the demise of [the] Protestant dominance [of the field] as professors of religion became increasingly uncomfortable with their religious identification … By striving to make their discipline more scientific, religion scholars not only embraced the ideals of the academy but also freed themselves from the Protestant establishment' (198). (Hart recapitulates the argument in his more recent book, *The University Gets Religion: Religious Studies in American Higher Education* (2000).)

Were this picture true, scholars would be hard-pressed to explain why the so-called new discipline is still held in suspicion by the rest of the academic and scientific community. What does account for the suspicion, however, is the fact that the notion of religious studies is not in fact carried out within a naturalistic and scientific framework, but more nearly resembles the academic field as it first emerged in the US – namely, as an inchoate enterprise not easily distinguishable from theology and characterized primarily by apologetic and moral concerns. This is clearly evident in the review of the field produced for the AAR by Ray Hart, entitled 'Religious and Theological Studies in American Higher Education' (1991), even though he admits that the term 'religious studies' is now generally used to refer to 'the scholarly, neutral and non-advocative study of multiple religious traditions' (716). Hart notes that many in the AAR are extremely uncomfortable with 'the nomenclature that discriminates "religious" from "theological studies"' (716), and points out that the members of the Academy are divided between the terms 'study of religion' (gaining knowledge *about* religion) and 'practice of religion' (*understanding* the truth of religion) (734, 778); he then claims, however, that by far the majority of the members favor a style of scholarship that combines the two activities, or one that at the very least eschews a clear demarcation between them. Joseph Kitagawa's essays, 'The History of Religions in America' (1959) and 'Humanistic and Theological History of Religion with Special Reference to the North American Scene' (1983), strengthen Hart's contention considerably. In the first essay, he maintains that the religious liberalism of the World's Parliament of Religions served as the fundamental impetus for the establishment of the study of comparative religions – which later became religious studies – in American universities, even though he acknowledges that the participants at the Parliament meeting in 1893 for the most part gathered together representatives of the world's faiths rather than scholars of religion. In drawing attention to this, Kitagawa underlines the fact that the academic study of religion in the US has more than one dimension; it has involved historical and social scientific analysis, but it has also moved beyond what such analyses can provide. Consequently he distinguishes the 'History of Religions' (as a scientific enterprise) from the 'theological History of Religions' – but with the implication that neither can do without the other. And he insists that the *Religionswissenschaft* later destined to become 'religious studies' is not simply scientific but rather 'religio-scientific,' being obliged to 'view that data "religio-scientifically"' (1959: 21). In the second essay, Kitagawa suggests that the scientific Enlightenment principles behind the scholarship of the members of the International Association for the History of Religions (IAHR) have greatly affected the development of the field in the US, and yet – in keeping with his earlier analysis of *Religionswissenschaft* – he refers to the discipline as 'autonomous[,] situated between normative studies … and descriptive studies' (1983: 559). Unlike other social sciences, then, for Kitagawa this discipline does not simply seek descriptions or explanations of events and processes; rather, it enquires after the meaning of religious data and is therefore a mode of 'research' linking descriptive with normative concerns (560). He contrasts this kind of study of religion with the more explicitly normative 'theological History of Religions' cited in his earlier essay, but it is clear that this 'humanistic History of Religions' also stands in contrast to the purely social-scientific study of religion represented by scholars affiliated to the IAHR. As one historian of the development of religious studies in the US puts it, despite the claim of having become an independent scientific enterprise in addition to the other social sciences, it has remained haunted by religious aspirations (Reuben 1996: 142). The religious studies of the post-1960s, in particular has always been concerned with more than scientific description and explanation of religion. As D. G. Hart echoes (1992: 207–8), post-1960s religious studies in the US is a discipline imbued with spiritual value; and the students of religion (as represented by the AAR) draw support from the humanities for their enterprise by stressing the spiritual relevance of their studies to the natural sciences.

The confusion that characterizes the post-war notion of 'religious studies' in the American context is rather clearly documented in Walter H. Capps's *Religious Studies: The Making of a Discipline* (1995). Although Capps refers to religious studies as an intellectual discipline which 'provides training and practice ... in directing and conducting inquiry regarding the subject of religion' (xiv), whereby the subject of religion can be made intelligible, he also claims that 'religious studies is a relatively new subject-field concerning those whose intellectual composition there is as yet no consensus' (xv). He maintains that this is partly because the principal contributions to the field have been made by persons in other disciplines such as history and the social sciences, and because 'convictional goals' have affected the processes of interpretation applied (XXII).

Scientific inquiry, therefore, is secondary to the fundamental questions about meaning and value that provide a coherent framework within which the multiplicity of disciplines making up the field operate. Capps argues that it ought not to surprise anyone to see such a religious goal characterize this academic study. For, as he notes, not only was the historical and comparative study of religion established in the universities in the late nineteenth century and until the Second World War undertaken largely by scholars involved both in the study and the practice of religion (325), but one can also make a strong case that the subsequent flowering of the study of religion in the university context – and especially so in the US – was due to its character as a liberal theological undertaking. According to Capps, that is, it is largely because of the Tillichian conceptualization of the theological enterprise that students of religion gained 'forceful and clear access to the more inclusive cultural worlds, and in ways that could be sanctioned religiously and theologically' (290). He rejects the view that the perpetuation of theological reflection in the religious studies enterprise undermines its academic or scientific respectability (325). Instead, the student of religion must recognize that religious studies, insofar as it is merely the sum of the analytical and interpretive achievements of the various constituent fields of research, does not do full justice to the subject of religion. Furthermore, the polymethodic and multidisciplinary character of the academic study of religion today constitutes 'religious studies' only if all these fields are working together to show 'that religion has a necessary and proper place within the inventory of elements of which the scope of knowledge is comprised' (345). 'In sum,' he concludes broadly, 'religious studies recognizes that religion is not fully translatable into religious studies, and this is an analytical and interpretive truth' (347).

More recent work in America concurs with Capps's conclusion. In his introduction to *Critical Terms for Religious Studies* (1998a), Mark C. Taylor claims both that prior to the

1960s, religious studies was essentially a Christian (Protestant) undertaking and that the *raison d'être* of the new religious studies since that time is still essentially religious but neither particularly Protestant or Christian. At that time, 'departments and programs in religion tended to be either extensions of the chaplain's office, which was almost always Christian and usually Protestant, or affiliated with philosophy departments, which were primarily if not exclusively concerned with Western intellectual history;' whereas after the 1960s they are associated not with science, but rather with 'the flowering of the 1960s counter culture' (Taylor 1998a: 11). Although he admits that religious studies has been 'profoundly influenced by developments dating back to the Enlightenment' (10), its new incarnation in university departments in the US was predominantly influenced by multicultural sensibilities created by the civil rights and anti-war movements of the late 1950s and early 1960s. If the 'how' of religious studies has changed because of the increased influence of the social sciences in cultural studies during this period, he avers nevertheless that this has not altered the essence of the discipline; that is, even if a social scientific study of religion has somehow displaced the old theology, it has not displaced the fundamental religious concern that has always – and always will – characterize the field. Taylor notes elsewhere (1994) that it is precisely for this reason that religious studies is an academically suspect discipline in secular colleges and universities (1994: 950). Yet even though the field of religious studies became captive to other methodologies, he argues, it cannot be reduced to them (951), because the secular approach of the sciences absolutize their understanding of religion and are themselves, therefore, simply another form of theology.

For Taylor, there is no appropriate procedure for a comprehensive scientific study of religion, and religious studies must therefore be both multidisciplinary and multicultural. But if he seems to discern the complexity of his stance, he nevertheless does not assist the scholarly study under question by his fluid description. Postmodernism, he maintains, undermines all possibility of a fundamental method or comprehensive explanatory approach to the data of the field. Consequently its quarry cannot be cognition; rather it must seek to understand religion by applying a multiplicity of notions and concepts that might act as 'enabling constraints' (1998a: 16) for a discourse of a different kind: 'for exploring the territory of religion' (17) by means of a 'dialogue between religious studies and important work going on in other areas of the arts, humanities, and social sciences' (18). Such a religious studies, he points out, properly transcends scientific reductionism and, like the study of religion antedating it, recognizes that '[r]eligion … is not epiphenomenal but sui generis' (6; see also 1999: 4). Stated differently, scientific theory is not not-theological, as Taylor might express it, because theory itself is theo-logical and onto-theological in character, given that it is a search either for an 'overarching or underlying unity' that will coherently frame the data. As he puts it:

> The gaze of the theorist strives to reduce differences to identity and complexity to simplicity. When understood in this way, the shift from theology to theory does not, as so many contemporary theorists think, escape God but exchanges overt faith for covert belief in the One in and through which all is understood. (1999: 76)

The new post-1960s study of religion in the American context on this reading of the situation is not new in its fundamental orientation from the traditional study of religion in the university. The religious discourse of traditional studies is replaced not by scientific discourse but rather by a different form of religious discourse – namely, the discourse of 'responsible inquiry' that 'neither demands answers nor believes in progress but seeks to keep the future open by a relentless questioning that unsettles everything by settling nothing. To settle nothing is to leave nothing unanswered. Forever unanswered' (Taylor 1994: 963). This kind of 'responsible discourse,' it is quite apparent, is not primarily concerned with obtaining knowledge about religions and religion, but rather with the well-being of the individual.

'Religious studies' globally

That there is no general convergence of opinion about the nature of religious studies among students of religion in the Anglo-American university context is clearly demonstrated by the analyses of the various Canadian, British, and American views presented above. The same can be said about religious studies globally. Although a 'thick description' of the global situation cannot be given, I will nevertheless attempt a brief sketch of similar problems raised in 'religious studies' discussions elsewhere in the world. Eric J. Sharpe, for example, notes that although the study of religion in Australian universities and colleges was from its inception free from confessional attachments, '[that is] not to say ... that those involved in teaching these various programmes were without theological interests' (1986b: 249).

He continues:

> On the whole, rather few [Australian students of religion] could be regarded as 'secular' scholars, and many held a form of dual citizenship, being 'theological' and 'scientific' at the same time ... All in all, the positions occupied by Australian scholars in the field by the late 1970s mirrored fairly accurately the divisions observable anywhere in the world ... (249)

In an essay entitled 'South Africa's Contribution to Religious Studies,' Martin Prozesky claims that the discipline has made a significant contribution to society because of the peculiarity of its being both scientific and 'more than' science. The student of religion, he insists, must go beyond merely seeking an explanation of religious phenomena to 'a genuinely liberative practice' (Prozesky 1990: 18). According to Prozesky, the student of religion is able to do this because religion itself is a humanizing force, which, when properly understood, will have a transformative effect upon those who study it.

Another striking example is provided by Michael Pye, in his 'Religious Studies in Europe: Structures and Desiderata' (1991), where he points out that the ambiguities and confusions that plague the notion of 'religious studies' in the Anglo-American context also have their counterpart in Europe. He points out that in Germany, for example, 'the term *Religionswissenschaft* in the singular (science of religion, which for Pye is the same as religious studies) is rivalled in some universities by the plural *Religionswissenschaften* (sciences of religion) which tends to mean religious sciences with a religious motivation, including Catholic and Protestant theology' (41). The evidence, then, regarding the diversity of perceptions, claims, and proposals about 'religious studies' as an enterprise carried out in the context of the modern university cannot be ignored, and would seem to lead to only one conclusion – that 'religious studies,' as Michael Pye has suggested, is 'a flag of convenience' (1994: 52) used by scholars, programs, and institutions to 'legitimate' the aims, methods, and procedures they adopt in their study of religions. A more recent survey of the field by a team of international scholars titled *Religious Studies: A Global* View (Alles 2008) not only attests to the versatility of the designation for the field but also confirms the continuing influence of religion and theology on it.

I do not think matters are quite as bleak as Pye paints it, however, and, in concluding this discussion, I will attempt to set out what general agreements might be reached as to the meaning and use of the term 'religious studies' by those involved in an academic study of religion in the context of the modern university.

'Religious studies': a summary and proposal

The term 'religious studies' it appears from this discussion, is used in two quite different yet not wholly unconnected ways. In one sense, as the state-of-the-art reviews of 'religious studies' in universities around the world suggest, the term includes whatever study of religion and religions is undertaken in any post-secondary institution of education, whether religious or secular, and regardless of the methodology adopted. Here the term is often taken to be commensurate with 'the academic study of religion' and 'the scholarly study of religion,' which notions themselves are often used synonymously. In this case, then, as Michael Pye puts it, the notion of religious studies 'covers a multitude of possibilities' (1991: 42), although it excludes outright confessional and apologetic studies of religion or of a particular religious tradition. Nevertheless, as the 'methodological' literature in the field shows, Pye's multitude of possibilities does involve studies that have a good deal of 'continuity' with such confessional studies including forms of religious education that provide an 'experiential understanding' of religion (Holley 1978; Bischoff 1975; Hull 1984; Prothero 2007), as well as 'revised,' non-confessional forms of theology (Novak 1971; Thiemann 1990; Ford 1999) and postmodern theology (see Wiebe 2008). The second, more common use of the term, however, is as a designation for a particular kind of approach to the study of religion with a particular aim, methodology, or style that distinguishes it from the type of (religious/confessional) study of religion antedating it. And when used in this sense, it still refers to the study of religion undertaken in the academy, but now designates an enterprise legitimated by the academy – in this case the modern research university – because it measures up to the received criteria of scientific study in the other university disciplines. Identification of religious studies with the academic study of religion in this instance, therefore, does not apply to all post-secondary research carried out under that rubric. 'Religious studies' as an academic undertaking, therefore, ought to connote a scientific enterprise even though it does not, as some would argue, constitute a scientific discipline (see, for example, Pye 1991). I use the notion of 'enterprise' here as defined by Robert A. McCaughey (1984) as 'any organized understanding of sufficient magnitude and duration to permit its participants to derive a measure of identity from it' (xiii).

As 'scientific,' the enterprise is chiefly characterized by an epistemic intention, taking for granted that the natural and social sciences are the only legitimate models for the objective study of religion; but it does not itself constitute a distinct scientific discipline. The primarily epistemic focus in this version of religious studies clearly distinguishes it from the types referred to above. It is not that earlier types of religious studies wholly reject the contributions made by the natural and social sciences to their understanding of religion, but just that the epistemic intention that informs the sciences is subordinated to religious commitments or theological assumptions; that it is placed in the service of other goals, such as the formation of character or the achievement of some form of religious enlightenment. The earlier exercises are nevertheless 'academic enterprises,' because they are pursued by scholars in the context of the university, but they might be appropriately considered 'mixed genre enterprises' because they attempt to blend scientific and extra-scientific goals. Religious studies as a 'scientific enterprise,' however, is a naturalistic study of religion carried out in several complementary disciplines. And the review of the literature above provides evidence of the widely held view that the field is polymethodic and multidisciplinary – as does the volume in which this essay appears. Religious studies, in this view, therefore, is not a separate discipline but instead a general rubric for empirical and scientific studies of religion which alone are appropriate in the context of a modern research university dedicated to the advancement of objective knowledge about the world, both natural (physical) and social.

Bibliography

Alles, Gregory D. 2008 *Religious Studies: A Global View*, London: Routledge.

Anderson, Charles P., 1972 *Guide to Religious Studies in Canada*, (3rd edn), Toronto: Corporation for the Publication of Academic Studies in Canada.

Badertscher, John M., Gordon Harland, and Roland E. Miller, 1993 *Religious Studies in Manitoba and Saskatchewan*, Waterloo: Wilfrid Laurier University Press.

Benson, Thomas L., 1987 'Religious Studies as an Academic Discipline,' in Mircea Eliade (ed.), *Encyclopedia of Religion*, New York: Macmillan Press, Vol. XIV, pp. 88–92.

Bischoff, Guntrum G., 1975 'The Pedagogy of Religiology,' in Anne Carr and Nicholas Piediscalzi (eds), *Public Schools Religion-Studies: 1975*, Missoula: American Academy of Religion, pp. 127–35.

Bowlby, Paul W. R., 2001 *Religious Studies in Atlantic Canada: A State-of-the-Art Review*, Waterloo: Wilfred Laurier University Press.

Braybrooke, Marcus, 1990 'Religious Studies and Interfaith Development,' in Ursula King (ed.), *Turning Points in Religious Studies*, Edinburgh: T. & T. Clark, pp. 132–41.

Cahill, Joseph, 1982 *Mended Speech: The Crisis of Religious Studies and Theology*, New York: Crossroad.

Cain, Seymour, 1987 'History of Study,' in Mircea Eliade (ed.), *The Encyclopedia of Religion*, New York: Macmillan Press, Vol. XIV, pp. 64–83.

Capps, Walter H., 1995 *Religious Studies: The Making of A Discipline*, Minneapolis: Fortress Press.

Cole, W. Owen, 1990 'The New Educational Reform Act and Worship in County Schools of England and Wales,' in Ursula King (ed.), *Turning Points in Religious Studies*, Edinburgh: T. & T. Clark, pp. 117–31.

Crites, Stephen (*et al.*), 1990 'Liberal Learning and the Religion Major' (an AAR Task Force on the Study in Depth of Religion), Syracuse: American Academy of Religion.

Cunningham, Adrian, 1990 'Religious Studies in the Universities: England,' in Ursula King (ed.), *Turning Points in Religious Studies*, Edinburgh: T. & T. Clark, pp. 21–31.

Davis, Charles, 1974–5 'The Reconvergence of Theology and Religious Studies,' *Studies in Religion*, 4, pp. 205–21.

Eliade, M., (1987) *Encyclopedia of Religion*, New York: Macmillan.

Ford, David, 1999 *Theology: A Very Short Introduction*, Oxford: Oxford University Press.

Ford, David, Ben Quash and Janet Martin Soskice, 2005 *Fields of Faith and Religious Studies for the Twenty-first Century*, Cambridge: Cambridge University Press.

Fraser, Brian J., 1995 *The Study of Religion in British Columbia: A State-of-the-Art Review*, Waterloo: Wilfrid Laurier University Press.

Hart, D. G., 1992 'American Learning and the Problem of Religious Studies,' in G. M. Marsden and B. J. Longfield (eds), *The Secularization of the Academy*, Oxford: Oxford University Press, pp. 195–233.

—— 2000 *The University Gets Religion: Religious Studies in American Higher Education*, Baltimore: Johns Hopkins University Press.

Hart, Ray, 1991 'Religious and Theological Studies in American Higher Education,' *Journal of the American Academy of Religion*, 69, pp. 715–827.

Holley, Raymond, 1978 *Religious Education and Religious Knowledge: An Introduction to the Philosophy of Religious Education*, London: Routledge.

Hull, John, 1984 'Religious Education in a Pluralistic Society,' in John Hull, *Studies in Religion and Education*, London: The Falmer Press, pp. 45–55.

Jackson, Robert, 1990 'Religious Studies and Developments in Religious Education,' in Ursula King (ed.), *Turning Points in Religious Studies*, Edinburgh: T. & T. Clark, pp. 102–16.

King, Ursula (ed.), 1990 *Turning Points in Religious Studies*, Edinburgh: T. & T. Clark.

Kitagawa, Joseph M., 1959 'The History of Religions in America,' in Mircea Eliade and Joseph M. Kitagawa (eds), *The History of Religions: Essays in Methodology*, Chicago: University of Chicago Press, pp. 1–30.

—— 1983 'Humanistic and Theological History of Religion With Special Reference to the North American Scene,' in Peter Slater and Donald Wiebe (eds), *Traditions in Contact and Change: Selected Proceedings of the XIVth Congress of the International Association for the History of Religions*, Waterloo: Wilfrid Laurier University Press, pp. 553–63.

Klostermaier, Klaus K. and Larry W. Hurtado (eds), 1991 *Religious Studies: Issues, Prospects, and Proposals*, Winnipeg: University of Manitoba and Scholars Press.

Laporte, Jean-Marc, 1993 'Review of *Religious Studies in Ontario: A State-of-the-Art Review*,' Toronto Journal of Theology, 9/2, p. 249.

McCaughey, Robert A., 1984 *International Studies and Academic Enterprises: A Chapter in the Enclosure of American Learning*, New York: Columbia University Press.

Myscofski, Carol and Richard Pilgrim (*et al.*), 1993 'Religious Studies and the Redefining Scholarship Project: A Report of the AAR Committee on "Defining Scholarly Work",' *Religious Studies News*, 8/3, September, pp 7–8.

Nesbitt, Eleanor, 1990 'Sikhism,' in Ursula King (ed.), *Turning Points in Religious Studies*, Edinburgh: T. & T. Clark, pp. 168–79.

Neufeldt, Ron W., 1983 *Religious Studies in Alberta: A State-of-the-Art Review*, Waterloo: Wilfrid Laurier University Press.

Nicholson, Ernest, 2003 *A Century of Theological and Religious Studies in Britain*, Oxford: Oxford University Press.

Novak, Michael, 1971 *Ascent of the Mountain, Flight of the Dove: An Introduction to Religious Studies*, New York: Harper & Row.

Ogden, Schubert M., 1986 (1975) 'Theology in the University,' in Schubert M. Ogden, *On Theology*, San Francisco: Harper & Row, pp. 121–33.

Olson, Alan M., 1990a 'Religious Studies,' in *Encyclopedia of Religious Education*, Iris V. Cully and Kendig Brubaker Cully (eds), San Francisco: Harper & Row, pp. 549–51.

Olson, Alan M., 1990b 'University,' in *Encyclopedia of Religious Education*, Iris V. Cully and Kendig Brubaker Cully (eds), San Francisco: Harper & Row, pp. 673–4.

Prothero, Stephen, 2007 *Religious Literacy: What Every American Needs to Know*, San Francisco: HarperSanFrancisco.

Prozesky, Martin, 1990 'South Africa's Contribution to Religious Studies,' *Journal of Theology of Southern Africa*, 70, pp. 9–20.

Pye, Michael, 1991 'Religious Studies in Europe: Structures and Desiderate,' in Klaus K. Klostermaier and Larry W. Hurtado (eds), *Religious Studies: Issues, Prospects and Proposals*, Winnipeg: University of Manitoba and Scholars Press, pp. 39–55.

—— 1994 'Religion: Shape and Shadow,' *Numen*, 41, pp. 51–75.

—— 1999 'Methodological Integration in the Study of Religions,' in Tore Ahlbäck (ed.), *Approaching Religion* (Vol. I), Åbo: Åbo Akademic University Press, pp. 189–205.

Remus, Harold E., 1988 'Religion as an Academic Discipline' (Part I: 'Origins, Nature and Changing Understandings'), in Charles H. Lippy, Peter M. Williams (eds), *Encyclopedia of the American Religious Experience*, Vol III, New York: Charles Scribners Sons, pp. 1653–65.

—— William Closson James, and Daniel Fraikin (eds), 1992 *Religious Studies in Ontario: A State-of-the-Art Review*, Waterloo: Wilfrid Laurier University Press.

Reuben, Julie, 1996 *The Making of the Modern University: Intellectual Transformation and the Marginalization of Morality*, Chicago: Chicago University Press.

Riley, Philip Boo, 1984 'Theology and/or Religious Studies: A Case Study of *Studies in Religion/Sciences Religieuses* 1971–1981,' in *Studies in Religion*, Vol. 13, pp. 423–44.

Rousseau, Louis, and Michel Despland (eds), 1988 *Les sciences religieuses au Québec depuis 1972*, Waterloo: Wilfrid Laurier Press.

Sharpe, Eric J., 1986a *Comparative Religion: A History*, (2nd edn), London: Duckworth.

—— 1986b '"From Paris 1900 to Sydney 1985" (An Essay in Retrospect and Prospect),' in Victor C. Hayes (ed.), *Identity Issues and World Religions: Selected Proceedings of the Fifteenth Congress of the International Association for the History of Religions*, Redford Park: Flinders University Press, pp. 245–52.

—— 1987 'Methodological Issues', in Mircea Eliade (ed.), *Encyclopedia of Religion*, Vol XIV, pp. 84–8.

Shepard, Robert S., 1991 *God's People in the Ivory Tower: Religion in the Early American University*, New York: Carlson Publishing Inc.

Smart, Ninian, 1973 *The Science of Religion and the Sociology of Knowledge*, Princeton: Princeton University Press.

—— 1990 'Concluding Reflections: Religious Studies in Global Perspective,' in Ursula King (ed.), *Turning Points in Religious Studies*, Edinburgh: T. & T. Clark, pp. 299–306.

—— 1995 'The Study of Religions', in John R. Hinnells (ed) *The New Penguin Dictionary of Religions*, London: Penguin Books, pp. 498–500.

—— 1996 'Some Thoughts on the Science of Religion,' in Arvind Sharma (ed.), *The Sum of our Choices: Essays in Honor of Eric J. Sharpe*, Atlanta: Scholars Press, pp. 15–25.

—— 1997 'Religious Studies in Higher Education,' in John R. Hinnells (ed.), *The New Penguin Dictionary of Religions*, London: Penguin, pp. 420–1.

—— 1998 'Methods in My Life,' in Jon R. Stone (ed.), *The Craft of Religious Studies*, New York: St. Martin's Press, pp. 18–35.

—— 1999 'Foreward,' in Peter Connolly (ed.), *Approaches to the Study of Religion*, London: Cassell, pp. ix–iv.

Taylor, Mark C., 1994 'Unsettling Issues,' *Journal of the American Academy of Religion*, Vol. LXII/4, pp. 949–63.

—— 1998a 'Introduction,' in Mark C. Taylor (ed.), *Critical Terms for Religious Studies*, Chicago: University of Chicago Press, pp. 1–19.

—— 1998b 'Retracings,' in Jon R. Stone (ed.), *The Craft of Religious Studies*, New York: St. Martin's Press, pp. 258–76.

—— 1999 *About Religion: Economics of Faith in Virtual Culture*, Chicago: University of Chicago Press.

Thiemann, Ronald F., 1990 'The Future of an Illusion: An Inquiry Into the Contrast Between Theological and Religious Studies,' *Theological Education*, 26/2, pp. 66–85.

Walls, Andrew F., 1990 'Religious Studies in the Universities: Scotland,' in Ursula King (ed.), *Turning Points in Religious Studies*, Edinburgh: T. & T. Clark, pp. 32–45.

Ward, Keith, 1990 'The Study of Truth and Dialogue in Religion,' in Ursula King (ed.), *Turning Points in Religious Studies*, Edinburgh: T. & T. Clark, pp. 221–31.

Wiebe, Donald, 2006 'The Learned Practice of Religion: A Review of the History of Religious Studies in Canada and Its Portent for the Future,' *Studies in Religion/Sciences Religieuses*, 35/3–4, pp. 475–501.

Wiebe, Donald, 2008 'Secular Theology Is Still Theology, Not the Academic Study of Religion,' *Bulletin of the Council of Societies for the Study of Religion*, 37/3, pp. 77–81.

Williams, Cyril, 1990 'Religious Studies in the Universities: Wales,' in Ursula King (ed.) *Turning Points in Religious Studies*, Edinburgh: T. & T. Clark, pp. 46–56.

Suggested reading

Hjelde (ed.) 2000 *Man, Meaning, and Mystery: Hundred Years of History of Religions in Norway. The Heritage of W. Brede Kristensen*, Leiden: Brill.
Focuses on the emergence of the field of the history of religions in Europe at the turn of the twentieth century, paying special attention to scholarly developments in the Netherlands, Sweden, Norway, and Denmark.

Jakelic, Slavica and Lori Pearson (eds) 2004 *The Future of the Study of Religion: Proceedings of Congress 2000*, Leiden: Brill.
Provides a wide array of perspectives on the nature of the field of religious studies and points to the problems facing the field, especially regarding the proper relations among the various sub-disciplines of the field.

Jensen, Jeppe Sinding 2003 *The Study of Religion in a New Key: Theoretical and Philosophical Soundings in the Comparative and General Study of Religion*, Aarhus: Aarhus University Press.
Examines the present conditions and future possibilities of the academic study of religion and is concerned to defend a theoretically oriented, comparative, and general study of religions.

Jensen, Jeppe Sinding and Luther H. Martin (eds) 2003 [1997] *Rationality and the Study of Religion*, London: Routledge.
Contributors argue that religious studies, like other disciplines in the university, must work within the framework of scientific rationality.

Kippenberg, Hans 2002 *Discovering Religious History in the Modern Age*, Princeton: Princeton University Press.
Looks at the rise of religious studies in Europe and Britain as a response to modernization. Covers all the main figures who contributed to the emergence of a 'science of religion.'

McCutcheon, Russell 1997 *Manufacturing Religion: The Discourse on Sui Generis Religion and the Politics of Nostalgia*, New York: Oxford Press.
Gives serious attention to the question of the nature of the theoretical object of religious studies with arguments against the notion that it is anything but a human phenomenon.

Massimo, Faggioli, and Alberto Melloni (eds) 2006 *Religious Studies in the Twentieth Century: A Survey on Disciplines, Cultures, and Questions*, Berlin: LIT. Verlag.
Proceedings of an international colloquium on religious studies with essays on the field in the twentieth century with a particular focus on methodology in the study of religious phenomena.

Molendijk, Arie L. and Peter Pels (eds) 1998 *Religion in the Making: The Emergence of the Sciences of Religion*, Leiden: Brill.
Proceedings of a conference that focused attention on the diversity of disciplines the field encompasses and on the boundary disputes among them. Special focus is given to the Netherlands, France, and Britain.

Preus, S. 1987 *Explaining Religion: Criticism and Theory from Bodin to Freud*, New Haven, CT: Yale University Press.
A clear analysis of the prehistory of the development of the field of religious studies, providing a history of the creation of a new intellectual ethos within which such an enterprise could thrive.

Reuben, Julie 1996 *The Making of the Modern University: Intellectual Transformation and the Marginalization of Morality*, Chicago: University of Chicago Press.
Provides a brilliant account of the emergence of the study of religion in relation to the marginalization of moral concerns in the curriculum of the modern research universities in the US.

Wiebe, Donald 1999 *The Politics of Religious Studies: The Continuing Conflict with Theology in the Academy*, New York: St. Martin's Press.

The primary concern of the essays in this volume is the political character of the academic context of religious studies in North America today.

Wiegers, Gerard A. 2002 *Modern Societies and the Sciences of Religion: Studies in Honour of Lammert Leertouwer*, Leiden: Brill.

Essays here are focused on developments in modern societies and how those changes influenced the scientific study of religions. In addition to European and Anglo-American developments, serious attention is given to religious studies in the Middle East, Africa, China, Indonesia, and Japan.

Chapter 9

Sociology of religion

Martin Riesebrodt and Mary Ellen Konieczny

Until the end of the 1970s most sociologists of religion seemed rather confident about their understanding of religious phenomena. We all more-or-less knew that modern societies were undergoing a process of secularization. Of course, this process could take different forms in different societies depending on their institutional order or religious culture. Certainly, very few sociologists expected religion to totally disappear. Most assigned to religion a legitimate space in the private sphere. Many assumed that religious institutions would undergo a process of internal secularization and would increasingly adapt to the requirements of modern institutions while maintaining their religious symbolism. Others expected religious values to permeate modern societies, leaving behind traditional forms of religion. Some imagined that national ideologies or civil religions would functionally replace religious traditions. But hardly anybody was prepared for the dramatic resurgence of religion that we have witnessed over the last three decades in which religion has re-emerged as a relatively autonomous public force, a marker of ethnic identities, and a shaper of modern subjects and their ways of life.

The renewed global importance of religion from North and South America to South and East Asia, from Europe to the Middle East and Africa has had a profound impact on the sociology of religion. It not only provided the discipline with an opportunity to revive the empirical study of religious phenomena on a global scale – more importantly, it challenged its conventional theoretical perspectives. Social theorists had to cope with their own cognitive dissonance between their expectation of secularization on the one hand and the actual resurgence of religion on the other.

The two most typical reactions to this challenge have been denial and instant conversion. Some authors have simply insisted that their expectations of modernization and secularization are basically sound. Focusing on the resurgence of religion in 'third world' countries has allowed them to pretend that these revivals of religion are part of an ongoing 'modernization' process. Not surprisingly, many have taken pains to detect a 'Puritan spirit' or an 'inner-worldly asceticism' in such movements. Other authors have chosen the opposite route of instant conversion, denying any general trend towards secularization in the West and elsewhere. According to them, secularization, generally understood as 'disenchantment,' is not a necessary outcome of social differentiation and the rationalizing processes of capitalism, science, and bureaucracy as most theories had assumed, but is just an effect of the absence of a religious market and competition between exclusive voluntary associations. This present state of uncertainty and confusion in the sociology of religion offers a good opportunity to review the development of the discipline from its nineteenth century origins to the present, and to point towards a future research agenda.

Three classical paradigms

The sociology of religion emerged from the philosophy of the Enlightenment on the one hand and its Romantic critique on the other. Although it attempts to make religion the object of scientific study, sociology has inherited certain presuppositions from the philosophical discourse that have shaped its perspectives on religion in different ways. In order to better understand the development of the sociology of religion, one has to consider how social scientific understandings of religion are informed by basic assumptions about Western modernity, the course of history, and the place of human beings in this world. Three classical paradigms had the strongest impact on the discipline: the approaches of Karl Marx, Émile Durkheim, and Max Weber.

Karl Marx (1818–1883)

For Marx, as for his teacher Hegel, history follows a logic through which human beings emancipate themselves from the realm of necessity to the realm of freedom and self-realization. However, for Marx, unlike Hegel, the engine of this development is not the dialectics of the 'world spirit' but that of the material conditions of existence. Human beings realize themselves in the process of the production and reproduction of their concrete lives. This takes place through actors' engagements in the technical and technological control of nature, in conjunction with the social relations through which humans exercise this process of control. An increasing control of nature leads to an increasing division of labor, creating class distinctions initially based almost exclusively upon gender. The differentiation between manual and intellectual labor causes drastic inequality based on the ownership of private property. In early socioeconomic stages, 'nature' seems rather mysterious, whereas with increasing control of natural forces and increasing class differentiation, 'society' becomes more unfathomable.

In other words, modern science and technology have produced an unprecedented rational understanding and practical control through which nature has become widely demystified. However, capitalism has produced an extreme class differentiation between manual and intellectual labor, as well as between owners of the means of production and workers. These social relations are usually not comprehended as they actually are, but are misunderstood, misrepresented, and mysticized.

The reasons for this mystification are manifold, but all based upon the alienating structures of modern socioeconomic relations. There are the privileged, who have an interest in legitimation. They produce and spread an ideology of self-justification, which is in part strategic – perhaps even cynical – and in part self-deluding. Then there are the workers, who are alienated from each other through competition, and deprived of their creativity and self-realization through the mechanical character of their work and the loss of control over the means of production as well as their own products. Finally, misrecognition lies in the very nature of commodity production itself, since the interaction between social actors appears in the form of an exchange relation between products.

For Marx, religion plays an obvious role in these processes. In early socioeconomic stages, religion consists mainly in a response to the mysteriousness of nature and expresses humanity's lack of understanding and control. But in more advanced stages, religion increasingly distorts the understanding of the true nature of social relations by expressing the alienation inscribed into class structures. Religion, by creating the illusion of a transcendental power of perfection which demands submission to the *status quo*, also prevents social actors from collectively establishing a social order that would allow them to realize their full potential as social and creative human beings.

In order to overcome alienation, it is not sufficient to criticize religious consciousness. Rather, one has to overturn the class structure of capitalism and change the mode of production. Once this has happened, religion would disappear and people would be able to understand and control society as rationally as they do nature, and they would be free to realize their true natures as social and creative beings.

Since for Marx religion does not represent the source of human alienation, but just expresses it, this approach does not pay much attention to the study of religion *per se*. Although the Marxian view that religions reflect the structures of social relations holds true for all social scientists to a certain degree, a rather narrow reading of Marx has led to a long and unfortunate neglect of the study of religion from a Marxian perspective. Only recently have social scientists recaptured the fruitful aspects of the Marxian tradition while giving up the teleological view of history (Comaroff and Comaroff 1991, 1995).

Émile Durkheim (1858–1917)

While Marx's understanding of history and humanity is based on a model of human and social emancipation, Durkheim's is based on social order and its civilizing, moralizing, and socializing mission. According to Durkheim, human beings have a double nature consisting of body and soul. On the one hand, they are driven by bodily needs, following their egoistic natural drives and desires; on the other, they have souls, which are social and moral. The task of any social order is to keep the egoistic drives of individuals in check, and to transform these individuals into social and moral agents who conform to group norms (Durkheim 1914/1960).

Although civilization progresses for Durkheim, the basic problem stays in many respects the same. What changes is the division of labor, and with it, modes of thought and methods of social integration. An increasing division of labor, which according to Durkheim has been institutionalized not for its unforeseeable greater efficiency but for the social regulation of competition, makes people much more interdependent than they were in segmentary societies. This explains why segmentary societies rely much more on integration through rituals than modern ones.

Nevertheless, any social order works only when people share basic categories of thought and moral beliefs, and reinforces them through collective rituals. All categories of thought and moral beliefs originate in religion, which is based on the distinction between sacred and profane. Differentiations of space, time, cause, and number originate out of this basic distinction. Religion, therefore, is the source of thought and knowledge but, following Comte, Durkheim argues that with the progress of civilization other modes of thought, especially science, replace religion at least in part. However, this is only a difference in degree, not in kind; since scientific knowledge also becomes obligatory it is, so-to-speak, a higher form of religion. Nevertheless, religion is still needed since science cannot replace the emotional side of religion, which attaches people to each other via symbolic representations. This can be generated only by dense interactions in extraordinary and often ecstatic situations, such as public ceremonies.

Durkheim's understanding of religion assumes a basic identity between the political and the religious unit and appears to be heavily informed by the modern Western idea of the nation. Durkheim's theory directly jumps from tribal religion to civic religion – omitting all examples of religiously pluralistic empires, conflicts between and within religious traditions, and disintegrative effects of religions. Durkheim suggests via his study of Australian totemism that all societies need a unifying system of thought, symbols, norms, and values, identifying nationalism as the new 'civic religion' adequate to modern industrial societies (1912/1995). However, Durkheim is not a nationalist. For him nationalism represents only a necessary intermediary stage in the emergence of human universalism. Durkheim's understanding of religion has been the most dominant theoretical influence in both sociology and anthropology.

Max Weber (1864–1920)

For Weber, neither human emancipation nor social order and integration are the central points of departure. Neither does history have an intrinsic goal, nor does modernity's central problem lie in the control of egoistic individualism. For Weber, modern Western societies are not underregulated but rather overregulated. In the modern bureaucratic age there is hardly any space left to lead a meaningful life according to any principles other than utilitarian ones. Weber shared the Marxian insight that people make their own history but do not control it. Weber's sociology is full of examples of how social actions have led to unintended and often paradoxical historical outcomes. Weber's central question, therefore, is how this modern rationalist system of external social control and internalized self-control has developed historically, and how modern individuals as cultural beings can respond to it with dignity and responsibility. Although himself religiously 'unmusical,' Weber sees a certain dignity in religious attempts to transcend the narrow boundaries of utilitarian interests through the dramatization of ultimate values and the principled shaping of one's life according to them.

Weber's sociology of religion begins with an inquiry into the religious sources of modern capitalist culture and ends with a cross-culturally comparative study of rationalisms embedded in the religious traditions of China, India, and ancient Judaism. Weber draws the conclusion that the modern West is the result of a unique rationalization process, which has affected not only its economic system and its principles of bureaucratic organization but also its culture – especially its science, music, and art.

While 'primitive' religions were hardly differentiated from the pursuit of 'this-worldly' interests, the rise of 'salvation' religions formulated by religious intellectuals and *virtuosi* defined religion as a separable sphere of interests. The very idea of salvation and the different paths to salvation defined the world in relation to an ultimate value, and restructured the attitudes and life conduct of social actors towards worldly spheres of interest. Of course, this did not take place independent of political and economic structures and developments, but it added a dimension of interests, which in turn could exert influence upon economic and political institutions and actors. According to Weber, religious ideas and interests are mediated by institutions, which develop their own dynamics in conjunction with the everyday needs of their followers.

In the West, a unique type of rationalism of 'world mastery' developed out of the confluence of the rationalism of Judaic ethical prophecy, Greek philosophy, Roman law, Christian monasticism and the emerging bourgeois economy of independent cities. This rationalism was taken up by parts of the Protestant Reformation, particularly by Calvinism and ascetic Protestant sects, and systematized into an attitude of inner-worldly asceticism. The ethos of these groups is characterized by self-control, methodical life conduct directed towards work in a calling, and acquisition through a regularly and rationally pursued business. This religious ethos of inner-worldly asceticism matched perfectly with a socially upwardly mobile class of small entrepreneurs and a wider economic interest in docile workers. It became a model that was adopted eventually by wider society, contributing to the shaping of a bourgeois, modern Western type of capitalism. Ironically, this originally religious ethos has been transformed in the course of capitalist development into our modern, religiously empty work habits and utilitarian attitudes.

Challenged by critics that his view of religion in the shaping of modern capitalist culture is not well founded, Weber engaged in a cross-culturally comparative study of *The Economic Ethics of the World Religions*. Studying the religions of China (Weber 1920/1951) and India (Weber 1920/1958) he concludes that they offered to their practitioners very different psychological incentives from Western religions, especially ascetic Protestantism. Confucianism basically affirms the world and does not create the inner tensions which motivated ascetic Protestants to shape the world. And although Indian religions certainly reject the world, they have cultivated techniques to escape from it, rather than transforming it. Moreover, Weber observes that the spread of a religious elite's ethos to the masses requires institutions of transmission; in the case of ascetic Protestantism, the intense involvement of the laity in congregational forms of prophetic religions was key to the development and spread of an ethic of innerworldly asceticism. But according to Weber, these were absent in China and India.

The Western rationalization processes set in motion by this religiously motivated ethos contributed to the disenchantment of the world by rejecting all irrational means of attaining salvation, and promoted the emergence of rationally organized institutional orders and ethics. According to Weber, this process of disenchantment and secularization removed the religious ethic from central economic, political, and cultural institutions, freeing them from religious control. Whoever chooses to live a life based on religious principles can do so only against the institutionalized logic of 'unbrotherly' bureaucratic regimes that no longer recognize religious morality but instead value efficiency, performance, and utility. Therefore, in Western modernity, religion can only survive in more central social institutions if it adapts to their logics and more-or-less sanctifies them. It is only in small voluntary associations at the social margins that religion can preserve an ethos of universal brotherhood. According to Weber, there exists the possibility of new charismatic upheavals that can change people's inner attitudes – but given the rigidity and efficiency of bureaucratic systems, these revolutionary possibilities are rather unlikely to succeed in the modern West.

Religion, modernity, secularization

Unlike Marx, neither Durkheim nor Weber expected religion to disappear, but both certainly assumed that it would be transformed in the modern world. The next generations of scholars elaborated these arguments in more detail, usually fusing the traditions of Durkheim and Weber as they understood them. Whereas those working in the Durkheimian tradition tended to focus more on the integrative role of religion at the social center, Weberians turned instead to religious movements at the margins of society.

Modernization and civil religion

Talcott Parsons and his students elaborated the Durkheimian perspective on religion, inquiring into the integration of modern societies through generalized religious values and civil religions. Parsons (1902–1979) focused on the interpenetration of Christian (specifically sectarian Protestant) values into the very fabric of modern industrial (specifically American) society. According to Parsons, the generalization of voluntarism and individualism made the modern US the most Christian society ever (Parsons 1963).

Robert Bellah's work typifies this view, especially in his evolutionary theory of religion (Bellah 1970). According to Bellah, humanity's need for religious symbols is a constant factor in social life – but as human societies have evolved over time, so have the content and dynamics of religious symbol systems. Historically, religion developed alongside of social and self-development, and as societies acquired greater knowledge and achieved greater capacity for social and self-transformation, religious belief concurrently has become characterized by individual choice. Bellah argues for a five-stage schema of the evolution of religion, ranging from primitive to modern. This schema views religion in the modern West – paradigmatically the Protestant US – as more highly developed and normatively better than other less rationalized and more magical forms. Bellah claims that the doctrinal diversity of Protestantism and the freedom of individuals to choose belief are not evidence of secularization, but rather evidence of human progress.

Following ideas of civil religion earlier explored by Rousseau and Durkheim, Bellah sought institutional settings where essential American values such as civic activism and individualism were interpreted, dramatized, and ritually enacted. Focusing on Presidential addresses at certain decisive moments in American history, he identified expressions of nationally shared ultimate values and a vision of the nation's calling, and claimed civil religion's continuing if fragile existence in America. According to Bellah, the particulars of American civil religion have incorporated Protestant Christian themes of covenant, death, and resurrection or rebirth, and its ritual calendar emphasizes the central importance of family and local community in American democracy. Civil religion, through narrative and collective ritual experience, creates a moral and affective consensus for democratic participation.

In later works, Bellah expresses concern that the actual practice of civil religion in the US has diminished to the point where it no longer provides moral cohesion, and worries that individualism threatens to undermine the moral consensus for participation upon which American democracy is built (Bellah 1975). In *Habits of the Heart* (1985), Bellah and his colleagues conclude that an individualistic ethos cannot supply the moral cohesion needed for democracy, and relocates the affective and cognitive resources necessary for democratic participation back within institutional churches, especially liberal Protestant ones.

Building on Bellah's approach, Robert Wuthnow (1988) presents an alternative characterization of religion in the contemporary US. Wuthnow argues that, in contrast to the early twentieth-century US when religion was primarily allied with and supportive of the state, religion since the Second World War is increasingly politically polarized and often mobilized against government and other political actors. Brought about by post-war economic expansion and a strong and active state, and catalyzed by special purpose groups, the religious landscape in the contemporary US has been restructured: a cleavage between liberal and conservative religionists has replaced denominationalism as the primary source of identification and religio-political engagement.

The Parsons School also sought to elaborate aspects of Max Weber's sociology of religion, but their reception of it was rather unfortunate. As translator of Max Weber's *Protestant Ethic*, Talcott Parsons encouraged his students to look for its analogs all over the world. The idea was to identify carriers of inner-worldly asceticism, which would promote the passage of 'underdeveloped' societies into a Western type of modernity. This represents a rather peculiar reading of Weber. Weber was not an evolutionist thinker, but a historicist one; he placed no credence in stage theories of societal development, nor did he believe that social scientists could identify significant general 'laws' of social life. Moreover, this approach ignores Weber's very ambiguous judgment on Western modernity, and transforms it into an optimistic theory of modernization and progress. It also leaves aside Weber's analysis of the affinity between certain classes and status groups with particular types of religious plausibility structures. Accordingly, scholars using this approach identified such diverse classes as reform bureaucrats and the military as potential carriers of modernization, classes which have little to do with the attitudes Weber has ascribed to ascetic Protestantism. Nevertheless, the Parsons School has produced some impressive studies, most importantly Robert Bellah's (1957) *Tokugawa Religion* (see also Shmuel Eisenstadt 1968).

Collapsed canopies and various paths of secularization

Peter Berger's (1967) articulation of a theory of secularization represents an alternative school of thought. Berger claims that religion's power to shape social life has largely diminished in Western modernity because of institutional differentiation, the pluralization of worldviews, and a loss of plausibility structures. Berger grounds his theory in a phenomenological perspective, according to which religious worldviews provide shields from the chaotic, uncontrollable aspects of the world which humans inhabit. A religious worldview is reproduced through socialization; since it dominates the social contexts individuals are born into, they take it for granted and learn to interpret their experiences according to this cognitive structure. But religion can remain strong in societies only where it is supported by a dialectical, mutually sustaining, and mutually determining relationship with a social base or plausibility structure. Further, religion is at its strongest when it has a monopoly in a relatively stable society – when it comprises a 'sacred canopy' within which individuals understand and interpret their social existence, and where there is an absence of competing interpretations.

It follows from this characterization that secularization is an inevitable result of change within the economic and social contexts upon which religious worldviews depend. Secularization occurs when a religious worldview and the social reality no longer coincide because its plausibility structures erode, and a formerly monopolistic religious worldview becomes open to revision and a plurality of interpretations. Once the sacred canopy collapses, religion progressively loses its power to shape social life. Although Berger no longer holds these views, they represent his most influential contribution to the sociology of religion; they have had a major impact on scholars like Nancy T. Ammerman (1987) and James D. Hunter (1983).

Whereas Berger sees secularization as a necessary consequence of modernization on an abstract and general level, David Martin (1978) has focused on secularization from a concrete and historical, comparative institutional perspective. Rather sceptical about the concept of secularization, Martin shows in an admirable comparative study how secularization was conditioned by the character of religious institutions and their relationships to the state. Martin locates the occurrence of secularization at three different social levels of analysis: at the level of social institutions, at the level of belief, and at the level of a people's ethos. He then proposes an ideal-typical schema that classifies the characteristics of nation states along several dimensions, and uses this schema to show how variation in the historical position of religion during state formation, the level of pluralism, and the logics embedded within religions practiced in particular settings, together produce different patterns of secularization. Martin's work does not simply assume secularization as a fact, but shows how different historical conditions produce secularization at different levels of society. For example, historically France's religious monopoly was politically challenged by secular institutions, which led to a comprehensive victory of secularism. In contrast, the separation of church and state and the pluralistic organization of religion in the US prevented conflict at the political level, and therefore, secularization primarily occurred on the level of the religious ethos. Martin's work remains among the most sophisticated of empirical and theoretical studies of secularization.

Lively margins

Bryan R. Wilson's (1982) studies of sectarianism, executed mostly in the interpretive tradition of Weber, explore an important aspect of secularization theories: the marginalization of religion. Wilson understood the central institutions of modern Western societies to be thoroughly secularized, but demonstrated that religious belief and practice endure among socially marginalized groups. He theorized the distinctiveness of these sectarian forms of religious practice.

Wilson observes that, whereas many in modern societies neither believe nor practice religion and the behaviors of mainline church members are rarely driven by religiosity, within modern sects one can yet observe the powerful social consequences of religion in individual lives. Sects shape in their adherents undifferentiated religious identities, which spill over and suffuse the whole of their lives. For the socially marginalized – for example, for temporal or generational groups such as adolescents and young adults – sects offer reassurance and comfort in the form of salvation beliefs. And with strong ethical norms and distinctive styles of life, sects bring their converts into a social world in which they can perceive themselves as integral to a social group, and in which they are aided in reinterpreting painful experiences of marginality.

Consistent with secularization theory, sectarian religion is withdrawn from the public sphere; sectarians do not engage in public discourse and have little effect on society as a whole. While incorporating aspects of modernity's rational procedures in their organization and practices, they distinguish themselves from modern society by constituting themselves in opposition to it in their creation of undifferentiated identities and distinctive ways of life. It is Wilson's view that social conditions for sectarian adherence include not only social marginality in its modern forms, but also the prerequisite of the lack of previous religious socialization.

Other scholars have paid attention to religion on society's margins in studies of the emergence of new religious movements. Many recent religious movements of Asian origin, such as Hare Krishna, the Unification Church of Reverend Moon, and Soka Gakkai have been well studied, with several of these studies making important theoretical contributions to the study of religion, and especially to understanding conversion processes (Lofland and Stark 1965, 1985; Beckford 1976; Snow and Phillips 1980; Lofland and Skonovd 1983; Barker 1984; Snow and Machalek 1984; Snow 1993).

Privatization

Toward the end of the 1960s and through the 1970s, secularization theories further crystallized and affirmed the view that religious decline in the modern West would inevitably progress. Empirical evidence of secularization was abundant in religion's increasing loss of power within political and cultural institutions, as well as in declining church attendance and aging congregations in many of the countries of Europe. Religion no longer occupied a place at modern societies' centers, and scholars took for granted that this state of affairs was a necessary consequence of modernization. Even where churches thrived, as they did in the US, it seemed clear that much of this practice, especially within liberal churches, was not so much religiously as socially motivated, reflecting the internal secularization of religious institutions. For some scholars, however, this clear evidence of the decline of religion at the center of modern society propelled them to look for authentic religious expression in more hidden and less public arenas.

Thomas Luckmann's (1967) work was a harbinger of this turn: he proposed a theory of secularization as privatization which claimed that religion was not disappearing in modernity, but that its locus had shifted from the public sphere to the inner personal experience of individuals. In Luckmann's view, religion arises as a necessary part of the social-psychological, meaning-making process in which humans are individuated and selves created. Although religious institutions are historically common, it is not necessary that religion be institutionalized for it to endure. Rather, religion endures in human history because it is a constitutive element of the formation of selves; it is the anthropological conditions giving rise to religion that are indeed universal.

Luckmann describes the historical process of secularization in the West as a consequence of the endurance, growth, and internal workings of religious institutions. As churches grew, they developed secular interests and did not remain exclusively determined by their religious functions. Specialization within these institutions required that religious norms become differentiated from secular norms, and the disjuncture between the two generated inconsistencies between doctrine and its institutional expression. Therefore, where previously religion was merely taken for granted, people were given cause to reflect upon it. Human reflection thereby transformed religion into an increasingly subjective reality.

In this process, institutional religion became progressively emptied of meaning, and the erosion of public religion was replaced by its increased importance in the private sphere. In modern societies, then, religions exist in ever more privatized forms and their meanings become properties of individual selves, and thus 'invisible.' In this view, secularization is the process of religious institutions' decline, but religion still endures as its social locations shift. Therefore, the new locus of religion in modernity is individuals' inner lives, even if this inner experience is largely unavailable to empirical scrutiny.

Grace Davie (1994, 2000) has built on this perspective by analyzing the discrepancy between believing and belonging. She shows that the majority of Europeans, and the British in particular, are neither secular nor atheist. Quite the contrary, many do believe in a God or other higher powers, and membership in religious associations is rather high. It is Davie's view that it is not Europeans' religious believing, but only their relatively infrequent participation in religious practices compared to those in non-European countries, that has declined.

Danièle Hervieu-Léger (1999) has likewise focused on the endurance of religious belief in modernity as religion has become increasingly privatized – but interestingly, she attempts a middle way between functional and substantive definitions of religion such that she can both affirm the reality of 'invisible religions' and account for many empirical instances of apparent religious revitalization. She observes that, although religion has declined in modernity because of scientific rationality and the concomitant autonomy and importance accorded to the self, questions of meaning and desire for experiences of sacredness are still common among modern societies. Following the Weberian insight that religion is fundamentally transformed in modernity, she theorizes this transformation as one in modes of belief, thereby defining religion as a way of believing whose authority practitioners legitimize by appeal to a tradition in a 'chain of memory.' Although Hervieu-Léger's definition of religion is still quite broad, it allows her to helpfully distinguish modern effervescent expressions of sacredness, such as are found in sport, from instances of religiousness which, whether collective or privatized, constitutively involve people making use of narratives – often fragmentary ones, given the nature of high modernity – to connect their beliefs and practices to a lineage.

Inspired by Luckmann or perhaps by a partial appropriation of Durkheim, other sociologists have proposed an even broader understanding of religion in modernity, where nearly any form of self-transcendence may constitute 'religion,' from banal everyday activities to 'effervescent' social gatherings. In this view, even private hobbies, shopping in a supermarket, barbecues, or soccer games can be religious phenomena, with still other quotidian experiences and practices classified as implicitly or quasi- religious. This view reveals one of the primary problems in attempting to take functional definitions of religion to their logical conclusion.

Secularism, pluralism, and religious resurgence

By the late 1970s it had become apparent that a resurgence of religion was taking place globally, evident from the United States to the Middle East, from South Asia and Africa even to parts of Europe. A revitalization of religion was underway in the US, as new religious movements spread across the Bay area in California and conservative religious forces – Protestant, Catholic, Jewish, Mormon – got organized in order to be saved from the 1960s (Tipton 1982). At the same time, religious revivals were taking place across the globe: Islam returned as a public force in the Middle East and beyond, religion was playing a forceful role in the shaping of ethnic identities and the fueling of ethnic conflicts from India and Sri Lanka (Tambiah 1992, 1996) to the Sudan and Ireland, and religious movements challenged the secular state in several areas of the world (Juergensmeyer 1993). This overwhelming empirical evidence of religious resurgence in modernity challenged the old paradigm of the classics and their revisionist readings and new syntheses.

Structural conditions of secularization

In the wake of empirical evidence of religious revitalization, the problematic aspects of older secularization theories became the subject of increasing criticism, revision, and reformulation, resulting in a clearer definition of the conditions of secularization and an extended elaboration of secularization as a theory of social differentiation. Recognizing the empirical reality of religious resurgence, those working within secularization theory strove to theorize secularization in ways that did not entail its inevitability and irreversibility, and moved towards conceptualizations of secularization as an historical process to be located and explored.

Following upon Martin's groundbreaking study, scholars sought to elaborate and distinguish secularization at different levels of analysis and to systematize characteristics of secularization within a larger conceptual framework. Among those taking this synthetic approach, Karel Dobbelaere's (1981) work is perhaps the most comprehensive. Dobbelaere's argument for a multidimensional concept of secularization proposes that secularization be studied through the examination of interrelated processes at three different levels of analysis. Secularization can occur through laicization – the societal differentiation of religion from other social formations and institutions – through organizational religious change, such as may occur within denominations, and in the religious involvement of individuals. Dobbelaere suggests that the relations between secularizing tendencies at each of these three levels do not have determinate outcomes and should be empirically investigated in order to more clearly theorize them. Although Dobbelaere believes that secularization is a contingent process, not a necessary or irreversible one, his canvas of empirical studies led him to conclude that secularization is empirically, if not theoretically, linearly progressive in the modern West.

Dobbelaere's theory has been influential in recent years, especially among those interested in analyzing organizational religious change. His formulation has been used successfully to elaborate the occurrence of organization-level secularization in the US through analyses of denominational leadership (Chaves 1993). Unlike the earlier comprehensive narratives, the newer frameworks have allowed scholars to explore the structural conditions of secularization at various levels of analysis, and have the capacity to provide explanations for empirically specific instances of secularization in modern societies.

Homo religionomicus

Concurrent with work advancing secularization theory in the 1970s and 1980s, other scholars began a move towards its wholesale rejection, and reinterpreted evidence of varying levels of religious participation among nation states and across religious denominations under a utilitarian rubric. These mostly North American scholars have been led by Rodney Stark and William S. Bainbridge (1979), who first used rational choice principles to construct a theory of religion. Stark and Bainbridge begin with the utilitarian assumption that individuals act to attain preferred ends while minimizing costs in an environment of opportunities and constraints. But the benefits desired by individuals are sometimes unattainable, either because of their social structural contexts, or because of the physical human limitations imposed by illness, disability, and the inevitability of death. In these life situations, religious rewards – such as doctrines promising salvation and eternal life, or religious experiences providing comfort and emotional benefits – can be sought as substitutes. In this view then, religion is conceptualized as a system of compensators for benefits unattainable to individuals. And since the human condition is such that the need for compensators – especially as a substitute for the avoidance of death – does not change, demand for religion is understood as relatively constant.

Since individual preferences are left unproblematized and the demand for religious goods are assumed to be constant, the behavior of religious institutions, frequently theorized as following the laws of market dynamics, becomes a primary locus of investigation for those working within this school of thought. Some studies, such as Iannaccone's (1994) work on the vitality of strict churches, offer explanations for why particular religious organizations are especially attractive to seekers on the religious market. Others, like the historical study of church membership in the US by Finke and Stark (1992), focus on the market behavior of religious organizations, claiming that variations in religious practice should be understood primarily as supply side phenomena. In their view, the amount of freedom allowed in the market, the degree of regulation, and the resulting level of competition among religious organizations determine levels of religious vitality in a given society.

Rational choice theories of religion have gained broad currency among sociologists of religion in recent years. At the same time, this approach has provoked heated criticism (Chaves 1995; Ammerman 1998; Neitz and Mueser 1998; Bruce 1999), especially for its use of a utilitarian psychology, which long ago was demonstrated to be an inadequate theory of human motivations. These theories also have been criticized for their general disinterest in problematizing religious preferences, whose social constructedness is obviously of critical interest in explaining religiously motivated behavior; in particular Max Weber, and subsequent scholars working within the framework of his sociology of religion, have emphasized the ways in which religions can shape and change people's preferences.

A related recent development within sociology of religion in the US is the appropriation of the economic metaphor, combined with a functionalist perspective, as the ground of a 'new paradigm' for the study of religion (Warner 1993). Scholars working within this perspective reject the idea that the US has undergone secularization over time, claiming instead that the disestablishment of religion in the US is causally related to high rates of church attendance and other forms of religious vitality. This new approach has fuelled a lively debate around the hypothesis that religious pluralism causes higher levels of religious practice than monopolistic situations – a debate that has rested in large part upon the technical evaluation of statistical evidence supporting the hypothesis (Land *et al.* 1991; Olson 1999; Voas *et al.* 2002). And in fact, empirical evidence from countries like Ireland, Poland, and Iran suggests that accounting for religious vitality requires a more complex explanation than internal religious pluralism.

Deprivatization and the resurgence of religion

Global evidence of religious resurgence has also been studied with particular attention to politics (Casanova 1994), ethnicity and nationalism (Juergensmeyer 2003; Zubrzycki 2006; Lybarger 2007), and the construction of gendered identities (Stacey 1990; Gallagher 2003; Chong 2008). This strand of research has yielded some interesting empirical studies and promising theoretical developments.

James Beckford has done important work directing attention to the re-emergence of religion in the public sphere, examining not longstanding churches, but rather the endurance of sects (Beckford 1975) and the emergence of new religious movements (Beckford 1985). His work is characterized by a careful evaluation of the limits of theories of religion. Beckford (1989) argues that the categories and distinctions used, the questions asked and the conclusions reached by Durkheim, Marx, Weber, and their descendants were profoundly shaped by the context of emergent industrial capitalism. The progression of industrial capitalism and the diminution of power and influence of old religious institutions are linked empirically in this historical period, and also are linked philosophically in the tradition of liberal thought. And while the present context of late industrial capitalism is both continuous with and distinguishable from that earlier variant, its discontinuous characteristics are critical for understanding religion in the present historical period. The analysis of religion in late industrial societies, therefore, must decisively move beyond conceptualizations of religion that emphasize its capacity to create values and socialize individuals and focus instead upon secularization and religion's marginality.

Beckford pays particular attention to the social structural features of advanced industrial capitalism that differ from its earlier historical form, and to emergent forms of religion in the modern West. The new sociological significance of religion, according to Beckford, includes its capacity to present the perception of new social realities in symbolic forms, and the potential of religion as a tool of mobilization against political establishments. He predicts that, in late industrial societies, the use of religious symbols is likely to be contested and controversial, since religion is no longer exclusively the domain of long enduring social institutions. Religion, then, often will be put to work outside the framework of religious organizations and state relations. He argues that the analysis of religion in contemporary societies will be most fruitful when religion is conceptualized not as a social institution, but as a cultural form or resource. Beckford's studies of new religious movements support and inform this perspective. Though new religious movements are very small in terms of the numbers of people who are shaped by them, and their ability to influence political actors is negligible, they have yet created a disproportionate amount of public controversy. Analysis of this public controversy draws attention to the way in which new religious forms in late industrial societies can serve as a barometer of issues of value and concern to broader segments of these societies.

Beckford has more recently explored related aspects of contemporary religion's marginality and capacity for public controversy in a study of religion in UK prisons (Beckford and Gilliat 1998). Interestingly, this research examines the power and roles of Church of England chaplains as they broker chaplaincy for the growing numbers of Buddhists, Hindus, Jews, Muslims, and Sikhs in these prisons. The study presents an extreme case of the more general problems of religious inequality in a society where swiftly increasing religious diversity exists alongside of a powerful but increasingly irrelevant established church.

José Casanova (1994) likewise examines the re-emergence of religion, concentrating not on marginalized religion but instead on the recent activities of churches in the public sphere. He interprets the re-emergence of religion in the public sphere as a reverse movement, or deprivatization, of the historical pattern of secularization in the modern West. Like David Martin and Karel Dobbelaere, Casanova problematizes the concept of secularization, but moves beyond other theories by rearticulating secularization in such a way as to account for the re-emergence of religion in the public sphere.

In his critical review of secularization theories, Casanova distinguishes between a central thesis – secularization as one instance of differentiation processes defining and driving modernization – and two subtheses – the decline of religion, and its privatization. He argues that, while secularization as differentiation is structurally bound to modernization, religious decline and privatization are historically contingent processes. Religious privatization is historically common because of religion's internal workings, the influence of liberalism, and external constraints upon religion brought about through the process of differentiation. But religion also can be deprivatized, as he shows in case studies including the liberation theology movement in Brazil, Catholicism in Poland during the rise of Solidarity, the public pronouncements of American Catholic bishops in the 1980s, and US Protestant fundamentalist activities in the political sphere. Interrogating the public–private distinction through these cases, Casanova theorizes the deprivatization of modern religion and convincingly shows that secularization is not only *not* a structurally inevitable consequence of modernity, but also one whose reversibility can be theoretically understood.

Steve Bruce and Martin Riesebrodt also have studied religious resurgence, directing their attention mostly at conservative and fundamentalist forms of religious revival. In analyses of Ulster Protestantism, Bruce shows how religion was historically important in the creation of politically mobilized ethnic identities, and how religion continues to play a vigorous role in shaping the ways in which Protestants and Catholics perceive their positions within society. He elaborates the attraction of evangelical Protestantism and its agenda among non-evangelicals as an aspect of ethnic identity, and shows how these religio-ethnic identities are sustained through continued conflict in Northern Ireland (Bruce 1992, 1994). And Martin Riesebrodt (1993), in his cross-culturally comparative study of the emergence of Protestant fundamentalism in the US and Shi'ite fundamentalism in Iran, has conceptualized fundamentalism as a specific type of social movement. He argues that a central feature of fundamentalist movements across traditions consist in their emphasis on patriarchal structures of authority and social morality, with the strict control of the female body often perceived to be the solution to the problems of modernity. Riesebrodt claims that issues of patriarchal authority and morality are not just symbolizations of other, 'real' problems, but of central concern. However, because of their centrality, they also often come to symbolize the general protest against dramatic social change, marginalization, disappointed expectations of upward social mobility, and fears and experiences of downward mobility.

Explorations of religious resurgence have included a number of studies of the success of mostly charismatic forms of Christianity in non-Western countries. It is again David Martin who set the example, with his groundbreaking comparative study of the global spread of charismatic Protestantism (Martin 1990). In this work he also draws an interesting historical parallel to the rise of Methodism in England during the Industrial Revolution.

Recent work on the re-emergence of religion as a social force has also included a new emphasis on religion and gender. This body of work includes work both by sociologists and anthropologists and traverses a broad range of topics from women's religious participation and the construction of gendered identities (Stacey 1990; Davidman 1991; Konieczny 2005), to the study of organizational processes surrounding denominations' ordination of women ministers (Chaves 1997; Nesbitt 1997), to some very sophisticated theoretical work on Latin American men's conversion to Evangelicalism (Smilde 2007).

Perhaps the most promising studies executed under this broad rubric investigate modern women's adherence to conservative, evangelical, and fundamentalist religious groups articulating patriarchal gender ideologies (Kaufman 1991; Griffith 1997; Gallagher 2003). Moving beyond explanations that view these women as passive victims of male domination or false consciousness, they explore women's active roles in the appropriation and transformation of traditionalist forms of religion that, from a progressive Western point of view, are contrary to their real interests. They argue that participation in traditionalist religious associations often enables women to restructure and remoralize domestic social relations. These studies also make it clear that these women live under conditions in which gender equality does not present itself as a realistic option. However, not all studies agree with this rather benign view of religious traditionalism's effect on women and argue that, in cases where patriarchal structures of authority have not yet broken down, they tend to reinforce female submission under patriarchal authority (Chong 2008).

Sociology of religion's future

As we have seen, sociology's founding fathers have written some of their most important studies on religion, and several generations of scholars have made their living off the classics' theoretical capital. At the same time, the sociology of religion has become a rather marginal field within sociology. Since it predicted the decline of its object of study, scholars understandably doubted its significance. With the global resurgence of religion, however, the sociology of religion not only seems to have a future – it also has a responsibility to make attempts at cognitively ordering and explaining the role religion plays in our present world. In order to live up to this responsibility several steps seem advisable.

First of all, a thorough revision of its theoretical perspectives is urgently needed. On the one hand, the resurgence of religious movements and personal piety on a global scale has shed serious doubt on the secularization thesis, which has strongly shaped most previous sociological theories of religion. On the other hand one cannot deny that secularization, as a process of institutional differentiation, has actually taken place. Modern states are widely secular, and neither capitalism and bureaucracy, nor modern science and modern culture, are based on religious principles; at times they are not even compatible with them. At the same time, almost no society has consistently separated church and state, especially not European ones. Privileged churches still exist in many European countries; for example, state universities entertain Protestant and Catholic theology departments where appointments have to be approved by the churches, and the German state collects taxes for all large religious denominations. Obviously, even institutional differentiation is rather incomplete.

But the problem with secularization theories runs deeper. Secularization is an overly complex concept based on problematic assumptions about causal connections between three processes: institutional differentiation, disenchantment, and privatization. Secularization theorists have long assumed that these three processes are expressions of one underlying grand, linear historical process. However, it seems increasingly obvious that there is no one metaphysical process of 'secularization;' rather, there exist historical trends towards institutional differentiation and de-differentiation, disenchantment and re-enchantment, and privatization and de-privatization. The sociology of religion must come to grips with these seemingly contradictory trends and revise its theoretical frame to better explain whether and how these processes are interrelated (Riesebrodt 2003, 2008).

Although the secularization debate has long dominated theoretical debates in the sociology of religion, it is worth emphasizing that theories of religion are more than theories of secularization. Functional definitions and explanations of religion have not contributed much to the understanding of religion in the contemporary world, since they diffuse the object of study and lack specificity in their explanation; religions cannot be adequately understood or explained when seen as a reflection of other, 'real' interests, or studied only in terms of the unintended consequences they produce. Rather, their existence should be understood, first of all, for their own sake. And it is important to emphasize that religions' actual effects often have been demonstrated to be by no means identical with the supposed functions that functionalist theories claim. Riesebrodt (2007, 2008) has therefore proposed an interpretative theory of religion which focuses on religious practices, and meanings institutionalized in 'liturgies.'

The sociology of religion, moreover, should attempt to account for the subjective side of religion as well as its objective side, analyzing and theorizing the individual religious actor along with the institutional order. With regard to the subjective side of religion, sociology should resist utilitarian simplifications in the explanation of social action. In their intentions and effects, religious practices – like those in other spheres – are neither exclusively rational and instrumental, nor exclusively irrational, but more often than not follow cultural patterns and social expectations. Therefore, the rational choice model, which assumes a rarely existing ideal market situation where individuals act consistently according to the results of cost-benefit analyses, turns out to be either tautological or empirically false. Moreover, since rational calculation is usually not a pleasurable task, but often a rather painful one, people should not even be expected to rationally calculate unless the possible gain outweighs the pain of calculating. Ultimately, the rational choice model might be most useful for religious market research where relatively exclusive voluntary associations actually compete for the same customers.

Second, the sociology of religion must overcome its rampant parochialism. It must move beyond theoretical paradigms that work just for one 'exceptional' country, or a particular group of Western nations or religious traditions. There is at present a pervasive tendency in the sociology of religion for scholars to limit their studies either to their country of citizenship or to the religious tradition of their own affiliation – except for Islam, ironically, in which case almost anybody seems to claim competency. This provincialism must be overcome.

And while the great majority of sociologists of religion have studied their own backyard, they have left the study of religion in non-Western countries mostly to scholars in disciplines outside sociology. With few exceptions, cross-culturally comparative work is absent from the sociology of religion. For example, the roles played by religion in colonial and post-colonial situations and in processes of globalization have become the domain of anthropologists and historians of religion, not sociologists. Sociology, whose founders' legacies and contemporary subdisciplinary diversity includes ample theoretical resources for the study of religion's relation to such processes and situations, should take its distinctive place in the development of knowledge in these areas.

The sociology of religion would be well advised to leave the tiring debate on secularization behind, and turn instead to contemporary issues of real concern. Religion and gender has been studied empirically, but there is still plenty of theoretical work to do. In addition, important new topics of study have emerged or reappeared, such as religion and the legitimation of violence against oneself and others (Hall 2000; Juergensmeyer 2000), the impact of new technologies on the forms and spread of religion, and the globalization of religion (Beyer 2006). Such investigations promise to contribute to realizing the foundational objectives and intellectual promise of the sociological study of religion. A good example is Peter Beyer's theory of religion in a globalizing world (Beyer 2006). Drawing upon Niklas Luhmann (1984/1995), Beyer's conceptualization of religion as a functional system of communication (one system among others including law, politics, science, art, and sport) is able to account for the diverse expressions and structures of religion in the contemporary world, as well as the very existence of this heterogeneity. His approach provides insight into the reasons for some of the enduring difficulties that have stymied previous debates concerning the nature and endurance of religion in modernity, and accounts for religion's frequently contested and ambiguous nature in historical conditions of globalization. Beyer's study is one example of how the sociological study of religion can be revitalized through the serious theoretical exploration of urgent contemporary questions.

In order to live up to its responsibility to cognitively order and explain the world we live in to the best of its abilities, the sociology of religion must eschew parochialism, broaden its perspective, and revisit its theories in light of these global historical processes and contemporary events. The sociology of religion needs to become once again a theoretically sophisticated, empirically grounded, universal social science; otherwise, it will be superfluous.

Bibliography

Ammerman, Nancy T. 1987. *Bible Believers: Fundamentalists in the Modern World*. New Brunswick, NJ: Rutgers University Press.

—— 1998. 'Religious Choice and Religious Vitality: The Market and Beyond.' In Lawrence A. Young, (ed.) 1998: 119–32.

Barker, Eileen. 1984. *The Making of a Moonie: Choice or Brainwashing?* New York: Oxford.

Beckford, James. 1975. *The Trumpet of Prophecy: A Sociological Study of Jehovah's Witnesses*. New York: John Wiley & Sons.

—— 1976. 'Accounting For Conversion.' *British Journal of Sociology* 29 (1978): 249–62.

—— 1985. *Cult Controversies: The Societal Response to New Religious Movements*. London and New York: Tavistock.

—— 1989. *Religion and Advanced Industrial Society*. London: Unwin Hyman.

Beckford, James and Sophie Gilliat. 2005. *Religion in Prison: 'Equal Rites' in a Multi-Faith Society*. Cambridge: Cambridge University Press.

Bellah, Robert N. 1957. *Tokugawa Religion*. New York: Free Press.

—— 1970. *Beyond Belief*. New York: Harper & Row.

—— 1975. *The Broken Covenant*. New York: Seabury Press.

—— Richard Madsen, William M. Sullivan, Ann Swidler and Steven M. Tipton. 1985. *Habits of the Heart: Individualism and Commitment in American Life*. Berkeley: University of California Press.

Berger, Peter. 1967. *The Sacred Canopy: Elements of a Sociological Theory of Religion*. Garden City, NY: Doubleday.

Beyer, Peter. 2006. *Religion in Global Society*. New York: Routledge.

Bruce, Steve. 1992. *The Red Hand: Protestant Paramilitaries in Northern Ireland*. Oxford and New York: Oxford University Press.

—— 1994. *The Edge of the Union: The Ulster Loyalist Political Vision*. Oxford: Oxford University Press.

—— 1999. *Choice and Religion: A Critique of Rational Choice Theory*. Oxford and New York: Oxford University Press.

Casanova, José. 1994. *Public Religions in the Modern World*. Chicago: University of Chicago Press.

Chaves, Mark. 1993. 'Intraorganizational Power and Internal Secularization in Protestant Denominations.' *American Journal of Sociology* 99(1): 1–48.

—— 1995. 'On the Rational Choice Approach to Religion.' *Journal for the Scientific Study of Religion* 34(1): 98–104.

—— 1997. *Ordaining Women: Culture and Conflict in Religious Organizations*. London: Harvard University Press.

Chong, Kelly H. 2008. *Deliverance and Submission: Evangelical Women and the Negotiation of Patriarchy in South Korea*. Boston: Harvard University Press.

Comaroff, Jean and John Comaroff. 1991. *Of Revelation and Revolution: Christianity, Colonialism and Consciousness in South Africa*. Chicago: University of Chicago Press.

Comaroff, John and Jean Comaroff. 1995. *Of Revelation and Revolution: The Dialectics of Modernity on a South African Frontier*. Chicago: University of Chicago Press.

Davidman, Lynn. 1991. *Tradition in a Rootless World*. Berkeley and Los Angeles: University of California Press.

Davie, Grace. 1994. *Religion in Britain since 1945*. Oxford: Blackwell.

—— 2000. *Religion in Modern Europe*. Oxford: Oxford University Press.

Dobbelaere, Karel. 1981. 'Secularization: A Multidimensional Concept.' *Current Sociology* 29: 1–216.

Durkheim, Émile. 1912/1995. *The Elementary Forms of the Religious Life*. Translated by Karen Fields. New York: Free Press.

—— 1914/1960. 'The Dualism of Human Nature.' In Kurt H. Wolff (ed.) *Émile Durkheim, 1858–1917: A Collection of Essays*. Columbus: Ohio State University 1960: 325–40.

Eisenstadt, Shmuel N. (ed.) 1968. *The Protestant Ethic and Modernization. A Comparative View*. New York: Basic Books.

Finke, Roger and Rodney Stark. 1992. *The Churching of America, 1776–1990: Winners and Losers in Our Religious Economy*. New Brunswick, NJ: Rutgers University Press.

Gallagher, Sally. 2003. *Evangelical Identity and Gendered Family Life*. New Brunswick, NJ: Rutgers University Press.

Griffith, R. M. 1997. *God's Daughters: Evangelical Women and the Power of Submission*. Berkeley and London: University of California Press.

Hall, John R. 2000. *Apocalypse Observed*. London and New York: Routledge.

Hervieu-Léger, Danièle. 2000. *Religion as a Chain of Memory*. New Brunswick, NJ: Rutgers University Press.

Hunter, James D. 1983. *American Evangelicalism: Conservative Religion and the Quandary of Modernity*. New Brunswick, NJ: Rutgers University Press.

Iannaccone, Laurence. 1994. 'Why Strict Churches are Strong.' *American Journal of Sociology* 99(5): 1180–211.

Juergensmeyer, Mark. 1993. *The New Cold War? Religious Nationalism Confronts the Secular State.* Berkeley: University of California Press.

—— 2000. *Terror in the Mind of God.* University of California Press.

Kaufman, D.R. 1991. *Rachel's Daughters: Newly Orthodox Jewish Women.* New Brunswick, NJ: Rutgers University Press.

Konieczny, Mary Ellen. 2005. *The Spirit's Tether: Orthodoxy, Liberalism and Family Among American Catholics.* University of Chicago Ph.D. Dissertation.

Land, Kenneth C., Glenn Deane and Judith Blau. 1991. 'Religious Pluralism and Church Membership: A Spatial Diffusion Model.' *American Sociological Review* 56(April): 237–49.

Lofland, John and Rodney Stark. 1965. 'Becoming a world-saver: a theory of conversion to a deviant perspective.' *American Sociological Review* 30, no. 6: 862–75.

Lofland, John and Norman Skonovd. 1983. 'Patterns of Conversion.' In Eileen Barker, (ed.) *Of Gods and Men.* Macon, GA: Mercer University Press, pp. 1–24.

Luckmann, Thomas. 1967. *The Invisible Religion.* New York: Macmillan.

Luhmann, Niklas. 1984/1995. *Social Systems.* Translated by John Bednarz, Jr. with Dirk Baecker. Stanford, CA: Stanford University Press.

Lybarger, Loren. 2007. *Religion and Identity in Palestine.* Princeton, NJ: Princeton University Press.

Martin, David. 1978. *A General Theory of Secularization.* Oxford: Blackwell.

—— 1990. *Tongues of Fire: The Explosion of Protestantism in Latin America.* London: Blackwell.

Neitz, Mary Jo. 1987. *Charisma and Community.* New Brunswick, NJ: Transaction Press.

—— and Peter R. Mueser. 1998. 'Economic Man and the Sociology of Religion: A Critique of the Rational Choice Approach.' In Lawrence A. Young (ed.) 1998: 105–18.

Nesbitt, Paula. 1997. *Feminization of the Clergy in America.* New York and Oxford: Oxford University Press.

Olson, Daniel V. 1999. 'Religious Pluralism and US Church Membership: A Reassessment.' *Sociology of Religion* 60: 149–74.

Parsons, Talcott. 1963. 'Christianity and Modern Industrial Society.' In E. Tiryakian (ed.) *Sociological Theory, Values, and Sociocultural Change.* New York: The Free Press, pp. 13–70.

Riesebrodt, Martin. 1993. *Pious Passion: The Emergence of Fundamentalism in the United States and Iran.* Berkeley: University of California Press.

—— 2003. 'Religion in Global Perspective.' In Mark Juergensmeyer (ed.) *Global Religions: A Handbook.* Oxford: Oxford University Press.

—— 2007. *Cultus und Heilsversprechen. Eine Theorie der Religionen.* Muenchen: C.H. Beck (English translation forthcoming, University of Chicago Press 2009).

—— 2008. 'Theses on a Theory of Religion.' *International Political Anthropology* 1 (no. 1): 25–41.

Smilde, David. 2007. *Reason to Believe: Cultural Agency in Latin American Evangelicalism.* Berkeley: University of California Press.

Snow, David A. 1993. *Shakubuku: A Study of the Nichiren Shoshu Buddhist Movement in America, 1960– 1975.* New York: Garland Press.

Snow, David and Cynthia Phillips. 'The Lofland-Stark Conversion Model: A Critical Reassessment.' *Social Problems* 27 (1980): 430–47.

Snow, David A. and Richard Machalek. 'The sociology of conversion.' *Annual Review of Sociology* 10 (1984): 167–90.

Stacey, Judith. 1990. *Brave New Families: Stories of Domestic Upheaval in Late Twentieth Century America.* New York: Basic Books.

Stark, Rodney and William Sims Bainbridge. 1979. *A Theory of Religion.* New York: P. Lang.

Swatos, William H., Jr (ed.) 1999. 'The Secularization Debate'. Special Issue of *Sociology of Religion*, Vol. 60, No. 3, Fall 1999.

Tambiah, Stanley J. 1992. *Buddhism Betrayed? Religion, Politics and Violence in Sri Lanka*. Chicago: University of Chicago Press.

—— 1996. *Leveling Crowds: Ethnonationalist Conflicts and Collective Violence in South Asia*. Berkeley: University of California Press.

Tipton, Steven. 1982. *Getting Saved from the Sixties: Moral Meaning in Conversion and Cultural Change*. Berkeley: University of California Press.

Tucker, Robert C. (ed.) 1978. *Marx-Engels Reader*. London: W.W. Norton.

Voas, David, Daniel V.A. Olson and Alasdair Crockett. 2002. 'Religious Pluralism and Participation: Why Previous Research is Wrong.' *American Sociological Review* 67: 212–30.

Warner, R. Stephen. 1993. 'Work in Progress Toward a New Paradigm of the Sociological Study of Religion in the United States.' *American Journal of Sociology* 98(5): 1044–93.

Weber, Max. 1904/1958. *The Protestant Ethic and the Spirit of Capitalism*. Translated by Talcott Parsons. London: Allen and Unwin.

—— 1920/1951. *The Religion of China: Confucianism and Taoism*. Translated and edited by Hans H. Gerth. New York: Free Press.

—— 1920/1958. *The Religion of India: The Sociology of Hinduism and Buddhism*. Translated and edited by Hans H. Gerth and Don Martindale. New York: Free Press.

—— 1922/1993. *The Sociology of Religion*. Boston: Beacon Press.

—— 1946. *From Max Weber: Essays in Sociology* (ed.) Hans H. Gerth and C. Wright Mills. New York: Oxford University Press.

Wilson, Bryan R. 1982. *Religion in Sociological Perspective*. New York: Oxford University Press.

—— 1990. *The Social Dimensions of Sectarianism: Sects and New Religious Movements in Contemporary Society*. Oxford: Clarendon Press.

Wuthnow, Robert. 1988. *The Restructuring of American Religion*. Princeton, NJ: Princeton University Press.

Young, Lawrence A. (ed.) 1998. *Rational Choice Theory and Religion: Summary and Assessment*. New York: Routledge.

Zubrzycki, Genevieve. 2006. *The Crosses of Auschwitz: Nationalism and Religion in Post-Communist Poland*. Chicago: University of Chicago Press.

Suggested reading

Beckford, James A. 1989. *Religion and Advanced Industrial Society*. London: Unwin Hyman.
 In this book, Beckford argues that the significance of religion in advanced industrial society is conditioned by secularization and religion's marginality. Among religion's most distinctive features in the contemporary West are its status as a site of contest and controversy, its capacity to express people's perceptions of new social realities symbolically, and its potential as a tool of mobilization against political establishments.

Beyer, Peter. 2006. *Religion in Global Society*. New York: Routledge.
 Beyer elaborates a theory of religion and globalization. In describing religion in globalizing world as a functional system of communication existing along other systems, such as law, politics, and science, Beyer accounts for the multitude of practices and worldviews and the frequent ambiguity and conflict that comprise contemporary religion.

Casanova, José. 1994. *Public Religions in the Modern World*. Chicago: University of Chicago Press.
 Casanova's project is to theoretically account for both secularization and the resurgence of religion in modernity. He argues that although some aspects of secularization are a structural consequence of modernity, religious decline and privatization are historically contingent processes. Religion, therefore, can be deprivatized; Casanova explores this re-emergence of religion in the public sphere in cases including the liberation theology movement in Brazil and Catholicism in Poland during the rise of Solidarity.

Hervieu-Léger, Danièle. 2000. *Religion as a Chain of Memory*. New Brunswick, NJ: Rutgers University Press.

Hervieu-Leger argues that although religion has declined in modernity because of science and the importance of personal autonomy, questions of meaning and desires for the experience of the sacred are common in modern societies. She theorizes religion in modern life as a way of believing whose appeal to authority is grounded in a tradition through a 'chain of memory.'

Martin, David. 1978. *A General Theory of Secularization*. Oxford: Blackwell.

Martin presents a comparative-historical and institutional theory of secularization, locating the occurrence of secularization at three levels of analysis: at the social institutional level, at the level of religious belief, and in a people's ethos. Through a comparative analysis of nations, Martin shows how secularization is conditioned by the character of religious institutions and their relation to the state.

Riesebrodt, Martin. 2008. 'Theses on a Theory of Religion.' *International Political Anthropology* 1 (no.1): 25–41.

In this short version of his book *Cultus und Heilsversprechen* (2007), Martin Riesebrodt proposes an interpretative theory of religion which focuses on religious practices and their meanings as institutionalized in 'liturgies.' He also argues that the concept of secularization needs to be disaggregated and analyzed in terms of three relatively independent and contradictory processes of institutional differentiation (and de-differentiation), disenchantment (and re-enchantment), and privatization (and de-privatization) of religion.

Stark, Rodney and William Sims Bainbridge. 1979. *A Theory of Religion*. New York: P. Lang.

Stark and Bainbridge present a deductive theory of religion constructed on rational choice principles, beginning with the utilitarian assumption that people's actions can be understood as choices made by weighing their options in terms of costs and benefits. Religion in this theory is presented as a system of 'compensators' for benefits that, for social or other reasons, are unattainable to individuals.

Chapter 10

Anthropology of religion

Rosalind I. J. Hackett

The (sub-)field of enquiry known as anthropology of religion has been enjoying some long overdue renewal and recognition over the last decade or so, with the development of new texts and research areas, and new communities of scholars.[1] This renewal of interest is related in part to the growing salience of religion on the world stage, not least as a marker of identity and source of conflict at the local, translocal, and transnational levels. This in turn has generated a greater need for those with specialized knowledge of religious actors and formations in diverse and changing contexts.

The scholarship of today, whether conducted by anthropologists who specialize in religion (e.g. Glazier 1999; Lambek 1993; Coleman 2000), or scholars of religion who employ anthropological theory and method (e.g. Brown 1991; Johnson 2002b; Geertz 2003), has come a long way from those early landmark texts of E. E. Evans-Pritchard on *Witchcraft, Magic and Oracles among the Azande* (1937) and *Nuer Religion* (1974 [1956]), and Émile Durkheim's *The Elementary Forms of the Religious Life* (1912). The new look anthropology of religion can be traced to three general factors: first, the changing nature and location of the subject matter (e.g. movement of peoples, influence of mass-mediated religion, and market forces); second, greater inter-disciplinarity among academic disciplines; and third, the critical insights derived from post-colonialism, post-structuralism, and postmodernism.[2] In particular, the once discernible distinction between ethnography (empirical research on particular cultures/peoples/regions conducted through fieldwork and participant observation), and more generalized, theoretical reflection (anthropology or ethnology), is now blurred. Some would attribute this merging of the empirical, and cross-cultural, comparative approaches to the work of Clifford Geertz whose body of writings has been influential far beyond the bounds of traditional anthropology.

As a way of offsetting the current difficulties of delineating academic boundaries due to the shared body of social and cultural theory, and the growing diversification of 'topics' or 'sub-fields,' Henrietta Moore argues that it is to the history of a discipline that we should look for its defining characteristics, rather than specific objects of inquiry (1999: 2). Similarly, many scholars consider that it is now more appropriate to treat 'religion,' 'politics,' and 'economics' as pervasive rather than bounded categories (see, e.g. Herzfeld 2001: xi). Thus, it will behove us to trace briefly some of the roads traveled by anthropologists since the nineteenth century, in their quest to identify and interpret religious ideas, symbols, and practice. This will provide the backdrop needed to consider some of the more promising current and future developments in anthropological approaches to religion. A comprehensive, representative synthesis of the 'master narratives,' (Moore 1999: 10) as well as the conceptual basics of the anthropology of religion is not feasible in the present context, so the emphasis is more on salient highlights, updates, and productive areas of debate. More extensive overviews and resources are available in the various texts/ textbooks, and readers on the subject.[3]

Pioneering the discipline

Anthropology enjoys an ongoing dialectical tension between its scientific and humanistic sides. This is well characterized by James Peacock in his valuable introductory text on the anthropological enterprise: 'Emphasis on culture and recognition of the subjective aspect of interpretation link anthropology to the humanities, yet its striving for systematization, generalization, and precise observation reflects the inspiration of the sciences' (1986: 92). When Sir Edward Tylor (1832–1917) was appointed to the first chair in anthropology in Britain (in the United States, Franz Boas [1858–1942] is regarded as the founding father of cultural anthropology), the field was then described as the 'science of man.' Influenced by the rationalist and evolutionist views of the nineteenth century, Tylor speculated that humans developed the idea of a soul, and from that, spirits, who might also inhabit natural phenomena, in their attempt to rationalize mysterious experiences such as dreams, trances, and hallucinations (1970 [1871]). He postulated that this early human belief, which he termed animism, eventually gave way to polytheism and monotheism, although traces of spiritualism persisted in beliefs such as reincarnation and immortality of the soul.

French sociologist Emile Durkheim saw religious beliefs and concepts as the product of particular social conditions, rather than in intellectualist terms. In his classic work, *Les Formes Elémentaires de la Vie Religieuse* (Durkheim 1965 [1912]), he argued that religion, predicated on a distinction between the sacred and the profane, was an essentially social phenomenon. Like many of the pioneering functionalist and evolutionist scholars, he turned to what he perceived to be some of the earliest and most elemental forms of religion, namely the totemic beliefs of the hunting and gathering Australian Aborigines. He argued that totemic symbols were mystically charged emblems of group loyalties, and that ritual expressed and strengthened the social organism. In fact, the 'collective effervescence' experienced at these ritual events was, he proposed, at the heart of the religious impulse. Durkheim's insistence on the holistic approach was critiqued by I. M. Lewis, who viewed it as a type of 'social determinism' that trumped any 'historical determinism' or questions about the origins of social institutions (1976: 52). It did, however, constitute a significant advance over the decontextualized, comparative approach of Sir James Frazer, in his landmark study of ritual and magic from classic texts around the world, *The Golden Bough* (1996 [1890]). Frazer believed there was an evolution in the ways in which people made sense of, and tried to control, their worlds, from magic, through religion, to science.

Frazer's lack of recognition of the scientific knowledge of 'primitive humanity' was roundly criticized by subsequent scholars. For example, Mary Douglas argued that the primitive worldview was not compartmentalized, but far more integrated and holistic than modern thought (Douglas 1975). Moreover, Bronislaw Malinowski (1884–1942) challenged the 'armchair anthropology' of Frazer and other scholars of the time and became, in I. M. Lewis' words, 'the pioneer, bush-whacking anthropologist' who turned fieldwork in exotic cultures into a doctrine and tenet of professionalism (Lewis 1976: 55–56). Based on the two years that he spent among the Trobriand Islanders in the Pacific, Malinowski explained religion and science in light of his functionalist theory of human needs (1954 [1925]). Magical rituals were performed when the situation was dangerous and unpredictable, such as fishing at sea, while religious rituals offered psychological assurance in the face of death.

Malinowski's contemporary A. R. Radcliffe-Brown (1881–1955) was more theoretically inclined and he developed the idea of 'structural-functionalism' (1952). From his viewpoint, social life was predicated on an orderly, organized foundation, and social organizations functioned in order to sustain social solidarity. His work spawned a whole generation of scholars. Drawing more on structural linguistics, French scholar Claude Lévi-Strauss (1963) promoted the idea of structures or patterns of culture existing at various levels of consciousness. These structures have functional significance, serving to resolve contradictions and binary oppositions in human life (Lewis 1976: 65–66). Later scholars, such as Luc de Heusch, have adapted structuralist principles to the complexities of religion elsewhere in the world (Heusch 1982).

With E. E. Evans-Pritchard's still influential work on the thought of the Azande people of central Africa came a shift in focus from that of 'structure' to that of 'meaning' (Evans-Pritchard 1937). He was particularly interested in how their beliefs in witchcraft, oracles, and magic translated into the actions of their everyday lives and social relations. His study raised important questions about rationality and cultural translation, subsequently generating a body of literature on the similarities or differences between unfalsifiable, so-called primitive belief systems and supposedly rational scientific worldviews (see Gellner 1999: 29). Some of this discussion centered on the rationality of millenarian movements such as the 'cargo cults' of the Pacific region, in achieving political ends (Worsley 1968; Lattas 1998). Rodney Needham questioned the use of the term 'belief' in many non-Western cultures (Needham 1972). He preferred the notion of 'idea,' since it conveyed the embedded aspect of cosmologies, and did not connote distance between 'observers' and 'informants.'

The intellectualist interpretation was given a new lease of life with Robin Horton's classic, and much debated, article, 'African traditional thought and Western science' (Horton 1993). In it he demonstrates the ways in which traditional African cultures and Western cultures both seek to explain, predict and control events. In addition to the continuities, he argues that the former thought-system is more closed than the latter. Ultimately, Horton's intellectualism and Malinowski's functionalism were more positive about the role of religion than French philosopher Lucien Lévy-Bruhl, who contended that the thought of primitive people was pre-logical, as it did not distinguish between cause and effect.

From modes of thought to modes of practice

Viewing cosmologies as resources for, rather than determinants of, action can help lessen the persistence of evolutionist or binary thinking, argues Michael Herzfeld (2001: 192f.). It may also undermine the tendency to treat cosmologies in isolation, along with 'religion.' He advocates greater recognition of the role of choice and agency in how people (whether 'primitives,' ethnographers, or scientists) organize their ideas about the universe. Addressing the question of myth, Herzfeld is troubled by the ongoing distinction between mythical and historical narratives, as held by Mircea Eliade and Claude Lévi-Strauss among others, as it leads to larger social distinctions between primitive or archaic and modern, and literate and non-literate societies. It also fails to recognize the ideological manipulation in both, as in nationalist myths of origin. So, while drawing on the insights of some of the early functionalist accounts of myth as providing models for human behavior, explaining disorder and failure (theodicy), and creating 'timeless temporalities,' anthropology must be true to its comparativism, and turn its lens onto the cosmology of the West itself, revealing its own cultural specificities (Herzfeld 2001: 206).

In his remarks on ritual, Herzfeld again underscores the need to not get too predicated on rites as reordering and instrumental (ibid.: 257f.). He states that all rituals are about time and the passage of existence. This is well illustrated by Arnold van Gennep's (1960) three-stage model of rituals (separation, marginality or liminality, and aggregation) which Victor Turner (1974) then gave more of a social interpretation. The latter argued that ritual could generate 'communitas' (the realm of anti-structure and the leveling of differences), allowing people to overcome uncertainty and ambiguity at the key transitional moments in their lives. Turner's work remains very popular with religion scholars because of its attention to indigenous cultural notions, notably Ndembu symbolism and ritual, and broader humanist concerns (Gellner 1999: 30).

Current scholarship on ritual evidences the shift in focus from structure to agency, and the influence of practice theory. Catherine Bell prefers the term 'ritualization' over a more objectified notion of ritual, viewing it as 'a matter of variously culturally specific strategies for setting some activities off from others, for creating and privileging a qualitative distinction between the 'sacred' and the 'profane,' and for ascribing such distinctions to realities thought to transcend the powers of human actors' (Bell 1992: 74). Thomas Csordas' analysis of the Catholic Charismatic Renewal movement serves as a fine example of the imaginative and complex ways in which ritual life can be interpreted (Csordas 1997).

From meaning to power

The emphasis on religion as a social institution by earlier anthropologists, notably of the British school, was given a new orientation in the 1970s by the American anthropologist, Clifford Geertz, in an influential essay entitled, 'Religion as a Cultural System' (Geertz 1973). Michael Lambek characterizes Geertz as 'the major exponent of a Weber-inspired interpretive anthropology which attempts to understand religion within a broadly cultural/symbolic domain, but also with reference to public circumstances in all their messiness' (Lambek 2008: 57). Geertz is well known for his advocacy of the need for 'thick description,' that is, interpretation of 'natives'' own interpretations of events, based on the anthropologist's empirical knowledge. As noted by David Gellner (1999: 20), this change marked the move from 'etic' (looking at cultures from the outside and in the light of broader principles) to 'emic' (viewing cultures from the inside and in terms of their own categories) approaches.

An important counterpoint to Geertz's interpretivist approach is the work of Talal Asad, notably in his well-known piece, 'The Construction of Religion as an Anthropological Category' (1993: 27–54). In this trenchant critique of essentialist definitions of religion, he claims that 'there cannot be a universal definition of religion, not only because its constituent elements and relationships are historically specific, but because that definition is itself the historical product of discursive processes' (ibid.: 29). To insist that religion has an autonomous essence, and is conceptually separate from the domain of power, is, he argues, a modern Western norm generated by post-Reformation history. This account, Lambek states, is 'indicative of a shift away from a symbolic anthropology toward a poststructuralist one that is more centrally concerned with power and discipline and with the way that religious subjects (i.e. practitioners) are formed' (Lambek 2008: 110). It also reflects efforts to contextualize ethnographic knowledge, notably in terms of the various colonial settings in which such knowledge was generated.

Historicizing and problematizing

Similar concerns to problematize and locate dominant anthropological concepts are found in the historical anthropology of Jean Comaroff and John Comaroff. For example, in their edited volume on *Modernity and its Malcontents*, they state decisively at the outset that the concept of modernity 'is profoundly ideological and profoundly historical' (Comaroff and Comaroff 1993: xi). As with much of their influential output, they tie their theoretical strengths into exciting empirical explorations that relate to the subject matter of 'religion' – generally situated in colonial and/or post-colonial Africa (Comaroff and Comaroff 1991, 1992). The authors in the volume on modernity, all former students of the Comaroffs, share a common orientation,

> that tries to dissolve the division between synchrony and diachrony, ethnography and historiography; that refuses to separate culture from political economy, insisting instead on the simultaneity of the meaningful and the material in all things; that acknowledges – no, stresses – the brute realities of colonialism and its aftermath, without assuming that they have robbed African peoples of their capacity to act on the world.
>
> (ibid.: xi)

Their 'analytic gaze' is turned upon the role of ritual in African modernity/modernities. It yields some excellent studies of the persistence, even efflorescence, of occultism, magic, and witchcraft in late twentieth-century African communities, as paradoxical consequences of 'modernity' and 'development' (ibid.). For example, based on her field studies of reports about witchcraft and other supernatural activities in the popular press in Onitsha, a large Igbo-speaking market town in south-eastern Nigeria, Misty Bastian argues that witchcraft is not seen as solely associated with the 'traditional' or the 'village' (Bastian 1993). In fact, it may even gain new power and meanings from the urban context, as it constitutes a useful medium for making sense of the complexity of West African life experiences (cf. Meyer 1999). Anthropologists have long believed that one of the most distinguishing characteristics of a society is the way that it deals with affliction and suffering. Witchcraft beliefs and practices offer a particularly illuminating window onto such existential questions. Building on, as well as contesting, the earlier analytical foundations laid by Evans-Pritchard (1937), and I. M. Lewis (1986), recent scholarship has generated some insightful analyses of the ways in which ideas about occult practice inform contemporary African social, political, and religious life (for example, Geschiere 1997; Bongmba 2001; Niehaus 2001; Ciekawy 1998; Hackett 2003).

The rethinking of the traditional/modern dichotomy in anthropological research is linked to the renewed appreciation for the historical dimension. Johannes Fabian argues that suppressing temporality allows investigators to ignore the fact that the people they study are actually living in the same time period as they are (1983). Contemporary anthropologists tend to be more interested in how various populations and interest groups *use* their images of the past to constitute or strengthen present interests, and also how far those who study such groups are themselves implicated in such processes. Herzfeld reminds us, in no uncertain terms, that '[t]he idea that we somehow stand outside our object of study is *preposterous*' (Herzfeld 2001: 55, emphasis added). The adjudication of the accuracy of historical accounts is controlled by the powerful, whose own 'literal' records need also to be read as 'interpretational devices' (ibid.: 62).

The reproduction of the past, or its suppression, through social and ritual performance, allows people to come to terms with 'a discomfiting present' (Herzfeld 2001: 58). In her illuminating and multi-layered work on West African slavery (which Herzfeld alludes to), Rosalind Shaw describes how ritual practices, namely divination, and images of pernicious occult powers, may be understood as 'memories of temporally removed processes created by an Atlantic commercial system that spanned three continents' (2002: 3). Interestingly, Shaw notes that, while divinatory skills lost favor in the light of the hegemony of a twentieth-century Western education, they enjoyed renewed salience with the catastrophic failure of Sierra Leone's economy and infrastructure during the 1980s and 1990s, and the emergence and entrenchment of the rebel war. She shows how mnemonic stories of European cannibalism under colonialism and present-day popular stories of 'big persons,' namely national politicians and top civil servants, rumored to have gained their prestige through evil ritual practices prescribed by diviners, serve as social critiques. These stories draw on colonial and pre-colonial memories of power and its abuses. It is noteworthy that the memories of suffering and exploitation detailed in her study are condensed and expressed via ritual means, as well as highly charged sacred objects and locations. Stephan Palmié's riveting study of Afro-Cuban religious culture also discloses how local forms of moral imagination constitute a response to the violent slave-trading past, rivaling Western understandings of modernity and rationality (2002).

Experience and experiencing

As with many other disciplines in the human sciences, anthropology experienced a 'crisis of representation' and the 'postmodern turn' in the 1980s and 1990s. In the wake of this critique, authors tend to be more transparent about their field experiences, even life trajectories. This is more than understanding positionality – frequently theoretical exploration is involved in trying to factor in the voices, or better still, knowledge, of women and indigenous peoples, or negotiate a balance between subjectivism and objectivism, for instance.[4] Research on religion appears to compound these ethical and epistemological issues, yet such methodological reflection by scholars of religion has been less forthcoming (see, however, Spickard et al. 2002; Dempsey 2000).

As an anthropologist with comparative religion and philosophy strings to his bow, Michael Jackson has been exemplary on this question of reflexivity. In his much-praised book *Paths Toward a Clearing* (1989), he reflects on 'the presumed coevalness that permits an ethnographer to have an understanding of the people he or she lives with and the images of radical otherness that pervade much anthropological writing' (ibid.: x). Drawing on his skills as novelist and poet, and on theoretical ideas from the existentialist and pragmatist traditions, Jackson focuses on experiences which are shared by both ethnographers and the people they study. He sets out to probe the dialectic at the heart of the anthropological project, namely the tensions between the search for universal cultural patterns and the empirical diversity of social life. He does this in the context of his experiences both among the Kuranko of Sierra Leone and the Walpiri of Central Australia (Jackson 1995).

In the course of twelve years of intensive research and collaboration with a Haitian Vodou priestess and her family in Brooklyn, Karen McCarthy Brown felt the need for more integrity, honesty, as well as imagination in her work (Brown 1991). Coming to the conclusion that fieldwork was more of a 'social art' than a social science, she wove fictional and autobiographical threads into the overall ethnographical analysis.[5] Similarly, Sam Gill, a professor of religious studies known for his work on the religions of indigenous peoples, develops 'storytracking' as an approach which allows him to trace the 'colonialist underbelly' of academic accounts of the Arrente, a Central Australian people, as well as to examine critically his own life and the challenge of living 'responsibly and decisively in a postmodern world' (Gill 1998).[6]

The anthropological study of experience and its inter-subjective expressions was seen by Victor W. Turner as a way of revitalizing a field that had become stultified by structural-functional orthodoxy. He drew inspiration for this new hermeneutical and humanistic direction from the German philosopher Wilhelm Dilthey. In *The Anthropology of Experience*, edited by Turner and Edward M. Bruner (but which appeared after Turner's death in 1983), several leading scholars discuss the intersections and disjunctures between life as lived, life as experienced, and life as told (V. W. Turner and Bruner 1986; see, also, E. Turner 1985). Drawing on their own ethnographic experiences, they document and analyze the symbolic manifestations and processual activities that are the 'structured units of experience,' such as the enactment of rituals, manipulation of images, performance of drama, or recitation of texts.

Experience is arguably central to the rich body of literature on spirit possession and shamanism. These staple topics of the field have generated a variety of cross-cultural and multi-perspectival accounts.[7] Paul Stoller's own experiences of sorcery and possession among the Songhay of Niger inform his body of writings (Stoller 1995, 1997). He is particularly attentive to the neglected senses (smell, taste, and touch) in Western anthropology (Stoller 1989, 1997), as is Constance Classen, who calls for a 'sensory anthropology' (Classen 1993; see also Meyer 2006). In fact, it could be argued that all issues of importance to a culture, including religious beliefs and practices, are infused with sensory values, while not forgetting that these same values may be used to express and reinforce divisions and hierarchies pertaining to race, gender and religion (Herzfeld 2001: 252–253). Dutch anthropologists Rijk van Dijk and Peter Pels underscore the need to deconstruct the 'politics of perception' at play in the relationship between anthropologist and interlocutor(s) (Dijk and Pels 1996). This lies behind the Western privileging of natural over supernatural, or observation over occultism or secrecy, rather than any given 'objectivity.' In fact, they provocatively, yet persuasively, claim that 'the anthropological study of religion tends to reflect, more than any other anthropological topic, the preconceptions of the Western observer' (ibid.: 247). This is probably the reason, they suggest, why so little has been written (except autobiographically) about fieldwork on religion.

Focusing more on the experiences of those who are petitioners and practitioners, Adeline Masquelier explores the 'ritual economy' of *bori* spirit possession cults (albeit a small minority) in the town of Dogondoutchi in south-western Niger, as they contest the rapidly growing Muslim community which has taken control of the trade networks and village affairs (Masquelier 2001). She demonstrates how *bori* allows people to remember an idealized past as to articulate and negotiate the problems of contemporary life: 'to transform the experience of novel, ambiguous, or threatening realities into symbols of a shared consciousness' (ibid.: 10–11). Masquelier, in searching for the appropriate interpretive lens for her case study, provides a helpful overview of the rich literature on spirit possession (Masquelier 2001: 11–31; see, also, Boddy 1994). She rejects those approaches which explain possession in pathological, biological, or functionalist terms, as in I. M. Lewis's well-known claim that both spirit possession and shamanism must be studied as social phenomena primarily to do with power and marginality (Lewis 1989). Masquelier opts instead for an approach which does justice to the therapeutic and performative aspects of possession, and which analyzes both its 'cultural logic' and wider historical and political contexts.

Engendering and embodying the field

At the outset of *Feminism and Anthropology*, Henrietta Moore stresses that '[t]he basis for the feminist critique is not the study of women, but the analysis of gender relations, and of gender as a structuring principle in all human societies' (1988: vii). For example, she looks at the relation between pollution beliefs and sexual antagonism in Melanesian societies (ibid.: 16–21). Susan Sered articulates well why anthropologists cannot ignore the role of religion in this and other areas of social life, '[t]he 'natural' and the 'supernatural' serve as complementary tools for naturalizing and sanctifying difference, prestige, and hierarchy' notably in regard to questions of gender (1999: 9). In some societies, the ritual context provides for much greater fluidity and reversal of gender roles (Sered 1999: 231–245).

'Mutually toxic' is the way Rosalind Shaw described the relationship between feminism and mainstream religious studies (in the early 1990s) (Shaw 1995). She saw a collision between the 'view from below,' contextual approach of feminist anthropology, and the 'view from above,' *sui generis* tradition of religious studies, with its privileging of texts and beliefs. However, Fiona Bowie argues that it is both possible and productive to accommodate the contested (Western origins, pro-women) and contesting (critical, deconstructive) nature of feminism in the study of religion (Bowie 2006: 82–106). Dorothy Hodgson's rich and cogent ethnography of the encounter of the Maasai and Catholic missionaries in Tanzania, *The Church of Women* (2005), proves that gender is a non-negotiable element of any such study.

One of the positive offshoots of the feminist impulse in anthropological scholarship has been a heightened attention to the social and cultural significance of the body (Lock 1997). Earlier social scientists, such as Durkheim, were interested in the relationship between the physical, social, and psycho-social domains. Mary Douglas stimulated an appreciation of the body for its symbolic properties (Douglas 1970). Michael Lambek and Andrew Stathern, in their inter-regional study of the relations between persons and bodies in Africa and Melanesia, attribute the burgeoning interest in the body to its 'increased visibility and objectification within late capitalist consumer society,' as well to shifts in academic focus to the domain of lived experience and the effects of the social realm on the body, to the body as signifier, and to mind/body holistic issues (Lambek and Strathern 1998: 5). So, as they rightly suggest, the body constitutes a type of centripetal concept around which current academic interests can be organized. They underscore the significance of embodiment as the model (supported by current scientific findings in brain/body studies) for discussing the interactions of body and mind, notably in the context of illness and health.

Michael Jackson is critical of prevailing tendencies in anthropology to interpret embodied experience in terms of belief and language, and to treat the body as inert and passive (1989: 122). Reviewing his earlier analysis of Kuranko rituals of initiation, which was unduly abstract and intellectualist, he now holds that 'what is done with the body is the ground of what is thought and said' (1989: 131; cf. Moore 1996: 3–12, 79–97). He also maintains that this focus on bodily praxis is more empathic and in line with indigenous interpretations, rather than being dependent on external experts in symbolic analysis.

Some studies highlight the intersections between the body, religious symbols, and political and economic power. Jean Comaroff shows how Zionist Christians in South Africa appropriated symbols of power from the dress of colonialists and missionaries, transforming these into messages of dissent and self-empowerment (Comaroff 1985). Two edited collections (Arthur 1999; Arthur 2000) provide a fascinating range of examples of how religious dress may be used, especially in the case of women, to negotiate new social environments, or to control sexuality and social behavior.

Closely tied to studies of the body are studies of illness and healing from a range of different perspectives (see Csordas 2002). René Devisch's detailed analysis of a healing cult, *mbwoolu*, among the Yaka of Congo (formerly Zaire) demonstrates how, through the use of liturgy and figurines, an ill person is ritually induced to die in his former condition and be reborn into a new one (1998). The imaginary, transgressive, and intimate qualities of this esoteric trance-possession cult differ from the more public, daytime ceremonies of initiation. Bruce Kapferer's impressive study of Sinhalese exorcism rituals in Sri Lanka stresses the critical importance of performance and ceremony (1991 [1983]). Some studies address the impact of exogenous forces. For example, Stacey Pigg's original, multi-level analysis of local theories of sickness and healing practices in Nepal weaves in the role of the state and international development agencies (1996).

In a lucid theoretical piece, 'Body and Mind in Mind, Body and Mind in Body' (1998), Michael Lambek stresses that it is important not to view the mind–body relationship reductively or incommensurably, but as a 'central dialectic in the ongoing constitution of human culture, society, and experience (and hence of anthropological theory)' (ibid.: 120). The celebration of the body, and the turn to practice theory, as useful as they have been in transcending problematic dichotomies, should not, he insists, lead us to forget that 'contemplative reason' is a fundamental characteristic of the human condition, regardless of time and place (ibid.: 119). This assertion seems especially pertinent to the study of religious worlds, still haunted as they are by the specters of essentialism, reductionism, and Orientalism (unintended or otherwise).

New moves and movements

Because of the quest for holistic analysis, anthropologists have been drawn over the years to the study of small-scale societies. This is where they find what Peacock calls 'the interrelatedness of meaning and life, culture and existence' (1986: 18). However, to downplay the exoticism and primitivism commonly associated with the work of Western anthropologists, and to address new social and cultural flows, many younger anthropologists have shifted their focus to new locations and phenomena. Some may still retain an interest in qualitative research on smaller, popular groups of other societies (as opposed to sociology's more traditional emphasis on the quantitative analysis of [our own] large-scale societies), but they are increasingly attuned to the national and global forces which shape communal identity and survival. Diaspora, travel, tourism, and transnationalism are now on the agenda, reflecting the fluid, multi-sited nature of contemporary anthropology (Vertovec 2000; Johnson 2002a; Tsing 1993). Syncretism and fetishism have also been experiencing a revival of interest in the post-colonial world of hybridized and creolized cultures (Shaw and Stewart 1994; Apter and Pietz 1993).

The rich body of work now emerging on global Pentecostalism and its local manifestations illustrates these new trends exceptionally well (Corten and Marshall-Fratani 2001; Harding 2000; Coleman 2000; Meyer 1999), building on earlier work on religious change and innovation (e.g. MacGaffey 1983). Evangelicalism and (Christian) fundamentalism have also been subject to anthropological analysis (DeBernardi 1999; Nagata 2001), and there is ongoing interest in missionary activities (Hackett 2008; Hodgson 2005; Buckser and Glazier 2003), and the problematic of conversion and cultural translation (Veer 1996). Joel Robbins has been instrumental in formulating an anthropology of Christianity (Robbins 2003, 2004; see, also Engelke and Tomlinson 2006; Cannell 2004). There is no shortage of works on Islam in a host of different contexts, whether in the public spheres of the Middle East (Eickelman and Salvatore 2002), Indonesia (Hefner 2000; Bowen 2003), Egypt (Starrett 2003), or Mali (Soares 2005). Anthropologists have also ventured into the worlds of neo-pagan/Wicca (Luhrmann 1989) and new age religions (Brown 1997), while Talal Asad has recently called for an anthropology of the secular (2003). Some have turned to cognitive anthropology for naturalistic explanations about religion (see, e.g. Whitehouse and Laidlaw 2004).

Material and media cultures

One of the most significant new areas in the anthropological study of religion is that of the visual and performing arts (Hackett 1996; Coote and Shelton 1994).[8] Theorists in this field have done much to problematize the concept of 'primitive.' An early landmark text, linking ritual and cosmology to art and architectonics, was James Fernandez's dense study of a Central African religious movement, *Bwiti* (Fernandez 1982). This has been followed by other scholars who have explored the relationship between the materiality and spirituality of place (see, e.g. Low and Lawrence-Zuniga 2003).

The French anthropologists who conducted extensive research on the Dogon of Mali were also attentive to the intersections of their elaborate masking and cosmological traditions (Griaule 1938). Greater attention to material and performance culture elucidates hidden cosmological and philosophical meanings (see, e.g. Abiodun 1994), although much more needs to be done on music and dance. Studies on secrecy (Nooter 1993) and on divination (Pemberton III 2000) illustrate this well. In fact, the findings have served to challenge prevailing Western understandings of power and aesthetics, for in some African art forms the least visible and least attractive art works may be the most spiritually charged. The magnificent study, *A Saint in the City* (and museum exhibition), of the urban arts associated with Sheikh Amadou Bamba, the Senegalese Sufi mystic, illustrates the devotional power of his sacred images for members of the Mouride order the world over (Roberts *et al.* 2003).[9] *Ways of the Rivers* is a stunning example of the intersections of art, religion, and the environment in the Niger Delta (Anderson and Peek 2002).[10]

Analyzing the growing interest in Australian Aboriginal visual culture, Fred Myers and Howard Morphy reveal how contemporary Australian Aboriginal spirituality is (re)constructed in the commodification of contemporary Aboriginal paintings (Myers 2002; Morphy 1992). These and other studies consider how indigenous art works circulate transculturally due to the art and tourist trades, and museum exhibitions, and how this affects their (original) ritual meanings and use, and present-day artistic production.

An exciting new area of investigation for anthropologists in general, and especially for those who focus on religion – notably the newer and/or minority movements seeking recognition and expansion – is the burgeoning mass media sector. Long absent from the purview of mainstream anthropology because of their perceived hegemonic and homogenizing tendencies, the media, particularly local and indigenous forms, are now the subject of conferences and publications (Ginsberg *et al.* 2002; Herzfeld 2001: 294–315). An important new volume assembles the work of several scholars who are engaged on the intersections of religion and media in a variety of locations (Meyer and Moors 2005; see, also, Meyer 2006; Witte 2003).[11] It is in the area of audience reception, practice, and agency that anthropologists, with their professed interest in everyday experience, can make their contribution to media studies (Herzfeld 2001: 17, 302f.). Comparative scholarship on Islam and the media is particularly well developed both substantively and theoretically (Anderson 2003).

Perduring and maturing debates

The changes in focus and content, adumbrated above, serve to raise old and new questions about the conscience of present-day anthropologists, and their purpose in a world plagued by conflict and injustice. The first of these perduring concerns is *epistemological*, in that it problematizes the relations of power and authority (both at the empirical and representational level) between anthropologist and the 'other' (Moore 1999: 5). A methodological stance of 'principled modesty' (2001: 67) and 'reflexive comparativism' (ibid.: 65), are favored by Herzfeld as they keep the core issue of sameness and difference in creative tension, obviating any lapse into reductive or hegemonic interpretations. Armin Geertz believes that ethnographically oriented scholars of religion should not capitulate to those voices that privilege insider authority, knowledge, and cultural competence. He opts for a dialogical relationship between scholar and consultant, which he terms 'ethnohermeneutics' (2003).

The critical insights of cultural anthropologists on these ethical and methodological questions should give pause for reflection, and perhaps, encouragement, to all those who engage in ethnographic work on religion. In his appropriately titled *Anthropology with an Attitude* (2001), Johannes Fabian expresses his frustration that his anthropologist colleagues seem more preoccupied with how they represent their data than with how they obtain it. He acknowledges that the application of hermeneutics and literary criticism to anthropology has produced valuable critical insights, but finds that texts, as produced by the ethnographer as records of verbal interaction in the field, have generated false assurances of objectivity. He would like to see more emphasis on how cultural knowledge is imparted through performance and action, rather than as discursive information. He is critical of the privileging of concepts and images derived from vision, namely, participant *observation*, in the production of 'objective' ethnographic knowledge. A more materialist, and inter-subjective approach in fieldwork can, in his estimation, erase the hierarchy between knower and known.

In his inimitably provocative way, Fabian also asks why 'ecstasis,' should not be included in our theories of knowledge. By this he means (and this links to the section on experience above) ecstatic initiation rituals, hallucinogens, alcohol, exhausting dances, and all-night vigils and wakes.[12] For that matter, he adds, there should be room for 'passion,' or referring to Michael Taussig's work on shamanism and colonialism in Bolivia (1987), 'terror' or 'torture.' For how, Fabian asks, 'can we hope to deal objectively with peoples and cultures whom Western imperialism made the subjects of brutal domination as well as of ethnographic inquiry?' (Fabian 2001: 32). Kirsten Hastrup, who is equally concerned with issues of discrimination and toleration (Hastrup and Ulrich 2001), argues in favor of the use of the 'ethnographic present' to go beyond the dichotomy of subjectivism and objectivism (Hastrup 1995: 9–25). She believes that it can convey both the creativity and inter-subjectivity of the fieldwork *process* and the written, more theoretical *presenting* of the ethnography, and their mutual imbrications.

The second ongoing area of debate is more *teleological* in that it addresses the purpose and outcomes of anthropological research. This is more than just applied anthropology, argues Henrietta Moore, it relates to the 'reconfiguration of the boundaries between academic and non-academic practice' and the recognition that anthropology is a disciplinary project which is part of 'the practice of governmentality' (1999: 3). In other words, there can be no more retreating into cultural relativism. Anthropologists still have to engage with theories that treat the *commonalities*, and not just the *differences*, between all human beings (ibid.: 17). Michael Jackson is concerned to find 'ways of opening up dialogue between people from different cultures or traditions, ways of *bringing into being* modes of understanding which effectively go beyond the intellectual conventions and political ideologies that circumscribe us all' (1989: x [author's emphasis]; cf. van Binsbergen 2003). Similarly, Michael Herzfeld believes that 'history from below,' i.e. detailed ethnography or thick description, can offer 'daily challenges to the dominance of certain political structures' (and, we should add, religious structures) (2001: 75). Faye Harrison and her contributors to *Decolonizing Anthropology* are even more proactive in exploring how, as 'organic intellectuals,' they can contribute toward 'social transformation and human liberation' (Harrison 1991).

Some scholars are translating their concerns regarding ethics and pragmatics into new arenas or objects of interrogation, such as development, discrimination, or violence and conflict. It is well known that anthropologists have served in an advisory capacity to governments, and development and humanitarian organizations. Some are now reviewing this practice, and analyzing these institutions, occasionally with a focus on religious agencies (see, e.g. Bornstein 2005). However, only two of these emergent areas can be highlighted here, namely violence and conflict, and human rights.

There is no shortage of texts these days on the ethnography and theory of violence and suffering (Das *et al.* 2001; Herzfeld 2001: 217–239; Tambiah 1996). In Cynthia Mahmood's estimation, the new interest of anthropologists in war and peace is generating 'a much richer understanding of how human beings experience violence' (Mahmood 2003). The area of conflict resolution has been particularly open to insights on culture. Clearly, the context of war and conflict compels the fieldworker to consider most carefully methods of communication, knowledge production, and representation. Such extreme contexts also tend to subvert conventional concepts and categories. For example, Swedish anthropologist Sverker Finnström, seeking to investigate the cultural practices whereby people in Northern Uganda both engage and try to comprehend existentially the realities of war and violence, and also struggle continuously to build hope for the future, opted for 'participant reflection' over 'participant observation' to reflect his more engaged relationship with his informants (Finnström 2008). Carolyn Nordstrom's groundbreaking work on war-torn regions and the strategies people adopt to (re)generate meaning and community in situations of extreme suffering is germane here (Nordstrom 1997). Marc Sommers, an anthropologist who works on Rwandan and Burundian refugee communities in Tanzania, states revealingly, '[p]erhaps no aspect of African refugee society and culture is as overlooked by researchers and most humanitarian relief agencies as their religious lives' (Sommers 2000: 18). Indeed, this aspect is often under-analyzed in otherwise praiseworthy works on social suffering (Das *et al.* 2001). However, in studies of the plight of indigenous peoples the religious or spiritual dimension may be more apparent (Adelson 2001).

Now that human rights constitute the new global *lingua franca* for victims of injustice and oppression the world over, anthropologists have to overcome their relativist leanings and respond to the call to 'anthropologize' and 'historicize' human rights (Booth 1999).

This may necessitate more attention to the religious uses and interpretations of the human rights idea. Several European scholars have indeed set out in their volume, *Culture and Rights: Anthropological Perspectives*, to develop more 'empirical, contextual analyses of specific rights struggles' (Cowan *et al.* 2001: 21). They rightly argue that such an intellectual strategy permits them 'to follow how individuals, groups, communities and states use a discourse of rights in the pursuit of particular ends, and how they become enmeshed in its logic.' Empirical studies also raise important questions about who subscribes to and who benefits from this or that version of culture, community, or tradition – all of which can have significant ethical and legal consequences. Minority religious and ethnic groups continue to serve as the interface for the increasingly legalized and politicized battles over cultural identity and survival (Barry 2001; Nye 2001; Hepner 2008; Hussain and Ghosh 2002). More research is needed to understand the ways in which the human rights concept is generating new discourses of sameness and difference among religious groups. In other words, against the backdrop of rights culture, identity politics, and the logic of the market, religious formations are more differentiated, yet in another vein, also more standardized, in ever more competitive public spheres (Hackett 2005).[13] Moreover, the current anthropological emphasis on practice is needed to compensate for the Western propensity for 'belief' in interpreting religious freedom issues, and to mediate rights conflict, such as between women's rights and religious rights.

Conclusion

Current scholarship in the anthropology of religion is undoubtedly still indebted to those early monographs and frameworks developed by the likes of Sir Edward Evans-Pritchard, Emile Durkheim, Mary Douglas, and Clifford Geertz. However, the postmodern and post-colonial turns, compressions of time and space with globalization, and rise of 'multiculturalist' issues, have occasioned some significant rethinking and realignment. Determining the general provenance or parameters of religion in 'exotic' small-scale societies has ceased to preoccupy contemporary anthropologists. Some now see their contribution as being rather to reconsider modern, secular society as symbolically and culturally constituted, and as much based on the religious impulse as on reason.

Arguably, then, the increasingly composite nature of anthropological theorizing bodes well for more creative and critical explorations of religious expression, practice, and transformation in a variety of contemporary locations. Current notions of (anthropological) theory as emphasizing the salience of holism, context, practice, and relations of power, and incorporating 'a critique of its own locations, positions and interests' (Moore 1999: 9–10), are clearly invaluable for the academic study of religion more generally. In sum, as stated at the outset, anthropological theory and method appear increasingly well positioned to respond to such pressing social and cultural issues as identity, difference, conflict, and survival as they are mediated by religion(s) in our globalizing world.

Acknowledgments

I would to acknowledge the helpful feedback on this chapter provided by such good colleagues and friends as Allen Roberts, Mark Hulsether, Tricia Hepner, Omri Elisha, and Michael Lambek.

Notes

1 The Society for the Anthropology of Religion was formally created in the American Anthropological Association in 2000 (http://www.uwgb.edu/sar/). Shortly after that, an Anthropology of Religion Consultation was inaugurated in the American Academy of Religion.

2 It may also derive from personal 'stock-taking' by individual authors at the conclusion of their careers, and their concern to transcend latent interpretations of religion as irrational, as Sarah Caldwell indicates in her insightful review of five major publications in the 1990s (Caldwell 1999).

3 For an historical survey of the field, see Morris 1987, and for accessible recent textbooks, see Bowie 2006; Morris 2006; Klass 1995; Klass and Weisgrau 1999; Bowen 1998; and for readers, see Glazier 1999; Glazier and Flowerday 2003; Lambek 2008; Hackett 2001. Note: there is a new attention to 'world religions' in the books by Bowen 1998 and Morris 2006.

4 See, also, the various essays on their field experiences by religion scholars in a special issue of *Method and Theory in the Study of Religion* 13,1 (2001). A new journal, *Fieldwork in Religion*, also began in 2004 http://www.equinoxjournals.com/ojs/index.php/FIR.

5 Cf. my own reflections on the limitations of my early training in the academic study of religion for conducting field-based research on religion in Nigeria (Hackett 2001).

6 Cf. Robert M. Baum's piece on the ethical considerations of doing fieldwork on a secessionist religious movement in the context of a religiously intolerant state (Baum 2001).

7 For helpful overviews of shamanism and neo-shamanism, see Vitebsky 1995; Johnson 1995 and van Binsbergen 1991.

8 *African Arts*, published quarterly for academics and the market, is a rich indication of the current vitality and diversity of the field.

9 http://www.fmch.ucla.edu/passporttoparadise.htm (last accessed March 11, 2009).

10 The cross-cultural study of religion and nature has received a major boost from Bron Taylor's and Jeffrey Kaplan's *Encyclopedia of Religion and Nature* project (New York: Cassell, 2005) http://www.religionandnature.com.

11 The *Journal of Religion in Africa* has two thematic issues on media (26,4: 1998) (33,2: 2003).

12 See, in this regard, the work of anthropologist/*sangoma* (diviner-healer), Wim van Binsbergen (van Binsbergen 1991) http://www.shikanda.net/index.htm (last accessed March 11, 2009).

13 See the guest edited issue of *Culture and Religion* on 'Law and Human Rights,' edited by Rosalind I. J. Hackett and Winnifred F. Sullivan (6,1: 2005).

Bibliography

Abiodun, Rowland. 1994. 'Ase: Verbalizing and Visualizing Creative Power through Art.' *Journal of Religion in Africa* 24 (4): 294–322.

Adelson, Naomi. 2001. 'Reimagining Aboriginality: An Indigenous People's Response to Social Suffering.' In *Remaking a World: Violence, Social Suffering, and Recovery*, edited by V. Das, A. Kleinman, M. Lock, M. Ramphele, and P. Reynolds. Berkeley and Los Angeles: University of California Press.

Anderson, Jon W. 2003. 'New Media, New Publics: Reconfiguring the Public Sphere of Islam.' *Social Research* 70 (3): 887–906.

Anderson, Martha G., and Philip M. Peek, eds. 2002. *Ways of the Rivers: Arts and Environment of the Niger Delta*. Los Angeles: UCLA Fowler Museum of Cultural History.

Apter, Emily, and William Pietz. 1993. *Fetishism as Cultural Discourse*. Ithaca, NY: Cornell University Press.

Arthur, Linda Boynton, ed. 1999. *Religion, Dress and the Body*. Oxford: Berg.

— 2000. *Undressing Religion: Commitment and Conversion from a Cross-Cultural Perspective*. Oxford: Berg.

Asad, Talal. 1993. *Genealogies of Religion: Discipline and Reasons of Power in Christianity and Islam*. Baltimore: Johns Hopkins University Press.

— 2003. *Formations of the Secular: Christianity, Islam, Modernity*. Stanford: Stanford University Press.

Barry, Brian. 2001. *Culture and Equality: An Egalitarian Critique of Multiculturalism*. Cambridge, MA: Harvard University Press.

Bastian, Misty. 1993. '"Bloodhounds Who Have No Friends": Witchcraft and Locality in the Nigerian Popular Press.' In *Modernity and its Malcontents: Ritual and Power in Postcolonial Africa*, edited by J. Comaroff and J. Comaroff. Chicago: University of Chicago Press.

Baum, Robert M. 2001. 'The Ethics of Religious Studies Research in the Context of the Religious Intolerance of the State: An Africanist Perspective.' *Method and Theory in the Study of Religion* 13 (1): 12–23.

Bell, Catherine. 1992. *Ritual Theory, Ritual Practice*. New York: Oxford University Press.

Boddy, Janice. 1994. 'Spirit Possession Revisited: Beyond Instrumentality.' *Annual Review of Anthropology* 24: 407–434.

Bongmba, Elias Kifon. 2001. *African Witchcraft and Otherness: A Philosophical and Theological Critique of Intersubjective Relations*. Albany, NY: State University of New York Press.

Booth, Ken. 1999. 'Three Tyrannies.' In *Human Rights in Global Politics*, edited by T. Dunne and N. J. Wheeler. New York: Cambridge University Press.

Bornstein, Erica. 2005. *The Spirit of Development: Protestant NGOs, Morality, and Economics in Zimbabwe*. Palo Alto, CA: Stanford University Press.

Bowen, John R. 1998. *Religions in Practice: An Approach to the Anthropology of Religion*. Boston: Allyn and Bacon.

— 2003. *Islam, Law, and Equality in Indonesia: An Anthropology of Public Reasoning*. New York: Cambridge University Press.

Bowie, Fiona. 2006. *The Anthropology of Religion*. Oxford: Blackwell, second edition.

Brown, Karen McCarthy. 1991. *Mama Lola: A Vodou Priestess in Brooklyn*. Berkeley: University of California Press.

Brown, Michael F. 1997. *The Channeling Zone: American Spirituality in an Anxious Age*. Cambridge, MA: Harvard University Press.

Buckser, Andrew, and Stephen D. Glazier, eds. 2003. *The Anthropology of Religious Conversion*. Lanham, MD: Rowman and Littlefield.

Caldwell, Sarah. 1999. 'Transcendence and Culture: Anthropologists Theorize Religion.' *Religious Studies Review* 25 (3): 227–232.

Cannell, Fenella, ed. 2006. *The Anthropology of Christianity*. Durham, NC: Duke University Press.

Ciekawy, Diane. 1998. 'Witchcraft in Statecraft: Five Technologies of Power in Coastal Kenya.' *African Studies Review* 41:119–141.

Classen, Constance. 1993. *Worlds of Sense: Exploring the Senses in History and Across Cultures*. New York: Routledge.

Coleman, Simon. 2000. *The Globalization of Charismatic Christianity*. Cambridge: Cambridge University Press.

Comaroff, Jean. 1985. *Body of Power, Spirit of Resistance*. Chicago: University of Chicago Press.

— and John L. Comaroff. 1991. *Of Revelation and Revolution*. Vol. 1. *Christianity, Colonialism, and Consciousness in South Africa*. Chicago: University of Chicago Press.

— 1992. *Ethnography and the Historical Imagination*. Boulder, CO: Westview.

— eds. 1993. *Modernity and Its Malcontents: Ritual and Power in Postcolonial Africa*. Chicago: University of Chicago Press.

Coote, Jeremy and Anthony Shelton, eds. 1994. *Anthropology, Art and Aesthetics, (Oxford Studies in the Anthropology of Cultural Forms)*. New York: Oxford University Press.

Corten, André, and Ruth Marshall-Fratani, eds. 2001. *Between Babel and Pentecost: Transnational Pentecostalism in Africa and Latin America*. Bloomington, IN: Indiana University Press.

Cowan, Jane K, Marie-Benedicte Dembour, and Richard A. Wilson, eds. 2001. *Culture and Rights: Anthropological Perspectives*. New York: Cambridge University Press.

Csordas, Thomas J. 1997. *Language, Charisma, and Creativity: The Ritual Life of a Religious Movement*. Berkeley and Los Angeles: University of California Press.

— 2002. *Body/Meaning/Healing (Contemporary Anthropology of Religion)*. New York: Palgrave Macmillan.

Das, Veena, Arthur Kleinman, Margaret Lock, Mamphela Ramphele, and Pamela Reynolds, eds. 2001. *Remaking a World: Violence, Social Suffering, and Recovery*. Berkeley and Los Angeles: University of California Press.

DeBernardi, Jean. 1999. 'Spiritual Warfare and Territorial Spirits: The Globalization and Localization of a Practical Theology.' *Religious Studies and Theology* 18 (2): 66–96.

Dempsey, Corinne. 2000. 'Religion and Representation in Recent Ethnographies.' *Religious Studies Review* 26 (1):37–42.

Devisch, René. 1998. 'Treating the Affect by Remodelling the Body in a Yaka Healing Cult.' In *Bodies and Persons: Comparative Perspectives from Africa and Melanesia*, edited by M. Lambek, and A. Strathern. New York: Cambridge University Press.

Dijk, Rijk van, and Peter Pels. 1996. 'Contested Authorities and the Politics of Perception: Deconstructing the Study of Religion in Africa.' In *Postcolonial Identities in Africa*, edited by R. Werbner and T. Ranger. London and New Jersey: Zed Books.

Douglas, Mary. 1970. *Natural Symbols: Explorations in Cosmology*. New York: Pantheon Books (Random House).

— 1975. *Implicit Meanings*. London: Routledge.

Durkheim, Émile. 1965 [1912]. *The Elementary Forms of the Religious Life*. New York: The Free Press.

Eickelman, Dale F., and Armando Salvatore. 2002. 'The Public Sphere and Muslim Identities.' *European Journal of Sociology* 43: 92–115.

Engelke, Matthew, and Matt Tomlinson, eds. 2006. *The Limits of Meaning: Case Studies in the Anthropology of Christianity*. New York: Berghahn Books.

Evans-Pritchard, E. E. 1937. *Witchcraft, Oracles and Magic Among the Azande*. Oxford: Clarendon Press.

— 1974 [1956]. *Nuer Religion*. New York: Oxford University Press.

Fabian, Johannes. 1983. *Time and the Other: How Anthropology Makes its Object*. New York: Columbia University Press.

— 2001. *Anthropology with an Attitude: Critical Essays*. Stanford: Stanford University Press.

Fernandez, James W. 1982. *Bwiti: An Ethnography of the Religious Imagination in Africa*. Princeton, NJ: Princeton University Press.

Finnström, Sverker. 2008. *Living with Bad Surroundings: War, History, and Everyday Moments in Northern Uganda, The Cultures and Practice of Violence*. Raleigh-Durham, NC: Duke University Press.

Frazer, James. 1996 [1890]. *The Golden Bough*. New York: Touchstone Books.

Geertz, Armin. 2003. 'Ethnohermeneutics and Worldview Analysis in the Study of Hopi Indian Religion.' *Numen* 50 (3):308–348.

Geertz, Clifford. 1973. 'Religion as a Cultural System.' In *The Interpretation of Cultures*, edited by C. Geertz. New York: Basic Books.

Gellner, David N. 1999. 'Anthropological Approaches.' In *Approaches to the Study of Religion*, edited by P. Connolly. London: Cassell.

Geschiere, Peter. 1997. *The Modernity of Witchcraft: Politics and the Occult in Postcolonial Africa*. Charlottesville: University Press of Virginia.

Gill, Sam D. 1998. *Storytracking: Texts, Stories, and Histories of Central Australia*. New York: Oxford University Press.

Ginsberg, Faye, Lila Abu-Lughod, and Brian Larkin, eds. 2002. *Media Worlds: Anthropology on New Terrain*. Los Angeles and Berkeley: University of California Press.

Glazier, Stephen D., ed. 1999. *Anthropology of Religion: A Handbook*. New York: Praeger.

— and Charles A. Flowerday, eds. 2003. *Selected Readings in the Anthropology of Religion: Theoretical and Methodological Essays*. New York: Praeger.

Griaule, Marcel. 1938. *Masques Dogons*. Vol. 33. Paris: Université de Paris, Travaux et Mémoires de l'Institut d'Ethnologie.

Hackett, Rosalind I. J. 1996. *Art and Religion in Africa*. London: Cassell.

— 2001. 'Field Envy: Or, the Perils and Pleasures of Doing Fieldwork.' *Method and Theory in the Study of Religion* 13 (1): 98–109.

— 2003. 'Discourses of Demonisation in Africa.' *Diogenes* 50 (3): 61–75.

— 2005. 'Mediated Religion in South Africa: Balancing Air-time and Rights Claims.' In *Media, Religion and the Public Sphere*, edited by B. Meyer, and A. Moors. Bloomington, IN: Indiana University Press.

— ed. 2008. *Proselytization Revisited: Rights Talk, Free Markets, and Culture Wars*. London: Equinox Publishers.

Harding, Susan. 2000. *The Book of Jerry Falwell*. Princeton, NJ: Princeton University Press.

Harrison, Faye V., ed. 1991. *Decolonizing Anthropology: Moving Further Toward an Anthropology for Liberation*. Washington, DC: Association of Black Anthropologists/American Anthropological Association.

Hastrup, Kirsten. 1995. *A Passage to Anthropology*. New York: Routledge.

— and George Ulrich, eds. 2001. *Discrimination and Toleration: New Perspectives, International Studies in Human Rights*. The Hague: Martinus Nijhoff.

Hefner, Robert W. 2000. *Civil Islam: Muslims and Democratization in Indonesia*. Princeton, NJ: Princeton University Press.

Hepner, Tricia Redeker. 2008. Transnational Governance and the Centralization of State Power in Eritrea and Exile. *Ethnic and Racial Studies* 31 (3):476–502.

Herzfeld, Michael. 2001. *Anthropology: Theoretical Practice in Culture and Society*. Oxford: Blackwell.

Heusch, Luc de. 1982. *The Drunken King Or, the Origin of the State*. Bloomington, IN: Indiana University Press.

Hodgson, Dorothy L. 2005. *The Church of Women: Gendered Encounters between Maasai and Missionaries*. Bloomington: IN: Indiana University Press.

Horton, Robin. 1993. 'African Traditional Thought and Western Science.' In *Patterns of Thought in Africa and the West: Essays on Magic, Religion and Science*, edited by R. Horton. New York: Cambridge University Press.

Hussain, Monirul, and Lipi Ghosh, eds. 2002. *Religious Minorities in South Asia: Selected Essays on Post-Colonial Situations*. New Delhi: Manak.

Jackson, Michael. 1989. *Paths Toward a Clearing: Radical Empiricism and Ethnographic Inquiry*. Bloomington, IN: Indiana University Press.

— 1995. *At Home in the World*. Raleigh, NC: Duke University Press.

Johnson, Paul C. 1995. 'Shamanism from Ecuador to Chicago: A Case Study in New Age Ritual Appropriation.' *Religion* 25: 163–178.

— 2002a. 'Migrating Bodies, Circulating Signs: Brazilian Candomblé, the Garifuna of the Caribbean, and the Category of Indigenous Religions.' *History of Religions* 41 (4): 301–327.

— 2002b. *Secrets, Gossip, and Gods: The Transformation of Brazilian Candomblé*. New York: Oxford University Press.

Kapferer, Bruce. 1991 [1983]. *A Celebration of Demons: Exorcism and the Aesthetics of Healing in Sri Lanka*. 2nd edn. Providence, RI/ Washington, DC: Berg/Smithsonian Institution Press.

Klass, Morton. 1995. *Ordered Universes: Approaches to the Anthropology of Religion*. Boulder, CO: Westview Press.

— and Maxine K. Weisgrau, eds. 1999. *Across the Boundaries of Belief*. Boulder, CO: Westview Press.

Lambek, Michael. 1993. *Knowledge and Practice in Mayotte: Local Discourses of Islam, Sorcery, and Spirit Possession*. Toronto: University of Toronto Press.

— 1998. 'Body and Mind in Mind, Body and Mind in Body: Some Anthropological Interventions in a Long Conversation.' In *Bodies and Persons: Comparative Perspectives from Africa and Melanesia*, edited by M. Lambek and A. Strathern. New York: Cambridge University Prss.

— ed. 2008. *A Reader in the Anthropology of Religion*. Malden, MA: Blackwell, second edition.

— and Andrew Strathern, eds. 1998. *Bodies and Persons: Comparative Perspectives from Africa and Melanesia*. New York: Cambridge University Press.

Lattas, Andrew. 1998. *Cultures of Secrecy: Reinventing Race in Bush Kaliai Cargo Cults*. Madison, WI: University of Wisconsin Press.

Lévi-Strauss, Claude. 1963. *Structural Anthropology*. New York: Basic Books.

Lewis, I. M. 1976. *Social Anthropology in Perspective*. Harmondsworth, Middlesex, UK: Penguin.
— 1986. *Religion in Context*. Cambridge: Cambridge University Press.
— 1989. *Ecstatic Religion*. 2nd ed. New York: Routledge.
Lock, Margaret. 1997. 'Cultivating the Body: Anthropology and Epistemologies of Bodily Practice and Knowledge.' *Annual Review of Anthropology* 22: 133–155.
Low, Setha M., and Denise Lawrence-Zuniga, eds. 2003. *The Anthropology of Space and Place: Locating Culture*. New York: Blackwell.
Luhrmann, Teresa M. 1989. *Persuasions of the Witch's Craft: Ritual Magic in Contemporary England*. Cambridge, MA: Harvard University Press.
MacGaffey, Wyatt. 1983. *Modern Kongo Prophets: Religion in a Plural Society*. Bloomington, IN: Indiana University Press.
Mahmood, Cynthia Kepley. 2003. 'Agenda for an Anthropology of Peace.' *Anthropology News*: 8.
Malinowski, Bronislaw. 1954 [1925]. *Magic, Science and Religion and Other Essays*. Garden City, NY: Doubleday.
Masquelier, Adeline. 2001. '*Prayer Has Spoiled Everything': Possession, Power, and Identity in an Islamic Town of Niger*. Durham, NC: Duke University Press.
Meyer, Birgit. 1999. *Translating the Devil: Religion and Modernity among the Ewe in Ghana*. Edinburgh: Edinburgh University Press.
— 2006. Religious Revelation, Secrecy and the Limits of Visual Representation. *Anthropological Theory* 6 (4):431–453.
— and Annelies Moors, eds. 2005. *Religion, Media, and the Public Sphere*. Indiana: Indiana University Press.
Moore, Henrietta. 1988. *Feminism and Anthropology*. London: Polity Press.
— 1996. *Space, Text, and Gender: An Anthropological Study of the Marakwet of Kenya*. New York: The Guildford Press.
— ed. 1999. *Anthropological Theory Today*. Cambridge: Polity Press.
Morphy, Howard. 1992. *Ancestral Connections*. Chicago: University of Chicago Press.
Morris, Brian. 2006. *Religion and Anthropology: A Critical Introduction*. New York: Cambridge.
— 1987. *Anthropological Studies of Religion: An Introductory Text*. New York: Cambridge University Press.
Myers, Fred. 2002. *Painting Culture: The Making of an Aboriginal High Art*. Durham, NC: Duke University Press.
Nagata, Judith. 2001. 'Beyond Theology: Toward an Anthropology of "Fundamentalism".' *American Anthropologist* 102 (2): 481–498.
Needham, Rodney. 1972. *Belief, Language and Experience*. Oxford: Blackwell.
Niehaus, Isak. 2001. 'Witchcraft in the New South Africa.' In *Witchcraft, Power and Politics: Exploring the Occult in the South African Lowveld*, edited by I. Niehaus, E. Mohlala and K. Shokane. Sterling, VA: Pluto Press.
Nooter, Mary (Polly) H., ed. 1993. *Secrecy: African Art that Conceal and Reveals*. New York: The Museum for African Art.
Nordstrom, Carolyn. 1997. 'The Eye of the Storm: From War to Peace-Examples from Sri Lanka and Mozambique.' In *Cultural Variation in Conflict Resolution: Alternatives to Violence*, edited by D. P. Fry and K. Bjorkqvist. Mahwah, NJ: Lawrence Erlbaum Associates.
Nye, Malory. 2001. *Multiculturalism and Minority Religions in Britain: Krishna Consciousness, Religious Freedom, and the Politics of Location*. London: Curzon.
Palmié, Stephan. 2002. *Wizards and Scientists: Explorations in Modernity and Afro-Cuban Tradition*. Durham, NC: Duke University Press.
Peacock, James L. 1986. *The Anthropological Lens: Harsh Light, Soft Focus*. New York: Cambridge University Press.
Pemberton III, John, ed. 2000. *Insight and Artistry in African Divination*. Washington, DC: Smithsonian Institution.

Pigg, Stacy Leigh. 1996. 'The Credible and the Credulous: the Question of "Villagers' Beliefs" in Nepal.' *Cultural Anthropology* 11 (2): 160–201.

Radcliffe-Brown, Arthur Reginald. 1952. *Structure and Function in Primitive Society*. Glencoe, IL: The Free Press.

Robbins, Joel. 2003. 'What is a Christian? Notes Toward an Anthropology of Christianity.' *Religion* 33 (3): 191–291.

— 2004. *Becoming Sinners: Christianity and Moral Torment in a Papua New Guinea Society*. Berkeley and Los Angeles: University of California Press.

Roberts, Allen F., Mary Nooter Roberts, Gassia Armenian, and Ousmane Gueye. 2003. *A Saint in the City: Sufi Arts of Urban Senegal*. Los Angeles: Fowler Museum of Cultural History, University of California Los Angeles.

Sered, Susan. 1999. *Women of the Sacred Groves: Divine Priestesses of Okinawa*. New York: Oxford University Press.

Shaw, Rosalind. 1995. 'Feminist Anthropology and the Gendering of Religious Studies.' In *Religion and Gender*, edited by U. King. Cambridge, USA: Blackwell.

— 2002. *Memories of the Slave Trade: Ritual and the Historical Imagination in Sierra Leone*. Chicago: The University of Chicago Press.

— and Charles Stewart, eds. 1994. *Syncretism/Anti-Syncretism: The Politics of Religious Synthesis*. New York: Routledge.

Soares, Benjamin F. 2005. *Islam and the Prayer Economy: History and Authority in a Malian Town*. Edinburgh: Edinburgh University Press.

Sommers, Marc. 2000. 'Urbanization, Pentecostalism, and Urban Refugee Youth in Africa.' Boston: Boston University African Studies Center.

Spickard, James V., S. Shawn Landres, and Meredith B. McGuire, eds. 2002. *Personal Knowledge and Beyond: Reshaping the Ethnography of Religion*. New York: New York University Press.

Starrett, Gregory. 2003. 'Violence and the Rhetoric of Images.' *Cultural Anthropology* 18 (3): 398–428.

Stoller, Paul. 1989. *The Taste of Ethnographic Things*. Philadelphia: University of Pennsylvania Press.

— 1995. *Embodying Colonial Memories: Spirit Possession, Power and the Hauka in West Africa*. New York: Routledge.

— 1997. *Sensuous Scholarship*. Philadelphia: University of Pennsylvania Press.

Tambiah, Stanley J. 1996. *Leveling Crowds: Ethnonationalist Conflicts and Collective Violence in South Asia*. Berkeley and Los Angeles: University of California.

Taussig, Michael. 1987. *Shamanism, Colonialism and the Wild Man*. Chicago: Chicago University Press.

Tsing, Anna Lowenhaupt. 1993. *In the Realm of the Diamond Queen*. Princeton, NJ: Princeton University Press.

Turner, Edith, ed. 1985. *On the Edge of the Bush: Anthropology as Experience*. Tucson, AZ: University of Arizona Press.

Turner, Victor W. 1974. *Dramas, Fields and Metaphors: Symbolic Action in Human Society*. Ithaca, NY: Cornell University Press.

— and Edward M. Bruner, eds. 1986. *The Anthropology of Experience*. Urbana, IL: University of Illinois Press.

Tylor, Edward B. 1970 [1871]. *Religion in Primitive Society*. Gloucester, MA: Peter Smith.

van Binsbergen, Wim. 1991. 'Becoming a Sangoma: Religious Anthropological Field-Work in Francistown, Botswana.' *Journal of Religion in Africa* 21 (4): 309–344.

— 2003. *Intercultural Encounters: African and Anthropological Lessons towards a Philosophy of Interculturality*. Berlin/Muenster: LIT.

Van Gennep, Arnold. 1960. *The Rites of Passage*. Translated by M. B. Vizedom and G. L. Caffee. Chicago: University of Chicago Press.

Veer, Peter van der, ed. 1996. *Conversion to Modernities: the Globalization of Christianity*. New York: Routledge.

Vertovec, Steve. 2000. *The Hindu Diaspora: Comparative Patterns*. New York: Routledge.

Vitebsky, Piers. 1995. *The Shaman: Voyages of the Soul, Trance, Ecstasy and Healing from Siberia to the Amazon*. London and Basingstoke: Macmillan in association with Duncan Baird Publishers.

Whitehouse, Harvey, and James Laidlaw. 2004. *Ritual and Memory: Toward a Cognitive Anthropology of Religion*. Walnut Creek, CA: AltaMira.

Witte, Marleen de. 2003. Televised Charismatic Christianity in Ghana. *Journal of Religion in Africa* 33 (2):171–202.

Worsley, Peter. 1968. *The Trumpet Shall Sound: A Study of 'Cargo' Cults in Melanesia*. New York: Schocken Books.

Suggested reading

Asad, Tahal. 1993. The Construction of Religion as an Anthropological Category, *The Genealogy of Religion: Discipline and Reasons of Power in Christianity and Islam*. Johns Hopkins University Press.
One of the best examples of the critical questioning an anthropologist can bring to categorizations and interpretations of religion.

Brown, Karen McCarthy. 1991. *Mama Lola: A Vodou Priestess in Brooklyn*. Berkeley: University of California Press.
Popular and imaginative study of Haitian vodou as experienced through the everyday lives and rituals of a Brooklyn-based family. A creative portrayal of a powerful Haitian priestess, with important reflections on participant-observation.

Evans-Pritchard, E. S. 1976. *Witchcraft, Oracles, and Magic among the Azande*. Oxford, Clarendon Press (especially Chapter 4: The Notion of Witchcraft Explains Unfortunate Events).
This classic work by one of the founding fathers of the field examines how the Azande of Sudan interpret, and take ritual action to deal with, evil and misfortune.

Hefner, R. 1998. Multiple Modernities: Christianity, Islam and Hinduism in a Globalizing Age. *Annual Review of Anthropology* 27: 83–104.
Examines from an anthropological perspective the changes impacting world religions in an age of globalization and late modernity.

Hodgson, Dorothy L. 2005. *The Church of Women: Gendered Encounters between Maasai and Missionaries*. Bloomington: IN: Indiana University Press.
Excellent case study that cogently demonstrates how to do anthropology in situations of religious encounter (in this study, the Maasai and Spiritan Catholic fathers in Tanzania). Her work also illustrates well how to frame a research question, methodology, and theoretical concepts and follow them all through in a thorough and engaging manner.

Lambek, Michael. ed. 2008. *A Reader in the Anthropology of Religion*. Malden, MA: Blackwell, second edition.
Provides extensive resources, both classic and contemporary, on how anthropologists have investigated and interpreted religion.

Lewis, I. M. 1986. *Religion in Context*. Cambridge: Cambridge University Press.
Short, insightful, and never lacking in humor, this study both informs and provokes the budding anthropologist of religion.

Lowenhaupt, Tsing, Anna. 1993. *In the Realm of the Diamond Queen: Marginality in an Out-of-the-Way Place*. Princeton, NJ: Princeton University Press.
Original, dense, and widely cited ethnography on the mountain peoples who inhabit a South Kalimantan rain forest in Indonesia that weaves together a fascinating array of topics: marginality, movement, state and regional power, globalization, shamanism, and women. A very instructive and reflexive treatment of the construction of self and Other.

Moro, Pamela, James Myers, and Arthur Lehmann. 2006. *Magic, Witchcraft, and Religion: An Anthropological Study of the Supernatural*. McGraw-Hill, seventh edition.

Useful resource for a range of accessible articles on the subject in terms of methodological approaches and topics (e.g. myth, ritual, and the various types of religious specialists).

Omri, Elisha. 2008. Moral Ambitions of Grace: The Paradox of Compassion and Accountability in Evangelical Faith-Based Activism. *Cultural Anthropology* 23 (1): 154–189.

Perceptive and clearly written study that exemplifies the merits of exploring new areas (domestic US) and new topics (evangelical mega-churches and humanitarian activism) for anthropologists of religion.

Chapter 11

Psychology of religion

Dan Merkur

The psychology of religion studies the phenomena of religion in so far as they may be understood psychologically. Religions and their denominations differ regarding the extent of the psychologizing that they each embrace, tolerate, and reject. For many religious devotees, psychological understanding is inherently antagonistic to religion because it ascribes to the human mind what those devotees credit to more-than-human agencies. They view the psychology of religion as a program that reduces religion to psychology. Other devotees are instead sympathetic to the psychology of religion. They value critical research as an irreplaceable means for the purification of religion from idolatry of the merely human.

Like psychology in general, the psychology of religion is an umbrella term for the findings of several, mutually exclusive schools of thought, each with its own research agenda and methodology. The major disciplinary affiliations include: the academic study of religion; academic psychology; psychoanalysis; analytic psychology; and transpersonal psychology. These several approaches to the psychological study of religion tend to be pursued in isolation from each other, as non-communicating and mutually disdainful subdisciplines. A useful way to comprehend both their strengths and their differences is to attend to the questions that they seek to answer. The overall project of each school of thought determines both what data it addresses and what methodologies it considers appropriate.

Psychology in the service of the history of religion

Psychologically oriented studies by historians of religion adhere to the methodological phenomenology of the history of religion in general. The manifest contents of religious experience are discussed, but no mention is ever made of the unconscious. The question of primary interest for this school of research has been whether psychology can explain otherwise inexplicable features of the historical record of the world's many and diverse religions. The psychology of religion, so conceived, subserves the writing of the history of religion, addresses the religious past more frequently than the religious present, and has been minutely attentive to cross-cultural findings in world religions.

Rejecting theories of cultural evolution that contrasted 'magic' and 'religion', Rudolf Otto (1932) suggested that experiences of the holy or 'numinous' were the defining characteristics of religion. For Otto (1950 [1917]), the numinous was a *sui generis* category of human experience. The quality of numinosity is sometimes experienced as awe and urgency at the mystery and immanent majesty of the Wholly Other; it may alternatively be known as a fascination at an august and transcendent 'Something More'. Otto's student and colleague, Nathan Söderblom (1933), argued that experiences of the numinous explained the veneration of sacred books. The world's scriptures are not held to be holy merely because of the ideas that they contain. Rather, the texts are sacred because their ideas concern living powers. Scriptures pertain to spirits, gods, or God that people encounter in personal religious experiences. When the numina cease to be experienced, interest in the books fails.

Many historians of religion pursued similar lines of inquiry with increasing detail. Söderblom's student Ernst Arbman (1939) argued that myths are venerated because the gods that they portray are credited with invisible responsibility for the fortuitous events of everyday life. Should belief in providential miracles fail, however, the myths decline into folktales. Biblical scholars noted that some Israelite prophets were described in fashions consistent with physically active trance states. Other ancient prophets were clearly not in trances. Some biblical data pointed to hypnagogic states, which occur between waking and falling asleep. Other prophets may have experienced inspirations during dream-like states of deep trance. Attention was also called to the ecstatic, experiential side of classical Greek religion; and the distinctive features of shamanism were noted in a variety of contexts. Zoroaster, the prophet who reformed ancient Iranian religion, was alleged to have been a shaman; and the legend of the opening of Muhammad's breast was treated as a folklore motif that described a shamanic initiation. The character of Vainamoinen in the Finnish national epic, *The Kalevala*, was identified as a shaman; and detailed studies were made of Siberian, Lapp, Native American, and other cultural variations of shamanism, past and present.

Underlying these psychologically oriented studies in the history of religion is the axiomatic assumption that most people are religious because they personally have religious experiences. Good and bad fortune may be attributed to demons, spirits, gods, God, karma, or what you will. Both conversions and subsequent encounters with numinous beings and numinous states of existence may proceed through dreams, visions, voices, or mystical unions. Notice needs also to be taken of occasional, highly emotionally charged rites. These orders of religious experience are, for those who have them, the very core of religion itself. In this approach to religion, people believe in myths, they subscribe to theologies, they engage in rites, precisely because they have religious experiences. For devotees, religious experiences confirm, prove, modify, extend – in short, motivate – the balance of what religion entails.

Two Swedish scholars who were trained by Söderblom formalized the axiomatic assumption with detailed psychological theories. Ernst Arbman argued that religious trance states, which he documented on a worldwide basis, varied in their contents in accord with the religious beliefs and expectations of the devotee. The religious belief complex was converted by the trance state from a series of ideas into a vivid, dream-like experience. Differences among visions, voices, automatic behavior, stigmata, solipsistic mystical unions, and all other trance phenomena, reflected differences in the pre-trance beliefs and expectations.

Hjalmar Sundén instead adapted the notion of a 'social role' from its original context in reference to interpersonal behavior as observed by social psychologists. The term had greater application in the study of religion, he maintained, than in explaining the roles of shaman, prophet, priest, lay person, mystic, and so forth. Sundén applied the concept to the apparent behavior of a greater-than-human personality, such as a spirit, angel, or God, as it manifests in a religious experience. Sundén proposed that people may learn a variety of roles that may manifest in the course of their religious experiences.

The theories of Arbman and Sundén both imply that religious experiences are learned behavior, whose differences are to be sought in the contents of the learning. It then follows that whether discussion is to be made of belief complexes or religious roles, analysis of the learned materials can be pursued competently by historians, without need for special training in psychology. This conclusion is a product of historians' methods, however. Only when the psychology of religion is limited to the identification of patterns in historical religious data does psychological expertise become unnecessary.

Religion as group pathology

Sigmund Freud (1856–1939), the founder of psychoanalysis, once privately remarked, 'Mankind has always known that it possesses spirit: I had to show it that there are also instincts'. A few sentences later, he went on to reject the validity of religion. 'Religion originates in the helplessness and anxiety of childhood and early manhood. It cannot be otherwise'. The apparent contradiction is to be explained by the special senses in which Freud referred to spirit and religion. For Freud, spirit (in German, *Geist*, which also means 'intellect') was an objectively existing intellectual power abroad in the cosmos that is responsible for life, reason, self-consciousness, and telepathy. Echoing Aristotle, Freud named 'the psychological ideal, the primacy of the intellect' and spoke of 'the voice of the intellect' as an intrapsychic manifestation of 'our God Logos.'

Freud used the criterion of evidence as a basis for defining religion in a contrasting manner.

> Critics persist in describing as 'deeply religious' anyone who admits to a sense of man's insignificance or impotence in the face of the universe, although what constitutes the essence of the religious attitude is not this feeling but only the next step after it, the reaction to it which seeks a remedy for it. The man who goes no further, but humbly acquiesces in the small part which human beings play in the great world – such a man is, on the contrary, irreligious in the truest sense of the word.

For Freud, spirituality pertained to the reality of the universe, inclusive of belief in its scientific knowledge. Speculation beyond the limits of intellect involved unproven and unprovable beliefs that he called religious. Freud further defined religion in conformance with liberal nineteenth-century Christian and Jewish theologies, as a 'system of doctrines and promises' concerning 'a careful Providence' that is imagined 'in the figure of an enormously exalted father'. Freud saw both magic and religion as misunderstandings of the nature of spirit that substituted infantile hopes and wishes for a scientifically valid appreciation. In likening magic and religion to childhood neuroses, he was both likening them to premodern beliefs such as astral myths and Ptolemy's geocentric astronomy, and suggesting that they derived their contents from the same infantile fantasies that shape neuroses.

As a clinician who wrote very little of mental health but extensively of psychopathology, Freud mentioned spirit only in passing but discussed magic and religion at length. He regularly addressed the questions: What are magic and religion? And why do people engage in them? He expressed his basic view of religion in a dense paragraph in 'Leonardo da Vinci and a Memory of His Childhood' (1957 [1910]):

> Psycho-analysis has made us familiar with the intimate connection between the father-complex and belief in God; it has shown us that a personal God is, psychologically, nothing other than an exalted father, and it brings us evidence every day of how young people lose their religious beliefs as soon as their father's authority breaks down. Thus we recognize that the roots of the need for religion are in the parental complex; the

almighty and just God, and kindly Nature, appear to us as grand sublimations of father and mother, or rather as revivals and restorations of the young child's ideas of them. Biologically speaking, religiousness is to be traced to the small human child's long-drawn-out helplessness and need of help; and when at a later date he perceives how truly forlorn and weak he is when confronted with the great forces of life, he feels his condition as he did in childhood, and attempts to deny his own despondency by a regressive revival of the forces which protected his infancy.

With very few changes, Freud maintained the same position for the remainder of his life. Religion functions primarily to offer consolation for human helplessness. The consolation is fictional. God is a fantasy that is based on infantile memories of father and mother and motivated by human helplessness.

In an essay entitled 'Obsessive Actions and Religious Practices' (1959 [1907]), Freud noted several parallels between personal rites that occur as symptoms of neurosis and the public rites of religions. He suggested that both arise as symbolic substitutes for unconscious guilt. In neurotic rites, the unconscious guilt is sexual; in religious rites, it is a response to egoism. Freud likely had in mind patients whose self-righteousness about ritual observances misdirected attention from ethical failings.

In *Totem and Taboo* (1958 [1913]), Freud expanded his argument to book length. He began by summarizing the anthropological evidence that incest is prohibited in aboriginal Australian cultures. Noting widespread practices of avoiding mothers-in-law, Freud suggested that extreme forms of avoidance had been added to a core prohibition of incest, in much the same irrational manner that obsessional neurotics multiply inhibitions. Because no one bothers to prohibit anything that is not desired, the two basic taboos of aboriginal Australian religions – not to kill the totem animal, and not to marry within the clan – indicated the content of the oldest and most powerful human desires. These desires are to kill the ancestral totem animal and to commit incest. Freud also connected guilt over the desire for patricide with the widespread belief in, fear of, and devotion toward ancestral spirits. In this way, Freud located the Oedipus complex – a boy's unconscious wish to kill his father and have sex with his mother – at the core of totemism, which was widely regarded at the time as the most primitive form of religion worldwide. Freud further argued that Christianity presents a similar ambivalence. Its God, who is explicitly called Father, is both murdered in the gospel narrative and consumed ritually in the mass; and Christianity's emphasis of virginity and celibacy can be seen as extreme forms of incest avoidance. The centrality of irrational Oedipal themes in both totemism and Christianity attested to the human origin and neurotic character of religion.

Freud maintained that magic was to be explained by the 'omnipotence of thoughts', a phenomenon that is found in obsessional neurosis in which thoughts are projected onto and substituted for reality. Magic is narcissistic in that it attributes supernatural power to the self, rather than to ancestral ghosts, totem spirits, and so forth. Because magic does not presuppose the existence of personal spirits, as religion does, Freud treated it as an older, pre-Oedipal stage in cultural evolution. Freud also demonstrated that the chief features of animism and magic occur normally in childhood; and he concluded with a speculative reconstruction of how the Oedipus complex may have evolved in the species.

In *Group Psychology and the Analysis of the Ego* (1955 [1921]), Freud created a theoretic bridge between individual and group psychology. He suggested that group members share an ego ideal that consists of or is embodied by the group leader. The devotion to the leader provides cohesion to the group, despite the rivalry that is also inevitably present. To illustrate the processes of group psychology, Freud used the examples of an army and the Roman Catholic Church.

Freud's next major statement on religion, *The Future of an Illusion* (1961 [1927]), added several new points. Civilization depends on coercion and the renunciation of instinct. Prohibitions are initially external and imposed on the individual, but are internalized during childhood as the superego. In addition to performing self-observation and conscience, the superego houses both personal and group ideals that are the basis for forming cultural units. Religious ideals promote civilization through their internalization in the superego.

The valuable socializing function of religion does not mitigate its fallacies, however. Religion anthropomorphizes nature. Religion asserts that external reality is subject to personal spirits and gods, on whom one may depend as one depended on one's parents in childhood. The belief that nature is benign and parental is an illusion. The illusion can be neither verified nor falsified; its treatment as true proceeds out of the wish that it were so, rather than through logical necessity. The illusion is maintained at the cost of denying the corresponding reality. Freud deplored religion, 'the universal obsessional neurosis of humanity', for intimidating the intelligence in order to maintain its illusions.

Responding to *The Future of an Illusion*, Theodor Reik observed that religion is perhaps the single most difficult source of resistance to psychotherapeutic change. Psychonalysts are able to help many people with disturbances in love and work, but make little progress on topics that religious beliefs and practices oppose. Talk therapy is still less effective with religious fanaticism. In private conversation, Freud told Reik that the solution to the problem of religion would likely not prove clinical, but would instead depend on the promotion of psychoanalytic ideas through public education.

Beginning with *Civilization and Its Discontents* (1961 [1930]), Freud struggled to comprehend the clinical problem of religion. Where he had earlier written of the superego internalizing civilization, he now stated that the superego turns aggression against the self in the form of guilt that makes civilization possible. Art, religion, and other illusions flourish under the protection, as it were, of the superego. Religion compares badly with art, however, 'since it imposes equally on everyone its own path to the acquisition of happiness and protection from suffering. Its technique consists in depressing the value of life and distorting the picture of the real world in a delusional manner – which presupposes an intimidation of the intelligence'. Freud now called religion a 'mass-delusion' – a malignancy significantly greater than the merely fanciful error of an 'illusion'.

Freud also acknowledged that religion has a third function, additional to consolation and socialization. Religion permits instinctual wishes to be 'sublimated' through their diversion to social valued and refined ends. Freud viewed religion as second only to art in promoting culture through transformations of sexuality and aggression into civilized behavior. At the same time, Freud suggested that the 'oceanic feeling' of mystical experience was not religious, but was connected with religion only secondarily.

In 'Constructions in Analysis' (1964 [1937]) Freud returned to his re-evaluation of religion as a delusion. He theorized that just as the fantasies of psychotics have delusional force because they distort underlying truths, so too the delusional quality of religions – their imperviousness to rational argument, and intractability to psychotherapy – must owe to their containing some manner of underlying truth. In *Moses and Monotheism* (1964 [1939]), Freud supposed this truth to be historical. The text's rejection by modern Bible critics has been unequivocal; and its thesis that Moses was an Egyptian whose imposition on the Jews induced them to murder him, overstated Freud's case that the many irrational aspects of Mosaic religion betray its human, neurotic, and Oedipal origin. The book's addition to Freud's theory of religion consists of its analysis of the Mosaic commandment that prohibits the making of Divine images. Freud took the commandment to imply that Moses conceived of a God who has no form. Proceeding from this premise, Freud suggested that the abstract concept of God is derived from concrete images of God, through a 'triumph of intellectuality over sensuality or, strictly speaking, an instinctual renunciation'. Freud remarked that 'all such advances in intellectuality have as their consequence that the individual's self-esteem is increased' (p. 115).

Object relations and the revalorization of religion

Freud's questions – what is religion? why are people religious? is religion healthy? – have remained the major concerns of psychoanalytic writings on religion. Although most psycho-analysts outdid Freud in pathologizing religion, Oskar Pfister (1923, 1948), a Lutheran pastor, psychoanalyst, and personal friend of Freud, saw psychoanalysis as a means to purify religion by identifying its morbid components. The neurotic aspects of religion could then be abandoned, and only healthy aspects retained.

Pfister's orientation was given powerful support by the clinical studies of Ana-Maria Rizzuto (1979), who noted that psychoanalytic patients' relations with God are complex, nuanced, and in process of continuous development, in a fashion that is consistent with their relations with other people. Rizzuto's finding has been amply confirmed by other psychoanalysts. It is inconsistent, however, with Freud's theory that God is the exalted father. Were God a symbol that displaces memories of the father as he was seen by the young child, a person's relation with God would be fixated and unchanging in its infantilism. It would not be in process of continuing growth and development.

Contemporary psychoanalysts favor an 'object relations' approach to religion that revises Freud's diagnosis. D. W. Winnicott drew attention to the infant's special attachment to its 'first not-me possession', a cloth, teddy bear, or doll that the infant cannot bear to be without. Its importance for the infant is accepted by the family, given social validation through tolerant regard, and surrounded with appropriate ritualized behaviors. Winnicott contended that a 'transitional object' is, for the infant, both part of the infant and an external reality. Logically paradoxical, it is experientially coherent, for it belongs to 'an intermediate area of *experiencing* … which is not challenged, because no claim is made on its behalf except that it shall exist as a resting-place for the individual'.

Winnicott was primarily concerned with infancy, but in a remarkable intuitive leap he extrapolated from the clinical evidence to a general theory of culture. Alluding to Freud's designation of religion as an illusion, Winnicott revalorized illusion:

> *Illusion* … is allowed to the infant, and … in adult life is inherent in art and religion, and yet becomes the hallmark of madness when an adult puts too powerful a claim on the credulity of others, forcing them to acknowledge a sharing of illusion that is not their own. We can share a respect for *illusory experience*, and if we wish we may collect together and form a group on the basis of the similarity of our illusory experiences.

Winnicott asserted that illusory experiences range from the transitional objects of infancy through play to creativity and the whole of cultural life. Because illusory experiences are unavoidable, they must be considered normal and healthy. They remain projections that buffer the individual from reality. However, Freud's either/or distinction between inner (psychic) and external (physical) reality is overly simplistic. Illusory experiences form a third class of phenomena.

Paul W. Pruyser (1974) added that an individual's capacity for illusory experience determines 'a disposition or a talent for the numinous', as is also the case for artistic creativity and art appreciation. Not everyone needs or likes to develop the transitional sphere. Among those who do, differences in taste – which are partly constitutional and partly acquired – lead to different preferences among art, literature, drama, music, religious ideas, metaphysical speculation, and ethical propositions. Arguing in the tradition of the historians of religion Otto and van der Leeuw, Pruyser asserted the intrinsically religious character of 'limit situations' because they involve '*transcendence* and *mystery* ... charged with cognitive, ontological, epistemological, and emotional implications'.

Pruyser emphasized that 'adequate reality-testing is needed to keep the transitional sphere properly bounded, and its content and language consensually validated'. Religions have historically permitted illusions to shade over into hallucination and delusion whenever 'excessive fantasy formation' has led to 'flagrant disregard of the obvious features of outer reality'. In Pruyser's view, the truth claims of religions may be valid if they are maintained as illusions – that is, as matters of faith – but they are definitely and necessarily false if they are presented as theological certainties.

Pfister's concern with the questions, 'What is sick? and what healthy in religion?', remains a major focus of clinical interest. The impact of religion on psychotherapy and the handling of religious issues in psychotherapy are pressing concerns for psychotherapists who work with religious clientele.

Spiritual awakening

A third major trend in the psychology of religion was begun by two founders of academic psychology, Edwin Diller Starbuck (1911 [1899]) and William James (1958 [1902]), but went into eclipse during the heyday of behaviorism. Familiar as Starbuck and James were with the evangelical tradition of American Protestantism, they conceptualized the psychology of religion, above all else, as the study of the process by which a non-religious person becomes religious. Where Freud had asked, 'What religious phenomena become coherent through their resemblance to psycho-pathology?', Starbuck and James implicitly asked, 'How does religion differ from irreligion? What psychological phenomena are uniquely religious, that is, are unlike any and all non-religious phenomena?' These questions led them to study religious experiences.

In Starbuck's opinion, the spiritual path begins with conversion but culminates in a further experience termed sanctification. Because sin ceases to be tempting, evil habits are abandoned, altruism increases, and there is a sense of having achieved complete union with one's spiritual ideals.

James expanded Starbuck's model to address Catholicism as well as evangelical Protestantism. According to James, 'healthy-minded religion' develops straightforwardly, without dramatic processes. Because the healthy-minded are at peace with their own imperfections, they feel no need to undergo spiritual development in any meaningful sense of the term. It is only the sick soul that must be twice-born in order to attain its natural inner unity and peace. The divided self gains unity through conversion. Some conversions occur during mystical moments. Others do not. When conversion is not followed by backsliding but is permanent, the individual achieves saintliness – a quality that is characterized by asceticism, strength of soul, purity, and charity.

Following Starbuck and James, many studies were made of conversion, but the treatment of a theological category, 'conversion', as though it were a psychological one has proved unworkable. Discussions of religious conversion address three separate psychological phenomena: (1) a change from irreligiosity to religiosity; (2) a change of existing religiosity from conventional routine to personal and devout; and (3) a change of affiliation from one religion to another. Because studies of conversion often proceeded at cross-purposes with each other, the larger topic of spiritual transformation was neglected until the rise of humanistic and transpersonal psychology in the 1960s and 1970s.

A pioneer of humanistic psychology, Abraham Maslow (1964) suggested that people have a hierarchy of motives, that commences with physiological needs, safety, belongingness and love, and progress to less necessary objects of desire, such as self-esteem, satisfaction striving or growth motivation, the need to know, aesthetic needs, and Being-values. Maslow identified Being-values through an analysis of peak experiences, including mystical. The values included: truth, goodness, beauty, wholeness, dichotomy-transcendence, aliveness, uniqueness, necessity, completion, justice, order, simplicity, richness, effortlessness, playfulness, and self-sufficiency.

Maslow contended that psychological changes conform with progress along the hierarchy of values. The changes that are sought through psychotherapy serve to heal deficiencies in the areas of belongingness, love, and self-esteem. Their function is to end existing psychic pain. Psychotherapy may be considered successful when these motives are satisfied. It is also possible, however, for the personality to move beyond health into excellence, when the further motives for growth, knowledge, aesthetics, and Being-values come to the fore. Maslow adopted the term 'self-actualization' in order to discuss the achievement of these goals.

Maslow argued, and quantitative studies have since confirmed, that traditional religious beliefs and observances are obstacles to self-actualization, particularly if they are conservative. On the other hand, because self-actualized people tend to have mystical peak experiences, Maslow and several other psychologists assumed the converse, that the world's mystical paths are techniques, among other matters, for self-actualization. The term 'transpersonal' denoting progress beyond self, to achieve something more than self alone, was introduced by Roberto Assagioli, who had founded psychosynthesis decades earlier. As it was defined in the 1970s, the project of transpersonal psychology was to place spiritual transformation and spiritual direction, so far as possible, on cross-cultural and scientific footing.

Assagioli (1991) developed a longitudinal, psychodynamic account of a clinically observable process that he termed 'self-realization' or 'spiritual awakening'. The process begins with an existential crisis regarding the meaning of life that is often attended by resistance of all solutions. One or more religious experiences occur next. The experiences are typically euphoric and profoundly meaningful. Their occurrence terminates the existential crisis, but frequently precipitates a crisis of another sort. The newly discovered meaningfulness of spirituality is made the pretext of narcissistic inflation or grandiosity. Once the inflation wanes, depression may set in. The depression often has an ethical content of remorse over past moral failings. If the depression is intolerable, the religious experiences may be denied, much as ideas born of alcoholic intoxication are discounted during subsequent sobriety. Alternatively, the newly appreciated spiritual values may be made the basis of behavioral change to embody the values. The reformation or transformation of character inevitably proceeds gradually, by small increments.

In many and perhaps most cases, spiritual awakenings do not proceed in uncomplicated fashions that would be consistent with Maslow's concept of a growth from mental health toward excellence. Most awakenings are complicated by pathological symptoms that arise out of unresolved conflicts within the personality. Christina and Stanislav Grof (1990) introduced the term, 'spiritual emergency', to denote a spiritual awakening that is complicated by psychopathology. The differences between a spiritual emergency and a psychiatric disorder include: absence of physical disease; absence of brain pathology; absence of organic impairment; intact, clear consciousness and coordination; continuing ability to communicate and cooperate; adequate pre-episode functioning; ability to relate and cooperate, often even during religious experiences; awareness of the intrapsychic nature of the process; sufficient trust to accept help and cooperate; ability to honor basic rules of therapy; absence of destructive or self-destructive ideas and tendencies; good cooperation in things related to physical health, basic maintenance, and hygienic rules. Spiritual emergencies are among the syndromes that have been recognized in the *Diagnostic and Statistical Manual* IV of the American Psychiatric Association as 'V62.89 Religious or Spiritual Problem'.

The conceptualization of single religious experiences in terms of creativity, commensurate with scientific and artistic achievement, was suggested by the social psychologists Daniel Batson and Larry Ventis (Batson *et al.* 1997). Merkur compared the longitudinal process of spiritual awakening with Wallas's classic model of four phases of creativity: (1) the establishment of a problem, for example, an existential crisis, or an advance in maturity; (2) the unconscious incubation of the problem's solution; (3) the manifestation of a creative solution as the content of one or more religious experiences, possibly precipitating a spiritual emergency; and (4) the refinement of the solution through its practical, behavioral implementation. In Merkur's (1999) model, religious experiences differ from the creative inspirations of painters, writers, musicians, scientists, and so forth, in having numinous 'limit situations' as their subject matter.

Some writers conceptualize spiritual awakening as spiritual in a metaphysical sense. In other cases, it is psychologized, for example, as self-actualization in Maslow's model or, alternatively, from Merkur's psychoanalytic perspective as a process of positive superego manifestation and integration.

Transpersonal psychotherapy

Because transpersonal psychology was unable to find a home in the academy, many practitioners came to depend for their income on private practices as psychotherapists. These financial constraints motivated a change in many transpersonalists' agendas. Rather than to research spiritual awakening, transpersonalists who were therapists came to promote spiritual practices as adjuncts to psychotherapy. Meditations, visualizations, prayer, and other religious practices were found to be useful in psychotherapy, for example, in learning self-observation, in cultivating self-discipline, and in building self-esteem.

Valuable as the procedures are clinically, the results are inevitably sectarian. Whichever meditations, visualizations, prayers, and so forth that a therapist enjoins on a client inevitably belong to one particular religion or another. The practices never belong to religion in general. Some transpersonal therapists are syncretistic in their borrowings; others confine themselves to the practices of a particular religious tradition.

The slippage of transpersonal psychology from the study into the practice of religion has given rise to a genre of apologetic literature. The writings claim that one or another tradition of religious mysticism (Zen, Sufism, Kabbalah, and so forth) is inherently therapeutic. Although the writings are published as psychology, they are better considered as theology.

Religious development

All authorities agree that religiosity takes different forms at different ages. No consensus has emerged, however, regarding the contents and duration of the stages. William W. Meissner, a Jesuit and a psychoanalyst, has argued that a person's religion reflects whatever may be the person's developmental stage at the time. Meissner suggested that faith and hope are issues in infancy. Contrition comes to the fore in early childhood. The central issues in later years are: penance and temperance in the kindergarten years; fortitude in grade school; humility in adolescence; the love of neighbors in young adulthood; service, zeal, and self-sacrifice in adulthood; and charity in maturity.

Recognizing that people's experiences are not necessarily limited to their current developmental issues, but may involve reversions to previous concerns, Meissner (1984) later proposed a typology of five modes of religious experience. The first is dominated by an absence of subject–object distinctions. The second reflects the worldview of toddlers. The veneration of idealized religious figures is necessary to sustain and maintain the sense of self. Faith is 'riddled with a sense of utter dependence, a terror of the omnipotence of the godhead, and a superstitious and magical need to placate by ritual and ceremonial'. The third mode reflects the anal stage of psychoanalytic theory. The self is cohesive, but efforts must be made to secure self-esteem. Concepts tend to be concrete, literal, and one-dimensional. Religious figures are authoritative, and myths tend to be anthropomorphic. Religious concerns address the permitted and the prohibited, the fear of punishment for transgressions, and the dutiful performance of obligations and rituals. The fourth mode presupposes the consolidation of the superego and, with it, the internalization of conscience around age six. Ethics and social concerns are at a premium. Recognition is made of the diversity of authorities. Conflicts are resolved partly through compartmentalization but partly through reliance on one's own judgment. Meissner remarked that 'by far the largest portion of adult religious behavior falls into this modality'.

Meissner's fifth and final mode of religious experience becomes possible when still greater maturity has been attained. In the fifth mode, instinctual drives are managed successfully, so that the ego enjoys considerable autonomy. Anxiety is lessened dramatically and is largely restricted to realistic external concerns. Wisdom, empathy, humor, and creativity come to the fore, and conflicts tend to be resolved through synthesis rather than compartmentalization. 'The religious belief system and its tradition are seen in increasingly realistic terms that affirm their inherent tensions and ambiguities and accept the relativity, partiality, and particularity of the beliefs, symbols, rituals, and ceremonials of the religious community'.

A significantly different developmental scheme was offered by James W. Fowler (1981), who worked with a Piagetian model of cognitive development. Fowler postulated a preverbal stage of undifferentiated faith and counted six further stages through the life span. He attributed a fantasy-filled, imitative 'intuitive-projective' faith to children between 3 and 7 years of age, a 'mythic-literal' faith to grade schoolers, and a 'synthetic-conventional' faith' to adolescents. After remarking that many adults never progress beyond synthetic-conventional faith, Fowler listed 'individuative-reflective' faith in young adulthood when people take responsibility for themselves, 'conjunctive faith' in mid-life when exceptions and compromises seem most realistic, and a 'universalizing' faith in rare individuals, martyrs among them.

Whether psychoanalytic or cognitive in the stages that they discern in the life span, existing accounts of religious development have regularly treated liberal, church-going Christianity as normative. Their descriptions of optimal development are inconsistent with the literalism of Christian fundamentalism; they are equally inconsistent with a personal practice of mystical experiences. Spiritual awakenings typically lead to beliefs in clairvoyance, precognition, and providential miracles.

Religion as psychotherapy

Analytic psychology, which Carl G. Jung developed following his break with Freud in 1912, is the approach to the psychology of religion that has been most favored by religious devotees, both in the academy and in the public at large. It was the first of the modern systems of psychology to be premised on the question, 'Is religiosity not inherently therapeutic?'

Jung (1969) premised analytic psychology on the assumption that the 'collective unconscious' or 'objective psyche' is universal in compass. The objective psyche is responsible, among other phenomena, for astrology, telepathy, prophecy, and fortuitous physical events – all of which Jung summarized under the term 'synchronicity'. The objective psyche is cosmic, yet it is simultaneously a component of the personal psyche of each human individual. Dreams manifest materials that originate from both the personal and the collective unconscious.

The objective psyche is composed of archetypes. Archetypes exist in the personal psyche as inborn clusters of form and motivation that constitute 'mentally expressed instincts'. However, the forms and behavioral urges have their source in the objective psyche and not in human genetics alone. Archetypes are personal entities that exist independently of human beings. Jung described them as 'autonomous *animalia* gifted with a sort of consciousness and psychic life of their own'.

Archetypes are always unconscious. They are unable to become conscious. What manifests is not an archetype but a mental image that expresses an archetype. The major archetypal images are three: the anima, which represents the feminine; the animus, which represents the masculine; and the shadow, which represents all that is rejected as evil and projected as other. Jung counted the sage, the father, the mother, the child, the hero, and the trickster as archetypal images of lesser importance.

Jung held that the unconscious manifests to consciousness in a compensatory manner. Should an archetype's manifestations be undervalued or repressed, or its opposite be overemphasized in consciousness, the psyche's need for equilibrium causes the archetype to manifest a compensatory quantity of appropriate archetypal images. Because every spontaneous manifestation of an archetypal image is compensatory, archetypal manifestation is intrinsically therapeutic. Although the design of the objective psyche is intelligent and purposive, the process of compensatory manifestation is itself regulated automatically in a quantitative manner.

In Jung's view, both dreams and religious experiences are instances of direct and unmediated manifestations of archetypal images. Although they are compensatory, dreams are irrational, while religious experiences consist of 'passionate conflicts, panics of madness, desperate confusions and depressions which were grotesque and terrible at the same time'.

Jung provided no criteria for distinguishing acute psychosis from a spiritual emergency; he seems to have made no such distinction.

For Jung, myths were to be seen in parallel, as culturally shared manifestations of the archetypes that give expression to the instinctual structures of the objective psyche. Like dreams, myths are compensatory. Although the archetypes that they manifest are eternal, myths are historical phenomena that provide correction for 'the inadequacy and one-sidedness of the present' in fashions appropriate to their eras and cultures.

Therapy consists of 'individuating' or achieving psychic distance from archetypal images. One may then be able to experience the images without being compelled to act on their basis. Organized religion is semi-therapeutic. Through 'a solidly organized dogma and ritual', Jung wrote, 'people are effectively defended and shielded against immediate religious experience'. A complete therapy moves beyond dogma and ritual into innovative, creative manipulations of archetypal images.

Jung also explained the individuation process in developmental terms. A child's worldview consists of a naive realism, an unreflecting and uncritical assumption that the habitual has the objective status of truth and law. This stage is succeeded by a maturing worldview whose rational and critical character liberates consciousness to a measure of autonomy. In its autonomy, however, critical consciousness suffers from the relativism of its own subjectivity. With a variety of differing subjectivities equally tenable, the psyche is driven into illness. The third and final developmental stage consists of the compensatory intervention of the unconscious. The pathogenic isolation of consciousness is interrupted by the manifestation of archetypal images. The images collectively alert consciousness to its grounding in the unconscious. Stability is regained, but with the naive ontological assumptions of the first stage replaced by the self-consciously psychological considerations of the third. In the process, consciousness becomes aware of, and makes its adjustment to, the unconscious. Because the unconscious is both personal and collective, the individuation process is inherently religious. Psychological health is not possible without religiosity.

Jung considered God and the Self to be archetypes. In some passages, he acknowledged that the two were indistinguishable. His concept of Self was adapted from the Hindu *atman*, which is one with God (*Brahman*) and equivalent to the mind and substance that are the cosmos. For Jung, the Self was an archetype that represents the unity of consciousness and the unconscious, and individuation was not complete until the Self was realized and psychic integration achieved.

Because Jung insisted that the 'God within' was a psychological phenomenon that was not to be confused with an external spiritual being intended by theologians, the case has sometimes been made that Jung psychologized religion and was ultimately concerned only with psychology. Analytic psychology may alternatively be seen as a psychologically informed practice of religion, whose rejection of theologians' God in favor of human self-deification is consistent with its roots in Romanticism and Western esotericism.

Academic psychology

Academics' concern in the 1920s for a scientific psychology, engaged in quantification and independently duplicable results, led the discipline of psychology to replace mental experience with behavior as its primary datum. Mental experience is accessible only through introspection and self-reports, both of which are unavoidably subjective. Behavior can instead be measured, as it were objectively, by external observers.

Due to its methodological concerns, the discipline of psychology largely abandoned the study of religion upon the rise of behaviorism. Behaviorism was incapable of discussing any of the aspects of religion that were of keenest interest to other schools of research. Behaviorism could not ask: what are the subjective phenomena of religion? why are people religious? what are the processes of becoming religious? what in religion is morbid, wholesome, and therapeutic?

Academic psychologists were unable to engage in the study of religion until the monopoly of behaviorism was broken in the 1950s and the methods of social psychology gained prominence. The methods of cognitive behaviorism followed soon afterward. Like psychology in general, however, the academic psychology of religion uses its research methods to determine which data will and will not be examined. It is not prepared to adapt its research methods to whatever the data may happen to be. Methodological purity, rather than practicality, remains the scientific standard. Psychology addresses data that it alone generates (via questionnaires, experiments, and so forth) and it fails to address data generated by academic students of religion. It also uses common terms in eccentric ways that are 'operational' methodologically. For these reasons, the academic psychology of religion has developed an extensive body of knowledge that has not contributed significantly to the academic study of religion. Psychologists nevertheless claim exclusive title to the name of 'science' and dismiss as unscientific and 'unempirical' all other approaches to the psychology of religion.

The major question that psychologists ask of religion is: 'What aspects of religion can be quantified statistically and correlated with other religious statistics?' This preoccupation with measurable variations means that psychologists end up addressing the implicit question, 'When, or under what circumstances, are people more and less religious?'

Because questions concerning measurable variations take for granted the definitions of whatever is being measured, the research program conceals two methodological flaws. As Benjamin Beit-Hallahmi remarked, the psychology of religion is a historical psychology. It is a historically and culturally limited body of findings concerning social behavior in the twentieth and twenty-first centuries, and almost entirely in the various societies of Western culture. Its findings cannot responsibly be considered universal. Nor are the findings reliable so far as they go. Most have been skewed by amateurism as well as by ethnocentricity. When psychologists circulate a survey questionnaire, the responses are limited both by the questions asked, and by the respondents' understanding of the questions. The scoring of experimental behavior is similarly constrained by the experimenters' subjectivity. Although some psychologists are competent in the study of religion, the majority are not. Accordingly, many of the questions that psychologists have asked, together with almost all of the answers that they have received on questionnaires, have been naive as well as ethnocentric. When, for example, the frequency of church attendance is used as a measurable index of religiosity, the findings are not merely limited to Christianity. They are skewed, in that they have to do with church attendance and not necessarily with religiosity.

With the warning, then, that psychologists' findings on religion are as subjective, speculative, and as little 'scientific' as anyone else's, let us review some of the more interesting results. People are religious because they have been taught to be so. Parental religiosity is the most important influence. Most studies show a positive correlation between religiosity and self-esteem. Religiosity is associated with life satisfaction and subjective well-being. Religiosity can increase optimism and a sense of control. There is also a correlation with self-ideal conflicts and guilt feelings. Religiosity does not affect suicidal behaviors.

In general, religiosity correlates positively with both subjective or self-rated health, and objective measures of physical health. In some cases, however, religions cause physical harm, for example, through physical punishment, asceticism, and the denial of medical help. The findings regarding religion and mental health are inconclusive.

Religion is socially cohesive. Religious people divorce less frequently, commit fewer crimes, work harder, and are more socially integrated than non-religious people. Religious people are more likely to be women, over the age of 50, and lower class. The greater religiosity of women may correlate with women's greater ease with being dependent, or with men's aversion to loving a masculine deity. Women report more religious experiences than men do. Parapsychological experiences are more frequent for people who are or have been unhappy and socially marginal; whereas mystical experiences correlate with positive affect and life satisfaction. Contact with the dead correlates with being widowed. On the other hand, there is a 99 percent probability that psychedelic drugs use will induce a religious experience in anyone, if the setting is engineered to promote one. Music, prayer and meditation, group worship, experiences of nature, emotional distress, and sensory deprivation are all less effective.

Freud's claim that God is the exalted father has been examined repeatedly. Some studies have found that God is described as more similar to father, but others noted a similarity to mother. Still others noted a similarity to whichever was the preferred parent. Cultures that favor accepting, loving, and nurturing parenting styles tend to favor benevolent deities, while rejecting parenting styles correlate with malevolent deities. Catholics find God more maternal than Protestants do.

There is a decline in religiosity during adolescence. Conversion experiences are nevertheless most frequent at 15 years of age. Conversion experiences correlate with socially isolated individuals and also with a strong emotional attraction to the proselytizer whose ideas and practices are accepted. Loss of religious faith or conversion from one religion to another is frequently associated with a rejection of parents. Conversion through coercion or 'mind control' is a fiction.

Unmarried people are more active religiously than married people. Religious involvement declines in the third decade of life. Religious involvement increases after age 30 and continues into old age.

Clinical psychology

The 1990s saw a major shift in clinical attitudes toward religion. After decades of one-sided antipathy to religion, psychiatrists, psychoanalysts, and clinical psychologists adopted more nuanced views, only to find themselves confronted by a new research question: how to distinguish healthy and morbid forms of religion. Psychologists established a statistically significant correspondence between religious involvement and mental health and went on to investigate with increasing specificity when and for whom religion is most healthy. The new paradigm came together, above all, in Kenneth I. Pargament's *The Psychology of Religious Coping* (1997). After noting that most people routinely turn to religion in one fashion or another in coping with the challenges of events, Pargament systematically reviewed a very considerable part of the academic psychology of religion for its pertinence to the topic of coping. Pargament arrived at the unremarkable finding that 'religious coping is more common among blacks, poor people, the elderly, women, and those who are more troubled' (p. 143). Pargament also established in equal detail that religion is variously helpful, harmful, and irrelevant to coping. Having normalized the discussion through a massive presentation of empirical findings, Pargament approached the potentially explosive question: 'What forms of religious coping are helpful, harmful, or irrelevant?' He distinguished four 'control-related' coping styles. In the self-directing approach, both religious and non-religious people rely on their own efforts. In the collaborative approach, people regard God as a partner who augments their own efforts to help themselves. In the deferring approach, people rely entirely on God, making no efforts on their own behalf. Lastly, in the pleading approach, peoples' efforts consist of petitioning God to provide. Pargament and his colleagues found that the collaborative approach is the most effective of the four, but 'overall…studies do not show that religious copers experience more benefits than their nonreligious counterparts.' The superior effectiveness of collaborative coping validated the conclusion, however, that 'religion does appear to add a unique dimension to the coping process.' Subsequent research suggests that religious copers have less stress over their failures to cope, when compared with non-religious copers; and the reduction of stress facilitates greater eventual accuracy in coping.

A score of books and hundreds of articles have since proceeded from the assumption that because people commonly resort to religious coping, and some kinds of coping are more effective than others, clinicians do well to encourage religious patients to use the more effective means of religious coping. Slippage from a phenomenological attitude to patients' religiosity, to proactive function as a spiritual counselor or director who is expert in religious coping, is frequent in the literature, which belongs more to the practice of religion than its study. The pragmatic necessities of clinical work have nevertheless brought a new and important research question to the fore: how to distinguish healthy and morbid religiosity on criteria that are academically or scientifically responsible. Answering this question will likely occupy many contributors for decades to come.

Concluding reflections

The humanistic psychologist David Bakan (1996) noted that psychology, in all of its major schools, has conceptualized human beings on the model of machines that are regulated exclusively by causal determinism. The psychological models abolished such older categories as origination, causativity, will, virtue and vice, heroism, cowardice, and so forth. As a consequence, what is currently being presented as psychology is inconsistent with our experience of ourselves.

We today possess a variety of psychologies of people imagined as machines. They are not psychologies of people as we are, nor are they what psychology must someday become. All of our current psychologies are arbitrarily and artificially truncated. The portions omitted may very well be the most significant of all. Need we be surprised that a bridge to theology has yet to be found?

Bibliography

Arbman, Ernst. 'Mythic and religious thought'. *Dragma: Martin P. Nilsson … Dedicatum*. Lund, 1939.
Assagioli, R. *Transpersonal Development: The Dimension Beyond Psychosynthesis*. London: HarperCollins, 1991.
Bakan, David. 'Origination, self-determination, and psychology'. *Journal of Humanistic Psychology* 36(1): 9–20, 1996.
Batson, C. D., Schoenrade, P. and Ventis, W. L. *Religion and the Individual: A Social Psychological Perspective*. London: Oxford University Press, 1997.

Beit-Hallahmi, B. and Argyle, M. *The Psychology of Religious Behaviour, Belief and Experience*. London and New York: Routledge, 1997.

Fowler, III, James W. *Stages of Faith: The Psychology of Human Development and the Quest for Meaning*. San Francisco: Harper & Row, 1981.

Freud, S. 'Group psychology and the analysis of the ego'. *Standard Edition*, 18: 69–143. London: Hogarth Press, 1955 [1921].

—— 'Leonardo da Vinci and a memory of his childhood'. *Standard Edition*, 11: 63–137. London: Hogarth Press, 1957 [1910].

—— 'Totem and taboo: Some points of agreement between the mental life of savages and neurotics'. *Standard Edition*, 13: 1–161. London: Hogarth Press, 1958 [1913].

—— 'Obsessive acts and religious practices'. *Standard Edition*, 9: 117–27. London: Hogarth Press, 1959 [1907].

—— 'The future of an illusion'. *Standard Edition*, 21: 5–56. London: Hogarth Press, 1961 [1927].

—— 'Civilization and its discontents'. *Standard Edition*, 21: 64–145. London: Hogarth Press, 1961 [1930].

—— 'Constructions in analysis'. *Standard Edition*, 23: 257–69. London: Hogarth Press, 1964 [1937].

—— 'Moses and monotheism: three essays'. *Standard Edition*, 23: 6–137. London: Hogarth Press, 1964 [1939].

—— *The Standard Edition of the Complete Psychological Works of Sigmund Freud*, 24 vols. Ed. James Strachey, with Anna Freud, Alix Strachey, and Alan Tyson. London: Hogarth Press, 1966 (cited elsewhere as *Standard Edition*).

Grof, C. and Grof, S. *The Stormy Search for the Self: A Guide to Personal Growth through Transformational Crisis*. Los Angeles: Jeremy P. Tarcher, 1990.

James, William. *The Varieties of Religious Experience: A Study in Human Nature*. Reprinted New York: New American Library, 1958 [1902].

Jung, C. G. *Psychology and Religion: West and East*, 2nd edn. Trans. R. F. C. Hull. Princeton: Princeton University Press, 1969.

Maslow, A. H. *Religions, Values, and Peak Experiences*. 1964; rpt. Harmondsworth: Penguin Books Ltd, 1976.

Meissner, W. W. *Psychoanalysis and Religious Experience*. New Haven: Yale University Press, 1984.

Merkur, D. *Mystical Moments and Unitive Thinking*. New York: State University of New York Press, 1999.

Otto, Rudolf. 'The sensus numinis as the historical basis of religion'. *Hibbert Journal* 30: 283–97, 415–30, 1932.

—— *The Idea of the Holy: An Inquiry into the Non-rational Factor in the Idea of the Divine and its Relation to the Rational*, 2nd edn. Trans. John W. Harvey. London: Oxford University Press, 1950 [1917].

Pargament, Kenneth I. *The Psychology of Religion and Coping: Theory, Research, Practice*. New York & London: Guilford Press, 1997.

Pfister, Oscar. *Some Applications of Psycho-Analysis*. London: George Allen & Unwin Ltd, 1923.

—— *Christianity and Fear: A Study in History and in the Psychology and Hygiene of Religion*. Trans. W. H. Johnston. London: George Allen & Unwin Ltd, 1948.

Pruyser, P. W. *Between Belief and Unbelief*. New York: Harper & Row, 1974.

Rizzuto, A.-M. *The Birth of the Living God: A Psychoanalytic Study*. Chicago: University of Chicago Press, 1979.

Söderblom, Nathan. *The Living God: Basal Forms of Personal Religion*. Gifford Lectures 1931. London: Oxford University Press, 1933.

Starbuck, Edwin Diller. *The Psychology of Religion: An Empirical Study of the Growth of Religious Consciousness*, 3rd edn. London, New York and Melbourne: Walter Scott Publishing Co., Ltd, 1911 [1899].

Suggested reading

Bakan, David, Merkur, Dan, and Weiss, David S. (2009), *Maimonides' Cure of Souls: Medieval Precursor of Psychoanalysis*. Albany, NY: State University of New York Press.
The posthumously completed final work of David Bakan, a major figure in the psychology of religion, is a historical study of Rabbi Moses Maimonides' twelfth century cure of souls, as evaluated from perspectives in humanistic psychology and psychoanalysis, and highlighting the many parallels with Freud's psychoanalysis; Freud was exposed to Maimonides during his religious education as a teenager.

Haartman, Keith. (2004), *Watching and Praying: Personality Transformation in Eighteenth Century British Methodism*. Amsterdam & New York: Rodopi.
A historical study of John Wesley's method and early British Methodist progress from conversion through sanctification, as evaluated from a contemporary psychoanalytic perspective, and interpreted as a historical achievement of psychotherapeutic personality change.

Jones, James W. (2002), *Terror and Transformation: The Ambiguity of Religion in Psychoanalytic Perspective*. Hove, UK & New York: Brunner-Routledge/Taylor & Francis Group.
An application of contemporary psychoanalytic theory that explores the roles of healthy and morbid ideals and idealization processes in the formation of different religious phenomena.

Pargament, Kenneth I. (1997), *The Psychology of Religion and Coping: Theory, Research, Practice*. New York & London: Guilford Press.
A paradigm-shifting contribution to the academic psychology of religion, that has pioneered the empirical evaluation of health and morbidity in religion.

Rubin, Jeffrey B. (2004), *The Good Life: Psychoanalytic Reflections on Love, Ethics, Creativity, and Spirituality*. Albany: State University of New York Press.
A psychoanalyst and advocate of Buddhist meditation reflects candidly on the humanistic wisdom to which a 'contemplative psychoanalysis' may aspire.

Safran, Jeremy D. (Ed.). (2003), *Psychoanalysis and Buddhism: An Unfolding Dialogue*. Boston: Wisdom Publications.
One of the better recent collections that brings together psychoanalysts and Buddhists to explore the intersection of these Western and Eastern approaches to the mind and its processes of change.

Spilka, Bernard, Hood, Jr., Ralph W. Hunsberger, Bruce, and Gorsuch, Richard. (2003), *The Psychology of Religion: An Empirical Approach*, 3rd ed. New York and London: Guilford Press.
A current and magisterial survey of the academic psychology of religion.

Chapter 12

Phenomenology of religion

Douglas Allen

'The phenomenology of religion' became one of the major twentieth-century disciplines and approaches to religion. Readers may have some sense of what is involved in other disciplines and approaches to religion, such as 'history of religion,' 'anthropology of religion,' 'psychology of religion,' 'sociology of religion,' or 'philosophy of religion,' even if some initial ideas are inaccurate. Few readers will have any clue as to what the term 'phenomenology of religion' means or what this discipline and approach describe.

An introductory exercise

The following exercise will help illustrate the rationale for phenomenology of religion and several of its major characteristics. Most societies and cultures have been described as 'religious.' Several billion human beings today describe themselves as 'religious.' Some of our most common language – emphasizing such terms as 'God,' 'soul,' 'heaven,' 'salvation,' 'sin,' and 'evil' – is 'religious.' Even human beings who claim that they are not 'religious' usually think that they know what they reject.

Scholarly approaches to religion involve critical reflection. When we reflect critically on such common terms as 'religion' and 'religious,' it becomes apparent that we usually use these terms in vague ways. This exercise is an attempt to begin such critical reflection as key to understanding phenomenology of religion.

The exercise

This exercise will work best for a class or group of participants. If there are more than 20 participants, divide into smaller groups allowing for more individual participation. This exercise will also work well through internet group communication. If you are alone, you can do the exercise by yourself, but it will work much better if you ask others for their responses. Each class or group should ask for one person to record responses and summarize results.

Phenomenology of religion starts with the view that religion is based on religious experience. Human beings have experiences that they describe as religious. These may be traditional or nontraditional. They may focus on inner feelings or outward forms and relations. They may be institutional and involve organized religion, or they may be highly personal and outside any institutional framework. They may involve prayer, worship, rituals, nature, or cosmic experiences.

In this exercise, many participants will state that they are religious and that they have had religious experiences. Religious participants should be encouraged to describe their religious experiences. What kind of an experience was it? What did it mean to the person who had such an experience? It may take time for participants to feel comfortable sharing their experiences. It is important to be nonjudgmental and to emphasize that there is no right or wrong answer. It is important to maintain an atmosphere in which others, even when they personally disagree, are respectful and attempt to empathize with and understand what religious participants are expressing.

As a variation, after all participants have had the opportunity to describe their religious experiences, the group may focus on respondents whose expressions refer to 'God.' These religious participants may be asked to describe at greater length the nature of such an experience of God and what is intended by their use of the term God.

After eliciting as many responses as possible, compile the results. Do not include or exclude responses based on agreement or disagreement. Summarize the major ways of describing religious experience and possibly the more restrictive descriptions in terms of experiences of God.

Results of the exercise

After compiling the results, reflect critically on them and analyze the data. Phenomenology of religion involves certain kinds of analysis.

When considering the major features expressed by religious participants, are there common characteristics in all or most of the descriptions? What are they? In reflecting on the tremendous variety of religious expressions, phenomenologists of religion claim that there are common general characteristics, structures, and patterns revealed only in religious experiences.

Religious people do not believe that their religious experiences are nothing more than subjective psychological feelings. They believe that they have experienced some religious reality: the experience of X. Based on your descriptions, what is the content or nature of X? How have participants described X? As God? In other terms? This points to the phenomenological doctrine of 'intentionality' emphasizing that all consciousness or experience is experience of something. Is there a common religious object or referent in your descriptions? If not one, are there several essential patterns and variations?

Phenomenologists of religion focus on language. We never have direct access to experiences of others. Instead we have expressions of others as they try to describe their religious experiences and realities. How do religious participants use language to describe experiences? Is there a specific or unique religious language? If the intended religious referent or reality transcends human attempts at definition and conceptual analysis, does this mean that religion cannot be studied in a critical, reflective, scholarly way?

In reflecting on the assembled data, here are several likely questions and concerns. On the one hand, are descriptions of 'religion,' 'religious,' and 'religious experience' too narrow? Some religious participants will be uncomfortable with other descriptions. For example, Buddhists may be uncomfortable identifying with certain God expressions. Even some participants using God expressions may feel that other God formulations, expressing personal anthropomorphic views or traditional exclusivistic views, have little to do with their experiences. To the extent that participants reflect religious, ethnic, class, and other differences, there will be a great plurality and diversity in responses. From the perspective of phenomenology of religion, which attempts to uncover universal or general structures and meanings, think about whether various expressions can be broadened.

On the other hand, are some descriptions too broad in the sense that they are also true of experiences and beliefs that are not religious? For example, some may describe religion as consisting of whatever is true or real for the experiencer. But don't nonreligious people also experience what they consider true or real? From the perspective of phenomenology of religion, our general descriptions must allow us to distinguish religious phenomena from nonreligious phenomena and analyze the religious as a specific kind of experience.

Reflecting on the assembled data, do some descriptions reveal a clear ethnocentrism, expressing one's own background, socialization, and beliefs but not adequate to describe the religious experiences and phenomena of others? Do some descriptions reflect normative positions, based on value judgments, that do not do justice to religious others?

This is not meant to criticize such ethnocentric and normative formulations. Such formulations are inadequate for providing a general phenomenological description of 'religion' and 'religious.' On theological, philosophical, or some faith-based grounds, Christian fundamentalists may describe religious experience as consisting only in the experience of Jesus Christ, and they may argue that those who do not experience and accept this reality are doomed to Hell. Many Muslims may describe religious experience as submitting to Allah and recognizing Muhammad as the true Messenger, and they may argue that others are nonbelievers whose experiential referents are unreal or demonic.

Phenomenology of religion attempts to avoid such narrow, overly broad, ethnocentric, and normative approaches. It attempts to describe religious experiences with their religious phenomena as accurately as possible. In its descriptions, analysis, and interpretation of meaning, it attempts to suspend value judgments about what is real or unreal in experiences of others. It attempts to describe, understand, and do justice to the religious phenomena as they appear in religious experiences of others.

The term 'phenomenology of religion'

Although 'phenomenology' and 'phenomenology of religion' are not part of ordinary language, they are popular terms in various scholarly disciplines. Starting in the early twentieth century, philosophical phenomenology became one of the major philosophical approaches. Phenomenology of religion emerged as one of the most influential modern approaches to religion. Scholars sometimes identify phenomenology of religion as a discipline and approach within the general field of *Religionswissenschaft*, the scientific study of religion. We shall use the term 'religious studies' to identify modern scholarly approaches to religion that include phenomenology as well as history, anthropology, sociology, psychology, linguistics, cognitive science, and other disciplines.

It is possible to differentiate four groups of scholars who use the term *phenomenology of religion*. First, there are works in which the term means nothing more than an investigation of phenomena or observable objects, facts, and events of religion. Second, from the Dutch scholar P. D. Chantepie de la Saussaye to such contemporary scholars as the Scandinavian historians of religions Geo Widengren and Åke Hultkrantz, phenomenology of religion means the comparative study and the classification of different types of religious phenomena.

Third, numerous scholars, such as W. Brede Kristensen, Gerardus van der Leeuw, Joachim Wach, C. Jouco Bleeker, Mircea Eliade, and Jacques Waardenburg, identify phenomenology of religion as a specific branch, discipline, or method within *Religionswissenschaft* or religious studies. This is where the most significant contributions of phenomenology of religion have been made.

Fourth, there are phenomenologists of religion influenced by philosophical phenomenology. A few scholars, such as Max Scheler and Paul Ricoeur, explicitly identify much of their work with philosophical phenomenology. Others use a phenomenological method and are influenced, at least partially, by phenomenological philosophy. There are also influential theological approaches, as seen in the works of Friedrich Schleiermacher, Paul Tillich, and Jean-Luc Marion, which utilize phenomenology of religion as a stage in the formulation of theology.

The terms *phenomenon* and *phenomenology* are derived from the Greek word *phainomenon* (that which shows itself, or that which appears). The term phenomenology has both philosophical and nonphilosophical roots.

One finds nonphilosophical phenomenologies in the natural and social sciences in which scientists want to emphasize the descriptive, as contrasted with the explanatory, conception of their science. A second nonphilosophical use of phenomenology appears in descriptive, systematic, comparative studies of religions in which scholars assemble groups of religious phenomena in order to disclose their major aspects and to formulate their typologies.

In the late eighteenth century, the German philosopher Immanuel Kant devoted considerable analysis to 'phenomena' as the data of experience, things that appear to and are constructed by human minds. Such phenomena, which Kant distinguishes from 'noumena,' or 'things-in-themselves' independent of our knowing minds, can be studied rationally, scientifically, and objectively. For example, I can give a causal explanation of why the frisbee was thrown at a certain direction, velocity, and distance. However, I cannot give the same kind of spatial, temporal, causal analysis to explain noumena such as 'God.'

Of all the uses of phenomenology by philosophers before the twentieth-century phenomenological movement, the term is most frequently identified with the German philosopher G. W. F. Hegel and his *Phenomenology of Spirit*. Hegel was determined to overcome Kant's phenomena-noumena bifurcation. Phenomena are actual stages of knowledge – manifestations in the development of Spirit – evolving from undeveloped consciousness of mere sense experience and culminating in forms of absolute knowledge. Phenomenology is the science by which the mind becomes aware of the development of Spirit and comes to know its essence – that is, Spirit as it is in itself – through a study of its appearances and manifestations.

This background led to two distinct senses of phenomenology that have shaped phenomenology of religion: there is the older, wider sense of the term as any descriptive study of a given subject matter of observable phenomena, and there is a narrower twentieth-century sense of the term as a philosophical approach utilizing a phenomenological method.

Some background to the phenomenology of religion

It is helpful to examine the context within which philosophical phenomenology and the phenomenology of religion originated and developed. By having a sense of other approaches and what phenomenology was reacting against, the rationale for phenomenology of religion becomes evident.

Phenomenologists of religion, emphasizing religious experience, recognize that being religious is not identical with studying religion. There is a first, foundational level of experience for the religious believer. Phenomenology and other scholarly approaches always involve some distance between the scholar and the subject matter necessary for critical reflection, analysis, interpretation, and verification of findings. While disagreeing on the relation between being religious and studying religion, scholars agree that scholarly study is not identical with being religious or having religious experience.

For thousands of years, scholars have attempted to assemble religious data and interpret their meaning. This often arose from exposure to new religious phenomena from expeditions of explorers, military and political conquests, economic exploitation, and missionary work. Studies were usually shaped by self-serving, apologetic, religious, political, and economic assumptions and judgments. Comparative religion often became competitive religion in which scholars studied others in order to demonstrate the superiority of their own religion or culture. From the perspective of phenomenology of religion, these earlier studies did not do justice to religious phenomena of religious others.

The origin of the modern scholarly study of religion is usually traced to the nineteenth century and especially to influences of the Enlightenment. Modern scholars were determined to free their approaches and disciplines from pre-modern investigations with their subjective and normative assumptions and judgments, their dependence on supernatural and other external authority, and their lack of concern for rigorous standards of objective knowledge. By insisting on unbiased impartial investigations, careful accumulation of data or facts, and the authority of human reason to analyze and interpret the meaning of phenomena, modern scholars had confidence in the human capacity to make progress and arrive at objective, verifiable knowledge.

From the perspective of phenomenology of religion, these modern studies also were limited and did not do justice to the religious phenomena of the other. Built into their scientific or scholarly studies were all kinds of unacknowledged normative assumptions and judgments. For example, most of these philologists, ethnologists, and other modern scholars adopted a positivistic view of 'facts' and 'objective' knowledge. Phenomenologists of religion assert that our approach must be commensurate with the nature of our subject matter. An approach yielding factual, objective knowledge when dissecting a worm may not provide objective knowledge of religious experience.

Nineteenth-century scholars often adopted from Darwin a notion of evolution and then applied it to language, culture, and religion. Typically, they arranged religious data in a unilinear framework, starting with the most undeveloped stage of 'primitive' religions and evolving to the evolutionary apex of Western monotheism, especially Christianity. In some frameworks, humans evolved beyond all religion to a higher rational, scientific stage. For phenomenology of religion, imposing such an evolutionary scheme on religious phenomena prevents us from accurately describing and understanding the meaning of phenomena.

Phenomenologists assert that scholarly approaches have been normative, applying their standards to make disciplinary value judgments. Human beings claim that they have 'experiences of God.' Psychologists of religion analyze and explain such phenomena psychologically. Sociologists of religion analyze and explain such phenomena in terms of social needs, functions, and structures. Philosophers of religion ask questions about meaning, truth, and reality as expressed in propositions about God's existence and the problem of evil. Phenomenologists of religion react against such approaches. Human beings claim to have experiences of God. What are the meaning and significance of such experienced phenomena? Other approaches, with their assumed norms and methodological framework, do not do justice to religious phenomena. How can we describe the religious phenomena and religious meaning of others as accurately as possible?

Philosophical phenomenology

As one of the major schools, movements, or approaches in twentieth-century philosophy, phenomenology takes many forms. The primary aim of philosophical phenomenology is to investigate and become directly aware of phenomena that appear in immediate experience, and thereby to allow the phenomenologist to describe the essential structures of these phenomena. In doing so, phenomenology attempts to free itself from unexamined presuppositions, avoid causal explanations, utilize a method for describing that which appears, and intuit essential meanings.

Edmund Husserl, founder and most influential philosopher of the modern phenomenological movement, aimed to establish phenomenology as an objective science. The early phenomenologists worked at German universities, especially at Göttingen and Munich. Other significant German phenomenologists include Max Scheler and Martin Heidegger. In the 1930s, the center of the movement began to shift to France. Leading French phenomenologists include Jean-Paul Sartre, Maurice Merleau-Ponty, Gabriel Marcel, and Paul Ricoeur.

One may delineate five characteristics of philosophical phenomenology that have particular relevance for the phenomenology for religion. Most phenomenologists have upheld a descriptive phenomenology that is antireductionist, involves phenomenological bracketing, focuses on intentionality, and aims at insight into essential structures and meanings.

Descriptive nature

Phenomenology aims to be a rigorous, descriptive science, discipline, or approach. The phenomenological slogan 'Zu den Sachen!' ('To the things themselves!') expresses the determination to turn away from philosophical theories, rational analysis and explanations, toward direct intuition and description of phenomena as they appear to consciousness. Phenomenology attempts to describe the nature of phenomena, the way appearances manifest themselves, and the essential structures at the foundation of human experience. A descriptive phenomenology, attempting to avoid reductionism and insisting on the phenomenological *epoché*, focuses on accurately describing the totality of phenomenal appearances in human experience.

Antireductionism

Phenomenological antireductionism is concerned with freeing us from uncritical preconceptions that prevent us from becoming aware of the specificity and diversity of phenomena, thus allowing us to broaden and deepen immediate experience and provide more accurate descriptions of experience. Husserl attacked forms of reductionism, such as 'psychologism,' which attempts to derive laws of logic from psychological laws and, more broadly, to reduce all phenomena to psychological phenomena. In opposing the oversimplifications of traditional empiricism and other forms of reductionism, phenomenologists aim to deal faithfully with phenomena as phenomena and to become aware of what phenomena reveal in their full intentionality.

Intentionality

A subject always 'intends' an object, and intentionality refers to the property of all consciousness as consciousness of something. All acts of consciousness are directed toward the experience of the intentional object. For Husserl, who took the term from his teacher Franz Brentano, intentionality was a way of describing how consciousness constitutes phenomena. In order to identify, describe, and interpret the meaning of phenomena, phenomenologists must be attentive to the intentional structures of their data; to the intentional structures of consciousness with their intended referents and meanings.

Bracketing

The antireductionist insistence on the irreducibility of intentional experience usually entails the adoption of a 'phenomenological *epoché.*' This Greek term literally means 'abstention' or 'suspension of judgment' and is often defined as a method of 'bracketing.' We must bracket the uncritically accepted 'natural world' by suspending beliefs and judgments about existence and reality based on an unexamined 'natural standpoint.' We must suspend ontological questions, as raised by philosophical idealism and materialism, about the reality behind phenomenal appearances. Only then can phenomenologists become aware of experiential phenomena as phenomena and gain insight into their essential structures. Many phenomenologists now interpret such bracketing not as part of a completely presuppositionless science, but as freeing one from unexamined presuppositions and as rendering explicit and clarifying such presuppositions.

Eidetic vision

The intuition of essences, often described as 'eidetic vision' or 'eidetic reduction,' is related to the Greek term *eidos*, which Husserl adopted from its Platonic meaning to designate 'universal essences.' Diverse phenomena, as intentional objects of consciousness, can be reduced to their essence that expresses the necessary and invariant features of the phenomena. The following is a brief formulation of a general phenomenological procedure for gaining insight into essential structures and meanings.

In the 'intuition of essences' (*Wesensschau*), the phenomenologist begins with particular data: specific phenomena as expressions of intentional experiences. The central aim of the phenomenological method is to disclose the essential structure embodied in the particular data.

One gains insight into meaning by the method of 'free variation.' After assembling a variety of particular phenomena, the phenomenologist searches for the invariant core that constitutes their essential meaning. The phenomena, subjected to a process of free variation, assume certain forms or relations of parts that are considered inessential in the sense that the phenomenologist can go beyond the limits imposed by such forms without destroying the basic character or intentionality of one's data. For example, the variation of a great variety of religious phenomena may disclose that unique structures of monotheism do not constitute the essential core or universal structure of all religious experience.

The phenomenologist gradually sees that phenomena assume forms that are regarded as essential in the sense that one cannot go beyond or remove such structures without destroying the basic 'whatness' or intentionality of the data. For example, variation might reveal that certain intentional structures of 'transcendence' constitute an invariant core of religious experience. When the universal essence is grasped, the phenomenologist achieves the eidetic intuition or the fulfilled *Wesensschau*.

Most phenomenologists using a method of *Wesensschau* propose that historical phenomena have a kind of priority, that one must substitute for Husserl's purely imaginary variation an actual variation of historical data, and that particular phenomena are not constituted by an individual but are the source of one's constitution and judgment.

The phenomenology of religion

The first major figure in the post-Enlightenment scholarly study of religion was F. Max Müller (1823–1900), who intended *Religionswissenschaft* to be a descriptive, objective science free from the normative theological and philosophical studies of religion.

For P. D. Chantepie de la Saussaye (1848–1920), who was the first to use the phrase 'phenomenology of religion,' phenomenology of religion is a special discipline of classification that occupies an intermediary position between history and philosophy. It is a descriptive, comparative approach collecting and grouping religious phenomena. The Dutch historian C. P. Tiele considered phenomenology the first stage of the philosophical part of the science of religion.

Scholars point to phenomenology of religion's sense of generality, with its approach characterized as systematic. For Widengren, phenomenology of religion aims at a coherent account and provides the systematic synthesis of the historical phenomena of religion. The Italian historian of religions Raffaele Pettazzoni viewed phenomenology and history as two complementary aspects of the integral science of religion. Phenomenology provides a deeper understanding of the religious meaning of historical data.

Major phenomenologists of religion

What follows are brief formulations of the approaches and contributions of seven influential phenomenologists of religion: Max Scheler, W. Brede Kristensen, Rudolf Otto, Gerardus van der Leeuw, C. Jouco Bleeker, Mircea Eliade, and Ninian Smart. Included are criticisms of Otto, van der Leeuw, and Eliade.

Max Scheler

Of the major philosophers who founded and developed philosophical phenomenology, Scheler (1874–1928) had the greatest focus on religion. In many ways, he can be considered the most significant early phenomenologist of religion. Influenced by Brentano, Husserl, Kant, Nietzsche, Dilthey, and Bergson, Scheler developed his own original phenomenological approach. His books *On the Eternal in Man* and *Formalism in Ethics and Non-Formal Ethics of Values* bring out his phenomenological method, his description and analysis of sympathy, love, and other values, and key characteristics of his phenomenology of religion.

Reminiscent of Schleiermacher and Otto, Scheler focuses on a phenomenological description and analysis of the unique religious human mode of experience and feeling; the being of the human being for whom structures and essences of religious values are presented to consciousness. Phenomenological disclosure, focusing on what is 'given' to consciousness as the Absolute, the Divine Person, or God, is not achieved through reason but only through the love of God orienting one toward experiential realization of the Holy. The turn to religion in some continental philosophy at the end of the twentieth century often exhibits characteristics similar to Scheler's phenomenological orientation.

W. Brede Kristensen

Much of the field has been dominated by a Dutch tradition of phenomenology of religion. Kristensen (1867–1953), who opposes evolutionist and positivist approaches to religion, attempts to understand religious documents in terms of religious values proper to the religious phenomena. Phenomenology of religion attempts to understand religious phenomena by classifying them into groups according to the essential characteristics of the religion. Similar to Otto, van der Leeuw, and Eliade, Kristensen considers the sacred or holy as the central transcendent object or essence around which religious material is organized. Kristensen attempts to integrate historical knowledge of facts with phenomenological 'empathy' and 'feeling' for the data in order to grasp 'inner meaning' and religious values in texts.

Descriptive phenomenology, the medium whereby philosophy and history of religion interact, seeks the 'meaning' of religious phenomena. This is 'the meaning that the religious phenomena have for the believers themselves.' Phenomenology does not end with classification of phenomena according to their meaning, but always involves 'understanding.' In order to achieve phenomenological understanding, scholars must avoid imposing their own value judgments on experiences of believers and must accept the faith of believers as sole 'religious reality.' The focus of phenomenology is the description and understanding of how believers understand their own faith.

Rudolf Otto

Two interdependent methodological contributions made by Rudolf Otto (1869–1937) deserve emphasis: his experiential approach, which involves the phenomenological description of the universal, essential structure of religious experience, and his antireductionism, which respects the unique, irreducible, 'numinous' quality of all religious experience.

In *Das Heilige* (translated as *The Idea of the Holy*), Otto presents what may be the best-known phenomenological account of religious experience. Otto describes the universal 'numinous' element as a unique a priori category of meaning and value. By numen and numinous, Otto means the concept of 'the holy' minus its moral and rational aspects. This constitutes the universal essence of religious experience. Since the unique nonrational experience cannot be defined or conceptualized, symbolic and analogical descriptions are meant to evoke within the reader the numinous experience that can be reawakened or recognized by means of our innate sense of the numinous.

Otto formulates a universal phenomenological structure of religious experience for distinguishing religious phenomena by their numinous aspect and for organizing and analyzing specific religious manifestations. He points to our *sui generis* religious experience of 'creature feeling' of absolute dependence in the experiential presence of the holy, the 'wholly other' that is qualitatively unique and transcendent.

Insistence on the unique a priori quality of religious experience points to Otto's antireductionist, autonomous, numinous approach. Otto rejects the one-sidedly intellectualistic and rationalistic bias of most interpretations and the reduction of religious phenomena to the interpretive schema of linguistic analysis, anthropology, sociology, psychology, and historicist approaches.

Various interpreters have criticized Otto's phenomenological approach for being too narrowly conceived. According to these critics, Otto's approach focuses on nonrational aspects of certain mystical and other 'extreme' experiences, but it is not sufficiently comprehensive to interpret the diversity and complexity of religious data, nor is it sufficiently concerned with the specific historical and cultural forms of religious phenomena. Critics also object to the a priori nature of Otto's project and influences of personal, Christian, theological, and apologetic intentions on his phenomenology.

Gerardus van der Leeuw

In his *Comparative Religion*, Eric J. Sharpe writes that 'between 1925 and 1950, the phenomenology of religion was associated almost exclusively with the name of the Dutch scholar Gerardus van der Leeuw (1890–1950), and with his book *Phänomenologie der Religion*.' In *Phänomenologie der Religion* (translated as *Religion in Essence and Manifestation*), van der Leeuw defines assumptions, concepts, and stages of his phenomenological approach. Focusing on phenomenological bracketing and empathy and influenced by Wilhelm Dilthey's formulations on hermeneutics and 'understanding' (*Verstehen*), van der Leeuw emphasizes the need to respect the specific intentionality of religious phenomena and to describe the phenomenon as 'what appears into view.' The phenomenon is given in the mutual relations between subject and object; that is, its 'entire essence' is given in its appearance to someone.

Van der Leeuw proposes a complex phenomenological-psychological method of systematic introspection. This involves 'the interpolation of the phenomenon into our lives' as necessary for understanding religious phenomena. Phenomenology must be combined with historical research, which provides phenomenologists with sufficient data. Van der Leeuw's emphasizes the religious aspect of 'power' as the basis of every religious form and as defining what is religious. Phenomenology describes how humans have religious experiences in relating to such extraordinary power, and how 'all understanding rests upon self-surrendering love.' Van der Leeuw considered himself a theologian and asserted that phenomenology of religion leads to both anthropology and theology.

Critics, while often expressing admiration for *Religion in Essence and Manifestation* as an extraordinary collection of religious data, offer many objections to van der Leeuw's phenomenology of religion: His phenomenological approach is based on numerous Christian theological and metaphysical assumptions and value judgments; it is often too subjective and highly speculative; and it neglects the historical and cultural context of religious phenomena.

C. Jouco Bleeker

Bleeker (1898–1983) distinguished three types of phenomenology of religion: descriptive phenomenology that restricts itself to systematization of religious phenomena, typological phenomenology that formulates different types of religion, and the specific sense of phenomenology that investigates the essential structures and meanings of religious phenomena. In terms of this specific sense, phenomenology of religion has a double meaning: it is an independent science that creates monographs, such as van der Leeuw's *Religion in Essence and Manifestation* and Eliade's *Patterns in Comparative Religion*, but it is also a scholarly method that utilizes such principles as the phenomenological *epoché* and eidetic vision. Although Bleeker frequently used technical terms borrowed from Husserl and philosophical phenomenology, he claimed that they were used by phenomenology of religion in only a figurative sense.

According to Bleeker, phenomenology of religion combines a critical attitude and concern for accurate descriptions with a sense of empathy for phenomena. It is an empirical science without philosophical aspirations, and it should distinguish its activities from those of philosophical phenomenology and of anthropology. Phenomenology of religion systematizes historical facts in order to understand their religious meaning.

Bleeker analyzes phenomenology of religion as inquiry into three dimensions of religious phenomena: *theoria*, *logos*, and *entelecheia*. The *theoria* of phenomena discloses the essence and significance of the empirical facts. The *logos* of phenomena provides a sense of objectivity by showing that hidden structures 'are built up according to strict inner laws' and that religion 'always possesses a certain structure with an inner logic.' The *entelecheia* of phenomena reveals the dynamics and development of religious life as 'an invincible, creative and self-regenerating force.'

Mircea Eliade

As one of the major interpreters of religion, symbol, and myth, the Romanian Eliade (1907–1986) submits that religion 'refers to the experience of the sacred.' The phenomenologist works with historical documents expressing *hierophanies*, or manifestations of the sacred, and attempts to decipher the existential situation and religious meaning expressed through the data. The sacred and the profane express 'two modes of being in the world,' and religion always entails the attempt of religious beings to transcend the relative, historical, temporal, 'profane' world by experiencing a 'superhuman' sacred world of transcendent values.

Eliade's phenomenology of religion includes morphological studies of different kinds of religious symbolism; interpretations of the structure and function of myth, with the cosmogonic and other creation myths functioning as exemplary models; treatments of rituals, such as those of initiation, as reenacting sacred mythic models; structural analysis of sacred space, sacred time, and sacred history; and studies of different types of religious experience, such as yoga, shamanism, alchemy, and other 'archaic' phenomena.

Key methodological principles underlying Eliade's phenomenological approach are, first, his assumption of the 'irreducibility of the sacred,' a form of phenomenological *epoché*. Only an antireductionist method, using a religious frame of reference or 'scale' of interpretation, does not distort the specific, irreducible religious intentionality expressed in the data.

Second, Eliade's emphasis on the 'dialectic of the sacred', as universal structure of sacralization, provides essential criteria for distinguishing religious from nonreligious phenomena. For example, there is always a sacred-profane dichotomy, and the sacred, expressing transcendent structures and meanings, paradoxically limits itself by incarnating itself in something ordinarily finite, temporal, and historical.

Third, Eliade formulates structural systems of religious symbols that constitute the hermeneutical framework underlying his phenomenology of religion. These symbols are 'multivalent' and through their 'function of unification' form autonomous, universal, coherent symbolic systems that provide the phenomenological framework for Eliade's interpretation of religious meaning.

Although Eliade was extremely influential, many scholars ignore or are hostile to his history and phenomenology of religion. The most frequent criticism is that Eliade is methodologically uncritical, often presenting sweeping generalizations and nonhistorical essences not based upon specific historical and empirical data. Critics charge that his approach is influenced by various normative judgments and an assumed ontological position that is partial to a religious, antihistorical, antimodern mode of being and to certain Eastern and archaic phenomena.

Ninian Smart

Born in Cambridge, England to Scottish parents, Smart (1927–2001) had a major impact on religious studies. Phenomenology, for Smart, is the best way to study religion and avoids two dominant approaches: (1) ethnocentric, normative, especially Christian, theological approaches in the study of religion; and (2) normative philosophical approaches with their exclusive focus on belief and conceptual analysis to the exclusion of other dimensions of religious phenomena.

Smart emphasized many points that became easily recognizable and widely accepted in phenomenology of religion and other approaches to religious phenomena. He emphasized suspension of one's own value judgments, a 'methodological agnosticism' regarding religious truth claims, and the need for phenomenological empathy in understanding and describing religious phenomena of others. He endorsed a liberal, humanistic, phenomenological approach that upholds pluralism and diversity and recognizes that religion expresses many dimensions of human experience. Such an approach is 'polymethodic,' multiperspectival, comparative, and cross-cultural. The phenomenologist of religion needs to take seriously the contextual nature of diverse religious phenomena; to ask questions, engage in critical dialogue, and maintain an open-ended investigation of religion; and to recognize that religions express complex, multidimensional, interconnected worldviews.

Characteristics of phenomenology of religion

The following features, some already mentioned, characterize much of phenomenology of religion: a comparative, systematic, empirical, historical, descriptive discipline and approach; antireductionist claims and its autonomous nature; adoption of philosophical phenomenological notions of intentionality and *epoché*; insistence on empathy, sympathetic understanding, and religious commitment; and claim to provide insight into essential structures and meanings.

Comparative and systematic approach

There is widespread agreement that phenomenology of religion is a very general, comparative approach concerned with classifying and systematizing religious phenomena. Phenomenologists are able to gain insight into essential structures and meanings only after comparing a large number of documents expressing a great diversity of religious phenomena.

Empirical approach

Most phenomenologists of religion insist that they use an empirical approach that is free from a priori assumptions and judgments. Such an empirical approach, often described as 'scientific' and 'objective,' begins by collecting religious documents and then goes on to describe just what the data reveal. A frequent attack on phenomenology of religion is that it is not empirically based and is therefore arbitrary, subjective, and unscientific. Critics charge that the universal structures and meanings are not found in the empirical data and are not subject to empirical tests of verification.

Historical approach

Phenomenologists of religion usually maintain not only that their approach must cooperate with and complement historical research but also that phenomenology of religion is profoundly historical. Phenomenologists must be aware of the specific historical, cultural, and socioeconomic contexts within which religious phenomena appear. Critics charge that phenomenology of religion is not historical, both in terms of a nonhistorical phenomenological method and the primacy it grants to nonhistorical and nontemporal universal structures.

Descriptive approach

Almost all phenomenologists of religion today do not restrict themselves to mere description of religious phenomena. Phenomenologists go beyond the severe methodological restrictions of descriptive phenomenology. And yet phenomenologists invariably regard their phenomenology of religion as descriptive, using a descriptive approach and providing descriptive classifications, typologies, and structures.

Antireductionism

Phenomenologists oppose reductionism, which imposes preconceptions and judgments on phenomena, in order to deal with phenomena as phenomena and to provide more accurate descriptions of just what phenomena reveal. Phenomenology of religion insists that investigators approach religious data as phenomena that are fundamentally and irreducibly religious. Otto, Eliade, and others criticize the reductions of religious data to fit nonreligious perspectives, such as those of sociology, psychology, or economics. Such reductionisms, it is argued, destroy the irreducibly religious intentionality of religious phenomena.

Autonomy

Directly related to this antireductionist claim is the identification of phenomenology of religion as an autonomous discipline and approach. If there are certain irreducible modes by which religious phenomena are given, then one must utilize a specific method of understanding commensurate with the religious nature of the subject matter. Phenomenology of religion is autonomous but not self-sufficient. It depends heavily on historical research and on data supplied by philology, ethnology, psychology, sociology, and other approaches. But it must always integrate the contributions of other approaches within its own unique phenomenological perspective.

Intentionality

Phenomenology analyzes acts of consciousness as consciousness of something and claims that meaning is given in the intentionality of the structure. For Otto, the a priori structure of religious consciousness is consciousness of its intended 'numinous object.' Van der Leeuw's phenomenological-psychological technique and Eliade's dialectic of the sacred are methods for capturing the intentional characteristics of religious manifestations. Phenomenologists of religion criticize reductionist approaches for denying the unique intentionality of religious phenomena.

Religious experiences reveal structures of transcendence in which human beings intend a transcendent referent, a supernatural meta-empirical sacred meaning. Religious language points to intended sacred structures and meanings that transcend normal spatial, temporal, historical, and conceptual categories and analysis. That is why religious expressions are highly symbolic, analogical, metaphorical, mythic, and allegorical.

At the same time, no intentional referent and meaning is unmediated. For meaningful religious experience and communication, intended transcendent referents must be mediated and brought into an integral relation with our limited spatial, temporal, historical, cultural world with its intended objects and meanings. This is why symbolism is essential for revealing, constituting, and communicating religious intentional meaning. Religious symbolic expressions serve as indispensable mediating bridges. On the one hand, they always point beyond themselves to intended transcendent meanings. On the other hand, by necessarily using symbolic language drawn from the spatial, temporal, natural, historical world of experience, they mediate the transcendent referent, limit and incarnate the sacred, allow disclosure of transcendent as imminent, and render sacred meanings humanly accessible and relevant to particular existential situations.

This specific religious intentionality ensures that the structures of experience, as well as interpretations and understandings, remain open-ended. The necessary structural conditions for religious experience, disclosure of phenomena, construction of texts, and formulation of interpretations ensure that meaningful human understandings necessarily reveal limited intentional perspectives. And such relative, situated, intentional, religious perspectives always point beyond themselves to structures of transcendence; to inexhaustible possibilities for revalorizing symbolic expressions, for bursting open self-imposed perspectival closures, and for new, creative, self-transcending experiences, interpretations, and understandings.

Epoché, empathy, and sympathetic understanding

By bracketing and suspending our unexamined assumptions and ordinary preconceptions and judgments, we become attentive to a much fuller disclosure of what manifests itself and how it manifests itself in experience. This allows for greater awareness of phenomena experienced on prereflective, emotive, imaginative, nonconceptual levels of intentional experience, thus leading to new insights into the specific intentionality and concrete richness of experience.

The phenomenological *epoché*, with an emphasis on empathy and sympathetic understanding, is related to methodological antireductionism. By suspending all personal preconceptions as to what is real and insisting on the irreducibility of the religious, phenomenologists attempt sympathetically to place themselves within the religious 'life-world' of others. This phenomenological orientation, different from the ideal of detached, impersonal scientific objectivity, recognizes limitations to such personal empathetic participation, since the other always remains to some extent 'other.' Critics charge that phenomenologists often give little more than vague appeals to abstain from value judgments and for empathetic participation.

In assuming a sympathetic attitude, the phenomenologist is not claiming that religious phenomena are not 'illusory' and that the intentional objects are 'real' as existing behind the phenomenal appearance. (As a matter of fact, many phenomenologists make such theological and metaphysical assumptions and judgments, but these usually violate the limits of their phenomenological perspectives.) The phenomenological bracketing entails suspension of all such value judgments regarding whether or not God, the holy, or sacred is actually an experience of ultimate reality.

Many phenomenologists argue for the necessity of religious commitment, a personal religious faith, or at least personal religious experience in order for a scholar to be capable of empathy, participation, and sympathetic understanding. Other phenomenologists argue that such personal religious commitments generally produce biased descriptions. A particular faith or theological commitment is not a precondition for accurate phenomenological descriptions. Rather it is a commitment, manifested in terms of intellectual curiosity, sensitivity, and respect, that is indispensable for participation and understanding. Believers and nonbelievers alike may share such a commitment.

Insight into essential structures and meanings

No subject matter is more central to philosophical phenomenology than analyses of eidetic reduction and eidetic vision, intuition of essences, method of free variation, and other techniques for gaining insight into essential structures and meanings. By contrast, phenomenology of religion, even in the specific sense of an approach concerned with describing essential structures and meanings, has usually avoided such methodological formulations.

One generally finds that most phenomenologists of religion accept both Bleeker's qualification that such terms as 'eidetic vision' are used only in a figurative sense and his warning that phenomenology of religion should not meddle in difficult philosophical questions of methodology. The result is that one is frequently presented with phenomenological typologies, 'universal structures,' and 'essential meanings' that lack a rigorous analysis of just how the phenomenologist arrived at or verified these discoveries.

Phenomenologists aim at intuiting, describing, and interpreting the essence of religious phenomena, but there is considerable disagreement as to what constitutes an essential structure. For some phenomenologists, an 'essential structure' is the result of an empirical inductive generalization expressing a property that different phenomena have in common. In the sense closest to philosophical phenomenology, essence refers to deep or hidden structures, which are not apparent on the level of immediate experience and must be uncovered and interpreted through the phenomenological method. These structures express the necessary invariant features allowing us to distinguish religious phenomena and to grasp religious phenomena as phenomena of a certain kind.

Controversial issues

The examination of major characteristics of phenomenology of religion raises many controversial issues.

Descriptive versus normative claims

Controversial issues arise from phenomenology of religion's claim that it is a descriptive discipline with a descriptive method, especially since most phenomenologists go beyond a mere description of the data, offering comparisons and evaluations, universal structures, and essential meanings.

Some of these issues arise from the adoption by many phenomenologists of religion of a traditional, at times absolute, descriptive–normative dichotomy consistent with classical empiricism of such philosophers as David Hume, with the Kantian philosophical framework, and with most nineteenth and twentieth-century approaches to religions.

Even phenomenologists of religion who go beyond Kristensen's descriptive restrictions frequently adopt a clear distinction between collection and description of religious data, which is objective and scientific, and interpretation of meaning, which is at least partially subjective and normative. Phenomenology of religion, despite its rejection of positivism, has sometimes unintentionally retained positivistic assumptions regarding the description of unconstructed, uninterpreted, objective 'facts.'

Recent scholarship challenges this absolute dichotomy. What is taken as objective and scientific is historically, culturally, and socially situated and constructed in terms of implicit and explicit value judgments. For example, how does one even begin the investigation? What facts should be collected as religious facts? One's principles of selectivity are never completely value-free. Philosophical phenomenologists have never accepted this sharp dichotomy, since the phenomenological project is founded on possibilities of describing meanings. The challenge to phenomenology of religion is to formulate a phenomenological method and framework for interpretation that allows the description of essential structures and meanings with some sense of objectivity.

Understanding versus explanation claims

Many controversial issues involve a sharp understanding–explanation dichotomy. This 'understanding' often has the sense of *Verstehen* as formulated by Dilthey as the method and goal of hermeneutics. Phenomenologists aim at understanding, describing and interpreting the nature and meaning of religious and other 'human' phenomena, as opposed to scientific, reductionistic approaches that give historical, psychological, and other explanations but do not grasp the irreducibly human and irreducibly religious dimensions of phenomena.

Critics challenge such methods and goals as unscientific and question whether phenomenological understanding and nonphenomenological explaining can be so completely separated. Explanatory approaches involve understanding, and understanding involves critical explanatory reflection. For example, for phenomenological understanding, expressions of religious others are not the absolute final word. The other may have a limited understanding of her or his phenomena, provide false explanations, and engage in blatantly unethical behavior. Phenomenology of religion necessarily involves critical reflection, including contextual awareness and scholarly interpretations, understandings, and explanations that go beyond describing expressed positions of religious others.

This in no way denies the value of phenomenological approaches that are self-critical in rendering explicit one's presuppositions, suspend one's value judgments, empathize, and describe phenomena and intended meanings of the religious other. Such phenomenology of religion aims at allowing other voices to be heard and is informed by a history of dominant, normative approaches and explanations that ignore, silence, and misinterpret the religious phenomena of others.

Antireductionist claims

Many critics attack phenomenology of religion's antireductionism, arguing that it is methodologically confused and often arises from the theological intention of protecting religion from secular analysis. All methodological approaches are perspectival, limiting, and necessarily reductionistic. The assumption of the irreducibility of the religious limits what phenomena will be investigated, what aspects of the phenomena will be described, and what meanings will be interpreted. Phenomenologists of religion cannot argue that other reductionistic approaches are necessarily false and that their approach does justice to all dimensions of religious phenomena.

Phenomenology of religion must show that its religious antireductionism is not methodologically confused and does not beg serious questions by simply avoiding scholarly challenges. It can argue for an antireductionist methodological primacy on the basis of such key notions as intentionality and insight into essential structures and meanings. It must show that its particular perspective is essential for shedding light on religious structures and meanings.

Empirical and historical claims

Much of philosophical phenomenology, even when described as radical empiricism, is conceived in opposition to traditional empiricism. Husserl called for a 'phenomenological reduction' in which the phenomenologist 'suspends' the 'natural standpoint' and its empirical world in order to become more attentive to phenomena and to intuit the deeper phenomenological essences.

Critics claim that phenomenology of religion starts with a priori nonempirical assumptions, utilizes a method that is not empirically based, and detaches religious structures and meanings from historical and cultural contexts. Critics often assume a clear-cut dichotomy between empirical, inductive, historical approaches and nonempirical, often rationalist, deductive, antihistorical approaches. They identify phenomenology of religion with the latter and argue that it cannot meet minimal empirical, historical, scientific, inductive criteria, including rigorous criteria for verification and falsification.

Controversies arise from criticisms that phenomenology of religion makes nonempirical, nonhistorical, a priori, theological, and other normative assumptions and grants an ontologically privileged status to religious phenomena and to specific kinds of religious experience. Critics charge that Otto, van der Leeuw, Eliade, and others have nonempirical and nonhistorical, extraphenomenological, theological, and other normative assumptions, intentions, and goals that take them beyond descriptive phenomenology and any rigorous scientific approach.

The status granted to essential religious structures and meanings is also controversial insofar as they exhibit the peculiarity of being empirical, based on investigating a limited sample of historical data, and, at the same time, universal. These structures are therefore empirically contingent and yet also the essential necessary features of religious phenomena.

Finally, there is controversy regarding the insistence by many phenomenologists of religion that they proceed by empirical inductive inference. Critics charge that they cannot repeat this inductive inference, that phenomenological structures do not appear in the empirical data, and that phenomenologists read into their data all kinds of essential meanings. Some, such as Douglas Allen in *Structure and Creativity in Religion*, respond by formulating a method of 'phenomenological induction' different from classical empirical induction, in which essential structures and meaning are based on, but not found fully in, the empirical data.

Questions of verification

Many criticisms of phenomenology of religion as methodologically uncritical involve questions of verification. Phenomenological 'intuition' does not free one from responsibility of ascertaining which interpretation of given phenomena is most adequate. Different phenomenologists, using a phenomenological method to investigate the same phenomena, present different eidetic intuitions. How does one resolve this contingency introduced into phenomenological insights? How does one verify interpretations and decide between different interpretations?

Such questions pose specific difficulties for a phenomenological method of *epoché* and intuition of essences. A phenomenological method often suspends the usual criteria of 'objectivity' that allow scholars to verify interpretations and choose between alternative accounts. Does this leave phenomenology of religion with a large number of personal, subjective, hopelessly fragmented interpretations of universal structures and meanings, each relativistic interpretation determined by the particular temperament, situation, and orientation of the phenomenologist?

Phenomenologists of religion submit that past criteria for verification are inadequate and offer a false sense of objectivity, but phenomenology of religion must also overcome the charges of subjectivity and relativism. It must formulate procedures for testing its claims of essential structures and meanings that involve criteria for intersubjective verification.

Response to controversial issues

Many writers describe phenomenology of religion as in a state of crisis. They usually minimize the invaluable contributions made by phenomenology to the study of religion, such as the impressive systematization of so much religious data and the raising of fundamental questions of meaning.

If phenomenology of religion is to deal adequately with controversial issues, the following are several of its future tasks. First, it must become more aware of historical, philological, and other specialized approaches to, and different aspects of, its religious data. Second, it must critique various approaches of its critics, thus showing that its phenomenological method is not obliged to meet inadequate criteria for objectivity. And most importantly, it must reflect more critically on questions of methodology so that it can formulate a more rigorous method, allowing for description of phenomena, interpretation of their structures and meanings, and verification of its findings.

Recent developments in phenomenology of religion

Developments within phenomenology of religion during the last decades of the twentieth century and early years of the twenty-first century convey a very mixed and confusing picture about the present status and future prospects for the field.

Within religious studies

Phenomenology of religion continues as a discipline and approach within the general scholarly study of religion. Earlier phenomenologists influence phenomenologists of religion, and they share the general phenomenological orientation defined by major characteristics previously delineated. Phenomenology of religion has also been successful to the extent that many other scholars, who do not consider themselves phenomenologists, adopt a phenomenological approach during early stages of their investigations because it has great value in allowing them to assemble data and do justice to the perspectives of religious persons.

At the same time, phenomenology of religion is sometimes described as being stagnant and in a state of crisis. There has been a recent renewal of interest in religion in French philosophical phenomenology and in phenomenological theology, but it is not clear how this relates to phenomenology of religion within religious studies. There are no contemporary phenomenologists of religion who enjoy the status and influence once enjoyed by a van der Leeuw or an Eliade. Some scholars are uncomfortable with the term since it carries so much baggage from Husserlian philosophical foundations and from Eliadean and other phenomenology of religion. In general, contemporary phenomenologists of religion attempt to be more contextually sensitive and more modest in their phenomenological claims.

Within philosophical and theological phenomenology

The emphasis in this chapter has been on phenomenology of religion as a discipline and method within religious studies and not on philosophical phenomenology with its limited focus on religion. Special mention may be made of two influential European philosophers. Emmanuel Levinas, a student of Husserl, became an influential continental philosopher in the late twentieth century. With his major focus on ethics, spirituality, and Jewish philosophy, Levinas emphasizes radical alterity and the primacy of the 'other,' thus reversing earlier phenomenological self–other emphasis on the privileged status of the constituting self or ego. Ricoeur, also with deep roots in Husserl, has made invaluable contributions to our understanding of religious phenomena with his analysis of philosophy as hermeneutical interpretation of meaning and with his focus on religious language, symbolism, and narrative.

Beginning in the late twentieth century, continental philosophy, especially French phenomenology, often takes a religious turn. Scholars such as Michel Henry and especially Jean-Luc Marion are often identified as part of 'the new phenomenology' and 'theological phenomenology.' However, it is not always clear whether to classify such developments under 'the phenomenology of religion.' Most of these scholars have been deeply influenced by Husserl's phenomenology, but they often seem to transgress phenomenology's boundaries and express ambiguous relations to phenomenology.

While significant developments in continental philosophy increasingly focus on religion, it is not yet clear whether such phenomenological and theological developments will have a significant influence on phenomenology of religion within religious studies.

Recent challenges

Most scholarly challenges to phenomenology of religion continue major criticisms previously described. Robert Segal and other scholars of religion, usually identified with social scientific and reductionist approaches, criticize phenomenology of religion for being unscientific, highly subjective, and lacking scholarly rigor. Scholars identifying with reductionistic cognitive science and neuroscience provide recent challenges.

There are also challenges to phenomenology of religion that offer opposite criticisms. Scholars criticize phenomenology of religion's claim to uncover universal structures and essences as being too reductionistic in denying the diversity and plurality of religious phenomena. Included here are a variety of approaches often described as postmodernist, deconstructionist, post-structuralist, narrativist, pragmatist, feminist, and relativist.

Gavin Flood and other scholars identified with critical theory, postmodernism, and other recent approaches criticize essentialist phenomenology of religion for being nonhistorical and nontemporal; for ignoring the situated contextualism of all phenomena and all approaches; for presenting a false view of human consciousness, experience, and language; and for romanticizing and defending religious phenomena and religious faith while ignoring the exploitative and oppressive dimensions of religious phenomena reflecting ideologies and power relations of domination.

Several recent contributions

Finally, there are three, recent, interrelated contributions to phenomenology of religion that often contrast with earlier characteristics: focus on the 'other,' 'givenness,' and contextualization.

Philosophical phenomenology and phenomenology of religion emphasize the need to become aware of one's presuppositions, suspend one's value judgments, and accurately describe and interpret the meaning of phenomena as phenomena. Earlier approaches have been critiqued for ignoring or distorting intentional structures and meanings of religious phenomena of the 'other.' More recent phenomenologists recognize that earlier phenomenology, with its essentializing projects and universalizing claims, often did not pay sufficient attention to diverse experiences and meanings of others. One sometimes learns more about the scholar's phenomenological theory of religion than about the particular religious phenomena of others. Recent phenomenology has been more sensitive to providing an approach for becoming attentive to the tremendous diversity of religious voices of others.

Related to this is the focus on givenness. There is the more ontological, theological, and controversial move by Marion and others to emphasize a phenomenological reduction of phenomena to a primary experience of givenness. In a more widespread and less controversial contribution, philosophical phenomenology and phenomenology of religion emphasize the need for an active openness and deeper kind of attentiveness to how religious phenomena appear or are given to us in experience. Over the decades, phenomenology of religion has become much broader, more self-critical, and more sophisticated in recognizing the complexity, ambiguity, and depth of our diverse modes of givenness. For example, in their very dynamic of givenness, religious phenomena both reveal and conceal structures and meanings; are multidimensional and given meaning through pre-understandings, the prereflective, the emotive, and the imaginative, as well as rational and conceptual analysis; are not disclosed as bare givens but as highly complex, inexhaustible, constituted, self-transcending givens; and are given in ways that affirm the open-ended perspectival nature of all knowledge and the nonclosure of descriptions, interpretations, and explanations.

Phenomenologists of religion are much more sensitive to the complex, mediated, interactive, contextual situatedness of their phenomenological tasks. Often criticized for claiming to uncover nonhistorical, nontemporal, noncontextualized, essential structures and meanings, phenomenologists of religion tend to be more sensitive to the perspectival and contextual constraints of their approach and more modest in their claims. There is value in uncovering religious essences and structures, but as embodied and contextualized, not as fixed, absolute, ahistorical, eternal truths and meanings.

These three contributions in phenomenology of religion of greater focus on the other, givenness, and contextualization can be related to a significant development in 'the late Husserl.' In his *Crisis of European Science* (1936), Husserl revisions his phenomenological project, especially by introducing the concept of the *Lebenswelt* or Lifeworld. He turns away from his earlier pure absolute idealism in which all judgments about phenomena are bracketed so that intentional phenomena are reduced to the consciousness of the constituting transcendental ego. Husserl now begins to rethink the pre-epistemological ground of his phenomenology in terms of the shared, intersubjective givenness of the lifeworld of lived experience. In such an intersubjective universe of what is given in lived experience, the dynamic horizon within which phenomena appear, consciousness is already embedded in the lifeworld of meanings and pre-judgments that are contextually, historically, socially, and culturally situated and constituted. Although Husserl did not develop this concept adequately, later philosophical phenomenology and some recent contributions in phenomenology of religion can be seen as ways of broadening and deepening this Husserlian orientation.

By now, it may be clear that phenomenology of religion has had a profound impact on religious studies, sometimes overtly and sometimes almost imperceptibly. Many scholars within religious studies, who would never call themselves phenomenologists, have had their teaching and research shaped by the contributions of phenomenology of religion. Their concerns about uncritical presuppositions and reductionism, empathy and essential structures, as well as their focus on such topics as sacred space and time, myth and ritual, have been influenced by their exposure to phenomenology of religion.

Within its specific discipline and approach, a more self-critical and modest phenomenology of religion has much to contribute to the study of religion. In providing descriptions and interpretations of phenomena, it will include awareness of its presuppositions, its historical and contextualized situatedness, and its limited perspectival knowledge claims. But it will not completely abandon concerns about essential structures, commonality and unity of human beings, as well as differences. Such a phenomenology of religion will attempt to formulate essential structures and meanings through rigorous phenomenological methods, while also attempting to formulate new, dynamic, open-ended, contextually sensitive projects involving creative encounter, contradiction, and synthesis.

Bibliography

Allen, D. (1978) *Structure and Creativity in Religion*, The Hague: Mouton.

Bleeker, C. J. (1963) *The Sacred Bridge*, Leiden: Brill.

Eliade, M. (1963) *Patterns in Comparative Religion*, trans. R. Sheed, New York: World.

—— (1969) *The Quest*, Chicago: University of Chicago Press.

Flood, G. (1999) *Beyond Phenomenology*, London: Cassell.

Husserl, E. (1970) *The Crisis of European Science and Transcendental Phenomenology*, trans. D. Carr, Evanston: Northwestern University Press.

Idinopulos, T. A. and E. A. Yonan, eds. (1994) *Religion and Reductionism*, Leiden: Brill.

Kristensen, W. B. (1960) *The Meaning of Religion*, trans. J. B. Carman, The Hague: Nijhoff.

Leeuw, G. van der (1963) *Religion in Essence and Manifestation*, 2 vols., trans. J. E. Turner, New York: Harper & Row.

Otto, R. (1950) *The Idea of the Holy*, trans. J. W. Harvey, New York and London: Oxford University Press.

Scheler, M. (1960) *On the Eternal in Man*, trans. B. Noble, London: SCM. New York: Harper.

Sharpe, E. J. (1986) *Comparative Religion*, La Salle, IL: Open Court.

Smart, N. (1973) *The Science of Religion and the Sociology of Knowledge*, Princeton: Princeton University Press.

Suggested reading

Eliade, M. (1963) *Patterns in Comparative Religion*, trans. R. Sheed, New York: World.
Morphological work illustrating Eliade's phenomenological framework for interpreting religious meaning.

—— (1969) *The Quest*, Chicago: University of Chicago Press.
Essays on Eliade's phenomenological method and discipline.

Leeuw, G. van der (1963) *Religion in Essence and Manifestation*, 2 vols., trans. J. E. Turner, New York: Harper & Row.
Classic work in phenomenology of religion.

Otto, R. (1950) *The Idea of the Holy*, trans. J. W. Harvey, New York and London: Oxford University Press.
Influential phenomenological account of religious experience.

Chapter 13

Comparative religion

William E. Paden

Comparative religion originated as an academic movement in the late nineteenth century. It signified then, as today, the cross-cultural study of all forms and traditions of religious life, as distinguished from the study or exposition of just one. As such, it entails the disciplined, historically informed consideration of any commonalities and differences that appear among religions.

Seeing similarities and differences is a basic activity of the human mind. The perception of relationships and patterns is the way individuals and cultures organize their experience of the world. It is a process without which there would be undifferentiated chaos, or at best only isolated facts. Likewise, specialized knowledge in any field advances by finding or constructing concepts and categories that give order and intelligibility to otherwise unrelated data. Comparison, among other things, is the process by which generalizations and classifications are produced, and is the basis of scientific and interpretive enterprises of every kind. The very concept 'religion,' as an academic definition of a certain area of culture, is such a cross-cultural, comparative category.

There can be no systematic study of religion as a subject matter without cross-cultural perspective. Lacking this, studies of religion would amount either to separate collections of unrelated historical data, or to speculative generalizations based only on the perspective of one culture. Modern generations of scholars have therefore tried to build an objective, or at least transcultural, vocabulary for describing a subject matter that is found in very different times, places and languages. For one cannot generalize about religion on the basis of the language and norms of just a single case, just as geologists do not construct a geology on the basis of the rocks that merely happen to be in one's neighborhood. The neighborhood rocks, analogues to one's own local religion, are themselves instances of certain common, universal properties of geological formations, chemical structures, and evolutionary development. Accordingly, without knowing these 'comparative' elements, one cannot know what is common and what is different about any particular religious phenomenon. Without them, one might not be able to see certain transcultural structures and functions in a given religious system.

Comparative analysis, then, both builds and applies the perspectives, reference points, and materials for any cumulative, interpretive study of religion. Moreover, these resources must necessarily be the collective, synthetic result of the contributions of many specialists, as no single person will have first-hand and technical knowledge of all of the world's religious cultures. While comparison is a tool that can be applied locally or among restricted historical and regional data, this essay focuses mostly on its cross-cultural, generalizing functions.

Comparison: the factor of selectivity

The process of comparison has a basic structure. First, there must be a point of commonality that allows for the comparison of two or more objects. Notably, the very term 'comparison' contains this idea, deriving from the Latin elements com, 'with,' and par, 'equal.' But comparison does not have to be limited to seeing commonalities. It can also perceive difference with respect to some aspect of what is otherwise in common. In everyday terms, for example, one can compare new houses (= the common factor) with regard to price (= the chosen criterion or aspect of difference). Likewise, one could compare religions (= the broad common factor) with regard to their population size, or their types of authority, or their views on gender; or compare purification rites with regard to their specific methods of removing impurity. The history of the comparative study of religion is the history and application of what its scholars have taken these common factors and these criteria of difference to be. Whether similarities or differences are emphasized will depend on the purposes at hand.

Comparison in itself is an activity, and not a theory or ideology, but it has been a tool of many different theories and hence employed for a range of interpretive or historical purposes. Consider two different 'comparative' approaches to the biblical story of creation. For the believer, to whom the account may present itself as the unique, authoritative Word of God, any comparison with other 'origins' accounts might be to show the superiority of Genesis. In that case, the ancient Babylonian account of creation, the *Enuma Elish*, could be shown to represent a more primitive 'polytheistic' idea of the world, compared to the Bible's ostensibly 'pure' monotheism. The scenarios in the *Enuma Elish* that describe many gods and goddesses generating offspring and having to fend off chaos, would be picked out to contrast unfavorably with the Genesis version of one supreme god who is in charge of creation from the beginning and has no equals. But for those interested in goddess mythologies, the Genesis story has been presented quite differently. Here the biblical account has been viewed as a latter-day, patriarchal version of mythologies that once honored a primal goddess with her sacred tree and companion serpent. In this comparative sequence, the Hebrew account has been construed as a story that demoted the power of the goddess – who in Genesis becomes the very human Eve, the source of man's fall, and the prototype of female subservience to males.

While the present article focuses mainly on academic, secular comparativism, rather than on matters of inter-religious relationships where 'truth' is typically the concern, the traditional role of religious approaches has been so pervasive that it requires some preliminary attention.

Religious forms of comparison

For those approaching comparison with religious motivation, their own beliefs are understandably used as a standard of interpretation. Historical Christian versions of comparative endeavors provide a range of examples of this. Here the rest of the world and its religions are all seen through the filters of patterns and prototypes set forth in the Bible. Here the overall motif is to demonstrate the superiority of Christianity.

Examples of Christian 'comparative religion'

Christian theologians needed to account for the existence of other religions and their gods, and traditional strategies included a whole spectrum of negative and positive interpretations that may be summarized briefly.

Demonic origins

Who or what were these 'pagan' gods that received so much devotion? Perhaps they were not really gods at all but demons seeking their own worshippers? How were missionaries to explain the presence of sculpted 'crosses' in Mayan temples that pre-dated the arrival of Christianity? Such overt parallels were easily seen as the mocking work of Satan, understood to be aping or imitating the true religion.

Historical diffusion

A second Christian strategy of explanation was the idea of 'historical' diffusion. Insofar as nonbiblical religions appeared to have anything truly religious about them, like the belief in a creator god, this could be explained as having been ultimately derived from the original pure monotheism of the biblical patriarchs. Likewise, where there was 'idolatrous' religion, such as the worship of forces of nature, this could be interpreted as a historical 'degeneration' from that same once pure source. Thus, any religious expression could be seen in terms of a unified theory of historical diffusion which assumed that all religions, as all cultures, could be traced to and from the survivors of the Great Flood. Sometimes etymologies were relied on to explain the transmission of these 'survivals' or 'remnants' of the patriarchal times. For example, the Hindu god Brahma was understood as a latter-day historical transformation of the biblical name, 'Abraham.' On other occasions, the idea of travel contact, perhaps via the lost tribes of Israel, was used to explain how religions like those of the Native Americans were able to obtain their ideas about a creator god.

Allegorical truths

A third mode of Christian comparison was to view other religions as containing *symbols* of Christian truths. Christians were already used to the idea that the Hebrew Bible contained images and events that allegorically prefigured the coming of the Christian messiah. Ancient Hebraic sacrifices, for example, were interpreted as symbolizing the sacrifice of Christ. Likewise, deities of other religions could be seen as representing attributes of the true God – for example, the goddess Athena was interpreted as pointing to God's 'wisdom.'

Natural vs. revealed religion

Christians also developed the idea of natural vs. revealed religion. This is the notion that all humans, by being made in the divine image, have a natural potential to know God. Such endowment could therefore account for the presence of other religions. Yet, while all humans have access to a basic knowledge of God, 'revealed' knowledge was God's *full* revelation through Christ to the biblical communities. In comparison, Christ could naturally be seen as the fulfillment of the innate yearnings of other religious peoples, and Christianity would be understood as religion in its highest, most complete, and universal form.

Dialogue

From modern theology has come the idea of 'dialogue' between religions. This means adopting a 'listening' stance toward others, and not merely a dogmatic, prejudging position that stereotypes others. For example, a statement of the Roman Catholic Church (from the Second Vatican Council, 1962–1965), urged its members to appreciate the presence of 'the holy' in other traditions, and also established a permanent commission to study the other faiths and explore their meaning through open dialogue. Wilfrid Cantwell Smith (1916–2000), an influential comparativist and specialist in Islam, emphasized that the comparative study of religion needs to responsibly describe the living qualities of other peoples' faiths in a way that those other persons themselves would be able to recognize as their own position.

Universalism

In contrast to Christian comparisons, there is another religious approach that may be termed universalism. This affirms that all religions refer to the same underlying spiritual reality, but do so through different cultural forms and languages. Just as water is water, regardless of what it is called, so, in universalistic thinking, God is God, regardless of name. Even in the world of ancient Greece, there was a well-known doctrine of 'the equivalence of the gods.' Thus, the fifth-century BC Greek historian Herodotus reported that the gods of Egypt were basically Egyptian names for Greek divinities: Ammon was but another name for Zeus, Horus was the same as Apollo, and Isis was taken as equivalent to the goddess Demeter.

Universalism became highly developed in classical Stoicism and during the European Renaissance, and was later fostered by the Romantic, Transcendentalist, and New Age movements. It has been a basic premise of many Asian and mystical traditions. In the Far East, Buddhists commonly interpreted native Chinese and Japanese gods as 'manifestations' of cosmic buddhas. Buddhas were the 'originals,' and the local gods were their 'appearances.'

Universalism has variants. For some, it is motivated by a sense that all humans are basically alike. Many find a common set of precepts undergirding the world's religions, such as the need to honor a divine being and assume ethical responsibility. Some look for common affirmations about peace or nonviolence. Still others understand the universal basis of religion in terms of a core spiritual experience or revelation of the divine. In that outlook, institutional and doctrinal differences are merely seen as the secondary, outward elaborations of a shared, intuitive sense of the 'wholly other' mystery that grounds all life.

The rise of comparative religion as an academic field

Interpreting and comparing religions evolves along with expanding knowledge of other cultures. One can only compare what lies within one's horizon of information. One can only study 'others' on the basis of the *kind* of knowledge of other cultures that is available at the time. In the Hebrew Bible, for example, references to other religions are always citations of other Near Eastern religions, not of Chinese, Japanese, or Indian religion. As recently as the early nineteenth century, Western Christendom still basically classified all religion into only four kinds, namely the three biblical monotheisms (Judaism, Christianity, Islam) and all others, lumped together as 'idolatry,' or 'paganism,' a derogatory term referring to those who supposedly worshipped false gods. Accounts brought back by missionaries and travelers continued to support the stereotype of the benighted state of non-Western or non-biblical peoples.

By the mid to late nineteenth century, however, the comparative study of religion, by that name, was being put forth as a modern academic field of knowledge. Several developments made this possible. One was the expanding knowledge of Asian religions, particularly through access to translations of their scriptures. A second was the emerging knowledge of pre-literate cultures, produced partly by the new field of anthropology. A third was a new idea of history, namely that the whole of human culture had undergone a long evolution from primitive origins (in contrast to the biblical account of human origins). And a fourth was the general trend toward classifying and mapping the data of the world's various subject matters. Together, these factors created a broad, new canvas for the study of religion.

The most influential nineteenth-century advocate of comparative religion was F. Max Müller (1823–1900). A native of Germany and then scholar at Oxford University from age 23, Müller was an authority on Sanskrit, the classical religious language of India. He edited an important 50-volume translation series termed *The Sacred Books of the East*. He urged that the study of religion should no longer be limited to the religions of the Mediterranean and that the great civilizational religions of the East, and their scriptures, should be taken seriously. Asian religions were to be brought into a horizon of respectful comparability with biblical religions. Here the older, parochial Western view of religious history as a simple contest of biblical vs. pagan traditions was to become obsolete.

Along these lines, more accurate histories of religion were produced. These replaced the previous provincial notions that all human languages derive from Hebrew, that all cultures and religions were traceable to the family of Noah, and that the dating of scriptures – whether biblical or nonbiblical – should be taken at face value.

Müller and others held that comparative religion is to any one religion as comparative philology is to the study of any particular language, and as comparative anatomy is to the anatomy of any one species. As the life sciences made progress through application of this method, so too would religious inquiry. The study of one religion would throw light on the study of another. Müller liked to apply to religion what the poet Goethe said of language: 'he who knows one ... knows none.' In addition, Müller also outlined a broad program and methodology of comparative study. This included principles like gaining knowledge of others through their own writings, grouping religions according to their regional, linguistic contexts, and avoiding the common distortion of comparing the positive aspects of one religion with the negative aspects of another (Müller 1872).

Toward an academic comparativism

In principle, though not always in practice, academic comparativism does not presuppose the value or truth of any one religion, but sets out to investigate religion as a patterned phenomenon of human culture and behavior. The rise of comparativism as a concern of the human sciences required in the first place that all religion would be studied by the same criteria. No religion would be privileged. No religious version of history would be used as normative. While all religions professed their own ancestral accounts of the past, the new, panhuman, naturalistic worldview now showed quite a different story of origins – a long, complex evolution of culture that did not coincide with the self-interested accounts of the various world scriptures. Religion – once the norm in terms of which all history and culture was perceived – now itself became an object to be interpreted in terms of wider patterns of human history.

Again, one source of this new knowledge was so-called primitive cultures, and anthropologists looked to these to find the origin of the fundamental structures of religious belief and practice and to identify universal laws about their evolution. The English scholar Edward B. Tylor (1832–1917) found 'belief in spiritual beings' (which he worked into a theory he called 'animism') to originate in the experience of dreams and of deceased relatives, and thence to evolve into forms of polytheism and monotheism. Others focused on the universal role of 'power' or *mana* (Melanesian term for supernatural force) in religions. The influential French sociologist Émile Durkheim (1858–1917) advocated that the source and structuring principle of religious life was 'the totemic principle.' In this theory, sacred objects were maintained as sacred because they symbolized each group's own social identity and tradition. Arnold van Gennep's classic, *Rites of Passage* (original French edition, 1908), showed the universality of ritual patterns by which social and life-cycle transitions were performed, and became part of the currency of comparative thinking. An influential application of comparativism to biblical religion was W. Robertson Smith's *The Religion of the Semites* (1889). Smith located ancient Hebrew practices in terms of common 'primitive' categories of totemic communion, sacrificial rites, sacred places, and taboos. The suggestion that biblical religion could be seen in such contexts was a scandal to many in his day.

The best known of these pre-modern comparativists was James G. Frazer (1854–1941), particularly through his book, *The Golden Bough*, first published in two volumes in 1890, and later to grow to twelve volumes. *The Golden Bough* was a vast compendium of examples of ritual, myth, and religion, organized by patterns and themes, and presented as an instance of comparative method. Frazer made extensive use of sources from primitive and folk cultures. The work began by citing an obscure Roman rite about the practice of succession to the priesthood of the goddess Diana, an institution that appeared to involve a ritual killing of the old priest by a new priest who would then assume the office. As a way of throwing comparative light on this, Frazer marshaled extensive illustrations from around the world that addressed the theme and subthemes of the ritual renewal of life, thus providing a universal context to the original Roman example. *The Golden Bough* became a study of the transcultural themes of sacred kingship, rites of succession, seasonal renewal festivals, mythologies of dying and rising gods, rites of scapegoating and expulsion, various forms of sympathetic and 'contagious' magic, and substitutionary ritual deaths, among other topics. Frazer thought that these showed the patterned way that the premodern human mind worked – a kind of archaeology of mentality. He held that once these universal patternings were understood, then many otherwise obscure or unusual cultural practices and beliefs – including many of those found in the Bible – would become more intelligible.

Psychologists Sigmund Freud (1856–1939) and C.G. Jung (1875–1961) also began to interpret religious patternings as expressions of the way the human psyche works. In particular, Jung correlated stages of the development of the human ego/self with what he took to be the equivalent of those stages expressed in the projection and history of mythological symbols. Hence certain psychological patterns or 'archetypes' could be found in religion – expressed, for example, in images of a primal paradise, a Great Mother, the journey of the 'hero,' or the reconciling 'union of opposites.' 'God-images' were understood to represent various features of the 'archetype of the self,' in all its stages. The writings of Joseph Campbell (1904–1987) – including the classic, *The Hero with a Thousand Faces* – would bring much of this approach into the public domain.

If recurring religious representations and practices appear independently in different cultures, with no explanation for their resemblances in terms of historical influence, then that might suggest that the parallels express something common to the human condition. But what? What is it that the patternings of religious life ultimately express? What are they patterns *of*? The human psyche? Social bonding? Political power? Gender empowerments? Varying environments? Social class? Are there stages of development that religious history goes through, and do the stages of the development of society and consciousness explain the varieties of religion? All of these trajectories of explanation utilized, indeed, required, comparative data. All have served as frameworks for pursuing and organizing the cross-cultural study of religion. Here, then, comparison ultimately involves more than description. It is guided by issues of explanation, too, and becomes a testing ground for theories of human behavior.

Inventories, taxonomies, phenomenologies

In late nineteenth-century Europe, the general 'science of religion' included two principal components: historical and phenomenological. The latter referred mainly to a description of types and forms of religious experience. Its task was to collate and organize all the data of religious history into groupings or classes of religious expressions – that is, to identify an overall taxonomy or anatomy of religious life. This was an inventorial enterprise that resulted in encyclopedic catalogues illustrating all the common forms of religion. An example was the influential work of P.D. Chantepie de la Saussaye published in 1887 (in German) and translated as Manual of the Science of Religion. Chantepie classed kinds of religious 'phenomena' together, along with subclasses. For example, the class, 'objects of veneration,' included stones, trees, animals, sky, earth, sun, moon, fire, ancestors, saints, heroes, and gods. He grouped together 'practices' under rubrics like divination, sacrifice, prayer, sacred dance and music, processions, rites of purification, sacred times and places, and described categories such as priests (and other religious specialists), scriptures, types of religious communities, myths, and theologies. Chantepie illustrated each category with examples from different cultures, and summarized the research that had been done on it. What naturalists like Linnaeus had done for the botanical world was now to be done for religion. The religious world had to be mapped, and its many species, here its 'classes of phenomena,' named and typed.

The phenomenology of religion tradition also went beyond just mapping. It began to look for an understanding of how religious forms function in the worlds of the adherents. Two major figures that developed this were Gerardus van der Leeuw in his *Religion in Essence and Manifestation* (German original, 1933), and Mircea Eliade. Van der Leeuw's book, which described religion as a relationship to an 'other power,' focused on some 106 patterns of religious life. For each one he tried to bring out the essential religious values, structure, and meanings connected with it.

Mircea Eliade's comparative patterns

The best-known comparative religion scholar of the last generation was the Rumanian-born Mircea Eliade (1907–1986), who came to the University of Chicago in 1956. Eliade's interest was in the recurring patterns and symbolisms by which religious cultures construct and inhabit their particular kinds of 'worlds,' through the language of myth and ritual. Such systems are structured, for the insider, by the belief in a sacred dimension to life, which makes them different from the nonreligious worlds which lack that factor. Eliade used the term hierophany, which literally means 'a manifestation of the sacred,' to refer to any object or form believed to convey spiritual power and value. Examples include trees, places, hunting, eating, one's country, personal gods, cosmic gods, or yogic techniques that aim at liberation from the human condition. Moreover, 'To many a mystic,' Eliade writes, 'the integrated quality of the cosmos is itself a hierophany' (Eliade 1958: 459). Some particularly distinctive comparative 'modalities of the sacred' as interpreted by Eliade include the following:

Sacred space

All humans have the experience of space, but religious cultures endow special places as gateways or connectors to the world of the sacred. Religious systems orient life around certain fixed points that form a site of communication with the gods. The sites may be natural, provided by the environment, like certain rivers or mountains, or they may be human constructions like shrines and temples. Sometimes these linkages are explicitly understood to connect heaven and earth, the above and the below. Around such an axis, or 'Centre of the World,' the rest of the world, the ordinary world, rises up and receives its value. A grand-scale example would be the great shrine at Mecca, the Ka'ba, the spiritual point on earth that Muslims believe God ordained as a bond with humanity. But local altars may also comprise an axis mundi (world axis), too.

The history of religion will show innumerable 'centers of the world,' each of which is absolute for the respective believers. Eliade's point is that this kind of language should not be judged literally or geographically, but as illustrative of a common religious way of structuring one's world through concentrative, centripetal points of focus (objects, places, mountains, shrines). That is, because a 'world' is relative to a people, these centers are not superstitious beliefs, but examples of a way the mind orients itself in space. Traditional Christian beliefs that placed Jerusalem's Church of the Holy Sepulcher (the traditional site of the tomb of Christ) at the center of the world and world maps, or the equivalent claims in other traditions, may be then understood in this wider comparative context. In Eliadean usage, such comparative perspective on sacred space gives context, dimensionality and universal humanity to any particular version of religious places and orientations.

Mythic time

A related religious pattern featured in Eliade's work is 'sacred time.' These are ritual or festival occasions when believers step into the revered 'Great Time' of the founders and gods. Religious cultures see themselves in terms of their own foundational sacred histories – accounts of primal, originary times when the world was created by the actions of the great beings of the past. However, it is not just past, chronological time. It is time that always underlies present time, and can be accessed periodically and reenacted through ritual 'openings'. In this way, one's world is renewed and re-empowered.

Sacrality of nature

Eliade held that for homo religiosus ('religious man') sacrality is often revealed through the very structures of nature. These include patterns connected with the infinity and transcendence of the sky, the fecundity of the earth, the power of the sun, the waxing and waning cycle of the moon and of life and death, the durability of stones, and the solubility and creativity of water. As such, these 'systems of symbolism' form connections with various religious motifs. Examples are the association of creator deities with the sky, goddesses with earth and moon, and baptismal rebirth with water. These and other complexes are described at length in Eliade's *Patterns in Comparative Religion* (first French edition 1949).

Eliade's approach, which he referred to as the 'History of Religions,' provided a set of comparative categories that cut across the particular religious traditions. At the same time, for Eliade the study of religion was a study in human creativity, on the analogy that religions are complex symbolic universes like great works of art. Studying these 'creations,' he thought, would have a culturally de-provincializing and rejuvenating effect.

In most respects Eliade's work is representative of both the strengths and weaknesses of traditional academic comparative religion. Many of the contemporary critiques of comparativism are critiques of Eliadeanism, and typically include the charge that cross-cultural categories illegitimately override significant cultural contexts and differences. This and other issues will be addressed next.

Issues and critiques

Comparativism is not without its problems and critics. Especially when it claims cross-cultural patterns, it can indulge in superficial parallels, false analogies, misleading associations, egregious stereotyping, and wholly unscientific or imaginative projections. As well, many historians believe that the best way to study religion is to avoid the application of abstract, generic concepts, with their preestablished meanings, and to build a knowledge of a particular religious tradition on its own terms, through its own primary sources. Critics of comparativism therefore often claim that it is always the specific, not the general, that is 'the real,' and that religious phenomena are indelibly embedded in unique sociocultural settings and hence are incomparable. The 'same' theme – such as ritual ablution or sacred space – may have different meanings and functions in different historical contexts. The distinctiveness of religious cultures, in this sense, would seem to remain elusively off the comparative grid. Briefly, here is a summary of these and other critical issues.

Comparativism as suppressing difference

Perhaps the most common criticism of cross-cultural categorizations is that they suppress or conceal significant difference, giving the illusion of homogeneity by making the expressions of other cultures conform to the concepts used by the scholar. The comparativist's concepts, the critic maintains, are themselves cultural, for example, European or Christian. Other societies are then reduced to instances of Euro-Christian classifications. Vague and dubious resemblances are abstracted from rich diversity, and the representation of others is limited to only those points which illustrate the scholar's own vocabulary. If a Westerner sets out to compare different ideas of 'God' around the world, he already has a standard of what to look for and it may be inadequate to describing non-Western representations of the superhuman.

A major advocate of the need for more rigorous contextual analysis in the comparative enterprise is the University of Chicago scholar, Jonathan Z. Smith. Many of his works (Smith 1982, 1987, 1990, 2004) challenge traditional categories and methods of comparison. To take one instance, Smith critiques Eliade's interpretation of the sacred 'pole' of a certain aboriginal Australian tribe. Eliade had maintained that the pole represented a kind of world axis that could nevertheless be carried from place to place. This portable link with the world above would allow the tribe to remain 'in its universe.' Smith's careful examination of the evidence showed that Eliade had superimposed the notion of a 'World Center' onto a culture which had very different notions of space and no notions of ritual linkages with a world above. The world axis idea, Smith pointed out, belonged to other kinds of cultures, like those of ancient Near Eastern city states, where political power was highly centralized and manifest in temples linking the human and the gods. But the Australian notion of space and environment lacked these elements. Smith concluded that 'The "Center" is not a secure pattern to which data may be brought as illustrative; it is a dubious notion that will have to be established anew on the basis of detailed comparative endeavors' (Smith 1987: 17).

Comparativism not only has been accused of inaccuracy of representation, but has been charged with political arrogance: appropriating 'others' to one's worldview and depriving them of their own voices. So-called cross-cultural thought can thus become a form of colonialist ideology – a means of extending one's own values over all and at the same time suppressing the 'subjectivity' of those who differ. According to this criticism, comparativism amounts to a kind of conceptual imperialism exercised by one culture, class, or gender over others.

So-called postmodern thinking challenges the notion of objectivity and maintains that comparative accounts are grounded in ideologies and used for the scholar's own theoretical purposes. Thus, what the comparativist takes as patterns 'out there,' should really be seen as strategies for manipulating data for subjective or cultural goals.

Comparativism as untheoretical

There is also the charge that the generalizations of comparative religion lack scientific value. Anyone, for example, can make claims about the existence of certain patterns, but it could be argued that this is just another form of mythmaking, fiction, metaphor, play. What, in contrast, is the scientific basis of comparison? Are its claims verifiable by evidence and falsification? For example, what social or historical conditions explain the differences and similarities contained in the comparison? Anthropologists, for their part, have a long scholarly tradition of comparative analysis – including statistical analysis – of cross-cultural topics (like kinship), with attention to complex variables and co-variables (cf. Naroll and Cohen 1970: 581–1008); and sociologists of religion have comparable analyses of new religious movements. But, it is charged, comparative religion scholarship has yet to incorporate and apply the canons of empirical and analytical methods (Martin 2000). A 'strong program' of comparative study would have 'scientific consequentiality' because it would advance evidence that can be falsified or tested; the act of placing a particular phenomenon as a member of a comparative 'class' would have to be defensible and shown to be necessary, much as particular languages could be shown to be logical instances of a certain language family (cf. Ivan Strenski, 'The Only Kind of Comparison Worth Doing,' in Idinopulos 2006: 271–292). Recent applications of cognitive and evolutionary models to the comparative study of religion point to more rigorous models of evidence and determination of variables (cf. Whitehouse 2004).

Regional comparison

Many would want to limit comparison to historically contiguous cultures, where there are already some common structural features and values. Exponents contrast that with what is taken to be the dubious practice of comparison between unrelated cultures or religions. The first. regional type, is based on a degree of historical genealogy in the form of continuity, diffusion, or contact.

Some elements of contemporary comparativism

The critiques have meant that the methods and process of cross-cultural concept formation have had to be qualified and defined in more careful ways. Hence, the post-Eliadean phase of comparativism has seen emergent articulations and emphases that in some ways address and remediate the problems just listed (Smith 1982, 1987, 1990; Poole 1986; Martin *et al.* 1996; Doniger 1998; Martin 2000; Patton and Ray 2000; *Numen* 2001; Braun 2004; Idinopulos *et al.* 2006). The following summarizes some of the elements and affirmations found in contemporary comparativism.

First, as mentioned above and as will be shown in the next sections, is that comparison is not only a matter of describing commonality, but a tool that may be used either to find similarity or difference. Insofar as comparison can also be used to highlight particulars, it is less subject to the above criticisms. Patterns are then not simply reductions to common types, as though forcing all differences into stereotypic boxes and erasing all particularity, but also have the effect of calling attention to differences, variations or innovations relative to the common theme. Arguably, you cannot have difference or distinctive attributes without some point of commonality in relation to which something is then different or distinctive.

Second, 'common factors' or patterns can be understood as matters to be *tested* rather than assumed or taken for granted. As such, a comparative pattern would be like a hypothesis to be explored or a question to be asked in relation to each of its supposed cultural examples (cf. Neville 2001, for a thorough review of this). Counter-evidence would be examined, complexity acknowledged. The cultural bias of the pattern would be taken into account. Thematic inquiry – like the use of any concept that might guide a historian's work – would then amount to a starting point for the complexities of research, leading toward areas of unforeseen possibilities, rather than an ideological gridwork imposed on history once and for all. Certainly comparative analysis is not a substitute for historical analysis. They go together.

Third, comparison can and should be clearly based on defined *aspects* of that which is compared. By focusing on and controlling the exact point of analogy, the comparativist understands that the objects may be quite incomparable in other respects and for other purposes. Because two or more things do not appear 'the same' on the surface, or as wholes, does not mean that they are not comparable in *some* ways (cf. Poole 1986). There is folk wisdom to the phrase, 'You can't compare apples and oranges,' because on the surface and as a whole, they are not 'the same,' yet they *are* comparable *in some aspects*: both belong to the class 'fruit,' both are edible, both are round and similar in size, and so forth. Proper comparison does not equate similarity with identity. Moreover, comparativists then must stipulate not only which feature of the data they are comparing, but also for what purpose (cf. Smith 1982, 2004; Carter 1998). Some outstanding, exemplary case studies illustrate this (Holdrege 1996, comparing Hinduism and Rabbinic Judaism, and Jones 2000, comparing sacred architectures).

Fourth, another qualifier is that 'cross-cultural' does not necessarily mean universal. A comparative pattern can be widespread, general, a matter of resemblance, or a 'near-universal' (a familiar anthropological concept), without being universal. A cross-cultural pattern does not need to appear in *all* cultures, but only needs to *recur* in relation to certain types or conditions of culture and religious systems. For example, not all religions have shamans, priests, savior figures, animal sacrifices, or scriptures. But the ones that do have certain recurrent social patterns in common.

Fifth, comparison may legitimately proceed by the use of clear cultural norms or prototypes, as long as the terms and purpose of comparison are understood. For example, one could take something like the Hebrew sacrificial system of the biblical period, and without assuming that it is an adequate basis for understanding all other sacrificial cults, one could investigate other systems that have some resemblances or likeness to it. The resemblance could be a matter of degree, not identity. In fact, if one examines any comparative pattern carefully, one can often find that it is implicitly based on a particular cultural version or prototype *of* that pattern. This is typically the case with the concept 'religion' itself. When Westerners use the term, what they often have in mind is a version of the Christian religion, so that, for example, religion signifies a system with a scripture, a creator god, and a concept of salvation. While this would be too narrow a way by which to describe everything religious, it is not in itself a faulty or uncontrolled comparative enterprise. The problem would be if there was no awareness that one was in fact limiting the analysis to the use of a particular historical norm or prototype (on the prototype issue see Saler 1993).

Sixth, academic comparativism should recognize a distinction between the perspectives, purposes and language of the comparativist and those of the insider. This is not to assert that the comparativist approach is better or more genuine in some absolute sense. Rather, the committed insider and the observing comparativist have different purposes. The object of the student of comparative religion is not simply to reiterate, replicate or 'understand' what particular religions say or do, though she must also be able to do that, but to find relationships and differences among religious traditions and to hold these up to view with a more wide-angled lens. These would be linkages that the insider, as insider, may neither see, be able to see, or be interested in.

To use the famous example of the philosopher William James, a crab does not see itself as a crustacean (the latter being an 'outsider's' concept). But the biologist does. The scientist sees all the crustacean features (and against a broad evolutionary background) that the crab shares with over 40,000 other subspecies. The comparative anatomy scholar therefore sees continuities and differences unobservable to the single organism, and builds a new vocabulary to describe them. Likewise, comparativists in religion generate a terminology about 'types' of religious behaviors and representations, using the whole history of religion as the 'context' for making comparisons.

Seventh, if religion should be studied from all angles, then comparative themes should not be limited to religious patterns only. Comparison needs to be versatile – as complex as its subject matter. Religion can be analyzed in terms of any concept or topic. The 'common factor' in comparison can even be a complex combination of factors. For example, the relation of sacrifice to patterns of male authority; or the relation of ideas of deity to changes in technology in developing countries; or the cross-culturally patterned ways fundamentalist movements respond to modernist governments.

Comparative religion thereby extends its repertory of concepts and patterns, the better to do justice to the subject's intimate connection with complex social realities, and to connect with some of the same theoretical concerns and perspectives found in other human and social sciences.

Eighth, in the face of the criticism that religion is always unique to culture and incomparable, there is a recent counter trend to reach behind culture in order to ground cross-cultural thinking in shared behavioral and cognitive patterns of the human species per se. The next section illustrates that approach.

Human-level commonality

Behind all cultures are human beings. One could therefore look for continuities in the kinds of things people do as humans and in the processes by which humans organize experience, rather than only in the specific content or context of what they believe as insiders to their respective cultures.

Commonality among humans is not merely physical. All humans engage in common activities not only by their shared bodily make-up but also by their mental, social, and linguistic nature (cf. Brown 1991). They not only sleep, eat, reproduce, and react to pain, but they also create societies that form 'kin'-like bonds, maintain moral order and codes of behavior, socialize the young, transmit ancestral tradition, distinguish between insiders and outsiders, set and defend boundaries, perform periodic rites, endow objects and persons with special prestige and authority, punish transgressions, experiment with alternative forms of consciousness, recite sacred histories and genealogies, interpret events and objects, form communicative systems with culturally postulated immaterial beings, classify the universe, and fashion their own worlds of time, space, language, and obligation. In these and many other ways, all human societies build, inhabit and maintain world-environments (Brown 1991: 130–141; cf. also the W. Paden essay in Idinopulos 2006: 59–76). Behaviors such as those just cited form common building blocks for the construction of diverse expressions of religious life. In turn, the religious systems play out these behavioral infrastructures with their local languages and values. Each of these mappings, for the insider, constitutes the way the world 'is.' To the comparativist, however, these are so many world *versions*.

The distinction of common, transcultural forms of human behavior and different cultural content (including meanings to the insider) then becomes important. Consider three illustrations:

Sacred histories

Each religion forms its own history of the world, its own memory system. The comparativist observes that there are as many of these 'origins' – with their prestigious founders and special founding events – as there are religious groups. For insiders to these traditions, such 'historical' origins are absolute. Every past rises up around key events and figures, not because it is objectively true by standards of modern historiography, but because it represents the given operating tradition and memory of a particular community. Even within the large Christian and Buddhist traditions, each sub-denomination has its own special lineages of authority, signature beliefs and models of history, just as villages, neighborhoods and families will have their own patron saints and ancestral icons.

These histories share common functions. They account for that on which the life of the group depends and the self-identity of the society; they create lines of transmission and authorization of power from the founders and exemplars; and they provide exemplary, idealized models for how to live.

But difference comes into the picture insofar as each group sees the past in terms of its own idea of what life is based on – its own idea of what is sacred. Navaho myths link the origin of humans with the origin of corn; Masai myths address the origin of the gift of cattle; ancient Babylonian myths deal with the founding deeds of their god-king Marduk; mystical sects describe their versions of the fall and redemption of the soul.

Sacred histories also showcase different social structures. They give superhuman authorization to particular social boundaries and roles, imperial descent, ethnic identity, or collective destinies. Many, such as the Judeo-Christian scriptures, include detailed genealogies. A well-known Hindu myth describes the origin of the four main castes from the body of a primal being, the brahmans emerging from the head, and the manual labor caste from the feet. The miraculous appearance of the 'Virgin of Guadalupe' to an indigenous Indian in 1531 is at once a national, ethnic, and religious 'foundation account' for Mexican identity.

Thus, 'myths of the past,' or 'sacred histories,' encoded either in scripture, oral tradition or ritual reenactments, not only have the common functions of indexing memory and guiding or inspiring behavior, but may also be read as representations of different social values and meanings to be investigated in contextual detail.

Periodic renewal rites

Cultures not only represent pasts; they also recollect them in recurring rituals. Here, the values and venerated objects of the culture are celebrated and are imprinted on the life of the group's members through the participatory media of the festival – such as unusual forms of fasting, feasting, music, dance, or other impressive collective performances.

Again, while the general function of these celebrative actions is similar, the content is not. In fact, only when the common factor is identified can the differences become appreciated. One of the important areas of difference is that of the social values that are meshed with the rites. For example, in traditional China the New Year festival highlighted the foundational role of family tradition and relationships. But in traditional South Asian Buddhist communities, major annual observances feature the mutually supportive relationship of the monks and laity. Annual rites in Pygmy culture feature the sanctity of the forest, but in Eskimo cultures the focus of honor is the sea mammals, and in ancient Athens the festivities celebrated the patron of the city, Athena. The Passover tradition for Jews focuses on the distinctive historical identity of that people; and for Christians, Easter celebrates the transformative power of their founder.

As renewal rites are not just expressions of religion, but of the broad activity by which humans construct time, they naturally appear in nonreligious versions, too, such as in national celebrations which honor the founders and accomplishments of one's country.

Again, any one of these festivals can be read for the way it reveals different meanings to different social classes within the society. Festivals often show patterns of status, social inclusion and exclusion, kinship, gender roles, local traditions, and other forms of social identity, thus encoding a variety of significations.

Sacred order

A third example of a general human disposition that serves comparative study while highlighting 'difference' is the notion of sacred order. All religious groups draw lines, identify boundary transgression, and punish violations. All establish categories that require defense and monitoring. All maintain and defend a system of allowable and unallowable behavior; all have some version of authority, law and tradition.

But no two orders are the same. The content of what constitutes order and disorder is relative to the sociocultural system. Boundaries and their negotiation are mingled with complex social norms related to ideas of honor, obligation, kinship, sexuality, selfhood and any number of value configurations peculiar to any society. While there are some specific, recurring patterns of restrictive behavior among diverse cultures, such as the prohibition against incest, murder, and theft, it remains that much that is obligatory or violative pertains to each culture's own norms. These might include notions of purity about food, social status, ritual, or protocols of the hunt.

Thus, at this broad level, comparative perspective *can* allow for a move 'downward' toward shared, panhuman features of behavior, and at the same time 'upward' to cultural specifics and differences, with all their particular inflections of texture and signification. Either or both directions may serve the comparativist's purposes.

There is some contrast here, then, to Eliadean comparativism. The latter cited examples of 'sacred space' (for example) in order to show how they embodied patterns like 'the Center,' or the 'world axis.' But the examples typically illustrated what one already knew about those spatial archetypes; the many listed examples of a theme tended to be essentially replicas of the same concept. By contrast, a sociologically sensitive comparativism looks also for why spaces are different and for the ways they show nuances of social, ethnic and political identities. Thus, Hopi kivas, Quaker meeting houses, modern suburban megachurches, Mormon Temples, Buddhist relic shrines, and Australian aboriginal 'markings' can be of interest for showing very specific cultural values and worldviews.

Religious patterns in secular life

From the above, it would follow that comparative religion has implications for the general understanding and explanation of human behavior; and also the other way around, because religious patterns are in many ways 'natural' human behaviors writ large and given a sacred basis. All cultures, not just religious ones, have special histories, places and times; all have renewal rites, sacred order and boundary marking. Even more specific 'forms' like pilgrimage, sacrifice, rites of passage, rites of purification, states of trance, ethical precepts, are not limited to religious domains. The notion of sacredness itself is a broader concept than religion: modern arenas where the factor of sacredness can be found include social justice, individual rights, and national sovereignty.

In these ways, the comparative religion endeavor invites reflection about any cultural system and its continuities with human worldmaking generally. The anthropologist Colin Turnbull thus discovered revealing aspects of adolescent 'passage' customs of British school boys *after* he had lived in the Pygmy culture and observed its puberty rites. Studying other cultures can thus have the reflexive effect of noticing the myths and rituals of one's own for the first time.

Traditionally, American college religion departments offered just one course on the 'Non-Christian Religions,' while all the other offerings would be on theological and historical facets of the ruling Judeo-Christian tradition. Today, in many academic settings, and particularly in secular public universities, this disproportion is being redressed. Indeed, one of the challenges of the comparative study of religion now is to be able to evenhandedly apply its perspectives to the study of biblical traditions.

The comparative study of religion is evolving. It develops along with our knowledge of the world and with the relevance of different kinds of theories and patterns applied to the world. Hence it is not something fixed for all time, but an ongoing process of discovery.

Summary

- Comparison is a basic activity of the human mind. All thought, all concepts, involve comparison.
- The comparative study of religion has evolved historically according to different worldviews and purposes.
- Comparison can either focus on commonality or on differences relative to a point of commonality, or both.
- Comparative perspective uncovers relationships between phenomena that would otherwise be unseen, and links those patterns to a broader interpretive theme or concept.
- Critiques of comparativism typically claim that it overrides interesting and important differences among cultures.
- A revival of interest in comparison has brought more clarification about its methods and goals, affirming, for example, that generalizations are corrigible, that they can achieve controlled focus on specific aspects of religion while still respecting context, and that they can help highlight cultural differences.
- Cross-cultural and historical (or culture-specific) perspectives are both part of the general study of religion.

Bibliography

Braun, Willi, ed., 2004, 'Comparison in the History of Religions: Reflections and Critiques,' special issue of *Method and Theory in the Study of Religion* 16/1.

Brown, Donald E., 1991, *Human Universals*, McGraw-Hill, New York.

Carter, Jeffrey, 1998, 'Description is Not Explanation: A Methodology of Comparison,' in *Method and Theory in the Study of Religion*, 10/2: 133–148.

Doniger, Wendy, 1998, *The Implied Spider: Politics and Theology in Myth*, Columbia University Press, New York.

Eliade, Mircea, 1958, *Patterns in Comparative Religion*, trans. Rosemary Sheed, World Publishing Company, Cleveland.

—— 1959, *The Sacred and the Profane: The Nature of Religion*, trans. Willard R. Trask, Harcourt, Brace, Jovanovich, New York.

Frazer, James G., 1963, *The Golden Bough*, abridged edn, Macmillan, New York.

Holdrege, Barbara, 1996, *Veda and Torah: Transcending the Textuality of Scripture*, State University of New York Press, Albany, NY.

Idinopulos, Thomas Athanasius, Brian C. Wilson, and James Constantine Hanges, eds. 2006, *Comparing Religions: Possibilities and Perils?* Brill, Leiden.

Jones, Lindsay, 2000, *The Hermeneutics of Sacred Architecture; Experience, Interpretation, Comparison*, 2 Vols., Harvard University Press, Cambridge.

Martin, Luther H., 2000, 'Comparison,' in Willi Braun and Russell T. McCutcheon, eds, *Guide to the Study of Religion*, 45–56. Cassell, London.

——, M. Hewitt, E.T. Lawson, W. Paden and D. Wiebe, 1996, 'The New Comparativism in the Study of Religion: A Symposium,' in *Method and Theory in the Study of Religion*, VIII/1: 1–49.

Müller, F. Max, 1872, *Lectures on the Science of Religion*, Charles Scribner Co., New York.

Naroll, Raoul and Ronald Cohen, eds, 1970, *A Handbook of Method in Cultural Anthropology*, The Natural History Press, New York.

Neville, Robert Cummings, ed. 2001, *Ultimate Realities: A Volume in the Comparative Religious Ideas Project*, The State University of New York Press, Albany, NY.

Numen: International Review for the History of Religions 2001, vol. 48, no. 3. Brill, Leiden (special issue on comparativism).

Paden, William E., 1994, *Religious Worlds: The Comparative Study of Religion*, 2nd edn, Beacon Press, Boston.

Patton, Kimberley C. and Benjamin C. Ray, eds, 2000, *A Magic Still Dwells: Comparative Religion in the Postmodern Age*, The University of California Press, Berkeley.

Poole, Fitz John Porter, 1986, 'Metaphors and Maps: Towards Comparison in the Anthropology of Religion,' *Journal of the American Academy of Religion* 54: 411–457.

Saler, Benson, 1993, *Conceptualizing Religion: Immanent Anthropologists, Transcendent Natives, and Unbounded Categories*, Leiden, Brill.

Sharpe, Eric C., 1986, *Comparative Religion: A History*, 2nd edn, Open Court, La Salle, Ill.

Smith, Jonathan Z., 1982, *Imagining Religion: From Babylon to Jonestown*, University of Chicago Press, Chicago.

—— 1987, *To Take Place: Toward Theory in Ritual*, University of Chicago Press, Chicago.

—— 1990, *Drudgery Divine: On the Comparison of Early Christianities and the Religions of Late Antiquity*, University of Chicago Press, Chicago.

—— 2004, Relating Religion: Essays in the Study of Religion, University of Chicago Press, Chicago.

Whitehouse, Harvey, 2004, *Modes of Religiosity: A Cognitive Theory of Religious Transmission*, Altamira Press, Walnut Creek, CA.

Suggested reading

Braun, Willi, ed., 2004, 'Comparison in the History of Religions: Reflections and Critiques,' *Method and Theory in the Study of Religion* 16/1.
Special issue, with essays by religious studies scholars responding to the Patton (2000) volume.

Eliade, Mircea, 1959, *The Sacred and the Profane: The Nature of Religion,* trans. Willard R. Trask, Harcourt, Brace, Jovanovich, New York.
Widely read classic on such themes as sacred space and sacred time by the leading comparativist of the last generation. (A condensation of many of the themes from his larger volume, *Patterns in Comparative Religion*, 1958.)

Idinopulos, Thomas Athanasius, Brian C. Wilson, and James Constantine Hanges, eds., 2006, *Comparing Religions: Possibilities and Perils?* Brill, Leiden.
Essays by thirteen religious studies scholars on the nature and aims of comparison.

Jones, Lindsay, ed. 2004, *Encyclopedia of Religion*, 2nd edn, 15 vols, Macmillan, Detroit, MI.
Major source of articles, with bibliographies, on comparative topics, and a thorough updating of the original 1987 edition (ed. by Mircea Eliade).

Müller, F. Max, 1872, *Lectures on the Science of Religion*, Charles Scribner Co., New York.
Seminal lectures on the importance of comparative perspective by a founder of the discipline.

Paden, William E., 1994, *Religious Worlds: The Comparative Study of Religion*, 2nd edn, Beacon Press, Boston.
An introduction to comparative perspective in the study of religion and to key patterns and variations in the formation of religious 'worlds.'

Patton, Kimberley C. and Benjamin C. Ray, eds., 2000, *A Magic Still Dwells: Comparative Religion in the Postmodern Age,* The University of California Press, Berkeley.
Essays by fourteen contemporary scholars on the ongoing importance of comparative work in relation to the challenge of postmodernism.

Poole, Fitz John Porter, 1986, 'Metaphors and Maps: Towards Comparison in the Anthropology of Religion,' *Journal of the American Academy of Religion* 54: 411–457.

Influential analysis of comparative method by an anthropologist of religion (for more advanced students).

Sharpe, Eric C., 1986, *Comparative Religion: A History*, 2nd edn, Open Court, La Salle, IL.
Remains a usefully informative overview of the development of comparative religion as a modern field.

Smart, Ninian, 1996, *Dimensions of the Sacred: An Anatomy of the World's Beliefs*, University of California Press, Berkeley.
Accessible demonstration of seven key categories by which religion can be studied (ritual, mythic, experiential, doctrinal, ethical, social, and material).

Smith, Jonathan Z., 1982, *Imagining Religion: From Babylon to Jonestown*, University of Chicago Press, Chicago.
Highly influential work raising critical issues on the methodology of comparison.

——, 2004, *Relating Religion: Essays in the Study of Religion*, Chicago University Press, Chicago.
Numerous articles on issues of comparison by the best-known contemporary comparativist.

Part 2
Key topics in the study of religions

Chapter 14

Gender

Darlene M. Juschka

What is gender? What is sex? What is gender/sex?

Historical prelude

Gender as a category of analysis has operated in a variety of ways depending on pedagogical location or historical period. For example, in sociological studies gender consists of the study of sex roles in pre-industrial and industrial societies. Or, historically in Europe, gender has simply been the natural designation of the sexes as opposite since the eighteenth century. However, in the 1960s gender became a central category of feminist studies. So for example, in feminist language studies gender becomes the means by which to look at the erasure of women by the generic term 'man' and the thingification of women as the object of the male gaze.

The development of gender as a category of analysis can be seen in the work of Margaret Mead and Catherine Berndt, for example, as a slow transformation of the belief in natural sex-roles and sex-role assignments to an analysis of the social construction of these roles. In other words, people like Mead and Berndt began to think about how the labor and roles given to men and women may have less to do with biological certainties and more to do with societal demands. These anthropologists examined women's ritual activities and beliefs among pre-industrial peoples, a focus that had been hitherto overlooked by their more androcentric colleagues. They found that the women they investigated tended to operate in a separate female sphere with rituals, symbols, and myths centered on such concerns as fertility and birth, economics, healing, or the well-being of the society, e.g. tending ancestors, the land, or myth cycles. They also became aware of two significant issues in the study of human society: one, the erasure of women and their activities from all fields of knowledge; and two, that women and men's gendered practices, e.g. work, parenting, status, were in fact social roles that were secondarily assigned as sex roles. Under the influence of first- and second-wave feminism,[1] then, the analysis of women as gendered, gender relating to both the oppression of women and creating a new subject of study based upon women, was established.

What is gender?

Gender is something we all know, or think we know. We immediately categorize people (and most everything, e.g. language, animals, planets, or inanimate objects) on the basis of their gender. We categorize ourselves repeatedly by ticking the appropriate box on a form to indicate our gender. We are careful to enter the proper washroom, and we choose particular apparel appropriate to our gender. We presuppose gender as it is manifested in all aspects of our lives. As such, we do not question gender. However, under the influence of second-wave feminism, gender as a category of analysis emerged. Gender, in this formulation, was seen to be a way to understand the oppression of women by men. The category of gender, then, was developed in order to think about how social systems, cultures, and religions, for example, were gender coded and how these codes impacted upon women and men. This coding was seen to define, regulate, and circumscribe the group named/marked women. Equally the coding was seen to define and regulate the group called men, but as man and human were synonymous, it afforded this group privileges it did not afford women, e.g. men as priests in Catholicism.

From here, then, gender ideology, which was seen to construct and mystify (locate in nature) inequalities between men and women, became an operative analytical tool in feminist theorizing. It was used to examine religious, social, national formations and operations, and further, under the sign of postcolonialism and/or international feminisms, to examine political, social, cultural relations between nations and countries. For example, in feminist postcolonial theorizing it became apparent that often countries and their populations colonized by the Eurowest were feminized and, as such, were understood as irrational and highly sexual in comparison to the masculinized Eurowest. A good example of this is Rudyard Kipling's poem 'The White Man's Burden' published in 1897. In response to this feminization, the elite men of colonialized locations often demanded the subjugation of the women of their nation via a strict gender differentiation. A good example of this is the discourse around the veil in twentieth-century Middle Eastern identity politics. Gender ideology was also used to examine economic, historical, medical, and ethical discourses, to name but a few, and their contribution to the production of knowledge. This knowledge, then, that seeks to explain human social, political, cultural organization, and production was determined to be gender coded.

In the development of gender as a category of analysis, gender was separated from sex. Sex, male and female, or the two-sex model, was seen to be a natural fact or the biological reality that gender overlays. What is assumed in such a formulation of gender is that sex is real and gender is artificial, or sex is an ahistorical (outside history) natural fact of human nature, while gender is a social and historical construction built upon that natural fact. Linda Nicholson (1994) comments that when gender and sex are thus formulated, sex is not dealt with as a conceptual category, but a biological truth. As such, then, gender becomes the conceptual category that is hung upon the 'coat-rack' of sex. Formulated as such, sex is fixed and immutable while gender is social, historical, and mutable.

In this perspective, then, an assumption resides: that sex is neutral or carries no inherent value. Gender, however, carries value and this value is subsequently placed on 'normatively' sexed bodies. Indeed, these sexed bodies are not just human bodies, but can include all plants and animals. When such proofs as plants and animals are used, they are then called upon secondarily to uphold the truth of the naturalness of the category of sex. However, in due time, the mid- to late 1980s, this kind of understanding of sex and gender, or what is call the gender/sex dimorphism was called into question (see Gilbert Herdt 1994).

Complicating the category of gender

Judith Butler (1990) and Christine Delphy (1996) also argued that treating sex as a fixed and immutable truth of human existence not only confuses the analysis, but also expresses a necessity to adhere to a closely organized system of beliefs, values and ideas without question or thought. In Delphy's effort to make apparent how taxonomies are products of the social and therefore equally socially encoded, she pushed the analysis to include sex, male and female and the variations therein, as a social construct. She argues that sex, like gender, is a social and historical category and not a natural category. Sex is not a natural category because we already understand it in accordance with gender. We read sex through the lens of gender. As such, sex is a social and historical category. She further argued, as we read sex through a gender lens, gender precedes sex and not the reverse (1996: 30). Therefore, our understanding of men as physically strong and women as physically weak is a socially created truth enforced by, for example, girls being discouraged from developing muscles and boys being encouraged to develop muscles.

Such an argument would appear to be counterintuitive. But following the development of the category of gender in academic discourses, Delphy suggested that gender as a concept was founded upon 'sex roles' – a line of analysis that looks at the division of labor and the differing statuses of men and women. This line of thinking, developed primarily in sociology and anthropology, was picked up and used by feminists. The category of sex, then, in this reasoning, consisted of biological differences between the male and female while gender was the cultural manifestation of these differences or, as she states, 'a social dichotomy determined by a natural dichotomy' (1996: 33). Delphy asked why it is assumed that sex would give rise to any sort of classification. Her argument proceeded from the position that:

> sex itself simply marks a social division: that it serves to allow social recognition and identification of those who are dominants and those who are dominated. That is that sex is a sign, but that since it does not distinguish just any old thing from anything else, and does not distinguish equivalent things but rather important and unequal things, it has historically acquired a symbolic value.
>
> (1996: 35)

Delphy's position was clear: both gender and sex are social constructions.

Speaking of sex and its history

In 1978 the first volume of Michel Foucault's *Histoire de la Sexualité* (Paris: Gallimard, in French) and *The History of Sexuality* (New York: Pantheon, in English) was released. The series in the end would consist of three published volumes, and as the title promises, the category of sexuality would itself be historicized. To historicize sex and sexuality was to recognize that different periods of time produced different conceptualizations of sex and sexuality. Foucault's work has implications for all those who think about the categories of gender and sex. Following Foucault have been many writers who continue to think about changes and breaks in the discourses of sex, sexuality, and gender.

Thomas Laqueur (1990), influenced by Foucault, examines the social and historical nature of the category of sex. He argued that a one-sex Aristotelian-Galenic model of human sexuality was operative prior to the 1800s in Europe. In this model of sexuality, female was misbegotten and genitally inverted and male properly begotten and genitally extroverted. A one-sex model, then, was used to define the natural state of the female and male of the human species. Subsequent to this the two-sex model emerged wherein female and male sexes are understood to be opposite:

By around 1800, writers of all sorts were determined to base what they insisted were fundamental differences between the male and female sexes, and thus between man and woman, on discoverable biological distinctions and to express these in a radically different rhetoric ... Thus the old model, in which men and women were arrayed according to their degree of metaphysical perfection, their vital heat, along an axis whose telos was male, gave way by the late eighteenth century to a new model of radical dimorphism, of biological divergence.

(1990: 5–6)

The implication of Foucault and Laqueur's (see also Blackwood 1999, Brown 1988) historicizing of sex and sexuality was the dislodging of sex from the realm of nature to locate it in the realm of the social, at least for those who were convinced. Foucault made apparent that sexuality, and sex therein, as much as gender, was a politically charged category that was intimately related to power. Foucault (and Laqueur), in his historical–political foray into sex, wished to discover or rather uncover how sex and sexuality were discursively formed: 'What is at issue, briefly, is the over-all "discursive fact," the way in which sex is "put into discourse"' (Vol. 1, 1990: 11). Sex, then, like gender is a discursive construction with implications of power. Although Foucault does not read sex through the sign of gender as Delphy does, he equally recognizes that sex is a category that is central to 'the order of things' and as such is a way that we organize ourselves. Like gender, then, sex has intimate relations to the dissemination of power in discourses, and religions have often been powerful and authoritative disseminators of the 'truth' of gender and sex. For example, in Christianity during the witch-craze or witch-hunt in Europe (1450–1700) women were understood to be more inclined toward evil because of their 'normative' femaleness. Signed as inclined toward evil and in league with the devil, females of all ages were tortured and murdered in numbers estimated conservatively to be 200,000. And during the same period in India, women who outlived their spouses were encouraged or forced to commit Sati. Sati is the act of a widow being burned alive with the body of her dead husband.

Elaborating a model of gender and sex

Gender, as an academic category of analysis, has been greatly debated since the 1980s. The majority of analyses focused on two categories, gender and sex, as indicated above. In this kind of analysis, gender is examined as a social category and sex as a biological category. Although this split rendered gender very useful as a category of analysis for purposes of the study of religions, the theoretical difficulties this split raised began to be discussed in studies of sexuality, under the influence of Foucault, and in feminist theorizing. With theorists like Foucault it became apparent that sex was itself socially constructed and demonstrated a historicity of its own. The work produced by feminist academics in religious studies called into question the biological givenness of sex (e.g. the female as inherently evil and weak and the male as inherently good and strong) as a category of analysis and, furthermore, sought to theorize gender and sex as produced in and by the social (e.g. male as inherently good meant he was closer to deity and therefore naturally in positions of power such as a religious leader). But, by grounding gender/sex in the social and material two significant problems have emerged.

The first difficulty encountered, notably discussed in the 1970s, was that gender and sex were dealt with as separate formative elements of human identity so that sex was seen to establish kinds of bodies, while gender was thought to subsequently shape those bodies. In this understanding, sex marked bodies as differentiated (fixed) while gender invested such marking with meaning (mutable). Here gender is seen to follow naturally from sex, or gender and sex are seen as superficially connected in a consecutive fashion, e.g. male is to man and female is to woman. What is not clearly theorized, then, is how gender and sex are interrelated and dependent upon each other for definition. Understanding that gender and sex are interrelated and dependent means they need to be understood as related to each other by the tension and interaction (dialectics) between the two categories. In this kind of understanding, gender and sex are related in a formative and primary fashion, e.g. man is to male as woman is to female.

The second problem that emerged in the 1980s was an absence of theorizing the interdependence of the categories of gender and sex. Instead gender and sex were presented as if they were interchangeable categories or simply synonyms. In this kind of analysis the dialectical (tension and interaction) mechanisms of gender and sex are erased. This theoretical position meant that gender ideology, or the power operations of social inequalities based on gender and sex, could not be adequately analyzed.

Understanding gender and sex as oppositional categories, the layering of gender and sex, or the blurring of gender and sex are all equally problematic. Without a clear theorizing of the dialectical relationship between gender and sex, studies continue to produce work wherein one or both the categories are reified (understood as things rather than concepts) and therefore resistant to a thoroughgoing analysis.

The difficulties encountered in the theorizing of gender as a category of analysis can be related to two basic issues: (1) essentialism (the sexed body remains fixed according to evolutionary requirements, e.g. man the hunter, female the gatherer) versus constructionism (the sexed body is mutable reflecting social roles and lives situated in particular social and historical surroundings); and (2) the lack of a theory of gender and sex.

Some of the most successful studies of gender/sex have emerged from two areas of study: feminist cultural studies (the study of cultural productions from a feminist deconstructive perspective, e.g. film, media, and written text) and queer theory (deconstruction of the discursive production of sexuality and gender, e.g. challenge to heterosexuality as normative sexuality as presented in Genesis 1:27 'So God created man in his own image, in the image of God he created him; male and female he created them'). In both of these locations there has been the recognition that the categories of gender and sex each require careful delineation and intersection. Feminist theorists in the study of religion have directed their attention toward this challenge and the analysis of gender and sex, as ideology (gender/sex), should prove a fruitful trajectory for the continued development of the categories of gender and sex.

The importance of gender/sex in the study of religion

If, in the study of religion, the scholar is to understand the structural development of the system under study, and is to understand the means by which that system is communicated, if s/he is to grasp why deity in the *Tanakh* (Hebrew Bible), for example, takes on both masculine and feminine attributes, then certainly how gender and sex are understood and used to express belief about existence in ancient Hebrew systems of religious belief is necessary to know. Examining the complexities of gender/sex, as produced in the social (e.g. myth) and signed on the level of the metaphysical (e.g. symbol) and enacted on the level of the biological (e.g. ritual), means engaging the study of religion as a human signing system. A human signing system refers to language, art, stories, and traditional ritual practices and the like used to express beliefs about existence, the world, the human, male and female, or deity.

To engage religions as human signing systems requires paying attention to such things as who is speaking; in other words, the person, the group or institution that is generating the discourse, and to whom the discourse is directed. By tracking the who and the whom in the communicative event, by paying attention to what is at stake and investigating what kinds of persuasions proliferate, one is better able to elucidate their understanding of social systems. Toward this end, then, one will want to examine gender/sex as they are delineated through religious discourses. An example of this kind of analysis is Helen Hardacre's study of a Japanese new religious movement, Buddhist *RisshōKōseikai*.

In her study Hardacre relates how Buddhist *RisshōKōseikai* had been co-founded by a woman, Naganuma Myōkō, but after her death in 1957 there was an internal power struggle. Out of this struggle emerged a new myth of origin, one that erased Myōkō as a co-founder of the group. Instead her male co-founder was given sole recognition. At one particular gathering of the women of the *RisshōKōseikai*, who had come together in order to celebrate the anniversary of their female founder's death, the importance of Myōkō within the movement was undercut directly by reference to her gender/sex. At this gathering a male elder, in support of the new male genealogy of *RisshōKōseikai*, spoke to these women about gender/sex and to do so drew on gender ideology to validate the new male genealogy. This was done, of course, in order to assert the legitimacy of masculine domination. To do this he naturalized men's domination over women via reference to femaleness and maleness in the 'state of nature':

> You women know that in the animal world, it is the males who are the most powerful. Take the gorilla for example – did you ever hear of a female gorilla leading the pack? … And it is the males who are prettiest. Whoever paid any attention to a drab female duck? … Being the stronger and most powerful, naturally the males are the most attractive as well. What I'm trying to tell you today is that it's the same way with human beings. It's the men who are superior, and the women who are behind all the trouble in the world.
>
> (Hardacre 1994: 111)

Delineated in a specific gender-based narrative, there is a necessity to understand how gender/sex operate on the sociopolitical level in order to know what is at stake for the speaker and the listeners. Clearly the male elder was attempting, via his use of biology, to locate men over women. But equally that the women of the group had come together to celebrate their female founder's death anniversary indicates that they were resisting the new myth of origin that located the founding of *RisshōKōseikai* with only its male co-founder.

Equally, when doing a gender/sex analysis another aspect that requires attention is awareness that the discourse of the hegemonic elite (those limited few who have control and power over the social, economic, political, cultural, and religious domains) is not the sole or only representation of the religion or culture. Often the views, perspectives, religious activities, and so forth of a small elite group of men have been, and continue to be, used as representative of the entire group. In this formulation any contestation and differences within the group related to class, race, or gender/sex are erased. To ignore such social categories as status, gender/sex, sexuality, race, or class that speak about power and that point to the particulars of social formations is to ignore the social and historical parameters of the system of belief and practice under study. Engaging gender and sex as interrelated categories of analysis (gender/sex) in the study of religion clarifies the object of one's study.

In the past, under the influence of Enlightenment epistemology, wherein the category of the human was the origin and basis for much theorizing done in the study of religion, complexity and diversity within an analysis were erased in order to ensure the subject of European philosophy, man. This man haunted, and in some measure continues to haunt, theorizing in religious studies, anthropology, sociology, philosophy, history, and science. At the same time, those studies that have shifted from this perspective continue to remain marginal in the university. Focusing solely on this man not only misses the social complexity and the structures that hold the religious edifices in place, but also distorts the analysis. Paying attention to gender/sex, sexuality, race, and class allows us to theorize the structures and understand better the multifaceted complexity of human social bodies.

The gendering of religions

The intersection of gender/sex and religions has been of interest to a number of theorists who study religions. Over the last five decades excellent work that looks at the ideological implications of gender/sex in the study of religion, or how gender and sex effect and affect the practice of religion, has been produced. These studies share a common interest in examining how religion has been one method to ensure the subordination of women in a variety of social and cultural locations, and the absence of women as living persons within the development and dissemination of religions. Such studies have sought to reveal the power imperatives, to bring women as subjects back into the various religions under study, and to examine men as gendered subjects. From here those interested in the intertwining of gender/sex and religion have developed analyses that examine historical and social shifts in a variety of cultures as registered by gender/sex, the political efficaciousness of gender/sex, and linked to this, the intersection of gender/sex with colonization. The interrelated categories of gender and sex provide a means and a way to understand not only the how and why of religions, but equally the how and why of social organization and the manufacturing of culture in and of itself.

Gender/sex and religious ideologies

The work of gendering religions has been taken up by a variety of feminists studying religions and theology. In the late 1960s and into the 1970s the work of Mary Daly, Rosemary Radford Ruether, and Elisabeth Schüssler Fiorenza presented some of the earlier gender interventions into the study of religion. Each of these feminists did triple duty in terms of their work in the study of religion. First, they brought tools of analysis to the study of religion in order to think about how these systems of belief and practice were used to legitimate and shape the social body. Second, each then focused on women in the religious system under analysis in order to make apparent women's activities and contributions. Third, each then furthered their analyses by interrelating patriarchal imperatives with women's contributions and activities in order to think about religion.

Daly's approach, after her rejection of Christianity, was to propose a two-world system located in most if not all societies. One part of this two-world system she named the foreground, which was a patriarchal construction operating in terms of patriarchal relations. The foreground was the site of women's exploitation and oppression, and detrimental to women's well-being. The second aspect of this two-world system was the Background, which was the real world that was obscured by the patriarchal world of the foreground. It is, Daly argued, in the Background that women can find their true being. This dualist world system, in large measure, reflects aspects of what is called feminist standpoint epistemology.

Feminist standpoint epistemology developed by Nancy Hartsock, Dorothy Smith, Patricia Hill-Collins (black feminist standpoint), and Mary Daly, among others, takes the position that women, as an oppressed group, are in a position to have a clearer and less distorted picture of reality as they are outside, or marginal to, the dominant system of power relations and therefore considerably less invested in maintaining it. According to standpoint theory, the picture of reality developed in patriarchy (and all oppressive systems) is an inversion of reality, and those who are marginal to the system are able to see this inversion. Further to this, as patriarchy is invested in maintaining its vision of the world, which empowers it, it is unable to see beneath the surface. Only the oppressed can clearly determine the operations of this inversion, based upon their experiences, and envision a means to move beyond it. Institutionalized religion, understood as patriarchal religion, Daly argues, is one of the pillars that supports the foreground. God the father is merely an inversion of the reality of the Goddess and a means and a way to ensure that the patriarchal reality of the foreground continues to endure.

Schüssler Fiorenza's contribution to the gendering of religion came in the form of uncovering patriarchal imperatives found in the New Testament and other texts related to the study of early Christianities. This method she called a feminist hermeneutics of suspicion, which exposes the intention to locate in the heavens and in nature the gender ideologies produced by the group. So for example, Paul's letter to the Corinthians (I Corinthians 11: 1–16), when discussing men's and women's hair related to normative male and female being, makes apparent Paul's operative gender ideology, which is his own and is one that emerges from his social location and has little to do with either deity or nature. Certainly Paul supports his understanding of normative male and female being by making recourse to deity and nature. Much as in the Buddhist *RisshōKōseikai* example, Paul's understanding of normative male and female appearance and behavior calls on nature to legitimate his view. In this passage Paul understands that it is a disgrace for women to have short hair and dishonorable for men to have long hair. Working within the honor–shame oriented culture of ancient Rome, the maintenance of social standing is intimately linked to honor, and for women to attempt to appear masculine (short hair) and therefore elevate their status is a disgrace, while for men to appear feminine (long hair) means a loss of social status and therefore dishonor. Male and female hairstyles, then, are culturally coded and reflect a gender ideology.

Second, she sought to make apparent women's activities in the early Christian communities through a feminist hermeneutics of remembrance. In this gender-sensitive methodology she examined not only the actions and contributions of men, but also those of women in these communities. Finally, by combining the hermeneutics of suspicion and remembrance, she developed what she termed a feminist critical hermeneutics of liberation. Through this model she hoped to be able to reclaim Christian history for concerned women and men of all nations, colors, and sexual orientation without engaging in Christian apologetics.

Rosemary Radford Ruether's gendering of religion also challenged patriarchal imperative of religions, particularly Judaism and Christianity. She too noted the absence of women and set upon a project of reclaiming and reconstructing women's Christian histories. She too developed a project of rereading and rewriting in order to reconceptualize a new Catholic Christianity as a system of belief and practice that creates a positive space for concerned women and men of all nations, colors, and sexual orientation. By gendering religion she, like Daly and Schüssler-Fiorenza, sought not only to understand the ideological impact of religion on women, and construct histories of women and religion, but also to move the study of religion toward developing analyses that reflected more honestly the social and historical realities of human systems of meaning.

Gender/sex and religious practices

The kinds of analyses indicated above represent some of the work of feminists in the study of religion through the 1970s and 1980s. Feminists, having learned the need to reread and rethink religious and historical texts, went on to think about how the interrelated categories of gender/sex shaped the knowledge and the systems of belief and practice that women produced. A particularly influential thinker working in this frame is Susan Starr Sered and her comparative text *Priestess, Mother, Sacred Sister: Religions Dominated by Women* published in 1994. There were of course other texts published in a similar vein, for example, Diane Bell's text *Daughters of the Dreaming* published in 1983. In such texts, theorists took gender/ sex as their cue and began to examine the religious orientations, creations, and inclinations of women. At the center of their studies was an interest in women's symbolic discourses and how women's symbolic discourses might differ from men's.

Sered's introductory chapter in *Priestess, Mother, Sacred Sister* briefly relates how the author engages specifically the category of gender in order to think about what might be central to women's religiosity and how it might be different from men's religiosity. This question, circling around the category of gender/sex, assumes from the outset that if indeed there is a difference between men's and women's religious beliefs and actions, that this difference could be related to their differing social lives. She notes that cross-culturally women of differing social groups share concerns such as childbearing and motherhood, which of course intersect with economic, social, physiological, and psychological concerns. Connected to this explicitly is child rearing and related to child rearing is healing. These appear to be issues that are often at the center of women's religiosity and as such suggest a gender/sex difference.

However, as Sered notes, men and women's religiosity are more alike than they are unalike. Although concerns may demonstrate gender/sex differences, both women and men make recourse to superordinate beings (singular or plural), both use ritual to imaginatively interact with these beings, and both have central myths that organize the system of belief and practice. As female and male are not opposite in sex, so women's and men's religions are not opposite in religion. Sered (1994: 8–9) suggests that when women and men's religiosity do differ, it is related to how superordinate beings are imagined, e.g. Jesus as feminine as among the Shakers of the American Colonies; the how and why of engagement with superordinate beings, e.g. through possession to heal the afflicted as with the *Zar* cult in the northern Sudan; the shaping and understanding of ritual actions, e.g. women as ritual leaders; and the way that they engage such issues as existence, e.g. women's ritual power as social power as with the *Sande* secret society in Sierra Leone and Liberia. But equally important to women and men's religiosity is the issue of power. Religiosity can and does confer power, whether on the basis of gender/sex, status, race, prestige, or age and is a means by which power is circulated or contested. Because of the propensity of gender/sex to be related to power, it is necessary to analytically engage gender/sex head-on when studying religion.

Gender/sex and performance

Judith Butler in her formative text *Gender Trouble*, first published in 1990 (10th anniversary edition 1999), equally suggests that it is gender that supports the category of sex and not the reverse. Following up on this, she makes an extended and complex argument demonstrating what is at stake politically when the category of sex is left as fixed and immutable beneath the category of gender, heterosexism. Linked to heterosexism, she argues, is the idea that individuals are trapped, not by biological imperatives as feminism had challenged this by socializing the category of gender, but now by cultural imperatives, since feminists had left the category of sex untheorized. She states that '[t]he institution of a compulsory and naturalized heterosexuality requires and regulates gender as a binary relation in which the masculine term is differentiated from a feminine term, and this differentiation is accomplished through the practices of heterosexual desire' (30). Butler clearly and succinctly demonstrated how gender in feminist theorizing continued to uphold 'normative' ideas concerning sex and gender to the peril of a feminist analysis and its claims to be liberating.

Added to this keen observation, Butler made another equally important observation; that gender/sex is performed. Butler, a feminist poststructuralist, underscored in her text the political imperative affiliated with the categories of gender/sex, and asked what might be the effects of such an imperative. This question allowed her to conjecture how identity itself was a political category with gender/sex central to this identity. Linked to this, then, was the necessity to perform gender/sex, so that those who ascribe to (are ascribed to) the category of female must perform as feminine or those who ascribe to (are ascribed to) the category male must perform as masculine. Furthermore, those ascribed as male, but desiring to the female, could perform as feminine and those ascribed as female, but desiring to the male, could perform as masculine; although this was done at their peril since they would be disciplined for transgressing gender boundaries. Butler argued '[t]here is no gender identity behind the expressions of gender; that identity is performatively constituted by the very "expressions" that are said to be its results' (33).

In the field of religious studies, particularly ritual, the instability and performativity of gender/sex are eminently apparent. Most visible in rites such as female and male circumcision, one sees the instability of sex as a natural category since the cutting of the body's genitals, the primary site of gender/sex, is used to properly fix the sex of the initiate. Furthermore, one notes the necessity to perform as woman or man in the acceptance of the cut that moves the child who would shriek to the adult who would capture said shriek between clenched teeth.

Gender/sex and historicity

In the text *Spirited Women: Gender, Religion and Cultural Identity in the Nepal Himalaya* (1996) Joanne C. Watkins, an anthropologist, is concerned with the 'interplay between changing trade patterns, gender meanings, and cultural identity in Nyeshang society' (4). Her concern, among other things, is to chart the changing gender ideology under the pressure of trade with the larger world. The interrelated categories of gender and sex, formulated in relation to religious beliefs, cultural systems and imperatives of kinship relations, are shifting and these shifts, then, register change in the social body and in the social identity of the group (Buddhist). In this kind of formulation, gender/sex, then, provides a window not only into understanding a cultural system, but provides a way to chart changes within a cultural system. It is this latter function, a window for understanding social and cultural change, for example, that has led some to assume that gender/sex was a means by which to determine religious fundamentalism, rather than a means by which to chart change. In other words, rather than assume a change toward more austere gender relations marks a shift toward fundamentalism, one should recognize that gender/sex actually becomes a means and a way to mark change in itself. Gender and sex, then, as they are both social categories are historical categories that reflect changes in the belief system over time (see also Laura L. Vance, *Seventh-day Adventism in Crisis: Gender and Sectarian Change in an Emerging Religion* (1999) who also registers changes in the social body by using the category of gender/sex).

Gender/sex and politics

The categories of gender/sex are a central concern in Patricia Jeffery and Amrita Basu's edited text *Appropriating Gender: Women's Activism and Politicized Religion in South Asia* (1998). In this text, as the title suggests, gender ideology acts as a category to register political activism. Basu states that 'in the past decade or so, religion and gender have become increasingly intertwined in the political turmoil that envelops South Asia' (3). Women, the gendered category, have, in some locations, become the repository of 'religious beliefs, and the keepers of the purity and integrity of the community' (3) felt to be under attack by the increasing globalization generated by such institutions as the World Bank, the World Trade Organization, the International Monetary Fund, and the United Nations. As noted above, gender and sex are not static categories and indeed register shifts and change in social bodies and, as the authors note, can become the means by which to initiate or resist social change. For example, the state, which can take on the masculine in relation to the feminized social body, can act as a paternalistic force that oversees the social body ensuring its proper functioning. It can be the state, as evinced in the United States in the early twenty-first century, that calls upon a particular gender ideology, heterosexual and masculine in this instance, to shore up and protect a social body it perceives to be under attack. The twin towers, symbols of American masculinity, attacked and felled in September of 2001, initiated a hypermasculine response of excessive militarism that was launched against the feminized Middle Eastern 'other.' 'Gender provides,' as Basu rightly comments, 'an extremely fruitful lens through which to interpret the actions of the state and of ethnic and religious communities' (5–6).

Gender/sex: where to from here?

As I hope I have made clear in the above, the interrelated categories of gender and sex are infinitely useful toward interrogating and understanding religions. In many ways gender/sex is a signing system that acts as a window that allows the viewer to see the complexities of human existence. Gender/sex, although still not a central category of analysis in the study of religions for many theorists, must be further sounded to push further our understanding of human social and cultural systems.

For example, in my own work I have sought to make apparent the mythological ground of gender ideology. This has been a process of revealing or bringing to consciousness the binarism that continues to fuel the ways in which we understand gender/sex. To first uncover the logic of binarism, noting that a significant root binary in most cultural systems is the male/female binary, and then to underscore the linguisticality of binarism allow for the socialization and historicization of binaries and subsequently, gender/sex. Yet this does not fully reveal just what is at stake in gender ideology.

First, gender ideology includes sex as a mythologized discourse. The foundational quality of myth – its apparent rootedness in nature – means that the social, historical, and political aspects of gender *and* sex are elided. As I have indicated, *both* gender and sex, as dialectically related categories, must be submitted to a thoroughgoing social and historical analysis. Second, what is at stake in gender ideology is power. Although this would seem evident, evidently it is not. 'I am a man' or 'I am a woman' seem not to be political statements that mark power. But indeed they do; such terms mark social power. Therefore to analytically engage gender/sex is to understand a significant aspect of the complexity of human signing systems mapped through that which we call religion.

Note

1   First-wave feminism refers to women's political and social action to provide women with both political and civil rights in the Eurowest during the mid-1800s and early 1900s. Second-wave feminism refers to women's political, social, cultural, and legal activities and analyses, beginning in the late 1950s and continuing to the present, toward addressing the oppression on women. Both first- and second-wave feminisms are terms used to designate the rise and resurgence of Eurowestern feminism and do not refer to the rise and resurgence of feminisms of the nineteenth and twentieth centuries in, for example, India, the Middle East, or Latin and South America. Third-wave feminism is a current term that is used to reflect a shift toward representation, technology, globalization, and international feminisms that began in the mid-1990s.

Bibliography

Bell, Diane (1993 [1983]). *Daughters of the Dreaming.* 2nd edn. Minnesota: University of Minnesota Press.
   Bell's comprehensive and thoughtful text is an ethnographic study of Australian Aboriginal women's rites, symbols, and myths. What Bell makes apparent is the importance of Australian Aboriginal women's ritual work toward the development and maintenance of the Dreamtime.
Blackwood, Evelyn and Saskia E. Wieringa (eds) (1999). *Same Sex Relations and Female Desires: Transgender Practices Across Cultures.* New York: Columbia University Press.
   This text is a fine collection of historical, sociological and ethnographic studies of transgendered practices. Focused upon women's same-sex desire, the category of gender is shown to be intimately connected with and foundational for the category of sex, while sexuality intersects with both sex and gender in a definitive fashion.
Brown, Peter (1988). *The Body and Society: Men, Women and Sexual Renunciation in Early Christian Society.* New York: Columbia University Press.
   Brown's text is a wonderful engagement with the category of gender/sex in the formative years of Christianity. Under the influence of theorists such as John Winkler, Brown makes apparent the historicity of the categories of gender and sex, and how these categories, understood differently in the ancient world, were central to the ideological formation of a 'normative' Christianity.
Butler, Judith (1999 [1990]). *Gender Trouble: Feminism and the Subversion of Identity.* New York and London: Routledge.
   This is a formative and pivotal text that is understood to be one of the founding texts of queer theory. This text engages the feminist category of gender, pointing to the short-comings of the theorizing of the category of gender and underscoring the heterosexism that is prevalent in this theorizing.
Delphy, Christine (1996 [1993]). 'Rethinking Sex and Gender.' In Diana Leonard and Lisa Adkins (eds), *Sex in Question: French Materialist Feminism*, 30–41. London: Taylor & Francis.
   Delphy's article is a logical and coherent analysis of the category of gender as it has operated in feminist theorizing from 1970 until 1990. She engages the concept of gender and demonstrates the limited nature of ignoring sex as a social and historical category.

Foucault, Michel (1990 [1978–1984]). *The History of Sexuality*. 3 vols. Robert Hurley (trans.). New York: Vintage.

Foucault's published trilogy intersects with the category of sexuality toward historicizing and politicizing it. Beginning with seventeenth-century Europe in volume one, he then interrogates sexuality and erotic literature in volume two and ends by interrogating sexuality in relation to Greco-Roman philosophy in the third.

Hardacre, Helen (1994). 'Japanese New Religions: Profiles in Gender.' In John Stratton Hawley (ed.), *Fundamentalism and Gender*, 111–133. New York: Oxford University Press.

This article is an interesting and well-documented discussion of the category of gender/sex and how it is used to limit the political and social power of women in Buddhist *Risshō Kōseikai*.

Herdt, Gilbert (ed.) (1994). *Third Sex, Third Gender: Beyond Sexual Dimorphism in Culture and History*. New York: Zone Books.

This anthology of articles is a marvellous delineation of the multiplicity of the categories of gender, sex, and sexuality. Linking all three categories in an effort to make apparent how each is reliant upon the other, this anthology is a cross-cultural and multi-historical analysis of human systems of meaning and social organization.

Jeffrey, Patricia and Amrita Basu (eds) (1998). *Appropriating Gender: Women's Activism and Politicized Religion in South Asia*. New York and London: Routledge.

This is a nicely developed anthology of articles that examine the political aspects of both gender/sex and religion. In these articles authors note, for example, how the state and women's groups employ the categories of gender/sex, linked to religious beliefs, for political purposes.

Laqueur, Thomas L. (1990). *Making Sex: Body and Gender from the Greeks to Freud*. Cambridge, MA and London: Harvard University Press.

Laqueur's text engages the categories of gender and sex and examines how their understanding shifted in the period of the 1800s in medical discourses. He links this shift to political change in Europe during this time period and changes in the conceptualization of the human under the influence of enlightenment philosophy.

Lincoln, Bruce (1989). *Discourse and the Construction of Society: Comparative Studies of Myth, Ritual and Classification*. New York: Oxford University Press.

A pivotal text that engages ritual, myth, and classification demonstrating their historicity, their political potency, and their importance toward constructing social bodies that subsequently impact on individual bodies.

Nicholson, Linda (1994). Interpreting Gender. *Signs*, 20, 1: 79–105.

A well-developed analysis of the use of the category of gender in the work of second-wave feminists. Nicholson makes apparent the unexamined idea of the immutability of sex as a biological category which resides beneath the concept of gender as a socialized category.

Sered, Susan Starr (1994). *Priestess, Mother, Sacred Sister: Religions Dominated by Women*. New York and Oxford: Oxford University Press.

Sered's cross-cultural examination through ethnographic literature of women's religiosity is a well-informed and thoughtful text. Her clear description of the multiplicity of women's religions and the rituals, symbols, and myths developed and utilized by women, allows her to speculate on common threads that link these variegated practices toward answering the question of how gender/sex intersects with and shapes religious beliefs.

Vance, Laura L. (1999). *Seventh-day Adventism in Crisis: Gender and Sectarian Change in an Emerging Religion*. Urbana and Chicago, IL: University of Illinois Press.

This study, based on official and unofficial publications and interviews, examines gender, sex, and sexuality and their relations to the worldview of Seventh-day Adventists. In line with this, the author examines concepts of femininity, masculinity, and sexuality and their relation to social practices.

Watkins, Joan (1996). *Spirited Women: Gender, Religion and Cultural Identity in the Nepal Himalaya*. New York: Columbia University Press.

This interesting ethnographic study examines the changing gender ideology among the Nyeshangte, a Tibetan Buddhism group found in the Himalayan Highlands. The author theorizes upon the intersection of modernism and capitalism with the cultural of the Nyeshangte and the subsequent changes in their understanding of gender and sex.

Suggested reading

Alsop, Rachel, Annette Fitzsimons, and Kathleen Lennon (2002). *Theorizing Gender*. Cambridge: Polity Press.

Butler, Judith (2004). *Undoing Gender*. New York: Routledge.

Goheen, Miriam (1996). *Men Own the Fields, Women Own the Crops: Gender and Power in the Cameroon Grassfields*. Madison, Wisconsin: Wisconsin University Press.

Joyce, Rosemary A. (2000). *Gender and Power in Prehistoric Mesoamerica*. Austin, TX: University of Texas Press.

McClintock, A. (1995). *Imperial Leather: Race, Gender, and Sexuality in the Colonial Contest*. New York: Routledge.

Ortner, Sherry B. (1996). *Making Gender: the Politics and Erotics of Culture*. Boston, MA: Beacon Press.

Penner, Todd and Caroline Vander Stichele (eds.), (2006). *Mapping Gender in Ancient Religious Discourses*. Biblical Interpretation Series 84. Leiden: Brill Academic Publishers.

Stratton, Kimberley (2007) *Naming the Witch: Magic, Ideology and Stereotype in the Ancient World*. New York: Columbia University Press.

Chapter 15

Insider/outsider perspectives

Kim Knott

Some years ago students who came to study religions at my university were introduced to the subject through a course called 'Religious Lives'. The purpose of the course was to develop an understanding of religions and their study by means of an examination of the autobiographies and biographies of a variety of religious people – what we might here call 'religious insiders'. The students came as 'outsiders' to these stories; but they also had their own stories, their own subjective experiences which they were asked to reflect on and write about. They were the 'insiders' in these accounts. The process of thinking about other people's religious lives as well as their own raised many critical questions and issues for discussion (Comstock 1995). Can we ever fully understand someone else's experience? What is the difference between an account of a religion by an insider and one by an outsider? Does translation from one language to another bridge a gap or create a barrier between the person telling the story and the one reading it? Additionally, we find ourselves considering the nature and limits of objectivity and subjectivity, 'emic' and 'etic' positions, 'experience-near' and 'experience-distant' concepts, empathy and critical analysis, the effect of personal standpoint, and the process of reflexivity. We even find that some of the lives we read about make us ask whether it is actually helpful to distinguish between insider and outsider perspectives. We will come to these matters in more detail shortly, but my purpose in listing them here is to show the range of concerns that are related to the insider/outsider debate, many of which have been at the heart of the study of religions since its inception as a discipline distinct from theology (Knott 2008). The debate challenges us by raising questions about the extent and limits of our knowledge and understanding. It invites us to consider whether or not our field of study is scientific. It is central to our methodology. It has an ethical dimension, and a political one.

Insider/outsider perspectives in the history of the study of religions

These questions came to the fore from the mid-1980s in a highly charged debate about the nature of Sikh studies and the contribution and motivation of particular scholars writing on Sikh religion (Grewal 1998; McLeod 2000; Shackle et al 2001). Who could understand and represent Sikh traditions? What were the personal motivations, epistemological standpoints and ideological interests of those who studied Sikh history and theology (King 1999)? As we shall see towards the end of this chapter, the issues in this debate eventually extended beyond the problem of the insider/outsider, but the problem was certainly of central importance early on. For example, in 1986, a collection of papers entitled *Perspectives on the Sikh Tradition* was published. Several of its authors strongly criticised Western scholarship on Sikhism, focusing particularly on the work of W. H. McLeod, who was held to have undermined the Sikh faith as a result of his historical and critical-textual approach to Sikh traditions (Singh 1986: 10; Grewal 1998: 126–31). Then, in 1991, in a review of the work of several Western scholars, including McLeod, Darshan Singh raised a key issue:

> The Western writers' attempt to interpret and understand Sikhism is an outsider's or non-participant's endeavour ... Primarily, religion is an area which is not easily accessible to the outsider, foreigner or non-participant. The inner meaning of a religion unfolds only through participation; by following the prescribed path and discipline.
>
> (1991: 3)

As we see from this case, the question of who can reliably understand and present a religion is contested. Darshan Singh and the authors of *Perspectives*, while accepting that Western outsiders have played a significant role in the development of Sikh studies, are suspicious of their motives (whether Christian or secular in origin), critical of their academic methods, and favour – by extension – the contribution of insiders to such studies. The strengths and weaknesses of participation and non-participation by scholars in the religions they study is a subject I shall return to shortly, but first I shall consider how, from the mid-nineteenth century onwards, Western scholars of the kind criticised above tackled the question of studying religions – both their own and those of others.

Emerging in the West as a field of enquiry with different objectives and methods to theology, the proponents of the early study of religions (also known as Religionswissenschaft and the history of religions) drew attention to its scientific, objective and comparative character (Waardenburg 1973; Sharpe 1975; Whaling 1995). They stressed the value of impartial scholarly accounts, and the development of appropriate conceptual tools, theories and methods. Writing in 1873, Max Müller stated that, as the object of study, religion should be shown reverence, but that it should also be subjected to critical scholarship. Twenty years later Cornelius Tiele, stressing the need among scientists of religion for objectivity but not judgement about the forms of religion, considered whether such scholarship was best done by believers or non-believers, concluding that, 'It is an error to suppose that one cannot take up such an impartial scientific position without being a sceptic; that one is disqualified for an impartial investigation if one possesses fixed and earnest religious convictions of one's own' (Tiele from *Elements of the Science of Religion* (1897–9), in Waardenburg 1973: 99). He distinguished between the private religious subjectivity of the individual and his or her outward impartiality as a scholar of religion. Tiele was not asserting that only sceptical non-believers or outsiders could study religions; rather, he was suggesting that those who were themselves religious were fully able to be impartial in their studies. This view, that those studying religion should set to one side their subjective experience and cultural baggage, and take an objective position with regard to the other, prevailed for nearly a century.

These issues were given consideration by other scholars, especially those associated with the phenomenology of religion, particularly Kristensen, van der Leeuw and Otto in Northern Europe, and later Eliade and Cantwell Smith in North America and Ninian Smart in Britain. They held the view, to quote Kristensen, that all religious phenomena were 'unique, autonomous and incomparable', yet capable of understanding by means of empathy, that is, by reliving in one's own experience that which appears to be alien (Kristensen from *The Meaning of Religion* in Waardenburg 1973: 391). While it was impossible to apprehend religion or the sacred in and of itself, it was possible to understand its manifestations or appearances (van der Leeuw 1963). The underlying aim of the phenomenological approach was to understand – by empathetic and imaginative re-experience – the insider position while refraining from forming a judgement about its truth or falsity (that being the domain of the theologian or philosopher).

The contemporary form of the insider/outsider debate, which has focused on the limits and desirability of such an approach, has raised different issues. A number of critics have argued that the phenomenology of religion has been implicitly theological (Segal 1983; Wiebe 1985), even a spiritual technique in its own right (McCutcheon 1997). Its assumptions about the essential, fundamental and totalising nature of the sacred, and its frequent adoption of Christian categories and types for the theorisation of religion have been deemed to be problematic (Fitzgerald 2000). Critics have questioned the rhetoric of impartiality and critical distance associated with phenomenology (Flood 1999).

Two rather different approaches to the study of religions have emerged in the West in recent decades. One is avowedly secular and scientific (Segal 1983; Wiebe 1985; McCutcheon 1997). It values an objective, outsider stance. It starts from the view that we cannot assume a common human nature across which categories such as religion and experiences of the sacred are shared. Instead, the social nature of religion and its capacity to be studied like other ideologies and institutions must be acknowledged. The aim of the scholar of religion should not be to get inside the experience and meaning of religious phenomena, but to build upon the benefits of critical distance to explain religion from the outside. The second approach focuses upon reflexivity (Brown 1991; Hufford 1995; King 1995; Flood 1999). Rather than requiring greater objectivity, as the previous approach does, it requires greater awareness on the part of the scholar about the dialogical nature of scholarship. While not being necessarily opposed to phenomenology, its criticism of that approach has been that the exponents of the latter were insufficiently aware of their intellectual and personal standpoint vis-à-vis others. They failed to take sufficient account of the effect of their position – either as individuals, often themselves religious, or as members of privileged groups of scholars, often Western and male – on their understanding of religion. Critics of this take a reflexive stance which requires that, as scholars, they research and write consciously from within their context and standpoint, whether as insiders or outsiders. Some couch this criticism in terms of post-colonialism, stressing the importance of a scholarly engagement with issues of identity, power and status (Shaw 1995; Flood 1999; King 1999; Donaldson and Pui-Lan 2002).

In his sourcebook on the insider/outsider problem – which may be consulted in association with this chapter – McCutcheon (1999) sought to categorise responses to the problem as follows: (i) the autonomy of religious experience, which he associated with the phenomenological approach; (ii) reductionism, exemplified by those taking a scientific, objective outsider stance; (iii) neutrality and methodological agnosticism, as adopted by those such as Ninian Smart who relied on insider accounts without evaluating their truth or falsity; and (iv) reflexivity. McCutcheon's presentation and discussion of these responses was introduced with reference to two terms which derive from the work of the linguist, Kenneth Pike. The *emic* perspective arises 'from studying behaviour as from inside the system' (Pike 1967: 37); the *etic* perspective, as from the outside. The former, then, is an attempt,

> to produce as faithfully as possible – in a word, to describe – the informant's own descriptions ... The etic perspective is the observer's subsequent attempt to take the

descriptive information they have already gathered and to organize, systematize, compare – in a word redescribe – that information in terms of a system of their own making …

(McCutcheon 1999: 17)

These terms are of central importance for understanding the perspectives of insider and outsider scholars.

Researching religious groups: insider/outsider perspectives and participant observation

Having dealt briefly with how some of the issues relating to the insider/outsider debate have been theorised, I shall turn now to a range of examples in order to investigate how these issues have been dealt with in practice. Our focus moves, then, from the theoretical to the methodological. For this purpose, I have developed a diagram to portray insider and outsider positions based on a model of participant/observer roles from the social sciences. The term 'participant observation' has commonly been used in anthropology to refer to the process of conducting research by living within a community over a period of time, participating in its life and observing its activities and use of symbols in order to develop an understanding of its meaning and structures (Davies 1999). This anthropological strategy need not detain us here. Rather, it is the four role conceptions of complete participant, participant-as-observer, observer-as-participant, and complete observer – first identified by two sociologists called Junker and Gold in the 1950s – that we shall consider here with reference to insider and outsider perspectives (Gold 1958: 217). They may be plotted on a continuum as follows:

OUTSIDER			INSIDER
Complete—————	Observer as —————	Participant—————	Complete
observer	participant	as observer	participant

If we take this diagram as illustrating the roles of those involved in researching religious groups, we can see that a number of positions are possible (though Gold's view was somewhat different as he took all researchers to be outsiders by default). I shall take the polar opposites first, followed by the two mid-way positions. At one end are those who are fully involved in religious activity as participants. They write about religion as insiders. Objectivity is not their purpose; critical distance is not their aim. They are scholars who write about their religion, with the benefit of an insider's faith and knowledge, as engaged participants (see Stringer 2002). They are unapologetic about this position, often believing that insiders like themselves provide the most informed and reliable accounts of their religion. I will look to the work of Fatima Mernissi, a Muslim scholar, for an example of this. Mernissi (1991) does not make a general case for the value of participant insider accounts, but rather shows how such accounts arise from particular standpoints and motivations. There is no single, uncontested view of what constitutes a religion like Islam; there are many differing participant accounts.

Moving to the far left of the diagram, we will turn to the role of the complete observer. Here we might expect to find a scholar who researches and writes about religion from the outside, eschewing any kind of participation. This is a position often associated with the psychology and sociology of religion, particularly with studies in which the researcher observes by means of the scientific use and analysis of questionnaires or structured interviews. My example is the fascinating study by Festinger, Riecken and Schachter carried out in the mid-1950s that revealed what happened to a religious group when its prophecy failed. We shall see how the researchers attempted to reproduce the complete observer stance in a situation where participation turned out to be unavoidable.

The role of the observer-as-participant will be examined in relation to Eileen Barker's stance in *The Making of a Moonie* (1984). From this we will discern a line of continuity with the phenomenological approach outlined earlier, particularly with the strategy of 'methodological agnosticism' commonly associated with the work of Ninian Smart (1973).

We will turn finally to those scholarly participants who adopt the role of observer in the midst of their own religious communities. They generally adopt a more critical stance than those who are complete participants, while remaining of the faith and sharing in the benefits of an insider's knowledge of the beliefs and practices of the community. For an understanding of this role we will examine the reflections of Samuel Heilman, a modernist Jew and sociologist writing in the 1980s before turning to those scholarly participants who have developed a reflexive and postmodernist critique of the insider/outsider problem (Pearson 2002; Collins 2002; Mandair 2001).

Fatima Mernissi: a complete but contentious participant?

OUTSIDER   INSIDER
                                                                                    Complete
                                                                                    participant

The majority of books written about religions are written by those who participate in them. There are numerous publishing houses associated with religious institutions; many groups have in-house newsletters and journals. In all of these, people of faith share with their co-religionists accounts of religious experience, religious ideas, responses to scripture, and thoughts about religious behaviour, ethics and the public demonstration of their faith. In addition, most religions have a class of scholars who reflect on, speak and write about their doctrinal, philosophical, legal or textual traditions, and may interpret them according to the needs of the time, or codify them so that they may be remembered and used in the future. Those who comprise such classes of scholars (theologians, rabbis, muftis, pandits and so on), often men, are by definition participants and insiders.

I have chosen Fatima Mernissi to illustrate the complete participant role, notably the stance she takes in *Women and Islam: An Historical and Theological Enquiry* (1991). As a Muslim feminist sociologist, she is hardly the obvious choice. Mernissi herself cites a case where she was denounced, by the editor of an Islamic journal, as a liar and misrepresentative of Islamic tradition. She is certainly not an authorised Islamic leader nor a trained theologian, but, as one who writes as a Muslim with the deliberate intention of recovering the Islamic past in order to understand women's rights, she evidently counts herself as an insider. What is more, she has a clear sense that this is not just a matter of private belief, but of legal requirement and communal identity:

> It is time to define what I mean when I say 'we Muslims'. The expression does not refer to Islam in terms of an individual choice, a personal option. I define being Muslim as belonging to a theocratic state ... Being Muslim is a civil matter, a national identity, a passport, a family code of laws, a code of public rights.

(20–1)

It is the denial of such rights to women in Muslim states that is of concern to Mernissi and that passionately engages her as a Muslim, a feminist and a scholar, as a result of which she turns her intellectual powers and scholarly training to the Hadith, the collections by later scholars of the sayings of the Prophet Muhammad. She is a critical religious insider tackling an issue of significance to contemporary Muslim women by recovering the foundational stories of the women around Muhammad and interrogating the misogynism of later interpretative accounts. In the preface to the English edition to her book, she writes:

> We Muslim women can walk into the modern world with pride, knowing that the quest for dignity, democracy, and human rights, for full participation in the political and social affairs of our country, stems from no imported Western values, but is a true part of the Muslim tradition.
>
> (viii)

Mernissi's is an emic, but not uncritical perspective. Rather than using the 'experience-distant' language of either comparative religion or sociology, she uses the 'experience-near' language of Islam (Geertz 1974), stressing, in particular, the centrality of the concept of *hijab* for an understanding of Muslim civilisation. Although she has not received the training associated with the *ulama*, she draws on the same sources of authority, though emphasising different stories and offering variant readings.

Although her book is not directed explicitly at a non-Muslim audience, Mernissi is clearly aware of the dominant Western critique, which has tended to see Islam as undemocratic and oppressive of women, and is keen to show that, in its foundational stories, there are 'matters dangerous to the establishment, of human dignity and equal rights' (Mernissi 1991: ix). She wishes to make clear to other Muslims that taking up the cause of women's rights does not place her outside Islamic tradition or Muslim society. She eschews the role of the secular feminist outsider and embraces that of participant in the narration of Islamic memory (10).

Can a single example, like that of Mernissi, point to a plurality of cases? I believe so. In choosing Mernissi – an insider who cites and disputes the views of many other Muslim insiders – I have indicated the complexity of insider perspectives. Choosing a feminist insider as an example has raised the issue of contestation between different insider-scholars within a single religion.

The struggle to be the complete observer

OUTSIDER   INSIDER
Complete——
observer

From an emic account in which experience-near concepts are to the fore, we now move to an etic one in which the language of social science is used to explain psychological behaviour resulting from religious belief. In the final part of their study of what happens to a messianic group when prophecy fails, Festinger, Riecken and Schachter (1956) examined the methodological difficulties that arose when trying to sustain the stance of the complete observer in a qualitative study of a dynamic religious community. At the time when they conducted their study, the key principles of social scientific research were objectivity, neutrality, the ability to repeat experiments, to demonstrate the validity of their results and to generalise from them. Many sociologists and psychologists used a quantitative approach, for example, by developing and administering a questionnaire (Beit-Hallahmi and Argyle 1996). Festinger and his co-researchers decided that such an approach was inappropriate for examining the cognitive and behavioural responses of a group of believers to 'undeniable disconfirmatory evidence' (1956: 4). Rather, it was essential to observe a group closely during such a process. Had it been possible to set up an experiment of this kind in a laboratory, behind glass, the researchers would no doubt have done so.

In fact, what they did was to await signs (in the media) of prophetic group activity, gain covert admittance to a group, and then observe the behaviour of its members from the inside. They adopted insider roles, as seekers who were 'non-directive, sympathetic listeners, passive participants who were inquisitive and eager to learn whatever others might want to tell us' (234). Such undercover work was deemed necessary to avoid alerting the group to the fact that it was being researched, and thus to avoid influencing the very beliefs, attitudes and responses they wished to observe.

Although the researchers were scientific outsiders, to the prophet, Mrs Keech, and her followers, they appeared to be complete participants. They were, however, students and staff from a variety of university psychology and sociology departments trained in observational methods. As such, they were conscious of the need to satisfy social scientific conditions, though they found themselves departing from 'the orthodoxy of social science in a number of respects', notably, in being unable 'to subject the members of the group to any standardised measuring instrument, such as a questionnaire or structured interview' (249). Further, they unintentionally reinforced members' beliefs, e.g. by seeming to confirm the view that they had been sent to join the group for a special purpose. They found it impossible to avoid discussing the belief system with members, answering calls from enquirers, and being seen by the movement's leaders as messengers from the Guardians (supernatural beings thought by members to be guiding the movement). All of these put them in a position of influencing those people they were supposed to be observing.

Despite these difficulties, *When Prophecy Fails* is an etic account as its purpose, hypothesis, methods, analysis, reporting and audience are evidently social scientific and not religious. While the researchers took seriously members' beliefs and responses, they did so only in so far as these were data to be collected and evaluated. The issue of their truth or falsity was not mentioned. Neither did the authors formally reflect on whether they accepted any of the beliefs of the group. Rather, they pretended 'to be merely interested individuals who had been persuaded of the correctness of the belief system' (249). Their pretence as insiders raises ethical questions about whether and in what ways the subjects of research should be informed and involved in decisions about the research process. The use in the book of terms such as 'covert', 'detective' and 'surveillance' heightens the distinction between the outsider-observer on the one side (in control, invisible, investigating), and the insider-observed on the other (passive, highly visible, exposed to detailed investigation), thereby raising the issue of power in the scholarly study and presentation of religious groups.

Arguably, this case fails to do full justice to the observer role because the demands of the research required the scholars involved to compromise their position as outsiders (by necessitating that they pretend to be participants). Nevertheless, we have been able to see how difficult it is for even the most determined observers to remain uninvolved, impartial and scientific when examining the subject of religious belief at close quarters. In the next section, we will consider whether an observer-as-participant who is known to and accepted by insiders encounters fewer problems. What are the characteristics of this stance? What difference does it make to the research if the participating observer owns up to being an outsider?

In neutral: the observer-as-participant

OUTSIDER   INSIDER
————————————————— Observer as —————————————————
                                participant

From the start of her investigation, Eileen Barker rejected the possibility of undertaking covert research on the Unification Church on both practical and ethical grounds: 'It was known that I was not a Moonie. I never pretended that I was, or that I was likely to become one' (1984: 20; see Lauder (2003) for a defence of covert research).

> I usually found my time with the movement interesting, and I grew genuinely fond of several individual Moonies, but at no time could I believe in the Unification version of reality. On the other hand, I could not accept the picture of the movement that outsiders kept telling me I ought to be finding.
>
> (1984: 21)

Barker's purpose in investigating the Unification Church, or 'Moonies' as they were frequently called, was to answer the question, 'Why should – how could – anyone become a Moonie?' (1). Little was known about them in the mid-1970s (despite the fact that the movement had been founded in 1954, in Korea), except for what was gleaned from negative media coverage about the leader and the conversion strategies of the movement which tended to stimulate fear and fascination rather than a desire to learn or to be informed. Sceptical of both the movement's self-image and the media account, Barker became an authorised observer whose research method was one of engaged participation. She lived in Unification centres, attended workshops, listened to members, engaged in conversations, asked questions and interviewed ex-members. Her stance, by her own admittance, had its strengths and weaknesses.

> Being known to be a non-member had its disadvantages, but by talking to people who had left the movement I was able to check that I was not missing any of the internal information which was available to rank-and-file members. At the same time, being an outsider who was 'inside' had enormous advantages. I was allowed (even, on certain occasions, expected) to ask questions that no member would have presumed to ask either his leaders or his peers.
>
> (21)

Barker borrowed a term from the work of Max Weber to identify her approach to understanding why people became Moonies: '*Verstehen* is a process of inquiry during which the researcher tries to put himself in other people's shoes or ... to see the world through their glasses' (20). Although she contextualised this with reference to the social sciences, it had much in common with the empathetic approach favoured by the phenomenologists of religion reviewed earlier in this account: Kristensen, van der Leeuw and, latterly, Ninian

Smart. It was Smart who first used the term 'methodological agnosticism' to signal the need for neutrality and the bracketing-out of truth claims and judgements in research on religion. Barker shared this view, believing that 'passing value judgements should be an enterprise that is separate from social science' (36). Rather, she hoped to bring together what she saw as 'an objective factual account of the history and beliefs of the movement' (10) with diverse voices from within and outside it.

Barker's etic account, interspersed with the experiences of Moonies, ex-Moonies, non-Moonies and anti-Moonies, represented a conscious attempt to *translate* Moonie reality and values for those unfamiliar with them. She found that she was able to stay in touch with outsiders' often unsympathetic and quizzical attitudes while becoming engrossed in Moonie reality by regularly re-reading her research diary. She was reminded of her own journey from ignorance to knowledge about the movement. She believed in the attempt to bridge the divergent perpectives of insiders and outsiders, and saw this as an appropriate scholarly task. Furthermore, she held that it was 'perfectly possible to see things from other people's points of view without necessarily agreeing that they are right' (35). At the same time, she recognised that there were those on both sides who believed that neutrality was impossible, even immoral.

The methodological agnosticism identified by Smart – and pursued by Barker – dominated the study of religion in the 1970s and 1980s. It upheld the dichotomy between inside and outside, positing the need for a value-free translator who would bridge the two perspectives. Barker exemplified the role of observer-as-participating translator. But could an outsider ever fulfil this role? Could such a scholar really be agnostic, or would his or her act of observation necessarily call such a stance into question?

The participant-as-observer comes of age

OUTSIDER   INSIDER
———Participant———————————————————
as observer

As we saw in the 1890s with Tiele and in the 1980s with Barker, many scholars of religion – with personal religious convictions or with none – have held that an impartial stance is possible. Indeed, many religious people have sought to research and write about their own religion *as if* they were observers, with objectivity and critical distance. It has often been the aim of such participants-as-observers to provide an entrée into their religion, its beliefs and practices, for outsiders; to make comprehensible, often through the use of 'experience-distant' concepts and commonly accepted scientific methods, the esoteric world from which they come. They have often shared this aim with observers-as-participants (like Barker), and have sought to exercise a bridge-building role with the purpose of communicating what is thought or practised within the religion to those outside it.

Many participants-as-observers have commented sensitively on their own position and purpose in writing as believers and practitioners. This has been especially true since the 1990s, with the impact of a critical postmodernist and reflexive stance. Several examples which exemplify this will be considered later in the section. First, we will look at an example from the 1980s in which orthodox religiosity and modernist sociology met in an autobiographical account by Samuel Heilman, *The Gate Behind the Wall* (1984, partially reproduced in Comstock 1995).

> I live in two worlds ... In one, I am attached to an eternal yesterday – a timeless faith and ritual, an ancient system of behavior. In that world, I am an Orthodox Jew. In my other world, there is little if any attachment to the enchantment of religion or sacred practice, and what is happening today or tomorrow matters far more than the verities embedded in the past. In that domain, I am a university professor of sociology.
>
> (Comstock 1995: 214)

Heilman describes this as 'a double life' in which the two aspects are compartmentalised, and which is generally maintained by forgetting one aspect while living out the other. He proceeds, though, to describe the attempt he made 'to collapse the boundaries between these two worlds and find a way to make myself whole' (214).

Starting out as a modern Orthodox Jewish sociologist, Heilman undertook a sociological study of his own synagogue community,

> believing that as an insider I could supply, through both introspection and a sense of the relevant questions to ask, information about dimensions of inner life not readily available to other researchers ... I would be able to give a fuller picture of the synagogue than could any outsider, however well prepared and trained he might be.
>
> (218)

Reflecting back on this exercise, he discovered that he had 'found my way back into the traditional synagogue from my new home in the University via the tools of my social science' (218). However, he harboured a further ambition, to fulfil his sacred duty to engage in *lemen*, the Yiddish term for the Orthodox Jewish practice of reviewing the sacred texts with devotion and awe (216). On the advice of his rabbi, he further utilised his professional skills as a participant observer in seeking out and participating in a traditional study circle or *chavruse* in Jerusalem. We see in this a desire both to fulfil personal religious commitments and to describe and explain the world of the *chavruse* to outsiders. What is of interest in Heilman's powerful account is, first, the way in which his position as participant-as-observer is demonstrated through the use of spatial imagery and specialist concepts, and, second, the way in which he reflects upon that position.

Heilman's title, *The Gate Behind the Wall*, in addition to situating us in Jewish Jerusalem at or near the Wailing Wall, promises us entry into a traditional and esoteric world from which, as outsiders, we are normally excluded, but to which, as an insider/outsider Jew, he was powerfully attracted. Further, he uses the imagery of walls, gates, rooms and doors to describe his modernist journey: 'Old walls made new through a process of uncovering seemed the right metaphor for my own quest' (221). In distinguishing between the compartmentalisation from which he was trying to escape and the wholeness he sought, he used the metaphor of rooms: in the former, 'one simply learns to dim the lights in one room while passing into the other'; in the *chavruse*, 'compartments collapse, and rooms open into one another' (229). Despite his most fervent efforts, though, as a modernist Jew, he felt unable to transcend his sense of distance; unable to escape 'the barriers of biography' (230).

Heilman's two purposes (and two worlds) are mirrored in his use of both 'experience-near' and 'experience-distant' concepts. He does not shy away from using Yiddish and Hebrew terms, but he also uses the language of religious studies and the social sciences in order to move his account beyond the descriptive and ethnographic to the analytical and theoretical. Repeatedly, he uses terms such as tradition, culture, liturgy and sacred text (rather than equivalent terms from Orthodox Judaism), and also introduces social scientific concepts such as liminality (227), authenticity (225) and organising principle (228). As autobiographical scholarship, Heilman's account is subjective in character. However, it goes beyond description of the participant's experience by offering an examination of the limits of Heilman's role as a modernist Orthodox Jewish sociologist. He suggests that the process of observation – of others and the self – by one who is an insider produces a feeling of separation. His repeated references to walls, borders, gates, barriers, doors and limits demonstrate this seemingly unalterable affliction: 'As if by some sort of biological rejection process, the strangeness in me was forcing me out (of the *chavruse*)' (230).

How have participants-as-observers since Heilman found this role? Have their purposes in writing from the inside out been comparable to his? Have their experiences of observation and the practice of writing about it been similar? Two authors, writing in a recent book on the insider/outsider problem, reveal the way in which the understanding of this role is changing. Both authors are critical of the juxtaposition of insiders and outsiders, and see the value of the critical insider stance. However, the first asserts the benefits of the both/and principle; the second commends the dissolution of the distinction between the two positions.

Jo Pearson (2002), whose study of British Wicca is entitled 'Going native in reverse', notes that there are some religions, requiring initiation, which are largely inaccessible to outsiders. For an understanding of these, we are dependent upon insiders who act as a bridge between the inside and outside, and facilitate the two aspects of involvement and distance. Such an insider-researcher acts as both insider and outsider, and the movement back and forth opens him or her up to a range of types of information: that which is available to outsiders, that which is only available to those within the researched community (insiders), and that which becomes available to the researcher through his or her reflexive participation in the research process.

At the end of an ethnographic account of his own Quaker meeting, Peter Collins (2002) disputes the notions of self and society which underlie the dualism of insider and outsider. He uses imagery similar to Heilman's to invoke the modernist perspective which sees society 'as a series of buildings each with a single door which serves both as entrance and exit: either one is in or one is out, and if one is in one building then one cannot at the same time be in another' (93). Collins's view, of a more processual society and a more dynamic self, in which worlds are overlapping and interactive rather than isolated and separate, makes the distinction between insider and outsider largely redundant. All participants create social meaning through the common practice of story telling, and this, in turn, dissolves the boundaries between inside and out.

Heilman writes of the unresolved tension of being between two worlds as a Jew who is also a sociologist. Pearson suggests that, whatever its difficulties, the both/and position of the insider-scholar is productive, the reflexive nature of its stance giving it the edge over outsider scholarship. Collins concludes that the distinction between insider and outsider becomes irrelevant when we recognise that all those who participate, whether of the faith or not, contribute to the co-construction of the story. The insider/outsider dichotomy is an unhelpful consequence of a modernist view of self and society.

Where does the problem lie, and what is the way forward?

This last view is similar to one expressed by Arvind-Pal Singh Mandair, a participant in the Sikh studies debate with which I began. In an attempt to understand its ideological contours, Mandair (2001) locates the problem in 'the current intellectual and methodological crisis or rupture in the human and social sciences' (49) in which 'secular reason has been placed in a position of supervision in respect of any possible inquiry into religion' (50). As he sees it, the Sikh studies debate is not so much a function of the insider/outsider problem (as suggested by Darshan Singh) as of the modernist turn from religious to secular thinking. In the case of Sikh studies, this has had the effect of making insider critiques of Western scholarship look like traditionalist, even fundamentalist, attacks.

Mandair is not merely being defensive here; there is a case to answer. Most twentieth-century studies of religions – whether they be historical, in the case of Sikh studies, phenomenological or sociological, in the case of our other examples – were rooted in the discourse of secular reason and scientific enquiry. Their authors spoke the language of neutrality, impartiality, objectivity, observation, reductionism, methodological agnosticism and atheism (Hufford 1995). Both outsiders and scholarly insiders sought to articulate their positions in these terms. With the latter, as we saw with Heilman, this led to a sense of tension, the result of being an insider subjectively caught up in an experience while endeavouring to maintain the appropriate level of critical distance required by the scholarly establishment.

Both Collins and Mandair invite us to step away from the imprisonment of this modernist position, but their diagnoses are different. Collins offers a postmodern response: the abandonment of dichotomous views of insider/outsider in favour of a more dynamic view in which everyone is a co-participant in the formulation of a narrative about religion. Mandair favours the move to a study of religion (Sikhism) that 'is at once a form of self-discovery, no less spiritual than political, no less therapeutic than classificatory' (68–9), in short, an antidote to the dominant objectivist, secularist approach.

Collins and Mandair invite us in different ways to reconceptualise the terms of our discipline in such a way that we are no longer compelled to compartmentalise the world of faith and the world of scholarship. For some scholars this would be a step too far, one which undermines the distinction between those doing religion and those observing it, between theology and the study of religions, indeed the very *raison d'être* of the latter as a field of study with its own terms of reference (Flood 1999; Fitzgerald 2000; McCutcheon 2003). In his attempt to think 'beyond phenomenology', however, Gavin Flood offers a strategy for reconfiguring critical distance, 'outsideness' and situated observation in the study of religions which depends not upon modernist notions of objectivity and the phenomenological assertion of non-confessionalism, but rather upon a dialogical and reflexive engagement between scholars and the religious people they study. My own view, formed in the context of developing a spatial methodology for the study of religion, is that *all* interlocutors – whether secular observers, religious participants, or those who strategically move between the two positions – are actors within a single knowledge-power field (Knott 2005). Despite their differing goals and interests, they have together defined, constituted and criticised 'religion' in general, particular 'religions' and their beliefs and practices, and the secular or non-religious domain beyond religion. The 'secular' (which has constituted the 'outside' in this discussion about scholarly positioning on religion) is indeed within the same field of action and discourse as the 'religious', and, although the field contains operational boundaries, groups and factions, all those within it are in one sense 'insiders', although as they go about their business they variously constitute themselves and others as 'insiders' or 'outsiders' in accordance with their ideological and social purposes.

The scholars discussed in this chapter have not only shown us the centrality of the insider/outsider problem in the study of religions, they have also highlighted the complex issues of subjectivity and objectivity, emic and etic perspectives, the politics and ethics of researching and writing about religion (whether as an outsider or an insider), the epistemological and methodological implications of the problem, and its ideological location within Western secular modernism. These are profound matters for anyone studying religions. What more recent perspectives show is that the problem of the insider and outsider is as vital now for understanding the theory and method of religious studies as it was when the latter first emerged as a discipline separate from theology more than a century ago.

Bibliography

Barker, Eileen, 1984, *The Making of a Moonie: Brainwashing or Choice?*, Oxford, Blackwell.

Beit-Hallahmi, B. and Argyle, Michael, 1996, *The Social Psychology of Religion*, London, Routledge.

Brown, Karen McCarthy, 1991, *Mama Lola: A Vodou Priestess in Brooklyn*, Berkeley CA, University of California Press.

Collins, Peter J., 2002, 'Connecting anthropology and Quakerism', in Elisabeth Arweck and Martin Stringer, eds, *Theorising Faith: The Insider/Outsider Problem in the Study of Ritual*, Birmingham, Birmingham University Press, pp. 77–95.

Comstock, Gary L., 1995, *Religious Autobiographies*, Belmont CA, Wadsworth.

Davies, Charlotte Aull, 1999, *Reflexive Ethnography: A Guide to Researching Selves and Others*, London, Routledge.

Donaldson, Laura E. and Pui-lan, Kwok, eds, 2002, *Postcolonialism, Feminism, and Religious Discourse*, New York and London, Routledge.

Festinger, Leon, Riecken, Henry W. and Schachter, Stanley, 1956, *When Prophecy Fails: A Social and Psychological Study of a Modern Group that Predicted the Destruction of the World*, New York, Harper & Row (reprinted 1964).

Fitzgerald, Timothy, 2000, *The Ideology of Religious Studies*, New York, Oxford University Press.

Flood, Gavin, 1999, *Beyond Phenomenology: Rethinking the Study of Religion*, London, Cassell.

Geertz, Clifford, 1974, '"From the native's point of view": on the nature of anthropological understanding', *Bulletin of the American Academy of Arts and Sciences*, 28: 1.

Gold, Raymond L., 1958, 'Roles in sociological field observations', *Social Forces*, 36, 217–23.

Grewal, J. S., 1998, *Contesting Interpretations of the Sikh Tradition*, New Delhi, Manohar.

Heilman, Samuel, 1984, *The Gate Behind the Wall*, Georges Bourchardt.

Hufford, David J., 1995, 'The scholarly voice and the personal voice: reflexivity in belief studies', *Western Folklore*, 54, 57–76.

King, Richard, 1999, *Orientalism and Religion: Postcolonial Theory, India and the Mystic East*, London, Routledge.

King, Ursula, ed., 1995, *Religion and Gender*, Oxford, Blackwell.

Knott, Kim, 2005, *The Location of Religion: A Spatial Analysis*, London, Equinox.

—— 2008, 'A spatial analysis of the relationship between theology and religious studies: Knowledge-power strategies and metaphors of containment and separation, insider and outsider', in Darlene Bird and Simon Smith, eds, *Theology and Religious Studies in Higher Education: Global Perspectives*, London, Continuum, pp. 117–38.

Kristensen, William Brede, 1960, *The Meaning of Religion*, The Hague, Martinus Nijhoff.

Lauder, M. A, 2003, 'Covert participant observation of a deviant community: Justifying the use of deception', *Journal of Contemporary Religion*, 18:2, pp. 185–96.

McCutcheon, Russell T., 1997, *Manufacturing Religion: The Discourse of Sui Generis Religion and the Politics of Nostalgia*, New York and Oxford, Oxford University Press.

—— ed., 1999, *The Insider/Outsider Problem in the Study of Religion: A Reader*, London and New York, Cassell.

—— 2003, *The Discipline of Religion*, London and New York, Routledge.

McLeod, W. H., 2000, *Exploring Sikhism: Aspects of Sikh Identity, Culture and Thought*, Oxford, Oxford University Press.

Mandair, Arvind-Pal Singh, 2001, 'Thinking differently about religion and history: issues for Sikh Studies', in Christopher Shackle, Gurharpal Singh and Arvind-Pal Mandair, eds, *Sikh Religion, Culture and Ethnicity*, Richmond, Curzon, pp. 47–71.

Mernissi, Fatima, 1991, *Women and Islam: An Historical and Theological Enquiry*, Oxford, Blackwell [1987].

Müller, Max F., 1873, *Introduction to the Science of Religion*, London, Longmans, Green & Co.

Pearson, Jo, 2002, '"Going native in reverse": the insider as researcher in British Wicca', in Elisabeth Arweck and Martin Stringer, eds, *Theorising Faith: The Insider/Outsider Problem in the Study of Ritual*, Birmingham, Birmingham University Press, pp. 97–113.

Pike, Kenneth, 1967, *Language in Relation to a Unified Theory of the Structure of Human Behaviour*, 2nd edn, The Hague, Mouton.

Segal, Robert A., 1983, 'In defense of reductionism', *Journal of the American Academy of Religion*, 51, 97–124.

Shackle, Christopher, Singh, Gurharpal and Mandair, Arvind-Pal, eds, 2001, *Sikh Religion, Culture and Ethnicity*, Richmond, Curzon.

Sharpe, Eric, 1975, *Comparative Religion: A History*, London, Duckworth.

Shaw, Rosalind, 1995, 'Feminist anthropology and the gendering of religious studies', in Ursula King, ed., *Religion and Gender*, Oxford, Blackwell, pp. 65–76.

Singh, Darshan, 1991, *Western Perspective on the Sikh Religion*, New Delhi, Sehgal Publishers Service.

Singh, Gurdev, ed., 1986, *Perspectives on the Sikh Tradition*, Patiala, Siddharth Publications.

Smart, Ninian, 1973, *The Science of Religion and the Sociology of Knowledge: Some Methodological Questions*, Princeton, Princeton University Press.

Stringer, Martin D., 2002, 'Introduction: Theorizing faith', in Elisabeth Arweck and Martin Stringer, eds, *Theorising Faith: The Insider/Outsider Problem in the Study of Ritual*, Birmingham, Birmingham University Press, pp. 1–20.

Tiele, Cornelius P., 1897–9, *Elements of the Science of Religion*, 2 vols, Edinburgh/London, Blackwood and Sons.

van der Leeuw, Gerardus, 1963, *Religion in Essence and Manifestation*, 2 vols, New York, Harper Torchbooks [1938].

Waardenburg, Jacques, 1973, *Classical Approaches to the Study of Religion*, The Hague, Mouton.

Whaling, Frank, ed., 1995, *Theory and Methods in Religious Studies: Contemporary Approaches to the Study of Religions*, Berlin, Mouton de Gruyter.

Wiebe, Donald, 1985, 'Does understanding religion require religious understanding?', in Witold Tyloch, ed., *Current Progress in the Methodology of the Science of Religions*, Warsaw, Polish Scientific Publishers.

Suggested reading

Arweck, Elisabeth and Stringer, Martin, eds, *Theorising Faith: The Insider/Outsider Problem in the Study of Ritual*, Birmingham, Birmingham University Press.
Useful introduction and collection of essays on insider/outsider issues which includes cited articles by scholarly insiders, Collins and Pearson.

Davies, Charlotte Aull, 1999, *Reflexive Ethnography: A Guide to Researching Selves and Others*, London, Routledge.
Major work from the methodological literature on insider/outsider issues and reflexivity.

Flood, Gavin, 1999, *Beyond Phenomenology: Rethinking the Study of Religion*, London, Cassell.
Important study which questions the adequacy of the phenomenology of religion and suggests that insiders and outsiders are dialogical partners in the study of religion.

Hufford, David J., 1995, 'The scholarly voice and the personal voice: reflexivity in belief studies', *Western Folklore*, 54, 57–76.
Article on insider/outsider issues and reflexivity.

McCutcheon, Russell T., ed., 1999, *The Insider/Outsider Problem in the Study of Religion: A Reader*, London and New York, Cassell.
Key text for understanding the issues involved in the insider/outsider problem; includes readings on all aspects of the problem and an excellent introduction.

Chapter 16

Post-structuralism and the study of religion

Jeremy Carrette

The study of religion is shaped by successive waves of critical and theoretical thought that redefine the subject and its practice in each historical period. The waves of phenomenology, feminism, structuralism and social construction have all shaped thinking about religion through the twentieth century. Some of these theoretical shifts cause threats to any desire to hold a simple correspondence theory of truth, where observation of the object of study is assumed to be neutral, direct and immediate – a form of rationalism. It is because of this radical questioning that many scholars of religion have shown ambivalence to theory and many wish to avoid the implications of the various waves of thinking. Theory, however, provides the unavoidable epistemological ground of any discipline. The situation is made even more complex in the study of religion because theoretical questions emerge through the multi-disciplinary formation of the subject. This means that theoretical shifts are embraced through the various changes in philosophy, sociology, psychology and anthropology, to mention a few areas, rather than through any coherent engagement within the study of religion.

The emergence of post-structuralist thinking in the 1960s, and its critical developments since that time, is not linked to any one method, but has implications for all methods in the study of religion and its central categories of knowledge. Post-structuralism is a trans-disciplinary critical examination of how we represent the world through language and ways of thinking. It is a diverse set of techniques for questioning the assumptions behind our thinking. Post-structuralism is therefore important as an intellectual development because it takes the subject back to the central problem of knowledge and intellectual practice. It presents a challenge to how we formulate truth and understanding in the study of religion. It raises questions about the very foundations of the subject. Post-structuralism takes us back to the history of philosophy and the question of how we know and what determines or shapes the categories of our knowledge. Whether one agrees or disagrees with post-structuralism, it poses important questions about the nature of language, representation, culture and history. It engages scholars of religion to think about how they make their knowledge claims and it presents a direct challenge to empiricism, rationalism and *positivism* within the field of study. If scholars of religion are concerned with presenting their work with accuracy and precision then post-structuralism cannot be ignored, because it demands consideration of the very language and concepts we use to make empirical claims.

The impact of post-structuralist theory on the study of religion – or rather the work of the people associated with the term – can be seen as one of the key critical horizons that emerged in the late twentieth and early twenty-first centuries. It is, as Antes, Geertz and Warne's

(2008: 1) contemporary survey suggests, one of the 'new approaches' in the study of religion after the preoccupation with phenomenological and social science methods; although in Antes, Geertz and Warne's work many of the potential insights are restricted to the domain of literary theory, as a separate 'approach' rather than integrated in all forms of knowledge (see McCance 2008). After the separation of the study of religion from theology, the domination of phenomenology and the marking of social scientific methods, post-structuralism displaces the field of knowledge by taking knowledge back to how we use signs in language and the politics of knowledge. It emerges in the epistemic and linguistic revolution following the reception of the Swiss linguistic Ferdinand de Saussure's posthumously published *Cours de Linguistique Générale* (Course in General Linguistics) in 1916 and the political development of related ideas in France in the 1960s (Saussure [1916] 1974). It subsequently transforms thinking in every field of knowledge and starts to have an impact on scholarship in the study of religion from the 1980s onwards.

The influence of post-structuralist thinking can now be seen in every area of the study of religion. To give some examples, by no means exhaustive, we can see post-structuralist ideas in biblical studies (Moore 1994; Sherwood 2004); the study of Buddhism (Coward 1990; Faure 1998); feminist theory and religion (Jantzen 1998; Joy 2006); the study of Hinduism (Urban 2003; King 1999a); the study of Islam (Almond 2004; Mahmood 2005); the study of Judaism (Boyarin 1996, 1997); the study of mysticism (Jantzen 1995; King 1999a; Hollywood 2002); the psychology of religion (Carrette 2007; Jonte-Pace 2001); Sikh studies (Mandair *et al.* 2001; Bhogal 2007); the sociology of religion (Turner 1991; Lehmann 1993); studies of the category of religion (McCutcheon 1997; King 1999a); theory and method (Taylor 1998; Flood 1999; Braun and McCutcheon 2000) and in theology (Caputo 1997; Ward 2000). It is perhaps more accurate to say that these scholars of religion use the works of thinkers associated with post-structuralism rather than outwardly deploy the sign of post-structuralism, which itself tells us something about the problem of capturing thought under fixed categories. They, as Hugh Urban (2003: 2) suggests in relation to his use of Foucault, are '[b]orrowing insights from' post-structuralist literature. Arvind Mandair (2006: 658) also uses the term 'borrow' in his use of ideas from the French post-structuralist thinker Jacques Lacan to make sense of Sikh texts. In both cases, this 'borrowing' is combined with all sorts of other strands of critical thinking from feminism, post-colonial theory, social theory and a range of other continental philosophers. Post-structuralism is therefore one critical discourse among many and becomes part of a longer critical tradition of thinking from the Enlightenment. The sense of 'borrowing' reflects the fact that ideas from post-structuralism serve a critical function. They are deployed to illuminate something concealed in normative modes of the study of religion. The post-structuralist hermeneutic appreciates text, context, history and power and provides critical strategies to disrupt the certainties of knowledge and reveal the values behind such thinking. The other sense of 'borrowing' is that the ideas are often isolated and extracted from the wider work of post-structuralist writers; although there have been detailed studies of individual post-structuralists and their use of religious ideas (see Anderson 1989; Carrette 2000; Hollywood 2002).

Following the work of Barthes (1963), I will argue that what holds the group of scholars of religion using post-structuralist ideas together is not a systematic approach, or a new method of post-structuralism, but the deployment of a new lexicon – a new vocabulary or set of expressions – in the study of religion and that this vocabulary brings us back to the problems of epistemology (the nature of knowledge), semiotics (the nature of signs) and *ideology* (the nature of power). I will first explore the key theoretical aspects of the term post-structuralism and its emergence from structuralism and then identify the key strategies employed in the field of religion by some of the above scholars and examine the implications of this method for future studies in religion. Needless to say, in the limits of this presentation, I can only skim the surface of the post-structuralist literature to provide a 'trace' of its critique, focusing on a few key ideas from the foundational texts. I will, however, contend that the engagement with post-structuralism is one of the most significant developments in the study of religion, because this critical perspective raises important questions about the legitimacy and authority of knowledge claims in the field.

The complexity of the term: emerging themes in 1960s French thought

Post-structuralism is a difficult term and like all 'isms' needs to be used as a marker for a set of ideas and then critically suspended as a term, because it reflects a holding of ideas that are constantly in process and exchange: it is like trying to catch a single point in a moving stream of historical thought. Ideas are constantly in exchange and motion, and only for strategic reasons are terms frozen and thinkers positioned to achieve certain temporary shorthand clarifications or political objectives in the intellectual and social world. Few writers claim to be post-structuralist and are often labelled as such by other writers attempting to identify trends and patterns of thinking, or even simply to dismiss them. It is also true that the specificity of a writer always reveals greater complexity and multiple strands of thought than any one term can convey. Nonetheless, the term post-structuralism can be used to identify a broad set of intellectual patterns of thought emerging from 1960s France, which had major importance on the late twentieth century and early twenty-first century in almost every intellectual discipline.

The term post-structuralism is used in a variety of different ways by its exponents and opponents and it is thus useful to identify a strict and general use. In its strict sense, it is used to identify a number of French intellectuals in the 1960s and their emergence within and development of structuralism. The work of Roland Barthes (1915–1980), Jacques Lacan (1925–1980), Michel Foucault (1926–1984), Jacques Derrida (1930–2004) and Julia Kristeva (1941–), who came to France from Bulgaria, are most commonly associated with this theoretical challenge. In its general usage post-structuralism has been used to embrace a wider movement of critical theory and continental philosophy and is often fused – and confused – with postmodernism. Postmodernism is a misleading term that tends to obfuscate the specificity of intellectual thought rather than provide any useful insight. Postmodernism suffers from even greater imprecision than post-structuralism and has more to do with the marketing of a broad set of ideas and thoughts in the late modern Anglo-Saxon world; it is a term of excitement or revulsion that hides the historical specificity of the texts and people it captures. However, it has been employed more effectively in Christian theology to identify partisan affiliations between different stylised positions of pre-modern, modern and late-modern theological thought (Ward 1997).

It is also important to recognise that the term postmodernism is often used by those who wish to assert clear statements of truth and fact from sense experience (positivism) to dismiss certain types of thinking as anti-Enlightenment relativism, which seriously distorts and does great injustice to the specific writers associated with post-structuralism. The reason for this confusion is related to the way French thinkers often associated with postmodernism, such as Jean-François Lyotard (1924–1998) and Jean Baudrillard (1929–2007), are wrongly linked with a different set of French thinkers connected to the more strict idea of post-structuralism. On the whole, it is best to separate the specific historical emergence of post-structuralism from the more enigmatic term postmodernism, while being aware that some confusingly use these terms interchangeably to identify wider trends of French intellectual thought. The specificity of post-structuralism will thus allow us to appreciate the historical context of French thought in the 1960s and move the discussion away from simple charges of relativism and anti-modernism. I will maintain that post-structuralism to some extent develops the critique of the Enlightenment – even in its suspicion of such thinking – by extending the critical platform of knowledge to the problem of representation. It arguably rests in the longer philosophical tradition of epistemology.

Structuralism and post-structuralism

It is not possible to understand post-structuralism without some understanding of structuralism and to understand why Barthes, Lacan, Foucault, Derrida and Kristeva are positioned by *both* terms at the same time. John Sturrock (1993: 137) rightly argues that post-structuralism is an extension rather than a complete break with structuralism. As he puts it: 'Post-structuralism is a critique of Structuralism conducted from within: that is, it turns certain of Structuralism's arguments against itself and points to certain fundamental inconsistencies in their method which Structuralists have ignored.' The problem here is that structuralism is best understood as an intellectual 'moment' in French academic history rather than a clear set of principles and an identified school. In François Dosse's (1997) comprehensive two volume *History of Structuralism* it is clear that '[w]hat Americans call poststructuralism existed even before the structural paradigm waned. In fact, it was contemporary with its triumph' (Dosse 1997: 17). At the very moment that structuralism reached its historical pinnacle in France – 1966 – it fragmented. Post-structuralism was thus part of the 'disparate fabric' of structuralism (Dosse 1997: xiii). It was embedded in the atmosphere and discourse of the historical context of structuralism and carried over much of its language.

The problematic nature of the situation can be illustrated by considering a famous cartoon by Maurice Henry in the French journal *La Quinzaine littéraire* in July 1967. The cartoon known as 'the structuralist picnic on the grass', depicts four structuralists (Foucault, Lacan, Barthes and Lévi-Strauss) sitting on the ground beneath tropical trees, wearing grass skirts, and having a conversation. The cartoon captured the intellectual moment of 1966 in French thought, with Foucault's successful *Les Mots et les choses* (The Order of Things), Lacan's *Écrits* (Writings) and Barthes's *Critique et vérité* (Criticism and Truth), in the context of Lévi-Strauss's 1958 text *Anthropologie structurale* (Structural Anthropology); the tropical setting echoes the work on primitive civilisations. However, as the cartoon appeared it also witnessed the artificial positioning of the thinkers. Only Lévi-Strauss would hold on to the term structuralism while the others would seek to distance themselves from it, especially Foucault. Soon after the cartoon the work of Derrida would come to the intellectual foreground and Kristeva would in time also emerge with her own contributions to *semiotic* theory after her arrival in France in 1965 (see Dosse 1997: 17ff; 54).

It important to note that French linguistic structuralism from the Parisian Left Bank is not the only type of structuralism. As Barthes (1966: 5) correctly asks: 'What structuralism are we talking about?' Barthes recognised that the idea had been discussed for a hundred years and it is, therefore, possible to find longer histories of structure. Derrida (1966: 278) makes the same point in his 1966 critical essay decentring the idea of structure in Lévi-

Strauss's work by showing it is 'as old as Western science and Western philosophy'. The idea that there are *given structures* can be found at all levels of analysis and in different types of knowledge. The post-structuralist linguistic type of structuralism should not obscure the fact that structures have also played a key part in wider scientific thinking, as Jean Piaget's (1968 [1971]) seminal text, *Structuralism*, argued. Types of structure can be seen in philosophy from Platonic forms to Kantian *a priori* synthetic forms and in science from general algebra to Newtonian physics. Piaget pointed out that despite the various types of structuralism there was an underlying synthesis. Although his concern was to explore structuralism within mathematics and social science, he mapped three key features. First, there is the determining feature of wholeness. The various elements always exist within a law or order. Second, these systems of wholeness are 'transformations', they are 'simultaneously *structuring* and *structured*', because in static form they would collapse. Piaget's third and final form is that structures are 'self-regulating'. They have a '*rhythm, regulation*' and '*operation*' that maintains the system and creates a closure by setting a boundary (Piaget 1968 [1971]: 3–16). Piaget's general insights allow the linguist Terence Hawkes (1977: 17) eloquently to capture something of the general nature of structuralism by considering the relationship between things. It is, for Hawkes, a 'way of thinking about the world which is predominantly concerned with the perception and description of structures'. It is a 'way of thinking' that does not examine the object itself, because 'the world is made up of *relationships not things* ...' [my emphasis]. This structural relationship emerged across all fields of study: anthropology (Lévi-Strauss), psychology (Piaget) and linguistics (Saussure), but it is the Saussurean tradition of structural thinking that leads to the insights of post-structuralism in France.

Saussure and semiotics

Ferdinand de Saussure's great insight in his 1916 *Cours de linguistique générale* was to study language from the *synchronic* rather than *diachronic* perspective; that is, to study language as a complete system at a given moment rather than its historical changes and variations. Saussure's first principle, according to Jameson's (1972: 7, 21) critical reading of the relation of the synchronic and diachronic, is 'an anti-historical one' that reacts against the dominant view of the time. This marking out of the underlying feature of language enables Saussure to see language as a 'system' with its own intrinsic relations. As Sturrock (1993: 6, 26) indicates, the word 'system' carries the meaning of 'structure', which oddly does not appear in Saussure and does not emerge until 1928 in the context of phonetics. From this basis of the *synchronic*, the central parts of language are then analysed. First, according to *langue* (the system of language) and *parole* (individual speech acts), something which has its source in Durkheim's sociological distinction between the collective and the individual (Doroszewski 1933, noted in Jameson 1972: 27, note 23). Language thus exists as a collective reservoir and is appropriated by the individual users who do not have complete assimilation of all its elements. As Saussure ([1916]: 1974 14) writes: 'For language is not complete in any speaker; it exists perfectly only within a collectivity.' He continues: 'In separating language from speaking we are at the same time separating: (1) what is social from what is individual; and (2) what is essential from what is accessory and more or less accidental' ([1916]: 1974 14).

The next major insight that sets the ground for post-structuralism is the marking out of the parts in language. The radical insight of Saussure was to mark out these parts not in terms of words as such, but in terms of *signs*. The basic element of the sign challenged the natural correspondence between words and things and set up the key notion of the arbitrariness of the sign.

> The bond between the signifier and the signified is arbitrary. Since I mean by sign the whole that results from associating of the signifier with the signified, I can simply say: *the linguistic sign is* arbitrary ... The word *arbitrary* also calls for comment. The term should not imply that the choice of the signifier is left entirely to the speaker ... I mean that it is unmotivated, i.e. arbitrary in that it actually has no natural connection with the signified.
>
> (Saussure [1916] 1974: 67, 69)

This famous assertion means that language is not a clear and transparent set of meanings but a system of signs and their structural relation. The sign has two aspects, the concept or signified (*signifié*) and the sound-image or signifier (*signifiant*). The relation is arbitrary because there is no natural link between – for example – the signifier 'cat' and the concept of the physical animal sitting on the mat (the signified), other than inside the structure of the language. There are two general types of relation between signs, echoing, as Jameson (1972: 37) notes, the diachronic and synchronic. First, the *syntagmatic*, those held in a time sequence as they are positioned alongside other signs (a 'horizontal' link) and, second, the *associative* or 'vertical' link, where there is a link through a shared meaning or sound, such as synonyms. What this technical outline of language indicates is that it is the *relation* between signs that is important. As Saussure indicates: 'language is a form and not a substance' (Saussure [1916] 1974: 122). Language thus depends on the differences and oppositions between signs. Structuralism extends Saussure's insights to other sign systems, such as myth and ritual.

The relationships between the sign and signified opens a key problem of what shapes, or determines, the relation. Jameson's (1972: 102, 106) political consciousness jumps on this dimension within linguistic structuralism and not only makes the point that French structuralists were 'the beneficiaries of a Marxist culture' but also shows how *ideology* rests within the 'idealistic tendencies' of the relation. As Jameson argues: '[I]n practice, all the Structuralists ... *do* tend to presuppose, beyond the sign-system itself, some kind of ultimate reality which, unknowable or not, serves as its most distant object of reference' (109–110). Here we see what will be a central struggle within structuralism: the relation between history and structure and what determines structure. The post-structuralists expose these tensions and this represents one of the radical extensions of the theory.

Structuralism and constructivism: the shift to post-structuralism

The shift to post-structuralism from within structuralism is a complex one and something obfuscated in Anglo-Saxon commentaries. As Dosse (1997: xiii) shows, the public reception of structuralism occurred at a time when it was already in a 'period of deconstruction, dispersion and ebb'. This internal shift reflects something of the very nature of structuralist logic. Although Fredric Jameson (1972: ix) tends to dismiss Piaget as appropriating structuralism, Piaget's wider perspective in the history of ideas surprisingly offers an insight into a more unified extension thesis between structuralism and post-structuralism. He makes the point, from mathematical and scientific domains, that structuralism contains its own *internal* problem that requires an *external* theory. This point arises when he discusses the work of Foucault. In discussion of Foucault's *Les Mots et les choses* (1966) he believes that Foucault's 'corrosive intelligence has performed a work of inestimable value' (Piaget 1968 [1971]: 135), one that supports Piaget's general insight: 'There is no structure apart from constructivism' (Piaget 1968 [1971]: 140).

The logical outcome of structuralism is a question about its own formation and the post-structuralists provide various ways of thinking about this problem. Foucault, like other post-structuralists, takes the structure – the given or what we assume is evident – and questions its assumptions through historical knowledge and the limitations of thinking. In a fascinating alignment of ideas, Piaget (Piaget 1968 [1971]: 13, 33, 135) links such ideas with the philosophy of Kurt Gödel and his 1931 critique of formal mathematics, which provided important insights into the limits of knowledge. According to Piaget, Gödel showed that any system of reasoning cannot demonstrate its own consistency or validity, because it requires a higher system of knowledge outside itself to provide its own justification. There was in the end a 'formally undecidable' nature to knowledge, and the foundation of mathematics. What this meant was that knowledge was 'essentially incomplete' (Piaget [1968] 1971: 33). The link between Gödel and Foucault is an important one in showing how the incompleteness of structure is the 'construction' of 'structure', which for Piaget 'is no longer avoidable' (Piaget 1968 [1971]: 13).

We have already noted in passing that Derrida (1966) was critical of the limitations of the idea of structure. For Derrida contemporary structuralism was an 'event' that asserted a metaphysical centre and presence with the idea of structure. He refers to its historical emergence as the 'structuralist invasion', but resists the historian making it an 'object', because its whole aim was to question how something is perceived and made into an object (Derrida 1963: 3). Derrida reveals the contradictions and tensions inherent not only in metaphysics but also in the metaphysics of structuralist theory. He shows how structuralism privileges the very concepts of sign and structure in a Saussurean displacement of the sign. Derrida's reading of structure shows his resistance and reconfiguration of structuralism. As he argues in his essay on Rousset:

> A structural realism has always been practiced, more or less explicitly. But never has structure been the exclusive *term* – in the double sense of the word – of critical description. It was always a *means* or relationship for reading or writing, for assembling significations, recognising themes, ordering constants and correspondences.
>
> (Derrida 1963: 15)

One tactic Derrida employs to undermine the notion of structure is to show how it operates as a metaphor rather than a thing itself. It constructs a relation rather than discovers it. 'Structuralism', for Derrida (1963: 26), 'lives within and on the difference between its promise and its practice.' For Dosse (1977: 19), Derrida was a paradoxical figure who was both 'inside and outside' structuralism. As Dosse went on to argue: 'But he might just as well have been considered to be the person who pushed the structuralist logic to its limit and toward an even more radical interrogation of all *substantification* or founding essence, in the sense of eliminating the signified.'

Derrida's reading of structuralism shows how the language of Saussure persists in post-structuralism and is made more complex as it is interrogated in different ways. Mark Taylor (1999: 106) aptly captures this critical transition: 'Structures, which seem to be complete, are inevitably constituted by processes of exclusion, which render them unavoidably incomplete.' Derrida, for example, questions the *logocentrism* of Saussure's idea of the sign – that is, the assumption that the world presents itself to consciousness in a clear and transparent manner, that it is immediately present. Derrida's approach is to provide close readings of parts of texts to reveal their incoherence and hidden tensions. He applies his deconstructive reading to the key texts of structuralism (Saussure and Lévi-Strauss), discovering the paradox and limits of their logic and their metaphysic of presence (Derrida [1967] 1976; 1972). In wishing to show how metaphysics holds a 'defense against the threat of writing', Derrida ([1967] 1976: 101–102) questions, for example, the *phonologism* of Lévi-Strauss. Derrida is questioning the priority of speech over writing, because speech gives the illusion of immediacy and presence (from the reality of the spoken word). By showing that speech is a form of writing he questions the opposition of the terms and creates a new set of concepts to explore the implications of this insight. Post-structuralism thus extends structuralism by both pushing and questioning its logic and revealing the inherent construction of structure. Post-structuralist thinking questions the authority of our intellectual assumptions. It extends what Derrida (1963: 3) calls 'an anxiety of language, within language' to its philosophical, historical and political formation.

This critical engagement with structure is the mark of post-structuralism. The historical moment of structuralism disappears when the critique of structuralism is located in a wider epistemological critique. The 'post' of post-structuralism is an intellectual transformation of the language of structuralism, increased, not least, by the student riots in Paris in May 1968 (historic protests against the traditional education system and employment in France that led to a political rethinking of knowledge). As Lacan famously declared: 'If the events of May demonstrated anything at all, they showed that it was precisely that structures had taken to the streets!' (Dosse 1997: 122). The political mutation was already apparent before, in so far as structuralism was always concerned with a hidden logic and relation, but the post-structuralists carry the language of structuralism into wider domains of knowledge. Barthes takes Saussure's linguistic ideas into *ideology* and *semiotics*; Foucault returns structuralism to history and the politics of knowledge; Lacan joins structuralism and psychoanalysis and rethinks the unconscious as language, and Kristeva radicalises structuralism by revealing the semiotics of gender. The post-structuralist literature, as Leonard Jackson (1991: 242) has argued, slowly increased the 'magnitude' of the philosophical claims from Saussure's more limited science.

We can find a way to understand the problem of structuralism and post-structuralism and make sense of post-structuralism in the field of religious studies by framing the discussion in terms of Roland Barthes' 1963 essay 'The Structuralist Activity'. Like Derrida, Barthes sees the 'overworked' nature of the idea of 'structure' and seeks rather to see the idea as an '*activity*', originated by Saussure, rather than a specific 'structuralist work'. The structuralist seeks to 'reconstruct' the object. For Barthes, the structuralist 'makes something appear which remained invisible or, if one prefers, unintelligible in the natural object' (Barthes 1963: 215). Post-structuralism develops this critical 'activity' using the structuralist lexicon but embellishes it within other forms of critical awareness of what Foucault called 'a positive unconscious of knowledge' (Foucault 1966: xi; 1969: 60). The post-structuralist is therefore engaging language, history and ideology in ways Saussure's model restricted critique. It reveals the hidden within the normative.

Post-structuralism and the study of religion

The post-structuralist radicalisation of structuralism provides religious studies with strategies of critique: ways of reading texts (Derrida and Kristeva), ways of exposing ideological structures (Barthes and Foucault), ways of uncovering the historical formation of ideas (Foucault) and ways of revealing hidden desires and the construction of subjectivity (Lacan and Kristeva). The scholars of religion who utilise these strategies – not methods because they are more fragmented – are doing a number of things. First, they are supporting and appealing to the authority of the associated French authors and their ideas, diverse as they may be within the intellectual space of French thought. Second, they are deploying the critical lexicon of these writers to question the assumptions operating in the field. Finally, they are using the ideas to expose the excluded issues within religious studies, not least in the ways we see postcolonial theory appeal to post-structuralism (King 1999a). There are various ways of mapping the critical literature of post-structuralism and the way it pervades scholarship in religious studies but I will map three key domains of this new lexicon for the field of religion: first, language and text; second, history, power and knowledge; and, third, subject and the body.

Language and text: the rethinking of categories

The lexicon of post-structuralism within religious studies is first and foremost an extension of the 'anxiety about language' in a post-Saussurean world. It is the concern about signification and representation and the way the text has become destabilised. In the study of religion in the last twenty years there has been increased critical concern with deployment of basic categories such as 'religion', 'Hinduism' and 'mysticism' as essential unchanging referents, which hold some fixed, natural, stable or essential meaning. Post-structuralists, and Derrida in particular, have supported this critical exercise, although the issues related to the philosophy of language are wider than the post-structuralist turn, as can be seen in Timothy Fitzgerald's *The Ideology of Religious Studies* (2000), which uses a range of analytical categories to make similar critical claims. This underlines how post-structuralism returns us to wider questions of epistemology.

Derrida provides a way of questioning the normative concepts within religious studies by showing how meaning is not present in the text but rather differed in a chain of signification (*différance*) and held by assumptions of power. *Différance* is created from the words 'differential' and 'deferred'; it implies meaning is never fully present in the text. Derrida's thinking therefore allows a disturbance of certainty. As he states in his 1967 study *Of Grammatology*, his intention in the book is to 'make enigmatic what one thinks one understands by the terms "proximity", "immediacy" and "presence"' (Derrida [1967] 1976: 70). Ideas are no longer clear or immediate in use and do not present themselves in a *metaphysics of presence*. Irritating as this may be to those following the dominant systems of knowledge, it has allowed the study of religion to question the hierarchy of meanings and the exclusion of the Other, not least in relation to issues of race, gender and colonialism. In the text we have only what Derrida calls the 'trace': no point of origin, an absence, tensions and the elusive nature of the sign. It is important to realise – to the annoyance of those wanting 'deconstruction' to be a method – that Derrida's readings of texts are not fixed procedures but a way of entering into each text on its own terms and finding within the text the points where it unravels itself. To many this is just a form of relativistic 'play' (a word in which Derrida delights), but it presents profound questions to how we assert various claims and the limits of representation. Derrida's deconstructive reading, as Barbara Johnson (1981: xv) notes, connects what a writer sees to what a writer does not see in their writing. As Johnson continues: 'The critique reads backwards from what seems natural, obvious, self-evident, or universal, in order to show that these things have their history, their reasons for being the way they are, their effects on what follows from them, and that the starting point is not a (natural) given but a (cultural) construct, usually blind to itself' (Johnson 1981: xv–xvi).

The appeal to Derrida has allowed the field of religion to suspend critically many of the accepted terms of the phenomenological tradition and the methods of structuralism, but it also raises important questions about translation. This anxiety about translation can be seen within postcolonial studies. As Mandair (2003: 91) recognises from his context of Sikh studies: 'To invoke the untranslatable is to invoke what Derrida calls the pharmakonomy of deconstruction as a simultaneously destructive/constructive movement.' The idea of the *pharmakon* emerges in Derrida's close reading of Plato's *Phaedrus*, or rather the translators of Plato, because it explores the problem of how the Greek word *pharmakon* can be translated as both 'remedy' and 'poison'. It reflects the fundamental undecidability of the text and in this sense the *pharmakon* is writing. '[T]he *pharmakon*, or if you will, writing, can only go around in circles: writing is only apparently good for memory, seemingly able to help it from within, through its own motion, to know what is true' (Derrida [1972] 2008: 105).

Derrida draws attention to the assumptions within the text and reveals the values behind the meaning of terms, concepts and ideas in the history of philosophy. As Grace Jantzen's (1999: 66) post-structuralist feminist philosophy of religion always makes clear, it requires the critical question of 'whose interests are being served' in the ways we stabilise our knowledge, concepts and terms. Such critique reveals the excluded Other – not least the gendered and culturally excluded. Not surprisingly, Derrida's techniques and his deconstructive approach have also been linked to the limits of knowledge in Buddhist philosophy, negative theology and mysticism (Magliola 1984; Silverman 1989). Since Magliola's (1984) linking of Nagarjuna's philosophy with Derridean deconstruction there has been much debate about the kind of correspondence of Derrida's thinking with Buddhist philosophy. As Coward and Foshay (1992: 227) argue:

> What Derrida says about philosophy, that it 'always re-appropriates for itself the discourse that delimits it', is equally true of Buddhism. Like all religions, Buddhism includes a strong onto-theological element [a theological philosophy about the nature of being], yet it also contains the resources that have repeatedly deconstructed this tendency.

Foucault's thinking has also been linked to non-western philosophical traditions, and wider elements of French post-structuralist thinking remain engaged with negative theology (Bradley 2004). Post-structuralism, therefore, offers not only a critical question of categories and method but a philosophical opportunity for cross-cultural philosophy of religion (King 1999b: 230–244).

History, power and knowledge: the will to authority

If Derrida explores the concealed elements of metaphysics through textual analysis, it is Foucault who exposes the hidden elements of ideas in their 'field of use' (Foucault 1969:

100); that is, in the 'network of institutions' and social structures where they take on their operational power (Foucault 1970: 217). The use of Foucault within the study of religion has been evident since David Chidester's (1986) mapping of his key concepts for the subject. Like Derrida, Foucault maintains the structuralist features within his work, even when he is not bound by its governing rules (Carrette 2000: 88). Foucault's reading of the institutions of madness, medicine and the prison provide various strategies for showing how 'discourses' are instruments of social engineering. Discourses are the practices of institutions. They are 'a body of anonymous historical rules, always determined in the time and space that have defined a given period' (Foucault 1969: 117). Foucault, following in part Heidegger, explores the historical conditions for the ideas governing our lives. He explores how at different moments of history, problems and issues arise as reflections of the orders of power, although power for Foucault is always mobile and non-hierarchical, because it shifts and always involves forms of resistance (Foucault 1976: 92ff).

Echoing structuralism, Foucault called his approach 'archaeological' in the 1960s, to show the layers of historical discourse and the hidden epistemic structures, not unlike Kuhn's paradigms in scientific knowledge. However, under the renewed influence of Nietzsche, in the 1970s he renamed his approach 'genealogical', because he recognised the importance of the 'non-discursive', that is how discourse always takes place within institutions and involved a relation of power mapped onto the body (Foucault 1971). Foucault has enabled scholars of religion to show how concepts are deployed in different historical contexts and how they are related to power and the body. For example, he showed how 'sexuality' was created through the 'deployment' or 'apparatus' (*dispositif*) of a 'subtle network of discourses, special knowledges, pleasures and powers', including the Christian confessional and psychiatric knowledge (Foucault 1976: 71). The complex emergence of ideas of sexuality has led scholars of religion to show how concepts like religion and Hinduism are shaped through what Foucault called a 'complex political technology' (Foucault 1976: 71). Foucault thus breaks the 'positivity' of knowledge; that is, the assumption that knowledge has an essential givenness. In this sense, where Derrida finds logocentrism in the text, Foucault finds it in social order. Here we see how the post-structuralist move is to reveal the hidden order of knowledge.

Foucault also allowed scholars of religion to raise suspicion over the construction of its own disciplinary knowledge. He showed how knowledge is bound by rules of utterance and that there is a sense of permitting and restricting ideas within different domains of thought. As he stated in his augural lecture at the Collège de France in 1970: 'Disciplines constitute a system of control in the production of discourse, fixing its limits through the action of an identity taking the form of a permanent reactivation of the rules.' The field of religious studies thus becomes a system of regulated statements around the object of 'religion'. The institutional domains of the study of religion interact to establish a disciplinary history, a nomenclature, a canon of texts, an agreement of interlocking methods and the codes of textbooks around the idea of religion as an object of study. These disciplinary practices, as Foucault continued in his 1970 lecture, 'exercise a sort of pressure, a power of constraint upon other forms of discourse' (Foucault 1970: 219).

The link between discourse and power is not far from the work of Roland Barthes and his more overt ideological analysis of semiotics (the science of signs) and his critique of the normative concepts of literary criticism. In his 1966 essay *Criticism and Truth*, Barthes marked out the constraints on thought in bourgeois criticism. As he declared: 'What does good taste forbid us to speak of?' (Barthes 1966: 7). According to Barthes, his form of 'new' criticism 'produced' new meanings with a new set of value judgments (Barthes 1966: 32). Barthes's critique provokes questions of method in the study of religion, but his ideological analysis of signs has also had an influence on thinking about myth, not least because of his influential structuralist text *Mythologies* published in 1957 (McCutcheon 2000). Even more than Foucault and Derrida, Barthes bridges both structuralism and post-structuralism. For example, in *Mythologies* we see the same critical lexicon of language, politics and power that Foucault would exploit, but in Barthes there is a distinct Marxist tone.

In *Mythologies* Barthes examined various cultural phenomena in terms of the ideological codes they carried. One such essay, for example, examined the marketing of the new Citroën D.S. 19 car, the *Déesse* (the goddess), introduced at the Paris Motor Show in 1955. The car is transformed from matter, from 'a primitive to a classical' form, in what Barthes calls a 'spiritualisation' of pressed-metal and the 'exaltation' of glass. As Barthes explains: 'We must not forget that an object is the best messenger of a world above that of nature: one can easily see in an object at once a perfection and an absence of origin, a closure and a brilliance, a transformation of life into matter (matter is much more magical than life), and in a word a *silence* which belongs to the realm of fairy-tales' (Barthes [1957] 1973: 88).

Barthes's conclusion to this brief essay indicates the way the goddess is 'mediatised' from the heavens in exhibition halls, but what is 'actualised', for Barthes, is the 'essence of petit-bourgeois advancement' (Barthes [1957] 1973: 90). The bridging of spiritualisation, mediatisation and actualisation are key ideological processes in the advertising of an object. Barthes's association of ideology and spirit in his essay on the Citroën D.S. can be seen as an early critique of marketing and spirituality, which Carrette and King (2005) unfolded in the later context of neo-liberal capitalism. This is another example of how post-structuralism provides a critique of the hidden politic of knowledge in the study of religion.

Subject and the body: the return of the other

Post-structuralist theory in the study of religion has been used to deconstruct texts and expose the alliance of power-knowledge inside institutions, but wrapped inside these critical perceptions is how post-structuralism brings increased awareness to the dynamics that shape subjectivity and the body. These ideas have been explored most powerfully in the post-structuralist feminist theory of Judith Butler (1990) who reveals the important relation between power, subjectivity and agency. Following Butler, Saba Mahmood (2005) uses Foucault's 'paradox of subjectification' – that is, the capacity of power to subject one to authority and create skills of ethical response – to read the ethical-political nature of Muslim women of Egypt. While Foucault's thinking has had a significant impact on studies of the body and religion (Turner 1991; Boyarin 1997), scholars of religion, in line with feminist writers, have turned to the psychoanalytically informed post-structuralist writings of Jacques Lacan and Julia Kristeva to make sense of the complexity of religious practices.

Jacques Lacan linked Saussure with Freud and inverted Saussure's signifier and signified to reinvigorate psychoanalytical ideas in France with his claim that 'what the psychoanalytical experience discovers in the unconscious is the whole structure of language' (Lacan [1966] 1977: 147). While, according to Nobus (2003: 53ff), Lacan's 'erroneous' reading of Saussure had more to do with Lévi-Strauss than Saussure, it enabled Lacan to react against ego-psychology and unfold a divided subject. Lacanian theory also reshaped psychoanalysis with the concepts 'Symbolic' (the order of language, social and cultural symbolism), 'Imaginary' (the order of phantasies and images) and the 'Real' (the impossible to represent, that which goes through you, throws you out of yourself). It provided a new meta-theory for reading the orders of domination and suppression in religious subjectivity, not least seen in later feminist deployments (see Joy *et al.* 2003).

Rejecting ego-psychology, Lacan showed how identity was divided as other, through the 'mirror stage', between six and eighteen months, where recognition is given through the other person (the mother) and our construction through the Symbolic order of language. There is a double edge to language. Speech, as Lacan noted, 'is founded in the existence of the Other, the true one, language is so made as to return us to the objectified other ...' (Lacan [1978] 1991: 244). The divided subject of Lacan is extended by Kristeva to recover a gendered and embodied political order. For Kristeva, the self is linguistic (the Symbolic) but also pre-lingustic (embodied), which she maps out in her idea of the semiotic. In her critical project the semiotic is linked with Plato's idea of the *chora* (the receptacle, a space where forms materialise) in the *Timaeus*; it is the pre-linguistic and pre-Oedipal which disrupts but is inseparable from the Symbolic order of Lacan (Kristeva 1974: 94; 1980: 133). The semiotic carries something prior to the Symbolic order and brings back a maternal and embodied dimension (Kristeva 1974: 94). This uncovering of an underlying container led Kristeva to define her approach of *semanalysis* as trying 'to describe the signifying phenomenon, or signifying phenomena, while analysing, criticising, and dissolving 'phenomenon', 'meaning' and 'signifier'' (Kristeva 1980: vii). This dissolving was also at the heart of the individual subject. According to Kristeva, we are subjects in 'process, ceaselessly losing our identity, destabilised by fluctuations in our relation to the other, to whom we nevertheless remain bound by a kind of homeostasis [a balanced regulation]' (Kristeva 1987: 9).

After her initial works on semiotics, Kristeva addressed more directly questions of religious history and thought. For example, in her 1982 work *Powers of Horror* she argued that her notion of abjection (the somatic and symbolic feeling of revulsion) 'accompanies all religious structurings and appears to be worked out in a new guise at the time of their collapse' (1982: 17). The fascination with religious thinking can be seen in much post-structuralist literature (see, for example, Foucault 1999 and Derrida 2002) and it creates not only a double analysis (the use of theoretical ideas to read religion and the use of religion by post-structuralists), but a double critique of post-structuralism. Hollywood (2002) and Jantzen (1999), for example, are critical of the gendered analysis within Lacan's *Seminar XX* (1974), where he explores female 'jouissance' (the ecstatic beyond enjoyment/pleasure) and St Teresa of Avila. The very conceptual space of post-structuralism facilitates a critique of the categories of religion and gender deployed by post-structuralists. As Kristeva ([1969] 1986: 77–78) argued in an early essay on semiotics: 'Semiotic research remains a form of enquiry that ultimately uncovers its own ideological gesture, only in order to record and deny it before starting all over again.' The self-reflexive critique remains the hallmark of post-structuralism and opens knowledge to its temporary and provisional nature.

The future challenge to religious studies

We have seen that scholars of religion employ a range of ideas and theories from the key thinkers associated with French post-structuralism and it is therefore important to recognise the distinctive contribution to the field and understand what is at stake in engaging with this set of ideas. As I have already highlighted, it is my argument in this essay that what underlies all these theories is a central question of epistemology. This confirms that while these questions emerge in 1960s France under a renewed political and intellectual context, they are evident in a longer tradition of critical thinking from the Enlightenment and indeed could be seen to reflect longer philosophical concerns with knowledge.

The shift from, or rather extension of, structuralism to post-structuralism is not just something that occurs in the texts of Derrida and Foucault on the Left Bank of Paris; it is not just the decentring of Saussure's sign or the deconstructing of Lévi-Strauss's phonologism. The shift from structuralism to post-structuralism is the constant activity of critique. It is to suspend the structures we construct to critique the structures we despise as constructions. Critique demands that we unravel what we do not see in our activity of seeing. It demands we constantly enact the ritual of disappearance. But this is not disappearance into the quagmire of relativism; it is the constant critique of change within life itself, which seeks the justice of greater understanding. It demands that we root out the tendency within us to build intellectual empires which blind to us to what we conceal in the assertion of our authority. Post-structuralism is a particular historical moment of critique but its critical strategies become waves of the impulse to yet more unravelling of the unseen in every new age of thought. Foucault and Derrida moved beyond the sign of post-structuralism as they found greater refinements of their thinking, but what remains is critique, endowed to us from the Enlightenment. As Foucault (1984: 42) underlined: 'I have been seeking to stress that the thread that may connect us with the Enlightenment is not faithfulness to doctrinal elements, but rather the permanent reactivation of an attitude – that is, of a philosophical ethos that could be described as a permanent critique of our historical era.'

Post-structuralism gives renewed energy to the critique of knowledge and practice in the study of religion. In the end what post-structuralism marks out in the history of ideas is the end of innocence. After this point the study of religion can no longer hide its own value judgements, investments and interests. It can no longer disguise its neutrality in terms of gender, culture, power, and ideology. Post-structuralism is the critical consciousness of our time, disturbing forever what we do not see in the knowledge claims of the study of religion.

Bibliography

Almond, I. 2004 *Sufism and Deconstruction: A Comparative Study of Derrida and Ibn'Arabi* (London: Routledge) .

Anderson, K. 1989 'Towards a New Reason: Guilt, Language and Nature in the Work of Roland Barthes and Francis Ponge' in *Ideology and Religion in French Literature: Essay in Honour of Brian Juden* ed. Cockerham, H. and Ehrman, E. (Camberley, Surrey: Porphyrogenitus).

Antes, P., Geertz, A. W. and Warne, R. R. eds. 2008 *New Approaches to the Study of Religion 2: Textual, Comparative, Sociological and Cognitive Approaches* (Berlin: Walter de Gruyter).

Barthes, R. [1957] 1973 *Mythologies* (London: Grafton Books).

Barthes, R. 1963 'The Structuralist Activity' in *Critical Essays* (Evanston: Northwestern University Press, 1972) pp.213–220.

Barthes, R. [1966] 2007 *Criticism and Truth* (London: Continuum) .

Bhogal, B. S. 2007 'Ghostly Disorientations: Translating the Adi Granth as the Guru Granth' in *Sikh Formations: Religion, Culture, Theory* Vol. 3; No.1, June 2007, pp.13–31.

Boyarin, D. 1996 *Thinking in Jewish* (Chicago: University of Chicago Press).

Boyarin, D. 1997 *Unheroic Conduct: The Rise of Heterosexuality and the Invention of Jewish Man* (Berkeley: University of California Press).

Bradley, A. 2004 *Negative Theology and Modern French Philosophy* (London: Routledge).

Braun, W. and McCutcheon, R. 2000 *Guide to the Study of Religion* (London: Cassell).

Butler, J. 1990 *Gender Trouble* (New York: Routledge).

Caputo, J. 1997 *The Prayers and Tears of Jacques Derrida: Religion Without Religion* (Indiana University Press).

Carrette, J. 2000 *Foucault and Religion: Spiritual Corporality and Political Spirituality* (London: Routledge).

Carrette, J. 2007 *Religion and Critical Psychology: Religious Experience in the Knowledge Economy* (London; Routledge).

Carrette, J. and King, R. 2005 *Selling Spirituality: The Silent Takeover of Religion* (London: Routledge).

Chidester, D. 1986 'Michel Foucault and the Study of Religion' in *Religious Studies Review*, Vol.12, No. 1, pp.1–9.

Coward, H. G. 1990 *Derrida and Indian Philosophy* (Albany, NY: SUNY Press).

Coward, H. and Foshay, T. 1992 *Derrida and Negative Theology* (Albany, NY: SUNY Press).

Derrida 1963 'Force and Signification' in Derrida [1967] 1990 pp.3–30.

Derrida, J. 1966 'Structure, Sign and Play in the Discourse of the Human Sciences' in Derrida [1967] 1990 pp.278-293.

Derrida, J. [1967] 1976 *Of Grammatology* (Baltimore: Johns Hopkins University Press).

Derrida, J. [1967] 1990 *Writing and Difference* (London: Routledge).

Derrida, J. [1972] 2008 *Dissemination* (London: Continuum).

Derrida, J. 2002 *Acts of Religion* ed. Gil Anidjar (London: Routledge).

Doroszewski, W. 1933 'Quelques remarques sur les rapports de la sociologie et de la linguistique: Durkheim et F. de Saussure' in *Journal de psychologie*, Vol. xxx (1933), pp.82–91.

Dosse, F. 1997 *History of Structuralism: Volume 2 The Sign Sets, 1967–Present* (Minneapolis: University of Minnesota Press).

Faure, B. 1998 *The Red Thread: Buddhist Approaches to Sexuality* (Princeton, NJ:, Princeton University Press).

Fitzgerald, T. 2000 *The Ideology of Religious Studies* (New York: Oxford University Press).

Flood, G. 1999 *Beyond Phenomenology: Rethinking the Study of Religion* (London: Cassell).

Foucault, M. 1966 *The Order of Things: An Archaeology of the Human Sciences* (London,: Routledge, 1991).

Foucault, M. 1969 *The Archaeology of Knowledge* (London: Routledge, 1991).

Foucault, M. 1970 'The Discourse on Language' in *The Archaeology of Knowledge* (New York: Pantheon) pp.215–237.

Foucault, M. 1971 'Nietzsche, Genealogy, History' in Michel Foucault *Language, Counter-Memory, Practice: Selected Essays and Interviews* ed. Donald Bouchard (Ithaca, NY: Cornell University Press).

Foucault, M. 1976 *The History of Sexuality Volume 1: An Introduction* (London: Penguin, 1990).

Foucault, M. 1999 *Religion and Culture* selected and edited by Jeremy Carrette (Manchester: Manchester University Press).

Goodchild, P. ed. 2003 *Difference in Philosophy of Religion* (Aldershot, Hants: Ashgate).

Hart, K. 1989 *The Trespass of the Sign: Deconstruction, Theology and Philosophy* (Cambridge: Cambridge University Press).

Hawkes, T. 1977 *Structuralism and Semiotics* (London: Methuen).

Hollywood, A. 2002 *Sensible Ecstasy: Mysticism, Sexual Difference and the Demands of History* (Chicago: University of Chicago Press).

Jackson, L. 1991 *The Poverty of Structuralism: Literature and Structuralist Theory* (London: Longman).

Jameson, F. 1972 *The Prison-House of Language: A Critical Account of Structuralism and Russian Formalism* (Princeton, NJ: Princeton University Press).

Jantzen, G. 1995 *Power, Gender and Christian Mysticism* (Cambridge: Cambridge University Press).

Jantzen, G. 1998 *Becoming Divine: Towards a Feminist Philosophy of Religion* (Manchester: Manchester University Press).

Johnson, B. 1981 'Translator's Introduction' in Derrida, J. [1972] 2008 *Dissemination* (London: Continuum) pp.vii–xxxv.

Jonte-Pace, D. 2001 *Speaking the Unspeakable: Religion, Misogyny and the Uncanny Mother in Freud's Cultural Texts* (Berkeley: University of California Press).

Joy, M. 2006 *Divine Love: Luce Irigaray, Women, Gender and Religion* (Manchester: Manchester University Press).

Joy, M., O'Grady, K. and Poxon, J.L. ed. 2003 *Religion in French Feminist Thought: Critical Perspectives* (London: Routledge).

King, R. 1999a *Orientalism and Religion: Post-Colonial Theory, India and the Mystic East* (London; Routledge).

King, R. 1999b *Indian Philosophy: An Introduction to Hindu and Buddhist Thought* (Edinburgh: Edinburgh University Press).

Kristeva, J. 1969 'Semiotics: A Critical Science and/or a Critique of Science' in *The Kristeva Reader* ed. Toril Moi 1986(Oxford: Blackwell) pp.74–88.

Kristeva, J. 1974 'Revolution in Poetic Language' in *The Kristeva Reader* ed. Toril Moi 1986 (Oxford: Blackwell) pp.89–136.

Kristeva, J. 1980 *Desire in Language: A Semiotic Approach to Literature and Art* (Oxford: Basil Blackwell).

Kristeva, J. 1982 *Powers of Horror: An Essay on Abjection* (New York: Columbia University Press).

Kristeva, J. 1987 *In the Beginning Was Love: Psychoanalysis and Faith* (New York: Columbia University Press).

Lacan, J. [1966] 1977 *Écrits: A Selection* (London: Tavistock).

Lacan, J. [1974] 1998 *Encore, the Seminar of Jacques Lacan Book* (New York: Norton).

Lacan, J. [1978] 1991 *The Seminar of Jacque Lacan Book 2: The Ego in Freud's Theory and in the Technique of Psychoanalysis 1954–1955*, Miller, J-A. ed. (New York: W.W. Norton & Company).

Lehmann, J. M. 1993 *Deconstructing Durkheim: A Post-post-structuralist Critique* (London: Routledge).

Lévi-Strauss, C. [1958] 1963 *Structural Anthropology* (New York: Basic Books).

McCance, D. 'New Approaches: Literary Theory' in Antes, Geertz, and Warne (2008) pp.59–73.

McCutcheon, R. 1997 *Manufacturing Religion: The Discourser on Sui Generis Religion and the Politics of Nostalgia* (Oxford & New York: Oxford University Press).

Magliola, R. 1984 *Derrida on the Mend* (West Lafayette, IN: Purdue University Press).

Mahmood, S. 2005 *The Politics of Piety: The Islamic Revival and the Feminist Subject* (Princeton, New Jersey: Princeton University Press).

Mandair, A. 2006 'The Politics of Nonduality: Reassessing the Work of Transcendence in Modern Sikh Theology' in *Journal of the American Academy of Religion* September 2006, Vol. 74, No. 3, pp.646–673.

Mandair, A-P., Shackle, C. and Singh, G. 2001 *Sikh Religion, Culture and Ethnicity* (Richmond, Surrey: Curzon Press).

Moore, S. D. 1994 *Poststructuralism and the New Testament: Derrida and Foucault at the Foot of the Cross* (Minneapolis: Augsburg Fortress).

Nobus, D. 2003 'Lacan's Science of the Subject: Between Linguistics and Topology' in *The Cambridge Companion to Lacan* ed. J-M Rabaté 2003 (Cambridge: Cambridge University Press), pp.50–68.

Piaget 1968 [1971] *Structuralism* London: Routledge, Kegan and Paul.

Saussure, F. [1916] 1974 *Course in General Linguistics* (London: Peter Owen).

Sherwood, Y. ed. 2004 *Derrida's Bible: Reading a Page of Scripture with a Little Help from Derrida* (London: Palgrave Macmillan).

Silverman, H. J. ed. 1989 *Derrida and Deconstruction* (New York: Routledge).

Sturrock, J. ed. 1979 *Structuralism and Since: From Lévi-Strauss to Derrida* (Oxford: Oxford University Press).

Sturrock, J. 1993 *Structuralism* (London: Fontana Press).

Taylor, M. ed. 1998 *Critical Terms for Religious Studies* (Chicago: University of Chicago Press).

Taylor, M. 1999 *About Religion: Economies of Faith in Virtual Culture* (Chicago: University of Chicago Press).

Turner, B. 1991 *Religion and Social Theory* (2nd edition) (London: Sage) .

Urban, H. 2003 *Tantra: Sex, Secrecy, Politics and Power in the Study of Religion* (Berkeley: University of California Press).

Ward, G. 1997 *The Postmodern God* (Oxford: Blackwell).

Ward, G. 2000 *Theology and Contemporary Critical Theory* (London: Palgrave Macmillan)

Suggested reading

Derrida, J. 1963 'Force and signification' in Derrida 1963, pp 3–30.

This text provides a useful point of access to the strategies Derrida employs to question structuralist thinking, in this case the work of Lévi-Strauss.

Foucault, M. 1970 'The Discourse on Language' in *The Archaeology of Knowledge* (New York: Pantheon) pp.215–237.

Foucault's inaugural lecture at the Collège de France in 1970 is a useful introduction to the rules behind disciplinary thinking. It shows the restrictions and limits of a discourse.

Kristeva, J. 1969 'Semiotics: A Critical Science and/or a Critique of Science' in *The Kristeva Reader* ed. Toril Moi 1986 (Oxford: Blackwell) pp.74–88.

This essay by Kristeva shows the way knowledge questions its own structures and illustrates clearly how Saussure's method is extended and developed by post-structuralists.

Sturrock, J. ed. 1979 *Structuralism and Since: From Lévi-Strauss to Derrida* (Oxford: Oxford University Press).

This introduction to the key post-structuralist thinkers is one of the most accessible secondary commentaries, providing outlines of Barthes, Foucault, Lacan and Derrida.

Chapter 17

Orientalism and the study of religions

Richard King

Introduction

How often have you watched a news report on television, read a newspaper article or been exposed to an advertisement conveying some image of 'Eastern' culture? Whether it is a scene of crowds of angry Muslims burning an American flag, a shaven-headed Buddhist monk clothed in a saffron robe and quietly meditating, militant Hindus attacking a mosque or a billboard promoting a perfume that evokes the 'mystic sensuality' of India, what all of these images have in common is their involvement in a long history of Western representations and stereotypes of Asia as an 'other' – that is as essentially different from the West. One consequence of such images, whether positive or negative in their connotations, is that 'we' (the West) become clearly separated from 'them' (the East). The acceptance of a basic opposition between Eastern and Western cultures characterizes what has been called 'Orientalism.'

Indeed images of the East have often functioned as a means of defining the cultural identity of the West, however differently that has been conceived throughout history. The Christian identity of medieval Europe was bolstered by concerns about the incursion of Turkish Muslims. In the eighteenth and nineteenth centuries, Asia represented both a mysterious and timeless realm of wisdom and spirituality, but also the site of unspeakable social depravities and primitive religious practices. In this regard the West was able to comfort itself that it was progressive, civilized and thoroughly modern in contrast to an ahistorical and unchanging Orient. Widespread beliefs about the indolent and despotic nature of Oriental societies also justified a Western sense of superiority and the belief that it was the duty of the West to civilize the savage and aid the Oriental in their progression away from tradition and dogmatism and towards modernity and civilization. In the modern era, whether it is the threat of the 'yellow peril' (Chinese communism) in the 1970s, or the militant Islamic fundamentalist of the 1980s and 1990s, the West has always maintained its own sense of cultural identity by contrasting itself with a radically different 'Orient'.

The latter part of the twentieth century has seen the demise of Western political rule of Asia and the emergence of countries such as India, Pakistan and Sri Lanka as independent nation-states. The British Empire, for instance, has become the British Commonwealth. However, many still question whether the world has really entered a 'post-colonial' era, arguing that Western political, economic and cultural dominance represents continuity rather than a fundamental break with the colonial past. Are we living today in a *post*-colonial or a *neo*-colonial age? Although the influence of Britain and the rest of Europe has receded to a significant degree since the end of the Second World War, it is clear that with the demise of Eastern European communism, the United States of America is the new global power in the West. Capitalism, consumerism and multi-national corporations continue to influence an increasingly global marketplace. Western dominance is apparent not only on an economic and political level, but on a cultural one also, having an inevitable impact upon traditional beliefs and practices in non-Western societies. What are we to make of the cultural impact of the 'new technologies'? When American television soap operas are beamed into middle-class Asian homes via satellite, punctuated by advertisements for Coca-Cola and McDonald's, where does one draw the line between the modernization of Asia and its Westernization? Is the 'global network' of cyberspace a realm in which Asian and Western cultures can meet as equal participants in a worldwide celebration of human diversity or does the rhetoric of 'globalization' mask the continued dominance of 'the rest' by the West?

What is Orientalism?

Orientalism refers to the long-standing Western fascination with the East and the tendency to divide the world up into East and West, with the East acting as a kind of mirror or foil by which Western culture defines itself. The question of the complicity between Western scholarly study of Asia – the discipline of Orientalism, and the imperialistic aspirations of Western nations – became a subject of considerable attention in Western academic circles after the publication of Edward Said's work, *Orientalism* (1978). In this book, Said offered a stinging indictment of Western conceptions of and attitudes towards the Orient. According to Said 'Orientalism' refers to three inter-related phenomena (1978: 2–3):

1   the academic study of the Orient;
2   a mind-set or 'style of thought' founded upon a rigid dichotomy of 'East' and 'West';
3   the corporate institution authorized to dominate, control and subjugate the peoples and cultures of the East.

For Said the mutual intersection of these three dimensions of Orientalism demonstrates the complicity between Western discourses about the Orient and Western colonialism. Orientalism then is primarily a 'Western style for dominating, restructuring, and having authority over the Orient' (Said 1978: 3). Although credit has usually been given to Said for highlighting this dimension of the Orientalist enterprise, his work was certainly not the first to suggest complicity between scholarly analysis of the East and Western imperialist aspirations. Said's work is also clearly indebted to earlier studies (Schwab 1950; Pannikar 1959; Abdel-Malek 1963; Steadman 1970).

The study of religion, both in the concern to explore comparative and cross-cultural issues and themes, and in the more specific attempt to understand and examine the religions and cultures of Asia, has had a seminal role to play in the development of Western conceptions of and attitudes towards the Orient, particularly from the nineteenth century onwards. Western intellectual interest in the religions of the East developed in a context of Western political dominance and colonial expansionism. It is perhaps surprising then to discover that it is only in recent years that the discipline of religious studies has begun to take seriously the political implications and issues involved when Western scholars and institutions claim the authority to represent and speak about the religions and cultures of others. Recent collections of scholarly articles such as *Orientalism and the Post-colonial Predicament* (1993) and *Curators of the Buddha* (1995), explore the impact of Western colonialism upon South Asia and the study of Buddhism respectively. Such developments have occurred in response to the growing post-colonial agenda to be found in other academic disciplines such as literary studies, anthropology and history. Specific studies such as Philip Almond's *The British Discovery of Buddhism* (1988), Talal Asad's *Genealogies of Religion* (1993) and Richard King's *Orientalism and Religion* (1999) have taken up the mantle left by Edward Said and applied it to the disciplines of Buddhist Studies (Almond), anthropology (Asad) and religious studies/ Indology (King). It is likely that the trend toward post-colonial approaches to the study of religion will continue, if only because the issues highlighted by such an orientation remain central to international politics and debates about globalization, modernity and the future of cross-cultural analysis in a post-colonial world.

Knowledge and power

Edward Said (1935–2003) was a diaspora Palestinian educated according to Western conventions and standards. He was a professor of English and Comparative Literature at Columbia University from 1963 until his death in 2003. This background in Western literary studies is reflected in Said's work, which displays the influence of a number of Western theorists and writers, most notably the French poststructuralist Michel Foucault (1926–84). The importance of Foucault in this context resides in his comprehensive analysis of the relationship between power and knowledge. In a number of critical studies on the history of madness, the birth of the clinic and the history of sexuality in the West, Foucault argued that all claims to knowledge involve an attempt to establish a particular set of power relations. Foucault described his method as a 'genealogy of knowledge' (supplementing what he describes in his earlier works as an 'archaeology of knowledge'). This involves an examination of the socio-historical roots of an ideology or institution in order to highlight the ways in which certain groups within society have constructed discourses which have promoted their own authority (Carrette 1999).

The impact of Foucault's work has grown as postmodernist and poststructuralist approaches have gained support in contemporary academic circles. Critics of Foucault's approach have questioned his apparently relativistic stance towards all knowledge and truth claims. Foucault seems to be arguing not just that knowledge is always associated with power, but that knowledge *is* power, i.e. that what we call knowledge is merely a manifestation or reflection of the will-to-power within any given society. It is this aspect of his approach, clearly influenced by the German philosopher Friedrich Nietzsche (1844–1900), which has drawn the fiercest criticism of his work, with the suggestion that Foucault's approach makes it impossible to establish any definitive truth about the nature of reality. From Foucault's perspective the concern is to overturn the modern ideal of an objective and value-free knowledge of universally applicable truths. But as other critics have argued there are many notions of truth at work in Foucault's writings (Prado 1995: 119). Nevertheless, in place of the notion of absolute and universal 'truths', Foucault advocates an approach that focuses upon a diversity of localized 'truths' and a concern to explore their complicity with power structures within that specific locality. Thus, for Foucault:

> Truth is a thing of this world: it is produced only by virtue of multiple forms of constraint. And it induces regular effects of power. Each society has its own régime of truth, its

'general politics' of truth: that is, the types of discourse which it accepts and makes function as true.

(Foucault 1977, translation in Gordon 1980: 131)

Said found Foucault's analysis and his equation of power and knowledge useful conceptual tools for articulating his own conception of Orientalism as the West's exercising of its will-to-power over the East. He remained unwilling, however, to adopt Foucault's general stance since it seemed to allow no room for ethical judgements based upon universal truths and humanistic principles. Moreover, if there is no truth 'out there' one can offer no basis for a critique of Western representations of the Orient on the basis of their *unrepresentative* nature. Thus, Said argued that:

> It would be wrong to conclude that the Orient was *essentially* an idea, or a creation with no corresponding reality … But the phenomenon of Orientalism as I study it here deals principally, not with a correspondence between Orientalism and Orient, but with the internal consistency of Orientalism and its ideas about the Orient (the East as career) despite or beyond any correspondence, or lack thereof, with a 'real' Orient.

(Said 1978: 5)

The truth is out there or is it?

The ambiguities of Said's analysis and methodology have been a central theme of many of the responses to his work. Some critics have argued that *Orientalism* reflects theoretical inconsistencies in Said's account (al-'Azm 1981; Lewis 1982; Clifford 1988; Ahmed 1992), with the author arguing on the one hand that 'the Orient' is constructed in Western imaginations and yet attacking Western characterizations of the East as misrepresentations of a real Orient 'out there'. Other reviewers have celebrated such ambiguities as deliberately disruptive and anti-theoretical (Behdad 1994; Prakash 1995), a position that Said himself came to endorse when reflecting, some years later, upon his own work (Said 1995: 340). Indeed, Said's reluctance to offer an alternative representation of 'the Orient' is grounded in his firmly held belief that the division between 'East' and 'West' is an act of the imagination, and a pernicious one at that. This, however, does not mean that the social and human realities that these images of 'the Orient' are meant to refer to are also imaginary. Far from it, it is precisely because representations of the Orient are essentially imaginary that they can be said to be unrepresentative of the diversity of Asian peoples and cultures (King 1999: 209). Said's challenge to his successors, therefore, is to find alternative and ever more nuanced ways of representing cultural diversity to replace those founded upon a simplistic and oppositional logic of 'Occident vs. Orient' – of 'us' and 'them':

> Can one divide human reality, as indeed human reality seems to be genuinely divided, into clearly different cultures, histories, traditions, societies, even races, and survive the consequences humanly? By surviving the consequences humanly, I means to ask whether there is any way of avoiding the hostility expressed by the division, say of men into 'us' (Westerners) and 'they' (Orientals).

(Said 1978: 45)

Other scholars, however, have been more willing to embrace a postmodernist or poststructuralist view of knowledge, with its rejection of any unproblematic appeal to a reality 'out there' beyond the play of representations. Anthropologist Ronald Inden, for instance, agrees with Foucault in rejecting a representational view of knowledge. There is no privileged or unmediated access to reality.

> [K]nowledge of the knower is not a disinterested mental representation of an external, natural reality. It is a construct that is always situated in a world apprehended through specific knowledges and motivated by practices in it. What is more, the process of knowing actively participates in producing and transforming the world that it constructs intellectually.
>
> (Inden 1990: 33)

Inden maintains that the study of South Asia has been based upon a misleading search for essences such as 'the Hindu mind,' 'the Indian village,' 'caste' and 'divine kingship' – as if entire cultures could be represented by such basic categories. These approaches also imply that the Western scholar has some special ability to discern the central features of Asian cultures in a way that is unavailable to Asians themselves. Inden advocates the abandonment of approaches that search for cultural essences and 'fundamental natures' because they ignore historical change and cultural diversity and therefore provide stereotypes of Asian culture. In their place Inden proposes an emphasis upon the historical agency of indigenous Asians. This approach, he suggests, would avoid the tendency to conceive of the Orient as an unchanging and timeless realm – as if Asian cultures and peoples were *subject to* rather than *agents of* historical change. The critical response to Inden's work has been varied. Some scholars have questioned his universal indictment of Western scholarship on the East as an example of the very essentialism that he attacks: 'If, as Inden says, India and the Indians were "essentialized" by the Indologists, it is certainly no less true and obvious that Indology and Indologists are being essentialized by his own sweeping statements' (Halbfass 1997: 19).

Other critics such as the Marxist literary theorist Aijaz Ahmad (1991) worry that Inden's appeal to indigenous agency lends itself too easily to appropriation by right wing Hindu groups in contemporary India. Indeed, the work of scholars such as Robert Sharf (1994; 1995) and King (1999) demonstrate that indigenous spokesmen for Asian religious traditions, such as D. T. Suzuki (Zen Buddhism) and Swami Vivekananda (Hinduism) were implicated in their own forms of 'internal colonialism' in the manner in which they represented their respective religious traditions at home and abroad. Moreover, many scholars have highlighted Western colonial influences upon contemporary forms of Hindu nationalism and communalism (Pandey 1990; Thapar 1992; Chatterjee 1986; van der Veer 1994).

Questions have also been raised about the poststructuralist theory of knowledge expounded by Inden. Is it possible, following Inden, to make any sort of appeal to a 'real India' underlying the various representations of it? In a similar fashion David Ludden criticizes Edward Said for believing that 'there is to be found in the East a real truth' (1993: 271). What we are dealing with are more or less powerful images of the Orient and not a 'real Orient' out there. Indologists such as Wilhelm Halbfass (1997: 16–17) have been quick to reject this approach on the grounds that it is self-refuting. Such a claim, he argues, prevents any critique of Orientalism based upon the misleading and *unrepresentative* nature of Orientalist accounts. How can one offer a critique of representations if there is no way of appealing to a real Orient or India 'out there'?

Orientalism in South Asia: the Asiatic Society of Bengal

Such has been the influence of Said's work in the decades succeeding the publication of his study that 'Orientalism' has now become a pejorative term, suggesting academic complicity with Western colonialism, rather than a neutral designation for the Western study of the East. For critics such as Bernard Lewis and David Kopf, Said's work has meant that the term 'Orientalist' is now 'polluted beyond salvation' (Lewis 1982: 50), representing 'a sewer category for all the intellectual rubbish Westerners have exercised in the global marketplace of ideas' (Kopf 1980: 498). Indeed before the publication of Said's study, the term 'Orientalism' had a specific meaning in a South Asian context, referring to the academic discipline which came into being as a result of the work of Sir William Jones, judge of the East India Company. Orientalism began with the formal establishment of the Asiatic Society of Bengal in Calcutta in 1784. The administrative and academic work of the Asiatic Society has been credited as the prime instigator for the Bengali Renaissance, a resurgence of intellectual interest in Hindu culture and reform among the Hindu intelligentsia of Bengal in the nineteenth century.

William Jones, the first President of the Asiatic Society of Bengal, is best known for his early work on Sanskrit – the ancient sacred language of the Hindus. Jones was a founding father of comparative linguistics and established links between Sanskrit and the European family of languages. In this sense he was an important catalyst for the explosion of interest in the cultural splendor of India's past, and also in the Romanticist tendency to conceive of India as the cradle of European civilization. Indeed under the influence of Romanticism India increasingly functioned as the canvas upon which a number of idealized representations and images were painted in the eighteenth and nineteenth centuries. India represented 'the childhood of humanity', an image which had positive as well as negative connotations. For the German writer Schlegel, India was 'the real source of all tongues, of all thoughts and utterances of the human mind. Everything – yes, everything without exception has its origin in India' (cited in Iyer 1965: 194). For his contemporary the German philosopher G. W. F. Hegel, however, the infantile nature of Indian culture meant that it had nothing to teach Europeans about modernity. India remained lost in an ancient fog of unprogressive mythologies and superstitions.

The Anglicists and the Orientalists

Assessment of the role, impact and motivations of Western Orientalists in India has become a subject of considerable debate in South Asian studies in response to Said's indictment of the Orientalist project. Historian David Kopf suggests that Said has missed his target with reference to the South Asian context. The Asiatic Society of Bengal, far from being a handmaiden to European colonialism, 'helped Indians to find an indigenous identity in the modern world' (Kopf 1980: 498). Early Orientalist scholarship on India, Kopf argues, was overwhelmingly attracted to and fascinated by its object, and defended the study of the indigenous traditions and languages of Asia when criticized by anti-Orientalist groups such as the Anglicists. This latter group, best exemplified by Thomas Babington Macauley (1800–59), argued that the most expedient means of educating Indians was to introduce them to Western ideas and literature and to teach these through the medium of the English language. Babington believed that 'a single shelf of a good European library was worth the whole native literature of India and Arabia', a view that he claimed would not be refuted by the Orientalists themselves. In his famous 'Minute on Indian Education' (1835) Macauley declared his vision for the transformation of India under British imperial rule:

We must at present do our best to form a class who may be interpreters between us and the millions whom we govern; a class of persons, Indian in blood and colour, but English in taste, in opinions, in morals, and in intellect.

(Harlow and Carter 1999: 59)

Affirmative Orientalism

Kopf contrasts the attitude of Anglicists such as Macauley with the more enthusiastic and positive attitude towards India to be found in the writings of Orientalists such as Sir William Jones, Max Müller and Henry Thomas Colebrooke. The ensuing debate between these two positions, he argues, demonstrates the diversity of motivations and attitudes towards India at this time. Said's sweeping generalizations about the complicity of Orientalist scholarship with a Western colonial agenda wildly overstep the mark. Many Western Orientalists were often deeply sympathetic towards the object of their study (Clifford 1988; Fox 1992). Richard G. Fox argues, for instance, that Said's own analysis ignores the fact that 'resistance to Orientalist domination proceeds from within it' (Fox 1992: 153). A similar point is made by Bernard Lewis when he argues that 'The most rigorous and penetrating critique of Orientalist scholarship has always been and will remain that of the Orientalists themselves' (Lewis 1982: 56). However, as Ulrike Freitag notes, this response by Lewis reiterates 'the exclusivist Orientalist stance'. This only serves to reconfirm 'the idea that only outsiders – that is, Orientalists – could really represent "rhe Orient" and [are] the only ones competent to review their own scholarship' (Freitag 1997: 630).

Despite its obvious fascination and affirmation of Oriental culture, Ronald Inden (1990) describes examples of 'affirmative Orientalism' as 'the Loyal Opposition' precisely because they do not question the basic opposition between Eastern and Western cultures that underlies the Orientalist enterprise. Many of the stereotypical presuppositions of the Orientalist project remain intact, even if treated sympathetically. What this demonstrates is that it is misleading to see the critique of Orientalism initiated by scholars such as Said and Inden as a simple rejection of the negativity of Western attitudes towards the East. The love affair that Western Romanticism has had with the Orient (and which persists to this day in New Age conceptions of 'eastern mysticism and philosophy') is equally problematic because it continues to represent the diversity of Oriental cultures in terms of homogenized stereotypes.

Furthermore, in India the nationalist struggle for home rule (*swaraj*) and independence from British rule often built upon the legacy of colonial stereotypes rather than uprooting them. This has led some (mainly diaspora) Indian historians to advocate the writing of a 'history from below' that focuses upon the meanings and actions of 'subaltern' (non-elite) groups within Indian society. The subalternist movement has similarities with Marxist approaches but rejects the universalism of the Marxist theory of 'class consciousness'. Instead the subalternist historians examine the localized context and aims of oppressed groups rather than reduce their history to the grand narrative of Marxism. According to subalternists such as Ranajit Guha (1988) and Partha Chatterjee (1986), Indian nationalist (and Marxist) accounts, like those written by the European colonialist, represent an elitist approach to history because they ignore or suppress the specific agency of non-elite groups within Indian society. The subalternist approach therefore offers a potential 'third way' beyond the options of Orientalism and Occidentalism ('Orientalism-in reverse'). This is achieved by rejecting the elitism of both Western colonial histories and indigenous nationalist histories. The latter, although usually anti-colonial in nature, exercises its own form of domestic or internal colonialism by replacing colonial rulership with a new elite – that of indigenous elite groups.

Hybridity and the diversity of Orientalist discourses

Recent scholarship has also emphasized the diversity of Orientalist accounts. Lisa Lowe (1991) rejects Said's portrayal of Orientalism as a monolithic project. She argues that there are a number of factors impinging upon Western representations of the East, including race, nation, gender and sexuality. Similarly, Homi Bhabha (1996: 42) questions Said's one-sided emphasis upon the power of the colonizer. This, he argues, gives too much power to the Western Orientalist and ignores the role played by the colonized subject in the production and interpretation of Orientalist discourses (see also Hallisey 1995: 32–3). For Bhabha the encounter between the Western colonizer and the colonized Asian subject is complex, producing a hybrid representation that is always beyond the control of both the colonialist and the native. Influenced by the French poststructuralist Jacques Derrida, Bhabha's point is that the authors of texts cannot hope to control the meaning attributed to their writings once they enter the public domain. Once an author provides an account of the Orient it can be interpreted in a variety of ways and pressed into the service of a number of different agendas. Bhabha makes much of the example of the English educated Indian. For Angliclists such as Macauley this figure represented the ideal for the future of India – civilized according to British cultural standards. However, in his mimicry of the English colonizer the Anglo-Indian represents a hybrid form of 'Englishness' that confronts the colonizer in unexpected ways. Frankenstein has created a monster that he can no longer control!

A good example to illustrate Bhabha's point is the 'discovery' of the *Ezourvedam*. This text, circulated in the form of a French 'translation', was said to be an ancient Hindu scripture and caught the attention of a number of eighteenth-century European intellectuals. The *Ezourvedam* proclaims the superiority of monotheism and rejects the polytheism and ritualism of the uneducated Hindu masses. Voltaire vigorously promoted the text as a testament to the superiority of ancient Hindu culture in comparison to the decadence of Christianity. However, the *Ezourvedam* was a 'fake', produced by French Jesuits in Pondicherry with the probable aim of discrediting Hindu beliefs and practices and convincing Hindus of the superiority of the Christian message. Thus, a text that was initially produced by missionary Christians to spread the 'good news' of the Gospel, was adopted by French intellectuals such as Voltaire and used to demonstrate the inferiority and decadence of Christianity. How ironic! Similarly, Western notions of India as 'backward' and undeveloped in comparison to the material and technological might of the modern West were adopted and transformed by Hindu intellectuals such as Swami Vivekananda in the anti-colonial struggle for Indian independence. The West may be materially prosperous, Vivekananda argued, but this only serves to highlight that it lacks the spirituality of India. In one simple move Vivekananda took a standard Western stereotype about India and used it to counteract Western claims to superiority. What examples like the *Ezourvedam* and Vivekananda illustrate rather well is the multiple meanings and directions that can be attributed to Orientalist discourses.

Problems with the notion of 'religion'

The colonial domination of the West over 'the rest' in recent centuries has caused many Western categories and ideas to appear more universal than they might otherwise have seemed. An important feature of recent scholarship, therefore, has been to cast doubt upon the universal application of Western ideas and theories. Even the appropriateness of the notion of 'religion' in a non-Western context has been questioned on the grounds that it is the product of the cultural and political history of the West. For Talal Asad (1993), the modern Western tendency to conceive of religion in terms of belief – that is as something located in the private state of mind of a believer, leads Westerners to think of religion as something that is essentially private and separate from the public realm of politics. When Islamic or Hindu leaders in Asia express political views, this is often seen in the West as a dangerous mixture of two separate realms of human life. Next time you watch a television news report about politics in the Middle East or India notice the style, presentation and reporting of events. How does the media portray foreign religious leaders in positions of political authority? Often news reports contain implicit assumptions about the 'normality' of the separation of religion from politics. However, as ex-BBC journalist Mark Tully suggests in his discussion of religion and politics in modern India:

> If we are really serious about coping with India's poverty we too have to show far greater respect for India's past and perhaps even learn from it ourselves … Many will say I am trying to drag India backwards – to deny it the fruits of modern science and technology and to rob it of the freedom of democracy. Such critics are, I believe, in effect accepting the claim that there is now only one way: that Western liberal democracy has really triumphed.
>
> (Tully 1991: 12)

We should bear in mind then that the separation of religion from politics is a feature of modern Western societies, reflecting eighteenth-century northern European disputes and the eventual separation of Church and State in modern Western nations. It is problematic therefore to impose this model of religion onto Asian cultures. Indeed for Asad all attempts to find a universal definition or 'essence' of religion are to be avoided because they imply that religion is somehow able to operate in isolation from other spheres of human cultural activity such as politics, law and science (1993: 28). Moreover, the sheer diversity of human cultures mean that the search for universal definitions of terms like 'religion' is fruitless. In its place, Asad advocates an approach to the study of cultures that focus upon embodied practices and the specific power-relations in which they operate.

King (1999) has also questioned the usefulness of the category of religion in the study of non-Western cultures. Modern notions of religion reflect Christian theological assumptions, in particular the preoccupation with orthodoxy and truth (rather than practice and forms of life) and with a canon of authorized scriptures as the location of the true essence of religion (King 1999: Chapters 2 and 3). As a consequence of colonial influence, world religions such as 'Hinduism' and 'Buddhism' have come to the fore in the colonial and modern periods, reflecting Western (Protestant and secular) assumptions about the nature of religion (see also Almond 1988; Fitzgerald 1990). It is not that these religions were simply 'imagined' by Westerners without the input of indigenous elite groups, but rather that their representation and subsequent developments within South Asian culture continue to reflect Western Orientalist concerns and assumptions. King argues that academic disciplines such as religious studies and Indology (the study of India) should work to extricate themselves from the Christian categories and secular assumptions, which continue to influence representations of the Orient, particularly the emphasis that is placed upon the so-called 'world religions'.

Orientalism and the study of Islam

Given that Said's work in this area focused almost exclusively upon the Middle Eastern and Islamic dimensions of Western Orientalist writings it is not surprising to find that his work has had a great deal of influence upon modern debates about the role and impact of Western Orientalism upon modern representations of Islam and Muslims. The debate has generally focused upon the legacy of Western colonialism in the Middle East and the continued existence of a number of negative stereotypes of Islam in the West. What is the relationship between modernity and Western culture? In Western culture modernity and traditionalism are usually seen as opposed to one another. Can one be modern and still align oneself with Islamic traditions? How is Islam to respond to the economic and political dominance of the West and the legacy of Western colonial rule in the Middle East?

Broadly speaking, there have been two main responses to these issues and the challenge laid down by the work of Edward Said. Some Arabic intellectuals and scholars of Islam have argued that Western scholarship should be abandoned in favor of an Islamicization of knowledge. Why, such proponents argue, should Muslims feel obliged to conform to the intellectual conventions and secular presuppositions of Western scholarship? This strand of Islamic scholarship has increasingly described itself as 'Islamism' as an indigenous alternative to the negative connotations of the Western term 'fundamentalism'. The Islamists tend to reject Western scholarship as a cultural attack upon Islam. In its place they advocate continuity with older traditions of Islamic scholarship, the use of Arabic as the primary linguistic mode of expression and an ongoing exploration of the truth expressed in the holy words of the Qur'an. Critics of this approach argue that Islamism represents the development of Occidentalism – a reversal of the Orientalist approach and a denigration of the West as inferior. Edward Said made it clear, however, that this was not the intention of his own analysis, concerned as he was to overturn and reject the dichotomy between Occident and Orient rather than reverse it. Nevertheless, for writers such as Akbar Ahmed this has been the result of Said's analysis:

> One inevitable consequence is the rejection of Western scholarship by Muslims. Muslim scholars in the West, whether Arab or Pakistani, are deeply suspicious of Western Orientalism. They are thus pushed into the hole, Said has unwittingly dug for them. For Muslims in Africa and Asia, imperfectly grasped bits of Marxist dogma, nationalism, and religious chauvinism create incorrect images of the West ... Said has left us with what he sets out to denounce: stereotypes and large blocks – Orientalist, Oriental, Orient.
>
> (Ahmed and Donnan 1994: 5)

Islamism represents a contemporary response to what has been called 'westoxification' (the pollution of Islamic culture by Western influences) and a reassertion of Islamic values and beliefs in a context of Western economic, political and cultural dominance. Scholars such as Mahmûd Hamdî Zaqzûq (1983) for instance, have called for a scientific response to Western Orientalism founded upon the truth of Islam. Others, such as Hasan Hanafi

(1991), call for the creation of Occidentalism, that is the academic study of the West, as a post-colonial response to the cultural and intellectual dominance of Western scholarship.

In contrast to the Islamists, there are also a number of Arabic intellectuals engaging with the concerns and issues of Western scholarship. In most cases such scholars are migrants, often educated *by* and now working *in* Western universities. The main concern for such writers remains the mutual proliferation of stereotypes about Arabs and Westerners and the question of the impact of globalization, cultural interaction and politics upon representations of Islam. Clearly these two strands of contemporary Arabic scholarship do not sit easily with each other. The Islamists direct much of their criticism towards those Arab intellectuals who have adopted or utilized Western methodologies in their analysis. This is seen as a rejection of Islam and complicity with the secularism of the Western colonial aggressor. Similarly, Western influenced Arabic scholars tend to reject Islamist approaches as 'Orientalism in reverse', questioning the privileged insulation of Arabic culture from wider international debates concerning modernism, postmodernism and globalization.

Orientalism, gender and religion

In the concern to highlight politics and the marginalization of the Other, the post-colonial agenda in scholarship has much in common with the development of feminist approaches to the study of religion (King 1999: 111–16). It is not surprising then to find that recent works have shown an increasing awareness of gender as a factor relevant to the Orientalist debate (Miller 1990). Lata Mani (1987) argues that nineteenth-century debates about the legality of *sati* (the ritual burning of a Hindu widow on her deceased husband's funeral pyre) – a practice abolished by the British in 1829 – did not allow the women concerned to emerge as either 'subjects' or 'objects'. Instead the Hindu widow became the 'site of contestation' in a debate which centered instead upon the question of whether or not the burning of widows was sanctioned by ancient Hindu sacred texts. All participants in this debate, whether abolitionists or preservationists, accepted without question the authority of Hindu brahmanical scriptures as the definitive source for 'the Hindu position'. The location of the 'essence' of Hinduism in ancient texts clearly reflects the Protestant presuppositions of the early Orientalists and gained further support from their reliance upon the scholarly community of brahmanical pandits as the authorized spokesmen for Hinduism (King 1999: Chapters 5 and 6).

Similarly, recent work has also paid attention to the images of the 'sexualized Orient' found in Western fantasies about the Oriental 'harem' and 'the veil' (Lewis 1996; Mabro 1996; Yegenoglu 1998). Notions of the seductive and sensual nature of the Orient and of the Oriental woman in particular also continue to this day in media advertising and popular culture. Whether this involves popularized accounts of the 'secrets of the *Kama Sutra*' (which is thereby transformed from an ancient Hindu text on the etiquette of courtship and lovemaking into an exotic manual of sexual positions), or the commodification and sexualization of Thai therapeutic massage, modern Western consumer culture continues to build upon much older colonial legacies and Orientalist stereotypes.

Attention has also turned to the role played by women in the Orientalist and imperial enterprises. Reina Lewis (1996), taking her lead from the work of Lisa Lowe (1991), argues that an examination of the location of female Orientalists in a complicated and sometimes contradictory network of power-relations demonstrates the diversity of the Orientalist project. Female Orientalists took up a variety of stances with regard to Western imperial superiority over the East at the same time as being involved in a complex series of domestic debates about the status and role of women in Western society. Her analysis suggests that an adequate critique of Orientalism should avoid the tendency to focus upon the expressed intentions and motivations of individual Orientalists and consider instead the broader structural relations of power that Orientalist discourses maintain: 'When we look at European women's representation of and participation in processes of othering, we are looking at representations made by agents who are themselves partially othered (as the symbolic feminized other of men in Europe)' (Lewis 1996: 238).

The most recent work within the field of post-colonial studies has focused upon the mutual involvement of a variety of factors (including race, class, gender and sexuality) in the study of the cultures, histories and religions of Asia. Anne McClintock (1995: 6–7) argues for instance that 'imperialism cannot be understood without a theory of gender power'. Similarly, Mrinalini Sinha (1995) has examined the ways in which nineteenth-century British notions of 'masculinity' developed in opposition to the perceived 'effeminacy' of the Bengali male. Sinha's work demonstrates rather well the complex interaction of Hindu and British notions of gender, race and sexuality in the colonial period. Attention has also turned in recent works to the existence of manipulative strategies and representations in pre-colonial Asian societies (Pollock 1993: 96–111; Killingley 1997; King 1999). These works suggest that the Orientalist tendency to stereotype and diminish the 'Other' is by no means an exclusively Western practice.

Concluding remarks

One of the most important insights to be drawn from the Orientalist debate is an awareness of the political nature of knowledge itself. Fundamentally, what post-colonial approaches teach us is to be more aware of the ongoing influence of colonialism upon the representation of others, and also of ourselves. Like feminist scholarship, post-colonialism is diverse but remains grounded in an awareness of the politics of knowledge, that is the involvement of scholarship in issues of power, authority and justice. This is especially relevant when dealing with the cultures and traditions of others, but 'indigenous' accounts by cultural 'insiders' are no less implicated by issues of authority and representation. Moreover, such has been the impact of Western domination over the last few centuries that indigenous traditions have themselves been transformed by the material and cultural violence of Western colonialism. Rejecting the separation of religion and its study from political concerns, post-colonial analysis opens up the possibility, indeed for such theorists the *necessity*, of exploring alternative ways of understanding and representing human diversity. How are we to make sense of differences between people in a *pluralistic* rather than an *oppositional* way? How might we try to understand the diverse ways of living that represent our common global heritage? This is perhaps the central issue confronting humanity today and no doubt will continue to influence debates within the study of religion. In this regard the comparative study of religion has a key role to play in the quest for greater understanding of the various cultures, peoples and forms of life that make up the world in which we live.

Bibliography

Abdel-Malek, Anouar (1963), 'Orientalism in Crisis' in *Diogenes*, 44: 103–40.

Ahmad, Aijaz (1991), 'Between Orientalism and Historicism: Anthropological Knowledge of India' in *Studies in History*, 7.1: 135–63.

—— (1992), *In Theory: Classes, Nations, Literature*, London: Verso.

Ahmed, Akbar S. and Hastings Donnan (eds) (1994), *Islam, Globalization and Postmodernity*, London: Routledge.

al-'Azm, Sadiq Jalal (1981), 'Orientalism and Orientalism in Reverse' in *Khamsin*, 8: 5–26.

Almond, Philip (1988), *The British Discovery of Buddhism*, Cambridge: Cambridge University Press.

Behdad, Ali (1994), *Belated Travelers: Orientalism in the Age of Colonial Dissolution*, Durham and London: Duke University Press.

Bhabha, Homi (1996), 'The Other Question,' in Padmini Mongia (ed.), *Contemporary Postcolonial Theory. A Reader*, London, New York, Sydney and Auckland: Arnold (Hodder Headline Group), 37–54. This article was first published in *Screen*, 24.6 (1983).

Carrette, J. R. (ed.) (1999), *Religion and Culture by Michel Foucault*, Manchester: Manchester University Press.

Chatterjee, Partha (1986), *Nationalist Thought and the Colonial World – A Derivative Discourse*, London: Zed Books.

Clifford, James (1988), *The Predicament of Culture: Twentieth Century Ethnography, Literature and Art*, Cambridge: Cambridge University Press.

Fitzgerald, Timothy (1990), 'Hinduism and the "World Religion" Fallacy' in *Religion*, 20: 101–18.

Foucault, Michel (1977), 'Truth and Power,' in Gordon, Colin (ed.) (1980), *Michel Foucault, Power/Knowledge. Selected Writings and Interviews 1972–1977, by Michel Foucault*, New York, London, Toronto: Harvester Wheatsheaf: 109–33.

Fox, Richard G. (1992), 'East of Said' in Michael Sprinker (ed.), *Edward Said. A Critical Reader*, Cambridge, MA and Oxford, UK: Blackwell.

Freitag, Ulrike (1997), 'The Critique of Orientalism' in Michael Bentley (ed.), *Routledge Companion to Historiography*, London and New York: Routledge, 620–38.

Guha, Ranajit (1988), 'On Some Aspects of the Historiography of Colonial India' in *Subaltern Studies*, vol. 1, Delhi: Oxford University Press.

Halbfass, Wilhelm (1997), 'Beyond Orientalism? Reflections on a Current Theme' in Eli Franco and Karin Preisendanz (eds), *Beyond Orientalism. The Work of Wilhelm Halbfass and its Impact on Indian and Cross-Cultural Studies*, Amsterdam and Atlanta, GA: Rodopi, Poznan: *Studies in the Philosophies of the Sciences and the Humanities*, vol. 59: 1–28.

Hallisey, Charles (1995). 'Roads Taken and Not Taken in the Study of Theravada Buddhism' in Donald Lopez Jr (ed.) *Curators of the Buddha*, Chicago: University of Chicago Press, 31–62.

Hanafi, Hasan (1991), *Prolegomena to the Science of Orientalism*, Cairo (in Arabic).

Harlow, Barbara and Mia Carter (eds) (1999), *Imperialism and Orientalism. A Documentary Sourcebook*, Oxford: Blackwell.

Iyer, R. (ed.) (1965), *The Glass Curtain between Asia and Europe. A Symposium on the Historical Encounters and Changing Attitudes of the Peoples of East and West*, London: Oxford University Press.

Killingley, Dermot (1997), 'Mlecchas, Yavanas and Heathens: Interacting Xenologies in Early Nineteenth Century Calcutta' in Eli Franco and Karin Preisendanz (eds), *Beyond Orientalism. The Work of Wilhelm Halbfass and its Impact on Indian and Cross-Cultural Studies*, Amsterdam and Atlanta GA: Rodopi, Poznan: *Studies in the Philosophies of the Sciences and the Humanities*, vol. 59: 123–40.

Kopf, David (1980), 'Hermeneutics versus History' in *Journal of Asian Studies*, vol. 39, no. 3.

Lewis, Bernard (1982), 'The Attack on Orientalism' in *New York Review of Books*, 24 June 1982: 49–56.

Lewis, Reina (1996), *Gendering Orientalism. Race, Femininity and Representation*, London and New York: Routledge.

Lowe, Lisa (1991), *Critical Terrains: French and British Orientalism*, Ithaca, NY and London: Cornell University Press.

Ludden, David (1993), 'Orientalist Empiricism: Transformations of Colonial Knowledge' in Carol Breckenridge and Peter van der Veer (eds), *Orientalism and the Postcolonial Predicament*, Philadelphia: University of Pennsylvania Press, 250–78.

Mabro, Judy (1996), *Veiled Half-Truths. Western Traveller's Perception of Middle Eastern Women*, New York: New York University Press.

Macauley, Thomas Babington (1835), 'A Minute on Indian Education' in Baubara Harlow and Mia Carter (eds) (1999), 56–62.

McClintock, Anne (1995), *Imperial Leather: Race, Gender and Sexuality in the Colonial Context*, London and New York: Routledge.

Mani, Lata (1987), 'Contentious Traditions. The Debate on Sati in Early Nineteenth Century Bengal' in *Cultural Critique*, 7: 119–56.

Miller, Jane (1990), *Seductions: Studies in Reading and Culture*, London: Virago.

Pandey, Gyanendra (1990), *The Construction of Communalism in Colonial North India*, Delhi and Oxford: Oxford University Press.

Panikkar, K. M. (1959), *Asia and Western Dominance*, London: George Allen & Unwin.

Pollock, Sheldon (1993), 'Deep Orientalism? Notes on Sanskrit and Power beyond the Raj' in Carol Breckenridge and Peter van der Veer (eds), *Orientalism and the Postcolonial Predicament*, Philadelphia: University of Pennsylvania Press, 73–133.

Prado, C. G. (1995), *Starting with Foucault. An Introduction to Genealogy*, Boulder, CO and Oxford, England: Westview Press Inc.

Prakash, Gyan (1995) 'Orientalism Now. A Review of Reviews' in *History and Theory*, 34(3): 199–212

Sardar, Ziauddin (1998), *Postmodernism and the Other. The New Imperialism of Western Culture*, London: Pluto Press.

Schwab, Raymond (1950), *The Oriental Renaissance: Europe's Discovery of India and the East, 1680–1880*, English translation, New York: Columbia University Press, 1984.

Sharf, Robert (1994), 'Whose Zen? Zen Nationalism Revisited' in James S. Heisig and John C. Maraldo (eds), *Rude Awakenings: Zen, the Kyoto School, and the Question of Nationalism*, Honolulu: University of Hawaii Press, 40–51.

—— (1995), 'The Zen of Japanese Nationalism' in Donald Lopez Jr (ed.), *Curators of the Buddha*, Chicago: University of Chicago Press, 107–60.

Sinha, Mrinalini (1995), *Colonial Masculinity. The 'Manly Englishman' and the 'Effeminate Bengali;' in the Late Nineteenth Century*, Manchester: Manchester University Press.

Steadman, John M. (1970), *The Myth of Asia*, London: Macmillan.

Thapar, Romila (1992), *Interpreting Early India*, Oxford: Oxford University Press.

Tully, Mark (1991), *No Full Stops in India*, London: Penguin.

van der Veer, Peter (1994), *Religious Nationalism: Hindus and Muslims in India*, Berkeley: University of California Press.

Yegenoglu, Meyda (1998), *Colonial Fantasies. Towards a Feminist Reading of Orientalism*, Cambridge: Cambridge University Press.

Zaqzûq, Mahmûd Hamdî (1983), *Orientalism and the Intellectual in the Cultural Struggle*, Doha (in Arabic).

Suggested reading

Asad, Talal (1993), *Genealogies of Religion. Discipline and Reasons of Power in Christianity and Islam*, Baltimore, MD: Johns Hopkins University Press.
A scholarly examination of Christian monastic discipline, the history of anthropological concepts of religion, and the Salman Rushdie affair from a post-colonial perspective. Not for the general reader.

Batchelor, Stephen (1994), *The Awakening of the West. The Encounter of Buddhism and Western Culture*, London: Aquarian Press.

A readable account of the interaction and reception of Buddhism in Western culture. Highly recommended.

Inden, Ronald (1990), *Imagining India*, Cambridge, MA and Oxford, England: Blackwell.
Inden is an anthropologist specializing in South Asia. This book offers a wide-ranging critique of the study of South Asian religion and society, and is strongly influenced by Edward Said and poststructuralist theory. An important work.

King, Richard (1999), *Orientalism and Religion. Post-colonial Theory, India and 'the Mystic East'*, London and New York: Routledge.
An exploration of 'the Orientalist debate', postcolonial theory and their implications for the comparative study of religion. Chapters explore the nature of religious studies, Orientalism, the study of Hinduism and Buddhism and the comparative study of mysticism.

Lopez Jr, Donald (ed.) (1995), *Curators of the Buddha. The Study of Buddhism Under Colonialism*, Chicago: University of Chicago Press.
A collection of six scholarly articles examining the Orientalism question in relation to various aspects of the study of Buddhism. The work presupposes a great deal of knowledge of Buddhism and its study and is aimed at the academic scholar rather than the student or general reader.

Mongia, Padmini (ed.) (1996), *Contemporary Postcolonial Theory: A Reader*, London, New York, Sydney and Auckland: Arnold (Hodder Headline Group).
A collection of important contributions to contemporary postcolonial theory, though with no specific reference to religion.

Said, Edward (1981), *Covering Islam. How the Media and the Experts Determine How We See the Rest of the World*, London: Routledge.
A readable discussion of Western media portrayals of Islam.

Said, Edward (1978; 2nd edn 1995), *Orientalism. Western Conceptions of the Orient*, London and New York: Penguin.
The classic text examining the link between Western colonialism and representations of the Orient.

Turner, Bryan (1994), *Orientalism, Postmodernism and Globalism*, London and New York: Routledge.
An examination of the impact of postmodernism and globalism on Western sociological studies of Islam.

Chapter 18

Secularization

Judith Fox

> The Sea of Faith
> Was once, too, at the full, and round earth's shore
> Lay like the folds of a bright girdle furl'd.
> But now I only hear
> Its melancholy, long, withdrawing roar,
> Retreating, to the breath
> Of the night-wind, down the vast edges drear
> And naked shingles of the world.
> (From *Dover Beach* by Matthew Arnold, 1867)

Many sociologists of religion in the 1970s believed that the world was becoming increasingly secular, and that fewer people were religious than before. This view was consistent with the predictions of some theologians. Western cultural commentators often talked of the 'death of God'. And this seemed to fit with a growing indifference to established religion in Western Europe. Those making the argument explained that social forces associated with 'modernity' were responsible for the progressive secularization occurring. Since then, however, increasing numbers have questioned the validity of this thesis. Today, only a minority support the view that progressive secularization is taking place. Yet the whole issue of secularization has by no means been settled, and still manages to generate substantial debate.

There are a number of reasons for the continuing disagreement between scholars on the subject of secularization. One is that there has been much confusion over the definition of terms. Another is that the arguments have been founded on rather different ideological assumptions. So this account begins by introducing the different ways in which the terms 'secular', 'secularization' and 'secularism' have been used. Next, I draw attention to the historical antecedents of the arguments put forward today, and to some presuppositions inherent in the notion of secularization. After sketching out the key elements of the various arguments, and summarizing some critiques of the thesis, I finish by reconsidering some of its more problematic aspects.

A question of definitions

A useful starting point is to review the proposition contained in the first sentence of this chapter. It appears to be saying, in rather general terms, that during the 1970s sociologists believed that religiosity was in decline. But appearances can be deceptive. In fact, the statement is, deliberately, somewhat less than straightforward. For the reading I have just suggested to be the case, one would have to equate the proposition that 'far fewer people were religious than before' with the idea that 'the world was becoming increasingly secular'. However, on closer inspection, I would like to suggest that these two phrases are not necessarily synonymous. And this is, in part, due to the disparity between the meanings attributed to the term 'secular' and its derivatives.

According to the Oxford English Dictionary (OED), the term 'secular' is derived from the same etymological root (L. *sæculum*) as the French word *siècle*, meaning 'century', or 'age'. Interestingly, this derivation is evident in the astronomical use of the word secular to talk about processes of change over long periods of time, such as changes in planetary orbits. However, most people are perhaps more familiar with the usage that originated in early ecclesiastical texts, in which the term 'secular' was commonly opposed to 'regular'. 'Regular', in this context, was a term applied to those persons subject to the rule of a monastic order. Thus, its opposite – 'secular' – was used to denote worldly affairs. Today, this is the most commonly understood meaning of 'secular'.

The principal entry for the term 'secularization' in the OED emphasizes its institutional character. There, secularization is described as: 'the conversion of an ecclesiastical or religious institution or its property to secular possession and use'. In contrast 'secularism', some sociologists of religion have argued, has a more personal orientation. It is the belief that morality should only take into account human and visible considerations. Secularists do not consider that moral codes should take into account, for instance, the existence of God, or of an afterlife. Whereas secularization is supposed to take place in the 'public' arena, secularism is a 'private' affair. Secularization, they have said, refers only to the diminishing of the public significance of religion. It does not refer to private levels of religiosity. It is, therefore, not synonymous with secularism. In fact, they have argued that the withdrawal of religion from the public domain might well imply an increase in personal forms of religiosity.

But, to complicate matters, this distinction between private religiosity and public religion has not been held universally by sociologists of religion. Peter Berger made the suggestion early on that: 'As there is a secularization of society and culture, so is there a secularization of consciousness' (Berger 1969: 107–8). He felt that secularization could have a private as well as a public component. It should also be noted that some who have insisted on the existence of secularization have not defined it as an irrevocable and irreversible trend. Instead, they have asserted that secularization ebbs and flows. Old religious forms die out, but they are replaced. Yet others have used the term secularization to describe a shift from 'other-worldly' to 'this-worldly' concerns within religious organizations, rather than in society at large.

Secularization theory, in other words, is one of those topics where the same word has been used in various ways on different occasions. However, as already noted, this confusion over meaning has not been the only reason for the disagreements over secularization. So, to complete our preparations for an examination of these debates, we should become conversant with the ideological antecedents of the different views being argued. To do so, we shall look briefly at the work of the two men widely regarded as the founding fathers of the sociology of religion, Max Weber (1864–1920) and Émile Durkheim (1858–1917), and at the goals of 'the Enlightenment project'.

The antecedents of contemporary secularization theories

The Enlightenment project that matured in the eighteenth century represented a revolutionary intellectual movement. Enlightenment thinkers such as Immanuel Kant, Voltaire and Thomas Paine believed that there was an underlying order to the world that could be progressively understood through the use of the rational faculties of men. Intellectual progress would be achieved by abandoning articles of faith, by rising above instinctual drives, and by renouncing irrationality. They assumed that men could lift themselves out of the mire of received wisdom and become autonomous human subjects. Men were capable of discovering foundational truths about the nature of reality by relying on intelligence rather than on divine revelation. These discoveries would come about by focusing on the objective facts of the world, and so discerning the laws governing life. Everything could ultimately be understood through science and rational thought. Then, once this understanding had been achieved, humanity would be able to control both Nature and its own destiny.

These assumptions permeated the intellectual milieu in which Max Weber lived, and the works of Karl Marx (1818–1883) and Friedrich Nietzsche (1844–1900) also represented major influences. Weber did not uncritically accept all of the tenets of Enlightenment thinking. He believed, for example, that there are some spheres in which science has no role to play. Nevertheless, Enlightenment assumptions are clearly visible in a number of his key ideas. Weber assumed that the foremost trend in Western society was towards increasing rationalization. He felt that social progress involved a move away from traditional, localized and sentimental ways of life and towards ordered bureaucracies and centralized control. Weber found this modern trend profoundly disturbing, but also inevitable. He saw it as the logical outcome of the rise of the nation state, and of capitalism. In particular, he believed, modernizing forces such as urbanization, the specialization of labour, and industrialization would have a profound impact on religion.

Weber argued – nostalgically, it has been said – that traditional life was permeated with a magical enchantment. Rationalization, he predicted, would lead to a progressive 'disenchantment' and, ultimately, to a world in which religion would no longer play a role in public life. This was not to say that religion would necessarily disappear altogether. However, it would increasingly become a matter of private choice. Weber believed this secularization would gradually occur because religion would no longer be able to exist in a state of unquestioned authority. Weber also suggested that Protestantism carried within itself the seeds of secularization. First, this was because it encouraged the idea that brotherly love could be manifested through 'a peculiarly objective and impersonal character, that of service in the interest of the rational organization of our social environment' (Weber 1930: 109). Thus, it promoted rationalization and, therefore, disenchantment. Second, he argued, Protestantism encouraged scientists to reflect upon the natural laws of divine creation as a way of knowing God. Since it allowed scientific explanations to undermine religious ones, its own internal logic would eventually undercut itself.

Weber has been described by a number of biographers as a brilliant scholar and a troubled soul. Unlike some contemporaries, he did not see the decline of religious influence as a liberating outcome of modernity. He simply saw it as unavoidable, given the social forces at play. Durkheim's position was very different. He was an atheist, and as influenced by Enlightenment thinking as Weber. But his assessment of the future of religion was far more optimistic. His view was that religious sentiment was essential to society, whether traditional or modern. Religion, he argued, enhances feelings of social solidarity. He, therefore, did not see it as something that could ever be outgrown by mankind, or as something that could be fully separated from society.

So Durkheim believed that religion would never lose its social significance. Instead, he maintained that: 'there is something eternal in religion that is destined to outlive the succession of particular symbols in which religious thought has clothed itself' (Durkheim 1912: 429). Religion would persist, not because it was necessarily true but because it had a public function to perform. Society required religion in order to maintain social cohesion and to strengthen collective feelings and ideas. He believed that forms of religion could be expected to change as society changes. But, Durkheim concluded, religion itself could never be extinguished or pushed to the margins, even when disputed by science. Science had the capability to challenge outmoded religious dogmas. But new religious forms, more in keeping with the times, would inevitably arise to take their place. Durkheim acknowledged that religion was apparently in decline during his lifetime. But he felt that a resurrection was imminent: 'In short, the former gods are growing old or dying, and others have not been born … [but] A day will come when our societies once again will know hours of creative effervescence during which new ideals will again spring forth and new formulas emerge to guide humanity' (ibid.: 429).

The ideas of these two men have, at least implicitly, dominated more recent debates over secularization. Part of their legacy is evident in the type of grand theorizing involved. Weber explicitly rejected the notion that religion is generalizable in an ahistorical sense. But both men sought to understand the underlying laws governing religion, and offered large-scale explanatory models based on the trends they observed. Contemporary theories of secularization fit neatly into this genre. Their influence is also visible in the assumptions underpinning contemporary arguments. All presume that social conditions have an impact on religion. But some, including Bryan Wilson and Roy Wallis, are explicitly Weberian in orientation. Others, such as Rodney Stark, Grace Davie and Charles Taylor, exhibit elements of Durkheimian thought in their challenges to the views of the former. To review the later perpetuation of the ideas of Weber and Durkheim, I shall turn first to the classic secularization thesis outlined by the Oxford sociologist Bryan Wilson. I will then examine the reactions of other scholars, before making some more general observations on the debate.

The great secularization debate

Bryan Wilson was seen by many to be the foremost British sociologist of religion of his day. His book *Religion in Secular Society*, published in 1966, laid out the principles of his secularization thesis and became a founding document of the contemporary debate. Wilson defined secularization as 'the process whereby religious thinking, practice and institutions lose social significance' (Wilson 1966: 14). His argument was that religion had formerly occupied a central position in society but, by the twentieth century, this was no longer the case. Wilson largely confined his analysis to Western society and, especially, to the position of religion in Britain and the United States. He agreed with Weber's view on the secularizing character of the Protestant ethos. He also maintained, like his august intellectual predecessor, that religion must be examined in terms of its historico-social context. Wilson allowed that in countries like Japan, concomitant with industrialization, secularizing processes were discernible. However, following Weber, he asserted that secularization was more markedly evident in Christianity than in other religions around the world. The effects of secularization were, therefore, also more in evidence in Christian, and especially Protestant, countries.

Wilson's adoption of a Weberian conceptual framework was unambiguously evident in his view that the onset of modernizing processes in the West were linked to the emergence of Protestantism. Before the advent of Protestantism, he believed, religious understandings were adopted as axiomatic. After it, they began to be seen as matters of faith rather than universals. The Church could no longer claim to hold sway over the hearts, minds and lives of the general populace, as it had in earlier times. Institutions that had previously been ecclesiastically governed, such as hospitals, schools and universities, began to be transferred to secular authorities. By the twentieth century, Western man was increasingly more rational than before:

> It seems to me difficult to maintain that man in western society is not more rational than ever he was, within the normal usage of the term 'rational'. So much more of his ordinary behaviour is controlled by cause-and-effect thinking, even if only because he knows more about the workings of the physical and social worlds ... The dominance of economic costing over spiritual aspiration in modern society, is the evidence of the growth of rationality in our social affairs, and consequently, at least in some measure, in our own habits of thought.
>
> (ibid.: 17)

Like Weber, Wilson regarded rationalizing processes as consequences of modernity that were both inevitable and inexorable. Due to their onslaught, religion would become increasingly marginalized and lacking in social significance. This had already happened in many parts of Europe, he said, where religion had been relegated from public life. It existed mainly on the periphery of society, where it continued to flourish in the form of socially insignificant sectarian religious organizations. Indeed, sects were evidence for secularization: 'it is in conditions in which the sacred order has been suborned to the secular – usually the religious institution to the political – as in the Roman Empire or Europe from the sixteenth to the nineteenth century, or in twentieth century Japan, that sectarianism becomes most manifest and institutionalized' (ibid.: 207). Wilson conceded that religious organizations had managed to remain in mainstream public life in the United States. However, he believed they were doomed to become increasingly bureaucratic and rationalized.

In this early book, Wilson included empirical evidence of processes of secularization. Although these processes were present in both countries, he argued, they followed different paths in Britain and the United States. In Britain, he used statistics published by a range of Protestant churches in England. The figures appeared to support his theme of a decline in religious membership and 'the general standing of the Church in society'. Wilson chose infant baptism, confirmation, church weddings, and attendance at Sunday school and Easter communion, as indices of levels of religious participation. His conclusion was that a decline was statistically evident. Turning his attention to America, he was not convinced that the statistics he was given were fully accurate. But he allowed that religion appeared far more resilient in the United States, and that the numbers indicated that religious membership was increasing rapidly. The main thrust of his argument for secularization taking place in America, therefore, differed from that which he used for Britain. Instead, he began by querying the authenticity and depth of religious commitment in America:

> The travellers of the past who commented on the apparent extensiveness of Church membership, rarely omitted to say that they found religion in America to be very

superficial. Sociologists generally hold that the dominant values of American society are not religious.

(ibid.: 112)

Religious affiliation in the United States, he argued, was part and parcel of 'being an American'. Public American religiosity, therefore, signified a social commitment rather than a sacred one. He theorized that the United States had needed to forge a common identity during the formative years of the Union, despite the plurality of its religious organizations. This need had led to the downplaying of religious difference. Religious values had thereby been eroded. Wilson suggested: 'though religious practice has increased, the vacuousness of popular religious ideas has also increased: the content and meaning of religious commitment has been acculturated' (ibid.: 122).

Wilson did not see the secularization he observed in both countries as being entirely dissimilar in kind. He linked secularization, wherever it occurred, to the increasingly mobile, urban and impersonal society he associated with the modern world. Looking at Britain and the United States, he also identified two other secularizing tendencies they had in common: denominationalism and ecumenicalism. Each new denomination, he said, eroded the notion of a unitary religious authority and so fuelled further secularization. Increasing numbers of denominations meant more competing views and an increase in doctrinal tension that undermined the basis of religious control. Some scholars saw ecumenicalism as a sign of a vigorous Church ready to engage with the doctrines and practices of others. For Wilson, however, ecumenicalism was a symptom of weakness rather than a sign of strength. This was because, he argued, organizations are most likely to amalgamate when they are weak. The desire for alliance leads to compromise and the amendment of commitment.

Some scholars saw the new religious movements that appeared in the West in the 1970s and 1980s as heralding the kind of religious regeneration envisaged by Durkheim. During this period, however, Wilson continued to affirm the view that, in common with sects in general, these movements were of little social consequence. In the 1990s, in a more conciliatory tone, he commented that new religions might indeed have positive benefits for individuals, and had significance on that basis. However, he saw no indication that any of them would or could transform the structure of society. They were, therefore, private forms of religion, and not to be taken as signs of the revival of public religion.

Wilson did not particularly distinguish between religious thinking and religious institutional presence in his earlier work on secularization. He believed that both, at different rates and in different ways, were under attrition in Western society. In his later work, however, he consistently reaffirmed the public character of the religious decline he was describing. In response to reactions to his earlier work, he emphasized that his own model of secularization did not necessarily imply the growth of a secular consciousness. It did not even necessarily entail the idea that most individuals living in secular societies have relinquished their interest in religion. Secularization simply meant that religion had ceased to be significant in public life.

Responses to Bryan Wilson's theory of secularization

Wilson was far from the first to argue that secularization was taking place in the modern world. But it is his work that was most often referred to by other sociologists as 'the classic thesis'. And it is his writings that are seen to have initiated the contemporary debate. Before

I turn to some alternative models that have been put forward in response, it is worth first reviewing briefly a few of the criticisms made about the specific content of his argument.

In an early rebuttal of the thesis, David Martin called for the concept of secularization to be abandoned, on the grounds that it was: 'less a scientific concept than a tool of counter-religious ideologies' (Martin 1969: 9). Martin went on to produce an important later comparative contribution to the debate, *A General Theory of Secularization*, but in this early work he objected to Wilson's position on a number of counts. One was that the notion of secularization implied a definition of religion, but religion is notoriously difficult to define. Another was that the thesis appeared to suggest that there once existed a 'Golden Age' of religion from whose norms we have subsequently diverged. This 'Golden Age', in his view, was an ideal based on representations of eleventh- to thirteenth-century Catholicism. However, said Martin, no such utopian period ever existed. A third objection he raised was that the view of 'modern man' put forward by Wilson was 'over-secularized'. Instead, Martin argued that contemporary society 'remains deeply imbued with every type of superstition and metaphysic' (ibid.: 113).

Other commentators, including Andrew Greeley, questioned the validity of the empirical evidence Wilson had marshalled (Greeley 1972). Greeley, an American priest and scholar, argued that statistics about church membership were not necessarily accurate indicators of levels of religious practice. He pointed out that many parishes did not keep records, and noted that the concept of membership is open to a number of interpretations. Different figures can be arrived at depending upon which interpretation is used. Greeley was also one of the scholars who objected to Wilson's view of ecumenicalism as a sign of weakness. He commented that engaging in dialogue with other Churches could equally well be seen as a response to plurality, and as a sign of strength. Generally, he rejected Wilson's suggestion that America was increasingly secular, along with the notion that modernity has a deleterious effect on religion. Agreeing with the misgivings raised by Greeley, other scholars described Wilson's attitude towards American religiosity and, indeed, towards sectarian religion, as unduly dismissive. They took exception to his assumption that a localized European model of religious 'authenticity' could be taken as a universal norm. It is worth noting, however, that in this, Wilson was not alone. A number of the early sociologists who supported his thesis assumed the European model of secularization as the norm, and evidence to the contrary as merely exceptions to the rule (Casanova 1994: 22).

The 'religious economies' model

It was two other American scholars, Rodney Stark and William Sims Bainbridge, who began the formulation of an alternative to Wilson's thesis. Their model was predicated on the existence of 'religious economies'. Notably, unlike Wilson, they defined secularization as both a public and private matter. For them, it was not only as a process affecting societies, but also one to which individual religious organizations were susceptible. Stark and Bainbridge suggested that religion arises through basic social exchanges. Within social exchanges, which are economic in nature, people attempt to gain rewards and avoid costs. Religion offers rewards in the form of 'compensators', these being rewards that are accepted as a matter of faith. Stark's and Bainbridge's view was that science alone does not offer sufficient rewards to individuals. This is because, they said, science is incapable of solving the central problems of human existence. For this reason, they argued, humans have continued to postulate supernatural entities able to meet their demands.

Stark and Bainbridge believed that religious revival and innovation was stimulated by supply and demand. Because of secularizing forces within organizations, they argued, religious entities that can offer powerful enough compensators are sometimes in short supply. This is because, over time, religious organizations tend to become more rational and secular. In so doing, they lose supernatural credibility. Human beings, however, have a fairly constant need for powerful religious compensators. When these compensators are in short supply, new forms of religion emerge that can meet the demand by offering the rewards necessary. In other words, the two American scholars agreed with Wilson that there was evidence of secularization. But they suggested that the history of religion exhibited patterns of cyclic decline and regeneration rather than a linear decline:

> Viewed in this way, secularization is not something new under the sun. It did not begin with the rise of science. . . . [and] secularization *does not bring the end of religion*. Rather, secularization is self-limiting in that it stimulates significant processes of reaction in other sectors of any religious economy.
>
> (Stark 1985: 302; italics in original)

Stark and Bainbridge also challenged Wilson's claim that new religious movements are proof of the withdrawal of religion from public life. The two pointed to European data that showed that cults – groups inspired from somewhere besides the primary religion of the culture in which they were located – were more numerous and stronger in those regions where conventional churches were weak. The data also indicated that sects – breakaway Christian groups – abounded in areas where the Church was stronger. In Stark's and Bainbridge's view, these facts undermined Wilson's thesis that there was a declining interest in religion in Europe. In fact, Europe, according to them, was not secular at all in the way envisaged by Wilson.

Stark and Bainbridge, in other words, were following a far more Durkheimian theoretical trajectory. They assumed that religion had an enduring function and that it would therefore always be needed. Disagreeing with Wilson, they saw religion as a universal that was more or less constant, and rejected the notion that it would be inexorably removed from the public sphere over time. Instead, like Durkheim, they believed that religious innovation and renewal are inevitable. They parted company from Durkheim in that the latter held that society requires religion. For Stark and Bainbridge, religion was an enduring phenomenon because of individuals' need for compensators. Nevertheless, they still clearly owed him a substantial intellectual debt.

Perhaps at least partly because of their theoretical divergence with Weber's vision, their thesis met with friendly ridicule on the other side of the Atlantic. Their most vocal adversary was the sociologist Roy Wallis, a former student of Wilson's. He accepted their premise that sectarian religious organizations become more rational with the passage of time. But Wallis argued that the figures offered by Stark to substantiate the view that revival and innovation was taking place in Europe were founded on too few cases. He also cast doubt on the accuracy of Stark's statistics, and suggested they were skewed. Wallis said that Stark should not have used numbers of cult movements in Europe as a basis for his claims that the continent was still religious. His objection was that just because someone opens an office 'does not mean that he has any customers' (Wallis 1986: 497). In so doing, he managed to convey the impression that the Americans had no idea about the religious situation in Europe. Therefore, their views on secularization were not to be accorded any degree of seriousness.

The 'rational choice' model

Stark, however, had only just begun his amicable assault on the bastions of European sociological expertise. Following other collaborative work, he reformulated his model along more sophisticated lines with Laurence Iannaccone (Stark and Iannaccone 1994). Like that of Stark and Bainbridge before, the framework of the revamped model was economic. It assumed a fairly constant need for religion since, they said, there is always human suffering that cannot be satisfactorily addressed by other means. It also assumed religious change to be a cyclic rather than a linear process. It differed from the earlier model, however, in that it focused on supply rather than demand.

Stark and Iannaccone attributed variations in devotion to discrepancies in the supply of religious services rather than to different levels of demand, or indeed to secularizing tendencies. In fact, the model dispensed with the need to posit processes of secularization entirely. Instead, it incorporated elements of rational choice theory. Consequently, it was predicated on the assumption that a free market is always more active and efficient than one dominated by a monopoly. The two presumed that this assumption holds good when applied to the religious as well as the commercial arena. Stark and Iannaccone predicted that in those countries where there is a monopoly on religion, there is little interest in religion on the part of its population, and demand is low. Conversely, in those countries where religious organizations must compete for members, such as America, a higher degree of religious enthusiasm could be expected.

Like David Martin before them, but for different reasons, Stark and Iannaccone disagreed with the notion that there had been 'a golden age of faith'. They rejected the received wisdom that medieval Europe was an era in which religiosity was high, because it went against what their own model predicted should have been the case. As the Church had a monopoly during that period, their theory suggested that religious enthusiasm should have been correspondingly low. The two scholars also pressed the case, as Stark had before with Bainbridge, that modern Europe was more religious than British sociologists were prepared to admit. In other words, they turned the Wilsonian version of events on its head. Their view was that a more religious Europe had not given way to an increasingly secular one. Instead, they argued that Europeans had been less interested in religion in the past. This was because Europe had been dominated by a religious monopoly. More recently, they said, this situation had given way to a more devout contemporary Europe, as it was supplied by a plurality of religious organizations. And they presented historical as well as contemporary data to support their argument.

Their critics were not slow to respond. Some took exception to the model because of its economic orientation. It was suggested that models of behaviour linked to commercial monopolies and the free market could not, and should not, be unproblematically applied to religion. Others poured scorn on the idea that religious affiliation could ever be the result of 'rational choice'. Seeing the two as a contradiction in terms was in part perhaps because of the way in which religion has been associated with irrationality in dominant European discourses. The most vociferous critic of the new model in Britain, however, was Steve Bruce, a former student of Roy Wallis. A Professor at the University of Aberdeen, Scotland, he, too, presented historical and contemporary data in support of his argument. Describing their 'iconoclasm' as 'misplaced', he, in by now time-honoured tradition, suggested that it was unfortunate that Stark and Iannaccone '… are not better acquainted with the work of British historians or with recent survey data. Only by making unreasonably light of the many signs of religiosity in pre-modern British culture and making unreasonably much of the very slight evidence of religious sentiment beyond the churches in contemporary Britain are they able to claim that Britain's religious climate has not changed drastically. Britain was once religious, it is now secular' (Bruce 1995: 428). The dismissal, once more, conveyed the distinct impression that the Americans had got 'the Brits', and so by implication the whole of Europe, all wrong.

Secularization and confusion

A year later, Sharon Hanson, then engaged in postgraduate work at King's College, London, conducted an examination of the arguments over secularization. Her analysis exposed weaknesses in both camps (Hanson 1996). First, she drew attention to the fact that Bruce, Stark and Iannaccone were often talking at cross-purposes, and for this reason were not always as opposed as they appeared. One camp, she said, would often critically evaluate the claims of the other without taking into account that they were using different definitions of both secularization and religion. The result was confusion. Second, she noted that at times they seemed to use evidence to support their own view that could be more readily used to support the opposing side.

Third, said Hanson, the work she examined often relied heavily on historical data to legitimate claims. However, the data tended to be used without much circumspection: 'Historical data is presented as unproblematic, often juxtaposed to contemporary data, without any attempt to note the difficulty of comparing contemporary and historical data. Using historical data in this way lacks rigour, sources are not properly investigated and generalisations are hastily reached' (ibid.: 164). Hanson, additionally, pointed out that data that appears to suggest religion has lost social significance does not tell us *why* this might be so. Nevertheless, she said: 'Both Stark and Iannaccone (1994) and Bruce (1995, 1996) use their purported statistical proofs and historical narrative to speak of the why. They then use this rationale as proof that religion has, indeed, lost its significance or has not done so. Thus, a cyclical self-supporting argument is set up on weak proofs and propositions, gaining artificial credibility by mere repetition'(ibid.: 164).

Notwithstanding these observations, Hanson was by no means entirely condemnatory of the positions of Bruce, Stark and Iannaccone. And all three have maintained their original allegiances thereafter (Bruce 2002; Swatos and Olson 2000). However, during the course of her critique she made a further point deserving of mention. Hanson, as others have done, noted that both critics and proponents of secularization have had a markedly 'christo-centric' understanding of 'religion'. The equation of Christianity with religion means that if the former appears to be in decline then so does the latter. But religious affiliation has become increasingly plural throughout the world. In some areas, it might be the case that Christianity is undergoing a decline in influence in the public sphere. Given the multitude of faiths and beliefs, however, this fact does not necessarily signal the disappearance of religion altogether.

Religious pluralism

Pursuing this line of reasoning, a third group of scholars, albeit working independently of each other, have focused on the increasingly diverse religious 'landscape' rather than on processes of secularization. Advocates of this approach include Peter Berger and Grace Davie. Instead of continuing the debate in terms of decline or persistence, they have identified pluralism, diversity and fragmentation as more fruitful ways of thinking about religion today. Wilson used the contemporary proliferation of new religious movements to argue that religion was becoming an increasingly private, and often less 'authentic', affair. Stark and his associates invoked new religious movements to argue for the persistence of religious innovation. Grace Davie has cited them simply as multiple religious constituencies in her broader argument that, while more people may believe rather than belong these days, religion still has an important, if less visible, function as a source of identity in multi-faith Britain (Davie 1994).

Two new interventions

Alongside such work, Charles Taylor and Talal Asad, each using quite different approaches, have recently made new and substantive contributions to the debate over secularization and its conditions. In *A Secular Age* (2007), a formidable book in both length and scope, Taylor pointed out that the scholars we have examined so far chose to look at secularization either in terms of institutions and practices or the falling away of religious belief and behaviour. As a philosopher and social theorist – not a sociologist by training – he suggested the possibility of a new direction. This was to focus on the changing 'conditions of belief' that have underpinned the shift from a pre-modern sense of God as an unchallengeable reality to the current climate in which God is optional. Some key assumptions running through Taylor's book were, first, that all human beings have a common religious capacity and are engaged in a search for an experience of joy or fullness to give meaning to their lives, however diverse this search might appear in form. Second, as Peter Berger had done a couple of decades earlier, Taylor assumed that human consciousness and social structures and institutions are interrelated. Lastly, his endeavour to trace 'changing conditions of belief' was founded on the premise that access is possible to 'the different kinds of lived experience involved in understanding your life one way or another' (Taylor 2007: 5). Accordingly, he concluded, accounting for why we live in a secular age is a matter of accounting for 'the whole context of understanding in which our moral, spiritual or religious experience and search takes place' (ibid.: 3).

Taylor drew on a number of aspects of Weber's work in order to make his argument. For instance, in order to solidify the relationship between individual consciousness and society that was at the crux of his thesis, he made extensive use of Weber's idea of disenchantment by coupling it with his own earlier work on historical ideas of selfhood. He posited that in 'enchanted' times and places, in which religion is all encompassing and unquestioned, people experience themselves as having 'porous' selves and are therefore open to being influenced by external entities such as spirits and deities. Conversely, as disenchantment increases in any society, selves become increasingly 'buffered'. People experience firmer boundaries between their selves and other entities, and feel less vulnerable to supernatural invasion. Taylor also agreed with Weber that the Reformation and Protestantism were prime contributors to this disenchantment. But he vigorously criticized what he called 'subtraction stories' of linear religious decline, and the assumption that modernity inevitably heralds the 'death of God'. Instead, he advocated a theory of re-enchantment. While conceding that secularization and secularity both exist today in limited senses, Taylor argued 'religious longing … remains a strong independent source of motivation in modernity' (2007: 530), and that new forms of religious searching are in the making.

Taylor's book won the 2007 Templeton prize – awarded annually for 'progress toward research or discoveries about spiritual realities' – and despite its nods to Weber was unabashedly Durkheimian in spirit. This particular scholarly debt was made explicit in the classificatory system of different types of religion and society he put together. Taylor associated his first type, called the 'paleo-Durkheimian', with pre-modern societies in which 'the force which inheres in social obligations comes from the sacred of which the Church is guardian and articulator' (ibid.: 442). He categorized nations in which 'religious belonging is central to political identity' (ibid.: 455) under his second type, the 'neo-Durkheimian'. Lastly, he linked his third type, the 'post-Durkheimian', to contemporary pluralistic societies in which each person can conduct their spiritual search according to their personal inclinations, without reference to orthodoxies and hierarchies or an overarching social framework. Furthermore, throughout the book, and like his intellectual predecessor, he spoke optimistically of relationships between the sacred and human beings and of 'new ways of existing both in and out of relation to God' (ibid.: 437).

It is instructive to juxtapose the writings of Taylor and Asad, as the longstanding aims of the latter have been to unsettle received wisdom and to undercut the apparent coherence of unitary narratives. His writings have therefore offered a rather different perspective, both to Taylor and to that of the other scholars covered so far. In *Formations of the Secular* (2003), for example, Asad problematized categories – such as 'religion' and 'the sacred' – through which Western scholars and others have tried to make sense of the world and our place in it, saying,

> I assume … that there is nothing *essentially* religious, nor any universal essence that defines 'sacred language' or 'sacred experience'.
>
> (Asad 2003: 25; italics in original)

Agreeing with the French sociologist François Isambert, he argued that Durkheim's school was complicit in the creation of the scholarly narrative of the 'sacred' as a homogenous and universal essence (ibid.: 32–3). And he suggested that Weberian disenchantment, rather than being evidence of secularizing processes, '… is, arguably, a product of nineteenth century romanticism, partly linked to the growing habit of reading imaginative literature – being enclosed within and by it – so that images of a "pre-modern" past acquire in retrospect a quality of enchantment' (ibid.: 13–4).

Asad has also offered specific critiques of Taylor's work. Like Peter Berger and Grace Davie, he has sought to move away from the question of whether the classic secularization thesis is correct. But, unlike them, his interest has been in the political dimensions of the secular: 'If the secularization thesis no longer carries the conviction it once did,' he has said, 'it is because the categories of "politics" and "religion" turn out to implicate each other more profoundly than we thought' (ibid.:200). Influenced by the French philosopher and historian Michel Foucault, Asad's attention has been concentrated on unmasking subtle political efforts to dominate and establish control. For instance, he has criticized Taylor's attempts to define religion, on the grounds that such definitions are ways of forcing commentary along certain prescribed paths:

> What are the stakes in wanting a fixed definition of 'religion', whether in terms of 'a sense of fullness', as Taylor suggests, or of 'transcendence', or of 'something beyond what has yet been achieved or will ever be achieved' – and so on?
>
> (Asad 2007)

He has also rejected Taylor's description of contemporary 'secularity' – Taylor's third religious type – as overly-optimistic. Instead of viewing secular states as spaces within which all are free to express themselves, and where plurality is tolerated, Asad's position is that the nation-state is inherently coercive. Since secularism arises within nation-states, therefore, it 'is not simply an intellectual answer to a question about enduring social peace and toleration' (Asad 2003:5), nor the vacuum that is left when religion has vacated the premises, but involves the inequalities and exclusions that are forcibly imposed in any political system.

Some closing thoughts

Many scholars have lately come to agree with the spirit of Thomas Luckmann's early comment that the secularization thesis is best described as a mythological account of the emergence of the modern world (Luckmann 1967). However, even if one's intellectual commitments are akin to those of Asad, it is not easy to dispense with the theory. This is because the historical particularity he has championed in opposition to the universalist claims of the Enlightenment only became intelligible through the intellectual developments of the latter. As Casanova has noted, it 'is so intrinsically interwoven with all the theories of the modern world and with the self-understanding of modernity that one cannot simply discard the theory of secularization without putting into question the entire web, including much of the self-understanding of the social sciences' (Casanova 1994: 18). In other words, it cannot be rejected without implicitly calling into question a host of other theories and assumptions commonly taken for granted. For instance, the idea that a benign trajectory of Progress, brought about by intellectual accomplishment rather than by articles of faith, will eventually lead to a complete and rational understanding of the laws underpinning nature and society.

Because it is such a pervasive theory, it is also practically impossible to refute empirically, whatever form it takes. For example, Wilson and others have suggested that the inexorable process they envisage might not be entirely linear. It could hypothetically occur at very different rates in different locations, depending on local conditions. At times, it might even seem to be reversed in the short term. So it is possible for a scholar interested in so doing to challenge specific elements of their argument, for instance the unreflective adoption of a Christian idea of religion. But it is difficult to know what evidence could be brought to bear that would convincingly rebut the argument in its entirety. A confirmed believer could always dismiss contrary evidence as a temporary setback, an insignificant exception to the rule, or as evidence of something other than 'religion' being at work: 'superstition', 'nationalism', or 'ethnic identity'.

It is also the case that, even if one accepts that religion has generally been removed from the public sphere, other scenarios than its decline can equally well explain this trend. For instance, a gender-sensitive account might find that there has been a shift away from public, 'male-centred' religion. Individuals have moved towards private religious activity that is more 'female' in character, reflecting the increased value attached to 'the feminine' in the West. Or, as some have argued, it could be said that public Christianity has retreated because of immigration and competition resulting from increased global communication, rather than through secularization. Such an argument would be that it has been replaced by less traditional religious forms, reflecting the increasingly multicultural and option-ridden world in which we live.

As Karl Popper pointed out, millions of people believe in astrology because it is possible to assemble a wealth of evidence indicating that it 'really works' (1989). He reflected that believers believe in astrology, and many other theories, because of the propensity of human beings to see confirming instances all around them once they have adopted a particular perspective. But confirming instances cannot be used as proofs, since any particular situation can be interpreted in light of a particular theory. So Popper concluded that only a theory couched in such a way as to be open to indisputable refutation can be properly tested, and be said to be scientific. It is not possible to prove that astrology definitively works, said Popper, since its statements cannot be unequivocally falsified. The same can be said of the secularization thesis. Both appear to have explanatory power, but cannot be subjected to rigorous scrutiny and refutation. Following Popper's argument, neither astrology nor secularization may be properly considered a scientific theory.

Steve Bruce, in particular, might protest at what I have just said. Indeed, in a 1995 article, Bruce put forward a number of statements in opposition to his own view. These included such hypotheses as: 'Insofar as it can be measured or gauged, compared with 1800, 1850, 1900, or 1950, there is now greater competition to join the clergy'. He then set about dispatching each one in order to show that secularization was occurring (Bruce 1995). But each of his arguments can be disputed, and in no case is his refutation unequivocal. For example, regarding the question of numbers joining the clergy, Bruce discounted the recent ordination of women in the UK and elsewhere as irrelevant. Instead, he focused on the fact that the younger sons of British gentry, who often chose to join the Church in centuries past, do not become ordained today in the same numbers as before. But it is equally possible to conclude that economic changes have meant that other career options have opened up to such individuals rather than to conclude that this is evidence of secularization. Further, just because the constituencies of the would-be ordained have shifted is not proof of secularization either. Arguably, it is merely evidence of changing class structures and of women's increasing public participation. In other words, despite his hypotheses and testing, Bruce did not produce conclusive evidence for secularization over some other explanation. Yet those who have championed a more Durkheimian view of secularization, suggesting that religious innovation works in cyclic fashion, have not always been persuasive in making their case either. Their arguments have often rested on highlighting of instances of religion flourishing in contemporary society. On occasion, this has involved overlooking, or explaining away, apparent examples of religion in decline.

However, as in the case of astrology, this does not necessarily mean that any of the theories of secularization that have been considered are wrong. It simply means that they are impossible to test rigorously, should we desire to do so. We can take a persuasive and informed view in relation to secularization. We can even try to think about religion without invoking this term. But we cannot know beyond doubt whether the theory is correct or not, in any of its forms. And, as with astrology, the view that we do adopt is likely to be coloured by our ideological and personal predilections and prejudices. Having said this, while the utility of traditional secularization theory may be under dispute, one thing is certain: if anyone in the future asks for your view on whether secularization is occurring, you should require him or her first to explain exactly what is meant by the question.

Summary

There has been considerable disagreement between scholars on the subject of secularization, due to confusion over the definition of terms and because their arguments have been founded on rather different ideological assumptions. This chapter traces the historical antecedents of the arguments put forward today, and the positions of key contributors to the debate.

Bibliography

Asad, T. (2003) *Formations of the Secular: Christianity, Islam, Modernity*. Stanford, CA: Stanford University Press.

Asad, T. (2007) 'Secularism, hegemony and fullness'. Posted 11/17/2007 on *The Immanent Frame*. http://www.ssrc.org/blogs/immanent_frame/

Berger, P. (1969) *The Sacred Canopy: Elements of a Sociological Theory of Religion*. Garden City, NY: Anchor Books.

Bruce, S. (1995) 'The Truth About Religion in Britain' in *Journal for the Scientific Study of Religion* 34: 417–430.

Bruce, S. (1996) *Religion in the Modern World: From Cathedrals to Cults*. Oxford: Oxford University Press.

Bruce, S. (2002) *God Is Dead: Secularization in the West*. Oxford: Blackwell.

Casanova, J. (1994) *Public Religions in the Modern World*. Chicago: University of Chicago Press.

Davie, G. (1994) *Religion in Britain since 1945: Believing Without Belonging*. Oxford: Blackwell.

Durkheim, E. (1912) *The Elementary Forms of Religious Life* trans. Karen Fields 1995. New York: Free Press.

Greeley, A. (1972) *Unsecular Man: The Persistence of Religion*. New York: Schocken.

Hanson, S. (1997) 'The Secularization Thesis: Talking at Cross Purposes' in *Journal of Contemporary Religion* 12,2: 159–180.

Luckmann, T. (1967) *The Invisible Religion*. New York: Macmillan.

Martin, D. (1969) *The Religious and the Secular*. London: Routledge & Kegan Paul.

Popper, K. (1989) *Conjectures and Refutations: The Growth of Scientific Knowledge*. London: Routledge. 5th edition (revised).

Stark, R. (1985) 'Europe's Receptivity to Religious Movements' in R. Stark ed. *Religious Movements: Genesis, Exodus and Numbers*. New York: Paragon.

Stark, R. and L. R. Iannaccone (1994) 'A Supply-side Re-interpretation of the "Secularization" of Europe' in *Journal for the Scientific Study of Religion* 33: 230–252.

Swatos, W. H. and Olson, D. V. ed. (2000) *The Secularization Debate*. Lanham, MD: Rowman & Littlefield.

Taylor, C. (2007) *A Secular Age*. Cambridge, MA and London: The Belknap Press of Harvard University Press.

Weber, M. (1930) *The Protestant Ethic and the Spirit of Capitalism* trans. by Talcot Parsons. London: Allen & Unwin.

Wallis, R. (1986) 'Figuring Out Cult Receptivity' in *Journal for the Scientific Study of Religion*. 25:494–503.

Wilson, B. (1966) *Religion in Secular Society*. Harmondsworth: Penguin.

Suggested reading

Asad, T. (2003) *Formations of the Secular: Christianity, Islam, Modernity*. Stanford, CA: Stanford University Press.

An examination of the genealogies of the 'secular' and the political dimensions of secularism.

Asad, T. (2007) 'Secularism, hegemony and fullness'. Posted 11/17/2007 on *The Immanent Frame* http://www.ssrc.org/blogs/immanent_frame/

The SSRC blog, The Immanent Frame, has hosted a vigorous debate on Taylor's work, including comments from Bellah, Asad, and a number of other distinguished contributors.

Berger, P. (1969) *The Sacred Canopy: Elements of a Sociological Theory of Religion.* Garden City, NY: Anchor Books.
Berger examined the phenomenon of secularization in the second half of this classic work. In more recent works, Berger has rejected the notion of secularization.

Bruce, S. (1995) 'The Truth About Religion in Britain' in *Journal for the Scientific Study of Religion* 34: 417–430.
The article comprised a succinct example of Bruce's argument.

Bruce, S. (2002) *God Is Dead: Secularization in the West.* Oxford: Blackwell.
The book covered the arguments of major contributors to the secularization debate and includes a restatement of Bruce's position.

Casanova, J. (1994) *Public Religions in the Modern World.* Chicago, IL: University of Chicago Press.
An informative and well-researched book in which Casanova looked at what he termed the 'deprivatization' of religion in the modern world.

Davie, G. (1994) *Religion in Britain since 1945: Believing Without Belonging.* Oxford: Blackwell.
Davie argued that religious belief persists, but not necessarily in traditional forms, hence her use of the phrase 'believing without belonging'.

Durkheim, É. (1912) *The Elementary Forms of Religious Life* trans. Karen Fields 1995. New York: Free Press.
Durkheim's classic work on religion, in which he concluded that, because it is essential to society, religion will not disappear.

Greeley, A. (1972) *Unsecular Man: The Persistence of Religion.* New York: Schocken.
The book was an early rebuttal of Wilson's thesis, and especially its applicability to the United States.

Hanson, S. (1997) 'The Secularization Thesis: Talking at Cross Purposes' in *Journal of Contemporary Religion* 12,2: 159–180.
A concise account of problems arising from the way terms and data are deployed in the secularization debate.

Martin, D. (1969) *The Religious and the Secular.* London: Routledge & Kegan Paul.
David Martin has produced a number of important works on secularization. This early work comprised another rebuttal to Wilson's thesis.

Popper, K. (1989) *Conjectures and Refutations: The Growth of Scientific Knowledge.* London: Routledge. 5th edition (revised).
In which Popper set out the conditions under which a theory is properly scientific.

Stark, R. (1985) 'Europe's receptivity to religious movements' in R. Stark ed. *Religious Movements: Genesis, Exodus and Numbers.* New York: Paragon.
A classic account of Stark and Bainbridge's thesis, in which Stark argued that Europe was far more religious than proponents of secularization suggested.

Stark, R. and L. R. Iannaccone (1994) 'A Supply-side Re-interpretation of the "Secularization" of Europe' in *Journal for the Scientific Study of Religion* 33: 230–252.
The article outlines rational choice theory and their understanding of its contribution to the secularization debate.

Swatos, W. H. and Olson, D. V. ed. (2000) *The Secularization Debate.* Lanham, MD: Rowman & Littlefield.
A collection of essays from critics and supporters of the secularization thesis.

Taylor, C. (2007) *A Secular Age.* Cambridge, MA and London: The Belknap Press of Harvard University Press.
  Taylor's analysis of the historical emergence of secular thought, and argument for a contemporary secularity that involves the multiplication of religions and spiritualities.

Weber, M. (1930) *The Protestant Ethic and the Spirit of Capitalism* trans. by Talcot Parsons. London: Allen & Unwin.
  Weber's classic work on Protestantism and its secularizing impact.

Wallis, R. (1986) 'Figuring Out Cult Receptivity' in *Journal for the Scientific Study of Religion* 25: 494–503.
  Roy Wallis's reply to Rodney Stark's 1985 article that argued that Europe was not as secular as had been suggested.

Wilson, B. (1966) *Religion in Secular Society.* Harmondsworth: Penguin.
  Wilson's classic account of the removal of religion from the public sphere.

Chapter 19

Mysticism and spirituality

Richard King

What do we mean by mysticism and spirituality?

'Mysticism' and 'spirituality' have proven particularly difficult concepts to define for a number of reasons. First, such terms tend to be used in a rather woolly and ill-defined manner in everyday language. The adjective 'mystical', for instance, is commonly used to describe any object, person, event or belief, which has a vaguely mysterious aspect to it. It is also applied to extraordinary experiences of union, whether religious or not, and to the supernatural, the magical and the occult in general. 'Spiritual' is similarly vague in its popular usage. The term 'mysticism' as a specific category is of more recent origin, reflecting the modern love of '-isms', and did not come into use until the end of the nineteenth century when it was used to denote that aspect of the Christian tradition which emphasised the indescribable (ineffable) nature of God and the importance of attaining an experiential union with the divine. Both terms are related to the term 'la mystique', which, as Michel de Certeau (1992) has demonstrated, first came to the fore in seventeenth-century France.

In the modern era mysticism has also been closely associated with the notion of spirituality and with the religions of the East. Today it is not uncommon for people to say that they are spiritual or that they have spiritual beliefs but that they are not religious, meaning of course that they do not affiliate with a particular religious institution or movement but still have some experience of the sacred. This association reflects modern shifts in Western understandings of religion since the Enlightenment and a tendency for many to distinguish between an inward and personal experience of the sacred (spirituality or mysticism) and allegiance to a particular form of organised religion (Carrette and King 2005). In a comparative context mysticism has come to denote those aspects of the various religious traditions which emphasise unmediated experience of oneness with the ultimate reality, however differently conceived. However, in the late twentieth century, the term of choice for those wishing to emphasise a more individualistic and less tradition-bound approach to the mystical, has been the notion of 'spirituality'. This reflects cultural trends related to secularization and the 'de-traditionalization' of contemporary religious forms (as in much of 'the New Age') in the West. However, for the sake of understanding the trajectory of twentieth-century scholarship within this field of study, this chapter will generally refer to the phenomenon under discussion as 'mysticism' rather than 'spirituality' since this was the preferred term within scholarship until fairly recently. The contemporary preference for the language of 'spirituality' will be briefly addressed at the end of this chapter.

Within Christian theological circles mysticism has often been viewed with great suspicion, being seen as a potential source of heresy and schism. If left unchecked, it has been argued, the unitive aspects of the mystical experience can lead to the adoption of heretical doctrines such as monism (everything is one), pantheism (everything is divine) and antinomianism (the claim to have transcended conventional moral guidelines). The mystic's claim to have experienced an unmediated experience of the divine has also been seen by many theologians as a direct threat to the authority of the Church as the sole mediator between the divine and human realms. Nevertheless, many of the most revered figures in the Christian tradition have been described as mystics, representing a vibrant tradition of orthodox spiritual teachings. In the twentieth century, interest in the cross-cultural dimensions of mysticism has also been seen by many as evidence of a spiritual common core at the centre of all world religions, providing a basis for inter-faith dialogue between religious traditions for some, and the hope of a truly globalised spirituality for others.

Origins of the term 'mystical'

Although the category of mysticism is relatively modern, its adjectival form – 'the mystical' has a much longer history. In the pre-Christian era the Greek term *mystikos* was used by the various mystery religions of the early Roman Empire. These movements usually focused upon specific deities, such as the Goddess Isis, or the God Mithras. In this context, the mystical seems primarily to have been concerned with the secrecy of ritual practices performed by initiates of these movements. The secrecy of *mystikos* functioned to exclude outsiders. Etymologically, both 'mysticism' and 'mystical' seem to derive from the Greek *muo*, meaning to close. This derivation reflects the esoteric nature of the Graeco-Roman mystery religions. The mystical therefore denotes the practice of closing one's eyes or of closing one's lips (i.e. remaining silent). In the modern study of mysticism both relate to different ways of understanding the nature of mysticism. On the one hand the mystical is often taken to be an experience which goes beyond the range and scope of everyday sensory experiences (such as visions). On the other hand, mysticism is often associated with the ineffable – that about which one should not, or perhaps cannot, speak.

As Louis Bouyer (1990) has demonstrated, there are three aspects to the early Christian understanding of 'the mystical' – all of which remain intertwined in their usage:

1 *Hermeneutics* – the mystical as the allegorical, spiritual or hidden meaning of scripture.
2 *Liturgy* – the mystical as a description of the mysterious power of Christian liturgy, in particular the Eucharist as the act of communion with the Body and Blood of Christ.
3 *Experience* – the mystical as an experiential knowledge of the divine.

Medieval conceptions of the mystical

In the sixth century CE we also find the development of the notion of a mystical theology in the works of Pseudo-Dionysius (so named because of the false attribution of his works to Dionysius the Areopagite, a disciple of St Paul mentioned in Acts 17: 34). For Dionysius there are two fundamental ways of speaking about the divine: kataphatic or affirmative theology, which speaks of God in terms of positive attributes ('God is good', God is love', etc.) and apophatic or negative theology, which takes seriously the mysterious, and indescribable nature of the divine. Negative theology, therefore, involves rejecting all affirmative statements about God and, for Dionysius, is also to be known as 'mystical theology'.

The path of negation involves an ascent of the hierarchy of reality, until one reaches the ineffable and divine Oneness that is the source of all things. One can speak positively about the things that God creates but not about the transcendent Cause Himself. Indeed it is Dionysius who first coined the term 'hierarchy' to denote a graduated conception of creation with God at the summit and various angelic beings acting as mediators between the divine and human realms. However, for Dionysius positive and negative theologies are intrinsically related and cannot occur in isolation from each other. Negation cannot occur unless one first makes an affirmation. Similarly, affirmative statements about God must be negated at a higher level if one is to avoid making a false image out of one's own limited conception of God. Negative theology is necessary therefore if we are to take seriously the transcendent nature of the divine. Moreover, as one ascends the celestial hierarchy towards God, words fall away, whilst at lower levels words become more and more effective in their representation of reality. The goal, argued Dionysius, was for the Christian to aspire to the highest realm and achieve a knowledge of God which left all conventional knowledge behind in a mystical 'darkness of unknowing':

> We would be like sculptors who set out to carve a statue. They remove every obstacle to the pure view of the hidden image, and simply by this act of clearing aside (*aphairesis*, denial) they show up the beauty which is hidden.
>
> (*Mystical Theology* Ch. 2, Pseudo-Dionysius, 1987: 138)

Negative theology, that is the idea that the divine being is too magnificent to be approached or described in any form, has come to be regarded as one of the defining features of mysticism and displays the unmistakable influence of Greek Neoplatonic philosophy. Medieval works such as the anonymously authored English text *The Cloud of Unknowing*, and the writings of figures such as the German Dominican Meister Eckhart (1260–1328) and the highly intellectual path of negation, involves the renunciation of all images of God as inadequate. God must always transcend the limitation of our human conception of the divine if He (She/It) is truly the supreme Creator of everything. As Eckhart explains:

> Unsophisticated teachers say that God is pure being. He is as far above being as the highest angel is above a gnat. I would be speaking incorrectly in calling God a being as if I called the sun pale or black. God is neither this nor that. A master says 'Whoever imagines that he has understood God, if he knows anything, it is not God that he knows.' However, in saying that God is not a being and is above being, I have not denied being to God, rather I have elevated it in him.
>
> (German Sermon 9 in McGinn, 1986: 256)

Although ultimately rejecting all intellectual attempts to represent the divine, the popularity and practice of negative (apophatic) theology tended to presume significant theological training and a knowledge of Christian and neoplatonic philosophical arguments. To identify mysticism in general and Christian mysticism in particular exclusively with these apophatic trends would be to ignore the diversity of trends encompassed by this term. As well as the highly intellectual path of negation there were also more affective strands of Christian mysticism represented by figures like Bernard of Clairvaux (1090–1153), Hildegard of Bingen (1098–1179) and Julian of Norwich (b. 1342). This trend placed a much greater emphasis upon love and the emotions as a means of encountering God rather than a highly abstract and intellectual path to the divine.

The scriptural basis for these more affective types of mysticism was the Song of Songs (*Song of Solomon*), a romantic poem that forms part of the Hebrew Bible/Old Testament. Although originally a composition outlining the loving relationship between God and Israel, early Christian writers tended to interpret the Song of Songs as a poetic exploration of the relationship between God (the Bridegroom) and the Church (the Bride). However, from the time of Origen (c. 185–254 CE), the Song of Songs has also been given a 'mystical interpretation' as an exposition of the loving intimacy that characterises God's relationship with the soul. Bernard of Clairvaux composed an extensive commentary upon the Song of Songs, outlining a three-fold path of pilgrimage in the soul's path to God. This began with the kiss on the feet and culminated in a union with the divine which he describes, following the Song of Songs, as 'the kiss on the mouth' (*Song of Solomon* 1: 2). The apparent eroticism of much of this literature has caused some controversy in Christian theological circles, with scholars such as Dean Inge (1899) and Anders Nygren (1953) criticising what they see as a confusion of the carnality of *eros* with the spiritual love of *agape*.

The medieval period in particular, however, also saw an explosion of activity by female mystics. Mostly excluded from formal theological training and therefore uninitiated in the abstract intellectualism of the mysticism of negation, many of these women placed a great deal of emphasis upon visions as a source of spiritual knowledge and authority, and in some cases were persecuted and even executed for their claims. Modern feminist scholarship has become increasingly interested in the resurgence of female spirituality during this period, and the historical task of recapturing some of the silenced voices of these remarkable women has only just begun (Bynum 1982; Petroff 1986; Beer 1992; Jantzen 1995).

William James and the modern study of mysticism

In the modern era the hermeneutic and liturgical dimensions of the mystical have been largely forgotten, as has the complex network of social forces and power-relations that constituted all claims to mystical insight. As a result the experiential dimensions of the category have come to the fore, often to the exclusion of broader understandings of the subject matter. An excellent example of this is the influential work of the philosopher, psychologist and early scholar of the mystical, William James (1842–1910). In his 1901–2 Gifford Lectures (subsequently published as *The Varieties of Religious Experience*), James provides the classic exposition of mysticism in terms of mystical experience.

James was interested in establishing an intellectual framework for the comparative study of mysticism and religious experience in general. For him this framework was provided by the emerging discipline of psychology, though James remained critical of reductionist approaches which interpreted religious experiences either in terms of neurological functions of the brain or as repressed sexual desires projected in the form of an erotic encounter with the divine. An important dimension of James' approach was his sensitivity to the mystical impulse within humans. For James, however, institutional and organised religion was 'second hand' in the sense that the true core of religion resided in individual religious experiences. Accounts of such experiences therefore provided the basic data for James' psychological analysis.

While the emphasis upon the study of private and extraordinary experiences has come to dominate the modern study of mysticism since James it is important to realise the influence of the European Enlightenment in the development of this approach to the subject matter. In the modern era the separation of the Church and State and the process of secularisation has precipitated a movement away from traditional patterns of organised religion. Migration of ethnic groups as a result of colonial expansion, the rise of individualism and modern capitalism have also resulted in a much greater awareness of the multi-cultural nature of society and an emphasis upon personal choice with regard to issues of religious affiliation. One consequence of these trends within the Western world has been the tendency to conceive of religion as essentially a *private* rather than a public matter. We can see the emergence of this orientation for instance in James' understanding of the mystical, which is now almost exclusively related to the extraordinary and private experiences of individuals, thereby ignoring or at least underplaying the social, communal and, some might argue, political dimensions of the mystical in the history of Christianity (see Jantzen 1995; King 1999; Carrette and King 2005).

The study of mysticism since James has taken a peculiarly psychological turn and has often been seen as the study of 'altered states of consciousness' and the phenomena associated with their attainment. James suggests that although such states are inaccessible to the ordinary rational mind (as it is often called), but such experiences may impart exceptional meaning and truth-giving quality to the agent: '[O]ur normal waking consciousness, rational consciousness as we call it, is but one special type of consciousness, whilst all about it, parted from it by the filmiest of screens, there lie potential forms of consciousness entirely different' (James 1977: 374).

James' characterisation of mysticism continues to have a powerful influence upon contemporary conceptions of the subject matter. Mystical experiences, he argued, exhibit four basic attributes: ineffability, noetic quality, transiency and passivity. In offering this account James was not arguing for some trans-cultural common core that might be thought to underlie the different forms of mystical experience, rather he was interested in providing a theoretical framework for exploring the rich diversity of mystical texts and traditions throughout the world. The first quality, ineffability, refers to the indescribable nature of the mystical experience. Such experiences, James felt, were so extraordinary in nature that ordinary language struggles to express their innermost nature. The first attribute, ineffability, has clearly been an important dimension of the mystical throughout history and in this regard James is following in the tradition of figures such as Pseudo-Dionysius and Eckhart in the association of the mystical with negative theology. Nevertheless, as recent scholarly work has suggested (Turner 1995; Jantzen 1995), when pre-modern Christian mystics made claims of ineffability they were invariably referring to the transcendent nature of the Creator and not to a transient and extraordinary state of consciousness.

Second, noetic quality refers to the impact mystical experiences have upon the mystic. Such experiences strike one as undeniably true, as the acquisition of some insight or knowledge of reality – the way things really are. James stresses this dimension of the mystical to distinguish such experiences from hallucinations and delusions. There is something about mystical experiences that provide their own self-validation for the experiencer. However, James is quick to point out, the cognitive authority of such experiences is only applicable to the individual concerned. One cannot expect those who have not had such an experience to take such insights on faith alone. This reflects James' own interest in the role of philosophical analysis as a publicly accountable arbiter of such experience. This issue of course brings up a number of interesting questions. What authority should one ascribe to mystical experiences per se? How might one distinguish between authentic and inspirational experiences and delusional or demonic ones? Traditionally, the Church adopted a variety of criteria for assessing the validity of mystical experiences ranging from conformity to orthodoxy and scripture to an examination of the effects of such experiences on the conduct of the individual. The proof of the pudding is in the eating, and an authentic mystical experience, it was argued, should at least result in moral behaviour and actions in accordance with the Church. Such criteria, of course, will not satisfy those who do not feel bound by traditional ecclesiastical authority, especially those living in a modern secular era where the Church no longer holds sway. Hence James' interest in the role of philosophy as a rational arbiter for such truth claims.

The third quality of mystical experiences in James's account is transiency. Such experiences are limited in duration. Of course one is entitled to point out that all states of consciousness (including everyday 'waking' consciousness) are also transient if only in the rather trivial sense that we regularly enter dream and deep sleep states throughout our lives. Moreover, it would seem that we enter a number of different states of consciousness even whilst awake, reflecting mood changes, levels of concentration, daydreaming, etc. James has made the assumption here that so-called 'normative' states of mind predominate throughout our lives and that they should be regarded as normative. Interesting work has been pursued in this regard by transpersonal psychologists such as Charles Tart (1969) and Arthur Deikman (1980, 1982) in an attempt to take seriously the insights to be gained from an analysis of so-called 'altered states of consciousness'.

The fourth and final feature of mystical experiences, according to James, is their passivity. Such experiences tend to render the subject immobile in the face of an overwhelming presence or sense of the unity of all things. Part of James's point here is to acknowledge the sense in which such episodes are experienced as 'given' rather than the result of an overly active imagination. However, passivity implies that the experience is given by some external power rather than being a consequence of the agency of the mystic. In theistic traditions such as Christianity and devotional forms of Hinduism and Sufism it is often believed that such raptures are a gift from God, but this ignores traditions such as Buddhism and some forms of Hinduism where the highest states of meditative concentration (*samadhi*) are the result of sustained yogic practice and the cultivation of a receptive mind. Such traditions advocate the explicit cultivation of meditative states as a prerequisite on the path to enlightenment and need not imply passivity on the part of the mystic. Moreover, although James does not wish to imply this in his own analysis, the association of mysticism with passivity, otherworldliness and quietism is flagrantly contradicted by the countless examples of figures such as Teresa of Avila, Francis of Assisi, Hildegard of Bingen and Mahatma Gandhi, all of whom were inspired to social activism by their mystical experiences and not in spite of them.

The mystical and the numinous

Another important figure in the early study of mysticism was Rudolf Otto (1869–1937). In 1917 Otto published *Das Heilige* (translated into English as *The Idea of the Holy* in 1923), an attempt to outline the central features of mystical and religious experiences. Otto was heavily influenced by the German theologian Friedrich Schleiermacher for whom religion was best characterised by the 'feeling of creatureliness' when confronted with the awesome power of the Wholly Other. Otto, like Schleiermacher and James before him, believed that the core of religion resided in experience; more specifically, the experience of the holy or the sacred (Latin: *numen*). Otto characterised this 'numinous feeling' using the Latin terms *mysterium tremendum et fascinans*. Religious experiences involve a sense of being overpowered by a wholly other or transcendental presence. They induce in the subject a sense of mystery, awe, dread and fearfulness and yet at the same time are strangely attractive and fascinating. These features of the religious impulse are neither rational nor irrational, Otto argued, but constitute the non-rational feeling that provides the basis for all subsequent religious expression.

Otto believed that the non-rational dimensions of religion were too easily overlooked in theological discussions about the notion of God. Indeed, it is this non-rational aspect which constitutes the essential core of all religious experiences. Otto then was something of an apologist for the mystical within Protestant circles, arguing explicitly against the association of the mystical with the irrational (as opposed to the non-rational). Otto accepted that religion requires rationalism, which for him means theological orthodoxy, but it also requires the *mysterium* element in religion, that is the non-rational or supra-rational. It is this which orthodoxy attempts to express in rational terms. The problem with mysticism (and for many Protestant theologians, mysticism has often been seen as a problem!) is that it often results either in the identification of oneself with the transcendent creator (pantheism), or a complete negation of the reality of the self when compared to the magnificence of the wholly other. Both positions are indeed erroneous, Otto argued, because they over-emphasise the non-rational dimension of the experience and therefore do not take seriously enough the role of reason (and orthodoxy) in the interpretation and framing of the numinous experience: '[E]ssentially mysticism is the stressing to a very high degree, indeed the overstressing, of the non-rational or supra-rational elements in religion; and it is only intelligible when so understood' (Otto 1959: 22).

Mysticism then is fundamentally grounded in something akin to Schleiermacher's feeling of creatureliness – described by Otto as *mysterium tremendum et fascinans* – and involves either an explicit *identification with* or an *obliteration of* the subject in relation to God – the wholly other. This means of course that mystical experiences are not *essentially* different from the broader range of religious experiences available to humanity, being little more than an over-emphasised sense of the numinous.

Two of the best illustrations of the numinous feeling in religious literature are Arjuna's vision of Krishna in the Hindu text the *Bhagavad Gita* and Isaiah's vision of the throne of God from the Old Testament:

> I see you everywhere, many-armed, many-stomached, many-mouthed, many-eyed, infinite in form; I cannot find out your end, your middle or your beginning – Lord of the universe form of everything … This space between heaven and earth is filled by you alone, as is every direction. Having seen this, your marvellous terrible form – the three worlds totter – great Self! … Vishnu, seeing you touching the sky, shining, rainbow-hued, cavern-mouthed, with luminous distended eyes, I am shaken to the core; I can find neither resolution nor rest … Seeing your mouths dancing with tusks, like the flames of universal dissolution, I am disorientated and without shelter. Have mercy, lord of gods, home of the world!
>
> (*Bhagavad Gita* Ch. 11: 16, 20, 24, 25, Johnson 1994: 50–1)

> I saw the Lord sitting upon a throne, high and lifted up; and his train filled the temple. Above him stood the seraphim; each had six wings: with two he covered his face, and with two he covered his feet, and with two he flew. And one called to another and said:

'Holy, holy, holy is the Lord of hosts; the whole earth is full of his glory.'
And the foundations of the thresholds shook at the voice of him who called, and the house was filled with smoke.

(The Book of Isaiah, 6: 1–4, *Revised Standard Version of the Bible*, 1973: 604)

For Otto, the numinous feeling is present to varying degrees in a variety of religious experiences, from the sense of awe when gazing at the stars at night, a sense of the presence of God when taking part in a religious act (e.g. the Eucharist), to the sense of wonder and majesty when 'communing with nature'. Otto, however, was clear that the numinous is a category in its own right and should not be reduced to or explained in terms of profane terms or categories. This clearly is one reason why Otto describes the numinous using Latin terminology in order to distinguish it from everyday feelings of fear, mystery, fascination and awe. The numinous is an irreducible category. In other words, religious experience cannot simply be explained in terms of 'profane' and everyday emotions. In this sense Otto is putting forward a phenomenological account of the numinous experience – that is one which purports to describe the phenomena of religious experience without attempting to reduce it into non-religious categories (i.e. in terms of everyday feelings and emotions). This is an important aspect of Otto's approach since as a Protestant theologian he believes in the Christian God. Consequently, he is at pains to avoid any form of reductionism – that is any attempt to explain religion and religious impulses in terms of non-religious categories. Otto explains the similarities between numinous and profane feelings as an analogy of associated feelings, but he warns readers that if you cannot direct your mind to a moment of deeply-felt religious experience then you should not bother to read his book since you will not be able to understand its significance (Otto 1959: 8)!

Scholars have drawn attention to a number of problems with Otto's account of the numinous. Although Otto describes the mystical as an overstressing of the non-rational, he nowhere questions this neo-Kantian assumption and its explicit polarisation of the mystical and the rational. Many of the world's great mystics have also been great systematisers and philosophers. Furthermore, despite Otto's great interest in the mystical systems of the East (e.g. Otto 1932), his work remains fundamentally framed by his own liberal Protestantism. Consequently, Otto's account of the numinous experience fits rather well with the theistic experiences of the Judaeo-Christian and Islamic traditions (and also one might argue with theistic elements within other religions such as Hinduism), but does not work so well when applied to non-theistic traditions such as Buddhism, Jainism and Daoism where experiences are not seen as an encounter between a creature and an overpoweringly majestic wholly other. Indeed, even within the Christian tradition, Otto's account is problematic when applied to figures such as Eckhart where theism appears to shade into monism. Otto's response of course would be that here the overpowering nature of the numinous can indeed fool the mystic into thinking that the duality between Creator and Created has been completely obliterated. Such theological pronouncements, however, will not satisfy those who do not feel bound by Otto's allegiance to traditional notions of Christian orthodoxy. It has also been suggested that Otto's account is patriarchal and gender exclusive, insofar as it ignores experiences of the divine which emphasise not an overpowering Father but an intimate and loving mother-goddess (Raphael 1994).

Concern about the universal applicability of Otto's conception of the numinous has led others to construct typologies for the different types of mysticism. Ninian Smart (1965) for instance, has argued that the numinous and the mystical actually represent radically different types of religious experience. The numinous is an experience of a transcendent otherness and tends to be dualistic, theistic and prophetic in nature. In stark contrast mystical experiences involve an overwhelming appreciation of the underlying unity of existence and an overcoming of dualistic boundaries between self and other. Smart argues that recognition of the difference between these two types of religious experience allows us to appreciate the relative role and significance of such experiences within the various world religions. Traditions which privilege the numinous such as mainstream Judaism, Islam (except Sufism) and mainstream Protestantism tend to devalue, or at least accord far less value to, mystical experiences. On the other hand some traditions explicitly favour mystical experiences of union, according them more authority than numinous experiences of a wholly other. For Smart this category is represented by Theravada Buddhism, Jainism and Samkhya-Yoga.

However, there are a number of religions that accept the validity of both the numinous and the mystical, though usually with one placed above the other according to the dominant doctrinal stance of the tradition. Thus, for the Advaita Vedanta, the Hindu school or radical monism, a theistic appreciation of the divine is accorded provisional status but only for as long as one has not achieved a direct realisation of the identity of oneself with Brahman – the absolute ground of all being. Similarly, in some Mahayana forms of Buddhism there is an acceptance of devotional beliefs and practices, though these are ultimately to be relinquished once one realises that everything is empty of inherent existence (*shunya-svabhava*). On the other hand, Roman Catholicism generally values the numinous (as Christianity in general has done throughout its history), but does accord some validity to the mystical path, so long as it remains within the boundaries of orthodoxy. As Smart's analysis suggests then, the problem for the Christian mystic historically has been explaining how an experience of union with the divine remains within the boundaries of an orthodoxy founded upon the truth of the numinous experience. This has led most Christian mystics to provide analogies and descriptions of their experiences which safeguard the numinous regard for dualism, whilst at the same time emphasising the unity of God and the soul. Thus, the predominant Christian analogy for such experiences has been of a loving communion between a bridegroom (God) and his bride (the soul). Those mystics who have offered a more straightforward monistic interpretation of their experiences (such as the Muslim al-Ghazali and the Dominican theologian Meister Eckhart) have incurred the wrath of their respective religious authorities and been branded heretics by their critics. Similarly, in Theravada Buddhism, faith (*shraddha*) and devotion to the Buddha is accorded less authority than an experience of one of the higher *jhanas*, where distinctions between subject and object are relinquished.

How many types of mysticism are there?

Much of the literature on the study of mysticism, particularly in the 1970s and 1980s, has been concerned with questions of classification. How many different types of mysticism are there? Some writers, most notably Aldous Huxley, have argued that mysticism represents a common core or thread that is present in all of the major world religions. As that which unites all religions, mysticism therefore constitutes a perennial philosophy which occurs in a variety of different cultural and religious contexts throughout human history. In his book, *The Perennial Philosophy* (1944), Huxley provides selections from the writings of a variety of mystics the world over (in English translation) as a means of demonstrating their fundamental unanimity. Other scholars, such as R. C. Zaehner, have rejected this view arguing that the doctrinal differences between these figures are too profound to be ignored or pushed under the carpet. Zaehner suggests that there are three fundamental types of mysticism: theistic, monistic and panenhenic ('all-in-one') or nature mysticism. The theistic category includes most forms of Jewish, Christian and Islamic mysticism and occasional Hindu examples such as Ramanuja and the *Bhagavad Gita*. Theistic mysticism is considered by Zaehner to be superior to the other two categories not only in its appreciation of God and His creation but also in the strong moral imperative that it provides. The monistic type, which Zaehner argues is based upon an experience of the unity of one's own soul, includes Buddhism and Hindu schools such as Samkhya and Advaita Vedanta. Finally, panenhenic or nature mysticism seems to refer to those examples that do not fit easily into his theistic or monistic categories. For Zaehner any experience of unity or fusion with the outside world, whether induced by drugs, the animistic experiences of (so-called) 'primitive' religions, or the writings of poets such as Wordsworth and Blake can be placed in this category. A number of scholars, notably Ninian Smart (see Woods, 1980: 78–91) and Frits Staal (1975: 73–5), have criticised Zaehner for the theological violence his approach does to non-theistic traditions, forcing them into a framework which privileges Zaehner's own liberal Catholicism. Buddhism, for instance, rejects monism as a philosophical position along with any notions of a permanent soul, and the Hindu school of Samkhya is avowedly dualistic in nature.

Zaehner is also criticised by Walter T. Stace in his book *Mysticism and Philosophy* (1960) on similar grounds. Stace argues that doctrinal differences between religious traditions are inappropriate criteria when making cross-cultural comparisons of mystical experiences. Mystics of course are predisposed to describe their experiences according to their own cultural and doctrinal background. These differences in interpretation do not necessarily represent differences in the nature of the experiences themselves. Nevertheless, for Stace mystical experiences can be classified into two basic types: introvertive and extrovertive. Introvertive experiences constitute the mystical core of religion, being an introspective and non-sensory awareness of the unity of all things. The extrovertive experience is only a partial realisation of this union, being an outwardly focused and sensory apprehension of the harmony of the universe.

Mystical experience and interpretation

The question of the relationship between mystical experiences and their interpretation has become one of the central concerns of the contemporary study of mysticism. For scholars such as Stace and Smart mystical experiences are phenomenologically the same cross-culturally but differ as a result of the specific interpretations or doctrinal ramifications that are subsequently applied to them by mystics. However, scholars such as Steven Katz reject any attempt to drive a wedge between experiences and their interpretations. Katz argues that it is not just the interpretation but the *experience itself* which is conditioned by the cultural and religious background of the mystic. Christian mystics have Christian mystical experiences and Buddhists have Buddhist ones. This should not surprise us, Katz argues, since this is precisely what the culture and traditions of these mystics condition them to experience (1978: 26–7).

According to Katz – it is not possible to have a pure or unmediated experience. There is no such thing, he argues, as an experience that is free from interpretation or any recognisable content. Katz describes his work as a 'plea for recognition of differences'. There is no perennial philosophy or cross-cultural unanimity between mystics of different religious traditions. Contrary to perennialists such as Huxley and Stace, Katz argues that when a Buddhist

experiences gained through the sacramental use of peyote than one would find in the case of a purely recreational use of drugs to achieve a temporary high. As the Hindu text, *Yoga Sutra* 1.12 suggests, states of higher awareness require the cultivation of detachment and vigilant practice to have any lasting impact. Staal (1975: 157) makes a similar point by drawing attention to the impact modern modes of transport can have on religious pilgrimages:

> In many religions, pilgrimages are considered meritorious, partly because they require a certain amount of sacrifice or at least discomfort. But they also lead to a certain place, generally an inaccessible spot where a temple or other sacred structure or object exists. With the improvement of modern transportation most inaccessible places have become rather accessible ... The difficult way has become the easy way ... Of course, the physical result, viz. the presence of the worshipper-cum-traveller at a certain place, is just the same ... But expectations grow and the subjective experience is generally not the same. This analogy indicates that we cannot eliminate the possibility that the physical and brain states of a college-kid who has taken a drug are in relevant respects the same as those of a Buddha. Yet their mental states (which might have physical correlates too) need not for that reason be identical.

Expectation and the duration of the path, therefore, can be instrumental factors in the depth of impact, long-term effects and nature of the final experience. Staal, however, remains critical of arguments based upon the immorality or dangerous nature of drug use. Many drugs have no chemically habitual aspect and although some may have long-term side effects if overused, so does staring through a telescope if done too often. Should we give up astronomy? Why, Staal asks, are activities such as the exploration of outer space or climbing Mt Everest to be admired, but the exploration of inner space through the careful and structured use of drugs to be rejected as dangerous and life threatening?

> It is not surprising that the religious use of drugs has not met with the approval of the religious establishments. Institutionalised religions are not so much concerned with religious or mystical experience as with ethics, morality and the continuation of the *status quo*.
>
> (Staal 1975: 176)

Nevertheless, Staal remains non-committal on the question of whether drugs clarify or distort our perception of reality. He argues, however, that mysticism should be investigated scientifically and critically, under controlled conditions. Such work must take seriously the mystical traditions and techniques being examined rather than subsuming them under a secular and reductionistic framework. 'If mysticism is to be studied seriously', Staal argues, 'it should not merely be studied indirectly and from without, but also directly and from within' (Staal 1975: 125). This requires an initial suspension of doubt concerning the truthfulness of the mystical system or technique being explored, but should also be followed at some stage by analysis and critical evaluation (1975: 135).

Questioning modern notions of mysticism and spirituality

Although it is often difficult to distinguish between accounts of drug-induced and non-drug-induced mystical experiences, the debate about the role of drugs in the cultivation of mystical states suggests that the phenomena of the mystical is more than a matter of simply inducing an altered state of consciousness. As we have seen, the explicit identification of mysticism with extraordinary and transient states of consciousness is an approach that began in earnest with the work of William James at the beginning of the twentieth century and continues to the present day in debates concerning the relationship between mystical experiences and their interpretation and the question of the possibility (or not) of an unmediated or 'pure' experience of reality.

However, the modern privatisation of 'the mystical' has come under increasing criticism in some of the most recent scholarship in this field. The privatization of the phenomenon of mysticism is most obviously demonstrated in the emergence of 'spirituality' in the late twentieth century to denote some kind of interiorised experience or apprehension of reality. Such approaches are increasingly oriented towards the individual self rather than religious traditions as the source of their authority. Such contemporary shifts have affected the way in which we as 'moderns' understand the spiritual traditions of the past, in both the East and the West. Deny Turner (1994), Grace Jantzen (1995) and Richard King (1999) have all questioned the modern tendency to approach classical and medieval mystical texts as if they were offering psychological accounts of extraordinary experiences. Ineffability in the modern study of mysticism and spirituality has become a question of the indescribable nature of intense and private experiences rather than a reflection of the traditional exploration of the transcendental majesty of God or the ultimate reality. This reflects the tendency to read such historical material in terms of modern psychological theories of the self. This 'psychologisation' of the religious has been an important step in the unhinging of 'the mystical' from its roots in the world's religious traditions, and its reformulation in terms of privatised and 'custom-made' spiritualities oriented towards the concerns of modern individual consumers searching for meaning in a marketplace of religions (Hanegraaff 1996; see also Carrette and King (2005) for a critical discussion of this trend). In response to such criticisms of modern forms of 'spirituality', some scholars (notably Forman 2004, Lynch 2007 and Heelas 2008) have argued that we are in fact seeing the emergence of a 'progressive spirituality' that is potentially transformative and socially-conscious rather than merely accommodating of contemporary consumerism and capitalism.

In her feminist analysis of Christian mysticism, Jantzen points to the shifting meanings of 'the mystical' throughout history, highlighting both the power struggles involved in all attempts to define the category and the ways in which women have been excluded by men from positions of authority in this process. Similarly, King (1999) offers an analysis of the colonial origins of the notion of 'the mystic East', arguing that the representation of Hinduism and Buddhism as mystical religions has functioned to reinforce Western Orientalist stereotypes of eastern religion and culture as world denying, amoral and lacking an impulse to improve society. This has allowed the West to define itself as progressive, scientific and liberal in contrast to the superstitious, tradition-bound and 'underdeveloped' Third World nations of Asia. In this regard the stability of the categories of 'spirituality' and 'the mystical' and the way in which they have been adopted has itself become subject to critical analysis as emphasis has shifted towards the power relations involved in attempts to classify particular religious figures, movements or traditions as mystical or spiritual in nature. At the same time, the emergence of contemporary forms of eclectic 'religiosity' in the Western world and the increasing popularity of the term 'spirituality' as an indicator of many people's sense of the 'transcendent' in the late twentieth and early twenty-first centuries is seen by some as the development of a kind of 'post-secularity' and has begun to attract the attention of sociologists of religion, seeking to map, classify and understand such contemporary trends in a way that moves beyond the secularisation debates of a previous generation of scholars.

Bibliography

Beer, Frances (1992), *Women and Mystical Experience in the Middle Ages*, Rochester, New York and Woodbridge, Suffolk: Boydell.

Bouyer, Louis (1990), *The Christian Mystery: From Pagan Myth to Christian Mysticism*, Edinburgh: T. & T. Clark.

Bynum, Caroline Walker (1982), *Jesus as Mother: Studies in the Spirituality of the High Middle Ages*, Berkeley: University of California Press.

Carrette, Jeremy and Richard King (2005), *Selling Spirituality. The Silent Takeover of Religion*, London and New York: Routledge.

Certeau, Michel de (1992), *The Mystic Fable Volume 1. The Sixteenth and Seventeenth Centuries*, trans. by Michael B. Smith, Chicago: University of Chicago Press.

Deikman, Arthur J. (1980), 'Deautomatization and the Mystic Experience,' in R. Woods (ed.) *Understanding Mysticism*, London: Athlone Press; Garden City, NY: Image Books.

—— (1982), *The Observing Self: Mysticism and Psychotherapy*, Boston: Beacon Press.

Evans, Donald (1989), 'Can Philosophers Limit What Mystics Can Do? A Critique of Steven Katz' in *Religious Studies* 25: 53–60.

Forman, Robert K. C. (2004), *Grassroots Spirituality. What It Is, Why It Is Here, Where It Is Going*, Imprint Academic.

Hanegraaff, Wouter J. (1996), *New Age Religion and Western Culture: Esotericism in the Mirror of Secular Thought*, Numen Book Series, Leiden, New York, Köln: E. J. Brill.

Heelas, Paul (2008), *Spiritualities of Life. New Age Romanticism and Consumptive Capitalism*, Oxford: Blackwell.

Huxley, Aldous (1954), *The Doors of Perception*, London: Grafton Books (Collins).

Inge, Dean (1899), *Christian Mysticism*, London: Methuen.

James, William (1977), *The Varieties of Religious Experience*, The Gifford Lectures 1901–2, Glasgow: Collins.

Jantzen, Grace (1995), *Power, Gender and Christian Mysticism*, Cambridge: Cambridge University Press.

Johnson, W. J. (1994), *The Bhagavad Gita*, Oxford and New York: Oxford University Press.

Katz, Steven (1978), 'Language, Epistemology and Mysticism,' in Katz (ed.) *Mysticism and Philosophical Analysis*, Oxford: Oxford University Press.

King, Richard (1999), *Orientalism and Religion. Postcolonial Theory, India and 'the Mystic East'*, London and New York: Routledge.

King, Sallie B. (1988), 'Two Epistemological Models for the Interpretation of Mysticism,' in *Journal of the American Academy of Religion* 61(2): 275–9.

Lynch, Gordon (2007), *The New Spirituality. An Introduction to Progressive Belief in the Twenty-first Century*, UK: I. B. Tauris; US: Palgrave-Macmillan.

McGinn, Bernard (ed.) (1986), *Meister Eckhart. Teacher and Preacher*, London: SPCK and New York: Paulist Press.

Nygren, Anders (1953), *Agape and Eros*, Philadelphia: Westminster.

Otto, Rudolf (1932), *Mysticism East and West. A Comparative Analysis of the Nature of Mysticism*, New York: MacMillan, 1970; London: Quest Edition, 1987.

—— (1959), *The Idea of the Holy* (original, 1917, *Das Heilige*), 2nd edn, London: Penguin.

Petroff, Elizabeth (ed.) (1986), *Medieval Women's Visionary Literature*, Oxford: Oxford University Press.

Pseudo-Dionysius (1987), *The Complete Works*, trans. by Colm Luibheid *et al.*, New York: Paulist Press.

Raphael, Melissa (1994), 'Feminism, Constructivism and Numinous Experience' in *Religious Studies* 30: 511–26.

Revised Standard Version of the Bible (1973), London/New York/Toronto: Collins.

Schimmel, Anne-Marie (1975), *Mystical Dimensions of Islam* (Chapel Hill: University of North Carolina Press.

Sells, Michael (1996) *Early Islamic Mysticism*. New York: Paulist Press.

Smart, Ninian (1965), *Reasons and Faiths. An Investigation of Religious Discourse, Christian and Non-Christian*, London: Routledge & Kegan Paul.

Stace, Walter (1960), *Mysticism and Philosophy*, London: Jeremy P. Tarcher Inc.

Tart, Charles (1969), *Altered States of Consciousness*, New York: Wiley.

Turner, Denys (1995), *The Darkness of God: Negativity in Christian Mysticism*, Cambridge: Cambridge University Press.

Watts, Alan (1965), *The Joyous Cosmology*, New York: Vintage Books.

Zaehner, R. C. (1957), *Mysticism Sacred and Profane*, Oxford: Clarendon Press.

Suggested reading

Robert Forman (ed.) (1990), *The Problem of Pure Consciousness*, New York, Oxford University Press.
Scholarly articles responding critically to the constructivist position of Katz and others.

Aldous Huxley, (1945) *The Perennial Philosophy*, New York: Harper Brothers.
Wide range of mystical quotations (in English translation) from the major religious traditions, with commentarial remarks by Huxley. A classic anthology and example of the perennialist position.

Steven Katz (ed.) (1983), *Mysticism and Religious Traditions*, New York: Oxford University Press.
Scholarly articles on various mystical traditions, mostly espousing the constructivist position.

Frits Staal (1975), *Exploring Mysticism*, Harmondsworth: Penguin.
Quality study, though rather difficult when dealing with Staal's own specialist area of Hindu and Buddhist mysticism.

Richard Woods (ed.) (1980), *Understanding Mysticism*, London: Athlone Press; Garden City, NY: Image Books.

Chapter 20

New religious movements

Judith Fox

So many people, so many opinions; his own a law to each.
(Terence 190–159 BCE)

In April 2008 law enforcement authorities raided the Texan ranch of the Fundamentalist Church of Jesus Christ of Latter Day Saints (the FLDS Church). A tip had been received that women and children inside the polygamous community were being abused. The group, which had broken away from the main Mormon Church in the 1930s, led an isolated existence. On the basis that they were in imminent danger, and under the watchful eyes of the media networks, who knew good television when they saw it, Child Protective Services took more than 400 children into custody. Over one hundred of the women voluntarily chose to leave the ranch with them. Stories rapidly circulated of under-age sex and marriage, and of harsh physical punishments being meted out, even to babies. But in addition to the debates over whether these individuals had ever really been under threat – on May 29 2008 the Texas Supreme Court ruled that all of the children must be returned as their removal had not been justified – there was another, more basic, question. How best to characterize this religious organization? For, as an article posted on the American news channel MSNBC's website on April 9 2008 pointed out, there was no consensus between 'the experts' as to its status. Was it a cult, a sect or a new religious movement (NRM)?

The lack of agreement evident on this particular occasion mirrored a more general absence of agreement that has existed among those who study NRMs. The first reason for this is that that scholars on different sides of the question have come from diverse academic backgrounds, including sociology, psychology and the history of religion. These different disciplines, based on somewhat different presuppositions, have given rise to different approaches and degrees of contact that, in turn, have led at times to markedly different views.

Another reason has been that there are substantial dissimilarities between the many groups that have been labeled by scholars under the blanket heading of NRM. Some are breakaway groups from earlier religious organizations, others coalesce around new charismatic leaders. Most teach that it is wrong to injure either oneself or others. Several groups, however, mostly apocalyptic in tone, have been responsible for violence against both followers and outsiders, resulting in injury and death. The vast majority of people in NRMs have not been interested in indulging in any type of criminal activity. Nevertheless, there have also been a small number who have engaged in reprehensible and illegal activities. Most followers enjoy normal mental health, but some have suffered breakdowns and emotional trauma. Hence, scholars have found themselves in sharp disagreement when seeking to provide generalized answers about, for example, the social relevance of the groups and the degree of danger NRMs pose to their members and the rest of the world.

An additional reason for why consensus on such a fundamental question as 'what is the nature of the beast/s we are studying' has not been forthcoming is that the study of NRMs has taken place in a strongly contested and politically charged arena, contributing to the discord. NRMs have often been the sites of arguments that tend to provoke passionate debate, such as the nature of 'free will', 'authenticity' and even 'religion' itself. Among researchers, some of these debates have taken the form of methodological concerns. There have been emotionally charged exchanges, for instance, over the kinds of relationships that scholars should adopt with the groups with which they work; and allegations have been made that some academics have been either duped by or have become complicit with NRMs, and that their research has consequently lacked 'objectivity'. Other arguments have centered on whether members of NRMs are 'freethinking' members of society, and so entitled to practice their religion as they see fit, or, alternatively, whether they are victims in need of rescue.

To shed further light on the difficulties in achieving academic consensus with regard to NRMs, this chapter will begin with a discussion of the widespread adoption by researchers of the category of 'new religious movement'. This will be followed by a brief outline of some of the common characteristics of NRMs that have been identified by scholars, along with the explanations that have been offered for the emergence and features of NRMs. After this, we will take a closer look at the conditions under which scholarship in the field has taken place by examining in more detail the debates over the relationships scholars have had with NRMs that have occurred, as well as the impact the prevailing cultural milieu has had on their research. Finally, we will look at the rather different public perceptions of NRMs around the world, and close with the question of whether NRMs are as ubiquitous as has been suggested, or whether it may be more useful to understand them as emerging from and operating under very particular historical conditions.

Labeling 'new religious movements'

'New religious movement' (NRM) is the label generally used today by scholars in Europe and America to designate a religious group which has either arrived in the West after 1950, and so is new to Westerners, or that has originated in the West since that time. By contrast, in Africa as well as in South and Southeast Asia, most scholars have tended to use the end of the nineteenth century as the cut-off point between 'new' and 'older' religious movements. In Japan, which has seen successive waves of new religions since that time, there has been a further differentiation made, between the 'new religions' of the early twentieth century and the 'new new religions' that have emerged since 1970 or so. In other words, there has been no single understanding of which groups come under this umbrella designation. As a result, movements as disparate as Teen Witches, Kundalini Yoga, African Charismatic Churches, Satanism, Tibetan Buddhism and UFO groups, to name but a few, have all been classified as NRMs.

This confusion has its source in the reason why the phrase NRM was coined in the first place. It was not the result of the identification of common elements between different religious groups that primarily led to them being grouped together. Instead, scholars agreed upon the term because of their burgeoning anxiety over the disparate ways in which other terms that had been used until then to designate such groups were being deployed. In particular, it was employed to serve as a counter-measure to the pejorative associations that had became associated with the label 'cult'.

Until the introduction of the name NRM, sociologists of religion had been accustomed to using the terms 'sects' and 'cults' to talk about small religious movements. Even between sociologists, however, there were differing opinions as to how these terms should be defined (Dawson 2003). For example, the American scholars Rodney Stark and William Sims Bainbridge used the criteria of doctrinal distinctiveness to classify sects as breakaways from older religious groups. Cults, they said, were movements that drew their inspiration from somewhere besides the primary religion of the culture in which they were located, and so were culturally innovative. The Oxford sociologist Bryan Wilson, by contrast, defined cults and sects on the basis of their social organization. He characterized sects as exclusive and elitist groups offering salvation through membership, with lifestyles and concerns which were markedly different from those of mainstream society (1992). His student Roy Wallis followed with a redefinition of cults as loosely organized groups seen by their members to be just one of a variety of paths to salvation, rather than as the only path. According to Wallis, sects were usually authoritarian and run by a single leader. Cults, he argued, had no clear organizational boundaries and the locus of authority was vested in the members rather than in the leadership. Some cults eventually coalesced into sects, as, for instance, in the case of the self-help oriented Dianetics courses, which transformed into the Church of Scientology. However, many other cults simply dissolved after a short period of time.

Psychologists of religion tended to use the term 'cult' quite differently again. They applied it to designate authoritarian religious groups that combine group processes with hypnotic techniques, resulting in what has often been called 'mind control'. It was this usage that found its way into popular discourse in the 1970s. The word 'cult' gradually took on more sinister connotations, no longer indicating just an enthusiastic and relatively unorganized following, but something deviant and potentially dangerous.

An active coalition of small groups in America and Europe, working against what they perceived as the exploitation of NRM members, became known as 'the anti-cult movement'. These 'anti-cultists' adopted the definition that was in use among psychologists and, with the help of the media, disseminated their own experiences – and suspicions – to the public. Their narrative began to dominate newspaper, television and other media representations. Cults were suspect and subversive, and run by power-crazed leaders intent on exploiting the vulnerable. Those under their sway could be persuaded to do things that no thinking person would do voluntarily. Hapless followers who naively became involved with them were at risk of sexual and psychological abuse, coercion, financial destitution, and the break up of their families. They were 'pseudo-religions', moneymaking schemes or criminal 'rackets' operating under the guise of religion. The menacing associations that became linked to the term 'cult' were further legitimated and reinforced by the catastrophic events surrounding groups as diverse as the People's Temple at Jonestown in Guyana, the Branch Davidians at Waco, members of the Solar Temple and Heaven's Gate in North America and Europe, and Aum Shinrikyo in Japan.

Most psychologists and a handful of sociologists are still happy to retain the label 'cult', and some continue to see it as analytically useful. By the 1980s, however, a feeling grew among other scholars in the field that the term 'cult' had become so politicized that it was unusable, and that the time had come for a new name for the groups they studied. Scholars of religion at the time often looked to how the people they studied represented themselves when attempting to choose an appropriate label. But, with groups from all major (and minor) religious, spiritual and alternative traditions being included in this category, there was consensus only in one important respect: by now, nobody – perhaps for obvious reasons – wanted to be called a member of a 'cult', or saw themselves as such. These days the term 'cult' is still sometimes used in mainstream society to describe groups such as direct marketing companies like Amway, therapeutic and self-help organizations and other small religious and political groups with charismatic leaders. It has even been deployed in relation to Al-Qaeda (see Gallagher 2007). However, among academics themselves the term 'new religious movement' – chosen for its apparent neutrality – is now more frequently used, with only a few preferring to continue to use the terms 'cult' and 'sect'.

Some pros and cons of the new label

The adoption of the phrase 'new religious movement', however, generated its own issues, the first of which hung on the word 'new'. As well as the confusion that was experienced over dating, it was not always obvious to scholars at what point in the development of a religion that something 'new' had evolved. When a church splintered, for instance, and new breakaway groups were formed, were the latter 'NRMs'? Should the term still be used even if the 'new' splinter group retained much of the original doctrine and practice? Similarly, it was often also unclear at what point a 'new religious movement' became a 'not so new religious movement'. Was it when the founder died, when records started to be kept and a complex organization emerged? Was it when a new wave of religious movements became apparent in that region? Or was it when a second and third generation was established, or when a movement was no longer associated with controversy? Protests over the use of the word 'new' were also made by a number of the groups usually put into this category. The International Society for Krishna Consciousness (ISKCON), for example, argued that it was only new in the West, and could trace its origins back to sixteenth-century Bengal, and even earlier. Like a number of other groups, ISKCON did not accept that they were 'new', and complained that the label was misleading.

There were also objections to the description 'religious' being applied to some of the movements placed in this category, as they did not normally describe themselves in those terms. For example, followers from South Asian groups such as the Brahma Kumaris, and followers of gurus such as Sathya Sai Baba, Mother Meera and Amritanandamayi protested that they belonged to 'spiritual' movements. For a short while in the 1980s, followers of the guru Osho Rajneesh presented themselves as members of a religion, Rajneeshism. The religion was probably deliberately created to assist wide-scale entry into the United States. But for most of the history of his movement, his followers did not articulate their affiliation in religious terms, and Osho spent a good deal of his life denouncing 'religion'. Falun Gong, a movement that recently gained a high profile in China for publicly protesting against the government, identified itself on its official web page as an organization whose members 'simply seek to maintain a strong and healthy body, improve their Xinxing (heart-mind-moral nature) and be good people.' Denounced as a cult by the authorities, the organization strongly rejected the claim that it was either a cult or a religion. This raised the question in some minds of whether it was appropriate and even ethical to label a group as religious if the group itself did not do so.

Scholars also noted that the phrase 'new religious movements' began to accumulate many of the negative connotations previously ascribed to 'cults'. Opponents of the phrase charged that academics introduced it in order to deflect what they considered to be legitimate criticism about these movements. In the face of such considerations, one suggestion was that scholars of religion abandon the label and return to using the technical terms 'sect' and 'cult', once having first agreed on their definition. However, most believed that it would be impossible to turn back the clock in this manner. Another proposal was to extend the phrase 'religious minority' to cover NRMs as well as diaspora communities (Introvigne 1997). But, though this might have had legal advantages, the suggestion had drawbacks of its own. Some groups described as 'religious minorities' in Europe – especially Islamic communities – have experienced themselves as threatened, marginalized and vulnerable. Hence, being called a 'religious minority' might not necessarily have placed those previously designated as 'cults' and 'NRMs' in a more comfortable position in relation to the mainstream. Further, since the meanings of terms are never definitively fixed, pejorative connotations could have been taken from the term 'NRM' and applied to 'religious minority', just as has happened between the terms 'cult' and 'NRM'. There are also groups who, despite being comparatively small, do not recognize themselves as a 'minority'. Instead, they believed that the truths that they have discovered will affect the majority of humankind in the longer term.

Despite such problems associated with 'new religious movement', advocates for the scholarly retention of the phrase pointed out that the label was still not as negatively charged as 'cult'. The phrase, they said, spoke to the fact that, although many groups defined in this way have their roots in older traditions, almost all do see themselves as new in some way. Indeed, it is this experience of newness that allowed them to offer their own unique message to humanity. Eileen Barker is one of a number of sociologists who has argued that many of these movements, whether they see themselves as 'religious' or not, also exhibit characteristics that are usually associated with 'new religion'. These characteristics include communal ownership of property, charismatic leadership, relationships based on personal trust rather than on institutional regulation, a message of salvation, liberation or transformation, a high turnover of members, and deviance from the wider community. In her view, therefore, the label 'new religious movement' does have some analytical merit (Barker 2004). In the face of all these considerations, and despite its methodological problems, 'new religious movement' has indeed prevailed as the label most commonly employed by scholars of religion.

Characteristics of NRMs

If there has been considerable debate over the labeling of NRMs, there has been less disagreement over the characteristics scholars have commonly ascribed to such groups. In some countries, especially but not exclusively in Southeast Asia, groups with millions of members have been classified as new religions. However, NRMs are usually characterized as small, the majority of them having no more than a few hundred members, and the larger ones usually being able to claim only memberships in the tens of thousands. Their converted are attracted for disparate reasons, depending on the particular movement. Some speak of the sense of purpose and community their membership gives them, and the opportunity to develop spiritually that they have not found elsewhere. Others say they are attracted by the promise of healing or prosperity, or stronger religious experiences than they have had before. Members talk of the feeling that they had of 'coming home' when they first made contact with the NRM, and of the trust they have in the claims of their leader.

The connection felt with a leader of an NRM is usually also seen as a very influential factor in conversion. Followers of NRMs commonly consider their leaders divine or enlightened or, at the very least, much closer to such a state than they are themselves. They are often thought to possess the ability to work miracles and heal the sick. Frequently being skilled orators, they are seen as having a singular capability to articulate the will of the divine, and have a charismatic and convincing allure for their followers. Often capricious in behavior, and contradictory in teaching, many appear to revel in flouting rules and in inconsistency, or in pushing their followers beyond what is considered 'normal'. Paradoxically and simultaneously, nevertheless, their word is usually final and absolute, and they can be accorded tremendous control over aspects of their followers' lives. Leaders can be given the power to regulate matters of dress, diet, hygiene, finances, friendships and family relationships, sexual relations and marriage, procreation and even – in rare instances – to decide whether it is time for their followers to end their mortal existence.

The coupling of stringent regulation and effervescent spontaneity characteristic of many NRMs has been seen to come about through the relationship between the members and the leader. The devotee trusts that the leader is able to deliver the promised spiritual rewards. It is thought that it is this sense of trust that encourages them to offer their wholehearted commitment. It is as a result that relations with leaders are often experienced as personal and intimate by members, even if they have never met the head of their movement in person. Members' commitment may be reinforced if the religion offers them ways of looking at the world that are radically different from the mainstream. These new perspectives sometimes undercut commitment to concerns other than those of the movement, and promote rupture between new and old.

Scholars say that this rupture may be reinforced by other attributes commonly found in NRMs. One is that these groups are rarely just about accepting received wisdom from others. Instead, they usually offer powerful new experiences to followers. These experiences convince members of the truthfulness of the teaching and the significance of the path. Following the example of the leadership, converts often adopt a vocabulary only used in their movement, allowing them to share the unique experiences of membership with each other. Their sexual norms are also often observed to be different from those of the mainstream, whether they advocate celibacy, arranged marriages for Westerners, polygamy in a monogamous society, or complete sexual 'freedom' (Chryssides and Wilkins 2006).

Gordon Melton has gone so far as to argue that these differences from the 'mainstream' are what constitute NRMs as a category: 'What new religions share is a common deficiency that pushes them into contested space at the fringes of society. New religions are assigned their fringe status by the more established and dominant religious culture, and by various voices within the secular culture (government officials, watchdog groups, the media, etc.)' (Melton 2004, 73). However, not all NRMs that have been studied have been found to be new in all senses. Many 'break-away' NRMs continue with at least some of the practices of the groups from which they have split. Others combine elements from multiple traditions in order to highlight the way they see themselves as embracing, and thereby transcending, all other religions. Having said that, the theme of rupture is often continued in teachings relating to the rapidly approaching emergence of a new social order, with which the group in question is associated in some significant way. A number also develop political agendas that explicitly challenge social norms, and are public and active in their pursuit. NRMs usually hope to enjoy a reputation based on their spiritual contribution to humanity. At least some, however, are more likely to have one founded unwittingly on whether their behavior can be tolerated by the wider society in which it is located.

The academic study of NRMs

A recent and useful overview of research on NRMs is *Cults and New Religious Movements: A Reader* (Dawson 2003), a compilation of some of the most influential articles written by contemporary scholars in the field. The voice that scholars of NRMs have perhaps drawn on most heavily is that of the early sociologist Max Weber (1864–1920). His writings (e.g. Weber 1968) have been brought to bear on the question of why the number of NRMs in the West appeared to increase substantially in the 1960s, and beyond; on the dynamics involved in conversion to NRM; and with regard to how commitment is maintained. Most studies of charismatic leadership, the most common form of leadership found in NRMs, have used Weber's portrayal of charismatic leaders as revolutionary and set apart by what are seen as exceptional qualities. Bryan Wilson relied heavily on Weber's portrayal of modernity and its rationalizing momentum for his own argument that NRMs are examples of private forms of religion. Wilson argued that privatised forms of religion appear when religion disappears from the public sphere, this disappearance being due to processes of modernization. Following Weber, he also said that such groups tend to emerge during times of social and political unrest, or when a country is subjected to foreign invasion. Other scholars have utilized Weber's notion of 'routinization' – the premise that practices tend to become routine and fixed over time – to try to understand how and why groups become increasingly institutionalized.

The most popular typology of NRMs so far devised has been that of Roy Wallis (Dawson 2003). Here Weber's influence is also discernible, especially in Wallis' assumption that groups tend to become increasingly more accommodating towards the mainstream over time. Additionally, Wallis divided his typology into three 'ideal types', another Weberian strategy. Earlier typologies were primarily descriptive, concentrating on the classification of groups in terms of doctrine. By contrast, Wallis sought to put together a predictive typology that could be used to forecast what kinds of features, such as recruitment patterns, different NRMs would be likely to display.

The first type he proposed was that of *world-rejecting* groups, which perhaps most closely conforms to popular images of new religions. World-rejecting groups, according to Wallis, typically took the form of closed communities of followers who believe that the outside world is impure, degenerate and sometimes dangerous, and that contact with it should be minimized. These communities tended to be run along authoritarian lines, and the needs of the group took precedence over those of the individual member. Income and property were often shared. Such movements usually anticipated an imminent transformation of the world, followed by a 'new world order' in which they would play a significant role. Wallis included ISKCON and the Children of God as examples.

Wallis' second type was that of *world-affirming* groups. These were not so recognizably religious, and were more individualistic than the first category. These groups may have had reservations about the existing social order. However, unlike their world-rejecting counterparts, they did not tend to view themselves as a refuge of purity in an impure world. Groups located in this category were oriented towards the attainment of 'human potential' through the release of the innate divinity or creativity of the person. They included seminar-oriented organizations such as The Forum and Insight. The last category identified by Wallis contained *world-accommodating* groups. These were movements who did not necessarily see themselves as an all-encompassing or unique path. Instead, they offered highly experiential techniques that could be utilized by people in order to revitalize their spirituality more generally. Wallis included organizations such as the charismatic churches and Subud in this category.

Wallis' typology has been criticized on numerous grounds. First, its detractors have pointed to its elevation of social orientation over doctrine as a serious shortcoming. Ignoring doctrine, they have contended, unhelpfully allows groups from entirely different traditions, with entirely different histories, to be put together. Critics have also argued that the Wallis typology does not allow for diversity within a particular movement, diversity that would place it in more than one category simultaneously. Sahaja Yoga for example, appears, on casual contact, to be *world-affirming*. However, the group has also displayed *world-rejecting* characteristics in certain circumstances. But, despite such criticisms, the typology remains the most cited in the field to this day.

NRMs and rapid social change

Another sociologist frequently referred to by scholars of NRMs, especially during the 1970s and 1980s, was Weber's contemporary, Émile Durkheim (1858–1917). According to Durkheim, social norms and values, especially those of religion, function as a kind of 'glue' to hold society together. In times of rapid social change, existing rules, habits, and beliefs no longer hold. New religious alternatives are, therefore, likely to be sought in order to provide new stability. On the basis that social change is always with us in one form or another, researchers used this idea to explain, at least in part, the emergence of what was estimated to be five new religions per day in different parts of the world. More broadly, a shared assumption of all the explanations put forward was that social change brings about religious change.

Researchers noted that in Africa most NRMs are based in urban areas, those typically populated with displaced families from rural villages, having to cope with new challenges and uncertainties. Over 6,000 Independent Churches have been counted, almost all of West African origin, the majority of which are said to have begun with a dream, a vision, or sickness. Their focus is on prophecy, prayer, and the Holy Spirit. Additionally, there are many new evangelical and charismatic churches that have recently been established by missionaries from North America. Africa has also imported some controversial new movements from other regions, including the Unification Church and the Children of God. But whether a movement is indigenous or imported, commentators have attributed its popularity to the need for stability experienced by members. The new groups have been seen as functioning to provide cohesion and a new sense of purpose after the throwing off of years of colonial repression, and following rapid urbanization (Jules-Rosette 1979).

Similarly, scholars of Southeast Asia have written of numerous NRMs emerging since the turn of the last century, a few of which have millions of followers, such as Cao Dai in Vietnam. Japanese scholars have pointed to diverse NRMs flourishing in urban areas in their country as well. Most of these movements are Buddhist, and it has been estimated that between 10 percent and 30 percent of the population belong to one or more of these groups. It is worth remembering that having multiple religious affiliations is not unusual in this region. In South Asia, NRMs have been described as coming into being all the time, coalescing around *avatars*, incarnations of the divine, and *self-realized* human beings, *gurus* and *swamis*, *sants* and Sufi *pirs*. Most of these groups are small, but some, like the Sai Baba movement, are substantial in size and have a considerable international following. The rapid social changes that came about following the end of colonial – or in the case of Japan, feudal – government were regularly invoked in explanations for the emergence of NRMs in all these regions. The concurrent increase in urbanization, communications and other forms of infrastructure was also seen as a contributing factor in the proliferation of new forms of religion.

In the West as well, rapid social change was put forward, either implicitly or explicitly, as the most significant factor behind the rise in the number of NRMs from the 1950s onwards. Increasing globalization, scholars argued, led to an increased access to knowledge about religions, the net result being an increase of religious choice. Europe saw waves of immigration from South Asia, the Middle East, and East Africa. Due to prohibitive legislation being lifted, there was also a marked increase in immigration from South Asia to the United States in the mid-1960s. Scholars additionally pointed to an increase in the number of travelers abroad, and to increased information from television and, more recently, the Internet. Some argued that, because this increase of information took place within a capitalist system, it gave rise to a situation in which a plethora of new and older religious movements sold their wares in a 'spiritual supermarket'.

A different group of scholars emphasized the psychological and emotional effects of the rapid economic and cultural changes the West has undergone. Some early studies, in a move reminiscent of the psychologist Abraham Maslow's theory of a 'hierarchy of needs', pointed to the increase in economic growth and leisure time in the 1960s. They explained that the 'baby boomers' of that era could afford to, and had the time to, indulge in the often 'narcissistic' pursuit of the spiritual. This pursuit was possible because their other, material, needs had already been satisfied. Such narcissism included far more widespread use of narcotics than before. The ingestion of psychedelic substances during the 1970s added to an already existing climate of questioning and 'seekership'. Against this backdrop, some individuals were motivated to join NRMs that offered them clear-cut messages, be they about gender, or morality, or purpose, about the world.

Studies conducted by psychologists from the 1960s onward tended to find that such conversions resulted in damage. By contrast, a few sociologists speculated that NRMs, at times, act as a means by which people actually resolve personal and emotional confusion, and are rehabilitated. They pointed out that a number of groups in the 1960s emphasized that meditation could offer a better 'trip' with more 'highs' for those searching for Truth. The groups, they said, enabled 'dropouts' to re-integrate with mainstream society. Members were re-inculcated with respect for community values and were supported in breaking their addictive patterns of behavior. Nevertheless, most scholarly explanations for the emergence of NRMs during that period tended to assume that young people join NRMs because they were deprived in some way. Individuals who could not cope with the stresses and strains of modern life converted to them as a retreat from the 'real world'.

More recent sociological commentators usually acknowledge that a complex of factors led to the increase in numbers from the 1950s onwards. But they affirm that new religion is hardly anything really new, or even particularly unusual. There are now well over 2,000 NRMs in North America, at least 2,000 in Europe, and over 700 in Britain alone. These NRMs have almost all been inspired by earlier religious forms (Melton 2009). Some are global organizations, and are represented in most major countries. Others have remained small and geographically limited, and have a low survival rate beyond one or two generations.

Researchers and new religious movements

Against the background of the strong feelings aroused by NRMs, a few of their researchers have been accused of being over-involved with their subject matter. Inspired by the desire to 'set the record straight' and to promote religious tolerance, they have been drawn into the role of public defenders of NRMs. They have attempted to counter publicly the depiction of NRMs as 'brainwashing cults'. These scholars have argued their case in the press and on television, as well as in academic circles. Some have advised NRMs on how to improve their public profile, and have supported them as expert witnesses in court cases. As a result, outraged critics of NRMs have branded them as 'apologists'. They have blamed them for being insufficiently aware that they have been used unscrupulously by cults for public relations purposes, and of unfairly using their academic credentials to invalidate opposing views from other expert witnesses. Some researchers have also been denounced on the basis that they have gained financially from their association with groups to which they gave their support. This issue is one to which scholars on all sides of the debate periodically return, in an attempt either to defend themselves, air grievances, or re-affirm the need for careful and well thought out research not driven by unacknowledged agendas (*Sociological Analysis* 1983; *Nova Religio* 1998; Zablocki and Robbins 2001).

One of the most well-known critics of academic-NRM relations has been Margaret Singer, an American psychologist, who concluded that academics should have no prolonged contact with NRMs for fear of undue influence. She has been publicly highly critical of the close relations other scholars have sometimes established with those they study. Rejecting the view that most people do not feel the attraction of cults, Singer argued that everyone is potentially susceptible, including those she termed 'co-opted academics' (Dawson 2003). Those who have disagreed with Singer and her supporters have pointed out that NRMs are often distrustful of outsiders. For this reason, in-depth participant observation is the best – and sometimes the only – way of gaining access. This method requires that scholars spend considerable time with members, in order to get behind the public relations façade that may exist, and to gain their trust. Those in favor of this kind of research have cast doubt on the assumption that all academics are at risk of becoming converts, or uncritical advocates. They have protested that scholars who have engaged in participant observation have mostly found the agendas of the movements they have studied, as Eileen Barker has put it, 'eminently resistible'.

Cultural assumptions and NRMs

The scholarly advocacy of religious tolerance toward NRMs has reflected broader sentiments within the academic milieu and society in which such advocacy has been situated. Similarly, trends in popular areas of new religious scholarship – for example the increased study of gender and violence – have reproduced the increase of interest in these topics outside the study of religions rather than any change in NRMs themselves. Arguably, too, both scholarly consensus and controversy about these movements has been influenced at least as much by outside factors as by the NRMs. Larger cultural narratives and debates have had an impact on what kinds of questions are asked of NRMs. To examine the consequences of certain cultural assumptions is not to belittle the findings and conclusions of scholars. The point is that perceptions of NRMs held by the interest groups involved in debating them arise out of wider social contexts and concerns that need to be taken into account in an analysis.

For example, the hostility that has been generated towards NRMs in the West from the 1970s onwards cannot be divorced from Western cultural associations applied to the word 'new'. This is especially when it is used in a religious context. Partly since the Western monotheistic religions uphold the notion of having one faith to the exclusion of all others, traditional religion is often represented as both 'authentic' and 'orthodox'. As non-traditional movements, NRMs are therefore assumed to be 'inauthentic' and 'unorthodox', regardless of their merits or failings. Arguably, the upshot of this has been that similarities between the activities of new, and so 'inauthentic', religious movements, and older, 'authentic' traditions have largely gone unnoticed. Christian monks and nuns have often risen at dawn to chant or say prayers without fear of reproof. Members of NRMs, rising at the same time for the same purpose, have been vulnerable to the charge of 'mind control' resulting from sleep deprivation and sensory overload. It is seen as acceptable, and sometimes praiseworthy, that monks and nuns in most of the world's religious traditions should give all their worldly goods to their respective organizations. Members of NRMs are likely to be described, at least in some quarters, as having been swindled for doing the same.

The concept of the 'free individual' upheld in both secular and religious narratives in the West has given rise to another arena of disagreement. Supporters of embattled NRMs have fought to ensure that the 'religious liberty' of members is protected. Critics have accused NRMs of removing freedom from individuals, and so have concluded that they are patently dangerous and subversive. The practice of 'deprogramming', common in the 1980s, was a by-product of this rhetoric of subversion and danger. It involved anti-cultists in Europe and the United States being paid by anxious families and friends to 'liberate' converted loved ones. Deprogramming typically meant the kidnap and forcible holding of a cult member until they had renounced their allegiance to their movement.

These antagonisms have spilled over into the research arena. The most vexed debates between scholars have been on the issue of 'brainwashing', and on the related question of whether those who join new religions are victims of 'mind-control'. Probably the best-known work on the subject is the comparative study of the Unification Church produced by Eileen Barker. In *The Making of a Moonie*, Barker concluded that the Unification Church members she studied were not simply the victims of insidious techniques of persuasion. However, there have been hundreds of other books and journal articles devoted to the issue. Some have taken a firm stand against the possibility of brainwashing occurring in religious movements, while others have argued strongly that the concept of brainwashing is a useful analytic tool of investigation (Zablocki and Robbins 2001; Dawson 2003).

Moving away from monoliths

Reference has already been made to the tendency to portray NRMs in oppositional terms. Often, members have been seen as *either* passive receptacles of pseudo-religious teachings, *or* as genuine spiritual seekers. Critics have been depicted as *either* champions against damaging and fascist religious regimes, *or* unreasonable bigots. Scholars who study them have been represented as *either* objective arbiters, *or* complicit dupes. Such depictions have served as rhetorical devices for deployment in order to legitimate or sanction. On the back of such rhetoric, NRMs are not always treated in the same way by civil governments, regardless of their location. Their treatment, instead, has depended on which country they are in, the relationship that religion enjoys with the state, the information networks between that country and others, and the degree of rupture the groups manifest with prevailing norms.

Indeed NRMs, depending on where they are located, have been seen very differently. They have been viewed as co-contributors to a healthy, pluralistic society. They have been seen as groups intent on subverting the very fabric of society, or as eccentric. Or they have been largely ignored as peripheral – but not necessarily dangerous – organizations. ISKCON, for example, has been viewed as a very controversial movement in Russia. The country has only a small South Asian population and a cautious attitude in its post-communist years to religions other than the Orthodox Church. In continental Europe, ISKCON is commonly viewed as a somewhat suspicious cult. In Britain and America, by contrast, it has recently successfully distanced itself from its earlier more controversial reputation. Instead it has developed a public image as an authentic upholder of traditional Indian religion in the West, and garnered widespread support from South Asian communities.

Similarly variously perceived, by the year 2000 the Church of Scientology had a number of Hollywood celebrities among its followers in the United States, including Tom Cruise and John Travolta. It was being seen as just one more acceptable spiritual path amongst many. In Britain, Scientology was allowed to promote its message on television. But it was being identified as a dangerous and subversive movement in a number of countries in continental Europe. Switzerland's Supreme Court, for instance, dismissed an appeal in 1999 by Scientology. They upheld a Basel edict aimed at punishing 'anyone who recruits or tries to recruit passers-by in a public place using deceptive or dishonest methods'. Tribunals in both Belgium and France have included the movement on their lists of disreputable cult organizations. In Germany, too, Scientology has been seen as sinister and overly aggressive in its methods of recruitment. The movement has never been allowed to apply for tax-exempt status there as a religious organization. In 1996, the German Social Democrat Party passed the measure that applicants for public service had to declare in writing that they were not Scientologists. They also decided that local politicians should not award contracts to companies owned or operated by members of the movement, and that companies applying for such contracts had to give written assurances that they were not associated with Scientology. Over a decade later, resistance has hardly eased. In January 2009, for example, a poster with a large stop sign went up outside the German headquarters of Scientology. It declared that the district of Charlottenburg-Wilmersdorf 'expresses its opposition to the activities of the Scientology sect in this district and in Berlin, and hopes that responsible parties in Berlin will watch the Scientology sect with a critical eye in the near future' (Der Spiegel 2009).

The discrepancies in the treatment of NRMs by national governments are partly due to political and cultural differences that exist between countries. But they are also due to the diversity that scholars have noted exists within the movements themselves, especially those with an international following. Belying the uniformity of their popular image, this diversity is often visible at national and sometimes even local levels. Differences in emphasis and outlook are apparent due to particular local leaders, the closeness of the relationship with the international leadership, and the societies from which followers have come. Additionally, variety is apparent when one takes a closer look at the quite radical changes in course that can occur within movements, and at the degree of commitment an individual has to the norms of the movement to which he or she belongs. So, some degree of divergence is usually evident. This is so even in the face of common teachings, shared vocabularies, and, sometimes, considerable social pressure to conform. In the 1980s, for example, Rajneeshism went through a period in which its communes were ordered to abide by strict codes of conduct issued by the main commune in Oregon. Consequently, the breakfast bowls at the main commune in England were required to be set out in the exact manner in which they were arranged at all the other communes. Similarly, toilets were cleaned according to a rigidly prescribed directive. Despite such enforced consistency, commune members saw themselves as 'the British' manifestation of Rajneeshism, and distinct from their German, Italian, or American counterparts. Many followers, moreover, did not live in the communes and had a more relaxed approach to their allegiance to the guru.

Scholars have noted a further reason for differences between the ways NRMs are viewed in different countries. This is the decision some take to accommodate their message to new environments when they expand. Dada Lekraj, the leader of the Brahma Kumaris, taught initially that the world would soon be devastated by nuclear holocaust. He believed that his followers had a spiritual mission to prepare humanity for its aftermath. Over time, and with the expansion of his movement into Europe, however, this message has been downplayed. The group now emphasizes its association with the United Nations. It encourages newcomers to try its meditations in order to bring peace and wholeness into their lives, aiming to foster love and peace on a global level. Another example is Mahikari, a Japanese movement. Mahikari tends to emphasize its links with Christianity to its Western converts more strongly than to its Japanese ones. The popular image of NRMs is that they are homogeneous entities peopled with followers who indiscriminately adopt the norms of the international leadership. However, everyday practices usually reveal a degree of differentiation once a movement has expanded abroad, or even within national borders. The differences that can occur are often then fed back into the variety of ways in which they are regarded across the world.

Concluding remarks

If NRMs look very different depending on the historical conditions under which they are constituted, can this argument be taken one step further to query the assumption that NRMs are always with us? In the 1970s and 1980s, social change was seen as being responsible for their appearance. More recently, Gordon Melton has argued that the emergence of NRMs is simply 'a normal, ongoing process in a free society'. In his view, ' It may be that the type of new religions may change from era to era, but the production is fairly steady relative to population and urbanization. The emergence of new religions seems to be one sign of a healthy and free society' (Melton 2007: 109).

It may be that Melton is correct. However, evidence for the steady creation of NRMs is debatable. Fewer NRMs appear to be starting up in contrast to thirty or even twenty years ago and, with some significant exceptions, the majority that have been set up are led by older teachers rather than by a new young generation of spiritual leaders. In other words, it is not clear that the early twenty-first century, despite the freedoms many are said to enjoy and the rapid social change occurring is as fertile a ground for the appearance of NRMs as was the case at the end of the previous century. This point, ironically however, may save NRMs as a critical category. For if it is the case that specific historic conditions have given rise not only to the waves of NRMs that have been identified but indeed to their very identification itself, that is an interesting and suggestive point of departure for further enquiry. In other words, rather than being bound together by shared characteristics, NRMs become a coherent field of study when using a historical approach that engages with how and why groups have been socially constituted in this way at very particular times and places. Whether this kind of historical scholarship will be pursued remains to be seen. It is to be hoped, however, that fruitful new avenues for research on contemporary religion will ensure that scholars of NRMs are not doomed to spend twenty more years debating the contours and merits of the category.

Summary

Scholarship on new religious movements (NRMs) has taken place in a hotly contested arena. Disagreements over the nature of these groups and the levels of danger they pose are apparent among academics as well as other interested parties. The chapter comprises a discussion of the history of the category of 'new religious movement', examining the characteristics that have been attributed to NRMs, explanations offered for their emergence, and the conditions under which scholarship in the field has taken place. It ends by looking at the different public perceptions of NRMs around the world, and closes with a suggestion of how the term NRMs might be retained as a critically useful category.

Bibliography

Barker, E. (1984) *The Making of a Moonie: Choice or Brainwashing?* New York: Basil Blackwell.
—— (2004) 'What are we studying? A Sociological case for keeping the "Nova"' in *Nova Religio* 8, 1: 88–102.
Bryner, J. (2008) 'Is Texas group a religious sect or clear-cut cult?' MSNBC.com April 9 2008.
Chryssides, G. E. and Wilkins, M. Z. (eds) (2006) *A Reader in New Religious Movements: Readings in the Study of New Religious Movements.* London, Continuum International Publishing Group.
Dawson, L. L. (ed.) (2003) *Cults and New Religious Movements: A Reader.* Second edition. Oxford and Boston: Blackwell.
Der Spiegel online (2009) 'Berlin District Posts Warning About Scientology.' Jan. 23, 2009.
Gallagher, E. (2007) 'Compared to What? "Cults" and "New Religious Movements"' in *History of Religions* 47,2:205–220.
Introvigne, M. (1997) 'Religious Liberty in Europe' in *ISKCON Communications Journal* 5, 2: 37–48.
Jules-Rosette, B. (ed.) (1979) *The New Religions of Africa.* Norwood, NJ: Ablex Publishing Company.
Melton, J. G. (2004) 'Toward a definition of "New Religion"' in *Nova Religio* 8, 1: 73–87.
—— 2007) 'New New Religions: Revisiting a Concept' in *Nova Religio* 10, 4: 103–112.
—— (ed.) (2009) *Encyclopedia of American Religions,* 8th Edition. Detroit: Gale Research Inc.
Nova Religio Symposium (1998) 'Academic Integrity and the Study of New Religious Movements'. 2, 1: 8–54.
Sociological Analysis (1983), 44, 3.
Weber, M. (1968) *Economy and Society: An Outline of Interpretive Sociology.* Volumes One and Two. G. Roth and C. Wittich (eds). New York: Bedminster Press.
Wilson, B. (1992) *The Social Dimensions of Sectarianism.* New York: Oxford University Press.
Zablocki, B. and Robbins, T. (2001) *Misunderstanding Cults: Searching for Objectivity in a Controversial Field.* Toronto: University of Toronto Press.

Suggested reading

Barker, E. (1984) *The Making of a Moonie: Choice or Brainwashing?* New York: Basil Blackwell.
   A comparative and widely cited study of conversion to the Unification Church by a leading scholar in the field.

Chryssides, G. E. and Wilkins, M. Z. (eds) (2006) *A Reader in New Religious Movements: Readings in the Study of New Religious Movements.* London: Continuum International Publishing Group.
   A very useful reader offering not only selected writings from NRMs but also passages from pertinent legislation and publications about NRMs by outside agencies.

Dawson, L. L. (ed.) (2003) *Cults and New Religious Movements: A Reader.* Second edition. Oxford and Boston: Blackwell.
   An excellent and readable compilation of some of the most influential scholarly work on new religious movements, including articles by Wallis, Beckford, Stark and Bainbridge, Barker, Singer and Wuthnow, among others.

Introvigne, M. (1997) 'Religious Liberty in Europe' in *ISKCON Communications Journal* 5, 2: 37–48.
An argument by the Director of CESNUR, a centre for the academic study of new religions, for such movements to be seen as religious minorities and studied in those terms.

Jules-Rosette, B. (ed.) (1979) *The New Religions of Africa*. Norwood, NJ: Ablex Publishing Company.
An edited volume offering a good overview of the diversity of new religion in Africa.

Melton, J. G. (ed.) (2009) *Encyclopedia of American Religions*, 8th Edition. Detroit: Gale Research Inc.
A formidable three volume reference work offering detailed profiles of over two thousand religions in North America.

Nova Religio Symposium (1998) 'Academic Integrity and the Study of New Religious Movements'. 2, 1: 8–54.
The symposium comprised a debate between scholars with close relationships with new religions and their critics.

Sociological Analysis (1983). 44, 3.
The issue was devoted to articles on the relationships academics have with the groups they study.

Weber, M. (1968) *Economy and Society: An Outline of Interpretive Sociology*. Volumes One and Two. G. Roth and C. Wittich (eds). New York: Bedminster Press.
The volumes include Weber's classic writings on charismatic authority.

Wilson, B. (1992) *The Social Dimensions of Sectarianism*. New York: Oxford University Press
The book is a characteristically careful and wide-ranging example of the work of this major proponent of the 'secularization thesis'.

Zablocki, B. D. and Robbins, T. (2001) *Misunderstanding Cults: Searching for Objectivity in a Controversial Field*. Toronto: University of Toronto Press.
An edited volume presenting different scholarly opinions on objectivity and 'brainwashing'.

Chapter 21

Fundamentalism

Henry Munson

On May 24, 2001, the *Jerusalem Post* printed an article entitled 'THINK AGAIN: God didn't say "You might want to …"'. In this article, 'ultra-Orthodox' columnist Jonathan Rosenblum castigates a prominent Conservative rabbi for asserting that the exodus from Egypt did not in fact occur. 'No plagues, no splitting of the sea – all a fairy tale', as Rosenblum puts it. He suggests that what the Conservative rabbi is actually saying is that 'It doesn't really matter that the Torah's claim to be the word of God to man is false', because the Torah is nevertheless 'divinely inspired' and embodies important 'spiritual values'. Rosenblum asks why should Jews look to the Torah (the first five books of the Hebrew Bible) for moral guidance if it consists of 'some really huge whoppers – the Exodus from Egypt, the giving of the Torah at Sinai, the stories of the alleged Patriarchs'. Rosenblum notes that the president of the Jewish Theological Seminary, the principal seminary of Conservative Judaism, which is in fact less conservative than Orthodox Judaism, has dismissed the book of Leviticus as having being superseded by our 'modern sensibility'. Rosenblum observes that if the Torah is simply the product of human authors, and if Jews can discard those parts of it they regard as incompatible with their 'modern sensibility', they can pick and choose those aspects of religious law they want to follow much as shoppers pick and choose in a supermarket. The result is moral chaos. This critique of Conservative Judaism would be qualified by many as 'fundamentalist' insofar as it insists on strict conformity to a sacred text believed to be in some sense the word of God.

Some scholars argue that the term *fundamentalism* should be used only to refer to those conservative Protestants who refer to themselves as fundamentalists. To speak of fundamentalism in other contexts, they argue, is to confuse analysis and attack, scholarship and polemic. This argument is made by people on both the theological and political right and left. From the right, scholars argue that religious liberals (those who pick and choose the commandments they will obey) use the term *fundamentalist* to denigrate those who insist on adhering to and upholding the traditional doctrines of a religion. From the left, scholars often argue that Westerners speak of 'Islamic fundamentalism' in order to undermine the legitimacy of Islamic movements that seek to overcome Western domination of the Islamic world. From both perspectives, the term 'fundamentalist' is seen as illegitimate because it serves to delegitimize.

Conservative Lutheran sociologist Peter Berger suggests that what needs to be explained is not that many people insist on defending their traditional religious beliefs, but that many liberal academics find this strange (Berger 1997). Sociologist Steve Bruce elaborates on this theme as follows:

In the broad sweep of human history, fundamentalists are normal. What we now regard as religious 'extremism' was commonplace 200 years ago in the Western world and is still commonplace in most parts of the globe. It is not the dogmatic believer who insists that the sacred texts are divinely inspired and true, who tries to model his life on the ethical requirements of those texts, and who seeks to impose these requirements on the entire society who is unusual. The liberal who supposes that his sacred texts are actually human constructions of differing moral worth, whose religion makes little difference in his life, and who is quite happy to accept that what his God requires of him is not binding on other members of his society: this is the strange and remarkable creature.

(Bruce 2000: 116–17)

Bruce goes on to say that 'Fundamentalism is a rational response of traditionally religious peoples to social, political and economic changes that downgrade and constrain the role of religion in the public world' (Bruce 2000: 117).

Edward Said approaches the subject of fundamentalism from a different perspective. He has argued that the terms *terrorism* and *fundamentalism* are both 'derived entirely from the concerns and intellectual factories in metropolitan centers like Washington and London':

They are fearful images that lack discriminate contents or definition, but they signify moral power and approval for whoever uses them, moral defensiveness and criminalization for whomever they designate … By such means the governability of large numbers of people is assured …

(Said 1993: 310)

Despite this condemnation of fundamentalism as an artifact of the Western imperial imagination, Said has himself used the term. In discussing Karen Armstrong's *Islam: A Short History* in a review essay published in 1992, he writes:

Her book's most valuable section is that in which she discusses the varieties of modern fundamentalism without the usual invidious focus on Islam. And rather than seeing it only as a negative phenomenon, she has an admirable gift for understanding fundamentalism from within, as adherence to a faith that is threatened by a strong secular authoritarianism. As an almost doctrinaire secularist myself, I nevertheless found myself swayed by her sympathetic and persuasive argument in this section …

(Said 1992: 74)

So here we find Said using the very term and concept he has often condemned as an egregious example of Western 'Orientalism'. Yet in this same essay, and on the same page, he reverts to his more usual position regarding 'Islamic fundamentalism' in particular:

above all, look with the deepest suspicion on anyone who wants to tell you the real truth about Islam and terrorism, fundamentalism, militancy, fanaticism, etc. . . . leave those great non-subjects to the experts, their think tanks, government departments, and policy intellectuals, who get us into one unsuccessful and wasteful war after the other.

(Said 1992)

So here we have one of the most influential intellectuals of the late twentieth century insisting that fundamentalism, like terrorism, is a 'non-subject' conjured up by Western imperialists to discredit Middle Eastern resistance to foreign domination. Yet this same intellectual speaks of 'varieties of fundamentalism', thus suggesting that he believes that fundamentalism really does exist outside the intellectual factories of the West. This contradiction illustrates a basic fact: most scholars are uncomfortable with the concept of fundamentalism when used outside its original Protestant context, but they often find themselves falling back on it for lack of a better alternative – when describing conservative religious movements of which they disapprove.

In addition to the common criticism that the term *fundamentalist*, when used outside its original Protestant context, denigrates those who adhere to and defend the orthodox tenets of their religion, another common criticism is that the imposition of the originally Christian term *fundamentalist* on other religious traditions tends to force a wide variety of movements into a Procrustean model that ignores many of their distinctive features. This is in turn related to the argument that the very fact of using an originally Christian term in other religious contexts entails some degree of Christocentric distortion.

Despite such criticisms, some scholars defend the use of the term *fundamentalism* as a useful tool for comparative purposes. Martin E. Marty and R. Scott Appleby argue that the use of the term outside the Protestant context has become so common, in the West at least, that it would be impossible to eradicate this usage. They argue that no alternative term has been found for comparative purposes, and that comparison is essential if we wish to transcend the description of specific cases. Moreover, they argue, 'all words have to come from somewhere', therefore the Christian origin of the term *fundamentalism* is not an insurmountable obstacle so long as the comparative use of the term does not involve forcing all movements called fundamentalist to resemble Protestant fundamentalism (Marty and Appleby 1991a: viii). They insist that they do not want to force all movements into a Procrustean bed. They define fundamentalism as follows:

> In these pages, then, fundamentalism has appeared as a tendency, a habit of mind, found within religious communities and movements, which manifests itself as a strategy, or set of strategies, by which beleaguered believers attempt to preserve their distinctive identity as a people or group. Feeling this identity to be at risk in the contemporary era, they fortify it by a selective retrieval of doctrines, beliefs, and practices from a sacred past. These retrieved 'fundamentals' are refined, modified, and sanctioned in a spirit of shrewd pragmatism: they are to serve as a bulwark against the encroachment of outsiders who threaten to draw the believers into a syncretistic, areligious, or irreligious cultural milieu …
>
> (Marty and Appleby 1991a: 835)

We shall see that this very broad conception of fundamentalism ignores many important distinctions among the movements Marty and Appleby describe as fundamentalist. In this essay, we shall speak of movements having a fundamentalist dimension only if they insist on strict conformity to sacred scripture and a moral code ostensibly based on it. These movements articulate moral outrage provoked by the violation of traditional religious values. This is also true of many politicized forms of religious conservatism, notably Catholic conservatism, that do not insist on strict conformity to sacred scripture *per se*.

Moreover, and this is crucial, some movements that have a fundamentalist dimension also articulate secular grievances. To focus only on their fundamentalist dimension is to ignore some of the principal sources of their political significance. We should not reduce moral outrage provoked by the violation of traditional religious values to a mere epiphenomenon of ethnic, nationalistic or other social grievances, but we should also avoid ignoring such grievances when the available evidence suggests that they are in fact important sources of the appeal of some movements commonly called 'fundamentalist'.

In *Strong Religion: The Rise of Fundamentalisms around the World*, Gabriel Almond, R. Scott Appleby, and Emmanuel Sivan argue that 'fundamentalist movements form in reaction to, and in defense against, the processes and consequences of secularization and modernization' (2003: 93). If the rejection of the marginalization of religion is not a movement's 'original impulse and a recurring reference', they argue, it is not in fact a fundamentalist movement (2003: 94). They muddy the definitional waters, however, by declaring:

> In short, the threat to the religious tradition may come from the general processes of modernization and secularization, from other religious groups and/or ethnic groups, from a secular state (imperial or indigenous) seeking to secularize and delimit the domain of the sacred, or from various combinations of these.
>
> (Almond *et al.* 2003: 94)

This passage blurs the important distinction between a conservative religious movement that rejects innovations that violate its traditional beliefs and a movement in which religion serves primarily as a marker of identity. In the first case, moral outrage provoked by the violation of traditional religious values is of central importance. In the second case, it is not.

Identity trumps belief: Protestant Unionism in Northern Ireland and Sikh militancy in India

If we take the case of Northern Ireland, for example, religion serves primarily as a marker of collective identity for both Catholic and Protestant, rather than as a set of beliefs to be defended in the face of secularization. This point is illustrated by the following joke. One night, a distinguished gentleman was walking down a dark alley in Belfast. Suddenly a masked man jumped out in front of him, waved a gun in his face, and asked, 'Are you a Catholic or a Protestant?' The terrified gentleman stammered, 'W-w-w-well, I-I-I am actually an atheist.' 'Well now', responded the gunman, with what appeared to be a twinkle in his eye, 'would you be a Catholic atheist or a Protestant atheist?' Similarly, when rioting Hindus pull men's pants down to see if they are circumcised, they are not interested in whether or not circumcised men are believing or practicing Muslims. A circumcised penis marks a man as the killable 'Other' regardless of what he actually believes or does. Religion serves as a distinctive marker of identity, and notably of national identity, even in the absence of belief.

There are movements in which religion serves primarily as a marker of ethnic or national identity, but which nonetheless have a clear fundamentalist dimension, in the sense that some of their most prominent adherents insist on strict conformity to sacred scripture and a moral code ostensibly based on it. Protestant Unionism in Northern Ireland, for example, is basically an expression of the fears of Protestants who are afraid of losing their identity and their rights in a predominantly Catholic Ireland. Many Unionists are in fact quite secular and only about a quarter, or at most a third, are fundamentalists (Bruce 1998: 68). Yet the fundamentalist Reverend Ian Paisley's Democratic Unionist Party (DUP) won more votes than any other party in Northern Ireland's legislative elections of November 26, 2003. Since

1979, Paisley has also consistently won more votes than any other candidate in Northern Ireland's elections to the parliament of the European Union – despite the fact that Paisley has portrayed the European Union as a Catholic plot to undermine Protestantism (Bruce 1998: 63–4, 67). From May 2007 through June 2008, Paisley served as Northern Ireland's 'first minister', with Sinn Féin's Martin McGuinness serving as deputy first minister. This is an important example of how militant fundamentalists can sometimes be induced to embrace moderate positions they once condemned. But for present purposes, the crucial point is that many non-fundamentalist Protestants in Northern Ireland regularly voted for Paisley. Steve Bruce has argued that this is because of the basic role conservative evangelicalism has played in shaping Ulster Protestant identity (1998: 73). It may also reflect Paisley's ability to articulate Protestant concerns in an earthy, populist language everyone can understand. The important point is that Protestant Unionism is primarily about identity rather than about conformity to scripture even though its most famous leader is a fundamentalist.

The case of Protestant Unionism is strikingly similar to Sikh militancy in India insofar as its fundamentalist dimension is subordinate to its nationalist dimension. The militant Sikh movement first attracted attention in 1978, when the fiery preacher Sant Jarnail Singh Bhindranwale led a march to break up a gathering of the Sant Nirankari sect considered heretical by orthodox Sikhs (Oberoi 1993: 273).

Bhindranwale's movement definitely had a fundamentalist dimension to it insofar as it stressed the need for conformity to a sacred text. But Sikh militancy was primarily an ethnic and nationalist movement, with religion serving as the principal marker of Sikh identity. That is, the Sikh militants of the late twentieth century fought primarily for an independent Sikh state in the Indian province of Punjab. While Bhindranwale and his followers did condemn Sikhs who violated the traditional Sikh moral code, the primary enemy of all the Sikh militants, some of whom were more religious than others, was the state of India rather than secularism *per se*. The militants condemned the government of India not for being secular, but for being biased in favor of Hindus (Mahmood 1996).

Hindu nationalism

At first glance, and even second and third, the notion of 'Hindu fundamentalism' seems preposterous. Hinduism does not have a single sacred text to which conformity can be demanded. Another important objection to the characterization of Hindu groups such as the Bharatiya Janata Party (BJP) as 'Hindu fundamentalists' is that conformity to a religious code of conduct is not of particular importance to them. They do speak of establishing a truly Hindu state and society, but for these people, Hinduism is above all a symbol of national identity rather than a set of rules to be obeyed (Raychaudhuri 1995).

The primarily nationalistic orientation of the Bharatiya Janata Party is reflected in its name, which means 'the Party of the Indian People'. Similarly, the name of a related group, the Rashtriya Swayamsevak Sangh (RSS) means 'the Association of National Volunteers'. In the Hindu nationalist literature, the emphasis is generally on the threat posed by Muslims and, more recently, converts to Christianity. The Hindu nationalist obsession with Muslims is reflected in the slogan 'For Muslims, there are only two places, Pakistan or the grave' (*Musulmanan ke do-hi shtan, pakistan aur kabristan* (Halliday 1995: 47).

Hindu nationalists do not stress strict conformity to sacred scripture or to a moral code based on it. It is true that members of the militant Hindu nationalist party Shiv Sena have attacked billboards for a film about a lesbian relationship between two Hindu women. They have also vandalized stores selling Valentine's Day greeting cards (Sengupta 2002). But by and large, puritanical insistence on conformity to a strict moral code has not been a distinctive feature of Hindu nationalism.

The activism of the people Marty and Appleby call 'Hindu fundamentalists' was triggered by the conversion to Islam of thousands of untouchables in southern India in the early 1980s. Coupled with the emergence of militant Sikh separatism, the resurgence of Muslim separatism in Kashmir, and the increasingly vocal demands of untouchables and lower-caste Hindus, some high-caste Hindus began to feel that their status in Indian society, and indeed the very survival of Hindu India, was at risk. This sense of vulnerability rather than a sense that divine law was being violated led to the increased political significance of the BJP and related groups in the late 1980s and early 1990s. In short, the basic impulse of groups like the RSS and the BJP is unquestionably nationalistic rather than 'fundamentalist'.

Given the close relationship between religious and national identity in much of the world, it is not surprising that we do find a nationalist dimension in some of the Christian, Jewish, and Muslim movements often called 'fundamentalist'. But the Hindu case differs radically from Christian fundamentalism, for example. Christian fundamentalists do tend to see the United States as God's chosen land, a 'city on a hill.' During the First World War, the evangelist Billy Sunday argued that 'Christianity and Patriotism are synonymous terms' (Marsden 1991: 51). However, late-twentieth-century Christian fundamentalism in the United States was fueled primarily by the moral outrage provoked by abortion, the banning of school prayer, feminism, gay rights, the teaching of evolution, and similar issues. Such moral issues do not dominate the rhetoric of Hindu nationalism.

Among the most salient issues associated with Hindu nationalism is that of the destruction of the Babri Mosque in Ayodhya and the rebuilding of the Hindu temple said to have existed on this site before its destruction by the Muslim Mughal dynasty. While there was undoubtedly some real religious fervor associated with the belief that Ayodhya was the birthplace of Ram (avatar of Vishnu and hero of the *Ramayana*), the impact of the conflict at Ayodhya was above all a reflection of the Hindu nationalists' emphasis on the essentially Hindu character of India and their view of Muslims as inherently alien enemies of Hindu India. The destruction of the mosque at Ayodhya on December 6, 1992 led to widespread rioting in which Hindus killed several thousand Muslims.

Rather than insist on strict doctrinal purity, Hindu nationalists try to encourage Sikhs and Jains to think of themselves as Hindus despite the distinctiveness of many of their beliefs. Some Hindu militants have admittedly tried to systematize Hinduism in the manner of the Western monotheisms. One group has proposed, for example, a uniform code of conduct for all Hindus, with the *Bhagavad Gita* serving as the sacred text of all Hindus. But the fact remains that the defense of the Hindu community, seen as synonymous with the Indian nation, has been the main theme of Hindu militancy rather than the goal of creating a Hindu state and society based on strict conformity to Hindu religious law. Referring to Hindu nationalism as 'fundamentalism' is thus misleading.

This does not mean that there is no point in comparing Hindu nationalism with movements in which the insistence on conformity to a strict moral code is of primary importance. On the contrary, such comparison is indispensable insofar as it helps us understand the distinction between nationalistic movements in which religion serves primarily as a badge of national identity and movements of militant religious conservatism which are fueled primarily by outrage by the violation of traditional religious values – 'fundamentalist' movements being a specific kind of militant religious conservatism in which strict conformity to a sacred text is stressed. (Militant Catholic and Eastern Orthodox conservatism are not characterized by this insistence on strict conformity to a specific sacred text although they do focus on strict conformity to traditional religious values.) We should bear in mind that we are speaking of a continuum of movements rather than a sharp dichotomy between religiously-tinged nationalism and militant religious conservatism. As the Unionist and Sikh cases demonstrate, nationalism and militant religious conservatism are often intertwined and careful analysis is required to determine their relative weight in specific cases. That is what we shall now attempt to undertake with respect to the best-known Christian, Jewish, and Muslim movements commonly referred to as 'fundamentalist.'

Christian fundamentalism in the United States

Fundamentalism the thing existed long before the word did. One could speak of the Maccabean revolt of the second century BCE as having a fundamentalist impulse insofar as it insisted on strict conformity to the Torah and Jewish religious law (Munson 2003b). Similarly, Calvin's sixteenth-century Genevan polity could be called fundamentalist insofar as it insisted on strict conformity to the Bible and a moral code ostensibly based on it. But the term *Fundamentalist* (traditionally written with an upper-case F) was only coined in 1920 by Curtis Lee Laws, the conservative editor of the Baptist newspaper *The Watchman-Examiner*. Laws created the word to refer to militantly conservative evangelical Protestants ready 'to do battle royal for the fundamentals' of Christianity (Beale 1986: 195).

Modern Christian fundamentalism emerged as a revolt against the tendency to rationalize and demythologize Protestant Christianity in the late nineteenth and early twentieth centuries. In response to Protestant liberalism that watered down the basic tenets of Christianity, conservative evangelicals published a series of pamphlets entitled *The Fundamentals* from 1910 to 1915. The central theme of *The Fundamentals* is that the Bible is the inerrant word of God. That is to say that it is without error. Associated with this idea is the belief that believers should live their lives according to a strict Biblically based moral code.

Evangelical Christians believe that the Bible is the word of God, that one can only be saved from eternal damnation by accepting Jesus Christ as one's savior, and that the Christian is obliged to 'evangelize', that is, to spread the 'good news' of Christ's death and resurrection for the sake of humanity. The acceptance of Jesus as one's savior is linked to the idea of being 'born again' through an experience of the Holy Spirit. George Marsden has described Christian fundamentalists as evangelicals who are 'angry about something' (Marsden 1991: 1).

In the nineteenth century, Christian evangelicals of a fundamentalist orientation (again, the thing preceded the word) had been politically active on both sides of the slavery issue, in anti-Catholic nativism, in the fight to maintain Sunday as a day of rest, and in the temperance movement. This political activism continued in the early twentieth century, with evolution becoming a major issue in the 1920s.

Some Christian fundamentalists ran for public office in the 1930s and 1940s on platforms that combined anti-Semitism, anti-communism, populism, and Christian revivalism (see Ribuffo 1983). From the 1950s through the 1970s, fundamentalist preachers like Billy James Hargis combined similar themes, minus the explicit anti-Semitism, with opposition to racial integration.

Although Christian fundamentalist ministers were active in opposing the civil rights movement and communism in the 1960s, they remained politically marginal. In 1979, however, the Reverend Jerry Falwell formed the Moral Majority in collaboration with important mainstream conservatives in the Republican party to defend religious Christian values. This marked the emergence of the 'New Christian Right,' which has become an important factor in American pilitics. Falwell, like most fundamentalists and some other Americans, felt that the feminist movement, the prohibition of school-sponsored prayer in public schools, the teaching of sex education, the gay rights movement, and the legalization of abortion all represented a process of moral decay that had to be halted. While most liberal intellectuals would see opposition to these developments as a rejection of secular 'modernity', most religious conservatives would see them as a fight to save their nation's moral integrity.

The federal government's attempt to deny the tax-exempt status of many Christian schools founded to circumvent the federally mandated racial integration of public schools was also one of the reasons for the formation of the Moral Majority, but in the 1980s many southern Christian fundamentalists disavowed their earlier opposition to civil rights. The Christian Right nevertheless remained an overwhelmingly white movement that was viewed with suspicion by most African Americans.

While it is true that Christian fundamentalism in the US has often been linked to religious bigotry, by the late twentieth century, Christian fundamentalists worked closely with conservative Catholics, Mormons, and sometimes even Orthodox Jews on moral issues such as abortion, prayer in schools, homosexuality, and the teaching of 'creationism' or 'intelligent design'. They saw themselves as defending their values in the face of the onslaught of liberal and secular values in American society rather than as trying to impose their values on others.

Politicized Jewish Orthodoxy in Israel

Three politicized forms of Orthodox Judaism in Israel (and elsewhere) have often been called 'fundamentalist': militant religious Zionism, Ashkenazi ultra-Orthodoxy, and the Shas party, which represents Jews of Middle Eastern origin. These groups are called 'fundamentalist' by their critics, not their supporters (Aran 1991; Heilman and Friedman 1991; Hirschberg 1999; Lustick 1988; Sprinzak 1991, 1999; Viorst 2007; see also Munson 2008).

Since the fall of Jerusalem's second temple in CE 70, most Jews have lived in the diaspora, that is, dispersed far from the Land of Israel promised by God to the Jewish people according to the Hebrew Bible. During their prolonged 'exile' (galut) from the Land of Israel, Jews all over the world prayed daily for the coming of the Messiah who would bring the Jews back to the Land of Israel and deliver them from their gentile oppressors. Zionism secularized this traditional messianic theme. Instead of waiting for God and the Messiah to bring the Jews back to the Land of Israel, Zionists argued that Jews should take it upon themselves to return to this land.

Most Orthodox rabbis opposed Zionism on the grounds that it involved humans doing what only God and the Messiah could do. In traditional Judaism, the return to the Land of Israel was inseparable from the messianic redemption of the people of Israel. For humans to return to this land and create a state there was to defy God's will and postpone the real redemption and the real ingathering of the exiles. Another reason for Orthodox hostility to Zionism was that most of the early Zionist leaders were clearly not interested in a state based on strict conformity to Jewish religious law.

In speaking of Orthodox Judaism, we should distinguish between the 'modern Orthodox' and the 'ultra-Orthodox'. (The ultra-Orthodox themselves generally object to the latter term.) The modern Orthodox insist on strict conformity to Jewish law, but they have nonetheless devised ways to participate in modern society in both the diaspora and Israel. The ultra-Orthodox are more traditional and insist on strict separation from gentile society as well as separation from Jews who do not follow Jewish law as strictly as they do. Hostility toward Zionism prevailed among both modern Orthodox and ultra-Orthodox rabbis in the late nineteenth and early twentieth centuries, though it virtually disappeared among the former when the Holocaust appeared to confirm the Zionist argument that Jews could only be safe in their own state.

Some modern Orthodox rabbis sought to legitimate Orthodox participation in the Zionist movement by severing it from the idea of the Messiah. Rabbi Isaac Jacob Reines (1839–1915), who founded the Mizrahi religious Zionist movement in 1902, agreed with the ultra-Orthodox that Jews should not try to 'force the End' on their own initiative. He embraced the traditional belief that Jews should passively await the coming of the Messiah, but, unlike the ultra-Orthodox, he argued that the Zionist settlement of the Land of Israel had nothing to do with the future messianic redemption of the Jews and thus did not constitute a heretical defiance of God's will. This form of religious Zionism was soon displaced by a radically different view, namely that Zionism was itself part of the gradual messianic redemption of the Jewish people and the Land of Israel. The secular Zionists were doing the work of God and the Messiah but they did not yet know it. This argument was made by Rabbi Avraham Kook (1865–1935), and it has remained a basic theme in religious Zionism (Ravitzky 1996).

Religious Zionists are usually referred to as the 'national religious' (*datim le'umim*) in Hebrew. This term captures the fusion of modern Orthodoxy and nationalism that has generally characterized religious Zionism. Many religious Zionists saw the Six-Day War of 1967 as a miracle and as a major step forward on the way toward the messianic redemption of the Jewish people. East Jerusalem, the Temple Mount, Judea, the very heart of ancient Israel, were now once again in Jewish hands. To return any of this land to the Arabs would be to defy God. The religious Zionists who felt this way began to settle in the territories occupied, or as they saw it, liberated, in the Six-Day War. There is also a religious Zionist peace movement, known as Meimad, which advocates giving up much of the territory won in 1967 in return for peace.

For the militant religious Zionists in the settler movement, settling the land won in 1967 and preventing the government from withdrawing from it took priority over anything else. These militant religious Zionists do advocate the creation of a state based on strict conformity to what they consider the laws of God and they did conform strictly to these laws in their everyday lives. But their political activities have focused primarily on settling and retaining the land won in 1967 rather than on creating a state and society based on strict conformity to religious law. Thus, while one can speak of militant religious Zionism as having a 'fundamentalist' dimension, it is also essential to remember its nationalist dimension. Militant religious Zionists tap some basic themes in mainstream Zionism, notably the idea that the goal of Zionism is to create a new Jew who will never submit to oppression. For militant religious Zionists, this involves a return to the Judaism of the Maccabees who fought Hellenism in the second century BCE much as religious Zionists fight decadent secularism today (Munson 2003b). Mainstream Zionism has always downplayed the religious and 'fundamentalist' dimensions of the Maccabean revolt while stressing its nationalistic aspect.

The ultra-Orthodox are often referred to in Hebrew as *Haredim*, or 'those who tremble' in the presence of God because they are 'God-fearing'. Unlike the modern Orthodox, who are virtually all religious Zionists, the ultra-Orthodox continue to reject Zionism, in principle at least, as a blasphemous attempt to bring about the return of the Jews to the Land of Israel by human means when God intended this to be effected by the Messiah. In practice, this rejection of Zionism results in a variety of different political positions ranging from that of the politically insignificant Neturei Karta to Haredi political parties that sometimes determine which of Israel's major parties gets to govern. (Israel's major parties often have to make concessions to small religious parties to win the support of a majority of the members of the Israeli parliament, the Knesset, and thereby form a government.)

The Ashkenazi Haredim, that is, the ultra-Orthodox of eastern European origin, differ from the ultra-Orthodox of Middle Eastern origin, who will be discussed below. Unlike the religious Zionists, whose political activities since 1967 have focused primarily on settling and preventing withdrawal from the territories occupied in the Six-Day War, the Haredi (ultra-Orthodox) political parties have continued to concentrate primarily on obtaining funding for their community and on enforcing strict conformity to their interpretation of Jewish religious law with respect to issues like observance of the Sabbath, conversion, Kosher dietary laws, and the desecration of the dead by archaeologists. Such issues clearly involve the defense of traditional religious values rather than nationalism. Since the Six-Day War, however, most Ashkenazi Haredim have tended to support the hard-line position of the militant religious Zionists regarding 'land-for-peace' despite their continued theoretical opposition to Zionism and the state it produced. This is a striking example of how changing social and political contexts can affect religious beliefs.

The Ashkenazi Haredim traditionally withdrew from surrounding gentile society in the diaspora and continue to separate themselves from mainstream Israeli society. Yet in the last few decades of the twentieth century, they became increasingly aggressive in trying to incorporate their moral code into Israeli law. Like Christian fundamentalists in the United States, they have been torn between the desire to withdraw from society and the desire to reform it. Because of their high birth rate, their numbers have grown, and this has meant greater electoral power. This has been especially evident in Jerusalem, which elected its first Haredi mayor in 2003. Israelis often use Jerusalem and Tel Aviv as metaphors to symbolize the 'culture war' between religious and secular Israelis (Faux 2008: 245–52).

The third major form of Jewish militant Orthodoxy in Israel often called fundamentalist is represented by the Shas party, Shas being an acronym for 'Sephardim Guardians of the Torah' in Hebrew. Shas is an interesting example of the fusion of militant religious conservatism with a sense of ethnic grievance. Although the term *Sephardim* originally referred to Jews of Spanish origin, it has come to be used to refer to Jews of Middle Eastern origin, or Mizrahim ('Orientals'). The Mizrahim are, by and large, less well educated and less well paid than the Ashkenazim, and many of them feel that Israelis of European origin discriminate against them. In addition to celebrating Sephardi/Mizrahi identity and advocating strict conformity to God's laws, Shas provides schools and other social services for poor Mizrahim. Shas is similar to some Islamic movements in this respect (Hirschberg 1999; Lehmann and Siebzehner 2006).

One can speak of a fundamentalist dimension to Shas insofar as it consistently supports legislation to enforce strict conformity to Jewish religious law. But much of its popular support is rooted in the frustration, resentment, and even rage of those Jews of Middle Eastern origin who feel they have been discriminated against by the Ashkenazi elite of European origin. Most Mizrahim who vote for Shas do not themselves conform to the strict moral code advocated by the party. Like the strongly nationalistic religious Zionist settlers, Shas demonstrates that movements often called fundamentalist often owe their political success to secular grievances as well as strictly religious ones. (Shas has tended to take an increasingly hawkish position on peace talks with the Palestinians.)

Islamic militancy in the Middle East

The term *Islamic fundamentalism* tends to conjure up images of fanaticism and terrorism. This is one reason most scholars of Islam prefer the more anodyne term *Islamist*. Islamist movements, like their Christian and Jewish counterparts, come in various forms. There are moderate, non-violent Islamist movements like the AK Party in Turkey. There are violent, extremist groups like al-Qa'ida (al Qaeda). And there are a number of Islamic movements that articulate specific ethnic and nationalist grievances, such as Hezbollah, which represents the Shi'a of Lebanon, and Hamas, which meshes Islamic fundamentalism with Palestinian nationalism (see Munson 2003a, 2004, 2008; Norton 2007; Pape 2005; Roy 2003).

Most militant Islamic movements clearly resort to violence far more often than do the Christian and Jewish movements commonly called fundamentalist. It is true that Christian fundamentalists were actively involved in the terrorism of the Ku Klux Klan and similar groups (Wade 1987). It is also true that Christian fundamentalists have been involved in attacking abortion clinics and killing doctors who perform abortions (Juergensmeyer 2000). Similarly, it is true that militant religious Zionists have engaged in some violence, notably Baruch Goldstein's massacre of 29 Palestinians praying in Hebron, Yigal Amir's assassination of Prime Minister Yitzhak Rabin in 1995, and regular attacks on Palestinians (Shulman 2007). But Christian and Jewish fundamentalists have not engaged in the same scale of violence as militant Islamic groups like Hizb Allah (Hezbollah), Hamas, and al-Qa'ida.

This does not mean that Islam is inherently more violent than Christianity. One can find many verses extolling the slaughter of the enemy in the name of God in the sacred scriptures of Judaism and Christianity (see Deuteronomy 7: 1–2, 7: 16 and 20: 10–18). The history of Christianity is full of holy wars and massacres of Jews condemned as 'Christ-killers' and the Holocaust was of course perpetrated by Christians (Carroll 2001). If violence is more commonly used by militant Islamic movements than by militantly conservative Christian and Jewish movements, this is because of the prevailing social and political situation in the Islamic world, and not because of some immutable trait of Islam (see Munson 2005).

One feature that distinguishes Islamism from conservative Christian and Jewish militancy is its anti-imperial dimension. When the European empires subjugated the Islamic world in the nineteenth and early twentieth centuries, Muslims perceived their wars against European imperialism as forms of *jihad*, or holy war. The distinction between Muslim and infidel became intertwined with the distinctions between the colonized and the colonizer and the oppressed and the oppressor. Thus traditional hostility toward the unbeliever as an unbeliever was now infused with new meaning. This had unfortunate consequences for religious minorities in the Islamic world (much as Irish Protestants suffered from sharing the religion of England).

This anti-imperial dimension persisted in the Islamist movements of the late twentieth century. On February 19, 1978, on the fortieth day of mourning for the 'martyrs' who had died in the first protests that eventually mushroomed into Iran's Islamic revolution, the revolution's leader the Ayatollah Khomeini declared, 'As for America, a signatory to the Declaration of Human Rights, it imposed this shah upon us, a worthy successor to his father. During the period he has ruled, this creature has transformed Iran into an official colony of America' (Khomeini 1981: 215). When Khomeini landed at Tehran airport on February 1, 1979, after fourteen and a half years of exile, he declared: 'Our triumph will come when all forms of foreign control have been brought to an end and all roots of the monarchy have been plucked out of the soil of our land' (1981: 252). On September 12, 1980, Khomeini told the Iranian pilgrims to Mecca, 'For more than fifty years, the Pahlavi puppet [the shah] has dragged our country down, filling the pockets of foreigners – particularly Britain and America – with the abundant wealth of our land …' (1981: 303).

All these fiery denunciations of the Western domination of 'our land' demonstrate that there was a nationalist dimension to Khomeini's militancy. We see this also in many of the slogans chanted during the marches that eventually coalesced into Iran's Islamic Revolution of 1978–9: 'We will destroy Yankee power in Iran! Death to the American dog! Shah held on a leash by the Americans! Hang this American king!' (Munson 1988: 63, 123). Iran's Islamic revolution was, among other things, a nationalist revolution against American domination.

For Khomeini, the goal of creating a strictly Islamic state and society based exclusively on Islamic law was inextricably intertwined with the goal of overcoming foreign domination. In 1972, he declared:

> If the Muslim states and peoples had relied on Islam and its inherent capabilities and powers instead of depending on the East (the Soviet Union) and the West, and if they had placed the enlightened and liberating precepts of the Quran before their eyes and put them into practice, then they would not today be captive slaves of the Zionist aggressors, terrified victims of the American Phantoms, and toys in the hands of the accommodating policies of the satanic Soviet Union. It is the disregard of the noble Quran by the Islamic countries that has brought the Islamic community to this difficult situation full of misfortunes and reversals and placed its fate in the hands of the imperialism of the left and the right.
>
> (Khomeini 1977: 156–7; Khomeini 1981: 210)

Passages like this are commonplace in the Islamist literature, though we do find some variation in this respect from country to country and group to group. In many cases, the resentment of foreign domination articulated in such passages is expressed in terms of preposterous theories that attempt to blame 'crusader' and Jewish plots for all the problems of the Islamic world. As nonsensical as such conspiracy explanations may be, the nationalistic and anti-imperial resentment that spawns them is real. And it is a major source of the appeal of Islamism.

For Islamists like Khomeini, the idea of a 'return to Islam' is linked to the goal of overcoming foreign domination as follows: the believers are suffering because they have deviated from the laws of God. To end their suffering, they have to conform to God's laws. God has allowed the infidels to dominate the believers because they have deviated from His laws. Once they conform, He will grant them victory. Such reasoning is often meshed with more subtle themes, notably that of cultural authenticity. The return to Islam becomes a means of regaining one's true cultural identity – as opposed to mimicry of the dominant West.

The anti-imperial dimension of Islamic militancy can also be seen in the rhetoric of Osama bin Laden. Given the common assertion, in the United States at any rate, that Bin Laden 'hates us because of our freedoms', it is important to note that he became politically active as a result of his resentment of Western domination. From 1979 to 1989, he actively supported armed resistance to the Soviet occupation of Afghanistan. He inevitably saw this struggle as a *jihad*. He felt it was his duty to help the oppressed believers of Afghanistan to fight the Russian infidels who were oppressing them. Once again, the distinction between believer and infidel was fused with the dichotomies of oppressed and oppressor and colonized and colonizer.

Resentment of the presence of American troops in Saudi Arabia and what bin Laden viewed as the subjugation of Saudi Arabia pervaded his early statements (see Munson 2004). Indeed, bin Laden has condemned the Saudi regime as heretical because of its subordination to the United States. This is significant. Saudi Arabia is viewed by most outsiders, including many Muslims, as a thoroughly fundamentalist state in which all aspects of society are governed by Islamic law. Yet bin Laden condemns the Saudi government for serving the interests of American imperialism!

As he became more famous, bin Laden downplayed the specifically Saudi grievances that dominated his early statements and focused more on the Palestinians and the deaths of Iraqi children because of sanctions. Thus in his videotaped message of October 7, 2001, after the attacks of September 11, he declared:

> What America is tasting now is nothing compared to what we have been tasting for decades. For over eighty years our umma [the Islamic world] has been tasting this humiliation and this degradation. Its sons are killed, its blood is shed, its holy places are violated, and it is ruled by other than that which God has revealed. Yet no one hears. No one responds …
>
> A million innocent children are being killed as I speak. They are being killed in Iraq yet they have done nothing wrong. Yet we hear no condemnation, no fatwa from the reigning sultans. And these days, Israeli tanks wreak havoc in Palestine, in Jenin, Ramallah, Rafah, Beit Jalah and elsewhere in the land of Islam, and we do not hear anyone raising his voice or moving.
>
> (bin Laden 2001)

Bin Laden's statements invariably focus on what he sees as oppression of Muslims by the United States and Israel, rather than on moral issues like the status of women or homosexuality. He would of course take very conservative, if not reactionary, positions on such issues, but he rarely mentions them in his public statements. His emphasis on the suffering of the Palestinians and Iraqis has made him a hero even in the eyes of many Muslims who might be unsympathetic to his goal of a totalitarian Islamic state. Gilles Kepel found that even Arab girls in tight jeans saw bin Laden as an anti-imperialist hero. A young Iraqi woman and her Palestinian friends told Kepel in the fall of 2001, 'He stood up to defend us. He is the only one' (Kepel 2002: 65–6). Bin Laden's heroic stature in the eyes of many Muslims is illustrated by the following joke often told after September 11, 2001. A woman is walking toward the men's room in a restaurant. Several employees of the restaurant try to stop her. She then asks, 'Is Bin Laden in this restroom?' They say no, and she responds, 'Then I can go in because there is only one man left in the Arab and Muslim world: him' (Kepel 2002: 41). This joke reflects the sense of impotence and the rage that pervade much of the Islamic world.

Such anecdotal evidence of the sources of bin Laden's appeal meshes with the evidence provided by public opinon surveys. For example, in March 2008, Professor Shibley Telhami and Zogby International surveyed 4,046 Arabs in Egypt, Jordan, Lebanon, Morocco, Saudi Arabia, and the United Arab Emirates (Telhami 2008). When asked, 'When you think about Al Qaeda, what aspect of the organization, if any, do you sympathize with most?' 30 percent answered 'That it confronts the US.' 21 percent said, 'I do not sympathize at all with this organization.' 18 percent said, 'That it stands for Muslim causes such as the Palestinian issue.' Only 7 percent said, 'That it seeks to create an Islamic state like that of the Taliban in Afghanistan.' In other words, most Arabs who sympathized with al-Qa'ida did so either because it defied the US or because it championed causes like that of the Palestinians. Such causes are essentially nationalistic, but are widely viewed – in the Islamic world – as involving Muslims fighting domination by infidels.

There are two common forms of myopia regarding the appeal of Islamic militancy. There is a tendency on the Right to focus only on the reactionary and anti-Semitic dimensions of such movements, while there is a tendency on the Left to focus only on the nationalistic, anti-imperialist, and social grievances they articulate. It is important to recognize that there is some truth to both perspectives. As a practical matter, diminishing the appeal of Islamic militancy entails addressing the nationalistic, anti-imperialist, and social grievances that fuel it. But it also entails encouraging a more tolerant interpretation of Islam.

Conclusion

The use of 'fundamentalism' as an analytical category for comparative purposes remains controversial. In fact, one good reason to avoid the term is to avoid having to waste time defending it. That said, we can discern a fundamentalist impulse in the Christian, Jewish, Muslim, and Sikh movements commonly called fundamentalist insofar as they insist on strict conformity to holy writ and to a moral code ostensibly based on it. (The actual links between moral codes and sacred scriptures are sometimes more tenuous than religious conservatives recognize.) Such an impulse is lacking in Hindu nationalism and it is not of equal significance in all Christian, Jewish, and Muslim movements.

We have seen that militant religious Zionism has a very strong nationalist dimension, with the Maccabees seen as models of the Jew who refuses to submit to the gentile. It is very hard to draw the line between the religious and national dimensions of religious Zionist militancy. This makes it possible for secular Zionists firmly committed to the retention of the territories Israel won in 1967 to cooperate with militant religious Zionist settlers despite their lack of interest in a Jewish state based on strict conformity to religious law. Militant religious Zionists would agree with most religious conservatives on issues like homosexuality and abortion, but their political activities have focused primarily on settling and retaining the land Israel won in 1967 rather than on moral issues involving the regulation of personal conduct.

There is also a nationalist and anti-imperial dimension to most Islamic militancy. Hamas is a fundamentalist movement in the sense that it advocates a state based on strict conformity to Islamic law, and the followers of Hamas are expected to follow a strictly Islamic code of conduct. At the same time, however, Hamas is clearly a Palestinian nationalist movement that echoes most of the traditional demands of the Palestinian Liberation Organization before it accepted the idea of the partition of pre-1948 Palestine into a Jewish state on 78 percent of the land and a Palestinian state on the remaining 22 percent (Munson 2003a). To speak of Hamas only in terms of its fundamentalist and anti-Semitic rhetoric while ignoring its nationalist dimension would be to distort the nature of the movement (see Roy 2003). But it is also wrong to ignore its fundamentalist and anti-Semitic dimensions (see Litvak 2005).

The case of Shas illustrates the fusion of politicized religious conservatism with demands on behalf of an ethnic group that believes it has been discriminated against. To speak of Shas only as a fundamentalist movement without reference to the sense of ethnic grievance that fuels it would be, once again, to ignore the social and political context that produced it. Just as religion often serves as a badge of national identity, so too does it often serve as a badge of ethnic identity within nations.

To speak of all groups that have a fundamentalist dimension simply as 'revolts against modernity' is inadequate insofar as it tends to downplay or ignore the nationalist and social grievances that often fuel such movements. This is not to suggest that religious outrage provoked by the violation of traditional religious values cannot induce people to undertake political action. If someone believes that abortion is murder, then it is perfectly natural that such a person would engage in political action to prevent abortion. And it is a mistake to attempt to ignore what people say when they explain their political acts in terms of their religious beliefs and assert that they really do what they do because of some sort of alleged disorientation caused by 'rapid modernization'. But while we should avoid reducing all apparently religious motivation to underlying secular causes, we should also recognize that moral outrage provoked by the violation of traditional religious values *is* sometimes meshed with outrage provoked by nationalistic and social grievances. (This too may be a form of moral outrage.)

Comparing the various politicized forms of religious conservatism and religiously tinged nationalism is useful. But this must be done with careful attention to the distinctive features of the movements in question and the specific historical contexts that have shaped them. The neglect of such features and contexts can transform comparison into caricature.

Bibliography

Almond, G. A., R. S. Appleby, and E. Sivan (2003) *Strong Religion: the Rise of Fundamentalisms around the World*. Chicago: University of Chicago Press.

Appleby, R. S. (1995) But All Crabs are Crabby: Valid and Less Valid Criticisms of the Fundamentalism Project. *Contention* 4 (3): 195–202.

Aran, G. 1991. Jewish Zionist Fundamentalism: The Bloc of the Faithful in Israel (Gush Emunim). In *Fundamentalisms Observed*, edited by M. E. Marty and R. S. Appleby. Chicago: University of Chicago Press.

    This is an excellent ethnographic overview of national-religious settlers.

Beale, D. O. (1986) *In Pursuit of Purity: American Fundamentalism since 1850*. Greenville, SC: Unusual Publications.

Berger, P. (1997) Secularism in Retreat. *The National Interest* (Winter 1996/97): 3–12.

bin Laden, O. (2001) The Arabic original of bin Laden's message of October 7, 2001 was at one time accessible at http://www.alitijahalakhar.com/archive/35/here35.htm (last accessed April 9, 2005). I have used my own translation. This message is also translated in Lawrence 2005: 103–5.

Bruce, S. (1998) *Conservative Protestant Politics*. New York: Oxford University Press.

—— (2000) *Fundamentalism*. Cambridge: Polity.

Carroll, J. (2001) *Constantine's Sword : The Church and the Jews, a History*. Boston: Houghton Mifflin.

Faux, E. (2008) *Le nouvel Israël: Un pays en quête de repères*. Paris: Seuil.

Halliday, F. (1995) Fundamentalism and the Contemporary World. *Contention* 4 (2): 41–58.

Heilman, S. C., and M. Friedman. (1991) Religious Fundamentalism and Religious Jews: The Case of the Haredim. In *Fundamentalisms Observed*, edited by M. M. E. and R. S. Appleby. Chicago: University of Chicago Press.

    This is an excellent introduction to the ultra-Orthodox, although it might be confusing to students with no knowledge of Judaism.

Hirschberg, P. (1999) *The World of Shas*. New York: The Institute on American Jewish–Israeli Relations of the American Jewish Committee.

    This is an excellent and readable introduction to Shas, although it does not cover the many important developments since 1999.

Juergensmeyer, M. (2000) *Terror in the Mind of God: The Global Rise of Religious Violence*. Berkeley, CA: University of California Press.

Kepel, G. (2002) *Chronique d'une guerre d'Orient*. Paris: Gallimard.

Khomeini, R. (1977) *Durus Fi Al-Jihad Wa-Al-Rafd: Yusatiruha Al-Imam Al-Khumayni Khilal Harakatihi Al-Nidaliyah Al-Ra'idah*. S.l.: s.n.

—— (1981) *Islam and Revolution in the Middle East: Writings and Declarations of Imam Khomeini*. Translated by H. Algar. Berkeley, CA: Mizan Press.

Lawrence, B., ed. (2005) *Messages to the World: The Statements of Osama Bin Laden*. London: Verso.
This is the best anthology of bin Laden's statements in English. It is essential reading for anyone seeking to understand bin Laden.

Lehmann, D. and B. Siebzehner (2006) *Remaking Israeli Judaism: The Challenge of Shas*. New York: Oxford University Press.

Litvak, M. The Anti-Semitism of Hamas, *Palestine-Israel Journal of Politics, Economics and Culture*, 2005 (http://www.pij.org/details.php?id=345, last accessed October 5, 2008).

Lustick, I. 1988. *For the Land and the Lord: Jewish Fundamentalism in Israel*. New York: The Council on Foreign Relations.
This remains a classic study of the militant national-religious movement in Israel.

Mahmood, C. K. (1996) *Fighting for Faith and Nation: Dialogues with Sikh Militants*. Philadelphia PA: University of Pennsylvania Press.
This presents a good overview of the militant Sikh perspective.

Marsden, G. M. (1991) *Understanding Fundamentalism and Evangelicalism*. Grand Rapids, MT: W. B. Eerdmans.
This is an excellent and readable introduction by a respected evangelical historian.

Martin, W. C. (1996) *With God on our Side: the Rise of the Religious Right in America*. 1st edn. New York: Broadway Books.
This is an excellent and readable narrative history. Broadway Books published a revised edition in 2005 with a brief 'Afterword' covering events since 1996.

Marty, M. E. and R. S. Appleby (1991a) The Fundamentalism Project: A User's Guide. In *Fundamentalisms Observed*, edited by M. E. Marty and R. S. Appleby. Chicago: University of Chicago Press.

—— and —— (1991b) Conclusion: An Interim Report on a Hypothetical Family. In *Fundamentalisms Observed*, edited by M. E. Marty and R. S. Appleby. Chicago: University of Chicago Press.

Munson, H. (1988) *Islam and Revolution in the Middle East*. New Haven, CT: Yale University Press.

—— (2003a) Islam, Nationalism, and Resentment of Foreign Domination. *Middle East Policy* 10 (2): 40–53.

—— (2003b) 'Fundamentalism' Ancient and Modern. *Daedalus* 132 (3): 31–41.

—— (2004) Lifting the Veil: Understanding the Roots of Islamic Militancy. *Harvard International Review* 25 (4): 20–23.

—— (2005) Religion and Violence: A Review Essay. *Religion* 35/4 (October 2005): 223–246.

—— (2008) 'Fundamentalisms' Compared, *Religion Compass* 2/4: 689–707.

Norton, R. A. (2007) *Hezbollah: A Short History*. Princeton: Princeton University Press. This is the best overview of Hezbollah in English.

Oberoi, H. (1993) Sikh Fundamentalism: Translating History into Theory. In *Fundamentalisms and the State*, edited by M. E. Marty and R. S. Appleby. Chicago: University of Chicago Press.

Pape, R. (2005) *Dying to Win: The Strategic Logic of Suicide Terrorism*. New York: Random House.
This is an influential study stressing that terrorism often assumed to be motivated primarily by Islamic fundamentalism is actually primarily aimed at resisting foreign occupation. Pape goes too far in downplaying the role of Islamic fundamentalism and he focuses too much on resistance to foreign occupation as opposed to resistance to foreign domination in general. This is, nonetheless, a very important book.

Ravitzky, A. (1996) *Messianism, Zionism, and Jewish Religious Radicalism*. Chicago: University of Chicago Press.

This is a classic intellectual history, but it is difficult reading for students with no knowledge of Judaism.

Raychaudhuri, T. (1995) Shadows of the Swastika: Historical Reflections on the Politics of Hindu Communalism. *Contention* 4 (2): 141–62.

This is very useful although some might argue that Raychaudhuri is unfairly critical of Hindu nationalism.

Ribuffo, L. P. (1983) *The Old Christian Right: The Protestant Far Right from the Great Depression to the Cold War.* Philadelphia: Temple University Press.

This is a valuable work.

Roy, S. (2003) Hamas and the Transformation(s) of Political Islam in Palestine. *Current History*, January, 13–20.

Said, E. W. (1992) Impossible Histories: Why the Many Islams Cannot be Simplified. *Harper's Magazine*, July. Accessed through Academic Search Premier.

—— (1993) *Culture and Imperialism.* 1st edn. New York: Knopf.

Sengupta, S. (2002) Oh, the Heartache! They Want Cupid Banished. *New York Times*, February 12, 2002.

Shulman, D. (2007) *Dark Hope: Working for Peace in Israel and Palestine.* University of Chicago Press.

This is an excellent account of how 'dovish' Israeli intellectuals have tried to prevent 'national-religious' settlers from attacking Palestinians.

Sprinzak, E. (1991) *The Ascendance of Israel's Radical Right.* New York: Oxford University Press.

This is an excellent and essential study of Israel's religious-nationalist settlers and their supporters, but it is difficult for students with little or no knowledge of Israeli politics.

—— (1999) *Brother Against Brother: Violence and Extremism in Israeli Politics from Altalena to the Rabin Assassination.* New York: The Free Press.

Like *The Ascendance of Israel's Radical Right*, this is excellent, but difficult for students with little or no knowledge of Israeli politics.

Telhami, S. (2008) 2008 Annual Arab Public Opinion Poll, Survey of the Anwar Sadat Chair for Peace and Development at the University of Maryland (with Zogby International). Accessible at http://sadat.umd.edu/surveys/index.htm (last accessed October 5, 2008).

Viorst, M. (2002) *What Shall I Do with This People?: Jews and the Fractious Politics of Judaism.* New York: Free Press.

This is an excellent and readable introduction to the political role of Judaism in modern Israel and to Jewish history in general.

Wade, W. (1987) *The Fiery Cross: The Ku Klux Klan in America.* New York: Simon and Schuster.

This remains an excellent and very readable source although it does not cover recent decades.

Suggested reading

Bergen, P. L. (2006), *The Osama Bin Laden I Know: An Oral History of Al-Qaeda's Leader.* New York: Free Press.

This is an insightful portrait of bin Laden based primarily on interviews with people who have known him.

Heilman, S. (1992), *Defenders of the Faith: Inside Ultra-Orthodox Jewry.* New York: Schocken Books.

This is a wonderfully human and readable ethnographic study of ultra-Orthodox Jews of European origin in Israel.

Hirschberg, P. (1999), *The World of Shas.* New York: The Institute on American Jewish–Israeli Relations of the American Jewish Committee.

This is an excellent and readable introduction to Shas, although it does not cover the many important developments since 1999.

Lawrence, B. ed. (2005), *Messages to the World: The Statements of Osama Bin Laden*. London: Verso.
This is the best anthology of bin Laden's statements in English. It is essential reading for anyone seeking to understand bin Laden and the way his anti-imperialism is meshed with reactionary fundamentalist Islam.

Lehmann, D. and B. Siebzehner (2006), *Remaking Israeli Judaism: The Challenge of Shas*. New York: Oxford University Press.
This is a valuable study of Shas.

Lustick, I. (1988), *For the Land and the Lord: Jewish Fundamentalism in Israel*. New York: The Council on Foreign Relations.
This remains a classic study of the militant national-religious movement in Israel.

Marsden, G. M. (1991), *Understanding Fundamentalism and Evangelicalism*. Grand Rapids MT: W. B. Eerdmans.
This is an excellent introduction by a respected evangelical historian.

Martin, W. C. (1996), *With God on our Side: the Rise of the Religious Right in America*. 1st edn. New York: Broadway Books.
This is an excellent and readable narrative history. Broadway Books published a revised edition in 2005 with a brief 'Afterword' covering events since 1996.

Norton, A. R. (2007), *Hezbollah: A Short History*. Princeton: Princeton University Press.
This is the best and most readable overview of Hezbollah available in English.

Pape, R. (2005), *Dying to Win: The Strategic Logic of Suicide Terrorism*. New York: Random House.
This is an influential study stressing that terrorism often assumed to be motivated primarily by Islamic fundamentalism is actually primarily aimed at resisting foreign occupation. Pape goes too far in downplaying the role of Islamic fundamentalism and he focuses too much on resistance to foreign occupation as opposed to resistance to foreign domination in general. This is, nonetheless, a very important book.

Peri, Y., ed. (2000), *The Assassination of Yitzhak Rabin*. Stanford, CA: Stanford University Press.
This is an important collection of essays on the significance of the assassination of Yitzhak Rabin in the context of Israel's 'culture war'.

Ravitzky, A. (1996), *Messianism, Zionism, and Jewish Religious Radicalism*. Chicago: University of Chicago Press.
This is a classic intellectual history, but students often complain that it is too 'dry', Dry or not, it is essential reading for anyone seeking to understand Israel's Religious Right.

Schattner, M. (2008), *Israël: L'autre conflit. Laïcs contre religieux*. Bruxelles: André Versaille.
This is an excellent history of the role of religion in Zionism and the modern state of Israel. For students seriously interested in such matters, it would be worth learning French just to read this book. The author, a secular Franco-Israeli journalist, begins his book by describing how his daughter became 'ultra-Orthodox' (*haredi*) and how now he cannot read the stories of Babar the elephant to his grandchildren. But he nonetheless does an excellent job of conveying a sense of how both the ultra-Orthodox and the national-religious Orthodox see the world.

Sprinzak, E, (1991), *The Ascendance of Israel's Radical Right*. New York: Oxford University Press.
This is a classic study of Israel's religious-nationalist settlers and their supporters, but it is difficult reading for students with little or no knowledge of Israeli politics.

—— (1999) *Brother against Brother: Violence and Extremism in Israeli Politics from Altalena to the Rabin Assassination*. New York: The Free Press.
Like Sprinzak's *The Ascendance of Israel's Radical Right*, this is excellent but difficult for students with little or no knowledge of Israeli history.

Chapter 22

Myth and ritual

Robert A. Segal

This chapter is divided into three sections: myth, myth tied to ritual, and ritual. The title of the chapter is meant to refer to myth by itself and to ritual by itself as well as to myth linked to ritual. The subject of each section is not actual myths or actual rites but theories of myths and theories of rituals as well as theories of the two combined.

Theories are accounts of some larger domain, of which myth or ritual or myth tied to ritual is a subset. For example, anthropological theories of myth or ritual are theories of culture applied to the case of myth or ritual. Psychological theories of myth or ritual are theories of the mind. Sociological theories are theories of society. Theories may go back to ancient times, but modern theories, which go back 150 years, come largely, though hardly entirely, from the social sciences, which themselves began to emerge as independent disciplines in the second half of the nineteenth century. Theories from outside the social sciences hail from the hoarier disciplines of philosophy, religious studies, and literature.

Myth

What unite theories across the disciplines are the questions asked. The three main questions are those of origin, function, and subject matter. By 'origin' is meant why and how myth arises. By 'function' is meant why and how myth persists. The answer to the why of origin and function is usually a need, which myth arises to fulfill and lasts by continuing to fulfill. What the need is, varies from theory to theory and from discipline to discipline. By 'subject matter' is meant the referent of myth. Some theories read myth literally, so that the referent is the straightforward, apparent one, such as gods. Other theories read myth symbolically, and the symbolized referent can be anything.

Theories differ not only in their answers to these questions but also in the questions they ask. Some theories, and perhaps some disciplines, concentrate on the origin of myth; others, on the function; still others, on the subject matter. Only a few theories tend to all three questions, and some of the theories that tend to origin or to function deal with either 'why' or 'how' but not both.

It is commonly said that theories of the nineteenth century focused on the question of origin and that theories of the twentieth century have focused on the questions of function and subject matter. But this characterization confuses historical origin with recurrent one. Theories that profess to provide the origin of myth claim to know not where and when myth first arose but why and how myth arises wherever and whenever it does. The issue of recurrent origin has been as popular with twentieth-century theories as with nineteenth-century ones, and interest in function and subject matter was as common to nineteenth-century theories as to twentieth-century ones.

There is one genuine difference between nineteenth- and twentieth-century theories. Nineteenth-century theories tended to see the subject matter of myth as the natural world and to see the function of myth as either a literal explanation or a symbolic description of that world. Myth was typically taken to be the 'primitive' counterpart to science, which was assumed to be wholly modern. Myth and science were not merely redundant but outright incompatible, and moderns, who by definition are scientific, therefore had to reject myth. By contrast, twentieth-century theories have tended to see myth as almost anything but an outdated counterpart to modern science, either in subject matter or in function. Consequently, moderns have not been obliged to abandon myth for science.

Besides the questions of origin, function, and subject matter, questions often asked about myth include: is myth universal? is myth true? The answers to these questions stem from the answers to the first three questions. A theory which contends that myth arises and functions to explain natural processes will likely restrict myth to societies supposedly bereft of science. By contrast, a theory which contends that myth arises and functions to unify society may well deem myth acceptable and perhaps even indispensable to all societies.

A theory which maintains that myth functions to explain natural processes is committed to the falsity of myth if the explanation given proves incompatible with a scientific one. A theory which maintains that myth functions to unify society may well circumvent the issue of truth by asserting that society is unified when its members *believe* that the laws they are obliged to obey were established long ago by revered ancestors, whether or not those laws really were established back then. This kind of theory sidesteps the question of truth because its answers to the questions of origin and function do.

Definition of myth

That myth, whatever else it is, is a story may seem self-evident. After all, when asked to name myths, most of us think first of *stories* about Greco-Roman gods and heroes. Yet myth can also be taken more broadly as a belief or credo – for example, the American 'rags to riches myth' and the American 'myth of the frontier.' Horatio Alger wrote scores of popular novels illustrating the rags to riches myth, but the credo itself rests on no story. The same is true of the myth of the frontier.

All of the theories considered here deem myth a story. But what is myth a story about? For folklorists above all, myth is about the creation of the world. In the Bible only the two creation stories (Genesis 1 and 2), the Garden of Eden story (Genesis 3), and the Noah story (Genesis 6–9) would qualify as myths. All other stories would instead constitute either legends or folktales. Other disciplines are less rigid and instead define myth as simply a story about something significant. Some theories insist that the story take place in the past. Others allow the story to take place in the present or in the future too.

For theories from, above all, religious studies, the main characters in myth must be gods or near-gods. Other disciplines tend to be more flexible. But all disciplines insist that the main figures be personalities – divine, human, or even animal. Excluded would be impersonal forces like Plato's Good.

Save for Rudolf Bultmann and Hans Jonas, all of the theorists considered here tend to the function of myth, and Bronislaw Malinowski tends to it almost exclusively. Theorists differ over what the function of myth is, but for all of them the function is weighty – in contrast to the lighter functions of legend and folktale. Myth accomplishes something significant for adherents.

In today's parlance, myth is false. Myth is 'mere' myth. But the 'mere' is misleading. Used negatively, 'myth' still captures the strength of the false conviction, and does so more fully than would tamer phrases like 'erroneous belief' and 'popular misconception.' A myth is a conviction false yet tenacious.

By contrast, the phrase 'rags to riches myth,' which sums up the traditional American conviction that anyone with determination can succeed, uses the term myth positively. Ironically, some Americans who continue to espouse the rags to riches credo may no longer refer to it as a 'myth' *because* the term has come to connote falsity. Let, then, myth here be deemed a story that expresses a tenaciously held conviction, be the conviction true or false.

The obvious way to classify theories of myth is by the disciplines from which they come. But this categorization turns out to be less than clear-cut, for a theory that formally falls within one discipline can seemingly also fall within another. For example, the anthropologist Malinowski entitles his classic essay on myth *Myth in Primitive Psychology*. The theory of the literary critic René Girard rests on a psychology that is pitted against Freud's. The categorization used in this chapter ignores disciplinary boundaries. Theories are classified by their positions on the relationship of myth to science.

Whether or not myths are as old as humanity, challenges to myth are as old, or almost as old, as myths themselves. In the West the challenge to myth goes back at least to Plato (c. 428–348 or 347 BCE), who rejected Homeric myth on, especially, moral grounds. It was above all the Stoics who defended myth against this charge by reinterpreting it allegorically. The chief modern challenge to myth has come not from ethics but from science. Here myth is assumed to explain how gods control the physical world rather than, as for Plato, to describe how gods behave among themselves. Where Plato bemoans myths for presenting the gods as models of immoral behavior, modern critics dismiss myths for explaining the world unscientifically.

Myth as true science

One form of the modern challenge to myth has been to the scientific credibility of myth. Did creation really occur in a mere six days, as the first of two creation stories in Genesis (1:1–2:4a) claims? Was there really a worldwide flood? Is the earth truly but six or seven thousand years old? Could the ten plagues on the Egyptians actually have happened? The most unrepentant defense against this challenge has been to claim that the biblical account is correct, for after all, the Pentateuch was revealed to Moses by God. This position, known as 'creationism,' assumes varying forms, ranging, for example, from taking the days of creation to mean exactly six days to taking them to mean 'ages.'

At the same time creationists vaunt their views as scientific. 'Creationism' is shorthand for 'creation science,' which appropriates scientific evidence of any kind both to bolster its own claims and to refute those of secular rivals such as evolution. Doubtless 'creation scientists' would object to the term 'myth' to characterize the view they defend, but only because the term has come to connote false belief. If the term is used neutrally for a firmly held conviction, creationism is a myth that claims to be scientific. For creation scientists, it is evolution that is untenable scientifically. In any clash between the Bible and modern science, modern science must give way to biblical science, not vice versa. Creationism, which may have its counterparts in other religions, thus goes beyond other versions of fundamentalism in claiming to be both religious *and* scientific, not religious *rather than* scientific.

Myth as modern science

A much tamer defense against the challenge of modern science has been to reconcile myth with modern science. Here elements at odds with modern science are either removed or, more cleverly, reinterpreted as in fact scientific. Myth is credible scientifically because it *is* science. There might not have been a Noah able single-handedly to gather up all living species and to keep them alive in a wooden boat sturdy enough to withstand the strongest seas that ever arose, but a worldwide flood did occur. What thus remains in myth is true because scientific. This approach is the opposite of that called 'demythologizing,' which separates myth from science.

In their comment on the first plague, the turning of the waters of the Nile into blood (Exodus 7:14–24), the editors of the *Oxford Annotated Bible* epitomize this rationalizing approach: 'The plague of blood apparently reflects a natural phenomenon of Egypt: namely, the reddish color of the Nile at its height in the summer owing to red particles of earth or perhaps minute organisms' (May and Metzger 1977: 75). Of the second plague, that of frogs (Exodus 8:1–15), the editors declare similarly: 'The mud of the Nile, after the seasonal overflowing, was a natural place for frogs to generate. Egypt has been spared more frequent occurrence of this pestilence by the frog-eating bird, the ibis' (May and Metzger 1977: 75). How fortuitous that the ibis must have been away on holiday when Aaron stretched out his hand to produce the plague and must have just returned when Moses wanted the plague to cease![1] Instead of setting myth *against* science, this tactic turns myth *into* science – and not, as is fashionable today, science into myth.

Likewise for the American Near Eastern scholar Samuel Noah Kramer (1897–1990), Sumerian creation myths evince observations about the physical world and scientific-like hypotheses drawn to account for them:

> It cannot be sufficiently stressed that the Sumerian cosmogonic concepts, early as they are, are by no means *primitive*. They reflect the mature thought and reason of the thinking Sumerian as he contemplated the forces of nature and the character of his own existence. When these concepts are analyzed; when the theological cloak and polytheistic trappings are removed, ... the Sumerian creation concepts indicate a keenly observing mentality as well as an ability to draw and formulate pertinent conclusions from the data observed.
>
> (Kramer 1961: 73)

Gods are mere personifications of natural phenomena, and their actions are mere metaphors for natural processes. Thus the mythic pronouncement that 'The union of [the male heaven-god] *An* and [the earth-goddess] *Ki* produced the air-god *Enlil*, who proceeded to separate the heaven-father *An* from the earth-mother *Ki*' is to be translated as follows: 'Heaven and earth were conceived as *solid* elements. Between them, however, and *from them*, came the gaseous element *air*, whose main characteristic is that of expansion. Heaven and earth were thus separated by the expanding element *air*' (Kramer 1961: 74, 73). Again, myth is science – modern science.[2]

Myth as primitive science

By far the most common response to the challenge of science has been to abandon myth for science. Here myth, while still an explanation of the world, is now taken as an explanation of its own kind, not a scientific explanation in mythic guise. The issue is therefore not the scientific *credibility* of myth but the *compatibility* of myth with science. Myth is considered to be 'primitive' science – or, more precisely, the pre-scientific counterpart to science, which is assumed to be exclusively modern. Myth is here part of religion. Where religion apart from myth provides the belief in gods, myth fills in the details of how gods cause events. Because myth is part of religion, the rise of science as the reigning modern explanation of physical events has consequently spelled the fall of not only religion but also myth. Because moderns by definition accept science, they cannot also have myth, and the phrase 'modern myth' is self-contradictory. Myth is a victim of the process of secularization that constitutes modernity.

The key exponents of this challenge to myth have been the pioneering English anthropologist E. B. Tylor (1832–1917) and the Scottish classicist and fellow pioneering anthropologist J. G. Frazer (1854–1941). For Tylor, myth provides knowledge of the world: 'When the attention of a man in the myth-making stage of intellect is drawn to any phenomenon or custom which has to him no obvious reason, he invents and tells a story to account for it ...' (Tylor 1871: I, 392). For Frazer, the knowledge that myth provides is a means to control of the world, especially of crops. For both, the events explained or effected by myth are those in the external world such as rainfall, not social phenomena such as customs, laws, and institutions. Myth is the primitive counterpart to natural, not social, science.

For Tylor and Frazer, science renders myth not merely redundant but incompatible. Why? Because the explanations myth and science give are incompatible. It is not simply that the mythic explanation is personalistic and the scientific one impersonal. It is that both are *direct* explanations of the *same* events. Gods operate not behind or through impersonal forces but in place of them. According to myth, the rain god, let us say, collects rain in buckets and then chooses to empty the buckets on some spot below. According to science, meteorological processes cause rain. One cannot stack the mythic account atop the scientific one, for the rain god, rather than utilizing meteorological processes, acts in place of them.

Strictly, causation in myth is never entirely personalistic. The decision of the rain god to dump rain on a chosen spot below presupposes physical laws that account for the accumulation of rain in heaven, the capacity of the buckets to retain the rain, and the direction of the dumped rain. But to maintain their rigid hiatus between myth and science, Tylor and Frazer would doubtless reply that myths themselves ignore physical processes and focus instead on divine decisions.

Because Tylor and Frazer assume that myth and science are incompatible, they take for granted not merely that primitives have only myth but, even more, that moderns have only science. Rather than an eternal phenomenon, as the theorists Mircea Eliade, C. G. Jung, and Joseph Campbell grandly proclaim, myth for Tylor and Frazer is merely a passing, if slowly passing, one. Especially for Tyler, myth has admirably served its function, but its time is over. Moderns who still cling to myth have simply failed either to recognize or to concede the incompatibility of it with science. While Tylor and Frazer do not date the beginning of the scientific stage, it is identical with the beginning of modernity and is therefore only a few centuries old. Dying in the first half of the twentieth century, Tylor and Frazer never quite envisioned a stage post the modern one.

In setting myth against science, Tylor and Frazer epitomize the nineteenth-century view of myth. In the twentieth century the trend has been to reconcile myth with science, so that moderns, who by definition espouse science, can still retain myth. Tylor's and Frazer's theories have been spurned by twentieth-century theorists on many grounds: for precluding modern myths, for subsuming myth under religion and thereby precluding secular myths, for deeming the function of myth scientific-like, and for deeming myth false. Nevertheless, Tylor's and Frazer's theories remain central to the study of myth, and twentieth-century theories can be seen as rejoinders to them. One rejoinder has been to take the function of myth as other than explanatory, in which case myth does not overlap with natural science and can therefore coexist with it. Another rejoinder has been to read myth other than literally, in which case myth does not even refer to the physical world and can therefore likewise coexist with natural science.[3] The most radical rejoinder has been to alter both the explanatory function and the literal reading of myth.

Myth as other than explanatory in function

The most important reinterpreters of the function of myth have been Bronislaw Malinowski, Lucien Lévy-Bruhl, Claude Lévi-Strauss, and Mircea Eliade. It is not clear whether for Malinowski (1884–1942), the Polish-born anthropologist, moderns as well as primitives have myth. What is clear is that for him primitives have science as well as myth, so that myth cannot be the primitive counterpart to modern science, theoretical or applied. Primitives use science both to explain and to control the physical world. They use myth to do the opposite: to reconcile themselves to aspects of the world that cannot be controlled.

Myth reconciles humans to the travails of life by rooting those travails in the primordial actions of gods or humans. Humans age because long ago a god or human did something that brought old age irremediably into the world: 'The longed-for power of eternal youth and the faculty of rejuvenation which gives immunity from decay and age, have been lost by a small accident which it would have been in the power of a child and a woman to prevent' (Malinowski 1926: 104). Myth pronounces the world not the best possible one but, in the wake of irreversible events, the only possible one.

Where for Tylor and Frazer myth deals almost exclusively with physical phenomena, for Malinowski it deals equally with social phenomena. Myth still serves to reconcile humans to the unpleasantries of life, but now to unpleasantries that, far from unalterable, can be cast off by members of society. Myth spurs members to accept the impositions of society by tracing them, too, back to a hoary past, thereby conferring on them the clout of tradition: 'The myth comes into play when rite, ceremony, or a social or moral rule demands justification, warrant of antiquity, reality, and sanctity' (Malinowski 1926: 36). Myths say, 'Do this because this has always been done.' A myth about the British monarchy would make the institution as ancient as possible, so that to tamper with it would be to tamper with tradition. In England today fox hunting is defended on the grounds that it has long been part of country life. In the case of physical phenomena the beneficiary of myth is the individual. In the case of social phenomena the beneficiary is society itself. The modern counterpart to myths of social phenomena, if moderns do not have myth, is ideology.[4]

To say that myth traces back the origin of phenomena is equivalent to saying that myth explains those phenomena. When, then, Malinowski denies strenuously that myths are explanations – primitives 'do not want to "explain," to make "intelligible" anything which happens in their myths' (Malinowski 1926: 41) – he is denying that they are, as for Tylor, explanations for their own sake. He cannot be denying that they are explanations at all, for it is exactly by explaining phenomena that myths serve their conciliatory function.

The French philosopher Lucien Lévy-Bruhl (1857–1939) does not contest Tylor's and Frazer's restriction of myth to primitives. Like Malinowski, he contests less Frazer's than Tylor's characterization of primitives and thus of myth. Where for Malinowski primitives are too overwhelmed by the world to have the luxury of reflecting on it, for Lévy-Bruhl primitives are too emotionally involved in the world to be capable of accounting for it. Their feelings shape the way they perceive as well as conceive the world. Rather than, as for Tylor, first experiencing a natural world of animals and plants and then postulating gods to account for their behavior, primitives project their 'collective representations' onto the world and thereby experience all things in the world as filled with a sacred, or 'mystic,' reality pervading the natural one: 'Primitive man, therefore, lives and acts in an environment of beings and objects, all of which, in addition to the properties that we recognize them to possess, are endued with mystic properties. He perceives their objective reality mingled with another reality' (Lévy–Bruhl 1926: 65). All phenomena, including humans, are mystically identical with one another.

Myth functions not to explain this mystical world view but to preserve it. As long as members experience oneness with the group, they experience oneness with the world, and myth is barely needed. But once members begin to experience themselves as individuals, they turn to myth to restore the feeling of oneness with society and the world:

> Where the participation of the individual in the social group is still directly felt, where the participation of the group with surrounding groups is actually lived – that is, as long as the period of mystic symbiosis lasts – myths are meagre in number and of poor quality … Where the aggregates are of a more advanced type, … there is, on the contrary, an increasingly luxuriant outgrowth of mythology. Can myths then likewise be the products of primitive mentality which appear when this mentality is endeavoring to realize a participation no longer directly felt – when it has recourse to intermediaries, and vehicles designed to secure a communion which has ceased to be a living reality?
>
> (Lévy-Bruhl 1926: 368–9)

For Lévy-Bruhl, myth is part of a mythic mentality, and from him comes the notion of a distinctively mythic, or 'mythopoeic,' way of thinking. Where for Tylor myth is as logical as science, for Lévy-Bruhl it is conspicuously illogical, or 'pre-logical.' For primitives, despite their yearning to re-experience the oneness of all things, simultaneously and inconsistently deem all things distinct. Theorists of myth influenced by Lévy-Bruhl include the German philosopher Ernst Cassirer (1955).

At first glance the French structural anthropologist Claude Lévi-Strauss (b. 1908) seems a throwback to Tylor. For Lévi-Strauss, myth is not only an exclusively primitive enterprise but, more, a rigorously intellectual one. Lévi-Strauss denounces nonintellectualists like Malinowski and Lévy-Bruhl as vigorously as they denounce intellectualists like Tylor. Indeed, in declaring that primitives, 'moved by a need or a desire to understand the world around them, … proceed by intellectual means, exactly as a philosopher, or even to some extent a scientist, can and would do' (Lévi-Strauss 1978: 16), Lévi-Strauss seems indistinguishable from Tylor. Yet he is in fact severely critical of Tylor. For Lévi-Strauss, primitives think differently from moderns rather than fail to think as well as moderns.

Primitive, or mythic, thinking is concrete. Modern thinking is abstract. Primitive thinking focuses on the observable, sensory, qualitative aspects of phenomena rather than, like modern thinking, on the unobservable, nonsensory, quantitative ones. Yet myth for Lévi-Strauss is no less scientific than modern science. It is simply part of the 'science of the concrete' rather than the science of the abstract. For Lévi-Strauss, myth *is* primitive science and not just the primitive counterpart to exclusively modern science. But because primitive and modern science concentrate on different aspects of the physical world, they are compatible rather than, like myth and science for Tylor, incompatible. And primitive science is not inferior to modern science, the way myth is to science for Tylor.

If myth is an instance of mythic thinking because it deals with concrete, tangible phenomena, it is an instance of thinking per se, modern and primitive alike, because it classifies phenomena. According to Lévi-Strauss, all humans think in the form of classifications, specifically pairs of oppositions, and project them onto the world. Many cultural phenomena express these oppositions, which Lévi-Strauss calls 'binary oppositions.' Myth is distinctive in resolving the oppositions it expresses: 'the purpose of myth is to provide a logical model capable of overcoming a contradiction' (Lévi-Strauss 1958: 105). Myth resolves a contradiction by providing either a mediating middle term or an analogous, but more easily resolved, contradiction. Either tactic narrows and thereby alleviates the contradiction, but, strictly, neither fully resolves it.

Like the contradictions expressed in other phenomena, those expressed in myth are for Lévi-Strauss apparently reducible to the fundamental contradiction between 'nature' and 'culture.' That contradiction stems from the conflict that humans experience between themselves as at once animal-like, hence a part of nature, and civilized, hence a part of culture. This conflict arises from the projection onto the world of the oppositional character of the mind. Humans not only think 'oppositionally' but, through projection, experience the world 'oppositionally' as well. By showing a way of diminishing that opposition, myth makes life more bearable and, even more, solves a logical conundrum.

In calling his approach to myth 'structuralist,' Lévi-Strauss distinguishes it from a 'narrative' approach, which adheres to the plot of myth. All other theories take for granted that the meaning of myth lies in its plot. Lévi-Strauss dismisses the plot and locates the meaning of myth in the structure. The plot is that element – say, event – A leads to event B, which leads to event C. The structure, which is identical with the expression and diminution of contradictions, is either that events A and B constitute an opposition mediated by event C or that events A and B are as opposed to each other as events C and D, an analogous opposition, are opposed.

Lévi-Strauss confines himself to, primarily, Native American myths, but other structuralists analyze modern myths. In *Mythologies* (1972) the French semiotician Roland Barthes (1915–80) takes as myths various cultural artifacts and shows how they serve to justify the bourgeois outlook of postwar France. The function of myth here is not intellectual but ideological. Myth has nothing to do with natural science. Where Lévi-Strauss largely analyzes myths independent of their social context – the grand exception is his analysis of the myth of Asdiwal – others inspired by him have, like Barthes, tied myths to their contexts. For the classicists Jean-Pierre Vernant (1983), Marcel Detienne (1977), Pierre Vidal-Naquet, and Nicole Loraux, the relationship between myth and society is much more malleable, subtle, and ironic than it is for Malinowski or even Barthes. Myth can as readily challenge as bolster existing ideology.

Unlike Malinowski and Lévy-Bruhl, the Romanian-born historian of religions Mircea Eliade (1907–86) has no hesitation in making one function of myth explanatory. For him, myth explains less how the gods presently control the world, as for Tylor and Frazer, than how they created it. Like Malinowski, Eliade includes myths of social phenomena as well as of physical ones. Explanation for Eliade is both an end in itself and, even more, a means to another end. To hear, to read, and above all to reenact a myth is magically to return to the time of the myth, the time of the origin of whatever phenomenon it explains. It is when the world is fresh that gods, the creators in myth, are belived to be closest at hand, as in the biblical case of 'the Lord God['s] walking in the garden of the cool of the day' (Genesis 3:8). The return to this 'primordial time' reverses the subsequent separation from gods, a separation that is equivalent to the fall, and is regenerative spiritually: 'What is involved is, in short, a return to the original time, the therapeutic purpose of which is to begin life once again, a symbolic rebirth' (Eliade 1968: 8). The ultimate benefit of myth is proximity to the gods, one or more.

Eliade ventures beyond the other respondents to Tylor and Frazer in proclaiming myth panhuman rather than merely primitive. Instead of showing how myth is logically compatible with science, he circumvents the issue by citing modern plays, novels, and movies with the mythic theme of yearning to escape from the everyday world into another, often earlier one:

> A whole volume could well be written on the myths of modern man, on the mythologies camouflaged in the plays that he enjoys, in the books that he reads ... Even reading includes a mythological function ... particularly because, through reading, the modern man succeeds in obtaining an 'escape from time' comparable to the 'emergence from time' effected by myths. Whether modern man 'kills' time with a detective story or enters such a foreign temporal universe as is represented by any novel, reading projects him out of his personal duration and incorporates him into other rhythms, makes him live in another 'history.'
>
> (Eliade 1968: 205)

If moderns, who by definition have science, also have myth, then for Eliade myth simply must be compatible with science – not quite the conclusion that Tylor and Frazer would draw. If even professedly atheistic moderns have myths, then myth must be universal. How modern myths, which do not involve gods, can still provide access to gods, Eliade never reveals. Likely for him, the agents in modern myths are merely human heroes, but heroes so elevated above ordinary mortals as to be virtual gods.

Myth as other than literal in meaning

The most prominent reinterpreters of not the function but the meaning of myth have been the German New Testament scholar Rudolf Bultmann (1884–1976) and the German-born philosopher Hans Jonas (1903–93). Both were students of the philosopher Martin Heidegger (1889–1976) in his earlier period and consequently offer existentialist readings of myth. While they limit themselves to their specialties, Christianity and Gnosticism, they apply a theory of myth per se.

Bultmann acknowledges that, read literally, myth is about the physical world and is incompatible with science. But unlike Malinowski and Eliade as well as Tylor, he reads myth symbolically. In Bultmann's exasperatingly confusing phrase, one must 'demythologize' myth, by which he means not eliminating, or 'demythicizing,' myth, the way Kramer does, but on the contrary extricating its true, symbolic subject matter. Once demythologized, myth is no longer about the external world but is instead about the place of human beings in that world. Myth no longer explains but instead describes, and it describes not the external world but humans' experience of that world: 'The real purpose of myth is not to present an objective picture of the world as it is, but to express man's understanding of himself in the world in which he lives. Myth should be interpreted not cosmologically, but anthropologically, or better still, existentially' (Bultmann 1953: 10). Myth depicts the human condition.

Read literally, the New Testament for Bultmann describes a cosmic battle between good and evil anthropomorphic gods for control of the physical world. These gods intervene miraculously not only in the operation of nature, as for Tylor and Frazer, but also in the lives of human beings. The beneficent beings direct humans to do good; the malevolent ones compel them to do evil. Taken literally, the New Testament presents a prescientific outlook:

> The world is viewed as a three-storied structure, with the earth in the centre, the heaven above, and the underworld beneath. Heaven is the abode of God and of celestial beings – the angels. The underworld is hell, the place of torment. Even the earth is more than the scene of natural, everyday events, of the trivial round and common task. It is the scene of the supernatural activity of God and his angels on the one hand, and of Satan and his daemons on the other. These supernatural forces intervene in the course of nature and in all that men think and will and do. Miracles are by no means rare. Man is not in control of his own life. Evil spirits may take possession of him. Satan may inspire him with evil thoughts. Alternatively, God may inspire his thought and guide his purposes.
>
> (Bultmann 1953: 1)

Demythologized, the New Testament still refers in part to the physical world, but now to a world ruled by a single, nonanthropomorphic, transcendent God. Satan does not even still exist. He becomes a symbol of one's own evil inclinations:

> Mythology expresses a certain understanding of human existence. It [rightly] believes that the world and human life have their ground and their limits in a power which is beyond all that we can calculate or control. Mythology speaks about this power inadequately and insufficiently because it speaks about it as if it were a worldly [i.e., physical] power. It [rightly] speaks of gods who represent the power beyond the visible, comprehensible world. [But] it speaks of gods as if they were men and of their actions as human actions ... Again, the conception of Satan as ruler over the world expresses a deep insight, namely, the insight that evil is not only to be found here and there in the world, but that all particular evils make up one single power which in the last analysis grows from the very actions of men, which form an atmosphere, a spiritual tradition, which overwhelms every man. The consequences and effects of our sins become a power dominating us, and we cannot free ourselves from them.
>
> (Bultmann 1958: 19, 21)

Damnation refers not to a future place but to one's present state of mind, which exists as long as one rejects God. There is no physical hell. Hell symbolizes despair over the absence of God. As John Milton's Satan declares, 'Which way I fly is Hell; myself am Hell.' Similarly, salvation refers to one's state of mind once one accepts God. Heaven refers not to a place in the sky but to joy in the presence of God. The eschatology refers not to the coming end of the physical world but to the personal acceptance or rejection of God in one's everyday life. The Kingdom comes not outwardly, with cosmic upheavals, but inwardly, whenever one embraces God.

Demythologized, myth ceases to be purely primitive, as for Tylor and Frazer, and becomes universal, as for Eliade. Myth ceases to be false, as for Tylor and Frazer, and becomes true. Where Eliade invokes the existence of modern myths as *ipso facto* evidence of the compatibility of myth with science, Bultmann actually labors to reconcile myth with science. Where Eliade claims that moderns have myths of their own, Bultmann claims that moderns can retain biblical myths.

Bultmann's boldest response to Tylor and Frazer is to circumvent the function of myth. In translating the meaning of myth into terms acceptable to moderns, he sidesteps the issue of why moderns, even if they can have myth, need it. Unlike other symbolic interpreters of myth such as the religious philosopher Paul Ricoeur (1967) and the philosopher Philip Wheelwright (1968), Bultmann never asserts that the meaning of myth is untranslatable into nonmythic terms and is therefore indispensable for expressing or even revealing its contents. Since he takes the meaning of myth from Heidegger's philosophy, he can hardly be doing so. He is thereby left with a theory that makes myth palatable to moderns but unnecessary for them. And even the palatibility of myth for moderns is tenuous, for myth still refers to God, albeit of a nonphysical kind. One must still believe in God to accept myth.

Like Bultmann, Jonas seeks to show that ancient myths have a meaning that continues to speak to moderns. For both Bultmann and Jonas, myth describes the alienation of humans from the world as well as from their true selves prior to their acceptance of God. Because Gnosticism, unlike mainstream Christianity, is radically dualistic, humans remain alienated from the physical world and from their bodies even after they have found the true God. And they find the true God only by rejecting the false god of the physical world.

Unlike Bultmann, who strives to bridge the divide between Christianity and modernity, Jonas acknowledges the divide between Gnosticism and modernity. In Gnosticism the state of alienation is temporary; in modern, secular existentialism alienation is permanent. Alienation *is* the human condition, not a fall from it. Jonas does not, then, seek to 'demythologize' either the source of alienation or the solution to it – as if alienation were temporary – but the fact of alienation. He translates Gnostic myths into existentialist terms not to make Gnosticism acceptable to moderns but only to show the similarity between the Gnostic and the existentialist outlooks: 'the essence of existentialism is a certain dualism, an estrangement between man and the world … There is only one situation … where that condition has been realized and lived out with all the vehemence of a cataclysmic event. That is the gnostic movement' (Jonas 1963: 325).

Like Bultmann, Jonas bypasses the function of myth and confines himself to the meaning. But he, like Bultmann, is thereby still left with finding a use for myth. Since he, too, takes his glossary from Heidegger, modern philosophy unlocks myth and not vice versa. What function, then, does myth serve?

Myth as both other than explanatory and other than literal

The most radical departures from Tylor and Frazer have transformed both the explanatory function and the literal meaning of myth. The most influential theorists here have been the Austrian physician Sigmund Freud (1856–1939) and the Swiss psychiatrist C. G. Jung (1875–1961). For both, the subject matter of myth is the unconscious, and the function of myth is to manifest the unconscious. The two differ sharply over the nature of the unconscious and in turn over the reason myth is needed to manifest it.

Because the Freudian unconscious is composed of repressed sexual and aggressive drives, myth functions to release those drives, but in a disguised way, so that the creator and the user of a myth need never confront its meaning and thereby their own nature. Myth, like other aspects of culture, serves simultaneously to reveal and to hide its unconscious contents. Compared with Jung, Freud wrote little on myth. His key discussion is his analysis of the myth of Oedipus in *The Interpretation of Dreams* (1953). The classical psychoanalytic study of myth is that of his one-time disciple, fellow Austrian Otto Rank (1884–1939). Focusing on myths of male heroes, Rank sees the myths as providing an unconscious, vicarious fulfillment of, above all, Oedipal drives. By identifying oneself with the named hero, whose own saga must be psychologized, one gains a partial fulfillment of lingering childhood desires. Myth serves neurotic adult males fixated at their Oedipal stage: 'Myths are, therefore, created by adults, by means of retrograde childhood fantasies, the hero being credited with the myth-maker's personal infantile history' (Rank 1914: 82).

By no means do Freudians still take myth so negatively. Spurred by ego psychology, contemporary Freudians such as the American Jacob Arlow (b. 1912–2004) take myth positively. For them, myth helps to solve the problems of growing up rather than to perpetuate them, is progressive rather than regressive, and facilitates adjustment to society and the physical world rather than childish flight from both. Myth may still serve to vent repressed drives, but it serves even more to sublimate them and to integrate them. Moreover, myth serves everyone, not just neurotics:

> Psychoanalysis has a greater contribution to make to the study of mythology than [merely] demonstrating, in myths, wishes often encountered in the unconscious thinking of patients. The myth is a particular kind of communal experience. It is a special form of shared fantasy, and it serves to bring the individual into relationship with members of his cultural group on the basis of certain common needs. Accordingly, the myth can be studied from the point of view of its function in psychic integration – how it plays a role in warding off feelings of guilt and anxiety, how it constitutes a form of adaptation to reality and to the group in which the individual lives, and how it influences the crystallization of the individual identity and the formation of the superego.
>
> (Arlow 1961: 375)

Jungians have taken myth positively from the outset. For them, the unconscious expressed in myth is not the Freudian repository of repressed, anti-social drives but a storehouse of innately unconscious 'archetypes,' or sides of the personality, that have simply never had an opportunity at realization: 'Contents of an archetypal character … do not refer to anything that is or has been conscious, but to something essentially unconscious' (Jung 1968: 156). Myth is one means of encountering this Jungian, or 'collective,' unconscious. The function of myth is less release, as for classical Freudians, than growth, as for contemporary ones. But where even contemporary Freudians see myth as a means of adjusting to the demands of the outer world, Jungians see myth as a means of cultivating the 'inner world.' The payoff is less adjustment than self-realization. Some Jungians and Jungian-oriented theorists such as the American Joseph Campbell (1904–87) (1949) so tout the benefit of myth that it becomes a panacea for humanity's problems. But Jung himself never goes this far. For Jung, myth works best as part of therapy. For Campbell, myth makes therapy unnecessary, and only the absence of myth makes therapy necessary.

For even contemporary Freudians, myth harks back to childhood. For Jungians, myth points forward. Myth especially serves adults already settled in the outer world but largely severed from the unconscious. Myth is to be read symbolically, as for Freudians, but not because its meaning has intentionally been disguised. Rather, the unconscious speaks a language of its own and simply awaits grasping. Understanding myth is less like breaking the Enigma code, as for Freudians, and more like deciphering the Rosetta Stone.

'Post,' or 'archetypal,' Jungians such as James Hillman (b. 1926) (1975) and David Miller (b. 1936) (1981) maintain that classical Jungian psychology, by emphasizing the therapeutic message of mythology, reduces myth to psychology and reduces god to a concept. They advocate the reverse: that psychology be viewed as irreducibly mythological. Myth is still to be interpreted psychologically, but psychology itself is to be interpreted mythologically. One grasps the psychological meaning of the myth of Saturn by imagining oneself to be the figure Saturn, not by translating Saturn's plight into clinical terms like depression. Moreover, the depressed Saturn represents a legitimate aspect of one's personality. Each god deserves its due. The psychological ideal should be pluralistic rather than monolithic – in mythological terms, polytheistic rather than monotheistic. Post-Jungians maintain that Jung's psychological ideal of a single, unified self (or 'Self') reflects a Western, specifically monotheistic, more specifically Christian, still more specifically Protestant, outlook. Instead of the Bible, Hillman and Miller take their mythic cues from the Greeks, however simplistic the equation of Greece with polytheism and of the Bible with monotheism may be. The title of Miller's key book says it all: *The New Polytheism* (1981).

Furthermore, the Western emphasis on progress is purportedly reflected in the primacy that Jung accords both hero myths and the ego, even in the ego's encounter with the unconscious. For the encounter is intended to abet development. According to Hillman and Miller, the ego is just one more archetype with its attendant kind of god, and it is the 'soul' rather than the ego that experiences the archetypes through myths. Myth serves to open one up to the soul's own depths. The payoff of mythology is aesthetic rather than moral: one gains a sense of wonder and contemplation rather than, as for classical Jungians, a guide to living. Consequently, the most apposite myths are those of the playful puer archetype and of the receptive anima archetype rather than, as for classical Jungians, those of the striving hero archetype and of the fully united, or integrated, wise old man archetype.

Myth and ritual

Myth is commonly taken to be words, often in the form of a story. A myth is read or heard. It says something. Yet there is an approach to myth that finds this view artificial. According to the myth and ritual, or myth-ritualist, theory, myth does not stand by itself but is tied to ritual. Myth is not just a statement but also an action. The most uncompromising form of the theory maintains that all myths have accompanying rituals and all rituals accompanying myths. In tamer versions some myths may flourish without rituals or some rituals without myths. Alternatively, myths and rituals may originally operate together but subsequently go their separate ways. Or myths and rituals may arise separately but subsequently coalesce. Whatever the tie between myth and ritual, the myth-ritualist theory differs from other theories of myth and from other theories of ritual in focusing on the tie.

The myth and ritual, or myth-ritualist, theory was pioneered by the Scottish biblicist and Arabist William Robertson Smith (1846–94), who argued that ritual came first and that myth arose to explain 'the circumstances under which the rite first came to be established, by the command or by the direct example of the god' (Smith 1894: 17). In Smith's version of myth-ritualism, myth is clearly subordinate to ritual.

The fullest development of the theory came in, especially, the second and third editions (1900, 1911–15) of J. G. Frazer's *Golden Bough*, itself dedicated to Smith. Frazer ties myth to magic, specifically to the first of his two laws of magic. The first law, that of homeopathy, is epitomized by voodoo, according to which the imitation of an action causes the action to occur. Ritual puts magic into practice. The aim is to get the crops to grow.

Frazer ties myth not only to ritual but also to kingship. In one version of his myth-ritualist scenario the king, merely human, plays the part of the god of vegetation, the key god of the pantheon, and acts out the myth of the god's death and rebirth. The ritualistic imitation of the death and rebirth of the god is believed to cause the same to happen to the god. And as the god goes, so go the crops. The ritual is performed at the end – the desired end – of winter, presumably when provisions are running low. The myth can be said to explain the ritual, as for Smith, but from the outset and in the form of the script of a play. Without the myth, there would be no ritual. At the same time the subject of myth is, as for Tylor, the world and not, as for Smith, the ritual: myth is about the death and rebirth of vegetation, not about the ritual used to effect that rebirth.

In the other version of Frazer's myth-ritualist scenario the king does not merely play the part of the god of vegetation but *is* the god, whose soul resides in the body of the incumbent. Here the king does not act out the death and rebirth of the god but is himself killed, with the god's soul then being transferred to the body of his successor. This ritualistic regicide occurs as often as annually or as infrequently and as unpredictably as at the earliest sign of the king's weakening. Now as the king goes, so goes the god and so in turn goes vegetation.

Strictly speaking, no magic is involved here. The replacement of the king does not imitate the revival of the god but effects it. In fact, no myth is involved either. The killing of the king is not the enactment of the myth of the death of the god of vegetation but the sheer killing of the king. The ritual – the killing – really stands alone, undirected by any mythic script. It is Frazer's English disciple Lord Raglan (1936) who provides a mythic script for the ritual: for him, hero myths describe ideal kings whose willingness to die for their community should be emulated by present-day kings. In both of Frazer's scenarios the ritual, whether with or without myth, is the primitive counterpart to *applied* science rather than, as for Tylor, the counterpart to scientific *theory*.

The classicists Gilbert Murray, F. M. Cornford, and A. B. Cook, all British or British-resident, applied the first version of Frazer's myth-ritualist scenario to such ancient Greek phenomena as tragedy, comedy, the Olympic games, science, and philosophy. These seemingly secular, even anti-religious phenomena are interpreted as latent expressions of the myth of the death and rebirth of the god of vegetation.

Among biblicists, the English S. H. Hooke, the Swede Ivan Engnell, the Welshman Aubrey Johnson, and the Norwegian Sigmund Mowinckel differed over the extent to which ancient Israel in particular adhered to a myth-ritualist pattern based on Frazer's first version. Engnell saw an even stronger adherence than the cautious Hooke. Johnson and especially Mowinckel saw a weaker one.

Invoking Frazer, Bronislaw Malinowski applied his own, qualified version of the theory to the myths of native peoples worldwide. Malinowski argues that myth, which for him, as for Smith, explains the origin of ritual, gives rituals a hoary origin and thereby sanctions them. Society depends on myth to spur adherence to rituals. But if all rituals depend on myth, so do many other cultural practices. They have myths of their own. Myth and ritual are therefore not coextensive.

Mircea Eliade applied a similar form of the theory but, going beyond Malinowski, applied the theory to modern as well as to 'primitive' cultures. Myth for Eliade, too, sanctions phenomena of all kinds, not just rituals, by giving them a primeval origin. For him, too, then, myth and ritual are not coextensive. But Eliade again goes beyond Malinowski in stressing the importance of the ritualistic enactment of myth in the fulfillment of the ultimate function of myth: when enacted, myth acts as a time machine, carrying one back to the time of the myth and thereby bringing one closer to God.

The most notable application of the myth-ritualist theory outside religion has been to the arts, especially literature. Jane Harrison (1913) daringly derived all art from ritual. She speculates that gradually people ceased believing that the imitation of an action caused the action to occur. Yet rather than abandoning ritual, they now practiced it as an end in itself. Ritual for its own sake became art, Harrison's clearest example of which is drama. More modestly than she, Murray and Cornford rooted specifically Greek epic, tragedy, and comedy in myth-ritualism. Murray then extended the theory to Shakespeare.

Other standard-bearers of the theory have included Jessie Weston on the Grail legend, E. M. Butler on the Faust legend, C. L. Barber on Shakespearean comedy, Herbert Weisinger on Shakespearean tragedy and on tragedy per se, Francis Fergusson on tragedy, Lord Raglan on hero myths and on literature as a whole, and Northrop Frye and Stanley Edgar Hyman on literature generally. As literary critics, these myth-ritualists have understandably been concerned less with myth itself than with the mythic origin of literature. Works of literature are interpreted as the outgrowth of myths once tied to rituals. For those literary critics indebted to Frazer, as the majority are, literature harks back to Frazer's second, not first, myth-ritualist version. 'The king must die' becomes the familiar summary line.

For literary myth-ritualists, myth becomes literature when myth is severed from ritual. Myth tied to ritual is religious literature; myth cut off from ritual is secular literature, or plain literature. When tied to ritual, myth can serve any of the active functions ascribed to it by myth-ritualists. Myth can even change the world. Bereft of ritual, myth is demoted to mere commentary.

Literary myth-ritualism is a theory not of myth and ritual themselves, both of which are assumed, but of their impact on literature. Yet it is a not a theory of literature either, for it firmly refuses to reduce literature to myth. Literary myth-ritualism is an explanation of the transformation of myth and ritual into literature.

The French-born literary critic René Girard (b. 1923) (1977) offers an ironic twist to the theory of Raglan. Where Raglan's hero is willing to die for the community, Girard's hero is killed or exiled by the community for having caused its present woes. Indeed, the 'hero' is initially considered a criminal who deserves to die. Only subsequently is the villain turned into a hero, who, as for Raglan, is heroic exactly for dying selflessly for the community. Both Raglan and Girard cite Oedipus as their fullest example. (Their doing so makes neither a Freudian. Both spurn Freud.) For Girard, the transformation of Oedipus from reviled exile in Sophocles's *Oedipus the King* to revered benefactor in Sophocles' *Oedipus at Colonus* typifies the transformation from criminal to hero.

Yet this change is for Girard only the second half of the process. The first half is the change from innocent victim to criminal. Originally, violence erupts in the community. The cause is the inclination, innate in human nature, to imitate others and thereby to desire the same objects as those of the imitated. Imitation leads to rivalry, which leads to

split into nonverbal and verbal behavior. Physical as well as verbal behavior conveys information.

The information conveyed by ritual concerns both the present and the ideal place of the individual in society and the cosmos alike: 'We are not dealing with information about a new agricultural technique or a better judicial procedure: we are concerned here with the crucial values of the believing community, whether it is a religious community, a nation, a tribe, a secret society, or any other type of group whose ultimate unity resides in its orientation towards transcendental and invisible powers' (Turner 1968: 2).

The Drums of Affliction focuses on Ndembu rituals of affliction, or rituals performed on behalf of persons whose illnesses or misfortunes are blamed on either ancestors or witches. Symptoms of affliction include backache, fever, boils, and difficulties in childbirth and hunting. The ritual tries to placate the spirits responsible. In the Ndembu village studied by Turner there loomed economic, political, and social decay in the wake of the colonial government's withdrawal of official recognition of the village chieftain. The loss of that recognition cost the village jobs, goods, and most of all clout. The village was also facing problems in hunting and farming.

The consequent frustration stirred previously suppressed tensions among individuals and among clans – tensions rooted ultimately in the clash between matrilineal descent and virilocal marriage. Because of both his particular lineage and his passive, effeminate personality, one villager, Kamahasanyi, became the scapegoat. Overwhelmed by the scorn of his relatives and neighbors, he developed various physical ills. His ancestors, he claimed, were punishing him for the failure of his line to retain the chieftainship, and his relatives and neighbors were bewitching him out of frustration at their own plight. Kamahasanyi demanded and received ritual curing. During the rituals all the personal antagonisms, which had been less unrecognized than ignored, were acknowledged and at least temporarily purged. Kamahasanyi himself was vindicated, and his ailments ceased, though the underlying tensions were scarcely eliminated.

On the one hand ritual for Turner serves to alleviate *social* turmoil: 'Ndembu ritual … may be regarded as a magnificent instrument for expressing, maintaining, and periodically cleansing a secular order of society without strong political centralization and all too full of social conflict' (Turner 1968: 21). On the other hand ritual for Turner also serves to alleviate *existential* turmoil:

> In the idiom of the rituals of affliction it is as though the Ndembu said: 'It is only when a person is reduced to misery by misfortune, and repents of the acts that caused him to be afflicted, that ritual expressing an underlying unity in diverse things may fittingly be enacted for him' … It is as though he were stripped of all possessions, all status, all social connections, and *then* endowed with all the basic virtues and values of Ndembu society.
>
> (Turner 1968: 22)

Ritual restores order to, at once, society and individuals' lives. Existential turmoil may grow out of social turmoil, but it is more than an expression of social turmoil.

Ritual alleviates both kinds of turmoil by acting out, by literally dramatizing, the situation it remedies. To use one of Turner's pet phrases, ritual is 'social drama.' As drama, ritual is not merely a part of social life but the depiction of it.[6] Where for Harrison drama is the legacy of ritual, for Turner drama is part of ritual.

Ritual for Turner describes not only how things are but also how they should be. It thereby serves as a model for altering society, not merely as a model of existing society:

> Ritual is a periodic restatement of the terms in which men of a particular culture must interact if there is to be any kind of a [sic] coherent social life … It has been more than once suggested that religious ritual is mainly 'expressive', that it portrays in symbolic form certain key values and cultural orientations. This is true as far as it goes, but it points to only one of many properties it possesses. More important is its creative function – it actually creates, or re-creates, the categories through which men perceive reality – the axioms underlying the structure of society and the laws of the natural and moral orders. It is not here a case of life being an imitation of art, but of social life being an attempted imitation of models portrayed and animated by ritual.
>
> (Turner 1968: 6–7)

Turner is claiming that ritual actually works, not merely is believed to work, and works by making sense of participants' experiences, not merely, as for Malinowski, Marx, and Freud, by releasing or redirecting their emotions. The individual ills treated by ritual are psychosomatic, and Turner often compares Ndembu rituals with psychoanalysis. But he is not thereby reducing the ills to feelings. On the contrary, he is elevating them to thoughts, or beliefs. Ndembu rituals work precisely because, like psychoanalysis, they make manifest not only repressed or, here, suppressed feelings but also suppressed beliefs.

Ritual as the alleviation of fear and guilt

The German classicist Walter Burkert (b. 1931) (1979, 1985, 1989) has developed a theory of ritual that derives from the ethology of Konrad Lorenz and, more recently, from the sociobiology of Edward O. Wilson. For Burkert, as for Turner, ritual is drama. It is 'as if' behavior. To take his central example, ritual, as he uses the term, is not the customs and formalities involved in hunting but the transformation of actual hunting into dramatized hunting. The function is no longer that of securing food, as for Frazer, since the ritual proper arises only in agricultural times, when farming has supplanted hunting as the prime source of food. Where for Frazer ritual is exactly a pre-scientific means of getting crops to grow, for Burkert ritual serves social and psychological ends – a shift in subject and function that applies as much to twentieth-century theories of ritual as to twentieth-century theories of myth and of myth plus ritual. Rather than rooted in agriculture, as for Frazer, ritual for Burkert is rooted in the prior stage of hunting and is simply preserved in the wake of agriculture: 'Hunting lost its basic function with the emergence of agriculture some ten thousand years ago. But hunting ritual had become so important that it could not be given up. Stability stayed with those groups who managed to make use of the social and psychological appeal of the ritual by transforming, by redirecting, it until the whole action became a ritual' (Burkert 1979: 55).

Hunting, according to Burkert, stirred feelings of fear and guilt. The fear was not merely of getting killed by the animal hunted but also of killing a fellow hunter and, too, of depleting the food supply: 'Killing to eat was an unalterable commandment, and yet the bloody act must always have been attended with a double danger and a double fear: that the weapon might be turned against a fellow hunter, and that the death of the prey might signal an end with no future, while man must always eat and so must always hunt' (Burkert 1985: 58). The even deeper fear was of one's own aggression and one's own mortality. The guilt was over the killing of a fellow living creature. The communal nature of hunting functioned to assuage the individual's fear and guilt, and at the same time functioned to cement a bond among hunters: 'From a psychological and ethological point of view, it is the communally enacted aggression and shared guilt which creates solidarity' (Burkert 1985: 58). The function of ritual for Burkert, as for Turner, Geertz, and Douglas, is social as well as individual.

Like Douglas above all, Burkert sharply contrasts the magical, practical, efficiacious, Frazerian view of ritual – ritual intended to secure rain, food, or fertility – to the symbolic, expressive one. Like Douglas as well, he dismisses the efficacious view and espouses the expressive one. For him, as for her, ritual makes a statement rather than carries out action. Where for Harrison ritual carries out an action and drama makes a statement, for Burkert and Douglas alike ritual, *as* drama, makes a statement rather than carries out an action. The shift in the study of ritual mirrors the shift in the study of myth and of myth plus ritual: for twentieth-century theorists, the efficacy of ritual is social, psychological, and existential, not physical.

Ritual as the reconciliation of contradictions

The English anthropologist Edmund Leach (1910–88) was well known for his structuralist analyses of, especially, biblical myths (1969). But unlike Claude Lévi-Strauss, who primarily analyzes myths, Leach analyzes rituals equally (1976). Also unlike Lévi-Strauss, who concentrates mostly on Native American myths – his programmatic structuralist analysis of the myth of Oedipus is an exception – Leach analyses modern rituals as often as 'primitive' ones. Still, as a Lévi-Straussian, he finds in rituals the same kinds of binary oppositions needing mediation that Lévi-Strauss finds in myths. For Leach, rituals are doing physically what myths are doing verbally.

In this later, structuralist phase Leach analyzes myths and rituals identically but separately. In his earlier, social functionalist phase he tightened the tie between myth and ritual beyond that of, so he assumed, even Harrison: 'Myth, in my terminology, is the counterpart of ritual; myth implies ritual, ritual implies myth, they are one and the same ... As I see it, myth regarded as a statement in words 'says' the same thing as ritual regarded as a statement in action' (Leach 1965, pp. 11–12). He claimed to be carrying myth-ritualism to its limits. In fact, Leach is really drawing the same close tie as Harrison and also Hooke.[7]

Ritual as the instillment of belief

Where Tylor and Frazer view ritual as the *application* of belief, and where Turner, Geertz, and Douglas view ritual as the *expression* or, at best, the *instillment* of belief, American anthropologist Roy Rappaport (1926–97) credits ritual with actually *creating* belief. Where for the others ritual is at most the key part of religion, for Rappaport it is nearly the whole. Rappaport does consider myth, but he subordinates it to ritual.

Rappaport's *Ritual and Religion in the Making of Humanity* (1999) represents an extraordinary venture beyond the approach to ritual in the work that made Rappaport's name, *Pigs for the Ancestors* (1968). There the function of ritual is ecological. The raising of pigs in abandoned gardens by the Tsembaga Maring farmers of New Guinea serves to clear the ground and make planting easier. The ritualistic killing of pigs serves to keep an increasing number from damaging the ground and making planting harder. The eating of pigs, which ordinarily happens only during rituals, provides protein to keep the people healthy. While Rappaport does note the social function of pig sacrifice – for example, the more pigs, the more dispersed the residents and so the less the social contact – he stresses the ecological function.

In *Ecology, Meaning, and Religion* (1979) Rappaport at once continues the ecological analysis of *Pigs* and moves radically beyond it. The key essay in the collection is 'The Obvious Aspects of Ritual.' Where, before, Rappaport had concentrated on the function of ritual, now he tends to the form of ritual. He tries to identify what makes ritual ritual by differentiating it from anything else. For example, ritual must be done precisely, repeatedly, and at set times and places. But an assembly line is equally formal yet scarcely a ritual. Ritual must, in addition, be performed. But so must dance. Ritual is a means to an end, not an end in itself. But so, too, is drama. Where, however, drama involves an audience, ritual requires a 'congregation,' which does not merely witness the action but also participates in it. Rappaport returns to the differentiation of ritual from drama found in Harrison. In *Pigs* Rappaport sees ritual as merely the human means of maintaining the ecosystem we share with animals. From 'Obvious' on, ritual becomes distinctly human.

Ritual and Religion in the Making of Humanity constitutes a grand elaboration of the 'Obvious' essay. Invoking concepts from fields as diverse as speech acts theory and cybernetics, Rappaport constructs one of the fullest and richest theories of ritual to be found. He claims that ritual does almost everything, not least things that others would automatically attribute to belief.

To take an example of which Rappaport would have approved, the biblical patriarch Isaac, wanting Esau, his firstborn son, to succeed in life, does not merely state his wish but utilizes the ritual of a blessing to ensure it (Genesis 27). Even when the blind Isaac discovers that he has been duped into bestowing his deathbed blessing on Jacob instead, the blessing cannot be undone. The ritual is itself efficacious, no matter what the intent of either party. To take a more positive example, most couples planning to spend their lives together still partake of the ritual of marriage. The ceremony binds the parties even if, let us say, one of them only pretends to be in love with the other.

Against Rappaport, one might note that even if Isaac's blessing, once offered, cannot be rescinded, it still does not transform Jacob into Isaac's firstborn or favorite. A wedding ceremony presupposes that the bride and groom are committed to each other and expresses, not establishes, that commitment. The ritual is hollow if the commitment is missing. And marriage, unlike Isaac's blessing, can be annulled, albeit by another ritual.

Rappaport roots other aspects of religion in ritual. To participate in a ritual is to accept it, so that acceptance spells obligation and therefore morality. Yet one might argue that just as ritual seemingly presupposes belief rather than dispenses with it, so ritual seemingly presupposes morality rather than creates it. When two parties ritually shake hands after agreeing to something, the faith that they have in each other does not stem from the handshake, which merely expresses, not establishes, their mutual trust.

Rappaport argues that not even homicide is always immoral – unless it violates a ritual: 'There are conditions, so common as to require no illustration, under which killing humans is laudable or even mandatory. What is immoral is, of course, killing someone whom there is an obligation, at least tacit, not to kill' (Rappaport 1999: 132).

Having rooted morality in ritual, Rappaport is prepared to conclude that ritual is the center of social life: 'In enunciating, accepting and making conventions moral, ritual contains within itself not simply a symbolic representation of social contract, but tacit social contract itself. As such, ritual … is *the* basic social act' (Rappaport 1999, p. 138). Ritual socializes in other ways, too. Notably, it links what is private to what is public. A rite of passage turns the physiological changes in an adolescent into a change in status.

Ritual ties human beings not only to one another but also to the external world. Ritual orders experience in many ways, with Rappaport emphasizing the experience of time over the experience of space. Most straighforwardly, ritual organizes time into clearcut divisions: the ritual of Christmas divides the year into two seasons. Above all, ritual, specifically religious ritual, connects humans to the cosmos. All rituals for Rappaport communicate, but religious rituals, which for him are the highest kind, convey something other than information since they are the most invariant and therefore the most repetitive. Their repetitiveness makes them ideal communicators of eternal, hence repetitive, 'sacred' truths. 'Sacred' truths are metaphysical. They provide certitude not only because they are unchanging but also because they lie beyond the realm of proof or disproof. Rappaport's originality is his claim that, once again, religious rituals do not merely assume, evince, or inculcate transcendent truths but somehow also establish and validate them.

Ritual as the ordering of the world

Where Burkert draws on ethology and sociobiology, where Leach draws on structuralism, and where Rappaport draws on cybernetics and other fields, cognitive theorists of ritual draw on cognitive psychology. Led by the French anthropologist Pascal Boyer (b. 1940) (1994, 2001), cognitive theorists have become so numerous and so organized as to constitute what the philosopher of science Imre Lakatos would have called a 'research program.' Cognitivists analyze the cognitive constraints that direct thinking, including religious thinking. Strikingly, they focus not on myth, which barely gets considered, but on ritual. Like Leach and others, they see ritual as a cognitive enterprise. In stressing the constraints under which thinking and in turn acting occurs, they really echo Tylor, for whom myth, despite appearances, has an orderliness that reflects the orderliness of the mind. In stressing the centrality of supernatural agents – gods – to religion, they again echo Tylor, for whom the distinctiveness of religion is exactly the postulation of gods rather than, as in science, natural processes (see Chapter 31 on Religion and Cognition).

In the nineteenth century ritual was assumed to be the 'primitive' counterpart to modern technology, which rendered it superfluous and, worse, impossible. In the twentieth century ritual has been seen as almost anything but the outdated counterpart to technology. Ritual, it has been maintained, is about the human world and not or not just about the physical world. Consequently, its function is not physical but social, psychological, or existential. Even for cognitive psychologists, the focus is now on how humans think ritually, not on what ritual is intended to do.

Notes

1 The classic attempt not to replace but to reconcile a theological account of the plagues and of succeeding events with a scientific account is that of the Jewish existentialist philosopher Martin Buber, for whom the believer, on the basis of faith, attributes to divine intervention what the believer acknowledges can be fully accounted for scientifically: see Buber 1958: 60–68, 74–79. Buber is the Jewish counterpart to the Protestant Rudolf Bultmann.

2 The classic work on finding science in myth is de Santillana and von Dechend (1969).

3 To be precise, Frazer, while assuming, like Tylor, that adherents read myth literally, himself reads it symbolically. The life – specifically, the death and rebirth – of the god of vegetation is a metaphorical description of the death and rebirth of the crops: '[T]he story that Adonis spent half, or according to others a third, of the year in the lower world and the rest of it in the upper world, is explained most simply and naturally by supposing that he represented vegetation, especially

the corn, which lies buried in the earth half the year and reappears above ground the other half' (Frazer 1922: 392). By contrast, Tylor insists that the only proper reading of myth is the literal one.

4   The classical theorist of myth as ideology is Georges Sorel 1961), for whom, to be sure, myth serves not to bolster society, as for Malinowski, but to foment revolution.

5   As Ronald Grimes, the organizer of the field of 'ritual studies,' writes of Turner's status, 'This academic generation's intellectual task seems to be that of getting beyond Victor Turner. His work has exercised considerable formative influence on the initial phases of ritual studies' (Grimes 1995: xvii).

6   Sometimes for Turner ritual is itself social drama. Other times ritual is a response to a social drama, in which case the drama refers to the turmoil itself and the ritual to the depiction of the turmoil. More precisely, ritual is here the last stage within a social drama, which begins with the turmoil and ends with what Turner calls 'redress.' Ritual is only one form of redress. A lawsuit is another.

7   Leach (1965: 13) lumps Harrison with Durkheim and Malinowski, neither of whom in fact brings myth and ritual so closely together, and is likely unaware of Hooke and other biblical myth-ritualists.

Bibliography

Arlow, Jacob A. 1961 'Ego Psychology and the Study of Mythology.' *Journal of the American Psychoanalytic Association* 9: 371–93.

Barthes, Roland 1972 *Mythologies*, trans. Annette Lavers. New York: Hill & Wang; London: Cape.

Bell, Catherine 1992 *Ritual Theory, Ritual Practice*. New York and Oxford: Oxford University Press.

Bell, Catherine 1997 *Ritual*. New York and Oxford: Oxford University Press.

Boyer, Pascal 1994 *The Naturalness of Religious Ideas*. Berkeley: University of California Press.

Boyer, Pascal 2001 *Religion Explained*. New York: Basic Books.

Buber, Martin 1958 [1946] *Moses*. New York: Harper Torchbooks.

Bultmann, Rudolf 1953 'New Testament and Mythology' (1944), in Hans-Werner Bartsch, ed. *Kerygma and Myth*, vol. 1, trans. Reginald H. Fuller (London: SPCK), 1–44. Reprinted, with rev. trans.: New York: Harper Torchbooks, 1961.

Bultmann, Rudolf 1958 *Jesus Christ and Mythology*. New York: Scribner's.

Burkert, Walter 1979 *Structure and History in Greek Mythology and Ritual*. Berkeley: University of California Press.

Burkert, Walter 1985 *Greek Religion*, trans. John Raffan. Cambridge, MA: Harvard University Press.

Burkert, Walter 1996 *Creation of the Sacred*. Cambridge, MA: Harvard University Press.

Campbell, Joseph 1949 *The Hero with a Thousand Faces*. New York: Pantheon Books. 2nd edn 1968.

Cassirer, Ernst 1955 *The Philosophy of Symbolic Forms*, vol. 2, trans. Ralph Manheim. New Haven, CT: Yale University Press.

De Santillana, Giorgio, and Hertha von Dechend 1969 *Hamlet's Mill*. Boston: Gambit.

Detienne, Marcel 1977 *The Gardens of Adonis*, trans. Janet Lloyd. Atlantic Highlands, NJ: Humanities Press.

Douglas, Mary 1970 *Purity and Danger*. (Original published 1966.) Baltimore, MD: Penguin Books.

Douglas, Mary 1973 *Natural Symbols*. 2nd edn (1st edn 1970). New York: Vintage Books.

Durkheim, Émile 1915 *The Elementary Forms of the Religious Life*, trans. Joseph Ward Swain. London: Allen and Unwin.

Eliade, Mircea 1968 [1959] *The Sacred and the Profane*, trans. Willard R. Trask. New York: Harvest Books.

Frazer, J. G. (James George) 1900 *The Golden Bough*. 2nd edn (1st edn 1890). 3 vols. London: Macmillan.

Frazer, J. G. (James George) 1911–15 *The Golden Bough*. 3rd edn. 12 vols. London: Macmillan.

Frazer, J. G. (James George) 1922 *The Golden Bough*. Abridged edn. London: Macmillan.

Freud, Sigmund 1953 [1913]. *The Interpretation of Dreams*. In *The Standard Edition of the Complete Psychological Works of Sigmund Freud*, eds. and trans. James Strachey *et al*. Vols 4 and 5. London: Hogarth Press and Institute of Psycho-Analysis.

Freud, Sigmund 1955 [1950]. *Totem and Taboo*. In *The Standard Edition of the Complete Psychological Works of Sigmund Freud*, eds. and trans. James Strachey *et al.* Vol. 13: ix–161. London: Hogarth Press and Institute of Psycho-Analysis.

Geertz, Clifford 1973 *The Interpretation of Cultures*. New York: Basic Books.

Geertz, Clifford 1983 *Local Knowledge*. New York: Basic Books.

Girard, René 1977 *Violence and the Sacred*, trans. Peter Gregory. London: Athlone Press; Baltimore, MD: Johns Hopkins University Press.

Grimes, Ronald L. 1995 *Beginnings in Ritual Studies*. Rev. edn (1st edn 1982). Columbia: University of South Carolina Press.

Harrison, Jane Ellen 1913 *Ancient Art and Ritual*. New York: Holt; London: Williams and Norgate.

Hillman, James 1975 *Re-Visioning Psychology*. New York: Harper & Row.

Krienath, Jens, Jan Snoek, and Michael Stausberg, eds. 2006 and 2007 *Theorizing Rituals*. 2 vols. Leiden: Brill.

Jonas, Hans 1963 'Gnostic, Existentialism, and Nihilism' (1952), in Jonas, *The Gnostic Religion*, 2nd edn (Boston: Beacon Press), 320–40.

Jung, C. G. 1968 *The Archetypes and the Collective Unconscious*, 2nd edn (1st edn 1959). *The Collected Works of C. G. Jung*, eds. Sir Herbert Read *et al.*, trans. R. F. C. Hull *et al.*, vol. 9, pt. 1. Princeton, NJ: Princeton University Press.

Kramer, Samuel Noah 1961 *Sumerian Mythology*, rev. edn (1st edn 1944). New York: Harper & Row.

Leach, Edmund 1965 *Political Systems of Highland Burma*. With new introduction. (Originally published 1954.) Boston: Beacon.

Leach, Edmund 1969 *Genesis as Myth and Other Essays*. London: Cape.

Leach, Edmund 1976 *Culture and Communication*. Cambridge: Cambridge University Press.

Lévi-Strauss, Claude 1958 'The Structural Study of Myth' (1955), in *Myth*, ed. Thomas A. Sebeok (Bloomington: Indiana University Press), 81–106. Reprinted in Lévi-Strauss, *Structural Anthropology*, vol. 1, trans. Claire Jacobson and Brooke Grundfest Schoepf (New York: Basic Books, 1963; London: Allen Lane, 1968), Chapter 11.

Lévi-Strauss, Claude 1978 *Myth and Meaning*. Toronto: University of Toronto Press.

Lévy-Bruhl, Lucien 1926 *How Natives Think*, trans. Lilian A. Clare. London: Allen & Unwin. Reprinted: Princeton, NJ: Princeton University Press, 1985.

Malinowski, Bronislaw 1925 'Magic, Science and Religion.' In *Science, Religion and Reality*, ed. Joseph Needham, 20–84. New York and London: Macmillan. Reprinted in Malinowski, *Magic, Science and Religion and Other Essays*, ed. Robert Redfield (Glencoe, IL, Free Press, 1948), 1–71.

Malinowski, Bronislaw 1926 *Myth in Primitive Psychology*. London: Kegan Paul; New York: Norton. Reprinted in Malinowski, *Magic, Science and Religion and Other Essays*, ed. Robert Redfield (Glencoe, IL, Free Press, 1948), 72–124.

Marx, Karl, and Friedrich Engels 1957 *On Religion*. Moscow: Foreign Languages Publishing.

May, Herbert G., and Bruce M. Metzger, eds. 1977 [1962] *The New Oxford Annotated Bible with the Apocrypha*, Revised Standard Version. New York: Oxford University Press.

Miller, David L. 1981 *The New Polytheism*. 2nd edn (1st edn 1974). Dallas: Spring.

Radcliffe-Brown, A. R. 1922 *The Andaman Islanders*. Cambridge: Cambridge University Press.

Raglan Lord 1936 *The Hero*. London: Methuen. Reprinted in Otto Rank, Lord Raglan, and Alan Dundes, *In Quest of the Hero* (Princeton, NJ: Princeton University Press, 1990), 89–175.

Rank, Otto 1914 *The Myth of the Birth of the Hero*. 1st edn. Trans. F. Robbins and Smith Ely Jelliffe. Nervous and Mental Disease Monograph Series, no. 18. New York: Journal of Nervous and Mental Disease Publishing. Reprinted in Otto Rank, Lord Raglan, and Alan Dundes, *In Quest of the Hero* (Princeton, NJ: Princeton University Press, 1990), 3–86.

Rank, Otto 2004 *The Myth of the Birth of the Hero*. 2nd edn. Trans. Gregory C. Richter and E. James Lieberman. Baltimore, MD: Johns Hopkins University Press.

Rappaport, Roy A. 1968 *Pigs for the Ancestors*. New Haven, CT: Yale University Press. Expanded edn 1984.

Rappaport, Roy A. 1979 *Ecology, Meaning, and Religion*. Richmond, CA: North Atlantic Books.

Rappaport, Roy A. 1999 *Ritual and Religion in the Making of Humanity*. Cambridge: Cambridge University Press.

Ricoeur, Paul 1967 *The Symbolism of Evil*, trans. Emerson Buchanan. New York: Harper & Row.

Segal, Robert A., ed. 1998 *The Myth and Ritual Theory*. Oxford, UK, and Malden, MA: Wiley-Blackwell.

Segal, Robert A. 1999 *Theorizing about Myth*. Amherst, MA: University of Massachusetts Press.

Segal, Robert A. 2004 *Myth: A Very Short Introduction*. Oxford: Oxford University Press.

Segal, Robert A., ed. 2008 *The Blackwell Companion to the Study of Religion*. Oxford, UK, and Malden, MA: Wiley-Blackwell.

Smith, William Robertson. 1894 *Lectures on the Religion of the Semites*. 2nd edn (1st edn 1889). London: Black.

Sorel, Georges A. 1961 [1950] *Reflections on Violence*, trans. T. E. Hulme and J. Roth. New York: Collier Books; London: Collier-Macmillan.

Turner, Victor W. 1967 *The Forest of Symbols*. Ithaca, NY: Cornell University Press.

Turner, Victor W. 1968 *The Drums of Affliction*. Oxford: Clarendon Press.

Turner, Victor W. 1969 *The Ritual Process*. Chicago: Aldine.

Tylor, E. B. (Edward Burnett) 1871 *Primitive Culture*. 2 vols. London: Murray. 5th edn 1913.

Van Hendy, Andrew 2001 *The Modern Construction of Myth*. Bloomington: Indiana University Press.

Vernant, Jean-Pierre 1983 *Myth and Thought among the Greeks*, trans. not given. London: Routledge & Kegan Paul.

Wheelwright, Philip 1968 *The Burning Fountain*. Rev. edn (1st edn 1954). Bloomington: Indiana University Press.

Suggested reading

For a short overview of modern theories of myth, see Robert A. Segal, 'Myth,' in *The Blackwell Companion to the Study of Religion*, ed. Segal, 337–55. For a book-length but still short overview, see Segal, *Myth: A Very Short Introduction*. For a much fuller presentation, see Andrew van Hendy, *The Modern Construction of Myth*. For a bibliography on theories of myth, see Thomas J. Sinekewicz, *Theories of Myth: An Annotated Bibliography* (Lanham, MD: Scarecrow Press, 1997). For a short overview of the myth-ritualist theory, see Segal, introduction to *The Myth and Ritual Theory*, ed. Segal, 1–13. This anthology provides selections from the leading exponents and critics of the theory. For a short overview of theories of ritual, see Catherine Bell, 'Ritual,' in *The Blackwell Companion to the Study of Religion*, ed. Segal, 397–411. For fuller overviews and assessments, see Bell's two books: *Ritual Theory, Ritual Practice* and *Ritual*. By far the fullest presentation of theories of ritual is to be found in Jens Kreinath, Jan Snoek, and Michael Stausberg, eds., *Theorizing Rituals*, volume 1. Volume 2 contains what is by far the fullest bibliography on theories of ritual.

Chapter 23

Religious authority

Scripture, tradition, charisma

Paul Gifford

Introduction

All human groups need some authority, some generally accepted means of resolving at least the major questions, merely to persist without disintegrating. However, authority is not a simple concept. It is not necessarily linked with power in any hard sense, although there are cases where the religious and secular realms may be so intertwined that the religion may take on some form of secular coercive power. Good analogues of religious authority are provided in the medical or academic fields. A doctor, for example, has authority: he is authorised by his training and professional expertise. With true authority he can say 'you must' or 'you must not'. Likewise an academic may have authority: her authority arises from her superior knowledge of the subject, which enables her to say 'this is so' or 'this is not so'. To maintain her credibility, she must continually vindicate this authority by evidence of competence, her ability to formulate new ideas, her capacity to stimulate students to new insights. Before clarifying further the kinds of authority influential in religious communities, some preparatory remarks are in order.

Religions are not all the same. There are distinct categories like 'primal' religions; the archaic religions of Egypt or Mesopotamia or Greece; and the founded ('world') religions like Islam. Furthermore, different religions within a single one of these categories can have surprisingly diverse internal dynamics; the role played by theology in Christianity, for example, is played within Judaism by law. Further, it is a mistake to presume any particular religion is a monolithic entity. Christianity has its divisions into Catholic, Protestant and Orthodox branches, to name just three, and in each of them authority is exercised significantly differently. Islam embraces Sunni, Shi'ite, Ahmadiyya, Ismaili – these branches all have different understandings of precisely where authority lies. But most importantly, religions are not static; they exist in living communities enduring through time, and thus continually change. Some of these changes can be profound. For example, we now think of Judaism as a religion centred on a book, but it was not always so. Judaism was for centuries centred on a sacrificial cult in the temple; it was the destruction of the first temple (587 BCE) that heightened its emphasis on its scriptures, and the definitive destruction of the third (70 CE) that carried this process to its ultimate conclusion. Other religions have undergone transformations just as profound. Zoroastrianism has been in turn the state religion of the Persian Empire, the religion of an oppressed and marginalised (and largely uneducated) minority under Muslim domination, the religion of a wealthy sector of modern India, and now increasingly the religion of influential professionals of a diaspora scattered throughout the West. The religion – its expression, its embodiment, its self-understanding – has not remained unaffected by these changing contexts. And the elements of authority within a religion, the way they are balanced, perceived, experienced, are among the things that have changed. This may be so, even if formal appearances mask this. Bishops have been authority figures within Christianity from its early years. Now, they would most naturally be perceived as part of the administrative bureaucracy. But they were not always best understood in that way. Medieval Europe was not a bureaucratically governed society; effective authority was exercised through the personal presence of an itinerant ruler, the exercise of patronage, the bonds established with dependents, the power to work miracles, the ceremonial projection of sacrality. In the last resort, a medieval bishop's authority may have more closely approximated the charismatic power of holy men (Mayr-Harting 1990: 124). Thus the office has persisted, but the kind of authority exercised has changed greatly.

These are some of the complications we will have to bear in mind in what follows. These factors will prevent us distinguishing neat categories of religious authority, or making any simple identification of certain forms of authority with particular religions. They will also prevent us from reaching much in the way of hard conclusions. However, even after this disclaimer, we can still raise many questions and shed some light in the general area of religious authority. In this chapter, we will focus on the three significant elements of scripture, tradition and charisma. We will ask in what way they are authoritative, how they are perceived to exert their influence, how their power is experienced and whether they function independently or in combination.

Scripture

We have already observed that different religions may have different internal dynamics. This is crucially so in the matter of sacred texts. Scripture (with cognates like 'écriture', 'scrittura', 'escritura') is a Western term (etymologically, from the Latin *scribere* 'to write') with its roots in the Christian West, and with its original reference to the Christian Bible. Initially, as 'Holy Scripture', the reference was exclusively to the Christian Bible, carrying connotations of inspiration, revelation, perhaps inerrancy. It is only in the last 150 years that the term has come to be applied in a less metaphysical and more descriptive sense to the sacred books of other religious traditions. (Max Müller's fifty-volume edition (1879–94) of *The Sacred Books of the East* was a milestone in this development.) Sometimes the connotations of the word as traditionally used in the West have been much less fitting when applied to other traditions. If the term is not unduly distorting when applied to the other founded religions of the Near East, to Judaism and Islam, its suitability to Eastern religions like Buddhism and Hinduism is less obvious. It is only in recent decades that serious efforts have been made to allow for the subtle distortions likely when a concept taken from one tradition is applied to others.

Nevertheless it is obviously characteristic of many religions to have sacred texts – which we will follow current convention and indiscriminately call 'scripture'. If we ask what it is that constitutes these particular texts scripture or sacred, we quickly see that it is not a matter of form or content. There is no essence, or intrinsic formal quality, or even set of family resemblances, that characterise all these diverse texts. As regards content, the diversity is enormous – from the hymns (*gathas*) of Zoroaster to the letters of Paul, the law codes of Deuteronomy and the sacrificial rituals of the Vedas. Even beauty or profundity is not an essential characteristic. Undoubtedly many have this sublimity – taken to its ultimate in Islam with its doctrine of the inimitability of the Qur'an (*i'jaz al-Qur'an*) – but alongside the sublime we can find other parts which may be genealogies, crude hagiography or fairly banal chronicles. It would be hard to list any criteria of form or content that could isolate precisely these texts and not others.

Likewise, authorship does not provide a criterion for elevating a text to the status of scripture, for here too there is enormous diversity. Although some (like the Qur'an) are intimately linked to the founder, others are by subsequent leaders (as is much of the Sikhs' Adi Granth), others have authors who are completely unknown (the case for a large part of the Jewish scriptures). In the case of the Hindu religion, with no individual founder, the scriptures are believed to have no author at all, not even God.

No, to label a text 'scripture' essentially involves none of these things. What makes a text or texts scripture is something of another register altogether, namely the text's relationship to a community. It is this relationship that is constitutive. Scripture is a relational term, like husband or mother; it has meaning only in relation to another. It is the community's persistence in according it an authoritative position in its life that constitutes a text scripture. Hence, as Smith well puts it, scripture is not an attribute of texts, but a 'human activity'. And it is an ongoing activity. 'No doubt, their scripture to a mighty degree makes a people what they are. Yet one must not lose sight of the point that it is the people who make it, keep making it, scripture' (Smith 1993: 18–19).

Thus authority over a community is built into the idea of scripture. Yet the various scriptures may exert their authority in many diverse ways. Scriptures (or parts of them) may provide the main prayers that adherents utilise throughout the day. In some forms of worship, the scriptures may become a sacred object; thus Jews may dance with the Torah in the synagogue. Most traditions have all kinds of significant popular uses – many Muslims use the Qur'an as a protective device against evil, even using a potion made from mixing water with the ink used to write a Qur'anic charm. Some religions regard scripture as the supreme source of their 'doctrine' or 'morals' or 'law'. However, a scripture's influence can be much more subtly pervasive; it is not always conscious or direct. Anyone familiar with medieval Europe will understand the role of the Bible in providing the source material for most European art; in this way the biblical narratives provided the images that fed the imagination and moulded cultural life. Within Islam, although pictorial representation is generally shunned, Qur'anic calligraphy has played a similar role. In such various ways, focused and diffuse, explicit and implicit, hard and soft, scriptures mould and direct their particular communities. The ability to guide and influence is there by definition, from the mere fact of being scripture.

However, for any living community the context changes over time. We have already drawn attention to the changes Zoroastrianism and Judaism have undergone in history, but change is universal. Islam has changed from a desert religion to the religion of the Abbasids and the Umayyads and the Ottomans. Christianity has transformed itself from a Jewish sect to the Byzantine state religion, to the cultural soul of Europe, to the religion of Latin American peasants. Continuity through change is a problem for any religion, and scripture is often one of the key things enabling the community to negotiate major transformations, providing the means of rendering changes explicable and manageable, thus ensuring some experience of identity over time.

Historical consciousness

The complexity of this process has become obvious only in relatively recent years. What has disclosed the complexity is the rise of a radical new perspective, historical consciousness. At its heart is the awareness that everything is relative, or related to the context in which it arose or in which it exists. Nothing human is supra-temporal, supra-cultural or supra-historical. Everything human is culturally conditioned. Where such a consciousness has taken root (notably in the West, especially Western academia), it has had important effects on the understanding of the past in general, and in particular has affected our attitude to historical texts.

It has altered our attitude to past 'authorities'. By and large, previous ages were incredibly respectful of past authorities. C.S. Lewis says of the European Middle Ages that they were 'ages of authority'.

> If their culture is regarded as a response to environment, then the elements in that environment to which they responded most vigorously were manuscripts. Every writer if he possibly can, bases himself on an earlier writer, follows an *auctour*, preferably a Latin one. This is one of the things that differentiates that period ... from our modern civilisation.

He remarks later of medieval people: 'They find it hard to believe that anything an old *auctour* has said is simply untrue' (cited in Nineham 1976: 45). The traditional Christian attitude to the Bible must be seen in this light, as part of a cultural disposition. That it is broadly cultural rather than narrowly religious is obvious from the fact that the same attitude was shown to classical authors. Indeed the Roman poet Virgil (Publius Vergilius Maro, 70–19 BCE) is an example of someone in the past whose work became almost mystically revered. It was repeated, commented on, embellished, used as an oracle, put into catenae and all sorts of legends grew up around the author. Virgil's writings, or (more correctly) what Virgil is supposed to have written, became part of the mental furniture of the European Middle Ages. Another example of an *auctour* given unquestioned status is Galen (131–201 CE), one of the founders of the Western medical tradition. He had described an organ in the human body called the *rete mirabile*. It is recorded that when medical dissection began, and this organ was not found, it seemed far more probable to those first clinical anatomists that there had occurred an organic change in the human body since his time than that Galen had made a mistake (see Nineham 1976: 268).

In the West, that attitude to the past has now changed radically. We can conveniently date the stirrings of change to about the time of the founding of the Royal Society, which received its charter in 1662 (Newton was to be its president from 1703 to 1727). The Royal Society's motto was: 'Nullius in verba'; in other words, 'We refuse to be bound by the words of any authority, however venerable or sacred' (Nineham 1976: 61). This change in mentality was linked to the rise of science, but came to be accepted far more widely. The newer understanding is succinctly encapsulated in Marx and Engels' reference in the 1848 Communist Manifesto to 'the burden of all the dead generations weighing like a nightmare on the mind of the living', and equally in Thomas Paine's claim that 'the vanity and presumption of governing beyond the grave is the most ridiculous and insolent of all tyrannies' (Paine 1798: 9).

An understanding of this change of mentality is crucial for the modern academic study of religion, and for understanding the role of scripture in particular. The 'clash of science and religion' arose not because Darwin had discovered a truth that 'disproved' some 'biblical' truth. The clash arose because the rise of science depended on a new view of truth; no longer as something revealed *back there* and enshrined in a text to which those coming after must continually refer. Now truth was seen as *out there ahead*, to be discovered by hypothesis, experiment and verification. Another cultural shift was at play here too. One of the reasons for the earlier respect for *auctours* was that most ages have been very aware of their own inferiority in regard to the past. Previous ages almost by definition deferred to their predecessors, sometimes because of the sentiment expressed by Plato: 'The ancients are better than we, for they dwelled nearer to the Gods' (*Philebus* 16c). With this perception, it was well nigh impossible to think of questioning the categories with which those earlier cultures had worked. However, it is much harder for the beneficiaries of the industrial and technological and information revolutions to 'feel' that previous ages were their superiors.

It is worthwhile unpacking some of the consequences of this new attitude to the past. Obviously, it tends to heighten the otherness of the past. Whereas even in relatively recent times people might have seen naturally the connections and similarities with antiquity, historical consciousness tends to flag up the strangeness, the discontinuities, the differences. When the world of a text from the distant past is perceived as so very different from our own, to take such a text as normative becomes much less natural, and the easy submission to a text, no matter how traditionally authoritative, less spontaneous. This is in marked contrast to many epochs that have naturally and spontaneously looked to the past for guidance.

Besides, quite often historical analysis has disclosed that a text was not really saying what it was claimed to say. This is not primarily because modern research shows that a text has been totally misunderstood (although this cannot be ruled out; the Zoroastrian *gathas* are a nightmare to interpret). It is much more likely that historical study shows that the traditionally accepted 'scriptural meaning' is just one among many views extractable from different portions of the scripture. In most cases, this is because although unicity (the presumption of one coherent interlocking whole) is almost invariably attributed to scripture, scripture in the vast majority of cases is in fact a compilation of pieces of quite diverse provenance. A rigorous historical approach often reveals that what has been taken to be *the* meaning has resulted from privileging one segment, and reading the whole through the spectacles provided by this privileged segment. In these cases it is evident that the scripture is far from self-interpreting: it is tradition or the living community that has been influential in ensuring that *this* is the received meaning of scripture. Examples abound, but the point is succinctly captured in this vignette of Africa's response to Christian missions:

> Protestant missionaries introduced the Bible to Africans as the ultimate earthly authority, but were bewildered when their African converts selected their biblical data so differently, highlighting the complex rituals, revelations through dreams and visions, the separation between clean and unclean animals, the practice of polygamy, the descent of God upon prophets, miraculous healings and exorcisms, and so on.
>
> (Hastings 1979: 70)

All these things so peripheral for the missionaries are just as clearly in the Christian Bible as the images, motifs and narratives that the missionaries stressed. It was only when other 'readings' were proffered that it became obvious that the received reading was a highly selective interpretation, even if traditionally authoritative.

Further, historical analysis often reveals that what the text has been traditionally taken to mean is, on closer inspection, found to be a later idea retrojected back into it. Judaism provides a classic example. The Mishnah and Talmud are widely viewed as commentaries on the Tanakh (the Torah, the Prophets, the Writings). They are presented in that way, as comment on or elaboration of the earlier text. On deeper inspection, however, the secondary or derivative appearance is revealed as just that – an appearance arising from the framework imposed on them. In fact both the Mishnah and the Talmud are deeply original works; in some cases their novelty is quite startling. It is the prior assumption that they must be expounding the 'more authoritative' Tanakh that has obscured this. In fact, rather than seeing it as a commentary on a preceding scripture, 'one might suggest rather that (the Mishnah) presents as it were that preceding scripture, if at all, as a commentary on itself' (Smith 1993: 114).

Authorship

The Mishnah and Talmud were the creation of so many (the former collated by Judah haNasi, the latter produced by the Amoraim) that they might be considered genuinely community products. But gifted or charismatic individuals within the community must often be viewed in the same light; the contribution of individual commentators has often been enormous. Their works, too, are often not best understood as commentaries at all, but more adequately as remarkably creative developments which might well have been celebrated as such except for the overriding assumption of the priority of the scripture, an assumption that functioned to disguise any innovation as a deeper elaboration of the text. Consider Augustine of Hippo (354–430 CE). His influence on subsequent Christianity is unparalleled, even though much of his influence is disguised by the fact that he did much of his theological work in terms of commentaries or homilies on scripture. His influence is so great that what subsequent Christian tradition has often understood as Paul, is really Augustine's reading of Paul. When subsequent Christians thought they were harkening to scripture they were in fact harkening to Augustine's understanding of scripture. Augustine's role or influence is underestimated because in the received understanding of scripture the canonical author Paul should be regarded as authoritative.

In Judaism, this phenomenon is perhaps even more salient. Until well into the twentieth century the Tanakh was hardly ever published without a key commentary, normally by Rashi (1040–1105 CE), Radak (1160–1235) or Ramban (1194–1270). It was through the often highly original lenses provided by these great commentators that the Tanakh was read. One observer perceptively catches the dynamics here: 'The bulk of Jewish literature is in the form of commentary on Scripture, whether this form is always justified or not (often the pretense of commentary disguises a full-fledged original personal viewpoint)' (Greenberg, cited in Smith 1993: 117).

Much the same could be said within Islam of jurists up to the Ayatollah Khomeini (1902–89 CE), of countless gurus within the Hindu tradition, and of masters within the Zen tradition. Under the rubric of interpreting their respective scriptures they were providing their community with new resources to meet new situations. In many cases they would have positively repudiated any idea that they exercised an authoritative role within a tradition, seeing themselves as simply servants of the text. But they were obviously far more than that, as historical criticism reveals.

The scripturalising of a text, therefore, has in many cases obscured as much as it has revealed the dynamics operative in the life of the religious community. By dint of scripturalising a text, the community has committed itself to presenting novelty in the form of exposition of or commentary on 'what was there already' in the community's scripture. In many cases this commitment has the effect of reducing the scripture almost to a *tabula rasa* on which the community can read what it wants to or has to. Barton has referred to this quality of 'semantic indeterminacy' of sacred texts. 'Sacred texts … tend to be semantically indeterminate, for they have to be read as supporting the religious system to which they belong, even at the expense of their natural sense' (Barton 1997: 61). The classic instance of this is in the Christian interpretation of the Jewish scripture as Christian. This was the result of a certain combination of presupposition and need: 'They [the Jewish Scriptures] were ostensibly the absolutely authoritative divine revelation; but in reality they functioned as a *tabula rasa* on which Christians wrote what they took (on quite other grounds) to be the meaning of Christ' (ibid.: 19). That this is more than something uniquely Christian is evident from the fact that the sectaries of the Dead Sea saw the Jewish scripture as referring to their Teacher of Righteousness (see especially their Habbakuk Commentary).

Interpretative techniques

This tendency to find in the scripture whatever the community needs for its continuing development is remarkably widespread. This is in effect the purpose of all forms of figurative or non-literal interpretation, namely to enable the community to find there what it must. In many traditions this approach has been taken to considerable lengths, often through elaborate theories of multiple senses of scripture. In Christianity, there were sometimes as many as seven, but most often four: the literal, the allegorical, the moral and the anagogic (or related to the end times). Judaism had its system of *pardes*, from the different forms of exegesis: *peshat* (literal), *remez* (allusive), *derash* (homiletical) and *sodh* (mystical). Islam has its *ta'wil* to explore symbolic and inner meanings (especially prominent in Shi'i and Sufi or mystical contexts). Once again, it is significant that this whole trajectory (through Judaism, Christianity and Islam) actually has its roots outside religion and in the world of classical literature. The techniques of allegory were introduced into the classics to avoid having to find in Homer and Hesiod meanings (the natural or common sense meanings) that were considered unworthy of them by scholars who looked back to them with awe and reverence. These approaches flourished in Alexandria, whence Philo introduced them into Judaism, Christian Fathers (again most notably of the Alexandrian school) adopted them, and later they found their way into Islamic scholarship. These multiple senses of the text, with the 'literal' not necessarily the most important, persisted right through until the rise of modern historical consciousness, when (at least in the West) the literal tended to become all-important, and the others largely fell away.

Layers of scripture

The scripturalising of a text has thus obscured much of the activity of the community in creatively addressing new issues and contexts. The theories constructed to explain the elevated role of scripture have most often reflected what was thought should have been the case, rather than what in fact was the case. Historical research has laid bare what was in fact occurring as the community utilised its scriptures. An additional aspect of this phenomenon is that the books that matter (in our sense, have authority) are in many cases not the theoretically acknowledged scripture at all, but others. In some religions there are evident layers of sacred books. The Avesta, Qur'an and the Tanakh are recognised in their respective religions as scripture par excellence, but these religions have other texts (respectively the Pahlavi texts, Hadith and Mishnah) as a subordinate or supporting layer. Historical criticism may reveal that in some cases it is not the primary but the secondary layer that is more authoritative. Much popular Hinduism is of this kind. In entire swathes of India the Mahabharata (especially the *Bhagavad-Gita*) and the *Ramayana* are far more significant than the Vedas, even though the former are *smrti* ('that which is remembered'), the secondary and derivative scriptural category, and the latter *sruti* ('that which is heard', namely by the seers) or scripture par excellence. Indeed, for Hinduism on Mauritius, the really authoritative works are the theoretically very subsidiary Ramcaritmanas of Tulsi Das and the religious poems of Kabir, as remembered by the indentured labourers taken there.

In all these ways, where on the face of it scripture seemed determinative and frequently enough was claimed to be determinative, it is at least as helpful to see the community determining its own shape in response to new needs, but portraying these responses as derived from the resources of the sacred text. It seems to be an essential element of scripture that it be used in this way.

Necessary reappraisal

This radical reappraisal arising from historical awareness does not mean that scripture is no longer of any significance for those religious communities where historical thinking has taken root. After all, the most fastidious historical scholar may worship in scriptural forms, and meditate on scriptural texts. For his or her personal religious life (indeed for the spiritual life of the community), all sorts of processes may be fruitful. One can do other things with scriptures than situate them in their context, find their 'original' meaning, analyse them historically (although the historical approach has become so dominant in the West that restricting significant enquiry to these issues is a real danger, particularly for academics). Nevertheless, in the West, it is widely agreed that if it is historical questions that are at issue – and the nature and extent of scripture's impact on a religious community over time is such a historical question – they must be answered with the strictest historical warrants. In such cases, even a believer cannot merely repeat the accepted doctrinal position in the face of historical evidence to the contrary.

No one should be in any doubt about the extent of the rethinking required by the rise of historical consciousness. (I repeat that in discussion here is the narrow historical point of the nature and extent of the influence of scripture on the community; broader questions of the impact of scientific or historical thinking on religion itself are beyond our present scope.) Two important Christian theologians, in an article entitled 'Scripture and Tradition', begin:

> Until recently, almost the entire spectrum of theological opinion would have agreed that the scriptures of the Old and New Testaments, together with their doctrinal interpretations, occupy a unique and indispensable place of authority for Christian faith, practice and reflection. But this consensus now seems to be falling apart.
>
> (Farley and Hodgson 1985: 61)

They then rethink the traditional view, in light of such considerations as have been raised above. Their conclusion is that the accepted theory is 'actually inappropriate' to Christianity 'when properly understood' (ibid.: 62).

It is Christianity and Judaism that are most affected by historical criticism because their centre of gravity has long been in the West, and the dominant strands of both are by and large committed to a general cultural relevance (as opposed to cultural isolation). Other religious traditions have been affected differently. Some have rejected the whole historical approach (Muslims tend to see the attempt to submit the Qur'an or Hadith to the same historical criticism as other books as yet another Western attempt to denigrate Islam). Some other traditions, still largely cocooned from the 'corrosion' of historical criticism, have been able to carry on relatively unchanged. Yet even in these latter instances, they have not proved totally impregnable; many have sizeable diasporas in the West, and their young, learning at school to approach texts historically, inevitably begin to address their scriptures in the same way.

This last point highlights a further complication hindering a simple correlation between kinds of authority and particular religions. We mentioned above the different attitudes to scripture within a single religion. Protestants have differed from Catholics (the difference usually expressed in the terms of precisely our problematic – 'Scripture versus Tradition'); Mahayana Buddhists differ from Theravada Buddhists; Shi'ites from Sunni Muslims. But the twentieth century saw a new phenomenon. Now Judaism and Christianity have a totally new division, between those who accept the legitimacy of historical criticism, and those who do not. In the West, most mainstream Christians, whether Catholic or Protestant, have come to accept it (officially as late as 1964 for Catholics). However, most Christians are now found in the Third World, where most are pre-critical and can maintain an unselfconscious attitude to scripture virtually impossible now for their Western co-religionists. In a further complication, some in the West positively deny the legitimacy of applying the historical approach to scripture, seeing this as destructive of Christianity itself. This is indeed a third and different stance, for such fundamentalists are not so much either critical or pre-critical as anti-critical. Despite the frequent claim of these fundamentalists to preserve the traditional attitude to scripture, their stance is every bit as modern as the critical approach to which they are reacting. Here then we have a profound three-way split within the one religion in attitudes to scriptural authority (and indirectly tradition).

Tradition

We should be clear what is being claimed here. We are not arguing that academic historical study of religion has 'destroyed' the authority of scripture in the sense of rendering scripture superfluous. The scriptures remain important, even where they are now understood to exert their influence as an originating repository of the images, myths, symbols, metaphors, narratives, laws, persons and paradigms that have given the community its identity, recalled it to its roots, anchored its legal structures, linked it with its founder, provided its classic access to the divine, created its general cultural ambiance, suggestively guided it through history, and exercised a crucial role in facing new challenges. These are, of course, the functions that scripture always played, although so often something rather more was claimed. So, in one sense, historical consciousness has merely brought theory into line with practice. Scripture has always functioned in a way that involved the living community. It never functioned in some absolute, unqualified, mechanical way, even though this was often presumed in theories about scripture (understood as blueprint, charter, constitution, inspired revelation, timeless word of God). You cannot talk of the authority of scripture apart from the religious community on its ongoing historical journey (that is, apart from its tradition). You cannot talk of authority, scripture or tradition in isolation. Graham has well expressed it: 'A text becomes scripture in living, subjective relationship to persons and to historical tradition. No text ... is sacred or authoritative in isolation from a community' (Graham 1987: 134).

It should be obvious that this historical consciousness has affected the understanding of tradition as much as of scripture. The awareness of inevitable change that constitutes this historical consciousness reveals that tradition persists only as a continual process of reinterpretation. The role of tradition, too, has been discovered to be anything but simple. In 1983 Hobsbawm and Ranger edited a remarkable book showing that so many 'time-honoured' and 'immemorial' traditions have been rather recently invented. They describe the overmastering impulse, beginning about 1870 and peaking around 1900 and spreading right across the world, to invent traditions in every aspect of national life – in politics, education, recreation as well as religion (again we meet a phenomenon broadly cultural rather than narrowly religious). National festivals, stamps and statues, anthems and flags, uniforms, military parades, monuments and jubilees are all quite modern. The creation of national symbolism where none before existed was not unconnected with the changing context. In the West there arose an urgent need to popularise traditional institutions as politics became mass politics. (The ritualism of the British monarchy increased in inverse proportion to the political power of the sovereign.) 'Traditions' were taking hold quite widely; around that time the British began to invent native 'African traditions' such as tribal divisions and customary law. Hobsbawm and Ranger's book focused on a particular period and Britain primarily, but it made a serious point of wide application; so often, in claims about the past, far more is going on than meets the eye. Very often the claim 'this is our tradition' is not a statement about the past at all (just as the claim 'our scripture says' is not necessarily a statement in any strict sense about the meaning of a document); it is a statement about the present – most often a statement of what the present might, or even should, be.

Charisma

I have spoken above of the living community, without specifying how a community operates. Here, obviously, due allowance must be made for the influence of the gifted individuals within a community, and we naturally move to our third focus of religious authority, charisma (from the Greek *charis*, 'grace' or 'favour', although the word is not widely found in profane Greek, the roots of our concept being in St Paul). The currency of the concept in contemporary study of religion comes from Weber, who treated the phenomenon at length (Weber 1978). Weber's concern was to distinguish types of leader: traditional, rational-legal and charismatic. The third type is based upon the perception of followers that an individual is endowed with exceptional (even divine) qualities. (Thus the concept of 'charisma' is just as much a relational term as 'scripture'.) Weber's ideal-type charismatic leader possesses authority based on his own qualities rather than on tradition or rational considerations. He offers a new revelation and way of life, demands obedience to his mission, and imposes new obligations. Charismatic leadership is unpredictable, personal and unstable, and hence normally must become 'routinised' if the mission of the originator is to persist.

This kind of authority is found most purely in shamanism or primal religions generally. In many religions of Africa, the most obvious religious figures are the healer-diviner, the witch and the medium. Some healer-diviners may be considered to have come by their skills through learning from their predecessors, but usually all three are considered to derive their exceptional gifts from the spirits. Some, particularly the spirit mediums, can even be taken over by their indwelling spirits in ecstatic trances. It is this possession that gives the charismatic religious figure his or her authority. Although charismatic authority is regarded with some suspicion in the increasingly bureaucratised West, it should not be thought that charisma is restricted to 'primal' religions. For one thing, for many scholars of religion it is the founders of the world religions that are the classic examples of this phenomenon. In Jewish tradition, Moses has been considered to have been endowed with the prophetic gifts to such a degree that he was 'the greatest of the prophets'. Jesus taught 'as one having authority, and not as the scribes' (Mk 1,22). Muhammad is understood to have possessed more *barakah* (blessing) than any other man. ('*Barakah*' is an important Islamic concept generally.) The Buddha was said to have had an aura surrounding his body, bringing all he met into submission. For another thing, it is the charismatic leaders of New Religious Movements (NRMs) who constitute a key focus of contemporary religious research.

Frequently charisma links with the other sources of authority considered above. As noted earlier, charisma must become routinised into standardised procedures and structures if the group is to persist beyond the life of the figure who triggered it, but in themselves charisma and tradition tend to tug in different directions. So charisma and tradition inevitably enjoy a somewhat conflictual relationship. With scripture, however, charisma often has an almost symbiotic relationship. Many charismatic leaders of NRMs ground their authority in texts. Someone like David Koresh of the 1993 Waco tragedy, in which 86 people died in a stand-off with US law enforcement agencies, possessed authority not just because of personal qualities, but because he was able to convince others that he was part of the end-time events supposedly predicted in scriptures. (His Branch Davidians were an offshoot of the millenarian Seventh Day Adventists.) American televangelists, the focus of so many studies of charisma, depend upon their own gifts but at the same time take care to anchor their authority in scripture. Scripture actually functions to reinforce their personal charismatic authority. Gurus of many religions win and hold their following to the extent that they are seen to reveal the 'real' meaning of scripture.

An example

As a concluding illustration of several of the foregoing points, consider Sikhism. The founder of Sikhism was Guru Nanak (1469–1539 CE), who was succeeded by nine other Gurus. The tenth Guru, Gobind Singh (1675–1708 CE) decreed that the line of Gurus would stop with him, ultimate authority being shared thereafter by both the Panth (community) and the Adi Granth (also known as the Guru Granth Sahib, the collection of writings of the Gurus – and some precursors – assembled essentially by the fifth Guru but given final form by the tenth).

Historical criticism shows that Guru Nanak, the undisputed founder of the religion, discounted outward observance, teaching that true religion is interior, and liberation is achieved through inward meditation directed to Akal Purakh (the 'Timeless Being') who reveals himself in the *nam* or divine name, and brings liberating karma, when transmigration comes to an end. This is achieved through *nam simaran*, a regular discipline of inner meditation that focuses on the omnipresence of the divine name. Such teaching was current among the Sants of North India at the time, thus 'effectively destroying any claims to significant originality' (McLeod 1989: 23). However, over time circumstances transformed Sikhism. The tenth Guru, Gobind Singh, institutionalised the community in the *Khalsa* in 1699, and began the formation of its special code of conduct (*Rahit*), which evolved throughout the eighteenth century. Over this time what had been a religion of interiority assumed an ever more exterior identity, marked particularly by uncut hair and the bearing of arms (militancy had first developed under the fifth, ninth and tenth Gurus especially). Under British occupation, a reform movement begun in the late nineteenth century attempted for the first time to distinguish Sikhs from Hindus. The self-understanding and marks of identity established over the late nineteenth and early twentieth centuries are still determinative today.

The Sikh scripture, the Adi Granth, is given enormous respect. Its mere presence constitutes any room or building a *gurdwara* (temple). No one may sit on a level higher than the lectern on which it is placed. Sikhs marry by circling it four times. Daily prayers are derived from it. Yet paradoxically, 'Within the Panth itself knowledge of the actual contents of the Adi Granth is very limited' (ibid.: 88). A second work, the Dasam Granth, had in the eighteenth century almost the same respect as the Adi Granth; now 'the Dasam Granth as a whole is seldom invoked and little understood' – probably because 'the material which dominates the narrative and anecdotal portion … is scarcely consonant with the preferred interpretation of the Sikh tradition' (ibid.: 90–1). On yet a third level of scripture are works by two distinguished Sikhs of the Guru period, Bhai Gurdas and Bhai Nand Lal. Both 'are explicitly approved for recitation in gurdwaras and as such they constitute a part of what we may regard as an authorized Sikh canon' (ibid.: 92). In practice, however, both are 'seldom read or heard' (ibid.: 94), probably because their spirit and content are so different from what the Khalsa came to be. A further class of scripture comprises the *Janam-sakhis*, cycles of narratives of the first Guru, very hagiographical, often miraculous. 'Although they have never been accepted as sacred scripture, their immense popularity has conferred on them a major role in the sustaining and transmission' of the Nanak tradition (ibid.: 97–8) – in our sense, made them enormously authoritative. Still another set of works, known as the Gurbalas, concentrates on tales of the two warrior Gurus, the sixth, Hargobind, and particularly the tenth, Gobind Singh, whose ideals inspired the eighteenth-century Khalsa. There is yet other literature, notably of the Singh Sabha or nineteenth-century reform movement, that offer the traditions reinterpreted in the light of Western ideals, but there is no space to elaborate on them here. I have merely outlined this history and this range of texts to illustrate the complex ways in which the community has regulated itself and (something slightly different) claimed it was regulating itself. The community has transformed itself over time. The 'traditional' practices and self-understanding have evolved in accordance with changing conditions. Revered and theoretically decisive scriptures are unstudied and neglected, because of their lack of harmony with later tradition; other books, not part of any canon, are far more influential or authoritative in determining the life of the community, because so compatible with later tradition.

Sikhism is a religion that is quite specific where authority lies: it is virtually undisputed that the mystically present Guru persists equally in the Panth and the Adi Granth. This theoretically precise doctrine, however, leaves much unresolved. Radical ambiguity persists in the translating of mystical authority into actual decisions. The Adi Granth provides 'little specific guidance on issues relating to the Rahit, and differences of opinion quickly emerge whenever the attempt is made to apply its general principles to particular cases' (ibid.: 75). However, in practice, the Panth has learnt to live with 'a radically uncertain theory of ultimate authority' (ibid.: 77). Undoubtedly there are stresses and strains, and certain issues continue to trouble the Panth, but the evolving tradition in most cases offers sufficient guidance to preserve an ongoing identity. We might complete our illustration by noting that it is the historical approach that enables scholars to establish the community's development (we have here followed McLeod, but our point about authority within a community is not narrowly dependent on his reconstruction), and to understand individual books in the light of particular contexts; yet Sikhism itself tends to reject this approach. However, the young Sikhs of the Western diaspora increasingly find such a historical approach unavoidable.

Conclusion

Religious authority, in practice, is thus a very complex reality. Understanding its various forms is rendered more difficult because so often the accepted theory does not so much reveal as obscure what is going on. We have drawn attention to three aspects or elements: scripture, or sacred books; tradition, or the living community itself as it survives through time; charisma, or exceptionally gifted individuals. Although it is legitimate to consider these separately, we have discovered so often an extremely complex interplay, not made less complex because so often the religion itself claims that there is in question a simple and transparent process. Here, as frequently elsewhere, theory can be one thing, practice another.

Summary

All human groups need some generally accepted means of resolving major questions, and for religious groups scriptures or authoritative texts, tradition or accepted precedents, and charismatic or gifted individuals have generally performed precisely these functions. These elements operate in very complex ways, often working together. They often function at considerable variance from the ways in which a religion claims they operate. The rise of historical consciousness over the last few centuries has revealed both the complexity and the variance. This chapter outlines the complicated and interrelated workings of scripture, tradition, charisma, with some examples from major religious traditions.

Bibliography

Barton, John, 1997, *People of the Book*, London: SPCK.

Farley, Edward and Hodgson, Peter C., 1985, 'Scripture and Tradition', in Peter C. Hodgson and Robert King (eds), *Christian Theology: an Introduction to its Tradition and Tasks*, Philadelphia PA: Fortress Press.

Graham, W.A., 1987, 'Scripture', in M. Eliade (ed.), *Encyclopedia of Religion*, New York: Macmillan; and London: Collier Macmillan.

Hastings, A., 1979, *A History of African Christianity, 1950–75*, Cambridge: Cambridge University Press.

Hobsbawm, Eric and Ranger, Terence (eds), 1983, *The Invention of Tradition*, Cambridge: Cambridge University Press.

McLeod, W.H., 1989, *The Sikhs: History, Religion and Society*, New York and Guildford: Columbia University Press.

Mayr-Harting, Henry, 1990, 'The West: The Age of Coversion (700–1050)', in John McManners (ed.), *The Oxford History of Christianity*, Oxford: Oxford University Press.

Müller, Max, 1879–94, *The Sacred Books of the East*, 50 vols, New Delhi: Motilal Banarsidass.

Nineham, Dennis, 1976, *The Use and Abuse of the Bible: A Study of the Bible in an Age of Rapid Cultural Change*, London: Macmillan.

Paine, Thomas, 1798, *Rights of Man*, London: Wordsworth Classics.

Plato, 360 BCE, *Philebus*. Trans. Robin Waterfield, 1982, London: Penguin Books.

Smith, Wilfred Cantwell, 1993, *What is Scripture?* Minneapolis, MN: Fortress Press.

Weber, Max, 1978, *Economy and Society*, Berkeley: University of California Press, especially I, 241–5; II, 1111–56.

Suggested reading

Barton, John, 1997, *People of the Book*, London: SPCK.
  A brief treatment of many of the issues, focusing on the Christian tradition.

Graham, W.A., 1987, 'Scripture', in M. Eliade (ed.), *Encyclopedia of Religion*, New York: Macmillan; and London: Collier Macmillan.
  Succinct summary of the issues.

Hobsbawm, Eric and Ranger, Terence (eds), 1983, *The Invention of Tradition*, Cambridge: Cambridge University Press.
  Shows the problematic nature of 'tradition'.

Smith, Wilfred Cantwell, 1993, *What is Scripture?* Minneapolis MN: Fortress Press.
  A magisterial treatment of all the issues involved, covering all traditions.

Weber, Max, 1978, *Economy and Society*, Berkeley: University of California Press, especially I, 241–5; II, 1111–56.
  The classic treatment of charismatic leadership.

Chapter 24

Hermeneutics

Garrett Green

For provisional purposes, one can define hermeneutics quite simply as the *theory of interpretation*. Although this straightforward definition may do as a point of entry into a subject notable for its complexity, controversy, and jargon-ridden discourse, it will need to be qualified in a number of ways before it can do justice to the field of hermeneutics as it impinges on the scholarly study of religion today.

Our provisional definition can be expanded, first of all, by identifying hermeneutics as theoretical reflection on the principles and rules of interpretation and understanding. Implicit in this still basic definition is a duality that reflects the disparate origins of modern hermeneutics and helps to account for its complexity. On the one hand are those who would think of hermeneutics primarily in terms of method and practice. Here the emphasis lies on the actual interpretation of texts by scholars, exegetes, or religious teachers. Hermeneutics in this sense articulates and codifies the principles and rules of textual interpretation – an activity that has enjoyed a long history under a variety of names and plays an important role in virtually all of the world's religions. On the other hand are those for whom the object of hermeneutics is not in the first instance the texts being interpreted so much as the human act of understanding that every interpretation presupposes and instantiates. Hermeneutics in this sense is more like a philosophy than a methodology. Indeed, in the influential modern tradition of hermeneutical speculation reaching from Schleiermacher to Gadamer, hermeneutics becomes the name for a comprehensive philosophy of understanding. When one thinks of hermeneutics as something to be 'applied,' one is using the term in the former (methodological) sense; when one uses it to describe a mode of reflection on the nature of human understanding, one is employing it in the latter (philosophical) sense. To make matters more complex, thinkers rarely adopt one or the other of these two types in its 'pure' form, so that the polarity represents not two kinds of hermeneutics but rather two tendencies or emphases within the modern hermeneutical discussion – tendencies that can take on endless variations and can be combined in myriads of ways.

Further clarification of hermeneutics requires that we look at the actual historical traditions that have led to our contemporary situation. The reason for this procedure should be plain from what has already been said: we cannot first establish the meaning of the term and then go on to describe the various ways of doing it, because every attempt at a formal definition already involves us in the controversial issues of the content of hermeneutical theory. The shape of the field today results not from the systematic unfolding of its conceptual meaning but rather from the interplay of concrete human personalities, cultures, and religious and philosophical traditions.

Origins and etymology

No one knows for certain the origins of the Greek verb *hermēneuein* ('to interpret'), from which our modern word derives, but most of the tendencies and controversies of later hermeneutical theory are foreshadowed in the ancient conversation about this term and its cognate noun *hermēneia*, which became a technical term and often appeared in titles – preeminently in Aristotle's treatise *On Interpretation* (*Peri Hermēneias*). Though the etymological connection is obscure, the most illuminating feature of ancient hermeneutics is its association with Hermes, the messenger of the gods. This connection underscores the fact that hermeneutics, while not a religious term per se, has always had an intrinsic relationship to religion. The archetypal problem of interpretation, one could say, is embodied in the mystery of the divine word that must first be translated (one of the root meanings of *hermēneuein*) into understandable human terms before it can be heard, obeyed, and appropriated. The most important texts calling forth the art of interpretation have long been religious texts, so that scriptural interpretation is not simply one category in a series of hermeneutical tasks but rather the source or model for all the others. Even in the highly secularized world of the modern academy one can find traces of this heritage in the continuing fascination and controversy aroused by issues of canon: how authoritative texts – pre-eminently the Bible in Western civilization – are to be interpreted.

The link between ancient Greek *hermēneia* and modern hermeneutical theory is found in the history of interpretation in the Jewish and Christian communities that were the successors to classical Greek and Roman culture and the forerunners of modern European and global culture. The shape of that history is largely determined by the texts whose interpretation was crucial for those communities. In classical culture the need to interpret Homer was the driving force behind hermeneutical thought, since the Iliad and the Odyssey functioned as foundational texts in those societies. The two main alternatives that developed were grammatical interpretation, which sought meaning in the structure and shape of the language in which the stories were told, and allegorical interpretation, in which the meaning of the text was sought in an external symbolic key. The grammatical interpreter looked at the way the text itself is put together, believing that the key to its meaning will be found within the structure of the text itself. Allegorical interpreters, on the other hand, believed that the meaning hidden in the text could only be deciphered with the help of an external key that would unlock its symbolism. First Jewish and then early Christian interpreters adapted and extended these methods for their own use in interpreting the Bible. The most important bridge figure is Philo of Alexandria (roughly a contemporary of Jesus, though the two were surely unaware of one another's existence), a Hellenistic Jewish philosopher who applied allegorical interpretation to the anthropomorphic narratives of the Torah, and whose ideas influenced the Christian thinkers who subsequently flourished in Alexandria. Rabbinic Judaism generally followed a different direction, which included several approaches to scripture, including literalist interpretations, midrashic exegesis, which tried to find meaning beyond the literal sense of the text, and others. Their overarching concern was to fit scripture into a theologically meaningful framework without succumbing to a dead literalism on the one hand or opening the floodgates to spiritualizing excesses on the other – interpretations which, by encouraging subjective or mystical readings, might endanger the identity and integrity of the community.

The Christian church fathers faced similar issues, compounded by the need to integrate the proclamation of Jesus with the Jewish scriptures. In addition to the kinds of interpretation already mentioned, the Christian fathers advocated the use of typological or figural interpretation, an approach often confused with allegory but in fact quite distinct from it. In this kind of interpretation, an earlier event (typically from the Old Testament) is taken as a figure or type for a later (New Testament) event. Unlike allegory, both figures, type and antitype, are real historical persons and events (e.g. Moses as figura of Jesus), whose meaning is found in the transcendent link between them. Figural interpretation has recently become the subject of renewed hermeneutical interest through the work of Erich Auerbach, whose book *Mimesis* (1953) describes the ancient practice, and through Hans W. Frei's book *The Eclipse of Biblical Narrative* (1974), which applies it to the modern history of theological hermeneutics.

The most important link between the hermeneutics of the early Christian church and the medieval period in Europe is the thought of Augustine of Hippo (354–430), whose importance for virtually every aspect of later Western thought can scarcely be exaggerated. Inheriting from the earlier church fathers the polarity between 'literal' and 'spiritual' senses of the scriptural text, he attempts to synthesize the legitimate concerns of both methods by investigating the role of signs (thereby becoming the precursor of the modern theory of signs, or semiotics). He sees the scriptures not as identical with the things to which they refer but rather as signifiers pointing to God. The upshot of this approach is a new stress on praxis – the living faith that is the goal of Christian teaching – as the proper context for interpretation of scripture. No mere theory can provide the conditions for right interpretation but only the faithful practice of reading the Bible in the context of the ongoing Christian community. In this way, scripture and tradition are linked in a dialectical relationship.

Of the many thinkers and schools of interpretation that might be mentioned in the long history of medieval interpretation of scripture, perhaps the most important for the later development of hermeneutics is the doctrine of the fourfold meaning of scripture. Earlier thinkers – following St Paul's admonition that 'the letter kills but the spirit gives life' (2 Cor. 3: 6) – had distinguished between two senses of the text, the literal and the spiritual. In medieval hermeneutics the spiritual came to be distinguished into three distinct senses: the allegorical, seen as the key to the content of faith; the tropological, which concerned the moral significance of the text; and the anagogical, which dealt with the relation between the text and the future hope of believers. The effect of this doctrine of the fourfold meaning of scripture was increasingly to separate the various theological disciplines – biblical studies, moral theology, eschatology, etc. – both from one another and from the practical life of faith. A shift in hermeneutical emphasis occurred after the rediscovery of Aristotle in the twelfth century and the founding of the first universities. In the Scholasticism that followed, theology became an academic discipline, and theologians took pains to give their speculations a scientific basis. The greatest of the medieval thinkers, Thomas Aquinas, formally retained the theory of the fourfold meaning of scripture while in fact de-emphasizing allegorical interpretation in favor of increased attention to the literal meaning of the text. The upshot of these developments was that theology (what Thomas called sacred doctrine) became an academic enterprise that concentrated on the literal text, while the spiritual meaning of the text became by default largely the concern of popular piety and spirituality.

Questions about the single or multiple meanings of texts, and about the relationships among the different senses, came to a head in the Protestant Reformation, with its insistence on the sole authority of scripture. It is no accident that the one who first galvanized the discontent of sixteenth-century Christians into the movement we know as the Protestant Reformation – Martin Luther (1483–1546) – was a professor of Bible, whose new theological direction was the direct result of a new interpretation of scripture. Hermeneutical issues thus stand at the heart of the Reformation and have continued to play a major role in Western Christianity ever since. Luther, together with the other leading Reformers – such as Ulrich Zwingli (1484–1531), the early leader of the Swiss Reformation, and John Calvin (1509–1564), who became the defining figure of the Reformed branch of the Protestant movement – all agreed that the church should be reformed in accordance with scripture, understood as the sole authority for faith and practice. Rejecting the claims of the Roman Catholic Church to be the final authority for the interpretation of the Bible, the Protestants insisted that 'scripture interprets itself.' This hermeneutical principle meant that the literal meaning of the words is primary and that obscure passages are to be understood in the light of those that are plain. Both Luther and Calvin rejected allegorical interpretation but supplemented a literal reading with figural interpretation, allowing them to read all of the scripture, Old and New Testaments, as one great text communicating the one Word of God. This hermeneutical approach should not be confused with the doctrine of direct verbal inspiration that has become so important and divisive in more recent Protestant debate. For the Reformers the Bible itself is not the final authority but rather communicates to us the Word of God, Christ himself, and its right interpretation thus requires not only the inspired text but also the internal inspiration of the Christian reader by the Holy Spirit. The issues of interpretation that first came to a head in sixteenth-century Europe have continued to arouse vigorous debate among Christians and Jews – and increasingly among other religious traditions as well – right up to the present day.

Beginning in the latter part of the seventeenth century in Europe, another cultural shift with hermeneutical implications began to take place. The movement that some of its proponents called Enlightenment was both a development with profound religious repercussions and also the beginning of the modern secular movement to shake off the restraints of theology and church. Wearied by a century of strife over religious issues unleashed by the Reformation, some European thinkers began searching for a new common basis, an authority that could unite, rather than divide people as religion seemed to have done. What they discovered was natural reason, understood to be the universal foundation of all truth, to which all human beings have access, and which could therefore adjudicate the many conflicting claims to truth and authority. In particular, Enlightenment thinkers developed the notion of a natural religion, based on the principles of universal reason and thus shared by human beings of all cultures and times. This natural religion was both the foundation and criterion for what they called the 'positive' religions, the existing historical traditions with their particular and arbitrary claims to authority. Immanuel Kant (1724–1804), whose monumental philosophical work represents the culmination of the Enlightenment, drew the hermeneutical implications of the commitment to natural reason in his proposal for a 'religion within the limits of reason alone' (the title of his book of 1794), whose principles and practices could be deduced by philosophical analysis and used to judge the truth of the positive religions. He interprets the narratives and commandments of scripture as mere pictorial representations of universal and rational religious truths.

The rise of modern hermeneutics

As we have seen, the issues that today we call hermeneutical have a long history. The ideas and activities comprising that history, however, only began to be called by the name hermeneutics with the rise of modernity in the West. Theoretical hermeneutics, in other words, is a product of modern culture, and its most distinctive and influential line of development has taken place in the context of Continental European philosophy over the past two centuries.

The thinker generally credited with being the founder of modern hermeneutical theory – Dilthey dubbed him the 'Kant of hermeneutics' – was the German theologian and Plato scholar F. D. E. Schleiermacher (1768–1834). As a major figure in the early Romantic movement, he articulated a hermeneutics in accordance with the notion of creativity, in which the work is understood as an expression of the creative genius of the author. Rejecting the traditional distinction between sacred and profane interpretation, he insisted that scripture can be understood in the same way as other texts. He argued that what is needed in both cases is a hermeneutics defined as the 'art of understanding' (*Kunstlehre des Verstehens*), thereby shifting attention away from the nature of the text itself to the nature of the understanding by which the text is read and interpreted. By focusing on the concept of understanding, Schleiermacher effectively re-conceives hermeneutics as an independent philosophical enterprise (though he insists upon calling it an 'art') rather than the handmaid of theology or literature studies. Though a theologian himself, he sought to minimize the distinction between general rules of textual interpretation and those rules appropriate to scriptural exegesis, insisting that the latter must remain subject to the former. Even the claim that the Bible is divinely inspired, therefore, cannot be invoked on behalf of a special theological hermeneutics. The theologian interprets texts according to the same general principles that apply in all situations of understanding. This move not only has significant consequences for the task of theology but also represents a major step in the direction of a disciplined study of religion distinct from the theology of Christianity or any other of the 'positive' religions. This contribution to the emerging field of religious studies is important in the light of another significant step taken by Schleiermacher: he, a Protestant clergyman and professor, was the first thinker in the European tradition to write a book on religion, understood as a phenomenon distinct from Christianity – his 1799 book *On Religion: Speeches to Its Cultured Despisers*.

Schleiermacher's hermeneutical 'art of understanding' has a bipolar structure, in which he distinguishes a grammatical (objective) dimension from a psychological or technical (subjective) aspect in the act of understanding. The former task requires that the interpreter be grounded in the linguistic and cultural modes of expression in which the author lived, while the technical-psychological aspect requires the interpreter to grasp the unique subjectivity of the author as expressed through the unified whole of the work. This latter task involves what Schleiermacher calls divination, a term that has provoked considerable controversy and misunderstanding. His intent is not to make understanding into a mysterious means of entry into the mind of the author, but he does believe that interpretation – though it entails an intuitive risk – can lead to understanding the mind of the author better than the author knows himself. The goal, like that of his fellow Romantics, is to grasp the universal in the individual, to do justice both to the uniqueness of particular expressions and to the general spirit of which they are incarnations. Schleiermacher's influence on his contemporaries was modest, especially in view of the immense influence his ideas eventually came to have on the development of hermeneutical theory. What made the difference was the subsequent discovery of Schleiermacher's hermeneutics by a man born the year before Schleiermacher's death.

Wilhelm Dilthey (1833–1911) became the main link between the Romantic hermeneutics of Schleiermacher in the early nineteenth century and the leading figures in the remarkable explosion of philosophical hermeneutics in the twentieth. Unlike Schleiermacher, Dilthey was not a theologian but a philosopher, and he had no hesitation about developing Schleiermacher's insights into a full-fledged philosophical hermeneutics. His most important accomplishment was to make hermeneutics into the foundational and definitive method of the human or cultural disciplines (*Geisteswissenschaften*) as distinguished from the natural sciences (*Naturwissenschaften*). Whether one believes this distinction to be a great achievement or a confusion with disastrous consequences, one can hardly deny the importance of Dilthey's conceptual innovations at this point. He argued that the human sciences differ from the natural sciences on the basis of their qualitatively different objects of inquiry. Natural scientists are able to observe their objects from an external perspective, so that the act of observation remains separate from the phenomena observed. The object of the human and cultural sciences, on the other hand, is not the outside world but what Dilthey calls *Erlebnis*, or lived experience, in which knower and known are related internally. Such an object one must understand, as it were, from the inside out, on the basis of one's own lived experience. Dilthey refers to the more objective task of the natural scientist as explanation (*Erklären*), which he contrasts with the hermeneutical task of understanding (*Verstehen*). In the study of religion today, as in other humanistic disciplines, scholars often divide sharply just at this point. Those who follow Dilthey in emphasizing the difference between natural scientific explanation and hermeneutical understanding are typically critical of scholars who seek the objectivity of scientific explanation in religious studies. The latter, on the other hand, often suspect the former of using questionable hermeneutical theories to legitimate apologetic or uncritical accounts of religion 'from the inside.' Most theorists today would acknowledge that in some way both explanation and understanding are required in any adequate approach to the study of religion, though they often disagree fundamentally about the methodological consequences of this hermeneutical situation.

Dilthey's ideas have been most influential in the continuing tradition of European hermeneutical speculation in the twentieth century, whose most important figures are Martin Heidegger, Hans-Georg Gadamer, and Paul Ricoeur. The entire philosophical program of Heidegger (1889–1976) can be characterized as hermeneutical (indeed, he originally did so himself), and his philosophy also lies behind the more specifically hermeneutical theories of Gadamer and Ricoeur. Despite his considerable debt to Dilthey, Heidegger believed that he, along with most of the other modern philosophers since Descartes, had failed to escape from psychologism and subjectivity. Heidegger's alternative is to propose a hermeneutical ontology, a philosophical analysis of Being, starting not from the subjectivity but rather from the existential situation of the interpreter. We humans find ourselves in a unique situation, because unlike other things in the world, which simply 'are,' we understand that we are. We exist, says Heidegger, 'stand out'; he especially likes the implications of the German word for existence, *Dasein*, since it literally means 'being there.' In other words, only humans can raise the question of Being Itself. In the resulting philosophy, interpretation does not appear merely as one among various human activities but rather takes on a foundational role in which existence itself is characterized as interpretation. In so doing, Heidegger revolutionized the meaning of philosophy, as has long been recognized. For our purposes, however, it is more important to note that he also changed the meaning of hermeneutics. By rejecting the Cartesian concept of the ego as thinking subject, he turns away from the Romantic focus on the creative individuality of the author expressed in the text. Since for Heidegger hermeneutics has become the cornerstone of philosophy, its focus shifts away from texts and their interpreters to ontology. Far from being an isolated methodological inquiry, hermeneutics on this account gives us access to the most universal and fundamental truths about human life in the world. Heidegger's approach has some particular implications that have profoundly influenced subsequent reflection on hermeneutics, even by thinkers who do not follow his philosophy in all its ramifications. Because of the existential situation of the human thinker, Heidegger emphasizes that understanding and interpretation never begin 'in neutral' without presuppositions but are always undertaken by people who are already involved, and who therefore have interests, presuppositions, and pre-understanding of the subject they are interpreting. But this situation implies that understanding is always circular in form; it can never begin in a hermeneutical vacuum. It is especially important to understand that for Heidegger and his successors this hermeneutical circle is not something negative; its circularity is not 'vicious.' Rather, it is a warning against any hermeneutical theory that tries to deny or ignore that necessary circularity of interpretation.

Heidegger's hermeneutical legacy

Relatively few students of religion are likely to master the difficult philosophy of Heidegger, but his ideas are nevertheless of major importance in religious studies, largely through the mediation of two thinkers who have appropriated significant aspects of his thought and presented them in works that are widely read, not only in philosophy and theology but also in religious studies.

A single book – *Truth and Method*, by Hans-Georg Gadamer (1900–2002), which first appeared in German in 1960 – catapulted hermeneutics into the center of discussion in theology and religious studies in the second half of the twentieth century and has made Gadamer's name synonymous with hermeneutical theory. While hardly an easy book to read, *Truth and Method* nevertheless makes accessible to non-philosophers an approach to hermeneutics that owes much to Heidegger. But Gadamer also returns hermeneutics to the traditional concerns of Schleiermacher and Dilthey: human understanding as it functions in the interpretation of authoritative texts. From Heidegger he takes his starting point within the hermeneutical circle; that is, he recognizes that understanding always and only takes place in the context of prior understandings – which is to say within a specific historic tradition of reading and interpreting texts. Gadamer's controversial way of making this basically Heideggerian point is by attempting to rehabilitate the term 'prejudice,' which the Enlightenment had seen as an entirely negative encumbrance to objective knowledge. Gadamer insists that every act of understanding begins in prejudice, in the original sense of pre-judgment: one is not simply neutral or detached from the object of understanding but rather already stands in some relationship to it. Far from constituting a barrier to be removed, such pre-judgments play an essential role in all acts of understanding. Unlike Schleiermacher, Gadamer does not see hermeneutics as a way of overcoming the historical distance between interpreter and text but rather insists on the historical nature of understanding itself, since interpretation always occurs within a concrete historical tradition and makes no sense when removed from this context. It is this common link with the overarching tradition that allows the modern interpreter to understand an ancient text, for the two are in fact already related to one another through a process that Gadamer calls *Wirkungsgeschichte*, 'effective history' – a history of the effects by which everything later in a tradition has been influenced by all that has gone before. The continuum constituted by this history of effective relationships allows Gadamer to conceive the goal of interpretation as a 'fusion of horizons' (*Horizontverschmelzung*), in which the horizon of the interpreter merges into that of the text. Gadamer believes that this phenomenological account of how understanding takes place is superior to every 'method' by which other theorists seek to arrive at the truth – a conviction alluded to in the title *Truth and Method*.

In an ongoing debate that has attracted widespread attention, Jürgen Habermas has accused Gadamer of failing to do justice to the limits of understanding. On Gadamer's account it would appear that understanding can always take place successfully as long as the interpreter acknowledges the context of tradition in which the text is embedded and is willing to enter into it. Habermas maintains that communication is often distorted in ways that the participants in a conversation do not and cannot recognize without the intervention of someone from the outside. An adequate hermeneutics must therefore be able to take into account the possibility and actuality of distorted communication. Otherwise the interpreter will be vulnerable to ideological bias, especially when he or she shares the bias of the text. The question raised by Habermas is whether or not Gadamer's traditionalist hermeneutics amounts in effect to a conservatism without critical resources for recognizing and combating ideology.

The other important theorist with roots in Heidegger's philosophy, Paul Ricoeur (1913–2005), is much more attuned to hermeneutical distortion and conflict than is Gadamer. Indeed, one of his major writings is titled *Conflict of Interpretations*. As the first major hermeneutical theorist since Schleiermacher to take a particular interest in religion, his work has been especially influential in theology and religious studies. Ricoeur is a philosopher, not a theologian, but he writes out of an explicit commitment to Reformed Christianity and divided his academic career between Paris and the Divinity School of the University of Chicago. His thought thus represents a bridge both between philosophical and religious hermeneutics and also between the Continental and Anglo-American academic worlds. His early work was devoted to an attempt to mediate the traditions of phenomenology and existentialism, which led him to develop a philosophical account of the symbol as the starting point for his hermeneutical theory. A symbol is any sign that contains, in addition to its direct or primary meaning, a secondary or hidden meaning that requires intellectual effort to uncover. In other words, symbol and interpretation become correlative terms. His hermeneutical point of departure is captured in the aphorism that he uses as a title for the conclusion to his 1967 book *The Symbolism of Evil*: 'The Symbol Gives Rise to Thought.' The problematic relationship between symbol and critical thought is epitomized in the hermeneutical circle, which Ricoeur puts this way: 'We must understand in order to believe, but we must believe in order to understand.' The way beyond circularity lies in taking the commitment to the truth of the symbol as a wager (borrowing a notion from his French predecessor Pascal). The interpreter must take the risk of assuming that the symbol offers the best way to human understanding, which means making his presuppositions explicit and then trying to demonstrate the power of the implicit symbolic truth through interpretation in the explicit form of articulate thought. In a schema that has appealed to many, Ricoeur conceives the modern hermeneutical situation in terms of three stages. The first is the pre-critical situation of original or primary naïveté: the world of myth in which symbols are experienced as immediately true. But for the modern interpreter this world has been shattered by criticism, which ushers in the second stage. Now the problem is to find a way to restore the power of the symbols without simply returning to primitive naïveté (something we would be unable to do in any event). Ricoeur calls this third stage a 'second naïveté,' for in one sense it is a return to the first stage. But unlike the original naïveté, this stage has been through the fires of criticism and is no longer simply an unreflective or immediate grasp of the symbols. Ricoeur is not always clear about just what second naïveté would consist of or how one might reach it, but the articulation of the goal itself has found resonance in other modern thinkers, including many who do not follow the specific path recommended by Ricoeur. What is at least clear is that the way to second naïveté is through interpretation, which means not a rejection of critical thought but rather a constructive application of criticism.

Ricoeur's most systematic attempt to work out his hermeneutical ideas in detail is contained in his 1976 book *Interpretation Theory*. Rather than seeking, like Schleiermacher, to go behind the text to find its meaning in the mind of the author, Ricoeur insists that the sense is to be found 'in front of' the text. Rather than seeking, like Gadamer, to fuse the horizons of text and interpreter, Ricoeur stresses the 'distanciation' from the author that first gives the text its autonomy and creates the hermeneutical situation. And rather than seeking, like Dilthey, to separate humanistic understanding from scientific explanation, Ricoeur sets the two in a dialectical relationship that forms the context for interpretation. He also seeks to go beyond Gadamer's uncritical acceptance of tradition by introducing a critical element into hermeneutics itself, so that interpretation includes both a retrieval of tradition and a critique of ideology. Like Heidegger, Ricoeur emphasizes the existential significance of interpretation; it is our primary means for understanding ourselves and our existence in the world. Texts – especially religious texts – disclose possible worlds, so that the interpretation of texts becomes a primary means of reflecting on the meaning of human existence. Once again it becomes apparent that hermeneutics as an enterprise has a special connection with the study of religion.

The hermeneutics of suspicion

Paul Ricoeur's attention to the *conflict* of interpretations has its roots in a historical thesis about the modern hermeneutical situation. He has coined the phrase 'the hermeneutics of suspicion' to designate a change that has taken place in the modern world, a hiatus in our relationship to texts, especially those authoritative texts that include the scriptures of the world's religions. Ricoeur identifies this rupture in our hermeneutical history with three figures from the late nineteenth century whom he dubs the 'masters of suspicion': Marx, Nietzsche, and Freud. Philosophers since Descartes had generally taken the ego, the thinking self, as a given – as the foundation and point of departure for understanding. With the masters of suspicion this assumption is subjected to scrutiny and found wanting. Marx, Freud, and Nietzsche – each in his own way – suggest that subjectivity may indeed be deceived, not from without, but from within: it is self-deceived. Marx's term 'false consciousness' could be extended to include the others as well: for all three of them, the goal of interpretation cannot simply be to establish the ground of an incorrigible self-consciousness; rather, the thinking subject must also be called into question, treated with suspicion. According to Marx, for example, class interest distorts both text and interpreter because both are unaware of its influence. The Marxist therefore engages in a critique of ideology in order to uncover the covert interests lurking behind the apparent meaning of the text. A Freudian is suspicious of received texts for quite different reasons, but the hermeneutical effect is comparable. Here the 'ideological' factor is not economic and social but unconscious and individual: to understand a text rightly the interpreter must take into account the unconscious motivations that may be at work behind the façade of rational discourse. With Nietzsche the situation is more complex, as we shall see shortly, but the need to take a kind of false consciousness into account links his position to that of Marx and Freud.

The true father of the hermeneutics of suspicion, the one from who the 'masters' first learned to identify false consciousness, is the philosopher Ludwig Feuerbach (1804–1872). Originally a student of Hegel's philosophy, Feuerbach rejected Hegelian idealism very early in favor of materialism, while nevertheless retaining the dialectical logic of the system. Whereas Hegel had identified thought and being, Feuerbach believed that material nature was the ground of human consciousness and therefore the origin of religion as well. His best-known work, *The Essence of Christianity*, attempts to demonstrate how religion arises out of a dialectic of self-alienation, whereby humans project their own essential worldly attributes onto an illusory heavenly subject or subjects, the gods. In his later work, especially his *Lectures on the Essence of Religion*, Feuerbach abandons even this inverted Hegelianism and argues that religion arises out of a misinterpretation of our experience with nature. In both versions of his critique, however, Feuerbach consistently identifies the imagination as the organ of religion, the source of all illusion. Religious people, he is convinced, 'misimagine' the world by reversing cause and effect, subject and predicate, of their experience. This account of religion entails that one cannot simultaneously understand the essence of religion and continue to be religious. The field of religious studies remains divided to this day between those who study religion as members of religious communities and those who, like Feuerbach, believe that understanding religion is incompatible with its practice. Both sides, however, can agree with Feuerbach that imagination is the organ of religious belief and practice while disagreeing on the question of truth. Feuerbach's hermeneutical legacy is the lingering suspicion that at least some forms of religion falsify reality by their very nature. A more problematic corollary of this legacy is the assumption that religion is false *because* it employs imagination.

The hermeneutics of suspicion has made important inroads into religion in recent decades – into both the religious traditions themselves, insofar as they participate in the intellectual debates of the modern academy, and into the scholarly study of religion. Liberation theologians, for example, have appropriated Marxist suspicion about religion by trying to use it as a critical tool for purifying traditional belief and practice of its unholy alliance with the forces of oppression and exploitation. Their program entails a revision of classical Marxism, of course, insofar as liberation theology assumes that only 'bad' religion is vulnerable to ideological critique. A similar development has taken place among religious feminists, who seek to expose the implicit patriarchy of many or all authoritative religious texts. One finds this approach both within religious traditions themselves – primarily Christianity and Judaism, but increasingly in other traditions as well, including especially Islam – in the form of feminist theology, and also among feminist scholars of religion, who apply a feminist hermeneutics of suspicion to the religious traditions they are investigating. These approaches, of course, have been controversial, not least because in some of their more extreme forms, the practitioners of suspicious hermeneutical theory often succumb to ideology themselves, making implicit historical, philosophical, or theological claims that are immune to criticism. In response, some members of the religious studies community have proposed submitting the hermeneutics of suspicion itself to a suspicious critique. The debate is one more reminder that the 'hermeneutical circle' is unavoidable – and not only within the religious traditions but also in the practice of religious studies. For the same reason it is unlikely that any hermeneutical theory will ever achieve the status of an accepted method to be applied universally by scholars of religion without reference to their own convictions.

Hermeneutics and postmodernism

The most recent and radical development in the hermeneutics of suspicion could be called the postmodern turn. So different is this variety of theory from the nineteenth-century 'masters of suspicion' identified by Ricoeur that it needs to be treated as a significant new departure in hermeneutics. Its historical connection with the older tradition is through Nietzsche, who plays a double role in modern interpretation theory. On the one hand, there is what we can call the 'modernist Nietzsche,' the one whom Ricoeur classifies together with Marx and Freud because he in effect identifies religion as a form of false consciousness. His variation on this theme locates the root of distortion in a Jewish and then Christian 'slave revolt of morality,' in which the weakest elements of society inverted the values of classical Greek nobility. What had been virtues – strength, valor, physical beauty – came to be represented as vices, while their opposites were exalted as virtues – that is, all the sickly values of the weak and diseased elements of society, above all pity. For Nietzsche this 'transvaluation of values' is epitomized in the cross of Christianity. This moralistic disease, Nietzsche believes, is not confined to religion but has its modern secular forms as well, such as socialism. The hermeneutical point is that texts, especially religious ones, cannot be taken at face value but must be subjected to radical critique. It is not only the misunderstanding of texts by interpreters that is the problem, one could say, but also the distortions of reality embodied in the texts themselves.

The other Nietzsche is the source of postmodern hermeneutics – the Nietzsche who declares that 'there are no facts, only interpretations.' (Whether or not the modern and postmodern Nietzsches can be reconciled is a serious question for Nietzsche scholars but one we need not address here, since both impulses flowing from this brilliant and bizarre mind have powerfully influenced hermeneutics in the century since he wrote.) Those recent thinkers who have come to be called 'postmodern' – especially Jacques Derrida (1930–2004) – have developed the 'other Nietzsche,' with help from Heidegger, into a powerful if controversial force in the contemporary intellectual world, one that has important consequences for hermeneutics. Derrida's position depends on a theory of language that emphasizes the instability of signs. Every linguistic sign refers, not to non-linguistic realities lying beyond language, but rather to other signs, which in turn refer to still other signs – and so on, in an endless deferral of meaning. The implication is not that communication is impossible but that it is always incomplete, continually in flux. The attempt to evade this situation, to appeal to some bedrock of certainty and meaning, constitutes the popular but ultimately futile quest for what Derrida calls a 'transcendental signified,' that is, a sign that refers to no further signs but only to itself. The hermeneutical implications of this state of affairs have particular importance for religious studies, since religions would appear to have a significant stake in interpretive stability and certainty – just what postmodernist hermeneutics denies is possible. Instead, interpretation appears endless and incapable of achieving closure. Another contemporary French theorist, Jean-François Lyotard, defines postmodernism as 'incredulity toward metanarratives' – a position that might appear to set all traditional religions in opposition to postmodernity.

The most important idea to emerge from Derrida's philosophy is *deconstruction*. For all its familiarity in the contemporary academic world, it is notoriously difficult to define – and the difficulty is presumably intentional on Derrida's part. Deconstruction is clearly the heart of his hermeneutics, yet he denies that it is a method or a technique for interpreting texts. In the hands of some of his devotees, however, it has in fact become a technique, a critical device (even a blunt instrument) for uncovering the covert ways in which texts try to stabilize meaning and disguise the flux of signs. Derrida intends deconstruction to be an antidote to what he calls 'logocentrism,' the prevalent assumption throughout Western thought that words have a fixed relationship to reality, that they can therefore put us in direct touch with a reality beyond or behind language. He labels the pursuit of such an essential reality the 'metaphysics of presence' and endeavors to show that it is based on the seductive but illusory 'myth of presence.'

The other French postmodernist whose influence on contemporary hermeneutics one can scarcely overlook is Michel Foucault (1926–1984). Mixing writing and lecturing with political activism and sexual experimentation, his life epitomized the Nietzschean postmodernism that he advocated in his writings. Even his academic discipline is difficult to pin down: trained in philosophy, psychology, and psychopathology, he focused much of his attention on the social sciences while calling himself an 'archaeologist of knowledge' and devoting much of his writing to historical studies. Although he did not choose the label postmodern, his passionate rejection of the Enlightenment and the modernism it produced has helped to define postmodernism. Like Derrida, Foucault rejects every attempt to establish a single meaning for a text, and opposes every theory that sees language as representing reality. Especially interested in anthropology, he opposes the typically modern assumption that 'man' has a 'human nature' that somehow persists through change. He prefers to follow Nietzsche by practicing 'genealogy,' the method of uncovering the historical layers underlying the present 'order' (another Enlightenment notion he criticizes). Genealogical analysis destroys the myth that there are laws or principles of development guiding the course of history, and shows the arbitrary and haphazard ways in which the present situation has emerged out of the conflicts of the past. His intent – virtually the opposite of Gadamer's at this point – is to call into question the legitimacy of the established order. But the point at which Foucault has had the greatest impact on hermeneutical thinking – including the study of religion – is his theory of the intimate relationship linking knowledge and power. Because knowledge is always embedded in actual social institutions and practices, it is never neutral but always involved in power relationships. So intimate is the relation between knowledge and power that the two virtually merge into a single concept in Foucault's thought (one of his books bears the title *Power/Knowledge*). The effect on hermeneutics is virtually to collapse the distinction between theory and practice: theorizing is the uncovering of the hidden sources of truth in specific power interests. The inevitable bias of this kind of theory is against every established order – a bias that Foucault, for whom the student uprising of 1968 was a defining event, by no means tries to deny. Consequently, his hermeneutic approach has been most eagerly adopted by those who see themselves as victims or outsiders to the established institutions of knowledge, and thus of power. Feminists, for example, in various fields, including theology and religious studies, have found Foucault's ideas useful in their attempt to wrest control of ideas and the institutions in which they are embedded from a patriarchal establishment. If Gadamer's hermeneutics portrays interpretation as a means for reclaiming tradition, Foucault makes the act of interpretation inherently subversive of every established order.

Ad hoc hermeneutics

The duality or ambivalence within contemporary hermeneutics that we noted at the outset can lead to very different overviews of its history and significance. It is perhaps inevitable that in writing about hermeneutics one will emphasize those thinkers who present their task explicitly in terms of hermeneutical theory. But we need to remind ourselves that most of the activity that would today be called hermeneutical – that is, the actual practice of interpreting texts in order to understand and use them in all kinds of social and individual ways – has been (and still is) carried out without the benefit of any theory of hermeneutics. Thus scholars of religion studying the 'hermeneutics' of various religious communities seldom encounter the kind of self-conscious reflection on the meaning of interpretation found in Schleiermacher and his successors right up through Gadamer, Ricoeur, and the postmodern philosophers. Religious studies needs to pay at least as much attention to the implicit hermeneutics of religious communities as to the explicit hermeneutical theories, both religious and secular, that dominate so much academic discussion.

Those who have tried to give theoretical voice to such an *ad hoc* approach to hermeneutics often appeal to the ideas of Ludwig Wittgenstein (1889–1951) for inspiration and support. Like most recent philosophers, Wittgenstein focused his attention particularly on language, which he believed to be the proper subject matter of philosophy. His posthumously published *Philosophical Investigations* (1953) supplied the original impulse for what came to be known as ordinary language philosophy. Wittgenstein is the champion of language as used non-technically in everyday situations, where communication typically takes place without benefit of formal theorizing. The negative correlate of this emphasis is the thesis that we – especially if we are academic philosophers and theoreticians – allow ourselves to be 'bewitched by language,' and Wittgenstein thought of his own philosophy as a kind of therapy for the linguistic conundrums of modern philosophers. His way of doing philosophy, in keeping with his point of view, is unsystematic and *ad hoc* – often aphoristic. He is the opponent of every essentialist theory that tries to understand phenomena by reducing them to a shared essence, something they all have in common. Using the example of family resemblances, he demonstrates that our recognition of kinship need not depend on any single shared trait. The notion has had considerable influence in religious studies, making scholars far more cautious about claims concerning the 'essence of religion.' We call phenomena religious for a variety of reasons and should be wary of over-schematizing their interrelationships. The implications of Wittgenstein for hermeneutics might be summed up by invoking one of his best-known aphorisms: 'Look and see!' Taken as a watchword, this non-theoretical advice is a reminder to keep one's eyes open, to look at the bewildering variety of religious phenomena without forcing them too quickly into preconceived theoretical molds. It is not that scholars ought to eschew theory altogether but rather that they should use it heuristically rather than systematically, that is, as a source of suggestion and a goad to new discovery, applying it in *ad hoc* ways as each situation requires.

An example of *ad hoc* hermeneutical practice within a religious community is found in the work of Karl Barth (1886–1968), a theologian in the Reformed tradition, and one of the major figures in twentieth-century Christian theology. Barth's chief opponents, including Rudolf Bultmann and Paul Tillich, were heavily influenced by Heidegger's existentialism. Bultmann in particular appeals to the notion of pre-understanding in his theological hermeneutics, a practice that caused Barth to accuse him of importing an alien philosophical criterion into theology instead of taking his hermeneutical bearings from the symbolic world of scripture itself. Their debate is far too complex to deal with here except to note that Barth's insistence on doing theology out of a theological perspective rather than basing it on prior acceptance of a philosophical theory represents a hermeneutical approach that one can find in many religious traditions and which ought to be given its due in religious studies. A classic statement of this approach is the Protestant Reformers' principle that 'scripture interprets itself,' meaning that the way to understand obscure or difficult passages of scripture is not by importing a hermeneutical theory from philosophy but rather by attending to the intratextual relations of the scriptural canon itself. Religious studies should resist the temptation to supply a supertheory, focusing instead on the implicit hermeneutical ideas and practices of the religious traditions themselves. After all, the notion of the hermeneutical circle – according to which one always interprets out of prior immersion in a tradition of reading texts and not as a 'neutral' outsider – has been a mainstay of the major hermeneutical theorists of the modern (and postmodern) age. Applied to religious studies, the hermeneutical circle implies that an *ad hoc* application of theory, hermeneutical and otherwise, is the wisest course to follow in studying the diverse phenomena of the world's religious traditions and practices, because it respects the unique features of those traditions while seeking to interpret them both sympathetically and critically.

Bibliography

Auerbach, E. (1953) *Mimesis: The Representation of Reality in Western Literature*. Princeton, NJ: Princeton University Press.

Caputo, J. D. (1987) *Radical Hermeneutics: Repetition, Deconstruction, and the Hermeneutic Project*. Bloomington and Indianapolis, IN: Indiana University Press.

Ebeling, G. (1959) 'Hermeneutik.' In *Die Religion in Geschichte und Gegenwart: Handwörterbuch für Theologie und Religionswissenschaft*. 3rd edn. Tübingen: J. C. B. Mohr (Paul Siebeck), 3: 242–62.

Ferraris, M. (1996), *History of Hermeneutics*. Translated by Luca Somigli. Atlantic Highlands, NJ: Humanities Press International.

Feuerbach, L. (1957 [1841]) *The Essence of Christianity*, New York: Harper.

—— (1967) *Lectures on the Essence of Religion*, New York: Harper.

Foucault, M. (1980) *Power/Knowledge: Selected Interviews and Other Writings, 1972–1977*. New York: Pantheon Books.

Fowl, Stephen E., ed., (1997) *The Theological Interpretation of Scripture: Classic and Contemporary Readings*. Cambridge, MA: Blackwell.

Frei, H. (1974) *The Eclipse of Biblical Narrative: A Study in Eighteenth and Nineteenth Century Hermeneutics*. New Haven, CT and London: Yale University Press.

Gadamer, H.-G. (1991) *Truth and Method*, 2nd rev. edn., translation revised by Joel Weinsheimer and Donald G. Marshall. New York: Crossroad.

Green, G. (2000) *Theology, Hermeneutics, and Imagination: The Crisis of Interpretation at the End of Modernity*. Cambridge: Cambridge University Press.

Grenz, S. J. (1996) *A Primer on Postmodernism*. Grand Rapids, MI, and Cambridge: William B. Eerdmans Publishing.

Jeanrond, W. G. (1991) *Theological Hermeneutics: Development and Significance*. London: Macmillan.

Kant, I. (1960 [1794]) *Religion within the Limits of Reason Alone*, translated by Theodore M. Greene and Hoyt H. Hudson, New York: Harper.

Ramm, B. L. (1976) *Protestant Biblical Interpretation: A Textbook of Hermeneutics*. Grand Rapids, MI: Baker Book House.

Ricoeur, P. (1974) *The Conflict of Interpretations: Essays in Hermeneutics*. Evanston, IL: Northwestern University Press.

—— (1976) *Interpretation Theory: Discourse and the Surplus of Meaning*. Fort Worth, TX: Texas Christian University Press.

Schleiermacher, F. (1977) *Hermeneutics: The Handwritten Manuscripts*, edited by H. Kimmerle, translated by J. Duke and J. Forstman. Missoula, MT: Scholars Press.

—— (1988 [1799]) *On Religion: Speeches to its Cultured Despisers*, translated by R. Crouter. Cambridge: Cambridge University Press.

Wittgenstein, L. (2001) *Philosophical Investigations: The German Text with a Revised English Translation*, translated by G. E. M. Anscombe. Oxford: Blackwell.

Suggested reading

Caputo, J. (1987) *Radical Hermeneutics: Repetition, Deconstruction, and the Hermeneutic Project*, Bloomington and Indianapolis: Indiana University Press.
  Hermeneutics reconceived in the light of postmodern philosophy.

Ebeling, G. (1959) 'Hermeneutik,' in *Die Religion in Geschichte und Gegenwart: Handwörterbuch für Theologie und Religionswissenschaft*, 3rd edn., Tübingen: J. C. B. Mohr (Paul Siebeck) 3: 242–62.
  A definitional essay by the leading proponent of the 'New Hermeneutic.'

Ferraris, M. (1996) *History of Hermeneutics*, translated by Luca Somigli, Atlantic Highlands, NJ: Humanities Press International.
  A comprehensive overview of philosophical hermeneutics.

Fowl, S., ed. (1997) *The Theological Interpretation of Scripture: Classic and Contemporary Readings*, Cambridge, MA: Blackwell.
  An anthology of primary texts in theological hermeneutics.

Green, G. (2000) *Theology, Hermeneutics, and Imagination: The Crisis of Interpretation at the End of Modernity*, Cambridge: Cambridge University Press.
  Hermeneutical issues in modern European religious and secular thought.

Grenz, S. (1996) *A Primer on Postmodernism*, Grand Rapids, MI, and Cambridge: Eerdmans.
  An introduction to postmodern philosophy for beginning students.

Jeanrond, W. (1991) *Theological Hermeneutics: Development and Significance*, London: Macmillan.
  A comprehensive history of theological hermeneutics.

Ramm, B. (1976) *Protestant Biblical Interpretation: A Textbook of Hermeneutics*, Grand Rapids, MI: Baker.
  A conservative Protestant account of biblical hermeneutics.

Ricoeur, P. (1995) *Figuring the Sacred: Religion, Narrative, and Imagination*, Minneapolis: Fortress.
  The best collection of Ricoeur's essays on religious themes.

—— (1991) *From Text to Action: Essays in Hermeneutics, II*, Evanston, IL: Northwestern University Press.
  A second collection of Ricoeur's essays on hermeneutics, supplementing *The Conflict of Interpretations* [1974].

Zimmermann, J. (2004) *Recovering Theological Hermeneutics: An Incarnational-Trinitarian Theory of Interpretation*, Grand Rapids, MI: Baker.
  A compelling argument against the secularization of hermeneutics.

Chapter 25

Religious pluralism

Michael Barnes

In a purely descriptive sense, religious pluralism is synonymous with the phenomenon of religious diversity or plurality, what is 'religiously other' within a given social context. In the last few decades, however, the term has acquired a very particular connotation. More often than not, it is used in a normative sense to refer to a specific stance in philosophy and theology, that associated with the name of John Hick and the thinkers of what might be called the 'Myth of Christian Uniqueness' school (a project developed in Hick and Knitter 1987 with an important set of counter-proposals in D'Costa 1990a). In its simplest form the thesis states that all religions are equally valid paths to the same transcendent reality.

This is how I use the term in this chapter, the first part of which is given over to a brief account and critique. My aim here is to identify some of the presuppositions which have led to the paradigm shift proclaimed by the Myth school. Hick's work is important because it raises many complex ethical and philosophical issues which attend the dialogue of religions. It is also extremely plausible, leading the reader away from what appears to be a narrow religious chauvinism to a more reasonable acceptance of the plurality of religions. It has, however, met with considerable opposition – not just because it sidelines the claims that religious traditions make to speak of truth but because it fails to address the crucial issue raised by the plurality of religions, namely *the significance for religious faith of the engagement with 'the other'*. Thus the second part of the chapter considers some responses which, in the wake of the Myth debate, religious traditions have themselves made to 'the other'. This will entail attention being given to a re-reading of the Christian theology of religions; the line developed here is in broad agreement with that espoused by Jacques Dupuis (1997, 2002), a position which Paul Griffiths (2001) refers to as 'open inclusivism'. But the normative thesis has not just met with predictable critique from within the world of orthodox mainstream Christian theology. Theologians and philosophers from other traditions have also waded into the fray. I intend, therefore, to add a brief account of religious plurality from Islamic and Buddhist perspectives.

The main concern of this chapter is not to examine the intra-systemic philosophical questions which the process of interreligious dialogue raises, nor to analyse the empirical 'results' of dialogue, the changes and formations which it encourages. (For the philosophical, theological and practical/political questions which arise from the debate about religious pluralism in the broad sense the reader is directed to an ever-growing literature (e.g. Tracy 1994; Di Noia 1992; Byrne 1995; O'Leary 1996; D'Costa 2000; Griffiths 2001; Heim 2001; Barnes 2002; Kaplan 2002; Marty 2005; Griffith-Dickson 2005.) The aim here is more limited: to consider how communities of faith deal with the interreligious relationship itself. This, of course, is a *theological* agenda and raises the question why it should find a place in a book largely devoted to Religious Studies. My point is that, in the multi-faith world which confronts students of religion from all religious backgrounds and none, theological questions about the internal coherence of a tradition cannot be separated from the more objective or academic questions put by those who are, strictly speaking, outsiders. Nor is 'theology' to be regarded any longer as the preserve of a few Christian intellectuals – as the recent phenomenon of 'Buddhist Theology' demonstrates (Jackson and Makransky 2000). As David Tracy has argued (1981), theology addresses different social realities or 'publics' – church and academy and wider society (in which category I would want to place 'other religions'). Theology is inter-disciplinary of its very nature – called to respond not just to the data which the academic study of religions raises but also to attend to the systems and strategies which communities of faith develop in responding to each other.

The growth of a hypothesis

Two major contributions to the growth of this normative hypothesis can be noted, if not completely distinguished. On the one hand, an awareness of the relativity of all religions invalidates claims to superiority and exclusiveness on the part of one. On the other, the greater contact between, and increasing knowledge of, particular traditions makes arguments for a common core or essence increasingly plausible. The growth of religious studies as an academic discipline committed to discerning the various dimensions of the world's religions has clearly been influential in uniting the two (Smart 1989:12–21). These developments are treated at length in other chapters in this volume.

The same two themes run consistently through Hick's work (Hick 1977, 1980a , 1980b, 1989). His version of the pluralist hypothesis builds on various considerations, especially the phenomenological 'family resemblance' argument, which rule out an *a priori* 'Christianity-centred' theology. One is an appreciation of the spiritual and moral values present in the world religions; the other an account of the destructive effect of Christian claims to superiority. Hick thus reads the history of theological accounts of the other as a move from intolerant 'exclusivism' through a more liberal 'inclusivism' to his own proposal, a 'theological crossing of the Rubicon' into what he considers the theologically more straightforward world of pluralism. Calling for a radical reconstruction or relativising of Christian claims, Hick argues persuasively that traditional christocentric and ecclesiocentric positions which have dominated the agenda for centuries need to be replaced by a theocentric position if theologians are to give an adequate account of the modern experience of the plurality of religions. According to Hick, the only appropriate way of understanding the plurality of religious beliefs and practices in today's world must be based on a reflection on the total religious experience of humankind.

This historical overview is backed up with a realist account of religious experience (Hick 1989:129–227). Rejecting both the sceptical view that religious experience is delusory and what he sees as a dogmatic view that it is delusory except for what is mediated through one's own tradition, Hick develops a third view – that all major religions are different ways of experiencing the Divine or Real. Religions are alternative soteriological 'spaces' through which people find the way from self-centredness to 'Reality-centredness', different configurations of divine phenomena which are instantiated as myths or stories that change or direct people's lives.

This thesis is developed on the basis of a distinction (noted in some form in all religions but as developed by Hick owing more to Kant) between the Real as such and the Real as humanly thought-and-experienced. Invoking Kant's thesis that the mind contributes to the character of the perceived environment, Hick distinguishes between the phenomenal world of the religions and the noumenal world which exists independent of our perception of it. Like Kant he seeks to be both a 'transcendental idealist' and an 'empirical realist'. But Hick goes beyond Kant – for whom God is postulated as the pre-supposition of *moral* obligation – by postulating the Absolute or the Real as the condition of possibility of all religious experience. Thus the Absolute in collaboration with the experiencing subject is responsible for the phenomenal world which religious persons experience. In Kantian terms, the Absolute or Real is the unknowable *noumenon* 'behind' the known *phenomena*. Faith affirms the Absolute – but only *that* it is, not *what* it is. The 'content' of the act of faith is derived from the particular language of a tradition – in Christianity the language which speaks of 'God in Christ', in Buddhism the language derived ultimately from the Buddha's enlightenment experience. While various developments in Hick's thought can be noted, particularly a nuancing of language about the Absolute, he adheres consistently to the terms of what he calls a 'Copernican Revolution' in the theology of religious pluralism (Hick 1973:120–132; D'Costa 1987). The same Absolute, however identified in personal or impersonal terms, is equivalently manifested in the various forms of human religiosity. Underlying all such forms is a common unthematised religious experience which the religions refer to in terms of the different languages of faith.

The plausibility of the hypothesis

There is no doubt about the attractiveness of a single hypothesis to explain the phenomenon of religious pluralism. But such a panoptic overview, however idealistic in its intentions, is by no means unproblematic. 'Universal' theologies and comprehensive theories generally raise the same questions about method and coherence as the *'philosophia perennis'*. (The classic account in its modern pluralist form is to be found in Schuon 1975; on 'universal theology' see the important collection in Swidler 1987). Whose 'data' are being considered? And from whose perspective? The very shift in meaning from a purely descriptive to a normative account of 'the other' raises political and ethical issues, about the nature of power and control in theological and philosophical discourse generally. Pluralists such as are represented by the 'Myth school' are right to draw attention to the innate chauvinism of much traditional Christian thinking; their call for respect, openness and understanding is the *sine qua non* of any theology of religions. There is, therefore, a strong ethical basis for some version of pluralism. But the extent to which the hypothesis can be made *normative*, that is to say can be held with philosophical consistency, let alone theological integrity, is open to doubt. Thanks in no small measure to the influence of Hick the topic of religious pluralism is now an important topic in the literature of philosophy of religion (e.g. Loughlin 1990; D'Costa 1996; Rowe 1999; Surin 1990; Wainwright 1999; Cheetham 2003; Cottingham 2005). Just a few of the more obvious points can be noted here.

In order to ensure that pluralism does not descend into some form of relativism it becomes necessary to abstract from the particularity of languages some sort of common 'meta-language'. But it quickly becomes problematic to argue for a correspondence between religious phenomena – the concepts, symbols or stories – and the Absolute to which they supposedly point. How does one *know* there is a correspondence? Might not all be as equally false as equally true? The not-so-hidden assumption is that religious languages are equivalent, equally effective *soteriologically*, since they appear to perform the same function in their respective traditions in pointing the way to the same unknowable Absolute.

But for this argument to work, the point of reference, the Absolute, must be capable of identification while yet remaining, by definition, the unknowable. It seems highly plausible to make different expressions of the Absolute identical; that is to say, to prescind from the particularity of the phenomenal names and to identify together the single noumenal reality to which they supposedly point. But the argument is invalid. One cannot make two 'unknowables' equivalent. As Keith Ward points out, 'it is rather like saying, "I do not know what X is; and I do not know what Y is; therefore X must be the same as Y." If I do not know what either is, I *ipso facto* do not know whether they are the same or different' (1990:5). The most that can be said is that very different languages and concepts may be speaking of the same unknowable. But again they may not. There is, in short, an important point to be made in using the term religious pluralism in its purely descriptive sense to signify a phenomenon of contemporary experience. But it is illegitimate to turn the 'given' into a theory which somehow accounts for the given.

The point is that there is no vantage-point 'above the action', as it were, which is not itself historically or culturally conditioned. This is where the apparent strength of the pluralist case masks real weakness; the assumption of the moral high ground can quickly become ideological. While it is not the case that pluralists hold that all religions are talking in different ways about the same thing, there is, nevertheless, a tendency to a certain sort of reductionist universalism. This determination to search out common values and essences tends almost inevitably to short-circuit the highly complex ways in which people of faith seek to identify themselves. Such a universalism fails to take seriously the variety of religions and the differences between them and turns out to be covertly élitist. In fact, on closer inspection what purports to be an objective, neutral and universal perspective looks suspiciously like a contradiction in terms. On the one hand, each religion is given equal soteriological value; on the other, a privilege is assumed for the pluralist 'system' itself.

Pluralists rightly draw attention to the way perceptions of specific religious traditions have been formed by Orientalist types of discourse; popular stereotypes, such as 'mystic India' or 'primitive Africa', not to mention reifications such as 'Hinduism' and 'Buddhism', have been largely constructed by eurocentric concerns. But a residual Orientalism, the tendency to project unexamined Western stereotypes on to what is properly 'other', is only too apparent in pluralist versions of the history of religions which seek to inscribe the plurality of creeds and culture within a single scheme.

There is an ambiguity here. This drive for theoretical mastery is quite at variance not just with the post-modern awareness of the historicity of all discourse about the other but with the much more diffuse and ill-defined practice of inter-faith relations. There can be little doubt about the influence of post-colonialist and post-Shoah discourse on the pluralist hypothesis; the challenge put to Western thought generally by the liberation movements of the past half-century has focussed attention on salvation and liberation themes as the single goal of all religions, thus giving rise to a more ethically nuanced approach to 'common essence' theories of religion. This 'liberationist perspective within the Myth school is represented particularly by the work of Paul Knitter and Aloysius Pieris (Hick and Knitter 1987:178ff.; Knitter 1995; Pieris 1988; Swidler 1990:19ff.; May 1998:75ff.; and for critique of Pieris Ramachandra 1996:38ff.). At the same time, the context within which liberation themes have been developed has now shifted from socio-economic analysis to broader cultural considerations, often of a sharply local dimension. Thus, for example, Pieris's more recent work places the familiar themes of the Buddhist-Christian dialogue within a more complex cultural-religious perspective (2004). Given that proponents of the normative hypothesis perceive the 'problem' of religious pluralism to lie with a 'Christianity-centred' view of reality and the false sense of superiority which it supposedly encourages, it is not altogether surprising that they have tended to ignore this dimension.

Identifying presuppositions

Two inter-related comments are in order here. The first is that there is nothing intrinsically dishonourable about the desire to mould others in one's own image; the properly ethical question, as Talal Asad indicates, is about the exercise of power and the means which are used in developing relations with the other (1993:12). Second, while it is obviously true that appalling things have been done in the name of religion – the Crusades and the conquest of the Americas are usually mentioned – it is one thing to recognise the failure of religious practice, another to lay it at the door of inherent defects within theory or the system of belief. There are, of course, significant links to be discerned between them, but any attempt to critique or re-read a religious tradition begs complex hermeneutical questions about language and method. Methods of correlation, bringing the texts of tradition into some sort of creative engagement with the exigencies of situation, are never value-free. Indeed the whole concept of a value-free universalism is itself deeply problematic. Self-confessedly neutral positions usually turn out, on closer inspection, to be dominated by very specific ideas of what makes for the 'humanum', human fulfilment or even the very nature of human being itself (Surin 1990; Loughlin 1990; D'Costa 1996).

Perhaps the most important – because intractable – of the unexamined presuppositions lurking behind the normative hypothesis is the concept of 'religion' itself. The idea that there are a number of identifiable entities called 'religions', different species of a common genus, is itself a construction of the Enlightenment (Lash 1996 drawing on the historical studies of Harrison 1990 and Cantwell Smith 1978). During the Age of Reason 'religion' came to designate not the life of faith and the proper worship offered to God, but the external 'system' of practice, an object of scientific study with all the paraphernalia of diverse transcendent beings, myths, rituals and other data of the category 'religion'. With the growth of knowledge of other continents the discovery of analogous systems of belief and practice created a religious geography – subsequently immortalised by Hick, using more astronomical terminology, as the 'Universe of Faiths'. The model by which the discrete 'religions' were identified, however, was the rationalist deism which dominated the debate about the nature of Christian faith in the seventeenth and eighteenth centuries. This, of course, gave a privileged place to a transcendent Absolute reality, the ultimate object of human understanding, and was rooted in what developed into an all-pervading dualism of sacred and profane. As God was set apart from the world, so the practices of religion came to be divorced from everyday living. The result has been, as Lash observes, that 'the role of religion as a medium of truth has been privatised' (1996:16).

The desire to map all forms of knowledge on to a single manipulable grid finds its most celebrated exponent in Descartes but runs through so much of modern culture (see especially Toulmin 1990; Pickstock 1998:47–61). The drive to develop a normative 'religious pluralism' shares in a similar foundationalism. Similar presuppositions are at work: that 'religious' phenomena can be distinguished and categorised, that all point toward a single overarching truth, and that a comprehensive theory of all religious phenomena is possible. Theories about what holds such phenomena together, whether emerging directly from a philosophical critique such as Feuerbach's, or finding a more derivative form in the psychology of Freud or the sociology of Durkheim, can all be traced back to the Enlightenment desire to impose a structure of thought on the data of consciousness. But, like the blander versions of the modern normative thesis, they are all more or less reductionist.

At least in theory the Enlightenment view of rationality encourages pluralism. In practice it can be quite limiting, espousing not a plurality of equally plausible positions but a neutral vantage-point, a 'view from nowhere'. A concept of truth defined largely in terms of abstract, timeless principles has little space for the broader uses to which human language is usually put – forms of rhetoric and poetics, for instance. Similarly the pluralist hypothesis ignores the diversity and richness of religious literature, obscuring the different purposes to which stories, parables and myths can be put, in favour of what D'Costa calls 'an entirely instrumental use of religious language' (D'Costa 1990b:532). All religion has but a single aim: to turn away from Self towards the Divine, or, in Hick's Kantian language, the noumenal Real. It is not difficult to recognise here an example of what Foucault defined as the aim of modern Western philosophy: to 'preserve, against all decenterings, the sovereignty of the subject' (1972:12). This tendency to define human selfhood in terms of self-knowledge makes God one more, albeit the supreme, human value, begging the question about the origin, not to say the interpretation of such values. Still less does it take into account the extent to which ethical value is to be understood within the particularity of distinct historical and cultural forms. There is always a danger, as Milbank observes, of an 'ascription to modern liberal Western values [which] does not acknowledge the traditional and continuing political sub-structures which perpetuate these values' (1990:175). Despite a degree of support, not just from a growing number of Asian theologians but also from a few Jewish and Muslim thinkers which give the hypothesis a certain moral force and plausibility, it remains very much a product of Anglo-American empiricist rationality.

In summary, what the pluralist hypothesis misses is a critical sense of itself as part of the historical and cultural complexity which has formed not just the different religious communities through their fraught and often destructive relations with each other but, more significantly, the particular post-Enlightenment universalist mind-set which it has inherited. The desire to 'stand above the action', the drive to replace the diffuseness of local diversity with the neatness of a comprehensive system, is itself bound up with ill-defined cultural shifts of consciousness about that most ancient of philosophical questions, the relationship between same and other. Thus McGrane, in his anthropological survey of European accounts of the other, concludes that in the twentieth century, due to the modern experience of the great diversity of cultures, the other is regarded as 'merely different' – thus opening the way to a form of cultural relativism, 'a great trivialization of the encounter with the Other' which reaffirms 'the Eurocentric idea of the progress of knowledge' (1989:129). In other words, the pluralist hypothesis, Hick's route across the Rubicon, is less a royal road cutting majestically through mountains of theological obfuscation than a short cut which misses the richness and variety of the landscape in its anxiety to get to the end of the journey. If McGrane is right, then it is clearly naive – not to say tautological – to regard the pluralist hypothesis as a solution to the 'problem' of pluralism.

Retrieving theological positions

In the first edition of this book what followed was a re-reading of a few aspects of the story of Christian relations with people of other faiths. My intention was to rescue the mainstream of the Christian theological tradition from being largely dismissed by pluralists as the outmoded

'Christianity-centred' positions of so-called 'exclusivism' and 'inclusivism'. I therefore argued for a retrieval of the more generous side of the Christian response to the other and for an account of the Christian tradition as genuinely 'other-centred', always charged with learning how to witness to what is discerned of God's purposes in the world of a rich and perplexing diversity. Something of that agenda remains. Even – perhaps especially – in the world of liberal modernity which Hick addresses, it is important that Christianity be not reduced to a series of more or less triumphalist answers to troublesome outsiders.

That world, however, is fast disappearing. The problem, as Cheetham observes, is that 'Hick's religious pluralism goes against the grain by seeking to be comprehensive rather than tradition-specific' (2003:168). It fits a liberal modern intellectual paradigm but is out of place in a more post-modern climate. In other words the normative hypothesis should be understood as a dimension of the history of inter-religious relations, but *not* as its explanation. Any work of critique is itself situated (including, of course, this one). In returning, therefore, to the question with which I began – about the *significance* of religious pluralism for people of faith – it is important not to repeat the fallacy of a magisterial view from nowhere. This does not, however, entail replacing theology with genealogical deconstruction. Surin's acerbic attack on all forms of Christian theology of religions, on the ground that they serve up abstract unitary theories instead of identifying political and cultural self-interest, is surely a polemic too far (Surin 1990). Nor does a post-modern account of religious pluralism leave no alternative but to 'out-narrate' the babble of competing voices. Theological questions are rooted not in the defence of some 'given' tradition which promises to explain the totality of truth, but in an originating sense of wonder before a world regarded as, at once, familiar and strange, same and other. In some sense, that must be true of all religious traditions.

Thus in this second edition I take a different line, one more in keeping with the rich development of interreligious dialogue in recent years – and indeed of a cross-religious or 'comparative' theology, one pursued in dialogue with the other. What is at stake is not the position of Christianity as some sort of fulfillment of all the others, but the claims of any religious tradition to its own specificity and integrity. Religions manifest significant differences, believe different things about the nature of ultimate reality, and teach different ways of human perfection. These are not to be reduced to some lowest common denominator without doing violence to the complex fabric of belief and practice which supports their claims to inject meaning into people's lives or diluting those claims by slipping into some kind of relativism. Increasingly, therefore, any theological response to 'the other' has had to take on board not just what Christianity has to say about other faith traditions but what other faith traditions have to say about their own 'others'. All traditions have both theoretical and practical resources for speaking of the other and for re-reading their own tradition when faced with the phenomenon of religious pluralism. I suggested in the introduction that religious pluralism raises hermeneutical and ethical questions about the meaning of inter-religious engagement. If that is correct, then the theological task is essentially a collaborative or dialogical exercise – speaking *and* listening to what the other has to say. It is at least arguable that a more theologically nuanced account of religious pluralism itself will give some intellectual credibility to the practical engagement of religious communities at a variety of levels.

The significance of difference

Much more is at stake than the cogency of a supposedly comprehensive meta-theory of religious diversity (Cheetham 2003:168). Strangely, perhaps, Hick is still very much dominated by the Christian 'salvation problematic' – can the non-Christian be saved? But for neither Barth nor Rahner (the usual suspects made to represent so-called 'exclusivism' and 'inclusivism' respectively) is salvation the central issue. Strictly speaking, the question of who is or who is not saved lies with God, and, although issues like grace and human freedom are very much at the heart of Christian anthropology, the Church has never pronounced upon soteriology *as such*. The ultimate state of the righteous individual is known only to God and may not be second-guessed by others, not even by the Church. The more pressing question is not *whether* people from other faith traditions can be saved – they always remain within the gracious providence of God, as do all human beings – but *how*. What part is played by the religions themselves? Are people saved *despite* their traditional beliefs and practice or precisely *through* them? The fact that such questions can be asked at all is an indication of how much Catholic theology in particular – admittedly in response to the reality of religious difference and the challenge of the pluralist hypothesis – has retrieved from its own tradition. At least three dimensions of this renewal should be noted in passing (pursued at much greater length in the first edition of this chapter): the Patristic notion of the 'seeds of the Word' (Saldanha 1984) which has opened up a sense of the continuing operative 'presence' of Jesus Christ as the revealed Word of God in the history of salvation; the ecclesiology of Vatican II which has restored to the Church a sense of its own identity as constituted by the *Missio Dei*, involving a participation in the work of God's Spirit sent into the world (Sullivan 1992; Burrows 1996); and finally the experience of dialogue itself which at a variety of levels has changed the way Christians think about mission and evangelisation (Panikkar 1978; Fitzgerald and Borelli 2006).

In an uncontroversial sense all Christian theology is concerned with pluralism, with the relationship of the Church to the other. In practice – and here the normative pluralist account of Christian theology does have a point – responses vary. Some theologians seek to maintain the integrity of the Church against non-Christians; others more openly affirm the identity of persons of faith and see them as representing at least the *possibility* that there exist outside the visible bounds of the Church 'truths of religious significance' (Griffiths 2001:63). The most influential advocate of post-Vatican II Catholic theology of religions, Jacques Dupuis, advocates the latter possibility. With his distinction between the religions as *de iure* rather than *de facto* (that is to say, having a proper role to play in the unfolding of the providential purposes of a beneficent God rather than being regarded as a purely contingent reality which will eventually be overcome) the 'great question of the other' is conceived no longer as a problem to be solved (which it remains within the terms of the normative pluralist hypothesis) but as a relationship to be explored (Dupuis 1997; 2002). The key issue is no longer about the salvation of the other; it is about the *theological significance of otherness*.

There is some irony in the fact that it is theology which, as the third millennium advances, is making the pluralist-dominated account of religious diversity look a little dog-eared. Even attempts to develop a 'fourth paradigm' (Ogden 1992; Di Noia 1992) seem way out of date. The reason for such dissatisfaction is to be sought not in nostalgia for the more comforting solutions of yester-year but in a growing awareness that modern 'possessive individualism' fails to address the political, and therefore theological, issues which are raised by the inter-action of different communities of faith in modern society. A pluralism which has already accepted a version of 'religion' as marginal to the public realm can produce little more than well-intentioned exhortations to a bland tolerance. Only by careful attention to the role religious practice plays in the formation and growth of communities of faith, and therefore to the ways it both encourages and discourages engagement and dialogue with others, can the significance of difference and otherness be appreciated. These are theological issues not because they are 'Christianity-centred' in the narrow sense, but because they address the challenge which inter-faith dialogue makes to all claims to self-sufficiency. In short: other persons disclose something of the mystery of *the* Other, of God – a point made with some cogency by David Tracy (1994:73ff., 95ff.).

The point to be stressed is that a normative account of religious pluralism does not encourage dialogue because it fails in the end to take otherness seriously. Whatever else religions may be about, they clearly respond to the human need for meaning. At some point all human beings, whether followers of recognized religious traditions or not, seek some sort of coherence in their living, what MacIntyre calls 'a life that can be conceived and evaluated as a whole' (1985:205). Supporters of the normative paradigm are undoubtedly correct that some theory of meaning is necessary to the understanding of religious diversity. Where the hypothesis appears curiously dated is in seeking to surmount diversity by assuming some sort of Archimedean 'place to stand'. My argument has been that there can be no such place which is not value and theory-laden. The question, therefore, is how to shift attention from particular theories, which tend almost inevitably to assume the position of all-encompassing master narratives, to the skills, dispositions and virtues which sustain persons in their pursuit of meaning. As MacIntyre has shown, where the practice of such virtues is learned is in the living out of the heritage which grounds and gives coherence to the faith of communities. This begins with the liturgical celebration of memories and the transmission and re-imaging of life-giving stories, which are passed from one generation to another. It continues with the various practices of faith – study and prayer as well as social exchange and dialogue with others – which they support and which give rise to a hermeneutical sensitivity to what in the Christian tradition have been referred to as 'seeds of the Word'.

The three-fold paradigm, the heart of the normative pluralist mis-reading of theological history, subordinates the life-giving practice of religious faith to a single value or virtue of tolerance, openness or respect. Admirable in its intentions, it nevertheless begs the question of motivation. There is a value in each of the three positions of the paradigm but it is distinctly *not* the value of the neat hierarchy. Rather than link so-called 'exclusivism', 'inclusivism' and 'pluralism' together as carefully graduated theological positions, ranked according to their openness to the other, it makes better sense to understand them as each embodying a theological virtue or value essential to the understanding of the relationship between *any* faith community and those which it perceives as other. Exclusivism witnesses to that faith which speaks of what it knows through the specificity of tradition. Inclusivism looks forward in hope to the fulfilment of all authentically religious truth and value. Pluralism expresses that love which seeks always to affirm those values in the present (Mathewes 1998; Barnes 2002:182ff.).

This shift of attention – from consideration of the specific *objects* of theological study to the nature of the theological *subject*, the community of faith which exists by seeking to articulate its relationship with God – makes for a more ethically and theologically nuanced account of the rich complexity of inter-religious relations than is allowed by a theory of normative religious pluralism. It also suggests how interreligious dialogue is to be conducted – with proper attention to those virtuous practices of faith which generate a community's sense of identity and quest for meaning.

Dialogue and the theology of religions

What has become known as theology of religions in recent years is less an attempt to work within or respond to the strictures laid down by the normative hypothesis, thus producing versions of a 'fourth model', than a reflection on the implications for Christian faith of the experience of *being in dialogue*. In his extraordinary and all too brief meditation on the Trinity Raimon Panikkar – described by Rowan Williams as an 'uncomfortable ally' for the pluralist case (2000:170) – has produced a remarkable exploration of human relationality spelt out in terms of certain interdependent and complementary spiritual attitudes (1973). More recently other writers have picked up the same theme (Heim 2001; Kärkkäinen 2004). The same sort of reflection on the dialogical experience is at work in Panikkar's better-known essay 'The Unknown Christ of Hinduism' (1981). This is more than an exercise in fulfilment theology. Panikkar is not trying to show how Christians 'know' something which Hindus do not. Rather, Christ – or, in his terms, the 'christic principle' – always remains in an important sense a mystery to *both* Christians and Hindus. Both are searching for the meaning of that Divine Mystery which Christians *name* in faith as Christ. For Panikkar a theology which emerges from interreligious dialogue with Hindus is about 'mutual fecundation'. It is not a matter of how Christians can go on defending 'their' name over against the names given by others, but of how *together* the name which Christians invoke can disclose to *both parties* what it has to say about the unnameable. Nor is such an approach to theology a purely Roman Catholic preserve. Kenneth Cragg's struggle to bridge the gap between the 'high prophetology' of the Church with the much more self-effacing version of mainstream Islam is intended to keep open a conversation with Islam in which Christians can learn how to speak of a God revealed in obedient discipleship, submitting to God's will and working for God's justice, while at the same time learning how to find God in experiences of suffering and loss (2002; 2004).

Perhaps the most interesting development within the broad movement of interreligious dialogue is the work of Francis Clooney in developing 'comparative theology'. This is spelled out in some detail as a practice of reading familiar Christian texts within a new context set by relatively unfamiliar non-Christian texts. Clooney argues that such an activity brings about a significant change in one's Christian perspective on 'the other'. A whole series of studies have juxtaposed Hindu devotional works and mainstream theology with familiar Christian texts, ranging from the *Spiritual Exercises* of St Ignatius of Loyola and the *Treatise on the Love of God* of St Francis de Sales to Rahner, von Balthasar and Richard Swinburne (1993; 2001; 2008). Meanwhile at a more inter-personal level the practice of Scriptural Reasoning builds on the experience, discernible at a variety of levels, of people of faith who exist in relationship with each other (Ford 2006). An extension of the shared study by Jews and Christians of Old and New Testaments to include the third of the Abrahamic religions, Scriptural Reasoning is intended to draw out the abundance of meaning from the 'plain sense' of the text, and introduce readers into the inherited 'prudential wisdom' of the tradition.

In other words, to pick up the distinction above, the focus is very much on theological subjects who act sometimes as host, sometimes as guest, sometimes taking the initiative, sometimes acting in a more responsive mode. This image of theological hospitality which involves thinkers *and* practitioners from across the religions is helpful in accounting for the shift away from a 'theology *for* dialogue' towards what might be called a 'theology *of* dialogue' – an exercise of responsible attention to the role which the other – what is 'not-self' – in all its forms, plays in the formation of faith. Although this dimension of Christian faith has always been present within the practice of the Church, it took the initiative of the Second

Vatican Council – and specifically the declaration, *Nostra Aetate*, on the relationship of the Catholic Church to Non-Christian Religions – to provide the momentum for a more open and dynamic approach to inter-religious relations. That hesitant statement, originally intended to address the legacy of Christian anti-Judaism, soon became a sort of 'inter-faith charter' for other Christian churches – many of whom have produced their own statements, such as *Generous Love*, published by the Anglican Consultative Council in 2008. In its wake have come two important initiatives from other faith communities. A group of influential Jewish academics in the USA produced *Dabru Emet* ('speak truth' from Zechariah 8.16), a brief yet generous statement on the state of Jewish-Christian relations (published in the New York Times on 10 September 2000). On 13 October 2007 a group of 158 Muslim leaders and teachers sent a more challenging letter called *A Common Word* to major Christian leaders throughout the world. Reacting originally to the Pope's Regensburg lecture, 12 September 2006, this remarkable statement has since led to a number of responses – including high-level meetings between Catholic and Muslim theologians in the Vatican and an important letter from the Archbishop of Canterbury.

Although not coming from 'official' authorities these two initiatives show how much the inter-faith climate has changed in recent years. They also witness to a growing consensus among theologians and thinkers across the religious spectrum that normative pluralism fails to reflect the lived reality of the faith communities themselves. While Hick's hypothesis has attracted some important support from outside the Christian tradition (Aslan 1998; Cohn-Sherbok 1994), others have voiced strong reservations. Muhammad Legenhausen, for instance, an American Shi'a theologian who teaches at the Imam Khomeini Institute in Qom, Iran, thinks Hick's normative pluralism a distinct improvement on prescriptive exclusivism and inclusivism (1999). But in his opinion it betrays a set of moral and political values and philosophical principles which are at odds with the mainstream of Islam. Legenhausen objects to the validation of religions in terms of personal religious experience – the argument that since all religions express a single interior truth it makes no difference which is followed. He finds Hick's account of Islam both ill-informed and patronising. From the beginning Islam has always allowed the message of Jesus while finding its theological elaboration in terms of the doctrines of Incarnation and Trinity objectionable. However, the normative pluralist case ends up reducing both traditions to something less than the single authentic revelation which Islam traces through the entire line of prophets, from Adam to Muhammad himself – the final Seal of the Prophets. It is not that Islam relativises all the previous prophets. On the contrary, the demand that the Holy Qur'an be accepted as the perfection of God's revelation validates rather than annuls all that has gone before.

Legenhausen agrees with Hick to this extent, that Christian theology needs to be rewritten in favour of the message of the *original* forms of Torah and Injil as God delivered them, not the adulterated forms in which, according to Islam, they are found today. But that does not imply that it makes no difference which religion is followed or that human beings should ever rest content with what has been bestowed by family and culture. This reads at first like the rigid form of exclusivism to which Hick so strongly objects. The reality is rather more nuanced. Distinguishing between the more spiritual perception of the *Sufi* and the task of the theologian, the one more attuned to the insights of other religions, the other more concerned with doctrinal detail, Legenhausen argues that both in their different ways hold that Islam brings to perfection all that was contained in the previously revealed religions. Non-reductive pluralism, as he calls it, comes close to what Christians have recently retrieved from an earlier tradition: that it is possible for a person to be saved by the grace of God even though what both traditions would uphold as the strict obligations of faith and practice are not fulfilled. The principle that no one can place any limit on the extent of the grace of God, common to both Catholic Christianity and Shi'a Islam, has about it a universalist generosity towards the other which makes the strictures of the threefold paradigm feel distinctly otiose.

Buddhism, as a non-theistic tradition, works with very different principles from those found in Christianity or Islam. Nevertheless similar religious instincts towards the other are discernible within both the Theravada and Mahayana traditions. In her account of Buddhist attitudes to religious others, Kristin Beise Kiblinger outlines various moves and strategies which illustrate a typically Buddhist form of accommodation to the religious claims of other traditions (2005). The Buddha himself warns against 'unskilful' forms of dogmatic attachment; other ways and practices are to be judged by what is 'profitable' or 'unprofitable' for enlightenment. No absolute distinction is possible, therefore, between the Dharma taught by the Buddha and what other teachers may say. In so far as their teaching coheres with the values inherent in the Noble Eightfold Path they are approved. The Buddha's teaching is always adapted to the needs of particular individuals. The famous boat metaphor, in which religious doctrines are likened to a raft which should be dumped once the river has been crossed, is a reminder that the form which Buddhist teachings takes makes them, as Paul Griffiths neatly puts it, 'instruments for transformation' rather than 'descriptions of reality' (1990b:137). The key is the concept of *upaya*, 'skilful means', that form of wisdom-and-compassion which the Buddhist cultivates in order to adapt the Dharma to different circumstances. Such an enlightened one can turn 'other' ideas and concepts, stories and parables, from their original context to some sort of preliminary to the fullness of the Dharma. Thus other ways can be considered as temporary stages, to be ranked like so many further lives which lead eventually to the final Nirvana. Just as the teachings of Upanisadic sages about ethical responsibility may be accepted, so the theistic teaching of Islam or Christianity may be approved as a proximate, if ultimately inadequate, version of Dharma. In the language of the *Samaññaphala Sutta*, the 'fruits' of other ways form a sort of hierarchy as the seeker after Dharma moves closer to the goal.

Nevertheless, this is very far from a Buddhist version of the systemic 'inclusivism' which normative pluralism attributes to Catholic Christianity. Kiblinger shows that there are any number of versions of what is, more exactly, an expression of the Buddhist conviction that all positions are ultimately 'empty'. The Middle Way avoids all extremes and all dogmatism. But that is not to say that Buddhism is just one teaching among others. Rather it transcends all views with 'a qualitative leap' (2005:52). In the light of this logic even the Dalai Lama, who often appears like a genial pluralist, is committed to the ultimate superiority of Buddhism (his 'pluralist-exclusivism' is analysed with great clarity in D'Costa 2000:72–95). Only the one who follows the teaching of the Buddha *to the end* can reach final enlightenment. In the final analysis, the *Buddhadharma* is non-negotiable and may not be reduced to the level of other teachings. For all its ethos of anti-dogmatic benign accommodation, Buddhism has its own specificity or 'difference'.

Non-reductive pluralism

In this chapter I have tried to make two main points. The first is to note the disconnect between theory and practice. Normative pluralism claims to provide a comprehensive yet tradition-neutral account of human religiosity, but fails to address the key question of the part religion plays in achieving a sense of self, let alone in maintaining identity under pressure from the other. Its rhetoric underscores the neuralgic points in interreligious relations but provides few resources for addressing them; tolerance *alone* is surely not enough to promote proper understanding of different faith communities or overcome the legacy of centuries of religiously inspired violence. I have, therefore, shifted attention to the communities of faith themselves and argued, with examples from the three great 'world religions' (those which are consciously concerned with promoting a truth for all people) that it is not just mainstream Christianity which is concerned to safeguard and articulate its sense of identity. This is the second point: a plea that outsiders (whether students of religion or practitioners from another faith tradition) try to understand religious traditions *as the insiders view them*. Islam and Buddhism as much as Christianity have few doubts about their own primacy over other traditions.

Is this just proof of religion's imperviousness to reason – the inevitable result of human intransigence? Is it likely to decrease with the growth of a globalised secularism? Will the harsher edges of religion be softened by the more acceptable forms of 'spirituality'? Or will harder economic climes cause religious communities to withdraw further into themselves? These are questions which are touched on elsewhere in this book. One thing is clear. Religions have been around for centuries and have constantly shifted and changed as they interact with each other. Alongside the virtues which have grown from a sense of loyalty and faithfulness to tradition, religion has developed less defensive strategies which seek to accommodate and adapt to the world of the other. With its focus on values of respect and openness the pluralist move has made its own contribution in this direction. The problem, however, is that it does little more than impose an artificial unity on an area of human endeavour and interaction which steadfastly resists such reduction. The alternative is to return to the wisdom of the religions themselves. As Jonathan Sacks puts it, in arguing for the 'Dignity of Difference', the remedy for tribalism does not have to be a bland universalism (2003). A dialogical non-reductive pluralism, which takes the truths and values of different faith communities with the utmost seriousness and seeks always to *learn* from them, may offer a better way forward.

Summary points

This chapter raises the following issues:

- religious pluralism as a normative and philosophically coherent account of the diversity of religions and cultures;
- the plausibility of the normative hypothesis and its presuppositions;
- the danger of reducing 'religion' to some generic essence and the obscuring of the complexity and richness of 'the religions';
- the impossibility of a comprehensive yet neutral account of religious diversity;
- a 'tradition-specific' account of the significance of religious pluralism and the meaning of what is 'other';
- the response of Christianity, Islam and Buddhism to other communities of faith;
- a practice of various forms of dialogue rooted not in *a priori* theory but emerging from practice and spirituality.

Bibliography

Aslan, Adnan (1998), *Religious Pluralism in Christian and Islamic Philosophy: the Thought of John Hick and Seyyed Hossein Nasr*, Richmond: Curzon.

Barnes, Michael (2002), *Theology and the Dialogue of Religions*, Cambridge, Cambridge University Press.

—— (2005), 'Theology of Religions' in Arthur Holder (ed.), *The Blackwell Companion to Christian Spirituality*, Oxford, Blackwell.

Byrne, Peter (1995), *Prolegomena to Religious Pluralism*, Basingstoke: Macmillan.

Cantwell Smith, Wilfred (1978), *The Meaning and End of Religion*, London: SPCK.

—— (1981), *Towards a World Theology*, Philadelphia, PA: Westminster.

Cheetham, David (2003), *John Hick: a Critical Introduction and Reflection*, Aldershot: Ashgate.

Clooney, Francis (1993), *Theology After Vedanta: an Experiment in Comparative Theology*, Albany, NY: SUNY Press.

—— (2001), *Hindu God Christian God*, Oxford: Oxford University Press.

—— (2008), *Beyond Compare*, Washington. DC: Georgetown University Press.

Cohn-Sherbok, Daniel (1994), *Judaism and Other Faiths*, London: Macmillan.

Cottingham, John (2005), *The Spiritual Dimension: Religion, Philosophy and Human Values*, Cambridge: Cambridge University Press.

Cragg, Kenneth (2002), *Am I Not Your Lord? Human Meaning in Divine Questioning*, London: Melisende.

—— (2004), *The Tragic in Islam*, London: Melisende.

D'Costa, Gavin (ed.) (1987), *John Hick's Theology of Religions, a Critical Evaluation*, Lanham, MD: University Press of America.

—— (1990a), *Religious Uniqueness Reconsidered: the Myth of a Pluralistic Theology of Religions*, Maryknoll, NY: Orbis.

—— (1990b), 'Taking Other Religions Seriously: Some Ironies in the Current Debate on a Christian Theology of Religions, *The Thomist*, 54; pp. 519–529.

—— (1996), 'The Impossibility of a Pluralist View of Religions', *Religious Studies*, 32; pp. 223–232.

—— (2000), *The Meeting of Religions and the Trinity*, Edinburgh: T and T Clark.

di Noia, Joseph (1992), *The Diversity of Religions: A Christian Perspective*, Washington, DC: Catholic University of America Press.

Dupuis, Jacques (1997), *Toward a Christian Theology of Religious Pluralism*, Maryknoll, NY: Orbis.

—— (2002), *Christianity and the Religions: From Confrontation to Dialogue*, Maryknoll, NY: Orbis.

Fitzgerald, Michael and Borelli, John (2006), *Interfaith Dialogue: a Catholic View*, London: SPCK.

Ford, David (ed.) (1997), *The Modern Theologians*, Oxford: Blackwell.

—— (2006), 'An Interfaith Wisdom: Scriptural Reasoning between Jews, Christians and Muslims', *Modern Theology*, 22.3, July, 2006; pp. 345–366.

Foucault, Michel (1972), *The Archaeology of Knowledge*, New York: Harper and Row.

Griffith-Dickson, Gwen (2005), *Philosophy of Religion*, London: SCM.

Griffiths, Paul (1990a), *An Apology for Apologetics: a Study in the Logic of Inter-religious Dialogue*, Maryknoll, NY: Orbis.

—— (1990b), *Christianity through Non-Christian Eyes*, Maryknoll, NY: Orbis.

—— (2001), *Problems of Religious Diversity*, Oxford: Blackwell.

Halbfass, Wilhelm (1988), *India and Europe: an Essay in Understanding*, Albany: State University of New York Press.

Harrison, Peter (1990), *'Religion' and the Religions in the English Enlightenment*, Cambridge: Cambridge University Press.

Heim, S. Mark (2001), *The Depth of the Riches*, Grand Rapids: Eerdmans.

Hewitt, Harold (ed.) (1991), *Problems in the Philosophy of Religion: Critical Studies of the Work of John Hick*, Basingstoke: Macmillan.

Hick, John (1973), *God and the Universe of Faiths*, London: Macmillan.

—— (1977), *God and the Universe of Faiths*, London: Fount.

—— (1980a), *God has Many Names*, London: Macmillan.

—— (1980b), 'Whatever Path Men Choose is Mine', in Hick and Brian Hebblethwaite (eds), *Christianity and Other Religions: Selected Readings*, London: Fount.

—— (1989), *An Interpretation of Religion*, Basingstoke: Macmillan.

Hick, John and Knitter, Paul (eds) (1987), *The Myth of Christian Uniqueness*, London: SCM.

Jackson, Roger and Makransky, John (2000), *Buddhist Theology*, Richmond: Curzon.

Kaplan, Stephen (2002), *Different Paths, Different Summits: A Model for Religious Pluralism*, Lanham, MD: Rowman and Littlefield.

Kärkkäinen, Veli-Matti (2004), *Trinity and Religious Pluralism*, Aldershot: Ashgate.

Kiblinger, Kristin Beise (2005), *Buddhist Inclusivism: Attitudes Towards Religious Others*, Aldershot: Ashgate.

Knitter, Paul (1995), *One Earth Many Religions: Multifaith Dialogue and Global Responsibility*, Maryknoll, NY: Orbis.

Lash, Nicholas (1996), *The Beginning and the End of 'Religion'*, Cambridge: Cambridge University Press.

Legenhausen, Muhammad (1999), *Islam and Religious Pluralism*, London: Al-Hoda.

Loughlin, Gerard (1990), 'Prefacing Pluralism: John Hick and the Mastery of Religion', *Modern Theology*, 7.1; pp. 29–55.

McGrane, Bernard (1989), *Beyond Anthropology: Society and the Other*, New York: Columbia University Press.

MacIntyre, Alasdair (2nd ed. 1985), *After Virtue*, London: Duckworth.

Marty, Martin (2005), *When Faiths Collide*, Oxford: Blackwell.

Mathewes, Charles T. (1998), 'Pluralism, Otherness and the Augustinian Tradition', *Modern Theology*, 14.1; pp. 83–112.

May, John D'Arcy (1998), *Pluralism and the Religions: the Theological and Political Dimension*, London: Cassell.

Milbank, John (1990), 'The End of Dialogue', in *Christian Uniqueness Reconsidered*, edited by Gavin D'Costa, Maryknoll, NY: Orbis; pp. 174–91.

Ogden, Schubert (1992), *Is There Only One True Religion or Are There Many?* Dallas: Southern Methodist University Press.

O'Leary, Joseph S. (1996), *Religious Pluralism and Christian Truth*, Edinburgh: Edinburgh University Press.

Panikkar, Raimon (1973), *The Trinity and the Religious Experience of Man*, London: Darton, Longman and Todd.

—— (1978), *The Intra-religious Dialogue*, New York: Paulist.

—— (1981), *The Unknown Christ of Hinduism*, London: Darton, Longman and Todd.

—— (1984), *Myth, Faith and Hermeneutics*, Bangalore: Asian Trading Corporation.

—— (1993), *The Cosmotheandric Experience*, Maryknoll, NY: Orbis.

Pickstock, Catherine (1998), *After Writing: on the Liturgical Consummation of Philosophy*, Oxford: Blackwell.

Pieris, Aloysius (1989), *An Asian Theology of Liberation*, Edinburgh: T & T Clark.

—— (2004), *Prophetic Humour in Buddhism and Christianity*, Colombo: Ecumenical Institute.

Ramachandra, Vinoth (1996), *The Recovery of Mission*, Carlisle: Paternoster.

Rowe, William (1999), 'Religious Pluralism', *Religious Studies*, 35; pp. 129–150.

Sacks, Jonathan (revised edn 2003), *The Dignity of Difference*, London: Continuum.

Saldanha, Chrys (1984), *Divine Pedagogy: a Patristic View of Non-Christian Religions*, Rome: Libreria Ateneo Salesiano.

Schuon, Frithjof (1975), *The Transcendent Unity of Religions*, New York: Harper and Row.

Smart, Ninian (1989), *The World's Religions*, Cambridge: Cambridge University Press.

Smith, Jonathan Z. (1998), 'Religion, Religions, Religious', in *Critical Terms for Religious Studies*, edited by Mark C. Taylor, Chicago: Chicago University Press; pp. 269–284.

Sullivan, Francis (1992), *No Salvation Outside the Church? Tracing the History of the Catholic Response*, London: Chapman.

Surin, Kenneth (1990), 'A Certain "Politics of Speech": "Religious Pluralism" in the Age of the McDonald's Hamburger', *Modern Theology*, 7.1; pp. 67–100.

Swidler, Leonard (ed.) (1987), *Toward a Universal Theology of Religion*, Maryknoll, NY: Orbis.

—— (ed.) (1990), *Death or Dialogue? From the Age of Monologue to the Age of Dialogue*, London: SCM.

Talal Asad (1993), *Genealogies of Religion*, Baltimore: Johns Hopkins University Press.

Toulmin, Stephen (1990), *Cosmopolis: the Hidden Agenda of Modernity*, Chicago: Chicago University Press.

Tracy, David (1981), *The Analogical Imagination: Christian Theology and the Culture of Pluralism*, London: SCM.

—— (1990), *Dialogue with the Other: the Inter-religious Dialogue*, Louvain: Peeters Press; Grand Rapids: Eerdmans.

—— (1994), *On Naming the Present: God, Hermeneutics and Church*, Maryknoll, NY: Orbis.

Troeltsch, Ernst (1921), *The Absoluteness of Christianity and the History of Religions*, SCM: London.

Wainwright, William (2nd ed. 1999), *Philosophy of Religion*, Belmont, CA: Wadsworth.

Ward, Keith (1990), 'Truth and the Diversity of Religions', *Religious Studies*, 26; pp. 1–18.

Williams, Rowan (2000), *On Christian Theology*, Oxford: Blackwell.

Yandell, Keith (1999), *Philosophy of Religion*, London: Routledge.

Suggested reading

Barnes, Michael (2002), *Theology and the Dialogue of Religions*, Cambridge, Cambridge University Press.
   Outlining the terms of a theology of dialogue.

Cheetham, David (2003), *John Hick: a Critical Introduction and Reflection*, Aldershot: Ashgate.
   Accessible, straightforward yet judicious overview of Hick's philosophy of religion.

Clooney, Francis (1993), *Theology After Vedanta: an Experiment in Comparative Theology*, Albany, NY: SUNY Press.
   One of the first examples of the author's approach to comparative theology with excellent introduction.

Cottingham, John (2005), *The Spiritual Dimension: Religion, Philosophy and Human Values*, Cambridge: Cambridge University Press.
   A refreshingly different approach to the 'traditional' topics of philosophy of religion.

Dupuis, Jacques (2002), *Christianity and the Religions: From Confrontation to Dialogue*, Maryknoll, NY: Orbis.
   Catholic theology of religions.

Griffiths, Paul (1990), *Christianity through Non-Christian Eyes*, Maryknoll, NY: Orbis.
   Invaluable collection of texts on Christianity from other faith perspectives.

Griffith-Dickson, Gwen (2005), *Philosophy of Religion*, London: SCM.
   Unique approach to philosophy of religion from a consciously interreligious angle.

Hick, John (1989), *An Interpretation of Religion*, Basingstoke: Macmillan.
   The most important of all Hick's texts on religious pluralism.

Part 3

Religions in the modern world

Chapter 26

Religion and politics

George Moyser

One of the most interesting features of the study of religion in recent years has been the resurgence of interest in its relationship with the political world. Many scholars now recognize that earlier assumptions, at least in Western academic circles, about the fading of religion from political life have not been borne out (Westerlund 1996). To the contrary, instead of a gradual marginalization and privatization of religion, in many parts of the world the opposite has occurred. Even in the West, religion has retained or even reasserted its presence in public debate, not least in the United States.

The result has been a substantial reassessment of the relationship of religion and politics in the modern world. Studies have appeared examining the way in which religious phenomena – ideas, symbols, individuals, institutions – influence the whole system of governance at local, national and international levels. Equally, attention is now being given to the ways in which the political system – leaders and institutions – respond to these religious claims. In short, the issue of the relationship between religion and politics is now a matter of serious academic attention. There is a growing recognition that religion and politics are not now, and in fact never have been, separate and hermetically sealed spheres of human thought and action. In the modern world, albeit in different ways from earlier times, religion and politics continue to combine in important ways to shape the public arena in which the many issues about the human predicament are debated and acted upon.

'Religion' and 'politics'

The intertwining of religion and politics, both as a descriptive reality and as a subject for prescriptive reflection, has an exceedingly long history that extends back to the earliest eras of intellectual discussion. This reflects the inherent qualities of 'religion' and 'politics' that seemingly inevitably drive them together into a complex, varied and dynamic relationship. From an historical point of view, as Finer points out, in the earliest times, religion formed part of a 'vast cosmology … into which all things are fitted' (Finer 1997: 23). This cosmology included matters religious, having to do with the divine, and matters political, having to do with the exercise of power. Within this context, those who monopolized political power also typically claimed religious authority. This arrangement appears, in various forms, in many ruler cults and sacral kingdoms across the ancient Middle East, Asia, and South America, as well as in Hellenistic Greece and Imperial Rome. In this way, a pattern evolved bringing religion into the most intimate association with politics, the two forming a single or monistic whole.

With the advent of historical religions, such as Judaism, Islam, Buddhism and Christianity, a more complex pattern began to emerge. Here, the religious sphere was gradually differentiated as being concerned with a supernatural order associated with the divine, as distinguished from a secular and natural order associated with mortal humanity. In short, a cosmological dualism appeared. Now, religious activity and belief began to carry with it the idea that there was a higher and better reality above and beyond ordinary reality to which all were in principle subject, including the king, the wielder of political power within that natural order. Thus there arose the possibility for some separation between the religious and political spheres, but also the possibility of tension and rivalry. For in articulating the imperatives of the divine and supernatural, the religious sphere prescribed specific values and behaviours within what was viewed as a subordinate order. In response, there emerged a variety of religio-political patterns. Some entailed very close relationships indeed where each supported and reinforced the claims of the other, or at least an accommodation was reached not to undermine the other's position. In other contexts, an adversarial pattern developed whereby religion provided an institutional framework or ideological rationale for political revolution or reform by invoking the superiority of the divine and supernatural reality.

Within and between the two, many variations have arisen in the course of human history, as all the major religions have had a concern for the political realm. In so doing, of course, this has led the political realm to have a concern for religion. This dialectic has been particularly intense where the religious sphere has articulated its concerns through specific institutions such as churches, temples, mosques and synagogues, and expressed them through religious functionaries such as rabbis, mullahs, monks or priests. How all this worked out in specific historical patterns has been the intent of scholars through the ages to understand and explain, or to advocate for particular idealized relationships.

Religion and politics in the pre-modern period

In the lengthy era between the advent of the historical religions and modern times, much was written about the relationship between religion and politics, largely of a prescriptive variety. Religion loomed large in the wider culture and society and hence its manifestations were of considerable moment for the political realm.

In Judaism, a very substantial tradition exists of reflection on ideal political relationships from a religious perspective. These have their origins in the understandings of the nature and role of politics and religion as set out by the authors of the Hebrew Bible. Those authors were writing for a people who felt themselves in a close relationship with the divine and formed a community which, for much of its history, had a degree of political autonomy. As a result, much was written about the way that political life should be ordered, political affairs conducted, public policies formed and rulers rule (see Bauckham 1989). Fundamental was the idea that God was the sole creative source of all reality, supernatural and natural, and had entered into a special relationship with the people through a covenant, spelt out in laws set out in the Pentateuch, that governed all aspects of life, religious, social, economic and political. Provision was made, in other words, for a very close and intimate relationship between the religious sphere and the political. Indeed, the notion of the divine covenant was the main principle of cohesion for what was otherwise a relatively loosely articulated tribal confederation. Political power was exercised in different specific forms, an assembly of adult males in earlier times, judges and kings later. But all operated within a framework that was substantially religious. Kings, however, were not of the pharaonic type – they were primarily secular political figures confirmed and legitimated by religiously conveyed gifts. This in turn allowed some prophetic writers to be highly critical of the way in which kingly political leadership was undertaken.

Later Jewish political organization and prescriptive political writing built on this tradition. Ben Joseph Gaon Saadiah (882–942), for example, set out prescriptive principles for Jewish life, in his *Book of Beliefs and Opinions* (1948), which sustained the idea of the Torah as the appropriate framework for a Jewish political constitution (see Elazar and Cohen 1985). Later still, other Jewish writers such as Moses Maimonides (1135–1204) advocated a form of prophetic political leadership. The common pattern of such writings, however, is the idea of a nation or community that was both political and religious, thereby closely interweaving religious and political ideas within one overarching system of thought.

The immediate context for writings in the Christian tradition was the presence of the Roman Empire, bitterly resented by many Jews. Within this emerged a Galilean Jew, Jesus, with remarkable gifts as a prophet and teacher whose attacks on established Jewish religious codes embroiled him in political as well as religious controversy. Some scholars, indeed, have cast him pre-eminently as a political revolutionary (Brandon 1967). From the New Testament record, however, his political views were essentially accommodationist, or neutralist, rather than adversarial. He is depicted as espousing a certain separation between politics and religion, and as expressing little direct interest in political affairs, and certainly not as encouraging nationalistic rebellion against the Romans.

In this vein, early Christian writings, represented by Paul (Romans 13: 1–13) and Peter (1 Peter: 2–3), reflect a fundamentally positive, or at least neutral, view of the Roman state (Cullmann 1957). Their concerns were with an 'other-worldly' agenda of conversion and awaiting the *Parousia*, Christ's soon-expected second coming. In this framework, mundane politics played little part. But, as the Church spread and grew, it increasingly attracted the attention of the governmental authorities as an unauthorized and potentially seditionist association. Some interpret passages in the Book of Revelation as cryptic responses to the persecution of the Church under Nero and Domitian (Rev. 17: 3–6, 18). As such attacks were periodically renewed, Christian writers such as Justin Martyr sought to explain and defend the Church, attacking the injustice and irrationality of the state in punishing believers. These 'apologists' claimed that the Church was not seeking to undermine Roman authority but looked to promote peace and decency in building 'God's Kingdom'. Their posture, in short, was largely apolitical and pacifist (Bainton 1960: 53–84) but, as in other historical and religious contexts, this does not always produce a policy of neutralism or benign neglect on the part of government.

In any event, the whole context changed radically with the coming to power of Constantine. In contrast to his predecessor Diocletian who had pursued a policy of persecution under Constantine (312–37), the State and Church entered into a most intimate and mutually supportive relationship (Armstrong 1993). In short, there emerged in Western culture the model of the sacralized Christian polity, or 'Christendom', which has provided the framework for debates about Church–State relations ever since, not least in the United States where public religious observances and favourable tax treatment of religious groups, for example, remain topics of public debate.

Reactions to this Constantinian settlement varied. Eusebius of Caesarea (c.260–c.340) occupies an important place as perhaps the first Christian political theologian in that his central problem was to expound the virtues of a Christianized civilization and polity. To him, the close association of Church and Empire allowed for the possibility of realizing the image of the heavenly city on earth (Cranz 1993). In practice, however, by espousing Christianity, Constantine had moved to co-opt and control the Church for his own political purposes. In reaction, St Gelasius, Pope from 492 to 496, developed his notion of 'two swords', one to the emperor as a symbol of secular power, but the other to the Pope and Church as a symbol of spiritual authority. Indeed, he not only denied that secular power could be exerted over the Church, but also asserted the superiority of the ecclesiastical power to the civil, in the tradition of Israelite theocracy (Ziegler 1942). As such, his writings became the basis for later medieval papal claims to both religious and political authority – to hold both swords simultaneously.

Yet another response came from St Augustine of Hippo (354–430) in his celebrated *De Civitate Dei* (On the City of God). This, however, was heavily influenced by an Empire already falling into disarray with the collapse of Rome before the pagan Visigoths in 410. Augustine posited two 'cities', the 'City of God', which entails the establishment of a perfect peace and justice through fellowship with God, and a 'City of man', instanced for Augustine by the Roman Empire. Rooted, in his view, in materialism, violence and injustice, the 'City of man' can never be the subject of Christian sacralization. At best it is capable of only a partial and temporary good. As such, his position on Church–State relations was a mixed one, advocating what might be called a semi-accommodationist posture.

The theocratic claims of the medieval papacy in their turn produced a reaction, most notably perhaps in the writings of Marsilius (or Marsiglio) of Padua (c.1275–1342). In his *Defensor Pacis* (1522), he argued that it was the State, not the Church, which should be the unifying presence in society. Indeed, the Church should be subordinated to the State, not the other way around, with the Church's decisions made through conciliar, rather than Papal, institutions. However, by this period, the whole medieval religio-political system was beginning to break down by the onset of the Reformation and the emergence of secular national political power.

What was unleashed was a whole range of arrangements and prescriptions about the relationship of Christianity to politics. On the one hand, in the Lutheran and Anglican traditions, close relationships were advocated with the Church typically subordinated to the State. This is known as Erastianism after the Swiss theologian Thomas Erastus who defended the supremacy of the secular power in his *Ecclesiastical Polity* (1594). But the Reformation also gave rise to more radical ideas about Church–State patterns. Calvin's political views, for example, influenced developments in many parts of Protestant Europe including Scotland, England and Holland that in turn influenced Puritan politics in New England and later the founding of the American republic (Kelly 1992). What all of this demonstrates is that, within the historic Christian tradition, a wide variety of Church–State patterns have been both advocated and institutionalized. These range from a monistic closeness and accommodation, on the one hand, to a dualistic tension and even adversarial separation, on the other, representing a diversity that persists through to the modern period.

The other major historical religions also developed distinctive views about the political realm. In traditional Islam, its core idea was the sovereignty of God over the entire community (the *Ummah Wahida*), manifested in public witness through prayer, fasting, tithing and pilgrimage. In other words, it emphasized a whole way of life embracing all facets of society, both 'religious' and 'political'. As such, the Islamic tradition is analogous to biblical Judaism in that the two spheres, though distinguishable in principle, are in practice brought into a very close monistic relationship. Governing that relationship is a body of Holy Scripture (the *Qur'an*) and a body of sacred law (the *sharia*).

Over the centuries since Muhammad (c.570–632), a number of writers developed these ideas in various ways. Ibn Khaldun (1332–1406), in his *Muqaddimah*, for example, argued that political rule was not *directly* drawn from divine sources, but arose from social solidarity within the *ummah* (Gibb 1962). Thus, while not espousing theocracy, he nevertheless saw a close relationship of politics, religion and law through their common roots in the *ummah*. Ahmad Ibn Taimiyya (1263–1328), on the other hand, developed a more direct and superordinate relationship between Islam and politics in which the *Qur'an*, the *sharia*, and *hadith* (collections of Muhammad's sayings and actions) provided the framework for government. For Taimiyya, religion provided legitimacy to Islamic rulers while the state provided security and protection to the religious authorities. His ideas have since inspired the political ideas of modern Islamic religious leaders such as Hasan al-Banna (1906–49), founder of the Muslim Brethren movement, Abu-l-Ala al-Mawdoodi (1903–79) who established Pakistan's Islamic Party and, not least, Ruholla Musavi Khomeini (1902–89), who inaugurated a theocratic system of government in Iran in 1979.

Buddhism also has a lengthy history of close entanglements with the political sphere. Buddha was himself, according to tradition, a political leader from Northern India who turned to an ascetic lifestyle and developed a set of teachings or truths about human existence (the *Dharma*). Critically, for its relationship with the political realm, Buddha attracted a set of followers, or 'sons', committed to the 'Noble Eightfold Path', a disciplined way of attaining the Buddhist ideal of Nirvana. These monks or clergy, known as the *Sangha*, formed the core of Buddhism as an institutionalized religion. However, Buddha's emphasis on ascetic detachment from worldly possessions led the *Sangha* into dependency on worldly leaders with wealth and power to provide them support. Thus in Buddhist societies too there arose a close and mutually supportive relationship between the religious and political domains. The religious sphere, the *Sangha*, provided political rulers with moral legitimacy while the political rulers provided Buddhist clergy with protection.

Such arrangements emerged in areas of South and Southeast Asia where Buddhism gained ascendancy. The earliest model is provided in India by Asoka who provided patronage to the *sangha* during his rule from 270 to 230 BCE. It was further realized elsewhere, notably in Ceylon (Sri Lanka), Burma (Myanmar), Siam (Thailand) and Tibet. In Sri Lanka, for example, a Buddhist dynasty was, according to tradition, established by Asoka's son and survived until its abolition by British colonialist intervention in 1815. But the tradition of a close association between Buddhism and polity has remained and become a major element within modern Sinhalese nationalism (see Smith 1978).

Similarly close ties developed in Tibet where Mahayana Buddhism became the central motif of political rule. Tibetan rulers came together with religious leaders (lamas) in a close system of mutual accommodation. The Dalai Lama emerged as the most powerful among the latter to become a cornerstone of state rule in Lhasa, the Tibetan capital, from the seventeenth century onwards. Until the arrival of the Communist Chinese after the 1949 Revolution, Buddhist monks formed a core part of Tibetan government, with the Dalai Lama acting as spiritual guide to the lay political leadership. Not surprisingly, therefore, after his flight to India in 1959, Tenzin Gyatso, the fourteenth Dalai Lama (1935–), set up a Tibetan government-in-exile, upholding Tibetan culture and the traditional association of Buddhism with the exercise of political power (see Goldstein 1989).

In Hinduism, the religion of some 800 million adherents mainly in India, there is also a tradition of very close associations with the political realm. Indeed, as in Islamic and Buddhist thought, Hinduism sees no clear distinction between the two. Both are part of a common overarching set of cultural assumptions. Politics is seen as a moral activity and morality is a matter of religion. Hence, religion has a legitimate claim over the political order. In Hindu thought, this comes about through the concept of the *purushartha* – that all action should conform to a set of moral or spiritual values that form the controlling framework for individual economic, social and political pursuits.

Such traditions, set out in classical Hindu texts as the *Arthashastra* of Kautilya from around 300 BCE, provided the basis for Hindu princely states right down to the modern period of British colonial rule. They also informed Hindu revivalist movements in the nineteenth century, such as the *Arya Samaj*, or Society of the Aryas, founded in 1876, which helped establish the Indian nationalist movement. Subsequent writers such as Bankimchandra Chattopadhyay (1839–94) and Bal Gangadhar Tilak (1856–1920) explicitly used religious ideas to link Hindu resurgence with political aspiration (see Jones 1989). And, of course, Mohandas K. Gandhi, who led the independence movement in the twentieth century, was himself a deeply spiritual Hindu and espoused a strong personal moral code as the basis for his political activity (see Parekh 1989).

What these historical circumstances reveal is a common pattern in which religion, be it Jewish, Christian, Islamic, Buddhist or Hindu, has typically, but not uniformly, maintained a prescriptive claim over the workings of the political sphere. Similarly, such claims have aroused strong political responses, again often resulting in the religious sphere being drawn within the orbit of the state. As such, in the pre-modern period, there is a wide, indeed global, pattern of intense if varying relationships between the religious and the political in which at times any demarcation between the two seems hard to discern. It is in the context of that legacy that the relationship between religion and politics in the modern period must be situated.

Religion and politics in the modern period

Amidst all the immense changes that mark off the modern context, religion still continues its claim to political relevance as the prescriptive arbiter of political and public morality and the repository of received, indeed, divinely inspired wisdom. Indeed, there has been much in the history of modern politics that has provoked, and continues to provoke, an affirmation of that claim. The scale and destructive capacity of modern warfare, the invention of nuclear weapons, the experience of the Holocaust and ethnic cleansing, the invention of new medical reproductive technologies, the recent phenomenon of global warming, the chronic disparities of material conditions within and between societies, are all examples of issues that have evoked a strong religious concern for the direction of public policy. Not least, the modern phenomenon of secularization has itself provoked a political response from the religious sphere. The whole movement of fundamentalism has been seen as a confrontation by traditionalists of those believed to be responsible for replacing a religious moral framework for politics and government by one that is humanistic and materialistic, and therefore, in their view, anti-religious (see Marty and Appleby 1991 and 1995).

Christian fundamentalism has been a significant presence in the United States throughout the twentieth century. First emerging in response to Darwin's evolutionist ideas, the movement's political influence rose but then declined following the 1925 Scopes Monkey Trial in Tennessee. Until the 1960s, fundamentalists focused on building up educational and media institutions within their sub-culture. Then, with the rise of new issues evidencing a further erosion of the traditional religious and moral fabric of public life in the banning of prayer in public (state) schools by the Supreme Court in 1962–3, and the legalization of abortion on demand in 1973, they re-entered the political arena led initially by Jerry Falwell's Moral Majority. Since then, Christian fundamentalism has been a significant political and electoral presence, forming an important part of the Republican Party's base and motivated most recently by the question of legalizing same-sex marriage.

In taking, generally speaking, a strictly literalist and inerrant view of Holy Scripture, emphasizing being 'born again' as a marker of faith, and adopting uncompromisingly conservative political stances, Christian fundamentalists form at best a large minority of America's Protestant constituency, and far less than that in other Western countries. Nevertheless, there is no doubt that, contrary to the expectations of many scholars, it is a form of politicized religion that maintains a wide appeal (see Wilcox 1996).

Fundamentalist religious perspectives also have had a significant resonance within a number of contemporary Islamic countries (see Esposito 1997). Here, they have been associated with political opposition to the uncritical importation and adoption of Western secular values, which are viewed as having corrupted the community. Hence, to Muslim fundamentalists, what is needed is a rigorous re-establishment of Islamic law (Qur'an and Shari'a) as the sole framework for national political life. In pursuing such goals, they have been viewed on the one hand as passionate and dedicated believers but, on the other hand, they have also been seen as legalistic, intolerant, and authoritarian.

Such perspectives were first articulated by Hasan al-Banna who decried Western influence in Egyptian culture in the inter-war period. Through the Muslim Brotherhood, his ideas have since spread throughout the Islamic world to countries such as Pakistan, Algeria and Afghanistan. But perhaps their most enduring and notable resonance has been seen in the regime established in Iran by Ayatollah Khomeini in replacement of the modernizing leadership of the shahs. Under their rule, a French-based legal code was substituted for the Shari'a and the educational system partly secularized. Khomeini then led a revolution in 1979 that brought him to power as 'Supreme Leader' and enabled him to put into effect his traditional Islamic ideas, set out in his Islam and Revolution (1981). To him, Islamic teaching demanded the merging of religion and politics and the establishment of a theocratic state. In this way, in Iran as in many other countries, fundamentalism has been a major modality for religion's seeking a central place in contemporary politics and public life.

The present era has also seen the development of a renewed relationship between Christianity and the political sphere through 'political theology' (Forrester 1988). Its founder was Johannes B. Metz whose Theology of the World (1969) was an attempt to correct the privatizing influence of modern Western culture which had led, in his view, to a neglect of the public and political sphere in favour of the private and individual. It also was an attempt to provide a faith-based assessment of the basic precepts that should govern the public pronouncements of religious institutions and leaders. For Metz, the Church has always been a political force in history and to him all theology, being in part a critique of the 'political implicatedness' of the Church, is necessarily political. In the past, he argued, the Church allowed itself to become politically engaged too uncritically with Constantinian Christendom being not the outcome of an evangelizing imperative but the product of a process of co-optation by the state presented as if it were the will of God. Similar but more contemporary examples of the potential for the political exploitation of Christianity can be found in Nazi Germany, in apartheid South Africa and even perhaps, in a democratic context, the association of evangelicals with the political Right in the United States. In the latter case, what such Christians see as the political expression of authentic religious commitments can also be viewed as a conservative political coalition co-opting religion to legitimate its power-seeking goals.

Religiously-inspired critiques of political arrangements have also arisen in a number of other strands of Christian thought, notable examples being black theology (Cone 1975) and feminist theology (Ruether 1983) both of which have been influential in shaping new understandings of racial and gender issues in America. Those understandings have focused around the theme of liberation, which has itself become a significant theological and political current in its own right. The term 'liberation theology' originated in Latin America with the publication of A Theology of Liberation by Gustavo Gutiérrez (1974). With Bonino, Segundo, Boff and others, a powerful and radical religious critique of economic and social conditions was developed, focused on a commitment to the materially poor and the urgent need for political action to transform a fundamentally unjust society. Through the development of religious and social networks among the non-elite in Latin America called 'base communities' and strategic alliances with Marxist-inspired groups, liberation theology gave a whole new dimension to the way religion engaged with the Latin American political process.

A high-point was the Second General Conference of the Latin American Bishops (CELAM) in Medellín, Colombia in 1968, which approved documents articulating a preferential option for the poor (1970). At the same time, however, it resulted in a clash with conservative religious and political leaders. Indeed, the linkage with Marxist analyses aroused opposition from the Vatican and the late Pope John Paul II whose experience of Communism in his Polish homeland had made him extremely hostile to such associations. For these and other reasons, since then the political impact of liberation theology in Latin America has diminished. Nevertheless, it has left a legacy in providing religious legitimacy for human rights that has resonated in other parts of the world, for example in Asia (Kee 1978: 127–50) and in South Africa.

In the latter case, there was a long history of human rights abuse, racism and oppression through the system of apartheid set up by the Nationalist Party when it came to power in 1948 and legitimated by the (white) Dutch Reformed Church in documents such as *Human Relations and the South African Scene in the Light of Scripture* (1976). Gradually, however, seeing this as a 'pseudo-gospel', religious groups became engaged with the resistance movement led by the African National Congress. Liberationist ideas influenced their contribution, especially in the *Kairos Document* (1985), which rejected both a 'State theology' of support for (white) political authority and a quietist 'Church theology' of focusing exclusively on saving souls. Instead, it called on the churches to engage directly in political action to challenge the satanic evil of apartheid (see Elphrick and Davenport 1997).

Outside of South Africa, however, liberation theology has had only a limited influence in African politics (Gifford 1998: 30). Instead, as in Latin America, Pentecostalism has recently had much greater sway and its political influence has generally been indirect, operating more within the cultural than the political arena (see Martin 1990). In its American roots at the turn of the twentieth century, Pentecostal movements were concerned above all with the imminent end of the world in divine judgement and the consequent need to evangelize (see Bloch-Hoell 1964). As such, Pentecostal Churches, such as the Assemblies of God and the Church of God in Christ, were little concerned with worldly politics.

Since World War II, however, and the non-arrival of judgement day, Pentecostalists became more open to political action, broadly defined. Black Pentecostalists, such as Al Sharpton and Eugene Rivers, stimulated by the 1960s Civil Rights Movement, turned to community involvement, tackling problems of juvenile delinquency and social welfare.

But white Pentecostalists, such as Oral Roberts and Pat Robertson, inclined towards supporting the Christian Right, advocating prayer in public schools, and opposing abortion and homosexuality. It is this latter tradition which has had, through missionary action, a greater influence on the shape of Pentecostalism elsewhere. In Brazil, Guatemala and Chile, for example, Pentecostal leaders have tended to support conservative agendas, although a minority has also associated itself with calls for social and economic justice. In Africa, the 'Faith Gospel' of Kenneth Copeland and Kenneth Hagin has also led to a stress on individualistic and personalized prosperity, this-worldly success through faith now, rather than on any directly political agenda. By default, therefore, it has had a substantially conservative influence.

Of course, the contemporary relationship between religion and politics has not only been influenced by ideas and issues emanating from the religious sphere. Modern political thought has also had an immense influence, not the least being liberalism. Stressing, at its core, the value of liberty and, in particular, a conception of personal freedom from external interference, liberalism provided much of the ideological framework within which Western Church–State relations are now conducted. Through its roots in the Reformation and the Enlightenment, liberalism developed a powerful critique of traditional arrangements. The idea of an established church, for example, was seen in the emergent pluralistic culture as a threat to individual religious freedom. What was needed was a disentangling of Church and State and the creation of a private sphere in which religion could prosper.

These ideas found their strongest expression in the United States where figures such as Thomas Jefferson and James Madison were instrumental in providing for both the disestablishment of churches and the protection of religious freedom in the First Amendment to the Constitution. But, as the decisions of the Supreme Court in subsequent years have made clear, it is an ambiguous and tension-ridden provision. Weber (1998), for example, articulates five distinct interpretations of what separation of Church and State might mean, various combinations of which have been used to justify differing judicial outcomes. Thus, the Court tolerates paid chaplains for Congress and state legislatures, and official prayers at the opening of their daily sessions, but has prohibited similar prayers in state schools. Indeed, the school prayer issue is still alive as the Court continues to strive for a reasoned balance between the twin imperatives of non-establishment and religious freedom. All in all, the whole American model remains much contested, in part for the confusion and uncertainty it has produced, in part for the way it seems in practice to support secularism by restricting a public place for religion which puts in jeopardy the very religious freedom separation is supposed to procure.

Not surprisingly, therefore, other countries have adopted Church–State models based upon neutrality through pluralism rather than neutrality through separation, that is an acceptance by the state of a public role for religion but competing alongside other secular ideas for influence (see Monsma and Soper 1997). At the same time, however, American liberalism has clearly influenced constitutional arrangements concerning religion in many parts of the world including Turkey, India and Japan, all cases where the constitutions have been secularized and religious freedom mandated. Indeed, its pervasive influence is attested to by the rise of fundamentalism.

Marxism represents another modern political ideology that has had a major impact on the relationship between religion and politics. For Marx, the central value was equality, or rather the absence of it within capitalism, which engendered gross inequality, exploitation and alienation. To him, religion was a symptom of more fundamental social and economic problems, it was 'the opium of the people', a form of cultural distortion that veiled a deeper material alienation. Such a fundamental antipathy toward religion led communists in the Soviet Union to espouse a policy of hostile Erastian control over, and restriction of, all public religious activity. Under Stalin, religious liberty was effectively dissolved. All churches had to be registered, public religious education was barred, many seminaries closed and much church property confiscated. The Russian Orthodox Church was reduced to the role of a political puppet (Ramet 1988).

Following the Soviet lead, the communist countries of Eastern Europe adopted similarly hostile state religious policies. Albania became the extreme case with the communist authorities proclaiming the abolition of religion in 1967. But the collapse of communist rule in 1989–91 has led to an institutional revitalization of religion and a renewal of its autonomy and political presence throughout the region. In Russia, the Orthodox Church has sought to provide support and legitimacy for the new regime as well as seeking the reassertion of its traditional privileges amidst the flowering of religious pluralism. In Poland, the Czech Republic and the former East Germany, the churches entered the post-communist era with considerable prestige and influence, having actively assisted in the overthrow of Communist rule. In Romania, Hungary and Bulgaria, however, such was the compliant closeness of the churches' relationship with the communist state that the new political era has been less accommodating.

Meanwhile, the Marxist legacy continues in a number of countries still communist ruled. In Cuba, after the Castro Revolution of 1959, the new regime expelled priests, shut down churches, nationalized private schools and inducted seminarians into the military. And though Church–State tensions have eased in recent years, culminating in a papal visit in 1998, the political authorities still remain wary of any Church comment that might be deemed critical (see Kirk 1989). Similarly in the People's Republic of China, a hostile Erastian religious policy is still largely in place. The State tightly controls religious institutions and restricts religious liberty. Indeed, the Cultural Revolution of 1966–76 led to thousands of religious adherents being jailed or killed. With the subsequent ascent to power of reformists, however, a slightly more liberal approach has gradually been taken. But the recent resurgence of religious activity, notably in the 'Buddhist Law' cult and the *Falun Gong* movement, has ensured that the State still maintains very strict limits on what is permitted. In short, though now muted and even transformed, Marxism retains an important indirect influence over contemporary relationships between religion and politics.

The Enlightenment also gave birth to nationalism which similarly contributes much to current relationships between religion and politics. For nationalism, the central value is 'nationhood' and loyalty to its manifestation in the nation-state. It has witnessed myriad different relationships with the religious sphere. In some cases, nationalism has remained largely secular, for example in Scotland, the Basque Country and Quebec. In other countries, however, religion has been woven into it. In the United States, Christian (and especially Protestant) religious symbols and images have been used to help form a 'civil religion', a political culture in which connections are drawn between national identity and the sacred. These range from mythic religious ideas about America's founding, through religiously defined views of political authority, to religiously informed political rituals and discourse.

In other contexts, religion has clashed violently with secular nationalism and the State by being the basis for a radical form of avowedly religious nationalism. Such has been the outcome in many parts of the Muslim world. For example, in Egypt an attempt was made by the Muslim Brethren to assassinate Gamal Abdel Nasser for his brand of secular nationalism in 1954. A radical offshoot of the Brethren succeeded in killing his successor, President Anwar al-Sadat, in 1981. Similar tense confrontations occurred in Afghanistan where Muslim groups overthrew the communist government in 1992, to then be replaced by the even more radical Taliban who established a strict and autocratic Muslim state (Rashid 2000) that was only overthrown by American military intervention following the terrorist attacks of September 11, 2001. Equally, in the Palestinian territories, a civil war took place following legislative elections in 2006 between Hamas (Islamic Resistance Movement), a movement of militant Muslim nationalists, and the more secular nationalist organization Fatah (Palestine Liberation Organization). The result left Hamas in effective control of the Gaza Strip in 2007 while Fatah was left in charge of Palestinian territory in the West Bank.

In South Asia, religious nationalism is at the root of continuing international tension between Pakistan and India over Kashmir. In India itself, Hindu nationalism has long been a militant force confronting both the religiously accommodationist nationalism of Mohandas K. Gandhi (who was assassinated) and the once-dominant Congress Party he led. In recent years, operating through a cultural organization, the Rashtriya Swayamsevak Sangh, and the powerful Bharatiya Janata Party (Indian People's Party), Hindu nationalists have also been in bloody confrontations with Sikhs in the Punjab, and with Muslims at Ayodya in Northern India (Van der Veer 1994).

Religious nationalism is also an important element in the politics of Israel that arose historically through Zionism, a nineteenth-century movement to attract Jewish settlement in the Biblical Promised Land. While itself largely secular, being rooted in European anti-Semitism and persecution, its religious elements have been represented in modern Israeli electoral politics by the National Religious Party (*Mafdal*) which is dedicated to Israel as a Jewish state – 'the Land of Israel for the People of Israel according to the Torah of Israel' – and by Shas and United Torah Judaism, dedicated to an even more theocratic conception of the Israeli polity. A particularly extreme form of Jewish nationalism was developed by Rabbi Meir Kahane, founder of the now banned Kach Party, who argued for the Torah being the basis for Israeli law and clashed with both secularized Jews and all he perceived to oppose the establishment of a Jewish nation-state. In 1995, Prime Minister Yitzak Rabin was assassinated by a follower of Rabbi Kahane for being too accommodating to the Palestinians.

Christianity too has been appropriated for nationalist causes in Europe for many centuries. Orthodoxy played a role in nationalist movements of Eastern Europe. In nineteenth-century Bulgaria, for example, nationalist ideas were linked to the desire for an independent Bulgarian Church. Equally, in Greece, the Orthodox Church has long played a part in the nurturing of Hellenic national identity, and is represented in modern Greek electoral politics by the People's Orthodox Rally. Perhaps most notably, the Orthodox Church, and the Moscow Patriarchate in particular, have been influential in the development of post-Soviet Russian politics.

In the West, Protestantism helped form British national identity and undergirded wars with Catholic France. Nationalism and religion also became closely interwoven within the politics of Northern Ireland. The nationalism of the Protestant majority took the form of loyalty to the British Crown while many in the Roman Catholic community aspired to join a reunified Ireland. The presence of a major religious element in these two rival national identities deepened the sense of mutual distrust, and provided symbols and rhetoric to castigate the opposition. Not least, it made the search for peaceful reconciliation both protracted and challenging, although some resolution seems to have been finally achieved in 2007.

Similar problems afflicted Yugoslavia. The legacy of history left the country with three rival religious traditions, each intertwined with local communal identities. Orthodoxy has been an element of Serbian nationalism; Roman Catholicism has historically been linked with Croatian and Slovenian identities, and Islam in Bosnia and Kosovo. After the collapse of Communism in 1990, these antagonistic forces surfaced again and the country fell apart amidst intense conflict and programmes of ethnic cleansing. The worst experiences were in Bosnia-Herzegovina, now effectively partitioned between the three communities under United Nations and NATO auspices. Kosovo too remains a source of inter-communal nationalist tensions. Although with a Muslim majority, it contains a Serb minority together with holy orthodox sites strongly associated with Serb nationalism. This led the Yugoslav (Serb) government to try to evict the Muslim population by force in order to maintain its grip on the province. The genocidal carnage that resulted was stopped only through NATO military action and presence as peacekeepers on the ground after which it then proclaimed itself a still-disputed independent country in 2008.

It is clear that, while secularizing tendencies are discernible within contemporary politics, especially in the West, religion remains a significant element within modern politics, locally, nationally and internationally. Contrary to the expectations of those who thought religion would fade from political life, this has not happened in the modern era. Religion continues as a source of authority and guidance for political action around the globe, while political leaders, for their part, have to devise strategies that take those religious claims into account. The result is to perpetuate the relationship between religion and politics in ever-changing and complex patterns in the present and, no doubt, in the future.

At the international level, this can, perhaps, be seen most dramatically in the recent rise of the fundamentalist Islamic group, al Qaeda, led by a Saudi exile, Osama bin Laden. Their orchestrated attacks on the World Trade Center in New York and the Pentagon in Washington DC signalled a new era in international affairs, dubbed by President George W. Bush 'the War on Terrorism'. The response of the United States, in initiating armed intervention in Afghanistan, the base of operations for al Qaeda, in late 2001, followed by the war to depose the regime of Iraqi president Saddam Hussein in 2003, brought religiously motivated violence to new heights of concern within the international community.

As later detailed analysis clearly shows, however (The 9/11 Commission Report 2004: 47–70), the historical roots and religious dimensions of this act of immense violence are substantial. For bin Laden and al Qaeda, the struggle is not just against the infidels of the West but, perhaps more importantly, it is also to promote 'the cause of Islamic revolution within the Islamic world itself, in the Arab lands especially and in Saudi Arabia above all' (Doran 2001). Regimes like that of Saudi Arabia, in allying themselves with the United States, have in their view betrayed Islam itself. Al Qaeda is itself part of a broader fundamentalist religious movement called Salafiyya, whose adherents, Salafis, encompassing Saudi Wahhabis, the Taliban and the Muslim Brotherhood, among others, share a common desire to see the restoration of a stricter and more literalist form of Islamic law throughout the Muslim world – for some of the more extreme by jihad (holy war) and martyrdom, if necessary. In doing so, they draw on a tradition of criticism of corrupt rulers that extends back centuries. It is that corruption that, again in their view, led to Islam's decline leaving it vulnerable to infidel regimes from the West 'eager to steal their land, wealth, and even their souls' (The 9/11 Commission Report 2004: 50).

It is perhaps doubtful that, in engaging in the war in Iraq, the leaders of the United States and allied Western powers were fully cognizant of the religious ramifications of their actions. On the contrary, it seemed that President Bush, for one, was eager to downplay this element in favour of justifications cast almost entirely in military and political terms. But, fully recognized or not, the world of the twenty-first century is now embroiled in an open-ended international conflict that has deep connections to the religious sphere. As such it is but the latest manifestation of the abiding association of religion and politics in the affairs of human society.

Politics and the study of religion

Religion has an individual and interior character to it – it is about personal spiritual practices, personal beliefs about the numinous, and personal values about how to lead one's life in a religiously appropriate way. All this is a part, an essential part, of the study of religion. But religion also has a communal or exterior character, embodied in religious institutions, sacred texts and symbols, religious leaders and activists. This too is part of the study of religion, and it is a part that is particularly illuminated by the study of the relationship between politics and religion. On the one hand, we can study how religion has impacted the wider society and, in particular, its political processes. For, as this chapter has argued, historically, religion has generally had an immense and sustained impact on a community's identity, values and understandings. To put it another way, religion has carried a relatively high degree of cultural power. To study how that power has spilled into, and helped shape, the political realm, is therefore to illuminate some of the broader consequences of religion's claims. By the same token, religion's social and cultural saliency has, again historically, drawn the attention of the political realm. For the exercise of power, even if primarily social and cultural, is the business of politics. Hence, the study of the way that realm has reacted to such power also adds to our understanding of religion.

When looked at in the round, as both the effect of religion on politics and that of politics on religion, the result has been, in particular contexts, a relationship so close as to make very difficult the drawing of distinctions between the two. The historical experience of such a monistic and sacralized political realm is, of course, to affirm the importance of the political for the study of religion. When the two realms can be empirically distinguished, a far more common historical phenomenon, especially in modern times, the resulting relationship has often been both complex and dynamic. For religious leaders and institutions have often sought to exercise significant political influence as a way of furthering their religious mission while political leaders have at times tried to rely on religious institutions and leaders to buttress and legitimize their political authority. At times, the result has been a relatively harmonious and symbiotic relationship but, in other contexts, it has led to a degree of tension and conflict, particularly where rival religious traditions exist side-by-side within a given community. Here, politics may be used to accentuate and extend that conflict as much as to resolve or repress it. Again, how all this operates forms part of the study of religion. In the modern world, at least in some Western contexts, religion clearly has lost some of its cultural power leading to the relationship becoming rather tenuous and atrophied. At the same time, the complex dynamics whereby this process has occurred is yet a further part of the dynamics and complexities of religion's place in human society and is, too, an essential part of the whole story. But, while this disengagement has occurred, it is also clear that in many other parts of the world, and not least at the international level, the relationship today remains a vital one. As such, the study of that relationship continues to contribute much to the understanding of religion as an abiding feature of the human condition.

Bibliography

Armstrong, G.T., 'Church and State Relations: The Changes Wrought by Constantine,' in E. Ferguson (ed.), *Church and State in the Early Church* (New York, Garland, 1993).

Bainton, R.H., *Christian Attitudes toward War and Peace: a Historical Survey and Critical Re-evaluation* (New York, Abingdon Press, 1960).

Bauckham, R., *The Bible in Politics: How to Read the Bible Politically* (Louisville, Westminster/John Knox Press, 1989).

Bloch-Hoell, N., *The Pentecostal Movement: Its Origin, Development and Distinctive Character* (New York, Humanities Press, 1964).

Brandon, S.G.F., *Jesus and the Zealots: a Study of the Political Factor in Primitive Christianity* (Manchester, Manchester University Press, 1967).

Cone, J.H., *God of the Oppressed* (New York, Crossroad Books, 1975).

Cranz, F.E. 'Kingdom and Polity in Eusebius of Caesarea', in E. Ferguson (ed.), *Church and State in the Early Church* (New York, Garland Publishing, 1993).

Cullmann, O., *The State in the New Testament* (London, SCM Press, 1957).

Doran, Michael Scott, 'Somebody Else's Civil War', in James F. Hoge, Jr and Gideon Rose (eds), *How Did This Happen? Terrorism and the New War* (New York, Public Affairs, 2001).

Elazar, D. and S.A. Cohen, *The Jewish Polity: Jewish Political Organization from Biblical Times to the Present* (Bloomington, Indiana University Press, 1985).

Elphrick, R. and T. Davenport, *Christianity in South Africa: A Political, Social and Cultural History* (Cape Town, David Philip Publishers, 1997).

Esposito, J.L. (ed.), *Political Islam: Revolution, Radicalism or Reform?* (Boulder, Lynne Rienner Publishers, 1997).

Finer, S., *The History of Government from the Earliest Times*, 3 vols (Oxford, Oxford University Press, 1997).

Forrester, D., *Theology and Politics* (Oxford, Blackwell, 1988).

Gibb, H.A.R., 'The Islamic Background of Ibn Khaldun's Political Theory,' in S.J. Shaw and W.R. Polk (eds.), *Studies on the Civilization of Islam: Collected Essays* (London, Routledge and Kegan Paul, 1962).

Gifford, P., *African Christianity: Its Public Role* (London, Hurst, 1998).

Goldstein, M., *A History of Modern Tibet* (Berkeley, University of California Press, 1989).

Gutiérrez, G., *A Theology of Liberation: History, Politics and Salvation* (Maryknoll, NY, Orbis, 1974).

Human Relations and the South African Scene in the Light of Scripture (Cape Town, Dutch Reformed Church Publishers, 1976).

Jones, K.W., *Socio-religious Reform Movements in British India* (Cambridge, Cambridge University Press, 1989).

Kairos Document: Challenge to the Church: a Theological Comment on the Political Crisis in South Africa (Braamfontein, The Kairos Theologians, 1985).

Kee, A., *The Scope of Political Theology* (London, SCM Press, 1978).

Kelly, D.F., *The Emergence of Liberty in the Modern World: The Influence of Calvin on Five Governments from the Sixteenth through the Eighteenth Centuries* (Phillipsburg, Presbyterian and Reformed, 1992).

Khomeini, R.M., *Islam and Revolution: Writings and Declarations of Imam Khomeini*, translated and edited by H. Algar (Berkeley, Mizan Press, 1981).

Kirk, J.M., *Between God and the Party: Religion and Politics in Revolutionary Cuba* (Tampa, University of South Florida Press, 1989).

Martin, D. *Tongues of Fire: The Explosion of Protestantism in Latin America* (Oxford, Basil Blackwell, 1990).

Martin, W., *With God on Our Side: The Rise of the Religious Right in America* (New York, Broadway Books, 1996).

Marty, M.E. and R.S. Appleby (eds), *Fundamentalisms Observed* (Chicago, University of Chicago Press, 1991).

—— *Fundamentalisms Comprehended* (Chicago, University of Chicago Press, 1995).

Metz, J.B., *Theology of the World* (London, Burns & Oates, 1969).

Monsma, S.V. and J.C. Soper, *The Challenge of Pluralism: Church and State in Five Democracies* (Lanham, MD, Rowman & Littlefield, 1997).

Parekh, B., *Ghandi's Political Philosophy* (London, Macmillan, 1989).

Ramet, P. (ed.), *Eastern Christianity and Politics in the Twentieth Century* (Durham, Duke University Press, 1988).

Rashid, Ahmed, *Taliban: Militant Islam, Oil and Fundamentalism in Central Asia* (New Haven, Yale University Press, 2000).

Ruether, R.R., *Sexism and God-Talk: Toward a Feminist Theology* (Boston, Beacon Press, 1983).

Second General Conference of Latin American Bishops, *Position Papers and Conclusions: The Church in the Present-Day Transformation of Latin America in the Light of the Council*, 2 vols (Bogotá, General Secretariat of CELAM, 1970).

Smith, B.L., *Religion and Legitimation of Power in Sri Lanka* (Chambersburg, Anima Books, 1978).

The 9/11 Commission Report: Final Report of the National Commission on Terrorist Attacks Upon the United States, (New York, W.W. Norton, 2004).

Van der Veer, P., *Religious Nationalism: Hindus and Muslims in India* (Berkeley, University of California Press, 1994).

Weber, P.J., 'Separation of Church and State: a Potent, Dynamic Idea in Political Theory', in R. Wuthnow (ed.), *The Encyclopedia of Politics and Religion* (Washington D.C., Congressional Quarterly, 1998).

Westerlund, D. (ed.), *Questioning the Secular State: The Worldwide Resurgence of Religion in Politics* (New York, St Martin's Press, 1996).

Wilcox, C., *Onward Christian Soldiers? The Religious Right in American Politics* (Boulder, Westview Press, 1996).

Ziegler, A.K., 'Pope Gelasius I and his Teaching on the Relation of Church and State', *Catholic Historical Review* 27 (1942), pp. 412–37.

Suggested reading

Ayoob, M. *The Many Faces of Political Islam: Religion and Politics in the Muslim World* (Ann Arbor: The University of Michigan Press, 2008).
Examines political Islam in its varied manifestations and the implications for Muslim politics and wider global relations.

Bruce, S. *Politics and Religion* (Cambridge: Polity Press, 2003).
A textbook for the field that examines religion's political role in historical empires, in forming national identity, in party politics, in political protest, and as an instrument of political control.

Hanson, E.O. *Religion and Politics in the International System Today* (Cambridge: Cambridge University Press, 2006).
Examines the increasing role of religion in influencing global politics, focusing on Christianity, Islam, Judaism, Hinduism, Buddhism, Confucianism, and Maoist Marxism.

Jelen, T.G. and C. Wilcox, *Religion and Politics in Comparative Perspective: The One, the Few and the Many* (Cambridge: Cambridge University Press, 2002).
Detailed case studies of politics and religion in specific countries and regions, illustrating linkages between the two spheres of varying closeness, and in contexts with either one dominant religion or competing traditions.

Journal of Church and State (Waco, TX: J.M. Dawson Institute of Church-State Studies).
A well-established scholarly journal with broad coverage, including brief notes on current Church–State affairs by country and listings of recent doctoral dissertations in the field.

Norris, P. and R. Inglehart, *Sacred and Secular: Religion and Politics Worldwide* (Cambridge: Cambridge University Press, 2004).
A major comparative study of religion and political culture, within the context of secularization and economic modernization, using the World Values Survey and European Values Survey.

Political Theology (London: Equinox Publishing).
An interdisciplinary journal that examines religious and political issues by drawing mainly on the disciplines of theology, religious studies, politics, philosophy and ethics. As such, it aims to reflect the diversity of religious and theological engagements with public and political life through contributions from scholars, practitioners and clergy.

Politics and Religion (Cambridge: Cambridge University Press).
A recent scholarly journal devoted to the field, published by the Religion and Politics Section of the American Political Science Association.

Wald, K.D. and A. Calhoun-Brown, *Religion and Politics in the United States* (Lanham, MD: Rowman & Littlefield Publishers, 2007).
An accessible and up-to-date study of one major country where religion has had a major political influence throughout its history.

Wuthnow, R. (ed.), *The Encyclopedia of Politics and Religion* (Washington, DC., Congressional Quarterly Press, 1998).
A major reference work that includes articles on broad themes, as well as specific religions, individuals, geographical regions, institutions, and events.

Chapter 27

Economics of religion

Laurence R. Iannaccone and
William Sims Bainbridge

In recent years there has been a revival of interest in economic explanations of religious behavior, backed up by extensive theoretical and empirical work that has placed this field on a solid footing. To be sure, topics such as church finances and giving have long been studied by economists, and many principles of management and marketing can be applied without much modification to religious organizations. However, the modern economics of religion is much broader and deeper than that, potentially addressing many of the topics covered by other social sciences and by religious studies. This essay will examine the major questions.

Economics is a rather technical science, fraught with mathematical equations and technical terminology, so we must translate into comprehensible language for a wider audience. Yet, we will use metaphors carefully, so they communicate accurately what economists of religion actually think. In particular, we organize this essay in terms of three familiar roles that people play in an economic system: *consumer*, *producer*, and *investor*. When we apply these three terms to religion we are not using analogies; the economics of religion really does assert that people primarily play these roles while engaged in religious behavior. We begin by describing each concept, then explain how they interact to form a *religious market*.

Consumers

Only humans manage money, but all vertebrate animals possess the fundamental prerequisite for economic behavior, decision-making on the basis of experienced and anticipated rewards (Skinner 1938). Like our mammalian forebears, we seek the things we desire and avoid the things we fear. Like them, we enter the world immature and dependent upon parental care-giving. Humans are a social species, but so too are bees and beavers, ants and elephants, and all social species have evolved complex mechanisms for resource sharing and defense. No other species appears to possess religious faith, but economic principles suggest that religion may be a natural human consequence of intelligent reward-seeking through social interaction in a world of uncertainty and deprivation.

In his classic, *The Wealth of Nations*, Adam Smith (1776) wrote brilliantly about the character of religious markets. Though these passages were long ignored, Smith's observations helped spark renewed interest in economic theories of religion fully two centuries after he wrote. Self-interest motivates many people to seek religious rewards, self-interest prompts other people to supply valued religious goods and services, and the combination yields a religious market in which the churches compete for customers.

Christian Churches and their non-Christian counterparts provide many of the same services as secular businesses (setting aside for the moment some special expected benefits peculiar to religion, which will be covered in the section on investors). Like a school or day-care center, Sunday school supervises and educates children. Like a theater or a symphony orchestra, church services provide drama and music. Like a country club or tourist resort, religious organizations host recreational activities. Religious charities can substitute for government welfare and social work (Gruber and Hungerman 2007). Many writers have drawn analogies between religious counseling or confession and their secular equivalents, professional or educational counseling and clinical psychology or psychotherapy (Bakan 1958; Frank 1961). In these latter examples, a client goes to a professional for a specialized service, whether the professional's credential is religious or secular, and the chief economic difference may be whether there is a set fee for a given service.

Different industries routinely compete to satisfy the same needs. Depending on relative costs, you may therefore drive your car to a conference, take a bus, fly on a plane, or use your computer to "meet" over the internet. But each industry provides products that differ from those provided by competing industries, and these products often come bundled in very different packages. With respect to social services, most religious organizations operate like department stores, providing one-stop sources of an array of different goods and services demanded by individuals and households.

Religious organizations can sometimes provide ordinary products more efficiently than secular organizations. A familiar example is moral education for children. Political pressures and legal rulings limit the extent to which public schools can inculcate values, but as voluntary organizations largely insulated from politics, religious organizations indoctrinate quite openly. Religion's ability to attract customers seeking cure of physical or mental illnesses depends on how well secular organizations are doing that job, which differs dramatically across ailments. One traditional function attributed to religion is that it authenticates members as good and trustworthy members of the community, a function that credit rating agencies also perform but not always as well (Klein 1997).

Renewed interest in economic theories of religion can be traced in large part to the work of Nobel-prize winning economist, Gary Becker. In one of his most famous essays, Becker (1976:5) argued that "the heart of the economic approach" lies in "the combined assumptions of maximizing behavior, market equilibrium, and stable preferences, used relentlessly and unflinchingly." Market dynamics are easier to address after separately reviewing religious production and consumption, but the other two assumptions can be illustrated by consumption alone. A formal statement of the maximizing principle is this:

> Individuals act rationally, weighing the costs and benefits of potential actions, and choosing those actions that maximize their net benefits.

Maximizing behavior is simply the point made earlier, that humans seek to gain the most reward at least cost. Given two alternatives whose contingencies are well known, a person will rationally choose the more advantageous one. Thus, the economic perspective on religion, and Becker's work in general, is often called *rational choice* theory (Stark and Iannaccone 1993; Iannaccone 1997).

This term has two disadvantages. Most obviously, it emphasizes just one of the three fundamental economic assumptions. One might just as well have focused on either of the others, for example calling this the *religious markets* approach (Jelen 2002). More subtly, "rational choice" ignores comparable terms used by people in other disciplines, thus obscuring the extent to which the theory enjoys a broader scientific basis than just economics. For example, operating from almost identical assumptions and giving great prominence to concepts from economics, the sociologist George Homans (1974) used the term *learning theory*, and thereby emphasized connections to behavioral psychology as well. But whatever name we use, the assumption that humans maximize is key to an economic understanding of religion. *Rational choice* has the advantage of making it clear from that start that religious behavior is often quite rational, rather than a consequence of mere ignorance, superstition, or wishful thinking.

The maximizing assumption is often criticized as tautological. An economist asserts that "customer A buys brand X rather than brand Y because the former maximizes the customer's expected utility." And how does the economist *know* it maximizes the customer's utility? Because he observed him choosing it! This certainly sounds like a tautology, which many declare a waste of words. But some tautologies, including those derived from mathematical definitions and axioms, turn out to be tremendously useful. Euclidean geometry is a case in point. Although one can derive illuminating alternative systems of geometry, this does not negate the relevance of standard geometry for describing the vast majority of situations encountered by humans. In a similar manner, the system of "tautologies" derived from standard economic assumptions yields one of the most valuable intellectual structures ever developed for social-scientific description, analysis, and theorizing.

In connection with religion, the chief substantive objection to maximization is the claim that it ignores altruistic behavior. This argument has also been raised in connection with simplistic theories that biological evolution is "survival of the fittest." Altruistic behavior, from the standpoint of sociobiology, represents *inclusive fitness* (Wilson 1975), action that helps the individual's genes survive and reproduce through benefit to close family relatives, not necessarily to the individual who takes the action.

Economists need not adopt this principle from sociobiology, because they have two other legitimate responses. First of all, altruism seems paradoxical only because we presume to fully know what a rational individual's preferences and reward contingencies should be. Yes, nobody wants to die, but a parent may value the lives of their children sufficiently to risk their own lives, and most examples of altruism in fact involve relatively minor sacrifices of momentary personal benefit to help exchange partners who will reciprocate in future. Second, the function of a scientific theory is not to explain everything, but rather to explain much with great clarity and to provide some guidance as to what phenomena fall beyond the scope of the theory. If empirical research turns up cases where the maximizing assumption really fails to apply, then economists will be motivated to search for new principles that do provide an explanation – as is in fact the case in the new and rapidly growing fields of behavioral economics, neuroeconomics, and experimental economics.

Turning to the assumption of stable preferences, the third core assumption in Becker's list, one cannot but wonder how economists deal with the fact that it is a rare (and strange) person indeed who always maintains the same tastes, values, beliefs, and behavior. However, a little more detail will help us understand what economists mean by "stable preferences," and how they handle behavioral change. Here is a formal statement of the principle:

The ultimate preferences (or "needs") that individuals use to assess costs and benefits tend not to vary systematically from person to person or time to time.

Note, first of all, that the principle is hedged by the phrase "tend not to vary systematically," which acknowledges that variations do occur but often can be ignored. More importantly, the stable "tastes" or "preferences" in question are *ultimate* preferences (Becker 1996).

Much of what people seek in life is but a means to an end. Consider, for example, the aphorism "in for a penny, in for a pound." What does *pound* mean? It refers to British currency. Americans should properly say, "in for a penny, in for a dollar." People in Britain prefer pounds while Americans prefer dollars, not because their ultimate preferences differ, but simply because they employ different currencies. Pounds and dollars facilitate the exchanges that enable people to satisfy their wants. Their value is instrumental not ultimate, and external conditions can change how valuable they are as means to achieve people's ultimate goals.

The real import of the stable preferences assumption is that it focuses our attention on external, market conditions that shape behavior by changing the relative costs and benefits associated with different actions. Economists leave to psychologists and neurobiologists the task of studying substantial differences in the mental apparatus of different individual people. As a social science, economics concerns what happens between people more than what happens inside them. This is not blindness, but the division of labor across the human sciences, and economists need to focus their vision on the factors that create and sustain markets, to discover new insights. We do not fault the Palomar and Hubble telescopes for failing to detect radio waves, because they were the best optical telescope of their eras, and wholly different designs were required for radio telescopes. Similarly, we should ask how far we can see with the tools of the economics of religion, not whether we can see absolutely everything in every direction.

One example of how economic thinking helps us understand religious behavior is the differences in what people with different incomes contribute to their religious organizations. For sake of simplicity, conceptualize each person's contribution as a combination of time and money that together constitutes his or her total "payment" for religious goods and services. People differ in the wage rates they can command for their work time, so the time of high wage earners truly has more monetary value, and it is only natural that they seek to obtain religious rewards through actions that require relatively less time and relatively more money. Though other considerations routinely influence people's contributions, this simple tradeoff accounts for many of the differences between rich and poor congregations – differences that are rarely even noted by non-economic researchers (Iannaccone 1990).

Producers

Producers are human beings, so their behavior follows the same principles as that of consumers. They too maximize, but the relevant maximizing now relates to the supply-side of the religious economy. Whether pastors, priests, rabbis, or imams – religious producers will tend to adjust behavior so as to maximize the return to their efforts. They are in this sense *profit maximizers*, even though the profits in question may derive from a complex mix of monetary and social rewards. The profit motive and entrepreneurial spirit is most clearly visible in new religious movements, but by no means absent in established denominations.

In a survey of alternative theories, Bainbridge and Stark (1979: 288) sketched the entrepreneur model of cult formation. They employed the concept of *compensator*, which will be considered more closely in the section on investors. This word refers to expectations of future rewards from religion, especially supernatural rewards promised in another life. Religious cults emphasize new supernatural hopes, manufactured and sold by their founders:

1   Cults are businesses that provide a product for their customers and receive payment in return.

2   Cults are mainly in the business of selling novel compensators.

3   Therefore, a supply of novel compensators must be manufactured.

4   Both manufacture and sales are accomplished by entrepreneurs.

5   These entrepreneurs, like those in other businesses, are motivated by the desire for profit, which they can gain by exchanging compensators for rewards.

6   Motivation to enter the cult business is stimulated by the perception that such businesses can be profitable, an impression likely to be acquired through prior involvement with a successful cult.

7   Successful entrepreneurs require skills and experience, which are most easily gained through a prior career as the employee of an earlier successful cult.

8   The manufacture of salable new compensators (or compensator-packages) is most easily accomplished by assembling components of pre-existing compensator-systems into new configurations, or by the further development of successful compensator-systems.

9   Cults tend therefore to cluster in lineages. They are linked by individual entrepreneurs who begin their careers in one cult and then leave to found their own. They bear strong "family resemblances" because they share many cultural features.

10 Ideas for completely new compensators can come from any cultural source or personal experience whatsoever, but the skillful entrepreneur experiments carefully in the development of new products and incorporates them permanently in his cult only if the market response is favorable.

Because most religious organizations incorporate as non-profits and describe their activities with a distinctive, non-economic vocabulary, the extent to which they operate like commercial firms and reward their leaders is obscured. But most cults are too new to have developed institutional arrangements that cover (or constrain) the worldly benefits desired by their leaders, and thereby witness to a broad truth: successful religions are businesses that yield a steady stream of rewards for their employees, and especially their top managers.

As in the world of commercial business, compensation can come in different forms. The New Thought religious organization called Unity was set up originally as a business, then morphed into a non-profit organization (Vahle 2002:147). David Berg (Moses David), founder of the Children of God (The Family) displayed substantial interest in sexual rewards, whereas L. Ron Hubbard seemed more interested in money (Bainbridge 2002b; Lewis 2009). Alternately, it could be that Berg and Hubbard adapted their business models to different segments of the religious market, with Hubbard targeting the wealthy and Berg selling to those who could only pay with time and services. The obvious entrepreneurial orientation of many cults routinely leads to accusations that they exploit their followers, but as in the secular business world, unsatisfied customers soon become ex-customers (Barker 1984).

The idea of clergy as profit-maximizers is probably the most controversial part of the economic theory of religion. Yet, clergy do benefit from their jobs (Bainbridge 2002a). Well-established denominations provide a good deal of economic security, considerable status in the community, and the pleasures of sociability. Some of these benefits, notably economic security, may have been even more important in earlier centuries, when few people in secular society enjoyed them. Some of the historical controversies about the churches precisely concern how much of which rewards clergy should enjoy, for example how much luxury versus asceticism and even celibacy. One possible explanation for the difficulty the Roman

Catholic Church faces in its current efforts to recruit nuns and priests is that the cost–benefit calculus has changed to the church's disadvantage, as increased economic security in the wider society means that security no longer offsets the personal cost of celibacy.

In most mainstream religious organizations, production is by no means limited to paid professionals. All active members of the laity participate in production, as is seen most clearly in worship services and group rituals but is no less true of the social activities, study groups, friendship networks, and even the faith maintained by congregations. As these examples suggest, most of the benefits of religion are *club goods* (Iannaccone 1992). These are goods that are *non-rivalrous*, in the sense that one person's use of them does not diminish another person's use of them, but *excludable*, in the sense that people who do not belong to the "club" cannot use them. Above all, they are *collectively produced*.

Prior to the historical development of commercial markets and industries, much human wealth production took place in households, and Iannaccone has shown how the combination of the economic concepts of club good and household production combine to explain the amateur producer role in religious groups:

> *Churches as clubs.* Club models of religion may be framed as an extension of the household production approach. The religious commodities that enter a household's utility function now depend not only upon their own inputs of time, goods, and capital, but also upon the inputs of fellow church members. So, for example, the pleasure and edification that I derive from a worship service does not depend solely on what I bring to the service (through my presence, attentiveness, public singing, and so forth); it also depends on how many other people attend, how warmly they greet me, how well they sing, how enthusiastically they read and pray, how deep their commitment, and so forth.
>
> (Iannaccone 1998: 1482)

Because both laity and clergy produce religious goods, both require *religious capital* (Iannaccone 1984; 1990), although clergy require more. James Coleman (1988) introduced the concept of *social capital* to rational choice theory, thereby increasing the social-scientific sophistication of the approach. *Religious capital* is the accumulated stock of skills, sensitivities, and social relationships that affect a person's net benefits from religious activities. Capital is a *stock* that augments the flow of goods and services that people create with their inputs of time and money. In contrast to time and money inputs, capital is durable and remains useful over time. In fact, some religious activities tend to augment the very capital that makes them productive. Religious capital and religious production can thus be mutually reinforcing, some might even say *addictive* (Iannaccone 1984). As the entrepreneur model of cult formation above already noted, founders of religions tend to apprentice in other successful religions. Like all other forms of capital – physical, financial, human, and social – stocks of religious capital must be built up over time.

Investors

A distinctive feature of religious organizations is that they promise attainment of rewards, such as eternal life in Heaven, that cannot be delivered in the here and now. Notice the use of economic terminology when Stark and Bainbridge (1987: 36) defined these promises as *compensators*: "When humans cannot quickly and easily obtain strongly desired rewards they persist in their efforts and may often accept explanations that provide only compensators.

These are intangible substitutes for the desired reward, having the character of I.O.U.s, the value of which must be taken on faith." Consumers who give their church time and money in hopes of earning entry into Heaven are essentially *investing* in it. When they die, and "go to their reward," then they believe they can cash in on this investment.

In the first formal economic model of religious activity, Corry Azzi and Ronald Ehrenberg (1975) placed heavy emphasis on the perceived supernatural benefits of religion. In particular, they saw the chief goal of religious activity as *afterlife consumption*, a supernatural return on natural investments. Religion requires major investments and promises the highest possible return, typically eternal life or some comparable form of transcendence. Like secular stocks and bonds, however, compensators come in all *denominations* – in the monetary sense of the term – both small and large. In their formal derivations, Stark and Bainbridge (1987:36, 39) distinguished specific from general compensators:

> Compensators are treated by humans as if they were rewards.
> For any reward or cluster of rewards, one or more compensators may be invented.
> Compensators vary according to the generality, value, and kind of the rewards for which they substitute.
>> Compensators which substitute for single, specific rewards are called *specific compensators*.
>> Compensators which substitute for a cluster of many rewards and for rewards of great scope and value are called *general compensators*.
> ...
> The most general compensators can be supported only by supernatural explanations.
>> *Supernatural* refers to forces beyond or outside nature which suspend, alter, or ignore physical forces.
>> *Religion* refers to systems of general compensators based on supernatural assumptions.

When Stark and Bainbridge coined the term *compensator*, they were thinking in terms of psychological compensation to assuage unsatisfied desires, but they could just as well have used the term *compensation* in the economic sense, as payment for work. Similarly, setting aside bad puns confusing *profit* with *prophet*, religion explicitly offers the hope of profit. The Bible often uses metaphors of profit and loss when discussing the benefits of religion. Here are just seven of the thirty-seven passages using the word *profit* in the King James Version:

> Samuel 12:21 And turn ye not aside: for then should ye go after vain things, which cannot profit nor deliver; for they are vain.
> Job 21:15 What is the Almighty, that we should serve him? and what profit should we have, if we pray unto him?
> Job 22:2 Can a man be profitable unto God, as he that is wise may be profitable unto himself?
> Proverbs 11:4 Riches profit not in the day of wrath: but righteousness delivereth from death.
> Jeremiah 7:8 Behold, ye trust in lying words, that cannot profit.
> Matthew 16:26 For what is a man profited, if he shall gain the whole world, and lose his own soul? or what shall a man give in exchange for his soul?
> James 2:14 What doth it profit, my brethren, though a man say he hath faith, and have not works? can faith save him?

Profit refers to benefit from actions, especially from exchanges. Interestingly, Bible passages often employ the language of profit and exchange to justify *religious* behavior. Should you try to gain the whole world, even at the cost of your soul, or seek to preserve your soul while forgoing the opportunity to gain the world? Religion is like a life insurance policy. Indeed, Azzi and Ehrenberg (1975) explicitly modeled religion as an after-life insurance policy, and Viviana Zelizer (1978) has documented how the emergence of the life insurance industry stimulated debates about whether it was sacrilegious.

Many secular investments can be bought and sold, but this is not usually the case for spiritual investments in religion. Stocks, bonds, and most physical assets can readily be exchanged for money, which provides a simple means of calculating their current value and ultimate profitability. The same is not true for general compensators of religion, nor is it true for most investments in relationships or even one's skills. To some extent, the difference is a matter of constraints on exchange and time. An owner of (term) life insurance cannot collect the death benefits while still alive, nor can the policy be redeemed in the event of some other person's death. Similarly, my investments in church-going and Christian virtue do not yield a ticket to Heaven that I can sell to others. But a more fundamental difference separating religious investments from most secular investments is *information*. We can determine whether a life insurance company has fulfilled its obligations when other people die, whereas we have no objective information about a religion's afterlife payouts to its investors, nor can we adduce much objective evidence for many other religious claims. The payoffs rest on faith.

This information problem helps us understand many seemingly strange features of religion, including the historical tension between pluralism and exclusivity (Iannaccone 1995). Stock market uncertainty prompts people to hedge their bets, investing in a diversified portfolio of assets. This same strategy arises in some religious markets especially those of Asia with the most familiar example being Japan where a given family might practice both Shinto and Buddhism, and more recently may even turn to Christianity for some services such as weddings. This risk reduction strategy leads to private production, diversified consumption, and fee-for-service transactions. In the west, however, the dominant strategy is quite different. The great monotheistic faiths – Judaism, Christianity, and Islam – reinforce trust through collective (club) production, exclusivity, and high levels of commitment. Collective production tends to reduce the perceived risk and raise the perceived value of religious activities, although also promotes free-rider problems in which some laity and even clergy may seek to gain religious rewards without making a commensurate investment (Iannaccone 2002).

Markets

Now that we have considered three main economic roles that people play in religion – consumers, producers, and investors – we can examine how these roles fit together to create markets. To this point we have deferred discussion of Becker's third basic assumption, which is often expressed as the principle that markets tend to reach equilibrium. We prefer a somewhat more cautious statement, but one that we think explains rather more:

> Social outcomes constitute the equilibria that emerge from the aggregation and interaction of individual actions.

Whenever we see relatively stable social forms, they probably reflect a market of one kind or another that has achieved a fairly durable equilibrium. Hence, we begin our discussion of religious markets by considering forces that produce equilibrium, despite our awareness that real social units are never truly in equilibrium and that small changes can sometimes trigger radical transformations both in secular and religious markets.

In ancient days, and in less economically developed parts of the world today, religion was local and conducted by religious professionals who did not belong to geographically widespread organizations. Indeed, *pagan* really means local. The modern analogy would be highly specialized service professionals, like dentists or psychoanalysts, who may belong to loose confederations but operate as tiny local businesses. The decisive transition to a more modern model was taken by the Roman Catholic Church, which inherited bureaucratic forms from the Roman Empire and operated rather like an industrial corporation or *firm* (Ekelund et al. 1996).

In a free market with easy entry and innovation, producers will not thrive unless they adjust their products in response to changes in technology, customer wants, and market conditions. A minister, who sees empty pews on a Sunday morning, will try various tactics to increase attendance, such as church picnics, inviting celebrity preachers to visit, and calling on parishioners at their home to offer spiritual benefits. Other things being equal, a denomination as a unit will adjust itself to attract customers. As local churches and denominations compete with each other for customers, the market as a whole becomes more vigorous. Customers receive more benefits from religion and more readily invest in it.

Every industry produces a range of products, brands, and firms, and there is some degree of segmentation in all markets. Earlier we explained that this results primarily from differences in the resources the various customers possess, and in other external factors, rather than differences in their fundamental preferences. However, to the extent that differences in fundamental preference do exist, they tend to reinforce market segmentation. Throughout the modern world, competing denominations offer different and distinctive bundles of goods and services tailored both to the different external conditions and internal tastes of their customers.

Social class has long been of major concern of sociologists of religion. Economists, by contrast, emphasize that individuals with different levels of income and education naturally demand different combinations of goods and services. Put crudely, poor people are attracted to deviant *sects*, whereas rich people flock to mainstream *churches and denominations* (Pope 1942). Earlier we noted that people with lower wage rates will tend to invest proportionately more time rather than money in religion, compared with rich people who invest proportionately more money. To the extent that prosperous people can afford to buy more of their ordinary rewards from secular business, they will demand less from their churches. People who are not prosperous will need to create many of the same rewards as club goods within their congregations. Thus, sects tend to attract customers from the margins of society – the segments poorly served by commercial markets and secular governments (Iannaccone and Berman 2006).

The diversity of firms in a free religious market will serve the needs of a larger fraction of the population, but there is also a second economic reason why a free market better mobilizes the population for religion. By the sheer fact of needing to compete with each other, clergy in different denominations will be forced to seek customers more vigorously. This was explicitly explained half way back to Adam Smith by social scientist of religion, William Folwell Bainbridge (1882b) in his observational study of American Protestant missions in Asia. Some leaders of international missions wanted to divide the Orient up among denominations, so they would not get in each others' way, but his research visiting missions in Japan, China, Burma and India suggested to him that this was a mistake. In another book from the same research (Bainbridge 1882a), but focusing on northern Baptist missions, he explained it was usually worthwhile concentrating efforts in areas where local religions were weak and potential customers could more readily be won over. Although he expressed this idea in terms of the military concept of *concentration of forces*, it could as easily be expressed in terms of concentrating marketing of a new religious product on *early adopter market segments*, comparable to those who first tend to buy new technologies (Katz and Lazarsfeld 1955; Rogers 2003).

Two decades ago, one of the first debates in the revived economics of religion centered on two opposing arguments about the relationship between religious pluralism and commitment (Warner 1993). In a series of publications, Roger Finke, Rodney Stark, and Laurence Iannaccone pictured religion as a market economy in which denominations compete with each other for members (Finke and Stark 1988, 1989a, 1989b, 1992; Finke 1989; Iannaccone 1991). Different individuals and groups in society have different needs, cultures, and non-religious affiliations, so therefore religious pluralism should increase commitment by offering each person the style of religion that suits him or her best. In their empirical work, they tried to show that rates of church membership are higher where there are more denominations in the religious marketplace.

In contrast, other researchers argued that religious pluralism has a negative effect on church membership (Breault 1989a, 1989b; Land *et al.* 1991; Blau *et al.* 1992; Blau *et al.*, cf. Christiano 1987). Religious monopoly might be associated with higher rates of religious involvement, if individual affiliations are chiefly the result of social influence, and if social influence is most effective when it is monolithic.

Thus, the narrow debate over denominational diversity and religious mobilization contrasted two distinctive general models of group process. The diversity-mobilization argument conceptualized group affiliation in terms of individual choices among competing suppliers, with individuals maximizing their satisfaction by selecting the suppliers that best meet their personal needs. The monopoly-mobilization argument saw affiliation in terms of the net power of social influences operating within a diffuse social network, wherein persons are more strongly impelled to join a group the greater the proportion of their consociates who are members. Empirical evidence at first seemed contradictory. It is possible to resolve this debate, first by acknowledging that both perspectives are correct, representing real competing forces in social life that produce different empirical outcomes depending upon which force is stronger under the circumstances (Bainbridge 1995). But the second theory like the first can be conceptualized in terms of the economics of religion.

If we realize that the customers of religion are also investors, then we can ask where they get the confidence to invest in one brand of religion or another. Brand loyalty is a very real phenomenon in commercial markets, as anyone would know who has compared the cost of national brand products in the grocery store with generics. Brands benefit from advertising, from personal testimonials, and from the perception that they must be good or they would not have survived in the market. Major brands really do have an advantage, whether they are breakfast cereals or churches, but market segmentation also works against them.

Note that one firm can have many brands, as General Motors sold both Pontiacs and Chevrolets built from similar designs with many of the identical parts. Thus, for example, the Roman Catholic church could have an ethnic Irish church in one part of Chicago, and an ethnic Polish church in another part, enjoying the benefits of diversity while remaining a single organization. On a higher level of abstraction, one could describe all Christian churches as different brands of the same faith. This in fact may be the best strategy. By agreeing about many fundamentals, all these Christian churches support faith in each other, even as they compete with each other. The analogy from secular markets might be the New York Stock Exchange. All the stocks listed on "the big board" benefit from the confidence the investing public has in the stock exchange, even as the individual listed companies compete for investors.

There were a number of methodological problems with the statistical studies of monopoly and mobilization (Voas et al. 2002). But their chief drawback was that they did not start with an appropriate theoretical model of where variations in religious diversity came from, or how much would be optimal in a given community. Studies tended to measure the religious diversity of metropolitan areas or US states, on rare occasions of different nations, then correlate this statistic with the fraction of the population who were formal members of religious organizations. In the United States, much diversity comes from the immigration patterns of a century or two earlier, when ethnic groups brought their traditional faiths to wherever they settled. As H. Richard Niebuhr (1929) noted, it would have been rational for many of these ethnic denominations to merge as their customers assimilated into the wider society, but in order to compete with each other they had actually emphasized minor differences just as ordinary corporations struggle over niche markets, product differentiation, and any other competitive advantages they can find to help them stay in business.

The optimal number of firms in the religious market could be rather small, if socioeconomic differences among the customers were the only marketing factor. It is not surprising, therefore, that some studies would fail to find a correlation between the number of denominations and the total membership rate – because everywhere there might be a sufficient number of diverse firms to satisfy the customers. In secular industries, the number of firms can decline as successful firms buy up others, but this is less likely to happen among religious organizations. There certainly are cases in which denominations merge, and in some cases like the United Church of Canada the motivation may have been a conscious realization that there were too many similar competitors for the size of the market.

It is possible there is a degree of asymmetry in the speed with which a free religious market clears, depending upon whether it begins below or above the optimal number of firms. New firms may enter a free market quickly; many of these new firms take a generation or two to fail, and well-established firms leave the market very, very slowly. This would especially be the case when competing firms offer products of roughly equal customer value, and when large firms do not enjoy economies of scale. Stark (1996) has argued that Christianity triumphed over classical paganism because it offered a much more satisfactory product, but innovations that markedly increase customer satisfaction may be rare in religion. Thus, the number of denominations in the market may not be a proper measure of whether it has reached equilibrium in terms of prices and the value to customers.

Because local congregations are like household economies producing club goods, they may not be very dependent upon the denomination they belong to, and indeed some very successful denominations such as the Southern Baptists are relatively loose confederations with much local autonomy comparable to business franchises. Unlike local automobile dealers, they are not highly dependent upon the fortunes of the manufacturer, and it is even possible for a local congregation to survive without a denomination, as many community churches in fact do. The point is that in the religion business very large firms may not have the advantage of economies of scale anywhere near as much as an automobile company does, and therefore smaller denominations are not doomed to being out-competed quickly by the large ones.

If a spectrum of faiths already exists in the society, then competition between religious organizations would rather quickly move toward equilibrium of costs and benefits with a high degree of mobilization of the public in religion, and a high level of customer satisfaction. As secular society changes, affected by such factors as new technology and political shifts, the segmentation of the market will change, but the religious market should adjust fairly smoothly. Widespread economic prosperity should move more people into mainstream churches, and economic decline or increased inequality would favor the sects, for example. Yet we know that some features of religion seem to change at a pace that rivals the glaciers for slowness.

The year 1776, in which Adam Smith essentially established the economics of religion, was notable also for the American Revolution and the first really practical steam engine developed by James Watt. In a loose sense, the modern era could be dated from that year, yet Judaism is something like fifteen times as old as *The Wealth of Nations*. Languages change only very slowly, but Christianity is about three times as old as the English language. The first thing to observe here is that religion is about the most powerful example of equilibrium we can discern in human affairs!

However, the example of Christianity does remind us there can be something new under the sun. Religious innovation does sometimes occur. Although based in the entire heritage of an ethnic group, Judaism emerged through entrepreneurial acts by individual leaders, notably Abraham leading his people into Egypt, and Moses leading them out again. Christianity began with the proverbial dozen disciples and remained small for a century or two. Islam entered the picture later, founded by Mohammad and his immediate successors. Thus one important topic relevant to religious equilibrium is the relative ease or difficulty with which new firms may enter the market.

Industries differ greatly, from one to another and over time, in terms of how easy or difficult it is to enter the market. Starting a new automobile company from scratch today is prohibitively costly, but that was not the case in 1900. Apple and Microsoft began as small groups of friends with few resources in the 1970s, but you would need a huge infusion of investment capital to launch a computer company to compete with them today. (We should not stretch our metaphors too far, but we might need to recognize that the open-source Linux operating system is analogous to a religious sect competing with the Microsoft church, relying as it does upon volunteer efforts in an intense but disorganized community not unlike a sect congregation.) What are the costs of successful entry into the religious market? How does a new firm enter the religious market?

In post-industrial society, as in the ancient world, there are few impediments to entry into the religious market, so cults abound. If the modern experience is any guide, much religious innovation is generated by small firms, as is the case in many other industries. Only a handful of people with a place to meet and the beginnings of a new faith are required. The low cost of entry into a free religious market is offset by the high likelihood of failure, however. One explanation is that cults are clubs, and religious club goods that are initially designed to serve the original members in their possibly unique circumstances may not market well to other people in the neighborhood, many of whom are already satisfied with the religion they have. Another explanation is that most tiny new religions cannot reach their market effectively, because potential customers may be strewn thinly over a wide area and can be reached only by extreme marketing exertions. Thus, any chance of success depends upon an unusual degree of entrepreneurship, which we already noted is required to start the novel religion in the first place. The main reason, however, is simply that over time innovation and entrepreneurship tends to fill all the profitable niches in a stable and open religious market. After more than two centuries of religious *laissez faire*, the U.S. market is not likely to see much *major* religious change absent equally major changes in technology, demography, or government.

Conclusion: consequences

The most famous social-scientific theory about the economic impact of religion is probably Max Weber's (1904–1905) century-old thesis that Protestantism stimulated the birth of capitalism by encouraging thrift and thus investment, and perhaps by encouraging rationalism as well. Many subsequent economic historians have disagreed with Weber, pointing out that capitalist institutions had already been established prior to the Reformation and thrived in Catholic areas (Samuelsson 1993; Delacroix 1995). Weber himself actually stated his thesis rather tentatively, writing about an elective affinity between the Protestant ethic and capitalism, rather than asserting that the former caused the latter, and specifically saying that Protestantism probably lost this function once capitalism was well launched. However, subsequent Weberians seem determined to be more Weberian than Weber himself, and introductory sociology students get the impression that capitalism could not exist without the continuing support of a particular kind of religion.

This conceivably could be true if a given religion enjoyed a monopoly through an alliance with the political elite of the society and exerted pressures on the secular economy for the benefit of the elite, but it would do so at the risk of losing many of its non-elite customers. However, in a free religious market, it is hard to see how a major religion could push the secular economy in any direction that its customers did not want to go. During historical dislocations, like the Reformation, religion might operate for a time as an independent force in society, but it would lose this power as equilibrium was reestablished. This is not to say that religion is unimportant in a free society, merely that it tends to operate like other free institutions. The pressure to survive constrains it to maximize the satisfactions of its customers and thus limits its power to force them toward goals they do not desire.

A free market of religion harmonizes with the free market of material goods and secular services, with the free market of ideas that is science and scholarship, and the free market of public decision-making that is democracy. Religion may contribute to the functionality of the entire society, by supporting interpersonal trust and suppressing criminal behavior, by compensating deprived populations for that portion of their deprivations that is unavoidable, and by supporting the production of the most important product of household labor, namely children (Bainbridge 2007). These are benefits that people want, rather than impositions upon them. Religion thus helps people achieve their valued goals on Earth, whatever rewards it may also provide in Heaven.

Bibliography

Azzi, Corry, and Ronald G. Ehrenberg. 1975. 'Household Allocation of Time and Church Attendance.' *Journal of Political Economy* 83: 27–56.

Bainbridge, William Folwell. 1882a. *Along the Lines at the Front: A General Survey of Baptist Home and Foreign Missions*. Philadelphia: American Baptist Publication Society.

——. 1882b. *Around the World Tour of Christian Missions*. New York: C. R. Blackall.

Bainbridge, William Sims. 1995. 'Social Influence and Religious Pluralism,' *Advances in Group Processes*, 12: 1–18.

—— . 2002a. 'A Prophet's Reward: Dynamics of Religious Exchange.' Pp. 63–89 in *Sacred Canopies, Sacred Markets*, edited by Ted G. Jelen. Lanham, MD: Rowman-Littlefield.

—— . 2002b. *The Endtime Family: Children of God*. Albany, NY: State University of New York Press.

—— . 2007. *Across the Secular Abyss*. Lanham, MD: Lexington.

Bainbridge, William Sims, and Rodney Stark. 1979. 'Cult Formation: Three Compatible Models.' *Sociological Analysis* 40: 285–295.

Bakan, David. 1958. *Sigmund Freud and the Jewish Mystical Tradition*. Princeton, NJ: Van Nostrand.

Barker, Eileen. 1984. *The Making of a Moonie: Choice or Brainwashing?* Oxford: Basil Blackwell.

Becker, Gary S. 1976. *The Economic Approach to Human Behavior*. Chicago: University of Chicago Press.

Becker, Gary S. 1996. *Accounting for Tastes*. Cambridge, MA: Harvard University Press.

Blau, J. R., K. C. Land, and K. Redding. 1992. 'The Expansion of Religious Affiliation: An Explanation of the Growth of Church Participation in the United States, 1850–1930.' *Social Science Research* 21: 329–352.

Blau, J. R., K. Redding, and K. C. Land. 1993. 'Ethnocultural Cleavages and the Growth of Church Membership in the United States, 1860–1930.' *Sociological Forum* 8: 609–637.

Breault, Kevin D. 1989a. 'New Evidence on Religious Pluralism, Urbanism, and Religious Participation.' *American Sociological Review* 54: 1048–1053.

—— . 1989b. 'A Reexamination of the Relationship between Religious Diversity and Religious Adherents.' *American Sociological Review* 54: 1056–1059.

Christiano, K. J. 1987. *Religious Diversity and Social Change*. Cambridge: Cambridge University Press.

Coleman, James. 1988. 'Social Capital in the Creation of Human Capital.' *American Journal of Sociology* 94(supplement): s95–s120.

Delacroix, Jacques. 1995. 'Religion and Economic Action: The Protestant Ethic, the Rise of Capitalism, and the Abuses of Scholarship.' *Journal for the Scientific Study of Religion* 34: 126–127.

Ekelund, Robert B., Robert D. Tollison, Gary M. Anderson, and Robert F. Hebert. 1996. *Sacred Trust: The Medieval Church as an Economic Firm*. New York : Oxford University Press.

Finke, R. 1989. 'Demographics of Religious Participation: An Ecological Approach, 1850–1980.' *Journal for the Scientific Study of Religion* 28: 45–58.

Finke, R. and R. Stark. 1988. 'Religious Economies and Sacred Canopies: Religious Mobilization in American Cities, 1906.' *American Sociological Review* 53: 41–49.

—— . 1989a. 'How the Upstart Sects Won America: 1776–1850.' *Journal for the Scientific Study of Religion* 28: 27–44.

—— . 1989b. 'Evaluating the Evidence: Religious Economies and Sacred Canopies.' *American Sociological Review* 54: 1054–1056.

—— . 1992. *The Churching of America: 1776–1990*. New Brunswick, NY: Rutgers University Press.

Frank, Jerome D. 1961. *Persuasion and Healing*. Baltimore: Johns Hopkins Press.

Gruber, Jonathan and Hungerman, Daniel M., 2007. 'Faith-based Charity and Crowd-out During the Great Depression.' *Journal of Public Economics*, Elsevier, 91(5–6): 1043–1069.

Homans, George C. 1974. *Social Behavior: Its Elementary Forms*. New York: Harcourt Brace Jovanovich.

Iannaccone, Laurence R. 1984. 'Consumption Capital and Habit Formation with an Application to Religious Participation'. Ph.D. Dissertation, University of Chicago.

—— . 1988. 'A Formal Model of Church and Sect.' *American Journal of Sociology* 9(supplement): s241–s268.

—— . 1990. 'Religious Participation: A Human Capital Approach.' *Journal for the Scientific Study of Religion* 29(3): 297–314.

—— . 1991. 'The Consequences of Religious Market Structure: Adam Smith and the Economics of Religion.' *Rationality and Society* 3: 156–177.

—— . 1992. 'Sacrifice and Stigma: Reducing Free–Riding in Cults, Communes, and Other Collectives.' *Journal of Political Economy* 100: 271–291.

—— . 1995. 'Risk, Rationality, and Religious Portfolios.' *Economic Inquiry* 38(2): 285–95.

——— . 1997 'Rational Choice: Framework for the Social Scientific Study of Religion.' Pp. 25–44 in *Rational Choice Theory and Religion: Summary and Assessment*, edited by Lawrence A. Young. New York: Routledge.

——— . 1998. 'Introduction to the Economics of Religion.' *Journal of Economic Literature* 36: 1465–1496.

——— . 2002. 'A Marriage Made in Heaven? Economic Theory and Religious Behavior.' Pp. 203–223 in *The Expansion of Economics – Toward a More Inclusive Social Science*, edited by Shoshana Grossbard–Schechtman and Christopher Clague. Armonk, NY: M. E. Sharpe.

Iannaccone, Laurence R., and Eli Berman. 2006. 'Religious Extremism: The Good, the Bad, and the Deadly.' *Public Choice*. 28: 109–29.

——— . 2008 'Economics of Religion.' In *The New Palgrave Dictionary of Economics*, edited by Stephen Durlauf and Lawrence Blume, London: Palgrave.

Jelen, Ted. G. (ed.) 2002. *Sacred Markets, Sacred Canopies*. Lanham, MD: Rowman and Littlefield.

Jelen, Ted G., and Clyde Wilcox. 2002. *Religion and Politics in Comparative Perspective: The One, the Few, and the Many*. Cambridge, UK: Cambridge University Press.

Katz, Elihu, and Paul F. Lazarsfeld. 1955. *Personal Influence*. Glencoe, IL: Free Press.

Klein, Daniel B. 1997. 'Knowledge, Reputation, and Trust, By Voluntary Means.' Pp. 1–9 in *Reputation: Studies in the Voluntary Elicitation of Good Conduct*, edited by Daniel B. Klein. Ann Arbor: University of Michigan Press.

Land, K. C., G. Deane, and J. R. Blau. 1991. 'Religious Pluralism and Church Membership: A Spatial Diffusion Model.' *American Sociological Review* 56: 237–249.

Lewis, James R. (ed.) 2009. *Scientology*. Oxford: Oxford University Press.

Niebuhr, H. Richard. 1929. *The Social Sources of Denominationalism*. New York: Henry Holt.

Pope, Liston. 1942. *Millhands and Preachers*. New Haven, CT: Yale University Press.

Rogers, Everett M. 2003. *Diffusion of Innovations*. New York: Free Press.

Samuelsson, Kurt. 1993. *Religion and Economic Action: The Protestant Ethic, the Rise of Capitalism, and the Abuses of Scholarship*. Toronto: University of Toronto Press.

Skinner, B. F. 1938. *The Behavior of Organisms*. New York: D. Appleton-Century.

Stark, Rodney. 1996. *The Rise of Christianity*. Princeton, NJ: Princeton University Press.

Stark, Rodney, and Laurence R. Iannaccone. 1993. 'Rational Choice Propositions About Religious Movements.' Pp. 241–261 in *Handbook on Cults and Sects in America*, edited by David G. Bromley and Jeffrey K. Hadden. Greenwich, CT: JAI Press.

Stark, Rodney and William Sims Bainbridge. 1985. *The Future of Religion*. Berkeley: University of California Press.

——— . 1987. *A Theory of Religion*. New York: Toronto/Lang.

Vahle, Neal. 2002. *The Unity Movement*. Philadelphia: Templeton Foundation Press.

Voas, David, Daniel V. A. Olson, and Alasdair Crockett. 2002. 'Religious Pluralism and Participation: Why Previous Research is Wrong.' *American Sociological Review* 67: 212–230.

Warner, R. Stephen. 1993. 'Work in Progress toward a New Paradigm for the Sociological Study of Religion in the United States.' *American Journal of Sociology* 98: 1044–1093.

Weber, Max. 1904–1905. *The Protestant Ethic and the Spirit of Capitalism*. New York: Scribner's [1958].

Wilson, Edward O. 1975. *Sociobiology*. Cambridge: Harvard University Press.

Zelizer, Viviana A. 1978. 'Human Values and the Market: The Case of Life Insurance and Death in 19th Century America.' *American Journal of Sociology* 84: 591–610.

Chapter 28

Geography, space and the sacred

Kim Knott

Religion takes place in space. Religious people are distributed globally and locally in various patterns at different times and according to various factors such as mission and conversion, religious growth or decline, migration and population change, war and natural disaster. Religions – whether 'indigenous', 'world' or 'new' religions – are more or less closely identified with particular continents, countries or localities. Religious groups occupy social spaces, gathering in mosques, churches, temples, community centres and other buildings, and meeting at times in the open in places denoted or apprehended as sacred. Families and individuals practise their religions at home, sometimes setting apart a room or area for worship or meditation, chanting or dancing. Religious and cosmological beliefs often have a spatial character, such as ideas about where certain religious activities should occur or where objects should be placed, which lands or places are deemed to be holy, or how heavenly cities or spiritual landscapes appear and are spatially organised. Furthermore, the location of religion in secular spaces is important too. Is it confined to particular times and places by the secular state? Is this reflected in distinctions between public and private spheres, in planning regulations or in the ritual and discourse of state and civic life? Religions and religious groups change over time, and this affects their spatial arrangements. They change across space too: they may appear and be situated quite differently in the US, India and Indonesia, for example. As we can see, religions and places are mutually influential.

There are many reasons, then, for the study of religions to be concerned with matters geographical and spatial. The history of this concern has been intermittent, as I shall show in a later section, but in the first decade of the twenty-first century there has been a revitalisation of interest among both geographers and scholars of religion in each other's subject matter. This follows what is now referred to as the 'spatial turn' in late-modern theory and methodology across the humanities and social sciences. Since the mid-1980s the spatial interests of continental social theorists, such as Henri Lefebvre, Michel Foucault and Michel de Certeau, and radical geographers, such as Doreen Massey, David Harvey and Edward Soja, have had an impact on academics in many disciplines, including the study of religions. New perspectives on the geography of religion have begun to emerge in Europe, Asia and the US, and innovative theoretical engagements between religion, space and territory have been formulated by scholars of religion. Theologians have also turned their attention to place and space (Sheldrake 2001; Gorringe 2002; Inge 2003; Bergmann 2007).

Later in this chapter, I will set the study of geography, space and the sacred in historical context, and examine the new perspectives and innovative engagements mentioned above. After that I will look at several themes that have attracted the interest of contemporary geographers and scholars of religion: pilgrimage and mobility; diasporas and migration; bodies and space; death and dying; and religion in secular spaces. I will illustrate these with examples from recent research and hope to generate ideas for potential projects and dissertations. First let me begin with an illustration from the work of students at my own university. Their research shows what can be learnt by undertaking studies of religion in the local area.

Local studies of religion

In recent years small groups of students at the University of Leeds have undertaken a teamwork project called 'The Religious Mapping of Leeds' (Knott 1998, 2000, 2009). Over one semester they work together to research the religious life of a neighbourhood and to examine the way religion intersects with, influences and is influenced by other local conditions, such as demographic, social, economic and political factors, education, crime, health and social provision. Over the years teams have studied various inner-city and suburban districts of Leeds – a multicultural city in northern England with a population of approximately 720,000 – such as Beeston, Moortown, Armley, Burley, Chapeltown, Harehills and Headingley (see Community Religions Project website). Working with a university supervisor and local community partner – these have included a police inspector, ministers and other religious specialists, and chairs of interfaith and other voluntary bodies – the team undertakes fieldwork in the area, visiting churches, chapels, mosques, synagogues, temples, attending services and interviewing congregation members and leaders, as well as identifying key local institutions and interviewing their representatives. Team members often conduct a street survey and speak to people in shops, restaurants, bars and other public places about their views on the area and the place of religion within it.

As well as learning a great deal about the history of local religious groups and the way religion functions within the area, they become aware of the way in which locality informs religion. One Baptist church is not just like any other, neither in its internal and external appearance, nor in its concerns. Baptist theological interests and commitments, and Baptist sacramental and ministerial practices may provide continuity from one church to another, but the way they are lived out is informed by the church's situation, the demographic profile of its congregation and local community, the type of neighbourhood, the built environment, the local economy and local resources of various kinds. This is equally true of mosques and gurdwaras. Furthermore, the role and place of religion differs from one neighbourhood to another. Religious leaders and members may be key players in local politics or active in social provision in some areas, or well known for their festivals or their contribution to fighting crime in others.

In many places in Leeds, as in other European cities, religion seems to have disappeared behind a lively façade of pizza take-aways, supermarkets, bars and boutiques, but when the students look more closely local charity shops come into focus, elderly people can be seen in day centres run by religious communities; mothers and toddlers make their way to groups held in church buildings; immigration advice and support services for asylum seekers can be witnessed in mosques and temples, and health food shops and libraries reveal the alternative spiritual life of the neighbourhood in posters and advertisements for local healers, meditation and yoga groups. Religious books, posters of deities, gurus and the Virgin Mary, prayer mats, tapes, CDs and videos of religious songs, films and festivals can be found vying for a little local space in bookshops or hardware stores. Focusing in still further reveals religion represented on mobile bodies – in hijabs and turbans, Christian crosses, Sikh *kara* and *kirpan* (symbolic bangle and sword), Hindu *Aum* (letter or syllable), Jewish star of David, the colours of rasta – and in devotional music, alongside the songs of Bollywood, through open car windows.

Once the students have described and analysed their data, and considered key themes of local importance – such as religion and ethnicity, the role of religion in social work, youth provision or education, religious responses to crime and policing, the religious contribution to community and sustainability, or ecumenical and inter-faith relations in the area – they go ahead and prepare a report and directory, and give a public presentation and answer questions about their findings in a local venue. This requires them to engage, negotiate and be accountable to local people.

Local studies of religion have other advantages too. By starting from the particular rather than the general and by focusing on what happens to religions within designated local spaces, they challenge the 'World Religions' approach with its focus on discrete, generic traditions and normative beliefs and practices that is so common in religious studies. Students reason inductively from their examination of particular Methodist churches and Sikh gurdwaras rather than reasoning deductively from their reading of textbooks about Christianity and Sikhism. Local studies require a multidisciplinary and polymethodic approach that brings student researchers into contact with a variety of ways of working within and beyond the study of religions. Furthermore, because of the nature of late-modern urban neighbourhoods, such studies necessitate an investigation not only of local but also national and global communications and interconnections. Religious and ethnic plurality, diasporic relationships, global identity politics, national as well as local government support for faith-based initiatives, inter-faith ventures, and new spiritual collaborations can all be witnessed and studied (Stausberg 2009; Knott 2009).

Geography and the spatial study of religion: a brief history

Within the study of religions there has been a history of interest in religious places and movements – sacred landscapes, pilgrimage routes, places of worship, missionary activities, global religious developments and cyber-religious networks – but, except in a few cases to which I shall return, there has been a lack of concern with the explicitly geographical or spatial implications of such places and movements. Similarly, despite earlier interest within geography, religion has remained a fairly marginal object of study since the 1960s, though a change can now be discerned. In this section I will consider the history of these two separate, but interconnected, fields of study.

In the sixteenth and seventeenth centuries, in Germany and England, the discipline of geography was forged overtly in a Christian mould, in part to demonstrate the 'visible side of the Divine revelation' (Park 1994: 9) but also to justify the superiority of Christianity in the context of other religions. However, despite Christian missionary interest in the relationship between religion and different geographical contexts, it was not until the late eighteenth century that the two were formally engaged in the scholarly project of *Religionsgeographie* by Gottlieb Kasche, and the possibility of a rational, non-confessional geography was addressed by Immanuel Kant (Büttner 1980; Park 1994). In the twentieth century several major geographical studies of religion were published, most notably by Deffontaines (1948), Sopher (1967), and Park (1994), with the latest addition by Stump (2008). Paul Fickeler is accredited with developing the modern agenda of the geography of religions in an article in German in

1947 (Fickeler 1962). He suggested that 'the science of religion should tackle the question of how environment affects religion, and that the geography of religion should tackle the question of how religion affects people and landscape' (Park 1994: 16–17), and identified a range of themes appropriate for geographical study (Fickeler 1962). The division of duties he proposed has since been challenged, with scholars on both sides breaching the disciplinary boundary. Furthermore, a number of geographers (e.g. Büttner 1974; Kong 1990; Cooper 1992) have called for an informed understanding and study of the dialectical *reciprocity* of religion and the environment.

Since the late 1990s the geographical study of religion has moved away from some of its old spheres of interest in denominational studies, religious demography, the landscape of death and pilgrimage, to new ones in the poetics and politics of the sacred, identity and community, and religion in relation to diaspora and postcolonial spaces, body and gender, global and local, political and ethical geographies, and theoretical considerations. Key contemporary contributors are Lily Kong, a major reviewer of recent trends in the geography of religion (Kong 1990, 2001), two British geographers, Julian Holloway and Oliver Valins (Holloway and Valins 2002; Valins 2003; Holloway 2006), Hans Knippenberg, editor of *The Changing Religious Landscape of Europe* (2005) and fellow European contributors, and those scholars with essays in the 2006 *Annals of the Association of American Geographers* who have sought to move the field forward with new conceptual and empirical interventions, including James Proctor (2006) and Adrian Ivakhiv (2006). The American scholar, Roger Stump, has made a significant contribution in recent years to developing the geography of religion for a student audience. Following earlier work on the geography of religious fundamentalism (Stump 2000), a later book organises the field according to four frames: the spatial dynamics of religious distributions, the contextuality of religions, religious territoriality in secular space, and the meanings and uses of sacred space (Stump 2008). This framework enables him to bring up to date subjects that preoccupied earlier geographers (religious distribution, sacred space and the spatial diversification of belief and practice in the major religions), whilst acknowledging and exploring the operation of religious territoriality within the secular spaces of everyday life, including the communal scale, body, home, the state and the global arena.

Despite the early development of *Religionsgeographie*, little significant reciprocal interest by religious studies scholars in space, place and geography can be witnessed before the mid-twentieth century. The content of Jacques Waardenburg's anthology of the first hundred years of the non-theological study of religions (1973) suggests that scholars of religion outside the discipline of geography gave little credence to these issues. The exception was Gerardus van der Leeuw in the mid-1930s who was the first to take an explicit interest in the role of different places and scales for religion. In a chapter on sacred space in his book, *Religion in Essence and Manifestation*, he identified a series of homologies (home, temple, settlement, pilgrimage site, human body) and linked synecdoches (hearth, altar, sanctuary, shrine and heart) which have since become key terms for a scholarly discussion of the location of the sacred (van der Leeuw 1938: 393–402; Chidester and Linenthal 1995: 6–7).

It was with the work of Mircea Eliade, however, that sacred space really became a significant subject of theoretical and critical enquiry, with its meaning, characteristics and functions being examined and typologised. His ideas have provided a frame of reference for subsequent scholars of sacred geography, both followers and critics. Eliade is known for positing several axioms, of sacred space as set apart from ordinary, profane space, as the 'Center' or *axis mundi* through which communication between different domains is possible, and as the manifestation of the 'Real' (hierophany) (Eliade 1959: 26). Scholars investigating the meaning and power of sacred space and time have often used these axioms as a reference point. Belden C. Lane, for example, adopted and developed them in his phenomenological enquiry into the poetics of American sacred landscape as 'storied place' (Lane 1988: 11–20), whilst Chidester and Linenthal, accusing Eliade of mystifying the sacred and ignoring its politics, overturned them in their subversive, critical approach to the contested nature of American sacred space (Chidester and Linenthal 1995: 16–18).

These scholars were as indebted to Jonathan Z. Smith as they were to Eliade. In a lecture in 1971 entitled 'The Wobbling Pivot', Smith had queried Eliade's focus on the Center at the expense of the periphery, and went on to elucidate what was to become an influential dichotomy between two existential possibilities, 'a *locative* vision of the world (which emphasises place) and a *utopian* vision of the world (using the term in its strict sense: the value of being in no place)' (Smith 1978a: 101). He developed these perspectives in his later essay, 'Map Is Not Territory', as an imperial, ideologically-orientated map, and a utopian map which reverses the locative and seeks to escape to a new world (1978b: 308–9). Smith's use of the metaphor of the map in the context of investigating these cosmological perspectives simultaneously de-territorialised the sacred and showed how space operates as an organising principle beyond the material world in the arena of belief and ideology. Smith continued to employ spatial terminology in his 1987 book, *To Take Place: Toward a Theory of Ritual*, in which he moved beyond earlier phenomenological conceptions of the 'sacred' and 'place', in favour of anthropological and sociological approaches. He argued that 'human beings are not placed, they bring place into being' (Smith 1987: 28), using ritual to do so. People do not so much respond to sacred place, as Eliade suggested, as create it through their ritual activity (105).

One further scholar requires our attention before we turn to the current theoretical and methodological agenda and that is Manfred Büttner, a German scholar who, in the 1970s, strove to instruct a largely ignorant audience of religious studies peers of the importance of the geography of religion. Writing in English as well as German and in well known scholarly journals, including *Religion* and *Numen*, he charted the history of the engagement between geography and religion and sought to develop an agenda for field study that would bring scholars together from both sides to further their mutual understanding of the way in which settlement and landscape are moulded by religion and the way the environment influences religions and religious groups. He called for a 'synthetic geography of religion' within the meta-science of all disciplines concerned with religion (Büttner 1974: 84; 1980). Despite his valiant efforts, this has yet to be fully realised.

The spatial study of religion: theory and method

Before turning to some of the major themes that have preoccupied scholars writing about geography, religion and space, I will first review recent advances of a theoretical and methodological kind. As I suggested earlier, a spatial turn in the humanities and social sciences has focused attention on space, place and location. It has challenged previous Cartesian perspectives, has considered space in its engagement with discourse, representation, power, identity and practice, as well as in both its physical and social aspects. Despite his interest in genealogy and the historical outworking of power relations, Foucault referred to modernity as the epoch not of time but space (1986: 22). Following Lefebvre's ground-breaking work, *La production de l'espace* (1974), social relations and culture have been understood as having their existence in and through space (Lefebvre 1991: 404), with social divisions and cultural classifications often being spatialised (Shields 1991: 29). These ideas can be seen to underpin the work of several scholars writing on space and religion to whom I shall now turn (Knott 2005a, 2008).

Contributing to the body of work developed by Eliade and Smith, and building on Durkheimian scholarship on the 'sacred', the Finnish scholar, Veikko Anttonen, engaged space and the sacred in two different ways. He used spatial concepts (of body and territory) to develop his theory of the 'sacred' as a category boundary, and also examined the topographical use of 'sacred' names and references within various landscapes and other contexts (1996, 2000, 2005). He saw body and territory, and the boundary between them, as pre-conceptual structures which humans use in generating discourse and practice about the 'sacred'. As bounded entities, they are co-extensive (1996: 41): the human body has both an inside and an outside, the latter being co-extensive with the inside of the territory. The boundaries between these pre-conceptual structures of body, territory and the wilderness beyond it have the potential to become markers for distinguishing between things on the basis of their value as well as for establishing rules for their engagement and transformation (1996: 42). This cognitive capacity for using spatial structures to distinguish certain things, events, persons and places as 'sacred' is culturally dependent. Anttonen demonstrated this in his work on territorial boundaries in the Baltic Sea area, commenting that the Finno-Ugric word *pyhä* was used of places that people wanted 'to demarcate from the rest of the environment as "separate", "designated", "prohibited", "dangerous"' (2005: 192). But he also noted that, in other cultural contexts, whether religious, national or ideological, a similar process of 'sacred' attribution was at work (2000: 280–1). Anttonen's theory unravels the cognitive and cultural relationship between space (body and territory), language and the process of sacralisation – making things 'sacred'.

Focusing explicitly on religion, rather than the 'sacred' as a category that crosses the boundary between the religious and the secular, Thomas Tweed used spatial tropes to develop 'a theory that made sense of the religious life of transnational migrants and addressed three themes – movement, relation and position', a theory with the potential to be applied to other (non-migrant) religious lives (2006: 5).

Starting with a spatialised understanding of theory in which he suggested that 'theories are embodied travels ..., positioned representations ..., and proposed routes' (Tweed 2006: 9), Tweed stressed the particular, located nature of his own and others' theories (18). At the heart of his work lies a definition of religion which employs spatial and aquatic tropes: 'Religions are confluences of organic-cultural flows that intensify joy and confront suffering by drawing on human and suprahuman forces to make homes and cross boundaries' (54). Breaking this down, he discussed the orienting spatial metaphors of 'dwelling' and 'crossing' and the aquatic metaphors of 'confluence' and 'flow', drawing on the theoretical insights of Deleuze and Guattari (hydraulic model), Latour (circulating fluids), Appadurai (cultural flows), Long (religion as orientation; one's place in the world), and Clifford (dwelling-in-travel) (Tweed 2006: 57–61, 74). Following an examination of 'dwelling', Tweed turned to 'crossing', developing the three aspects of 'terrestrial crossing', 'corporeal crossing' and 'cosmic crossing'. He revealed the potential of this spatial term to connect geographical, embodied and imagined movements and transformations (123–63), concluding that 'religions are flows, translocative and transtemporal crossings' (158).

Tweed's theoretical project shows the rich possibilities of rethinking religion through spatial (and aquatic) metaphors, and – following Smith's contribution that 'map is not territory' – may also provide geographers with a new perspective on the relevance of religion for their discipline. Religions facilitate 'crossings', movements from one position to another; such crossings are not confined to geographical scales, but may also be corporeal and cosmic.

Moving from theory to methodology now, I turn to my own work, *The Location of Religion: A Spatial Analysis* (Knott 2005a). In writing it, my intention was to develop a spatial methodology for locating religion, particularly in ostensibly secular places, things, communities and objects. Whilst this also required theorising a field of religious-secular relations, which I shall not discuss here, it chiefly involved extrapolating tractable 'tools' from cultural and social theories of space for the study of religions. I developed a set of terms for analysing the location of religion: (1) the body as the source of space, (2) the dimensions of space, (3) the properties of space, (4) the aspects of space, and (5) the dynamics of space (Knott 2005a: 12–58; 2005b: 156–66; 2008: 1108–11). These analytical terms – which together constitute a spatial methodology – allow for the close and detailed examination of a place, object, body or group by means of its spatial attributes. Beginning with the foundational role of the body for our experience and representation of space, in particular with signs of the body inscribed in the object or place of our investigation, the methodology then requires a consideration of that object's or place's physical, social and mental dimensions. The next step involves a study of its spatial properties, that is its diachronic extensiveness and synchronic interconnections, its configuration (the way in which the research object or place is formed by its constituent parts), and its power relations. The final stages entail a consideration of the dynamic aspects of the object or place, first by means of its spatial aspects – the way in which it is practised, represented and lived – and, second, by means of the processes of production and reproduction that form it and allow it to generate new spaces. A methodology based on these spatial elements is an interpretive process which may be employed systematically, though its various elements can also be applied in isolation. It has the effect of opening up the object or place of study to in-depth enquiry whilst at the same time taking seriously its interconnections, whether diachronic or synchronic. As such, it enables a thorough contextualisation of religion. Examples of the application of this methodology can be found in relation to the location of religion in the left hand (Knott 2005a), an English medical centre (Knott and Franks 2007), and an urban high street (Knott 2009).

Reconceived in contemporary theory as dynamic, 'space' is no longer merely the passive container or backdrop for human activity that it was once thought to be. It is thoroughly enmeshed in embodiment and everyday practice, in ritual, knowledge and discourse, and consequently it is enmeshed in religion no less than in other areas of social and cultural life. Considering pre-conceptual spatial structures for people's attribution of the 'sacred' as a category boundary (Anttonen), exploring the application of spatial metaphor for theorising religion (Tweed), and opening up 'space' and its constituent elements to closer scrutiny in order to examine the location of religion in secular contexts (Knott) are all examples of what thinking spatially has added to the theoretical and methodological resources of the study of religion. However, from the side of geography, it is important to note a complementary process. Adrian Ivakhiv, in an article subtitled 'Mapping the distribution of an unstable signifier', calls for geographers to adopt a deconstructive approach to 'religion' and the 'sacred', and to consider them as 'ways to distribute a certain kind of significance across geographic spaces' (2006: 169). Citing Foucault on the recent invention of 'religion' and the possibility of its erasure, he suggests that 'it is the task of geographers of religion to trace the changing orchestrations of those significances across space and place' (169), noting their relationship to other forms of significance, whether ideological, cosmological or political

(171). Geographers, he says, are particularly well suited to tracing the '(re)distribution and (re)configuration' (173) of such significances, for example of religious sacrality and irreligious profanity, and their relationship to ethnic or national sacralities. Starting from a base in geography rather than cognition, Ivakhiv nevertheless comes close to Anttonen in recommending a study of the incidence and distribution of the 'sacred' in its many forms and contexts.

Geography, space and religion: some contemporary themes

All academic disciplines have their own traditions and bodies of knowledge. Alister McGrath has referred to theology as having an organising 'architecture', to which theologians have historically deferred (2001: 141). The agenda of geographers of religion is insufficiently systematic or stable to be referred to in this way. The subject matter of geography of religion has reflected broader intellectual trends, though – as is the case in many disciplines – it has lagged behind them. I shall consider five contemporary themes, several of which have established roots in the discipline whilst others have appeared on the agenda more recently: pilgrimage and movement; diasporas and migration; bodies and space; death and dying; and religion in secular spaces.

Pilgrimage and movement

I begin with pilgrimage because it has repeatedly been drawn on as a theme for treatment by geographers, as well as anthropologists and scholars of religion. From Deffontaines' consideration of it in 1948 and the ground-breaking study on Hindu pilgrimage by Bhardwaj in 1973, up to the more recent attempt to re-frame it as 'cultures in motion' (Coleman and Eade 2004a), it has continued to attract significant scholarly attention (see Park 1994: 258–85; Stump 2008: 334–45). In the past the focus was on pilgrim distribution, types and levels of sacred space, and motivation for pilgrimage, with scholars from the late 1970s onwards responding in particular to the theoretical contribution of Victor and Edith Turner in *Image and Pilgrimage in Christian Culture* (1978). Focusing on the popular and anarchic aspects of pilgrimage, the Turners introduced concepts of 'anti-structure', 'liminality' and 'communitas' which have since become an important focus for the comparative study of both pilgrimage and tourism and for challenging the boundary between religious and secular travel. Nevertheless, they worked within what Coleman and Eade have referred to as a 'largely place-centred approach to the culture of sacred travel' (2004b: 2). More recent studies have turned from a focus on place to one on movement to, in and from places, on the journey itself and on mobility.

The instability of place was signalled by the geographer Yi-Fu Tuan who suggested that, both socially and individually, people need to go beyond their own places and their routine experience of place, to be 'out of place' and to realise place as 'a temporary abode, not an enduring city' (Tuan cited in Park 1994: 260). Articulating the centrality of mobility, however, fell to Morinis (1992) who noted both the intersection of journeying with the embodiment of an ideal, and the structural opposition of stasis and movement as defining features of pilgrimage. Developing these ideas, Coleman and Eade sought to reframe pilgrimage in the context of several interlocking notions of movement (2004b:16–17). In terms of *movement as performative action*, pilgrimage could be seen as bringing about transformations of various kinds, such as invoking the idea of a pan-Hindu sacred space, more than the sum of separate local sites. *Movement as embodied action* saw pilgrimage as producing bodily effects, practices and experiences: the focus of contemporary travellers en route to Santiago de Compostela was on walking the journey and feeling the journey in the body, rather than on getting to the pilgrimage destination by the quickest route. Pilgrimage, they suggested, was best understood in the context of local conceptions of mobility, place and space (*movement as part of a semantic field*), there being no fixed, generic notion of movement that could be drawn on to explain different pilgrimages and pilgrim experiences. The final aspect, *movement as metaphor*, was important to pilgrimage irrespective of whether an actual physical journey occurred. References to the journeying soul, the inner pilgrimage, cosmic crossings, and life as quest all make metaphorical use of movement (see also Tweed 2006).

Coleman and Eade's reframing of pilgrimage with reference to movement can be illustrated using Paul Basu's study of 'roots-tourism' in the Scottish Highland diaspora (2004). Starting with *movement as metaphor*, many Scottish diasporic visitors from North America or Australasia describe travelling to and through Scotland in terms of the *route metaphors* of 'homecoming', 'quest' and 'pilgrimage', which together form a 'grammar for roots tourism' (154). In so doing they often draw on local myths of movement such as the Arthurian grail quest and other Celtic narratives as well as discourses of movement informed by their New World origins, such as 'diaspora' and 'return from exile' (*movement as part of a semantic field*). Working with the metaphors of quest and pilgrimage, in particular, enables Scottish diasporic travellers to draw on a related repertoire of behaviours and experiences, such as 'processing barefoot, kneeling, weeping, collecting relics, depositing *ex-votos*' (174) (*movement as embodied action*). Furthermore, in terms of *movement as performative action*, as Basu suggests, performing these journeys and seeing them through the route metaphors of homecoming, quest and pilgrimage enables Scottish diasporic travellers to imagine their destination as 'home', 'the indeterminate' and 'the sacred', and to experience it as profound, mysterious and enchanted (156).

Diasporas and migration

Basu's example evokes a second popular theme at the intersection of work on religion, geography and space, and that is diasporas and migration (Park 1994: 138–9, 153–8; Stump 2008: 63–77). The focus of another chapter in this volume, by Séan McLoughlin, this theme is now central for both geographers interested in religion and scholars of religion interested in space. As Kong made clear in her 2001 review of new geographies of religion, the multicultural contexts that arise as a result of population migration and diasporic identifications produce new religious landscapes, complex religious/secular relations and inter-religious contestations (2001: 214–5). The appearance and character of urban space may be changed as new communities transform existing buildings or build new ones; and disputes over planning, changes of usage, and heritage may arise. Different religious groups may vie over control of a particular space or its interpretation and significance; equally they may agree to share space. Kong's own work on Hindu *Thaipusam* processions in Singapore – which again highlights the importance of movement – brings to the fore the negotiation of religious and secular agencies, in particular the state's management of religion and regulation of time and space (2005).

Another important spatial consequence of the migration of religious people is the diasporic identification with and memory of the place of origin – sometimes referred to as 'home', as we saw in the case of those Americans and Australians who retained an affinity with Scotland. Sometimes what is remembered and longed for is not a physical place but a scattered socio-religious community, such as the Muslim *ummah* or the Parsi diaspora. Although tangible transnational relationships may be maintained through visits or electronic communications, the imaginative and emotional spaces and connections are just as important, if not more so.

Thomas Tweed – whose theoretical contribution I discussed earlier – provides an example in his poignant account of the Cuban Catholic diaspora in Miami and the hope they placed in 'Our Lady of the Exile' to liberate their homeland from communism and return it to the place of their memories (1997). His account of the annual feast day, that recalls the journey by boat in 1961 of Our Lady of Charity from Cuba to the US mainland, reveals a complex politics of identity with multiple spatial referents: the Cuba of the nationalist diasporic imagination, the real Communist Cuba, the socio-spatial gathering of like-minded Cuban Catholics, the memory of the sea journey, the procession and sacred space with Our Lady at the centre, and the moving bodies of the worshippers (1997: 116). In his later analysis of this event, Tweed focuses on the themes of dwelling and crossing (2006: 169–71). He notes that Cubans in Miami, in addition to living in the US, orient themselves around the shrine to Our Lady and around the annual events with which she is associated. They are grounded in their conception of the Cuban 'homeland' and use of its associated symbols, the flag, map and national anthem. But their beliefs and practices also involve terrestrial, corporeal and cosmic crossings (169). The crossing from Cuba to Miami by the Virgin and by the migrants themselves is recalled; Our Lady's help is sought for rites of passage involving bodily crossings; and the ultimate horizon of salvation both for the nation and the individual is invoked and becomes a focus for prayer.

Body

Tweed draws attention to the affective dimension of this event, the weeping, shouting and singing, the swaying and waving of handkerchiefs, the reaching out to touch Our Lady, the pride as the national anthem is sung. The space of the body, as a resource for the expression of love of God and participation in religious community, but also as a site where the order and power of religion may be played out, is important for geographers and other scholars of religion interested in the interface between individuals and religious institutions (Stump 2008: 239–49). Largely ignored in earlier geographies of religion, as Stump suggests, its importance lies in its relationship to religious identity – through dress, ornamentation and body markings – to personal purity, in being the site where religious prohibitions are enforced, to the observance of orthodoxy and orthopraxy, as well as to personal expressions of faith (240). All bodies are differently marked by their social and cultural contexts and inflected by personal preferences and tastes. Their observation and analysis can be productive for understanding larger geo-political and religious/ideological movements and forces, as well as for working at the micro-level of individuals, families, objects, rituals and habits.

A much-studied subject of embodiment in recent years has been the *hijab* and other aspects of Islamic veiling. In addition to the increased incidence of covering by Muslim women in the Middle East, Asia and Europe since the Iranian revolution, the subject has sparked anxiety in secular liberal societies, contention between Muslims as well as with non-Muslims, and generated public debates about the appropriateness of veiling in schools and other public places. Because of the Islamic association of *hijab* with *purdah*, meaning 'curtain or screen' – that which separates public from private, and women from the gaze of those who are not close family members – there are particular spatial considerations to be borne in mind, as well as those political ones which lead Islamist and feminist exponents to debate *hijab* and its importance for women.

The prominence and widespread nature of this debate has created a fertile ground for the discussion of other items of religious dress and bodily adornment, particularly the Christian cross and Sikh turban. The urban geographer Margaret Walton-Roberts, in an article on Sikh identity in the Vancouver area of Canada, critiqued essentialising notions of identity by examining the multiple meanings of the turban, whether in racialising discourse, as a strategic choice for a positive multiculturalism, or to affirm an ethno-nationalist agenda (1998). The turban in such cases may become a focus for scholars interested in the geography of body and identity, but also in the adorned body as part of a changing urban landscape (see also Knott 2005a: 40–2).

Death and dying

A spatial focus follows bodies through the dynamism of life to dying and death. As Park suggests, 'geographers have devoted more attention to landscapes of death than to landscapes of worship' even to the point of developing a new technical term, 'necrogeography' (1994: 213). This has occurred, at least in part, because religions themselves are so interested in the meaning of death, in the rituals that surround it, in its capacity to affect emotions and social relations, and in what happens afterwards – both in terms of disposing of the body and of any continuity of spirit or resurrection of the body. All of these aspects of death have spatial effects that are open to geographical study, the most common of which have been burial practices (see Park 1994: 213–26). The different ways in which religious groups have disposed of the dead – through burial, cremation or, in the case of Zoroastrians, exposure to sunlight and birds of prey – and what they do with the remains have been fertile subjects for study, with a particular focus on cemetery landscapes, their size, form and architecture. But beliefs and practices change, and in some Western societies – particularly in urban contexts where space is under pressure – cremation has become the norm and has produced its own geography. Furthermore, environmental issues have led to changes in the materials used for transporting bodies for cremation or burial, and to the sites selected for the scattering of ashes or internment, with woodland sites often favoured.

The mapping of deathscapes, the statistical and demographic study of socio-cultural patterns of death and dying (in relation to disease, accidents, old age, etc.) and the distribution of different religious practices vis-à-vis death and disposal all contribute to a complex necrogeography. But there are new areas too that are ripe for development, such as a shift of interest from the spaces of death to those associated with dying, bereavement, and relationships between the living and those who have 'passed over'. For example, the geography of the hospice movement, the architecture of hospices, and the movements of the terminally ill and those who take the journey with them provide a new focus. Another is the geography of belief and practice around contact with ancestors and other deceased people.

Holloway, in his work on Spiritualism and the geography of the séance, changes the focus from the fact of death to the spirit of vitality, to continuity beyond the grave and connections with the living. He considers the affects and sensations felt by those participating in the séance and the way in which they were touched by, possessed and haunted by ghosts and spirits (185). He charts the idea of 'enchanted space' and its possibility for focusing on bodies, feelings and vitality across the borderland between the living and dead, and in so doing contributes to reorienting the contemporary geography of religion, moving it away from its fixation on traditional subject matter.

Religion in secular context

A key change in geographical studies of religion has been in the scholarly attention now given to the engagement between religion and its secular context. The distribution of religious people, their beliefs and practices and impact on the landscape is interesting in and of itself, but is nonetheless best understood in relation to the relations between religion and state, and – in many countries – between religion and the secular conditions of modernity. Religious organisations and individuals have to negotiate their relationship with secular government and other agencies, sometimes seeking recourse in human rights legislation which protects religious as well as other interests. In terms of space and geography, this process of negotiation is often witnessed in the planning process and built environment, as well as in relation to public ritual, proselytising, processions, and matters of external symbols, dress and individual behaviour. As Stump suggests, however, the relationship works in the other direction too with religious bodies seeking to resist or protect themselves from secular society by constructing firm boundaries, or by seeking to extend their influence in public matters by challenging secular laws and policies, or through the activities of faith-based organisations (2008: 268–79). Public space, health and education are key arenas in which both religious and secularist exponents may seek to 'gain ground'. This metaphor is not inappropriate as success may well be measured territorially, in terms of the colonisation of public places and the recognition of the right to own or build property, and to mark the landscape. Pnina Werbner, with reference to the sacralisation of space by British Muslims, calls this process 'stamping the earth with the name of Allah' (1996: 167). Other writers in *Making Muslim Space in North America and Europe* (Metcalf 1996) refer to the 'islamization of space', to 'new Medinas' as well as the traditional socio-religious process of *da'wa* or propagation.

But secular spaces are interesting in their own right for geographers of religion, first, because such scholars have relevant tools and skills that enable them to examine these spaces with reference to the beliefs, practices and values that inform and shape them or that issue forth from them. Secondly, secular spaces are worthy of study precisely because they are places where religion is not present or which religious bodies are forced to negotiate or contest. In my own work with Myfanwy Franks on the location of religion in an English medical centre (Knott and Franks 2007), in addition to finding some surprising references to religion, we delved deeply into the range of secular values expressed and practised in its physical, social and discursive spaces. We saw how medical workers contested each other's interpretations of professional principles and practices, notions of vocation and code of conduct, sometimes drawing on metaphors of 'faith' and 'fundamentalism' for support or critique, and on notions of the 'sacred' to express those aspects of their work or working environment which were non-negotiable for them.

Sophie Gilliat-Ray, in her studies of what might be called 'secular sacred places' in British public institutions (such as hospitals and the Millennium Dome), considered the role they had for the people who use them, many of whom had not been nurtured in religious communities and have no formal religious affiliation. She suggested that,

> [S]ites of spiritual activity that are in some senses generic or universal and where there is an absence of explicit religious symbols or architecture associated with one single faith

community, allow space for people to explore their own sometimes muddled beliefs (or lack of them) ... People can undertake their own private interpretive work ... Such spaces are thus perfectly suited to the needs of an increasing number of people who have forgotten (or who may have never known) the protocols of visiting religious buildings.

(2005: 364–65)

Her examination of the affinity between such unconventional sacred sites and the needs of the people who may pass through them raises questions about both the nature and function of secular sacred space and the process of sacralisation in late-modernity that form a new context for debates in geography of religion and the wider study of religions about sacred space.

Summary

The spatial turn evident in the work of social and cultural theorists from the late 1960s to the end of the twentieth century had an impact on the geographical and spatial study of religion and the sacred, broadening the interests of scholars and increasing the focus on theory and method. Traditional themes, such as pilgrimage and deathscapes, were revisited and developed; new themes emerged as a result of global developments, population movements, the politics of identity, awareness of the importance of gender and embodiment, and the need for secular agencies to engage with religious institutions and to express their own beliefs and interests. Small and large scales were considered: from body and locality to transnational movements and the new scapes of globalisation.

After giving examples of the many reasons for the study of religions to be concerned with spatial and geographical data and issues, this chapter focused on the small scale by considering the religious mapping of urban neighbourhoods, an example of the way in which students can engage with the subject of religion in their own localities.

The history of the geography of religion and the study of sacred space was presented, with particular reference to the work of Fickeler and Stump, van der Leeuw, Eliade and Smith. Recent theoretical and methodological contributions – by Anttonen, Tweed and Knott – were then discussed, showing the way in which scholars outside geography have worked productively with spatial concepts and tropes to understand more about religion and the sacred and to hone tools for their study. Ivakhiv's call for geographers to use their disciplinary knowledge and skills to challenge the boundary between religion and other kinds of significance and sacrality was also considered.

In the final section I took five themes – pilgrimage and movement, diasporas and migration, body, death and dying, and religion in secular context – and examined their contemporary relevance for the geographical and spatial study of religion. Examples were given from recent ethnographic work that show how scholars are able to innovate and refresh old themes as well as develop new ones. They suggest fruitful topics that can be pursued in student projects.

Bibliography

Anttonen, V. (1996) 'Rethinking the Sacred: The Notions of "Human Body" and "Territory" in Conceptualizing Religion', in T. A. Idinopulos and E. A. Yonan (eds) *The Sacred and its Scholars: Comparative Religious Methodologies for the Study of Primary Religious Data*, Leiden: E. J. Brill.

Anttonen, V. (2000) 'Sacred', in W. Braun and R. T. McCutcheon (eds) *A Guide to the Study of Religion*, London: Cassell.

Anttonen, V. (2005) 'Space, Body, and the Notion of Boundary: A Category-Theoretical Approach to Religion', *Temenos* 41:2, 187–202.

Basu, P. (2004) 'Route Metaphors of "Roots Tourism" in the Scottish Highland Diaspora', in S. Coleman and J. Eade (eds) *Reframing Pilgrimage: Cultures in Motion*, London and New York: Routledge.

Bergmann, S. (2007) 'Theology in its Spatial Turn: Space, Place and Built Environments Challenging and Changing the Images of God', *Religion Compass* 1:3, 353–79.

Bhardwaj, S. (1973) *Hindu Places of Pilgrimage in India: A Study in Cultural Geography*, Berkeley: University of California.

Büttner, M. (1974) 'Religion and Geography: Impulses for a New Dialogue between *Religionswissenschaftlern* and Geography', *Numen* 21, 165–96.

Büttner, M. (1980) 'Survey Article on the History and Philosophy of the Geography of Religion in Germany', *Religion* 10:2, 86–119.

Chidester, D. and Linenthal, E. T. (eds) (1995) *American Sacred Space*, Bloomington and Indianapolis: Indiana University Press.

Coleman, S. and Eade, J. (eds) (2004a) *Reframing Pilgrimage: Cultures in Motion*, London and New York: Routledge.

Coleman, S. and Eade, J. (2004b) 'Introduction: Reframing Pilgrimage', in S. Coleman and J. Eade (eds) *Reframing Pilgrimage: Cultures in Motion*, London and New York: Routledge.

Community Religions Project, http://www.leeds.ac.uk//trs/irpl/crp.htm, accessed 16 March 2009.

Cooper, A. (1992) 'New Directions in the Geography of Religions', *Area* 24, 123–9.

Deffontaines, P. (1948) *Geographie et Religions*, Paris: Gallimard.

Eliade, M. (1959) *The Sacred and the Profane: The Nature of Religion*, San Diego: Harcourt Brace Jovanovitch.

Fickeler, P. (1962) 'Fundamental Questions in the Geography of Religions', in P. L. Wagner and M. W. Mikesell (eds) *Readings in Cultural Geography*, Chicago: Chicago University Press.

Foucault, M. (1986) 'Of Other Spaces' (Des espaces autres), *Diacritics* 16:1, 22–27.

Gilliat-Ray, S. (2005) 'Sacralising' Sacred Space in Public Institutions: A Case Study of the Prayer Space at the Millennium Dome', *Journal of Contemporary Religion* 20:3, 357–372.

Gorringe, T. (2002) *A Theology of the Built Environment: Justice, Empowerment, Redemption*, Cambridge: Cambridge University Press.

Holloway, J. (2006) 'Enchanted Spaces: The Séance, Affect and Geographies of Religion', *Annals of the Association of American Geographers* 96:1, 182–87.

Holloway, J. and Valins O. (2002) 'Placing Religion and Spirituality in Geography', *Social and Cultural Geography* 3:1, 5–9.

Inge, J. (2003) *A Christian Theology of Place*, Aldershot and Burlington, VT: Ashgate.

Ivakhiv, A. (2006) 'Toward a Geography of "Religion": Mapping the Distribution of an Unstable Signifier', *Annals of the Association of American Geographers* 96:1, 169–75.

Knippenberg, H. (ed.) (2005) *The Changing Religious Landscape of Europe*, Amsterdam: Het Spinhuis.

Knott, K. (1998) 'Issues in the Study of Religions and Locality', *Method and Theory in the Study of Religion* 10, 279–90.

Knott, K. (2000) 'Community and Locality in the Study of Religions', in T. Jensen and M. Rothstein (eds) *Secular Theories on Religion: Current Perspectives*, Copenhagen: Museum Tusculanum Press.

Knott, K. (2005a) *The Location of Religion: A Spatial Analysis*, London and Oakville CT: Equinox.

Knott, K. (2005b) 'Spatial Theory and Method for the Study of Religion', *Temenos: Nordic Journal of Comparative Religion* 41:2, 153–84.

Knott, K. (2008) 'Spatial Theory and the Study of Religion', *Religion Compass* 2:6, 1102–1116.

Knott, K. (2009) 'From Locality to Location and Back Again: A Spatial Journey in the Study of Religion', *Religion* 39:2, 154–60.

Knott, K. and Franks, M. (2007) 'Secular Values and the Location of Religion: A Spatial Analysis of an English Medical Centre', *Health and Place* 13:1, 224–37.

Kong, L. (1990) 'Geography of Religion: Trends and Prospects', *Progress in Human Geography* 14, 355–71.

Kong, L. (2001) 'Mapping "New" Geographies of Religion: Politics and Poetics in Modernity', *Progress in Human Geography* 25:2, 211–33.

Kong, L. (2005) 'Religious Processions: Urban Politics and Poetics', *Temenos: Nordic Journal of Comparative Religion* 41:2, 225–50.

Lane, B. C. (1988) *Landscapes of the Sacred: Geography and Narrative in American Spirituality*, New York: Paulist Press.

Lefebvre, H. (1974) *La production de l'espace*, Paris: Anthropos.

Lefebvre, H. (1991) *The Production of Space*, Oxford and Cambridge MA: Blackwell.

McGrath, A. E. (2001) *Christian Theology: An Introduction*, third edition, Oxford: Blackwell.

Metcalf, B. D. (1996) (ed.) *Making Muslim Space in North America and Europe*, Berkeley: University of California Press.

Morinis, E. A. (ed.) (1992) *Sacred Journeys: The Anthropology of Pilgrimage*, Westport CT: Greenwood Press.

Park, C. (1994) *Sacred Worlds: An Introduction to Geography and Religion*, London and New York: Routledge.

Proctor, J. (2006) 'Introduction: Theorizing and Studying Religion', *Annals of the Association of American Geographers* 96:1, 165–68.

Sheldrake, P. (2001) *Spaces for the Sacred: Place, Memory and Identity*, Baltimore, MD: Johns Hopkins University Press.

Shields, R. (1991) *Places on the Margin: Alternative Geographies of Modernity*, London and New York: Routledge.

Smith, J. Z. (1978a) 'The Wobbling Pivot', in J. Z. Smith, *Map is Not Territory: Studies in the History of Religions*, Chicago and London: Chicago University Press.

Smith, J. Z. (1978b) 'Map is Not Territory', in J. Z. Smith, *Map is Not Territory: Studies in the History of Religions*, Chicago and London: Chicago University Press.

Smith, J. Z. (1987) *To Take Place: Toward a Theory of Ritual*, Chicago and London: University of Chicago Press.

Sopher, D. E. (1967) *Geography of Religions*, New York: Prentice-Hall.

Stausberg, M. (2009) 'Exploring the Meso-Levels of Religious Mappings: European Religion in Regional, Urban, and Local Contexts', *Religion* 39:2, 103–8.

Stump, R. W. (2000) *Boundaries of Faith: Geographical Perspectives on Religious Fundamentalism*, Lanham, MD: Rowman and Littlefield.

Stump, R. W. (2008) *The Geography of Religion: Faith, Place and Space*, Lanham: Rowman and Littlefield.

Turner, V. and Turner, E. (1978) *Image and Pilgrimage in Christian Culture*, New York: Columbia University Press.

Tweed, T. A. (1997) *Our Lady of the Exile: Diasporic Religion at a Cuban Catholic Shrine in Miami*, New York and Oxford: Oxford University Press.

Tweed, T. A. (2006) *Crossing and Dwelling: A Theory of Religion*, Cambridge MA and London: Harvard University Press.

Valins, O. (2003) 'Stubborn Identities and the Construction of Socio-Spatial Boundaries: Ultra Orthodox Jews Living in Contemporary Britain', *Transactions of the Institute of British Geographers* NS 28, 158–75.

van der Leeuw, G. (1938) *Religion in Essence and Manifestation*, Princeton: Princeton University Press.

Waardenburg, J. (1973) *Classical Approaches to the Study of Religion: 1 Introduction and Anthology*, Leiden: Mouton.

Walton-Roberts, M. (1998) 'Three Readings of the Turban: Sikh Identity in Greater Vancouver', *Urban Geography* 19:4, 311–31.

Werbner, P. (1996) 'Stamping the Earth with the Name of Allah: Zikr and the Sacralizing of Space among British Muslims', in B. Daly Metcalf (ed.) *Making Muslim Space in North America and Europe*, Berkeley: University of California Press.

Suggested reading

Knippenberg, H. (ed.) (2005) *The Changing Religious Landscape of Europe*, Amsterdam: Het Spinhuis.
A collection of essays by geographers on religion in various European countries.

Knott, K. (2005) *The Location of Religion: A Spatial Analysis*, London and Oakville CT: Equinox.
A spatial methodology for the study of religion developed from social and cultural theories of space, with a case study on the location of religion in discourse and representations of the left hand.

Knott, K. (2008) 'Spatial Theory and the Study of Religion', *Religion Compass* 2:6, 1102–1116.
A discussion of spatial theory and its application in the study of religion.

Kong, L. (2001) 'Mapping "New" Geographies of Religion: Politics and Poetics in Modernity', *Progress in Human Geography* 25:2, 211–33.
A new agenda for the geography of religion in the context of modernity.

Park, C. (1994) *Sacred Worlds: An Introduction to Geography and Religion*, London and New York: Routledge.
A textbook which briefly charts the history of the geography of religion and reviews its many empirical studies up to the early 1990s.

Proctor, J. (2006) 'Introduction: Theorizing and Studying Religion', *Annals of the Association of American Geographers* 96:1, 165–68.
An essay which considers new theoretical directions for geographers studying religion. It is followed in the same volume by several exemplary articles.

Stump, R. W. (2008) *The Geography of Religion: Faith, Place and Space*, Lanham, MD: Rowman and Littlefield.
The most recent book to chart the scope and contemporary agenda of the geography of religion.

Tweed, T. A. (2006) *Crossing and Dwelling: A Theory of Religion*, Cambridge MA and London: Harvard University Press.
A new definition and theory of religion which uses spatial and aquatic tropes, particularly the concepts of crossing and dwelling.

Chapter 29

Religion and the environment

Roger S. Gottlieb

This chapter focuses on the way the environmental crisis is challenging and profoundly altering every aspect of religious life: theology, institutional self-definition, the everyday conduct of religious people, and ritual. Religious environmentalism as a global movement is described and some interesting problems which the movement faces are discussed.

What's the problem here?

Why does a book like this one need a chapter on religion and the environment? For two reasons: first, because humanity now faces an enormous challenge to its continued existence, a challenge it has created itself. Second, because responding to this challenge is profoundly altering every aspect of religious life: theology, institutional self-definition, the everyday conduct of religious people, and ritual. Along with these profound changes there arise serious questions the answers to which are deeply in doubt. All of these are the subject of this essay.

The environmental crisis has a number of by now familiar, frightening dimensions. Global climate change, species extinction, wildness loss, and the trillions of pounds of toxic chemicals we have pumped into the air, water, and earth. Future prospects of genetic engineering and nano-technology loom devastatingly larger than present and past consequences of other "miracle" developments such as nuclear engineering/armaments (uncounted tons of as yet undisposable long term poisons, massive contamination sites around nuclear labs, etc.). If the reader has become numb to these generalities (certainly a forgivable response given the overwhelming character of the crisis) one simple "fact" may help focus attention. In 2004 a test of the umbilical cord blood of a dozen randomly chosen newborns at a St. Louis hospital revealed a total of 270 toxic chemicals – with each infant averaging nearly two hundred: carcinogens, endocrine disrupters, substances which adversely affect neurological development or immune system functioning. No one can be sure how these affect developing foetuses – either singly or in concert. (Indeed, what would "experiments" to determine this look like?) But, the chemicals' track records in the labs and for adults are clear.

What does such a dreadful reality mean to *religious* people in particular? Well, for one thing it means something to all of us simply as people. Insofar as Christians or Jews or Muslims have bodies of their own and love their children, this should galvanize immediate and drastic action.

But there are other, specifically religious, reasons as well. First, as members of the Abrahamic tradition, Jews, Christians, and Muslims think of the world not simply as a collection of inert material lying around for human use, but as the gift of a loving God. The world is "creation" – an act of generosity. Even more, the traditions often teach that the world is ours only temporarily – it still belongs to God. Is this any way to treat the gift of the Master of the Universe?

Second, there are specifically religious practices which are called into doubt. Can Jews sanctify wine if they know it contains poisonous pesticide residues? Can the communion wafer really be the "body of Christ" if it was grown with destructive chemical fertilizers and the people who worked the farms on which it was grown suffer from disproportionate amounts of cancer from using those fertilizers?

Third, religions – all religions – share one basic belief: that *they* have some kind of privileged knowledge of what God wants and how a person should act. What happens to this theological and moral self-confidence when, for example, a fourth grader in religious school asks: "Why have you let this happen?" How much respect can religious teachers demand of a younger generation of future members of the faithful when the older generation seems, rather obviously, to have failed so dismally?

Finally, religions must ask themselves the embarrassing question of how they could have been so dumb about all this for so long. It was, after all, not the leading religious authorities or theologians who noticed that modern industrial practices had some real problems. It was freelance mystics and nature lovers, the single believer with no institutional clout, anti-communist western Marxists, and the occasional more or less pagan phenomenologist, who raised questions about what humanity was doing to nature and what that might presage in terms of humanity's treatment of itself. For their part, religions concentrated on whether or not the fruits of industrialization were being distributed with a modicum of social justice, that's all (see Berry 1988; Harrison 1998).

For (at least) all these reasons the environmental crisis is not just a crisis for our health care system, economy, politics, and recreation, but for religion as well. The good news, however, is that over the last twenty years or so religions have risen to this challenge. There now exists a vibrant, worldwide movement of religious environmentalism, one encompassing virtually every faith on every continent, and one which means that religions, even as they were and in some ways continue to be part of the problem, have become part of the solution as well.

Theology

The environmental crisis demands – and has occasioned – some profound theological changes.

In the most general terms these changes involve a denial of centuries-old ideas asserting that humans are different from, better than, or independent from nature. In turn, these changes are accomplished by four different types of theological strategies.

To begin, there has been an active attempt to recover ecologically promising, even powerful, elements of tradition that have been marginalized. To take but three examples: The Jewish philosopher and commentator Maimonides, a twelfth-century Egyptian generally thought of as the most important Jewish thinker in a millennium, cautioned Jews quite clearly: "Do not think that the rest of the earth was made only for you. Each created thing has its own purpose" (in Hadassah 1993: 110). St Francis, the thirteenth-century mystic and spiritual teacher whose life and teaching became the inspiration for an entire religious order, preached to flowers and would move worms out of the roadway to keep them from being trampled (Sorrel 1988). The Koran flatly declares that "Everything is a community like yours" (6:38) and "The creation of Heaven and Earth is of greater importance than humanity, yet most people realize this not."(40:57). Jains and Buddhists both have deep traditions of non-violence towards all of life.

Such statements, and many more that could be offered, provide an initial basis for ecotheology. They are undoubtedly part of the tradition, no fancy footwork of interpretation is needed to give them an ecological direction, and thus they can be (and have been) standard-bearers for a greener version of tradition.

More challenging is the need to reinterpret tradition. This does not mean the importation of essentially new ideas, but rather a significantly different orientation and emphasis in the understanding of what is there already. Ecological motifs in the Torah provide a convenient example, not only because of the centrality of the Torah in the Western tradition, but because a great deal of work has been done on it already.

The dominant theme in Biblical understanding of the human relation with nature has been (unfortunately) the classic passage Genesis 1: 26–28, in which God proclaims:

> Let us make man in our image, in our likeness, and let them rule over the fish of the sea and the birds of the air, over the livestock, over all the earth, and over all the creatures that move along the ground. So God created man in his own image, in the image of God he created him; male and female he created them. God blessed them and said to them, Be fruitful and increase in number; fill the earth and subdue it. Rule over the fish of the sea and the birds of the air and over every living creature that moves on the ground.

In the context of two millennia of a human struggle to survive with limited technological power, it is not surprising that this passage was generally taken as license to use nature in a purely instrumental fashion. Thus Nachmonides, an important thirteenth-century Spanish-Jewish commentator, argued that this passage gave people the right to mine the hills and plow the fields to get what we wanted.

However, there is a good deal more to the Bible and in fact to the Torah in particular, than this passage. For one thing "in our image" can be seen in a variety of ways – (particularly because virtually no one wants to take it literally!). Indeed some read it as conferring responsibility rather than simply unbridled power. We are to act, Lawrence Troster (Troster 2001) suggests, as God's representatives on earth, carrying out God's purposes here.

How then does God want us to treat nature? The mere term "dominion" does not tell us much. As a matter of fact many other passages in the Torah suggest that God has in mind both clear limits for what we may do and also a clear sense of moral concern that extends to the non-human.

For instance, when the Israelites rest on the Sabbath, they must rest their animals as well. If you see your enemy's donkey fallen under a heavy load, you must help raise it up – not just the donkey of your friend, but of someone you *really* do not like. And, to my mind best of all, during the Sabbatical year, when no crops are planted, the food that grows from last year's fallen seeds is to be left not only to the usual code names for the powerless – "the widow, the stranger, and the orphan" – but to "wild animals" as well (Exodus 23:5–12).

What these (and other) passages indicate is that the Bible often teaches respect for non-human nature, and that "care" (as in Adam and Eve's initial responsibility to care for the Garden of Eden, Genesis 2:15) rather than "dominion" is the rule. The point is not that this is the "true" interpretation, and that somehow theologians, rabbis, and popes missed it all these years. For clearly there are other biblical passages which support the dominion thesis quite easily. Rather, what is crucial is that one can, by focusing on passages which, even if they have not been used this way before, are legitimately part of the tradition, find a biblical basis for an ecological oriented religion. One does not have to invent new sacred texts or sweep away the past – one merely has to focus on parts of the tradition that are there already. This work of interpretation has been a central task of ecotheology, one so well performed by this time that there can be little doubt that the most conservative, "orthodox" religious person can also be an environmentalist. (Pope John Paul II used God's response to creation "And God said that it was very good" (Genesis 1:31) as a prooftext for his own ecological turn. Think of how many other Popes read that verse and made no ecological sense out of it whatsoever. Yet clearly the Pope was not inventing anything new, except the meaning that he was taking from a very old verse (Murphy 1989).)

That said it deserves mention that ecotheologians *also* do a fair amount of both rejection of the past and invention for the present and future. Not everything that has been part of the tradition will remain, and some important new concepts and values must emerge.

For example, we can note the position of Rabbi Ismar Schorsch, who helped create the National Religious Partnership for the Environment, an interfaith coalition with a wide range of educational programs for religious groups and society as a whole. Schorsch, for many years the chancellor of Conservative Judaism's leading educational institution, the Jewish Theological Seminary, is not hesitant to take Jewish tradition to task and advocate a fundamental transformation. It is a mistake, he argues, to use Judaism's rejection of paganism to propel Judaism into an "adversarial relationship with the natural world." When that is done

> the modern Jew is saddled with a reading of his tradition that is one-dimensional. Judaism has been made to dull our sensitivity to the awe inspiring power of nature. Preoccupied with the ghost of paganism, it appears indifferent and unresponsive to the supreme challenge of our age: man's degradation of the environment. Our planet is under siege and we as Jews are transfixed in silence.
>
> (Schorsch 1991)

This statement is all the more significant because Conservative Judaism was, as much as any other form of Judaism, a longstanding adherent of the very "one-dimensional reading" of tradition that Schorsch is criticizing. His claim, then, suggests that Jews have been theologically and ethically misguided.

In the Christian world, the long-standing tendency to make categorical distinctions between body and spirit, the world and the soul, the moral status of people and the non-moral status of everything else, has been sharply criticized. Protestant theologian Sallie McFague (2001), for example, urges us to imagine that far from being simply an immaterial transcendence outside the physical universe, God is also a part of our physical reality. The earth, she suggests, can be thought of as "The Body of God." After all, if God is not part of the world as we know it, how could we ever encounter Him/Her? John Cobb, one of the earliest voices in ecological theology, admits that with regard to anthropocentrism: "As a Protestant Christian I am impelled to move quickly to acknowledge that Protestant theology has been an extreme case." This anthropocentrism, he argues, must change (Cobb 2004: 249–50).

Given the different theological orientation of Eastern religions – which have not tended to make such rigid distinctions between humans and the rest of the natural world – the Buddhist and Hindu response to environmental issues necessarily takes a different form. Also, the technology and social forms which have brought about the environmental crisis have been predominantly Christian and Euro-American capitalist. That does not mean that in the present, Hindus and Buddhists are not cheerfully developing economically and polluting a great deal. It means that the practices which allow such pollution are much less rooted in their *religious* culture than they are in Western ones.

However, there is at least one fundamental change that Buddhism and Hinduism have to face, and which under the leadership of their respective environmental thinkers, they are facing. While these traditions lack the West's human-nature dualism, they also lack the tradition of prophetic social criticism which has been essential to Judaism, Christianity and (if to a lesser extent) Islam. That is, they have generally tended towards a kind of social passivity – or at least social quietism – which would make them less contributors to the environmental crisis than inactive witnesses to it. When Thich Nhat Hanh, Vietnamese Buddhist teacher who has become widely known in Europe and the U.S., advocated a kind of "socially engaged Buddhism" which *requires* social activism as much as it does meditation and psychological self-examination, he was roundly condemned by his fellow Buddhist leaders. Such activism, his critics taught, was profoundly unBuddhist! In response Nhat Hanh and other leaders, such as Thailand's Sulak Sivaraksa, have identified social commitment in general and ecological activism in particular as essential to developing Buddhist virtues (Kaza and Kraft 2000).

Institutional commitment

The new ecotheologies have helped religious people think the meaning of their faiths in new, ecologically responsible, ways. Yet religions are not defined by theologians and professors. Their public identity is determined most powerfully by their public leadership – by Popes and Bishops and large national and international councils and publicly recognized authorities. There may be many who differ with the recognized leadership, but that dissension can only be what it is because there are leaders to dissent from.

It is one of the great accomplishments of the world's religions that ecological responsibility has not been consigned to a handful of (probably liberal) thinkers. Rather, the world's religious leaders have stated unequivocally that environmental values are now an essential part of the faith.

Consider for example the dramatic 1997 statement by Bartholomew I, leader of 300 million Orthodox Christians from North and South America, Europe, and Asia.

> To commit a crime against the natural world is a sin ... to cause species to become extinct and to destroy the biological diversity of God's creation ... to degrade the integrity of the Earth by causing changes in its climate, stripping the Earth of its natural forests, or destroying its wetlands ... to contaminate the Earth's waters, its land, its air, and its life with poisonous substances – these are sins.
>
> (Bartholomew 2004: 229–230)

It is not just Bartholomew's authority which is critical here, but the fact that the powerful theological language he uses directly contradicts any presupposition that the environmental crisis is merely a technical problem or a flawed policy. His assertion that it is a sin (and that these sins should also be subject to criminal penalty) puts our relation to nature in the category of religious morality – along with sexuality and how we treat the poor. This is a direct expansion of both religion and environmental concern.

A similar expansion can be found in important statements by Catholic authorities, including Pope John Paul II in particular and various national councils of Catholic Bishops (Hart 2006). In his first year as Pope, John Paul declared St. Francis (one of those traditional yet marginalized ecological voices) the patron saint of those concerned with the environment. Over the next two decades a series of statements revealed two central principles: first, that concern with environmental issues was now to take its place alongside more familiar Catholic social justice concerns such as poverty, abortion, capital punishment, and war. It was now essential to Catholic teaching to resist the cultural and political failures which led to the environmental crisis. Second, that crisis is not defined solely in terms of how it affects people.

> This discovery of a transcendent presence in creation, must also lead us also to rediscover our *fraternity with the earth*, to which we have been linked since creation (cf. Gen 2:7). This very goal was foreshadowed by the Old Testament in the Hebrew Jubilee, when the earth rested and man gathered what the land spontaneously offered (cf. Lev 25:11–12). If nature is not violated and humiliated, it returns to being the *sister of humanity*.
>
> (John Paul II 2000)

We might note that this is not only a bold and non-human centered environmental declaration; it is also a groundbreaking move for a religious tradition which for many centuries did its best to destroy any religion which honored the earth.

Similar ideas, accompanied by awareness of the consequences of environmental destruction and the need for fundamentally changed values and policies, have been expressed in a series of statements by councils of Catholic Bishops in the Philippines, the Columbia River region of the U.S. and Canada, and America's Midwest. These statements do not rest with theological claims or moral imperatives, but include challenges to existing social structures. From the Philippines comes a serious questioning of the human costs of "development." Does all this destruction of rainforest and pollution of water resources really translate into a better life for the ordinary poor Filipino? From the Columbia River watershed comes a clear assertion that all sectors of society bear some responsibility for ecological threats to the area; and that in particular, corporations who clear cut or pollute are responsible for changing their ways and cleaning up the messes they have made (Gottlieb 2006a: 85–95; Hart 2004).

While Buddhism has no central authority structure the way Catholicism does, it does have some internationally recognized leaders. Of these probably the most important is the Dalai Lama. He has made many ecologically oriented pronouncements, linking environmental problems to more comprehensive problems of greed and attachment. And he has also proposed that Tibet be turned into an international ecological refuge and criticized the Chinese government for unecological practices – including the dumping of nuclear wastes – in Tibet (Kaza 2000).

It might well be asked what difference all this makes. For example: doesn't a good deal of Christian teaching, of whatever variety, stress the importance of humility, peacefulness, and voluntary poverty? Yet if we examine the U.S., an ostensibly Christian country, it is pretty hard to find these values in place. A huge military machine combines with hundreds of millions of guns in the hands of ordinary, "Christian" citizens. The pursuit and exercise of wealth is widely manifest and endlessly celebrated. If Catholic Bishops or the National Council of Churches or the Evangelical Environmental Network call on their parishioners to mend their ecological ways, why should we expect anything real to happen, any more than it does in these other areas?

This is an important point with a good deal of truth in it. No simple religious declaration will solve the environmental crisis. Most religious people, like most other people, spend their time taking care of themselves and their family without much conspicuous dedication to stringent moral demands. On the other hand, however, it is not a small thing that religious authorities, who have the ear of billions of people, and enormous financial and institutional resources and social capital, have embraced a green gospel. The religious presence in the anti-slavery and civil rights movements was momentous, and has been vital in anti-war efforts over the last century as well. If a few really good statements won't solve our environmental problems, they surely will be at least a little – and quite possibly more than a little – help.

Action

Our answer to these questions need not be purely speculative. The true test of religious environmentalism is the way in which religious environmentalists have been involved in environmental activism. This activism can take a wide variety of forms. Indeed on one end public statements, including books, films, and teaching, are themselves a kind of activism. But here I have in mind more focused efforts which can include lobbying governments or even taking part in governments, involvement in ecological restoration or clean up campaigns, public demonstrations and challenges to polluting corporations. Evaluating religious efforts in this context makes abundantly clear the simple fact that throughout the world religious people have joined – in throngs and for religious reasons – the environmental movement. Here is a sampling of cases (Gottlieb 2004, 2006a, b; Palmer 2003; Taylor 2006).

- In northern California the "Redwood Rabbis" engaged in a public struggle to protect one of the area's last remaining stands of Redwood trees. They challenged the logging company's head, a leader in his own Jewish community, with going against Jewish values. Violating legal orders, the group engaged in direct action by planting new Redwood seedlings in the grove.
- In Tanzania fishermen were dissuaded from their ecologically disastrous policy of dynamite fishing by a local sheik who ruled that the practice was un-Islamic. The fishermen had ignored government decrees and scientific cautions, but were convinced by a religious stricture.
- In the U.S. the Methodist Church engaged in a focused campaign to demand that Staples stores stop selling paper the production of which led to Dioxin pollution.
- In India the Sikh religion has committed itself to a *three hundred year* policy of responsible ecological practices. Since the Sikhs fulfill one of their religious commitments by giving food to the poor – providing tens of millions of meals a day – this means changing their patterns of energy use, packaging, clean up, etc.
- Religious Witness for the Earth, an interfaith activist environmental group centered in New England, engaged in civil disobedience protesting against the Bush administration's energy policy, demonstrated at the U.N., and held a 125 mile "Climate Walk" publicizing the dangers of and possible responses to global warming.
- In Taiwan the Shu Tzi organization, founded by a charismatic nun decades ago and concentrating on charity and relief work in Taiwan and abroad, has included ecological issues in its activities. One year it helped recycle millions of pounds of paper and metal.
- In the U.S. a loose network of nuns, the "Sisters of Earth," practice and teach organic agriculture, model low impact living, take part in local ecological efforts, save seeds,

and monitor and criticize the ecologically destructive practices of local and national governments and transnational institutions such as the World Bank and the World Trade Organization.

- In a fascinating instance of the intersection of religion, environmentalism, and political life, there is the case of Nambaryn Enkhbayar, the prime minister of Mongolia, who has led a Buddhist oriented attempt to combine economic development with real sustainability, particularly in regard to preserving forests, biodiversity, and Mongolia's unique seven foot long river fish (the Taimen). In Enkhbayar's words:

> Buddhism considers the creation of a good balance or, let us put it in a broader sense – of a healthy environment where everyone and everything can enjoy freedom to realize or improve its potential – is the condition for the qualitative development ...
> (Enkhbayar: nd)

The Mongolian population has responded favorably towards these conservation efforts, a remarkable fact given the country's severe poverty. Religious support for sustainability seems (at least for now) to have made the difference in garnering broad support for ecologically sound, rather than destructive, economic development.

When religions turn green

As I have stressed already, the examples offered here are only a small percentage of what is out there. And indeed the list is growing all the time. If we step back from this large array, and look for trends in what we have observed, some extremely interesting patterns emerge.

First, as religions become attuned to ecological problems and environmental issues they become increasingly open to ecumenical and interfaith efforts of all kinds. A good number of religious environmental organizations and actions have enlisted a variety of religious participants (Gottlieb 2006a, b). Interfaith Power and Light, for example, a national U.S. group focusing on local responses to climate issues, with more than 20 state chapters, includes Protestants, Catholics, Jews, Buddhists, and Muslims among its members. Well publicized statements by important religious figures on global warming have often been signed by leaders of widely different faiths. Religious Witness for the Earth included Jewish, Unitarian, and Episcopalian clergy in its leadership. Even in Israel-Palestine, perhaps the place one would least expect to find interreligious cooperation, Jewish and Muslim leaders have combined forces on common ecological concern, most notably the sadly deteriorated state of the Jordan River.

These cooperative, respectful efforts extend beyond the bounds of familiar, "major" religions. I have already mentioned the newfound Catholic respect for indigenous people's ecological knowledge. In a remarkable and hopeful story, southern Zimbabwe was the scene of a highly effective coalition of local Christian congregations and traditional spirit medium communities. Facing a landscape ravaged by logging and war, they joined together to plant over 8 million trees, change agricultural practices, and create a new sense of the sacredness of the earth and trees (Daneel 2001). These were religious traditions which in the past would have had virtually nothing to say to each other, nothing respectful in any case. On the Christian side, especially, there is a long and painful history of rejection and contempt for faiths outside the orbit of monotheism. Yet as a member of the Christian side of the coalition put it: "We must be respectful to the Krallheads and Chiefs – or else where will we plant our trees?" (Daneel 2001: 185).

Perhaps even more remarkably, there have been well publicized cases of religious cooperation with science. Given the long history of antagonism between these two cultural forces, this is no small matter. As a matter of course most of the new ecotheological writings include extensive references to scientific accounts of ecological problems from global warming to the presence of endocrine disruptors in the food chain. This is true not just for theologians but for statements by religious leaders as well. Science is no longer the "enemy" of truth, but a source of critically important knowledge which is essential if people are to fulfill their *religious* imperatives: in this case, to preserve God's creation and to love one's neighbor (or at least not poison him). This newfound openness goes both ways. In fact, the initial move in a process which led to a widely read "Joint Declaration on the Environment," which was signed by leading religious figures and leading scientists, was made by those on the scientific side (Gottlieb 2004). They publicly acknowledged that their own technical expertise was incomplete until it was joined with reflections on moral values and the ultimate meaning of human existence – resources, in short, that would be best obtained from religious leaders. Would not Galileo, imprisoned by the Bishops for offering an astronomy the Bishops didn't like, or John Scopes, who was put on trial for teaching evolution, not find the public cooperation of science and religion a remarkable turn?

The next quite interesting development in ecological religion is the tendency towards a leftist political orientation. It is perhaps inevitable that any serious environmentalism will come up against the tendency of global corporations and repressive governments to ecological destruction and unsustainable practices. Capitalism in particular has always structured ecological consequences as "externalities" – monetary and human costs that are outside the process of buying and selling commodities and making profits. The very idea that a global market – in which subsistence labor throughout the world is replaced by wage labor, local production is reoriented towards export, and what was heretofore accepted as "the commons" (land, water, even air) gets privatized – will meet human needs has been seriously questioned by environmentalists of all stripes, now including religious ones.

To take one example, consider some powerful statements by the World Council of Churches, an umbrella organization representing some 400 million Protestants. The WCC has been a frequent observer and at times participant in international meetings on climate change and in those contexts it has at times vigorously contested the conventional acceptance of economic globalization. For example, in 2003, in preparation for a meeting with the World Bank, WCC general secretary Konrad Raiser questioned "the allegedly irrefutable logic of the prevailing economic paradigm" (World Council of Churches 2003). Simultaneously representatives of 70 member churches signed a document stating that "nothing less than a fundamental shift in political-economic paradigms is necessary." The pieties of globalization have been rejected by the WCC, for it sees this sweeping change in the world social order as often leading to widespread poverty, more national debt, environmental distress, and increased polarization between rich and poor. Beyond these powerful generalities, in 2000 the WCC criticized British Petroleum, Shell and Exxon-Mobil as examples of "transnational corporations" which not only bore some responsibility for global warming, but which were trying to persuade the public that global warming was not real (Gottlieb 2006a: 125–126).

Perhaps even more impressively, a key concept of politically oriented environmentalism – the kind that connects environmental concerns to other dimensions of social justice rather than just focusing on conservation of wilderness and wildlife – is not only employed by religious environmentalists, but was in fact largely *generated* by a particular Christian denomination.

   This fascinating history begins with a 1984 struggle in Warren County, North Carolina, that state's most concentrated African-American region (Gottlieb 2006a: 134–138). The state government decided to locate a toxic waste facility there, which already had the largest number in the state. Fed up with the environmental effects of such facilities, and (rightly) surmising that the racial make-up of the area had something to do with the siting decision, the residents of Warren County mounted fierce resistance. The Social Justice committee of the United Church of Christ was an active participant in the protests, with some members of the Church going to jail for civil disobedience (along with a few congressmen as well!). Surmising that racial inequality in the distribution of toxic materials was not limited to one county in one state, the UCC then commissioned and helped prepare a nationwide, county by county study of *Toxic Wastes in the United States* (Commission for Racial Justice 1987). The 1987 study established that African Americans, Latinos, and Native Americans were more likely to live in an area damaged by toxic wastes than were whites, and that this was true even for middle class non-white communities. Out of this study came the now widely known concept of environmental racism, and the related term "environmental justice," which refers to what we would like to see replace the former. In 1991 the UCC sponsored a widely attended and publicized national meeting of People of Color Environmental Activists, which produced a document defining Principles of Environmental Justice. Interestingly the first of these principles, which have been disseminated throughout the world and helped define the parameters of a fundamentally new way of looking at both environmentalism and social justice, emphasizes the "sacredness of Mother Earth" (Gottlieb 2004: 729). In other words, this fusion of resistance to oppression, now combined with an awareness of how modern industrial society hurts both people and other forms of life, was initially couched in a spiritual vocabulary, and sponsored by, of all things, a particular Christian denomination.

   Finally, it is important to note that the activist involvement and the leftist (or at least *more* to the left) political orientation of religious environmentalists is not limited to what we might call the "usual suspects" of liberal Protestants, social justice oriented Catholics, and Reform Jews. In the U.S. there has been a significant, and generally increasing, presence of Evangelical Christians in the environmental movement. For over a decade now the Evangelical Environmental Network has issued some quite strong statements, signed by leaders of Evangelical seminaries, editors of newspapers, and widely respected ministers, making clear that humans have an obligation to protect God's creation and change their ways. In 2004 Evangelicals initiated the compelling campaign "What Would Jesus Drive?" They began with public events in Detroit, challenging America's auto manufacturers to produce more earth friendly cars, proceeded to cavalcade through the south and ended at the nation's largest Christian rock festival. The theme of the campaign was that basic *Christian* values – as familiar and essential as the Golden Rule – required basic *environmental* values. A few years later several Evangelical leaders held a joint press conference with (of all people) some leading lights of Harvard University's science departments, issuing a collective call for immediate and significant national action on global warming (Gottlieb 2006a 128–30).

   On one level, of course, this kind of expansion of social concern, ecumenism, and openness to the secular world is hardly surprising. The environmental crisis is the most equal opportunity of threats. Racism and class domination will afflict some groups more than others, wars can be localized, and human rights have a drastically unequal distribution. Yet while some regions and groups (as we saw in our account of environmental racism) will suffer more immediately from environmental damage than others, the crisis as a whole affects us all. Global climate change is, well, *global*. The enormous weight of pollutants affects the bloodstreams of the rich as well as the poor. The earth is precious to everyone. If there is anything that can bring human beings closer together, willing (for once) to focus on what unites us rather than what divides us, the environmental crisis might just be it. In the secular realm of international law, there are, after all, some 300 environmental treaties which did not exist thirty years ago. The few examples sketched above indicate that similar changes are happening in the religious world. Perhaps this crisis will also be, as the Chinese say, a great opportunity.

What religion brings to the table

As a human being who values my own health and that of my loved ones, and cares greatly about the fate of the rest of life, I would be truly delighted to see every religious person rush out and become an active member of some environmental organization. Yet religious environmentalism means a good deal more than that. Religions have distinct institutional, cultural, and moral resources which promise to make critical and very particular contributions to environmentalism, contributions which in many cases will be unlikely to come from other sources.

To begin, there is the rather obvious point that religion – if not always or always as strong as it might – is a powerful motivator of behavior. In an environmental context often plagued by the phenomenon of "everyone knows about it but no one does anything" a religious motivation can push people to act when other considerations – including economic and health motives – do not. As we saw in the example from Tanzania above, people will sometimes heed religious calls when they do not listen to anything else. Other examples range as far as Beijing, where appeals to traditional Taoist values allow Chinese medical authorities to authorize substitutes in remedies that used to call for parts of now endangered animals; and Saudi Arabia, where Islamic teachings are used to justify nature preserves; to the way even as anti-environmental a president as George W. Bush had to pay some attention to the environmental concerns of Evangelicals (Palmer 2003).

As well, there are important resources from what might be called the "culture" of religion: values and practices which are not necessarily limited to faith traditions, but which as a matter of fact are most widely present in them. For example, there are religious practices which stress the need to confront life's most difficult aspects, including deficiencies in one's own moral character. These practices are important because, in a sense, the most significant environmental problems are not present on the usual list of climate change, pollution, species loss, etc. Rather the worst threats are the *human* habits of avoidance and denial. It is above all our inability and unwillingness to face the truth that keeps the environmental crisis in play (Gottlieb 2003: Chapter 2). While in some ways religions – with their emphasis on other-worldly and after-death realities – are prime examples of socially passive escapism, there are in fact some powerful religious resources which move in the opposite direction. For example, the Catholic practice of Confession can be trivialized, but if it is not it provides a profound psychological and moral experience in real self-examination and commitment to personal moral improvement. The sincere Catholic really looks at him/herself, and is willing to acknowledge and change where s/he is doing wrong. In Buddhism, similarly, there is traditional training – e.g. meditating in graveyards to cultivate an awareness of the finitude of life – in being able to be emotionally present to distressing realities. This is a capacity of which anyone who studies environmental issues needs a great deal. Reading about something like the "Great Pacific Ocean Garbage Patch" – a thick soup-like collection of plastic refuse that is *larger than the United States* – takes an enormous amount of emotional strength.

Otherwise we simply blot out the distressing reality or imagine that surely "somebody else" will take care of it.

Religious culture is also a repository of values which stress that there is more to life than accumulation. A secularized, globalized world (more on this later) tacitly assumes that the goal of life is money, toys, pleasure and power. Religious values – rest on the Sabbath, the joys of contemplation, quiet enjoyment of family love, focused study of spiritual texts – are more reliable sources of human happiness. If environmentalism is to achieve the truly global level of support it needs, it cannot simply be the political movement whose catchwords are "No," "Do not," and "Stop." It must offer alternative forms of life which provide real pleasure and prospects of human fulfillment. Religious fellowship is – or should be – pretty cheap, and may involve no more consumption than a modest church supper or the cost of some long lasting hymnals.

Ritual

If rituals are not confined to the sphere of religion, they are among religion's most cultivated specialities. From the Passover Seder to the Hajj, cultures of faith have produced forms of prayer, meditation, celebration, contrition, and mourning that provide a sense that the world of human experience, no less than the physical world, can be ordered.

In the face of the environmental crisis ritual forms are being devised that meet the distinct emotional needs of our situation. These include special prayers which express our awareness of our individual and collective sins and our commitments to change. A new emphasis on celebrations (e.g. the Jewish practice of holding a special service-and-meal for Tu B'shvat, the new year of the trees) connecting humans with nature joins with the creation of specifically new forms. These latter include, for example, weekend workshops in which people try to imaginatively take on the identity of other forms of life, and engage in a Council of All Beings (Macy 1991) in which each of them will address humanity with their pain and hope that people can change their ways.

The new rituals are supported by religious authorities. For example both the National Council of Churches and the U.S. Council of Catholic Bishops have produced tens of thousands of copies of congregational resources which include prayers and services for Earth Day and other opportunities to focus attention on ecological issues. Leading Buddhist teachers such as Thich Nhat Hanh, have offered environmental "Gathas" – short meditative verbal formulas to raise awareness of our environmental situation.

If prayer is the opportunity to open our hearts to God, then the environmental crisis engenders prayers that have never been heard before. In Zimbabwe, one of the leaders of the remarkable tree planting coalition I described above, in the course of a "tree-planting Eucharist," offered the following:

> You, tree, I plant you. Provide us with clean air to breathe and all the other benefits which Mwari [God] has commanded. We in turn will take care of you, because in Jesus Christ you are one with us. He has created all things to be united in him. I shall not chop down another tree. Through you, tree, I do penance for all the trees I have felled.
> (Daneel 2001: 185)

Sadly, in the new green liturgy we can also find appeals to heaven that indicate the way victims of environmental suffering can come to feel that only God can help them. In Nigeria's

Niger Delta province, where oil extraction by global oil companies working in concert with local governments to repress resistance, has devastated the health and culture of the local population, a minister beseeched God in a way that may never have been done before:

> We pray to God on this holy morn that no petroleum oil will be discovered in our communities. Indeed, Lord, let the oil underneath our houses and farms drift away from us. Lord, spare us the pains and the misfortunes and diseases that petroleum oil brings to our people and to our farms and rivers. Lord, protect us from further harm in the hands of those who want our properties, Amen.
>
> (in Fields 2003)

What stands in the way?

The information sketched so far describes a dramatic shift in religion's moral values and public identity. Given the public commitment of its recognized, institutional leaders, there can be little doubt that religion's self-understanding now includes the obligation to value, and work to preserve, our planet's web of life.

As positive as these developments are, it is necessary to conclude this essay with a brief sketch of some powerful social forces which stand in the way of everything religious environmentalism stands for.

Perhaps most important is the force which obstructs every form of environmentalism: globalization. By this term I mean the generalized imposition of market relations throughout the world, the drastic erosion of subsistence labor in favour of wage labor and the orientation of production to global exchange rather than local consumption; the rise in scope and power of transnational corporations and globalizing institutions (World Bank, World Trade Organization, International Monetary Fund) which drastically limit political sovereignty of local communities or even national governments; and the spread of a media-dominated culture of spectacle and endless distraction. For globalization the whole world is a collection of resources to be bought, used in production and sold; and every human being is essentially a consumer and a wage worker. The value of both people and things is measured in money (Steger 2001; Stiglitz 2002).

Globalization has been an environmental disaster. Alliances between local and international economic and political elites make the force of globalization often impossible to resist. Local communities are devastated by the mammoth economic projects it favors: huge dams, ruthless oil and mineral extraction, export agriculture. Yet I believe that the struggle against the values and dynamic of globalization appears as the most important political struggle of our time. If its imperatives are not replaced by humane and sustainable ones, all forms of environmentalism are doomed to at best extremely limited success. For that reason it is at least a little comforting that through the widespread adoption of the concept of ecojustice most religious environmentalists are able to name and, as best they can, resist the forces of globalization. As religious environmentalism continues to develop, this will provide a basis for continued engagement among different religions and between religious environmentalists and a whole host of secular political groups. Such alliances will, if my analysis is correct, be a very strong element in the resistance to globalization.

On the personal level, religious environmentalism, again like all other forms of the movement, finds in an increasingly widespread consumerism a rigid barrier to needed personal and social change. While people have liked "stuff" for a very long time, and conspicuous consumption by the rich is nothing new, consumerism in the present is quite different from anything we have encountered in the past. First, what we have now is the identification of desired relationships and personal qualities with the acquisition of material objects. Health, sexual attraction, social acceptance, intelligence, love of family – these and other good things are represented and experienced as commodities you can buy. Second, an unending, addictive attraction to the very act of buying has been engendered. It is not the desired object which is the key, but the experience of desire itself. As a result of these two features, consuming is not simply a wanted pleasure, a pastime, or a benefit of a little disposable income, it has become a way of life, seemingly *essential* to one's sense of self. Against this entrenched attachment, this powerful addiction, calls to care about climate, cancer rates caused by pollution, or the vanishing rainforest may stand little chance (Miller 2003; Kaza 2003).

There is hope, however. A life defined by trips to the mall or one-clicks at Amazon.com simply does not make people happy. There is a growing realization of that fact in the West – and one hopes that some spread of this insight will spread to India, China and other developing nations before the human race completely overwhelms the biosphere. As I have argued above, religious environmentalism, often more than other kinds, is particularly fitted to offer an alternative to consumerism. Rather than represent itself as the stern voice of a judgmental divine force, it will be the task of religious environmentalists to remind people that a spiritually oriented life, if it is anything at all, offers more lasting happiness, contentment, and healthy loving human (and non-human) relationships than lives oriented solely to pleasure or status. In order to make this argument, however, religious environmentalists must themselves communicate – in their person and in the programs they support – precisely the values of calm acceptance, compassion for weakness, self-awareness, at least occasional joy and frequent sincere laughter. Only in this way can they really support their claim that a spiritual approach to living on this earth not only bodes well for forests and trout, but for us as well.

A few tough questions

Any large change in a cultural structure as significant as religion, especially when the change involves profound connections to the worlds of science, politics, economics, and health, is bound to raise all sorts of critical, difficult questions. I will conclude this essay by looking at two such questions.

First, there is the seven hundred pound gorilla in the room that people often ignore: the issue of capitalism. Can our environmental woes be significantly mitigated as long as the forces of production are privately owned, the economy is geared to continued growth, and an enormous political power flows from enormous wealth? Can capitalism be environmentally reformed by cap and trade schemes for greenhouse emission, or severe fines and jail terms for pollution? Or does the social influence which stems from corporate power require that such power be removed before anything but the most modest reforms occur? Can capitalism accommodate clean production? Can it limit its drive towards endless growth and the inculcation of limitless needs to consume?

On the other hand, non-capitalist economies have often been accompanied by economic stagnation, terrible human rights records, and the creation of political elites which function all too much like the ruling class of capitalist societies. Further, in much of the world, including and especially the U.S., the very idea of a serious attempt at socialism is simply not on the political landscape (though with the recent bailouts of major corporations, this might change a bit).

My own answer, which is that something quite different from global capitalism must be created if the web of life on this planet is to be preserved, is not really important here. I am, rather, simply indicating that this is a problem which must eventually be confronted by religious environmentalists. Interestingly, as this issue takes its place on the agenda, religious environmentalists will have to turn not to theology or scripture, but to the history of social movements in general and the left in particular for inspiration and example. This is, to say the least, no small irony.

Finally, in some ways at the opposite end of the spectrum from religion's confrontation with capitalism is its confrontation with the values which govern its own internal functioning. Consider the place of the lay leadership in religious institutions. Virtually every religion has its version of what Jews often call the "big givers," i.e. wealthy, interested and therefore influential members of the lay religious community who by virtue of their financial contributions end up in positions of leadership. But not just any rich donor can get a leadership position. If a well-known producer of hard-core pornography, no matter what the size of his bankroll was, endeavored to use his money to become a Deacon, a member of the board of Trustees, or a lay leader, chances are pretty good that he would be refused. Such a person, it would be said, is not the kind of leader we want.

But what if the case concerns not the psychic pollution of porn, but the physical pollution of toxic waste? Would a church refuse an important position to a wealthy CEO of a polluting chemical company? Or a lumber company prone to clear cutting? Or the head of a public relations firm that specializes in "greenwashing" dangerous power plants?

This is a particularly thorny problem because all the members of the church in question – no less than myself and virtually everyone quoted in this essay – *also* bear some responsibility for the environmental crisis. We all plug into the same grid, drive our cars, dispose of our old cell phones, and enjoy the cheap food produced by chemicalized, industrial agriculture.

While this problem has not yet really surfaced as yet, I have no doubt it will, probably reasonably soon. As the confrontation with capitalism raises issues of reform and revolution, so this one leads to a struggle between compassion and judgment, self-criticism and the need to draw moral boundaries, loving the sinner while hating the sin and saying, "No, this is simply not acceptable." This is a very old religious problem, and in the context of the environmental crisis it will be enormously interesting to see how the world's vibrant and diverse religious communities try to resolve it.[1]

Note

Many thanks to John Hinnells for valuable editorial suggestions.

Bibliography

Bartholomew, I. (2004) Address of His Holiness Ecumenical Patriarch Bartholomew at the Environmental Symposium, Santa Barbara, CA, November 8, 1997 in Gottlieb 2004.

Berry, Thomas (1988) *Dream of the Earth*, San Francisco: Sierra Club Books.

Cobb, John B., Jr., (2004) "Protestant Theology and Deep Ecology," in Roger S. Gottlieb, ed., *This Sacred Earth, Second Edition*, New York: Routledge.

Commission for Racial Justice (1987) *Toxic Wastes in the United States*, New York: United Church of Christ.

Daneel, Martinus L. (2001) *African Earthkeepers: Wholistic Interfaith Mission*, Maryknoll, NY: Orbis Books.

Enkhbayar, Narayan n/d "Prime Minister of Mongolia to be first International President of ARC," Alliance of Religion and Conservation Website: http://www.arcworld.org/news.asp?pageID=6.

Fields, Leslie (2003) *Friends of the Earth*, Vol. 33, #3, Fall.

Gottlieb, Roger S. (2003) *A Spirituality of Resistance: Finding a Peaceful Heart and Protecting the Earth*, Lanham, MD: Rowman and Littlefield.

Gottlieb, Roger S. (2004) *This Sacred Earth: Religion, Nature, Environment*, second edition, New York: Routledge.

Gottlieb, Roger S. (2006a) *A Greener Faith: Religious Environmentalism and our Planet's Future*, New York: Oxford University Press.

Gottlieb, Roger S. (2006b) *The Oxford Handbook of Religion and Ecology*, New York: Oxford University Press.

Hadassah (1993) *Judaism and Ecology, a Study Guide*, New York: Hadassah

Harrison, Peter (1998) *The Bible, Protestantism, and the Rise of Natural Science*, New York: Cambridge University Press.

Hart, John (2004) *What are they Saying about Environmental Theology?* NY: Paulist Press.

Hart, John (2006) "Catholicism," in Gottlieb (2006b).

John Paul II (2000) "Nature is our Sister," Catholic Conservation Website, http://conservation.catholic.org/pope_john_paul_ii.htm.

Kaza, Stephanie (2000) "To Save all Beings: Buddhist Environmental Activism," in Christopher S. Queen ed. *Engaged Buddhism in the West*, Somerville, MA: Wisdom Publications.

Kaza, Stephanie (2003) *Hooked! Buddhist Writings on Greed, Desire, and the Urge to Consume*, Boston: Shambala.

Kaza, Stephanie and Kraft, Kenneth (2000) *Dharma Rain: Sources of Buddhist Environmentalism*, Boston: Shambala.

McFague, Sallie (2001) *Life Abundant: Rethinking Theology and Economy for a Planet in Peril*, Minneapolis: Fortress Press.

Macy, Joanna (1991) *World as Lover, World as Self*, Berkeley, CA: Parallax Press.

Miller, Vincent (2003) *Consuming Religion: Christian Faith in a Consumer Culture*, London: Continuum.

Murphy, Charles (1989) *At Home on Earth: Foundations for a Catholic Ethic of the Environment*, NY: Crossroad.

Palmer, Martin (2003) *Faith in Conservation: New Approaches to Religion and the Environment*, Washington, DC: The World Bank.

Schorsch, Ismar (1991) "Tending to our Cosmic Oasis," Luminaries website: http://learn.jtsa.edu/topics/luminaries/monograph/tendingto.shtml.

Sorrell, Roger (1988) *St. Francis of Assisi and Nature: Tradition and Innovation in Western Christian Attitudes Toward the Environment*, Oxford, England: Oxford University Press.

Steger, Manfred B. (2001) *Globalism: The New Market Ideology*, Lanham, MD: Rowman and Littlefield.

Stiglitz, Joseph E. (2002) *Globalization and Its Discontents*, New York: Norton.

Taylor, Sarah MacFarland (2006) *Sisters of Earth*, Cambridge: Harvard University Press.

Troster, Lawrence (2001) "Created in the Image of God," in Martin Yaffe, ed. *Judaism and Environmental Ethics" A Reader*, Lanham, MD: Lexington Books.

World Council of Churches (2003): http://www2.wcc-coe.org/pressReleasesen.nsf/09c9d(2(2d54ad7a37c1(256d0a004ebd7d/c0cc4cb160ebf5b6c1(256da40051b7(2f?OpenDocument.

Suggested reading

Berry, Thomas (1987) *Dream of the Earth*, San Francisco: Sierra Books.
   Perhaps the single most influential work of ecotheology.

Gottlieb, Roger S. ed. (2004) *This Sacred Earth: Religion, Nature, Environment*, second edition, New York: Routledge.
   Updated version of first comprehensive collection on the topic, includes scripture, essays, institutional pronouncements, news articles, prayers, poetry.

Gottlieb, Roger S. ed. (2006) *The Oxford Handbook of Religion and Ecology*, New York: Oxford University Press.
Large collection with essays by leading scholars on every aspect of religious environmentalism.

Gottlieb, Roger S. (2006) *A Greener Faith: Religious Environmentalism and our Planet's Future*, New York: Oxford University Press.
Study of theological, institutional, political, and social aspects of religious environmentalism.

Grim, John ed. (2001) *Indigenous Traditions and Ecology: The Interbeing of Cosmos and Community*, Cambridge: Harvard University Press.
Excellent collection of articles.

Hart, John (2006) *Sacramental Commons*, Lanham, MD: Rowman and Littlefield.
Short, focused book from Catholic viewpoint by important scholar and writer for the church.

Izzi Dien, Mawil W. (2000) *The Environmental Dimensions of Islam*, Cambridge: Lutterworth.
Study of Islam on this topic by leading commentator.

Kaza, Stephanie ed. (2000) *Hooked! Buddhist Writings on Greed, Desire, and the Urge to Consume*, Boston: Shambala.
Using Buddhism to help understand and overcome consumerism.

Palmer, Martin (2003) *Faith in Conservation: New Approaches to Religion and Environment*, Washington, DC: World Bank.
Filled with wonderful accounts of practical connections between religion and environmental activism.

Tirosh-Samuelson, Havah (2002) *Judaism and Ecology: Created World and Revealed Word*, Cambridge: Harvard Divinity School.
Wide-ranging collection on Jewish theology and history on the topic.

Wallace, Mark (2001) *Fragments of the Spirit: Nature, Violence, and the Renewal of Creation*, New York: Trinity Press.
Evocative and poetic Christian ecotheology.

Chapter 30

Religion and science

Thomas Dixon

Introduction: the two books

From one point of view, religion and science simply have nothing to do with each other. Religions are concerned with scriptural traditions and rituals, with which all members of a community engage, in order to give themselves a sense of identity, history, moral values and spirituality; they are practised by billions of people worldwide, from the most to the least educated, richest to poorest. Science, in contrast, is an elite, educated, professional activity involving expensive high-tech instruments and complex mathematics; it is engaged in by a group of intellectual, expert researchers and theoreticians who push back the frontiers of human knowledge and discover the true nature of the universe. On this view, studying 'religion and science' might seem like studying 'football chants and electronic engineering' or 'modern dance and nuclear physics' – an absurd attempt to bring together and compare two totally unrelated subjects.

In fact, of course, religion and science have much more in common than this initial caricature suggests. Specifically, religion and science share an interest in the same fundamental questions about the origins and nature of the physical universe in general, and of human beings in particular. It is when religion and science have found themselves giving different answers to these questions, whether in Renaissance Italy or in modern-day America, that conflicts have arisen. Since modern science was born into a European culture in which the Christian Church and its teachings held considerable political and intellectual influence, it has largely been in Christian countries that conflicts between scripture and science have been keenly felt and contested. As a result, in this section and the one that follows, although I talk about 'religion' and science, the examples I use are cases of interaction specifically between Christian religion and science; I will discuss the problems this raises in the third section, on criticisms of the 'dialogue' project.

For some, the whole history of modern thought can be summarised as a battle between religion and science, which science has won. One of the most famous proponents of this idea was Thomas Huxley. Huxley was the archetypical Victorian agnostic and man of science. His determined assaults on Christian theology in the name of evolution earned him the nickname 'Darwin's bulldog'. In his review of Darwin's *On the Origin of Species* (1859), Huxley wrote:

> Extinguished theologians lie about the cradle of every science as the strangled snakes beside that of Hercules; and history records that whenever science and orthodoxy have

been fairly opposed, the latter has been forced to retire from the lists, bleeding and crushed if not annihilated; scotched, if not slain.

(Huxley 1893: 52)

It is not difficult to think of examples that seem to substantiate this idea of the history of religion and science as a perpetual battleground. We might think of Galileo's condemnation by the Roman Catholic Church in the seventeenth century. In this case, the Bible taught that the earth was stationary and the sun orbited around it. For example, the book of Joshua (10: 12–14) stated that God made the sun stand still in the middle of the sky until Joshua and his troops were victorious in battle against the Amorites. This seemed to contradict the claim of the new Copernican astronomy, that the sun was static at the centre of the cosmos, while the earth and the other planets orbited around it. If the scriptures were the word of an omniscient God, and it was true that the earth orbited round the sun, then surely the book of Joshua should have stated that God had made the earth stand still to prolong the day, rather than that he had made the sun stand still. Either the religious text or the scientific theory must be wrong.

Or we might think about a conflict that has been hotly contested in modern America, namely that between the Bible and the theory of evolution. The first chapter of Genesis says that God made all the creatures of the sea, the birds, the wild animals, the livestock and the creatures that move along the ground, each 'according to their kinds', and that he created human beings in his own likeness to rule over them. This picture of the separate creation of many distinct kinds is directly contradicted by the Darwinian claim that all living things, including we humans, are descended from a common ancestor, only gradually evolving into the myriad species we now see around us.

Studying 'religion and science', then, could seem to involve thinking about a long list of conflicts: Galileo versus the Church; Darwinism versus Creationism; Bible versus science; superstition versus rationality; dogma versus empirical evidence; and so on. Certainly, any serious attempt to think about this subject must involve some account of the true nature and causes of these apparent conflicts. However, equally, any such attempt would not rest content with such a simplistically polarised account. Historical studies reveal that more complicated issues were at stake, often to do not only with the interpretation of scripture, but also with the question of the relative authority of Church and state over science and education. Struggles over the relationship between religion and science have often been political, as well as intellectual. Knowledge is a form of power, and there is much at stake, for both Church and state, in settling what sorts of knowledge should be taught in schools and universities, and by whom.

The main focus of any book or university course on 'religion and science' is likely to be the modern period (from around the seventeenth century onwards), since it is that period that saw the birth of the institutions, methods and theories that are representative of modern 'science'. However, the fundamental questions at issue are ancient and enduring. Perhaps the most fundamental of all is the question of the relationship between the observable and the unobservable. The Nicene Creed states that God made 'all that is, seen and unseen'. The Apostle Paul wrote, in his letter to the Romans, that 'since the creation of the world God's invisible qualities – his eternal power and divine nature – have been clearly seen, being understood from what has been made' (Romans 1: 20). But what exactly can the observable world tell us about the unobservable? The desire to answer this question motivates the whole immense variety of enterprises that might come under the umbrella of 'religion and science'.

A second ancient question is about the relative authority of the different sources of human knowledge: our senses, our reason, the testimony of others and the testimony of scripture. This problem has surfaced in a number of different guises. Philosophers and theologians have written about the relationship between faith and reason, whether these are opposed routes to knowledge, and which should be given priority. Another way that this epistemological question has been discussed is to think about God's two books – the book of nature and the book of scripture. Do these books tell the same story? Do you need to be an expert to be able to read them properly, or can anyone understand them? Can they be read in the same way? Historians of science have shown that the way these two books were read, and by whom, underwent significant changes as the modern period unfolded, and that this was one of the central factors in developing relationships between religion and science.

The emergence of 'religion and science' as an academic field

Considerations of the ways to relate knowledge of nature and knowledge of God, prior to the nineteenth century, were frequently undertaken in works of 'natural theology'. Authors of such works, echoing the opening lines of Psalm 19, 'The heavens declare the glory of God; the skies proclaim the work of his hands', reassured their readers that new scientific experiments, theories and technologies were supports and not hindrances to religious faith (see Brooke 1991; Brooke and Cantor 1998). Such writers agreed with Galileo, who had said that the book of nature and the book of scripture, since they had the same divine author, could not contain contradictory truths. Any apparent contradiction must result from faulty reading. William Paley's celebrated work, entitled simply *Natural Theology* (2006; first published 1802), was the classic expression of the view that the study of natural contrivances confirmed what was already known through revelation, namely that the world was the product of a divine contriver. As the nineteenth century wore on, however, discussions about the relationship between religion and science became more urgent and agonised. Works of natural theology continued to be written, arguing that the scientific study of all aspects of nature revealed it to be the handiwork of a wise, powerful and benevolent God. But the tone was becoming increasingly defensive. Theologians confronted a bewildering array of perceived threats – to biblical chronology, to mind–body dualism, to the possibility of miracles – posed by developments in the sciences of geology, physiology, neurology, psychology, sociology and evolutionary biology. 'Religion and science' was emerging as a lively intellectual arena in which a variety of different contests could be played out.

The first half of the twentieth century saw a steady stream of books on the relationship between religion and science, produced by scientists, historians, philosophers and theologians. Dominating themes included philosophical and scientific interpretations of evolution, including Henri Bergson's influential *Creative Evolution* (first published in French in 1907) as well as debates specifically about Darwinism, and about new developments in physics and cosmology (Bowler 2001). However, it was only in the second half of the century that 'religion and science' became organised as a distinct and recognisable academic field, with its own university courses and textbooks, and a specialist journal. One year in particular – 1966 – might be considered the watershed. That was the year that saw both the foundation, in Chicago, of *Zygon: Journal of Religion and Science*, the first academic journal in the area, and also the publication of British physicist-theologian Ian Barbour's important and substantial book, *Issues in Science and Religion*.

Barbour's work set the agenda, the tone and the standard for much subsequent writing on the subject. *Issues in Science and Religion* was divided into three sections: 'Religion and the History of Science', covering Galileo, Newton, Enlightenment rationalism, Darwinian debates and twentieth-century 'process' thought; 'Religion and the Methods of Science', which looked at the roles of empirical evidence and authority in constructing and choosing between theories in both science and religion; and 'Religion and the Theories of Science', focusing on theological issues raised by developments in particular scientific areas including quantum physics, genetics and artificial intelligence. More recent books on religion and science (and, indeed, the rest of this chapter too) still tend to be organised along much the same lines. In his more recent work, Barbour (1997) has developed an analysis of four different possible ways of relating science and religion: conflict, independence, dialogue and integration. He argues in favour of 'dialogue' and 'integration' as his own preferred models. Like most writers in the field, Barbour's ethos is pluralist yet apologetic, rejecting the idea of an essential conflict between religion and science and seeking a more conciliatory and constructive interaction. Many authors have developed this approach further in the forty years since Barbour's seminal book. In Britain, John Polkinghorne (1994) and Arthur Peacocke (1984, 1993) have produced notable work in this tradition, as have Nancey Murphy (1990) and Robert J. Russell *et al.* (1999) in the United States. In recent years, very substantial financial and institutional support for work seeking creative 'dialogue' and 'integration' between science and religion has been provided by the John Templeton Foundation, and by the Center for Theology and the Natural Sciences (CTNS) in Berkeley, California, which, in 2003, launched the journal *Theology and Science*.

Criticisms of the 'dialogue' project

While recognising the importance, for many practical, ethical and political reasons, of encouraging constructive dialogue between scientists and representatives of religious traditions, there are nonetheless several important criticisms that have been made of this 'dialogue' project. I should say at the outset that advocates of such dialogue would be the first to acknowledge the weight of these criticisms, and have certainly recognised and responded to them. It will be useful to articulate them nonetheless. Perhaps the three most important are: that the supposed 'dialogue' is one-sided; that it neglects the plurality of both science and religion; and that it does not acknowledge the fact that it is largely just about Christianity.

The first concern challenges the idea that there is really a balanced 'dialogue' between religion and science, or that work on religion and science has built a two-way 'bridge', allowing traffic to cross between theological and scientific communities. The reality seems much less balanced than either of these metaphors suggests. If it is a conversation, it is one in which science does all the talking and theology all the listening; if it is a bridge, the traffic across it seems to go just one way (compare Russell (2003), who favours the 'bridge' metaphor, with Drees (2003) who is more critical). It is generally scientific theories, and the philosophy of scientific method, that set the terms of the interaction, and religion and theology that are required to fit in with the theories, and to mimic the methods. Professional theologians write books and organise conferences about how their work should be shaped and constrained by the latest developments in the sciences. Professional scientists, even those with a religious commitment and a sympathy for the 'dialogue' project, only rarely seem to find their decisions about experimental and theoretical work being affected by theological or religious considerations. And, following on from this, some might ask whether religious traditions should not, in any case, be seeking to take a more critical stance and speak in a more 'prophetic' voice when commenting on science and technology, rather than always seeking harmonious dialogue. It goes without saying that prominent scientific atheists, such as Richard Dawkins (2006), are also adamant for their own reasons that good-natured dialogue between science and religion is impossible (for the opposite point of view, see Ward 2008).

The second criticism – that the 'religion and science' project overlooks plurality – is a particularly important one. Too frequently in the pages of books about religion and science one encounters statements about 'the relationship' between two 'disciplines' called 'science' and 'religion', or, indeed, about building a bridge between 'the religious community' and 'the scientific community', as if these were all singular items. In reality, of course, there are, and have been historically, an almost infinitely wide array of different sciences and different religions. It is, further, virtually impossible to reach definitive answers to questions about what counts as 'science' and what as 'religion'. Although we can all agree that physics, chemistry and biology are sciences, what about psychology and sociology? Even if we agree about those, what about economics, history, psychoanalysis, philosophy, theology? Are any or all of these scientific disciplines? What about 'creation science' and 'Intelligent Design'? Similarly with 'religion': perhaps, from a Western perspective, the monotheistic faiths of Judaism, Christianity and Islam are what we have in mind when we talk about 'religion'. But what about Eastern traditions such as Buddhism and Confucianism? Is it accurate to put them into the same category? And what about New Age movements; or cults surrounding dead celebrities; or humanistic and atheistic traditions; or political ideologies such as Socialism or Nazism; or popular protest groups such as the anti-globalisation movement? Do any or all of these count as religions? Perhaps, for some people, science itself, or some form of scientific naturalism, can fulfil religious functions (Dixon 2002; Drees 1996; Midgley 2002). Not only is it difficult to know how far the boundaries of 'science' and 'religion' extend, but also some enterprises and individuals have been simultaneously religious and scientific. How, in these cases, can we construe the idea of a 'dialogue'? Finally, we must remember that 'science' and 'religion' are, in any case, not real things or agents that can literally engage in a dialogue. They are abstractions that stand for a plurality of individuals, communities, institutions and practices, as well as ideas and theories. Which of these are being brought together in a 'dialogue' or 'integration'? Although (as this chapter itself amply demonstrates) it is difficult to eliminate general statements about 'science' or 'religion' from one's writing altogether, more specific statements, and ones that replace singulars with plurals, will often be more accurate and informative.

The third criticism follows on from this point. One of the ways in which discussions of science and religion are in danger of talking in misleadingly general terms rather than attending to particularities is when the terms 'religion' or 'theology' are used when what is actually being discussed is exclusively Christian religion or Christian theology. The overwhelming majority of academic contributions to the area of 'religion and science' in the last forty years or so have been written by individuals who profess some form of Christian faith (and of these, many are members or ministers of Protestant churches, whether Anglican, Reformed or Lutheran). The problem is not that most discussions of 'religion and science' are parts of specifically Christian, often Protestant, theological projects. The problem arises only when it seems that this particular context is being obscured or hidden by the use of very general language. Although talking about 'religion' and 'theology' in general terms might help to foster inclusiveness and pluralism in academic discussions, it could also have quite the opposite effect. Non-Christian readers might feel that the usage implies not an openness to plurality, but rather an arrogant assumption that 'religion' and 'theology' are synonymous with a particular kind of Christianity. And, looking at it from the other direction, members of particular religious traditions might feel that the distinctive values and beliefs of their traditions are being obliterated in general statements about an all-purpose, lowest-common-denominator modern category of 'religion' (Harrison 2006). For these reasons, some would say that, if the subject at hand is essentially the relationship between modern physics and Anglican theology, or between evolutionary theory and American evangelicalism, it would be best simply to say so, rather than conducting a more general discussion about 'religion', or 'theology', and 'science'.

There is awareness in the academic field of 'religion and science' that non-Christian religions have generally been excluded. Members of the 'Abrahamic', monotheistic traditions (Judaism, Christianity and Islam), by virtue of having in common certain prophets, teachings, historical contexts and basic theological assumptions about the Creator and his creation, can engage in a degree of shared discussion about relationships between science and religion. The very general questions alluded to in the introduction to this chapter, for instance, about relationships between the book of nature and the book of scripture; between faith and reason; and between the seen and the unseen, would make some sense to Jews, Christians and Muslims alike. The answers given to those questions would differ widely, not only between these faiths, but also within each tradition, but the questions could be discussed with some integrity nonetheless. But can the dialogue be extended even further? Robert Russell, in the editorial of the first issue of *Theology and Science*, expresses the hope that it can. He envisages the bridge-building project being extended to connect 'cosmology, physics, biology, and genetics and other religious traditions, such as Buddhism, Taoism, and Hinduism' (Russell 2003: 3). However, it is hard to imagine that the preoccupations of writers in the field of 'religion and science' will be very easily exported beyond the pale of Western monotheism. As historians have shown, those preoccupations have arisen from a very particular set of intellectual, social and political circumstances in Western Europe and North America, especially from the seventeenth century onwards. It might be better for proponents of science–religion dialogue to focus on articulating more precisely their own particular political agendas and theological commitments, rather than trying to stretch the boundaries and the senses of 'science' and 'religion' yet further in an attempt to create a universal dialogue.

Religion and the history of science

Some of the most interesting academic work of recent years on relationships between religion and science has been produced by historians. Their work has often highlighted the sorts of concerns about the 'dialogue' project mentioned earlier. They have particularly warned against the tendency to over-general, essentialist and schematic treatments of religion and science (Brooke 1991; Brooke and Cantor 1998; Cantor and Kenny 2001; Harrison 2006). 'Serious scholarship in the history of science', John Hedley Brooke wrote, in his 1991 book, *Science and Religion: Some Historical Perspectives*, 'has revealed so extraordinarily rich and complex a relationship between science and religion in the past that general theses are difficult to sustain' (Brooke 1991: 5). Brooke is one of many historians who have used historical examples to falsify generalisations about science and religion. Simple overarching stories about either war or peace, about either the building of walls or the building of bridges, are no longer tenable. Historians have taught us to ask, when confronted with a statement about relations between science and religion, to whose religion, which science, and what time and place, the statement refers (or belongs). The conclusion we must draw, according to Brooke, is that there is 'no such thing as *the* relationship between science and religion. It is what different individuals and communities have made of it in a plethora of different contexts' (Brooke 1991: 321). Jews, Christians and Muslims at different times and in different places, have all contributed to the development of modern science, and have reacted to that development in particular ways (Brooke and Numbers 2009; Clayton and Simpson 2006: Part I; Ferngren 2000: Part IV). Pre-modern and early-modern Islamic culture, for example, provided a particularly fertile environment for the growth of the sciences of mathematics and astronomy, which were used, among other things, to calculate the correct times of prayer and the direction of Mecca from different locations. The experience of Jews in relation to modern science was different again. Excluded from the leading European universities in the early-modern period, Jews still developed a strong connection with the science and practice of medicine, and, once exclusions from academic institutions were finally removed, subsequently were able to contribute significantly in all areas of the sciences.

Complexity has become the key note of recent histories of science–religion engagements. Grand narratives are to be replaced with local histories; sweeping generalisations are to be falsified by way of thorough and historically sensitive case studies (Dixon 2003). The last twenty-five years have seen the production of an impressive array of studies, which together provide those interested in religion and science with the materials to throw doubt on almost any generalisation with a well-chosen counterexample (for a flavour of these, see Brooke 1991; Brooke and Cantor 1998; Dixon, Cantor and Pumfrey 2009; Ferngren 2000; Lindberg and Numbers 2003; Moore 1979).

Celebrated episodes that had previously been cited, by writers sympathetic to Huxley's 'extinguished theologians' history of science, as examples of a conflict between religion and science, have now been reappraised. The Galileo affair, for example, can be understood as comprising several different conflicts. There was a theological conflict: between those who thought that only bishops and church councils had the authority to reinterpret the scriptures, and those who, like Galileo, thought that an individual layman could decide that a particular passage, which seemed to conflict with scientific knowledge, should be read figuratively. This was a particularly sensitive issue in the wake of the Reformation. There was a scientific conflict: between believers in the old Aristotelian world-view and the Ptolemaic astronomy and defenders of the new Copernican system. There was a philosophical conflict: between those who thought that the Copernican system was merely a useful device for making astronomical calculations and predictions and those who thought that it actually described the true arrangement of the planets. There was a political conflict: between Galileo's friends, patrons and supporters and those who felt he was an arrogant and untrustworthy character whose influence needed to be curbed. Historians have thus looked for deeper causes of tension and conflict in the politics and theology of the seventeenth-century Roman Catholic Church. The Galileo affair, from this perspective, looks less like a conflict between a man of science on the one hand and church leaders on the other, and more like a tense and politically charged discussion among Catholics about biblical interpretation, Aristotelian science, and the relationship between individual believers and the church hierarchy (Brooke and Cantor 1998: Chapter 4; Lindberg 2003).

More recent conflicts about evolution have also been reinterpreted. Victorian confrontations between Darwinians and Anglicans have become legendary. At a packed meeting of the British Association for the Advancement of Science in 1860, in front of an audience composed of many leading men of science as well as other ladies and gentlemen with an informed interest in scientific questions, the bishop of Oxford, 'Soapy Sam' Wilberforce, sarcastically asked Thomas Huxley whether he was descended from an ape on the side of his grandmother or his grandfather. Huxley, apparently white with rage, rose to his feet and tremulously responded that he would rather be descended from an ape than from a bishop, especially one who used his intellectual abilities to try to block the progress of science. This exchange caused such excitement that one woman was reported even to have fainted and been carried from the room. Behind this colourful legend, however, was much more than a simple conflict between a champion of science and a conservative defender of religion. As in the Galileo case, there were theological, scientific, philosophical and political dimensions to the conflict. Liberal theologians had no problem with accepting the Darwinian theory as an explanation of how God had brought plants and animals into existence. But other Christian writers saw the acceptance of Darwinism as tantamount to atheism. Scientists disagreed over whether there was enough evidence to accept the Darwinian theory of evolution; and philosophers over whether it had been produced according to the proper inductive scientific method. There was also an important political dimension to the Victorian conflict: Huxley and others were engaged in a campaign to separate scientific research and teaching at schools and universities from the influence of the established Church of England. High-profile assaults on bishops and theologians were useful rhetorical weapons in this battle to create an autonomous and secular scientific profession (Brooke 1991, 2003; James 2005; Moore 1979; Turner 1993).

Turning to early twentieth-century America, a disturbance that appeared on the surface to be a conflict between science and religion again turns out to have resulted from tensions running along deeper social and political fault-lines. In Dayton, Tennessee in a sweltering hot courtroom in the summer of 1925, a local schoolteacher, John Scopes, was successfully prosecuted under new legislation for teaching his pupils that humans had evolved from lower animals. The prosecution was led by the three-times Democratic presidential candidate, William Jennings Bryan, and the defence by the most celebrated lawyer of the age, the agnostic Clarence Darrow. While many at the time (including Bryan and Darrow) saw the Scopes 'monkey trial' as a classic case of the conflict between religion and science, the reasons for the amount of political heat generated were more complicated. These included the continuing political hostilities between North and South, even sixty years after the Civil War; a popular resentment at the perceived autocracy of a Northern intellectual elite; tensions between the ideals of intellectual freedom and majoritarian democracy; and conflicts between the rights of individual states and the authority of the federal government (see Larson 1997).

What historians of science and religion have demonstrated is that for every individual who argues that a particular scientific advance is a threat to their religious faith, there will be another who can explain why, on the contrary, it is compatible or even confirmatory of that faith. One of the most interesting questions to ask, both historically and with reference to present-day debates, is what the broader political motives are for presenting such developments as either in conflict or in harmony with a particular kind of religion.

Philosophy of science and theological method

Philosophers of science interested in the project of demarcating science from other activities (including religion and theology) have often focused on the scientific method. Some have emphasised the inductive nature of scientific work – the way that it produces laws and generalisations only after painstakingly collecting empirical data from which to generalise. On this view, scientific theories can be verified by collecting a sufficient amount of confirmatory empirical evidence. Others, such as Karl Popper, have been less optimistic and argued that the hallmark of science is the quest not for verification but for falsification. No matter how many black ravens you observe, you cannot conclusively prove that all ravens are black simply by accumulating observations. The next one you see could be white. However, the observation of a single white raven is sufficient to falsify conclusively the hypothesis that all ravens are black. Thus the scientist can expect evidence to provide certain falsification of unsuccessful theories but, in the case of apparently successful hypotheses, the best that she can hope for is provisional corroboration. Even very well confirmed theories are sometimes eventually falsified, partially or completely. Imre Lakatos, and the highly influential Thomas Kuhn (1996; first published 1962), subsequently suggested more sophisticated accounts of falsification, which acknowledged that the lack of a match between theory and data more often results in a rejection (or at least reinterpretation) of the data, or a questioning of the competence of the experimenter, than in a rejection of the theory that was being tested. The way that Lakatos put this was to say that every research programme has a 'hard core' of assumptions that are never discarded, no matter what the empirical evidence, and a 'protective belt' of auxiliary assumptions (about calibration of measuring instruments, possible sources of interference in the experimental set-up, and so on). The latter are more likely to be modified or discarded when experimental observations fail to match up with theoretical predictions.

Popper, Kuhn and Lakatos are just three of many philosophers of science to whom theologians have looked when formulating their arguments about the differences and similarities between theological and scientific methods (Barbour 1966, 1997; Knight 2001; McGrath 1998; Scott and Moore 2007). One of the central issues has been the question of whether science and religion can both be considered rational activities. According to one familiar caricature, scientific theories are rational because they are based on the facts, but religious beliefs represent an irrational sort of wish-fulfilment; science demands strong empirical evidence, but religion encourages blind faith in the complete absence of evidence; the scientist is the very embodiment of objectivity and reason, but the religious practitioner is, by contrast, a creature of irrational emotions and obscure mystical experiences. There are some grains of truth in all this. Certainly there has been a strand of thought within Christian theology that has celebrated the rejection of worldly wisdom, and has emphasised the contrast between the logic of secular reason and the ineffability of religious faith. However, it is unfair to suggest that most religions encourage people to believe things in the absence of any good evidence. Most theologians would see faith and reason as being more closely connected than that.

Writers on 'religion and science' have tried to overcome the stereotyped idea that science is supremely rational and religion is the opposite in two ways: talking down the rationality of science, and talking up the rationality of religion. Appealing to post-positivist philosophers of science, including Popper, Lakatos and Kuhn, those following the first strategy have noted that science is not quite the value-free, fact-based, truth-producing machine that it was once thought to be. They point to the fact that scientific observations are more loaded with theoretical assumptions than was previously supposed, that scientists are sometimes prone to be as dogmatic and inflexible in the face of recalcitrant evidence as the most doctrinaire of theologians, and that non-scientific factors (such as social and political concerns) seem to have a considerable impact on theory-choice in scientific communities. Writers following the second strategy have tried to draw close analogies between theological and scientific methods. Arthur Peacocke and Nancey Murphy have argued, each in their own way, that theology is very much like a scientific discipline: it makes inferences from the observable realm to the unobservable; it deploys models and metaphors to represent the unobservable, just as the natural sciences do (for instance, when physicists use models of 'waves' and 'particles' to understand the subatomic realm); and it has a set of hard-core theoretical commitments, which, just as in the natural sciences, are surrounded and supported by a belt of more flexible 'auxiliary hypotheses' (see Murphy 1990; Peacocke 1984).

Taken together, these strategies would be self-defeating, since the former questions the superior rationality of science, while the latter takes it for granted. There are problems with each of the strategies taken on its own too. Most religious traditions have a strong commitment to the careful study of nature and the rigorous application of human reason. In such traditions it is important that the rationality and success of the sciences are nurtured and encouraged. Talking down the sciences, in any case, does nothing to enhance the rationality of religion and theology, which are equally vulnerable to critiques that draw attention to hidden assumptions, prejudices and political interests. The problem, on the other hand, with suggesting a close analogy between scientific and theological methods is that it can look too much as though theologians have abandoned the distinctive skills and prophetic voice of religion in an attempt to mimic the high-prestige methods of the sciences. For many, this represents too much of an intellectual and cultural surrender to an anti-theological and scientistic world-view.

Physics and divine action

Early modern debates about the physical sciences (specifically about astronomy and cosmology) provided the centrepiece for one of the most well-known controversies concerning religion and science, namely the Galileo affair. For most of the modern period, however, physical science has frequently provided the basis for a more positive engagement. One of the pre-eminent figures in the history of modern science, Isaac Newton, is a case in point. Newton's laws of motion and gravitation laid the foundations for modern physics and were taken, by some, to depict a deterministic universe from which God had been banished. Newton himself, however, was devoutly religious and believed that there were many points in the system he described at which divine intervention was not only possible, but absolutely essential. He invoked the hand of the Deity to explain, for example, the rotation of the planets on their own axes, and the fact that matter was spread evenly throughout the universe rather than collapsing into a single great mass through the force of gravity. In the eighteenth and nineteenth centuries, alongside the development of explicitly atheistic and deterministic cosmologies by some French Newtonians, more pious writers on the physical sciences continued to discern divine authorship in the elegant mathematical laws that governed the movements and interactions of terrestrial and celestial bodies. In the later nineteenth century, physicists interested in the ways that different sorts of energy could be converted into one another, and in the role of the 'ether' as a vehicle for electromagnetic forces, became fascinated by psychical research, and the controversial idea that the human spirit could be understood as some sort of physical or electromagnetic phenomenon. Physicists in late Victorian Britain accordingly undertook investigations of the fundamental forces of nature in darkened seance rooms as well as in experimental laboratories (Oppenheim 1985).

The twentieth century saw an explosion of new ideas in the physical sciences. The theory of relativity, quantum physics, chaos theory and 'Big Bang' cosmology all brought with them suggestive new religious and theological ideas. The fuzzy, indeterminate mathematics of quantum theory seemed to indicate that physical reality was not, after all, closed and deterministic. The central role of the observer in determining the outcome of quantum events challenged the modernist dichotomy between subject and object. Big Bang cosmology could be interpreted as confirming something like a biblical view of a moment of creation out of nothing, or alternatively as describing a closed system with no boundaries and no need for a Creator. This all opened up new possibilities in debates about divine activity, which continue to be discussed by theologians and scientists (Clayton1997; Drees 1990; Polkinghorne 1994; Russell *et al.* 1999; Saunders 2002). A key danger of which such writers are constantly aware is that they might end up constructing a 'God of the gaps' – in other words, locating God simply in gaps in current scientific knowledge. If those gaps turn out to be temporary ones that disappear with advances in science, rather than being permanent, metaphysical gaps, then the cause of theism will have been weakened rather than strengthened.

Darwinism and design

There is a stark contrast between the images of God and nature suggested by the physical sciences on the one hand and those conjured up by the biological sciences on the other. Physicists have often found it natural to infer the existence of an intelligent designer from the awesome scale and mathematical beauty of the universe, and from the apparent fine-tuning of its fundamental laws and constants, as discovered by modern physics. The biological sciences, on the other hand, deal not with immense expanses of space and time, nor with grand, elegant and satisfying mathematical proofs, but rather with the messy, violent realities of the Darwinian struggle for existence. A famously gruesome example of this struggle is to be found in the case of the parasitic ichneumon wasp. The female ichneumon lays her eggs inside the body of a caterpillar, with the result that, for their first meal, her offspring eat their host alive. Having observed this phenomenon, the young Charles Darwin wrote to a friend: 'What a book a devil's chaplain might write on the clumsy, wasteful, blundering, low, and horridly cruel works of nature!' And since the publication in 1859 of Darwin's book, *On the Origin of Species*, others too have found it harder to discern in the natural world the benign and intelligent Deity of Newton or Paley.

Indeed, for many, the question of evolution, especially human evolution, remains the central one in discussions of religion and science. It is certainly a question that polarises opinion, especially in the United States. Polls have found that about 45 per cent of the population of the US believe that man was created in roughly his present state at some time in the last 10,000 years; about 40 per cent prefer to say that humans were the result of a divinely guided process of evolution; and only about 10 per cent believe that human beings evolved in an entirely natural way over millions of years through a process in which God had no part. Among professional scientists, of course, the vast majority would believe in the minority view – that humans have a common ancestry with all other animals and have evolved in an entirely natural way. The philosophical question of the demarcation of science from pseudo-science takes on a new political urgency in the context of debates about creationism and evolutionism. Creationists, from the early twentieth century onwards, have claimed that the theory of evolution is scientifically unsound and, in reality, is merely a dangerous atheistic ideology dressed up in scientific clothing – a new pied piper leading the children of America into a pit of unbelief and immorality. Evolutionists return the compliment, arguing that 'creation science' is nothing more nor less than fundamentalist Christianity mischievously masquerading as science, in an attempt to confer on itself a bogus academic credibility. Arguments on both sides range from partisan bluster to careful philosophical and scientific argumentation. The most recent incarnation of this debate has focused on the scientific, philosophical and religious credentials of the new 'intelligent design' movement (Dembski and Ruse 2004; Sarkar 2007). The way that these confrontations are resolved has particularly important implications since what is most often at issue is the practical question of who should determine the content of the science curriculum in public schools, and what should be on it. Thus, deciding how to answer the question of whether the biological sciences reveal a world of design or of chance, of divine purpose or of meaningless strife, continues to have concrete political consequences, as has been evident in American court cases from the Scopes trial in Dayton, Tennessee in 1925 to the ruling against the teaching of 'intelligent design' in Dover, Pennsylvania in 2005 (Bowler 2007; Dixon 2008: Chapter 5; Larson 1997; Numbers 2006; Ruse 2003).

Science and the soul

While some reactions to Darwinism have centred on the difficulty of reconciling the theory of evolution by natural selection with the teachings of the Bible about the creation of separate species, the sticking point for others has been the question of the existence and status of the human soul. The problem of how to combine an evolutionary understanding of human origins with anything other than a materialistic understanding of the soul is a difficult one. If the brain is the organ of the mind, and the brain, like all our other organs, gradually evolved from much more basic beginnings, it is hard to see how an immaterial or supernatural 'soul' can be inserted into the process. If human beings are nothing more than large-brained apes who live in particularly complex and violent societies, what sense can be made of religious ideas about the dignity or even immortality of the human spirit? Scientific writers from Darwin himself, in *The Descent of Man* (1871), up to popular writers of more recent times such as E. O. Wilson, Richard Dawkins, and Steven Pinker have produced intriguing accounts of the evolutionary origins, and genetic basis, of moral and religious feelings. For many theologians, however, the human soul, created in the image of God, with its faculties of will and intellect, is something that marks human beings out as quite different sorts of creatures from other animals. For them, the soul is the seat of reason and morality, which are both lacked by non-human animals.

It is not only modern evolutionary science that has posed problems for traditional understandings of the soul. Developments in medicine, psychiatry, psychology and neuroscience during the eighteenth and nineteenth centuries had already illustrated ever-closer links between the physical structures of the brain and nervous system and the healthy or pathological functioning of the human mind. As these links were made with ever greater precision and certainty through the twentieth century, theologians were confronted with difficult questions about the relationship between the body, on the one hand, and the mind, soul or spirit on the other (Dixon 2008: Chapter 6; Dueck and Lee 2005; van Huyssteen 2006; Watts 2002). The simplest explanation, that all our thoughts and feelings were simply states of the brain, seemed incompatible with religious ideas about an immaterial soul and a freely acting will. One response to these questions was the development of a philosophical position termed 'non-reductive physicalism' (Brown *et al.* 1998). Proponents of this view favoured a holistic understanding of human nature instead of the sort of soul–body dualism that modern science seemed to make untenable. As well as seeking consonance with scientific views of mind and brain, these writers also invoked biblical teachings about the indissolubility of the soul–body unity to support their case for physicalism, seeing the doctrine of the bodily resurrection, for instance, as more authentically biblical than belief in an immortal and immaterial spirit. In short, Hebrew holism was to be preferred, they said, to Hellenistic dualism. Others still need further convincing that a totally physicalist understanding of human beings can really do justice to traditional religious teachings about the soul.

From theory to practice: technology, ethics, politics

Many academic discussions about religion and science have taken place at an intellectual level. Religion and science are both, however, fundamentally practical activities. They both seek not only to describe the world, but also to change it. The prophetic voice in religion denounces injustices and abuses of the present day and calls for personal and social regeneration, reform, rebirth. Similarly, one of the leading justifications of the funding of scientific research is that it will provide the means of material improvement, for both rich and poor, through all sorts of new technologies, especially in the areas of communications, agriculture and medicine. In their different ways, religion and science both offer salvation. The leading questions driving academic discussions of religion and science have therefore often been about technology, ethics and politics rather than simply about competing intellectual positions. Historically, it has frequently been the spokespeople of religious traditions who have led the way in raising ethical concerns about experimentation on animals, the use of contraceptives, the development of nuclear weapons, the cloning of human beings, the patenting of genes, or the causes and consequences of climate change. Religions can also provide resources for those concerned with ecology and the 'stewardship' of the natural world.

Religion and science both have fraught and ambiguous relationships with the political world. Scientists have often claimed to be ethically neutral creatures, driven only by the pursuit of truth. On this view, it is down to elected politicians or, indeed, religious leaders, to form committees and make decisions about moral and political questions arising from science. Such a view, however, does not stand very close scrutiny. All scientific research programmes have to be funded, either commercially or from public money. Such funding generally has strings attached. The decision to accept funding from a pharmaceuticals company, an arms manufacturer or even a charity, a campaign group or a government agency is always an ethical and political one. Scientists have a good deal of cultural and political clout as a result of the status of their profession. That status, in turn, rests very heavily on the belief that scientists are objective and detached, motivated by purer motives than, for instance, party politics or sectarian religious views. One of the most interesting lessons of the history of science is that in the modern world few more powerful rhetorical strategies exist than claiming scientific status for one's political ideology. Laissez-faire individualists, Socialists, Nazis and Communists have all claimed scientific authority for their political creeds. But while scientists and politicians today are quick to denounce such examples from history as perversions of both science and politics, they are not always so quick to notice cases in the present when science and politics have become closely intertwined. Interpreting scientific findings relating to physical and mental differences between people of different races, sexes, or sexual orientations, for instance, is inevitably a political activity, no matter how much people, on all sides, try to present their case as purely scientific or empirical, while depicting their opponent's case as ideologically loaded (Dixon 2008: Chapter 6).

Connections between religion and politics are similarly double-edged. One of the most important functions of religious leaders has been to draw attention to the failings of political rulers. For such complaints to seem authentic, they must be seen to come from outside the political system itself. While scientists can appeal to the authority of nature and of scientific objectivity, religious writers can invoke a moral, spiritual, even divine authority which is, like the authority of the scientists, based on something beyond and above the messy and corrupt world of human affairs. Indeed, if any single rhetorical strategy has been more effective in political debates through history than the appeal to nature or science, it has been the appeal to God and morality. Disputes over the teaching of evolution and creation science in schools in the United States in the twentieth century illustrate perfectly these complex relationships between religion, science and politics.

Concluding remarks

Even in this brief survey of issues arising in the study of interactions between the worlds of religion and science, we have seen how many different philosophical, theological, ethical and political interpretations can be given to the results of scientific research. From the gruesome habits of the ichneumon wasp to the mysteries of psychic phenomena – from parasitology to parapsychology – there has always been controversy about what the natural can reveal about the divine, and how such revelations should shape our actions. Scientific understandings of the universe and our place in it, together with the technological advances that come with them, will undoubtedly continue to provide material for a wide range of intellectual and political controversies as long as human civilisations survive. Students of 'religion and science', through their attempts to get to grips with the huge variety of engagements to which these fundamental human endeavours have given rise, will perhaps be less surprised than others to find, lying around the cradle of every science in the future, as the strangled snakes beside that of Hercules, extinguished scientists and their defunct research programmes, extinguished ethicists and their superseded philosophies, extinguished politicians and their exploded ideologies and, no doubt, one or two extinguished theologians too.

Bibliography

Barbour, Ian (1966), *Issues in Science and Religion*, London: SCM Press.
—— (1997), *Religion and Science: Historical and Contemporary Issues*, San Francisco: HarperSanFrancisco (in the UK as London: SCM Press, 1998). A thorough and wide-ranging survey by one of the central figures in the field.
Bowler, Peter J. (2001), *Reconciling Science and Religion: The Debate in Early Twentieth-Century Britain*, Chicago: University of Chicago Press.
—— (2007), Peter J. Bowler, *Monkey Trials and Gorilla Sermons: Evolution and Christianity from Darwin to Intelligent Design*, Cambridge MA and London: Harvard University Press.
Brooke, John H. (2003), 'Darwin and Victorian Christianity', in Jonathan Hodge and Gregory Radick (eds), *The Cambridge Companion to Darwin*, Cambridge and New York: Cambridge University Press, pp. 192–213.
—— and Geoffrey Cantor (1998), *Reconstructing Nature: The Engagement of Science and Religion*, Edinburgh: T. & T. Clark.

—— and Ronald Numbers (eds) (2009), *Science and Religion around the World*, Oxford: Oxford University Press.

Brown, Warren S., Nancey Murphy and H. Newton Malony (eds) (1998), *Whatever Happened to the Soul? Scientific and Theological Portraits of Human Nature*, Minneapolis: Fortress Press.

Cantor, Geoffrey and Chris Kenny (2001), 'Barbour's Fourfold Way: Problems with his Taxonomy of Science-Religion Relationships', *Zygon* 36: 765–81.

Clayton, Philip (1997), *God and Contemporary Science*, Edinburgh: Edinburgh University Press.

Dawkins, Richard (2006), *The God Delusion*, London: Bantam.

Dembski, William A. and Michael Ruse (eds) (2004), *Debating Design: From Darwin to DNA*, Cambridge: Cambridge University Press.

Dixon, Thomas (2002), 'Scientific Atheism as a Faith Tradition', *Studies in History and Philosophy of Biological and Biomedical Sciences*, 33: 337–59.

—— (2003) 'Looking Beyond "The Rumpus about Moses and Monkeys": Religion and the Sciences in the Nineteenth Century', *Nineteenth-century Studies* 17: 25–33.

——, Geoffrey Cantor, and Stephen Pumfrey (eds) (2009), *Science and Religion: New Historical Perspectives*, Cambridge: Cambridge University Press.

Drees, Willem B. (1990), *Beyond the Big Bang: Quantum Cosmologies and God*, La Salle, IL: Open Court.

—— (1996), *Religion, Science and Naturalism*, Cambridge and New York: Cambridge University Press.

—— (2003), '"Religion and Science" Without Symmetry, Plausibility, and Harmony', *Theology and Science* 1: 113–28.

Dueck, Alvin, and Cameron Lee (eds) (2005), *Why Psychology Needs Theology: A Radical-Reformation Perspective*, Grand Rapids: Eerdmans.

Ferngren, Gary B. (ed.) (2000), *The History of Science and Religion in the Western Tradition: An Encyclopedia*, New York and London: Garland.

Harrison, Peter (2006), '"Science" and "Religion": Constructing the Boundaries', *The Journal of Religion* 86: 81–106.

Huxley, Thomas H. (1893), *Collected Essays, Volume 2: Darwiniana*, London: Macmillan.

James, Frank (2005), 'An "Open Clash Between Science and the Church"? Wilberforce, Huxley and Hooker on Darwin at the British Association, Oxford, 1860', in David Knight and Matthew Eddy (eds), *Science and Beliefs: From Natural Philosophy to Natural Science*, Aldershot: Ashgate, pp. 171–93.

Knight, Christopher C. (2001), *Wrestling with the Divine: Religion, Science, and Revelation*, Minneapolis: Fortress Press.

Kuhn, Thomas (1996), *The Structure of Scientific Revolutions*, 3rd edition, Chicago: University of Chicago Press.

Larson, Edward J. (1997), *Summer for the Gods: The Scopes Trial and America's Continuing Debate over Science and Religion*, New York: Basic Books.

Lindberg, David C. (2003), 'Galileo, the Church, and the Cosmos', in David C. Lindberg and Ronald L. Numbers (eds), *When Science and Christianity Meet*, Chicago and London: University of Chicago Press, pp. 33–60.

McGrath, Alister E. (1998), *Science and Religion: An Introduction*, Oxford, UK; Malden, MA: Blackwell.

Midgley, Mary (2002), *Evolution as a Religion: Strange Hopes and Stranger Fears*, revised edition, London and New York: Routledge.

Moore, James R. (1979), *The Post-Darwinian Controversies: A Study of the Protestant Struggle to Come to Terms with Darwin in Great Britain and America, 1870–1900*, Cambridge: Cambridge University Press.

Murphy, Nancey (1990), *Theology in the Age of Scientific Reasoning*, Ithaca: Cornell University Press.

Numbers, Ronald L. (2006), *The Creationists: From Scientific Creationism to Intelligent Design*, 2nd edition, Cambridge, MA: Harvard University Press.

Oppenheim, Janet (1985), *The Other World: Spiritualism and Psychical Research in Britain, 1850–1914*, Cambridge: Cambridge University Press.

Paley, William (2006), *Natural Theology*, edited with an introduction by Matthew D. Eddy and David Knight, Oxford: Oxford University Press.

Peacocke, Arthur (1984), *Intimations of Reality: Critical Realism in Science and Religion*, Notre Dame, IN: University of Notre Dame Press.

—— (1993), *Theology for a Scientific Age: Being and Becoming – Natural, Divine, and Human*, enlarged edition, Minneapolis: Fortress Press (in the UK as London: SCM Press).

Polkinghorne, John (1994), *The Faith of a Physicist*, Princeton, NJ: Princeton University Press (in the UK as *Science and Christian Belief*, London: SPCK).

Ruse, Michael (2003), *Darwin and Design: Does Evolution Have a Purpose?* Cambridge, MA: Harvard University Press, 2003.

Russell, Robert J. (2003), 'Bridging Theology and Science: The CTNS Logo', *Theology and Science* 1: 1–3.

——, Nancey Murphy, Theo C. Meyering and Michael A. Arbib (eds) (1999), *Neuroscience and the Person: Scientific Perspectives on Divine Action*, Vatican City State: Vatican Observatory; Berkeley, CA: Center for Theology and the Natural Sciences.

Sarkar, Sahotra (2007), *Doubting Darwin? Creationist Designs on Evolution*, Oxford, UK; Malden, MA: Blackwell.

Saunders, Nicholas (2002), *Divine Action and Modern Science*, Cambridge: Cambridge University Press.

Scott, Michael and Andrew Moore (eds) (2007), *Realism and Religion: Philosophical and Theological Perspectives*, Aldershot: Ashgate.

Turner, Frank M. (1993), *Contesting Cultural Authority: Essays in Victorian Intellectual Life*, Cambridge: Cambridge University Press.

van Huyssteen, Wentzel (2006), *Alone in the World: Human Uniqueness in Science and Theology; The Gifford Lectures*, Grand Rapids: Eerdmans.

Ward, Keith (2008), *Why There Almost Certainly is a God: Doubting Dawkins*, Oxford: Lion.

Watts, Fraser (2002), *Theology and Psychology*, Aldershot: Ashgate.

Suggested reading

Brooke, John Hedley (1991), *Science and Religion: Some Historical Perspectives*, Cambridge: Cambridge University Press.
An excellent place to start: an erudite, engaging, informative and thought-provoking historical survey.

Clayton, Philip and Zachary Simpson (eds) (2006), *The Oxford Handbook of Religion and Science*, Oxford and New York: Oxford University Press.
A comprehensive collection of over fifty concise essays by leading experts on all the key issues.

Dixon, Thomas (2008), *Science and Religion: A Very Short Introduction*, Oxford: Oxford University Press.
An introductory book expanding at somewhat greater length on the historical, philosophical and theological issues touched on above.

Ferngren, Gary B. (ed.) (2000), *The History of Science and Religion in the Western Tradition: An Encyclopedia*, New York and London: Garland.
An invaluable reference work with contributions by leading scholars on historical, philosophical, religious and scientific themes coming right up to the present day and paying attention to particularities of time and place. Also available in condensed form as: Gary B. Ferngren (ed.) (2002), *Science and Religion: A Historical Introduction*, Baltimore, MD: Johns Hopkins University Press.

Larson, Edward J. (1997), *Summer for the Gods: The Scopes Trial and America's Continuing Debate over Science and Religion*, New York: Basic Books.

A Pulitzer Prize-winning study, combining a vivid account of the Scopes trial with perceptive broader reflections.

Lindberg, David C. and Ronald L. Numbers (eds) (2003), *When Science and Christianity Meet*, Chicago and London: University of Chicago Press.

A collection of studies by leading historians in the field, aimed at a broad readership.

Polkinghorne, John (1994), *The Faith of a Physicist*, Princeton, NJ: Princeton University Press (in the UK as *Science and Christian Belief*, London: SPCK).

An engaging and sophisticated study by an eminent theoretical physicist now ordained in the Anglican Church.

Post, Stephen G. *et al.* (eds) (2002), *Altruism and Altruistic Love: Science, Philosophy and Religion in Dialogue*, Oxford and New York: Oxford University Press.

A substantial interdisciplinary work seeking answers from scientists, philosophers and theologians to fundamental questions about human nature and human morality.

Watts, Fraser (2002), *Theology and Psychology*, Aldershot: Ashgate.

An engaging and accessible survey of the theological implications of scientific accounts of the human mind, from evolutionary psychology to artificial intelligence.

Chapter 31

Religion and cognition

Luther H. Martin

Whereas the twentieth century has been characterized in terms of biological achievement, culminating with the mapping of the human genome, the twenty-first century is forecast to be that of the brain. The understanding of this most complex of human organs is a daunting interdisciplinary project that includes, among others, evolutionary biologists and neuroscientists, researchers into cybernetics and artificial intelligence, philosophers and psychologists, social and cultural anthropologists, linguists and historians. Researchers from across this broad range of disciplines have already initiated major investigations into how our evolved genetic endowment expresses itself in the physiology of the brain and its various functional systems, the relationships and interactions of these systems, and the ways in which input from our environment is processed by these systems. Many of these researchers foresee that naturalistic explanations for the ways by which neurological structures and systems (brain) enable but also constrain our mental functions (mind) will be one of the outcomes of this research over the coming century. This prognosis of a material explanation for human cognition has been termed the identity of 'brain' and 'mind'. In the meantime, cognitive scientists are contributing to this long-term task by focusing on the general properties, functions and organization of human cognition, including those associated with 'religion'.

What is cognitive science?

Cognitive scientists seek to explain the kinds of perceptual and conceptual representations that the mental processing of sensory input allows, the memory, transmission and transformations of these mental representations, the relationships among them, and the ways in which some of these mental representations become public. Everything that we perceive and conceive is, of course, the outcome of processing by the human mind. Much mental processing occurs, however, below the threshold of consciousness and, consequently, has only recently become recognized as an area of investigation. For example, human beings perceive their environment as a rich tapestry of color and represent it as such – to ourselves and to others – in decorative and artistic expressions, etc. What we experience as color is, however, not a property of objects in our environment but is a mental representation of our optic discernment of a certain spectrum of light waves as they are differentially reflected from these objects. This mental capacity to code our environment for color is an adaptive and evolved function of the human brain to help describe and to discriminate among objects in the environment, for example, those fauna and flora that are good to eat, an ability upon which survival depends. The point is that the chromatic representation of our environment is the effect of a significant but non-conscious processing of sensory input by brains. And there is any number of additional non-conscious biocognitive processes upon which we depend every day and throughout our lives, for example, those that regulate physiological functions such as the regular patterning of heartbeat and breathing, mental functions such as those that orient us in space and time, or social proficiencies such as instantaneous face recognition or the capacity for empathetic response.

In addition to such non-conscious mental functionings, humans also have a conscious ability to recognize and represent objects or events from our environment, or to recall certain objects or events from our past (from explicitly learned information or from experienced events). And we have the ability to communicate such representations among ourselves and to transmit them over time. We even have the ability to represent objects and events that have no natural existence. Common examples of such fabricated and fabulous representations include monsters, unicorns, imaginary friends, the dramatis personae of novels and myths, UFOs and their alien personnel, etc. From the adaptive perspective of natural selection, this ability to imagine allows us to anticipate and plan for possibilities with which we might be confronted in a not yet existent future – an ability already detectable in our primate forebears (Gassaniga 2008: 54).

Finally, we have the ability to 'represent our representations' both to ourselves (constituting, thereby, a component of our self-consciousness) as well as to others (establishing, thereby, a basis for communication and sociality). This 'metarepresentational' ability allows us critically to reflect upon our representations, to categorize and to compare them with others, to judge them, and to discriminate, thereby, between 'fact' and 'fiction'. It is this discriminatory capacity that allows for an adaptive relationship to the realities of our environment while establishing a basis for the production and appreciation of the creative arts. When this metarepresentational ability is employed, it is, nevertheless, often uncritically biased by learned values or by ideological commitments rather than based upon intersubjective and lawful criteria, as is the ideal, for example, in scientific inquiry. To the extent that the representational processes of human cognition can be accurately explained and their effects mapped, we have a scientific basis for explaining the production of all human mental representations, whether reflexive or reflective, factual or fictive, past and present.

History of cognitive science

Most pre-scientific views of mental activity have considered the human brain to be a *tabula rasa*, or blank slate, upon which environmental/cultural input was writ, the output of which might be manipulated (by learning, by the exercise of reason, or by the strength of willpower). Simply put, understandings of workings of the mind were dominated by anecdotal evidence, a legacy of the philosophy of mind tradition that had long privileged first-person accounts of mental activity. This introspective tradition reached a psychological apogee in the psychoanalytic movements of the late nineteenth and early twentieth centuries and its philosophical zenith with twentieth-century phenomenology. With the increasing availability of more advanced medical care during the twentieth century, third-person accounts of mental capacities began to provide alternative, more accurate views of mental functions. These studies, initially based upon observations of subjects who suffered brain lesions, either from injury or disease, together with subsequent advances in experimental psychology, showed that first-person accounts were insufficient to explain the increasingly sophisticated insights into the nature of mental processes and were, in many cases, simply illusory.

First-person accounts as the basis for understanding mental activity were further challenged by the rise of behavioral psychology, which, despite its continuing assumptions about the brain as a *tabula rasa*, nevertheless insisted upon systematically observable evidence for human behavior. Scientific controls on the stimulus-response methodology upon which behaviorism depended proved to be, however, imperfect. Even simple sensory stimuli are subject to a wide variety of responses that are, consequently, not reproducible. And as long as stimuli are capable of arousing a range of human response, they are simply not experimentally neutral.

The most significant challenge to the 'mind-blind' premise of most traditional approaches to human mental activity was findings about the contributions of and constraints upon mental processing for the kinds of mental representations we are able to make. For example, by the mid-twentieth century linguists had concluded that young children exhibit a linguistic competency that is underdetermined by environmental input. For example, children from about the age of three begin to exhibit a consistent use of syntactic rules in their verbal constructions in the absence of any linguistically correct models in their environment from which they might learn these rules – the colloquial speech characteristic of most informal situations, such as the home, for example – and, of course, long before they receive any formal instruction about these rules. This conclusion about the constructive dynamic of human cognition is perhaps the single most well-known development contributing to what came to be termed the 'cognitive revolution'. In turn, this conclusion gave focus to findings that were emerging from other fields during this period. Advances in computer technology suggested that the human brain is a kind of non-conscious computational system for information processing. Developments in information theory, which explored how information is encoded and transmitted, offered analogies for the mental processing of sensory input. And a resurgence in memory research began to describe discrete systems of human memory and the workings and limitations of these different systems with greater precision than had previously been the case. Finally, the development of non-invasive technologies for directly imaging brain activity – positron emission tomography, magnetic resonance imagery and functional magnetic resonance imagery, magnetoencephalography and, most recently (though minimally invasive), therapeutic deep-brain stimulation – has contributed to an explosion in the understanding of brain functions during the final decades of the twentieth century.

Why a cognitive science of religion?

When an academic, in contrast to a theological, study of religion was first proposed in the late nineteenth century, it was envisioned as one of the new human sciences that would discover and describe universal laws of human behavior and change. While some social scientific studies of religion did embrace scientific paradigms such as Darwinian evolution (although generally misappropriated in terms of the social Darwinism of the time), scholars of religion steadfastly resisted as reductionistic any scientific approach to their work, preferring instead to retain their largely theological (confessional) agendas.

A general disenchantment with optimistic views of scientific and technological advances, and with concomitant views of social and cultural progress, followed upon the ravages of the First World War. This disillusionment, together with recognition of the fallacy of social

Darwinism, reinforced the anti-scientism of religious scholars. Ironically, it was again the effects of political history that gave rise to a new focus among the human sciences. As a consequence of the Cold War, many scholars turned their attention to 'area studies', especially to those areas considered of strategic concern to national securities, and to the unique histories of these areas, to the specificities of their cultures and to their subjectivities, including their religions.

But while human behaviors and representations are manifest in historically and regionally specific ways, they nevertheless seemed to some to express certain human universals. Mid-century phenomenologists of religion attempted to catalogue these human universals arguing that they were historically varied expressions of a *sui generis* (non-reducible) 'sacrality'. However, evolutionary biologists, cognitivists and anthropologists began to argue that such patterned universals were shaped, rather, by the ordinary capacities of and constraints upon human brain functions, which, like the panhuman functioning(s) of any of our organs or systems, are the naturally selected consequences of our evolutionary history (Tooby and Cosmides 1992; Mithen 1996; Atran 2002). Does this mean, then, that religion is an evolved adaptation of *H. sapiens* (see Bulbulia *et al.* 2008)?

Whereas cognitivists agree that many specifically human capacities, such as linguistic competence and sociality, are the adaptive products of our evolutionary history, most consider religion to be, like many other cultural activities, such as the ability to operate automobiles, an evolutionary by-product; that is, while 'religion' is not itself evolved, it is a social construction upon cognitive proclivities that are. 'Religion' is, in other words, not a natural kind, nor even a stable historical formation, upon which natural selection might act (see, however, D. S. Wilson 2002). This conclusion does not diminish the historical and social significance of religion. It does mean, however, that those cultural productions like 'religion' that are evolutionary by-products of our mental functions are subject to different levels of explanation than the biological. And it means that representations of religion are still constrained by the mental 'landscape' of evolved possibilities and are subject, therefore, to 'naturalistic' explanations (Atran 2002). It is this possibility of naturalistic explanations that lie at the core of the cognitive science of religion.

The cognitive science of religion

Although a cognitive science of religion was first suggested in 1980 (Guthrie), only a few systematically formulated cognitive *theories* of religion have been proposed. These theories are focused on the areas of religious rituals, religious claims and religious transmission. While there are, of course, significant differences among and within these three areas of theoretical attention, together they lay the foundation for a comprehensive study of religion from the cognitive perspective.

Religious actions

In 1990, the scholar of comparative religion, E. Thomas Lawson, and his colleague, the philosopher Robert N. McCauley, proposed a cognitive theory of religious ritual (Lawson and McCauley 1990; McCauley and Lawson 2002). Whatever else religious rituals might be, they argued, they are human actions. Consequently, religious rituals can be understood in terms of the ways by which humans represent any action. This 'human action representation system' is a set of formal relations that includes an 'actor' or 'agent', an 'act' and 'a recipient of the action' or 'the patient'. This formal representational structure, familiar also from syntactic expressions of action relations (i.e. subject, verb, object), generates the possibility for two categories of actions – those in which the agent acts upon the patient and those in which the agent is acted upon by the patient.

What qualifies either of these ordinary types of action as religious are claims about the presence of superhuman agents or of their authorized surrogates (a priest, for example) in the formal action structure. What qualifies agents as superhuman (whether understood in negative or in positive terms, e.g. as a god or as a demon) is an attribution to them of an ability to accomplish a result that is considered to be unobtainable by ordinary means. What qualifies either of these types of religious actions as ritual is that something significant is understood to have transpired in the act, again whether the result is viewed as positive (e.g. a blessing) or negative (e.g. a curse). Thus, for example, when a Roman Catholic priest, an authorized surrogate of Jesus (Son of God) through apostolic succession, baptizes an infant, the status of that infant is considered to be changed and he/she is henceforth recognized as a member of the Christian communion.

Lawson and McCauley further contend that the role assigned to superhuman agents predicts certain features of all religious rituals. When a superhuman agent, or its surrogate, is represented as the actor in the ritual – what Lawson and McCauley term 'special agent rituals' – then that act, as an action by a superhuman agent, is understood to be altogether effectual and, as such, requires little or no repetition. Its uniqueness and significance is, however, typically invested with a sensory pageantry and emotional salience that enhances long-term memorability, as is typically the case, for example, with weddings. If, on the other hand, a superhuman agent is not represented in the ritual as the actor but as the *recipient* of an action – what Lawson and McCauley term 'special patient rituals' – then the effects of that ritual, since it is performed by human agents, will be less effectual than those performed by a superhuman agent and, consequently, must be repeated. Periodic sacrifices or weekly offerings are examples of such rituals. And in contrast to the heightened sensory pageantry of special agent rituals, Lawson and McCauley predict that the regular performance and consequent routinization characteristic of special patient rituals will result in a diminution of their emotional salience and, consequently, of their memorability. The burden of memorability falls then to repetition, a process familiar from the rote memorization of, for example, the multiplication table

Lawson and McCauley readily acknowledge the limits of their theory. It addresses only religious rituals while (deliberately) avoiding wider issues in the study of religion, and it offers a view of religious ritual which may exclude other forms of religious action that do not conform to their model, such as prayer. Their very careful formulations, however, are the strength of the theory. Whereas religious scholars have heretofore understood ritual as an inclusive designation for virtually any set of patterned, repetitive behavior, the Lawson and McCauley theory differentiates religious from otherwise ordinary kinds of human behavior, while disclosing a common cognitive basis for both. Further, their theory differentiates among kinds of religious rituals that are often conflated, e.g. special agent rites of the Roman Catholic Mass (in which the same bread and wine may be transubstantiated into the body and blood of Jesus but once), and special patent rites of that Mass (in which the same patients repeatedly participate in Jesus' sacrifice over their lifetime). Such theories of ritual bring to the study of religion an analytical precision previously absent from religious studies (see e.g. Sørensen 2007).

Religious ideas

If ordinary human actions are predicated as 'religious' by claims to superhuman agents, then the basis for such claims must themselves be accounted for. The anthropologist Pascal Boyer has argued that representations of superhuman agency, documented from virtually every human society, are readily and easily produced by our ordinary cognitive equipment and are, consequently, as 'natural' as are the actions they predicate (Boyer 2001). For example, 'agents' as self-motivating, intentional objects in the world are readily distinguished from inanimate objects even by infants. Further, a surprisingly large number – perhaps a majority – of all young children claim to have imaginary friends. Such individuals, like those who are generally able to recognize but still enjoy fantasy (as fantasy) as adults tend to be particularly capable in their social understandings and abilities (Taylor 1999) – an attribute often associated with religion (e.g. Durkheim 1915). This innate – or at least developmentally early – ability to detect and/or imagine agency is generalized as a tendency to represent all objects in our environment anthropomorphically, i.e. in terms of human features and attributes, and, likewise, all occurrences in our environments as intentional (Guthrie 1993). Anthropomorphic representation is such an exquisitely tuned feature of our cognitive processing that we tend to conclude that there is agency all around us (which of course there is) but even when no agent may actually be present (e.g. faces in the clouds, bumps in the night, etc.). There is, of course, a survival advantage for any organism to be able to react reflexively to ambiguous information from its environment, such as a fleeting perception of movement, since this information may indicate the presence of a predator or foe. Even if it turns out, upon reflection, that the inferred presence was that of a friend or even incorrect – a blowing in the wind, as it were – 'it is better to be safe', the old adage holds, 'than sorry'.

There is, in other words, little cognitive difference between imputing agency to unambiguous data and to ambiguous data, such as movement, intention, certain shapes, etc., especially when those data are deemed to be potentially relevant for our lives, as a possible indication of the presence of danger, for example. And if otherwise ambiguous events are judged potentially significant for our lives, again whether those effects are positive or negative, it is also 'natural' to conclude that they may have been intentionally instigated. The human brain, of course, seeks explanations for such intuitive responses to environmental cues and they typically become rather quickly judged as fact or fiction. For others, such intuitive responses provide the occasions for metarepresentation, reflection and intellectual 'rationalization'.

The category of agency belongs to what cognitivists refer to as our 'intuitive ontology', that is to say, to our ordinary expectations about the world. Thus, when any information is represented in terms of or as the effects of agency – whether actual or presumed, whether superhuman or not – a great deal of information is inferred from these expectations apart from any specifically learned knowledge. Such ordinary agency expectations include, for example, intentionality, self-movement, some form of metabolism, response to external stimuli, etc. In the absence of complete information, such ontological categories as 'agency' are sometimes 'violated'. A common example is ghosts which are generally represented in terms of ordinary agents – they act and react in terms of ordinary sensory stimuli such as light, sound, smell, touch, they exist in time and hold memories of the past, they communicate and can be communicated with, etc. However, they are also represented as possessing a few characteristics that violate our ordinary expectations about agents, such as being capable of invisibility or of passing through physical barriers. Whereas such claims about ghosts violate ordinary expectations about agents, they are not so excessive as to be judged bizarre, like the Godzilla of Japanese film (even though they might still be enjoyed as popular diversion), or simply dismissed, at least by most (as are, for example, claims to the existence of aliens who abduct earthlings for titillating sexual experimentation). Rather the more minimalist violations, exemplified by ghosts, prove to be attention-grabbing and, consequently, highly memorable and readily transmissible while being, at the same time, ordinary enough to be readily understood and, thereby, easily accepted (Boyer 2001). Most of the Christian Bible, for example, contains a collection of rather mundane stories – genealogies, family intrigues, accounts of kings and battles, insightful but unexceptional teachings, etc. – rendered attractive and memorable, however, by their association with claims to miraculous 'acts of God' (or of His Son). It is these extraordinary acts that reportedly attracted the attention of the first Christians (e.g. The Gospel according to John 2:11; 6:12; Acts of the Apostles 2:22; the Epistles to the Romans 15:18–19 and to the Hebrews 2:3– 4) and that retain the attention of modern Christians, many of whom admit never having read most of the 'ordinary' portions of the Bible at all.

In addition to agency, cognitivists also refer to intuitive categories of 'substances' or 'physical objects', both natural and man-made, of 'animals' and 'plants' (Boyer 2001; Atran 2002). By investing any of these ordinary categories with some qualities that defy expectations, attention is drawn to the information embedded in or associated with them and that information tends, thereby, to be considered more valuable than others in the marketplace of possible human ideas and, consequently, selected for and transmitted.

Religious persistence

The original effects to which superhuman agency have been attributed often prove to be historically inaccessible or, if known, of little significance – that is to say, any number of ambiguous possibilities can evoke conclusions about and representations of superhuman intentionality. Is the hearing of voices, for example, to be interpreted as a divine call or as an auditory illusion? Are feelings of exaltation an indication of spirituality or of having a particularly good day? Whereas naturalistic explanations for such experiences garner little attention, their interpretations as 'religious' prove to be attention grabbing and, once introduced, are readily transmitted in predictable ways. Cognitivists are interested in these modes of transmission.

The cognitive anthropologist Harvey Whitehouse has identified two divergent modes of religious transmission which he terms 'imagistic' and 'doctrinal' (Whitehouse 2004). The 'imagistic mode of religiosity' does not refer, in Whitehouse's description, to religious traditions that trade in images – a trait of virtually all religions. Rather, 'imagistic' is Whitehouse's designation for a mode of religiosity whereby religious knowledge is transmitted through infrequently performed rituals that – like Lawson's and McCauley's special agent rituals – are rendered especially memorable through intense sensory pageantry and heightened emotionality. The dramatic, often traumatic, character of these rituals typically occasions a spontaneous exegesis of that experience by its participants as well as an enduring cohesion among them that is occasioned by the shared rigors of the ritual regimen and that result in closely-bound, face-to-face communities.

In contrast to the spontaneous exegetical reflections evoked by the emotionally salient rituals of the imagistic modality, religious knowledge in the doctrinal mode is formulated as a coherent set of shared beliefs or doctrines maintained by a strong, hierarchically organized leadership. Such coherently formulated sets of orthodox teachings allow for their ready transmission by authorized teachers and missionaries and for the relatively faithful reception and retention of such routinized catechetical instruction by followers. This widespread distribution of and adherence to a shared corpus of religious knowledge is characteristic of large, imagined communities in which individual affinities are mostly anonymous – large Protestant denominations, for example. While this doctrinal modality may be found in non-literate contexts, it is more often characteristic of literate societies or of those influenced by them.

The two modes of religious transmission proposed by Whitehouse rely on and are constrained by different systems of memory that are invoked by the different forms of ritual practice. The catechetical instruction in and the repetitive reinforcement of beliefs that are characteristic of the doctrinal mode of religiosity – and that are reminiscent of the encoding of memory associated with the repetitive character of special patient rituals – become encoded in the explicit memory system as generalized schemas of knowledge. The personalized experiences and exegeses characteristic of the imagistic mode are, on the other hand, encoded in the episodic or autobiographical memory system, the contents of which are only recalled when presented with stimuli associated with an individual's own participation in a particular event. This remembered material is organized (and transmitted) in terms of those personal associations and not in terms of any shared large-scale belief system.

A particularly salient type of episodic memory, sometimes referred to as 'flash-bulb' memory, often results from participation in an especially traumatic or consequential event. This effect is exemplified by the abrupt and overwhelming emotional experiences that are a feature of many initiation rites both ancient and modern, e.g. initiations into a number of tribal societies, the Hellenistic mystery cults, criminal organizations or revolutionary cells, contemporary pseudo-religious fraternal groups or 'fundamentalist' religious factions,. Such events tend to create especially strong memories that, while incomplete, nevertheless accurately retain many details.

The cognitive anthropologist Dan Sperber has emphasized that the transmission of religious knowledge – like that of any knowledge – is from mind to mind. Such transmission inevitably involves transformations by which 'remembered' traditions are, at the same time, the consequence of constructive cognitive processes (Sperber 1996). This transformative inevitability is illustrated, at a non-profound level, by the children's game known variously as 'Chinese Whispers' or 'Telephone' in which a message that is transmitted from one person to another around the room becomes transformed, sometimes radically, by the time it reaches the final participant. On the other hand, messages which resonate with innate cognitive proclivities are attracted to those mental structures and result in a certain stabilization of knowledge that may be shared and become public and that we know as 'culture'. Any knowledge significant enough to become stabilized and publicly shared may also be considered significant enough to be inscribed and conserved in material culture as well. Such inscribings – from the first flint tools to writing itself – provide cultural way stations for continuing mnemonic and reflexive traditions of cultural transmission and exegesis.

The significance of cognitive science for the study of religion

What exactly can a cognitive science of religion contribute to the study of religion that has otherwise been lacking? Cognitive science cannot, of course, explain all religious data. While, for example, cognitive science has little to say about the meanings claimed for specific cultural constructions, it *can* explain the ubiquity of religion among virtually all human societies, past and present. It can offer naturalistic explanations for recurring patterns that have long been noted among the diversities of religious expressions. It can offer explanations for the modes of conservation and transmission employed by those particular constructions and for individual commitments to them. And it can express these explanations with some precision in ways that may be assessed from the wealth of ethnographic and historical data controlled by scholars of religion. For example, the previously discussed cognitive theories of religious behavior, of religious ideas and of religious persistence have all been, and continue to be, systematically assessed by anthropologists, archaeologists and historians. Results of this research to date broadly confirm the predictions of cognitive theories of religion (Barrett 2004; Whitehouse 2004; Whitehouse and Laidlaw 2004; Whitehouse and Martin 2004).

In addition to proposing specifically *cognitive theories* of religion, the cognitive sciences can also contribute to three issues in the larger study of religion. They can help to stipulate the kinds of data that might be included – and excluded – from such an area of study, they can provide a framework for organizing and evaluating the history of religions, and they can offer a non-ethnocentric basis for comparing religions.

Defining 'religion'

A comprehensive definition of religion – and consequently the focus and scope of its study – has long been debated. Proposals for such a definition have ranged from those with parochial (theological or confessional) biases, to those with a universalizing but still quasi-religious ('sacred' or 'spiritual') basis, to those shaped, however unintentionally, by Western conceptual categories (such as philosophical dualism) and/or political policies (colonialism). On the other hand, some functionalist definitions of religion (such as 'ultimate concern') are so broad as to include virtually anything and exclude nothing. Some recent scholars have even conceded defeat in the definitional endeavor and advocate collapsing the study of religion into that of culture(s), posing then, of course, the even more daunting task of defining 'culture', or they simply disregard the issue altogether and pursue their work without any explicit delineation for the data their work might include. As with conceptions of 'religion' as a natural kind that might provide an object for natural selection, there is, of course, no natural 'thing' as 'religion' in the world for which a 'correct' definition might be agreed. 'Religion' is, however, no less susceptible to definition as an *analytic category* than are other domains of culture such as 'economics' or 'politics'. Analytic categories, in contrast to categories whose contents refer to natural kinds in the world, must be theoretically stipulated in a clear and explicit manner (which is not to say that referential categories don't present their own theoretical problems) and, consequently, be subject to assessment of their validity and utility rather than simply being idiosyncratically asserted or confessed.

What counts as 'religious' data can be stipulated from a cognitivist perspective, as we have seen, as those ordinary behaviors and mental representations that are, however, legitimated by claims to the authority of superhuman agents. This definition, adapted from E. B. Tylor's classic 'minimum definition of religion',[1] has the advantage of stipulating what religion is *not*. Ideologies such as Marxism or world views such as Freudianism, for example, are excluded from considerations as religion, as are those patterned, repetitive human acts characteristic of such sports as football and often analyzed as 'religious' ritual. Whatever the functional similarities to religious ideas and practices that may be exhibited by such cultural expressions, they make no claim upon superhuman agency.

Some may object that 'legitimating claims to the authority of superhuman agency' as a stipulation for what counts as 'religion' excludes certain forms of 'atheistic' religious thought, such as Buddhist, Taoist or Confucian. However, anyone with minimal experience 'in the field'– even as tourists – will recognize that the actual practices of the overwhelming majority of participants in such traditions involve an acknowledgment of and devotion to superhuman agency. Such positions of 'religious atheism' are espoused by a very small number of intellectuals in these traditions. In fact, cognitivists have demonstrated that a dissonance between intellectual formulations and actual practice is a common feature of religions (Barrett 2004; Slone 2004). Intellectual representation of a deity as omniscient, for example, does not negate a confessor's impulse regularly to convey information to that deity through prayer.

Further, the minimum definition of religion differentiates 'religious' behaviors and concerns from those associated with other social systems, whether or not such differentiations are made emically. Since 'religious' and 'political' systems, for example, both claim legitimacy by appeal to the power of authority, the one is often embedded in the other, as was the case with ancient Greece and Rome. And whereas 'religious' systems are often virtually identified with moral traditions, especially by biblically-based religions, this is not necessarily the case for other traditions, as is again exemplified by ancient Greece where representations of deities exhibited wide moral latitude in contrast to the ethical authority of the philosophers. Rather, evolutionary biologists have argued that distributions of power and systems of morality are elaborations upon and codifications of evolved behavioral tendencies, such as relationships of dominance-submission, reciprocal altruism, a concern and ability to detect cheaters, etc.

In addition to Tylor's minimal definition of religion, an additional 'Durkheimian' caveat stipulates that religious representations are those that are 'costly' (in terms of resources, time, labor, cognitive effort, etc.).[2] When, in other words, social elaborations of ordinary concerns and behaviors are legitimated by costly appeals to superhuman authority, we may consider them to be 'religious'

Still, questions for further research are posed by stipulating 'religion' as costly claims to the authority of superhuman agency. How are those superhuman agents deemed to have certain attributes worthy of that costly behavior within a particular culture to be distinguished from the proliferation of superhuman agents that are 'naturally' produced by the mind but held within that same culture to be insignificant? How are gods to be distinguished from figures of folklore such as fairies or trolls? How are the 'true' (culturally accepted) deities to be distinguished from 'false' gods, from newly revealed deities or from those imported from another cultural context? Are there cognitive predispositions for such valuations and differentiations or are they simply a matter of sociohistorical construction? But how then do we explain those constructions?

Nevertheless, the stipulation of religious data as those that are legitimated by claims of superhuman agency which result in costly behavior emphasizes that the study of religion requires no privileged approach or method but rather is the study of ordinary human activities, the 'supernatural' inflections of which prove to be quite natural (Boyer 2001). Ironically, this cognitively informed definition of religion returns to and builds upon proposals by the nineteenth-century proponents of a scientific study of religion (Tylor, Durkheim), but it contributes a naturalistic foundation, a theoretical formulation and an analytic precision that were previously unavailable to earlier definitions. It is this more precise definition that can provide a clearly stipulated theoretical object, heretofore absent, for historical and comparative studies of religion.

The historical study of religions

In addition to providing historians of religion with a clearly defined theoretical object, cognitive science can provide them with a theoretical framework for explaining and understanding past expressions of religion. Evolutionary psychologists and cognitive archaeologists have taught us that a fundamental architecture of human cognition is the product of our evolutionary history. The capacities and constraints that are characteristic of this organic architecture, consequently, can allow historians to discriminate between and organize their culturally variable data in ways that are consonant with processes that are common to all human cognition rather than conflating such data as the singular product of a common time and place. For example, a particular religious practice judged to be an example of Whitehouse's imagistic mode of religiosity might well have a history incommensurate with that of one judged to be doctrinal, even if those two histories have conventionally been considered to be of the 'same' tradition. Or the successful spread and establishment of one religion in the face of its alternatives might be explicable in terms of its adopted modality or its attraction to innate cognitive templates rather than in terms of its contents, which, in a common cultural context, are likely to be similar.

Further, cognitive science can contribute insights into how and why some historical events and representations but not others that may have been historically possible were selected, remembered and transmitted over time. For example, the acceptance of a new or imported religious practice might be attributed, in part at least, to its relative absence in the traditional ritual system and, therefore, provides a balance within that system. Or the successful spread of a new religion might simply be attributed to its attractiveness to intuitive cognitive proclivities rather than to similarities with traditional expressions.

The historical record, in other words, is not only limited by historical antecedents and cultural contingencies but is constrained by mental processes that are common to all humans. Based upon the predictable patterns of the latter, historians can construct historical trajectories that can help fill in the gaps of historical knowledge – especially when the data are incomplete or fragmentary, as of course, historical data mostly are. And they can do so with greater accuracy and with more nuance than they could if working from historical remains alone. Such a pursuit has already begun to produce significant research in the historical study of religion (see e.g. Whitehouse and Martin 2004).

The comparative study of religion

The nineteenth-century recognition of different religious traditions from around the world and the desire in some way to compare these traditions provided the very impetus for the founding of an academic study of religion. For many, this comparative perspective is what continues to inform and to motivate the academic study of religion. If, however, our own past is, as the saying goes, a foreign country, how much more so is the past – and the present – of others.

As scholars of religion began to amass detailed knowledge of the various cultures of the world and of their local religious expressions and traditions, they produced ever-growing compilations of their 'phenomenal' characteristics. Cultural studies in the latter half of the twentieth century have revealed that the innumerable traits catalogued in these 'phenomenographies' of religion were largely organized in Western, if not specifically Christian (colonial), categories. Such scholarly biases, together with an emphasis on the autonomy of particular cultural formations, correctly called the comparative method into question. The evolved capacities and constraints of human cognition can, however, provide a metric of universal human possibilities in terms of which the vast diversity of human cultures – and their religious expressions – might be measured and in terms of which they have been historically and socially constructed (see e.g. Whitehouse and Laidlaw 2004). A comparative study of religions cannot, in other words, be pursued productively at the level of their cultural expressions and meanings but must be based in the generative level of cognitive functions.

Related theoretical initiatives

Cognitive theories of religion have generated, and continue to generate, a wealth of experimental, analytic and applied research. Research from related social sciences remain, however, relatively unexploited by cognitive scientists of religion, e.g. that of ethology, sociobiology, and behavioral economics

Ethologists employ evolved animal behaviors as a basis for explaining the cultural behavior of humans – including the religious (e.g. Burkert 1996). Sociobiologists seek to explain both animal and human behavior on the basis of evolutionary history and genetic makeup (e.g. E. O. Wilson 1998, Chapter 11). Both ethologists and sociobiologists have, however, tended to overstate their case by suggesting direct relationships between their data and religious behaviors and expressions. In other words, they take little account of cognitive processing in the complex process of cultural production. On the other hand, ethological research, especially primatology, has offered insights into the evolutionary history of human cognitive potentials while fundamental conclusions by sociobiologists concur with similar conclusions by cognitivists – about evolved constraints upon human sociality, for example, such as those based on the limitations of short-term memory upon information processing or those governing optimal group size.

The role of emotion in religion should also be noted. Emotion (and its related senses of 'significant experience' or 'emotion-laden thought and perception') is, today, perhaps the most widespread popular 'theory' of religion. Religions have their origin, or their 'essence', according to this view, in religious experiences or in feelings of spirituality, the paradigm of which is mysticism. This popular view about the causal significance of an inward experience for the origin of or basis for religion in contrast to institutional externalities and practices is largely the consequence of Protestant theological claims. Nevertheless, religious claims and practices are universally correlated with (as opposed to caused by) heightened feelings and emotional display. Although the significance of emotion for religion has been acknowledged in connection with 'special agent rituals' and with the mnemonic strategies of the 'imagistic' mode of religious transmission, a comprehensive theory of the relation between emotion and religious cognition has yet to be fully undertaken (but see Pyysiäinen 2004: Chapter 5).

Economic models, such as rational choice theory, have also proposed useful and insightful explanations for religious behaviors and ideas (see Young 1997). Such models are based, however, in classic economic theorizing which assumes that individual humans are rational agents who act in their own self-interest. This view has recently been challenged by the revisionist work of behavioral economists in light of insights concerning cognitive and emotional constraints on human rationality (e.g. Ariely 2008); for example, little to no correlation has been found between moral reasoning and moral behavior. While behavioral economics is increasingly influential for an understanding of human decision making generally, it has not yet been employed in the study of religion.

Challenges and conclusion

The cognitive sciences are a relatively new area of study. They have, however, firmly established their basic principles and are poised to make dramatic breakthroughs over the coming century, both in new areas of discovery and application as well as in an integration of their fundamental theoretical premises. This is no less the case with the even more recent cognitive science of religion. As with any new discipline, however, basic challenges remain.

Challenges

If the cognitive sciences, including the cognitive science of religion, are to realize a comprehensive set of scientific explanations, then the relationship of cognitive functions to their neurological base, to neurochemical/hormonal effects, etc., must ultimately be identified. While cognitivists acknowledge the neurophysiological basis of cognition, the present state of knowledge does not yet allow for a close modeling of this relationship, although plausible theories are being proposed and significant research is beginning to emerge. Different mental functions, for example, have been associated with specific areas of the brain and the neural mechanisms of some of these functions, what we experience as memory, for example, have begun to be tracked at the molecular level.

On the other hand, caution must be exercised about interpreting neurophysiological functions – those revealed by brain imaging, for example – as causal rather than as correlative data for such 'states of mind' as 'religious' experiences. This identity of neurophysiological activity with particular mental representations neglects mediating levels of cognitive processing as well as the significance of environmental factors upon the expression of those mental representations and for their transmission. Such correlative data have even been evoked as proofs for the objective validity of specific religious claims, a fallacy of the so-called 'neurotheology' that is reminiscent of some sociobiological and ethological conclusions about religious practices and ideas.

If a comprehensive explanation for the organization and functions of human cognition based upon the material conditions of brain activity has not yet been fully realized, neither has a comprehensive explanation for the connection between cognition and culture, though scientific explanations for this connection is sometimes resisted. Least constructively, some have raised the old caveat of reductionism. Others, who have devoted their professional life to cultural studies but who nevertheless wish to include human cognition in their considerations, have been drawn to theories that are more congenial to conventional cultural studies, those associated with narrativity and imagination, for example (e.g. Fauconnier and Turner 2002).

Of the first, reductionistic, concern, it might simply be noted that, from a scientific perspective, theoretical reduction (in contrast to a reduction of the data) is what is recognized as progress in knowledge (Slingerland 2008: Chapter 6). The second concern arises from perceptions that cognitivists are neglecting culture in favor of brain research. This is a somewhat surprising concern since leading cognitive scientists of religion have, in fact, addressed and emphasized just this connection and have offered plausible suggestions for precisely this connection (e.g. Sperber 1996; Lawson and McCauley 1990; Boyer 2001; Atran 2002; Whitehouse 2004). If comprehensive suggestions for the exact connections between cognition and culture remain tentative, however, it is because cognitive science is a new science and it is important for this new science to map precisely the forms and functions of human cognition before they are related to the conclusions of the past 150 years of cultural studies.

If cognitive science is finally to be applicable to a study of 'religion', then those cognitive mechanisms and processes that generate cultural formations, such as the 'religious', must be specifically identified as must those that, in turn, may be altered by environmental factors, including the social and cultural (see now Smail 2008). Although social and cultural theorists may have to relinquish certain of their conventional presumptions, about the *sui generis* autonomy of culture, for example (Tooby and Cosmides 1992; Atran 2002), they are as capable of addressing the connection between cognition and culture as are cognitivists – a potential contribution presciently noted by one of the founders of sociological studies.[3]

Conclusion

Religious actions derive from the basic repertoire of ordinary human behaviors that are predicated by counterintuitive ideas, which are, however, also natural products of human cognition. The ready grasp of such behaviors and ideas from a very early age attests to this 'naturalness', i.e. to the cognitive ease whereby they are produced and to the readiness of our cognitive acceptance of, and even commitment to, their cultural valuations and manipulations. Because of this naturalness, it is unlikely that religiosity will ever wither away from the activities and ideas of our species. Despite the predictions of many social scientists, 'religious' ideas and behavior continue to persist as an 'intuitive' category that is documented from virtually all human societies. Because of this intuitive 'naturalness' of 'religion' – even among the community of religious scholars – cultural studies of 'religion' have also proven to be unreliable as an academic pursuit, especially in any scientific sense envisioned by its founders. The cognitive science of religion, on the other hand, can formulate hypotheses about behaviors and ideas deemed 'religious' as predictions that are intersubjectively testable, not only by experimentalists but, guided by their experimental designs and predictions, also by ethnographers and historians. Such study, like the cognitive sciences generally, will require broad interdisciplinary cooperation; its achievements will be those of a community of scholars working together scientifically over the coming decades.

Notes

1   E. B. Tylor's well-known 'minimum definition of Religion' is 'the Belief in Spiritual Beings' (Tylor 1958 [1871]: 8).

2   For Durkheim, religion 'always presupposes that the worshipper gives some of his substance or his goods to the gods' (Durkheim 1915: 385).

3 'Society exists and lives only in and through … individual minds', Durkheim wrote. 'If … the beliefs, traditions and aspirations of the group were no longer felt and shared by the individuals, society would die' (Durkheim, 1915: 359).

Bibliography

Ariely, Dan (2008) *Predictably Irrational: The Hidden Forces that Shape Our Decisions*. New York: HarperCollins. A popular introduction to experimental insights into everyday human behaviors from the perspective of behavioral economics.

Atran, Scott (2002) *In Gods We Trust: The Evolutionary Landscape of Religions*. Oxford and New York: Oxford University Press. A comprehensive view of religion as an evolutionary by-product, by a leading cultural anthropologist.

Barrett, Justin L. (2004) *Why Would Anyone Believe in God?* Walnut Creek, CA: AltaMira Press. An examination of religious ideas about god(s) by an experimental psychologist.

Boyer, Pascal (2001) *Religion Explained: The Evolutionary Origins of Religious Thought*. London: Heinemann and New York: Basic Books. A comprehensive view of religion, and one of the most important, by an anthropologist who is one of the pioneers of the cognitive science of religion.

Bulbulia, Joseph, Richard Sosis, Erica Harris, Russell Genet, Cheryl Genet, and Karen Wyman, eds. (2008) *The Evolution of Religion: Studies, Theories, and Critiques*. Santa Margarita, CA: The Collins Foundation Press. A recent and comprehensive discussion by 50 contributors concerning an evolutionary perspective on religion.

Burkert, Walter (1996). *Creation of the Sacred: Tracks of Biology in Early Religions*. Cambridge, MA: Harvard University Press. An examination of religious behaviors employing insights from ethology.

Durkheim, Émile (1915) *The Elementary Forms of the Religious Life*, trans. J. W. Swain. New York: The Free Press.

Fauconnier, Gilles and Mark Turner (2002) *The Way We Think: Conceptual Blending and the Mind's Hidden Complexities*. New York: Basic Books. A study of conceptual blending (and reblending) as the basis of human imagination.

Gassaniga, Michael S. (2008) *Human: The Science Behind What Makes Us Unique*. New York: HarperCollins. A comprehensive and accessible overview of most of the themes addressed in this article.

Guthrie, Stewart (1980) 'A Cognitive Theory of Religion', *Current Anthropology*, 21 (2): 181–203.

—— (1993) *Faces in the Clouds: A New Theory of Religion*. Oxford and New York: Oxford University Press. A view of religion as an innate tendency of humans to anthropomorphize their environment, by a cultural anthropologist.

Lawson, E. Thomas and McCauley, Robert N. (1990) *Rethinking Religion: Connecting Cognition and Culture*. Cambridge: Cambridge University Press. A cognitive theory of religious ritual and one of the most important theories for the cognitive science of religion, by two of the pioneers in the field.

McCauley, Robert N. and Lawson, E. Thomas (2002) *Bringing Ritual to Mind: Psychological Foundations of Cultural Forms*. Cambridge: Cambridge University Press. An important continuation and extension of the arguments presented in Lawson and McCauley 1990.

Mithen, Steven (1996) *The Prehistory of the Mind: The Cognitive Origins of Art and Science*. London: Thames & Hudson. A fascinating and highly plausible reconstruction of the evolution of the human mind, by a cognitive archaeologist.

Pyysiäinen, Ilkka (2004) *Magic, Miracles, and Religion: A Scientist's Perspective*. Walnut Creek, CA: AltaMira Press. A comprehensive overview of the cognitive science of religion to date.

Slingerland, Edward (2008) *What Science Offers the Humanities: Integrating Body and Culture*. Cambridge: Cambridge University Press. A historian of religion defends naturalistic and scientific studies of religion.

Slone, D. Jason (2004) *Theological Incorrectness: Why Religious People Believe What They Shouldn't*. Oxford and New York: Oxford University Press. A brief and accessible introduction to the cognitive science of religion, with examples and applications from Buddhism and Christianity.

Smail, Daniel Lord (2008). *On Deep History and the Brain*. Berkeley: University of California Press. A historian offers a view of how social institutions are created to respond to the dynamics of brain chemistry.

Sørensen, Jesper (2007) *A Cognitive Theory of Magic*. Lanham, MD: AltaMira. A recent cognitive study of ritual behaviors (magic); contains up-to-date bibliography.

Sperber, Dan (1996) *Explaining Culture: A Naturalistic Approach*. Oxford and Cambridge, MA: Blackwell. An important and influential theory of culture and of cultural transmission based on the micro-processes of human cognition, by a cultural anthropologist.

Taylor, Marjorie (1999) *Imaginary Companions and the Children Who Create Them*. New York: Oxford University Press.

Tooby, John and Cosmides, Leda (1992) 'The Psychological Foundations of Culture'. In *The Adapted Mind: Evolutionary Psychology and the Generation of Culture*, J. H. Barkow, L. Cosmides, J. Tooby, eds. Oxford and New York: Oxford University Press, pp. 19–136. This classic article is the 'charter' for an evolutionary approach to the study of cultural phenomena.

Tylor, E. B. (1958 [1871]) *Primitive Culture, Part II: Religion in Primitive Culture*. New York: Harper & Brothers.

Whitehouse, Harvey (2004) *Modes of Religiosity: A Cognitive Theory of Religious Transmission*. Walnut Creek, CA: AltaMira Press. An important and influential theory of different modes of culture and of cultural transmission, especially religious, by a leading cultural anthropologist.

—— and Laidlaw, James A., eds (2004) *Ritual and Memory: Towards a Comparative Anthropology of Religion*. Walnut Creek, CA: AltaMira Press. An exploration by anthropologists of comparative studies based in the cognitive sciences.

—— and Martin, Luther H., eds (2004) *Theorizing Religions Past: Archaeology, History, and Cognition*. Walnut Creek, CA: AltaMira Press. An exploration by archeologists and historians of historical approaches to religion based in the cognitive sciences.

Wilson, David Sloan (2002) *Darwin's Cathedral: Evolution, Religion, and the Nature of Society*. Chicago: The University of Chicago Press. An evolutionary argument for religious groups as culturally evolved adaptations, by an eminent biologist.

Wilson, Edward O. (1998). *Consilience: The Unity of Knowledge*. New York: Alfred A. Knopf. A recent if brief look at religion by the founder of socio-biology.

Young, Lawrence A., ed. (1997) *Rational Choice Theory and Religion: Summary and Assessment*. London: Routledge. A good introduction to the pros and cons of modelling religion in terms of classic economic theory, i.e. rational choice theory.

Suggested reading

As a relatively new field of study, few introductory works in the cognitive science of religion have been published. A brief introduction to the basic premises of the cognitive science of religion is Justin Barrett's 'Exploring the Natural Foundations of Religion', in *Trends in Cognitive Science* 4 (2000): 29–34. Longer introductions to the cognitive science of religion include Jason Slone's *Theological Incorrectness: Why Religious People Believe What They Shouldn't* (Oxford and New York: Oxford University Press, 2004), with examples from Christianity and Buddhism, and Todd Tremlin's *Minds and Gods: The Cognitive Foundations of Religion* (Oxford and New York: Oxford University Press, 2006), which emphasizes the evolutionary framework of the field. The most significant contributions to the field to date include Justin Barrett's *Why Would Anyone Believe in God?* (Walnut Creek, CA: AltaMira Press, 2004), Pascal Boyer's *Religion Explained: The Evolutionary Origins of Religious Thought* (London: Heinemann and New York: Basic Books (2001), and Ilkka Pyysiäinen's *How Religion Works: Towards a New Cognitive Science of Religion* (Leiden: E. J. Brill, 2001). Michael Gassaniga's *Human: The Science Behind What Makes Us*

Unique (New York: HarperCollins, 2008) is a good overview of the recent research into brain and cognitive functions generally.

For recent specialized studies in the cognitive science of religion, with good bibliographies, see Jesper Sørensen, *A Cognitive Theory of Magic* (Lanham, MD: AltaMira, 2007) and Emma Cohen, *The Mind Possessed: The Cognition of Spirit Possession in an Afro-Brazilian Religious Tradition* (Oxford and New York: Oxford University Press, 2007).

For specialized topics in the cognitive sciences, see *The MIT Encyclopedia of the Cognitive Sciences*, R. A. Wilson and F. C. Keil, eds. Cambridge, MA: MIT Press, 1999.

Chapter 32

Religion, media and cultures of everyday life

Gordon Lynch

Despite sometimes well-supported claims about the growing secularization of society, religion remains embedded in the media and cultures of everyday Western life. Religious figures and issues attract substantial interest in news media. Religious debates generate considerable interest through interactive media such as online discussion forums and blogs. Entertainment media continue to represent traditional religious figures and narratives in a variety of ways ranging from the reverent to the ironic, as well as addressing alternative spiritual traditions and broader forms of the supernatural. The rise of new media, and cheaper forms of media production and distribution, have supported the growth of a range of niche religious media including film, popular music, and educational materials. The internet, and other mobile communications technology, have also provided new opportunities for religious communication and the development of religious networks spread over wide geographical areas. Religious lifestyle media and products (which in mass-produced forms, date back well into the nineteenth century) have continued to evolve with the emergence of new religious lifestyle magazines and branded religious drinks, games, clothing and jewellery.

Whilst the numbers of active participants in religious services and institutions may therefore be low, and falling, in many Western societies, religion therefore remains a powerful presence in media and popular cultures. Public awareness of religion is framed through the media, and some of the deepest controversies around contemporary religion are bound up with the content and uses of media. The controversy over the publication of the Danish cartoons of the Prophet Muhammad was both a dispute over the content of particular media publications, but was also fuelled by media that circulated the cartoons around the world with the intention of encouraging Muslim protests or rallying people around support for principles of freedom of speech. Similarly the rise of the new atheism has been made possible by various global media that disseminate the ideas of Richard Dawkins, Christopher Hitchens, and others, and by various communications media (such as online discussion boards and social networking sites) that enable supporters of the new atheism to collaborate and campaign together with little face-to-face interaction. The media also increasingly become the key public space in which such religious issues are discussed and argued over.

Understanding how religion is bound up with media and cultures of everyday life is therefore essential for making sense of contemporary forms of lived religion, as well as how religion is encountered and negotiated by people who are not themselves active religious adherents. In this chapter, we will examine the growing academic literature that has developed in this field since the 1990s, noting the different concerns and approaches that scholars have brought to this work as well as the key questions that this work has addressed and continues to generate.

By the end of the chapter, we will also have discussed how the study of religion, media and cultures of everyday life has a central role to play in making sense of some of the most important questions in the study of contemporary religion. Before doing this, though, we will take a step back from specifically focusing on religion to examine why scholars have thought that media and popular culture is, or is not, worth studying, and consider the implications of wider scholarship on media and popular culture for work in the study of religion.

Just kitsch? Why study media and popular culture

Until the middle of the twentieth century – with a few exceptions such as the Mass Observation project in the UK – scholars paid little serious attention to mass forms of media and popular culture. A common assumption was that popular culture was devoid of any intellectual, moral or aesthetic value, and that it should be largely ignored as worthless kitsch or berated from a distance for its potential to produce moral decay (see Storey, 2003; Lynch, 2005, pp.1–11). Popular or mass culture was, from this perspective, typically contrasted with other, more valuable forms of culture; either the 'high' culture of the canon of great art, literature and philosophical thought (Arnold, 1869), or authentic 'folk' cultures passed down through generations which were now being replaced by superficial forms of mass entertainment (McDonald, 1957).

By the 1950s, however, more sustained academic attention was being paid to understanding media and popular culture. The early part of the twentieth century had seen the growing social impact of what were then new media, radio and film, and later, television. The role of these expanding media as a tool for propaganda before and during the Second World War, as well as its role in the growing advertising industry, generated interest and concern about the ways in which media could be used to influence the way in which the public thought, shopped and voted. Over time, this generated an increasingly sophisticated research literature on the effects of the media on its audiences (see, e.g. Brooker and Jermyn, 2003).

In the period after the Second World War, critical social theorists also increasingly turned their attention to issues of popular culture. Whilst earlier Marxist thought had focused on the importance of economic structures for determining how power was maintained in capitalist societies, a growing number of theorists began to explore how culture itself perpetuated particular power structures or ideological myths about the nature of society (Barthes, 1957; Lefebvre, 1961). Particularly influential in this regard was the work of Theodore Adorno (1991), a leading writer in the Frankfurt School of critical Marxist thought, which critiqued the ways in which various forms of popular culture (newspaper horoscopes, popular music, the Hollywood star system) provided consumers with illusory and unimportant choices that deflected them producing genuinely creative and participatory societies. This radical critique of contemporary cultures of everyday life was also evident in the work of the Situationist International, a group of intellectuals, artists and architects, who sought not only to identify oppressive structures in contemporary cultural life, but to develop new forms of cultural practice that enabled people to experience social spaces in radical and creative ways (Vaneigem, 1967; Debord, 1977). The intellectual and activist work of the Situationists played an important role in encouraging the student protests in France which led to the Paris uprising of May 1968, in which for a short time, it appeared that a revolutionary social movement might generate major political change in the country. The failure of workers' organizations to support this uprising led both to its political collapse, but also led a number of disappointed radical intellectuals to reflect on how it was that people oppressed by a particular social system would not be moved to rise up against it. Again, attention turned to the role that culture played in winning people's assent to existing power structures. A number of cultural theorists turned to both the work of Louis Althusser (1971), who proposed that ideological state apparatuses determined the ways in which people were able to think about themselves and their social world, and Antonio Gramsci (1972), another disappointed revolutionary from earlier in the century, who wrote about how power elites were able to win the assent of wider populations through processes of hegemony.

An important stimulus for the study of media and popular culture during this period came with the formation of the Centre for Contemporary Cultural Studies (CCCS) at the University of Birmingham in 1964. Whilst critical theorists such as Adorno regarded popular culture with suspicion, staff at the CCCS were increasingly interested in how culture operated as a system of power relations in which people were subjected to, but also able to resist, dominant forms of power and ideology (see Turner, 2003, pp.58ff.). The CCCS became particularly associated with the idea of sub-culture, typically focused on young, working-class people (and, as some critics of the concept later observed, men) who developed new cultural styles and practices to challenge dominant social structures and expectations (Hall and Jefferson, 1976; see also Bennett and Kahn-Harris, 2006). Dick Hebdige's (1979) study of the punk movement became a classic text of this kind of analysis. The CCCS played a foundational role in the development of cultural studies as a new academic discipline, and its interest in media and popular culture as a site of struggle provided an alternative approach to thinking about cultural texts and practices beyond the critique of popular culture as kitsch or opiate of the people.

Within this academic turn to the study of media and popular culture, important tensions have arisen which also frame the more specific study of religion, media and cultures of everyday life. The first of these is the tension between a critical view of popular culture which sees it as trapping its consumers into the assumptions and power structures of capitalist societies (e.g. Adorno, 1991), and a more optimistic view which sees in everyday cultural practices the potential to resist dominant power structures and assumptions about gender, ethnicity and sexuality (see, e.g. de Certeau, 1984; Fiske, 1989). One specific example of this tension is between the view of contemporary consumer culture as trapping people into an illusory sense of choice and freedom which obscures the real roots of their suffering (Williamson, 1986; Carrette and King, 2004), and the view that consumer culture can provide people with the freedom to challenge existing structures and assumptions and to live creatively (Nava, 1992; Ward, 2002). A second tension has arisen between approaches to the study of media and popular culture that are purely theoretical and those which emphasize the importance of empirical work (see Lynch, 2009). Advocates of theoretical approaches to the study of media and popular culture (who draw on Marxism, feminism, psychoanalysis, post-structuralism and queer theory) argue that such theoretical critiques are necessary because those involved in everyday cultural practices may well suffer from a false consciousness produced by particular psychological or social processes. Such false consciousness makes it very difficult for people to be able to detect the power structures and assumptions embedded in their cultural lives, and interviewing people about their perceptions will therefore simply generate accounts from this false consciousness. Conversely, other researchers have argued that without some real-world study, purely theoretical approaches are in danger of generating accounts of people's cultural lives that are inadequate, or in some cases, wholly wrong. One example of this debate focused on ideas developed by contributors to the film journal, *Screen*, in the 1980s, who drew on the work of theorists such as Althusser, and the film theorist,

Christian Metz, to argue that the structure and content of film narratives positioned their audiences to think and feel in particular ways (see Turner, 2003, pp.85–9). Against this, other scholars in media and cultural studies argued that such a view tends to depict audiences as passive recipients of the ideological content of film, and fails to recognize that audience research demonstrates that people retain considerable freedom in interpreting and making use of film in ways quite different from those intended by its producers or implied in the text of the film itself. These wider debates about how we think about and study media and popular culture remain important in setting the scene for how scholars of religion approach their work in this area.

The emergence of the study of religion, media and cultures of everyday life

The earliest academic literature exploring the relationship between religion, media and popular culture began to be published in the early 1970s (see, e.g. Butler, 1969; Cooper and Skrade, 1970; Hurley, 1970), and typically focused on how religion was represented in popular film or how film engaged with theological questions about the meaning and purpose of life (both issues which remain important in the current film and religion literature). This literature began to broaden in the 1980s as some writers started to think about other forms of media and popular culture, and the phenomenon of televangelism attracted particular interest in how religious groups were using media (see, e.g. Hoover, 1988). But it was not until the 1990s, that academic interest in this field consolidated and began to increase both in quantity and quality. In the early 1990s, the American Academy of Religion agreed to establish Religion and Popular Culture and Religion, Film and Visual Culture groups at its major annual meeting, which were later followed by the formation of a Religion, Media and Culture group. Work undertaken through these groups led both to a special issue of the *Journal of the American Academy of Religion* in 1996 on religion and American popular culture, and later to an influential edited book, *Religion and Popular Culture in America* (Forbes and Mahan, 2000). During the same period, a collaboration between Scandinavian and North American media scholars led to the first international media, religion and culture conference being held in Uppsala in 1993. This subsequently evolved into a bi-ennial international conference that, along with regular seminars run by the International Study Commission for Media, Religion and Culture, became the leading network through which scholars in this field met and discussed their ideas (Hoover and Lundby, 1997; Hoover and Schofield Clark, 2002; Mitchell and Marriage, 2003). Since the mid-1990s there has been a significant increase in the numbers of edited and authored books exploring issues of religion, media and popular culture (see Schofield Clark, 2007), with this literature now sufficiently well-developed for a second wave of publications to begin to reflect on what this academic literature has and has not achieved (Johnston, 2007; Lynch, 2007). This has also been supported by the emergence of specialist journals such as the online journals of *Religion and Film* and *Religion and Popular Culture*, as well as the more recent journal, *Material Religion*.

Within this growing literature, two relatively distinct bodies of work has emerged. The first of these is concerned with studying media and popular culture from the disciplines of biblical studies and theology. Much of this work has focused specifically on film. Biblical scholars have been particularly interested in the ways in which biblical characters and narratives have been represented in film (see, e.g. Baugh, 1997; Stern *et al.*, 1999). But they have also explored how particular biblical texts might help critical reflection on theological themes addressed in specific films (e.g. Jewett, 1993), how sensitivity to film texts might assist processes of biblical interpretatation (Kreitzer, 2002), how films form part of the reception history of biblical texts (Christianson, 2007), and how film theory might help us to analyse how characters are constructed in both film and biblical narratives (Exum, 1996). Theologians have also been interested in treating films as resources for theological reflection, although there has been some debate as to whether popular film can really be a suitable focus for serious theological work (see Jasper, 1997). Given that film narratives deal with themes such as suffering, violence, evil, meaning and redemption, a number of theologians have argued that they can stimulate theological discussion of these themes as effectively as any other piece of high art or literature (Marsh and Ortiz, 1997; Deacy, 2001; Deacy and Ortiz, 2007). The popularity of film amongst students has also made it an attractive method for raising theological questions in the classroom which can then be explored in more depth through other academic theological texts (Marsh, 2007). Another branch of theological interest in media and popular culture seeks to move beyond this kind of textual study to analyse the nature and structure of contemporary society. This missiological or practical theological work uses cultural analysis to diagnose the conditions of contemporary life in order to reflect on how best the Church might respond to these. A seminal text of this kind has been Tom Beaudoin's (1998) *Virtual Faith*, which considered missiological implications of the idea that young adults, increasingly alienated from institutional religion, were instead turning to media and popular culture as resources to construct their own personalized theologies around principles of authenticity, flexibility and creativity. Beaudoin (2008) has since refined this work further, developing a more reflexive approach to thinking about why theologians come to study popular culture, and how this academic activity can both disclose insights about the cultural contexts in which theologians work and serve as a form of therapy on the theologian's own sense of self.

This missiological branch of theological study shares more in common with the second main body of work to have emerged on religion, media and popular culture, which is primarily interested in theorizing and investigating lived religion. Important contributions have been made to this work by scholars in religious studies who have explored how concepts used elsewhere in this field might be used to analyse media and popular culture. Religious scholars have therefore discussed how film can be understood as a form of cultural myth (Martin and Ostwalt, 1995), sports events as a form of ritual (Price, 2005), dieting as a form of religious practice on the body (Lelwica, 2005), and the construction of consumer products such as Coca-Cola as a form of religious fetish (Chidester, 1996). Related to this work is the use of functionalist definitions of religion to examine whether particular forms of media and popular culture serve purposes typically associated with religion such as generating community, meaning, providing ritual and sacred space, and producing religious experiences. Robin Sylvan (2002) has, for example, argued that certain genres of popular music can be understood as religious in this functionalist sense in that they provide particular theologies, offer experiences of shared community at gigs and through fan networks, and generate experiences of transcendence through practices of listening and dancing. Whilst this functionalist approach has been a useful stimulus for thinking about the religious and sacred uses of media and popular culture, it also has significant limitations (see Lynch, 2006). Emphasizing the ways in which forms of culture operate in religion-like ways risks focusing our attention on particular issues (e.g. how culture produces community, meaning or ecstatic experience) and may turn our attention away from aspects of people's cultural lives that are in reality far more important for them, such as using a clubbing night out to meet friends or to find sexual partners. Similarly, functionalist definitions of religion can import theological assumptions into what appears to be social scientific analysis (see Lynch, 2009b). A good example of this is the idea that popular culture can be a source of religious experience, when what constitutes an authentic religious experience is essentially a matter of theological judgment. This means that when Robin Sylvan (2005) writes about the post-rave dance scene as a site of religious experience, he is not so much a neutral observer of the scene, as someone implicitly attempting to develop a theology of club culture which values particular clubbing experiences as having a sacred or transcendent significance.

Contributions to the study of media, popular culture and lived religion have also been made by writers from other disciplines. Sociologists of religion have been interested in how media and popular culture serve as mechanisms for the transmission and development of religious ideologies and identities (Partridge, 2005; Lovheim, 2007). Scholars in media studies have been interested in the religious uses that audiences make of popular media (e.g. Schofield Clark, 2005), the production and use of media to different religious ends (e.g. Hendershot, 2004), and the ways in which media act as a public space for the construction and discussion of particular religious questions and concerns (Lundby, 2006). The work of some anthropologists of religion has been influenced by the wider turn in anthropology to understanding the significance of media and popular culture for the everyday life-worlds of people in economically-developed societies (see, e.g. Miller, 1998, 2008). This has led anthropologists of religion to examine the ways in which people produce and consume religious media, as well as how the sensory engagement with media and popular culture forms part of religious subjectivities and shapes religious adherents' sense of public space and wider society (Meyer and Moors, 2005). Finally, scholars working in art history, and the study of visual and material culture, have also undertaken important work in studying the role that images and objects play in everyday, lived religion (McDannell, 1995; Morgan, 2005). Turning away from the traditional religious pre-occupations of art historians with the analysis of high religious art, these scholars have focused their attention on how people use religious images or objects that art historians have tended to think of as worthless kitsch. For example, Warner Sallman's portrait of Christ, one of the most re-reproduced images of the twentieth century, falls below the aesthetic standards demanded by the attention of traditional art history, but nevertheless has had a significant role in people's religious lives as a focus for devotion, source of personal and family memories, and gift given at important moments of struggle and change (Morgan, 1998). Scholars of visual and material culture have therefore drawn attention to the religious significance of everyday objects – pictures, clothing, family bibles – which form the stuff of lived religion yet have often been invisible to analyses of religion which focus narrowly on statements of belief and formal ritual.

From this brief overview of issues explored in this second body of work, it is clear that there is a considerable overlap of interests between scholars in these disciplines in understanding the place of media and popular culture in lived religion. Whilst these different disciplinary backgrounds mean that these scholars sometimes draw on different traditions of theory, or different methodological approaches, to pursue their interests, there is also considerable common ground that makes this an essentially multi-disciplinary field of study. At the micro level of individual's religious life-worlds, these scholars are interested in exploring the role of media and popular culture in the construction of religious identities and subjectivities – how they make religious life-worlds possible. This can involve thinking about how media and popular culture feature in the ways in which people imagine and negotiate their relations with other people within and beyond the boundaries of their family, friends, and broader social, religious and political communities. At a macro, social level, these scholars are also interested in the ways in which media and popular culture are implicated in wider patterns of religious change, framing the ways in which different religious and secular ideas and activities interact, and are bound up with the structures and processes of late capitalism, globalization and new forms of religious trans-national networks.

Key questions for the future study of religion, media and cultures of everyday life

As this work on lived religion, media and popular culture has developed and consolidated, a number of important questions have emerged which are still to be resolved. First, in what ways are particular forms of media and popular culture implicated in transforming contemporary religion? Discussion of this question has focused increasingly on the theory of the mediatization of religion, which has been explored in most detail by a network of Scandinavian media and religion scholars (see, e.g. Lundby, 2009). The wider theory of mediatization suggests that as particular social forms became increasingly dependent on the media in the twentieth century, both in terms of the ways in which they are practised and the ways in which the public is aware of them, so those social forms become increasingly shaped by the particular logics of those media. A good example of this is contemporary party politics, in which politicians' engagement with their public audiences is now so dependent on broadcast and print media that politicians' ideas are increasingly constructed as sound-bites tailored to the delivery formats of those media. Theories about the mediatization of religion thus consider how the increasing importance of media both in the lives of religious communities, and for public awareness of religion, changes the nature of lived religion itself. The presence of religious resources, rituals and networks from across the world on the internet could therefore play a role in undermining traditional religious authorities, weaken people's ties to local religious communities, create more opportunities for people to engage with alternative spiritual practices such as Wicca, and strengthen networks of people with similar religious views across wide geographical areas. The availability of a wide range of fatwas and Qur'anic reasoning online can, for example, expose Muslims to much broader resources of Islamic thought than would normally have been accessible to them simply in their local community or mosque, which can not only open up new ways of thinking but also require new practices of religious discernment in judging which online sources to follow (Echchaibi, 2008). Similarly the role of the internet in making it possible for people with similar views to come together across continents has not only energized new religious networks such as trans-national atheism, but also consolidated networks of progressives and conservatives that accelerate tensions within religious institutions (for example, over issues of gay sexuality in the Anglican Communion). Whilst there are some interesting examples of the ways in which media may be transforming religious practices and institutions, theories of the mediatization of religion also need to be treated with some caution. The idea that media transform religion suggests a linear process in which media act on religion, but religion does not act on media. This is clearly too simplistic, however. The role of media in lived religion is not determined simply by the nature of the media itself, but is also shaped by prior religious assumptions and practices. The development of a kosher mobile phone network for ultra-orthodox Jews in Israel is a good example of how media use is in this instance shaped by prior religious convictions about purity and the demands of the Torah (Campbell, 2007). Rather than demonstrating a one-way flow of influence, media and lived religion exist in a complex web of patterns of influence in which religious life-worlds both act upon, and are acted upon by, different forms of media (Schofield Clark, 2009). A further area for debate with theories of the mediatization of religion concerns the suggestion that the media transformation of religion is a modern phenomenon. Lived religion has always been a mediated phenomenon, though, in the sense that religious adherents' relations with each other and their sacred figures are made possible only through particular images or objects, whether texts, images, music, food or even the medium of bodily experience. In this sense, clear distinctions between what is 'religion' and what is 'media' can become somewhat problematic. But recognizing that religion always has been mediated raises the possibility that the influence of media on lived religion may not simply be a modern phenomenon but one that can also be traced in other periods of history – such as the importance of mass-produced, printed books in shaping the cultural and intellectual conditions for the Protestant Reformation. Whilst theories of the mediatization of religion are unlikely to be accepted wholesale by scholars of lived religion, understanding the ways in which these theories do and do not work will help us to think more clearly about the complex place of media in lived religion.

A second important area of study that is opening up concerns the role of the senses and aesthetics for the uses of media and popular culture in lived religion. Much of the early literature on religion, media and popular culture tended to treat media and popular culture as texts which contained meanings that people engaged with in different ways. What was often missing from this was the recognition that people's involvement with media and other cultural practices does not take the form of a disembodied encounter with information, but embodied processes of sensory and aesthetic engagement with images, sounds, objects, spaces, smells and tastes (see Morgan, in press). The study of religious visual culture is not therefore simply the analysis of religious images, but of the religious practices of seeing, through which these images become a part of people's everyday religious worlds (Morgan, 2005). Films of Hindu myth, for example, do not simply convey information to Hindu viewers, but may for some become a means of practising *darshan*, the experience of divine encounter through gazing on the image of the god (Dwyer, 2005). Anthropologists, religious historians and scholars of visual and material culture have played a leading role in raising questions about how the religious uses of media and popular culture are bound up with sensory and aesthetic regimes that people learn in particular religious contexts (Schmidt, 2002; Meyer, 2008). Their work has suggested that religious groups are therefore important not only (or even necessarily) in providing intellectual formation in relation to their particular beliefs and dogma, but in informally teaching new adherents how to see, feel or hear the divine through particular images, objects and sounds. The experience of feeling the presence of the Holy Spirit through the Gospel music of a black Pentecostal worship service is thus dependent on having learned how to recognize and experience the movement of the Spirit through particular changes in the music's timing, pitch and volume. This attention to the sensory and aesthetic regimes through which religious adherents make use of media and popular culture thus offers the potential for us to move beyond thinking about how people use these resources to construct conscious, narrated religious identities, to thinking about the place of media and popular culture in religious subjectivities based not only on thinking, but feeling, sensing and experiencing.

A third area of work requiring further study is that which examines media and popular culture in terms of the whole circuit of cultural production and consumption. The notion of the circuit of culture was first proposed by Richard Johnson (1986/7), a leading figure in the CCCS, who argued that research in cultural studies sometimes lacked a broader sense of cultural systems and processes. Johnson suggested that cultural studies researchers would therefore benefit by thinking about their work in terms of studying different stages of the circuit of cultural production and consumption. His ideas were later developed in a key textbook, *Doing Cultural Studies: The Story of the Sony Walkman* (Du Gay *et al.* 1997), in which the authors suggested that the circuit of culture involved processes of *production*, forms of *representation* in cultural texts and objects, the use of these cultural products in the *formation of social identities*, the wider ways in which these cultural products were used and *consumed*, and the *structures which regulated* how these forms of culture were produced, distributed and used. The point here is that these different points of the circuit of culture do not exist in isolation, but in complex patterns of inter-connection. For example, the decisions that media producers make about the representation of the content of their products is not simply their own autonomous decision, but influenced by their perceptions of what their audiences want as well as financial and other regulatory structures which encourage or prohibit particular forms of content. In the study of religion, media and popular culture, scholars have tended to pay attention to particular points in the circuit of culture. The study of religion and film is a good case in point, in which a considerable amount of work has been done on the representation of religious characters and narratives in film. There has been much less work done, by comparison, on the processes by which films relevant to religion are made, the ways such films are consumed by their audiences, and the legal, financial and cultural regulatory structures that shape these processes (see Lynch, 2009a). As we have seen, researchers interested in media, popular culture and lived religion, particularly in media studies, anthropology and visual and material culture studies, have done much more work on cultural consumption. But there is still relatively little work done on the processes by which media and popular culture relevant to religion are produced, or complex systems of cultural production, consumption and regulation as a whole. Part of the challenge for the field is methodological. Students and scholars in religious studies, for example, are not usually trained in the range of empirical methods that are needed to examine processes of cultural production and consumption in real-world settings, which means that ideas about the ritual or mythological functions of media and popular culture are generally left at the level of theoretical assertions rather than being examined through real-world investigation. Again, people trained in religious studies do not necessarily know how to access information about media and culture industries which is more familiar to those working in film and media studies. This suggests the value of cross-disciplinary training and collaboration, both for new students in the field and for more experienced researchers.

A final area of study that is just beginning to attract more sustained interest concerns religion and virtual realities. Electronically-constructed virtual worlds have become an increasing part of many people's cultural lives through the expansion of the video games market (annual income from which now exceeds that of Hollywood film), and the online virtual world of *Second Life*. Religion can be found up in the expanding world of console-based and online video games, both in the form of religions invented as part of the worlds constructed for fantasy games and in the form of games designed and marketed for niche religious audiences, such as the Evangelical video games, *Catechumen* and *Left Behind: Eternal Forces*. Video games have also been designed to encourage the development of particular kinds of spiritual practice, such as *The Night Journey*, produced in conjunction with the video artist Bill Viola, which seeks to encourage an attitude of contemplation in the game player. Different forms of religious institution and practice can also be found in the virtual world of *Second Life*, which includes not only meeting places for a wide range of traditional and alternative religious groups, but also virtual forms of real-world religious pilgrimage sites (such as a virtual Mecca). As the forms of interaction on *Second Life* become more complex (e.g. with the introduction of live voice communication), so richer possibilities emerge for different kinds of religious practice. These include practices which may not be available in a person's local community, such as opportunities to have a same-sex wedding in a progressive, virtual church. As the methods of interface with these virtual worlds also become more complex, this also raises possibilities for more sophisticated forms of aesthetic engagement with these virtual worlds. Future work in this area may consider in what ways existing religious power-structures and aesthetic regimes are imported into these virtual worlds, and in what ways these worlds make possible new forms of religious organization and practice.

The wider study of religion and contemporary society

As we have seen, then, the period since the 1990s has since undergone a significant expansion of academic work on religion, media and popular culture, which has made important advances in how we think about this field as well as raising important areas for future study. Thinking about media and cultures of everyday life in relation to religion is not simply a niche area of academic work for those with interests in cultural studies, but also has the potential to add to our understanding of some of the most important issues facing the study of religion and contemporary society.

First, the study of media and popular culture can help to clarify how religious groups and ideologies survive and even thrive in the cultural conditions of late modernity. The secularization thesis proposed that as societies became increasingly modernized, so the social significance of religion would decline. In Western Europe, there is considerable evidence to support this thesis. Yet at the same time, it is clear that this process of decline is uneven and that whilst some religious institutions are dying out, others are able to survive, find new members and influence wider public life. Some previous attempts to explain why some religious groups fare better than others have focused on the attraction of conservative religious beliefs in a cultural climate of risk and uncertainty, or on demographic trends (particularly birth rates) in specific religious communities. Another possibility worth considering is that the ability of religious groups to survive and thrive in late modernity is related to their ability to generate sub-cultural worlds of media and popular culture through which adherents feel part of a wider collective, learn and maintain particular sensory and aesthetic regimes for encountering their vision of the sacred, and find reinforcement for particular ways of seeing and acting in the world. This may be especially pertinent for the ability of religious groups to retain their younger members. There is considerable potential, then, for thinking both about how such religious sub-cultures operate, including analysing the ways in which they succeed and fail in maintaining hegemonic views of the world and how religious authority is reinforced or challenged through them. Understanding such sub-cultures in a wider social context might also give us greater insights into how some religious groups are more able than others to maintain a core of active adherents in a cultural climate that they experience as indifferent, or even hostile, to religion.

A second key issue for the study of contemporary religion is the relationship between religion and the wider public sphere, including the place of religion in relation to public institutions such as government, education, welfare and the legal system. The new atheism is part of a wider phenomenon of secularisms that seek to maintain clear boundaries between religion as a matter of private concern, and public life characterized by rational ways of thinking and arguing that are not conducted along the lines of narrow confessional assumptions. At the same time, many religious groups are attempting to maintain or expand their involvement in the delivery of school education, the recognition of religious conscience and beliefs in the legal system, and respect for religious sensitivities in public arts and media. Tensions around these issues in many Western societies have been fuelled by the growth of some religions linked to migration, notably Islam, associated liberal fears about the resurgence of fundamentalist religion, tensions within liberal thought between values of tolerance and equality of opportunity, as well as other sources of social and political grievance. These contentious issues about the place of religion in contemporary public life are particularly fought through the media. The media has become a key site for public awareness of religion, as fewer people have direct contact with religious institutions, and also provides a context for this debate to take place through news coverage and other interactive media. Media outrage over particular interventions in this debate, such as the pilloring of the Archbishop of Canterbury, Dr Rowan Williams, by some British tabloid newspapers for suggesting that there should be some recognition of Sharia law within the British legal system, also exemplifies how the media actively constructs shared beliefs around national identity, otherness, and the dangers of particular forms of religion. Understanding how the media represents, and makes possible, particular forms of interaction around the place of religion in public life is therefore another key area for study.

A third important area for study is the cultural circulation of religion beyond the traditional boundaries of religious institutions and personal piety. Whilst there is a long history of the subversion and re-working of institutional religious symbols in what is sometimes referred to as folk religion, the expansion of mass media in the twentieth century created new ways in which religious symbols and figures could be used and represented against the grain of religious orthodoxy. Schofield Clark (2005) has, for example, described the recent rise of the 'dark side of Evangelicalism', in which Evangelical beliefs and symbols acquire a wider cultural life and are used in ways far removed from Christian orthodoxy. Marilyn Manson's subversive use of Christian imagery in his music, learnt from his teenage years at a private Christian school, provide a good illustration of this. This cultural circulation of religion extends not only to figures and symbols from particular religious traditions, but also to the concept of religion itself. Some of the public commentary, for example, anticipating the introduction of Apple's new i-Phone used religious allusions to emphasize its significance, depicting it as a miraculous moment of salvation. Notions of religion can also circulate through media and popular culture to refer to practices not conventionally thought of in religious terms, with for example club nights being given religious names, or people referring to sporting venues as shrines or to sports fandom as a kind of religious devotion. What is interesting about such uses of religion is not necessarily whether popular music or sport could be thought of as religious in some sense. Functionalist concepts of religion are problematic in this context as we noted earlier. But the fact that religious language and imagery is being used in this way is illuminating both in terms of what people are attempting to do and say about their cultural practices, often in an ironic and knowing way, through such uses of religion, as well as suggesting what people imagine religion to be. The persistence of religious language and symbols in societies in which growing numbers of people have little formal religious involvement, and in which these religious resources are detached from their institutional moorings, invites further analysis. The unconventional circulation of religion through globalized media and popular culture also creates significant possibilities for conflict. The case of the international protests over the Danish cartoons of the Prophet Muhammad provides a good example of this. The fact that these protests were inspired, not by the original publication of the cartoons in a Danish language tabloid, but by their re-publication in news media in the Middle East intended to stimulate public protest, exemplifies that cycles of cultural representation and protest can occur through complex processes and can be shaped by a range of religious, cultural, commercial and political factors. These protests feed into wider controversies about freedom of speech, artistic freedom, the nature and limits of blasphemy, and respect for religious beliefs that further energizes conflict and debate concerning the place of religion in public life. Understanding more about the nature and effects of the circulation of religion within media and popular culture beyond the boundaries of piety therefore provides another important basis for understanding religion in the contemporary world.

Finally, the study of media and popular culture can also help to illuminate broader questions about operative forms of the sacred in contemporary society. Faced with the plurality of religious and secular life-worlds, some scholars of religion have returned to the concept of the sacred, examining what different religious and secular forms of the sacred shape contemporary life. The notion of the sacred used here is not that of some form of universal religious experience – as suggested by Rudolf Otto and Mircea Eliade – and which has since been criticized as a liberal, theological account of mysticism. It reflects, instead, a revision of Émile Durkheim's understanding of the sacred as a social form that shapes communal identity, values and experiences of collective effervescence, and concepts from cultural anthropology in which the sacred acts as a non-negotiable marker of essential values or boundaries (see Antonnen, 2000). As a social force that shapes communities and becomes a basis of social action, the sacred is generated not through some kind of pure inner experience of transcendence, but through social and cultural processes in which the sacred is remembered and made real in people's lives. Media and popular culture are central to such processes in everyday life. The mass production and consumption of images of gods, saints and shrines is, for example, an important point of connection between many people's lives and the vision of the sacred in a particular religious tradition. But it is not only religious forms of the sacred that are mediated in such ways. Secular forms of the sacred are also remembered, celebrated and fought over through media and popular culture. One such example is the periodic repetition of news stories concerning the abduction or abuse of children. Whilst the individual cases vary, the feelings which they are intended to evoke suggest that such news stories are not simply providing information, but serving as a kind of ritual for recognizing the sacrality of the care of children. We may well need complex ways of understanding the genealogies and forms of the sacred that shape contemporary life, discovering that religious and secular forms of the sacred are often more inter-twined than might at first appear. But an integral part of this task will also be to consider how these forms of the sacred take concrete form in people's lives through media and cultures of everyday life.

In summary, then, the study of religion, media and cultures of everyday life is a relatively recent field. Although informed in part by the more serious academic attention paid to the study of media and popular culture in the latter half of the twentieth century, this work has only grown significantly within the study of religion over the past two decades. We are already at a stage now where there is greater clarity about theories and methods that might help this work, as well some of the important questions that scholars in this area are turning to. Beyond this, though, we are beginning to see a growing recognition by a wider range of scholars interested in lived religion of how issues relating to media and popular culture are bound up with some of the most important questions for understanding contemporary religion. From its relatively recent growth, then, the study of religion, media and cultures of everyday life is starting to offer important ways of helping us to understand the cultural grounds on which contemporary forms of religion and the sacred are constructed and contested.

Bibliography

Adorno, Theodor (1991) *The Culture Industry: Selected Essays on Mass Culture*, London: Routledge.

Althusser, Louis (1971) *Lenin and Philosophy and Other Essays*, London: New Left Books.

Antonnen, Veikko (2000) 'Sacred', in W. Braun and R. McCutcheon (eds) *Guide to the Study of Religion*, London: Cassell, pp.271–82.

Arnold, M. (1869) *Culture and Anarchy*, Oxford: Oxford University Press.

Barthes, Roland (1957) *Mythologies*, London: Vintage.

Baugh, Lloyd (1999) *Imagining the Divine: Jesus and Christ-Figures in Film*. Kansas City: Sheed and Ward.

Beaudoin, Thomas (1998) *Virtual Faith: The Irreverent Spiritual Quest of Generation X*, Chichester: Jossey-Bass.

Beaudoin, Thomas (2008) *Witness to Dispossession: The Vocation of a Post-Modern Theologian*, New York: Orbis.

Bennett, Andy and Kahn-Harris, Keith (eds) (2004) *After Subculture: Critical Studies in Contemporary Youth Culture*, Basingstoke: Palgrave Macmillan.

Butler, Ivan (1969) *Religion in the Cinema*, New York: A.C. Barnes.

Brooker, Will and Jermyn, Deborah (eds) (2003) *The Audience Studies Reader*, London: Routledge.

Campbell, Heidi (2007) ' "What God hath wrought": considering how religious communities culture (or kosher) the cell phone', *Continuum: Journal of Media and Cultural Studies*, 21(2), pp.191–203.

Carrette, Jeremy and King, Richard (2004) *Selling Spirituality: The Silent Takeover of Religion*, London: Routledge.

Chidester, David (1996) 'The Church of baseball, The fetish of Coca-Cola, and the potlatch of rock-and-roll: theoretical models for the study of religion in American popular culture', *Journal of the American Academy of Religion*, vol. LXI, Fall, pp.743–65.

Christianson, Eric (2007) *Ecclesiastes Through the Centuries*, Wiley-Blackwell: Oxford.

Cooper, John and Skrade, Carl (1970) *Celluloid and Symbols*, Philadelphia: Fortress Press.

Deacy, Christopher (2001) *Screen Christologies: Redemption and the Medium of Film*, Cardiff: University of Wales Press.

Deacy, Christpopher and Ortiz, Gaye (2007) *Theology and Film: Challenging the Sacred/Secular Divide*, Oxford: Blackwell.

Debord, Guy (1977) *The Society of the Spectacle*, London: Black & Red.

De Certeau, Michel (1984) *The Practice of Everyday Life*, Berkeley: University of California Press.

Du Gay, Paul, Hall, Stuart, Janes, Linda, Mackay, Hugh, and Negus, Keith (1997) *Doing Cultural Studies: The Story of the Sony Walkman*, Milton Keynes: Open University Press.

Dwyer, Rachel (2006) *Filming the Gods: Religion and Indian Cinema*, London: Routledge.

Echchaibi, Nabil (2008) 'From audio-tapes to video-blogs: the delocalization of authority in Islam', paper presented at the international Media, Religion and Culture conference, São Paulo, Brazil.

Exum, C. (1996) *Plotted, Shot and Painted: Cultural Representations of Biblical Women*, JSOT supplement series, 215, Sheffield: Sheffield Academic Press.

Fiske, John (1989) *Understanding Popular Culture*, London: Unwin Hyman.

Forbes, Bruce and Mahan, Jeffrey (eds) (2000) *Religion and Popular Culture in America*, Berkeley: University of California Press.

Gramsci, Antonio (1972) *Selections from the Prison Notebooks*, London: International Press.

Hall, Stuart and Jefferson, Tony (1976) *Resistance Through Rituals: Youth Subcultures in Post-War Britain*, Birmingham: University of Birmingham Press.

Hebdige, Dick (1979) *Subculture: The Meaning of Style*, London: Routledge.

Hendershot, Heather (2004) *Shaking the World for Jesus: Media and Conservative Evangelical Culture*, Chicago: University of Chicago Press.

Hoover, Stewart (1988) *Mass Media Religion: The Social Sources of the Electronic Church*, London: Sage.

Hoover, Stewart and Lundby, Knut (eds) (1997) *Rethinking Media, Religion and Culture*, London: Sage.

Hoover, Stewart and Clark, Lynn Schofield Clark (eds) (2002). *Practicing Religion in the Age of the Media: Explorations in Media, Religion and Culture*, New York: Columbia University Press.

Hurley, Neil (1970) *Theology through Film*, New York: Harper & Row.

Jasper, David (1997) 'On systematizing the unsystematic: a response', in C. Marsh and G. Ortiz *Explorations in Theology and Film*, Oxford: Blackwell, pp.235–44.

Jewett, Robert (1993) *'St. Paul at the Movies': The Apostle's Dialogue with American Culture*, Louisville: Westminster/John Knox Press.

Johnson, Richard (1986/7) 'What is cultural studies anyway?', *Social Text*, 16, pp.38–80.

Johnston, Robert (ed.) (2007) *Reframing Theology and Film: New Focus for an Emerging Discipline*, Grand Rapids: Baker Academic.

Kreitzer, Larry (2002) *Gospel Images in Fiction and Film: On Reversing the Hermeneutical Flow*, Sheffield: Sheffield Academic Press.

Lefebvre, Henri (1961) *Critique of Everyday Life, vol.II*, London: Verso.

Lelwica, Michelle (2005) 'Losing their way to salvation: women, weight loss and the salvation myth of culture lite', in (eds) B. Forbes and J. Mahan *Religion and Popular Culture in America* , 2nd edition, Berkeley: University of California Press, pp.174–194.

Lovheim, Mia (2007) 'Virtually boundless? Youth negotiating tradition in cyberspace', in (ed.) N. Ammerman *Everyday Religion: Observing Modern Religious Lives*, New York: Oxford University Press, pp.83–101.

Lundby, Knut (2006) 'Contested communication: mediating the sacred', in J. Sumiala-Seppanen, K. Lundby and R. Salokangas (eds) *Implications of the Sacred in Post-Modern Media*, Göteborg: Nordicom, pp.43–62.

Lundby, Knut (ed.) (2009) *Mediatization: Concepts, Changes, Consequences*, New York: Peter Lang.

Lynch, Gordon (2005) *Understanding Theology and Popular Culture*, Oxford: Blackwell.

Lynch, Gordon (2006) 'The role of popular music in the construction of alternative spiritual ideologies and identities', *Journal for the Scientific Study of Religion*, 45(4), pp.481–8.

Lynch, Gordon (2007) *Between Sacred and Profane: Researching Religion and Popular Culture*, London: IB Tauris.

Lynch, Gordon (2009a) 'Cultural theory and cultural studies', in J. Lyden (ed.) *The Routledge Companion to Religion and Film*, London: Routledge, pp.275–91.

Lynch, Gordon (2009b) 'Religious experience and popular culture: towards a new frame of enquiry', in H. Zock (ed.) *Religion and Art at the Crossroads*, Leuven: Peeters, pp.71–84.

McDannell, Colleen (1995) *Material Christianity: Religion and Popular Culture in America*, New Haven, CT: Yale University Press.

McDonald, Dwight (1957) 'A theory of mass culture', in B. Rosenberg and D. White (eds) *Mass Culture: The Popular Arts in America*, London: Collier-Macmillan, pp.59–73.

Marsh, Clive (2007) *Theology Goes to the Movies: An Introduction to Critical Christian Thinking*, London: Routledge.

Marsh, Clive and Ortiz, Gaye (1997) *Explorations in Theology and Film*, Oxford: Blackwell.

Martin, Joel and Ostwalt Jr., Conrad (eds) (1995) *Screening the Sacred: Religion, Myth, and Ideology in Popular American Film*, Westport, CT: Greenwood Press.

Meyer, Birgit (2008) 'Religious sensations: why media, aesthetics and power matter in the study of contemporary religion', in H. de Vries (ed.) *Religion: Beyond a Concept*. New York: Fordham University Press, pp.704–23.

Meyer, Birgit and Moors, Anne-Lise (eds) (2005) *Religion, Media and the Public Sphere*, Bloomington: Indiana University Press.

Miller, Daniel (1998) *A Theory of Shopping*, Cambridge: Polity.

Miller, Daniel (2008) *The Comfort of Things*, Cambridge: Polity.

Mitchell, Jolyon and Marriage, Sophia (2003) *Mediating Religion: Conversations in Media, Religion and Culture*, London: Continuum.

Morgan, David (1998) *Visual Piety: A History and Theory of Popular Religious Images*, Berkeley: University of California Press.

Morgan, David (2005) *The Sacred Gaze; Religious Visual Culture in Theory and Practice*, Berkeley: University of California Press.

Morgan, David (ed.) (in press) *The Matter of Belief*, London: Routledge.

Nava, Mica (1992) *Changing Cultures: Feminism, Youth and Consumerism*, London: Sage.

Partridge, Christopher (2005) *The Re-Enchantment of the West: Alternative Spiritualities, Sacralization, Popular Culture and Occulture*, London: Continuum.

Price, Joseph (2005) 'An American apotheosis: sports as popular religion', in (eds) B. Forbes and J. Mahan *Religion and Popular Culture in America*, 2nd edition, pp.195–212.

Schmidt, Leigh Eric (2002) *Hearing Things: Religion, Illusion and the American Enlightenment*, Cambridge, MA: Harvard University Press.

Schofield Clark, Lynn (2005) *From Angels to Aliens: Teenagers, the Media and the Supernatural*, New York: Oxford University Press.

Schofield Clark, Lynn (2007) 'Why study popular culture?', in G. Lynch (ed.) *Between Sacred and Profane: Researching Religion and Popular Culture*, London: IB Tauris, pp.5–20.

Schofield Clark, Lynn (2009) 'Mediatization and media ecology', in K. Lundby (ed.) *Mediatization: Concepts, Changes, Consequences*, New York: Peter Lang, in press.

Stern, Richard, Jeffords, Clayton and Debona, Guerric (1999) *Savior on the Silver Screen*, New York: Paulist Press.

Storey, John (2003) *Inventing Popular Culture*, Oxford: Blackwell.

Sylvan, Robin (2002) *Traces of the Spirit: The Religious Dimensions of Popular Music*, New York: New York University Press.

Sylvan, Robin (2005) *Trance Formation: The Spiritual and Religious Dimensions of Global Rave Culture*, New York: Routledge.

Turner, Graeme (2003) *British Cultural Studies: An Introduction*, 3rd edition, London: Routledge.

Vaneigem, Raoul (1967) *The Revolution of Everyday Life*, London: Rebel Press.

Ward, Pete (2002) *Liquid Church*, Carlisle: Paternoster Press.

Williamson, Judith (1986) *Consuming Passions: The Dynamics of Popular Culture*, London: Marion Boyars.

Suggested reading

Forbes, Bruce and Mahan, Jeffrey (eds) (2005) *Religion and Popular Culture in America*, 2nd edition, Berkeley: University of California Press.

Hoover, Stewart (2006) *Religion in the Media Age*, London: Routledge.

Lynch, Gordon (2007) *Between Sacred and Profane: Researching Religion and Popular Culture*, London: IB Tauris.

Meyer, Birgit and Moors, Anne-Lise (eds.) (2005) *Religion, Media and the Public Sphere*, Bloomington: Indiana University Press.

Morgan, David (2005) *The Sacred Gaze; Religious Visual Culture in Theory and Practice*, Berkeley: University of California Press.

Morgan, David (ed.) (2008) *Keywords in Religion, Media and Culture*, London: Routledge.

Turner, Graeme (2003) *British Cultural Studies: An Introduction*, 3rd edition, London: Routledge.

Chapter 33

Religion and diaspora

Seán McLoughlin

Autobiographical out-takes: Irish Catholics and Punjabi Sikhs overseas

As an undergraduate student during the late 1980s, I encountered (what was still called) comparative religion for the first time. As part of the course, students were introduced to the religions and cultures of so-called ethnic minorities, especially South Asian heritage Muslims, Hindus, Sikhs and Parsis. While preparing for end-of-term examinations, I remember very clearly a long, early summer's day spent reading a study of migration from rural India. An educationalist's account of the significance of family, home, language and religion for the children of Indians overseas, it explores 'how far the social traditions of the Punjabi villages are being maintained in Sikh households' (James 1974: 2).[1] This early study of how religion and culture travel, how they alter and change as people move, mix and remake their lives in new settings, what they preserve, lose and gain, and the impact of all this on their identification with homes new and old, really captured my interest. Although, I did not consciously make such a connection at the time, I imagine now that it had much to do with my own sense of identity. As with so many people, in so many different places, during the modern period, my family history has been shaped by forces of international migration.

Like the Punjabi Sikhs described by James, I grew up with a strong sense of religious and cultural distinctiveness. In a small market town in the English Midlands I did not experience the overt hostility often shown to people of colour. However, against the general context of John Paul II's papal visits and a civil war in the North, growing up in a nationalist family from rural Ireland ensured a very ambiguous sense of belonging to Protestant England. My early life and socialisation in the 1970s and 1980s revolved around various Catholic institutions: a church with an Irish parish priest; three schools staffed mainly by Catholic teachers; and a social club where the navvies drank and Irish bands played folk ballads about rebellion and the migrant's sense of opportunity and loss. A deep connection with Catholic Ireland was reinforced by visits home every summer and the regular arrival, from across the water, of St Patrick's Day cards and religious paraphernalia from rosaries to relics. Broader but less intense links were maintained with 'the Yanks' (unfamiliar Irish-American relatives) who arrived periodically for weddings and funerals and Catholic missionaries who returned from India or Africa to raise funds and remind us that the poor would eventually be sending missions back to us.[2] The latter, in particular, pointed beyond attempts to reproduce and encapsulate Irish Catholic tradition in an alien setting, attempts that could not resist broader and more organic processes of cultural exchange and translation. My local community included some

Catholics who were not Irish – Italians, Poles, Yugoslavs, even one or two Africans and Pakistanis – and, as a teenager especially, I was acculturated to increasingly commodified and globalised forms of English working class popular culture (mostly music and football).

Deciding to study theology and religious studies at university opened up more cosmopolitan experiences. In multi-racial, multi-cultural, multi-faith Manchester I found myself embracing the diversity of the city both intellectually and emotionally and my intended focus on Christian theology was soon dropped in favour of comparative religion. Towards the end of a vacation spent packing eggs back in Nottinghamshire, inter-railing around Europe, and meeting my future (English, non-Catholic) wife, I was also given the chance to spend one week studying religion more intensively in the field. John Hinnells, Professor of Comparative Religion in Manchester at the time, had arranged for a small group of interested students to practise what John always preached, that is, 'get your hands dirty with religion'. We would stay at a United Reformed Church under the supervision of the resident minister, someone who was actively engaged in multi- and interfaith work in the West London suburb of Southall.

Doing comparative religion in 'chota (little) Punjab'

Southall, perhaps like parts of Houston, Washington DC or Northern California in the United States (Jurgensmeyer 2002: 3), is one of any number of the world's 'chota (little) Punjabs'. It is seen by some as a ghetto and by others as the busy, if slightly tatty, capital of South Asian Britain (Baumann 1996: 38). In 1991, just a few years after my stay, the decennial national census suggested that around 60 per cent of Southall's 61,000 population were of South Asian heritage (1996: 48). Sikhs are the largest single religious grouping in the town, representing around 40 per cent of the population (1996: 73). Like so many Chinatowns or Little Italys in today's global cities, institutions, organisations and businesses owned, and run, by people who trace their cultural heritage overseas have transformed the ecology of Southall's main streets. As well as *gurdwaras* (Sikh temples), *mandirs* (Hindu temples) and Muslim mosques, there are numerous Asian grocers, pubs, butchers, video and music stores, jewellers, curry houses, *sari* shops and the offices of *Des Pardes* (*Home and Abroad*), the largest Punjabi language newspaper in Britain. Southall, then, is what anthropologists sometimes call 'institutionally complete' – it is a home abroad to all things South Asian. Because of this, the town is a magnet for Asian families and visitors from the rest of England. It has even featured heavily in so-called 'Asian cool' movies, such as *Bend It Like Beckham* (2002).

With all this on the doorstep, and briefed with a little local knowledge, I was encouraged to go out into Southall and simply *do* comparative religion. I should attempt to produce, in outline, my own religious map of the area, visiting places of worship and community organisations, observing and talking to people as best I could about such matters as:

- the background to, and history of, their migration;
- the remaking of their congregations and places of worship, as well as associated beliefs and practices;
- the influence of diverse religious movements, organisations and their leaderships;
- the impact of social status, gender and generation;
- the extent of public recognition and multi-cultural/interfaith relations in a plural setting;
- and, finally, the consequences of continuing links with the Indian subcontinent and beyond.

Looking back now, there was a danger of becoming a comparative religion tourist and unreflectively consuming the difference and exotica around me. After all, why should people want to talk to me, what did I have to offer and could I possibly hope to give anything back? Nevertheless, somewhere in between the fear and the exhilaration of awkwardly made dialogues and connections, I was able to reflect that, given a general concern to reaffirm religious and cultural identifications while all the time adapting to new circumstances, something that set them apart from the (ir)religious ethnic majority in Britain, the people of South Asian heritage I had met in Southall probably had much in common with the parents and grandparents of the O'Sullivans, Passaseos and Heidukewitschs I had been to school with. Nevertheless, the whiteness of the latter kept the option of assimilation open in a way that was not true for the former.

Where do we go from here? Reflections, definitions and overview

My experiences as a Catholic of Irish heritage, and those of Southall Sikhs of Punjabi heritage, provide just two ethnographic snapshots of a diverse and complex global phenomenon, which, since the 1980s has increasingly been described in terms of the term diaspora. The examples I have given locate both me and my academic career firmly in England, however diasporas are, of course, everywhere. In the United States, for example, the Pluralism Project at Harvard University has sought to map the changing religious landscape of America since the early 1990s. As the director of the project, Diana L. Eck (2002) argues that diversity is now a feature of 'Main Street' USA.[3] In Boston, The Pluralism Project has documented the history of 13 traditions and interfaith groups. One of the most prominent and long-standing of these is, undoubtedly, Irish-American Catholicism. Between 1820 and 1920, a massive 4.5 million people left poverty and famine in Ireland for life in a modern American city in the making. Dominated by the New England Protestant establishment, Boston in the nineteenth century was nevertheless increasingly the home of Italian and other Catholics from Southern and Eastern Europe, as well as Jews and Orthodox Christians. Today, Irish Catholics in Boston are themselves part of the establishment, but they still share something of a transnational tradition with newcomers, such as the Vietnamese who have arrived in the city since the Immigration Act of 1965. While Irish Catholics in Boston and the English Midlands have quite different histories, I have no doubt that many of the themes in my story would still have much resonance there.

Whether taken in America or in England, my snapshots are intended to give a certain depth and texture to a topic that is very much concerned with the living religions of real people. Therefore, just as my own account reveals something of who I am and where I'm coming from, I hope readers will be prompted to reflect on how they and their families, or the neighbourhoods, cities and countries in which they live, have been impacted by diaspora. At its best, the study of religions and cultures should always provoke us to ponder the risks and rewards of learning about ourselves as we encounter the difference of others. Moreover, as we are beginning to see, diaspora is by no means confined to the experiences of people of colour or the visible minorities who have migrated from Asia, Africa and the Middle East in the post-war period. Discussions that mention both Irish and Vietnamese Catholics in the same breath, never mind Punjabi Sikhs, may be rare. However, such studies are beginning to emerge as Peggy Levitt's (2007) comparison of Irish, Brazilians, Indians and Pakistanis in America illustrates. Her work teaches us that diverse diasporas do share many continuities of experience for all their differences. Indeed, what remains perhaps most interesting are the outcomes of 'our' interactions in a globalised world, whoever 'we' may now be.

Before going any further some basic definitions are also in order. Steven Vertovec, for example, suggests that diaspora, migration and transnationalism are three separate, but related, terms. As such, scholars and students alike should seek to distinguish between them more carefully:

> Diasporas arise from some form of migration, but not all migration involves diasporic consciousness; all transnational communities comprise diasporas, but not all diasporas develop transnationalism.[4]

> (2004: 282)

For Vertovec, *migration* involves movement from one place to another, the challenges of relocation having prompted people throughout the ages to reconstruct or remake their life-worlds in new contexts. Migrants also very often form a minority, marked out from the ethnic majority in terms of 'race', language, culture and/or religion, as well as residential, educational and employment patterns. So, while *diaspora* also suggests dispersal from a homeland, Vertovec insists that it should be defined principally in terms of the continuing consciousness of a connection, real or imagined, to that homeland and a distinctive community of co-ethnics in other parts of the world, although not all migrants develop such consciousness. In the present age of accelerated globalisation, time and space are compressed with increasing intensity and extensity by advances in communications technology to such an extent that people increasingly experience the world as a global village or a single place. Under these conditions diasporas can become *trans-national*, in the sense that social, economic, political and cultural circulations or flows between the homeland and its diasporas become part of the fabric of everyday life. However, this was not always the case historically and diasporas may have struggled to maintain contact and communication with the homeland while still imagining a sense of connection to it.

In the first half of this chapter, then, I will explore in more detail how the study of diaspora has evolved and developed historically and how it can be mapped both in terms of different types of diasporas and some characteristics they seem to share in common. As we shall see, the term diaspora has a long history associated with the dispersal of ancient Jewry and, more recently, people of African descent as part of the far-reaching consequences of slavery. Nevertheless, the term's high profile in contemporary scholarship must be contextualised in terms of changing patterns of international mobility and developments in postmodern and postcolonial theory. Thus, as well as seeking to move beyond common-sense definitions of important related concepts, my overall emphasis is on a key contrast in the formation of cultural identity between twin processes of translation, intermixture and re-negotiation on the one hand, and re-traditionalisation, or maintaining boundaries of cultural distinctiveness, on the other.

In the second half of the chapter I show how the study of diaspora has impacted the study of religion. Ninian Smart (1987) is identified in current genealogies as the first to use the term. However, this should not obscure, as it sometimes does, that the roots of a distinctive research agenda for religious studies in this field actually lie in the early empirical and ethnographic work of scholars working on migration during the 1970s and 1980s. A key concern of that pioneering literature was to unpick the relationship between religion and ethnicity, as well as the factors affecting the transformation of transplanted religion. I continue by exploring the question of whether religions can truly be considered diasporas, reflecting on the utility of the distinctions that are sometimes made between so-called 'ethnic' and 'universal' traditions. However, I maintain that it is the mapping of empirical patterns and trends that stands as the field's major achievement in the last decade or so. By way of conclusion, I argue that the study of religion and diaspora – like the study of religion per se – should pay greater attention to critically analysing the different types of work done by the category 'religion' in differently configured locations.

Babylon and beyond: the study of diaspora

In the first edition of *Diaspora: A Journal of Transnational Studies*, editor Khachig Tölöyan (1991), argued that the new surge of popularity in diaspora studies had been accompanied by a decisive shift in focus for the field. In fact, as Robin Cohen (2008: 1) has argued in the second edition of his excellent survey, *Global Diasporas*, up to four phases of recent development can now be identified. For more or less 2,000 years the term diaspora was used mainly in relation to the 'prototypical' Jewish diaspora. However, from the 1960s and 1970s this usage came first to be extended to others with experiences of large-scale scattering due to homeland traumas. Then, second, during the 1980s, diaspora also came to encompass those groups hitherto identified as immigrants, ethnic minorities, exiles, expatriates, refugees, guest-workers and so on. Indeed, many members of such groups embraced the term, too, most likely because it had more positive overtones than some of these other terms. From the mid-1990s, Cohen highlights what he sees as a third phase in which postmodern and postcolonial critiques of the term deconstructed, re-appropriated (and sometimes rejected outright) the necessary relationship between, and scholarly focus upon, ethno-religious communities and their homeland origins. For some this also marked an unhelpful 'dispersal' of the term to encompass literally any far-flung collective – gay, deaf, digital, terrorist and so on (Brubaker 2005: 4). For others, an overwhelming emphasis on cultural identity in this new work distracted from the realities of political economy and the continuing power of the security-conscious state to regulate citizenship (Kalra *et al.* 2005). However, in the present fourth phase of 'reflective consolidation', Cohen remarks that the field has gone some way to acknowledging the validity of these critiques, most especially in terms of the more metaphorical and deterritorialised interpretations of diaspora as what Brah has called 'a homing desire' (1996: 179).

'The word "diaspora" is derived from the Greek verb *speiro* (to sow) and the preposition *dia* (over)' (Cohen 1997: ix). While the ancient Greeks thought of this 'sowing over' mainly in terms of migration and colonisation, in an authoritative contribution on semantic genealogies, Martin Baumann (2000: 316) insists that any suggestion that the term is of non-Jewish origin is 'fanciful'. For ancient Jewry, diaspora had the negative association of exile. Nevertheless, Cohen maintains that trauma and victimhood should not be unduly emphasised in conceiving diaspora, arguing that others who have lived 'at home abroad' can be categorised neither as victims (nor as colonists). As the experiences of peoples settled in specific places at specific points in time vary significantly, Cohen (1997: x; revised 2008: 18) produces a typology of diasporas, each exemplified by particular ethnic groups:

- *victim diasporas* (e.g. Jews, Africans, Armenians, Irish, Palestinians);
- *labour diasporas* (e.g. Indians, Chinese, Japanese, Turks, Italians, North Africans);
- *imperial diasporas* (e.g. British, Russian and other colonial powers);
- *trade diasporas* (e.g. Venetians, Chinese, Japanese, Lebanese, Indians);

- *deterritorialised diasporas* (e.g Caribbean peoples, Roma, Sindhis, Parsis, Muslims and other religious diasporas).

In fact, Cohen insists that Jews cannot only be regarded as a victim diaspora. At different times in history, they have been successful labour, trade and deterritorialised diasporas (1997: xi). Given the variety subsumed by the term, he judges 'a grand overarching theory ... impossible' (1997: xii). Nevertheless, building on the earlier work of others, Cohen still finds it important to develop a list of what he regards as diasporas' common features (1997: 26; revised 2008: 17). This is reproduced here in a somewhat abbreviated form:

1   dispersal from a homeland to two or more foreign regions;
2   or, expansion from a homeland in search of work, trade or empire;
3   a collective memory and myth about the homeland;
4   an idealisation of the ancestral home and collective commitment to it;
5   a return movement; even if this is only vicarious or based on intermittent visits home;
6   a strong and long-standing ethnic group consciousness of distinctiveness, for example, in terms of its common cultural and religious heritage and the belief in a common fate;
7   a troubled relationship with host societies, suggesting a lack of acceptance or possibility of further calamity;
8   a sense of empathy with, and co-responsibility for, co-ethnics elsewhere;
9   the possibility of enrichment in host countries tolerant of pluralism.

While Cohen and many others suggest that it is no longer necessary to take Jewish experiences as the only paradigm of diaspora, it is clear that Judaism still has a pivotal place in diaspora studies.[5] Of course, Jews were made captives and exiles after Jerusalem was captured by the Babylonians in the sixth century BCE and thereafter the idea of 'Babylon' became synonymous with oppression and exile in an alien land. However, as both Cohen and Ter Haar (1998) remark, even as the displaced Jews 'remembered Zion', there was eventually opportunity and creativity in Babylon as many made their home there. Indeed, 'the Jewish communities in Alexandria, Antioch, Damascus, Asia Minor and Babylon became centres of civilisation, culture and learning' (Cohen, 1997: 5). The term 'diaspora' itself became widely 'used in the Septuagint, the Greek translation of the Hebrew scriptures explicitly intended for the Hellenic Jewish communities in Alexandria (circa third century BCE)' (Braziel and Mannur 2003: 2). Yet, as Baumann notes, 'surprisingly, the Hebrew words for "exile", "banishment" and "deportation", *gola* and *galut*, were *not* rendered into Greek by "diaspora"' (2000: 316).[6]

Despite the integration of post-Babylonian Jewry, then, and the opportunity to travel to Palestine and Jerusalem as pilgrims, the thrust of the neologism remained unfavourable but was also deeply theological. Diaspora was 'an integral part of a pattern constituted by the fourfold course of sin or disobedience, scattering and exile as punishment, and finally return and gathering' (Baumann 2000: 317). In Rome, Antioch and Corinth, the early Christian church adopted theological notions of diaspora from Judaism, though altering 'its soteriological meaning according to Christian eschatology' (2000: 319). Before Christianity became fully institutionalised as the state religion of Rome in the fourth century, the nascent community saw itself as a travelling and wandering people, spreading the Gospel and awaiting the Kingdom of God. Interestingly, use of the term diaspora also reappears much later in Christian history to describe both the Protestant and Roman Catholic religious minorities created in the wake of shifts in the religious allegiance of states during the Reformation and Counter-Reformation (Baumann 2000: 20).

Before the 1960s, then, the study of diaspora was largely confined to more traditional approaches to Jewish (and to some extent) Christian studies. However, notably for the study of religion, Baumann suggests that much of this scholarship was 'historically descriptive' (2000: 320) and even now demonstrates little interest in, or even awareness of, the sort of theory or comparison that occupies many other scholars today. In other academic circles, the study of diaspora first came to prominence in African studies during the 1950s and 1960s although it took until the mid-1970s for this interest to mushroom (2000: 321). At a time of African states' postcolonial independence from Western powers, diaspora thus became associated with the racialised politics of remembering the transatlantic slave trade.[7] Clearly, a number of parallels with the Jewish experience could be made, including the appropriation of biblical symbolism to give expression to the experience of living under oppression in 'Babylon' or the emergence of modern religio-nationalist return movements such as Rastafarianism (see Cohen 2008: 132–3). Notably, it was from African studies, too, that the term diaspora entered the contemporary social sciences and humanities. During the 1980s and into the 1990s, for example, Cultural Studies scholars with a personal interest in the experiences of migrants of African descent from the Caribbean such as Stuart Hall and Paul Gilroy were at the forefront of postmodern and postcolonial critiques and re-appropriations of the term diaspora. In what follows, I provide an outline of these ideas and point forwards towards their implications for the study of religion.

Diaspora and the global postmodern: cultural identities, translation and re-traditionalisation

Hall (1992: 304–5) argues that while globalisation continues to reproduce uneven power relations between 'the Rest and the West', its impact on cultural identities in postmodernity has actually been contradictory. With the old certainties and universal claims associated with post-Enlightenment thinking in crisis, the seemingly stable narratives of identity associated with the nation-state have been undermined by telecommunications technology and consumer capitalism, as well as international migration. At the same time, because the global postmodern has heightened consciousness of difference and relativised the discreteness of all cultures, it has also given rise to a defence of particularistic identities including those once thought to have been entirely displaced and superseded by modernity (Hall 1992: 304). Hall suggests that contemporary cultural identities oscillate between reactive attempts to reinstate the boundaries of local, ethnic, national or religious community and a further outcome of globalisation, that is, greater cultural hybridity. He draws a neat contrast between tradition and translation; whereas tradition represents the attempt to imagine a sense of ongoing continuity with a memorialised past, translation suggests a more self-conscious embrace of the uncertainties and possibilities of greater cultural intermixture and fusion.

Contemporary genetics has shown that there are no separate 'racial' groups within humankind. In fact, the arguments of nineteenth-century 'scientific-racism', which maintained that there was a hierarchy of 'races' among the people of the world, each with their own hereditary characteristics, are entirely false. Nevertheless, it is still very common to find the suggestion that there are more or less innate, timeless and elementary *cultural*, as opposed to *biological*, differences between certain peoples, communities and civilisations (see, for example, Huntington 1993). In general terms, earlier anthropological theories of culture did tend to essentialise it as some*thing* unified and undivided in this way. The diverse skills, ideas and practices acquired and developed by human beings as members of social groups

(Eriksen 2001), it was often reduced to a list of unchanging traits and customs contained by the structures and boundaries of a given society. However, rather than a *characteristic* people *have*, today culture is understood more dynamically by anthropologists as a *practice*, something all people are in the continuous process of *making* and *remaking* (Baumann 1996, 1999). Indeed, in an age of deterritorialised or 'travelling' *culture* (Clifford 1994), any necessary linkage with place has been broken, while identities – self-identifications shaped and modified dialectially and contextually in relation to the ascriptions of others – are viewed as highly contingent, plural and criss-crossing (Hall 1992).

As migrants cross the borders of contemporary nation-states, then, they come to dwell in what postcolonial literary theorist, Homi Bhabha (1994), describes as an *in-between*, interstitial or third space. In the words of author, Salman Rushdie, this is where 'newness enters the world' (Bhabha 1994: 227). In his argument that 'It ain't where you're from, it's where you're at' (1991), Gilroy joins Bhabha and Rushdie in a clear retort to definitions of those labelled as 'immigrants' or 'ethnic minorities' as with*in* the nation but not *of* the nation. Here, diaspora theory disavows a preoccupation with connections to the homeland becoming instead 'a critique of discourses of fixed origins' (Brah 1996: 179–80). Rather than being 'caught between two cultures', second and third generation identifications cannot be confined by assumptions about 'roots' because their more or less skilful multicultural navigation of identity actively improvises novel 'routes' (Gilroy 1993; Clifford 1994; Ballard 1994).

In such work, then, there is a desire to escape not only from the outsider exclusions of hostland racisms and nationalisms but also from insider attempts to resist marginalisation with nostalgic appeals to cultural and religious authenticity. Certainly Gilroy's (1993; 2000) preference has ultimately been for a convivial cosmopolitanism which includes a capability to mediate 'between camps' based on a sense of 'planetary humanism'. However, while there is no doubt that diaspora theory during the 1990s offered a timely reminder that cultural identity is inevitably hybridising, its treatment of tradition was often much less nuanced. More productive was the work of several anthropologists including Pnina Werbner who maintains that 'cultures evolve historically through unreflective borrowings' (1997a: 4). It is this unconscious hybridising that makes the everyday integration of new ideas and practices possible. Therefore while amongst jet-setting intellectuals and artistic elites there is a more intentional and playful celebration of hybridity, a more organic and unintended hybridity tends to characterise the lives of the diasporic masses. Exposed to the inequalities and exclusions of the world's global cities, cultural difference and intermixture can for them be experienced in terms of crisis, alienation and doubt (1997a: 12).

Moreover, while we all have multiple identities, a politics that seriously challenges the uneven distribution of power and resources between majorities and minorities, has not emerged from the endless shifts of hybridity (Asad 1993). We must all speak from somewhere and, as Werbner again argues, being heard requires an act of prioritising, of naming and 're-presenting' oneself (1997b: 228). For many migrants, it is in a selective return to aspects of their own 'chains of memory' (Hervieu-Léger 2000) and social networks that many have discovered the moral resources to restore certainties in the face of translation and organise political resistance to exclusion (Hall 1991: 52–3; Werbner 1997a: 21). So, what anthropologists call ethnicity is never a simple or conservative reproduction of shared homeland custom, language or religion. Rather, with our interest in religion to the fore, what we might designate 're-traditionalisation', signals a dynamic, deeply contextual re-organisation of culture in novel settings to construct symbolic boundaries vis-à-vis others so as to enhance group distinctiveness.

It is the solidarities resulting from re-traditionalisation that help groups to advance their own interests in competition with others in plural societies. In many liberal democracies, for example, such 'fictions of *unity*' have been useful in binding migrants and diasporas together periodically, both when they have sought to transmit their traditions and when they have addressed themselves to the state or wider society (Werbner 1991; Baumann 1996). Indeed, for both pragmatic and political reasons, one of the main vehicles for the public recognition of such groups, multicultural policy-making, has tended to promote the idea of 'communities', each with its own distinctive 'culture'. Nevertheless, communities, whether ethnically, nationally or religiously marked, are routinely made up of complex individual differences, conflicting constituencies and relations of power that can silence women and young men especially. Indeed, as Anthony Cohen (1985) argues, it is only their 'symbolic form', and not their 'content', that is held in common. This means that the multiple interpretations and meanings attached to communal symbols by individuals can be reconciled.

Thus, as Gerd Baumann (1996; 1999) suggests, depending on the dynamics of any given context, and who one might be interacting with, people both routinely cross and dissolve, as well as re-make and fix the boundaries of cultural identity. Similarly, and with a more explicit concern for 'a theory of religion that made sense of the religious life of transnational migrants' (2006: 5), Thomas Tweed has suggested that 'religions involve two spatial practices – dwelling and crossing' (2006: 7). Intimately bound up with making sense of human joy and suffering, whether in terms of everyday struggles or more cosmic horizons, religion, he argues, can be characterised in terms of both i) (re)orientation, constraint and boundary marking, as well as ii) exchange, mixture and transformation. It is to the study of religion and diaspora that I turn now.

Diaspora and the study of religion

In his *New Handbook of Living Religions*, Hinnells explains why he thinks the study of religion should take diaspora seriously. In terms of promoting the relevance of the study of religion per se, both to potential students and those who fund education at all levels, he insists that the challenges posed to plural societies by recognising religious and cultural differences have been tremendously important (1997: 1–2). Indeed, Hinnells argues that the presence of 'world religions' in global cities has raised the profile of religion generally, both encouraging new religious movements and reinforcing the public position of historic Christian churches in the West (1997: 845). However, despite this, and the fact that, contrary to many expectations, 'migrants are more rather than less religious after migration' (1997: 683), Hinnells observes that scholars of migration and diaspora in other disciplines have tended to overlook the significance of religion. Baumann, too, remarks that, 'the history of religions was a real latecomer in making use of the diaspora term' (2000: 323). Many in this area of the field have been reluctant to embrace a term that they still associate with Jewish Studies: 'their caution was (and is) in many cases based on the knowledge of the term's origin and soteriological coinage, stirring up various theoretical problems for a cross-cultural, generalised application' (2000: 323).

Surveys of the literature on diaspora are unanimous in tracing the first discussion of contemporary diaspora religion to a slightly obscure publication by Ninian Smart (Baumann 2000; Vertovec 2004; Hinnells 2005). While Smart (1987) did not really differentiate religious homelands from ethno-national homelands or diaspora from globalisation, he underlined that, rather than assimilate or liberalise, even traditions characterised as essentially resistive of singular definitions such as 'Hindu-ism' tend to emphasise 'universalising' religious tendencies in a pluralising world. Self-conscious of difference – provoked by interactions with others, both with the state, wider society and a broader range of co-religionists – diasporas produce increasingly rationalised and homogenising accounts of their traditions. However, the study of diaspora was of only passing interest to Smart as was the empirical study of religion. Indeed, in the heyday of ethnic and migration studies, it was initiatives such as the Community Religions Project (CRP), founded in 1976 and based in my own department of Theology and Religious Studies at the University of Leeds, that were the real pioneers. Starting very much within the history and phenomenology of religions, the CRP's first wave of publications were concerned mainly with descriptions of how the content of Hinduism, Islam and Sikhism was changing, having been transplanted overseas.[8]

With its emphasis on lived experience, the work of the CRP and its contemporaries outside the UK did begin to take Religious Studies beyond the World Religions paradigm. As Flood notes, this paradigm presents 'constructed entities as if they are in some timeless realm (perhaps a realm of pure doctrine) outside wider cultural patterns and history (especially colonial history, the relation between religion and capitalism, and recently globalisation)' (1999: 3). However, given a continued tendency to emphasise objective description over critical explanation, theoretical discussions from this period can still appear somewhat parochial. Highlighting the consonance between religion as a reified scholarly construct and its articulation in religious fundamentalism, Searle-Chatterjee (2000), for example, argues that the ethnographic tradition in both Religious Studies and Anthropology uncritically reproduced 'Hindu-ism' and other traditions as normative categories, isolating them from wider social and political contexts. A close re-reading of the writing in question suggests a more nuanced picture than she presents (McLoughlin and Zavos 2009). Nevertheless, in urging greater vigilance in analysing just how, by whom and for what purposes religious discourse is deployed, polemics like that of Searle-Chatterjee are reflective of a much broader theoretical move in the field since the beginning of the 1990s. Building to some extent on issues first raised by Smith (1964), but influenced too by postmodernist and postcolonial thought, many scholars of religion have sought to deconstruct the idea of 'religion' as a cross-cultural and trans-historical phenomenon (McCutcheon 1997).

To trace the particularly modern and Western location of the category of religion one must turn to post Reformation Europe, and especially the seventeenth century, when a substantive definition of natural religion amongst Deists and others opened the way for comparison of a presumed universal in human societies. Rationalised and compartmentalised, individualised and privatised, 'religion' as a reified discourse eventually emerged as an autonomous and bounded essence 'segregated conceptually from power' (Asad 1993: 28–9). This modern attempt to confine and domesticate religion reflected the powerful secularising ideologies and interests of the equally modern nation state within Europe (Van der Veer and Lehmann 1999). However, this new construction of 'religion' was also exported beyond Europe as part of the colonial will to power. By the end of the nineteenth century, fundamental social change had produced new elites and new public spheres espousing a neo-orthodox episteme which mimicked Protestant Christianity. The impact of such processes continues to be felt, perhaps even more intensely, in diaspora.

In the context of such thinking, some like Fitzgerald (2001) go so far as to argue that 'religion' should be abandoned for what he sees as more precise analytical categories associated with Anthropology and Cultural Studies. However, all categories and frameworks of study (including culture) are of course contingent. Nevertheless, scholarly analyses of 'religion' must be reflexive and grounded in examining the ways in which discourses and practices associated with religious values, rituals, institutions and identities are actually used to both authorise and contest relations of power. In advocating such a realistic or 'worldly' model of religion, one which moves back and forth between detailed description of ethnographic contexts and theory, Sutcliffe (2004) highlight's Knott's emphasis on the importance of inductive rather than deductive reasoning. In an analysis which sees religion as deeply contextualised in the practice of locality and space, she examines how the category is produced both practically and discursively (2005: 81) and argues that the study of religion must always begin with particular locations. Stepping back from location to locality for the time being, however, what follows are some further reflections on Knott's earlier work at the CRP, both in terms of: i) problematising the relationship between religion, ethnicity and identity and ii) mapping the various factors contributing to 'new patterns and forms' (1986: 10) of religion amongst migrants.

Religion, migration and ethnicity: research agendas for religious studies

[T]here have been relatively few accounts of migration and settlement in which religion has been described as having any significance for individuals and communities beyond its role in assisting them to organise, to reap material benefit or to enter dialogue or competition with the wider society ... religions do perform these functions in many situations. However, they also have their own dynamics which, though related to social, political and economic contexts, are explained from within rather than from without (with recourse to their historical development, texts, value systems, ritual practices, socio-religious organisation etc.).

(Knott 1992: 13)

These comments represent a plea to religious studies scholars to be more active in the study of 'ethnic minority' religions, at least in part because the accounts of other disciplines have proved limited. Reflecting on the work of sociologists and anthropologists, Knott argues that 'with a few notable exceptions, they have failed to provide plausible accounts of the role and significance of religions in the lives of the groups they have described' (1992: 4–5). At the same time, she admits that, 'The discipline of Religious Studies in Britain or elsewhere has not so far developed a coherent perspective on ethnicity' (1992: 11). Knott suggests that this is partly because the study of migrant religion is still new to the discipline, as is the idea of taking the social context of religion seriously. As a result, social scientific assumptions about religion have often gone unchallenged.

In this respect Knott's main concern is that the literature on religion and ethnicity generally fails to distinguish sufficiently between the two. Indeed, in some of the classic works on ethnicity in North American sociology, religion is often seen merely 'as the passive instrument of ethnic identity' or 'in the service of ethnicity' (1992: 12). For Knott, while there is no doubt that religion can operate in this way, such an approach has obvious limitations: 'there are times when religion plays a more active role in the definition of an ethnic group's identity and behaviour than many of these accounts suggest' (1992: 12). Knott identifies the work of Hans Mol, a sociologist of religion, as of particular use here.

Revisiting his work today, Mol perhaps now appears too quick to generalise about the 'essential function of religion', its 'most universal form', 'basic human needs' and so on (1979:

34). Nevertheless, in his notions of religion as the 'harnesser of change' and the 'sacraliser of identity', he clearly elaborates the remarks we have encountered so far about the significance of tradition:

> Religion … seems to have more to do with an already established system of meaning, a stable tradition, an orderly delineation of a potentially disorderly existence. The essential function of religion cannot therefore be exhaustively summarized in terms of 'creative change'. Rather religion in its most universal form seems to function as an antidote to change, or as the 'harnesser' of change. If religion then somehow is bound up with a basic human need for delineation, order, one may define it as 'the sacralisation of identity'.
>
> (1979: 34)

> It directs the attention to the boundary maintenance of an embattled ethnic culture in a strange environment. Religion seems to be always bound up with the clearer delineation of a culture … it also provides … an island of meaning, tradition and belonging in the sea of anomie of modern industrial societies.
>
> (1979: 37)

For Mol, religion, as a resource with which to mark ethnic identity, offers something that other cultural stuff cannot. Backed by sacred authority, religious boundaries would seem to provide more universal, and so less readily negotiable, vehicles for the articulation of distinctiveness than those associated with the customs of particular peoples and places. According to Mol, the function of religion is at least as much to do with an 'orderly delineation' and 'harnessing of change' as opposed to 'creative change', a comment we might relate, once again, to the contrast between twin processes of tradition and translation, dwelling and crossing, discussed earlier. However, as has been suggested already, the reproduction of a 'stable tradition' is always a creative act; hence the emphasis on *re*traditionalisation. To say the same thing in a new context is always to say something different (Baumann 1996, 1999). Nevertheless, Mol's work very effectively underlines the fact that an emphasis on tradition among many migrants, at least initially, represents no simple 'refusal to change', as sometimes suggested, but rather a dynamic adaptation strategy in the undeniable face of change.

If Mol's emphasis is on the *function* of religion in contexts of migration, elsewhere Knott (1986) argues that religious studies scholars must also be attentive to what happens to its specific *content* in such circumstances. 'How does a religion and the religiousness of its people change in an alien milieu? How are they different from their parent traditions in the homeland?' (1986: 8). Further to this empirical 'comparative religion exercise' (1986: 8), Knott has proposed a framework, which begins to 'map' the range of *factors* that might contribute to 'new patterns and forms of religious behaviour, organisation, experience and self-understanding' (1986: 10). This has been much cited and elaborated; for example, Hinnells (1997) produces a ten-point framework and Vertovec (2000: 21–3) goes even further, reminding us of a seventeen-point framework he and others first devised back in 1990. In any case, Knott's factors can be summarised thus:

1   '*Home traditions*' – (i) the nature of the religion itself (e.g. its universality or ethnic particularity) and (ii) the nature [and impact] of other cultural factors such as language, customs, food and dress, etc.

2 'Host[land] traditions' – cultural, political, legal, educational, welfare, immigration and settlement procedures [e.g. the status of religion in the public sphere].

3 'Nature of migration process' – from the homeland or other migration contexts [e.g. people who are 'twice migrants']; are migrant sojourners or settlers, economic migrants, exiles or refugees?

4 'Nature of migrant group' – religious and ethnic diversity, group size, geographical dispersion, division and cohesion (origin, history of settlement, caste and kinship, [social class and educational background]).

5 'Nature of host response' – social attitudes [discourses and practices] rather than cultural traditions, e.g. racism, attitudes to assimilation and integration, ecumenism.

For Knott, it is the complex relationships between these different factors that begin to explain the sheer diversity of expressions and trajectories of religions in contexts of migration. As well as choosing 'to standardize their beliefs and practices, to reject their "little" traditions at the expense of their "great" traditions' (1986: 13), religious individuals and communities may opt for, 'Increased traditionalism, new sects, unlikely religious unions, conversion and mission' (1992: 10). All form part of the remaking of religious traditions in new contexts. Looking to the future, Knott argues that 'the Religious Studies approach ... [is] in great need of unleashing' (1986: 13). However, in the 1980s and early 1990s, the project of mapping the evolution of religious continuity and transformation had only just begun. In our penultimate two sections we trace how such agendas for the study of migration and ethnicity in religious studies has developed, first in theoretical terms and then in more empirical terms.

Theorising religion and diaspora: 'ethnic' and 'universal' traditions?

In general, I would argue that religions can provide *additional cement to bind* a diasporic consciousness, but they do not constitute diasporas in and of themselves ... an overlap between faith and ethnicity is likely to *enhance social cohesion* ... [but] The myth and idealization of a *homeland and a return movement are also conspicuously absent* in the case of world religions. Indeed one might suggest that their programmes are *extraterritorial* rather than territorial ... On the other hand ... spiritual affinity may generate a bond analogous to that of a diaspora.

(Cohen 1997: 189; my emphasis)

The question of whether a particular tradition, or religions in general, can properly be described in terms of diaspora has been one of the more obvious theoretical issues to occupy scholars in the last decade or so. Cohen's discussion quoted here from the first edition of *Global Diasporas* is immediately reminiscent of the social scientific conceptions of religion, migration and ethnicity examined by Knott (1986, 1992). In the same way that religion 'reinforced ethnicity', Cohen suggests that religion provides 'additional cement' to diasporas and 'is likely to enhance social cohesion'. In the second edition of his book, Cohen (2008) does adopt a more flexible approach to the definition of diaspora, one which can now include 'religious diasporas' as an example of deterritorialised diasporas with 'atypical' imaginings of 'home'. However, diaspora remains essentially an ethno-national phenomenon, something to do with peoples and places and 'theorizing the connection between religion and diaspora is [still] fraught with uncertainty' (2008: 153).

Referring to Hinnells' work on the Parsis, for example, Cohen maintained that those Zoroastrians who migrated from Persia to India so as to survive the Islamisation of early Muslim Iran, represented 'not so much a travelling nation then, as a travelling religion ... Parsees ... do not seek to return to, or to recreate, a homeland' (1997: 188–9). Hinnells (2005) takes issue with these arguments about both the Parsis and religion per se. First, he notes that orientation to the homeland can be manifest to various degrees of intensity and, for some, cultural identification with the homeland may be far more important than return (cf. Brah 1996). Hinnells insists that many Parsis do still speak of themselves as Persians and not Indians. Not least because of the Islamic Republic in contemporary Iran, few currently consider returning to live there. Nevertheless, the Parsis do express their love for Persia in various ways. For example, they furnish their homes with books, artefacts and symbols of ancient Iran and organise religious tours as and when possible. Second, Hinnells suggests that Cohen's comments also raise questions about what is meant by the term 'world religions'. If this simply identifies a tradition to be found in many countries around the world, and so is related to globalisation and international migration, then Zoroastrianism would 'qualify', as would most other 'faiths' today. However, if, as Cohen implies (1997: 188), a world religion is a tradition open to all people in the world, then Hinnells (2005) is clear that not only Zoroastrianism, but also Judaism, Hinduism and Sikhism are not really world religions.

Vertovec (2004) takes up this debate in a somewhat different way. He is less concerned with what constitutes a 'world religion' than the distinctions that can be made between different 'types' of traditions. For example, Vertovec reminds us that, given the existence of the Zionist and Khalistani movements, Judaism and Sikhism are both exceptions to Cohen's general rule about religions and homelands. Both 'religions' are in effect 'discrete ethnic groups' (2004: 281). Indeed, he argues that, if Judaism and Sikhism can be considered exceptions, as Cohen agrees they can, then so, too, can Hinduism. The emphasis here is on 'a place' as much as 'a people': 'no matter where in the world they live, most Hindus tend to sacralize India ... [as] a spiritual homeland' (Vertovec 2004: 281).[9] As Hinnells (2005) remarks, Cohen's rule is clearly one with a lot of exceptions. Nevertheless, if, following Knott (1986: 11) and others, we differentiate between so-called ethnic and universal traditions, then Vertovec's distinctions could make good sense. Ethnic religions may properly represent diasporas. However, for other, more universal and missionary religions, less obviously tied to particular peoples or places, for example Christianity, Islam and Buddhism, the relationship with ethnicity can be very different:

> It broadens the term far too much to talk – as many scholars do – about the "Muslim diaspora", "Catholic diaspora" ... and so forth. These are of course world traditions that span many ethnic groups and nationalities ... Hinnells (1997) himself flags up one problem ... are Muslims in Pakistan part of a diaspora religion because Islam is derived from and broadly centred on Mecca?
>
> (Vertovec 2004: 281)

Perhaps, in the case of universal religions, then, it would be better to speak only of migration or transnationalism. However, Vertovec does not make such a suggestion. Indeed, accounts that explicitly identify 'transnational religion', while having more than doubled in the last five years (see, for example, Levitt 2007), are still relatively few in number compared to those concerned with 'diaspora religion'.[10] Moreover, it also seems clear that apparently ethnic and universal traditions can behave like each other in different situations.

For example, we have seen already how Smart (1987) argues that under the conditions of the global postmodern plural Hindu traditions are exhibiting a tendency to universalise. Similarly, traditions such as Christianity and Islam have always been ethnicised in practice.[11] To spread their messages successfully and stay meaningful through time and across space, both have had to be flexible enough to adapt to local circumstances. Indeed, once people are gradually born into universal traditions, religion becomes indigenised and so, for many adherents, essentially a matter of custom and descent. Thus what we are actually seeing at work here – and within the quotation from Vertovec – is the ongoing dialectic of the global and the local, abstracted universal spaces and the unpredictability of everyday life rooted in the particular.

Despite the evident salience of such processes of glocalisation, where religious and cultural identities are both deterritorialised and reterritorialised, in diaspora especially, many second- and third-generation youth are prioritising what they see as the universals of religion from the localised custom they associate with their parents' and grandparents' homelands. One way of analysing this situation is to relate it to Mol's (1979) conception of religion as the 'sacralizer of identity' and 'harnesser of change'. Because religion, backed by the sacred authority of the past, has such great potential for articulating distinctiveness in its own right, this can open the way for other potential markers of ethnic identity to become more negotiable as time passes and those born in the diaspora establish their own priorities and 'routes'. So long as religious boundaries are maintained – and, recalling Cohen (1985), this does not require unchanging content – language and aspects of custom, as well as attachment to the homeland per se, can become relatively less important and perhaps eventually abandoned altogether. This opens up the possibility for a new, more mobile, religious 'homing desire' (Brah 1996: 179–80) without the risk of losing all sense of continuity in a 'chain of memory' (cf. Hervieu-Léger 2000). Indeed, the prioritisation of religion over custom, especially for those with most invested in new contexts, can facilitate adaptation and acculturation, while all the time retaining a sense of pride in distinctiveness and rejecting outright assimilation. Ter Haar (1998), for example, shows how many African Christians in Europe are forward, rather than backward, looking. They see themselves as part of an international, rather than an ethnic, church, deliberately using religion as a source of capital to bridge outwards and link upwards beyond the bonding provided by cultural heritage per se.

In a roundabout way then, Cohen's account of religion does actually begin to strike the right chord. On the one hand, religions can and do provide 'additional cement' and 'cohesion' to 'territorial' ethno-national diasporas (1997: 189; 2008: 153). However, in different contexts, the very same traditions, differently configured and deployed, can challenge and transcend ethnicity (as well as the nation-state – see Baumann 1999) by forging multi-ethnic and more universalising networks and linkages. They can point beyond the territorial to the extraterritorial (1997: 189), whether that be in terms of the convergences of a global ethics and civil society or the conflicts of transnational terrorism (Jurgensmeyer 2002). In our penultimate section I briefly summarise how religious studies' more empirical agenda, in terms of mapping contemporary patterns and trends, has evolved in the last decade or so.

Mapping religion and diaspora: summary patterns and trends

Perhaps the main characteristic of contemporary scholarship on religion and diaspora has been the growth of empirical studies. In many ways this is more representative of the research that has been completed than the theoretical debates considered in the previous section.

To give a flavour of this work, and provide an opportunity for further reading, indicative studies of contemporary Sikhs, Christians, Jews, Hindus, Zoroastrians, Buddhists, Muslims and others have all been cited in endnotes to this chapter. The majority focus on people resettled in North America and Europe, although the processes described are by no means confined to the West and increasingly reflect cross-border circulations. With just a few exceptions, all were written in the 1990s or 2000s. This reflects the fact that, in the last two decades or so, diasporas established in the post-war period have begun to mature and are increasingly visible in public life (Coward *et al.* 2000) as well as international politics. Most tend to focus on one religious tradition and/or ethnic community. However, Hinnells (2005) – in an account of Zoroastrianism in eleven countries – argues that comparative studies should be more of a priority.

Attention to comparative perspectives begins to reveal important differences within and between religious traditions, depending upon such factors as the dynamics of regional and national contexts and the nature of specific groups. Hinnells (1997), for example, elaborates an ambitious international comparison across the major religious traditions of South Asian diasporas in Australia, Britain, Canada and the United States.[12] Since the 1960s, when South Asian migration to Canada and the United States began, newcomers there have tended to be educated professionals more likely to integrate and produce innovative religious scholarship (1997: 837, 840). In Britain, by contrast, because of its colonial connections to the subcontinent, diasporas are longer-standing and comprise a higher percentage of unskilled workers, although this is rapidly changing, especially amongst Hindus and Sikhs (1997: 836). Whereas in Britain South Asian heritage Muslims predominate (1997: 841), in the United States and Canada the Muslim presence is more ethnically diverse. Of the Jains, Hinnells remarks that, given their low public profile and numbers in all contexts, for pragmatic reasons they will often tolerate the outsiders' perception of them as part of the Indian, or Hindu, scene rather than as something different' (1997: 843).

Clearly, it is extremely difficult in a general survey to do justice to the numerous empirical studies that have been conducted, or even Hinnells' more comparative synthesis of such material. Nevertheless, by way of drawing different threads together, and so dealing more systematically with the empirical realities only alluded to thus far, I present now a summary of the key factors, patterns and trends that need to be taken into account when beginning to study religion and diaspora. Such a summary might even function as an outline syllabus for a course of study. My starting point was the agenda for the religious mapping of Southall referred to at the beginning of this chapter. However, once I began to write it was, of course, impossible to exclude my subsequent experiences as a researcher and teacher across Islamic, South Asian and religious studies or, indeed, new insights gleaned from reading and re-reading the literature while preparing this piece.

1   The context of reception or settlement in terms of particular nation-states has very significant consequences in shaping the general dynamics of migration and diaspora. Factors deserving of consideration include: the legacy of colonialism; the extent of citizenship rights; the nature of immigration/security legislation; social attitudes to cultural pluralism and levels of protection from discrimination; the status and public recognition of religion; employment and educational opportunities; the numbers of co-ethnics and co-religionists settled in a particular area, and the relative size and presence of other religious and ethnic groups. For example, existing religion-state relations can determine the extent to which the public sphere is hospitable to other faiths.

2   The different resources that migrants can mobilise – their social or cultural 'capital' – are also important in moulding experiences in diaspora. Initially, these will largely be constrained by the social, economic and political structures of the context of migration, and as well as its timing and circumstances, and the nature and extent of continuing links to the homeland. Otherwise, this might include: levels of cohesion in the diaspora, including the shape and levels of organisational infrastructure, and the authority of leaderships and their ability to make alliances that bridge outwards and link upwards. For example, 'twice migrants', i.e. those who already have experience of migration, education and business in other parts of the diaspora, are very likely to succeed more quickly than unskilled, first time migrants, from rural areas.

3   Huge moral and economic investments are made by diasporic communities to establish and sustain more or less autonomous, associations including multi-functional religious institutions. Such investments were often accelerated as the need to transmit homeland traditions beyond the family was brought sharply into focus by the emergence of generations socialised, educated and/or born in the diaspora. The idea of a congregation can thus become more significant than in the homeland, as public meetings for worship also provide an opportunity for a range of socialising and organising in what is initially an alien context.

4   Facilitating an imagined sense of continuity with the past is an important function of religion and especially religious ritual in diaspora. The re-making of sacred spaces through familiar bodily performances of speech, music, dance, drama and art, are all a way of remembering and transmitting homeland culture as well as binding communities together in new settings. However, compared to what was commonplace in the homeland, ritual practices can also be much elaborated, standardised or reoriented, and even disappear overseas. Some aspects of religious practice travel better than others, while the public celebration of festivals can mark a growing confidence of diasporas to lay claim to their new home.

5   All such 'communities' are inevitably divided amongst themselves along various lines of cleavage, so much so that ethnic, denominational/sectarian and other divisions can result in open struggles for power over the control of institutions. So, while communal 'fusion' and cooperation is a feature of early settlement, 'fission' and fragmentation is quick to develop as groups mature, especially where the numbers settled locally allow the formation of new and distinct congregations. Notably, in these circumstances, religious ideologies can become a resource to sanctify the marking of social status hierarchies, including some and excluding others, for example, in terms of ethnicity and race.

6   Depending on the age and gender profiles of diasporas, dominant constituencies such as older men also often marginalise the interests of younger men and women. Despite young people's protestations about their lack of appropriate skills, elders may still prefer to import functionaries from the homeland to secure a form of transmission which emphasises cultural continuity. Yet, if conservative transmission is seen to be failing – and perhaps even creating a gap that could be filled by political radicals – it can increasingly become a matter for state intervention. The same is true of important gendered sites of struggle. While male leaderships are challenged by the public activities of women, issues such as education, sexuality, work and marriage can remain contentious.

7   Less institutionalised or more implicit forms of religiosity remain important in the private, domestic and individualised spaces of diaspora. Amongst women especially, intra-household rituals and rites of passage are a crucial aspect of reproducing the wider

community as well as the family. Although, they routinely lack the authority of public religious institutions and leaderships, with roots in hybrid homeland cultures, they often retain the potential to subvert orthodoxies, especially in these alternative spaces. Moreover, globalised trends toward the decentring of religious authority via the virtual communities of the new media open up endless possibilities for more fluid and dissenting religious forms.

8   While religion can undoubtedly reinforce ethnicity, the children and grandchildren of migrants increasingly produce their own local-global interpretations of traditions, often arguing for the separation of religious 'universals' from cultural 'particulars' in ways their parents and grandparents rarely did. A globalised tendency towards the modernisation, universalisation and Protestantisation of belief is in evidence here, although so too are processes of compartmentalisation and secularisation. Cosmopolitan encounters with 'others' of the same faith tradition in diaspora have broadened awareness and self-conscious explorations of global religious identities at the expense of ethnicity. However, this becomes manifest in new vernacular forms of religion, for example, in terms of dress, organisations and public engagement as well as thinking. Other factors to take into account in this regard include: translations of sacred texts (which allow access to their meaning); pluralism and the liberal project of interfaith relations; rationalised and decontextualised accounts of 'world religions' reproduced in school-based religious education.

9   As leaderships seek to present a common front to outsiders, especially when seeking recognition from the state in respect of planning permission, animal sacrifice, school uniforms, burial or cremation arrangements, 'fusion' reasserts itself contextually and temporally over 'fission', in the shape of local, national and international umbrella organisations. Given the manifest resources often associated with religious institutions in diaspora – buildings, people, voluntary giving, etc. – the local and/or national state may incorporate such organisations into projects seeking to manage minority populations. However, in so doing, communities risk their autonomy and the state runs the risk of endorsing particular versions of religious orthodoxy, while attempts at multiulturalism can reinforce difference as much as promote integration or critical dialogues. For good or ill, religion, at least as much as race or ethnicity, has become one of the main ways of identifying the 'difference' of migrants, diasporas and transnationals among both 'insiders' and 'outsiders' in contemporary Western societies.

10   Transnational flows between diasporas, ethno-national homelands and sacred centres of faith traditions constitute the everyday reality of a globalised network society. Such networks are sustained by pilgrimages and holidays, various media, including satellite television, and the visits of religious and political leaders, as well as international movements and world organisations. Indeed, in the form of the mass media and conumerism, late modern globalisation appears to have become a key means by which religion flourishes. Given its extraterritorial ability to trump the nation-state with non-locative as well as more evidently locative identifications, religions can also provide powerful resources for imagining alternatives to the moral and political order suggested by the West. Whether because of nostalgia, or a lack of access to power, diasporas have played a significant role in supporting not only homeland movements, but also religious nationalism and even transnational terrorism. Political crises 'there' continue to impact communities and identities 'here' and vice versa.

Conclusion

The project of empirical mapping remains a crucial one. To cite the editor of this collection one last time, all students of Comparative Religion should seek to 'get their hands dirty with religion'. Indeed, with its emphasis on the complex continuities and transformations of lived experience, the study of religion and diaspora has already played a significant, but rarely acknowledged, role in taking Religious Studies beyond the outdated World Religions paradigm. Nevertheless, as Hinnells (1997: 683) himself implies, compared to fieldwork based studies, theoretical discussions have not been taken up as vigorously as they might. For example, it is now much clearer that religion has become disembedded from, and can work against, ethnicity at least as much as it works with it (as it does with and against the nation-state). By way of conclusion, then, I want to argue that there is now an opportunity and a need for more intense theoretical reflection on the significant body of data that has been collected over the last twenty years or so.

Flood (1999) maintains that 'after Phenomenology', Religious Studies is at something of a theoretical and methodological crossroads and needs to engage more openly across disciplinary boundaries. Given the wide-ranging interest of other disciplines in migration, disapora and transnationalism, and the continuing salience of religion for these issues and related public policies, the study of religion and diaspora ought to be one area where the prospects for such engagement are good. However, it is striking that most of the literature considered here, whether produced by scholars of Religious Studies or the social sciences, *still* rarely theorises religion with the same level of sophistication as culture, hybridity, ethnicity and so on. Therefore while Religious Studies may begin to relocate in terms of broader disciplinary contexts it must also continue to export more sophisticated accounts of religion to those for whom such a task is less of a priority. Future success in this respect will involve building upon the empirical content of religion and thinking seriously about its relationships to other concepts discussed in this chapter. This could begin to reveal more clearly what work categories associated with religion 'do', that is, the 'uses' of religious symbols, discourses and practices in particular time-space configurations by embodied constituencies positioned very differently in terms of relations of power (Knott 2005).

Notes

1 For other accounts of the Sikh diaspora see the relevant chapters in Ballard (1994), Hinnells (1997; 2010), Cohen (1997; 2008) and Coward *et al.* (2000), as well as Tatla (1999), Nayar (2004) and Dusenbury (2007).

2 For an account of the Irish Catholic diaspora in England see Fielding (1993) and in America see McCaffrey (1997). See also O'Sullivan (2000).

3 A number of other resources have been produced including a CD Rom, *On Common Ground: World Religions in America*, Columbia University Press, 1996 / 2000. See http://www.pluralism.org.

4 A pre-publication version of Vertovec (2004) can be downloaded from http://www.transcomm. ox.ac.uk/ the site of the UK Economic and Social Research Council's completed research programme on transnational communities.

5 For the Jewish diaspora, historical and contemporary, see the relevant chapters in Cohen (1997; 2008) and Ter Haar (1998), as well as Barclay (1996), Kaplan (2000), Boyarin and Boyarin (2002) and Gilman (2003). See also the website of 'Beth Hatefutsoth', the Museum of the Jewish Diaspora, at http://www.bh.org.il.

6 For online copies of his research on diaspora and migration, as well as materials on Buddhism in the West and Tamil Hindus in Germany, see Baumann's homepage, http://www.baumann-martin. de/. See also Prebish and Baumann (2002) on Buddhism in the West.

7 Ter Haar (1998) notes that the African diaspora in Europe, as opposed to America and the Caribbean, has had rather different experiences. On the former, see also Harris (2006). On the latter, see also the chapters in Hinnells (1997; 2010), as well as Pitts (1993), Murphy (1994), McCarthy Brown (2001) and Trost (2008).

8 For a list of the Community Religions Project's publications see http://www.leeds.ac.uk//trs/irpl/crp.htm.

9 Vertovec's arguments are expanded in Vertovec (2000). For other accounts of the Hindu diaspora see the relevant chapters in Ballard (1994); Hinnells (1997; 2010), Coward et al. (2000), Alfonso et al. (2004) and Kumar (2006), as well as Burghart (1987) and Waghorne (2004).

10 While my search for 'diaspora religion' at Amazon online bookstore (24 March 2009) produced 247 results (compared with 106 in 2004), 'transnational religion' produced just 47 (compared with 20 in 2004). Of that 47, most were still studies of the more 'universalising' traditions, especially Islam and Christianity (mainly Catholicism in America, Europe and China, as well as Pentecostalism in Africa and Latin America). On Latin American Christianity, for example, see Tweed (1997) and Vásquez and Marquardt (2003).

11 For Muslim heritage diasporas and transnational Islam, see chapters in Ballard (1994), Hinnells (1997; 2010) and Coward et al. (2000), as well as Metcalf (1996), Mandaville (2001), Haddad and Smith (2002), Werbner (2002) and Cesari and McLoughlin (2005).

12 This comparison, minus its Australian dimension, where developments are at an earlier stage, is further developed in Coward et al. (2000). Elsewhere, Ter Haar (1998) attempts a smaller scale mapping of Africans in Europe (Germany, Britain and the Netherlands) and Vertovec (2000) Hindus in the Caribbean and Britain.

Bibliography

Asad, Talal, 1993, *Genealogies of Religion: Discipline and Reasons of Power in Christianity and Islam*, Baltimore and London, The Johns Hopkins University Press.

Ballard, Roger, (ed.) 1994, *Desh Pardesh: The South Asian Presence in Britain*, London, Hurst and Co.

Barclay, John, M.G. 1996, *Jews in the Mediterranean Diaspora: From Alexander to Trajan*, London and New York, Continuum International Publishing Group.

Baumann, Gerd, 1996, *Contesting Culture: Discourses of identity in multi-ethnic London*, Cambridge, Cambridge University Press.

Baumann, Gerd, 1999, *The Multicultural Riddle: Rethinking National, Ethnic and Religious Identities*, New York and London, Routledge.

Bhabha, Homi, 1994, *The Location of Culture*, London, Routledge.

Boyarin, Jonathan and Boyarin, Daniel, 2002, *Powers of Diaspora: Two Essays on the Relevance of Jewish Culture*, Minneapolis, MN, University of Minnesota Press.

Brah, Avtar, 1996, *Cartographies of Diaspora*, London, Routledge.

Braziel, Jana Evans and Mannur, Anita, (eds), 2003, *Theorizing Diaspora: A Reader*, Malden, MA and Oxford, Blackwell.

Brubaker, Rogers, 2005, 'The 'diaspora' diaspora', *Ethnic and Racial Studies*, 28 (1), pp. 1–19.

Burghart, Richard (ed.) 1987, *Hinduism in Great Britain: the Perpetuation of Religion in an Alien Cultural Milieu*, London and New York, Tavistock Publications.

Cesari, Jocelyne and McLoughlin, Seán, (eds) 2005, *European Muslims and the Secular State*, Aldershot, Ashgate.

Clifford, James, 1994, 'Diasporas', *Current Anthropology*, 9 (3), pp. 302–38.

Cohen, Anthony P., 1985, *The Symbolic Construction of Community*, London, Routledge.

Coward, Harold, Hinnells, John R. and Williams, Raymond Brady, 2000, *The South Asian Religious Diaspora in Britain, Canada, and the United States*, New York, State University of New York Press.

Dusenbery, Verne A., 2007, *Sikhs at Large: Religion, Culture and Politics in Global Perspective*, New Delhi, Oxford University Press India.

Eck, Diana L. 2002, *A New Religious America*, San Francisco, Harper.

Eriksen, Thomas H., 2001, *Small Places, Large Issues: An Introduction to Social and Cultural Anthropology*, London, Pluto Press.

Fielding, Steven, 1993, *Class and Ethnicity: Irish Catholics in England 1880–1939*, Buckingham, Open University Press.

Fitzgerald, Timothy, 2001, *The Ideology of Religious Studies*, Oxford and New York, Oxford University Press.

Flood, Gavin, 1999, *Beyond Phenomenology: Rethinking the Study of Religion*, London and New York, Cassell.

Gilman, Sander L. 2003, *Jewish Frontiers: Essays on Bodies, Histories and Identities*, London, Palgrave Macmillan.

Gilroy, Paul, 1991, '"It Ain't Where You're From, It's Where You're At …": The Dialectics of Diasporic Identification', *Third Text*, 13, pp. 3–16.

Gilroy, Paul, 1993, *The Black Atlantic: Modernity and Double Consciousness*, London, Verso.

Gilroy, Paul, 2000, *Between Camps*, Harmondsworth, Penguin.

Haddad, Yvonne Y. and Smith, Jane I. 2002, *Muslim Minorities in the West: Visible and Invisible* Lanham, MD, AltaMira Press.

Hall, Stuart, 1991, 'Old and New Identities, Old and New Ethnicities', in King, A.D. (ed.) *Culture, Globalization and the World-System*, Macmillan, Basingstoke, pp. 41–68.

Hall, Stuart, 1992, 'The Question of Cultural Identity', in Hall, S., Held, D. and McGrew, T. (eds) *Modernity and Its Futures*, Cambridge: Polity Press, in association with Blackwell Publishers, Oxford and The Open University, pp. 273–325.

Harris, Hermione, 2006, *Yoruba in Diaspora: An African Church in London*, New York and London, Palgrave Macmillan.

Hervieu-Léger, Danièle, 2000, *Religion as a Chain of Memory*, Cambridge, Polity Press.

Hinnells, John R. 2005, *The Zoroastrian Diaspora: Religion and Migration*, Oxford, Oxford University Press.

Huntington, Samuel, 1993, 'The Clash of Civilizations?' in *Foreign Affairs*, 72, (3), pp. 22–49.

James, Allan, G., 1974, *Sikh Children in Britain*, London and New York, Oxford University Press.

Jurgensmeyer, Mark, 2002, 'Thinking Globally About Religion', paper posted at the eScholarship Repository, University of California, Santa Barbara, http://repositories.cdlib.org/gis/1

Kalra, Virinder, Kaur, Raminder and Hutnyk, John (2005) *Diaspora and Hybridity*, London, Sage.

Kaplan, Yosef, 2000, *An Alternative Path to Modernity: The Western Sephardi Diaspora in the Seventeenth Century*, Leiden, Brill.

Knott, Kim, 1986, *Religion and Identity, and the Study of Ethnic Minority Religions in Britain*, Community Religions Project Research Papers No. 3, Department of Theology and Religious Studies, The University of Leeds.

Knott, Kim, 1992, *The Role of Religious Studies in Understanding the Ethnic Experience*, Community Religions Project Research Papers No. 7, Department of Theology and Religious Studies, The University of Leeds.

Knott, Kim, 2005, *The Location of Religion: A Spatial Analysis*, London, Equinox Books.

McCaffrey, Lawrence J. 1997, *The Irish Catholic Diaspora in America*, Washington DC, Catholic University of America Press.

McCarthy Brown, Karen, 2001, *Mama Lola: A Vodou Priestess in Brooklyn*, Berkeley, University of California Press (updated and expanded edition).

McCutcheon, Russell T. (1997) *Manufacturing Religion*, New York, Oxford Universtiy Press.

McLoughlin, Seán and Zavos, John, 2009, 'Writing Religion in Br-Asian Cities', working paper available from http://www.leeds.ac.uk/writingbritishasiancities

Mandaville, Peter, 2001, *Transnational Muslim Politics: Reimagining the Umma*, London and New York, Routledge.

Metcalf, Barbara Daly, (ed.) 1996, *Making Muslim Space in North America and Europe*, Berkeley, Los Angeles and London, University of California Press.

Mol, Hans, 1979, 'Theory and Data on the Religious Behaviour of Migrants', *Social Compass*, XXVI, (1), pp. 31–9.

Murphy, Joseph M., 1994, *Working the Spirit: Ceremonies of the African Diaspora*, Boston, Beacon Press.

Nayar, Kamala E. 2004, *The Sikh Diaspora in Vancouver: Three Generations Amid Tradition, Modernity, and Multiculturalism*, Toronto, University of Toronto Press.

O'Sullivan, Patrick, 2000, *Religion and Identity*: vol. 5, Irish Worldwide: History, Heritage, Identity, Leicester, Leicester University Press.

Pitts, Walter F., 1993, *Old Ship of Zion: Afro-Baptist Ritual in the African Diaspora*, Oxford and New York, University Press USA.

Prebish, Charles, S. and Baumann, Martin, (eds) 2002, *Westward Dharma: Buddhism Beyond Asia*, Berkeley, University of California Press.

Searle-Chatterjee, Mary, 2000, "World religions" and "ethnic groups": do these paradigms lend themselves to the cause of Hindu nationalism?' *Ethnic and Racial Studies* 23 (3), pp. 497–515.

Smart, Ninian, 1987, 'The importance of diasporas', in Shaked, S., Werblovsky, R. Y., Shulman, D. D. and Strounka, G. A. G. (eds) *Gilgul: Essays on Transformation, Revolution and Permanence in the History of Religions*, Leiden, Brill, pp. 288–95.

Smith, Wilfred Cantwell 1964, *The Meaning and End of Religion*, New York, New American Library.

Sutcliffe, Steven (ed.), 2004, 'Introduction', *Religion: Empirical Studies*, Aldershot, Ashgate.

Tatla, Darshan Singh, 1999, *The Sikh Diaspora: The Search for Statehood*, London, University College London Press.

Ter Haar, Gerrie (ed.), 1998, *Strangers and Sojourners: Religious Communities in the Diaspora*, Leuven, Peeters.

Tölölyan, Khachig 1991, 'The Nation State and its Other: In Lieu of a Preface', *Diaspora: A Journal of Transnational Studies*, 1: 1, pp. 3–7.

Trost, Theodore L. 2008, *The African Diaspora and the Study of Religion*, London, Palgrave Macmillan.

Tweed, Thomas A. 1997, *Our Lady of the Exile: Diaspora Religion at a Cuban Catholic Shrine in Miami*, New York, Oxford University Press.

Van der Veer, Peter and Lehmann, Hartmut 1999, *Nation and Religion*, Princeton, Princeton University Press.

Vertovec, Steven, 2000, *The Hindu Diaspora: Comparative Patterns*, London and New York, Routledge.

Waghorne, Joanne P. 2004, *Diaspora of the Gods: Modern Hindu Temples in an Urban Middle-Class World*, Oxford and New York, Oxford University Press.

Werbner, Pnina, 1991, 'The fiction of unity in ethnic politics', in Werbner, Pnina and Anwar, Muhammad (eds) *Black and Ethnic Leaderships*, Routledge, London, pp. 113–145.

Werbner, Pnina, 1997a, 'Introduction', in Werbner, P. and Modood, T. (eds) *Debating Cultural Hybridity*, London and New Jersey, Zed Books. pp. 1–26.

Werbner, Pnina, 1997b, 'Essentialising Essentialism, Essentialising Silence', in Werbner, P. and Modood, T. (eds) *Debating Cultural Hybridity*, London and New Jersey, Zed Books, pp. 226–254.

Werbner, Pnina, 2002, *Imagined Diasporas Among Manchester Muslims*, Oxford, James Currey Ltd.

Suggested reading

Alfonso, Carolin, Kokot, Waltraud and Tölölyan, Khachig (eds) (2004) *Diaspora, Identity and Religion*, London and New York, Routledge.
Edited collection with some contributions by leading scholars of diaspora including a number of chapters on religion and religions.

Baumann, Martin (2000) 'Diaspora: Genealogies of Semantics and Transcultural Comparison', *Numen*, 47, (3), pp. 313–337.
Key journal article by a specialist setting out some of the meanings and uses of the term diaspora in historical and contemporary aspects of the study of religion.

Cohen, Robin (1997) *Global Diasporas: An Introduction*, London, Routledge.
Essential overview of the various types of diaspora, both historical and contemporary, with significant updating in terms of approaches to the subject matter for the second edition in 2008.

Hinnells, John R. (ed.) (1997) *The New Penguin Handbook of Living Religions*, London, Penguin Books.
Perhaps the first introduction to the study of religion to include chapters mapping key patterns and trends in the study of 'diaspora religion' across various traditions and regions. A third edition with new chapters on diasporas in the West will be published in 2010.

Knott, Kim and McLoughlin, Seán (eds) (2010) *Diasporas: Concepts, Identities, Intersections*, London, Zed.
Comprehensive collection of concise articles by world-leading and new scholars on all aspects of the study of diaspora including key concepts, multi-disciplinary approaches, trans-regional case studies and new directions for research.

Kumar, Pratap (ed.) (2006) *Religious Pluralism in the Diaspora*, Leiden, Brill.
Edited collection notable especially for its contributions on Chinese and Japanese-Brazilian disaporas.

Levitt, Peggy (2007) *God Needs No Passport: Immigrants and the Changing American Religious Landscape*, New York and London, The New Press.
Accessible study of diverse aspects of transnationalism in the everyday cross border religious lives, practices and identities of Brazilian, Indian, Irish and Pakistani immigrants.

Tweed, Thomas A. (2006) *Crossing and Dwelling: A Theory of Religion*, Cambridge, Massachusetts, and London, Harvard University Press.
A new, challenging, theoretical approach to the study of religion informed by an emphasis on transnational flows of migration.

Vásquez, Manuel A. and Marquardt, Marie F. (2003) *Globalizing the Sacred: Religion Across the Americas*, New Brunswick, NJ, Rutgers University Press.
Study of transnational religion in the USA and Latin America which also provides a very useful bridge between contemporary cultural theory and the study of religion.

Vertovec, Steven (2004) 'Religion and diaspora', in P. Antes, A. W. Geertz and R. Warne (eds), *New Approaches to the Study of Religion: Textual, Comparative, Sociological, and Cognitive Approaches*, Berlin and New York, Verlag de Gruyter.
Probably the most comprehensive synthesis of key patterns and trends in the literature on religion and diaspora by one of the most prolific experts in the field of migration studies.

Glossary

A

A Common Word an open letter sent on 13 October 2007 by 158 Muslim leaders and teachers to Pope Benedict XVI and major Christian leaders throughout the world.

Academic or scientific enterprise any organized approach to understanding a set of data that involves a sizeable group of people over a sufficiently long period of time that permits them to gain an identity from it.

Academic theology seeking understanding, knowledge and wisdom in relation to questions theology raises, pursued through engagement with a range of academic disciplines.

Accommodationist (semi-) a person or institution who finds it expedient to adapt to the opinions or behaviour of another, for example, a religious movement seeking survival by adjusting their views and activities to prevailing political realities.

Ahriman the Middle Persian form of the older Angra Mainyu, the destructive evil spirit in Zoroastrianism.

Allegorical interpretation an interpretive practice in which the literal meaning of a text is taken to be a vehicle for the spiritual or moral level that represents the primary meaning of the text. Characters and events in the literal text are assumed to have a one-to-one correspondence to the higher symbolic meaning.

Analytic psychology the name that Carl G. Jung gave to his own school of psychotherapy, to differentiate it from Freud's psychoanalysis.

Anglicist-Orientalist Controversy a debate occurring mainly (though not exclusively) in Britain in the early to mid-nineteenth century over the direction British imperial policy should take with regard to the cultural and educational transformation of India under British rule. The Anglicist position, most famously taken by Thomas Babington Macauley, promoted Anglophone education and the promotion of English and European literature as the medium for the creation of a class of an Anglicized Indian elite, whilst the Orientalist position (exemplified by figures such as Warren Hastings) strongly advocated the promotion, study and exploration of Indian languages and literature.

Anthropocentrism treating only human beings (as opposed to, say, all of life) as having moral value.

Anthropic principle   the principle, sometimes utilized in cosmology and astrophysics, that life (especially embodied conscious life) existing in a universe will impose certain conditions that significantly restrict the physical properties of that universe.

Anthropology   more generalized, comparative and theoretical reflection on culture and human behaviour.

Antireductionism   concept used by many phenomenologists insisting on irreducibility of the religious and opposing reductionistic approaches that reduce religious phenomena to non-religious explanations.

Apophatic theology   an approach to speaking about the divine which involves the claim that the nature of the divine is beyond all linguistic forms of expression, hence the best way to speak about the divine is to say what it is not. A key aspect of many mystical traditions and literature (cf. Cataphatic/Kataphatic theology).

Autonomy   generally used in the study of religion to indicate that it is not wholly dependent on the techniques and methods of other fields and disciplines; in the strong sense of the term, it suggests that the scientific study of religions and religious phenomena transcends the 'integrated causal model' that ties together the other natural and social sciences.

B

Behaviourism   a school of academic psychology, greatly exercised by considerations of strict scientific method, that limited itself to the measurement of behaviour, to the exclusion of all considerations of mind and thought.

Bharatiya Janata Party   radical right wing political party in India.

Bracketing (epoché)   phenomenological suspension of preconceptions and judgements about what is real behind phenomena or appearances.

C

Cataphatic/Kataphatic theology   speaking about the divine using positive or affirmative attributes, to be distinguished from apophatic theology.

Charisma   the special gifts giving an individual influence.

Civil religion   the interpretations, dramatizations and ritual enactments of a nation's vision of its calling and shared ultimate values. The concept goes back to Jean Jacques Rousseau and was further developed by Émile Durkheim and more recently by Robert Bellah in the US context.

Clinical psychology   a specialization within academic psychology that is concerned with psychotherapy; the techniques of cognitive behavioural therapy are favoured.

Cognitive science   interdisciplinary research into how the brain and its functions (mind) produce just the kinds of mental representations that it does.

Commentary   an explanatory, critical or scholarly exposition of a text.

Community the symbolic aggregation of diverse individuals and constituencies in terms of their contested affiliation to a social group.

Comparative religion the cross-cultural study of forms and traditions of religious life.

Comparative theology a development within Christian (and especially Catholic) theology of religions which seeks to bring familiar Christian texts into a dialogue with texts from another religious tradition.

Comparativism the study of ways religious data are similar to, or different from, each other.

Confessional theology theology pursued according to the belief and practice of a particular religious community or 'confession' of faith.

Consumerism psychological and social state in which buying commodities promises personal happiness and virtue.

Copernican astronomy the theory that the sun rather than the earth is at the centre of the orbits of the other planets; put forward in *On the Revolutions of the Heavenly Spheres* (1543) by Nicolaus Copernicus, and developed further by Galileo Galilei in the seventeenth century.

Cosmological arguments arguments for the existence of God in which certain alleged facts about the world (its coming to be, its being contingent, etc.) are used to infer a cause beyond the world, namely God.

Cosmology study of the universe including space, time and humanity

Cosmopolitanism multiple, criss-crossing, affiliations which transcend narrow ties; openness and tolerance to others including a capability to mediate in-between traditions based on a sense of belonging to humanity as a whole.

Counterintuitive anything that violates ordinary expectations about the world or aspects of the world.

Creationism a term for the general belief that the world has a supernatural Creator; during the later twentieth century it became particularly associated with religiously motivated anti-evolutionary movements.

Crossing and dwelling key terms in Thomas Tweed's theory that point to the way in which religions enable people to cross territorial, corporeal and cosmic boundaries but also settle and make homes.

Cult until the 1970s, sociologists used the term 'cult' to indicate either a culturally innovative religious group or one that is loosely organized and ephemeral. However, the label came to be used – mainly by psychologists – to designate authoritarian groups that used 'mind-control'; the Anti-Cult Movement fostered the idea that 'cults' are dangerous. In response, most sociologists now use the term 'new religious movement' instead.

Culture the diverse skills, ideas and practices acquired and developed by human beings as members of society in different contexts; a key source of both human similarity and difference.

D

Dabru Emet (from the opening Hebrew words of Zechariah 8.16, 'speak truth')   a brief statement of eight theses produced by Jewish theologians in the USA, and signed by many more, commenting on the current state of Jewish–Christian relations (published in the New York Times on 10th September 2000).

Darwinism   taken loosely, any modern evolutionary theory, more properly the theory of evolution by natural selection as elaborated in Charles Darwin's *On the Origin of Species* (1859).

Deathscapes   with 'necrogeography', a key term in the geography of religion signifying the way in which rituals of death and dying mark and change the landscape.

Demography   the statistical study of the characteristics of human populations.

Denominational geography   a branch of the geography of religion that focuses on the distribution and movements of Christian or other religious denominations and on the landscapes they produce.

Diaspora   meaning 'scattering' or 'sowing', a term that refers to the movement of people away from their places of origin, and to the way in which those people retain real or imagined connections with such places.

Doctrinal religiosity   a mode of transmitting religious knowledge as a coherent set of shared beliefs or doctrines maintained by a strong, hierarchical leadership. Such coherently formulated sets of orthodox teachings allow for their widespread transmission by authorized teachers and missionaries and for the relatively faithful reception and retention of such knowledge through routinized instruction that encodes its content in the semantic memory of followers.

E

Ecotheology   transforming basic religious ideas in the light of the environmental crisis and concern for non-human forms of and conditions for life.

Eidetic vision (intuition of essences, eidetic reduction)   phenomenological insight into the necessary and invariant features, essential structures and meanings, of phenomena.

Embodiment   having a bodily form.

Environmental crisis   human-caused devastation of species and environment on earth.

Environmental justice   connection between social justice issues and environmental issues.

Environmental racism   disproportionate effect of environmental pollution on racial/ethnic minorities.

Erastianism   a view developed by Thomas Erastus that the state should be supreme over the church, even in ecclesiastical matters.

Ethnicity   the symbolic organization of boundaries of communal difference marked by signifiers such as language, custom and/or religion, often to advance group interest.

Ethnography empirical research on particular cultures/peoples/regions conducted through fieldwork and participant observation.

Ethology the study of animal behaviour.

Evangelical a Christian who believes that one must be 'born-again' by accepting Jesus as one's saviour to attain salvation and that a Christian is obliged to 'evangelize', that is, to spread the 'good news' (Greek *evangelion*)of Christ's death and resurrection.

F

Fatah a major and relatively moderate nationalist Palestinian political party, founded in 1954. It is the largest faction of the Palestine Liberation Organization (PLO) and a supporter of the government in the West Bank.

Figural interpretation a method of biblical exegesis in which one historical figure or event (usually in the Old Testament) is taken to signify not only itself but also a later figure or event (usually in the New Testament); also called typological interpretation.

Function the recurrent need that religion, once it arises, continues to fulfil. Religion lasts as long as it fulfils the need at least as well as anything else.

Functional definitions of religion conceptualizations that define religion according to its individual and/or societal purposes, for example, its capacity to produce social integration or experiences of self-transcendence. Functional definitions contrast with substantive definitions of religion, which define religion according to characteristic features including, for example, belief in higher powers or its organization in churches.

Fundamentalism fundamentalism refers to claims of religious groups to literally 'return' to the basic principles of a religious tradition. This usually implies an emphasis on patriarchal structures of authority and social morality, and strict control of the female body.

G

Gender ideology is the mystification of social relations so that they appear to be based in, and derived from, nature.

Gender performance is derived from the work of Judith Butler and speaks to how humans in multiple social and cultural locations perform, or act out without critical thought, what are believed to be normative and natural modes of femaleness/femininity and maleness/masculinity.

Gender/sex is a formation of a concept that understands both gender and sex to be social constructs, but furthermore insists that gender is the primary category that informs and shapes what has been understood as biological sex.

Geography of religion the study of religion and its effect on landscape, environment and population movements.

Globalization the effects of time–space compression allowed by communications technologies such that the world is increasingly experienced as a single place.

H

Hamas a paramilitary party in Palestine formed in 1987 that gained control of the Gaza Strip in 2007. It is otherwise known as the Islamic Resistance Movement and is dedicated to the overthrow of Israel.

Haredim Hebrew term for ultra-Orthodox Jews. It means 'those who tremble' in the presence of God because they are 'God-fearing'.

Hermeneutics the art of interpreting; originally the arts of interpreting literary, legal, and biblical texts, it is now used for the art of interpreting any meaningful content.

Heteronormativity is the view that the proper and normative form of sexuality is that between the group marked as men and the group marked as women.

Hierophany from the believer's perspective, a sense of the revelation of the sacred in or through a particular object or form.

Hindu nationalism a movement that insists that to be a 'real' Indian entails being a Hindu.

Historical consciousness the awareness that everything human is relative, or related to the context in which it arose or exists.

Homo Religiosus 'religious man', understood as that type of human who experiences the world as having a sacred dimension.

Humanistic psychology a school of academic psychology, influenced partly by existentialism, but more extensively by common sense, that reintroduced humanistic considerations, in reaction against behaviourism's exclusively mechanical vision of people.

Hybridity the constant and organic fusion, intermixture and translation of cultural practices.

I

Identity the dialectical interrelation of contextual identifications ascribed by the self and others.

Ideology a term used by Karl Marx to refer to the values and beliefs of the dominant class in society who produced a false consciousness in those excluded from the means of production.

Illusion an unprovable belief, unreliable for Freud, harmless for Winnicott.

Imagistic religiosity a mode of transmitting religious knowledge through infrequently performed but emotionally salient rituals that promote individual reflections by each participant and that become encoded in the episodic (autobiographical) memory of followers.

Indology the academic study of India, focusing on the philological analysis of its classical texts.

Ineffability   the quality of being inexpressible through words or concepts. This is a key idea about the nature of the ultimate reality propounded by many mystics from a variety of religious traditions. In modern discussions of mysticism this term is usually taken as referring to the inexpressible nature of mystical experiences.

Intelligent design   the name for the most recent version of anti-Darwinian creationism, presented by its defenders as a scientific theory about the inexplicability in naturalistic terms of certain forms of biochemical complexity.

Intentionality   phenomenological concept that consciousness is always consciousness of something; that consciousness always has an intentional object.

L

Lifeworld (Lebenswelt)   concept introduced by Husserl to indicate the pre-epistemological ground of phenomenology in terms of shared, intersubjective givenness of universe of lived experience.

Local and global   two important and interconnected scales of analysis for the spatial study of religion.

Logocentrism   Jacques Derrida's critique of privileging speech over writing.

M

Mediatization   the process by which social structures and practices, or public awareness of these, becomes so dependent on media use that those structures and practices are shaped by the 'logic' of that media (e.g. politicians' adapting their political messages to sound-bites to fit the format of contemporary print and broadcast news media). In the context of religion, the mediatization thesis suggests that religious practices and communities are shaped and transformed by the media on which they are dependent.

Mental representations   thoughts, beliefs or ideas formed by the mind in relationship to the world (whether correctly or not).

Metaphysics of presence   the assumption that reality is immediately present to consciousness rather than caught in the problems of language and representation.

Metarepresentations   second-order representations (of mental representations) which allow for self-reflection, critical thought or imaginative possibilities.

Methodological naturalism   a conceptual framework for the study of natural and social phenomena that precludes recourse to supernatural/non-natural sources of explanation.

Midrash   a mode of legal or homiletic biblical interpretation typically employed in Rabbinic Judaism.

Migration   mobility and relocation from one place to another for various reasons – whether voluntary or forced – often creating minorities marked out from majorities in terms of race, language, culture and/or religion.

Monistic   the view that a society or culture has essentially only one identity or character, as opposed to several (pluralistic).

Multiculturalism   the public recognition of difference including cultural and religious difference by the nation-state and civil society.

Muslim Brethren   a radical and fundamentalist group, founded in Egypt in 1929, to oppose secularization and promote a restoration of strict Islam.

Myth   a story, which can be about anything and which has as its characters gods, humans, or animals, that expresses a deeply cherished conviction.

Myth-ritualism   the theory of myth which contends that some or all myths were originally or subsequently linked to rituals, so that myth can only be understood in relation to ritual.

N

Natural theology   discourse about God based on the natural human faculties of observation and reason, rather than proceeding from supernatural sources such as revelation or religious experience; particularly applied to works seeking to infer the existence and attributes of God from the properties of the natural world.

Naturalism   a version of atheism in which it is held that the universe is a closed system which operates according to natural laws and the natural order of things; opposed to supernaturalism.

Neurotheology   an attempt by some to explain religion by correlating neural states with subjective religious experiences.

New new religions   the term 'new new religions', or '*shin-shin-shûkyô*' was used by scholars to designate new religious groups that emerged in Japan in the 1970s in order to differentiate them from earlier Japanese 'new religions'. More recently, it was applied by Melton (2007) to religious groups established in America after 1990.

New religious movement   the category of 'new religious movement' (NRM) has been adopted by the majority of scholars of new religion as an ostensibly neutral term that circumvents the pejorative associations of 'sect' and 'cult'.

Noological arguments   arguments for the existence of God in which it is claimed that certain mental states (including the notions of rationality or consciousness) imply God as their ground.

Numen   a Latin term referring to the powerful presence of a divine being. Made famous in the modern era by Rudolph Otto (1869–1937), who argued in his work *Das Heilige* (1917; English translation '*The Idea of the Holy*', 1923) that the essential and distinctive aspect of religious experiences is their 'numinous' quality. Otto defined the numinous experience as being a 'creaturely feeling' (following Lutheran theologian Friedrich Schleiermacher, 1768–1834) of *mysterium tremendum et fascinans*, a mysterious, awe-inspiring and deeply attractive experience of the power of the ultimate reality. Otto believed that this experience was the 'non-rational' root of all human experiences of the religious but that it needed to be tempered by an appeal to rationality and orthodoxy. Mystics, according to Otto, are those figures within a religious tradition who place particular emphasis upon the 'non-rational' aspects of religious experience.

O

Object relations theory   a school of psychoanalysis, initially developed in Britain, that emphasizes the role of unconscious relationships with the objects of love and hate.

Oedipus complex   boys' age-appropriate desires, between four and five-and-one-half, to kill their fathers and marry their mothers; in Freud's view, the inappropriate persistence of the Oedipus complex later in life characterized neurosis.

Ohmazd   the Middle Persian form of the older Ahura Mazda, God in Zoroastrianism.

Ontological arguments   a priori arguments for the existence of God in which it is argued that it is logically impossible that God does not exist.

Orientalism   originally a descriptive term denoting the academic enterprise of studying the Orient, the word has, under the influence of Edward Said, increasingly been used in a pejorative sense to denote academic/intellectual interest in the East that is tainted by its complicity with Western colonialism. Generally speaking, Orientalism denotes a paradigmatic 'style of thought' focused on an essentialized separation of 'East' and 'West'.

Origin   either the historical origin – when and where religion first arose – or the recurrent origin, the cause of religion whenever and wherever it arises. The recurrent origin, on which theories of religion, is a need that exists before religion and is the necessary or (less often) sufficient cause of the creation of religion.

P

Pantheism   the view that God and all that exists are the same; typically includes the notion that the 'all' is ultimately impersonal.

Parsis   literally the people from Pars or Persia, descendents of those refugees who migrated after the Islamic invasion of Iran probably in the seventh or eighth century. They settled in North West India and are now mainly found in Mumbai but there are important diaspora groups in most Western countries. Their religion is Zoroastrianism.

Phenomenology   in philosophy, an analysis not of things in themselves but of 'intentional' objects, that is, objects as they are presented to the mind; in religious studies, the word generally refers to the scholarly attempt to identify the basic features of religion.

Phenomenology of religion   scholarly approach and discipline that has a general sense of the descriptive study of observable phenomena and a narrower sense related to the philosophical approach that uses a phenomenological method.

Philology   the study of languages and texts, and more broadly, the use of texts to study cultural worlds, as in the study of ancient Chinese, Greek, Persian, or Sanskrit.

Phonologism   the priority of the spoken word, what Jacques Derrida called the 'exclusion or abasement of writing' (*On Grammatology* [1967] 1976, Johns Hopkins University Press, p. 102).

Pilgrimage   the movement of people to places held to be sacred; a metaphor for significant personal journeys and quests.

Plausibility structures   the social and economic structures and contexts in which religious worldviews are grounded and supported. The concept implies that religion remains strongest in societies where it is monopolistic and supported by a dialectical, mutually sustaining, and mutually determining relationship with a social base.

Polymethodic   the use of a number of methods in a study.

Polythetic   a kind of definition that does not define a word in terms of a single feature or essence (e.g. 'even numbers are divisible by two without remainder') but instead in terms of a variety of characteristics, a bundle of which makes an instance a member of the class, but none of which must be present in every instance.

Positivism   a philosophical assertion that reality and truth were immediately present to sense experience.

Postcolonialism   is a social and political movement that emerged in late 1950s in colonized locations sometimes known as the global south. It seeks to critically engage Eurowestern colonialization.

Primatology   the study by anthropologist, biologists, and psychologists, among others, of the order of mammals that includes monkeys, apes, and humans, and of their ancestors.

Privatization of religion   this term refers to the process by which the locus of religion shifts from the public sphere to the private lives or inner personal experience of individuals.

Process theology   a school of theology (originated by Alfred North Whitehead and further developed by Charles Hartshorne) in which God is understood to be interdependent with the world and is also affected by those in the world; God and the world evolve together.

Psychoanalysis   the school of psychotherapy that Sigmund Freud founded.

Purity laws   religious prescriptions to guard against the danger of pollution.

Q

Quantum theory   a branch of fundamental theoretical physics developed in the early twentieth century seeking especially to describe the properties of the smallest constituents of matter, which behave sometimes as waves and sometimes as particles.

R

Rational choice theory of religion   a deductive theory of religion based on the utilitarian assumption that people's preferences are stable across time and space and that actions can be understood as choices made by weighing options in terms of costs and benefits.

Reduction   the explanation of one domain in terms of another, such as the 'reduction' of biological processes in cells to chemical reactions or the explanation of religious elements in sociological or psychological terms.

Reflexivity   critical self-reflection on academic methods and theories.

Religion, minimal definition of costly behaviour or ideas or sets of costly behaviours or ideas that are legitimated by claims to the authority of superhuman agents provide necessary (if insufficient) attributes for analytically stipulating data that might be termed 'religious'.

Religiongeschichte comparative historical study of various religious traditions.

Religionswissenschaft a loan-word from the German language designating in a broad and general way the scientific study of religions and religious phenomena.

Religious authority the ability to influence or enforce, arising from office, knowledge or expertise.

Religious environmentalism response to the environmental crisis by religions of the world, including theological, institutional, political, and ritual developments.

Religious geography a branch of theology and religious studies in which scholars examine the effect of place, landscape and the environment on religious ideas and practices.

Religious history study of religious life in the past in its social, political, and cultural context on the basis of rigorous objective analysis of primary sources.

Religious mapping locating and surveying the presence of religions within a designated area and examining their manifestations, interconnections, functions and representations.

Religious pluralism a term used with a variety of connotations to refer to the diversity of religious forms, but in a normative sense applied particularly to the philosophical position, espoused by John Hick which claims that all religions are equally valid paths to the same divine reality.

Religious studies academic inquiry into questions such as the essence and origin of religion, its description and function, its language and the relation between religions, undertaken with a concern for academic autonomy from theological confession.

Ritual an action, which is usually public but which can also be private, that is prescribed and that cannot be altered in any way.

S

Sacralization to make something sacred, or imbue it with sacred character, such as a ruler or system of governance.

Sacred space space produced by a process of ritualization or sacralization; a place deemed to be imbued with special meaning, power and ritual significance; the study of sacred space has been an important sub-field within the study of religions, associated especially with Mircea Eliade and Jonathan Z. Smith.

Scriptural reasoning an open-ended practice of prayerful reading and dialogical reasoning by scholars, exegetes, commentators from the three Abrahamic traditions – Judaism, Christianity and Islam.

Scripture the privileged text(s) of a religious community.

Sect   'sect' has been applied by sociologists to breakaway groups from established religious organizations and to religious groups with high boundaries that offer exclusive paths to salvation. Because the term accumulated negative connotations, 'new religious movement' is now more commonly used by scholars.

Secularization   a sociological concept embodying various ideas about trends in human society that include the alleged marginalization of religious influences in the political and cultural spheres and/or the decline of individual religious belief and practice.

Secular space   often associated with the public realm of government and civil society, as opposed to the private domain of the individual, family and religious organizations; space claimed by secularists and, at times, contested by religious bodies.

Semiotics   the study of signs, the way meaning is constructed and conveyed in systems of social communication.

Senses of scripture   varieties of interpretative (especially non-literal) procedures applied to sacred texts.

Shamanism   a complex of ritual practices and symbols – stemming from Siberia, but found also in Central and East Asia and among native peoples in the Americas – centred on the mediatory figure of the shaman who is believed to be able to communicate with and travel to the spirit world for the purposes of healing communities.

Social Darwinism   an attempt to adapt Darwin's theory of natural selection to social processes. This attempt, especially popular in the nineteenth and early twentieth centuries, supposed that competition drives social evolution and that the strongest or fittest will survive. It was used to justify, among other ideologies, military conquest, colonialism, slavery, unregulated capitalism, and eugenics.

Soteriology   the Christian doctrine of salvation – the theological category within which the relationship of Christianity to other religions has traditionally been conceived.

Spatial study of religion   examining religion and religions through a spatial lens; applying a spatial approach or methodology to the study of religion.

Spatial turn   scholarly trend from the late 1960s onwards in which the concept of 'space' was redefined and reappropriated by social and cultural theorists, such as Foucault and Lefebvre, and radical geographers, such as Harvey, Massey and Soja.

Special agent ritual   a form of religious ritual in which a superhuman agent occupies the role of actor. Typically, a participant serves as the patient of such a ritual only once.

Special patient ritual   a form of religious ritual in which a superhuman agent is the recipient of the ritual actions. A participant serving in such a ritual typically participates in these rituals more than once.

Spirit possession   concept that religious practitioners may be possessed by spirits and deities – wittingly or unwittingly – to enable communication with the spirit world, and eventually healing, as well as spiritual and social transformation.

Substantification   the making of something into a substance or essence; the process of making something appear given with reality rather than constructed in history or through language.

Superego   a term invented by Freud to name the agency within the mind that accomplishes self-observation, judgements of conscience, and the formation and maintenance of ideals.

Superhuman agent, counterintuitive agent a representation of an ordinary or 'natural' actor to which is attributed, however, an ability to accomplish some result considered to be unobtainable by ordinary means.

Syncretism the creative synthesis of two or more systems of religious ideas and practices into a new system, as in the case of African-derived religions in the Americas.

Systematic theology theology pursued and organized according to a series of classical theological *loci*, themes or categories (such as creation, christology, soteriology, doctrine of God, pneumatology, eschatology, ecclesiology).

T

Taxonomy classification, as in the Linnaean system which classifies living organisms; in religious studies, the attempt to classify religions and their various elements.

Teleological arguments arguments for the existence of God in which certain observations of the world (apparent design, order, or purpose) are used to infer a designer of the world, namely God; also referred to as the 'design argument'.

Theocracy a system of governmental rule by religious leaders in a society where God or a deity is recognized as the supreme source of political power, and whose laws are interpreted and instituted by those religious authorities on the basis of their high religious status and/ or a divine commission.

Theology thinking and deliberating about questions raised by, about and between the religions, with a view to understanding, knowledge and wisdom.

Theology of religions a term applied to a variety of Christian theological positions and strategies which seek to respond to questions and challenges raised by the phenomenon of religious diversity or pluralism.

Theory an explanation of the origin and function of religion. Not a denial of differences among religions but a concentration on similarities.

The sacred Mircea Eliade's (and other) formulations of the universal, transcendent essence or structure of all religious experience.

Tradition an authoritative yet contested chain of memory which disciplines belief, practice and identity in the present with reference to a sacred vision of the past and/or future.

Transnationalism the social, cultural, economic, political and religious circulations and flows across the borders of nation-states made possible by late modern globalisation.

Twin Towers incident when airliners were flown by a group of radical Muslims into the World Trade Center in New York on 11 September 2001 killing thousands.

Typological interpretation *see* figural interpretation.

U

Universalism The belief that all religions point to the same spiritual reality, though through different cultural forms.

W

Westoxification   this idea, first popularized during the Iranian Revolution of 1979, refers to the processes of cultural, military and political influence exerted by the West on non-Western (specifically Islamic) societies, which are seen as polluting and 'toxic' for the integrity and independence of those societies and the values they seek to uphold. The term probably originated in Iran, where in Farsi it is *gharbzadegi*. Jalal Al-e Ahmad is sometimes credited with coining or popularizing it.

Wisdom   a wide-ranging term which may embrace describing, understanding, explaining, knowing and deciding, not only regarding matters of empirical fact but also regarding values, norms, beliefs and the shaping of lives, communities and institutions.

Z

Zionism   a modern movement and ideology of Jewish nationalism and political liberation, founded as a result of increased anti-Semitism in Europe and Russia in the late nineteenth century.

Zoroaster   the priestly prophet who revealed God's teachings in Zoroastrianism. He lived approximately in the thirteenth century BCE in north-east Iran.

Zoroastrianism   the religion of Zoroaster who lived in North East Iran probably in the thirteenth century BCE. It teaches that God (Ahura Mazda, the Wise Lord) created the world perfect but it is assaulted by evil (Angra Mainyu, the Destructive Spirit) with suffering, misery and death. It is an important human duty to fight evil and protect the Good Creation. Traditionally it taught there will be a last great conflict between good and evil when good will triumph, the dead will be raised and all dwell with God in a perfect existence.

Index

Page ranges in **bold** indicate where a subject is given a whole chapter's treatment.